ESSENTIAL READINGS IN

WORLD

POLITICS

7TH EDITION

ESSENTIAL READINGS IN

WORLD POLITICS

7TH EDITION

Karen A. Mingst, Heather Elko McKibben,
and Jack L. Snyder

W. W. NORTON & COMPANY
New York · London

W. W. Norton & Company has been independent since its founding in 1923, when William Warder Norton and Mary D. Herter Norton first published lectures delivered at the People's Institute, the adult education division of New York City's Cooper Union. The firm soon expanded its program beyond the Institute, publishing books by celebrated academics from America and abroad. By midcentury, the two major pillars of Norton's publishing program—trade books and college texts—were firmly established. In the 1950s, the Norton family transferred control of the company to its employees, and today—with a staff of four hundred and a comparable number of trade, college, and professional titles published each year—W. W. Norton & Company stands as the largest and oldest publishing house owned wholly by its employees.

Editor: Peter Lesser

Project Editor: Taylere Peterson

Assistant Editor: Anna Olcott

Managing Editor, College: Marian Johnson

Managing Editor, College Digital Media: Kim Yi

Production Manager: Eric Pier-Hocking

Marketing Manager, Political Science: Erin Brown

Director of College Permissions: Megan Schindel

Permissions Associate: Elizabeth Trammell

Composition: Westchester Publishing Services

Manufacturing: LSC Communications, Crawfordsville

Permission to use copyrighted material is included in the credits section of this book, which begins on page 725.

Library of Congress Cataloging-in-Publication Data

Names: Mingst, Karen A., 1947- editor.
Title: Essential readings in world politics / Karen A. Mingst, Heather Elko McKibben, and Jack L. Snyder.
Description: Seventh Edition. | New York : W.W. NORTON & COMPANY, [2019] |
    Series: The Norton Series in World Politics | Includes bibliographical references.
Identifiers: LCCN 2018053663 | ISBN 9780393664614 (paperback)
Subjects: LCSH: International relations. | World politics.
Classification: LCC JZ1305 .E85 2019 | DDC 327—dc23 LC record available at
    https://lccn.loc.gov/2018053663

ISBN: 978-0-393-66461-4 (pbk.)

W. W. Norton & Company, Inc., 500 Fifth Avenue, New York, NY 10110

wwnorton.com

W. W. Norton & Company Ltd., 15 Carlisle Street, London W1D 3BS

2 3 4 5 6 7 8 9 0

CONTENTS

3. INTERNATIONAL RELATIONS THEORIES 84

4. LEVELS OF ANALYSIS 154

PREFACE

This reader is the result of a collaborative effort between the three co-editors, with an evolving mix of classic and contemporary selections over seven editions.

The articles have been selected to meet several criteria. First, the collection is designed to augment and amplify the core text, *Essentials of International Relations,* Eighth Edition, by Karen A. Mingst, Heather Elko McKibben, and Ivan M. Arreguín-Toft. The chapters in this book follow those in the text. Second, the selections are purposefully eclectic; that is, key theoretical articles are paired with contemporary pieces found in the literature. When possible, articles have been chosen to reflect diverse theoretical perspectives and policy viewpoints. Finally, the articles are intended to be both readable and engaging to undergraduates. The co-editors worked to maintain the integrity of challenging pieces while making them accessible to undergraduates at a variety of colleges and universities, in some cases working closely with authors to translate technical material into highly accessible yet precise prose.

Special thanks go to those individuals who provided reviews of this book and offered suggestions and reflections based on teaching experience. Our product benefited greatly from these evaluations, although had we included all the suggestions, the book would have been thousands of pages! Peter Lesser, our editor at W. W. Norton, guided part of the process, compiling thorough evaluations from users of earlier editions and providing suggestions. Anna Olcott kept us "on task" and offered excellent suggestions as the book took final shape. Their professionalism and understanding made this process much more rewarding. We also thank W. W. Norton's copyediting and production staff for their careful work on this book.

ABOUT THE AUTHORS

Karen A. Mingst is Professor Emeritus at the Patterson School of Diplomacy and International Commerce at the University of Kentucky. She holds a PhD in political science from the University of Wisconsin. A specialist in international organization, international law, and international political economy, Professor Mingst has conducted research in Western Europe, West Africa, and Yugoslavia. She is the author or editor of seven books and numerous academic articles.

Heather Elko McKibben is an associate professor in the Department of Political Science at the University of California, Davis. She has been at Davis since 2009, after receiving her PhD from the University of Pittsburgh in 2008 and holding a postdoctorate position in the Niehaus Center for Globalization and Governance at Princeton University in the 2008-2009 academic year. In her research, Professor McKibben is interested in understanding when, why and how different countries negotiate with each other. When and why will countries come to the negotiating table to resolve problems instead of resorting to more coercive measures? What types of strategies do they use in those negotiations, and why do those strategies differ from country to country and negotiation to negotiation? When and why will countries be able to reach cooperative agreements, and what are the resulting agreements likely to look like? Examining international negotiations in a wide variety of settings, Professor McKibben seeks to answer these types of questions.

Jack L. Snyder is the Robert and Renee Belfer Professor of International Relations in the Department of Political Science and the Saltzman Institute of War and Peace Studies at Columbia University. He is the editor of the Norton Series in World Politics and his books including *From Voting to Violence: Democratization and Nationalist Conflict*. Professor Snyder is a Fellow of the American Academy of Arts and Sciences and an elected member and chair of Columbia's Arts and Sciences Policy and Planning Committee.

GUIDE TO THIS READER

Many of the selections included here are reprinted in their entirety. A number have been excerpted from longer works. A * * * indicates that word(s) or sentence(s) are omitted. A ■■■ indicates that paragraph(s) or section(s) are omitted. Brackets indicate text added by the editors for purposes of clarification. Complete bibliographic citations are included at the bottom of the first page of each selection. Readers who desire to delve deeper into the source material are encouraged to pursue these citations as well as those cited in the readings.

1

APPROACHES TO INTERNATIONAL RELATIONS

In *Essentials of International Relations*, Eighth Edition, Karen A. Mingst, Heather Elko McKibben, and Ivan M. Arreguín-Toft introduce theories and approaches used to study international relations. The readings in this section of *Essential Readings in World Politics* complement that introduction. Jack Snyder first provides an overview of rival theories and suggests how theories guide decision makers to respond to contemporary events. Originally written in the aftermath of the September 11, 2001 terror attacks, this essay is brought up to date with a new introduction and a new concluding commentary on the rise of China, populist political movements, and other new challenges to the prevailing international order.

Some of the conceptual approaches that shape international relations thinking today have a long track record. Thucydides (460 BCE–c. 395 BCE), in his history of the Peloponnesian War, presents a classic dialogue between Athenian imperialists and their Melian victims. The two sides debate the place of power and principle in international relations. The leaders of Melos ponder the fate of the island, deciding whether to risk defying the Athenians, and whether they can rely on the enemy of Athens, the Lacedaemonians (also known as Spartans), for protection.

Thomas Hobbes's *Leviathan*, published in 1651 at the time of the English Civil War, explains how fear and greed lead to endemic conflict in situations of anarchy, where there is no sovereign power to provide protection and enforce laws. This work expresses a central insight of contemporary realists about the root cause of war.

Immanuel Kant's *Perpetual Peace*, published in 1795, foreshadows the key arguments of today's liberal approach to international relations theory: liberal states with representative governments are unlikely to fight wars against each other, because government policy is accountable to the average citizen who bears the costs of war. This creates the potential to form a cooperative league of liberal states, embodied nowadays in international organizations such as the United Nations, international economic institutions, the North Atlantic Treaty Organization, and the European Union, which were established to a large extent through the efforts of the liberal great powers.

A newer approach to understanding international politics is called constructivism, based on the insight that social reality is constructed from ideas about values, norms, rules, and cultures that shape collective identities and interests. Ted Hopf's essay offers a crystal clear statement of this approach and why it is important for understanding international relations.

Jack Snyder

ONE WORLD, RIVAL THEORIES

The September 11, 2001, terrorist attacks provoked much handwringing among scholars of international relations. They worried that their accustomed approaches to understanding world politics had blinded them to this new type of threat and were becoming obsolete. Shortly thereafter, I wrote an essay for *Foreign Policy* arguing that the field's major theories were still yielding valuable insights, but also had some blind spots that clouded their vision in a rapidly changing world. That essay, which remains quite relevant in the face of continuing terrorist threats, is reproduced intact in the following pages.

It is high time, however, to once again take stock of dramatic new developments in world affairs and assess how well our theories are keeping up with them. One of the issues after 2001 was whether conventional approaches that focused on the central role of national states, such as realism, were ill-suited to understanding the rising significance of non-state actors, including transnational terrorist networks such as Al Qaeda or principled transnational activist networks such as Human Rights Watch. However, realists might note that the most prominent terror threat in recent years has called itself the "Islamic State," arguably confirming that territorial governance is what makes or breaks bids for international power.

Transformative new issues, barely envisioned in 2001, have subsequently emerged on the international agenda. One is the astonishingly rapid economic rise of China, which is striving to expand its regional influence in East Asia and could eventually become a peer competitor of the United States. This poses a set of issues to which international relations theories with a long track record—such as realism, liberalism, and normative approaches—should be well suited.

Several classic works on international relations excerpted in this volume offer historically tested hypotheses about strategic competition between rival great powers, including the particular dangers that loom when a rising power threatens to catch up with a previously dominant power. Well-vetted knowledge assesses tactics for containing a great power's attempts to expand its regional sphere of influence (see the selection by John Mearsheimer), the importance of leadership by a dominant state for the smooth functioning of multilateral economic and security institutions (Robert Gilpin), the effect of changes in material power on prevailing international norms (Robert Keohane and John Ikenberry), and frictions between democratic and authoritarian great powers that exacerbate strategic rivalry (Michael Doyle). Recent works by Thomas Christensen and Iain Johnston examine the rise of China in the light of long-established as well as newer approaches (adapting insights of selections from Robert Jervis, Thomas Schelling, and Alexander Wendt).

More perplexing to accustomed styles of analysis are intense challenges to the internal stability of the liberal democratic order. In 1989, Francis Fukuyama (excerpted in this volume) announced "the end of history" with the decisive victory of liberal democracy over its historical authoritarian competitors, communism and fascism. The rise of China, the assertiveness of Russia, the terrifying world financial crisis of 2008, and the wildfire spread of right-wing nationalist populism in many

From *Foreign Policy* (Nov./Dec. 2004): 53–62.

wealthy democracies in 2016–17 have shown that judgment to be premature (see Daniel Drezner and Fareed Zakaria). The usual set of theories I discussed in the wake of 9/11 has little to say about this systemic turbulence at the very core of the liberal global order. But that does not mean that the theoretical cupboard is bare of helpful resources. We just need to go back further, to the era of unstable global capitalism and disorderly mass nationalism in the first half of the twentieth century, to gain insight into the causes of these more recent predicaments. See, for example, Ikenberry's 2018 article, reprinted in Chapter 2, reflecting on Karl Polanyi's classic 1944 analysis of the collapse of the gold standard and the rise of populist fascism in Europe.

I will have more to say on these new challenges, and on some new theoretical approaches in the field of international relations, in a new conclusion following my reprinted 2004 *Foreign Policy* essay.

■　■　■

The U.S. government has endured several painful rounds of scrutiny as it tries to figure out what went wrong on September 11, 2001. The intelligence community faces radical restructuring; the military has made a sharp pivot to face a new enemy; and a vast new federal agency has blossomed to coordinate homeland security. But did September 11 signal a failure of theory on par with the failures of intelligence and policy? Familiar theories about how the world works still dominate academic debate. Instead of radical change, academia has adjusted existing theories to meet new realities. Has this approach succeeded? Does international relations theory still have something to tell policymakers?

[In 1998], political scientist Stephen M. Walt published a much-cited survey of the field in [*Foreign Policy*] ("One World, Many Theories," Spring 1998). He sketched out three dominant approaches: realism, liberalism, and an updated form of idealism called "constructivism." Walt argued that these theories shape both public discourse and policy analysis. Realism focuses on the shifting distribution of power among states. Liberalism highlights the rising number of democracies and the turbulence of democratic transitions. Idealism illuminates the changing norms of sovereignty, human rights, and international justice, as well as the increased potency of religious ideas in politics.

The influence of these intellectual constructs extends far beyond university classrooms and tenure committees. Policymakers and public commentators invoke elements of all these theories when articulating solutions to global security dilemmas. President George W. Bush promises to fight terror by spreading liberal democracy to the Middle East and claims that skeptics "who call themselves 'realists' . . . have lost contact with a fundamental reality" that "America is always more secure when freedom is on the march." Striking a more eclectic tone, National Security Advisor Condoleezza Rice, a former Stanford University political science professor, explains that the new Bush doctrine is an amalgam of pragmatic realism and Wilsonian liberal theory. During the recent presidential campaign, Sen. John Kerry sounded remarkably similar: "Our foreign policy has achieved greatness," he said, "only when it has combined realism and idealism."

International relations theory also shapes and informs the thinking of the public intellectuals who translate and disseminate academic ideas. During the summer of 2004, for example, two influential framers of neoconservative thought, columnist Charles Krauthammer and political scientist Francis Fukuyama, collided over the implications of these conceptual paradigms for U.S. policy in Iraq. Backing the Bush administration's Middle East policy, Krauthammer argued for an assertive amalgam of liberalism and realism, which he called "democratic realism." Fukuyama claimed that Krauthammer's faith in the use of force and the feasibility of democratic change in Iraq blinds him to the war's lack of legitimacy, a failing that "hurts

Figure 1.1. From Theory to Practice

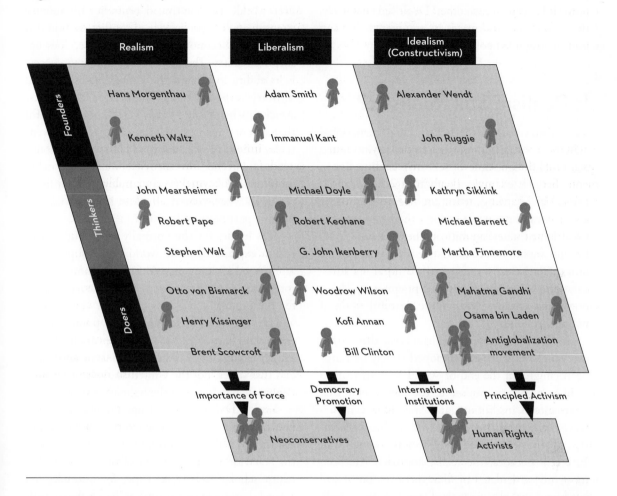

both the realist part of our agenda, by diminishing our actual power, and the idealist portion of it, by undercutting our appeal as the embodiment of certain ideas and values."

Indeed, when realism, liberalism, and idealism enter the policymaking arena and public debate, they can sometimes become intellectual window dressing for simplistic worldviews. Properly understood, however, their policy implications are subtle and multifaceted. Realism instills a pragmatic appreciation of the role of power but also warns that states will suffer if they overreach. Liberalism highlights the cooperative potential of mature democracies, especially when working together through effective institutions, but it also notes democracies' tendency to crusade against tyrannies and the propensity of emerging democracies to collapse into violent ethnic turmoil. Idealism stresses that a consensus on values must underpin any stable political order, yet it also recognizes that forging such a consensus often requires an ideological struggle with the potential for conflict.

Each theory offers a filter for looking at a complicated picture. As such, they help explain the assumptions behind political rhetoric about foreign policy. Even more important, the theories act as a powerful check on each other. Deployed effectively, they reveal the weaknesses in arguments that can lead to misguided policies.

Is Realism Still Realistic?

At realism's core is the belief that international affairs is a struggle for power among self-interested states. Although some of realism's leading lights, notably the late University of Chicago political scientist Hans J. Morgenthau, are deeply pessimistic about human nature, it is not a theory of despair. Clearsighted states can mitigate the causes of war by finding ways to reduce the danger they pose to each other. Nor is realism necessarily amoral; its advocates emphasize that a ruthless pragmatism about power can actually yield a more peaceful world, if not an ideal one.

In liberal democracies, realism is the theory that everyone loves to hate. Developed largely by European émigrés at the end of World War II, realism claimed to be an antidote to the naive belief that international institutions and law alone can preserve peace, a misconception that this new generation of scholars believed had paved the way to war. In recent decades, the realist approach has been most fully articulated by U.S. theorists, but it still has broad appeal outside the United States as well. The influential writer and editor Josef Joffe articulately comments on Germany's strong realist traditions. (Mindful of the overwhelming importance of U.S. power to Europe's development, Joffe once called the United States "Europe's pacifier.") China's current foreign policy is grounded in realist ideas that date back millennia. As China modernizes its economy and enters international institutions such as the World Trade Organization, it behaves in a way that realists understand well: developing its military slowly but surely as its economic power grows, and avoiding a confrontation with superior U.S. forces.

Realism gets some things right about the post-9/11 world. The continued centrality of military strength and the persistence of conflict, even in this age of global economic interdependence, does not surprise realists. The theory's most obvious success is its ability to explain the United States' forceful military response to the September 11 terrorist attacks. When a state grows vastly more powerful than any opponent, realists expect that it will eventually use that power to expand its sphere of domination, whether for security, wealth, or other motives. The United States employed its military power in what some deemed an imperial fashion in large part because it could.

It is harder for the normally state-centric realists to explain why the world's only superpower announced a war against Al Qaeda, a nonstate terrorist organization. How can realist theory account for the importance of powerful and violent individuals in a world of states? Realists point out that the central battles in the "war on terror" have been fought against two states (Afghanistan and Iraq), and that states, not the United Nations or Human Rights Watch, have led the fight against terrorism.

Even if realists acknowledge the importance of nonstate actors as a challenge to their assumptions, the theory still has important things to say about the behavior and motivations of these groups. The realist scholar Robert A. Pape, for example, has argued that suicide terrorism can be a rational, realistic strategy for the leadership of national liberation movements seeking to expel democratic powers that occupy their homelands. Other scholars apply standard theories of conflict in anarchy to explain ethnic conflict in collapsed states. Insights from political realism—a profound and wide-ranging intellectual tradition rooted in the enduring philosophy of Thucydides, Niccolò Machiavelli, and Thomas Hobbes—are hardly rendered obsolete because some nonstate groups are now able to resort to violence.

Post-9/11 developments seem to undercut one of realism's core concepts: the balance of power.

Standard realist doctrine predicts that weaker states will ally to protect themselves from stronger ones and thereby form and reform a balance of power. So, when Germany unified in the late nineteenth century and became Europe's leading military and industrial power, Russia and France (and later, Britain) soon aligned to counter its power. Yet no combination of states or other powers can challenge the United States militarily, and no balancing coalition is imminent. Realists are scrambling to find a way to fill this hole in the center of their theory. Some theorists speculate that the United States' geographic distance and its relatively benign intentions have tempered the balancing instinct. Second-tier powers tend to worry more about their immediate neighbors and even see the United States as a helpful source of stability in regions such as East Asia. Other scholars insist that armed resistance by U.S. foes in Iraq, Afghanistan, and elsewhere, and foot-dragging by its formal allies actually constitute the beginnings of balancing against U.S. hegemony. The United States' strained relations with Europe offer ambiguous evidence: French and German opposition to recent U.S. policies could be seen as classic balancing, but they do not resist U.S. dominance militarily. Instead, these states have tried to undermine U.S. moral legitimacy and constrain the superpower in a web of multilateral institutions and treaty regimes—not what standard realist theory predicts.

These conceptual difficulties notwithstanding, realism is alive, well, and creatively reassessing how its root principles relate to the post-9/11 world. Despite changing configurations of power, realists remain steadfast in stressing that policy must be based on positions of real strength, not on either empty bravado or hopeful illusions about a world without conflict. In the run-up to the recent Iraq war, several prominent realists signed a public letter criticizing what they perceived as an exercise in American hubris. And in the continuing aftermath of that war, many prominent thinkers called for a return to realism. A group of scholars and public intellectuals (myself included) even formed the Coalition for a Realistic Foreign Policy, which calls for a more modest and prudent approach. Its statement of principles argues that "the move toward empire must be halted immediately." The coalition, though politically diverse, is largely inspired by realist theory. Its membership of seemingly odd bedfellows—including former Democratic Sen. Gary Hart and Scott McConnell, the executive editor of the *American Conservative* magazine—illustrates the power of international relations theory to cut through often ephemeral political labels and carry debate to the underlying assumptions.

The Divided House of Liberalism

The liberal school of international relations theory, whose most famous proponents were German philosopher Immanuel Kant and U.S. President Woodrow Wilson, contends that realism has a stunted vision that cannot account for progress in relations between nations. Liberals foresee a slow but inexorable journey away from the anarchic world the realists envision, as trade and finance forge ties between nations, and democratic norms spread. Because elected leaders are accountable to the people (who bear the burdens of war), liberals expect that democracies will not attack each other and will regard each other's regimes as legitimate and nonthreatening. Many liberals also believe that the rule of law and transparency of democratic processes make it easier to sustain international cooperation, especially when these practices are enshrined in multilateral institutions.

Liberalism has such a powerful presence that the entire U.S. political spectrum, from neoconservatives to human rights advocates, assumes it as largely self-evident. Outside the United States, as well, the liberal view that only elected governments are legitimate and politically reliable has taken hold. So it is no surprise that liberal themes are constantly invoked as a response to today's security dilemmas. But the last several years have also produced a fierce tug-of-war between disparate strains of liberal thought. Supporters and critics of the Bush administration, in particular, have emphasized very different elements of the liberal canon.

For its part, the Bush administration highlights democracy promotion while largely turning its back on the international institutions that most liberal theorists champion. The U.S. National Security Strategy of September 2002, famous for its support of preventive war, also dwells on the need to promote democracy as a means of fighting terrorism and promoting peace. The Millennium Challenge program allocates part of U.S. foreign aid according to how well countries improve their performance on several measures of democratization and the rule of law. The White House's steadfast support for promoting democracy in the Middle East—even with turmoil in Iraq and rising anti-Americanism in the Arab world—demonstrates liberalism's emotional and rhetorical power.

In many respects, liberalism's claim to be a wise policy guide has plenty of hard data behind it. During the last two decades, the proposition that democratic institutions and values help states cooperate with each other is among the most intensively studied in all of international relations, and it has held up reasonably well. Indeed, the belief that democracies never fight wars against each other is the closest thing we have to an iron law in social science.

But the theory has some very important corollaries, which the Bush administration glosses over as it draws upon the democracy-promotion element of liberal thought. Columbia University political scientist Michael W. Doyle's articles on democratic peace warned that, though democracies never fight each other, they are prone to launch messianic struggles against warlike authoritarian regimes to "make the world safe for democracy." It was precisely American democracy's tendency to oscillate between self-righteous crusading and jaded isolationism that prompted early Cold War realists' call for a more calculated, prudent foreign policy.

Countries transitioning to democracy, with weak political institutions, are more likely than other states to get into international and civil wars. In the last fifteen years, wars or large-scale civil violence followed experiments with mass electoral democracy in countries including Armenia, Burundi, Ethiopia, Indonesia, Russia, and the former Yugoslavia. In part, this violence is caused by ethnic groups' competing demands for national self-determination, often a problem in new, multiethnic democracies. More fundamental, emerging democracies often have nascent political institutions that cannot channel popular demands in constructive directions or credibly enforce compromises among rival groups. In this setting, democratic accountability works imperfectly, and nationalist politicians can hijack public debate. The violence that is vexing the experiment with democracy in Iraq is just the latest chapter in a turbulent story that began with the French Revolution.

Contemporary liberal theory also points out that the rising democratic tide creates the presumption that all nations ought to enjoy the benefits of self-determination. Those left out may undertake violent campaigns to secure democratic rights. Some of these movements direct their struggles against democratic or semidemocratic states that they consider occupying powers—such as in Algeria in the 1950s, or Chechnya, Palestine, and the Tamil region of Sri Lanka today. Violence may also be directed at democratic supporters of oppressive regimes, much like the U.S. backing of the governments of Saudi Arabia and Egypt. Democratic regimes make attractive targets for terrorist violence by national liberation movements precisely because they are accountable to a cost-conscious electorate.

Nor is it clear to contemporary liberal scholars that nascent democracy and economic

Figure 1.2. The Leading Brands

Theories:	Realism	Liberalism	Idealism (Constructivism)
Core Beliefs	Self-interested states compete for power and security	Spread of democracy, global economic ties, and international organizations will strengthen peace	International politics is shaped by persuasive ideas, collective values, culture, and social identities
Key Actors in International Relations	States, which behave similarly regardless of their type of government	States, international institutions, and commercial interests	Promoters of new ideas, transnational activist networks, and nongovernmental organizations
Main Instruments	Military power and state diplomacy	International institutions and global commerce	Ideas and values
Theory's Intellectual Blind Spots	Doesn't account for progress and change in international relations or understanding that legitimacy can be a source of military power	Fails to understand that democratic regimes survive only if they safeguard military power and security; some liberals forget that transitions to democracy are sometimes violent	Does not explain which power structures and social conditions allow for changes in values
What the Theory Explains about the Post-9/11 World	Why the United States responded aggressively to terrorist attacks; the inability of international institutions to restrain military superiority	Why spreading democracy has become such an integral part of current U.S. international security strategy	The increasing role of polemics about values; the importance of transnational political networks (whether terrorists or human rights advocates)
What the Theory Fails to Explain about the Post-9/11 World	The failure of smaller powers to militarily balance the United States; the importance of non-state actors such as Al Qaeda; the intense U.S. focus on democratization	Why the United States has failed to work with other democracies through international organizations	Why human rights abuses continue, despite intense activism for humanitarian norms and efforts for international justice

liberalism can always cohabitate. Free trade and the multifaceted globalization that advanced democracies promote often buffet transitional societies. World markets' penetration of societies that run on patronage and protectionism can disrupt social relations and spur strife between potential winners and losers. In other cases, universal free trade can make separatism look attractive, as small regions such as Aceh in Indonesia can lay claim to lucrative natural resources. So far, the trade-fueled boom in China has created incentives for improved relations with the advanced democracies, but it has also set the stage for a possible showdown between the relatively wealthy coastal entrepreneurs and the still impoverished rural masses.

While aggressively advocating the virtues of democracy, the Bush administration has shown little patience for these complexities in liberal thought—or for liberalism's emphasis on the importance of international institutions. Far from trying to assure other powers that the United States would adhere to a constitutional order, Bush "unsigned" the International Criminal Court statute, rejected the Kyoto environmental agreement, dictated take-it-or-leave-it arms control changes to

Russia, and invaded Iraq despite opposition at the United Nations and among close allies.

Recent liberal theory offers a thoughtful challenge to the administration's policy choices. Shortly before September 11, political scientist G. John Ikenberry studied attempts to establish international order by the victors of hegemonic struggles in 1815, 1919, 1945, and 1989. He argued that even the most powerful victor needed to gain the willing cooperation of the vanquished and other weak states by offering a mutually attractive bargain, codified in an international constitutional order. Democratic victors, he found, have the best chance of creating a working constitutional order, such as the Bretton Woods system after World War II, because their transparency and legalism make their promises credible.

Does the Bush administration's resistance to institution building refute Ikenberry's version of liberal theory? Some realists say it does, and that recent events demonstrate that international institutions cannot constrain a hegemonic power if its preferences change. But international institutions can nonetheless help coordinate outcomes that are in the long-term mutual interest of both the hegemon and the weaker states. Ikenberry did not contend that hegemonic democracies are immune from mistakes. States can act in defiance of the incentives established by their position in the international system, but they will suffer the consequences and probably learn to correct course. In response to Bush's unilateralist stance, Ikenberry wrote that the incentives for the United States to take the lead in establishing a multilateral constitutional order remain powerful. Sooner or later, the pendulum will swing back.

Idealism's New Clothing

Idealism, the belief that foreign policy is and should be guided by ethical and legal standards, also has a long pedigree. Before World War II forced the United States to acknowledge a less pristine reality, Secretary of State Henry Stimson denigrated espionage on the grounds that "gentlemen do not read each other's mail." During the Cold War, such naive idealism acquired a bad name in the Kissinge-rian corridors of power and among hardheaded academics. Recently, a new version of idealism—called constructivism by its scholarly adherents—returned to a prominent place in debates on international relations theory. Constructivism, which holds that social reality is created through debate about values, often echoes the themes that human rights and international justice activists sound. Recent events seem to vindicate the theory's resurgence; a theory that emphasizes the role of ideologies, identities, persuasion, and transnational networks is highly relevant to understanding the post-9/11 world.

The most prominent voices in the development of constructivist theory have been American, but Europe's role is significant. European philosophical currents helped establish constructivist theory, and the *European Journal of International Relations* is one of the principal outlets for constructivist work. Perhaps most important, Europe's increasingly legalistic approach to international relations, reflected in the process of forming the European Union out of a collection of sovereign states, provides fertile soil for idealist and constructivist conceptions of international politics.

Whereas realists dwell on the balance of power and liberals on the power of international trade and democracy, constructivists believe that debates about ideas are the fundamental building blocks of international life. Individuals and groups become powerful if they can convince others to adopt their ideas. People's understanding of their interests depends on the ideas they hold. Constructivists find absurd the idea of some identifiable and immutable "national interest," which some realists cherish. Especially in liberal societies, there is overlap between constructivist and liberal approaches, but the two are distinct. Constructivists contend that their theory is deeper than realism and liberalism

because it explains the origins of the forces that drive those competing theories.

For constructivists, international change results from the work of intellectual entrepreneurs who proselytize new ideas and "name and shame" actors whose behavior deviates from accepted standards. Consequently, constructivists often study the role of transnational activist networks—such as Human Rights Watch or the International Campaign to Ban Landmines—in promoting change. Such groups typically uncover and publicize information about violations of legal or moral standards at least rhetorically supported by powerful democracies, including "disappearances" during the Argentine military's rule in the late 1970s, concentration camps in Bosnia, and the huge number of civilian deaths from land mines. This publicity is then used to press governments to adopt specific remedies, such as the establishment of a war crimes tribunal or the adoption of a landmine treaty. These movements often make pragmatic arguments as well as idealistic ones, but their distinctive power comes from the ability to highlight deviations from deeply held norms of appropriate behavior.

Progressive causes receive the most attention from constructivist scholars, but the theory also helps explain the dynamics of illiberal transnational forces, such as Arab nationalism or Islamist extremism. Professor Michael N. Barnett's 1998 book *Dialogues in Arab Politics: Negotiations in Regional Order* examines how the divergence between state borders and transnational Arab political identities requires vulnerable leaders to contend for legitimacy with radicals throughout the Arab world—a dynamic that often holds moderates hostage to opportunists who take extreme stances.

Constructivist thought can also yield broader insights about the ideas and values in the current international order. In his 2001 book, *Revolutions in Sovereignty: How Ideas Shaped Modern International Relations*, political scientist Daniel Philpott demonstrates how the religious ideas of the Protestant Reformation helped break down the medieval political order and provided a conceptual basis for the modern system of secular sovereign states. After September 11, Philpott focused on the challenge to the secular international order posed by political Islam. "The attacks and the broader resurgence of public religion," he says, ought to lead international relations scholars to "direct far more energy to understanding the impetuses behind movements across the globe that are reorienting purposes and policies." He notes that both liberal human rights movements and radical Islamic movements have transnational structures and principled motivations that challenge the traditional supremacy of self-interested states in international politics. Because constructivists believe that ideas and values helped shape the modern state system, they expect intellectual constructs to be decisive in transforming it—for good or ill.

When it comes to offering advice, however, constructivism points in two seemingly incompatible directions. The insight that political orders arise from shared understanding highlights the need for dialogue across cultures about the appropriate rules of the game. This prescription dovetails with liberalism's emphasis on establishing an agreed international constitutional order. And, yet, the notion of cross-cultural dialogue sits awkwardly with many idealists' view that they already know right and wrong. For these idealists, the essential task is to shame rights abusers and cajole powerful actors into promoting proper values and holding perpetrators accountable to international (generally Western) standards. As with realism and liberalism, constructivism can be many things to many people.

Stumped by Change

None of the three theoretical traditions has a strong ability to explain change—a significant weakness in such turbulent times. Realists failed to predict the end of the Cold War, for example. Even after it happened, they tended to assume that the new system would become multipolar ("back to the future," as the scholar John J. Mearsheimer put it). Likewise, the liberal theory of democratic peace is stronger on what happens after states become democratic than in predicting the timing of democratic transitions, let alone prescribing how to make transitions happen peacefully. Constructivists are good at describing changes in norms and ideas, but they are weak on the material and institutional circumstances necessary to support the emergence of consensus about new values and ideas.

With such uncertain guidance from the theoretical realm, it is no wonder that policymakers, activists, and public commentators fall prey to simplistic or wishful thinking about how to effect change by, say, invading Iraq or setting up an International Criminal Court. In lieu of a good theory of change, the most prudent course is to use the insights of each of the three theoretical traditions as a check on the irrational exuberance of the others. Realists should have to explain whether policies based on calculations of power have sufficient legitimacy to last. Liberals should consider whether nascent democratic institutions can fend off powerful interests that oppose them, or how international institutions can bind a hegemonic power inclined to go its own way. Idealists should be asked about the strategic, institutional, or material conditions in which a set of ideas is likely to take hold.

Theories of international relations claim to explain the way international politics works, but each of the currently prevailing theories falls well short of that goal. One of the principal contributions that international relations theory can make is not predicting the future but providing the vocabulary and conceptual framework to ask hard questions of those who think that changing the world is easy.

■   ■   ■

One of the weaknesses of international relations theories at the end of the millennium was analyzing processes of change. It is not surprising that this field, like the rest of the world, was taken unawares by the most consequential developments of the new century. What kinds of theories might be needed to do better in the future?

Several of the readings in this volume deal with processes of large-scale change. Kant, Doyle, Krasner, Keohane, and Ikenberry foresee or analyze the deepening and spread of democratic governance of states, the expansion of economic relations among them, and their formation of international organizations to maintain peace and cooperation. Fewer, most notably Fukuyama, trace the historically parallel development of authoritarian, economic protectionist, illiberal political systems in some modernizing states, including some of the great powers. One crucial task for international relations theory is to do as much work on the political development of illiberal states in their international context as has been done on the evolution of liberal states and their role in the international order.

A promising sign is the recent turn toward the study of the foreign policies of different types of authoritarian states, including China. For example, most authoritarian leaders are in some way accountable to various elite groups and sometimes need to consider mass popular opinion, with varying consequences for foreign policy.[1] So far, these theories are mostly static comparisons rather than dynamic analyses of change over time, but they are pointing in a fruitful direction.

Studies of the evolution of the international order as a whole will be needed to understand the broader context shaping the domestic evolution of states. In this volume, Krasner describes the impact of changing concentrations of power on states' free trade policies; Martha Finnemore describes change in prevailing global norms of humanitarian intervention. Even more ambitiously, other essays attempt to describe an underlying taproot that drives global political evolution over the long run. V. I. Lenin, a maker of history as well as an analyst of it, argues that inexorable economic competition drives capitalist states to imperial expansion and war.

At a comparable level of ambition, Polanyi, as paraphrased and updated by John Ruggie (and discussed in this volume by Ikenberry), argues with startling contemporary resonance that populist nationalism arises from a contradiction at the heart of liberalism: the incompatibility between mass political participation and the "creative destruction" wreaked by the "invisible hand" of unregulated market competition.[2] To protect themselves from the chaos of free markets, the masses demand political control over markets and economic resources by the state. This can take the form of state socialism in a totalitarian planned economy, fascist nationalism that counts on economic protectionism and military conquest of imperial territories, or the democratic welfare state that protects citizens from the vagaries of the market by a thick safety net of social insurance. Ruggie's extension of Polanyi argues that the Bretton Woods international economic institutions of the post–World War II period provided a complementary regulatory buffer at the international level that the welfare state provided at the domestic level. Today, economists such as Joseph Stiglitz and Dani Rodrik argue that the weakening of welfare state regulatory institutions at both levels explains rising levels of inequality, backlash against immigrants, and the political success of right-wing populists.[3]

One of the most pressing needs of contemporary international relations theory is a renovated version of modernization theory that works simultaneously at the international and domestic levels, and helps to explain the turmoil that uncontrolled international capital and labor mobility brings to wealthy established democracies as well as emerging transitional societies. Modernization theory has had a very poor reputation for decades, because many people associate it with the naive,

self-congratulatory, false notion that all states will proceed in a straight line from underdeveloped traditional society to modern liberal democratic state along the same path initially trod by Great Britain. What is needed now, however, is a more nuanced form of modernization theory that analyzes the dangerous detours that authoritarian modernizers take in their rocky, sometimes long-lasting transitional phase.[4] Whereas the field of comparative politics analyzes modernization mainly at the level of individual states, international relations needs to take on the task of understanding the political dynamic of this process at the global level.[5]

If this is what is needed from international theory, what have its most recent innovations actually provided? One strong trend has been a shift toward eclectic, problem-driven research. Twenty-plus years ago, the field of international relations was seized with the paradigm debates between and within realism, liberalism, and social constructivism. Since 9/11, however, younger scholars in particular have increasingly defined their research agendas not in terms of their primary theoretical commitments but in terms of contemporary real-world problems that they seek to understand and solve. This trend has been especially prominent in research on civil wars and terrorism. To be sure, a good deal of this research draws on insights and concerns related to the traditional international relations paradigms. These include the problem of insecurity and credible commitments in anarchy (see the selections by Robert Jervis, Barry Posen, and James Fearon), a staple of the realist approach. Social constructivism plays a key role in studying identity politics in violent conflict. Even liberalism comes into play in studies of democratic transition and conflict as well as the effects of forms of rebel wartime governance on forms of post-conflict regime.[6] What is different, however, is the increased willingness to mix conceptually diverse causal variables—military power, governance institutions, culture, norms, ideas, and bargaining—as complementary elements in the same research design as opposed to treating them as competing explanations. International relations course syllabi almost universally continue to teach the foundational works of realism, liberalism, and constructivism, though they may relabel them as something like "power politics and alliances," "regime type and institutions," and "ideas, norms, and transnationalism."

Ironically, some of the leading skeptics about the international relations field's past emphasis on competing paradigms have themselves advanced what amounts to a fourth paradigm based on rational bargaining as structured by institutionalized rules.[7] The definitive introduction to the study of international relations based on this approach is the W. W. Norton textbook *World Politics: Interests, Interactions, Institutions*, by Jeffry A. Frieden, David A. Lake, and Kenneth A. Schultz.[8] Selections in this volume include several foundational works in this vein. The works by Schelling, Jervis, and Fearon represent the key milestones in the development of the bargaining approach. Keohane's selection is the seminal work on international institutions as a key facilitator of bargaining among states. And Putnam's canonical essay on "two-level games" shows how international bargaining between national leaders interacts with veto powers built into domestic institutions to determine what political coalitions supporting international cooperation are possible.

This approach is often labeled "rationalism" for short. Sometimes a given article will stick to this strictly. For example, Fearon's rational bargaining theory of war explicitly sets aside possible nonrational psychological influences on decision making in order to study how leaders who are strictly rational might nonetheless fail to find a bargain they can agree on to avert the costs of resolving their dispute by war. Others, however, are keen to study how psychological limitations and biases can skew assessments of cost, benefits, the probability of success, and the nature of the adversary even when decision makers are trying hard to approach their problem rationally. Jervis, for example, studies how mental shortcuts that are nearly unavoidable in the face of complexity and uncertainty tend to exacerbate conflict when there is no guarantee that rivals will stick to an agreement. Verifiable arms control agreements, he says, can reduce uncertainty and solve these problems. Keohane similarly argues that uncertainty and complexity mean that decision makers can be at best "boundedly rational," so institutions can provide focal points or rules of thumb to guide cooperation based on reciprocity. This kind of marriage of rational decision making, bargaining, and cognitive psychology has been exceedingly popular in the fields of economics and public policy in recent years, bearing the label of "behavioral economics."

This shows that the relationship among the three (and now four) paradigms is characterized by overlap and complementarity, not just competition. One might be satisfied under the loose banner of eclecticism, picking and choosing as needed in problem-solving research. That said, one of the basic criteria for evaluating any scientific argument is whether it is logically consistent. Claims, for example, that decision makers are simultaneously rational and not rational might put any reader's warning antennae on alert. For this reason, it is worth expending some effort thinking about how eclecticism fits together coherently and maintains internal consistency.

As one beginning step in this direction, it might be noted that two of the paradigms, realism and liberalism, are arguably different in kind than the other two, rationalism and constructivism. Realism and liberalism encompass substantive theories of international relations. They are based on content-filled assumptions about the central driving forces of international affairs—who are the key actors, what are their motivations, how and why they interact the way they do. Moreover, they are anchored in deep philosophical traditions that have a long track record of resonance in public life.

Politicians, public intellectuals, and regular citizens talk in these categories. They lead quite directly to testable hypotheses about, say, the balance of power or relations between democracies.

In contrast, rationalism and constructivism are more like sets of methodological assumptions that can be applied to any type of social interaction. (See the article by Ted Hopf.) They make assumptions about how people approach problem solving and social relations in general. Their substantive connection to international politics per se requires making additional assumptions about actors, motives, and the structures within which interaction takes place. Sometimes this substantive connection is based on hypotheses provided by realism and liberalism. For this reason, it is possible to have scholars describe themselves as "constructivist realists" who believe that international power politics is a social convention based on a set of socially learned roles and shared norms. Thus, Wendt envisions a Hobbesian realist "culture of anarchy" as well as a Kantian liberal culture of anarchy.[9] Conversely, Mearsheimer is a rationalist realist who holds that strategic actors calculate how best to maximize power in the face of objective material constraints and opportunities. Kenneth Waltz, in contrast to both, argued from the premise that natural selection of effective over ineffective strategies for state survival in anarchy drove the process of socialization of states to adopt strategies that endlessly produced war and balances of power.[10]

In short, contemporary international relations theory remains innovative within the context of an enduring body of tested hypotheses that remain perennially relevant to broader public debates about current policy issues. As I argued in 2004, the area that needs the greatest attention is dynamic theories of change. Some older theories provide guidance on how to begin to construct such theories, but much work remains to be done on this difficult task. The readings in this volume should provide a strong point of embarkation for this quest.

NOTES

1. Jessica Weeks, *Dictators at War and Peace* (Ithaca: Cornell University Press, 2014); Jessica Chen Weiss, *Powerful Patriots: Nationalist Protest in China's Foreign Relations* (New York: Oxford University Press, 2014), discussed in the selections by Johnston.
2. John Gerard Ruggie, "International Regimes, Transactions, and Change: Embedded Liberalism in the Postwar Economic Order," *International Organization* 36 (Spring 1982), 379–416.
3. Joseph E. Stiglitz, *Freefall: America, Free Markets, and the Sinking of the World Economy* (New York: W. W. Norton, 2010); Dani Rodrik, *Straight Talk on Trade: Ideas for a Sane World Economy* (Princeton: Princeton University Press, 2017).
4. Samuel Huntington, *Political Order in Changing Societies* (New Haven: Yale University Press, 1968); Edward D. Mansfield and Jack Snyder, *Electing to Fight* (Cambridge: MIT Press, 2005).
5. An interesting recent attempt is Francis Fukuyama, *The Origins of Political Order* and *Political Order and Political Decay*, 2 vols. (New York: Farrar, Straus and Giroux, 2011 and 2014).
6. Aila M. Matanock, *Electing Peace: From Civil Conflict to Political Participation* (Cambridge, UK: Cambridge University Press, 2017); Reyko Huang, *The Wartime Origins of Democratization: Civil War, Rebel Governance, and Political Regimes* (Cambridge, UK: Cambridge University Press, 2016).
7. David Lake and Robert Powell, eds., *Strategic Choice and International Relations* (Princeton: Princeton University Press, 1999); David A. Lake, "Theory Is Dead, Long Live Theory: The End of the Great Debates and the Rise of Eclecticism in International Relations," *European Journal of International Relations* 19 (2013), 567–87.
8. Third edition, 2015.
9. Alexander Wendt, *Social Theory of International Politics* (Cambridge, UK: Cambridge University Press, 1999), chapter 6.
10. Kenneth Waltz, *Theory of International Politics* (Reading, MA: Addison-Wesley, 1979).

Thucydides
MELIAN DIALOGUE

Introduction by Suresht Bald

It was the sixteenth year of the Peloponnesian War, but for the last six years the two great feuding empires headed by Athens and Sparta (Lacedaemon) had avoided open hostile action against each other. Ten years into the war they had signed a treaty of peace and friendship; however, this treaty did not dissipate the distrust that existed between them. Each feared the other's hegemonic designs on the Peloponnese and sought to increase its power to thwart the other's ambitions. Without openly attacking the other, each used persuasion, coercion, and subversion to strengthen itself and weaken its rival. This struggle for hegemony by Athens and Sparta was felt most acutely by small, hitherto "independent" states who were now being forced to take sides in the bipolar Greek world of the fifth century B.C. One such state was Melos.

Despite being one of the few island colonies of Sparta, Melos had remained neutral in the struggle between Sparta and Athens. Its neutrality, however, was unacceptable to the Athenians, who, accompanied by overwhelming military and naval power, arrived in Melos to pressure it into submission. After strategically positioning their powerful fleet, the Athenian generals sent envoys to Melos to negotiate the island's surrender.

The commissioners of Melos agreed to meet the envoys in private. They were afraid the Athenians, known for their rhetorical skills, might sway the people if allowed a public forum. The envoys came with an offer that if the Melians submitted

and became part of the Athenian empire, their people and their possessions would not be harmed. The Melians argued that by the law of nations they had the right to remain neutral, and no nation had the right to attack without provocation. Having been a free state for seven hundred years they were not ready to give up that freedom. Thucydides captures the exchange between the Melian commissioners and the Athenian envoys:

* * * The Athenians * * * sent a fleet against the island of Melos. Thirty of the ships were their own, six were from Chios, and two were from Lesbos. Their own troops numbered twelve hundred hoplites, three hundred archers, and twenty mounted archers. There were also about fifteen hundred hoplites from their allies on the islands. The Melians are colonists from Sparta and would not submit to Athenian control like the other islanders. At first, they were neutral and lived peaceably, but they became openly hostile after Athens once tried to compel their obedience by ravaging their land. The generals Cleomedes, son of Lycomedes, and Tisias, son of Tisimachus, bivouacked on Melian territory with their troops, but before doing any injury to the land, they sent ambassadors to hold talks with the Melians. The Melian leadership, however, did not bring these men before the popular assembly. Instead, they asked them to discuss their mission with the council and the privileged voters. The Athenian ambassadors spoke as follows.

"We know that what you are thinking in bringing us before a few voters, and not before the popular assembly, is that now the people won't be deceived after listening to a single long, seductive, and unrefuted speech from us. Well, those of you who are sitting here can make things even safer

From Thucydides, *The Peloponnesian War,* trans. Walter Blanco, ed. Walter Blanco and Jennifer Tolbert Roberts (New York: W. W. Norton & Co., 1998). Introduction by Suresht Bald, Willamette University.

for yourselves. When we say something that seems wrong, interrupt immediately, and answer, not in a set speech, but one point at a time.—But say first whether this proposal is to your liking."

The Melian councillors said, "There can be no objection to the reasonableness of quiet, instructive talks among ourselves. But this military force, which is here, now, and not off in the future, looks different from instruction. We see that you have come as judges in a debate, and the likely prize will be war if we win the debate with arguments based on right and refuse to capitulate, or servitude if we concede to you."

ATHENIANS

Excuse us, but if you're having this meeting to make guesses about the future or to do anything but look at your situation and see how to save your city, we'll leave. But if that's the topic, we'll keep talking.

MELIANS

It's natural and understandable that in a situation like this, people would want to express their thoughts at length. But so be it. This meeting is about saving our city, and the format of the discussion will be as you have said.

ATHENIANS

Very well.

We Athenians are not going to use false pretenses and go on at length about how we have a right to rule because we destroyed the Persian empire, or about how we are seeking retribution because you did us wrong. You would not believe us anyway. And please do not suppose that you will persuade *us* when you say that you did not campaign with the Spartans although you were their colonists, or that you never did us wrong. No, each of us must exercise what power he really thinks he can, and we know and you know that in the human realm, justice is enforced only among those who can be equally constrained by it, and that those who have power use it, while the weak make compromises.

MELIANS

Since you have ruled out a discussion of justice and forced us to speak of expediency, it would be inexpedient, at least as we see it, for you to eradicate common decency. There has always been a fair and right way to treat people who are in danger, if only to give them some benefit for making persuasive arguments by holding off from the full exercise of power. This applies to you above all, since you would set an example for others of how to take the greatest vengeance if you fall.

ATHENIANS

We're not worried about the end of our empire, if it ever does end. People who rule over others, like the Spartans, are not so bad to their defeated enemies. Anyway, we're not fighting the Spartans just now. What is really horrendous is when subjects are able to attack and defeat their masters.—But you let us worry about all that. We are here to talk about benefiting our empire and saving your city, and we will tell you how we are going to do that, because we want to take control here without any trouble and we want you to be spared for both our sakes.

MELIANS

And just how would it be as much to our advantage to be enslaved, as for you to rule over us?

ATHENIANS

You would benefit by surrendering before you experience the worst of consequences, and we would benefit by not having you dead.

MELIANS

So you would not accept our living in peace, being friends instead of enemies, and allies of neither side?

ATHENIANS

Your hatred doesn't hurt us as much as your friendship. That would show us as weak to our other subjects, whereas your hatred would be a proof of our power.

MELIANS

Would your subjects consider you reasonable if you lumped together colonists who had no connection to you, colonists from Athens, and rebellious colonists who had been subdued?

ATHENIANS

They think there's justice all around. They also think the independent islands are strong, and that we are afraid to attack them. So aside from adding to our empire, your subjugation will also enhance our safety, especially since you are islanders and we are a naval power. Besides, you're weaker than the others—unless, that is, you show that you too can be independent.

MELIANS

Don't you think there's safety in our neutrality? You turned us away from a discussion of justice and persuaded us to attend to what was in your interest. Now it's up to us to tell you about what is to our advantage and to try to persuade you that it is also to yours. How will you avoid making enemies of states that are now neutral, but that look at what you do here and decide that you will go after them one day? How will you achieve anything but to make your present enemies seem more attractive, and to force those who had no intention of opposing you into unwilling hostility?

ATHENIANS

We do not think the threat to us is so much from mainlanders who, in their freedom from fear, will be continually putting off their preparations against us, as from independent islanders, like you, and from those who are already chafing under the restraints of rule. These are the ones who are most likely to commit themselves to ill-considered action and create foreseeable dangers for themselves and for us.

MELIANS

Well then, in the face of this desperate effort you and your slaves are making, you to keep your empire and they to get rid of it, wouldn't we, who are still free, be the lowest of cowards if we didn't try everything before submitting to slavery?

ATHENIANS

No, not if you think about it prudently. This isn't a contest about manly virtue between equals, or about bringing disgrace on yourself. You are deliberating about your very existence, about standing up against a power far greater than yours.

MELIANS

But we know that there are times when the odds in warfare don't depend on the numbers. If we give up, our situation becomes hopeless right away, but if we fight, we can still hope to stand tall.

ATHENIANS

In times of danger, hope is a comfort that can hurt you, but it won't destroy you if you back it up with plenty of other resources. People who gamble everything on it (hope is extravagant by nature, you see) know it for what it really is only after they have lost everything. Then, of course, when you can recognize it and take precautions, it's left you flat. You don't want to experience that. You Melians are weak, and you only have one chance. So don't be like all those people who could have saved themselves by their own efforts, but who abandoned their realistic hopes and turned in their hour of need to invisible powers—to prophecies and oracles and all the other nonsense that conspires with hope to ruin you.

MELIANS

As you well know, we too think it will be hard to fight both your power and the fortunes of war, especially with uneven odds. Still, we believe that our fortune comes from god, and that we will not be defeated because we take our stand as righteous men against men who are in the wrong. And what we lack in power will be made up for by the Spartan League. They will have to help us, if only because of our kinship with them and the disgrace they would feel if they didn't. So it's not totally irrational for us to feel hopeful.

ATHENIANS

Well, when it comes to divine good will, we don't think we'll be left out. We're not claiming anything or doing anything outside man's thinking about the gods or about the way the gods themselves behave. Given what we believe about the gods and know about men, we think that both are always forced by the law of nature to dominate everyone they can. We didn't lay down this law, it was there—and we weren't the first to make use of it. We took it as it was and acted on it, and we will bequeath it as a living thing to future generations, knowing full well that if you or anyone else had the same power as we, you would do the same thing. So we probably don't have to fear any disadvantage when it comes to the gods. And as to this opinion of yours about the Spartans, that you can trust them to help you because of their fear of disgrace—well, our blessings on your innocence, but we don't envy your foolishness. The Spartans do the right thing among themselves, according to their local customs. One could say a great deal about their treatment of others, but to put it briefly, they are more conspicuous than anyone else we know in thinking that pleasure is good and expediency is just. Their mindset really bears no relation to your irrational belief that there is any safety for you now.

MELIANS

But it's exactly because of this expediency that we trust them. They won't want to betray the Melians, their colonists, and prove themselves helpful to their enemies and unreliable to their well-wishers in Greece.

ATHENIANS

But don't you see that expediency is safe, and that doing the right and honorable thing is dangerous? On the whole, the Spartans are the last people to take big risks.

MELIANS

We think they'll take on dangers for us that they wouldn't for others and regard those dangers as less risky, because we are close to the Peloponnese from an operational point of view. Also, they can trust our loyalty because we are kin and we think alike.

ATHENIANS

Men who ask others to come to fight on their side don't offer security in good will but in real

fighting power. The Spartans take this kind of thing more into consideration than others, because they have so little faith in their own resources that they even attack their neighbors with plenty of allies. So it's not likely that they'll try to make their way over to an island when we control the sea.

MELIANS

Then maybe they'll send their allies. The sea of Crete is large, and it is harder for those who control the sea to catch a ship than it is for the ship to get through to safety without being noticed. And if that doesn't work, they might turn against your territory or attack the rest of your allies, the ones Brasidas didn't get to. And then the fight would shift from a place where you have no interest to your own land and that of your allies.

ATHENIANS

It's been tried and might even be tried for you—though surely you are aware that we Athenians have never abandoned a siege out of fear of anyone.

But it occurs to us that after saying you were going to talk about saving yourselves, you haven't in any of this lengthy discussion mentioned anything that most people would rely on for their salvation. Your strongest arguments are in the future and depend on hope. What you've actually got is too meager to give you a chance of surviving the forces lined up against you now. You've shown a very irrational attitude—unless, of course, you intend to reach some more prudent conclusion than this after you send us away and begin your deliberations. For surely you don't mean to commit yourselves to that "honor" which has been so destructive to men in clear and present dangers involving "dishonor." Many men who could still see where it was leading them have been drawn on by the allure of this so-called "honor," this word with its seductive power, and fallen with open eyes into irremediable catastrophe, vanquished in their struggle with a fine word, only to achieve a kind of dishonorable honor because they weren't just unlucky, they were fools. You can avoid this, if you think things over carefully, and decide that there is nothing so disgraceful in being defeated by the greatest city in the world, which invites you to become its ally on fair terms—paying us tribute, to be sure, but keeping your land for yourselves. You have been given the choice between war and security. Don't be stubborn and make the wrong choice. The people who are most likely to succeed stand up to their equals, have the right attitude towards their superiors, and are fair to those beneath them.

We will leave now. Think it over, and always remember that you are making a decision about your country. You only have one, and its existence depends on this one chance to make a decision, right or wrong.

Then the Athenians withdrew from the discussion. The Melians, left to themselves, came to the conclusion that had been implied by their responses in the talks. They answered the Athenians as follows: "Men of Athens, our decision is no different from what it was at first. We will not in this brief moment strip the city we have lived in for seven hundred years of its freedom. We will try to save it, trusting in the divine good fortune that has preserved us so far and in the help we expect from the Spartans and from others. We invite you to be our friends, to let us remain neutral, and to leave our territory after making a treaty agreeable to us both."

That was the Melian response. The talks were already breaking up when the Athenians said, "Well, judging from this decision, you seem to us to be the only men who can make out the future more clearly than what you can see, and who gaze upon the invisible with your mind's eye as if it were an accomplished fact. You have cast yourselves on luck, hope, and the Spartans, and the more you trust in them, the harder will be your fall."

Then the Athenian envoys returned to the camp. Since the Melians would not submit, the Athenian generals immediately took offensive action and, after dividing their men according to the cities they came from, began to build a wall around Melos. Later the Athenians left a garrison of their own and allied men to guard the land and sea routes and then withdrew with most of their army. The men who were left behind remained there and carried on the siege.

At about this same time, the Argives invaded the territory of Phlius, where they fell into an ambush set by the Phliasians and the Argive exiles, who killed about eighty of them. The Athenian raiders on Pylos took a great deal of booty from Spartan territory, but despite even this, the Spartans did not renounce the treaty and declare war. They did, however, announce that if any of their people wished to raid Athenian territory, they could do so. The Corinthians made war on the Athenians over some private quarrels, but the rest of the Peloponnesians held their peace. The Melians staged a night attack on the part of the Athenian wall opposite their market and captured it. They killed some men and withdrew into the city carrying grain and as many other useful provisions as they could, taking no further action. The Athenians kept a better watch from then on. And so the summer came to an end.

The following winter, the Spartans were about to march into Argive territory, but the omens from sacrifices made before crossing the border were unfavorable and they turned back. This balked expedition led the Argives to suspect some of their citizens. They arrested some, but others managed to escape. At about the same time, the Melians again captured yet another part of the Athenian wall when only a few men were on guard duty. Because of this, another contingent later came from Athens, under the command of Philocrates, son of Demeas. By now, the Melians were completely cut off, and there were traitors within the city itself. So, on their own initiative, they agreed to terms whereby the Athenians could do with them as they liked. The Athenians thereupon killed all the males of fighting age they could capture and sold the women and children into slavery. The Athenians then occupied the place themselves and later sent out five hundred colonists.

Thomas Hobbes
FROM *LEVIATHAN*

Of the NATURAL CONDITION *of Mankind, as Concerning Their Felicity, and Misery*

Nature hath made men so equal, in the faculties of body, and mind; as that though there be found one man sometimes manifestly stronger in body, or of quicker mind then another; yet when all is reckoned together, the difference between man, and man, is not so considerable, as that one man can thereupon claim to himself any benefit, to which another may not pretend, as well as he. For as to the strength of body, the weakest has strength enough to kill the strongest, either by secret machination, or by confederacy with others, that are in the same danger with himself.

And as to the faculties of the mind (setting aside the arts grounded upon words, and especially that skill of proceeding upon general, and infallible rules, called science; which very few have, and but in few things; as being not a native faculty, born with us; nor attained, (as prudence), while we look after somewhat else), I find yet a greater equality amongst men, than that of strength. For prudence, is but experience; which equal time, equally bestowes on all men, in those things they equally apply themselves unto. That which may perhaps make such equality incredible, is but a vain conceit of one's own wisdom, which almost all men think they have in a greater degree, than the vulgar; that is, than all men but themselves, and a few

others, whom by fame, or for concurring with themselves, they approve. For such is the nature of men, that howsoever they may acknowledge many others to be more witty, or more eloquent, or more learned; yet they will hardly believe there be many so wise as themselves: for they see their own wit at hand, and other men's at a distance. But this proveth rather that men are in that point equal, than unequal. For there is not ordinarily a greater sign of the equal distribution of any thing, than that every man is contented with his share.

From this equality of ability, ariseth equality of hope in the attaining of our ends. And therefore if any two men desire the same thing, which nevertheless they cannot both enjoy, they become enemies; and in the way to their end (which is principally their own conservation, and sometimes their delectation only), endeavour to destroy, or subdue one an other. And from hence it comes to pass, that, where an invader hath no more to fear, than an other man's single power; if one plant, sow, build, or possess a convenient seat, others may probably be expected to come prepared with forces united, to dispossess, and deprive him, not only of the fruit of his labour, but also of his life, or liberty. And the invader again is in the like danger of another.

And from this diffidence of one another, there is no way for any man to secure himself, so reasonable, as anticipation; that is, by force, or wiles, to master the persons of all men he can, so long, till he see no other power great enough to endanger him: And this is no more than his own conservation requireth, and is generally allowed. Also because there be some, that taking pleasure in contemplating their own power in the acts of

From Thomas Hobbes, *Leviathan,* ed. A. R. Waller (Cambridge: Cambridge University Press, 1904), 81–86. This excerpt has been edited to contemporary spelling and capitalization.

conquest, which they pursue farther than their security requires; if others, that otherwise would be glad to be at ease within modest bounds, should not by invasion increase their power, they would not be able, long time, by standing only on their defence, to subsist. And by consequence, such augmentation of dominion over men, being necessary to a man's conservation, it ought to be allowed him.

Again, men have no pleasure (but on the contrary a great deal of grief) in keeping company, where there is no power able to over-awe them all. For every man looketh that his companion should value him, at the same rate he sets upon himself: And upon all signs of contempt, or undervaluing, naturally endeavours, as far as he dares (which amongst them that have no common power to keep them in quiet, is far enough to make them destroy each other), to extort a greater value from his contemners, by dommage; and from others, by the example.

So that in the nature of man, we find three principal causes of quarrel. First, competition; secondly, diffidence; thirdly, glory.

The first, maketh men invade for gain; the second, for safety; and the third, for reputation. The first use violence, to make themselves masters of other men's persons, wives, children, and cattle; the second, to defend them; the third, for trifles, as a word, a smile, a different opinion, and any other sign of undervalue, either direct in their persons, or by reflexion in their kindred, their friends, their nation, their profession, or their name.

Hereby it is manifest, that during the time men live without a common power to keep them all in awe, they are in that condition which is called war; and such a war, as is of every man, against every man. For WAR, consisteth not in battle only, or the act of fighting; but in a tract of time, wherein the will to contend by battle is sufficiently known: and therefore the notion of *time,* is to be considered in the nature of war; as it is in the nature of weather. For as the nature of foul weather, lyeth not in a shower or two of rain; but in an inclination thereto of many days together; So the nature of war, consisteth not in actual fighting; but in the known disposition thereto, during all the *time* there is no assurance to the contrary. All other time is PEACE.

Whatsoever therefore is consequent to a time of war, where every man is enemy to every man; the same is consequent to the time, wherein men live without other security, than what their own strength, and their own invention shall furnish them withal. In such condition, there is no place for industry; because the fruit thereof is uncertain: and consequently no culture of the earth; no navigation, nor use of the commodities that may be imported by sea; no commodious building; no instruments of moving, and removing such things as require much force; no knowledge of the face of the earth; no account of time; no arts; no letters; no society; and which is worst of all, continual fear, and danger of violent death; And the life of man, solitary, poor, nasty, brutish, and short.

It may seem strange to some man, that has not well weighed these things; that nature should thus dissociate, and render men apt to invade, and destroy one another: and he may therefore, not trusting to this inference, made from the passions, desire perhaps to have the same confirmed by experience. Let him therefore consider with himself, when taking a journey, he arms himself, and seeks to go well accompanied; when going to sleep, he locks his doors; when even in his house he locks his chests; and this when he knows there be laws, and public officers, armed, to revenge all injuries shall be done him; what opinion he has of his fellow subjects, when he rides armed; of his fellow citizens, when he locks his doors; and of his children, and servants, when he locks his chests. Does he not there as much accuse mankind by his actions, as I do by my words? But neither of us accuse man's nature in it. The desires, and other passions of man, are in themselves no sin. No more are the actions, that proceed from those passions, till they know a law that forbids them: which till laws be made they cannot know: nor can any law be made, till they have agreed upon the person that shall make it.

It may peradventure be thought, there was never such a time, nor condition of war as this; and I believe it was never generally so, over all the world: but there are many places, where they live so now. For the savage people in many places of *America,* except the government of small families, the concord whereof dependeth on natural lust, have no government at all; and live at this day in that brutish manner, as I said before. Howsoever, it may be perceived what manner of life there would be, where there were no common power to fear; by the manner of life, which men that have formerly lived under a peaceful government, use to degenerate into, in a civil war.

But though there had never been any time, wherein particular men were in a condition of war one against another; yet in all times, kings, and persons of sovereign authority, because of their independency, are in continual jealousies, and in the state and posture of gladiators; having their weapons pointing, and their eyes fixed on one another; that is, their forts, garrisons, and guns upon the frontiers of their kingdoms, and continual spies upon their neighbours; which is a posture of war. But because they uphold thereby, the industry of their subjects; there does not follow from it, that misery, which accompanies the liberty of particular men.

To this war of every man against every man, this also is consequent; that nothing can be unjust. The notions of right and wrong, justice and injustice have there no place. Where there is no common power, there is no law: where no law, no injustice. Force, and fraud, are in war, the two cardinal virtues. Justice, and injustice are none of the faculties neither of the body, nor mind. If they were, they might be in a man that were alone in the world, as well as his senses, and passions. They are qualities, that relate to men in society, not in solitude. It is consequent also to the same condition, that there be no propriety, no dominion, no *mine* and *thine* distinct; but only that to be every man's, that he can get; and for so long, as he can keep it. And thus much for the ill condition, which man by mere nature is actually placed in; though with a possibility to come out of it, consisting partly in the passions, partly in his reason.

The passions that incline men to peace, are fear of death; desire of such things as are necessary to commodious living; and a hope by their industry to obtain them. And reason suggesteth convenient articles of peace, upon which men may be drawn to agreement. These articles, are they, which otherwise are called the laws of nature. * * *

Immanuel Kant
FROM *PERPETUAL PEACE*

The state of peace among men living in close proximity is not the natural state * * *; instead, the natural state is a one of war, which does not just consist in open hostilities, but also in the constant and enduring threat of them. The state of peace must therefore be *established,* for the suspension of hostilities does not provide the security of peace, and unless this security is pledged by one neighbor to another (which can happen only in a state of *lawfulness*), the latter, from whom such security has been requested, can treat the former as an enemy.

First Definitive Article of Perpetual Peace: The Civil Constitution of Every Nation Should Be Republican

The sole established constitution that follows from the idea * * * of an original contract, the one on which all of a nation's just * * * legislation must be based, is republican. For, first, it accords with the principles of the *freedom* of the members of a society (as men), second, it accords with the principles of the *dependence* of everyone on a single, common [source of] legislation (as subjects), and third, it

accords with the law of the equality of them all (as citizens). Thus, so far as [the matter of] right is concerned, republicanism is the original foundation of all forms of civil constitution. Thus, the only question remaining is this, does it also provide the only foundation for perpetual peace?

Now in addition to the purity of its origin, a purity whose source is the pure concept of right, the republican constitution also provides for this desirable result, namely, perpetual peace, and the reason for this is as follows: If (as must inevitably be the case, given this form of constitution) the consent of the citizenry is required in order to determine whether or not there will be war, it is natural that they consider all its calamities before committing themselves to so risky a game. (Among these are doing the fighting themselves, paying the costs of war from their own resources, having to repair at great sacrifice the war's devastation, and, finally, the ultimate evil that would make peace itself better, never being able—because of new and constant wars—to expunge the burden of debt.) By contrast, under a nonrepublican constitution, where subjects are not citizens, the easiest thing in the world to do is to declare war. Here the ruler is not a fellow citizen, but the nation's owner, and war does not affect his table, his hunt, his places of pleasure, his court festivals, and so on. Thus, he can decide to go to war for the most meaningless of reasons, as if it were a kind of pleasure party, and he can blithely leave its justification (which decency requires) to his diplomatic corps, who are always prepared for such exercises.

From Immanuel Kant, *Perpetual Peace and Other Essays on Politics, History, and Morals,* trans. Ted Humphrey (Indianapolis: Hackett Publishing Co., 1983), 107–17. The author's notes have been omitted.

Second Definitive Article for a Perpetual Peace: The Right of Nations Shall Be Based on a Federation of Free States

As nations, peoples can be regarded as single individuals who injure one another through their close proximity while living in the state of nature (i.e., independently of external laws). For the sake of its own security, each nation can and should demand that the others enter into a contract resembling the civil one and guaranteeing the rights of each. This would be a federation *of nations,* but it must not be a nation consisting of nations. The latter would be contradictory, for in every nation there exists the relation of *ruler* (legislator) to *subject* (those who obey, the people); however, many nations in a single nation would constitute only a single nation, which contradicts our assumption (since we are here weighing the rights of *nations* in relation to one another, rather than fusing them into a single nation).

Just as we view with deep disdain the attachment of savages to their lawless freedom—preferring to scuffle without end rather than to place themselves under lawful restraints that they themselves constitute, consequently preferring a mad freedom to a rational one—and consider it barbarous, rude, and brutishly degrading of humanity, so also should we think that civilized peoples (each one united into a nation) would hasten as quickly as possible to escape so similar a state of abandonment. Instead, however, each *nation* sees its majesty * * * to consist in not being subject to any external legal constraint, and the glory of its ruler consists in being able, without endangering himself, to command many thousands to sacrifice themselves for a matter that does not concern them. * * *

Given the depravity of human nature, which is revealed and can be glimpsed in the free relations among nations (though deeply concealed by governmental restraints in law governed civil-society), one must wonder why the word *right* has not been completely discarded from the politics of war as pedantic, or why no nation has openly ventured to declare that it should be. For while Hugo Grotius, Pufendorf, Vattel, and others whose philosophically and diplomatically formulated codes do not and cannot have the slightest legal force (since nations do not stand under any common external constraints), are always piously cited in justification of a war of aggression (and who therefore provide only cold comfort), no example can be given of a nation having foregone its intention [of going to war] based on the arguments provided by such important men. The homage that every nation pays (at least in words) to the concept of right proves, nonetheless, that there is in man a still greater, though presently dormant, moral aptitude to master the evil principle in himself (a principle he cannot deny) and to hope that others will also overcome it. For otherwise the word *right* would never leave the mouths of those nations that want to make war on one another, unless it were used mockingly, as when that Gallic prince declared, "Nature has given the strong the prerogative of making the weak obey them."

Nations can press for their rights only by waging war and never in a trial before an independent tribunal, but war and its favorable consequence, victory, cannot determine the right. And although a *treaty of peace* can put an end to some particular war, it cannot end the state of war (the tendency always to find a new pretext for war). (And this situation cannot straightforwardly be declared unjust, since in this circumstance each nation is judge of its own case.) * * * Nonetheless, from the throne of its moral legislative power, reason absolutely condemns war as a means of determining the right and makes seeking the state of peace a matter of unmitigated duty. But without a contract among nations peace can be neither inaugurated nor guaranteed. A league of a special sort must therefore be established, one that we can call a *league of peace* (*foedus pacificum*), which will be distinguished from a *treaty of peace* (*pactum pacis*) because the latter seeks merely to stop *one* war, while the former seeks to end *all* wars forever. This league does not seek any power of the sort possessed by nations, but only the maintenance and security of each nation's own freedom, as well as that of the other nations leagued with it, without their having thereby to subject themselves to civil laws and their constraints (as men in the state of nature must do). It can be shown that this *idea of federalism* should eventually include all nations and thus lead to perpetual peace. For if good fortune should so dispose matters that a powerful and enlightened people should form a republic (which by its nature must be inclined to seek perpetual peace), it will provide a focal point for a federal association among other nations that will join it in order to guarantee a state of peace among nations that is in accord with the idea of the right of nations, and through several associations of this sort such a federation can extend further and further.

Ted Hopf

THE PROMISE OF CONSTRUCTIVISM IN INTERNATIONAL RELATIONS THEORY

A challenger to the continuing dominance of neorealism and neoliberal institutionalism in the study of international relations in the United States, constructivism is regarded with a great deal of skepticism by mainstream scholars.[1] While the reasons for this reception are many, three central ones are the mainstream's miscasting of constructivism as necessarily postmodern and antipositivist; constructivism's own ambivalence about whether it can buy into mainstream social science methods without sacrificing its theoretical distinctiveness; and, related to this ambivalence, constructivism's failure to advance an alternative research program. In this article, I clarify constructivism's claims, outline the differences between "conventional" and "critical" constructivism, and suggest a research agenda that both provides alternative understandings of mainstream international relations puzzles and offers a few examples of what constructivism can uniquely bring to an understanding of world politics.

Constructivism offers alternative understandings of a number of the central themes in international relations theory, including: the meaning of anarchy and balance of power, the relationship between state identity and interest, an elaboration of power, and the prospects for change in world politics. Constructivism itself should be understood in its *conventional* and *critical* variants, the latter being more closely tied to critical social theory. The conventional constructivist desire to present an alternative to mainstream international relations theory requires a research program. Such a program includes constructivist reconceptualizations of balance-of-threat theory, the security dilemma, neoliberal cooperation theory, and the democratic peace. The constructivist research program has its own puzzles that concentrate on issues of identity in world politics and the theorization of domestic politics and culture in international relations theory.

Conventional Constructivism and Issues in Mainstream International Relations Theory

Since constructivism is best defined in relation to the issues it claims to apprehend, I present its position on several of the most significant themes in international relations theory today.

From *International Security* 23, no. 1 (Summer 1998): 171–200.

Actors and Structures Are Mutually Constituted

How much do structures constrain and enable the actions of actors, and how much can actors deviate from the constraints of structure? In world politics, a structure is a set of relatively unchangeable constraints on the behavior of states.[2] Although these constraints can take the form of systems of material dis/incentives, such as a balance of power or a market, as important from a constructivist perspective is how an action does or does not reproduce both the actor and the structure.[3] For example, to the extent that U.S. appeasement in Vietnam was unimaginable because of U.S. identity as a great power, military intervention constituted the United States as a great power. Appeasement was an unimaginable act. By engaging in the "enabled" action of intervention, the United States reproduced its own identity of great power, as well as the structure that gave meaning to its action. So, U.S. intervention in Vietnam perpetuated the international intersubjective understanding of great powers as those states that use military power against others.

Meaningful behavior, or action,[4] is possible only within an intersubjective social context. Actors develop their relations with, and understandings of, others through the media of norms and practices. In the absence of norms, exercises of power, or actions, would be devoid of meaning. Constitutive norms define an identity by specifying the actions that will cause Others to recognize that identity and respond to it appropriately.[5] Since structure is meaningless without some intersubjective set of norms and practices, anarchy, mainstream international relations theory's most crucial structural component, is meaningless. Neither anarchy, that is, the absence of any authority above the state, nor the distribution of capabilities, can "socialize" states to the desiderata of the international system's structure absent some set of meaningful norms and practices.[6]

A story many use in first-year international relations courses to demonstrate the structural extreme, that is, a situation where no agency is imaginable, illustrates the point. The scenario is a fire in a theater where all run for the exits.[7] But absent knowledge of social practices or constitutive norms, structure, even in this seemingly overdetermined circumstance, is still indeterminate. Even in a theater with just one door, while all run for that exit, who goes first? Are they the strongest or the disabled, the women or the children, the aged or the infirm, or is it just a mad dash? Determining the outcome will require knowing more about the situation than about the distribution of material power or the structure of authority. One will need to know about the culture, norms, institutions, procedures, rules, and social practices that constitute the actors and the structure alike.

Anarchy as an Imagined Community

Given that anarchy is structural, it must be mutually constituted by actors employing constitutive rules and social practices, implying that anarchy is as indeterminate as Arnold Wolfers's fire. Alexander Wendt has offered a constructivist critique of this fundamental structural pillar of mainstream international relations theory.[8] But still more fundamentally, this move opens the possibility of thinking of anarchy as having multiple meanings for different actors based on their own communities of intersubjective understandings and practices. And if multiple understandings of anarchy are possible, then one can begin to theorize about different domains and issue areas of international politics that are understood by actors as more, or less, anarchic.

Self-help, the neorealist inference that all states should prefer security independence whenever possible, is a structurally determined behavior of an actor only to the extent that a single particular understanding of anarchy prevails.[9] If the implications of anarchy are not constant across all relationships and issue areas of international politics, then a continuum of anarchies is possible. Where there are catastrophic consequences for not being able to rely on one's own capacity to enforce an agreement, such as arms control in a world of offensive military advantage, neorealist conceptualizations of anarchy are most apt. But where actors do not worry much about the potential costs of ceding control over outcomes to other states or institutions, such as in the enforcement of trade agreements, this is a realm of world politics where neorealist ideas of anarchy are just imaginary.

Identities and Interests in World Politics

Identities are necessary, in international politics and domestic society alike, in order to ensure at least some minimal level of predictability and order.[10] Durable expectations between states require intersubjective identities that are sufficiently stable to ensure predictable patterns of behavior. A world without identities is a world of chaos, a world of pervasive and irremediable uncertainty, a world much more dangerous than anarchy. Identities perform three necessary functions in a society: they tell you and others who you are and they tell you who others are.[11] In telling you who you are, identities strongly imply a particular set of interests or preferences with respect to choices of action in particular domains, and with respect to particular actors.

The identity of a state implies its preferences and consequent actions.[12] A state understands others according to the identity it attributes to them, while simultaneously reproducing its own identity through daily social practice. The crucial observation here is that the producer of the identity is not in control of what it ultimately means to others; the intersubjective structure is the final arbiter of meaning. For example, during the Cold War, Yugoslavia and other East European countries often understood the Soviet Union as Russia, despite the fact that the Soviet Union was trying hard not to have that identity. Soviet control over its own identity was structurally constrained not only by East European understanding, but also by daily Soviet practice, which of course included conversing with East Europeans in Russian.

Whereas constructivism treats identity as an empirical question to be theorized within a historical context, neorealism assumes that all units in global politics have only one meaningful identity, that of self-interested states. Constructivism stresses that this proposition exempts from theorization the very fundamentals of international political life, the nature and definition of the actors. The neorealist assumption of self-interest presumes to know, a priori, just what is the self being identified. In other words, the state in international politics, across time and space, is assumed to have a single eternal meaning. Constructivism instead assumes that the selves, or identities, of states are a variable; they likely depend on historical, cultural, political, and social context.

Constructivism and neorealism share the assumption that interests imply choices, but neorealism further assumes that states have the same a priori interests. Such a homogenizing assumption is possible only if one denies that interests are the products of the social practices that mutually constitute actors and structures.[13] Given that interests are the product of identity, that is, having the identity "great power" implies a particular set of interests different from those implied by the identity "European Union member," and that identities are multiple, constructivist logic precludes acceptance of pregiven interests.[14]

By making interests a central variable, constructivism explores not only how particular interests come to be, but also why many interests do not. The tautological, and therefore also true, most common, and unsatisfying explanation is that interests are absent where there is no reason for them, where promised gains are too meager. Constructivism, instead, theorizes about the meaning of absent interests. Just as identities and interests are produced through social practices, missing interests are understood by constructivists as produced absences, omissions that are the understandable product of social practices and structure. The social practices that constitute an identity cannot imply interests that are not consistent with the practices and structure that constitute that identity. At the extreme, an actor would not be able to imagine an absent interest, even if presented with it.[15]

The consequences of this treatment of interests and identities work in the same direction as constructivism's account of structure, agency, and anarchy: states are expected to have (1) a far wider array of potential choices of action before them than is assumed by neorealism, and (2) these choices will be constrained by social structures that are mutually created by states and structures via social practices. In other words, states have more agency under constructivism, but that agency is not in any sense unconstrained. To the contrary, choices are rigorously constrained by the webs of understanding of the practices, identities, and interests of other actors that prevail in particular historical contexts.

The Power of Practice

Power is a central theoretical element for both mainstream and constructivist approaches to international relations theory, but their conceptualizations of power are vastly different. Neorealism and neoliberal institutionalism assume that material power, whether military or economic or both, is the single most important source of influence and authority in global politics.[16] Constructivism argues that both material and discursive power are necessary for any understanding of world affairs. I emphasize both because often

constructivists are dismissed as unRealistic for believing in the power of knowledge, ideas, culture, ideology, and language, that is, discourse.[17] The notion that ideas are a form of power, that power is more than brute force, and that material and discursive power are related is not new. Michel Foucault's articulation of the power/knowledge nexus, Antonio Gramsci's theory of ideological hegemony, and Max Weber's differentiation of coercion from authority are all precursors to constructivism's position on power in political life.[18] Empirical work exists in both international relations theory and security studies that demonstrates the need to appreciate both the material and the discursive aspects of power.[19] Given that the operation of the material side of power is familiar from the mainstream literature, here I concentrate on the discursive side, the power of practice in constructivism.

The power of social practices lies in their capacity to reproduce the intersubjective meanings that constitute social structures and actors alike. The U.S. military intervention in Vietnam was consistent with a number of U.S. identities: great power, imperialist, enemy, ally, and so on. Others observing the United States not only inferred U.S. identity from its actions in Vietnam, but also reproduced the intersubjective web of meaning about what precisely constituted that identity. To the extent, for example, that a group of countries attributed an imperialist identity to the United States, the meaning of being an imperialist state was reproduced by the U.S. military intervention. In this way, social practices not only reproduce actors through identity, but also reproduce an intersubjective social structure through social practice. A most important power of practice is its capacity to produce predictability and so, order. Social practices greatly reduce uncertainty among actors within a socially structured community, thereby increasing confidence that what actions one takes will be followed by certain consequences and responses from others.[20]

An actor is not even able to act as its identity until the relevant community of meaning, to paraphrase Karl Deutsch,[21] acknowledges the legitimacy of that action, by that actor, in that social context. The power of practice is the power to produce intersubjective meaning within a social structure. It is a short step from this authorizing power of practice to an understanding of practice as a way of bounding, or disciplining interpretation, making some interpretations of reality less likely to occur or prevail within a particular community.[22] The meanings of actions of members of the community, as well as the actions of Others, become fixed through practice; boundaries of understanding become well known. In this way, the ultimate power of practice is to reproduce and police an intersubjective reality.[23] Social practices, to the extent that they authorize, discipline, and police, have the power to reproduce entire communities, including the international community, as well as the many communities of identity found therein.[24]

State actions in the foreign policy realm are constrained and empowered by prevailing social practices at home and abroad. Richard Ashley, for example, writes of a foreign policy choice as being a kind of social practice that at once constitutes and empowers the state, defines its socially recognized competence, and secures the boundaries that differentiate the domestic and international economic and political spheres of practice and, with them, the appropriate domains in which specific actors may secure recognition and act competently. Finally, Ashley concludes, foreign policy practice depends on the existence of intersubjective "precedents and shared symbolic materials— in order to impose interpretations upon events, silence alternative interpretations, structure practices, and orchestrate the collective making of history."[25]

Although I have necessarily concentrated on articulating how discursive power works in this section, the power to control intersubjective understanding is not the only form of power relevant to a constructivist approach to world politics. Having resources that allow oneself to deploy discursive power—the economic and military wherewithal to sustain institutions necessary for the formalized reproduction of social practices—is almost always part of the story as well.

Change in World Politics

Constructivism is agnostic about change in world politics.[26] It restores much variety and difference to world affairs and points out the practices by which intersubjective order is maintained, but it does not offer any more hope for change in world politics than neorealism. Constructivism's insight that anarchy is what states make of it, for example, implies that there are many different understandings of anarchy in the world, and so state actions should be more varied than only self-help. But this is an observation of already-existing reality, or, more precisely, a set of hypotheses about the same. These different understandings of anarchy are still rooted in social structures, maintained by the power of practice, and quite impervious to change. What constructivism does offer is an account of how and where change may occur.

One aspect of constructivist power is the power to reproduce, discipline, and police. When such power is realized, change in world politics is very hard indeed. These intersubjective structures, however, although difficult to challenge, are not impregnable. Alternative actors with alternative identities, practices, and sufficient material resources are theoretically capable of effecting change. Robert Cox's account of British and American supremacy, for example, perhaps best illustrates the extraordinary staying power of a well-articulated ideological hegemony, but also its possible demise. And Walker rightly observes that constructivism, to the extent that it surfaces diversity, difference, and particularity, opens up at least potential alternatives to the current prevailing structures.[27] Constructivism conceives of the politics of identity as a continual contest for control over the power necessary to produce meaning in a social group. So long as there is difference, there is a potential for change.

Thus, contrary to some critics[28] who assert that constructivism believes that change in world politics is easy, that "bad" neorealist structures need only be thought away, in fact constructivism appreciates the power of structure, if for no other reason than it assumes that actors reproduce daily their own constraints through ordinary practice. Constructivism's conceptualization of the relationship between agency and structure grounds its view that social change is both possible and difficult. Neorealism's position that all states are meaningfully identical denies a fair amount of possible change to its theoretical structure.

In sum, neorealism and constructivism share fundamental concerns with the role of structure in world politics, the effects of anarchy on state behavior, the definition of state interests, the nature of power, and the prospects for change. They disagree fundamentally, however, on each concern. Contra neorealism, constructivism assumes that actors and structures mutually constitute each other; anarchy must be interpreted to have meaning; state interests are part of the process of identity construction; power is both material and discursive; and change in world politics is both possible and difficult.

Constructivisms: Conventional and Critical

To the degree that constructivism creates theoretical and epistemological distance between itself and its origins in critical theory, it becomes "conventional" constructivism. Although constructivism shares many of the foundational elements of critical theory, it also resolves some issues by adopting defensible rules of thumb, or conventions, rather than following critical theory all the way up the postmodern critical path.[29] I situate constructivism in this way to highlight both its commonalities with traditional international relations theory and its differences with the critical theory with which it is sometimes misleadingly conflated.[30] Below I sketch out the relationship between conventional constructivism and critical social theory by identifying both those aspects of critical theory that constructivism has retained and those it has chosen to conventionalize. The result, conventional constructivism, is a collection of principles distilled from critical social theory but without the latter's more consistent theoretical or epistemological follow-through. Both critical and conventional constructivism are on the same side of the barricades in Yosef Lapid's characterization of the battle zone: the fixed, natural, unitary, stable, and essence-like, on the one (mainstream international relations theory) hand, and the emergent, constructed, contested, interactive, and process-like, on the other (constructivist) one.[31]

Conventional and critical constructivism do share theoretical fundamentals. Both aim to "denaturalize" the social world, that is, to empirically discover and reveal how the institutions and practices and identities that people take as natural, given, or matter of fact are, in fact, the product of human agency, of social construction.[32] Both believe that intersubjective reality and meanings are critical data for understanding the social world.[33] Both insist that all data must be "contextualized," that is, they must be related to, and situated within, the social environment in which they were gathered, in order to understand their meaning.[34] Both accept the nexus between power and knowledge, the power of practice in its disciplinary, meaning-producing, mode.[35] Both also accept the restoration of agency to human individuals. Finally, both stress the reflexivity of the self and society, that is, the mutual constitution of actor and structure.[36]

Perhaps where constructivism is most conventional is in the area of methodology and epistemology. The authors of the theoretical introduction to *The Culture of National Security*, for example, vigorously, and perhaps defensively, deny that their authors use "any special interpretivist methodology."[37] The authors are careful to stress that they do not depart from "normal science" in this volume, and none of the contributors either deviates from that ground or questions whether it is appropriate.[38] This position is anathema to critical theory which, as part of its constitutive epistemology, has a lengthy bill of particulars against positivism.

Conventional constructivism, while expecting to uncover differences, identities, and multiple understandings, still assumes that it can specify a set of conditions under which one can expect to see one identity or another. This is what Mark Hoffman has called "minimal foundationalism, accepting that a contingent universalism is possible and may be necessary." In contrast, critical theory rejects either the possibility or the desirability of a minimal or contingent foundationalism.[39] Ashley chides all noncritical approaches for "anticipating analysis coming to a close." In allowing for such premature closure, the analyst participates in the normalization or naturalization of what is being observed, and risks hiding the patterns of domination that might be revealed if closure could only be deferred.[40] To reach an intellectually satisfying point of closure, constructivism adopts positivist conventions about sample characteristics, methods of difference, process tracing, and spuriousness checks. In making this choice, critical theorists argue, constructivism can offer an understanding of social reality but cannot criticize the boundaries of its own understanding, and this is precisely what critical theory is all about.[41]

So, for example, Thomas Berger makes claims about Japanese and German national identities that imply a certain outcome for an indefinite period of time to come.[42] Such a claim requires the presumed nonexistence of relevant unobservables, as well as the assumption that the practices, institutions, norms, and power relations that underlay the production of those identities are somehow fixed or constant. Critical theorists would see this as an illusion of control; none of these factors can be so easily immobilized for either analysis or prediction.

This difference manifests itself as well in how critical and conventional constructivism understand identity. Conventional constructivists wish to discover identities and their associated reproductive social practices, and then offer an account of how those identities imply certain actions. But critical theorists have a different aim. They also wish to surface identities, not to articulate their effects, but to elaborate on how people come to believe in a single version of a naturalized truth. In other words, critical theory aims at exploding the myths associated with identity formation, whereas conventional constructivists wish to treat those identities as possible causes of action. Critical theory thus claims an interest in change, and a capacity to foster change, that no conventional constructivist could make.

In addition, and in a related vein, critical theorists self-consciously recognize their own participation in the reproduction, constitution, and fixing of the social entities they observe.[43] They realize that the actor and observer can never be separated. Conventional constructivists ignore this injunction, while largely adopting interpretivist understandings of the connectivity of subjects with other subjects in a web of intersubjective meaning. The observer never becomes a subject of the same self-reflective critical inquiry.

Conventional and critical constructivists also split over the origins of identity.[44] Whereas conventional constructivists accommodate a cognitive account for identity, or offer no account at all, critical constructivists are more likely to see some form of alienation driving the need for identity. As remarked above, conventional constructivism accepts the existence of identities and wants to understand their reproduction and effects, but critical constructivists use critical social theory to specify some understanding of the origin of identity.

Tzvetan Todorov and Ashis Nandy, for example, assume that European identities were incomplete (indeed, every self is incomplete without an other) until they encountered peoples in the Americas and India, respectively.[45] The necessity of difference with an other to produce one's own identity is found in Hegel's bondsman's tale, where the more powerful slaveowner can neither know his own identity nor exercise his superior power until his slave, his other, helps him construct that identity through practice. Perhaps conventional constructivism could accept this assumption: the need for others to construct oneself, but critical constructivism moves beyond this position with the aid of Nietzsche, Freud, and Lacan.[46] The former allows difference to reign, whereas the latter implies either the assimilation of the other, if deemed equal, or his oppression, if inferior.[47]

Critical theory's approach toward identity is rooted in assumptions about power.[48] Critical theorists see power being exercised in every social exchange, and there is always a dominant actor in that exchange. Unmasking these power relations is a large part of critical theory's substantive agenda; conventional constructivism, on the other hand, remains "analytically neutral" on the issue of power relations. Although conventional constructivists share the idea that power is everywhere, because they believe that social practices reproduce underlying power relations, they are not necessarily interested in interrogating those relations. Critical theory's assumption that all social relations are instances of hierarchy, subordination, or domination ironically appears similar to the expectations of realists and neorealists about world politics.[49] The different conceptualizations of power imply different theoretical agendas. Whereas conventional constructivism is aimed at the production of new knowledge and insights based on novel understandings, "critical theory analyzes social constraints and cultural understandings from a supreme human interest in enlightenment and emancipation."[50]

Although conventional and critical constructivism share a number of positions—mutual constitution of actors and structures, anarchy as a social construct, power as both material and discursive, and state identities and interests as variables—conventional constructivism does not accept critical theory's ideas about its own role in producing change and maintains a fundamentally different understanding of power.[51]

A Constructivist Research Agenda

This section aims at moving constructivism from the margins[52] by articulating a loosely Lakatosian research program for a constructivist study of international relations.[53] I present this research agenda in three sections. The first step is to show that constructivism offers competing understandings of some key puzzles from mainstream international relations theory. The second move is to suggest what new and innovative puzzles constructivism promises to raise. The last step is for constructivism to point out its own weaknesses.

Mainstream Puzzles, Constructivist Solutions

Constructivism can provide alternative accounts of the balance of threat, security dilemmas, neoliberal institutionalist accounts of cooperation under anarchy, and the liberal theory of the democratic peace.

BALANCE OF THREAT

Neorealism tells us that states ally against power. Steven Walt rightly observed that this is empirically wrong. He suggested, instead, that states ally against threats. The attempted fix was to claim that states will balance, not against power, but against particular kinds of power. The latter is the power possessed by a relatively capable, geographically proximate state with offensive military capabilities and perceived hostile intentions.[54] Whereas geographical proximity and offensive military capacity can be established a priori, perceived intentions threaten tautology. Several constructivist scholars have pointed to balance of threat as one of the mainstream accounts most susceptible to a constructivist alternative.[55] What is missing here is a theory of threat perception, and this is precisely what a constructivist account of identity offers.

Distribution of power cannot explain the alliance patterns that emerged after World War II; otherwise, the United States would have been balanced against, not the Soviet Union. Instead, the issue must be how France, Britain, Germany, and the United States came to understand Soviet military capabilities and geographical proximity as threatening. The neorealist account would be that the Soviet Union demonstrated by its behavior that it was an objective threat to Western Europe. A constructivist account would be that the state identities of Western Europe, the United States, and the Soviet Union, each rooted in domestic sociocultural milieus, produced understandings of one another based on differences in identity and practice. The potential advantage of this approach is that it is more likely to surface differences in how the Soviet threat was constructed in different sites than is the neorealist approach, which accords objective meaning to Soviet conduct.

Let us imagine, for example, that the United States balanced against the Soviet Union because of the latter's communist identity, and what that meant to the United States. If true, it means that other possible Soviet identities, such as an Asian, Stalinist, Russian, or authoritarian threat, were not operative. So what? First, how the United States understood the Soviet threat, as communist, not only explains the anticommunist direction of U.S. actions in the Cold War, but it also tells us that the United States understood itself as the anticommunist protector of a particular set of values both at home and abroad. Second, how the United States constructed the Soviet communist threat needs to be understood in relation to how Western Europeans understood that threat. If, for example, France understood the Soviet threat as a Russian threat, as an instance of superior Russian power in Europe, then France would not readily join in U.S. anticommunist ventures against the Soviet Union. In particular, whereas the United States saw the third world during the Cold War as an arena for battling communism, as in Vietnam, Europeans very rarely understood it in those terms, instead regarding third world states as economic actors or as former colonies.

SECURITY DILEMMAS

Security dilemmas are the products of presumed uncertainty.[56] They are assumed to be commonplace in world politics because states presumably cannot know, with sufficient certainty or confidence, the intentions of others. But as important as the security dilemma is to understanding conflictual relations among states, we do not see much evidence of security dilemmas among many pairs or groups of states: members of the same alliance, members of the same economic institution, perhaps two peaceful states or two neutral states, and so on. In the study of world politics, uncertainty might be best treated as a variable, not a constant. Constructivism can provide an understanding of what happens most of the time in relations between states, namely, nothing threatening at all. By providing meaning, identities reduce uncertainty.[57]

States understand different states differently. Soviet and French nuclear capabilities had different meanings for British decision makers. But of course certainty is not always a source of security. Knowing that another state is an aggressor resolves the security dilemma, but only by replacing it with certain insecurity, an increased confidence that the other state is in fact threatening. As Richard Ashley, bowing generously to Karl Deutsch, pointed out, politics itself is impossible in the absence of "a background of mutual understandings and habitual practices that orients and limits the mutual comprehension of practices, the signification of social action."[58] Constructivism's empirical mission is to surface the "background" that makes uncertainty a variable to understand, rather than a constant to assume.

NEOLIBERAL COOPERATION

Neoliberalism offers compelling arguments about how states can achieve cooperation among themselves. Simple iterative interaction among states, even when they prefer to exploit one another, may still lead to cooperative outcomes. The conditions minimally necessary for such outcomes include transparency of action, capacity to monitor any noncooperative behavior and punish the same in a predictable fashion, a sufficiently low discount (high appreciation) rate for future gains from the relationship, and an expectation that the relationship will not end in the foreseeable future.[59]

International institutions, whether in the form of regimes, laws, treaties, or organizations, help provide these necessary conditions for cooperation. By having rules about what constitutes a violation of a relationship, institutions help increase the confidence of each state that it will not be exploited and that its own cooperative move will be reciprocated. By establishing formal mechanisms of surveillance, institutions enable states to see what other states are doing, again enhancing confidence that a defection will be seen and a cooperative action will be followed by the same. By creating rules and procedures for surveillance and sanction, all parties can have greater confidence that violations will be punished. By formalizing these relationships, institutions help reduce each state's discount rate for future gains while increasing each state's expectation that the relationship will continue into the future.[60]

Constructivism shares neoliberalism's conclusion that cooperation is possible under anarchy, but offers a very different account of how that outcome emerges. Robert Keohane presents as the heart of neoliberalism two fundamental assumptions: there are potentially beneficial agreements among states that have not been reached, and they are hard to achieve.[61] A constructivist approach might begin by investigating how states understand their interests within a particular issue area. The distribution of identities and interests of the relevant states would then help account for whether cooperation is possible. The assumption of exogenous interests is an obstacle to developing a theory of cooperation.

Sitting down to negotiate a trade agreement among friends (as opposed to adversaries or unknowns) affects a state's willingness to lead with a cooperative move. Perhaps it would no longer understand its interests as the unilateral exploitation of the other state. Instead it might see itself as a partner in pursuit of some value other than narrow strategic interest. In *Logic of Collective Action*, Mancur Olson bracketed a host of situations where cooperation was relatively easy, despite large numbers of players, the absence of a group large enough to provide a public good, but sufficiently small to avert coordination problems (a *k*-group), no hegemonic leadership, and so on. These were situations where communities of identity existed such that the players were not in a noncooperative game in the first place. Too little attention has been paid to this insight. A constructivist account of cooperation would reconstruct such intersubjective communities as a matter of course.

When a neoliberal writes of difficulty in reaching an agreement, she usually has one particular problem in mind: uncertainty. Many of the institutional mechanisms described above are aimed at reducing uncertainty among states: provision of transparency; facilitation of iteration; enabling of decomposition; and of course the development of rules, monitoring capabilities, and adjudication procedures. A constructivist would agree that these are all very important, but that a prior issue must be raised: Is it not likely that the level of certainty is a variable associated with identity and practice, and that, ceteris paribus, the less certainty one has, the more institutional devices are necessary to produce cooperation, the harder that cooperation will be to achieve, and the more likely it will be to break down?

Neoliberalism has concluded that an important part of ensuring compliance with agreements is the development of reputations for reliability.[62] One of the most important components of discursive power is the capacity to reproduce order and predictability in understandings and expectations. In this respect, identities are a congealed reputation, that is, the closest one can get in social life to being able to confidently expect the same actions from another actor time after time. Identities subsume reputation; being a particular identity is sufficient to provide necessary diagnostic information about a state's likely actions with respect to other states in particular domains.[63]

On the other side of the life cycle, neoliberals argue that institutions die when members no longer "have incentives to maintain them."[64] But one of the more enduring puzzles for neoliberals is why these institutions persist past the point that great powers have an apparent interest in sustaining them. Their answers include lags caused by domestic political resistance to adjustment, the stickiness of institutional arrangements, and the transaction costs entailed in the renegotiation of agreements and the establishment of a new order.[65] An alternative constructivist hypothesis would be that if the identities being reproduced by the social practices constituting that institution have gone beyond the strategic game-playing self-regarding units posited by neoliberals, and have developed an understanding of each other as partners in some common enterprise, then the

institution will persist, even if apparent underlying power and interests have shifted.[66] Duncan Snidal, in his formal representation of what is most likely to happen as a hegemon falters, includes as an untheorized variable "interest in the regime," with the obvious positive relationship between interest in the regime and willingness to expend resources to maintain it after hegemonic decline.[67] Constructivist research, through exploring the nature of the norms, practices, and identities constituting membership in some institution, can provide some measurable substantive content for that variable.

Although constructivists and neoliberals agree that anarchy does not preclude cooperation among states, how they understand the emergence and reproduction of such cooperation yields very different accounts and research agendas.

THE DEMOCRATIC PEACE

The observation that democratic states have not fought each other is an empirical regularity in search of a theory. Neither structural nor normative accounts fare very well.[68] The former requires assuming a consistently bellicose executive being constrained by a pacific public and its duly-elected representative institutions—but only when democratic adversaries are about. The latter has more promise, but its naturalization of certain aspects of liberalism—the market, nonviolent resolution of differences, the franchise, the First Amendment—and its crucial assumption that these norms actually matter to decision makers in democratic states when making choices about war and peace with other democracies, are untenable and untested, respectively.

Constructivism is perfectly suited to the task of testing and fundamentally revising the democratic peace.[69] Its approach aims at apprehending how the social practices and norms of states construct the identities and interests of the same. Ergo, if democracies do not fight each other, then it must be because of the way they understand each other, their intersubjective accounts of each other, and the socio-international practices that accompany those accounts.[70] But constructivism could offer a more general account of zones of peace, one not limited to democracies. Different periods of the histories of both Africa and Latin America have been marked by long stretches of little or no warfare between states. These pacific periods are obviously not associated with any "objective" indicators of democracy. By investigating how African and Latin American states constructed themselves and others, it might be possible to understand these neglected zones of "authoritarian peace."

Constructivist Puzzles

Constructivism offers an account of the politics of identity.[71] It proposes a way of understanding how nationalism, ethnicity, race, gender, religion, and sexuality, and other intersubjectively understood communities, are each involved in an account of global politics. Understanding how identities are constructed, what norms and practices accompany their reproduction, and how they construct each other is a major part of the constructivist research program.

Although nationalism and ethnicity are receiving more attention in mainstream international relations theory, attention to gender, sexuality, race, and religion have received much less, and certainly none of them is part of either neorealist or neoliberal accounts of how the world works.[72] Constructivism promises to deal with these issues, not merely because they are topical or heretofore undervalued, but because as varieties of identity, they are central to how constructivism generates understandings of social phenomena. Constructivism assumes, a priori, that identities are potentially part of the constitutive practices of the state, and so, productive of its actions at home and abroad.[73]

One of the most important by-products of this concern with identity politics is the return of differences among states. The same state is, in effect, many different actors in world politics, and different states behave differently toward other states, based on the identities of each. If true, then we should expect different patterns of behavior across groups of states with different identities and interests.[74] Although it is tempting to assert that similarity breeds cooperation, it is impossible to make such an a priori claim. Identities have much more meaning for each state than a mere label. Identities offer each state an understanding of other states, its nature, motives, interests, probable actions, attitudes, and role in any given political context.

Understanding another state as one identity, rather than another, has consequences for the possible actions of both. For example, Michael Barnett has speculated that the failure of deterrence against Iraq in Kuwait in 1990 is because Saudi Arabia was seen as an "Arab," rather than a "sovereign," state. Iraq's understanding of Saudi Arabia as an Arab state implied that Riyadh would never allow U.S. forces to deploy on Arab territory. If, instead, Iraq had understood Saudi Arabia as a sovereign state, in a realist world, it would have perhaps expected Saudi balancing against Iraqi actions in Kuwait, including U.S. military intervention, and would have been deterred.[75] In other words, neorealist predictions of balancing behavior, such as that of Saudi Arabia, rely on a single particular identity being ascribed to that country by Iraq. But if alternative identities are possible, as constructivism suggests, the neorealist world is smaller than alleged.

Or another state may not be seen as another "state" at all, but instead as an ally, friend, enemy, co-guarantor, threat, a democracy, and so on.[76] Finally, constructivism's expectation of multiple identities for actors in world politics rests on an openness to local historical context. This receptivity to identities being generated and reproduced empirically, rather than resting on pregiven assumptions, opens up the study of world politics to different units altogether.[77] Hypothesizing differences among states allows for movement beyond the typical binary characterizations of mainstream international relations: democratic-nondemocratic, great power–non-great power, North-South, and so forth. While these common axes of analysis are certainly relevant, constructivism promises to explain many other meaningful communities of identity throughout world politics.

A third constructivist promise is to return culture and domestic politics to international relations theory. To the extent that constructivism is ontologically agnostic—that is, it does not include or exclude any particular variables as meaningful—it envisions no disciplinary divides between international relations and comparative subfields (or any fields for that matter). Constructivism has no inherent focus on "second image" accounts of world politics. In fact, an appropriate criticism would be that it has remained far too long at the systemic level of analysis.[78] Nevertheless, constructivism provides a promising approach for uncovering those features of domestic society, culture, and politics that should matter to state identity and state action in global politics. There are many different ways in which a constructivist account can operate at the domestic level. I mention only several here.

Any state identity in world politics is partly the product of the social practices that constitute that identity at home.[79] In this way, identity politics at home constrain and enable state identity, interests, and actions abroad. Ashis Nandy has written about the close connection between Victorian British generational and gender identities at home and the colonization of India. Victorian Britain drew a very strict line between the sexes and also between generations, differentiating the latter into young and old, productive and unproductive, respectively. British colonial dominance was understood as masculine in relationship to Indian's feminine submission, and Indian culture was understood as infantile and archaic. In these ways Victorian understandings of itself made India comprehensible to Britain in a particular way.[80] Whereas conventional accounts of colonialism and imperialism rely on disparities in relative material power to explain relations of domination and subordination, constructivists would add that no account of such hierarchical outcomes is complete without exploring how imperial identities are constructed both at home and with respect to the subordinated Other abroad.[81] Even if material power is necessary to produce imperialism, its reproduction cannot be understood without investigating the social practices that accompanied it and the discursive power, especially in the form of related identities, they wielded.

Within the state itself might exist areas of cultural practice, sufficiently empowered through institutionalization and authorization, to exert a constitutive or causative influence on state policy.[82] The state's assumed need to construct a national identity at home to legitimize the state's extractive authority has effects on state identity abroad. A more critical constructivist account might begin by positing the state's need for an Other in world politics, so as to justify its own rule at home.[83]

A last promise of constructivism concerns not so much research issues as research strategy. Constructivism offers a heterogamous research approach: that is, it readily combines with different fields and disciplines. Constructivism itself is the product of structural linguistics, postmodern political theory, critical theory, cultural and media studies, literary criticism, and no doubt others. Far from claiming primacy as a theory of international politics, constructivism lends itself to collaboration with other approaches, both within political science and outside. Literatures in decision making, political culture, socialization, and experimental cognitive and social psychology would seem to be most promising partners.

Constructivist Problems

A constructivist research program, like all others, has unexplained anomalies, but their existence need not necessitate the donning of protective belts of any sort. Conventional constructivism has one large problem that has several parts. Friedrich Kratochwil has observed that no theory of culture can substitute for a theory of politics.[84] Paul Kowert and Jeffrey Legro have pointed out that there is no causal theory of identity construction offered by any of the authors in the Katzenstein volume.[85] Both criticisms are as accurate as they are different, and imply different remedies.

Kratochwil's statement reinforces the point that constructivism is an approach, not a theory. And if it is a theory, it is a theory of process, not substantive outcome. In order to achieve the latter, constructivism must adopt some theory of politics to make it work. Critical theory is far more advanced in this regard than conventional constructivism, but it comes at a price, a price that one may or may not be willing to pay, depending on empirical, theoretical, and/or aesthetic interests. I have described how differently critical and conventional constructivism treat the origins of identity and the nature of power. It is here that critical theory finds its animating theory of politics. By assuming that the identities of the Self and Other are inextricably bound up in a relationship of power, and that the state is a dominating instrument, critical theorists can offer theoretically informed accounts of the politics of identity: at least along the dimensions specified, that of hierarchy, subordination, domination, emancipation, and state-society struggle.

The price paid for such theories of politics, however, is an ironic one that naturalizes certain "realities," privileging social relations of dominance and hierarchy. Of course, critical theory asserts its ultimate openness to variation and change, but the point here is that its theory of politics, a priori, is more closed than that of its conventional version, which stands accused of theoretical underspecification. The problem of underspecification exists because conventional constructivism, as a theory of process, does not specify the existence, let alone the precise nature or value, of its main causal/constitutive elements: identities, norms, practices, and social structures. Instead, constructivism specifies how these elements are theoretically situated vis-à-vis each other, providing an understanding of a process and an outcome, but no a priori prediction per se. The advantages of such an approach are in the nonpareil richness of its elaboration of causal/constitutive mechanisms in any given social context and its openness (and not just in the last instance, as in critical theory) to the discovery of other substantive theoretical elements at work. The cost here, however, is the absence of a causal theory of identity.

The dilemma is that the more conventional constructivism moves to furnish such a causal theory, the more it loses the possibility of maintaining the ontological openness that its interpretivist methods afford. But the dilemma is a continuum, not a binary opposition. Conventional constructivists can and do specify their theoretical elements in advance in practice. Just to take one example, not a single author in the Katzenstein volume assessed gender, class, or race in any of their analyses. This observation (not criticism) is intended to underline how conventional constructivists already bound their a priori theoretical domains according to empirical interest and theoretical priors. Moreover, conventional constructivists can make predictions, if they choose. Their only constraint is just how durable they believe the social structures to be that they have demonstrated are constraining the reproduction of identities, interests, norms, and practices, in some social context. For example, when Risse-Kappen argues that North Atlantic Treaty Organization (NATO) members regard each other as liberal allies, rather than as realist states balancing against a threat, he is making a prediction: if NATO members see each other as liberal allies, NATO will persist beyond the point where the threat disappears.

One obstacle to the development of a causal model of identity is conventional constructivism's silence on the issue of intentionality. Critical theorists confidently declare their indifference to the issue: establishing causality is an illusory goal. Kowert and Legro point out the failure of any author in the Katzenstein volume to establish more than a correlative relationship between an identity and an outcome. In fact, the authors do far more than that: they control for alternative explanations and they show the connection between norms and interests and outcomes. But what is missing is the decision based on the identity. Here again, constructivist heterogamy allows for an attempted fix. The answer may lie in trying to marry constructivist process to psychological process. Kowert and Legro discuss the possibility in terms of the experimental social psychological work of Marilyn Brewer and Jonathan Turner.[86] To the extent it is possible to establish a causal link between a particular identity, such as Japanese antimilitarism, and an interest in opposing Japanese military expenditures (or between belief in a norm, such as humanitarian interventionism, and an action to fulfill that norm), it might be attainable through ongoing work on the connection between identity and behavior in social psychology.

The last problem with constructivism is really not so much a problem as it is an advantage. Constructivism's theory of process and commitment to interpretivist thick description place extraordinary demands on the researcher to gather mountains of elaborate empirical data. To reconstruct the operation of identity politics, even in a limited domain for a short period, requires thousands of pages of reading, months of interviews and archival research, and a host of less conventional activities, such as riding public transportation, standing in lines, and going to bars and cafés to participate in local practices. (The latter need not be so onerous.) The point here is that the evidence necessary to develop an understanding of, say, a national identity, its relation to domestic identities, the practices that constitute both, implied interests of each, and the overall social structure is necessarily vast and varied. Constructivism is no shortcut.

The Constructivist Promise

The assumptions that underlay constructivism account for its different understanding of world politics. Since actors and structures are mutually constructed, state behavior in the face of different distributions of power or anarchy is unknowable absent a reconstruction of the intersubjective meaning of these structures and actors. Since actors have multiple identities, and these identities imply different interests, the a priori and exogenous attribution of identical interests to states is invalid. Since power is both material and discursive, patterned behavior over time should be understood as a result of material or economic power working in concert with ideological structures, social practices, institutionalized norms, and intersubjective webs of meaning. The greatest power of all is that which disciplines actors to naturally imagine only those actions that reproduce the underlying arrangements of power—material and discursive. Since constructivist social structures are both enduring and mutable, change in world politics is considered both difficult and possible.

A conventional constructivist recasting of mainstream international relations puzzles is based on the implications of its assumptions. Since what constitutes a threat can never be stated as an a priori, primordial constant, it should be approached as a social construction of an Other, and theorized at that level. Since identities, norms, and social practices reduce uncertainty, the security dilemma should not be the starting point for analyzing relations among states. Since states are already situated in multiple social contexts, any account of (non)cooperation among them should begin by exploring how their understandings of each other generate their relevant interests. Since communities of identity are expected to exist, patterns of behavior that spur scholars to consider a liberal peace should instead provoke us to consider zones of peace more generally.

A conventional constructivist account of politics operates between mainstream international relations and critical theory. Conventional constructivism rejects the mainstream presumption that world politics is so homogenous that universally valid generalizations can be expected to come of theorizing about it. It denies the critical constructivist position that world politics is so heterogeneous that we should presume to look for only the unique and the differentiating. Contrary to both these two approaches, conventional constructivism presumes we should be looking for communities of intersubjectivity in world politics, domains within which actors share understandings of themselves and each other, yielding predictable and replicable patterns of action within a specific context.

Mainstream international relations theory treats world politics as an integrated whole, undifferentiated by either time or territory. Critical theory regards world politics as an array of fragments that can never add up to a whole, and regards efforts to construct such a whole as a political move to impose some kind of rationalistic, naturalized order on irrepressible difference. Conventional constructivism, on the other hand, regards the world as a complicated and vast array of different domains, the apprehension of all of which could never yield a fully coherent picture of international politics. The failure to account for any one of them, however, will guarantee a theoretically unsatisfying understanding of the world. In effect, the promise of constructivism is to restore a kind of partial order and predictability to world politics that derives not from imposed homogeneity, but from an appreciation of difference.

NOTES

1. The canonical neorealist work remains Kenneth N. Waltz, *Theory of International Politics* (Reading, Mass.: Addison-Wesley, 1979). The debate between neorealism and neoliberal institutionalism is presented and summarized in David A. Baldwin, ed., *Neorealism and Neoliberalism* (New York: Columbia University Press, 1993). Constructivist challenges can be found in Nicholas Greenwood Onuf, *World of Our Making: Rules and Rule in Social Theory and International Relations* (Columbia: University of South Carolina Press, 1989); Peter J. Katzenstein, ed., *The Culture of National Security: Norms and Identity in World Politics* (New York: Columbia University Press, 1996); and Yosef Lapid and Friedrich V. Kratochwil, eds., *The Return of Culture and Identity in IR Theory* (Boulder, Colo.: Lynne Rienner, 1996).

2. Most important for this article, this is the neorealist conceptualization of international structure. All references to neorealism, unless otherwise noted, are from Waltz, *Theory of International Politics*.

3. Friedrich Kratochwil suggests that this difference in the understanding of structure is because structuralism entered international relations theory not through sociolinguistics, but through microeconomics. Friedrich V. Kratochwil, "Is the Ship of Culture at Sea or Returning?" in Lapid and Kratochwil, *The Return of Culture and Identity*, p. 211.

4. The critical distinction between action and behavior is made by Charles Taylor, "Interpretation and the Sciences of Man," in Paul Rabinow and William M. Sullivan, eds., *Interpretive Social Science: A Second Look* (Berkeley: University of California Press, 1987), pp. 33–81.

5. Ronald L. Jepperson, Alexander Wendt, and Peter J. Katzenstein, "Norms, Identity, and Culture in National Security," in Katzenstein, *The Culture of National Security*, p. 54.

6. David Dessler, "What's At Stake in the Agent-Structure Debate?" *International Organization*, Vol. 43, No. 3 (Summer 1989), pp. 459–460.

7. Arnold Wolfers, *Discord and Collaboration* (Baltimore, Md.: Johns Hopkins University Press, 1962).

8. Alexander Wendt, "Anarchy Is What States Make of It: The Social Construction of Power Politics," *International Organization*, Vol. 46, No. 2 (Spring 1992), 391–425.

9. Elizabeth Kier, for example, shows how the same "objective" external structural arrangement of power cannot account for French military strategy between the two world wars. Elizabeth Kier, "Culture and French Military Doctrine before World War II," in Katzenstein, *The Culture of National Security*, pp. 186–215.

10. The focus on identity does not reflect a lack of appreciation for other elements in the constructivist approach, such as norms, culture, and institutions. Insofar as identities are the most proximate causes of choices, preferences, and action, I concentrate on them, but with the full recognition that identities cannot be understood without a simultaneous account of normative, cultural, and institutional context.

11. Henri Tajfel, *Human Groups and Social Categories: Studies in Social Psychology* (Cambridge, U.K.: Cambridge University Press, 1981), p. 255. Although there are many accounts of the origin of identity,

I offer a cognitive explanation because it has minimal a priori expectations, assuming only that identities are needed to reduce complexity to some manageable level.

12. Dana Eyre and Mark Suchman, for example, find that, controlling for rational strategic need, domestic coalition politics, and superpower manipulation, countries in the third world prefer certain weapons systems over others because of their understanding of what it means to be "modern" in the twentieth century. Dana P. Eyre and Mark C. Suchman, "Status, Norms, and the Proliferation of Conventional Weapons: An Institutional Theory Approach," in Katzenstein, *The Culture of National Security*, pp. 73–113. Other examples of empirical research that have linked particular identities to particular sets of preferences are "civilized" identities driving attitudes toward weapons of mass destruction; notions of what constitutes "humanitarian" shaping decisions to intervene in other states; the identity of a "normal" state implying particular Soviet foreign policies; and "antimilitarist" identities in Japan and German shaping their post–World War II foreign policies. These arguments can be found in Richard Price and Nina Tannenwald, "Norms and Deterrence: The Nuclear and Chemical Weapons Taboos," pp. 114–152; Martha Finnemore, "Constructing Norms of Humanitarian Intervention," pp. 153–185; Robert Herman, "Identity, Norms, and National Security: The Soviet Foreign Policy Revolution and the End of the Cold War," pp. 271–316; and Thomas U. Berger, "Norms, Identity, and National Security in Germany and Japan," pp. 317–356. All of the above are in Katzenstein, *The Culture of National Security*. On identity and mutual intelligibility, see Roxanne Lynn Doty, "The Bounds of 'Race' in International Relations," *Millennium: Journal of International Studies*, Vol. 22, No. 3 (Winter 1993), p. 454.

13. Robert Keohane calls the failure to contextualize interests one of the major weaknesses of mainstream international relations theory. Robert O. Keohane, "International Institutions: Two Approaches," *International Studies Quarterly*, Vol. 32, No. 4 (December 1988), pp. 390–391.

14. Jeffrey Legro, for example, has shown how the preferences of great powers before and during World War II with respect to the use and nonuse of strategic bombing, and chemical and submarine warfare, are unfathomable without first understanding the identities of the military organizations responsible for shaping those preferences. Jeffrey W. Legro, "Culture and Preferences in the International Cooperation Two-Step," *American Political Science Review*, Vol. 90, No. 1 (March 1996), pp. 118–137.

15. See, for example, Tannenwald, "Norms and Deterrence," and Kier, "Culture and French Military Doctrine before World War II," p. 203. For a brilliant account of how social structure enables and impedes the construction of identity and interest, see Jane K. Cowan, "Going Out for Coffee? Contesting the Grounds of Gendered Pleasures in Everyday Sociability," in Peter Loizos and Evthymios Papataxiarchis, eds., *Contested Identities: Gender and Kinship in Modern Greece* (Princeton, N.J.: Princeton University Press, 1991), pp. 196–197.

16. A rare effort in the mainstream literature to break away from this focus on material power is Judith Goldstein and Robert O. Keohane, eds., *Ideas and Foreign Policy* (Ithaca, N.Y.: Cornell University Press, 1993).

17. As R.B.J. Walker has clarified, "To suggest that culture and ideology are crucial for the analysis of world politics is not necessarily to take an idealist position. . . . On the contrary, it is important to recognize that ideas, consciousness, culture, and ideology are bound up with more immediately visible kinds of political, military, and economic power." In R.B.J. Walker, "East Wind, West Wind: Civilizations, Hegemonies, and World Orders," in Walker, ed., *Culture, Ideology, and World Order* (Boulder, Colo.: Westview Press, 1984), p. 3. See also Onuf, *World of Our Making*, p. 64. Joseph Nye's conceptualization of "soft" power could be usefully read through a constructivist interpretation. See Joseph S. Nye, Jr., *Bound to Lead: The Changing Nature of American Power* (New York: Basic Books, 1991), esp. pp. 173–201.

18. Colin Gordon, ed., *Power/Knowledge: Selected Interviews and Other Writings, 1972–1997, by Michel Foucault* (Brighton, Sussex, U.K.: Harvester Press, 1980); Antonio Gramsci, *Selections from the Prison Notebooks*, trans. and ed., Quinton Hoare and Geoffrey Nowell Smith (New York: International Publishers, 1992); and Max Weber, *From Max Weber*, ed., Hans Gerth and C. Wright Mills (New York: Oxford University Press, 1946).

19. Price and Tannenwald show that even power as material as nuclear missiles and chemical artillery had to be understood and interpreted before it had any meaning. In Price and Tannenwald, "Norms and Deterrence." Robert Cox has provided an account of the rise, reproduction, and demise of nineteenth-century British supremacy, and the rise and reproduction of U.S. dominance in the twentieth century through a close reading of the interaction between material and discursive power. Robert W. Cox, "Social Forces, States, and World Orders: Beyond International Relations Theory," *Millennium: Journal of International Studies*, Vol. 10, No. 1 (Spring 1981), pp. 126–155.

20. Onuf sees these reproducible patterns of action as the product of "reflexive self-regulation," whereby agents refer to their own and other's past and anticipated actions in deciding how to act. Onuf, *World of Our Making*, p. 62.

21. Karl W. Deutsch, *Nationalism and Social Communication: An Inquiry into the Foundations of Nationality* (New York: MIT Press, 1953), pp. 60–80. Deutsch was a constructivist long ahead of his time to the extent that he argued that individuals could not engage in meaningful action absent some community-wide intersubjectivity. Another work constructivist in essence is Robert Jervis's *The Logic of Images in International Relations* (Princeton, N.J.: Princeton University Press, 1970). Applying Erving Goffmann's self-presentation theory to international politics, Jervis pointed out that state actions, such as gunboat diplomacy, were meaningless unless situated in a larger intersubjective community of diplomatic practice.

22. See Doty, "The Bounds of Race," p. 454; and Carol Cohn, "Sex and Death in the Rational World of Defense Intellectuals," *Signs: Journal of Women in Culture and Society*, Vol. 12, No. 32 (Summer 1987), pp. 687–718.

23. See Richard K. Ashley, "Untying the Sovereign State: A Double Reading of the Anarchy Problématique," *Millennium: Journal of International Studies*, Vol. 17, No. 2 (Summer 1988), p. 243, for a discussion of this process.

24. Richard K. Ashley, "The Geopolitics of Geopolitical Space: Toward a Critical Social Theory of International Politics," *Alternatives*, Vol. 12, No. 4 (October–December 1987), p. 409.

25. Richard K. Ashley, "Foreign Policy as Political Performance," *International Studies Notes* (1988), p. 53.

26. Critical constructivism denies this vigorously.

27. R.B.J. Walker, "Realism, Change, and International Political Theory," *International Studies Quarterly*, Vol. 31, No. 1 (March 1987), pp. 76–77.

28. See, for example, John J. Mearsheimer, "The False Promise of International Institutions," *International Security*, Vol. 19, No. 1 (Winter 1994/1995), pp. 5–49, esp. 37–47.

29. Jepperson, Wendt, and Katzenstein differentiate the kind of "sociological" analysis performed in their volume from the "radical constructivist position" of Richard Ashley, David Campbell, R.B.J. Walker, and Cynthia Weber. See Jepperson, Wendt, and Katzenstein, "Norms, Identity, and Culture," p. 46, notes 41 and 42.

30. As, for example, in Mearsheimer, "The False Promise of International Institutions," wherein constructivism, reflectivism, postmodernism, and poststructuralism are all reduced to "critical theory," p. 37, note 128.

31. Yosef Lapid, "Culture's Ship: Returns and Departures in International Relations Theory," in Lapid and Kratochwil, *The Return of Culture and Identity*, pp. 3–20.

32. Mark Hoffman, "Critical Theory and the Inter-Paradigm Debate," *Millennium: Journal of International Studies*, Vol. 16, No. 2 (Summer 1987), pp. 233–236.

33. Ashley, "The Geopolitics of Geopolitical Space," p. 403.

34. In this respect, both critical and conventional constructivism can be understood as sharing an interpretivist epistemology, more generally. See Taylor, "Interpretation and the Sciences of Man."

35. James Der Derian, *On Diplomacy. A Genealogy of Western Estrangement* (Oxford, U.K.: Basil Blackwell, 1987), p. 4.

36. R.B.J. Walker, "World Politics and Western Reason: Universalism, Pluralism, Hegemony," in Walker, *Culture, Ideology, and World Order*, p. 195; and Ashley, "The Geopolitics of Geopolitical Space," pp. 409–410.

37. Jepperson, Wendt, and Katzenstein, "Norms, Identity, and Culture," p. 67.

38. The only, even partial, exceptions are Price and Tannenwald, "Norms and Deterrence," and Michael N. Barnett, "Institutions, Roles, and Disorder: The Case of the Arab States System," *International Studies Quarterly*, Vol. 37, No. 3 (September 1993), pp. 271–296.

39. Mark Hoffman, "Restructuring, Reconstruction, Reinscription, Rearticulation: Four Voices in Critical International Theory," *Millennium: Journal of International Studies*, Vol. 20, No. 1 (Spring 1991), p. 170. David Campbell argues that no identity (or any other theoretical element for that matter) may be allowed to be fixed or final. It must be critically deconstructed as soon as it acquires a meaning. David Campbell, "Violent Performances: Identity, Sovereignty, Responsibility," in Lapid and Kratochwil, *The Return of Culture and Identity*, pp. 164–166. See also Stephen J. Rosow, "The Forms of Internationalization: Representation of Western Culture on a Global Scale," *Alternatives*, Vol. 15, No. 3 (July–September 1990), p. 289, for differences on this issue.

40. Ashley, "The Geopolitics of Geopolitical Space," p. 408.

41. Hoffman, "Restructuring, Reconstruction, Reinscription, Rearticulation," p. 232.

42. Berger, "Norms, Identity, and National Security in Germany and Japan."

43. Cynthia Weber points this out as a very important distinction between her approach to the state and more modernist approaches. Weber similarly separates conventional constructivists from critical theorists. Max Weber, *Simulating Sovereignty: Intervention, the State, and Symbolic Exchange* (Cambridge, U.K.: Cambridge University Press, 1995), p. 3.

44. For a review of this issue see Friedrich Kratochwil, "Is the Ship of Culture at Sea or Returning?" pp. 206–210.

45. The discussion of the work of Todorov and Nandy is in Naeem Inayatullah and David L. Blaney, "Knowing Encounters: Beyond Parochialism in International Relations Theory," in Lapid and Kratochwil, *The Return of Culture and Identity*, pp. 65–84.

46. For an account of identity based on these three theorists, see Anne Norton, *Reflections on Political Identity* (Baltimore, Md.: Johns Hopkins University Press, 1988).

47. Inayatullah and Blaney, "Knowing Encounters," pp. 65–66. For a very useful analysis of how different accounts of identity have made their way through feminist theorizing, see Allison Weir, *Sacrificial Logics: Feminist Theory and the Critique of Identity* (New York: Routledge, 1996).

48. My views on the differences separating critical and conventional constructivist positions on power were shaped in conversation with Jim Richter.

49. See Arturo Escobar, "Discourse and Power in Development: Michel Foucault and the Relevance of His Work to the Third World," *Alternatives*, Vol. 10, No. 4 (October–December 1984), esp. pp. 377–378.

50. This is taken from Andrew Linklater, "The Question of the Next Stage in International Relations Theory: A Critical-Theoretical Point of View," *Millennium: Journal of International Studies*, Vol. 21, No. 1 (Spring 1992), p. 91, and is based on his interpretation of Jürgen Habermas. For a view on precisely the point of the emancipator power of critical theory, see Chris Brown, "'Turtles All the Way Down': Anti-Foundationalism, Critical Theory, and International Relations," *Millennium: Journal of International Studies*, Vol. 23, No. 2 (Summer 1994), p. 219.

51. For an alternative account of international relations theory from a critical theory perspective in which conventional constructivism's positions can be found as well, see Richard K. Ashley, "Three Modes of Economism," *International Studies Quarterly*, Vol. 27, No. 4 (December 1983), pp. 477–491. On the construction of anarchy, in particular, see Ashley, "Untying the Sovereign State," p. 253. In addition, conventional constructivism is more willing to accept the ontological status of the state when theorizing, whereas critical theory demands that the state remain a zone of contestation, and should be understood as such; its autonomous existence should not be accepted. For the former conventional view, see Alexander Wendt, "Constructing International Politics," *International Security*, Vol. 20, No. 1 (Summer 1995), p. 72. For the critical view of the state, see Ashley, "Untying the Sovereign State," pp. 248–251.

52. For the challenge to constructivists to develop a research program or be marginalized, see Keohane, "International Institutions," p. 392. For criticism in a similar vein, see Thomas J. Biersteker, "Critical Reflections on Post-Positivism in International Relations,"

International Studies Quarterly, Vol. 33, No. 3 (September 1989), p. 266.

53. It is a loose adaptation because, while I adopt Lakatosian criteria for what constitutes a progressive and degenerative shift in a research program, I do not adopt his standards of falsificationism or their associated "protective belts" of auxiliary hypotheses. See Imre Lakatos, "Falsification and the Methodology of Scientific Research Programmes," in Imre Lakatos and Alan Musgrave, eds., *Criticism and the Growth of Knowledge* (Cambridge, U.K.: Cambridge University Press, 1970), pp. 91–196.

54. Stephen M. Waltz, *The Origins of Alliances* (Ithaca, N.Y.: Cornell University Press, 1987), p. 5. By acknowledging that "one cannot determine a priori . . . which sources of threat will be most important in any given case; one can say only that all of them are likely to play a role," Waltz does not offer a nontautological means for specifying threat. Quotation on p. 26.

55. See Thomas Risse-Kappen, "Collective Identity in a Democratic Community: The Case of NATO," in Katzenstein, *The Culture of National Security*, pp. 361–368; Barnett, "Identity and Alliances," pp. 401–404; Peter J. Katzenstein, "Introduction: Alternative Perspectives on National Security," in Katzenstein, *The Culture of National Security*, pp. 27–28; Jepperson, Wendt, and Katzenstein, "Norms, Identity, and Culture," p. 63; and Wendt, "Constructing International Politics," p. 78.

56. Robert Jervis, "Cooperation under the Security Dilemma," *World Politics*, Vol. 30, No. 2 (March 1978), pp. 167–214.

57. I thank Maria Fanis for bringing home to me the importance of thinking about world politics in this way.

58. Ashley, "Three Modes," p. 478; see also Ashley, "The Geopolitics of Geopolitical Space," p. 414.

59. Kenneth A. Oye, "Explaining Cooperation under Anarchy: Hypotheses and Strategies," in Kenneth A. Oye, ed., *Cooperation under Anarchy* (Princeton, N.J.: Princeton University Press, 1986), pp. 1–24.

60. The regimes literature is vast. For an early foundational volume that includes theoretical specification, empirical illustration, and some-self-critique, see Stephen D. Krasner, ed., *International Regimes* (Ithaca, N.Y.: Cornell University Press, 1983). Elaboration of the market failure logic is in Robert O. Keohane, *After Hegemony* (Princeton, N.J.: Princeton University Press, 1984).

61. Keohane, "International Institutions," p. 386.

62. On the critical importance of a theory of reputation to account for economic transactions, such as contracts, see David M. Kreps, "Corporate Culture and Economic Theory," in James E. Alt and Kenneth A. Shepsle, eds., *Perspectives on Positive Political Economy* (Cambridge, U.K.: Cambridge University Press, 1990), pp. 90–143. Formal game-theoretic work on reputation consistently shows that it should matter, and it does, but only when assumed to do so. Empirical work in international relations has shown that reputations do not work as hypothesized by most international relations theory. See Jonathan Mercer, *Reputation and International Politics* (Ithaca, N.Y.: Cornell University Press, 1996); Ted Hopf, *Peripheral Visions: Deterrence Theory and American Foreign Policy in the Third World, 1965–1990* (Ann Arbor: University of Michigan Press, 1994); Richard Ned Lebow, *Between Peace and War: The Nature of International Crisis* (Baltimore, Md.: Johns Hopkins University Press, 1981); and Jervis, *Logic of Images in International Relations*.

63. For a recognition that "shared focal points," à la Thomas Schelling, have much in common with intersubjective reality and its capacity to promote cooperative solutions to iterative games, see Geoffrey Garrett and Barry R. Weingast, "Ideas, Interests, and Institutions: Constructing the European Community's Internal Market," in Goldstein and Keohane, *Ideas and Foreign Policy*, pp. 173–206.

64. Keohane, "International Institutions," p. 387.

65. On lags and stickiness, see Stephen D. Krasner, "State Power and the Structure of International Trade," *World Politics*, Vol. 28, No. 3 (April 1976), pp. 317–343. On transaction costs, see Keohane, *After Hegemony*.

66. Another constructivist hypothesis offers itself here: institutionalized cooperation will be more likely to endure to the extent that the identities of the members of that institution are understood as common and they are reproduced by a thick array of social practices. This is meant as a continuum, with narrow self-interest being arrayed at one end of the spectrum, neoliberal institutionalization of self-interested cooperation in the middle, community of identity toward the other end, and harmony at the other pole.

67. Duncan Snidal, "The Limits of Hegemonic Stability Theory," *International Organization*, Vol. 39, No. 4 (Autumn 1985), esp. pp. 610–611.

68. For a comprehensive review of the most recent literature on the democratic peace, and an empirical test that shows that satisfaction with the status quo (a variable subject to constructivist interpretation) is the single most important factor affecting the use of force by democracies and authoritarian states alike, see David L. Rousseau, Christopher Gelpi, and Dan Reiter, "Assessing the Dyadic Nature of the Democratic Peace, 1918–1988," *American Political Science Review*, Vol. 90, No. 3 (September 1996), p. 527.

69. For a very well-developed research design to test constructivist versus mainstream accounts of the democratic peace, see Colin Kahl, "Constructing a Separate Peace: Constructivism, Collective Liberal Identity, and the Democratic Peace," *Security Studies*, Vol. 8, No. 2–3 (1998), pp. 94–144.

70. For accounts of the democratic peace that focus on its contextual intersubjective characters, see Ido Oren, "The Subjectivity of the 'Democratic' Peace: Changing U.S. Perceptions of Imperial Germany," *International Security*, Vol. 20, No. 2 (Fall 1995), pp. 147–184; Thomas Risse-Kappen, *Cooperation among Democracies*, p. 30; and Risse-Kappen, "Collective Identity in a Democratic Community," pp. 366–367.

71. I do not try to compile a comprehensive set of questions for constructivists, but instead merely elaborate general themes for research, themes that do not have a prominent place in mainstream international relations theory.

72. For a critical view of neorealism's belated efforts to capture nationalism, see Yosef Lapid and Friedrich Kratochwil, "Revisiting the 'National': Toward an Identity Agenda in Neorealism?" in Lapid and Kratochwil, *The Return of Culture and Identity*, pp. 105–126. For a most imaginative critical constructivist treatment of nationalism, see Daniel Deudney, "Ground Identity: Nature, Place, and Space in Nationalism," in ibid., pp. 129–145; see also Roxanne Lynn Doty, "Sovereignty and the Nation: Constructing the

Boundaries of National Identity," in Thomas J. Biersteker and Cynthia Weber, eds., *State Sovereignty as Social Construct* (Cambridge, U.K.: Cambridge University Press, 1996) pp. 121–147.

73. For example, J. Ann Tickner observes that contemporary masculinized Western understandings of themselves lead to feminized portrayals of the South as "emotional and unpredictable." Tickner, "Identity in International Relations Theory: Feminist Perspectives," in Lapid and Kratochwil, *The Return of Culture and Identity*, pp. 147–162.

74. For example, Risse-Kappen, "Collective Identity in a Democratic Community," finds a common identity within the North Atlantic Treaty Organization; see also Iver B. Neumann and Jennifer M. Welsh, "The Other in European Self-Definition," *Review of International Studies*, Vol. 17, No. 4 (October 1991), pp. 327–348, for an exploration of "Christian" and "European" states versus "Islamic" "Asiatic" Turkey.

75. Michael N. Barnett, "Institutions, Roles, and Disorder: The Case of the Arab States System," *International Studies Quarterly*, Vol. 37, No. 3 (September 1993), pp. 271–296.

76. See Risse-Kappen, "Collective Identity in a Democratic Community," and Michael N. Barnett, "Sovereignty, Nationalism, and Regional Order in the Arab System," *International Organization*, Vol. 49, No. 3 (Summer 1995), pp. 479–510, for examples.

77. Yale Ferguson and Richard Mansbach, for example, offer a rich variety of "polities," such as city-states, civilizations, polis, empires, kingdoms, caliphates, each of which had and, in some cases, has and will have, meaningful identities in world politics. Ferguson and Mansbach, "Past as Prelude," pp. 22–28, and Sujata Chakrabarti Pasic, "Culturing International Relations Theory," both in Lapid and Kratochwil, *The Return of Culture and Identity*, pp. 85–104.

78. Keohane, in "International Institutions," p. 392, has made this observation about "reflectivist" scholarship. For similar laments, see Dessler, "What's At Stake," p. 471; and Barnett, "Institutions, Roles, and Disorder," p. 276. Alexander Wendt acknowledges he

has "systematically bracketed" domestic factors in Wendt, "Anarchy Is What States Make of It," p. 423.

79. Two works that make the connection between domestic identity construction at home and state identity are Audie Klotz, *Norms in International Relations: The Struggle against Apartheid* (Ithaca, N.Y.: Cornell University Press, 1995); and Peter J. Katzenstein, *Cultural Norms and National Security* (Ithaca, N.Y.: Cornell University Press, 1996).

80. Inayatullah and Blaney, "Knowing Encounters," pp. 76–80.

81. Compare this, for example, to Richard Cottam's very interesting account of imperial British images of Egypt. The critical difference is that Cottam does not see British constructions of themselves or their society's parts as relevant to an understanding of British images of Egyptians, Richard Cottam, *Foreign Policy Motivation: A General Theory and Case Study* (Pittsburgh: University of Pittsburgh Press, 1977).

82. One might say this about the French military between World Wars I and II. See Kier, "Culture and French Military Doctrine before World War II."

83. This is done by David Campbell, *Writing Security: United States Foreign Policy and the Politics of Identity* (Minneapolis: University of Minnesota Press, 1992) and Jim George, *Discourses of Global Politics: A Critical (Re)Introduction to International Relations* (Boulder, Colo.: Lynne Rienner, 1994).

84. Kratochwil, "Is the Ship of Culture at Sea or Returning?" p. 206.

85. Paul Kowert and Jeffrey Legro, "Norms, Identity, and Their Limits: A Theoretical Reprise," in Katzenstein, *The Culture of National Security*, p. 469. For other critical reviews of constructivism and world politics, see Jeffrey T. Checkel, "The Constructivist Turn in International Relations Theory," *World Politics*, Vol. 50, No. 2 (January 1998), pp. 324–348, and Emanuel Adler, "Seizing the Middle Ground: Constructivism in World Politics," *European Journal of International Relations*, Vol. 3, No. 3 (1997), pp. 319–363.

86. Ibid., p. 479.

2 HISTORICAL CONTEXT

Core ideas about international politics, introduced in Chapter 2 of *Essentials of International Relations*, Eighth Edition, have emerged as responses to historic diplomatic challenges. The selections in this chapter were written at the historical and intellectual turning points of the twentieth century: the end of World War I, the end of World War II, and the end of the Cold War. These events spawned many of the ideas and trends that still shape debates about contemporary international politics.

The post–World War I peace process led to a clear statement of the liberal perspective. U.S. president Woodrow Wilson's Fourteen Points, in an address to Congress in January 1918, summarized some of the key ideas of liberal theory. Wilson blamed power politics, secret diplomacy, and autocratic leaders for the devastating world war. He suggested that with the spread of democracy and the creation of a "league of nations," aggression would be stopped.

At the end of the Cold War in 1989, Francis Fukuyama published a controversial essay, "The End of History?," speculating whether the victory of liberal ideas over communism and fascism had left no significant rival ideology in sight. Samuel Huntington, in what is probably the most discussed essay on world politics in recent decades, begged to differ: he foresaw the emergence of a "clash of civilizations" pitting "the West against the rest." In Huntington's subsequent book, *The Clash of Civilizations and the Remaking of World Order* (1996), he somewhat modified his earlier claim, acknowledging that conflicts within civilizations remained more common than conflicts between them. Despite criticism from many scholarly experts and political analysts, his thesis attracted huge attention, seemed relevant in an era of rising terrorist attacks, and appealed even to some non-Westerners, such as Chinese nationalists who agreed that a clash of civilizations was coming.

A key question for the future is whether the rise of illiberal China represents a new ideological rival to liberalism based on the principles of national sovereignty, mercantilist economic strategies, cultural conservatism, and authoritarian politics. If so, will these principles attract adherents among other rising powers? Is history beginning again? The final selection by John Ikenberry on contemporary challenges facing the liberal international order asks whether the world is again at a decisive turning point.

Woodrow Wilson
THE FOURTEEN POINTS

It will be our wish and purpose that the processes of peace, when they are begun, shall be absolutely open and that they shall involve and permit henceforth no secret understandings of any kind. The day of conquest and aggrandizement is gone by; so is also the day of secret covenants entered into in the interest of particular governments and likely at some unlooked-for moment to upset the peace of the world. It is this happy fact, now clear to the view of every public man whose thoughts do not still linger in an age that is dead and gone, which makes it possible for every nation whose purposes are consistent with justice and the peace of the world to avow now or at any other time the objects it has in view.

We entered this war because violations of right had occurred which touched us to the quick and made the life of our own people impossible unless they were corrected and the world secured once and for all against their recurrence. What we demand in this war, therefore, is nothing peculiar to ourselves. It is that the world be made fit and safe to live in; and particularly that it be made safe for every peace-loving nation which, like our own, wishes to live its own life, determine its own institutions, be assured of justice and fair dealing by the other people of the world as against force and selfish aggression. All the peoples of the world are in effect partners in this interest, and for our own part we see very clearly that unless justice be done to others it will not be done to us. The program of the world's peace, therefore, is our program; and

From Woodrow Wilson's address to the U.S. Congress, January 8, 1918.

that program, the only possible program, as we see it, is this:

I. Open covenants of peace, openly arrived at, after which there shall be no private international understandings of any kind but diplomacy shall proceed always frankly and in the public view.

II. Absolute freedom of navigation upon the seas, outside territorial waters, alike in peace and in war, except as the seas may be closed in whole or in part by international action for the enforcement of international covenants.

III. The removal, so far as possible, of all economic barriers and the establishment of an equality of trade conditions among all the nations consenting to the peace and associating themselves for its maintenance.

IV. Adequate guarantees given and taken that national armaments will be reduced to the lowest point consistent with domestic safety.

V. A free, open-minded, and absolutely impartial adjustment of all colonial claims, based upon a strict observance of the principle that in determining all such questions of sovereignty the interests of the populations concerned must have equal weight with the equitable claims of the government whose title is to be determined.

VI. The evacuation of all Russian territory and such a settlement of all questions affecting Russia as will secure the best and freest cooperation of the other nations of the world in obtaining for her an unhampered and unembarrassed opportunity for the independent determination of her own political development and national policy and assure her of a sincere welcome into the society of free nations under institutions of her own choosing; and, more than a welcome, assistance also of every kind that she may need and may herself desire. The treatment accorded Russia by her sister nations in the months to come will be the acid test of their good will, of their comprehension of her needs as distinguished from their own interests, and of their intelligent and unselfish sympathy.

VII. Belgium, the whole world will agree, must be evacuated and restored, without any attempt to limit the sovereignty which she enjoys in common with all other free nations. No other single act will serve as this will serve to restore confidence among the nations in the laws which they have themselves set and determined for the government of their relations with one another. Without this healing act the whole structure and validity of international law is forever impaired.

VIII. All French territory should be freed and the invaded portions restored, and the wrong done to France by Prussia in 1871 in the matter of Alsace-Lorraine, which has unsettled the peace of the world for nearly fifty years, should be righted, in order that peace may once more be made secure in the interest of all.

IX. A readjustment of the frontiers of Italy should be effected along clearly recognizable lines of nationality.

X. The peoples of Austria-Hungary, whose place among the nations we wish to see safeguarded and assured, should be accorded the freest opportunity of autonomous development.

XI. Rumania, Serbia, and Montenegro should be evacuated; occupied territories restored; Serbia accorded free and secure access to the sea; and the relations of the several Balkan states to one another determined by friendly counsel along historically established lines of allegiance and nationality; and international guarantees of the political and economic independence and territorial integrity of the several Balkan states should be entered into.

XII. The Turkish portions of the present Ottoman Empire should be assured a secure sovereignty, but the other nationalities which are now under Turkish rule should be assured an undoubted security of life and an absolutely unmolested opportunity of autonomous development, and the Dardanelles should be permanently opened as a free passage to the ships and commerce of all nations under international guarantees.

XIII. An independent Polish state should be erected which should include the territories inhabited by indisputably Polish populations, which should be assured a free and secure access to the sea, and whose political and economic independence and territorial integrity should be guaranteed by international covenant.

XIV. A general association of nations must be formed under specific covenants for the purpose of affording mutual guarantees of political independence and territorial integrity to great and small states alike.

In regard to these essential rectifications of wrong and assertions of right we feel ourselves to be intimate partners of all the governments and peoples associated together against the imperialists. We cannot be separated in interest or divided in purpose. We stand together until the end.

For such arrangements and covenants we are willing to fight and to continue to fight until they are achieved; but only because we wish the right to prevail and desire a just and stable peace such as can be secured only by removing the chief provocations to war, which this program does remove. We have no jealousy of German greatness, and there is nothing in this program that impairs it. We grudge her no achievement or distinction of learning or of pacific enterprise such as have made her record very bright and very enviable. We do not wish to injure her or to block in any way her legitimate influence or power. We do not wish to fight her either with arms or with hostile arrangements of trade if she is willing to associate herself with us and the other peace-loving nations of the world in covenants of justice and law and fair dealing. We wish her only to accept a place of equality among the peoples of the world—the new world in which we now live—instead of a place of mastery.

Neither do we presume to suggest to her any alteration or modification of her institutions. But it is necessary, we must frankly say, and necessary as a preliminary to any intelligent dealings with her on our part, that we should know whom her spokesmen speak for when they speak to us, whether for the Reichstag majority or for the military party and the men whose creed is imperial domination.

We have spoken now, surely, in terms too concrete to admit of any further doubt or question. An evident principle runs through the whole program I have outlined. It is the principle of justice to all peoples and nationalities, and their right to live on equal terms of liberty and safety with one another, whether they be strong or weak. Unless this principle be made its foundation no part of the structure of international justice can stand. The people of the United States could act upon no other principle; and to the vindication of this principle they are ready to devote their lives, their honor, and everything that they possess. The moral climax of this the culminating and final war for human liberty has come, and they are ready to put their own strength, their own highest purpose, their own integrity and devotion to the test.

Francis Fukuyama
THE END OF HISTORY?

In watching the flow of events over the past decade or so, it is hard to avoid the feeling that something very fundamental has happened in world history. The past year has seen a flood of articles commemorating the end of the Cold War, and the fact that "peace" seems to be breaking out in many regions of the world. Most of these analyses lack any larger conceptual framework for distinguishing between what is essential and what is contingent or accidental in world history, and are predictably superficial. If Mr. Gorbachev were ousted from the Kremlin or a new Ayatollah proclaimed the millennium from a desolate Middle Eastern capital, these same commentators would scramble to announce the rebirth of a new era of conflict.

And yet, all of these people sense dimly that there is some larger process at work, a process that gives coherence and order to the daily headlines. The twentieth century saw the developed world descend into a paroxysm of ideological violence, as liberalism contended first with the remnants of absolutism, then bolshevism and fascism, and finally an updated Marxism that threatened to lead to the ultimate apocalypse of nuclear war. But the century that began full of self-confidence in the ultimate triumph of Western liberal democracy seems at its close to be returning full circle to where it started: not to an "end of ideology" or a convergence between capitalism and socialism, as earlier predicted, but to an unabashed victory of economic and political liberalism.

The triumph of the West, of the Western *idea*, is evident first of all in the total exhaustion of viable systematic alternatives to Western liberalism. In the past decade, there have been unmistakable changes in the intellectual climate of the world's two largest communist countries, and the beginnings of significant reform movements in both. But this phenomenon extends beyond high politics and it can be seen also in the ineluctable spread of consumerist Western culture in such diverse contexts as the peasants' markets and color television sets now omnipresent throughout China, the cooperative restaurants and clothing stores opened in the past year in Moscow, the Beethoven piped into Japanese department stores, and the rock music enjoyed alike in Prague, Rangoon, and Tehran.

What we may be witnessing is not just the end of the Cold War, or the passing of a particular period of postwar history, but the end of history as such: that is, the end point of mankind's ideological evolution and the universalization of Western liberal democracy as the final form of human government. This is not to say that there will no longer be events to fill the pages of *Foreign Affairs*'s yearly summaries of international relations, for the victory of liberalism has occurred primarily in the realm of ideas or consciousness and is as yet incomplete in the real or material world. But there are powerful reasons for believing that it is the ideal that will govern the material world *in the long run*. To understand how this is so, we must first consider some theoretical issues concerning the nature of historical change.

I

The notion of the end of history is not an original one. Its best known propagator was Karl Marx,

From *The National Interest* 16 (Summer 1989): 3–18. Some of the author's notes have been omitted.

who believed that the direction of historical development was a purposeful one determined by the interplay of material forces, and would come to an end only with the achievement of a communist Utopia that would finally resolve all prior contradictions. But the concept of history as a dialectical process with a beginning, a middle, and an end was borrowed by Marx from his great German predecessor, Georg Wilhelm Friedrich Hegel.

For better or worse, much of Hegel's historicism has become part of our contemporary intellectual baggage. The notion that mankind has progressed through a series of primitive stages of consciousness on his path to the present, and that these stages corresponded to concrete forms of social organization, such as tribal, slave-owning, theocratic, and finally democratic-egalitarian societies, has become inseparable from the modern understanding of man. Hegel was the first philosopher to speak the language of modern social science, insofar as man for him was the product of his concrete historical and social environment and not, as earlier natural right theorists would have it, a collection of more or less fixed "natural" attributes. The mastery and transformation of man's natural environment through the application of science and technology was originally not a Marxist concept, but a Hegelian one. Unlike later historicists whose historical relativism degenerated into relativism *tout court,* however, Hegel believed that history culminated in an absolute moment—a moment in which a final, rational form of society and state became victorious.

It is Hegel's misfortune to be known now primarily as Marx's precursor, and it is our misfortune that few of us are familiar with Hegel's work from direct study, but only as it has been filtered through the distorting lens of Marxism. In France, however, there has been an effort to save Hegel from his Marxist interpreters and to resurrect him as the philosopher who most correctly speaks to our time. Among those modern French interpreters of Hegel, the greatest was certainly Alexandre Kojève, a brilliant Russian emigre who taught a highly influential series of seminars in Paris in the 1930s at the *Ecole Practique des Hautes Etudes*.[1] While largely unknown in the United States, Kojève had a major impact on the intellectual life of the continent. Among his students ranged such future luminaries as Jean-Paul Sartre on the Left and Raymond Aron on the Right; postwar existentialism borrowed many of its basic categories from Hegel via Kojève.

Kojève sought to resurrect the Hegel of the *Phenomenology of Mind*, the Hegel who proclaimed history to be at an end in 1806. For as early as this Hegel saw in Napoleon's defeat of the Prussian monarchy at the Battle of Jena the victory of the ideals of the French Revolution, and the imminent universalization of the state incorporating the principles of liberty and equality. Kojève, far from rejecting Hegel in light of the turbulent events of the next century and a half, insisted that the latter had been essentially correct. The Battle of Jena marked the end of history because it was at that point that the *vanguard* of humanity (a term quite familiar to Marxists) actualized the principles of the French Revolution. While there was considerable work to be done after 1806—abolishing slavery and the slave trade, extending the franchise to workers, women, blacks, and other racial minorities, etc.—the basic *principles* of the liberal democratic state could not be improved upon. The two world wars in this century and their attendant revolutions and upheavals simply had the effect of extending those principles spatially, such that the various provinces of human civilization were brought up to the level of its most advanced outposts, and of forcing those societies in Europe and North America at the vanguard of civilization to implement their liberalism more fully.

The state that emerges at the end of history is liberal insofar as it recognizes and protects through a system of law man's universal right to freedom, and democratic insofar as it exists only with the consent of the governed. For Kojève, this so-called "universal homogenous state" found real-life embodiment in the countries of postwar Western Europe—precisely those flabby, prosperous, self-satisfied, inward-looking, weak-willed states whose grandest project was nothing more heroic than the creation of the Common Market. But this was only to be expected. For human history and the conflict that characterized it was based on the existence of "contradictions": primitive man's quest for mutual recognition, the dialectic of the master and slave, the transformation and mastery of nature, the struggle for the universal recognition of rights, and the dichotomy between proletarian and capitalist. But in the universal homogenous state, all prior contradictions are resolved and all human needs are satisfied. There is no struggle or conflict over "large" issues, and consequently no need for generals or statesmen; what remains is primarily economic activity. * * *

II

For Hegel, the contradictions that drive history exist first of all in the realm of human consciousness, i.e., on the level of ideas—not the trivial election year proposals of American politicians, but ideas in the sense of large unifying world views that might best be understood under the rubric of ideology. Ideology in this sense is not restricted to the secular and explicit political doctrines we usually associate with the term, but can include religion, culture, and the complex of moral values underlying any society as well.

■   ■   ■

For Hegel, all human behavior in the material world, and hence all human history, is rooted in a prior state of consciousness—an idea similar to the one expressed by John Maynard Keynes when he said that the views of men of affairs were usually derived from defunct economists and academic scribblers of earlier generations. * * *

Hegel's idealism has fared poorly at the hands of later thinkers. Marx reversed the priority of the real and the ideal completely, relegating the entire realm of consciousness—religion, art, culture, philosophy itself—to a "superstructure" that was determined entirely by the prevailing material mode of production. Yet another unfortunate legacy of Marxism is our tendency to retreat into materialist or utilitarian explanations of political or historical phenomena, and our disinclination to believe in the autonomous power of ideas. A recent example of this is Paul Kennedy's hugely successful *The Rise and Fall of the Great Powers,* which ascribes the decline of great powers to simple economic overextension. Obviously, this is true on some level: an empire whose economy is barely above the level of subsistence cannot bankrupt its treasury indefinitely. But whether a highly productive modern industrial society chooses to spend 3 or 7 percent of its GNP on defense rather than consumption is entirely a matter of that society's political priorities, which are in turn determined in the realm of consciousness.

■   ■   ■

III

Have we in fact reached the end of history? Are there, in other words, any fundamental "contradictions" in human life that cannot be resolved in the context of modern liberalism, that would be resolvable by an alternative political-economic structure? If we accept the idealist premises laid out above, we must seek an answer to this question in the realm of ideology and consciousness. Our task is not to answer exhaustively the challenges to liberalism promoted by every crackpot messiah around the world, but only those that are embodied in important social or political forces and movements, and which are therefore part of world history. For our purposes, it matters very little what strange thoughts occur to people in Albania or Burkina Faso, for we are interested in what one could in some sense call the common ideological heritage of mankind.

In the past century, there have been two major challenges to liberalism, those of fascism and of communism. The former saw the political weakness, materialism, anomie, and lack of community of the West as fundamental contradictions in liberal societies that could only be resolved by a strong state that forged a new "people" on the basis of national exclusiveness. Fascism was destroyed as a living ideology by World War II. This was a defeat, of course, on a very material level, but it amounted to a defeat of the idea as well. What destroyed fascism as an idea was not universal moral revulsion against it, since plenty of people were willing to endorse the idea as long as it seemed the wave of the future, but its lack of success. After the war, it seemed to most people that German fascism as well as its other European and Asian variants were bound to self-destruct. There was no material reason why new fascist movements could not have sprung up again after the war in other locales, but for the fact that expansionist ultranationalism, with its promise of unending conflict leading to disastrous military defeat, had completely lost its appeal. The ruins of the Reich chancellory as well as the atomic bombs dropped on Hiroshima and Nagasaki killed this ideology on the level of consciousness as well as materially, and all of the proto-fascist movements spawned by the German and Japanese examples like the Peronist movement in Argentina or Subhas Chandra Bose's Indian National Army withered after the war.

The ideological challenge mounted by the other great alternative to liberalism, communism, was far more serious. Marx, speaking Hegel's language, asserted that liberal society contained a fundamental contradiction that could not be resolved within its context, that between capital and labor, and this contradiction has constituted the chief accusation against liberalism ever since. But surely, the class issue has actually been successfully resolved in the West. As Kojève (among others) noted, the egalitarianism of modern America represents the essential achievement of the classless society envisioned by Marx. This is not to say that there are not rich people and poor people in the United States, or that the gap between them has not grown in recent years. But the root causes of economic inequality do not have to do with the underlying legal and social structure of our society, which remains fundamentally egalitarian and moderately redistributionist, so much as with the cultural and social characteristics of the groups that make it up, which are in turn the historical legacy of premodern conditions. Thus black poverty in the United States is not the inherent product of liberalism, but is rather the "legacy of slavery and racism" which persisted long after the formal abolition of slavery.

As a result of the receding of the class issue, the appeal of communism in the developed Western world, it is safe to say, is lower today than any time since the end of the First World War. This can be measured in any number of ways: in the declining membership and electoral pull of the major European communist parties, and their overtly revisionist programs; in the corresponding electoral success of conservative parties from Britain and Germany to the United States and Japan, which are unabashedly pro-market and antistatist; and in an intellectual climate whose most "advanced" members no longer believe that bourgeois society is something that ultimately needs to be overcome. This is not to say that the opinions of progressive intellectuals in Western countries are not deeply pathological in any number of ways. But those who believe that the future must inevitably be socialist tend to be very old, or very marginal to the real political discourse of their societies.

One may argue that the socialist alternative was never terribly plausible for the North Atlantic world, and was sustained for the last several decades primarily by its success outside of this region. But it is precisely in the non-European world that one is most struck by the occurrence of major ideological transformations. Surely the most remarkable changes have occurred in Asia. Due to the strength and adaptability of the indigenous cultures there, Asia became a battleground for a variety of imported Western ideologies early in this century. Liberalism in Asia was a very weak reed in the period after World War I; it is easy today to forget how gloomy Asia's political future looked as recently as ten or fifteen years ago. It is easy to forget as well how momentous the outcome of Asian ideological struggles seemed for world political development as a whole.

The first Asian alternative to liberalism to be decisively defeated was the fascist one represented by Imperial Japan. Japanese fascism (like its German version) was defeated by the force of American arms in the Pacific war, and liberal democracy was imposed on Japan by a victorious United States. Western capitalism and political liberalism when transplanted to Japan were adapted and transformed by the Japanese in such a way as to be scarcely recognizable. Many Americans are now aware that Japanese industrial organization is very different from that prevailing in the United States or Europe, and it is questionable what relationship the factional maneuvering that takes place with the governing Liberal Democratic Party bears to democracy. Nonetheless, the very fact that the essential elements of economic and political liberalism have been so successfully grafted onto uniquely Japanese traditions and institutions guarantees their survival in the long run. More important is the contribution that Japan has made in turn to world history by following in the footsteps of the United States to create a truly universal consumer culture that has become both a symbol and an underpinning of the universal homogenous state. V. S. Naipaul travelling in Khomeini's Iran shortly after the revolution noted the omnipresent signs advertising the products of Sony, Hitachi, and JVC, whose appeal remained virtually irresistible and gave the lie to the regime's pretensions of restoring a state based on the rule of the *Shariah*. Desire for access to the consumer culture, created in large measure by Japan, has played a crucial role in fostering the spread of economic liberalism throughout Asia, and hence in promoting political liberalism as well.

The economic success of the other newly industrializing countries (NICs) in Asia following on the example of Japan is by now a familiar story. What is important from a Hegelian standpoint is that political liberalism has been following economic liberalism, more slowly than many had hoped but with seeming inevitability. Here again we see the victory of the idea of the universal homogenous state. South Korea had developed into a modern, urbanized society with an increasingly large and well-educated middle class that could not possibly be isolated from the larger democratic trends around them. Under these circumstances it seemed intolerable to a large part of this population that it should be ruled by an anachronistic military regime while Japan, only a decade or so ahead in economic terms, had parliamentary institutions for over forty years. Even the former socialist regime in Burma, which for so many decades existed in dismal isolation from the larger trends dominating Asia, was buffeted in the past year by pressures to liberalize both its economy and political system. It is said that unhappiness with strongman Ne Win began when a senior Burmese officer went to Singapore for medical treatment and broke down crying when he saw how far socialist Burma had been left behind by its ASEAN neighbors.

But the power of the liberal idea would seem much less impressive if it had not infected the largest and oldest culture in Asia, China. The simple existence of communist China created an alternative pole of ideological attraction, and as such constituted a threat to liberalism. But the past fifteen years have seen an almost total discrediting of Marxism-Leninism as an economic system. Beginning with the famous third plenum of the Tenth Central Committee in 1978, the Chinese Communist party set about decollectivizing agriculture for the 800 million Chinese who still lived in the countryside. The role of the state in agriculture was reduced to that of a tax collector, while production of consumer goods was sharply increased in order to give peasants a taste of the universal homogenous state and thereby an incentive to work. The reform doubled Chinese grain output in only five years, and in the process created for Deng Xiao-ping a solid political base from which he was able to extend the reform to other parts of the economy. Economic statistics do not begin to describe the dynamism, initiative, and openness evident in China since the reform began.

China could not now be described in any way as a liberal democracy. At present, no more than 20 percent of its economy has been marketized, and most importantly it continues to be ruled by a self-appointed Communist party which has given no hint of wanting to devolve power. Deng has made none of Gorbachev's promises regarding democratization of the political system and there is no Chinese equivalent of *glasnost*. The Chinese leadership has in fact been much more circumspect in criticizing Mao and Maoism than Gorbachev with respect to Brezhnev and Stalin, and the regime continues to pay lip service to Marxism-Leninism as its ideological underpinning. But anyone familiar with the outlook and behavior of the new technocratic elite now governing China knows that Marxism and ideological principle have become virtually irrelevant as guides to policy, and that bourgeois consumerism has a real meaning in that country for the first time since the revolution. The various slowdowns in the pace of reform, the campaigns against "spiritual pollution" and crackdowns on political dissent are more properly seen as tactical adjustments made in the process of managing what is an extraordinarily difficult political transition. By ducking the question of political reform while putting the economy on a new footing, Deng has managed to avoid the breakdown of authority that has accompanied Gorbachev's *perestroika*. Yet

the pull of the liberal idea continues to be very strong as economic power devolves and the economy becomes more open to the outside world. There are currently over 20,000 Chinese students studying in the U.S. and other Western countries, almost all of them the children of the Chinese elite. It is hard to believe that when they return home to run the country they will be content for China to be the only country in Asia unaffected by the larger democratizing trend. The student demonstrations in Beijing that broke out first in December 1986 and recurred recently on the occasion of Hu Yao-bang's death were only the beginning of what will inevitably be mounting pressure for change in the political system as well.

What is important about China from the standpoint of world history is not the present state of the reform or even its future prospects. The central issue is the fact that the People's Republic of China can no longer act as a beacon for illiberal forces around the world, whether they be guerrillas in some Asian jungle or middle class students in Paris. Maoism, rather than being the pattern for Asia's future, became an anachronism, and it was the mainland Chinese who in fact were decisively influenced by the prosperity and dynamism of their overseas co-ethnics—the ironic ultimate victory of Taiwan.

Important as these changes in China have been, however, it is developments in the Soviet Union—the original "homeland of the world proletariat"—that have put the final nail in the coffin of the Marxist-Leninist alternative to liberal democracy. It should be clear that in terms of formal institutions, not much has changed in the four years since Gorbachev has come to power: free markets and the cooperative movement represent only a small part of the Soviet economy, which remains centrally planned; the political system is still dominated by the Communist party, which has only begun to democratize internally and to share power with other groups; the regime continues to assert that it is seeking only to modernize socialism and that its ideological basis remains

Marxism-Leninism; and, finally, Gorbachev faces a potentially powerful conservative opposition that could undo many of the changes that have taken place to date. Moreover, it is hard to be too sanguine about the chances for success of Gorbachev's proposed reforms, either in the sphere of economics or politics. But my purpose here is not to analyze events in the short-term, or to make predictions for policy purposes, but to look at underlying trends in the sphere of ideology and consciousness. And in that respect, it is clear that an astounding transformation has occurred.

Emigres from the Soviet Union have been reporting for at least the last generation now that virtually nobody in that country truly believed in Marxism-Leninism any longer, and that this was nowhere more true than in the Soviet elite, which continued to mouth Marxist slogans out of sheer cynicism. The corruption and decadence of the late Brezhnev-era Soviet state seemed to matter little, however, for as long as the state itself refused to throw into question any of the fundamental principles underlying Soviet society, the system was capable of functioning adequately out of sheer inertia and could even muster some dynamism in the realm of foreign and defense policy. Marxism-Leninism was like a magical incantation which, however absurd and devoid of meaning, was the only common basis on which the elite could agree to rule Soviet society.

What has happened in the four years since Gorbachev's coming to power is a revolutionary assault on the most fundamental institutions and principles of Stalinism, and their replacement by other principles which do not amount to liberalism *per se* but whose only connecting thread is liberalism. This is most evident in the economic sphere, where the reform economists around Gorbachev have become steadily more radical in their support for free markets, to the point where some like Nikolai Shmelev do not mind being compared in public to Milton Friedman. There is a virtual consensus among the currently dominant school of Soviet economists now that central planning and the command system of allocation are the root cause of economic inefficiency, and that if the Soviet system is ever to heal itself, it must permit free and decentralized decision-making with respect to investment, labor, and prices. After a couple of initial years of ideological confusion, these principles have finally been incorporated into policy with the promulgation of new laws on enterprise autonomy, cooperatives, and finally in 1988 on lease arrangements and family farming. There are, of course, a number of fatal flaws in the current implementation of the reform, most notably the absence of a thoroughgoing price reform. But the problem is no longer a *conceptual* one: Gorbachev and his lieutenants seem to understand the economic logic of marketization well enough, but like the leaders of a Third World country facing the IMF, are afraid of the social consequences of ending consumer subsidies and other forms of dependence on the state sector.

In the political sphere, the proposed changes to the Soviet constitution, legal system, and party rules amount to much less than the establishment of a liberal state. Gorbachev has spoken of democratization primarily in the sphere of internal party affairs, and has shown little intention of ending the Communist party's monopoly of power; indeed, the political reform seeks to legitimize and therefore strengthen the CPSU's rule. Nonetheless, the general principles underlying many of the reforms—that the "people" should be truly responsible for their own affairs, that higher political bodies should be answerable to lower ones, and not vice versa, that the rule of law should prevail over arbitrary police actions, with separation of powers and an independent judiciary, that there should be legal protection for property rights, the need for open discussion of public issues and the right of public dissent, the empowering of the Soviets as a forum in which the whole Soviet people can participate, and of a political culture that is more tolerant and pluralistic—come from a source fundamentally alien to the USSR's Marxist-Leninist tradition, even if they are incompletely articulated and poorly implemented in practice.

■   ■   ■

If we admit for the moment that the fascist and communist challenges to liberalism are dead, are there any other ideological competitors left? Or put another way, are there contradictions in liberal society beyond that of class that are not resolvable? Two possibilities suggest themselves, those of religion and nationalism.

The rise of religious fundamentalism in recent years within the Christian, Jewish, and Muslim traditions has been widely noted. One is inclined to say that the revival of religion in some way attests to a broad unhappiness with the impersonality and spiritual vacuity of liberal consumerist societies. Yet while the emptiness at the core of liberalism is most certainly a defect in the ideology—indeed, a flaw that one does not need the perspective of religion to recognize—it is not at all clear that it is remediable through politics. Modern liberalism itself was historically a consequence of the weakness of religiously-based societies which, failing to agree on the nature of the good life, could not provide even the minimal preconditions of peace and stability. In the contemporary world only Islam has offered a theocratic state as a political alternative to both liberalism and communism. But the doctrine has little appeal for non-Muslims, and it is hard to believe that the movement will take on any universal significance. Other less organized religious impulses have been successfully satisfied within the sphere of personal life that is permitted in liberal societies.

The other major "contradiction" potentially unresolvable by liberalism is the one posed by nationalism and other forms of racial and ethnic consciousness. It is certainly true that a very large degree of conflict since the Battle of Jena has had its roots in nationalism. Two cataclysmic world wars in this century have been spawned by the nationalism of the developed world in various guises, and if those passions have been muted to a certain extent in postwar Europe, they are still extremely powerful in the Third World. Nationalism has been a threat to liberalism historically in Germany, and continues to be one in isolated parts of "post-historical" Europe like Northern Ireland.

But it is not clear that nationalism represents an irreconcilable contradiction in the heart of liberalism. In the first place, nationalism is not one single phenomenon but several, ranging from mild cultural nostalgia to the highly organized and elaborately articulated doctrine of National Socialism. Only systematic nationalisms of the latter sort can qualify as a formal ideology on the level of liberalism or communism. The vast majority of the world's nationalist movements do not have a political program beyond the negative desire of independence *from* some other group or people, and do not offer anything like a comprehensive agenda for socio-economic organization. As such, they are compatible with doctrines and ideologies that do offer such agendas. While they may constitute a source of conflict for liberal societies, this conflict does not arise from liberalism itself so much as from the fact that the liberalism in question is incomplete. Certainly a great deal of the world's ethnic and nationalist tension can be explained in terms of peoples who are forced to live in unrepresentative political systems that they have not chosen.

While it is impossible to rule out the sudden appearance of new ideologies or previously unrecognized contradictions in liberal societies, then, the present world seems to confirm that the fundamental principles of socio-political organization have not advanced terribly far since 1806. Many of the wars and revolutions fought since that time have been undertaken in the name of ideologies which claimed to be more advanced than liberalism, but whose pretensions were ultimately unmasked by history. In the meantime, they have helped to spread the universal homogenous state to the point where it could have a significant effect on the overall character of international relations.

IV

What are the implications of the end of history for international relations? Clearly, the vast bulk of the Third World remains very much mired in history, and will be a terrain of conflict for many years to come. But let us focus for the time being on the larger and more developed states of the world who after all account for the greater part of world politics. Russia and China are not likely to join the developed nations of the West as liberal societies any time in the foreseeable future, but suppose for a moment that Marxism-Leninism ceases to be a factor driving the foreign policies of these states—a prospect which, if not yet here, the last few years have made a real possibility. How will the overall characteristics of a de-ideologized world differ from those of the one with which we are familiar at such a hypothetical juncture?

The most common answer is—not very much. For there is a very widespread belief among many observers of international relations that underneath the skin of ideology is a hard core of great power national interest that guarantees a fairly high level of competition and conflict between nations. Indeed, according to one academically popular school of international relations theory, conflict inheres in the international system as such, and to understand the prospects for conflict one must look at the shape of the system—for example, whether it is bipolar or multipolar—rather than at the specific character of the nations and regimes that constitute it. This school in effect applies a Hobbesian view of politics to international relations, and assumes that aggression and insecurity are universal characteristics of human societies rather than the product of specific historical circumstances.

Believers in this line of thought take the relations that existed between the participants in the classical nineteenth century European balance of power as a model for what a de-ideologized contemporary world would look like. Charles Krauthammer, for example, recently explained that if as a result of Gorbachev's reforms the USSR is shorn of Marxist-Leninist ideology, its behavior will revert to that of nineteenth century imperial Russia. While he finds this more reassuring than the threat posed by a communist Russia, he implies that there will still be a substantial degree of competition and conflict in the international system, just as there was say between Russia and Britain or Wilhelmine Germany in the last century. This is, of course, a convenient point of view for people who want to admit that something major is changing in the Soviet Union, but do not want to accept responsibility for recommending the radical policy redirection implicit in such a view. But is it true?

In fact, the notion that ideology is a superstructure imposed on a substratum of permanent great power interest is a highly questionable proposition. For the way in which any state defines its national interest is not universal but rests on some kind of prior ideological basis, just as we saw that economic behavior is determined by a prior state of consciousness. In this century, states have adopted highly articulated doctrines with explicit foreign policy agendas legitimizing expansionism, like Marxism-Leninism or National Socialism.

The expansionist and competitive behavior of nineteenth-century European states rested on no less ideal a basis; it just so happened that the ideology driving it was less explicit than the doctrines of the twentieth century. For one thing, most "liberal" European societies were illiberal insofar as they believed in the legitimacy of imperialism, that is, the right of one nation to rule over other nations without regard for the wishes of the ruled. The justifications for imperialism varied from nation to nation, from a crude belief in the legitimacy of force, particularly when applied to non-Europeans, to the White Man's Burden and Europe's

Christianizing mission, to the desire to give people of color access to the culture of Rabelais and Molière. But whatever the particular ideological basis, every "developed" country believed in the acceptability of higher civilizations ruling lower ones—including, incidentally, the United States with regard to the Philippines. This led to a drive for pure territorial aggrandizement in the latter half of the century and played no small role in causing the Great War.

The radical and deformed outgrowth of nineteenth-century imperialism was German fascism, an ideology which justified Germany's right not only to rule over non-European peoples, but over *all* non-German ones. But in retrospect it seems that Hitler represented a diseased bypath in the general course of European development, and since his fiery defeat, the legitimacy of any kind of territorial aggrandizement has been thoroughly discredited. Since the Second World War, European nationalism has been defanged and shorn of any real relevance to foreign policy, with the consequence that the nineteenth-century model of great power behavior has become a serious anachronism. The most extreme form of nationalism that any Western European state has mustered since 1945 has been Gaullism, whose self-assertion has been confined largely to the realm of nuisance politics and culture. International life for the part of the world that has reached the end of history is far more preoccupied with economics than with politics or strategy.

The developed states of the West do maintain defense establishments and in the postwar period have competed vigorously for influence to meet a worldwide communist threat. This behavior has been driven, however, by an external threat from states that possess overtly expansionist ideologies, and would not exist in their absence. To take the "neo-realist" theory seriously, one would have to believe that "natural" competitive behavior would reassert itself among the OECD states were Russia and China to disappear from the face of the earth.

That is, West Germany and France would arm themselves against each other as they did in the 1930s, Australia and New Zealand would send military advisers to block each others' advances in Africa, and the U.S.-Canadian border would become fortified. Such a prospect is, of course, ludicrous: minus Marxist-Leninist ideology, we are far more likely to see the "Common Marketization" of world politics than the disintegration of the EEC into nineteenth-century competitiveness. Indeed, as our experience in dealing with Europe on matters such as terrorism or Libya prove, they are much further gone than we down the road that denies the legitimacy of the use of force in international politics, even in self-defense.

The automatic assumption that Russia shorn of its expansionist communist ideology should pick up where the czars left off just prior to the Bolshevik Revolution is therefore a curious one. It assumes that the evolution of human consciousness has stood still in the meantime, and that the Soviets, while picking up currently fashionable ideas in the realm of economics, will return to foreign policy views a century out of date in the rest of Europe. This is certainly not what happened to China after it began its reform process. Chinese competitiveness and expansionism on the world scene have virtually disappeared: Beijing no longer sponsors Maoist insurgencies or tries to cultivate influence in distant African countries as it did in the 1960s. This is not to say that there are not troublesome aspects to contemporary Chinese foreign policy, such as the reckless sale of ballistic missile technology in the Middle East; and the PRC continues to manifest traditional great power behavior in its sponsorship of the Khmer Rouge against Vietnam. But the former is explained by commercial motives and the latter is a vestige of earlier ideologically-based rivalries. The new China far more resembles Gaullist France than pre–World War I Germany.

The real question for the future, however, is the degree to which Soviet elites have assimilated the consciousness of the universal homogenous state that is post-Hitler Europe. From their writings and from my own personal contacts with them, there is no question in my mind that the liberal Soviet intelligentsia rallying around Gorbachev has arrived at the end-of-history view in a remarkably short time, due in no small measure to the contacts they have had since the Brezhnev era with the larger European civilization around them. "New political thinking," the general rubric for their views, describes a world dominated by economic concerns, in which there are no ideological grounds for major conflict between nations, and in which, consequently, the use of military force becomes less legitimate. As Foreign Minister Shevardnadze put it in mid-1988:

> The struggle between two opposing systems is no longer a determining tendency of the present-day era. At the modern stage, the ability to build up material wealth at an accelerated rate on the basis of front-ranking science and high-level techniques and technology, and to distribute it fairly, and through joint efforts to restore and protect the resources necessary for mankind's survival acquires decisive importance.

The post-historical consciousness represented by "new thinking" is only one possible future for the Soviet Union, however. There has always been a very strong current of great Russian chauvinism in the Soviet Union, which has found freer expression since the advent of *glasnost*. It may be possible to return to traditional Marxism-Leninism for a while as a simple rallying point for those who want to restore the authority that Gorbachev has dissipated. But as in Poland, Marxism-Leninism is dead as a mobilizing ideology: under its banner people cannot be made to work harder, and its adherents have lost confidence in themselves. Unlike the propagators of traditional Marxism-Leninism, however, ultra-nationalists in the USSR believe in their Slavophile cause passionately, and one gets

the sense that the fascist alternative is not one that has played itself out entirely there.

The Soviet Union, then, is at a fork in the road: it can start down the path that was staked out by Western Europe forty-five years ago, a path that most of Asia has followed, or it can realize its own uniqueness and remain stuck in history. The choice it makes will be highly important for us, given the Soviet Union's size and military strength, for that power will continue to preoccupy us and slow our realization that we have already emerged on the other side of history.

V

The passing of Marxism-Leninism first from China and then from the Soviet Union will mean its death as a living ideology of world historical significance. For while there may be some isolated true believers left in places like Managua, Pyongyang, or Cambridge, Massachusetts, the fact that there is not a single large state in which it is a going concern undermines completely its pretensions to being in the vanguard of human history. And the death of this ideology means the growing "Common Marketization" of international relations, and the diminution of the likelihood of large-scale conflict between states.

This does not by any means imply the end of international conflict *per se*. For the world at that point would be divided between a part that was historical and a part that was post-historical. Conflict between states still in history, and between those states and those at the end of history, would still be possible. There would still be a high and perhaps rising level of ethnic and nationalist violence, since those are impulses incompletely played out, even in parts of the post-historical world. Palestinians and Kurds, Sikhs and Tamils, Irish Catholics and Walloons, Armenians and Azeris, will continue to have their unresolved grievances. This implies that terrorism and wars of national liberation will continue to be an important item on the international agenda. But large-scale conflict must involve large states still caught in the grip of history, and they are what appear to be passing from the scene.

The end of history will be a very sad time. The struggle for recognition, the willingness to risk one's life for a purely abstract goal, the worldwide ideological struggle that called forth daring, courage, imagination, and idealism, will be replaced by economic calculation, the endless solving of technical problems, environmental concerns, and the satisfaction of sophisticated consumer demands. In the post-historical period there will be neither art nor philosophy, just the perpetual caretaking of the museum of human history. I can feel in myself, and see in others around me, a powerful nostalgia for the time when history existed. Such nostalgia, in fact, will continue to fuel competition and conflict even in the post-historical world for some time to come. Even though I recognize its inevitability, I have the most ambivalent feelings for the civilization that has been created in Europe since 1945, with its north Atlantic and Asian offshoots. Perhaps this very prospect of centuries of boredom at the end of history will serve to get history started once again.

NOTE

1. Kojève's best-known work is his *Introduction à la lecture de Hegel* (Paris: Editions Gallimard, 1947), which is a transcript of the *Ecole Practique* lectures from the 1930s. This book is available in English entitled *Introduction to the Reading of Hegel* arranged by Raymond Queneau, edited by Allan Bloom, and translated by James Nichols (New York: Basic Books, 1969).

Samuel P. Huntington

THE CLASH OF CIVILIZATIONS?

The Next Pattern of Conflict

World politics is entering a new phase, and intellectuals have not hesitated to proliferate visions of what it will be—the end of history, the return of traditional rivalries between nation states, and the decline of the nation state from the conflicting pulls of tribalism and globalism, among others. Each of these visions catches aspects of the emerging reality. Yet they all miss a crucial, indeed a central, aspect of what global politics is likely to be in the coming years.

It is my hypothesis that the fundamental source of conflict in this new world will not be primarily ideological or primarily economic. The great divisions among humankind and the dominating source of conflict will be cultural. Nation states will remain the most powerful actors in world affairs, but the principal conflicts of global politics will occur between nations and groups of different civilizations. The clash of civilizations will dominate global politics. The fault lines between civilizations will be the battle lines of the future.

Conflict between civilizations will be the latest phase in the evolution of conflict in the modern world. For a century and a half after the emergence of the modern international system with the Peace of Westphalia, the conflicts of the Western world were largely among princes—emperors, absolute monarchs, and constitutional monarchs attempting to expand their bureaucracies, their armies, their mercantilist economic strength, and,

From *Foreign Affairs* 72, no. 3 (Summer 1993): 22–49.

most important, the territory they ruled. In the process they created nation states, and beginning with the French Revolution the principal lines of conflict were between nations rather than princes. * * * [A]s a result of the Russian Revolution and the reaction against it, the conflict of nations yielded to the conflict of ideologies, first among communism, fascism-Nazism, and liberal democracy, and then between communism and liberal democracy. During the Cold War, this latter conflict became embodied in the struggle between the two superpowers, neither of which was a nation state in the classical European sense and each of which defined its identity in terms of its ideology.

* * * With the end of the Cold War, international politics moves out of its Western phase, and its centerpiece becomes the interaction between the West and non-Western civilizations and among non-Western civilizations. In the politics of civilizations, the peoples and governments of non-Western civilizations no longer remain the objects of history as targets of Western colonialism but join the West as movers and shapers of history.

The Nature of Civilizations

During the Cold War the world was divided into the First, Second, and Third Worlds. Those divisions are no longer relevant. It is far more meaningful now to group countries not in terms of their political or economic systems or in terms of their level of economic development but rather in terms of their culture and civilization.

What do we mean when we talk of a civilization? A civilization is a cultural entity. Villages, regions, ethnic groups, nationalities, religious groups, all have distinct cultures at different levels of cultural heterogeneity. The culture of a village in southern Italy may be different from that of a village in northern Italy, but both will share in a common Italian culture that distinguishes them from German villages. European communities, in turn, will share cultural features that distinguish them from Arab or Chinese communities. Arabs, Chinese, and Westerners, however, are not part of any broader cultural entity. They constitute civilizations. A civilization is thus the highest cultural grouping of people and the broadest level of cultural identity people have short of that which distinguishes humans from other species. It is defined both by common objective elements, such as language, history, religion, customs, institutions, and by the subjective self-identification of people. * * *

* * * Civilizations are nonetheless meaningful entities, and while the lines between them are seldom sharp, they are real. Civilizations are dynamic; they rise and fall; they divide and merge. And, as any student of history knows, civilizations disappear and are buried in the sands of time.

Westerners tend to think of nation states as the principal actors in global affairs. They have been that, however, for only a few centuries. The broader reaches of human history have been the history of civilizations. In *A Study of History*, Arnold Toynbee identified 21 major civilizations; only six of them exist in the contemporary world.

Why Civilizations Will Clash

Civilization identity will be increasingly important in the future, and the world will be shaped in large measure by the interactions among seven or eight major civilizations. These include Western, Confucian, Japanese, Islamic, Hindu, Slavic-Orthodox, Latin American, and possibly African civilization. The most important conflicts of the future will occur along the cultural fault lines separating these civilizations from one another.

Why will this be the case?

First, differences among civilizations are not only real; they are basic. Civilizations are differentiated from each other by history, language, culture, tradition and, most important, religion. The people of different civilizations have different views on the relations between God and man, the individual and the group, the citizen and the state, parents and children, husband and wife, as well as differing views of the relative importance of rights and responsibilities, liberty and authority, equality and hierarchy. These differences are the product of centuries. They will not soon disappear. * * *

Second, the world is becoming a smaller place. The interactions between peoples of different civilizations are increasing; these increasing interactions intensify civilization consciousness and awareness of differences between civilizations and commonalities within civilizations. * * *

Third, the processes of economic modernization and social change throughout the world are separating people from longstanding local identities. They also weaken the nation state as a source of identity. In much of the world, religion has moved in to fill this gap, often in the form of movements that are labeled "fundamentalist." Such movements are found in Western Christianity, Judaism, Buddhism, and Hinduism, as well as in Islam. * * * The "unsecularization of the world," George Weigel has remarked, "is one of the dominant social facts of life in the late twentieth century." * * *

Fourth, the growth of civilization-consciousness is enhanced by the dual role of the West. On the one hand, the West is at a peak of power. At the same time, however, and perhaps as a result, a return to the roots phenomenon is occurring among non-Western civilizations. Increasingly one hears references to trends toward a turning inward and "Asianization" in Japan, the end of the Nehru legacy and the "Hinduization" of India, the failure of Western ideas of socialism and nationalism and hence "re-Islamization" of the Middle East, and now a debate over Westernization versus Russianization in Boris Yeltsin's country. A West at the peak of its power confronts non-Wests that increasingly have the desire, the will, and the resources to shape the world in non-Western ways.

■   ■   ■

Fifth, cultural characteristics and differences are less mutable and hence less easily compromised and resolved than political and economic ones. In the former Soviet Union, communists can become democrats, the rich can become poor and the poor rich, but Russians cannot become Estonians and Azeris cannot become Armenians. * * * Even more than ethnicity, religion discriminates sharply and exclusively among people. A person can be half-French and half-Arab and simultaneously even a citizen of two countries. It is more difficult to be half-Catholic and half-Muslim.

Finally, economic regionalism is increasing. * * * On the one hand, successful economic regionalism will reinforce civilization-consciousness. On the other hand, economic regionalism may succeed only when it is rooted in a common civilization. The European Community rests on the shared foundation of European culture and Western Christianity. The success of the North American Free Trade Area depends on the convergence now underway of Mexican, Canadian, and American cultures. Japan, in contrast, faces difficulties in creating a comparable economic entity in East Asia because Japan is a society and civilization unique to itself. * * *

■   ■   ■

As people define their identity in ethnic and religious terms, they are likely to see an "us" versus "them" relation existing between themselves and people of different ethnicity or religion. The end

of ideologically defined states in Eastern Europe and the former Soviet Union permits traditional ethnic identities and animosities to come to the fore. Differences in culture and religion create differences over policy issues, ranging from human rights to immigration to trade and commerce to the environment. * * * Most important, the efforts of the West to promote its values of democracy and liberalism as universal values, to maintain its military predominance and to advance its economic interests engender countering responses from other civilizations. * * *

The clash of civilizations thus occurs at two levels. At the micro-level, adjacent groups along the fault lines between civilizations struggle, often violently, over the control of territory and each other. At the macro-level, states from different civilizations compete for relative military and economic power, struggle over the control of international institutions and third parties, and competitively promote their particular political and religious values.

The Fault Lines between Civilizations

The fault lines between civilizations are replacing the political and ideological boundaries of the Cold War as the flash points for crisis and bloodshed. The Cold War began when the Iron Curtain divided Europe politically and ideologically. The Cold War ended with the end of the Iron Curtain. As the ideological division of Europe has disappeared, the cultural division of Europe between Western Christianity, on the one hand, and Orthodox Christianity and Islam, on the other, has reemerged. The most significant dividing line in Europe, as William Wallace has suggested, may well be the eastern boundary of Western Christianity in the year 1500. This line runs along what are now the boundaries between Finland and

Russia and between the Baltic states and Russia, cuts through Belarus and Ukraine separating the more Catholic western Ukraine from Orthodox eastern Ukraine, swings westward separating Transylvania from the rest of Romania, and then goes through Yugoslavia almost exactly along the line now separating Croatia and Slovenia from the rest of Yugoslavia. In the Balkans this line, of course, coincides with the historic boundary between the Hapsburg and Ottoman empires. The peoples to the north and west of this line are Protestant or Catholic; they shared the common experiences of European history—feudalism, the Renaissance, the Reformation, the Enlightenment, the French Revolution, the Industrial Revolution; they are generally economically better off than the peoples to the east; and they may now look forward to increasing involvement in a common European economy and to the consolidation of democratic political systems. The peoples to the east and south of this line are Orthodox or Muslim; they historically belonged to the Ottoman or Tsarist empires and were only lightly touched by the shaping events in the rest of Europe; they are generally less advanced economically; they seem much less likely to develop stable democratic political systems. The Velvet Curtain of culture has replaced the Iron Curtain of ideology as the most significant dividing line in Europe. As the events in Yugoslavia show, it is not only a line of difference; it is also at times a line of bloody conflict.

Conflict along the fault line between Western and Islamic civilizations has been going on for 1,300 years. * * *

■ ■ ■

This centuries-old military interaction between the West and Islam is unlikely to decline. It could become more virulent. The Gulf War left some Arabs feeling proud that Saddam Hussein had attacked Israel and stood up to the West. It also left many feeling humiliated and resentful of the West's military presence in the Persian Gulf, the West's overwhelming military dominance, and their apparent inability to shape their own destiny. Many Arab countries, in addition to the oil exporters, are reaching levels of economic and social development where autocratic forms of government become inappropriate and efforts to introduce democracy become stronger. Some openings in Arab political systems have already occurred. The principal beneficiaries of these openings have been Islamist movements. * * *

Those relations are also complicated by demography. The spectacular population growth in Arab countries, particularly in North Africa, has led to increased migration to Western Europe. The movement within Western Europe toward minimizing internal boundaries has sharpened political sensitivities with respect to this development. * * *

■ ■ ■

Historically, the other great antagonistic interaction of Arab Islamic civilization has been with the pagan, animist, and now increasingly Christian black peoples to the south. In the past, this antagonism was epitomized in the image of Arab slave dealers and black slaves. It has been reflected in the on-going civil war in the Sudan between Arabs and blacks, the fighting in Chad between Libyan-supported insurgents and the government, the tensions between Orthodox Christians and Muslims in the Horn of Africa, and the political conflicts, recurring riots and communal violence between Muslims and Christians in Nigeria. The modernization of Africa and the spread of Christianity are likely to enhance the probability of violence along this fault line. Symptomatic of the intensification of this conflict was the Pope John Paul II's speech in Khartoum in February 1993 attacking the actions of the Sudan's Islamist government against the Christian minority there.

On the northern border of Islam, conflict has increasingly erupted between Orthodox and

Muslim peoples, including the carnage of Bosnia and Sarajevo, the simmering violence between Serb and Albanian, the tenuous relations between Bulgarians and their Turkish minority, the violence between Ossetians and Ingush, the unremitting slaughter of each other by Armenians and Azeris, the tense relations between Russians and Muslims in Central Asia. * * *

The conflict of civilizations is deeply rooted elsewhere in Asia. The historic clash between Muslim and Hindu in the subcontinent manifests itself now not only in the rivalry between Pakistan and India but also in intensifying religious strife within India between increasingly militant Hindu groups and India's substantial Muslim minority. The destruction of the Ayodhya mosque in December 1992 brought to the fore the issue of whether India will remain a secular democratic state or become a Hindu one. * * *

■　　■　　■

Groups or states belonging to one civilization that become involved in war with people from a different civilization naturally try to rally support from other members of their own civilization. * * *

■　　■　　■

Civilization rallying to date has been limited, but it has been growing, and it clearly has the potential to spread much further. As the conflicts in the Persian Gulf, the Caucasus, and Bosnia continued, the positions of nations and the cleavages between them increasingly were along civilizational lines. Populist politicians, religious leaders, and the media have found it a potent means of arousing mass support and of pressuring hesitant governments. In the coming years, the local conflicts most likely to escalate into major wars will be those, as in Bosnia and the Caucasus, along the fault lines between civilizations. The next world war, if there is one, will be a war between civilizations.

The West versus the Rest

The West is now at an extraordinary peak of power in relation to other civilizations. Its superpower opponent has disappeared from the map. Military conflict among Western states is unthinkable, and Western military power is unrivaled. Apart from Japan, the West faces no economic challenge. It dominates international political and security institutions and with Japan international economic institutions. Global political and security issues are effectively settled by a directorate of the United States, Britain, and France, world economic issues by a directorate of the United States, Germany, and Japan, all of which maintain extraordinarily close relations with each other to the exclusion of lesser and largely non-Western countries. Decisions made at the U.N. Security Council or in the International Monetary Fund that reflect the interests of the West are presented to the world as reflecting the desires of the world community. The very phrase "the world community" has become the euphemistic collective noun (replacing "the Free World") to give global legitimacy to actions reflecting the interests of the United States and other Western powers.[1] * * *

■　　■　　■

* * * V. S. Naipaul has argued that Western civilization is the "universal civilization" that "fits all men." At a superficial level much of Western culture has indeed permeated the rest of the world. At a more basic level, however, Western concepts differ fundamentally from those prevalent in other civilizations. Western ideas of individualism, liberalism, constitutionalism, human rights, equality, liberty, the rule of law, democracy, free markets, the separation of church and state often have little resonance in Islamic, Confucian, Japanese, Hindu, Buddhist, or Orthodox cultures. Western efforts to propagate such ideas produce instead a reaction against "human rights imperialism" and a reaffirmation of

indigenous values, as can be seen in the support for religious fundamentalism by the younger generation in non-Western cultures. The very notion that there could be a "universal civilization" is a Western idea, directly at odds with the particularism of most Asian societies and their emphasis on what distinguishes one people from another. Indeed, the author of a review of 100 comparative studies of values in different societies concluded that "the values that are most important in the West are least important worldwide."[2] In the political realm, of course, these differences are most manifest in the efforts of the United States and other Western powers to induce other peoples to adopt Western ideas concerning democracy and human rights. Modern democratic government originated in the West. When it has developed in non-Western societies it has usually been the product of Western colonialism or imposition.

The central axis of world politics in the future is likely to be, in Kishore Mahbubani's phrase, the conflict between "the West and the Rest" and the responses of non-Western civilizations to Western power and values.[3] Those responses generally take one or a combination of three forms. At one extreme, non-Western states can, like Burma and North Korea, attempt to pursue a course of isolation, to insulate their societies from penetration or "corruption" by the West, and, in effect, to opt out of participation in the Western-dominated global community. The costs of this course, however, are high, and few states have pursued it exclusively. A second alternative, the equivalent of "bandwagoning" in international relations theory, is to attempt to join the West and accept its values and institutions. The third alternative is to attempt to "balance" the West by developing economic and military power and cooperating with other non-Western societies against the West, while preserving indigenous values and institutions; in short, to modernize but not to Westernize.

■ ■ ■

Implications for the West

This article does not argue that civilization identities will replace all other identities, that nation states will disappear, that each civilization will become a single coherent political entity, that groups within a civilization will not conflict with and even fight each other. This paper does set forth the hypotheses that differences between civilizations are real and important; civilization-consciousness is increasing; conflict between civilizations will supplant ideological and other forms of conflict as the dominant global form of conflict; international relations, historically a game played out within Western civilization, will increasingly be de-Westernized and become a game in which non-Western civilizations are actors and not simply objects; successful political, security, and economic international institutions are more likely to develop within civilizations than across civilizations; conflicts between groups in different civilizations will be more frequent, more sustained, and more violent than conflicts between groups in the same civilization; violent conflicts between groups in different civilizations are the most likely and most dangerous source of escalation that could lead to global wars; the paramount axis of world politics will be the relations between "the West and the Rest"; the elites in some torn non-Western countries will try to make their countries part of the West, but in most cases face major obstacles to accomplishing this; a central focus of conflict for the immediate future will be between the West and several Islamic-Confucian states.

This is not to advocate the desirability of conflicts between civilizations. It is to set forth descriptive hypotheses as to what the future may be like. If these are plausible hypotheses, however, it is necessary to consider their implications for Western policy. These implications should be divided between short-term advantage and long-term accommodation. In the short term it is clearly in the interest of the West to promote greater cooperation and unity within its own civilization, particularly between its European and North American components; to incorporate into the West societies in Eastern Europe, and Latin America whose cultures are close to those of the West; to promote and maintain cooperative relations with Russia and Japan; to prevent escalation of local inter-civilization conflicts into major inter-civilization wars; to limit the expansion of the military strength of Confucian and Islamic states; to moderate the reduction of Western military capabilities and maintain military superiority in East and Southwest Asia; to exploit differences and conflicts among Confucian and Islamic states; to support in other civilizations groups sympathetic to Western values and interests; to strengthen international institutions that reflect and legitimate Western interests and values and to promote the involvement of non-Western states in those institutions.

In the longer term other measures would be called for. Western civilization is both Western and modern. Non-Western civilizations have attempted to become modern without becoming Western. To date only Japan has fully succeeded in this quest. Non-Western civilizations will continue to attempt to acquire the wealth, technology, skills, machines, and weapons that are part of being modern. They will also attempt to reconcile this modernity with their traditional culture and values. Their economic and military strength relative to the West will increase. Hence the West will increasingly have to accommodate these non-Western modern civilizations whose power approaches that of the West but whose values and interests differ significantly from those of the West. This will require the West to maintain the economic and military power necessary to protect its interests in relation to these civilizations. It will also, however, require the West to develop a more profound understanding of the basic religious and philosophical assumptions underlying other civilizations and the ways in which people in those civilizations see their interests. It will require an effort to identify elements of commonality between Western and other civilizations. For the relevant future, there will be no universal civilization, but instead a world of different civilizations, each of which will have to learn to coexist with the others.

NOTES

1. Almost invariably Western leaders claim they are acting on behalf of "the world community." One minor lapse occurred during the run-up to the Gulf War. In an interview on "Good Morning America," Dec. 21, 1990, British Prime Minister John Major referred to the actions "the West" was taking against Saddam Hussein. He quickly corrected himself and subsequently referred to "the world community." He was, however, right when he erred.
2. Harry C. Triandis, *The New York Times*, Dec. 25, 1990, p. 41, and "Cross-Cultural Studies of Individualism and Collectivism," *Nebraska Symposium on Motivation*, vol. 37, 1989, pp. 41–133.
3. Kishore Mahbubani, "The West and the Rest," *The National Interest*, Summer 1992, pp. 3–13.

G. John Ikenberry

THE END OF LIBERAL INTERNATIONAL ORDER?

For seven decades the world has been dominated by a western liberal order. After the Second World War, the United States and its partners built a multifaceted and sprawling international order, organized around economic openness, multilateral institutions, security cooperation and democratic solidarity. Along the way, the United States became the 'first citizen' of this order, providing hegemonic leadership—anchoring the alliances, stabilizing the world economy, fostering cooperation and championing 'free world' values. Western Europe and Japan emerged as key partners, tying their security and economic fortunes to this extended liberal order. After the end of the Cold War, this order spread outwards. Countries in east Asia, eastern Europe and Latin America made democratic transitions and became integrated into the world economy. As the postwar order expanded, so too did its governance institutions. NATO expanded, the WTO was launched and the G20 took centre stage. Looking at the world at the end of the twentieth century, one could be excused for thinking that history was moving in a progressive and liberal internationalist direction.

Today, this liberal international order is in crisis. For the first time since the 1930s, the United States has elected a president who is actively hostile to liberal internationalism. Trade, alliances, international law, multilateralism, environment, torture and human rights—on all these issues, President Trump has made statements that, if acted upon,

would effectively bring to an end America's role as leader of the liberal world order. Simultaneously, Britain's decision to leave the EU, and a myriad other troubles besetting Europe, appear to mark an end to the long postwar project of building a greater union. The uncertainties of Europe, as the quiet bulwark of the wider liberal international order, have global significance. Meanwhile, liberal democracy itself appears to be in retreat, as varieties of 'new authoritarianism' rise to new salience in countries such as Hungary, Poland, the Philippines and Turkey. Across the liberal democratic world, populist, nationalist and xenophobic strands of backlash politics have proliferated.[1]

How deep is this crisis? It might simply be a temporary setback. With new political leadership and renewed economic growth, the liberal order could bounce back. But most observers think there is something more fundamental going on. Some observers see a crisis of American hegemonic leadership. For 70 years, the liberal international order has been tied to American power—its economy, currency, alliance system, leadership. Perhaps what we are witnessing is a 'crisis of transition', whereby the old US-led political foundation of the liberal order will give way to a new configuration of global power, new coalitions of states, new governance institutions. This transition might be leading to some sort of post-American and post-western order that remains relatively open and rules-based.[2] Others see a deeper crisis, one of liberal internationalism itself. In this view, there is a long-term shift in the global system away from open trade, multilateralism and cooperative security. Global

From *International Affairs* 94, no. 1 (2018): 7–23.

order is giving way to various mixtures of nationalism, protectionism, spheres of influence and regional Great Power projects. In effect, there is no liberal internationalism without American and western hegemony—and that age is ending. Liberal internationalism is essentially an artefact of the rapidly receding Anglo-American era.[3] Finally, some go even further than this, arguing that what is happening is that the long era of 'liberal modernity' is ending. Beginning with the Enlightenment and running through the industrial revolution and the rise of the West, world-historical change seemed to be unfolding according to a deep developmental logic. It was a progressive movement driven by reason, science, discovery, innovation, technology, learning, constitutionalism and institutional adaptation. The world as a whole was in the embrace of this global modernizing movement. Perhaps today's crisis marks the ending of the global trajectory of liberal modernity. It was an artefact of a specific time and place—and the world is now moving on.[4]

No one can be sure how deep the crisis of liberal internationalism runs. In what follows, I argue that, despite its troubles, liberal internationalism still has a future. The American hegemonic organization of liberal order is weakening, but the more general organizing ideas and impulses of liberal internationalism run deep in world politics. What liberal internationalism offers is a vision of open and loosely rules-based order. It is a tradition of order-building that emerged with the rise and spread of liberal democracy, and its ideas and agendas have been shaped as these countries have confronted and struggled with the grand forces of modernity. Creating an international 'space' for liberal democracy, reconciling the dilemmas of sovereignty and interdependence, seeking protections and preserving rights within and between states—these are the underlying aims that have propelled liberal internationalism through the 'golden eras' and 'global catastrophes' of the last two centuries. Despite the upheavals and destruction of world war, economic depression, and the rise and fall of fascism and totalitarianism, the liberal international project survived. It is likely to survive today's crises as well. But to do so this time, as it has done in the past, liberal internationalism will need to be rethought and reinvented.

I make this argument in three steps. First, I offer a way of thinking about liberal internationalism. It is not simply a creature of American hegemony. It is a more general and longstanding set of ideas, principles and political agendas for organizing and reforming international order. In the most general sense, liberal internationalism is a way of thinking about and responding to modernity—its opportunities and its dangers. What has united the ideas and agendas of liberal internationalism is a vision of an open, loosely rules-based and progressively oriented international order. Built on Enlightenment foundations, it emerged in the nineteenth century with the rise in the West of liberalism, nationalism, the industrial revolution, and the eras of British and American hegemony. A conviction has run through nineteenth- and twentieth-century liberal internationalists that the western and—by extension—the global international order is capable of reform. This separates liberal internationalism from various alternative ideologies of global order—political realism, authoritarian nationalism, Social Darwinism, revolutionary socialism and post-colonialism.

Second, I trace liberal internationalism's crooked pathway into the twenty-first century, as it evolved and reinvented itself along the way. In the nineteenth century, liberal internationalism was seen in the movements towards free trade, international law, collective security and the functional organization of the western capitalist system. Along the way, liberal internationalism mixed and intermingled with all the other major forces that have shaped the modern global system—imperialism, nationalism, capitalism, and the shifting movements of culture and civilization. In the twentieth century and into the twenty-first, it moved through a sequence of golden eras, crises and turning points: Wilson and the League of Nations; the post–Second World War Anglo-American settlement and the building of the US-led postwar order; crises of capitalism and leadership in the world economy; the post–Cold War American 'unipolar' moment and the 'globalization' of liberalism and neo-liberal ideas; debates about the Responsibility to Protect (R2P) and liberal interventionism; and today's crisis of the western liberal order. Liberal internationalism came into its own as a political order during the Cold War, under American auspices. American liberal hegemony was essentially a western order built around 'free world' social purposes.

Third, I identify the sources of the contemporary crisis of liberal internationalism. These can be traced to the end of the Cold War. It is important to recall that the postwar liberal order was originally not a global order. It was built 'inside' one half of the bipolar Cold War system. It was part of a larger geopolitical project of waging a global Cold War. It was built around bargains, institutions and social purposes that were tied to the West, American leadership and the global struggle against Soviet communism. When the Cold War ended, this 'inside' order became the 'outside' order. As the Soviet Union collapsed, the great rival of liberal internationalism fell away, and the American-led liberal order expanded outwards. With the end of the Cold War, liberal internationalism was globalized. Initially, this was seen as a moment of triumph for western liberal democracies. But the globalization of the liberal order put in motion two shifts that later became the sources of crisis. First, it upended the political foundations of the liberal order. With new states entering the system, the old bargains and institutions that provided the sources of stability and governance were overrun. A wider array of states—with a more diverse set of ideologies and agendas—were now part of the order. This triggered what might be called a 'crisis of authority,' where new bargains, roles and responsibilities were now required. These struggles over authority and

governance continue today. Second, the globalization of the liberal order also led to a loss of capacity to function as a security community. This can be called a 'crisis of social purpose.' In its Cold War configuration, the liberal order was a sort of full-service security community, reinforcing the capacity of western liberal democracies to pursue policies of economic and social advancement and stability. As liberal internationalism became the platform for the wider global order, this sense of shared social purpose and security community eroded.

Taking all these elements together, this account of the crisis can be understood as a crisis of success, in the sense that the troubles besetting the liberal order emerged from its post–Cold War triumph and expansion. Put differently, the troubles today might be seen as a 'Polanyi crisis'—growing turmoil and instability resulting from the rapid mobilization and spread of global capitalism, market society and complex interdependence, all of which has overrun the political foundations that supported its birth and early development.[5] They do not, on the contrary, constitute what might be called an 'E. H. Carr crisis,' wherein liberal internationalism fails because of the return of Great Power politics and the problems of anarchy.[6] The troubles facing liberal internationalism are not driven by a return of geopolitical conflict, although conflicts with China and Russia are real and dangerous. In fact, the liberal international order has succeeded all too well. It has helped usher in a world that has outgrown its political moorings.

Liberal internationalism has survived its 200-year journey into the current century because, with liberal democracy at the core, it offered a coherent and functional vision of how to organize international space. The industrial revolution and the relentless rise of economic and security interdependence generated both opportunities and threats for liberal democracies. Liberal internationalism, in all its varied configurations, has provided templates for cooperation in the face of the grand forces of modernity. To do so again, the liberal international project will need to rethink its vision. It will either need to offer a 'small and thick' vision of liberal order, centred as it was during the Cold War on the western liberal democracies; or it will need to offer a 'large and thin' version of liberal internationalism, with global principles and institutions for coping with the dangers and vulnerabilities of twenty-first-century modernity—cascading problems of environmental destruction, weapons of mass destruction, global health pandemics and all the other threats to human civilization.

Liberal Internationalism and World Order

When the nineteenth century began, liberal democracy was a new and fragile political experiment, a political glimmering within a wider world of monarchy, autocracy, empire and traditionalism. Two hundred years later, at the end of the twentieth century, liberal democracies, led by the western Great Powers, dominated the world—commanding 80 per cent of global GNP. Across these two centuries, the industrial revolution unfolded, capitalism expanded its frontiers, Europeans built far-flung empires, the modern nation-state took root, and along the way the world witnessed what might be called the 'liberal ascendancy'—the rise in the size, number, power and wealth of liberal democracies.[7] Liberal internationalism is the body of ideas and agendas with which these liberal democracies have attempted to organize the world.

Liberal internationalism has risen and fallen and evolved. But its general logic is captured in a cluster of five convictions. One concerns openness. Trade and exchange are understood to be constituents of modern society, and the connections and gains that flow from deep engagement and integration foster peace and political advancement. An open international order facilitates economic growth, encourages the flow of knowledge and technology, and draws states together. Second, there is a commitment to some sort of loosely rules-based set of relations. Rule and institutions facilitate cooperation and create capacities for states to make good on their domestic obligations. This is what John Ruggie describes as 'multilateralism'—an institutional form that coordinates relations among a group of states 'on the basis of generalized principles of conduct.'[8] Third, there is a view that liberal international order will entail some form of security cooperation. This does not necessarily mean alliances or a formal system of collective security, but states within the order affiliate in ways designed to increase their security. Fourth, liberal internationalism is built on the idea that international society is, as Woodrow Wilson argued, 'corrigible.' Reform is possible. Power politics can be tamed—at least to some extent—and states can build stable relations around the pursuit of mutual gains. Fifth and finally, there is an expectation that a liberal international order will move states in a progressive direction, defined in terms of liberal democracy. The order provides institutions, relationships, and rights and protections that allow states to grow and advance at home. It is a sort of mutual aid and protection society.[9]

Seen in this way, a liberal international order can take various forms. It can be more or less global or regional in scope. The early postwar western liberal order was primarily an Atlantic regional community, while the post–Cold War liberal system has had a wider global reach. A liberal international order can be more or less organized around a hegemonic state—that is, it can be more or less hierarchical in character. It can be more or less embodied in formal agreements and governance institutions. Perhaps most importantly, the 'social purposes' of a liberal international order can vary. It can have a 'thin' social purpose, providing, for example, only rudimentary rules and institutions for limited cooperation and exchange among liberal democracies. Or it could have a 'thick' social purpose, with a dense set of agreements and shared commitments aimed at realizing more ambitious goals of cooperation, integration and shared security. Overall, liberal internationalism can be more or less open, rules-based and progressively oriented.[10] Liberal internationalism can be seen as breaking down or disappearing when international order is increasingly organized around mercantile blocs, spheres of influence, imperial zones and closed regions.

Taken as a whole, liberal internationalism offers a vision of order in which sovereign states—led by liberal democracies—cooperate for mutual gain and protection within a loosely rules-based global space. Glimmerings of this vision emerged in the late eighteenth and early nineteenth centuries, triggered by Enlightenment thinking and the emergence of industrialism and modern society. Over the next century, a variety of economic, political and intellectual developments set the stage for the reorganization of relations among western states. The Great Powers of Europe met as the patrons of western order in the Congress of Vienna. Led by Britain, these states entered into a period of industrial growth and expanding trade. Political reform—and the revolutions of 1848—reflected the rise of and struggles for liberal democracy and constitutionalism, the growth of the middle and working classes, and the creation of new political parties arrayed across the ideological spectrum from conservative to liberal and socialist. Nationalism emerged and became tied to the building of modern bureaucratic states. Britain signalled a new orientation towards the world economy with the repeal of the Corn Laws. Nationalism was matched with new forms of internationalism—in law, commerce and social justice. Peace movements spread across the western world. A new era of European industrial-age imperialism began, as Britain, France and other European states competed for colonial prizes. Along the way, new ideas of 'the global' emerged, intellectual and political visions of a rapidly developing global system.[11]

In this setting, liberal internationalism emerged as a way of thinking about western and world order. It began as a variety of scattered nineteenth-century internationalist ideas and movements. Liberal ideas in Britain began with Adam Smith's writings in the late eighteenth century and continued with thinkers such as Richard Cobden and John Bright in the nineteenth. A general view emerged—captured, for example, in the writings of Walter Bagehot and many others—that there was a developmental logic to history, a movement from despotic states to more rules-based and constitutional ones. Kant's ideas on republicanism and perpetual peace offered hints of an evolutionary logic in which liberal democracies would emerge and organize themselves within a wider political space. Ideas of contracts, rights and the law were developed by thinkers from John Locke to John Stuart Mill.[12]

The connections between domestic liberalism and liberal internationalism are multifaceted, and they have evolved over the last two centuries. It is hard to see a distinctive or coherent liberal international agenda in the nineteenth century. At this time, such notions were primarily manifest in ideas about world politics that emerged from thinkers and activists committed to liberalism within countries—in ideas about liberalization of trade, collective security, arbitration of disputes and so forth. What emerges during this era is a sense of an international sphere of action that was opening up within the liberal democratic world, and a conviction that collective efforts could and should be made to manage this expanding international space. As Mark Mazower has argued, what was new was the notion that a realm of 'the international' was growing and that 'it was in some sense governable.'[13]

In the twentieth century there emerged a much more full-blown sense of liberal internationalism, understood as a set of prescriptions for organizing and reforming the world in such a way as to facilitate the pursuit of liberal democracy at home. Beginning with Woodrow Wilson in 1919, liberal internationalism emerged as an agenda for building a type of order—a sort of 'container' within which liberal democracies could live and survive. In the hands of F. D. Roosevelt and his generation after 1945, liberal internationalism became to an even greater extent an agenda for building an international community within which liberal democracies could be stabilized and protected. Growing out of the New Deal experience, the postwar 'embedded liberal' order was designed in part to safeguard liberal democracies from growing risks of economic and political upheavals generated by modernity itself. In this way, liberal internationalism offered a vision of a reformed and managed western—and, eventually, global—order that would provide the organizational principles, institutions and capacities to negotiate the international contingencies and dislocations that threaten the domestic pursuit of liberal democracy.

The Era of American Liberal Hegemony

Liberal internationalism emerged after the Second World War as an organizing vision for the western-led order. As in 1919, so after 1945 the United States used its postwar position to lead in the building of a postwar order. But along the way, liberal internationalism took on a new shape and character—and with the rise of the Cold War, a U.S.-led liberal hegemonic order emerged. In the age of Wilson, liberal internationalism was a relatively simply vision. International order was to be organized around a collective security system in which sovereign states would act together to uphold a system of territorial peace. The Wilsonian vision was undergirded by open trade, national self-determination, and the expectation of the continuing spread of liberal democracy. As Wilson himself put it: 'What we seek is the reign of law, based on the consent of the governed and sustained by the organized opinion of mankind.'[14] It was an ambitious scheme of order, but one without a lot of institutional machinery for global economic and social problem-solving or the management of Great Power relations. It was to be an institutionally 'thin' system of order in which states—primarily the western powers—would act cooperatively through a shared embrace of liberal ideas and principles.[15] The great centerpiece and organizational embodiment of Wilsonian liberal internationalism was the League of Nations.

The dramatic upheavals of the Great Depression, the Second World War and the Cold War set the stage for another American-led attempt to build a liberal order. A new moment to remake the world had arrived. Basic questions about power, order and modernity had to be rethought. From the 1930s onwards, the viability of western liberal democracy was itself uncertain. The violence and instabilities of the 1930s and 1940s forced liberal internationalists—and indeed everyone else—to reassess their ideas and agendas. The First World War was a jolt to the optimistic narratives of western civilization and progress. But FDR and his generation—facing the even more frightening rise of fascism and totalitarianism, followed by the horrors of total war, the Holocaust and the advent of atomic weapons, not to mention the collapse of the world economy—seemed to face a far more formidable, even existential array of threats. Modernity itself showed its dark side.

In this setting, FDR and his contemporaries found themselves advancing a new—more world-weary—vision of liberal international order. Paradoxically, it became both more universalistic in its vision and more deeply tied to American hegemonic power. The universalism can be seen in the Charter of the United Nations and the Universal Declaration of Human Rights. In the 1940s, liberal internationalism was reframed. The liberal internationalism of the Woodrow Wilson era was built around civilizational, racial and cultural hierarchies. It was a creature of the western white man's world. It was a narrow type of principled internationalism. Wilson-era liberal internationalism did not challenge European imperialism or racial hierarchies. British liberals explicitly defended empire and continued to see the world in racial and civilizational terms. The 1940s saw a shift or reformulation of these ideas. Universal rights and protections became more central to the ideological vision. FDR's Four Freedoms (of speech and worship, from want and fear) were the defining vision for this new conception of liberal international order. The postwar order was to be a security community—a global space where liberal democracies joined together to build a cooperative order that enshrined basic human rights and social protections.

At the same time, these universal rights and protections were advanced and legitimated in terms of the American-led Cold War struggle. The United States would be the hegemonic sponsor and protector of the liberal order. With American leadership, the 'free world' would be a sort of 'security community.' It would have rules, institutions, bargains and full-service political functions. To join the western liberal order was to join a 'mutual protection' society. To be inside this order was to enjoy trade, expanding growth, and tools for managing economic stability. Inside, it was warm; outside, it was cold. Countries would be protected in alliance partnerships and an array of functional organizations. In other words, in the postwar era, liberal internationalism became both more universal in its ideas and principles and more tied to an American-led political order.[16]

Over the Cold War decades, American-led liberal internationalism emerged as a distinctive type of order. The United States came to take on a variety of functions and responsibilities. It came to have a direct role in running the order—and it also found itself increasingly tied to the other states within the order. The United States became a provider of public goods—or at least 'club goods.' It upheld the rules and institutions, fostered security cooperation, led the management of the world economy, and championed shared norms and cooperation among the western-oriented liberal democracies. In security affairs, the United States established an array of security partnerships, beginning with NATO and alliances in east Asia. In the management of the world economy, the Bretton Woods international financial institutions became tied to the American market and dollar. Together, in the shadow of the Cold War, the American domestic system—its market and polity—became 'fused' to the evolving and deepening postwar liberal order.

American liberal hegemony, as a type of international order, had several key characteristics. First, it was built around open multilateral trade. In many ways, this was the key vision of the postwar American architects of liberal order. During the war, the question was debated: how large a geopolitical market space would the United States need so as to remain a viable global power? This was the era when most of the world's regions were divided into imperial zones, blocs and spheres of influence. The American strategic judgement was that, on the contrary, the postwar world would need to be open and accessible to the United States. The worst outcome would be closed regions in Europe, Asia and the Middle East, dominated by hostile Great Powers. Out of these worries, the United States launched its efforts to open the world economy and build institutions and partnerships that would establish a durably open global order. At the core of this system would be the liberal democracies, facilitating trade through GATT and later the WTO.

Second, American liberal hegemony was also defined by its commitment to a 'managed' open world economy. This is what John Ruggie has called 'embedded liberalism.' International agreements, embodied in the Bretton Woods system, were designed to give governments greater ability to regulate and manage economic openness to ensure that it was reconciled with domestic economic stability and policies in pursuit of full employment.[17] The New Deal itself provided an inspiration for this new thinking about the organization of an open world economy. The visionary goal was a middle ground between openness and stability. Free trade was essential for the sort of economic recovery and growth that would support centrist and progressive postwar political leadership in the United States and Europe. But trade and exchange would need to be reconciled with government efforts to ensure economic stability and the security of workers and the middle class. Social and economic security went hand in hand with national security.

Third, the postwar liberal order was built around new and permanent international institutions. To a greater extent than in Wilson's day, post-1945 liberal internationalists sought to build order around a system of multilateral governance. This was a vision of intergovernmentalism more than supranationalism. Governments would remain the primary source of authority. But governments would organize their relations around permanent regional and global institutions. They would conduct relations on multilateral platforms—bargaining, consulting, coordinating. These institutions would serve multiple purposes. They would facilitate cooperation by providing venues for ongoing bargaining and exchange. They would reinforce norms of equality and non-discrimination, thereby giving the order more legitimacy. And they would tie the United States more closely to its postwar partners, reducing worries about domination and abandonment. The result was an unprecedented effort across economic, political and security policy spheres to build working multilateral institutions.

Fourth, there was a special emphasis on relations among the western liberal democracies. The core underlying principles and norms of the liberal order could be construed as 'universal.' FDR's Four Freedoms were of this sort, and so too were the principles of multilateralism embedded in the postwar economic institutions. But the order itself was organized around the United States and its liberal democratic allies and clients. The fact that it was built inside the larger Cold War–era bipolar system

reinforced this orientation. Architects of the order understood that there was a special relationship among the western liberal democracies. At first this encompassed essentially just western Europe and Japan; but in the aftermath of the Cold War a larger and more diverse community of democracies took hold. The essential premise of American global leadership was that there is something special and enduring about the alignment of democracies. They have shared interests and values. American presidents from Woodrow Wilson to Barack Obama have acted on the assumption that democracies have a unique capacity to cooperate. In building liberal order during the Cold War, there was an authentic belief—held in Washington but also in European and Asian capitals—that the 'free world' was not just a temporary defensive alliance ranged against the Soviet Union: it was a nascent political community—a community of shared fate.[18] In this sense, the American-led order was, at its core, a 'democratic alliance' to defend and support a shared liberal democratic political space.

This liberal hegemonic order flourished over the decades of the Cold War. It provided a framework for the liberalization of trade and decades of growth across the advanced industrial world. Incomes and life opportunities steadily increased for the postwar generations of Europeans, Japanese and Americans. This open system ushered in, as Paul Johnson argues, 'the most rapid and prolonged economic expansion in world history.'[19] But the postwar liberal order was more than a growth machine. It provided a 'container' within which liberal democracies could gain greater measures of security and protection as well. To be inside this liberal hegemonic order was to be positioned inside a set of full-service economic, political and security institutions. It was both a *Gesellschaft*—a 'society' defined by formal rules, institutions and governmental ties—and a *Gemeinschaft*—a 'community' defined by shared values, beliefs and expectations.[20] Liberal order was a sort of nascent security community—with 'security' defined broadly.

Crises and Transformations

The foundations of this postwar liberal hegemonic order are weakening. In a simple sense, this is a story of grand shifts in the distribution of power and the consequences that follow. The United States and its allies are less powerful than they were when they built the postwar order. The unipolar moment—when the United States dominated world economic and military rankings—is ending. Europe and Japan have also weakened. Together, this old triad of patrons of the postwar liberal order is slowly dwindling in its share of the wider global distribution of power. This shift is probably not best seen as a transition from an American to a Chinese hegemonic order, the 'return to multipolarity' or a 'rise of the non-West.' Rather, it is simply a gradual diffusion of power away from the West. China will probably not replace the United States as an illiberal hegemon, and the global South will probably not emerge as a geopolitical bloc that directly challenges the U.S.-led order. But the United States—and its old allies—will continue to be a smaller part of the global whole, and this will constrain their ability to support and defend the liberal international order.

The political troubles of western liberal democracies magnify the implications of these global power shifts. As noted above, democracies everywhere are facing internal difficulties and discontents. The older western democracies are experiencing rising inequality, economic stagnation, fiscal crisis, and political polarization and gridlock. Many newer and poorer democracies, meanwhile, are beset by corruption, backsliding and rising inequality. The great 'third wave' of democratization seems to have crested, and now to be receding. As democracies fail to address problems, their domestic legitimacy is diminished and increasingly challenged by resurgent nationalist, populist and xenophobic movements. Together, these developments cast a dark shadow over the democratic future.

During the Cold War, the American-led liberal order was lodged within the western side of the bipolar world system. It was during these decades that the foundations of liberal hegemonic order were laid. With the collapse of the Soviet Union, this 'inside' order became the nucleus of an expanding global system. This had several consequences. One was that the United States became the sole superpower—the world entered the unipolar moment. This made American power itself an issue in world politics. During the Cold War, American power had a functional role in the system: it served as a balance against Soviet power. With the sudden emergence of unipolarity, American power was less constrained—and it did not play the same system-functional role. New debates emerged about the character of American hegemonic power. What would restrain American power? Was the United States now an informal empire? The American war in Iraq and the global 'war on terror' exacerbated these worries.[21]

Ironically, the crisis of the US-led liberal order can be traced to the collapse of Cold War bipolarity and the resulting spread of liberal internationalism. The seeds of crisis were planted at this moment of triumph. The liberal international order was, in effect, globalized. It was freed from its Cold War foundations and rapidly became the platform for an expanding global system of liberal democracy, markets and complex interdependence. During the Cold War, the liberal order was a global subsystem—and the bipolar global system served to reinforce the roles, commitments, identity and community that were together manifest as liberal hegemony. The crisis of liberal internationalism can be seen as a slow-motion reaction to this deep transformation in the geopolitical setting of the postwar liberal international project. Specifically, the globalization of liberal internationalism put in motion two long-term effects: a crisis of governance and authority, and a crisis of social purpose.

First, with the collapse of the Soviet sphere, the American-led liberal international order became the only surviving framework for order, and a growing number and diversity of states began to be integrated into it. This created new problems for the governance of the order. During the Cold War, the western-oriented liberal order was led by the United States, Europe and Japan, and it was organized around a complex array of bargains, working relationships and institutions. (Indeed, in the early postwar years, most of the core agreements about trade, finance and monetary relations were hammered out between the United States and Britain.) These countries did not agree on everything, but relative to the rest of the world, this was a small and homogeneous group of western states. Their economies converged, their interests were aligned and they generally trusted each other. These countries were also on the same side of the Cold War, and the American-led alliance system reinforced cooperation. This system of alliance made it easier for the United States and its partners to make commitments and bear burdens. It made it easier for European and east Asian states to agree to operate within an American-led liberal order. In this sense, the Cold War roots of the postwar liberal order reinforced the sense that the liberal democracies were involved in a common political project.

With the end of the Cold War, these foundational supports for liberal order were loosened. More, and more diverse, states entered the order—with new visions and agendas. The post–Cold War era also brought into play new and complex global issues, such as climate change, terrorism and weapons proliferation, and the growing challenges of interdependence. These are particularly hard issues on which to reach agreement among states coming from very different regions, with similarly different political orientations and levels of development. As a result, the challenges to multilateral cooperation have grown. At the core of these challenges has been the problem of authority and governance. Who pays, who adjusts, who leads? Rising non-western states began to seek a greater voice in the governance of the expanding liberal order. How

would authority across this order be redistributed? The old coalition of states—led by the United States, Europe and Japan—built a postwar order on layers of bargains, institutions and working relationships. But this old trilateral core is not the centre of the global system in the way it once was. The crisis of liberal order today is in part a problem of how to reorganize the governance of this order. The old foundations have been weakened, but new bargains and governance arrangements are yet to be fully negotiated.[22]

Second, the crisis of the liberal order is a crisis of legitimacy and social purpose. During the Cold War, the American-led postwar order had a shared sense that it was a community of liberal democracies that were made physically safer and economically more secure by affiliating with each other. The first several generations of the postwar period understood that to be inside this order was to be in a political and economic space where their societies could prosper and be protected. This sense was captured in John Ruggie's notion of 'embedded liberalism.' Trade and economic openness were rendered more or less compatible with economic security, stable employment and advancing living standards. The western-oriented liberal order had features of a security community—a sort of mutual protection society. Membership of this order was attractive because it provided tangible rights and benefits. It was a system of multilateral cooperation that provided national governments with tools and capacities to pursue economic stability and advancement.

This idea of liberal order as a security community is often lost in the narratives of the postwar era. The United States and its partners built an order—but they also 'formed a community': one based on common interests, shared values and mutual vulnerability. The common interests were manifest, for example, in the gains that flowed from trade and the benefits of alliance cooperation. The shared values were manifest in a degree of public trust and ready capacity for cooperation rooted in the values and institutions of liberal democracy. Mutual vulnerability was a sense that these countries were experiencing a similar set of large-scale perils—flowing from the great dangers and uncertainties of geopolitics and modernity. This idea of a western security community is hinted at in the concept of 'risk society' put forward by sociologists Anthony Giddens and Ulrich Beck. Their argument is that the rise of modernity—of an advanced and rapidly developing global system—has generated growing awareness of and responses to 'risk.' Modernization is an inherently unsettling march into the future. A risk society is, as Beck defines it, 'a systematic way of dealing with hazards and insecurities induced and introduced by modernisation itself.'[23] The Cold War intensified this sense of risk, and out of a growing sense of shared economic and security vulnerabilities, the western liberal democracies forged a security community.

With the end of the Cold War and the globalization of the liberal order, this sense of security community was undermined. This happened in the first instance, as noted above, through the rapid expansion in the number and variety of states in the order. The liberal order lost its identity as a western security community. It was now a far-flung platform for trade, exchange and multilateral cooperation. The democratic world was now less Anglo-American, less western. It embodied most of the world—developed, developing, North and South, colonial and post-colonial, Asian and European. This too was a case of 'success' planting the seeds of crisis. The result was an increasing divergence of views across the order about its members, their place in the world, and their historical legacies and grievances. There was less of a sense that liberal internationalism was a community with a shared narrative of its past and future.

The social purposes of the liberal order were further undermined by rising economic insecurity and grievance across the western industrial world. Since the 2008 financial crisis at least, the fortunes of workers and middle-class citizens in Europe and the United States have stagnated.[24] The expanding opportunities and rising wages enjoyed by earlier postwar generations seem to have stalled. For example, in the United States almost all the growth in wealth since the 1980s has gone to the top 20 per cent of earners in society. The post–Cold War growth in trade and interdependence does not seem to have directly advanced the incomes and life opportunities of many segments of the western liberal democracies. Branko Milanovic has famously described the differential gains across the global system over the last two decades as an 'elephant curve.' Looking across global income levels, Milanovic finds that the vast bulk of gains in real per capita income have been made in two very different groups. One comprises workers in countries such as China and India who have taken jobs in low-end manufacturing and service jobs, and, starting at very low wage levels, have experienced dramatic gains—even if they remain at the lower end of the global income spectrum. This is the hump of the elephant's back. The other group is the top 1 per cent—and, indeed, the top 0.01 per cent—who have experienced massive increases in wealth. This is the elephant's trunk, extended upward.[25] This stagnation in the economic fortunes of the western working and middle classes is reinforced by long-term shifts in technology, trade patterns, union organization and the sites for manufacturing jobs.

Under these adverse economic conditions, it is harder today than in the past to see the liberal order as a source of economic security and protection. Across the western liberal democratic world, liberal internationalism looks more like neoliberalism—a framework for international capitalist transactions. The 'embedded' character of liberal internationalism has slowly eroded.[26] The social purposes of the liberal order are not what they once were. It is less obvious today that the liberal democratic world is a security community. What do citizens in western democracies get from liberal internationalism? How does an open and loosely rules-based international order deliver security—economic or physical—to the lives of the great middle class? Liberal internationalism across the twentieth century was tied to progressive agendas within western liberal democracies. Liberal internationalism was seen not as the enemy of nationalism, but as a tool to give governments capacities to pursue economic security and advancements at home. What has happened in the last several decades is that this connection between progressivism at home and liberal internationalism abroad has been broken.

Conclusions

For the past 70 years, liberal internationalism has been embedded in the postwar American hegemonic order. It is an order that has been marked by economic openness and security cooperation as well as collective efforts to keep the peace, promote the rule of law, and sustain an array of international institutions organized to manage the modern problems of interdependence. This expansive version of liberal order emerged in fits and starts during the twentieth century as the United States and Europe struggled with the great dangers and catastrophes that shocked and shook the world—world war, economic depression, trade wars, fascism, totalitarianism and vast social injustices. Today this American-led era of liberal internationalism looks increasingly beleaguered. To bet on the future of the global liberal order is a little bit like a second marriage—a triumph of hope over experience. But it is important to take the long view. The liberal international project has travelled from the eighteenth century to our own time through repeated crises, upheavals, disasters and breakdowns—almost all of them worse than those appearing today. Indeed, it might be useful to think about liberal international order the way John Dewey thought about democracy—as a framework for coping with the inevitable problems of modern society. It is not a blueprint for an ideal world order; it is a methodology or machinery for responding to the opportunities and dangers of modernity.

The future of this liberal order hinges on the ability of the United States and Europe—and increasingly a wider array of liberal democracies—to lead and support it. This, in turn, depends on the ability of these leading liberal democracies to remain stable, well functioning and internationalist. Can these states recover their stability and bearings as liberal democracies? Can they regain their legitimacy and standing as 'models' of advanced societies by finding solutions to the current generation's great problems—economic inequality, stagnant wages, fiscal imbalances, environmental degradation, racial and ethnic conflicts, and so forth? Global leadership hinges on state power, but also on the appeal and legitimacy of the ideals and principles that Great Powers embody and project. The appeal and legitimacy of liberal internationalism will depend on the ability of the United States and other states like it to re-establish their ability to function and to find solutions to twenty-first-century problems.

It is worth remembering that American liberal internationalism was shaped and enabled by the domestic programmes of the Progressives, the New Deal and the Great Society. These initiatives aimed to address American economic and social inequalities and reorganize the American state in view of the unfolding problems of industrialism and globalization. FDR and the New Deal were the critical pivot for America's liberal internationalist vision of order.

It was an era of pragmatic and experimental domestic and foreign policy. It was a moment when the regime principles of the American foundation and Civil War were once again renewed and updated. It was a time of existential crisis—but also of bold and visionary undertakings. The domestic progressive experience provides an important lesson for those seeking to grapple with the present generation's crisis of liberal democracy.

The liberal internationalism of the twentieth century was closely tied to domestic progressive policy and movements. The internationalism of Wilson's and FDR's generations emerged from their efforts to build a more progressive domestic order. Internationalism was put at the service of strengthening the nation—that is, the ability of governments and national leaders to make good on their promises to promote economic well-being and social advancement.

So the future of liberal internationalism hinges on two questions. First, can the United States and other liberal democracies recapture their progressive political orientation? America's 'brand'—as seen in parts of the non-western world—is perceived to be neo-liberal, that is, single-minded in its commitment to capital and markets. It is absolutely essential that the United States shatter this idea. Outside the West—and indeed in most parts of Europe—this is not the core of the liberal democratic vision of modern society. If there is an ideological 'centre of gravity' in the wider world of democracies, it is more social democratic and solidarist than neo-liberal. Or, to put it simply: it looks more like the vision of liberal democracy that was articulated by the United States during the New Deal and early postwar decades. This was a period when economic growth was more inclusive and was built around efforts to promote economic stability and social protections. If liberal internationalism is to thrive, it will need to be built again on these sorts of progressive foundations.

Second, can the United States and its old allies expand and rebuild a wider coalition of states willing to cooperate within a reformed liberal global order? It is a simple fact that the United States cannot base its leadership on the old coalition of the West and Japan. It needs to actively court and co-opt the wider world of developing democracies. It is already doing this, but it needs to make the enterprise integral to its grand strategic vision. The goal should be to reconfigure rights and responsibilities in existing institutions to reflect the diffusion of power in an increasingly multipolar world. This should be done in such a way as to cultivate deeper relations with democratic states within the rising non-western developing world. The global multilateral institutions—from the UN and IMF downwards—need to be reformed to reflect this new global reality.

In the end, the sources of continuity in the postwar liberal international order become visible when we look at the alternatives. The alternatives to liberal order are various sorts of closed systems—a world of blocs, spheres and protectionist zones. The best news for liberal internationalism is probably the simple fact that more people will be harmed by the end of some sort of global liberal international order than will gain. This does not mean it will survive, but it does suggest that there are constituencies—even in the old industrial societies of the West—that have reason to support it. Beyond this, there is simply no grand ideological alternative to a liberal international order. China does not have a model that the rest of the world finds appealing. Neither does Russia. These are authoritarian capitalist states. But this type of state does not translate into a broad set of alternative ideas for the organization of world order. The values, interests and mutual vulnerabilities that drove the rise and spread of liberal internationalism are still with us. Crises and transformations in liberal internationalism have marked its 200-year passage to the present. If liberal democracy survives this era, so too will liberal internationalism.

NOTES

1. On the troubles of western liberal democracy, see Edward Luce, *The retreat of western liberalism* (New York: Atlantic Monthly Press, 2017); Bill Emmott, *The fate of the West: the battle to save the world's most successful political idea* (New York: Public Affairs, 2017).

2. See G. John Ikenberry, *Liberal Leviathan: the origins, crisis, and transformation of the American world order* (Princeton: Princeton University Press, 2011); Amitav Acharya, *The end of American world order* (Cambridge: Polity, 2014).

3. See Robert Kagan, *The world America made* (New York: Vintage, 2013). For recent views, see Ian Buruma, 'The end of the

Anglo-American order', *New York Times Magazine*, 29 Nov. 2016; Ulrich Speck, 'The crisis of liberal order', *The American Interest*, 12 Sept. 2016; Michael J. Boyle, 'The coming illiberal era', *Survival* 58: 2, 2016, pp. 35–66.

4. On the crisis of liberal modernity, see Pankaj Mishra, *Age of anger: a history of the present* (New York: Farrar, Straus & Giroux, 2017).

5. Karl Polanyi, *The great transformation: the political and economic origins of our times* (Boston: Beacon, 1957).

6. E. H. Carr, *The twenty years crisis, 1919–1939: an introduction to the study of international relations* (London: Macmillan, 1951).

7. See Michael Doyle, 'Kant, liberal legacies, and foreign affairs', parts 1 and 2, *Philosophy and Public Affairs* 12: 1–2, 1983, pp. 205–35, 323–53.

8. John Gerard Ruggie, 'Multilateralism: the anatomy of an institution', in John Gerard Ruggie, ed., *Multilateralism matters: the theory and praxis of an institutional form* (New York: Columbia University Press, 1993), p. 11.

9. See Tim Dunne and Matt McDonald, 'The politics of liberal internationalism', *International Politics* 50: 1, Jan. 2013, pp. 1–17; Beate Jahn, *Liberal internationalism: theory, history, practice* (New York: Palgrave, 2013).

10. For a discussion of these various dimensions of liberal internationalism, see G. John Ikenberry, 'Liberal internationalism 3.0: America and the dilemmas of liberal world order', *Perspectives on Politics* 7: 1, March 2009, pp. 71–87.

11. For depictions of the theory and history of liberal internationalism, see Tony Smith, *America's mission: the United States and the worldwide struggle for democracy* (Princeton: Princeton University Press, 1994); Michael Mandelbaum, *The ideas that conquered the world: peace, democracy, and free markets in the twenty-first century* (New York: Public Affairs, 2004); Elizabeth Borgwardt, *A new deal for the world: America's vision for human rights* (Cambridge, MA: Harvard University Press, 2005); Frank Ninkovich, *Modernity and power: a history of the domino in the twentieth century* (Chicago: University of Chicago Press, 1994). For a portrait of liberalism within the wider array of classical theories of international relations, see Michael Doyle, *Ways of war and peace: realism, liberalism, and socialism* (New York: Norton, 1997).

12. See Edmund Fawcett, *Liberalism: the life of an idea* (Princeton: Princeton University Press, 2014).

13. Mark Mazower, *Governing the world: the history of an idea* (London: Allen Lane, 2012), p. 15.

14. Woodrow Wilson, speech at Mount Vernon, Virginia, 4 July 1918, https://archive.org/details/addressofpresideoowilsonw.

15. See Ikenberry, 'Liberal internationalism 3.0'.

16. For a depiction of the American liberal hegemonic order, see Ikenberry, *Liberal Leviathan*.

17. John Ruggie, 'International regimes, transactions, and change: embedded liberalism in the postwar economic order', *International Organization* 36: 2, Spring 1982, pp. 379–415.

18. Timothy Garton Ash, *Free world: America, Europe, and the surprising future of the West* (New York: Random House, 2004).

19. Quoted in Paul Ninkovich, *The global republic: America's inadvertent rise to world power* (Chicago: University of Chicago Press, 2014), p. 178.

20. These terms were introduced in the early twentieth century by the German sociologists Ferdinand Tonnies and Max Weber.

21. See Ikenberry, *Liberal Leviathan*, ch. 6. For debates about American unipolarity, see Steve Walt, *Taming American power: the global response to US primacy* (New York: Norton, 2005); Stephen G. Brooks and William C. Wohlforth, *World out of balance: international relations and the challenge of American primacy* (Princeton: Princeton University Press, 2008).

22. For an overview of these governance challenges, see Amitav Acharya, *Why govern? Rethinking demand and progress in global governance* (Cambridge: Cambridge University Press, 2016).

23. Ulrich Beck, *Risk society: towards a new modernity* (London: Sage, 1992), p. 7. See also Anthony Giddens and Christopher Pierson, *Making sense of modernity: conversations with Anthony Giddens* (Palo Alto, CA: Stanford University Press, 1998).

24. For evidence of stagnant and declining incomes among the working and middle classes in the US and Europe, and connections to the election of Donald Trump and Brexit, see Ronald Ingelhart and Pippa Norris, *Trump, Brexit, and the rise of populism: economic have-nots and cultural backlash*, working paper (Cambridge, MA: Harvard Kennedy School, 19 July 2016).

25. Branko Milanovic, *Global inequality: a new approach for the age of globalization* (Cambridge, MA: Harvard University Press, 2016), ch. 1.

26. See Jeff D. Colgan and Robert O. Keohane, 'The liberal order is rigged: fix it now or watch it wither', *Foreign Affairs* 96: 3, May–June 2017, pp. 36–44. For an account of the rise of neo-liberalism in the late twentieth century, see Mark Blyth, *Great transformation: economic ideas and institutional change in the twentieth century* (Cambridge: Cambridge University Press, 2002).

3 INTERNATIONAL RELATIONS THEORIES

Over the past century, the most prominent perspectives for understanding the basic nature of international politics have included realism, liberalism, various forms of idealism, such as social constructivism, and economic radicalism, including Marxism. These viewpoints have vied for influence both in public debates and in academic arguments.

The readings in this chapter constitute some of the most concise and important statements of these theoretical traditions. Hans J. Morgenthau, the leading figure in the field of international relations in the period after World War II, presents a realist view of power politics. His influential book, *Politics among Nations* (1948), excerpted here, played a central role in intellectually preparing Americans to exercise global power in the Cold War period and to reconcile power politics with the idealistic ethics that had often dominated American discussions about foreign relations.

In *The Tragedy of Great Power Politics* (2001), John J. Mearsheimer offers a contemporary interpretation of international politics that he calls "offensive realism." The chapter reprinted here is a marvel of clarity in describing international anarchy and its implications. States operate in a self-help system; to ensure their survival in that system, states must strive to become as powerful as possible. This competitive striving for security makes conflict the enduring and dominant feature of international relations, in Mearsheimer's view.

Michael W. Doyle, drawing inspiration from Kant, advances the liberal theory of the democratic peace. His 1986 article in the *American Political Science Review* points out that no two democracies have ever fought a war against each other—a finding that still holds true, as long as democracy is defined strictly enough. This sparked an ongoing debate among academics and public commentators on why this was the case, and whether it meant that the United States and other democracies should place efforts to promote the further spreading of democracy at the head of their foreign policy agendas.

Whereas realists like Mearsheimer argue that the condition of anarchy necessarily causes insecurity and fear among states, social constructivists such as

Alexander Wendt insist that behavior in anarchy depends on the ideas, cultures, and identities that people and their states bring to the anarchical situation. The excerpt here is drawn from his seminal piece in that debate, which has spawned influential research on such topics as the taboo against using nuclear weapons, changing norms of humanitarian military intervention, and the rise of powerful transnational human rights networks, some of which we excerpt in later chapters.

In addition to realism, liberalism, and constructivism, thinking about international politics has also been shaped by radical critiques of global capitalism. These include Marxist-Leninist doctrines propounded by the Soviet Union and theories about dependent economic development advanced by voices in the Global South. Perhaps the most consequential radical theory of international relations is V. I. Lenin's *Imperialism, the Highest Stage of Capitalism*, published in 1917, just months before Lenin's Bolshevik party seized power in the Russian Revolution. Lenin's arguments about global inequality, the privileged position of finance capital, competition for resources and markets, and the consequent armed rivalries between great powers continue to resonate today. Not only leftist radicals but also realists can still find much of interest in Lenin's insights.

Hans J. Morgenthau

A REALIST THEORY OF INTERNATIONAL POLITICS

This book purports to present a theory of international politics. The test by which such a theory must be judged is not *a priori* and abstract but empirical and pragmatic. The theory, in other words, must be judged not by some preconceived abstract principle or concept unrelated to reality, but by its purpose: to bring order and meaning to a mass of phenomena which without it would remain disconnected and unintelligible. It must meet a dual test, an empirical and a logical one: Do the facts as they actually are lend themselves to the interpretation the theory has put upon them, and do the conclusions at which the theory arrives follow with logical necessity from its premises? In short, is the theory consistent with the facts and within itself?

The issue this theory raises concerns the nature of all politics. The history of modern political thought is the story of a contest between two-schools that differ fundamentally in their conceptions of the nature of man, society, and politics. One believes that a rational and moral political order, derived from universally valid abstract principles, can be achieved here and now. It assumes the essential goodness and infinite-malleability of human nature, and blames the failure of the social order to measure up to the rational standards on lack of knowledge and understanding, obsolescent social institutions, or the depravity of certain isolated individuals or groups. It trusts in education, reform, and the sporadic use of force to remedy these defects.

The other school believes that the world, imperfect as it is from the rational point of view, is the result of forces inherent in human nature. To improve the world one must work with those forces, not against them. This being inherently a world of opposing interests and of conflict among them, moral principles can never be fully realized, but must at best be approximated through the ever temporary balancing, of interests and the ever precarious settlement of conflicts. This school, then, sees in a system of checks and balances a universal principle for all pluralist societies. It appeals to historic precedent rather than to abstract principles, and aims at the realization of the lesser evil rather than of the absolute good.

■　■　■

* * * Principles of Political Realism

* * * Political realism believes that politics, like society in general, is governed by objective laws that have their roots in human nature. In order to improve society it is first necessary to understand the laws by which society lives. The operation of these laws being impervious to our preferences, men will challenge them only at the risk of failure.

Realism, believing as it does in the objectivity of the laws of politics, must also believe in the

From Hans J. Morgenthau, *Politics among Nations: The Struggle for Power and Peace* (1948; reprint, New York: Knopf, 1985), 3–5, 12, 31–34, 36–39. Some of the author's notes have been omitted.

possibility of developing a rational theory that reflects, however imperfectly and one-sidedly, these objective laws. It believes also, then, in the possibility of distinguishing in politics between truth and opinion—between what is true objectively and rationally, supported by evidence and illuminated by reason, and what is only a subjective judgment, divorced from the facts as they are and informed by prejudice and wishful thinking.

■　■　■

For realism, theory consists in ascertaining facts and giving them meaning through reason. It assumes that the character of a foreign policy can be ascertained only through the examination of the political acts performed and of the foreseeable consequences of these acts. Thus we can find out what statesmen have actually done, and from the foreseeable consequences of their acts we can surmise what their objectives might have been.

Yet examination of the facts is not enough. To give meaning to the factual raw material of foreign policy, we must approach political reality with a kind of rational outline, a map that suggests to us the possible meanings of foreign policy. In other words, we put ourselves in the position of a statesman who must meet a certain problem of foreign policy under certain circumstances, and we ask ourselves what the rational alternatives are from which a statesman may choose who must meet this problem under these circumstances (presuming always that he acts in a rational manner), and which of these rational alternatives this particular statesman, acting under these circumstances, is likely to choose. It is the testing of this rational hypothesis against the actual facts and their consequences that gives theoretical meaning to the facts of international politics.

* * * The main signpost that helps political realism to find its way through the landscape of international politics is the concept of interest defined in terms of power. This concept provides the link between reason trying to understand international politics and the facts to be understood. * * *

We assume that statesmen think and act in terms of interest defined as power, and the evidence of history bears that assumption out. That assumption allows us to retrace and anticipate, as it were, the steps a statesman—past, present, or futures—has taken or will take on the political scene. We look over his shoulder when he writes his dispatches; we listen in on his conversation with other statesmen; we read and anticipate his very thoughts. Thinking in terms of interest defined as power, we think as he does, and as disinterested observers we understand his thoughts and actions perhaps better than he, the actor on the political scene, does himself.

■　■　■

* * * Political realism is aware of the moral significance of political action. It is also aware of the ineluctable tension between the moral command and the requirements of successful political action. And it is unwilling to gloss over and obliterate that tension and thus to obfuscate both the moral and the political issue by making it appear as though the stark facts of politics were morally more satisfying than they actually are, and the moral law less exacting that it actually is.

Realism maintains that universal moral principles cannot be applied to the actions of states in their abstract universal formulation, but that they must be filtered through the concrete circumstances of time and place. The individual may say for himself: "*Fiat justitia, pereat mundus* (Let justice be done, even if the world perish)," but the state has no right to say so in the name of those who are in its care. Both individual and state must judge political action by universal moral principles, such as that of liberty. Yet while the individual has a moral right to sacrifice himself in defense of such a moral principle, the state has no right to let its moral disapprobation of the infringement of liberty get in the way of successful political action, itself inspired by the moral principle of national survival. There can be no political morality without prudence; that is, without consideration of the political consequences of seemingly moral action. Realism, then, considers prudence—the weighing of the consequences of alternative political actions—to be the supreme virtue in politics. Ethics in the abstract judges action by its conformity with the moral law; political ethics judges action by its political consequences. * * *

■ ■ ■

POLITICAL POWER

What Is Political Power?

■ ■ ■

International politics, like all politics, is a struggle for power. Whatever the ultimate aims of international politics, power is always the immediate aim. Statesmen and peoples may ultimately seek freedom, security, prosperity, or power itself. They may define their goals in terms of a religious, philosophic, economic, or social ideal. They may hope that this ideal will materialize through its own inner force, through divine intervention, or through the natural development of human affairs. They may also try to further its realization through nonpolitical means, such as technical co-operation with other nations or international organizations. But whenever they strive to realize their goal by means of international politics, they do so by striving for power. The Crusaders wanted to free the holy places from domination by the Infidels; Woodrow Wilson wanted to make the world safe for democracy; the Nazis wanted to open Eastern Europe to German colonization, to dominate Europe, and to conquer the world. Since they all chose power to achieve these ends, they were actors on the scene of international politics.

■ ■ ■

* * * When we speak of power, we mean man's control over the minds and actions of other men. By political power we refer to the mutual relations of control among the holders of public authority and between the latter and the people at large.

Political power is a psychological relation between those who exercise it and those over whom it is exercised. It gives the former control over certain actions of the latter through the impact which the former exert on the latter's minds. That impact derives from three sources: the expectation of benefits, the fear of disadvantage, the respect or love for men or institutions. It may be exerted through orders, threats, the authority or charisma of a man or of an office, or a combination of any of these.

■ ■ ■

Political power must be distinguished from force in the sense, of the actual exercise of physical violence. The threat of physical violence in the form of police action, imprisonment, capital punishment, or war is an intrinsic element of politics. When violence becomes an actuality, it signifies the abdication of political power in favor of military or pseudo-military power. In international politics in particular, armed strength as a threat or a potentiality is the most important material factor making for the political power of a nation. If it becomes an actuality in war, it signifies the substitution of military for political power. The actual exercise of physical violence substitutes for the psychological relation between two minds, which is of the essence of political power, the physical relation between two bodies, one of which is strong enough to dominate the other's movements. It is for this reason that in the exercise of physical violence the psychological element of the political relationship is lost, and that we must distinguish between military and political power.

■   ■   ■

While it is generally recognized that the interplay of the expectation of benefits, the fear of disadvantages, and the respect or love for men or institutions, in ever changing combinations, forms the basis of all domestic politics, the importance of these factors for international politics is less obvious, but no less real. There has been a tendency to reduce political power to the actual application of force or at least to equate it with successful threats of force and with persuasion, to the neglect of charisma. That neglect * * * accounts in good measure for the neglect of prestige as an independent element in international politics. * * *

■   ■   ■

An economic, financial, territorial, or military policy undertaken for its own sake is subject to evaluation in its own terms. Is it economically or financially advantageous? * * *

When, however, the objectives of these policies serve to increase the power of the nation pursuing them with regard to other nations, these policies and their objectives must be judged primarily from the point of view of their contribution to national power. An economic policy that cannot be justified in purely economic terms might nevertheless be undertaken in view of the political policy pursued.

The insecure and unprofitable character of a loan to a foreign nation may be a valid argument against it on purely financial grounds. But the argument is irrelevant if the loan, however unwise it may be from a banker's point of view, serves the political policies of the nation. It may of course be that the economic or financial losses involved in such policies will weaken the nation in its international position to such an extent as to out-weigh the political advantages to be expected. On these grounds such policies might be rejected. In such a case, what decides the issue is not purely economic and financial considerations but a comparison of the political chances and risks involved; that is, the probable effect of these policies upon the power of the nation.

■   ■   ■

The Depreciation of Political Power

The aspiration for power being the distinguishing element of international politics, as of all politics, international politics is of necessity power politics. While this fact is generally recognized in the practice of international affairs, it is frequently denied in the pronouncements of scholars, publicists, and even statesmen. Since the end of the Napoleonic Wars, ever larger groups in the Western world have been persuaded that the struggle for power on the international scene is a temporary phenomenon, a historical accident that is bound to disappear once the peculiar historic conditions that have given rise to it have been eliminated. * * * During the nineteenth century, liberals everywhere shared the conviction that power politics and war were residues of an obsolete system of government, and that the victory of democracy and constitutional government over absolutism and autocracy would assure the victory of international harmony and permanent peace over power politics and war. Of this liberal school of thought, Woodrow Wilson was the most eloquent and most influential spokesman.

In recent times, the conviction that the struggle for power can be eliminated from the international scene has been connected with the great attempts at organizing the world, such as the League of Nations and the United Nations. * * *

* * * [In fact,] the struggle for power is universal in time and space and is an undeniable fact of experience. It cannot be denied that throughout historic time, regardless of social, economic, and political conditions, states have met each other in contests for power. Even though anthropologists have shown that certain primitive peoples seem to be free from the desire for power, nobody has yet shown how their state of mind and the conditions under which they live can be recreated on a world-wide scale so as to eliminate the struggle for power from the international scene.[1] It would be useless and even self-destructive to free one or the other of the peoples of the earth from the desire for power while leaving it extant in others. If the desire for power cannot be abolished everywhere in the world, those who might be cured would simply fall victims to the power of others.

The position taken here might be criticized on the ground that conclusions drawn from the past are unconvincing, and that to draw such conclusions has always been the main stock in trade of the enemies of progress and reform. Though it is true that certain social arrangements and institutions have always existed in the past, it does not necessarily follow that they must always exist in the future. The situation is, however, different when we deal not with social arrangements and institutions created by man, but with those elemental bio-psychological drives by which in turn society is created. The drives to live, to propagate, and to dominate are common to all men.[2] Their relative strength is dependent upon social conditions that may favor one drive and tend to repress another, or that may withhold social approval from certain manifestations of these drives while they encourage others. Thus, to take examples only from the sphere of power, most societies condemn killing as a means of attaining power within society, but all societies encourage the killing of enemies in that struggle for power which is called war. * * *

■　■　■

NOTES

1. For an illuminating discussion of this problem, see Malcolm Sharp, "Aggression: A Study of Values and Law," *Ethics*, Vol. 57, No. 4, Part II (July 1947).
2. Zoologists have tried to show that the drive to dominate is found even in animals, such as chickens and monkeys, who create social hierarchies on the basis of will and the ability to dominate. See, e.g., Warder Allee, *Animal Life and Social Growth* (Baltimore: The Williams and Wilkens Company, 1932), and *The Social Life of Animals* (New York: W. W. Norton and Company, Inc., 1938).

John J. Mearsheimer

ANARCHY AND THE STRUGGLE FOR POWER

Great powers, I argue, are always searching for opportunities to gain power over their rivals, with hegemony as their final goal. This perspective does not allow for status quo powers, except for the unusual state that achieves preponderance. Instead, the system is populated with great powers that have revisionist intentions at their core.[1] This chapter presents a theory that explains this competition for power. Specifically, I attempt to show that there is a compelling logic behind my claim that great powers seek to maximize their share of world power. I do not, however, test offensive realism against the historical record in this chapter. That important task is reserved for later chapters.

Why States Pursue Power

My explanation for why great powers vie with each other for power and strive for hegemony is derived from five assumptions about the international system. None of these assumptions alone mandates that states behave competitively. Taken together, however, they depict a world in which states have considerable reason to think and sometimes behave aggressively. In particular, the system encourages states to look for opportunities to maximize their power vis-à-vis other states.

How important is it that these assumptions be realistic? Some social scientists argue that the assumptions that underpin a theory need not

From *The Tragedy of Great Power Politics* (New York: Norton, 2001): 29–54. Some of the author's notes have been edited.

conform to reality. Indeed, the economist Milton Friedman maintains that the best theories "will be found to have assumptions that are wildly inaccurate descriptive representations of reality, and, in general, the more significant the theory, the more unrealistic the assumptions."[2] According to this view, the explanatory power of a theory is all that matters. If unrealistic assumptions lead to a theory that tells us a lot about how the world works, it is of no importance whether the underlying assumptions are realistic or not.

I reject this view. Although I agree that explanatory power is the ultimate criterion for assessing theories, I also believe that a theory based on unrealistic or false assumptions will not explain much about how the world works.[3] Sound theories are based on sound assumptions. Accordingly, each of these five assumptions is a reasonably accurate representation of an important aspect of life in the international system.

Bedrock Assumptions

The first assumption is that the international system is anarchic, which does not mean that it is chaotic or riven by disorder. It is easy to draw that conclusion, since realism depicts a world characterized by security competition and war. By itself, however, the realist notion of anarchy has nothing to do with conflict; it is an ordering principle, which says that the system comprises independent states that have no central authority above them.[4] Sovereignty, in other words, inheres in states because there is no higher ruling body in the international system.[5] There is no "government over governments."[6]

The second assumption is that great powers inherently possess some offensive military capability, which gives them the wherewithal to hurt and possibly destroy each other. States are potentially dangerous to each other, although some states have more military might than others and are therefore more dangerous. A state's military power is usually identified with the particular weaponry at its disposal, although even if there were no weapons, the individuals in those states could still use their feet and hands to attack the population of another state. After all, for every neck, there are two hands to choke it.

The third assumption is that states can never be certain about other states' intentions. Specifically, no state can be sure that another state will not use its offensive military capability to attack the first state. This is not to say that states necessarily have hostile intentions. Indeed, all of the states in the system may be reliably benign, but it is impossible to be sure of that judgment because intentions are impossible to divine with 100 percent certainty.[7] There are many possible causes of aggression, and no state can be sure that another state is not motivated by one of them.[8] Furthermore, intentions can change quickly, so a state's intentions can be benign one day and hostile the next. Uncertainty about intentions is unavoidable, which means that states can never be sure that other states do not have offensive intentions to go along with their offensive capabilities.

The fourth assumption is that survival is the primary goal of great powers. Specifically, states seek to maintain their territorial integrity and the autonomy of their domestic political order. Survival dominates other motives because, once a state is conquered, it is unlikely to be in a position to pursue other aims. Soviet leader Josef Stalin put the point well during a war scare in 1927: "We can and must build socialism in the [Soviet Union]. But in order to do so we first of all have to exist."[9]

States can and do pursue other goals, of course, but security is their most important objective.

The fifth assumption is that great powers are rational actors. They are aware of their external environment and they think strategically about how to survive in it. In particular, they consider the preferences of other states and how their own behavior is likely to affect the behavior of those other states, and how the behavior of those other states is likely to affect their own strategy for survival. Moreover, states pay attention to the long term as well as the immediate consequences of their actions.

As emphasized, none of these assumptions alone dictates that great powers as a general rule *should* behave aggressively toward each other. There is surely the possibility that some state might have hostile intentions, but the only assumption dealing with a specific motive that is common to all states says that their principal objective is to survive, which by itself is a rather harmless goal. Nevertheless, when the five assumptions are married together, they create powerful incentives for great powers to think and act offensively with regard to each other. In particular, three general patterns of behavior result: fear, self-help, and power maximization.

State Behavior

Great powers fear each other. They regard each other with suspicion, and they worry that war might be in the offing. They anticipate danger. There is little room for trust among states. For sure, the level of fear varies across time and space, but it cannot be reduced to a trivial level. From the perspective of any one great power, all other great powers are potential enemies. This point is illustrated by the reaction of the United Kingdom and France to German reunification at the end of the Cold War. Despite the fact that these three states had been close allies for almost forty-five years, both the

United Kingdom and France immediately began worrying about the potential dangers of a united Germany.[10]

The basis of this fear is that in a world where great powers have the capability to attack each other and might have the motive to do so, any state bent on survival must be at least suspicious of other states and reluctant to trust them. Add to this the "911" problem—the absence of a central authority to which a threatened state can turn for help—and states have even greater incentive to fear each other. Moreover, there is no mechanism, other than the possible self-interest of third parties, for punishing an aggressor. Because it is sometimes difficult to deter potential aggressors, states have ample reason not to trust other states and to be prepared for war with them.

The possible consequences of falling victim to aggression further amplify the importance of fear as a motivating force in world politics. Great powers do not compete with each other as if international politics were merely an economic marketplace. Political competition among states is a much more dangerous business than mere economic intercourse; the former can lead to war, and war often means mass killing on the battlefield as well as mass murder of civilians. In extreme cases, war can even lead to the destruction of states. The horrible consequences of war sometimes cause states to view each other not just as competitors, but as potentially deadly enemies. Political antagonism, in short, tends to be intense, because the stakes are great.

States in the international system also aim to guarantee their own survival. Because other states are potential threats, and because there is no higher authority to come to their rescue when they dial 911, states cannot depend on others for their own security. Each state tends to see itself as vulnerable and alone, and therefore it aims to provide for its own survival. In international politics, God helps those who help themselves. This emphasis on self-help does not preclude states from forming alliances.[11] But alliances are only temporary marriages of convenience: today's alliance partner might be tomorrow's enemy, and today's enemy might be tomorrow's alliance partner. For example, the United States fought with China and the Soviet Union against Germany and Japan in World War II, but soon thereafter flip-flopped enemies and partners and allied with West Germany and Japan against China and the Soviet Union during the Cold War.

States operating in a self-help world almost always act according to their own self-interest and do not subordinate their interests to the interests of other states, or to the interests of the so-called international community. The reason is simple: it pays to be selfish in a self-help world. This is true in the short term as well as in the long term, because if a state loses in the short run, it might not be around for the long haul.

Apprehensive about the ultimate intentions of other states, and aware that they operate in a self-help system, states quickly understand that the best way to ensure their survival is to be the most powerful state in the system. The stronger a state is relative to its potential rivals, the less likely it is that any of those rivals will attack it and threaten its survival. Weaker states will be reluctant to pick fights with more powerful states because the weaker states are likely to suffer military defeat. Indeed, the bigger the gap in power between any two states, the less likely it is that the weaker will attack the stronger. Neither Canada nor Mexico, for example, would countenance attacking the United States, which is far more powerful than its neighbors. The ideal situation is to be the hegemon in the system. As Immanuel Kant said, "It is the desire of every state, or of its ruler, to arrive at a condition of perpetual peace by conquering the whole world, if that were possible."[12] Survival would then be almost guaranteed.[13]

Consequently, states pay close attention to how power is distributed among them, and they make a special effort to maximize their share of world power. Specifically, they look for opportunities to alter the balance of power by acquiring additional increments of power at the expense of potential rivals. States employ a variety of means—economic, diplomatic, and military—to shift the balance of power in their favor, even if doing so makes other states suspicious or even hostile. Because one state's gain in power is another state's loss, great powers tend to have a zero-sum mentality when dealing with each other. The trick, of course, is to be the winner in this competition and to dominate the other states in the system. Thus, the claim that states maximize relative power is tantamount to arguing that states are disposed to think offensively toward other states, even though their ultimate motive is simply to survive. In short, great powers have aggressive intentions.[14]

Even when a great power achieves a distinct military advantage over its rivals, it continues looking for chances to gain more power. The pursuit of power stops only when hegemony is achieved. The idea that a great power might feel secure without dominating the system, provided it has an "appropriate amount" of power, is not persuasive, for two reasons.[15] First, it is difficult to assess how much relative power one state must have over its rivals before it is secure. Is twice as much power an appropriate threshold? Or is three times as much power the magic number? The root of the problem is that power calculations alone do not determine which side wins a war. Clever strategies, for example, sometimes allow less powerful states to defeat more powerful foes.

Second, determining how much power is enough becomes even more complicated when great powers contemplate how power will be distributed among them ten or twenty years down the road. The capabilities of individual states vary over time, sometimes markedly, and it is often difficult to predict the direction and scope of change in the balance of power. Remember, few in the West anticipated the collapse of the Soviet Union before it happened. In fact, during the first half of the Cold War, many in the West feared that the Soviet economy would eventually generate greater wealth than the American economy, which would cause a marked power shift against the United States and its allies. What the future holds for China and Russia and what the balance of power will look like in 2020 is difficult to foresee.

Given the difficulty of determining how much power is enough for today and tomorrow, great powers recognize that the best way to ensure their security is to achieve hegemony now, thus eliminating any possibility of a challenge by another great power. Only a misguided state would pass up an opportunity to be the hegemon in the system because it thought it already had sufficient power to survive.[16] But even if a great power does not have the wherewithal to achieve hegemony (and that is usually the case), it will still act offensively to amass as much power as it can, because states are almost always better off with more rather than less power. In short, states do not become status quo powers until they completely dominate the system.

All states are influenced by this logic, which means that not only do they look for opportunities to take advantage of one another, they also work to ensure that other states do not take advantage of them. After all, rival states are driven by the same logic, and most states are likely to recognize their own motives at play in the actions of other states. In short, states ultimately pay attention to defense as well as offense. They think about conquest themselves, and they work to check aggressor states from gaining power at their expense. This inexorably leads to a world of constant security competition, where states are willing to lie, cheat, and use brute force if it helps them gain advantage over their rivals. Peace, if one defines that concept as a state of tranquility or mutual concord, is not likely to break out in this world.

The "security dilemma," which is one of the most well-known concepts in the international relations literature, reflects the basic logic of offensive realism. The essence of the dilemma is that the measures a state takes to increase its own security usually decrease the security of other states. Thus, it is difficult for a state to increase its own chances of survival without threatening the survival of other states. John Herz first introduced the security dilemma in a 1950 article in the journal *World Politics*.[17] After discussing the anarchic nature of international politics, he writes, "Striving to attain security from . . . attack, [states] are driven to acquire more and more power in order to escape the impact of the power of others. This, in turn, renders the others more insecure and compels them to prepare for the worst. Since none can ever feel entirely secure in such a world of competing units, power competition ensues, and the vicious circle of security and power accumulation is on."[18] The implication of Herz's analysis is clear: the best way for a state to survive in anarchy is to take advantage of other states and gain power at their expense. The best defense is a good offense. Since this message is widely understood, ceaseless security competition ensues. Unfortunately, little can be done to ameliorate the security dilemma as long as states operate in anarchy.

It should be apparent from this discussion that saying that states are power maximizers is tantamount to saying that they care about relative power, not absolute power. There is an important distinction here, because states concerned about relative power behave differently than do states interested in absolute power.[19] States that maximize relative power are concerned primarily with the distribution of material capabilities. In particular, they try to gain as large a power advantage as possible over potential rivals, because power is the best means to survival in a dangerous world. Thus, states motivated by relative power concerns are likely to forgo large gains in their own power, if such gains give rival states even greater power, for smaller national gains that nevertheless provide them with a power advantage over their rivals.[20] States that maximize absolute power, on the other

hand, care only about the size of their own gains, not those of other states. They are not motivated by balance-of-power logic but instead are concerned with amassing power without regard to how much power other states control. They would jump at the opportunity for large gains, even if a rival gained more in the deal. Power, according to this logic, is not a means to an end (survival), but an end in itself.[21]

Calculated Aggression

There is obviously little room for status quo powers in a world where states are inclined to look for opportunities to gain more power. Nevertheless, great powers cannot always act on their offensive intentions, because behavior is influenced not only by what states want, but also by their capacity to realize these desires. Every state might want to be king of the hill, but not every state has the wherewithal to compete for that lofty position, much less achieve it. Much depends on how military might is distributed among the great powers. A great power that has a marked power advantage over its rivals is likely to behave more aggressively, because it has the capability as well as the incentive to do so.

By contrast, great powers facing powerful opponents will be less inclined to consider offensive action and more concerned with defending the existing balance of power from threats by their more powerful opponents. Let there be an opportunity for those weaker states to revise the balance in their own favor, however, and they will take advantage of it. Stalin put the point well at the end of World War II: "Everyone imposes his own system as far as his army can reach. It cannot be otherwise."[22] States might also have the capability to gain advantage over a rival power but nevertheless decide that the perceived costs of offense are too high and do not justify the expected benefits.

In short, great powers are not mindless aggressors so bent on gaining power that they charge headlong into losing wars or pursue Pyrrhic victories. On the contrary, before great powers take offensive actions, they think carefully about the balance of power and about how other states will react to their moves. They weigh the costs and risks of offense against the likely benefits. If the benefits do not outweigh the risks, they sit tight and wait for a more propitious moment. Nor do states start arms races that are unlikely to improve their overall position. As discussed at greater length in Chapter 3, states sometimes limit defense spending either because spending more would bring no strategic advantage or because spending more would weaken the economy and undermine the state's power in the long run.[23] To paraphrase Clint Eastwood, a state has to know its limitations to survive in the international system.

Nevertheless, great powers miscalculate from time to time because they invariably make important decisions on the basis of imperfect information. States hardly ever have complete information about any situation they confront. There are two dimensions to this problem. Potential adversaries have incentives to misrepresent their own strength or weakness, and to conceal their true aims.[24] For example, a weaker state trying to deter a stronger state is likely to exaggerate its own power to discourage the potential aggressor from attacking. On the other hand, a state bent on aggression is likely to emphasize its peaceful goals while exaggerating its military weakness, so that the potential victim does not build up its own arms and thus leaves itself vulnerable to attack. Probably no national leader was better at practicing this kind of deception than Adolf Hitler.

But even if disinformation was not a problem, great powers are often unsure about how their own military forces, as well as the adversary's, will perform on the battlefield. For example, it is sometimes difficult to determine in advance how new weapons and untested combat units will perform in the face of enemy fire. Peacetime maneuvers and war games are helpful but imperfect indicators of what is likely to happen in actual combat. Fighting wars is a complicated business in which it is often difficult to predict outcomes. Remember that although the United States and its allies scored a stunning and remarkably easy victory against Iraq in early 1991, most experts at the time believed that Iraq's military would be a formidable foe and put up stubborn resistance before finally succumbing to American military might.[25]

Great powers are also sometimes unsure about the resolve of opposing states as well as allies. For example, Germany believed that if it went to war against France and Russia in the summer of 1914, the United Kingdom would probably stay out of the fight. Saddam Hussein expected the United States to stand aside when he invaded Kuwait in August 1990. Both aggressors guessed wrong, but each had good reason to think that its initial judgment was correct. In the 1930s, Adolf Hitler believed that his great-power rivals would be easy to exploit and isolate because each had little interest in fighting Germany and instead was determined to get someone else to assume that burden. He guessed right. In short, great powers constantly find themselves confronting situations in which they have to make important decisions with incomplete information. Not surprisingly, they sometimes make faulty judgments and end up doing themselves serious harm.

Some defensive realists go so far as to suggest that the constraints of the international system are so powerful that offense rarely succeeds, and that aggressive great powers invariably end up being punished.[26] As noted, they emphasize that 1) threatened states balance against aggressors and ultimately crush them, and 2) there is an offense-defense balance that is usually heavily tilted toward the defense, thus making conquest especially difficult. Great powers, therefore, should be content with the existing balance of power and not try to change it by force. After all, it makes little sense for a state to initiate a war that it is likely to lose; that would be self-defeating behavior. It is better to concentrate instead on preserving the balance of power.[27] Moreover, because aggressors seldom succeed, states should understand that security is abundant, and thus there is no good strategic reason for wanting more power in the first place. In a world where conquest seldom pays, states should have relatively benign intentions toward each other. If they do not, these defensive realists argue, the reason is probably poisonous domestic politics, not smart calculations about how to guarantee one's security in an anarchic world.

There is no question that systemic factors constrain aggression, especially balancing by threatened states. But defensive realists exaggerate those restraining forces.[28] Indeed, the historical record provides little support for their claim that offense rarely succeeds. One study estimates that there were sixty-three wars between 1815 and 1980, and the initiator won thirty-nine times, which translates into about a 60 percent success rate.[29] Turning to specific cases, Otto von Bismarck unified Germany by winning military victories against Denmark in 1864, Austria in 1866, and France in 1870, and the United States as we know it today was created in good part by conquest in the nineteenth century. Conquest certainly paid big dividends in these cases. Nazi Germany won wars against Poland in 1939 and France in 1940, but lost to the Soviet Union between 1941 and 1945. Conquest ultimately did not pay for the Third Reich, but if Hitler had restrained himself after the fall of France and had not invaded the Soviet Union, conquest probably would have paid handsomely for the Nazis. In short, the historical record shows that offense sometimes succeeds and sometimes does not. The trick for a sophisticated power maximizer is to figure out when to raise and when to fold.[30]

Hegemony's Limits

Great powers, as I have emphasized, strive to gain power over their rivals and hopefully become hegemons. Once a state achieves that exalted position, it becomes a status quo power. More needs to be said, however, about the meaning of hegemony.

A hegemon is a state that is so powerful that it dominates all the other states in the system.[31] No other state has the military wherewithal to put up a serious fight against it. In essence, a hegemon is the only great power in the system. A state that is substantially more powerful than the other great powers in the system is not a hegemon, because it faces, by definition, other great powers. The United Kingdom in the mid-nineteenth century, for example, is sometimes called a hegemon. But it was not a hegemon, because there were four other great powers in Europe at the time—Austria, France, Prussia, and Russia—and the United Kingdom did not dominate them in any meaningful way. In fact, during that period, the United Kingdom considered France to be a serious threat to the balance of power. Europe in the nineteenth century was multipolar, not unipolar.

Hegemony means domination of the system, which is usually interpreted to mean the entire world. It is possible, however, to apply the concept of a system more narrowly and use it to describe particular regions, such as Europe, Northeast Asia, and the Western Hemisphere. Thus, one can distinguish between *global hegemons*, which dominate the world, and *regional hegemons*, which dominate distinct geographical areas. The United States has been a regional hegemon in the Western Hemisphere for at least the past one hundred years. No other state in the Americas has sufficient military might to challenge it, which is why the United States is widely recognized as the only great power in its region.

My argument, which I develop at length in subsequent chapters, is that except for the unlikely event wherein one state achieves clear-cut nuclear superiority, it is virtually impossible for any state to achieve global hegemony. The principal impediment to world domination is the difficulty of projecting power across the world's oceans onto the territory of a rival great power. The United States, for example, is the most powerful state on the planet today. But it does not dominate Europe and Northeast Asia the way it does the Western Hemisphere, and it has no intention of trying to conquer and control those distant regions, mainly because of the stopping power of water. Indeed, there is reason to think that the American military commitment to Europe and Northeast Asia might wither away over the next decade. In short, there has never been a global hegemon, and there is not likely to be one anytime soon.

The best outcome a great power can hope for is to be a regional hegemon and possibly control another region that is nearby and accessible over land. The United States is the only regional hegemon in modern history, although other states have fought major wars in pursuit of regional hegemony: imperial Japan in Northeast Asia, and Napoleonic France, Wilhelmine Germany, and Nazi Germany in Europe. But none succeeded. The Soviet Union, which is located in Europe and Northeast Asia, threatened to dominate both of those regions during the Cold War. The Soviet Union might also have attempted to conquer the oil-rich Persian Gulf region, with which it shared a border. But even if Moscow had been able to dominate Europe, Northeast Asia, and the Persian Gulf, which it never came close to doing, it still would have been unable to conquer the Western Hemisphere and become a true global hegemon.

States that achieve regional hegemony seek to prevent great powers in other regions from duplicating their feat. Regional hegemons, in other words, do not want peers. Thus the United States, for example, played a key role in preventing imperial Japan, Wilhelmine Germany, Nazi Germany, and the Soviet Union from gaining regional supremacy. Regional hegemons attempt to check aspiring hegemons in other regions because they fear that a rival great power that dominates its own region will be an especially powerful foe that is essentially free to cause trouble in the fearful great power's backyard. Regional hegemons prefer that there be at least two great powers located together in other regions, because their proximity will force them to concentrate their attention on each other rather than on the distant hegemon.

Furthermore, if a potential hegemon emerges among them, the other great powers in that region might be able to contain it by themselves, allowing the distant hegemon to remain safely on the sidelines. Of course, if the local great powers were unable to do the job, the distant hegemon would take the appropriate measures to deal with the threatening state. The United States, as noted, has assumed that burden on four separate occasions in the twentieth century, which is why it is commonly referred to as an "offshore balancer."

In sum, the ideal situation for any great power is to be the only regional hegemon in the world. That state would be a status quo power, and it would go to considerable lengths to preserve the existing distribution of power. The United States is in that enviable position today; it dominates the Western Hemisphere and there is no hegemon in any other area of the world. But if a regional hegemon is confronted with a peer competitor, it would no longer be a status quo power. Indeed, it would go to considerable lengths to weaken and maybe even destroy its distant rival. Of course, both regional hegemons would be motivated by that logic, which would make for a fierce security competition between them.

Power and Fear

That great powers fear each other is a central aspect of life in the international system. But as noted, the level of fear varies from case to case. For example, the Soviet Union worried much less about Germany in 1930 than it did in 1939. How much states fear each other matters greatly, because the amount of fear between them largely determines the severity of their security competition, as well as the probability that they will fight a war. The more profound the fear is, the more intense is the security competition, and the more likely is war. The logic is straightforward: a scared state will look especially hard for ways to enhance its security, and it will be disposed to pursue risky policies to achieve that end. Therefore, it is important to understand what causes states to fear each other more or less intensely.

Fear among great powers derives from the fact that they invariably have some offensive military capability that they can use against each other, and the fact that one can never be certain that other states do not intend to use that power against oneself. Moreover, because states operate in an anarchic system, there is no night watchman to whom they can turn for help if another great power attacks them. Although anarchy and uncertainty about other states' intentions create an irreducible level of fear among states that leads to power-maximizing behavior, they cannot account for why sometimes that level of fear is greater than at other times. The reason is that anarchy and the difficulty of discerning state intentions are constant facts of life, and constants cannot explain variation. The capability that states have to threaten each other, however, varies from case to case, and it is the key factor that drives fear levels up and down. Specifically, the more power a state possesses, the more fear it generates among its rivals. Germany, for example, was much more powerful at the end of the 1930s than it was at the decade's beginning, which is why the Soviets became increasingly fearful of Germany over the course of that decade.

This discussion of how power affects fear prompts the question, What is power? It is important to distinguish between potential and actual power. A state's potential power is based on the size of its population and the level of its wealth. These two assets are the main building blocks of military power. Wealthy rivals with large populations can usually build formidable military forces. A state's actual power is embedded mainly in its army and the air and naval forces that directly support it. Armies are the central ingredient of military power, because they are the principal instrument for conquering and controlling territory—the paramount political objective in a world of territorial states. In short, the key component of military might, even in the nuclear age, is land power.

Power considerations affect the intensity of fear among states in three main ways. First, rival states that possess nuclear forces that can survive a nuclear attack and retaliate against it are likely to fear each other less than if these same states had no nuclear weapons. During the Cold War, for example, the level of fear between the superpowers probably would have been substantially greater if nuclear weapons had not been invented. The logic here is simple: because nuclear weapons can inflict devastating destruction on a rival state in a short period of time, nuclear-armed rivals are going to be reluctant to fight with each other, which means that each side will have less reason to fear the other than would otherwise be the case. But as the Cold War demonstrates, this does not mean that war between nuclear powers is no longer thinkable; they still have reason to fear each other.

Second, when great powers are separated by large bodies of water, they usually do not have much offensive capability against each other, regardless of the relative size of their armies. Large bodies of water are formidable obstacles that cause significant power-projection problems for attacking armies. For example, the stopping power of water explains in good part why the United Kingdom and the United States (since becoming a great power in 1898) have never been invaded by another great power. It also explains why the United States has never tried to conquer territory in Europe or Northeast Asia, and why the United Kingdom has never attempted to dominate the European continent. Great powers located on the same landmass are in a much better position to attack and conquer each other. That is especially true of states that share a common border. Therefore, great powers separated by water are likely to fear each other less than great powers that can get at each other over land.

Third, the distribution of power among the states in the system also markedly affects the levels of fear.[32] The key issue is whether power is distributed more or less evenly among the great powers or whether there are sharp power asymmetries. The configuration of power that generates the most fear is a multipolar system that contains a potential hegemon—what I call "unbalanced multipolarity."

A potential hegemon is more than just the most powerful state in the system. It is a great power with so much actual military capability and so much potential power that it stands a good chance of dominating and controlling all of the other great powers in its region of the world. A potential hegemon need not have the wherewithal to fight all of its rivals at once, but it must have excellent prospects of defeating each opponent alone, and good prospects of defeating some of them in tandem. The key relationship, however, is the power gap between the potential hegemon and the second most powerful state in the system: there must be a marked gap between them. To qualify as a potential hegemon, a state must have—by some reasonably large margin—the most formidable army as well as the most latent power among all the states located in its region.

Bipolarity is the power configuration that produces the least amount of fear among the great powers, although not a negligible amount by any means. Fear tends to be less acute in bipolarity, because there is usually a rough balance of power between the two major states in the system. Multipolar systems without a potential hegemon, what I call "balanced multipolarity," are still likely to have power asymmetries among their members, although these asymmetries will not be as pronounced as the gaps created by the presence of an aspiring hegemon. Therefore, balanced multipolarity is likely to generate less fear than unbalanced multipolarity, but more fear than bipolarity.

This discussion of how the level of fear between great powers varies with changes in the distribution of power, not with assessments about each other's intentions, raises a related point. When a state surveys its environment to determine which states pose a threat to its survival, it focuses mainly on the offensive *capabilities* of potential rivals, not their intentions. As emphasized earlier, intentions are ultimately unknowable, so states worried about their survival must make worst-case assumptions about their rivals' intentions. Capabilities, however, not only can be measured but also determine whether or not a rival state is a serious threat. In short, great powers balance against capabilities, not intentions.[33]

Great powers obviously balance against states with formidable military forces, because that offensive military capability is the tangible threat to their survival. But great powers also pay careful attention to how much latent power rival states control, because rich and populous states usually can and do build powerful armies. Thus, great powers tend to fear states with large populations and rapidly expanding economies, even if these states have not yet translated their wealth into military might.

The Hierarchy of State Goals

Survival is the number one goal of great powers, according to my theory. In practice, however, states pursue non-security goals as well. For example, great powers invariably seek greater economic prosperity to enhance the welfare of their citizenry. They sometimes seek to promote a particular ideology abroad, as happened during the Cold War when the United States tried to spread democracy around the world and the Soviet Union tried to sell communism. National unification is another goal that sometimes motivates states, as it did with Prussia and Italy in the nineteenth century and Germany after the Cold War. Great powers also occasionally try to foster human rights around the globe. States might pursue any of these, as well as a number of other non-security goals.

Offensive realism certainly recognizes that great powers might pursue these non-security goals, but it has little to say about them, save for one important point: states can pursue them as long as the requisite behavior does not conflict with balance-of-power logic, which is often the case.[34] Indeed, the pursuit of these non-security goals sometimes complements the hunt for relative power. For example, Nazi Germany expanded into eastern Europe for both ideological and realist reasons, and the superpowers competed with each other during the Cold War for similar reasons. Furthermore, greater economic prosperity invariably means greater wealth, which has significant implications for security, because wealth is the foundation of military power. Wealthy states can afford powerful military forces, which enhance a state's prospects for survival. As the political economist Jacob Viner noted more than fifty years ago, "there is a long-run harmony" between wealth and power.[35] National unification is another goal that usually complements the pursuit of power. For example, the unified German state that emerged in 1871 was more powerful than the Prussian state it replaced.

Sometimes the pursuit of non-security goals has hardly any effect on the balance of power, one way or the other. Human rights interventions usually fit this description, because they tend to be small-scale operations that cost little and do not detract from a great power's prospects for survival. For better or for worse, states are rarely willing to expend blood and treasure to protect foreign populations from gross abuses, including genocide. For instance, despite claims that American foreign policy is infused with moralism, Somalia (1992–93) is the only instance during the past one hundred years in which U.S. soldiers were killed in action on a humanitarian mission. And in that case, the loss of a mere eighteen soldiers in an infamous firefight in October 1993 so traumatized American policymakers that they immediately pulled all U.S. troops out of Somalia and then refused to intervene in Rwanda in the spring of 1994, when ethnic Hutu went on a genocidal rampage against their Tutsi neighbors.[36] Stopping that genocide would have been relatively easy and it would have had virtually no effect on the position of the United States in the balance of power.[37] Yet nothing was done. In short, although realism does not prescribe human rights interventions, it does not necessarily proscribe them.

But sometimes the pursuit of non-security goals conflicts with balance-of-power logic, in which case states usually act according to the dictates of realism. For example, despite the U.S. commitment to spreading democracy across the globe, it helped overthrow democratically elected governments and embraced a number of authoritarian regimes during the Cold War, when American policymakers felt that these actions would help contain the Soviet Union.[38] In World War II, the liberal democracies put aside their antipathy for communism and formed an alliance with the Soviet Union against Nazi Germany. "I can't take communism," Franklin Roosevelt emphasized, but to defeat Hitler "I would hold hands with the Devil."[39] In the same way, Stalin repeatedly demonstrated that when his ideological preferences clashed with power considerations, the latter won out. To take the most blatant example of his realism, the Soviet Union formed a non-aggression pact with Nazi Germany in August 1939—the infamous Molotov-Ribbentrop Pact—in hopes that the agreement would at least temporarily satisfy Hitler's territorial ambitions in eastern Europe and turn the Wehrmacht toward France and the United Kingdom.[40] When great powers confront a serious threat, in short, they pay little attention to ideology as they search for alliance partners.[41]

Security also trumps wealth when those two goals conflict, because "defence," as Adam Smith wrote in *The Wealth of Nations,* "is of much more importance than opulence."[42] Smith provides a good illustration of how states behave when forced to choose between wealth and relative power. In 1651, England put into effect the famous Navigation Act, protectionist legislation designed to damage Holland's commerce and ultimately cripple the Dutch economy. The legislation mandated that all goods imported into England be carried either in English ships or ships owned by the country that originally produced the goods. Since the Dutch produced few goods themselves, this measure would badly damage their shipping, the central ingredient in their economic success. Of course, the Navigation Act would hurt England's economy as well, mainly because it would rob England of the benefits of free trade. "The act of navigation," Smith wrote, "is not favorable to foreign commerce, or to the growth of that opulence that can arise from it." Nevertheless, Smith considered the legislation "the wisest of all the commercial regulations of England" because it did more damage to the Dutch economy than to the English economy, and in the mid-seventeenth century Holland was "the only naval power which could endanger the security of England."[43]

Creating World Order

The claim is sometimes made that great powers can transcend realist logic by working together to build an international order that fosters peace and justice. World peace, it would appear, can only enhance a state's prosperity and security. America's political leaders paid considerable lip service to this line of argument over the course of the twentieth century. President Clinton, for example, told an audience at the United Nations in September 1993 that "at the birth of this organization 48 years ago . . . a generation of gifted leaders from many nations stepped forward to organize the world's efforts on behalf of security and prosperity. . . .

Now history has granted to us a moment of even greater opportunity. . . . Let us resolve that we will dream larger. . . . Let us ensure that the world we pass to our children is healthier, safer and more abundant than the one we inhabit today." [44]

This rhetoric notwithstanding, great powers do not work together to promote world order for its own sake. Instead, each seeks to maximize its own share of world power, which is likely to clash with the goal of creating and sustaining stable international orders.[45] This is not to say that great powers never aim to prevent wars and keep the peace. On the contrary, they work hard to deter wars in which they would be the likely victim. In such cases, however, state behavior is driven largely by narrow calculations about relative power, not by a commitment to build a world order independent of a state's own interests. The United States, for example, devoted enormous resources to deterring the Soviet Union from starting a war in Europe during the Cold War, not because of some deep-seated commitment to promoting peace around the world, but because American leaders feared that a Soviet victory would lead to a dangerous shift in the balance of power.[46]

The particular international order that obtains at any time is mainly a by-product of the self-interested behavior of the system's great powers. The configuration of the system, in other words, is the unintended consequence of great-power security competition, not the result of states acting together to organize peace. The establishment of the Cold War order in Europe illustrates this point. Neither the Soviet Union nor the United States intended to establish it, nor did they work together to create it. In fact, each superpower worked hard in the early years of the Cold War to gain power at the expense of the other, while preventing the other from doing likewise.[47] The system that emerged in Europe in the aftermath of World War II was the unplanned consequence of intense security competition between the superpowers.

Although that intense superpower rivalry ended along with the Cold War in 1990, Russia and the

United States have not worked together to create the present order in Europe. The United States, for example, has rejected out of hand various Russian proposals to make the Organization for Security and Cooperation in Europe the central organizing pillar of European security (replacing the U.S.-dominated NATO). Furthermore, Russia was deeply opposed to NATO expansion, which it viewed as a serious threat to Russian security. Recognizing that Russia's weakness would preclude any retaliation, however, the United States ignored Russia's concerns and pushed NATO to accept the Czech Republic, Hungary, and Poland as new members. Russia has also opposed U.S. policy in the Balkans over the past decade, especially NATO's 1999 war against Yugoslavia. Again, the United States has paid little attention to Russia's concerns and has taken the steps it deems necessary to bring peace to that volatile region. Finally, it is worth noting that although Russia is dead set against allowing the United States to deploy ballistic missile defenses, it is highly likely that Washington will deploy such a system if it is judged to be technologically feasible.

For sure, great-power rivalry will sometimes produce a stable international order, as happened during the Cold War. Nevertheless, the great powers will continue looking for opportunities to increase their share of world power, and if a favorable situation arises, they will move to undermine that stable order. Consider how hard the United States worked during the late 1980s to weaken the Soviet Union and bring down the stable order that had emerged in Europe during the latter part of the Cold War.[48] Of course, the states that stand to lose power will work to deter aggression and preserve the existing order. But their motives will be selfish, revolving around balance-of-power logic, not some commitment to world peace.

Great powers cannot commit themselves to the pursuit of a peaceful world order for two reasons. First, states are unlikely to agree on a general formula for bolstering peace. Certainly, international relations scholars have never reached a consensus on what the blueprint should look like. In fact, it seems there are about as many theories on the causes of war and peace as there are scholars studying the subject. But more important, policymakers are unable to agree on how to create a stable world. For example, at the Paris Peace Conference after World War I, important differences over how to create stability in Europe divided Georges Clemenceau, David Lloyd George, and Woodrow Wilson.[49] In particular, Clemenceau was determined to impose harsher terms on Germany over the Rhineland than was either Lloyd George or Wilson, while Lloyd George stood out as the hard-liner on German reparations. The Treaty of Versailles, not surprisingly, did little to promote European stability.

Furthermore, consider American thinking on how to achieve stability in Europe in the early days of the Cold War.[50] The key elements for a stable and durable system were in place by the early 1950s. They included the division of Germany, the positioning of American ground forces in Western Europe to deter a Soviet attack, and ensuring that West Germany would not seek to develop nuclear weapons. Officials in the Truman administration, however, disagreed about whether a divided Germany would be a source of peace or war. For example, George Kennan and Paul Nitze, who held important positions in the State Department, believed that a divided Germany would be a source of instability, whereas Secretary of State Dean Acheson disagreed with them. In the 1950s, President Eisenhower sought to end the American commitment to defend Western Europe and to provide West Germany with its own nuclear deterrent. This policy, which was never fully adopted, nevertheless caused significant instability in Europe, as it led directly to the Berlin crises of 1958–59 and 1961.[51]

Second, great powers cannot put aside power considerations and work to promote international peace because they cannot be sure that their efforts will succeed. If their attempt fails, they are likely to pay a steep price for having neglected the balance of power, because if an aggressor appears at the door there will be no answer when they dial 911. That is a risk few states are willing to run. Therefore, prudence dictates that they behave according to realist logic. This line of reasoning accounts for why collective security schemes, which call for states to put aside narrow concerns about the balance of power and instead act in accordance with the broader interests of the international community, invariably die at birth.[52]

Cooperation among States

One might conclude from the preceding discussion that my theory does not allow for any cooperation among the great powers. But this conclusion would be wrong. States can cooperate, although cooperation is sometimes difficult to achieve and always difficult to sustain. Two factors inhibit cooperation: considerations about relative gains and concern about cheating.[53] Ultimately, great powers live in a fundamentally competitive world where they view each other as real, or at least potential, enemies, and they therefore look to gain power at each other's expense.

Any two states contemplating cooperation must consider how profits or gains will be distributed between them. They can think about the division in terms of either absolute or relative gains (recall the distinction made earlier between pursuing either absolute power or relative power; the concept here is the same). With absolute gains, each side is concerned with maximizing its own profits and cares little about how much the other side gains or loses in the deal. Each side cares about the other only to the extent that the other side's behavior affects its own prospects for achieving maximum profits. With relative gains, on the other hand, each side considers not only its own individual gain, but also how well it fares compared to the other side.

Because great powers care deeply about the balance of power, their thinking focuses on relative gains when they consider cooperating with other states. For sure, each state tries to maximize its absolute gains; still, it is more important for a state to make sure that it does no worse, and perhaps better, than the other state in any agreement. Cooperation is more difficult to achieve, however, when states are attuned to relative gains rather than absolute gains.[54] This is because states concerned about absolute gains have to make sure that if the pie is expanding, they are getting at least some portion of the increase, whereas states that worry about relative gains must pay careful attention to how the pie is divided, which complicates cooperative efforts.

Concerns about cheating also hinder cooperation. Great powers are often reluctant to enter into cooperative agreements for fear that the other side will cheat on the agreement and gain a significant advantage. This concern is especially acute in the military realm, causing a "special peril of defection," because the nature of military weaponry allows for rapid shifts in the balance of power.[55] Such a development could create a window of opportunity for the state that cheats to inflict a decisive defeat on its victim.

These barriers to cooperation notwithstanding, great powers do cooperate in a realist world. Balance-of-power logic often causes great powers to form alliances and cooperate against common enemies. The United Kingdom, France, and Russia, for example, were allies against Germany before and during World War I. States sometimes cooperate to gang up on a third state, as Germany and the Soviet Union did against Poland in 1939.[56] More recently, Serbia and Croatia agreed to conquer and divide Bosnia between them, although the United States and its European allies prevented them from executing their agreement.[57] Rivals as well as allies cooperate. After all, deals can be struck that roughly reflect the distribution of power and satisfy concerns about cheating. The various arms control agreements signed by the superpowers during the Cold War illustrate this point.

The bottom line, however, is that cooperation takes place in a world that is competitive at its core—one where states have powerful incentives to take advantage of other states. This point is graphically highlighted by the state of European politics in the forty years before World War I. The great powers cooperated frequently during this period, but that did not stop them from going to war on August 1, 1914.[58] The United States and the Soviet Union also cooperated considerably during World War II, but that cooperation did not prevent the outbreak of the Cold War shortly after Germany and Japan were defeated. Perhaps most amazingly, there was significant economic and military cooperation between Nazi Germany and the Soviet Union during the two years before the Wehrmacht attacked the Red Army.[59] No amount of cooperation can eliminate the dominating logic of security competition. Genuine peace, or a world in which states do not compete for power, is not likely as long as the state system remains anarchic.

Conclusion

In sum, my argument is that the structure of the international system, not the particular characteristics of individual great powers, causes them to think and act offensively and to seek hegemony.[60] I do not adopt Morgenthau's claim that states invariably behave aggressively because they have a will to power hardwired into them. Instead, I assume that the principal motive behind great-power behavior is survival. In anarchy, however, the desire to survive encourages states to behave aggressively. Nor does my theory classify states as more or less aggressive on the basis of their economic or political systems. Offensive realism makes only a handful of assumptions about great powers, and these assumptions apply equally to all great powers.

Except for differences in how much power each state controls, the theory treats all states alike.

I have now laid out the logic explaining why states seek to gain as much power as possible over their rivals. * * *

NOTES

1. Most realist scholars allow in their theories for status quo powers that are not hegemons. At least some states, they argue, are likely to be satisfied with the balance of power and thus have no incentive to change it. See Randall L. Schweller, "Neorealism's Status-Quo Bias: What Security Dilemma?" *Security Studies* 5, No. 3 (Spring 1996, special issue on "Realism: Restatements and Renewal," ed. Benjamin Frankel), pp. 98–101; and Arnold Wolfers, *Discord and Collaboration: Essays on International Politics* (Baltimore, MD: Johns Hopkins University Press, 1962), pp. 84–86, 91–92, 125–26.

2. Milton Friedman, *Essays in Positive Economics* (Chicago: University of Chicago Press, 1953), p. 14. Also see Kenneth N. Waltz, *Theory of International Politics* (Reading, MA: Addison-Wesley, 1979), pp. 5–6, 91, 119.

3. Terry Moe makes a helpful distinction between assumptions that are simply useful simplifications of reality (i.e., realistic in themselves but with unnecessary details omitted), and assumptions that are clearly contrary to reality (i.e., that directly violate well-established truths). See Moe, "On the Scientific Status of Rational Models," *American Journal of Political Science* 23, No. 1 (February 1979), pp. 215–43.

4. The concept of anarchy and its consequences for international politics was first articulated by G. Lowes Dickinson, *The European Anarchy* (New York: Macmillan, 1916). For a more recent and more elaborate discussion of anarchy, see Waltz, *Theory of International Politics*, pp. 88–93. Also see Robert J. Art and Robert Jervis, eds., *International Politics: Anarchy, Force, Imperialism* (Boston: Little, Brown, 1973), pt. 1; and Helen Milner, "The Assumption of Anarchy in International Relations Theory: A Critique," *Review of International Studies* 17, No. 1 (January 1991), pp. 67–85.

5. Although the focus in this study is on the state system, realist logic can be applied to other kinds of anarchic systems. After all, it is the absence of central authority, not any special characteristic of states, that causes them to compete for power.

6. Inis L. Claude, Jr., *Swords into Plowshares: The Problems and Progress of International Organization*, 4th ed. (New York: Random House, 1971), p. 14.

7. The claim that states might have benign intentions is simply a starting assumption. I argue subsequently that when you combine the theory's five assumptions, states are put in a position in which they are strongly disposed to having hostile intentions toward each other.

8. My theory ultimately argues that great powers behave offensively toward each other because that is the best way for them to guarantee their security in an anarchic world. The assumption here, however, is that there are many reasons besides security for why a state might behave aggressively toward another state. In fact, it is

uncertainty about whether those non-security causes of war are at play, or might come into play, that pushes great powers to worry about their survival and thus act offensively. Security concerns alone cannot cause great powers to act aggressively. The possibility that at least one state might be motivated by non-security calculations is a necessary condition for offensive realism, as well as for any other structural theory of international politics that predicts security competition.

9. Quoted in Jon Jacobson, *When the Soviet Union Entered World Politics* (Berkeley: University of California Press, 1994), p. 271.

10. See Elizabeth Pond, *Beyond the Wall: Germany's Road to Unification* (Washington, DC: Brookings Institution Press, 1993), chap. 12; Margaret Thatcher, *The Downing Street Years* (New York: Harper-Collins, 1993), chaps. 25–26; and Philip Zelikow and Condoleezza Rice, *Germany Unified and Europe Transformed: A Study in Statecraft* (Cambridge, MA: Harvard University Press, 1995), chap. 4.

11. Frederick Schuman introduced the concept of self-help in *International Politics: An Introduction to the Western State System* (New York: McGraw-Hill, 1933), pp. 199–202, 514, although Waltz made the concept famous in *Theory of International Politics*, chap. 6. On realism and alliances, see Stephen M. Walt, *The Origins of Alliances* (Ithaca, NY: Cornell University Press, 1987).

12. Quoted in Martin Wight, *Power Politics* (London: Royal Institute of International Affairs, 1946), p. 40.

13. If one state achieves hegemony, the system ceases to be anarchic and becomes hierarchic. Offensive realism, which assumes international anarchy, has little to say about politics under hierarchy. But as discussed later, it is highly unlikely that any state will become a global hegemon, although regional hegemony is feasible. Thus, realism is likely to provide important insights about world politics for the foreseeable future, save for what goes on inside in a region that is dominated by a hegemon.

14. Although great powers always have aggressive intentions, they are not always *aggressors*, mainly because sometimes they do not have the capability to behave aggressively. I use the term "aggressor" throughout this book to denote great powers that have the material wherewithal to act on their aggressive intentions.

15. Kenneth Waltz maintains that great powers should not pursue hegemony but instead should aim to control an "appropriate" amount of world power. See Waltz, "The Origins of War in Neorealist Theory," in Robert I. Rotberg and Theodore K. Rabb, eds., *The Origin and Prevention of Major Wars* (Cambridge: Cambridge University Press, 1989), p. 40.

16. The following hypothetical example illustrates this point. Assume that American policy-makers were forced to choose between two different power balances in the Western Hemisphere. The first is the present distribution of power, whereby the United States is a hegemon that no state in the region would dare challenge militarily. In the second scenario, China replaces Canada and Germany takes the place of Mexico. Even though the United States would have a significant military advantage over both China and Germany, it is difficult to imagine any American strategist opting for this scenario over U.S. hegemony in the Western Hemisphere.

17. John H. Herz, "Idealist Internationalism and the Security Dilemma," *World Politics* 2, No. 2 (January 1950), pp. 157–80.

Although Dickinson did not use the term "security dilemma," its logic is clearly articulated in *European Anarchy*, pp. 20, 88.

18. Herz, "Idealist Internationalism," p. 157.

19. See Joseph M. Grieco, "Anarchy and the Limits of Cooperation: A Realist Critique of the Newest Liberal Institutionalism," *International Organization* 42, No. 3 (Summer 1988), pp. 485–507; Stephen D. Krasner, "Global Communications and National Power: Life on the Pareto Frontier," *World Politics* 43, No. 3 (April 1991), pp. 336–66; and Robert Powell, "Absolute and Relative Gains in International Relations Theory," *American Political Science Review* 85, No. 4 (December 1991), pp. 1303–20.

20. See Michael Mastanduno, "Do Relative Gains Matter? America's Response to Japanese Industrial Policy," *International Security* 16, No. 1 (Summer 1991), pp. 73–113.

21. Waltz maintains that in Hans Morgenthau's theory, states seek power as an end in itself; thus, they are concerned with absolute power, not relative power. See Waltz, "Origins of War," pp. 40–41; and Waltz, *Theory of International Politics*, pp. 126–27.

22. Quoted in Marc Trachtenberg, *A Constructed Peace: The Making of the European Settlement, 1945–1963* (Princeton, NJ: Princeton University Press, 1999), p. 36.

23. In short, the key issue for evaluating offensive realism is not whether a state is constantly trying to conquer other countries or going all out in terms of defense spending, but whether or not great powers routinely pass up promising opportunities to gain power over rivals.

24. See Richard K. Betts, *Surprise Attack: Lessons for Defense Planning* (Washington, DC: Brookings Institution Press, 1982); James D. Fearon, "Rationalist Explanations for War," *International Organization* 49, No. 3 (Summer 1995), pp. 390–401; Robert Jervis, *The Logic of Images in International Relations* (Princeton, NJ: Princeton University Press, 1970); and Stephen Van Evera, *Causes of War: Power and the Roots of Conflict* (Ithaca, NY: Cornell University Press, 1999), pp. 45–51, 83, 137–42.

25. See Joel Achenbach, "The Experts in Retreat: After-the-Fact Explanations for the Gloomy Predictions," *Washington Post*, February 28, 1991; and Jacob Weisberg, "Gulfballs: How the Experts Blew It, Big-Time," *New Republic*, March 25, 1991.

26. Jack Snyder and Stephen Van Evera make this argument in its boldest form. See Jack Snyder, *Myths of Empire: Domestic Politics and International Ambition* (Ithaca, NY: Cornell University Press, 1991), esp. pp. 1, 307–8; and Van Evera, *Causes of War*, esp. pp. 6, 9.

27. Relatedly, some defensive realists interpret the security dilemma to say that the offensive measures a state takes to enhance its own security force rival states to respond in kind, leaving all states no better off than if they had done nothing, and possibly even worse off. See Charles L. Glaser, "The Security Dilemma Revisited," *World Politics* 50, No. 1 (October 1997), pp. 171–201.

28. Although threatened states sometimes balance efficiently against aggressors, they often do not, thereby creating opportunities for successful offense. Snyder appears to be aware of this problem, as he adds the important qualifier "at least in the long run" to his claim that "states typically form balancing alliances to resist aggressors." *Myths of Empire*, p. 11.

29. John Arquilla, *Dubious Battles: Aggression, Defeat, and the International System* (Washington, DC: Crane Russak, 1992), p. 2. Also see

Bruce Bueno de Mesquita, *The War Trap* (New Haven, CT: Yale University Press, 1981), pp. 21–22; and Kevin Wang and James Ray, "Beginners and Winners: The Fate of Initiators of Interstate Wars Involving Great Powers since 1495," *International Studies Quarterly* 38, No. 1 (March 1994), pp. 139–54.

30. Although Snyder and Van Evera maintain that conquest rarely pays, both concede in subtle but important ways that aggression sometimes succeeds. Snyder, for example, distinguishes between expansion (successful offense) and overexpansion (unsuccessful offense), which is the behavior that he wants to explain. See, for example, his discussion of Japanese expansion between 1868 and 1945 in *Myths of Empire*, pp. 114–16. Van Evera allows for variation in the offense-defense balance, to include a few periods where conquest is feasible. See *Causes of War*, chap. 6. Of course, allowing for successful aggression contradicts their central claim that offense hardly ever succeeds.

31. See Robert Gilpin, *War and Change in World Politics* (Cambridge: Cambridge University Press, 1981), p. 29; and William C. Wohlforth, *The Elusive Balance: Power and Perceptions during the Cold War* (Ithaca, NY: Cornell University Press, 1993), pp. 12–14.

32. In subsequent chapters, the power-projection problems associated with large bodies of water are taken into account when measuring the distribution of power (see Chapter 4). Those two factors are treated separately here, however, simply to highlight the profound influence that oceans have on the behavior of great powers.

33. For an opposing view, see David M. Edelstein, "Choosing Friends and Enemies: Perceptions of Intentions in International Relations," Ph.D. diss., University of Chicago, August 2000; Andrew Kydd, "Why Security Seekers Do Not Fight Each Other," *Security Studies* 7, No. 1 (Autumn 1997), pp. 114–54; and Walt, *Origins of Alliances*.

34. See note 8 in this chapter.

35. Jacob Viner, "Power versus Plenty as Objectives of Foreign Policy in the Seventeenth and Eighteenth Centuries," *World Politics* I, No. 1 (October 1948), p. 10.

36. See Mark Bowden, *Black Hawk Down: A Story of Modern War* (London: Penguin, 1999); Alison Des Forges, *"Leave None to Tell the Story": Genocide in Rwanda* (New York: Human Rights Watch, 1999), pp. 623–25; and Gerard Prunier, *The Rwanda Crisis: History of a Genocide* (New York: Columbia University Press, 1995), pp. 274–75.

37. See Scott R. Feil, *Preventing Genocide: How the Early Use of Force Might Have Succeeded in Rwanda* (New York: Carnegie Corporation, 1998); and John Mueller, "The Banality of 'Ethnic War,'" *International Security* 25, No. 1 (Summer 2000), pp. 58–62. For a less sanguine view of how many lives would have been saved had the United States intervened in Rwanda, see Alan J. Kuperman, "Rwanda in Retrospect," *Foreign Affairs* 79, No. 1 (January–February 2000), pp. 94–118.

38. See David F. Schmitz, *Thank God They're on Our Side: The United States and Right-Wing Dictatorships, 1921–1965* (Chapel Hill: University of North Carolina Press, 1999), chaps. 4–6; Gaddis Smith, *The Last Years of the Monroe Doctrine, 1945–1993* (New York: Hill and Wang, 1994); Tony Smith, *America's Mission: The United States and the Worldwide Struggle for Democracy in the Twentieth Century* (Princeton, NJ: Princeton University Press, 1994); and

Stephen Van Evera, "Why Europe Matters, Why the Third World Doesn't: American Grand Strategy after the Cold War," *Journal of Strategic Studies* 13, No. 2 (June 1990), pp. 25–30.

39. Quoted in John M. Carroll and George C. Herring, eds., *Modern American Diplomacy*, rev. ed. (Wilmington, DE: Scholarly Resources, 1996), p. 122.

40. Nikita Khrushchev makes a similar point about Stalin's policy toward Chinese nationalist leader Chiang Kai-shek during World War II.

41. See Walt, *Origins of Alliances*, pp. 5, 266–68.

42. Adam Smith, *An Inquiry into the Nature and Causes of the Wealth of Nations*, ed. Edwin Cannan (Chicago: University of Chicago Press, 1976), Vol. 1, p. 487. All the quotes in this paragraph are from pp. 484–87 of that book.

43. For an overview of the Anglo-Dutch rivalry, see Jack S. Levy, "The Rise and Decline of the Anglo-Dutch Rivalry, 1609–1689," in William R. Thompson, ed., *Great Power Rivalries* (Columbia: University of South Carolina Press, 1999), pp. 172–200; and Paul M. Kennedy, *The Rise and Fall of British Naval Mastery* (London: Allen Lane, 1976), chap. 2.

44. William J. Clinton, "Address by the President to the 48th Session of the United Nations General Assembly," United Nations, New York, September 27, 1993. Also see George Bush, "Toward a New World Order: Address by the President to a Joint Session of Congress," September 11, 1990.

45. Bradley Thayer examined whether the victorious powers were able to create and maintain stable security orders in the aftermath of the Napoleonic Wars, World War I, and World War II, or whether they competed among themselves for power, as realism would predict. Thayer concludes that the rhetoric of the triumphant powers notwithstanding, they remained firmly committed to gaining power at each other's expense. See Bradley A. Thayer, "Creating Stability in New World Orders," Ph.D. diss., University of Chicago, August 1996.

46. See Melvyn P. Leffler, *A Preponderance of Power: National Security, the Truman Administration, and the Cold War* (Stanford, CA: Stanford University Press, 1992).

47. For a discussion of American efforts to undermine Soviet control of Eastern Europe, see Peter Grose, *Operation Rollback: America's Secret War behind the Iron Curtain* (Boston: Houghton Mifflin, 2000); Walter L. Hixson, *Parting the Curtain: Propaganda, Culture, and the Cold War, 1945–1961* (New York: St. Martin's, 1997); and Gregory Mitrovich, *Undermining the Kremlin: America's Strategy to Subvert the Soviet Bloc, 1947–1956* (Ithaca, NY: Cornell University Press, 2000).

48. For a synoptic discussion of U.S. policy toward the Soviet Union in the late 1980s that cites most of the key sources on the subject, see Randall L. Schweller and William C. Wohlforth, "Power Test: Evaluating Realism in Response to the End of the Cold War," *Security Studies* 9, No. 3 (Spring 2000), pp. 91–97.

49. The editors of a major book on the Treaty of Versailles write, "The resulting reappraisal, as documented in this book, constitutes a new synthesis of peace conference scholarship. The findings call attention to divergent peace aims within the American and Allied camps and underscore the degree to which the negotiators themselves considered the Versailles Treaty a work in progress." Manfred F. Boemeke, Gerald D. Feldman, and Elisabeth Glaser, eds.,

The Treaty of Versailles: A Reassessment after 75 Years (Cambridge: Cambridge University Press, 1998), p. 1.

50. This paragraph draws heavily on Trachtenberg, *Constructed Peace*; and Marc Trachtenberg, *History and Strategy* (Princeton, NJ: Princeton University Press, 1991), chaps. 4–5. Also see G. John Ikenberry, "Rethinking the Origins of American Hegemony," *Political Science Quarterly* 104, No. 3 (Autumn 1989), pp. 375–400.

51. The failure of American policymakers during the early Cold War to understand where the security competition in Europe was leading is summarized by Trachtenberg, "The predictions that were made pointed as a rule in the opposite direction: that Germany could not be kept down forever; that the Federal Republic would ultimately . . . want nuclear forces of her own; that U.S. troops could not be expected to remain in . . . Europe. . . . Yet all these predictions—every single one—turned out to be wrong." Trachtenberg, *History and Strategy*, pp. 231–32. Also see Trachtenberg, *Constructed Peace*, pp. vii–viii.

52. For more discussion of the pitfalls of collective security, see John J. Mearsheimer, "The False Promise of International Institutions," *International Security* 19, No. 3 (Winter 1994–95), pp. 26–37.

53. See Grieco, "Anarchy and the Limits of Cooperation," pp. 498, 500.

54. For evidence of relative gains considerations thwarting cooperation among states, see Paul W. Schroeder, *The Transformation of European Politics, 1763–1848* (Oxford: Clarendon, 1994), chap. 3.

55. Charles Lipson, "International Cooperation in Economic and Security Affairs," *World Politics* 37, No. 1 (October 1984), p. 14.

56. See Randall L. Schweller, "Bandwagoning for Profit: Bringing the Revisionist State Back In," *International Security* 19, No. 1 (Summer 1994), pp. 72–107. See also the works cited in note 59 in this chapter.

57. See Misha Glenny, *The Fall of Yugoslavia: The Third Balkan War*, 3d rev. ed. (New York: Penguin, 1996), p. 149; Philip Sherwell and Alina Petric, "Tudjman Tapes Reveal Plans to Divide Bosnia and Hide War Crimes," *Sunday Telegraph* (London), June 18, 2000; Laura Silber and Allan Little, *Yugoslavia: Death of a Nation*, rev. ed. (New York: Penguin, 1997), pp. 131–32, 213; and Warren Zimmerman, *Origins of a Catastrophe: Yugoslavia and Its Destroyers—America's Last Ambassador Tells What Happened and Why* (New York: Times Books, 1996), pp. 116–17.

58. See John Maynard Keynes, *The Economic Consequences of the Peace* (New York: Penguin, 1988), chap. 2; and J. M. Roberts, *Europe, 1880–1945* (London: Longman, 1970), pp. 239–41.

59. For information on the Molotov-Ribbentrop Pact of August 1939 and the ensuing cooperation between those states, see Alan Bullock, *Hitler and Stalin: Parallel Lives* (London: HarperCollins, 1991), chaps. 14–15; I.C.B. Dear, ed., *The Oxford Companion to World War II* (Oxford: Oxford University Press, 1995), pp. 780–82; Anthony Read and David Fisher, *The Deadly Embrace: Hitler, Stalin, and the Nazi-Soviet Pact, 1939–1941* (New York: Norton, 1988); Geoffrey Roberts, *The Unholy Alliance: Stalin's Pact with Hitler* (Bloomington: Indiana University Press, 1989), chaps. 8–10; and Adam B. Ulam, *Expansion and Coexistence: Soviet Foreign Policy, 1917–1973*, 2d ed. (New York: Holt, Rinehart, and Winston, 1974), chap. 6.

60. Waltz maintains that structural theories can explain international outcomes—i.e., whether war is more likely in bipolar or multipolar systems—but that they cannot explain the foreign policy behavior of particular states. A separate theory of foreign policy, he argues, is needed for that task. See *Theory of International Politics*, pp. 71–72, 121–23.

Michael W. Doyle

LIBERALISM AND WORLD POLITICS

Promoting freedom will produce peace, we have often been told. In a speech before the British Parliament in June of 1982, President Reagan proclaimed that governments founded on a respect for individual liberty exercise "restraint" and "peaceful intentions" in their foreign policy. He then announced a "crusade for freedom" and a "campaign for democratic development" (Reagan, June 9, 1982).

In making these claims the president joined a long list of liberal theorists (and propagandists) and echoed an old argument: the aggressive instincts of authoritarian leaders and totalitarian ruling parties make for war. Liberal states, founded on such individual rights as equality before the law, free speech and other civil liberties, private property, and elected representation are fundamentally against war this argument asserts. When the citizens who bear the burdens of war elect their governments, wars become impossible. Furthermore, citizens appreciate that the benefits of trade can be enjoyed only under conditions of peace. Thus the very existence of liberal states, such as the U.S., Japan, and our European allies, makes for peace.

Building on a growing literature in international political science, I reexamine the liberal claim President Reagan reiterated for us. I look at three distinct theoretical traditions of liberalism, attributable to three theorists: Schumpeter, a brilliant explicator of the liberal pacifism the president invoked;

Machiavelli, a classical republican whose glory is an imperialism we often practice; and Kant.

Despite the contradictions of liberal pacifism and liberal imperialism, I find, with Kant and other liberal republicans, that liberalism does leave a coherent legacy on foreign affairs. Liberal states are different. They are indeed peaceful, yet they are also prone to make war, as the U.S. and our "freedom fighters" are now doing, not so covertly, against Nicaragua. Liberal states have created a separate peace, as Kant argued they would, and have also discovered liberal reasons for aggression, as he feared they might. I conclude by arguing that the differences among liberal pacifism, liberal imperialism, and Kant's liberal internationalism are not arbitrary but rooted in differing conceptions of the citizen and the state.

Liberal Pacifism

There is no canonical description of liberalism. What we tend to call *liberal* resembles a family portrait of principles and institutions, recognizable by certain characteristics—for example, individual freedom, political participation, private property, and equality of opportunity—that most liberal states share, although none has perfected them all. Joseph Schumpeter clearly fits within this family when he considers the international effects of capitalism and democracy.

Schumpeter's "Sociology of Imperialisms," published in 1919, made a coherent and sustained argument concerning the pacifying (in the sense of

From *American Political Science Review* 80, no. 4 (Dec. 1986): 1151–69. The author's notes have been omitted.

nonaggressive) effects of liberal institutions and principles (Schumpeter, 1955; see also Doyle, 1986, pp. 155–59). Unlike some of the earlier liberal theorists who focused on a single feature such as trade (Montesquieu, 1949, vol. I, bk. 20, chap. 1) or failed to examine critically the arguments they were advancing, Schumpeter saw the interaction of capitalism and democracy as the foundation of liberal pacifism, and he tested his arguments in a sociology of historical imperialisms.

He defines *imperialism* as "an objectless disposition on the part of a state to unlimited forcible expansion" (Schumpeter, 1955, p. 6). Excluding imperialisms that were mere "catchwords" and those that were "object-ful" (e.g., defensive imperialism), he traces the roots of objectless imperialism to three sources, each an atavism. Modern imperialism, according to Schumpeter, resulted from the combined impact of a "war machine," warlike instincts, and export monopolism.

Once necessary, the war machine later developed a life of its own and took control of a state's foreign policy: "Created by the wars that required it, the machine now created the wars it required" (Schumpeter, 1955, p. 25). Thus, Schumpeter tells us that the army of ancient Egypt, created to drive the Hyksos out of Egypt, took over the state and pursued militaristic imperialism. Like the later armies of the courts of absolutist Europe, it fought wars for the sake of glory and booty, for the sake of warriors and monarchs—wars *gratia* warriors.

A warlike disposition, elsewhere called "instinctual elements of bloody primitivism," is the natural ideology of a war machine. It also exists independently; the Persians, says Schumpeter (1955, pp. 25–32), were a warrior nation from the outset.

Under modern capitalism, export monopolists, the third source of modern imperialism, push for imperialist expansion as a way to expand their closed markets. The absolute monarchies were the last clear-cut imperialisms. Nineteenth-century imperialisms merely represent the vestiges of the imperialisms created by Louis XIV and Catherine the Great. Thus, the export monopolists are an atavism of the absolute monarchies, for they depend completely on the tariffs imposed by the monarchs and their militaristic successors for revenue (Schumpeter, 1955, p. 82–83). Without tariffs, monopolies would be eliminated by foreign competition.

Modern (nineteenth-century) imperialism, therefore, rests on an atavistic war machine, militaristic attitudes left over from the days of monarchical wars, and export monopolism, which is nothing more than the economic residue of monarchical finance. In the modern era, imperialists gratify their private interests. From the national perspective, their imperialistic wars are objectless.

Schumpeter's theme now emerges. Capitalism and democracy are forces for peace. Indeed, they are antithetical to imperialism. For Schumpeter, the further development of capitalism and democracy means that imperialism will inevitably disappear. He maintains that capitalism produces an unwarlike disposition; its populace is "democratized, individualized, rationalized" (Schumpeter, 1955, p. 68). The people's energies are daily absorbed in production. The disciplines of industry and the market train people in "economic rationalism"; the instability of industrial life necessitates calculation. Capitalism also "individualizes"; "subjective opportunities" replace the "immutable factors" of traditional, hierarchical society. Rational individuals demand democratic governance.

Democratic capitalism leads to peace. As evidence, Schumpeter claims that throughout the capitalist world an opposition has arisen to "war, expansion, cabinet diplomacy"; that contemporary capitalism is associated with peace parties; and that the industrial worker of capitalism is "vigorously anti-imperialist." In addition, he points out that the capitalist world has developed means of preventing war, such as the Hague Court and that the least feudal, most capitalist society—the United States—has demonstrated the least imperialistic tendencies (Schumpeter, 1955, pp. 95–96). An example of the lack of imperialistic tendencies in the U.S., Schumpeter thought, was our leaving over half of Mexico unconquered in the war of 1846–48.

Schumpeter's explanation for liberal pacifism is quite simple: Only war profiteers and military aristocrats gain from wars. No democracy would pursue a minority interest and tolerate the high costs of imperialism. When free trade prevails, "no class" gains from forcible expansion because

> foreign raw materials and food stuffs are as accessible to each nation as though they were in its own territory. Where the cultural backwardness of a region makes normal economic intercourse dependent on colonization it does not matter, assuming free trade, which of the "civilized" nations undertakes the task of colonization. (Schumpeter, 1955, pp. 75–76)

Schumpeter's arguments are difficult to evaluate. In partial tests of quasi-Schumpeterian propositions, Michael Haas (1974, pp. 464–65) discovered a cluster that associates democracy, development, and sustained modernization with peaceful conditions. However, M. Small and J. D. Singer (1976) have discovered that there is no clearly negative correlation between democracy and war in the period 1816–1965—the period that would be central to Schumpeter's argument (see also Wilkenfeld, 1968, Wright, 1942, p. 841).

* * * A recent study by R. J. Rummel (1983) of "libertarianism" and international violence is the closest test Schumpeterian pacifism has received. "Free" states (those enjoying political and economic freedom) were shown to have considerably less conflict at or above the level of economic sanctions than "nonfree" states. The free states, the partly free states (including the democratic socialist countries such as Sweden), and the nonfree states accounted for 24%, 26%, and 61%, respectively, of the international violence during the period examined.

These effects are impressive but not conclusive for the Schumpeterian thesis. The data are limited, in this test, to the period 1976 to 1980. It includes, for example, the Russo-Afghan War, the Vietnamese invasion of Cambodia, China's invasion of Vietnam, and Tanzania's invasion of Uganda but just misses the U.S., quasi-covert intervention in Angola (1975) and our not so covert war against Nicaragua (1981–). More importantly, it excludes the cold war period, with its numerous interventions, and the long history of colonial wars (the Boer War, the Spanish-American War, the Mexican Intervention, etc.) that marked the history of liberal, including democratic capitalist, states (Doyle, 1983b; Chan, 1984; Weede, 1984).

The discrepancy between the warlike history of liberal states and Schumpeter's pacifistic expectations highlights three extreme assumptions. First, his "materialistic monism" leaves little room for noneconomic objectives, whether espoused by states or individuals. Neither glory, nor prestige, nor ideological justification, nor the pure power of ruling shapes policy. These nonmaterial goals leave little room for positive-sum gains, such as the comparative advantages of trade. Second, and relatedly, the same is true for his states. The political life of individuals seems to have been homogenized at the same time as the individuals were "rationalized, individualized, and democratized." Citizens—capitalists and workers, rural and urban—seek material welfare. Schumpeter seems to presume that ruling makes no difference. He also presumes that no one is prepared to take those measures (such as stirring up foreign quarrels to preserve a domestic ruling coalition) that enhance one's political power, despite determental effects on mass welfare. Third, like domestic politics, world politics are homogenized. Materially monistic and democratically capitalist, all states evolve toward free trade and liberty together. Countries differently constituted seem to disappear from Schumpeter's analysis. "Civilized" nations govern "culturally backward" *regions*. These assumptions are not shared by Machiavelli's theory of liberalism.

Liberal Imperialism

Machiavelli argues, not only that republics are not pacifistic, but that they are the best form of state for imperial expansion. Establishing a republic fit for imperial expansion is, moreover, the best way to guarantee the survival of a state.

Machiavelli's republic is a classical mixed republic. It is not a democracy—which he thought would quickly degenerate into a tyranny—but is characterized by social equality, popular liberty, and political participation (Machiavelli, 1950, bk. 1, chap. 2, p. 112; see also Huliung, 1983, chap. 2; Mansfield, 1970; Pocock, 1975, pp. 198–99; Skinner, 1981, chap. 3). The consuls serve as "kings," the senate as an aristocracy managing the state, and the people in the assembly as the source of strength.

Liberty results from "disunion"—the competition and necessity for compromise required by the division of powers among senate, consuls, and tribunes (the last representing the common people). Liberty also results from the popular veto. The powerful few threaten the rest with tyranny, Machiavelli says, because they seek to dominate. The mass demands not to be dominated, and their veto thus preserves the liberties of the state (Machiavelli, 1950, bk. 1, chap. 5, p. 122). However, since the people and the rulers have different social characters, the people need to be "managed" by the few to avoid having their recklessness overturn or their fecklessness undermine the ability of the state to expand (Machiavelli, 1950, bk. 1, chap. 53, pp. 249–50). Thus the senate and the consuls plan expansion, consult oracles, and employ religion to manage the resources that the energy of the people supplies.

Strength, and then imperial expansion, results from the way liberty encourages increased population and property, which grow when the citizens know their lives and goods are secure from arbitrary seizure. Free citizens equip large armies and provide soldiers who fight for public glory and the common good because these are, in fact, their own (Machiavelli, 1950, bk. 2, chap. 2, pp. 287–90). If you seek the honor of having your state expand, Machiavelli advises, you should organize it as a free and popular republic like Rome, rather than as an aristocratic republic like Sparta or Venice. Expansion thus calls for a free republic.

"Necessity"—political survival—calls for expansion. If a stable aristocratic republic is forced by foreign conflict "to extend her territory, in such a case we shall see her foundations give way and herself quickly brought to ruin"; if, on the other hand, domestic security prevails, "the continued tranquility would enervate her, or provoke internal disensions, which together, or either of them separately, will apt to prove her ruin" (Machiavelli, 1950, bk. 1, chap. 6, p. 129). Machiavelli therefore believes it is necessary to take the constitution of Rome, rather than that of Sparta or Venice, as our model.

Hence, this belief leads to liberal imperialism. We are lovers of glory, Machiavelli announces. We seek to rule or, at least, to avoid being oppressed. In either case, we want more for ourselves and our states than just material welfare (materialistic monism). Because other states with similar aims thereby threaten us, we prepare ourselves for expansion. Because our fellow citizens threaten us if we do not allow them either to satisfy their ambition or to release their political energies through imperial expansion, we expand.

There is considerable historical evidence for liberal imperialism. Machiavelli's (Polybius's) Rome and Thucydides' Athens both were imperial republics in the Machiavellian sense (Thucydides, 1954, bk. 6). The historical record of numerous U.S. interventions in the postwar period supports Machiavelli's argument (* * * Barnet, 1968, chap. 11), but the current record of liberal pacifism, weak as it is, calls some of his insights into question. To the extent that the modern populace actually controls (and thus unbalances) the mixed republic, its diffidence may outweigh elite ("senatorial") aggressiveness.

We can conclude either that (1) liberal pacifism has at least taken over with the further development of capitalist democracy, as Schumpeter predicted it would or that (2) the mixed record of liberalism—pacifism and imperialism—indicates that some liberal states are Schumpeterian democracies while others are Machiavellian republics. Before we accept either conclusion, however, we must consider a third apparent regularity of modern world politics.

Liberal Internationalism

Modern liberalism carries with it two legacies. They do not affect liberal states separately, according to whether they are pacifistic or imperialistic, but simultaneously.

The first of these legacies is the pacification of foreign relations among liberal states. * * *

Beginning in the eighteenth century and slowly growing since then, a zone of peace, which Kant called the "pacific federation" or "pacific union," has begun to be established among liberal societies. More than 40 liberal states currently make up the union. Most are in Europe and North America, but they can be found on every continent, as Appendix 1 indicates.

Here the predictions of liberal pacifists (and President Reagan) are borne out: liberal states do exercise peaceful restraint, and a separate peace exists among them. This separate peace provides a solid foundation for the United States' crucial alliances with the liberal powers, e.g., the North Atlantic Treaty Organization and our Japanese alliance. This foundation appears to be impervious to the quarrels with our allies that bedeviled the Carter and Reagan administrations. It also offers the promise of a continuing peace among liberal states, and as the number of liberal states increases, it announces the possibility of global peace this side of the grave or world conquest.

Of course, the probability of the outbreak of war in any given year between any two given states

is low. The occurrence of a war between any two adjacent states, considered over a long period of time, would be more probable. The apparent absence of war between liberal states, whether adjacent or not, for almost 200 years thus may have significance. Similar claims cannot be made for feudal, fascist, communist, authoritarian, or totalitarian forms of rule (Doyle, 1983a, p. 222), nor for pluralistic or merely similar societies. More significant perhaps is that when states are forced to decide on which side of an impending world war they will fight, liberal states all wind up on the same side despite the complexity of the paths that take them there. These characteristics do not prove that the peace among liberals is statistically significant nor that liberalism is the sole valid explanation for the peace. They do suggest that we consider the possibility that liberals have indeed established a separate peace—but only among themselves.

Liberalism also carries with it a second legacy: international "imprudence" (Hume, 1963, pp. 346–47). Peaceful restraint only seems to work in liberals' relations with other liberals. Liberal states have fought numerous wars with nonliberal states. (For a list of international wars since 1816 see Appendix 2.)

Many of these wars have been defensive and thus prudent by necessity. Liberal states have been attacked and threatened by nonliberal states that do not exercise any special restraint in their dealings with the liberal states. Authoritarian rulers both stimulate and respond to an international political environment in which conflicts of prestige, interest, and pure fear of what other states might do all lead states toward war. War and conquest have thus characterized the careers of many authoritarian rulers and ruling parties, from Louis XIV and Napoleon to Mussolini's fascists, Hitler's Nazis, and Stalin's communists.

Yet we cannot simply blame warfare on the authoritarians or totalitarians, as many of our more enthusiastic politicians would have us do. Most wars arise out of calculations and miscalculations of interest, misunderstandings, and mutual suspicions, such as those that characterized the origins of World War I. However, aggression by the liberal state has also characterized a large number of wars. Both France and Britain fought expansionist colonial wars throughout the nineteenth century. The United States fought a similar war with Mexico from 1846 to 1848, waged a war of annihilation against the American Indians, and intervened militarily against sovereign states many times before and after World War II. Liberal states invade weak nonliberal states and display striking distrust in dealings with powerful nonliberal states (Doyle, 1983b).

Neither realist (statist) nor Marxist theory accounts well for these two legacies. While they can account for aspects of certain periods of international stability (* * * Russett, 1985), neither the logic of the balance of power nor the logic of international hegemony explains the separate peace maintained for more than 150 years among states sharing one particular form of governance—liberal principles and institutions. Balance-of-power theory expects—indeed is premised upon—flexible arrangements of geostrategic rivalry that include preventive war. Hegemonies wax and wane, but the liberal peace holds. Marxist "ultra-imperialists" expect a form of peaceful rivalry among capitalists, but only liberal capitalists maintain peace. Leninists expect liberal capitalists to be aggressive toward nonliberal states, but they also (and especially) expect them to be imperialistic toward fellow liberal capitalists.

Kant's theory of liberal internationalism helps us understand these two legacies. * * * *Perpetual Peace*, written in 1795 (Kant, 1970, pp. 93–130), helps us understand the interactive nature of international relations. Kant tries to teach us methodologically that we can study neither the systemic relations of states nor the varieties of state behavior in isolation from each other. Substantively, he anticipates for us the ever-widening pacification of

a liberal pacific union, explains this pacification, and at the same time suggests why liberal states are not pacific in their relations with nonliberal states. Kant argues that perpetual peace will be guaranteed by the ever-widening acceptance of three "definitive articles" of peace. When all nations have accepted the definitive articles in a metaphorical "treaty" of perpetual peace he asks them to sign, perpetual peace will have been established.

The First Definitive Article requires the civil constitution of the state to be republican. By *republican* Kant means a political society that has solved the problem of combining moral autonomy, individualism, and social order. A private property and market-oriented economy partially addressed that dilemma in the private sphere. The public, or political, sphere was more troubling. His answer was a republic that preserved juridical freedom—the legal equality of citizens as subjects—on the basis of a representative government with a separation of powers. Juridical freedom is preserved because the morally autonomous individual is by means of representation a self-legislator making laws that apply to all citizens equally, including himself or herself. Tyranny is avoided because the individual is subject to laws he or she does not also administer (Kant, *PP* [*Perpetual Peace*], pp. 99–102 * * *).

Liberal republics will progressively establish peace among themselves by means of the pacific federation, or union (*foedus pacificum*), described in Kant's Second Definitive Article. The pacific union will establish peace within a federation of free states and securely maintain the rights of each state. The world will not have achieved the "perpetual peace" that provides the ultimate guarantor of republican freedom until "a late stage and after many unsuccessful attempts" (Kant, *UH* [*The Idea for a Universal History with a Cosmopolitan Purpose*], p. 47). At that time, all nations will have learned the lessons of peace through right conceptions of the appropriate constitution, great and sad experience, and good will. Only then will individuals enjoy perfect republican rights or the full guarantee of a global and just peace. In the meantime, the "pacific federation" of liberal republics—"an enduring and gradually expanding federation likely to prevent war"—brings within it more and more republics—despite republican collapses, backsliding, and disastrous wars—creating an ever-expanding separate peace (Kant, *PP*, p. 105). Kant emphasizes that

> it can be shown that this idea of federalism, extending gradually to encompass all states and thus leading to perpetual peace, is practicable and has objective reality. For if by good fortune one powerful and enlightened nation can form a republic (which is by nature inclined to seek peace), this will provide a focal point for federal association among other states. These will join up with the first one, thus securing the freedom of each state in accordance with the idea of international right, and the whole will gradually spread further and further by a series of alliances of this kind. (Kant, *PP*, p. 104)

The pacific union is not a single peace treaty ending one war, a world state, nor a state of nations. Kant finds the first insufficient. The second and third are impossible or potentially tyrannical. National sovereignty precludes reliable subservience to a state of nations; a world state destroys the civic freedom on which the development of human capacities rests (Kant, *UH*, p. 50). Although Kant obliquely refers to various classical interstate confederations and modern diplomatic congresses, he develops no systematic organizational embodiment of this treaty and presumably does not find institutionalization necessary (Riley, 1983, chap. 5; Schwarz, 1962, p. 77). He appears to have in mind a mutual nonaggression pact, perhaps a collective security agreement, and the cosmopolitan law set forth in the Third Definitive Article.

The Third Definitive Article establishes a cosmopolitan law to operate in conjunction with the pacific union. The cosmopolitan law "shall be limited to conditions of universal hospitality." In this Kant calls for the recognition of the "right of a foreigner not to be treated with hostility when he arrives on someone else's territory." This "does not extend beyond those conditions which make it possible for them [foreigners] to attempt to enter into relations [commerce] with the native inhabitants" (Kant, *PP*, p. 106). Hospitality does not require extending to foreigners either the right to citizenship or the right to settlement, unless the foreign visitors would perish if they were expelled. Foreign conquest and plunder also find no justification under this right. Hospitality does appear to include the right of access and the obligation of maintaining the opportunity for citizens to exchange goods and ideas without imposing the obligation to trade (a voluntary act in all cases under liberal constitutions).

Perpetual peace, for Kant, is an epistemology, a condition for ethical action, and, most importantly, an explanation of how the "mechanical process of nature visibly exhibits the purposive plan of producing concord among men, even against their will and indeed by means of their very discord" (Kant, *PP*, p. 108; *UH*, pp. 44–45). Understanding history requires an epistemological foundation, for without a teleology, such as the promise of perpetual peace, the complexity of history would overwhelm human understanding (Kant, *UH*, pp. 51–53). Perpetual peace, however, is not merely a heuristic device with which to interpret history. It is guaranteed, Kant explains in the "First Addition" to *Perpetual Peace* ("On the Guarantee of Perpetual Peace"), to result from men fulfilling their ethical duty or, failing that, from a hidden plan. Peace is an ethical duty because it is only under conditions of peace that all men can treat each other as ends, rather than means to an end (Kant, *UH*, p. 50; Murphy, 1970, chap. 3). * * *

In the end, however, our guarantee of perpetual peace does not rest on ethical conduct. * * *

The guarantee thus rests, Kant argues, not on the probable behavior of moral angels, but on that of "devils, so long as they possess understanding" (*PP*, p. 112). In explaining the sources of each of the three definitive articles of the perpetual peace, Kant then tells us how we (as free and intelligent devils) could be motivated by fear, force, and calculated advantage to undertake a course of action whose outcome we could reasonably anticipate to be perpetual peace. Yet while it is possible to conceive of the Kantian road to peace in these terms, Kant himself recognizes and argues that social evolution also makes the conditions of moral behavior less onerous and hence more likely (*CF* [*The Contest of Faculties*], pp. 187–89; Kelly, 1969, pp. 106–13). In tracing the effects of both political and moral development, he builds an account of why liberal states do maintain peace among themselves and of how it will (by implication, has) come about that the pacific union will expand. He also explains how these republics would engage in wars with nonrepublics and therefore suffer the "sad experience" of wars that an ethical policy might have avoided.

■ ■ ■

Kant shows how republics, once established, lead to peaceful relations. He argues that once the aggressive interests of absolutist monarchies are tamed and the habit of respect for individual rights engrained by republican government, wars would appear as the disaster to the people's welfare that he and the other liberals thought them to be. The fundamental reason is this:

> If, as is inevitability the case under this constitution, the consent of the citizens is required to decide whether or not war should be declared, it is very natural that they will have a great hesitation in embarking on so dangerous an enterprise. For this would mean calling down on themselves all the miseries of war, such as doing the fighting themselves, supplying the costs of the war from their own resources, painfully making good the ensuing devastation, and, as the crowning evil, having to take upon themselves a burden of debts which will embitter peace itself and which can never be paid off on account of the constant threat of new wars. But under a constitution where the subject is not a citizen, and which is therefore not republican, it is the simplest thing in the world to go to war. For the head of state is not a fellow citizen, but the owner of the state, and war will not force him to make the slightest sacrifice so far as his banquets, hunts, pleasure palaces and court festivals are concerned. He can thus decide on war, without any significant reason, as a kind of amusement, and unconcernedly leave it to the diplomatic corps (who are always ready for such proposes) to justify the war for the sake of propriety. (Kant, *PP*, p. 100)

Yet these domestic republican restraints do not end war. If they did, liberal states would not be warlike, which is far from the case. They do introduce republican caution—Kant's "hesitation"—in place of monarchical caprice. Liberal wars are only fought for popular, liberal purposes. The historical liberal legacy is laden with popular wars fought to promote freedom, to protect private property, or to support liberal allies against nonliberal enemies. Kant's position is ambiguous. He regards these wars as unjust and warns liberals of their susceptibility to them (Kant, *PP*, p. 106). At the same time, Kant argues that each nation "can and ought to" demand that its neighboring nations enter into the pacific union of liberal states (*PP*, p. 102). * * *

■ ■ ■

* * * As republics emerge (the first source) and as culture progresses, an understanding of the

legitimate rights of all citizens and of all republics comes into play; and this, now that caution characterizes policy, sets up the moral foundations for the liberal peace. Correspondingly, international law highlights the importance of Kantian publicity. Domestically, publicity helps ensure that the officials of republics act according to the principles they profess to hold just and according to the interests of the electors they claim to represent. Internationally, free speech and the effective communication of accurate conceptions of the political life of foreign peoples is essential to establishing and preserving the understanding on which the guarantee of respect depends. Domestically just republics, which rest on consent, then presume foreign republics also to be consensual, just, and therefore deserving of accommodation. * * * Because nonliberal governments are in a state of aggression with their own people, their foreign relations become for liberal governments deeply suspect. In short, fellow liberals benefit from a presumption of amity; nonliberals suffer from a presumption of enmity. Both presumptions may be accurate; each, however, may also be self-confirming.

Lastly, cosmopolitan law adds material incentives to moral commitments. The cosmopolitan right to hospitality permits the "spirit of commerce" sooner or later to take hold of every nation, thus impelling states to promote peace and to try to avert war. Liberal economic theory holds that these cosmopolitan ties derive from a cooperative international division of labor and free trade according to comparative advantage. Each economy is said to be better off than it would have been under autarky; each thus acquires an incentive to avoid policies that would lead the other to break these economic ties. Because keeping open markets rests upon the assumption that the next set of transactions will also be determined by prices rather than coercion, a sense of mutual security is vital to avoid security-motivated searches for economic autarky. Thus, avoiding a challenge to

another liberal state's security or even enhancing each other's security by means of alliance naturally follows economic interdependence.

A further cosmopolitan source of liberal peace is the international market's removal of difficult decisions of production and distribution from the direct sphere of state policy. A foreign state thus does not appear directly responsible for these outcomes, and states can stand aside from, and to some degree above, these contentious market rivalries and be ready to step in to resolve crises. The interdependence of commerce and the international contacts of state officials help create crosscutting transnational ties that serve as lobbies for mutual accommodation. According to modern liberal scholars, international financiers and transnational and transgovernmental organizations create interests in favor of accommodation. Moreover, their variety has ensured that no single conflict sours an entire relationship by setting off a spiral of reciprocated retaliation * * *. Conversely, a sense of suspicion, such as that characterizing relations between liberal and nonliberal governments, can lead to restrictions on the range of contacts between societies, and this can increase the prospect that a single conflict will determine an entire relationship.

No single constitutional, international, or cosmopolitan source is alone sufficient, but together (and only together) they plausibly connect the characteristics of liberal polities and economies with sustained liberal peace. Alliances founded on mutual strategic interest among liberal and nonliberal states have been broken; economic ties between liberal and nonliberal states have proven fragile; but the political bonds of liberal rights and interests have proven a remarkably firm foundation for mutual nonaggression. A separate peace exists among liberal states.

In their relations with nonliberal states, however, liberal states have not escaped from the insecurity caused by anarchy in the world political system considered as a whole. Moreover, the very constitutional restraint, international respect for individual rights, and shared commercial interests that establish grounds for peace among liberal states establish grounds for additional conflict in relations between liberal and nonliberal societies.

Conclusion

Kant's liberal internationalism, Machiavelli's liberal imperialism, and Schumpeter's liberal pacifism rest on fundamentally different views of the nature of the human being, the state, and international relations. Schumpeter's humans are rationalized, individualized, and democratized. They are also homogenized, pursuing material interests "monistically." Because their material interests lie in peaceful trade, they and the democratic state that these fellow citizens control are pacifistic. Machiavelli's citizens are splendidly diverse in their goals but fundamentally unequal in them as well, seeking to rule or fearing being dominated. Extending the rule of the dominant elite or avoiding the political collapse of their state, each calls for imperial expansion.

Kant's citizens, too, are diverse in their goals and individualized and rationalized, but most importantly, they are capable of appreciating the moral equality of all individuals and of treating other individuals as ends rather than as means. The Kantian state thus is governed publicly according to law, as a republic. Kant's is the state that solves the problem of governing individualized equals, whether they are the "rational devils" he says we often find ourselves to be or the ethical agents we can and should become. Republics tell us that

> in order to organize a group of rational beings who together require universal laws for their survival, but of whom each separate individual

is secretly inclined to exempt himself from them, the constitution must be so designed so that, although the citizens are opposed to one another in their private attitudes, these opposing views may inhibit one another in such a way that the public conduct of the citizens will be the same as if they did not have such evil attitudes. (Kant, *PP*, p. 113)

Unlike Machiavelli's republics, Kant's republics are capable of achieving peace among themselves because they exercise democratic caution and are capable of appreciating the international rights of foreign republics. These international rights of republics derive from the representation of foreign individuals, who are our moral equals. Unlike Schumpeter's capitalist democracies, Kant's republics—including our own—remain in a state of war with nonrepublics. Liberal republics see themselves as threatened by aggression from nonrepublics that are not constrained by representation. Even though wars often cost more than the economic return they generate, liberal republics also are prepared to protect and promote—sometimes forcibly—democracy, private property, and the rights of individuals overseas against nonrepublics, which, because they do not authentically represent the rights of individuals, have no rights to noninterference. These wars may liberate oppressed individuals overseas; they also can generate enormous suffering.

■   ■   ■

Perpetual peace, Kant says, is the end point of the hard journey his republics will take. The promise of perpetual peace, the violent lessons of war, and the experience of a partial peace are proof of the need for and the possibility of world peace. They are also the grounds for moral citizens and statesmen to assume the duty of striving for peace.

Appendix 1. Liberal Regimes and the Pacific Union, 1700–1982

PERIOD	PERIOD	PERIOD
18th Century	Chile, 1891–	Ireland, 1920–
Swiss Cantons[a]	Total = 14	Mexico, 1928–
French Republic, 1790–1795		Lebanon, 1944–
United States,[a] 1776–	**1900–1945**	Total = 29
Total = 3	Switzerland	
	United States	**1945–[b]**
1800–1850	Great Britain	Switzerland
Swiss Confederation	Sweden	United States
United States	Canada	Great Britain
France, 1830–1849	Greece, –1911;	Sweden
Belgium, 1830–	1928–1936	Canada
Great Britain, 1832–	Italy, –1922	Australia
Netherlands, 1848–	Belgium, –1940	New Zealand
Piedmont, 1848–	Netherlands, –1940	Finland
Denmark, 1849–	Argentina, –1943	Ireland
Total = 8	France, –1940	Mexico
	Chile, –1924; 1932–	Uruguay, –1973
1850–1900	Australia, 1901	Chile, –1973
Switzerland	Norway, 1905–1940	Lebanon, –1975
United States	New Zealand, 1907–	Costa Rica, –1948; 1953–
Belgium	Colombia, 1910–1949	Iceland, 1944–
Great Britain	Denmark, 1914–1940	France, 1945–
Netherlands	Poland, 1917–1935	Denmark, 1945
Piedmont, –1861	Latvia, 1922–1934	Norway, 1945
Italy, 1861–	Germany, 1918–1932	Austria, 1945–
Denmark, –1866	Austria, 1918–1934	Brazil, 1945–1954; 1955–1964
Sweden, 1864–	Estonia, 1919–1934	Belgium, 1946–
Greece, 1864–	Finland, 1919–	Luxembourg, 1946–
Canada, 1867–	Uruguay, 1919–	Netherlands, 1946–
France, 1871–	Costa Rica, 1919–	Italy, 1946–
Argentina, 1880–	Czechoslovakia, 1920–1939	Philippines, 1946–1972

(continued)

Appendix 1. Liberal Regimes and the Pacific Union, 1700–1982 (Continued)

PERIOD	PERIOD	PERIOD
1945–^b(cont.)	Turkey, 1950–1960;	Senegal, 1963–
India, 1947–1975; 1977–	1966–1971	Malaysia, 1963–
Sri Lanka, 1948–1961;	Japan, 1951–	Botswana, 1966–
1963–1971; 1978–	Bolivia, 1956–1969; 1982–	Singapore, 1965–
Ecuador, 1948–1963; 1979–	Colombia, 1958–	Portugal, 1976–
Israel, 1949–	Venezuela, 1959–	Spain, 1978–
West Germany, 1949–	Nigeria, 1961–1964;	Dominican Republic, 1978–
Greece, 1950–1967; 1975–	1979–1984	Honduras, 1981–
Peru, 1950–1962; 1963–	Jamaica, 1962–	Papua New Guinea, 1982–
1968; 1980–	Trinidad and Tobago, 1962–	Total = 50
El Salvador, 1950–1961		

Note: I have drawn up this approximate list of "Liberal Regimes" according to the four institutions Kant described as essential: market and private property economies; politics that are externally sovereign; citizens who possess juridical rights; and "republican" (whether republican or parliamentary monarchy), representative government. This latter includes the requirement that the legislative branch have an effective role in public policy and be formally and competitively (either inter- or intra-party) elected. Furthermore, I have taken into account whether male suffrage is wide (i.e., 30%) or, as Kant (*MM* [*The Metaphysics of Morals*], p. 139) would have had it, open by "achievement" to inhabitants of the national or metropolitan territory (e.g., to poll-tax payers or householders). This list of liberal regimes is thus more inclusive than a list of democratic regimes, or polyarchies (Powell, 1982, p. 5). Other conditions taken into account here are that female suffrage is granted within a generation of its being demanded by an extensive female suffrage movement and that representative government is internally sovereign (e.g., including, and especially over military and foreign affairs) as well as stable (in existence for at least three years). Sources for these data are Banks and Overstreet (1983), Gastil (1985), *The Europa Yearbook, 1985* (1985), Langer (1968), U.K. Foreign and Commonwealth Office (1980), and U.S. Department of State (1981). Finally, these lists exclude ancient and medieval "republics," since none appears to fit Kant's commitment to liberal individualism (Holmes, 1979).

^aThere are domestic variations within these liberal regimes: Switzerland was liberal only in certain cantons; the United States was liberal only north of the Mason-Dixon line until 1865, when it became liberal throughout.

^bSelected list, excludes liberal regimes with populations less than one million. These include all states categorized as "free" by Gastil and those "partly free" (four-fifths or more free) states with a more pronounced capitalist orientation.

Appendix 2. International Wars Listed Chronologically

British-Maharattan (1817–1818)

Greek (1821–1828)

Franco-Spanish (1823)

First Anglo-Burmese (1823–1826)

Javanese (1825–1830)

Russo-Persian (1826–1828)

Russo-Turkish (1828–1829)

First Polish (1831)

First Syrian (1831–1832)

Texas (1835–1836)

(continued)

Appendix 2. International Wars Listed Chronologically (Continued)

First British-Afghan (1838–1842)

Second Syrian (1839–1940)

Franco-Algerian (1839–1847)

Peruvian-Bolivian (1841)

First British-Sikh (1845–1846)

Mexican-American (1846–1848)

Austro-Sardinian (1848–1849)

First Schleswig-Holstein (1848–1849)

Hungarian (1848–1849)

Second British-Sikh (1848–1849)

Roman Republic (1849)

La Plata (1851–1852)

First Turco-Montenegran (1852–1853)

Crimean (1853–1856)

Anglo-Persian (1856–1857)

Sepoy (1857–1859)

Second Turco-Montenegran (1858–1859)

Italian Unification (1859)

Spanish-Moroccan (1859–1860)

Italo-Roman (1860)

Italo-Sicilian (1860–1861)

Franco-Mexican (1862–1867)

Ecuadorian-Colombian (1863)

Second Polish (1863–1864)

Spanish-Santo Dominican (1863–1865)

Second Schleswig-Holstein (1864)

Lopez (1864–1870)

Spanish-Chilean (1865–1866)

Seven Weeks (1866)

Ten Years (1868–1878)

Franco-Prussian (1870–1871)

Dutch-Achinese (1873–1878)

Balkan (1875–1877)

Russo-Turkish (1877–1878)

Bosnian (1878)

Second British-Afghan (1878–1880)

Pacific (1879–1883)

British-Zulu (1879)

Franco-Indochinese (1882–1884)

Mahdist (1882–1885)

Sino-French (1884–1885)

Central American (1885)

Serbo-Bulgarian (1885)

Sino-Japanese (1894–1895)

Franco-Madagascan (1894–1895)

Cuban (1895–1898)

Italo-Ethiopian (1895–1896)

First Philippine (1896–1898)

Greco-Turkish (1897)

Spanish-American (1898)

Second Philippine (1899–1902)

Boer (1899–1902)

Boxer Rebellion (1900)

Ilinden (1903)

Vietnamese-Cambodian (1975–)

Timor (1975–)

Saharan (1975–)

Ogaden (1976–)

Russo-Japanese (1904–1905)

Central American (1906)

Central American (1907)

Spanish-Moroccan (1909–1910)

Italo-Turkish (1911–1912)

First Balkan (1912–1913)

(continued)

Appendix 2. International Wars Listed Chronologically (Continued)

Second Balkan (1913)

World War I (1914–1918)

Russian Nationalities (1917–1921)

Russo-Polish (1919–1920)

Hungarian-Allies (1919)

Greco-Turkish (1919–1922)

Riffian (1921–1926)

Druze (1925–1927)

Sino-Soviet (1929)

Manchurian (1931–1933)

Chaco (1932–1935)

Italo-Ethiopian (1935–1936)

Sino-Japanese (1937–1941)

Changkufeng (1938)

Nomohan (1939)

World War II (1939–1945)

Russo-Finnish (1939–1940)

Franco-Thai (1940–1941)

Indonesian (1945–1946)

Indochinese (1945–1954)

Madagascan (1947–1948)

First Kashmir (1947–1949)

Palestine (1948–1949)

Hyderabad (1948)

Korean (1950–1953)

Algerian (1954–1962)

Russo-Hungarian (1956)

Sinai (1956)

Tibetan (1956–1959)

Sino-Indian (1962)

Vietnamese (1965–1975)

Second Kashmir (1965)

Six Day (1967)

Israeli-Egyptian (1969–1970)

Football (1969)

Bangladesh (1971)

Philippine-MNLF (1972–)

Yom Kippur (1973)

Turco-Cypriot (1974)

Ethiopian-Eritrean (1974–)

Ugandan-Tanzanian (1978–1979)

Sino-Vietnamese (1979)

Russo-Afghan (1979–)

Iran-Iraqi (1980–)

Note: This table is taken from Melvin Small and J. David Singer (1982, pp. 79–80). This is a partial list of international wars fought between 1816 and 1980. In Appendices A and B, Small and Singer identify a total of 575 wars during this period, but approximately 159 of them appear to be largely domestic, or civil wars.

This list excludes covert interventions, some of which have been directed by liberal regimes against other liberal regimes—for example, the United States' effort to destabilize the Chilean election and Allende's government. Nonetheless, it is significant that such interventions are not pursued publicly as acknowledged policy. The covert destabilization campaign against Chile is recounted by the Senate Select Committee to Study Governmental Operations with Respect to Intelligence Activities (1975, *Covert Action in Chile, 1963–73*).

Following the argument of this article, this list also excludes civil wars. Civil wars differ from international wars, not in the ferocity of combat, but in the issues that engender them. Two nations that could abide one another as independent neighbors separated by a border might well be the fiercest of enemies if forced to live together in one state, jointly deciding how to raise and spend taxes, choose leaders, and legislate fundamental questions of value. Notwithstanding these differences, no civil wars that I recall upset the argument of liberal pacification.

REFERENCES

Banks, Arthur, and William Overstreet, eds. 1983. *A Political Handbook of the World; 1982–1983*. New York: McGraw Hill.

Barnet, Richard. 1968. *Intervention and Revolution*. Cleveland: World Publishing Co.

Chan, Steve. 1984. Mirror, Mirror on the Wall . . . : Are Freer Countries More Pacific? *Journal of Conflict Resolution*, 28:617–48.

Doyle, Michael W. 1983a. Kant, Liberal Legacies, and Foreign Affairs: Part 1. *Philosophy and Public Affairs*, 12:205–35.

Doyle, Michael W. 1983b. Kant, Liberal Legacies, and Foreign Affairs: Part 2. *Philosophy and Public Affairs*, 12:323–53.

Doyle, Michael W. 1986. *Empires*. Ithaca: Cornell University Press.

The Europa Yearbook for 1985. 1985. 2 vols. London: Europa Publications.

Gastil, Raymond. 1985. The Comparative Survey of Freedom 1985. *Freedom at Issue*, 82:3–16.

Haas, Michael. 1974. *International Conflict*. New York: Bobbs-Merrill.

Holmes, Stephen. 1979. Aristippus in and out of Athens. *American Political Science Review*, 73:113–28.

Huliung, Mark. 1983. *Citizen Machiavelli*. Princeton: Princeton University Press.

Hume, David. 1963. Of the Balance of Power. *Essays: Moral, Political, and Literary*. Oxford: Oxford University Press.

Kant, Immanuel. 1970. *Kant's Political Writings*. Hans Reiss, ed. H. B. Nisbet, trans. Cambridge: Cambridge University Press.

Kelly, George A. 1969. *Idealism, Politics, and History*. Cambridge: Cambridge University Press.

Langer, William L., ed. 1968. *The Encyclopedia of World History*. Boston: Houghton Mifflin.

Machiavelli, Niccolo. 1950. *The Prince and the Discourses*. Max Lerner, ed. Luigi Ricci and Christian Detmold, trans. New York: Modern Library.

Mansfield, Harvey C. 1970. Machiavelli's New Regime. *Italian Quarterly*, 13:63–95.

Montesquieu, Charles de. 1949. *Spirit of the Laws*. New York: Hafner. (Originally published in 1748.)

Murphy, Jeffrie. 1970. *Kant: The Philosophy of Right*. New York: St. Martins.

Pocock, J. G. A. 1975. *The Machiavellian Moment*. Princeton: Princeton University Press.

Powell, G. Bingham. 1982. *Contemporary Democracies*. Cambridge, MA: Harvard University Press.

Reagan, Ronald. June 9, 1982. Address to Parliament. *New York Times*.

Riley, Patrick. 1983. *Kant's Political Philosophy*. Totowa, NJ: Rowman and Littlefield.

Rummel, Rudolph J. 1983. Libertarianism and International Violence. *Journal of Conflict Resolution*, 27:27–71.

Russett, Bruce. 1985. The Mysterious Case of Vanishing Hegemony. *International Organization*, 39:207–31.

Schumpeter, Joseph. 1955. The Sociology of Imperialism. In *Imperialism and Social Classes*. Cleveland: World Publishing Co. (Essay originally published in 1919.)

Schwarz, Wolfgang. 1962. Kant's Philosophy of Law and International Peace. *Philosophy and Phenomenonological Research*, 23:71–80.

Skinner, Quentin. 1981. *Machiavelli*. New York: Hill and Wang.

Small, Melvin, and J. David Singer. 1976. The War-Proneness of Democratic Regimes. *The Jerusalem Journal of International Relations*, 1(4):50–69.

Small, Melvin, and J. David Singer. 1982. *Resort to Arms*. Beverly Hills: Sage Publications.

Thucydides. 1954. *The Peloponnesian War*. Rex Warner, ed. and trans. Baltimore: Penguin.

U.K. Foreign and Commonwealth Office. 1980. *A Yearbook of the Commonwealth 1980*. London: HMSO.

U.S. Congress. Senate. Select Committee to Study Governmental Operations with Respect to Intelligence Activities. 1975. *Covert Action in Chile, 1963–74*. 94th Cong., 1st sess., Washington, DC: U.S. Government Printing Office.

U.S. Department of State. 1981. *Country Reports on Human Rights Practices*. Washington, DC: U.S. Government Printing Office.

Weede, Erich. 1984. Democracy and War Involvement. *Journal of Conflict Resolution*, 28:649–64.

Wilkenfeld, Jonathan. 1968. Domestic and Foreign Conflict Behavior of Nations. *Journal of Peace Research*, 5:56–69.

Wright, Quincy. 1942. *A Study of History*. Chicago: Chicago University Press.

Alexander Wendt

ANARCHY IS WHAT STATES MAKE OF IT
The Social Construction of Power Politics

The debate between realists and liberals has reemerged as an axis of contention in international relations theory.[1] Revolving in the past around competing theories of human nature, the debate is more concerned today with the extent to which state action is influenced by "structure" (anarchy and the distribution of power) versus "process" (interaction and learning) and institutions. Does the absence of centralized political authority force states to play competitive power politics? Can international regimes overcome this logic, and under what conditions? What in anarchy is given and immutable, and what is amenable to change?

■ ■ ■

* * * I argue that self-help and power politics do not follow either logically or causally from anarchy and that if today we find ourselves in a self-help world, this is due to process, not structure. There is no "logic" of anarchy apart from the practices that create and instantiate one structure of identities and interests rather than another; structure has no existence or causal powers apart from process. Self-help and power politics are institutions, not essential features of anarchy. *Anarchy is what states make of it.*

■ ■ ■

From *International Organization* 46, no. 2 (Spring 1992): 391–425. Some of the author's notes have been omitted.

Anarchy and Power Politics

Classical realists such as Thomas Hobbes, Reinhold Niebuhr, and Hans Morgenthau attributed egoism and power politics primarily to human nature, whereas structural realists or neorealists emphasize anarchy. The difference stems in part from different interpretations of anarchy's causal powers. Kenneth Waltz's work is important for both. In *Man, the State, and War,* he defines anarchy as a condition of possibility for or "permissive" cause of war, arguing that "wars occur because there is nothing to prevent them."[2] It is the human nature or domestic politics of predator states, however, that provide the initial impetus or "efficient" cause of conflict which forces other states to respond in kind.[3] Waltz is not entirely consistent about this, since he slips without justification from the permissive causal claim that in anarchy war is always possible to the active causal claim that "war may at any moment occur."[4] But despite Waltz's concluding call for third-image theory, the efficient causes that initialize anarchic systems are from the first and second images. This is reversed in Waltz's *Theory of International Politics,* in which first- and second-image theories are spurned as "reductionist," and the logic of anarchy seems by itself to constitute self-help and power politics as necessary features of world politics.[5]

This is unfortunate, since whatever one may think of first- and second-image theories, they have the virtue of implying that practices determine the character of anarchy. In the permissive view, only if human or domestic factors cause A to attack B will B have to defend itself. Anarchies may contain dynamics that lead to competitive power politics, but they also may not, and we can argue about when particular structures of identity and interest will emerge. In neorealism, however, the role of practice in shaping the character of anarchy is substantially reduced, and so there is less about which to argue: self-help and competitive power politics are simply given exogenously by the structure of the state system.

I will not here contest the neorealist description of the contemporary state system as a competitive, self-help world;[6] I will only dispute its explanation. I develop my argument in three stages. First, I disentangle the concepts of self-help and anarchy by showing that self-interested conceptions of security are not a constitutive property of anarchy. Second, I show how self-help and competitive power politics may be produced causally by processes of interaction between states in which anarchy plays only a permissive role. In both of these stages of my argument, I self-consciously bracket the first- and second-image determinants of state identity, not because they are unimportant (they are indeed important), but because like Waltz's objective, mine is to clarify the "logic" of anarchy. Third, I reintroduce first- and second-image determinants to assess their effects on identity-formation in different kinds of anarchies.

Anarchy, Self-Help, and Intersubjective Knowledge

Waltz defines political structure on three dimensions: ordering principles (in this case, anarchy), principles of differentiation (which here drop out), and the distribution of capabilities.[7] By itself, this definition predicts little about state behavior. It does not predict whether two states will be friends or foes, will recognize each other's sovereignty, will have dynastic ties, will be revisionist or status quo powers, and so on. These factors, which are fundamentally intersubjective, affect states' security interests and thus the character of their interaction under anarchy. In an important revision of Waltz's theory, Stephen Walt implies as much when he argues that the "balance of threats," rather than the balance of power, determines state action, threats being socially constructed.[8] Put more generally, without assumptions about the structure of identities and interests in the system, Waltz's definition of structure cannot predict the content or dynamics of anarchy. Self-help is one such intersubjective structure and, as such, does the decisive explanatory work in the theory. The question is whether self-help is a logical or contingent feature of anarchy. In this section, I develop the concept of a "structure of identity and interest" and show that no particular one follows logically from anarchy.

A fundamental principle of constructivist social theory is that people act toward objects, including other actors, on the basis of the meanings that the objects have for them.[9] States act differently toward enemies than they do toward friends because enemies are threatening and friends are not. Anarchy and the distribution of power are insufficient to tell us which is which. U.S. military power has a different significance for Canada than for Cuba, despite their similar "structural" positions, just as British missiles have a different significance for the United States than do Soviet missiles. The distribution of power may always affect states' calculations, but how it does so depends on the intersubjective understandings and expectations, on the "distribution of knowledge," that constitute their conceptions of self and other.[10] If society "forgets" what a university is, the powers and practices of professor and student cease to exist; if the United States and Soviet Union decide that they are no longer enemies, "the cold war is over." It is collective meanings that constitute the structures which organize our actions.

Actors acquire identities—relatively stable, role-specific understandings and expectations about self—by participating in such collective meanings.[11]

Identities are inherently relational: "Identity, with its appropriate attachments of psychological reality, is always identity within a specific, socially constructed world," Peter Berger argues.[12] Each person has many identities linked to institutional roles, such as brother, son, teacher, and citizen. Similarly, a state may have multiple identities as "sovereign," "leader of the free world," "imperial power," and so on.[13] The commitment to and the salience of particular identities vary, but each identity is an inherently social definition of the actor grounded in the theories which actors collectively hold about themselves and one another and which constitute the structure of the social world.

Identities are the basis of interests. Actors do not have a "portfolio" of interests that they carry around independent of social context; instead, they define their interests in the process of defining situations.[14] As Nelson Foote puts it: "Motivation . . . refer[s] to the degree to which a human being, as a participant in the ongoing social process in which he necessarily finds himself, defines a problematic situation as calling for the performance of a particular act, with more or less anticipated consummations and consequences, and thereby his organism releases the energy appropriate to performing it."[15] Sometimes situations are unprecedented in our experience, and in these cases we have to construct their meaning, and thus our interests, by analogy or invent them de novo. More often they have routine qualities in which we assign meanings on the basis of institutionally defined roles. When we say that professors have an "interest" in teaching, research, or going on leave, we are saying that to function in the role identity of "professor," they have to define certain situations as calling for certain actions. This does not mean that they will necessarily do so (expectations and competence do not equal performance), but if they do not, they will not get tenure. The absence or failure of roles makes defining situations and interests more difficult, and identity confusion may result. This seems to be happening today in the United States and the former Soviet Union:

without the cold war's mutual attributions of threat and hostility to define their identities, these states seem unsure of what their "interests" should be.

An institution is a relatively stable set or "structure" of identities and interests. Such structures are often codified in formal rules and norms, but these have motivational force only in virtue of actors' socialization to and participation in collective knowledge. Institutions are fundamentally cognitive entities that do not exist apart from actors' ideas about how the world works.[16] This does not mean that institutions are not real or objective, that they are "nothing but" beliefs. As collective knowledge, they are experienced as having an existence "over and above the individuals who happen to embody them at the moment."[17] In this way, institutions come to confront individuals as more or less coercive social facts, but they are still a function of what actors collectively "know." Identities and such collective cognitions do not exist apart from each other; they are "mutually constitutive."[18] On this view, institutionalization is a process of internalizing new identities and interests, not something occurring outside them and affecting only behavior; socialization is a cognitive process, not just a behavioral one. Conceived in this way, institutions may be cooperative or conflictual, a point sometimes lost in scholarship on international regimes, which tends to equate institutions with cooperation. There are important differences between conflictual and cooperative institutions to be sure, but all relatively stable self-other relations—even those of "enemies"—are defined intersubjectively.

Self-help is an institution, one of various structures of identity and interest that may exist under anarchy. Processes of identity-formation under anarchy are concerned first and foremost with preservation or "security" of the self. Concepts of security therefore differ in the extent to which and the manner in which the self is identified cognitively with the other,[19] and, I want to suggest, it is upon this cognitive variation that the meaning of anarchy and the distribution of power depends. Let me illustrate with a standard continuum of security systems.[20]

At one end is the "competitive" security system, in which states identify negatively with each other's security so that ego's gain is seen as alter's loss. Negative identification under anarchy constitutes system of "realist" power politics: risk-averse actors that infer intentions from capabilities and worry about relative gains and losses. At the limit—in the Hobbesian war of all against all—collective action is nearly impossible in such a system because each actor must constantly fear being stabbed in the back.

In the middle is the "individualistic" security system, in which states are indifferent to the relationship between their own and others' security. This constitutes "neoliberal" systems: states are still self-regarding about their security but are concerned primarily with absolute gains rather than relative gains. One's position in the distribution of power is less important, and collective action is more possible (though still subject to free riding because states continue to be "egoists").

Competitive and individualistic systems are both "self-help" forms of anarchy in the sense that states do not positively identify the security of self with that of others but instead treat security as the individual responsibility of each. Given the lack of a positive cognitive identification on the basis of which to build security regimes, power politics within such systems will necessarily consist of efforts to manipulate others to satisfy self-regarding interests.

This contrasts with the "cooperative" security system, in which states identify positively with one another so that the security of each is perceived as the responsibility of all. This is not self-help in any interesting sense, since the "self" in terms of which interests are defined is the community; national interests are international interests.[21] In practice, of course, the extent to which states' identification with the community varies, from the limited form found in "concerts" to the full-blown form seen in "collective security" arrangements.[22] Depending on how well developed the collective self is, it will produce security practices that are in varying degrees altruistic or prosocial. This makes collective action less dependent on the presence of active threats and less prone to free riding.[23] Moreover, it restructures efforts to advance one's objectives, or "power politics," in terms of shared norms rather than relative power.[24]

On this view, the tendency in international relations scholarship to view power and institutions as two opposing explanations of foreign policy is therefore misleading, since anarchy and the distribution of power only have meaning for state action in virtue of the understandings and expectations that constitute institutional identities and interests. Self-help is one such institution, constituting one kind of anarchy but not the only kind. Waltz's three-part definition of structure therefore seems underspecified. In order to go from structure to action, we need to add a fourth: the intersubjectively constituted structure of identities and interests in the system.

This has an important implication for the way in which we conceive of states in the state of nature before their first encounter with each other. Because states do not have conceptions of self and other, and thus security interests, apart from or prior to interaction, we assume too much about the state of nature if we concur with Waltz that, in virtue of anarchy, "international political systems, like economic markets, are formed by the coaction of self-regarding units."[25] We also assume too much if we argue that, in virtue of anarchy, states in the state of nature necessarily face a "stag hunt" or "security dilemma."[26] These claims presuppose a history of interaction in which actors have acquired "selfish" identities and interests; before interaction (and still in abstraction from first- and second-image factors) they would have no experience upon which to base such definitions of self and other. To assume otherwise is to attribute to states in the state of nature qualities that they can only possess in society.[27] Self-help is an institution, not a constitutive feature of anarchy.

What, then, *is* a constitutive feature of the state of nature before interaction? Two things are left if we strip away those properties of the self which presuppose interaction with others. The first is the material substrate of agency, including its intrinsic capabilities. For human beings, this is the body; for states, it is an organizational apparatus of governance. In effect, I am suggesting for rhetorical purposes that the raw material out of which members of the state system are constituted is created by domestic society before states enter the constitutive process of international society,[28] although this process implies neither stable territoriality nor sovereignty, which are internationally negotiated terms of individuality (as discussed further below). The second is a desire to preserve this material substrate, to survive. This does not entail "self-regardingness," however, since actors do not have a self prior to interaction with an other; how they view the meaning and requirements of this survival therefore depends on the processes by which conceptions of self evolve.

This may all seem very arcane, but there is an important issue at stake: are the foreign policy identities and interests of states exogenous or endogenous to the state system? The former is the answer of an individualistic or undersocialized systemic theory for which rationalism is appropriate; the latter is the answer of a fully socialized systemic theory. Waltz seems to offer the latter and proposes two mechanisms, competition and socialization, by which structure conditions state action.[29] The content of his argument about this conditioning, however, presupposes a self-help system that is not itself a constitutive feature of anarchy. As James Morrow points out, Waltz's two mechanisms condition behavior, not identity and interest.[30] This explains how Waltz can be accused of both "individualism" and "structuralism."[31] He is the former with respect to systemic constitutions of identity and interest, the latter with respect to systemic determinations of behavior.

Anarchy and the Social Construction of Power Politics

If self-help is not a constitutive feature of anarchy, it must emerge causally from processes in which anarchy plays only a permissive role.[32] This reflects a second principle of constructivism: that the meanings in terms of which action is organized arise out of interaction.[33] This being said, however, the situation facing states as they encounter one another for the first time may be such that only self-regarding conceptions of identity can survive; if so, even if these conceptions are socially constructed, neorealists may be right in holding identities and interests constant and thus in privileging one particular meaning of anarchic structure over process. In this case, rationalists would be right to argue for a weak, behavioral conception of the difference that institutions make, and realists would be right to argue that any international institutions which are created will be inherently unstable, since without the power to transform identities and interests they will be "continuing objects of choice" by exogenously constituted actors constrained only by the transaction costs of behavioral change.[34] Even in a permissive causal role, in other words, anarchy may decisively restrict interaction and therefore restrict viable forms of systemic theory. I address these causal issues first by showing how self-regarding ideas about security might develop and then by examining the conditions under which a key efficient cause—predation—may dispose states in this direction rather than others.

Conceptions of self and interest tend to "mirror" the practices of significant others over time. This principle of identity-formation is captured by the symbolic interactionist notion of the "looking-glass self," which asserts that the self is a reflection of an actor's socialization.

Consider two actors—ego and alter—encountering each other for the first time.[35] Each wants to survive and has certain material capabilities, but neither actor has biological or domestic imperatives for power, glory, or conquest (still bracketed), and there is no history of security or insecurity between the two. What should they do? Realists would probably argue that each should act on the basis of worst-case assumptions about the other's intentions, justifying such an attitude as prudent in view of the possibility of death from making a mistake. Such a possibility always exists, even in civil society; however, society would be impossible if people made decisions purely on the basis of worst-case possibilities. Instead, most decisions are and should be made on the basis of probabilities, and these are produced by interaction, by what actors *do*.

In the beginning is ego's gesture, which may consist, for example, of an advance, a retreat, a brandishing of arms, a laying down of arms, or an attack.[36] For ego, this gesture represents the basis on which it is prepared to respond to alter. This basis is unknown to alter, however, and so it must make an inference or "attribution" about ego's intentions and, in particular, given that this is anarchy, about whether ego is a threat.[37] The content of this inference will largely depend on two considerations. The first is the gesture's and ego's physical qualities, which are in part contrived by ego and which include the direction of movement, noise, numbers, and immediate consequences of the gesture.[38] The second consideration concerns what alter would intend by such qualities were it to make such a gesture itself. Alter may make an attributional "error" in its inference about ego's intent, but there is also no reason for it to assume a priori—before the gesture—that ego is threatening, since it is only through a process of signaling and interpreting that the costs and probabilities of being wrong can be determined.[39] Social threats are constructed, not natural.

Consider an example. Would we assume, a priori, that we were about to be attacked if we are ever contacted by members of an alien civilization? I think not. We would be highly alert, of course, but whether we placed our military forces on alert

or launched an attack would depend on how we interpreted the import of their first gesture for our security—if only to avoid making an immediate enemy out of what may be a dangerous adversary. The possibility of error, in other words, does not force us to act on the assumption that the aliens are threatening: action depends on the probabilities we assign, and these are in key part a function of what the aliens do; prior to their gesture, we have no systemic basis for assigning probabilities. If their first gesture is to appear with a thousand spaceships and destroy New York, we will define the situation as threatening and respond accordingly. But if they appear with one spaceship, saying what seems to be "we come in peace," we will feel "reassured" and will probably respond with a gesture intended to reassure them, even if this gesture is not necessarily interpreted by them as such.[40]

This process of signaling, interpreting, and responding completes a "social act" and begins the process of creating intersubjective meanings. It advances the same way. The first social act creates expectations on both sides about each other's future behavior: potentially mistaken and certainly tentative, but expectations nonetheless. Based on this tentative knowledge, ego makes a new gesture, again signifying the basis on which it will respond to alter, and again alter responds, adding to the pool of knowledge each has about the other, and so on over time. The mechanism here is reinforcement; interaction rewards actors for holding certain ideas about each other and discourages them from holding others. If repeated long enough, these "reciprocal typifications" will create relatively stable concepts of self and other regarding the issue at stake in the interaction.[41]

It is through reciprocal interaction, in other words, that we create and instantiate the relatively enduring social structures in terms of which we define our identities and interests. Jeff Coulter sums up the ontological dependence of structure on process this way: "The parameters of social organization themselves are reproduced only in and through the orientations and practices of members engaged in social interactions over time. . . . Social configurations are not 'objective' like mountains or forests, but neither are they 'subjective' like dreams or flights of speculative fancy. They are, as most social scientists concede at the theoretical level, intersubjective constructions."[42]

The simple overall model of identity- and interest-formation proposed in Figure 3.1 applies to competitive institutions no less than to cooperative ones. Self-help security systems evolve from cycles of interaction in which each party acts in ways that the other feels are threatening to the self, creating expectations that the other is not to be trusted. Competitive or egoistic identities are caused by such insecurity; if the other is threatening, the self is forced to "mirror" such behavior in its conception of the self's relationship to that other.[43] Being treated as an object for the gratification of others precludes the positive identification with others necessary for collective security; conversely, being treated by others in ways that are empathic with respect to the security of the self permits such identification.[44]

Competitive systems of interaction are prone to security "dilemmas," in which the efforts of actors to enhance their security unilaterally threatens the security of the others, perpetuating distrust and alienation. The forms of identity and interest that constitute such dilemmas, however, are themselves ongoing effects of, not exogenous to, the interaction; identities are produced in and through "situated activity."[45] We do not *begin* our relationship with the aliens in a security dilemma; security dilemmas are not given by anarchy or nature. Of course, once institutionalized such a dilemma may be hard to change (I return to this below), but the point remains: identities and interests are

Figure 3.1. The Codetermination of Institutions and Process

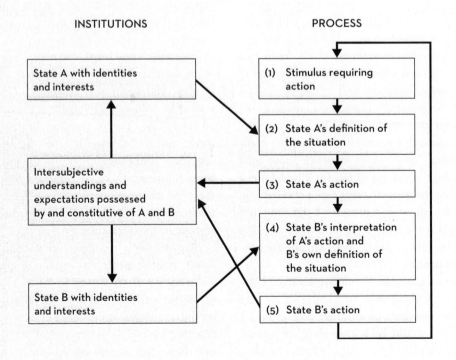

INSTITUTIONS   PROCESS

State A with identities and interests

Intersubjective understandings and expectations possessed by and constitutive of A and B

State B with identities and interests

(1) Stimulus requiring action

(2) State A's definition of the situation

(3) State A's action

(4) State B's interpretation of A's action and B's own definition of the situation

(5) State B's action

constituted by collective meanings that are always in process. As Sheldon Stryker emphasizes, "The social process is one of constructing and reconstructing self and social relationships."[46] If states find themselves in a self-help system, this is because their practices made it that way. Changing the practices will change the intersubjective knowledge that constitutes the system.

Predator States and Anarchy as Permissive Cause

The mirror theory of identity-formation is a crude account of how the process of creating identities and interests might work, but it does not tell us why a system of states—such as, arguably, our own—would have ended up with self-regarding and not collective identities. In this section, I examine an efficient cause, predation, which, in conjunction with anarchy as a permissive cause, may generate a self-help system. In so doing, however, I show the key role that the structure of identities and interests plays in mediating anarchy's explanatory role.

The predator argument is straightforward and compelling. For whatever reasons—biology, domestic politics, or systemic victimization—some states may become predisposed toward aggression. The aggressive behavior of these predators or "bad apples" forces other states to engage in competitive power politics, to meet fire with fire, since failure to do so may degrade or destroy them. One predator will best a hundred pacifists because anarchy provides no guarantees. This argument is powerful in part because it is so weak: rather than making the strong assumption that all states are inherently power-seeking (a purely reductionist theory of power politics), it assumes that just one is power-seeking and that the others have to follow suit because anarchy permits the one to exploit them.

In making this argument, it is important to reiterate that the possibility of predation does not in itself force states to anticipate it a priori with competitive power politics of their own. The possibility of predation does not mean that "war may at any moment occur"; it may in fact be extremely unlikely. Once a predator emerges, however, it may condition identity- and interest-formation in the following manner.

In an anarchy of two, if ego is predatory, alter must either define its security in self-help terms or pay the price. This follows directly from the above argument, in which conceptions of self mirror treatment by the other. In an anarchy of many, however, the effect of predation also depends on the level of collective identity already attained in the system. If predation occurs right after the first encounter in the state of nature, it will force others with whom it comes in contact to defend themselves, first individually and then collectively *if* they come to perceive a common threat. The emergence of such a defensive alliance will be seriously inhibited if the structure of identities and interests has already evolved into a Hobbesian world of maximum insecurity, since potential allies will strongly distrust each other and face intense collective action problems; such insecure allies are also more likely to fall out amongst themselves once the predator is removed. If collective security identity is high, however, the emergence of a predator may do much less damage. If the predator attacks any member of the collective, the latter will come to the victim's defense on the principle of "all for one, one for all," even if the predator is not presently a threat to other members of the collective. If the predator is not strong enough to withstand the collective, it will be defeated and collective security will obtain. But if it is strong enough, the logic of the two-actor case (now predator and collective) will activate, and balance-of-power politics will reestablish itself.

The timing of the emergence of predation relative to the history of identity-formation in the community is therefore crucial to anarchy's explanatory role as a permissive cause. Predation will always lead victims to defend themselves, but whether defense will be collective or not depends on the history of interaction within the potential collective as much as on the ambitions of the predator. Will the disappearance of the Soviet threat renew old insecurities among the members of the North Atlantic Treaty Organization? Perhaps, but not if they have reasons independent of that threat for identifying their security with one another. Identities and interests are relationship-specific, not intrinsic attributes of a "portfolio"; states may be competitive in some relationships and solidary in others. "Mature" anarchies are less likely than "immature" ones to be reduced by predation to a Hobbesian condition, and maturity, which is a proxy for structures of identity and interest, is a function of process.[47]

The source of predation also matters. If it stems from unit-level causes that are immune to systemic impacts (causes such as human nature or domestic politics taken in isolation), then it functions in a manner analogous to a "genetic trait" in the constructed world of the state system. Even if successful, this trait does not select for other predators in an evolutionary sense so much as it teaches other states to respond in kind, but since traits cannot be unlearned, the other states will continue competitive behavior until the predator is either destroyed or transformed from within. However, in the more likely event that predation stems at least in part from prior systemic interaction—perhaps as a result of being victimized in the past (one thinks here of Nazi Germany or the Soviet Union)—then it is more a response to a learned identity and, as such, might be transformed by future social interaction in the form of appeasement, reassurances that security needs will be met, systemic effects on domestic politics, and so on. In this case, in other words, there is more hope that process can transform a bad apple into a good one.

The role of predation in generating a self-help system, then, is consistent with a systematic focus on process. Even if the source of predation is entirely exogenous to the system, it is what states *do* that determines the quality of their interactions under anarchy. In this respect, it is not surprising that it is classical realists rather than structural realists who emphasize this sort of argument. The former's emphasis on unit-level causes of power politics leads more easily to a permissive view of anarchy's explanatory role (and therefore to a processual view of international relations) than does the latter's emphasis on anarchy as a "structural cause";[48] neorealists do not need predation because the system is given as self-help.

This raises anew the question of exactly how much and what kind of role human nature and domestic politics play in world politics. The greater and more destructive this role, the more significant predation will be, and the less amenable anarchy will be to formation of collective identities. Classical realists, of course, assumed that human nature was possessed by an inherent lust for power or glory. My argument suggests that assumptions such as this were made for a reason: an unchanging Hobbesian man provides the powerful efficient cause necessary for a relentless pessimism about world politics that anarchic structure alone, or even structure plus intermittent predation, cannot supply. One can be skeptical of such an essentialist assumption, as I am, but it does produce determinate results at the expense of systemic theory. A concern with systemic process over structure suggests that perhaps it is time to revisit the debate over the relative importance of first-, second-, and third-image theories of state identity-formation.[49]

Assuming for now that systemic theories of identity-formation in world politics are worth pursuing, let me conclude by suggesting that the realist-rationalist alliance "reifies" self-help in the sense of treating it as something separate from the practices by which it is produced and sustained. Peter Berger and Thomas Luckmann define reification as follows: "[It] is the apprehension of the products of human activity *as if* they were something else than human products—such as facts of nature, results of cosmic laws, or manifestations of divine will. Reification implies that man is capable of forgetting his own authorship of the human world, and further, that the dialectic between man, the producer, and his products is lost to consciousness. The reified world is . . . experienced by man as a strange facticity, an *opus alienum* over which he has no control rather than as the *opus proprium* of his own productive activity."[50] By denying or bracketing states' collective authorship of their identities and interests, in other words, the realist-rationalist alliance denies or brackets the fact that competitive power politics help create the very "problem of order" they are supposed to solve—that realism is a self-fulfilling prophecy. Far from being exogenously given, the intersubjective knowledge that constitutes competitive identities and interests is constructed every day by processes of "social will formation."[51] It is what states have made of themselves.

Institutional Transformations of Power Politics

Let us assume that processes of identity- and interest-formation have created a world in which states do not recognize rights to territory or existence—a war of all against all. In this world, anarchy has a "realist" meaning for state action: be insecure and concerned with relative power. Anarchy has this meaning only in virtue of collective, insecurity-producing practices, but if those practices are relatively stable, they do constitute a system that may resist change. The fact that worlds of power politics are socially constructed, in other words, does not guarantee they are malleable, for at least two reasons.

The first reason is that once constituted, any social system confronts each of its members as an objective social fact that reinforces certain behaviors and discourages others. Self-help systems, for example, tend to reward competition and punish altruism. The possibility of change depends on whether the exigencies of such competition leave

room for actions that deviate from the prescribed script. If they do not, the system will be reproduced and deviant actors will not.[52]

The second reason is that systemic change may also be inhibited by actors' interests in maintaining relatively stable role identities. Such interests are rooted not only in the desire to minimize uncertainty and anxiety, manifested in efforts to confirm existing beliefs about the social world, but also in the desire to avoid the expected costs of breaking commitments made to others—notably domestic constituencies and foreign allies in the case of states—as part of past practices. The level of resistance that these commitments induce will depend on the "salience" of particular role identities to the actor.[53] The United States, for example, is more likely to resist threats to its identity as "leader of anticommunist crusades" than to its identity as "promoter of human rights." But for almost any role identity, practices and information that challenge it are likely to create cognitive dissonance and even perceptions of threat, and these may cause resistance to transformations of the self and thus to social change.[54]

For both systemic and "psychological" reasons, then, intersubjective understandings and expectations may have a self-perpetuating quality, constituting path-dependencies that new ideas about self and other must transcend. This does not change the fact that through practice agents are continuously producing and reproducing identities and interests, continuously "choosing now the preferences [they] will have later."[55] But it does mean that choices may not be experienced with meaningful degrees of freedom. This could be a constructivist justification for the realist position that only simple learning is possible in self-help systems. The realist might concede that such systems are socially constructed and still argue that after the corresponding identities and interests have become institutionalized, they are almost impossible to transform.

In the remainder of this article, I examine three institutional transformations of identity and security interest through which states might escape a Hobbesian world of their own making. In so doing, I seek to clarify what it means to say that "institutions transform identities and interests," emphasizing that the key to such transformations is relatively stable practice.

Sovereignty, Recognition, and Security

In a Hobbesian state of nature, states are individuated by the domestic processes that constitute them as states and by their material capacity to deter threats from other states. In this world, even if free momentarily from the predations of others, state security does not have any basis in social recognition—in intersubjective understandings or norms that a state has a right to its existence, territory, and subjects. Security is a matter of national power, nothing more.

The principle of sovereignty transforms this situation by providing a social basis for the individuality and security of states. Sovereignty is an institution, and so it exists only in virtue of certain intersubjective understandings and expectations; there is no sovereignty without an other. These understandings and expectations not only constitute a particular kind of state—the "sovereign" state—but also constitute a particular form of community, since identities are relational. The essence of this community is a mutual recognition of one another's right to exercise exclusive political authority within territorial limits. These reciprocal "permissions"[56] constitute a spatially rather than functionally differentiated world—a world in which fields of practice constitute and are organized around "domestic" and "international" spaces rather than around the performance of particular activities.[57] The location of the boundaries between these spaces is of course sometimes contested, war being one practice through which states negotiate the terms of their individuality.

But this does not change the fact that it is only in virtue of mutual recognition that states have "territorial property rights."[58] This recognition functions as a form of "social closure" that disempowers nonstate actors and empowers and helps stabilize interaction among states.[59]

Sovereignty norms are now so taken for granted, so natural, that it is easy to overlook the extent to which they are both presupposed by and an ongoing artifact of practice. When states tax "their" "citizens" and not others, when they "protect" their markets against foreign "imports," when they kill thousands of Iraqis in one kind of war and then refuse to "intervene" to kill even one person in another kind, a "civil" war, and when they fight a global war against a regime that sought to destroy the institution of sovereignty and then give Germany back to the Germans, they are acting against the background of, and thereby reproducing, shared norms about what it means to be a sovereign state.

If states stopped acting on those norms, their identity as "sovereigns" (if not necessarily as "states") would disappear. The sovereign state is an ongoing accomplishment of practice, not a once-and-for-all creation of norms that somehow exist apart from practice.[60] Thus, saying that "the institution of sovereignty transforms identities" is shorthand for saying that "regular practices produce mutually constituting sovereign identities (agents) and their associated institutional norms (structures)." Practice is the core of constructivist resolutions of the agent-structure problem. This ongoing process may not be politically problematic in particular historical contexts and, indeed, once a community of mutual recognition is constituted, its members—even the disadvantaged ones[61]—may have a vested interest in reproducing it. In fact, this is part of what having an identity means. But this identity and institution remain dependent on what actors do: removing those practices will remove their intersubjective conditions of existence.

This may tell us something about how institutions of sovereign states are reproduced through social interaction, but it does not tell us why such a structure of identity and interest would arise in the first place. Two conditions would seem necessary for this to happen: (1) the density and regularity of interactions must be sufficiently high and (2) actors must be dissatisfied with preexisting forms of identity and interaction. Given these conditions, a norm of mutual recognition is relatively undemanding in terms of social trust, having the form of an assurance game in which a player will acknowledge the sovereignty of the others as long as they will in turn acknowledge that player's own sovereignty. Articulating international legal principles such as those embodied in the Peace of Augsburg (1555) and the Peace of Westphalia (1648) may also help by establishing explicit criteria for determining violations of the nascent social consensus.[62] But whether such a consensus holds depends on what states do. If they treat each other as if they were sovereign, then over time they will institutionalize that mode of subjectivity; if they do not, then that mode will not become the norm.

Practices of sovereignty will transform understandings of security and power politics in at least three ways. First, states will come to define their (and our) security in terms of preserving their "property rights" over particular territories. We now see this as natural, but the preservation of territorial frontiers is not, in fact, equivalent to the survival of the state or its people. Indeed, some states would probably be more secure if they would relinquish certain territories—the "Soviet Union" of some minority republics, "Yugoslavia" of Croatia and Slovenia, Israel of the West Bank, and so on. The fact that sovereignty practices have historically been oriented toward producing distinct territorial spaces, in other words, affects states' conceptualization of what they must "secure" to function in that identity, a process that may help account for the "hardening" of territorial boundaries over the centuries.[63]

Second, to the extent that states successfully internalize sovereignty norms, they will be more

respectful toward the territorial rights of others.[64] This restraint is *not* primarily because of the costs of violating sovereignty norms, although when violators do get punished (as in the Gulf War) it reminds everyone of what these costs can be, but because part of what it means to be a "sovereign" state is that one does not violate the territorial rights of others without "just cause." A clear example of such an institutional effect, convincingly argued by David Strang, is the markedly different treatment that weak states receive within and outside communities of mutual recognition.[65] What keeps the United States from conquering the Bahamas, or Nigeria from seizing Togo, or Australia from occupying Vanuatu? Clearly, power is not the issue, and in these cases even the cost of sanctions would probably be negligible. One might argue that great powers simply have no "interest" in these conquests, and this might be so, but this lack of interest can only be understood in terms of their recognition of weak states' sovereignty. I have no interest in exploiting my friends, not because of the relative costs and benefits of such action but because they are my friends. The absence of recognition, in turn, helps explain the Western states' practices of territorial conquest, enslavement, and genocide against Native American and African peoples. It is in *that* world that only power matters, not the world of today.

Finally, to the extent that their ongoing socialization teaches states that their sovereignty depends on recognition by other states, they can afford to rely more on the institutional fabric of international society and less on individual national means—especially military power—to protect their security. The intersubjective understandings embodied in the institution of sovereignty, in other words, may redefine the meaning of others' power for the security of the self. In policy terms, this means that states can be less worried about short-term survival and relative power and can thus shift their resources accordingly. Ironically, it is the great powers, the states with the greatest national means, that may have the hardest time learning this lesson; small powers do not have the luxury of relying on national means and may therefore learn faster that collective recognition is a cornerstone of security.

None of this is to say that power becomes irrelevant in a community of sovereign states. Sometimes states *are* threatened by others that do not recognize their existence or particular territorial claims, that resent the externalities from their economic policies, and so on. But most of the time, these threats are played out within the terms of the sovereignty game. The fates of Napoleon and Hitler show what happens when they are not.

Cooperation among Egoists and Transformations of Identity

We began this section with a Hobbesian state of nature. Cooperation for joint gain is extremely difficult in this context, since trust is lacking, time horizons are short, and relative power concerns are high. Life is "nasty, brutish, and short." Sovereignty transforms this system into a Lockean world of (mostly) mutually recognized property rights and (mostly) egoistic rather than competitive conceptions of security, reducing the fear that what states already have will be seized at any moment by potential collaborators, thereby enabling them to contemplate more direct forms of cooperation. A necessary condition for such cooperation is that outcomes be positively interdependent in the sense that potential gains exist which cannot be realized by unilateral action. States such as Brazil and Botswana may recognize each other's sovereignty, but they need further incentives to engage in joint action. One important source of incentives is the growing "dynamic density" of interaction among states in a world with new communications technology, nuclear weapons, externalities from industrial development, and so on.[66] Unfortunately, growing dynamic density does not ensure that states will in fact realize joint gains; interdependence also entails vulnerability and the risk of being "the sucker," which if exploited will become a source of conflict rather than cooperation.

This is the rationale for the familiar assumption that egoistic states will often find themselves facing prisoners' dilemma, a game in which the dominant strategy, if played only once, is to defect. As Michael Taylor and Robert Axelrod have shown, however, given iteration and a sufficient shadow of the future, egoists using a tit-for-tat strategy can escape this result and build cooperative institutions.[67] The story they tell about this process on the surface seems quite similar to George Herbert Mead's constructivist analysis of interaction, part of which is also told in terms of "games."[68] Cooperation is a gesture indicating ego's willingness to cooperate; if alter defects, ego does likewise, signaling its unwillingness to be exploited; over time and through reciprocal play, each learns to form relatively stable expectations about the other's behavior, and through these, habits of cooperation (or defection) form. Despite similar concerns with communication, learning, and habit-formation, however, there is an important difference between the game-theoretic and constructivist analysis of interaction that bears on how we conceptualize the causal powers of institutions.

In the traditional game-theoretic analysis of cooperation, even an iterated one, the structure of the game—of identities and interests—is exogenous to interaction and, as such, does not change.[69] A "black box" is put around identity- and interest-formation, and analysis focuses instead on the relationship between expectations and behavior. The norms that evolve from interaction are treated as rules and behavioral regularities which are external to the actors and which resist change because of the transaction costs of creating new ones. The game-theoretic analysis of cooperation among egoists is at base behavioral.

A constructivist analysis of cooperation, in contrast, would concentrate on how the expectations produced by behavior affect identities and interests. The process of creating institutions is one of internalizing new understandings of self and other, of acquiring new role identities, not just of creating external constraints on the behavior of exogenously constituted actors.[70] Even if not intended as such, in other words, the process by which egoists learn to cooperate is at the same time a process of reconstructing their interests in terms of shared commitments to social norms. Over time, this will tend to transform a positive interdependence of *outcomes* into a positive interdependence of *utilities* or collective interest organized around the norms in question. These norms will resist change because they are tied to actors' commitments to their identities and interests, not merely because of transaction costs. A constructivist analysis of "the cooperation problem," in other words, is at base cognitive rather than behavioral, since it treats the intersubjective knowledge that defines the structure of identities and interests, of the "game," as endogenous to and instantiated by interaction itself.

The debate over the future of collective security in Western Europe may illustrate the significance of this difference. A weak liberal or rationalist analysis would assume that the European states' "portfolio" of interests has not fundamentally changed and that the emergence of new factors, such as the collapse of the Soviet threat and the rise of Germany, would alter their cost-benefit ratios for pursuing current arrangements, thereby causing existing institutions to break down. The European states formed collaborative institutions for good, exogenously constituted egoistic reasons, and the same reasons may lead them to reject those institutions; the game of European power politics has not changed. A strong liberal or constructivist analysis of this problem would suggest that four decades of cooperation may have transformed a positive interdependence of outcomes into a collective "European identity" in terms of which states increasingly define their "self"-interests.[71] Even if egoistic reasons were its starting point, the process of cooperating tends to redefine those reasons by reconstituting identities and interests in terms of new intersubjective understandings and commitments. Changes in the distribution of power during the late twentieth century are undoubtedly a challenge to these new understandings, but it is not as if West European states have some inherent, exogenously given interest in abandoning collective security if the price is right. Their identities and security interests are continuously in process, and if collective identities become "embedded," they will be as resistant to change as egoistic ones.[72] Through participation in new forms of social knowledge, in other words, the European states of 1990 might no longer be the states of 1950.

Critical Strategic Theory and Collective Security

The transformation of identity and interest through an "evolution of cooperation" faces two important constraints. The first is that the process is incremental and slow. Actors' objectives in such a process are typically to realize joint gains within what they take to be a relatively stable context, and they are therefore unlikely to engage in substantial reflection about how to change the parameters of that context (including the structure of identities and interests) and unlikely to pursue policies specifically designed to bring about such changes. Learning to cooperate may change those parameters, but this occurs as an unintended consequence of policies pursued for other reasons rather than as a result of intentional efforts to transcend existing institutions.

A second, more fundamental, constraint is that the evolution of cooperation story presupposes that actors do not identify negatively with one another. Actors must be concerned primarily with absolute gains; to the extent that antipathy and distrust lead them to define their security in relativistic terms, it will be hard to accept the vulnerabilities that attend cooperation.[73] This is important because it is precisely the "central balance" in the state system that seems to be so often afflicted with such competitive thinking, and realists can therefore argue that the possibility of cooperation within one "pole" (for example, the West) is parasitic on the dominance of competition between poles (the East–West conflict). Relations between the poles may be amenable to some positive reciprocity in areas such as arms control, but the atmosphere of distrust leaves little room for such cooperation and its transformative consequences.[74] The conditions of negative identification that make an "evolution of cooperation" most needed work precisely against such a logic.

This seemingly intractable situation may nevertheless be amenable to quite a different logic of transformation, one driven more by self-conscious efforts to change structures of identity and interest than by unintended consequences. Such voluntarism may seem to contradict the spirit of constructivism, since would-be revolutionaries are presumably themselves effects of socialization to structures of identity and interest. How can they think about changing that to which they owe their identity? The possibility lies in the distinction between the social determination of the self and the personal determination of choice, between what Mead called the "me" and the "I."[75] The "me" is that part of subjectivity which is defined in terms of others; the character and behavioral expectations of a person's role identity as "professor," or of the United States as "leader of the alliance," for example, are socially constituted. Roles are not played in mechanical fashion according to precise scripts, however, but are "taken" and adapted in idiosyncratic ways by each actor.[76] Even in the most constrained situations, role performance involves a choice by the actor. The "I" is the part of subjectivity in which this appropriation and reaction to roles and its corresponding existential freedom lie.

The fact that roles are "taken" means that, in principle, actors always have a capacity for "character planning"—for engaging in critical self-reflection and choices designed to bring about changes in their lives.[77] But when or under what conditions can this creative capacity be exercised? Clearly, much of the time it cannot: if actors were constantly reinventing their identities, social order would be impossible, and the relative stability of identities and interests in the real world is indicative of our propensity for habitual rather than creative action. The exceptional, conscious choosing to transform or transcend roles has at least two preconditions. First, there must be a reason to think of oneself in novel terms. This would most likely stem from the presence of new social situations that cannot be managed in terms of preexisting self-conceptions. Second, the expected costs of intentional role change—the sanctions imposed by others with whom one interacted in previous roles—cannot be greater than its rewards.

When these conditions are present, actors can engage in self-reflection and practice specifically designed to transform their identities and interests and thus to "change the games" in which they are embedded. Such "critical" strategic theory and practice has not received the attention it merits from students of world politics (another legacy of exogenously given interests perhaps), particularly given that one of the most important phenomena in contemporary world politics, Mikhail Gorbachev's policy of "New Thinking," is arguably precisely that.[78] Let me therefore use this policy as an example of how states might transform a competitive security system into a cooperative one, dividing the transformative process into four stages.

The first stage in intentional transformation is the breakdown of consensus about identity commitments. In the Soviet case, identity commitments centered on the Leninist theory of imperialism, with its belief that relations between capitalist and socialist states are inherently conflictual, and on the alliance patterns that this belief engendered. In the 1980s, the consensus within the Soviet Union over the Leninist theory broke down for a variety of reasons, principal among which seem to have been the state's inability to meet the economic-technological-military challenge from the West, the government's decline of political legitimacy at home, and the reassurance from the West that it did not intend to invade the Soviet Union, a reassurance that reduced the external costs of role change.[79] These factors paved the way for a radical leadership transition and for a subsequent "unfreezing of conflict schemas" concerning relations with the West.[80]

The breakdown of consensus makes possible a second stage of critical examination of old ideas about self and other and, by extension, of the structures of interaction by which the ideas have been sustained. In periods of relatively stable role identities, ideas and structures may become reified and thus treated as things that exist independently of social action. If so, the second stage is one of denaturalization, of identifying the practices that reproduce seemingly inevitable ideas about self and other; to that extent, it is a form of "critical" rather than "problem-solving" theory.[81] The result of such a critique should be an identification of new "possible selves" and aspirations.[82] New Thinking embodies such critical theorizing. Gorbachev wants to free the Soviet Union from the coercive social logic of the cold war and engage the West in far-reaching cooperation. Toward this end, he has rejected the Leninist belief in the inherent conflict of interest between socialist and capitalist states and, perhaps more important, has recognized the crucial role that Soviet aggressive practices played in sustaining that conflict.

Such rethinking paves the way for a third stage of new practice. In most cases, it is not enough to rethink one's own ideas about self and other, since old identities have been sustained by systems of interaction with *other* actors, the practices of which remain a social fact for the transformative agent. In order to change the self, then, it is often necessary to change the identities and interests of the others that help sustain those systems of interaction. The vehicle for inducing such change is one's own practice and, in particular, the practice of "altercasting"—a technique of interactor control in which ego uses tactics of self-presentation and stage management in an attempt to frame alter's definitions of social situations in ways that create the role which ego desires alter to play.[83] In effect, in altercasting ego tries to induce alter to take on a new identity (and thereby enlist alter in ego's effort to change itself) by treating alter *as if* it already had that identity. The logic of this follows directly from the mirror theory of identity-formation, in which alter's identity is a reflection of ego's practices; change those practices and ego begins to change alter's conception of itself.

What these practices should consist of depends on the logic by which the preexisting identities were sustained. Competitive security systems are sustained by practices that create insecurity and distrust. In this case, transformative practices should attempt to teach other states that one's own state can be trusted and should not be viewed as a threat to their security. The fastest way to do this is to make unilateral initiatives and self-binding commitments of sufficient significance that another state is faced with "an offer it cannot refuse."[84] Gorbachev has tried to do this by withdrawing from Afghanistan and Eastern Europe, implementing asymmetric cuts in nuclear and conventional forces, calling for "defensive defense," and so on. In addition, he has skillfully cast the West in the role of being morally required to give aid and comfort to the Soviet Union, has emphasized the bonds of common fate between the Soviet Union and the West, and has indicated that further progress in East–West relations is contingent upon the West assuming the identity being projected onto it. These actions are all dimensions of altercasting, the intention of which is to take away the Western "excuse" for distrusting the Soviet Union, which, in Gorbachev's view, has helped sustain competitive identities in the past.

Yet by themselves such practices cannot transform a competitive security system, since if they are not reciprocated by alter, they will expose ego to a "sucker" payoff and quickly wither on the vine. In order for critical strategic practice to transform competitive identities, it must be "rewarded" by alter, which will encourage more such practice by ego, and so on.[85] Over time, this will institutionalize a positive rather than a negative identification between the security of self and other and will thereby provide a firm intersubjective basis for what were initially tentative commitments to new identities and interests.[86]

Notwithstanding today's rhetoric about the end of the cold war, skeptics may still doubt whether Gorbachev (or some future leader) will succeed in building an intersubjective basis for a new Soviet (or Russian) role identity. There are important domestic, bureaucratic, and cognitive-ideological sources of resistance in both East and West to such a change, not the least of which is the shakiness of the democratic forces' domestic position. But if my argument about the role of intersubjective knowledge in creating competitive structures of identity and interest is right, then at least New Thinking shows a greater appreciation—conscious or not—for the deep structure of power politics than we are accustomed to in international relations practice.

Conclusion

All theories of international relations are based on social theories of the relationship between agency, process, and social structure. Social theories do not determine the content of our international theorizing, but they do structure the questions we ask about world politics and our approaches to answering those questions. The substantive issue at stake in debates about social theory is what kind of foundation offers the most fruitful set of questions and research strategies for explaining the revolutionary changes that seem to be occurring in the late twentieth century international system. Put simply, what should systemic theories of

international relations look like? How should they conceptualize the relationship between structure and process? Should they be based exclusively on "microeconomic" analogies in which identities and interests are exogenously given by structure and process is reduced to interactions within those parameters? Or should they also be based on "sociological" and "social psychological" analogies in which identities and interests and therefore the meaning of structure are endogenous to process? Should a behavioral-individualism or a cognitive-constructivism be the basis for systemic theories of world politics?

This article notwithstanding, this question is ultimately an empirical one in two respects. First, its answer depends in part on how important interaction among states is for the constitution of their identities and interests. On the one hand, it may be that domestic or genetic factors, which I have systematically bracketed, are in fact much more important determinants of states' identities and interests than are systemic factors. To the extent that this is true, the individualism of a rationalist approach and the inherent privileging of structure over process in this approach become more substantively appropriate for systemic theory (if not for first- and second-image theory), since identities and interests are *in fact* largely exogenous to interaction among states. On the other hand, if the bracketed factors are relatively unimportant or if the importance of the international system varies historically (perhaps with the level of dynamic density and interdependence in the system), then such a framework would not be appropriate as an exclusive foundation for general systemic theory.

Second, the answer to the question about what systemic theories should look like also depends on how easily state identities and interests can change as a result of systemic interaction. Even if interaction is initially important in constructing identities and interests, once institutionalized its logic may make transformation extremely difficult. If the meaning of structure for state action changes so slowly that it becomes a de facto parameter within which process takes place, then it may again be substantively appropriate to adopt the rationalist assumption that identities and interests are given (although again, this may vary historically).

We cannot address these empirical issues, however, unless we have a framework for doing systemic research that makes state identity and interest an issue for both theoretical and empirical inquiry. Let me emphasize that this is *not* to say we should never treat identities and interests as given. The framing of problems and research strategies should be question-driven rather than method-driven, and if we are not interested in identity- and interest-formation, we may find the assumptions of a rationalist discourse perfectly reasonable. Nothing in this article, in other words, should be taken as an attack on rationalism per se. By the same token, however, we should not let this legitimate analytical stance become a de facto ontological stance with respect to the content of third-image theory, at least not until after we have determined that systemic interaction does not play an important role in processes of state identity- and interest-formation. We should not choose our philosophical anthropologies and social theories prematurely. By arguing that we cannot derive a self-help structure of identity and interest from the principle of anarchy alone—by arguing that anarchy is what states make of it—this article has challenged one important justification for ignoring processes of identity- and interest-formation in world politics. As such, it helps set the stage for inquiry into the empirical issues raised above and thus for a debate about whether communitarian or individualist assumptions are a better foundation for systemic theory.

I have tried to indicate by crude example what such a research agenda might look like. Its objective should be to assess the causal relationship between practice and interaction (as independent variable) and the cognitive structures at the level of individual states and of systems of states which constitute identities and interests (as dependent variable)—that is, the relationship between what actors *do* and what they *are*. We may have some a priori notion that state actors and systemic structures are "mutually constitutive," but this tells us little in the absence of an understanding of how the mechanics of dyadic, triadic, and *n*-actor interaction shape and are in turn shaped by "stocks of knowledge" that collectively constitute identities and interests and, more broadly, constitute the structures of international life. Particularly important in this respect is the role of practice in shaping attitudes toward the "givenness" of these structures. How and why do actors reify social structures, and under what conditions do they denaturalize such reifications?

The state-centrism of this agenda may strike some, particularly postmodernists, as "depressingly familiar."[87] The significance of states relative to multinational corporations, new social movements, transnationals, and intergovernmental organizations is clearly declining, and "postmodern" forms of world politics merit more research attention than they have received. But I also believe, with realists, that in the medium run sovereign states will remain the dominant political actors in the international system. Any transition to new structures of global political authority and identity—to "postinternational" politics—will be mediated by and path-dependent on the particular institutional resolution of the tension between unity and diversity, or particularism and universality, that is the sovereign state.[88] In such a world there should continue to be a place for theories of anarchic interstate politics, alongside other forms of international theory; to that extent, I am a statist and a realist. I have argued in this article, however, that statism need not be bound by realist ideas about what "state" must mean. State identities and interests can be collectively transformed within an anarchic context by many factors—individual, domestic, systemic, or transnational—and as such are an important dependent variable. Such a reconstruction of state-centric international theory is necessary if we are to theorize adequately about the emerging forms of transnational political identity that sovereign states will help bring into being. To that extent, I hope that statism, like the state, can be historically progressive.

■ ■ ■

NOTES

1. See, for example, Joseph Grieco, "Anarchy and the Limits of Cooperation: A Realist Critique of the Newest Liberal Institutionalism," *International Organization* 42 (Summer 1988), pp. 485–507; Joseph Nye, "Neorealism and Neoliberalism," *World Politics* 40 (January 1988), pp. 235–51; Robert Keohane, "Neoliberal Institutionalism: A Perspective on World Politics," in his collection of essays entitled *International Institutions and State Power* (Boulder, CO: Westview Press, 1989), pp. 1–20; John Mearsheimer, "Back to the Future: Instability in Europe after the Cold War," *International Security* 13 (Summer 1990), pp. 5–56.

2. Kenneth Waltz, *Man, the State, and War* (New York: Columbia University Press, 1959), p. 232.

3. Ibid., pp. 169–70.

4. Ibid., p. 232. This point is made by Hidemi Suganami in "Bringing Order to the Causes of War Debates," *Millennium* 19 (Spring 1990), p. 34, fn. 11.

5. Kenneth Waltz, *Theory of International Politics* (Boston: Addison-Wesley, 1979).

6. The neorealist description is not unproblematic. For a powerful critique, see David Lumsdaine, [*Moral Vision in International Politics:*] *The Foreign Aid Regime, 1949–1989* (Princeton, NJ: Princeton University Press, [1993]).

7. Waltz, *Theory of International Politics,* pp. 79–101.

8. Stephen Walt, *The Origins of Alliances* (Ithaca, NY: Cornell University Press, 1987).

9. See, for example, Herbert Blumer, "The Methodological Position of Symbolic Interactionism," in his *Symbolic Interactionism: Perspective and Method* (Englewood Cliffs, NJ: Prentice-Hall, 1969), p. 2. Throughout this article, I assume that a theoretically productive analogy can be made between individuals and states.

10. The phrase "distribution of knowledge" is Barry Barnes's, as discussed in his work *The Nature of Power* (Cambridge: Polity Press, 1988); see also Peter Berger and Thomas Luckmann, *The Social Construction of Reality* (New York: Anchor Books, 1966).

11. For an excellent short statement of how collective meanings constitute identities, see Peter Berger, "Identity as a Problem in the Sociology of Knowledge," *European Journal of Sociology,* vol. 7, no. 1, 1966, pp. 32–40.

12. Berger, "Identity as a Problem in the Sociology of Knowledge," p. 111.

13. While not normally cast in such terms, foreign policy scholarship on national role conceptions could be adapted to such identity language. See Kal Holsti, "National Role Conceptions in the Study of Foreign Policy," *International Studies Quarterly* 14 (September 1970), pp. 233–309; and Stephen Walker, ed., *Role Theory and Foreign Policy Analysis* (Durham, NC: Duke University Press, 1987). For an important effort to do so, see Stephen Walker, "Symbolic Interactionism and International Politics: Role Theory's Contribution to International Organization," in C. Shih and Martha Cottam, eds., *Contending Dramas: A Cognitive Approach to Post-War International Organizational Processes* (New York: Praeger, [1992]).

14. On the "portfolio" conception of interests, see Barry Hindess, *Political Choice and Social Structure* (Aldershot, UK: Edward Elgar, 1989), pp. 2–3. The "definition of the situation" is a central concept in interactionist theory.

15. Nelson Foote, "Identification as the Basis for a Theory of Motivation," *American Sociological Review* 16 (February 1951), p. 15. Such strongly sociological conceptions of interest have been criticized, with some justice, for being "oversocialized"; see Dennis Wrong, "The Oversocialized Conception of Man in Modern Sociology," *American Sociological Review* 26 (April 1961), pp. 183–93. For useful correctives, which focus on the activation of presocial but nondetermining human needs within social contexts, see Turner, *A Theory of Social Interaction,* pp. 23–69; and Viktor Gecas, "The Self-Concept as a Basis for a Theory of Motivation," in Judith Howard and Peter Callero, eds., *The Self-Society Dynamic* (Cambridge: Cambridge University Press, 1991), pp. 171–87.

16. In neo-Durkheimian parlance, institutions are "social representations." See Serge Moscovici, "The Phenomenon of Social Representations," in Rob Farr and Serge Moscovici, eds., *Social Representations* (Cambridge: Cambridge University Press, 1984), pp. 3–69.

17. Berger and Luckmann, *The Social Construction of Reality,* p. 58.

18. See Giddens, *Central Problems in Social Theory;* and Alexander Wendt and Raymond Duvall, "Institutions and International Order," in Ernst-Otto Czempiel and James Rosenau, eds., *Global Changes and Theoretical Challenges* (Lexington, MA: Lexington Books, 1989), pp. 51–74.

19. Proponents of choice theory might put this in terms of "interdependent utilities."

20. Security systems might also vary in the extent to which there is a functional differentiation or a hierarchical relationship between patron and client, with the patron playing a hegemonic role within its sphere of influence in defining the security interests of its clients. I do not examine this dimension here; for preliminary discussion, see Alexander Wendt, "The States System and Global Militarization," Ph.D. diss., University of Minnesota, Minneapolis, 1989; and Alexander Wendt and Michael Barnett, "The International System and Third World Militarization," unpublished manuscript, 1991.

21. This amounts to an "internationalization of the state." For a discussion of this subject, see Raymond Duvall and Alexander Wendt, "The International Capital Regime and the Internationalization of the State," unpublished manuscript, 1987. See also R. B. J. Walker, "Sovereignty, Identity, Community: Reflections on the Horizons of Contemporary Political Practice," in R. B. J. Walker and Saul Mendlovitz, eds., *Contending Sovereignties* (Boulder, CO: Lynne Rienner, 1990), pp. 159–85.

22. On the spectrum of cooperative security arrangements, see Charles Kupchan and Clifford Kupchan, "Concerts, Collective Security, and the Future of Europe," *International Security* 16 (Summer 1991), pp. 114–61; and Richard Smoke, "A Theory of Mutual Security," in Richard Smoke and Andrei Kortunov, eds., *Mutual Security* (New York: St. Martin's Press, 1991), pp. 59–111. These may be usefully set alongside Christopher Jencks' "Varieties of Altruism," in Jane Mansbridge, ed., *Beyond Self-Interest* (Chicago: University of Chicago Press, 1990), pp. 53–67.

23. On the role of collective identity in reducing collective action problems, see Bruce Fireman and William Gamson, "Utilitarian Logic in the Resource Mobilization Perspective," in Mayer Zald and John McCarthy, eds., *The Dynamics of Social Movements* (Cambridge, MA: Winthrop, 1979), pp. 8–44; Robyn Dawes et al., "Cooperation for the Benefit of Us—Not Me, or My Conscience," in Mansbridge, *Beyond Self-Interest,* pp. 97–110; and Craig Calhoun, "The Problem of Identity in Collective Action," in Joan Huber, ed., *Macro-Micro Linkages in Sociology* (Beverly Hills, CA: Sage, 1991), pp. 51–75.

24. See Thomas Risse-Kappen, "Are Democratic Alliances Special?" unpublished manuscript, Yale University, New Haven, CT, 1991.

25. Waltz, *Theory of International Politics,* p. 91.

26. See Waltz, *Man, the State, and War;* and Robert Jervis, "Cooperation Under the Security Dilemma," *World Politics* 30 (January 1978), pp. 167–214.

27. My argument here parallels Rousseau's critique of Hobbes. For an excellent critique of realist appropriations of Rousseau, see Michael Williams, "Rousseau, Realism, and Realpolitik," *Millennium* 18 (Summer 1989), pp. 188–204. Williams argues that far from being a fundamental starting point in the state of nature, for Rousseau the stag hunt represented a stage in man's fall. On p. 190, Williams cites Rousseau's description of man prior to leaving the state of nature: "Man only knows himself; he does not see his own well-being to be identified with or contrary to that of anyone else; he neither hates anything nor loves anything; but limited to no more than physical instinct, he is no one, he is an animal." For another critique of Hobbes on the state of nature that parallels my constructivist reading of anarchy, see Charles Landesman, "Reflections on Hobbes: Anarchy and Human Nature," in Peter Caws, ed., *The Causes of Quarrel* (Boston: Beacon, 1989), pp. 139–48.

28. Empirically, this suggestion is problematic, since the process of decolonization and the subsequent support of many Third World states by international society point to ways in which even the raw material of "empirical statehood" is constituted by the society of states. See Robert Jackson and Carl Rosberg, "Why Africa's Weak States Persist: The Empirical and the Juridical in Statehood," *World Politics* 35 (October 1982), pp. 1–24.

29. Waltz, *Theory of International Politics,* pp. 74–77.

30. See James Morrow, "Social Choice and System Structure in World Politics," *World Politics* 41 (October 1988), p. 89. Waltz's behavioral treatment of socialization may be usefully contrasted with the more cognitive approach taken by Ikenberry and the Kupchans in the following articles: G. John Ikenberry and Charles Kupchan, "Socialization and Hegemonic Power," *International Organization* 44 (Summer 1989), pp. 283–316; and Kupchan and Kupchan, "Concerts, Collective Security, and the Future of Europe." Their approach is close to my own, but they define socialization as an elite strategy to induce value change in others, rather than as a ubiquitous feature of interaction in terms of which all identities and interests get produced and reproduced.

31. Regarding individualism, see Richard Ashley, "The Poverty of Neorealism," *International Organization* 38 (Spring 1984), pp. 225–86; Wendt, "The Agent-Structure Problem in International Relations Theory"; and David Dessler, "What's at Stake in the Agent-Structure Debate?" *International Organization* 43 (Summer 1989), pp. 441–74. Regarding structuralism, see R. B. J. Walker, "Realism, Change, and International Political Theory," *International Studies Quarterly* 31 (March 1987), pp. 65–86; and Martin Hollis and Steven Smith, *Explaining and Understanding International Relations* (Oxford: Clarendon Press, 1989).

32. The importance of the distinction between constitutive and causal explanations is not sufficiently appreciated in constructivist discourse. See Wendt, "The Agent-Structure Problem in International Relations Theory," pp. 362–65; Wendt, "The States System and Global Militarization," pp. 110–13; and Wendt, "Bridging the Theory/Meta-Theory Gap in International Relations," *Review of International Studies* 17 (October 1991), p. 390.

33. See Blumer, "The Methodological Position of Symbolic Interactionism," pp. 2–4.

34. See Robert Grafstein, "Rational Choice: Theory and Institutions," in Kristen Monroe, ed., *The Economic Approach to Politics* (New York: Harper Collins, 1991), pp. 263–64. A good example of the promise and limits of transaction cost approaches to institutional analysis is offered by Robert Keohane in his *After Hegemony* (Princeton, NJ: Princeton University Press, 1984).

35. This situation is not entirely metaphorical in world politics, since throughout history states have "discovered" each other, generating an instant anarchy as it were.

36. Mead's analysis of gestures remains definitive. See Mead's *Mind, Self, and Society.* See also the discussion of the role of signaling in the "mechanics of interaction" in Turner's *A Theory of Social Interaction,* pp. 74–79 and 92–115.

37. On the role of attribution processes in the interactionist account of identity-formation, see Sheldon Stryker and Avi Gottlieb, "Attribution Theory and Symbolic Interactionism," in John Harvey et al., eds., *New Directions in Attribution Research,* vol. 3 (Hillsdale, NJ: Lawrence Erlbaum, 1981), pp. 425–58; and Kathleen Crittenden, "Sociological Aspects of Attribution," *Annual Review of Sociology,* vol. 9, 1983, pp. 425–46. On attributional processes in international relations, see Shawn Rosenberg and Gary Wolfsfeld, "International Conflict and the Problem of Attribution," *Journal of Conflict Resolution* 21 (March 1977), pp. 75–103.

38. On the "stagecraft" involved in "presentations of self," see Erving Goffman, *The Presentation of Self in Everyday Life* (New York: Doubleday, 1959). On the role of appearance in definitions of the situation, see Gregory Stone, "Appearance and the Self," in Arnold Rose, ed., *Human Behavior and Social Processes* (Boston: Houghton Mifflin, 1962), pp. 86–118.

39. This discussion of the role of possibilities and probabilities in threat perception owes much to Stewart Johnson's comments on an earlier draft of my article.

40. On the role of "reassurance" in threat situations, see Richard Ned Lebow and Janice Gross Stein, "Beyond Deterrence," *Journal of Social Issues*, vol. 43, no. 4, 1987, pp. 5–72.

41. On "reciprocal typifications," see Berger and Luckmann, *The Social Construction of Reality*, pp. 54–58.

42. Jeff Coulter, "Remarks on the Conceptualization of Social Structure," *Philosophy of the Social Sciences* 12 (March 1982), pp. 42–43.

43. The following articles by Noel Kaplowitz have made an important contribution to such thinking in international relations: "Psychopolitical Dimensions of International Relations: The Reciprocal Effects of Conflict Strategies," *International Studies Quarterly* 28 (December 1984), pp. 373–406; and "National Self-Images, Perception of Enemies, and Conflict Strategies: Psychopolitical Dimensions of International Relations," *Political Psychology* 11 (March 1990), pp. 39–82.

44. These arguments are common in theories of narcissism and altruism. See Heinz Kohut, *Self-Psychology and the Humanities* (New York: Norton, 1985); and Martin Hoffmann, "Empathy, Its Limitations, and Its Role in a Comprehensive Moral Theory," in William Kurtines and Jacob Gewirtz, eds., *Morality, Moral Behavior, and Moral Development* (New York: Wiley, 1984), pp. 283–302.

45. See C. Norman Alexander and Mary Glenn Wiley, "Situated Activity and Identity Formation," in Morris Rosenberg and Ralph Turner, eds., *Social Psychology: Sociological Perspectives* (New York: Basic Books, 1981), pp. 269–89.

46. Sheldon Stryker, "The Vitalization of Symbolic Interactionism," *Social Psychology Quarterly* 50 (March 1987), p. 93.

47. On the "maturity" of anarchies, see Barry Buzan, *People, States, and Fear* (Chapel Hill: University of North Carolina Press, 1983).

48. A similar intuition may lie behind Ashley's effort to reappropriate classical realist discourse for critical international relations theory. See Richard Ashley, "Political Realism and Human Interests," *International Studies Quarterly* 38 (June 1981), pp. 204–36.

49. Waltz has himself helped open up such a debate with his recognition that systemic factors condition but do not determine state actions. See Kenneth Waltz, "Reflections on *Theory of International Politics*: A Response to My Critics," in Robert Keohane, ed., *Neorealism and Its Critics* (New York: Columbia University Press, 1986), pp. 322–45. The growing literature on the observation that "democracies do not fight each other" is relevant to this question, as are two other studies that break important ground toward a "reductionist" theory of state identity: William Bloom's *Personal Identity, National Identity and International Relations* (Cambridge: Cambridge University Press, 1990) and Lumsdaine's *Ideals and Interests*.

50. See Berger and Luckmann, *The Social Construction of Reality*, p. 89. See also Douglas Maynard and Thomas Wilson, "On the Reification of Social Structure," in Scott McNall and Gary Howe, eds., *Current Perspectives in Social Theory*, vol. 1 (Greenwich, CT: JAI Press, 1980), pp. 287–322.

51. See Richard Ashley, "Social Will and International Anarchy," in Hayward Alker and Richard Ashley, eds., *After Realism*, work in progress, Massachusetts Institute of Technology, Cambridge, and Arizona State University, Tempe, 1992.

52. See Ralph Turner, "Role-Taking: Process Versus Conformity," in Rose, *Human Behavior and Social Processes*, pp. 20–40; and Judith Howard, "From Changing Selves toward Changing Society," in Howard and Callero, *The Self-Society Dynamic*, pp. 209–37.

53. On the relationship between commitment and identity, see Foote, "Identification as the Basis for a Theory of Motivation"; Howard Becker, "Notes on the Concept of Commitment," *American Journal of Sociology* 66 (July 1960), pp. 32–40; and Stryker, *Symbolic Interactionism*. On role salience, see Stryker, ibid.

54. On threats to identity and the types of resistance that they may create, see Glynis Breakwell, *Coping with Threatened Identities* (London: Methuen, 1986); and Terrell Northrup, "The Dynamic of Identity in Personal and Social Conflict," in Louis Kreisberg et al., eds., *Intractable Conflicts and Their Transformation* (Syracuse, NY: Syracuse University Press, 1989), pp. 55–82. For a broad overview of resistance to change, see Timur Kuran, "The Tenacious Past: Theories of Personal and Collective Conservatism," *Journal of Economic Behavior and Organization* 10 (September 1988), pp. 143–71.

55. James March, "Bounded Rationality, Ambiguity, and the Engineering of Choice," *Bell Journal of Economics* 9 (Autumn 1978), p. 600.

56. Haskell Fain, *Normative Politics and the Community of Nations* (Philadelphia: Temple University Press, 1987).

57. This is the intersubjective basis for the principle of functional nondifferentiation among states, which "drops out" of Waltz's definition of structure because the latter has no explicit intersubjective basis. In international relations scholarship, the social production of territorial space has been emphasized primarily by poststructuralists. See, for example, Richard Ashley, "The Geopolitics of Geopolitical Space: Toward a Critical Social Theory of International Politics," *Alternatives* 12 (October 1987), pp. 403–34; and Simon Dalby, *Creating the Second Cold War* (London: Pinter, 1990). But the idea of space as both product and constituent of practice is also prominent in structurationist discourse. See Giddens, *Central Problems in Social Theory;* and Derek Gregory and John Urry, eds., *Social Relations and Spatial Structures* (London: Macmillan, 1985).

58. See John Ruggie, "Continuity and Transformation in the World Polity: Toward a Neorealist Synthesis," *World Politics* 35 (January 1983), pp. 261–85.

59. For a definition and discussion of "social closure," see Raymond Murphy, *Social Closure* (Oxford: Clarendon Press, 1988).

60. See Richard Ashley, "Untying the Sovereign State: A Double Reading of the Anarchy Problematique," *Millennium* 17 (Summer 1988), pp. 227–62.

61. See, for example, Mohammed Ayoob, "The Third World in the System of States: Acute Schizophrenia or Growing Pains?" *International Studies Quarterly* 33 (March 1989), pp. 67–80.

62. See William Coplin, "International Law and Assumptions about the State System," *World Politics* 17 (July 1965), pp. 615–34.

63. See Anthony Smith, "States and Homelands: The Social and Geopolitical Implications of National Territory," *Millennium* 10 (Autumn 1981), pp. 187–202.

64. This assumes that there are no other, competing, principles that organize political space and identity in the international system and coexist with traditional notions of sovereignty; in fact, of course, there are. On "spheres of influence" and "informal empires," see Jan Triska, ed., *Dominant Powers and Subordinate States* (Durham, NC:

Duke University Press, 1986); and Ronald Robinson, "The Excentric Idea of Imperialism, With or Without Empire," in Wolfgang Mommsen and Jurgen Osterhammel, eds., *Imperialism and After: Continuities and Discontinuities* (London: Allen & Unwin, 1986), pp. 267–89. On Arab conceptions of sovereignty, see Michael Barnett, "Sovereignty, Institutions, and Identity: From Pan-Arabism to the Arab State System," unpublished manuscript, University of Wisconsin, Madison, 1991.

65. David Strang, "Anomaly and Commonplace in European Expansion: Realist and Institutional Accounts," *International Organization* 45 (Spring 1991), pp. 143–62.

66. On "dynamic density," see Ruggie, "Continuity and Transformation in the World Polity"; and Waltz, "Reflections on *Theory of International Politics*." The role of interdependence in conditioning the speed and depth of social learning is much greater than the attention to which I have paid it. On the consequences of interdependence under anarchy, see Helen Milner, "The Assumption of Anarchy in International Relations Theory: A Critique," *Review of International Studies* 17 (January 1991), pp. 67–85.

67. See Michael Taylor, *Anarchy and Cooperation* (New York: Wiley, 1976); and Robert Axelrod, *The Evolution of Cooperation* (New York: Basic Books, 1984).

68. Mead, *Mind, Self, and Society.*

69. Strictly speaking, this is not true, since in iterated games the addition of future benefits to current ones changes the payoff structure of the game at T1, in this case from prisoners' dilemma to an assurance game. This transformation of interest takes place entirely within the actor, however, and as such is not a function of interaction with the other.

70. In fairness to Axelrod, he does point out that internalization of norms is a real possibility that may increase the resilience of institutions. My point is that this important idea cannot be derived from an approach to theory that takes identities and interests as exogenously given.

71. On "European identity," see Barry Buzan et al., eds., *The European Security Order Recast* (London: Pinter, 1990), pp. 45–63.

72. On "embeddedness," see John Ruggie, "International Regimes, Transactions, and Change: Embedded Liberalism in a Postwar Economic Order," in Krasner, *International Regimes*, pp. 195–232.

73. See Grieco, "Anarchy and the Limits of Cooperation."

74. On the difficulties of creating cooperative security regimes given competitive interests, see Robert Jervis, "Security Regimes," in Krasner, *International Regimes*, pp. 173–94; and Charles Lipson, "International Cooperation in Economic and Security Affairs," *World Politics* 37 (October 1984), pp. 1–23.

75. See Mead, *Mind, Self, and Society.*

76. Turner, "Role-Taking."

77. On "character planning," see Jon Elster, *Sour Grapes: Studies in the Subversion of Rationality* (Cambridge: Cambridge University Press, 1983), p. 117.

78. For useful overviews of New Thinking, see Mikhail Gorbachev, *Perestroika: New Thinking for Our Country and the World* (New York: Harper & Row, 1987); and Allen Lynch, *Gorbachev's International Outlook: Intellectual Origins and Political Consequences* (New York: Institute for East–West Security Studies, 1989).

79. For useful overviews of these factors, see Jack Snyder, "The Gorbachev Revolution: A Waning of Soviet Expansionism?" *World Politics* 12 (Winter 1987–88), pp. 93–121; and Stephen Meyer, "The Sources and Prospects of Gorbachev's New Political Thinking on Security," *International Security* 13 (Fall 1988), pp. 124–63.

80. See Daniel Bar-Tal et al., "Conflict Termination: An Epistemological Analysis of International Cases," *Political Psychology* 10 (June 1989), pp. 233–55.

81. See Robert Cox, "Social Forces, States and World Orders: Beyond International Relations Theory," in Keohane, *Neorealism and Its Critics,* pp. 204–55. See also Brian Fay, *Critical Social Science* (Ithaca, NY: Cornell University Press, 1987).

82. Hazel Markus and Paula Nurius, "Possible Selves," *American Psychologist* 41 (September 1986), pp. 954–69.

83. See Goffman, *The Presentation of Self in Everyday Life*; Eugene Weinstein and Paul Deutschberger, "Some Dimensions of Altercasting," *Sociometry* 26 (December 1963), pp. 454–66; and Walter Earle, "International Relations and the Psychology of Control: Alternative Control Strategies and Their Consequences," *Political Psychology* 7 (June 1986), pp. 369–75.

84. See Volker Boge and Peter Wilke, "Peace Movements and Unilateral Disarmament: Old Concepts in a New Light," *Arms Control* 7 (September 1986), pp. 156–70; Zeev Maoz and Daniel Felsenthal, "Self-Binding Commitments, the Inducement of Trust, Social Choice, and the Theory of International Cooperation," *International Studies Quarterly* 31 (June 1987), pp. 177–200; and V. Sakamoto, "Unilateral Initiative as an Alternative Strategy," *World Futures,* vol. 24, nos. 1–4, 1987, pp. 107–34.

85. On rewards, see Thomas Milburn and Daniel Christie, "Rewarding in International Politics," *Political Psychology* 10 (December 1989), pp. 625–45.

86. The importance of reciprocity in completing the process of structural transformation makes the logic in this stage similar to that in the "evolution of cooperation." The difference is one of prerequisites and objective: in the former, ego's tentative redefinition of self enables it to try and change alter by acting "as if" both were already playing a new game; in the latter, ego acts only on the basis of given interests and prior experience, with transformation emerging only as an unintended consequence.

87. Yale Ferguson and Richard Mansbach, "Between Celebration and Despair: Constructive Suggestions for Future International Theory," *International Studies Quarterly* 35 (December 1991), p. 375.

88. For excellent discussions of this tension, see Walker, "Sovereignty, Identity, Community"; and R. B. J. Walker, "Security, Sovereignty, and the Challenge of World Politics," *Alternatives* 15 (Winter 1990), pp. 3–27. On institutional path dependencies, see Stephen Krasner, "Sovereignty: An Institutional Perspective," *Comparative Political Studies* 21 (April 1988), pp. 66–94.

V. I. Lenin

FROM *IMPERIALISM, THE HIGHEST STAGE OF CAPITALISM*

■ ■ ■

Chapter V

The Division of the World among Capitalist Combines

Monopolist capitalist combines—cartels, syndicates, trusts—divide among themselves, first of all, the whole internal market of a country, and impose their control, more or less completely, upon the industry of that country. But under capitalism the home market is inevitably bound up with the foreign market. Capitalism long ago created a world market. As the export of capital increased, and as the foreign and colonial relations and the "spheres of influence" of the big monopolist combines expanded, things "naturally" gravitated towards an international agreement among these combines, and towards the formation of international cartels.

This is a new stage of world concentration of capital and production, incomparably higher than the preceding stages. Let us see how this super-monopoly develops.

■ ■ ■

From V. I. Lenin, *Imperialism, the Highest Stage of Capitalism: A Popular Outline* (New York: International Publishers, 1939). The order of some passages has been changed. The author's notes have been omitted.

Chapter X

The Place of Imperialism in History

We have seen that the economic quintessence of imperialism is monopoly capitalism. This very fact determines its place in history, for monopoly that grew up on the basis of free competition, and precisely out of free competition, is the transition from the capitalist system to a higher social-economic order. We must take special note of the four principal forms of monopoly, or the four principal manifestations of monopoly capitalism, which are characteristic of the epoch under review.

Firstly, monopoly arose out of the concentration of production at a very advanced stage of development. This refers to the monopolist capitalist combines, cartels, syndicates and trusts. We have seen the important part that these play in modern economic life. At the beginning of the twentieth century, monopolies acquired complete supremacy in the advanced countries. And although the first steps towards the formation of the cartels were first taken by countries enjoying the protection of high tariffs (Germany, America), Great Britain, with her system of free trade, was not far behind in revealing the same basic phenomenon, namely, the birth of monopoly out of the concentration of production.

Secondly, monopolies have accelerated the capture of the most important sources of raw materials, especially for the coal and iron industries, which are the basic and most highly cartelised industries in capitalist society. The monopoly of the most important sources of raw materials has enormously increased the power of big capital, and has sharpened the antagonism between cartelised and non-cartelised industry.

Thirdly, monopoly has sprung from the banks. The banks have developed from modest intermediary enterprises into the monopolists of finance capital. Some three or five of the biggest banks in each of the foremost capitalist countries have achieved the "personal union" of industrial and bank capital, and have concentrated in their hands the disposal of thousands upon thousands of millions which form the greater part of the capital and income of entire countries. A financial oligarchy, which throws a close net of relations of dependence over all the economic and political institutions of contemporary bourgeois society without exception—such is the most striking manifestation of this monopoly.

Fourthly, monopoly has grown out of colonial policy. To the numerous "old" motives of colonial policy, finance capital has added the struggle for the sources of raw materials, for the export of capital, for "spheres of influence," *i.e.*, for spheres for profitable deals, concessions, monopolist profits and so on; in fine, for economic territory in general. When the colonies of the European powers in Africa, for instance, comprised only one-tenth of that territory (as was the case in 1876), colonial policy was able to develop by methods other than those of monopoly—by the "free grabbing" of territories, so to speak. But when nine-tenths of Africa had been seized (approximately by 1900), when the whole world had been divided up, there was inevitably ushered in a period of colonial monopoly and, consequently, a period of particularly intense struggle for the division and the redivision of the world.

The extent to which monopolist capital has intensified all the contradictions of capitalism is generally known. It is sufficient to mention the high cost of living and the oppression of the cartels. This intensification of contradictions constitutes the most powerful driving force of the transitional period of history, which began from the time of the definite victory of world finance capital.

Monopolies, oligarchy, the striving for domination instead of the striving for liberty, the exploitation of an increasing number of small or weak nations by an extremely small group of the richest or most powerful nations—all these have given birth to those distinctive characteristics of imperialism which compel us to define it as parasitic or decaying capitalism. More and more prominently there emerges, as one of the tendencies of imperialism, the creation of the "bond-holding" (rentier) state, the usurer state, in which the bourgeoisie lives on the proceeds of capital exports and by clipping coupons. It would be a mistake to believe that this tendency to decay precludes the possibility of the rapid growth of capitalism. It does not. In the epoch of imperialism, certain branches of industry, certain strata of the bourgeoisie and certain countries betray, to a more or less degree, one or other of these tendencies. On the whole, capitalism is growing far more rapidly than before. But this growth is not only becoming more and more uneven in general; its unevenness also manifests itself, in particular, in the decay of the countries which are richest in capital (such as England).

■   ■   ■

When free competition in Great Britain was at its zenith, *i.e.*, between 1840 and 1860, the leading British bourgeois politicians were opposed to colonial policy and were of the opinion that the liberation of the colonies and their complete separation from Britain was inevitable and desirable. M. Beer, in an article, "Modern British Imperialism," published in 1898, shows that in 1852, Disraeli, a statesman generally inclined towards imperialism, declared: "The colonies are millstones round our necks." But at the end of the nineteenth century the heroes of the hour in England were Cecil

Rhodes and Joseph Chamberlain, open advocates of imperialism, who applied the imperialist policy in the most cynical manner.

It is not without interest to observe that even at that time these leading British bourgeois politicians fully appreciated the connection between what might be called the purely economic and the politico-social roots of modern imperialism. Chamberlain advocated imperialism by calling it a "true, wise and economical policy," and he pointed particularly to the German, American and Belgian competition which Great Britain was encountering in the world market. Salvation lies in monopolies, said the capitalists as they formed cartels, syndicates and trusts. Salvation lies in monopolies, echoed the political leaders of the bourgeoisie, hastening to appropriate the parts of the world not yet shared out. The journalist, Stead, relates the following remarks uttered by his close friend Cecil Rhodes, in 1895, regarding his imperialist ideas:

> I was in the East End of London yesterday and attended a meeting of the unemployed. I listened to the wild speeches, which were just a cry for "bread," "bread," "bread," and on my way home I pondered over the scene and I became more than ever convinced of the importance of imperialism. . . . My cherished idea is a solution for the social problem, *i.e.,* in order to save the 40,000,000 inhabitants of the United Kingdom from a bloody civil war, we colonial statesmen must acquire new lands to settle the surplus population, to provide new markets for the goods produced by them in the factories and mines. The Empire, as I have always said, is a bread and butter question. If you want to avoid civil war, you must become imperialists.

This is what Cecil Rhodes, millionaire, king of finance, the man who was mainly responsible for the Boer War, said in 1895. * * *

■   ■   ■

* * * The unevenness in the rate of expansion of colonial possessions is very marked. If, for instance, we compare France, Germany and Japan, which do not differ very much in area and population, we will see that the first has annexed almost three times as much colonial territory as the other two combined. In regard to finance capital, also, France, at the beginning of the period we are considering, was perhaps several times richer than Germany and Japan put together. In addition to, and on the basis of, purely economic causes, geographical conditions and other factors also affect the dimensions of colonial possessions. However strong the process of levelling the world, of levelling the economic and living conditions in different countries, may have been in the past decades as a result of the pressure of large-scale industry, exchange and finance capital, great differences still remain; and among the six powers, we see, firstly, young capitalist powers (America, Germany, Japan) which progressed very rapidly; secondly, countries with an old capitalist development (France and Great Britain), which, of late, have made much slower progress than the previously mentioned countries; and, thirdly, a country (Russia) which is economically most backward, in which modern capitalist imperialism is enmeshed, so to speak, in a particularly close network of pre-capitalist relations.

■   ■   ■

Colonial policy and imperialism existed before this latest stage of capitalism, and even before capitalism. Rome, founded on slavery, pursued a colonial policy and achieved imperialism. But "general" arguments about imperialism, which ignore, or put into the background the fundamental difference of social-economic systems, inevitably degenerate into absolutely empty banalities, or into grandiloquent comparisons like "Greater Rome and Greater Britain." Even the colonial policy of capitalism in its *previous* stages is essentially different from the colonial policy of finance capital.

The principal feature of modern capitalism is the domination of monopolist combines of the big capitalists. These monopolies are most firmly established when *all* the sources of raw materials are controlled by the one group. And we have seen with what zeal the international capitalist combines exert every effort to make it impossible for their rivals to compete with them; for example, by buying up mineral lands, oil fields, etc. Colonial possession alone gives complete guarantee of success to the monopolies against all the risks of the struggle with competitors, including the risk that the latter will defend themselves by means of a law establishing a state monopoly. The more capitalism is developed, the more the need for raw materials is felt, the more bitter competition becomes, and the more feverishly the hunt for raw materials proceeds throughout the whole world, the more desperate becomes the struggle for the acquisition of colonies.

■   ■   ■

The bourgeois reformists, and among them particularly the present-day adherents of Kautsky, of course, try to belittle the importance of facts of this kind by arguing that it "would be possible" to obtain raw materials in the open market without a "costly and dangerous" colonial policy; and that it would be "possible" to increase the supply of raw materials to an enormous extent "simply" by improving agriculture. But these arguments are merely an apology for imperialism, an attempt to embellish it, because they ignore the principal feature of modern capitalism: monopoly. Free markets are becoming more and more a thing of the past; monopolist syndicates and trusts are restricting them more and more every day, and "simply" improving agriculture reduces itself to improving the conditions of the masses, to raising wages and reducing profits. Where, except in the

imagination of the sentimental reformists, are there any trusts capable of interesting themselves in the condition of the masses instead of the conquest of colonies?

Finance capital is not only interested in the already known sources of raw materials; it is also interested in potential sources of raw materials, because present-day technical development is extremely rapid, and because land which is useless today may be made fertile tomorrow if new methods are applied (to devise these new methods a big bank can equip a whole expedition of engineers, agricultural experts, etc.), and large amounts of capital are invested. This also applies to prospecting for minerals, to new methods of working up and utilising raw materials, etc., etc. Hence, the inevitable striving of finance capital to extend its economic territory and even its territory in general. In the same way that the trusts capitalise their property by estimating it at two or three times its value, taking into account its "potential" (and not present) returns, and the further results of monopoly, so finance capital strives to seize the largest possible amount of land of all kinds and in any place it can, and by any means, counting on the possibilities of finding raw materials there, and fearing to be left behind in the insensate struggle for the last available scraps of undivided territory, or for the repartition of that which has been already divided.

■   ■   ■

The necessity of exporting capital also gives an impetus to the conquest of colonies, for in the colonial market it is easier to eliminate competition, to make sure of orders, to strengthen the necessary "connections," etc., by monoplist methods (and sometimes it is the only possible way).

The non-economic superstructure which grows up on the basis of finance capital, its politics and its ideology, stimulates the striving for colonial conquest. "Finance capital does not want liberty, it wants domination," as Hilferding very truly says. * * *

■ ■ ■

Since we are speaking of colonial policy in the period of capitalist imperialism, it must be observed that finance capital and its corresponding foreign policy, which reduces itself to the struggle of the Great Powers for the economic and political division of the world, give rise to a number of *transitional* forms of national dependence. The division of the world into two main groups—of colony-owning countries on the one hand and colonies on the other—is not the only typical feature of this period; there is also a variety of forms of dependent countries; countries which, officially, are politically independent, but which are, in fact, enmeshed in the net of financial and diplomatic dependence. We have already referred to one form of dependence—the semi-colony. Another example is provided by Argentina.

"South America, and especially Argentina," writes Schulze-Gaevernitz in his work on British imperialism, "is so dependent financially on London that it ought to be described as almost a British commercial colony."

■ ■ ■

Chapter VII

Imperialism as a Special Stage of Capitalism

We must now try to sum up and put together what has been said above on the subject of imperialism. Imperialism emerged as the development and direct continuation of the fundamental attributes of capitalism in general. But capitalism only became capitalist imperialism at a definite and very high stage of its development, when certain of its fundamental attributes began to be transformed into their opposites; when the features of a period of transition from capitalism to a higher social and economic system began to take shape and reveal themselves all along the line. Economically, the main thing in this process is the substitution of capitalist monopolies for capitalist free competition. Free competition is the fundamental attribute of capitalism, and of commodity production generally. Monopoly is exactly the opposite of free competition; but we have seen the latter being transformed into monopoly before our very eyes, creating large-scale industry and eliminating small industry, replacing large-scale industry by still larger-scale industry, finally leading to such a concentration of production and capital that monopoly has been and is the result: cartels, syndicates and trusts, and merging with them, the capital of a dozen or so banks manipulating thousands of millions. At the same time monopoly, which has grown out of free competition, does not abolish the latter, but exists over it and alongside of it, and thereby gives rise to a number of very acute, intense antagonisms, friction and conflicts. Monopoly is the transition from capitalism to a higher system.

If it were necessary to give the briefest possible definition of imperialism we should have to say that imperialism is the monopoly stage of capitalism. Such a definition would include what is most important, for, on the one hand, finance capital is the bank capital of a few big monopolist banks, merged with the capital of the monopolist combines of manufacturers; and, on the other hand, the division of the world is the transition from a colonial policy which has extended without hindrance to territories unoccupied by any capitalist power, to a colonial policy of monopolistic possession of the territory of the world which has been completely divided up.

But very brief definitions, although convenient, for they sum up the main points, are nevertheless inadequate, because very important features of the phenomenon that has to be defined have to be especially deduced. And so, without forgetting the conditional and relative value of all definitions, which can never include all the concatenations of a phenomenon in its complete development, we must give a definition of imperialism that will embrace the following five essential features:

1. The concentration of production and capital developed to such a high stage that it created monopolies which play a decisive role in economic life.
2. The merging of bank capital with industrial capital, and the creation, on the basis of this "finance capital," of a "financial oligarchy."
3. The export of capital, which has become extremely important, as distinguished from the export of commodities.
4. The formation of international capitalist monopolies which share the world among themselves.
5. The territorial division of the whole world among the greatest capitalist powers is completed.

Imperialism is capitalism in that stage of development in which the dominance of monopolies and finance capital has established itself; in which the export of capital has acquired pronounced importance; in which the division of the world among the international trusts has begun; in which the division of all territories of the globe among the great capitalist powers has been completed.

■　　■　　■

Another special feature of imperialism, which is connected with the facts we are describing, is the decline in emigration from imperialist countries, and the increase in immigration into these countries from the backward countries where lower wages are paid. As Hobson observes, emigration from Great Britain has been declining since 1884. In

that year the number of emigrants was 242,000, while in 1900, the number was only 169,000. German emigration reached the highest point between 1880 and 1890, with a total of 1,453,000 emigrants. In the course of the following two decades, it fell to 544,000 and even to 341,000. On the other hand, there was an increase in the number of workers entering Germany from Austria, Italy, Russia and other countries. According to the 1907 census, there were 1,342,294 foreigners in Germany, of whom 440,800 were industrial workers and 257,329 were agricultural workers. In France, the workers employed in the mining industry are, "in great part," foreigners: Polish, Italian and Spanish. In the United States, immigrants from Eastern and Southern Europe are engaged in the most poorly paid occupations, while American workers provide the highest percentage of overseers or of the better paid workers. Imperialism has the tendency to create privileged sections even among the workers, and to detach them from the main proletarian masses.

It must be observed that in Great Britain the tendency of imperialism to divide the workers, to encourage opportunism among them and to cause temporary decay in the working class movement, revealed itself much earlier than the end of the nineteenth and the beginning of the twentieth centuries; for two important distinguishing features of imperialism were observed in Great Britain in the middle of the nineteenth century, *viz.*, vast colonial possessions and a monopolist position in the world market. Marx and Engels systematically traced this relation between opportunism in the labour movement and the imperialist features of British capitalism for several decades. For example, on October 7, 1858, Engels wrote to Marx:

The English proletariat is becoming more and more bourgeois, so that this most bourgeois of all nations is apparently aiming ultimately at the possession of a bourgeois aristocracy, and a bourgeois proletariat *as well as* a bourgeoisie.

For a nation which exploits the whole world—this is, of course, to a certain extent justifiable.

Almost a quarter of a century later, in a letter dated August 11, 1881, Engels speaks of ". . . the worst type of English trade unions which allow themselves to be led by men sold to, or at least, paid by the bourgeoisie." In a letter to Kautsky, dated September 12, 1882, Engels wrote:

> You ask me what the English workers think about colonial policy? Well, exactly the same as they think about politics in general. There is no workers' party here, there are only Conservatives and Liberal-Radicals, and the workers merrily share the feast of England's monopoly of the colonies and the world market. . . . [Engels expressed similar ideas in the press in his preface to the second edition of *The Condition of the Working Class in England,* which appeared in 1892.]

We thus see clearly the causes and effects. The causes are: 1) Exploitation of the whole world by this country. 2) Its monopolistic position in the world market. 3) Its colonial monopoly. The effects are: 1) A section of the British proletariat becomes bourgeois. 2) A section of the proletariat permits itself to be led by men sold to, or at least, paid by the bourgeoisie. The imperialism of the beginning of the twentieth century completed the division of the world among a handful of states, each of which today exploits (*i.e.,* draws super-profits from) a part of the world only a little smaller than that which England exploited in 1858. * * *

The distinctive feature of the present situation is the prevalence of economic and political conditions which could not but increase the irreconcilability between opportunism and the general and vital interests of the working class movement. Embryonic imperialism has grown into a dominant system; capitalist monopolies occupy first place in economics and politics; the division of the world has been completed. On the other hand, instead of an undisputed monopoly by Great Britain, we see a few imperialist powers contending for the right to share in this monopoly, and this struggle is characteristic of the whole period of the beginning of the twentieth century. Opportunism, therefore, cannot now triumph in the working class movement of any country for decades as it did in England in the second half of the nineteenth century. But, in a number of countries it has grown ripe, over-ripe, and rotten, and has become completely merged with bourgeois policy in the form of "social-chauvinism."

■　　■　　■

Chapter IX

The Critique of Imperialism

By the critique of imperialism, in the broad sense of the term, we mean the attiude towards imperialist policy of the different classes of society as part of their general ideology.

The enormous dimensions of finance capital concentrated in a few hands and creating an extremely extensive and close network of ties and relationships which subordinate not only the small and medium, but also even the very small capitalists and small masters, on the one hand, and the intense struggle waged against other national state groups of financiers for the division of the world and domination over other countries, on the other hand, cause the wholesale transition of the possessing classes to the side of imperialism. The signs of the times are a "general" enthusiasm regarding its prospects, a passionate defence of imperialism, and every possible embellishment of its real nature. The imperialist ideology also penetrates the working class. There is no Chinese Wall between it and the other classes. The leaders of the so-called "Social-Democratic" Party of Germany are today justly called "social-imperialists," that is, socialists in words and imperialists in deeds; but as early as 1902, Hobson noted the existence of "Fabian imperialists" who belonged to the opportunist Fabian Society in England.

Bourgeois scholars and publicists usually come out in defence of imperialism in a somewhat veiled form, and obscure its complete domination and its profound roots; they strive to concentrate attention on partial and secondary details and do their very best to distract attention from the main issue by means of ridiculous schemes for "reform," such as police supervision of the trusts and banks, etc. Less frequently, cynical and frank imperialists speak out and are bold enough to admit the absurdity of the idea of reforming the fundamental features of imperialism.

■　■　■

4 LEVELS OF ANALYSIS

A typical framework for organizing the different theoretical traditions is the "levels of analysis." These levels are arrayed on a continuum starting with the international system as a whole, then continuing down through the type of domestic political system of individual states (democratic or authoritarian), the various interest groups and bureaucracies within the state, and finally individual decision making and psychology.

Different theoretical traditions place different bets on which level is likely to explain more about international politics. Realists such as Hans J. Morgenthau and John Mearsheimer normally start by looking as the structure of the international system as a whole. Morgenthau writes in *Politics among Nations* that the international system is characterized by competition among states, each seeking to enhance its power. As a consequence of this competition, a balance of power tends to emerge. In the selection in this chapter, Morgenthau discusses what states can do to stabilize the balance. However, not only realists prioritize the level of the international system; so does constructivist Alexander Wendt, who writes about "cultures of anarchy" that characterize the structure of the international system as a whole.

As we saw in the previous chapters, liberal theorists such as Michael Doyle prioritize the domestic regime type of states and the distinctive patterns of diplomatic relations this creates, most notably the absence of war between democracies. The liberal multilateralist John Ikenberry prioritizes the distinctive pattern of international organizations that are created by powerful liberal states to sustain cooperation among them.

Individual psychology is also important in shaping international relations. Individuals include not only foreign policy elites—the leaders who move the world—but also the diplomats, warriors, activists, and voters whose attitudes and perceptions animate the politics of international issues. In a now-classic piece originally published in 1968, Robert Jervis articulates hypotheses on the origins of misperceptions. Drawing heavily on psychology, he suggests strategies for decision makers to mitigate the effects of misperception.

One of the most consequential tasks of political judgment is inferring the intentions of a state's adversaries. In her article "In the Eye of the Beholder," Keren Yarhi-Milo surveys three theories of how leaders and their intelligence services approach this problem. The first two are based on variants of a rational theory of decision making: the first posits that actors base their judgments on the adversary's costly behavior, ignoring "cheap talk," while the second expects them to focus mainly on the adversary's capabilities. Yarhi-Milo proposes a third theory based on psychological research about selective attention to information. In case studies of the Carter administration's response to the Soviet invasion of Afghanistan and the Reagan administration's response to Mikhail Gorbachev's diplomacy, she finds that leaders focus inordinately on vivid information gained in personal encounters, whereas intelligence services focus narrowly on data that can be compiled routinely, such as weapons capabilities.

While some theoretical traditions and scholars disproportionately emphasize one level of analysis, many scholars believe that painting a well-rounded picture of a state's foreign relations requires drawing on all of the levels of analysis, tracing their interactions. This chapter includes works by two authorities on contemporary Chinese foreign policy who integrate insights from diverse levels of analysis.

Thomas J. Christensen, an academic China specialist and a prominent theorist of international relations, served as Deputy Assistant Secretary of State for East Asian and Pacific Affairs with responsibility for relations with China from 2006 to 2008. In *The China Challenge* he draws on both his experience in government and his scholarly roots to argue in favor of a balanced strategy that will "channel China's nationalist ambitions into cooperation rather than coercion." In presenting his case, Christensen makes use of the arguments of some contributors to *Essential Readings in World Politics*, including Thomas Schelling and Robert Jervis, and rebuts the arguments of others, such as John Mearsheimer.

Alastair Iain Johnston draws on constructivist international relations theory in a series of three related articles that probe some insufficiently examined conventional wisdoms about China's "newly assertive" foreign policy, its supposedly "rising nationalism," and the reaction of China's public opinion to different rhetorical justifications of international rivalry. In studying these very practical topics of contemporary political concern, Johnston moves seamlessly across levels of analysis, taking into account shifts in international power, the nature of democratic and authoritarian regimes, the political influence of governmental bureaucracies, and the dynamics of mass psychology. Excerpts from these articles are also noteworthy for their creative use of survey research in a challenging environment, including experiments embedded in the surveys.

Hans J. Morgenthau
THE BALANCE OF POWER

The aspiration for power on the part of several nations, each trying either to maintain or overthrow the status quo, leads of necessity to a configuration that is called the balance of power[1] and to policies that aim at preserving it. We say "of necessity" advisedly. For here again we are confronted with the basic misconception that has impeded the understanding of international politics and has made us the prey of illusions. This misconception asserts that men have a choice between power politics and its necessary outgrowth, the balance of power, on the one hand, and a different, better kind of international relations on the other. It insists that a foreign policy based on the balance of power is one among several possible foreign policies and that only stupid and evil men will choose the former and reject the latter.

It will be shown * * * that the international balance of power is only a particular manifestation of a general social principle to which all societies composed of a number of autonomous units owe the autonomy of their component parts; that the balance of power and policies aiming at its preservation are not only inevitable but are an essential stabilizing factor in a society of sovereign nations; and that the instability of the international balance of power is due not to the faultiness of the principle but to the particular conditions under which the principle must operate in a society of sovereign nations.

From Hans J. Morgenthau, *Politics among Nations: The Struggle for Power and Peace* (1948; reprint, New York: Knopf, 1985), pp. 187–89, 198–201, 213–14, 222, 227–28. Some of the author's notes have been omitted.

Social Equilibrium

Balance of Power as Universal Concept

The concept of "equilibrium" as a synonym for "balance" is commonly employed in many sciences—physics, biology, economics, sociology, and political science. It signifies stability within a system composed of a number of autonomous forces. Whenever the equilibrium is disturbed either by an outside force or by a change in one or the other elements composing the system, the system shows a tendency to re-establish either the original or a new equilibrium. Thus equilibrium exists in the human body. While the human body changes in the process of growth, the equilibrium persists as long as the changes occurring in the different organs of the body do not disturb the body's stability. This is especially so if the quantitative and qualitative changes in the different organs are proportionate to each other. When, however, the body suffers a wound or loss of one of its organs through outside interference, or experiences a malignant growth or a pathological transformation of one of its organs, the equilibrium is disturbed, and the body tries to overcome the disturbance by re-establishing the equilibrium either on the same or a different level from the one that obtained before the disturbance occurred.[2]

The same concept of equilibrium is used in a social science, such as economies, with reference to the relations between the different elements of the economic system, e.g., between savings and investments, exports and imports, supply and demand, costs and prices. Contemporary capitalism itself has been described as a system of "countervailing power."[3] It also applies to society as a whole. Thus we search for a proper balance between different geographical regions, such as the East and the West, the North and the South; between different kinds of activities, such as agriculture and industry, heavy and light industries, big and small businesses, producers and consumers, management and labor; between different functional groups, such as city and country, the old, the middle-aged, and the young, the economic and the political sphere, the middle classes and the upper and lower classes.

Two assumptions are at the foundation of all such equilibriums: first, that the elements to be balanced are necessary for society or are entitled to exist and, second, that without a state of equilibrium among them one element will gain ascendancy over the others, encroach upon their interests and rights, and may ultimately destroy them.

Consequently, it is the purpose of all such equilibriums to maintain the stability of the system without destroying the multiplicity of the elements composing it. If the goal were stability alone, it could be achieved by allowing one element to destroy or overwhelm the others and take their place. Since the goal is stability plus the preservation of all the elements of the system, the equilibrium must aim at preventing any element from gaining ascendancy over the others. The means employed to maintain the equilibrium consist in allowing the different elements to pursue their opposing tendencies up to the point where the tendency of one is not so strong as to overcome the tendency of the others, but strong enough to prevent the others from overcoming its own. * * *

■   ■   ■

DIFFERENT METHODS OF THE BALANCE OF POWER

The balancing process can be carried on either by diminishing the weight of the heavier scale or by increasing the weight of the lighter one.

Divide and Rule

The former method has found its classic manifestation, aside from the imposition of onerous conditions in peace treaties and the incitement to treason and revolution, in the maxim "divide and rule." It has been resorted to by nations who tried to make or keep their competitors weak by dividing them or keeping them divided. The most consistent and important policies of this kind in modern times are the policy of France with respect to Germany and the policy of the Soviet Union with respect to the rest of Europe. From the seventeenth century to the end of the Second World War, it has been an unvarying principle of French foreign policy either to favor the division of the German Empire into a number of small independent states or to prevent the coalescence of such states into one unified nation. * * * Similarly, the Soviet Union from the twenties to the present has consistently opposed all plans for the unification of Europe, on the assumption that the pooling of the divided strength of the European nations into a "Western bloc" would give the enemies of the Soviet Union such power as to threaten the latter's security.

The other method of balancing the power of several nations consists in adding to the strength of the weaker nation. This method can be carried out by two different means: Either B can increase its power sufficiently to offset, if not surpass, the power of A, and vice versa; or B can pool its power with the power of all the other nations that pursue identical policies with regard to A, in which case A will pool its power with all the nations pursuing identical policies with respect to B. The former alternative is exemplified by the policy of compensations and the armament race as well as by disarmament; the latter, by the policy of alliances.

Compensations

Compensations of a territorial nature were a common device in the eighteenth and nineteenth centuries for maintaining a balance of power which had been, or was to be, disturbed by the territorial acquisitions of one nation. The Treaty of Utrecht of 1713, which terminated the War of the Spanish Succession, recognized for the first time expressly the principle of the balance of power by way of territorial compensations. It provided for the division of most of the Spanish possessions, European and colonial, between the Hapsburgs and the Bourbons *"ad conservandum in Europa equilibrium,"* as the treaty put it.

■   ■   ■

In the latter part of the nineteenth and the beginning of the twentieth century, the principle of compensations was again deliberately applied to the distribution of colonial territories and the delimitation of colonial or semicolonial spheres of influence. Africa, in particular, was during that period the object of numerous treaties delimiting spheres of influence for the major colonial powers. Thus the competition between France, Great Britain, and Italy for the domination of Ethiopia was

provisionally resolved * * * by the treaty of 1906, which divided the country into three spheres of influence for the purpose of establishing in that region a balance of power among the nations concerned. * * *

Even where the principle of compensations is not deliberately applied, however, * * * it is nowhere absent from political arrangements, territorial or other, made within a balance-of-power system. For, given such a system, no nation will agree to concede political advantages to another nation without the expectation, which may or may not be well founded, of receiving proportionate advantages in return. The bargaining of diplomatic negotiations, issuing in political compromise, is but the principle of compensations in its most general form, and as such it is organically connected with the balance of power.

Armaments

The principal means, however, by which a nation endeavors with the power at its disposal to maintain or re-establish the balance of power are armaments. The armaments race in which Nation A tries to keep up with, and then to outdo, the armaments of Nation B, and vice versa, is the typical instrumentality of an unstable, dynamic balance of power. The necessary corollary of the armaments race is a constantly increasing burden of military preparations devouring an ever greater portion of the national budget and making for ever deepening fears, suspicions, and insecurity. The situation preceding the First World War, with the naval competition between Germany and Great Britain and the rivalry of the French and German armies, illustrates this point.

It is in recognition of situations such as these that, since the end of the Napoleonic Wars, repeated attempts have been made to create a stable balance of power, if not to establish permanent peace, by means of the proportionate disarmament of competing nations. The technique of stabilizing the balance of power by means of a proportionate reduction of armaments is somewhat similar to the technique of territorial compensations. For both techniques require a quantitative evaluation of the influence that the arrangement is likely to exert on the respective power of the individual nations. The difficulties in making such a quantitative evaluation—in correlating, for instance, the military strength of the French army of 1932 with the military power represented by the industrial potential of Germany—have greatly contributed to the failure of most attempts at creating a stable balance of power by means of disarmament. The only outstanding success of this kind was the Washington Naval Treaty of 1922, in which Great Britain, the United States, Japan, France, and Italy agreed to a proportionate reduction and limitation of naval armaments. Yet it must be noted that this treaty was part of an over-all political and territorial settlement in the Pacific which sought to stabilize the power relations in that region on the foundation of Anglo-American predominance.

Alliances

The historically most important manifestation of the balance of power, however, is to be found not in the equilibrium of two isolated nations but in the relations between one nation or alliance of nations and another alliance.

■ ■ ■

Alliances are a necessary function of the balance of power operating within a multiple-state system. Nations A and B, competing with each other, have three choices in order to maintain and improve their relative power positions. They can increase their own power, they can add to their own power the power of other nations, or they can withhold the power of other nations from the adversary. When they make the first choice, they embark upon an armaments race. When they choose the second and third alternatives, they pursue a policy of alliances.

Whether or not a nation shall pursue a policy of alliances is, then, a matter not of principle but of expediency. A nation will shun alliances if it believes that it is strong enough to hold its own unaided or that the burden of the commitments resulting from the alliance is likely to outweigh the advantages to be expected. It is for one or the other or both of these reasons that, throughout the better part of their history, Great Britain and the United States have refrained from entering into peacetime alliances with other nations.

■ ■ ■

The "Holder" of the Balance

Whenever the balance of power is to be realized by means of an alliance—and this has been generally so throughout the history of the Western world— two possible variations of this pattern have to be distinguished. To use the metaphor of the balance, the system may consist of two scales, in each of which are to be found the nation or nations identified with the same policy of the status quo or of imperialism. The continental nations of Europe have generally operated the balance of power in this way.

The system may, however, consist of two scales plus a third element, the "holder" of the balance or the "balancer." The balancer is not permanently identified with the policies of either nation or group of nations. Its only objective within the system is the maintenance of the balance, regardless of the concrete policies the balance will serve. In consequence, the holder of the balance will throw its weight at one time in this scale, at another time in the other scale, guided only by one consideration—the relative position of scales. Thus it will put its weight always in the scale that seems to be higher than the other because it is lighter. The balancer may become in a relatively short span of history consecutively the friend and foe of all major powers, provided they all consecutively threaten the balance by approaching predominance over the others and are in turn threatened by others about to gain such predominance. To paraphrase a statement of Palmerston: While the holder of the balance has no permanent friends, it has no permanent enemies either; it has only the permanent interest of maintaining the balance of power itself.

The balancer is in a position of "splendid isolation." It is isolated by its own choice; for, while the two scales of the balance must vie with each other to add its weight to theirs in order to gain the overweight necessary for success, it must refuse to enter into permanent ties with either side. The holder of the balance waits in the middle in watchful detachment to see which scale is likely to sink. Its isolation is "splendid"; for, since its support or lack of support is the decisive factor in the struggle for power, its foreign policy, if cleverly managed, is able to extract the highest price from those whom it supports. But since this support, regardless of the price paid for it, is always uncertain and shifts from one side to the other in accordance with the movements of the balance, its policies are resented and subject to condemnation on moral grounds. Thus it has been said of the outstanding balancer in modern times, Great Britain, that it lets others fight its wars, that it keeps Europe divided in order to dominate the continent, and that the fickleness of its policies is such as to make alliances with Great Britain impossible. "Perfidious Albion" has become a byword in the mouths of those who either were unable to gain Great Britain's support, however hard they tried, or else lost it after they had paid what seemed to them too high a price.

The holder of the balance occupies the key position in the balance-of-power system, since its position determines the outcome of the struggle for power. It has, therefore, been called the "arbiter" of the system, deciding who will win and who will lose. By making it impossible for any nation or combination of nations to gain predominance over the others, it preserves its own independence as well as the independence of all the other nations, and is thus a most powerful factor in international politics.

The holder of the balance can use this power in three different ways. It can make its joining one or the other nation or alliance dependent upon certain conditions favorable to the maintenance or restoration of the balance. It can make its support of the peace settlement dependent upon similar conditions. It can, finally, in either situation see to it that the objectives of its own national policy, apart from the maintenance of the balance of power, are realized in the process of balancing the power of others.

■   ■   ■

EVALUATION OF THE BALANCE OF POWER

■ ■ ■

The Unreality of the Balance of Power

[The] uncertainty of all power calculations not only makes the balance of power incapable of practical application but leads also to its very negation in practice. Since no nation can be sure that its calculation of the distribution of power at any particular moment in history is correct, it must at least make sure that its errors, whatever they may be, will not put the nation at a disadvantage in the contest for power. In other words, the nation must try to have at least a margin of safety which will allow it to make erroneous calculations and still maintain the balance of power. To that effect, all nations actively engaged in the struggle for power must actually aim not at balance—that is, equality—of power, but at superiority of power in their own behalf. And since no nation can foresee how large its miscalculations will turn out to be, all nations must ultimately seek the maximum of power obtainable under the circumstances. Only thus can they hope to attain the maximum margin of safety commensurate with the maximum of errors they might commit. The limitless aspiration for power, potentially always present * * * in the power drives of nations, finds in the balance of power a mighty incentive to transform itself into an actuality.

Since the desire to attain a maximum of power is universal, all nations must always be afraid that their own miscalculations and the power increases of other nations might add up to an inferiority for themselves which they must at all costs try to avoid. Hence all nations who have gained an apparent edge over their competitors tend to consolidate that advantage and use it for changing the distribution of power permanently in their favor. This can be done through diplomatic pressure by bringing the full weight of that advantage to bear upon the other nations, compelling them to make the concessions that will consolidate the temporary advantage into a permanent superiority. It can also be done by war. Since in a balance-of-power system all nations live in constant fear lest their rivals deprive them, at the first opportune moment, of their power position, all nations have a vital interest in anticipating such a development and doing unto the others what they do not want the others to do unto them. * * *

NOTES

1. The term "balance of power" is used in the text with four different meanings: (1) as a policy aimed at a certain state of affairs, (2) as an actual state of affairs, (3) as an approximately equal distribution of power, (4) as any distribution of power. Whenever the term is used without qualification, it refers to an actual state of affairs in which power is distributed among several nations with approximate equality. * * *

2. Cf., for instance, the impressive analogy between the equilibrium in the human body and in society in Walter B. Cannon, *The Wisdom of the Body* (New York: W. W. Norton and Company, 1932), pp. 293, 294: "At the outset it is noteworthy that the body politic itself exhibits some indications of crude automatic stabilizing processes. In the previous chapter I expressed the postulate that a certain degree of constancy in a complex system is itself evidence that agencies are acting or are ready to act to maintain that constancy. And moreover, that when a system remains steady it does so because any tendency towards change is met by increased effectiveness of the factor or factors which resist the change. Many familiar facts prove

that these statements are to some degree true for society even in its present unstabilized condition. A display of conservatism excites a radical revolt and that in turn is followed by a return to conservatism. Loose government and its consequences bring the reformers into power, but their tight reins soon provoke restiveness and the desire for release. The noble enthusiasms and sacrifices of war are succeeded by moral apathy and orgies of self-indulgence. Hardly any strong tendency in a nation continues to the stage of disaster; before that extreme is reached corrective forces arise which check the tendency and they commonly prevail to such an excessive degree as themselves to cause a reaction. A study of the nature of these social swings and their reversal might lead to valuable understanding and possibly to means of more narrowly limiting the disturbances. At this point, however, we merely note that the disturbances are roughly limited, and that this limitation suggests, perhaps, the early stages of social homeostasis." (Reprinted by permission of the publisher. Copyright 1932, 1939, by Walter B. Cannon.)

3. John K. Galbraith, *American Capitalism, the Concept of Countervailing Power* (Boston: Houghton Mifflin, 1952).

Robert Jervis
HYPOTHESES ON MISPERCEPTION

In determining how he will behave, an actor must try to predict how others will act and how their actions will affect his values. The actor must therefore develop an image of others and of their intentions. This image may, however, turn out to be an inaccurate one; the actor may, for a number of reasons, misperceive both others' actions and their intentions. * * * I wish to discuss the types of misperceptions of other states' intentions which states tend to make. * * *

■   ■   ■

Theories—Necessary and Dangerous

* * * The evidence from both psychology and history overwhelmingly supports the view (which may be labeled Hypothesis 1) that decision-makers tend to fit incoming information into their existing theories and images. Indeed, their theories and images play a large part in determining what they notice. In other words, actors tend to perceive what they expect. Furthermore (Hypothesis 1a), a theory will have greater impact on an actor's interpretation of data (a) the greater the ambiguity of the data and (b) the higher the degree of confidence with which the actor holds the theory.[1]

■   ■   ■

From *World Politics* 20, no. 3 (April 1968), 454–79. Some of the author's notes have been omitted.

* * * Hypothesis 2: scholars and decision-makers are apt to err by being too wedded to the established view and too closed to new information, as opposed to being too willing to alter their theories. Another way of making this point is to argue that actors tend to establish their theories and expectations prematurely. In politics, of course, this is often necessary because of the need for action. But experimental evidence indicates that the same tendency also occurs on the unconscious level. * * *

However, when we apply these and other findings to politics and discuss kinds of misperception, we should not quickly apply the label of cognitive distortion. We should proceed cautiously for two related reasons. The first is that the evidence available to decision-makers almost always permits several interpretations. It should be noted that there are cases of visual perception in which different stimuli can produce exactly the same pattern on an observer's retina. Thus, for an observer using one eye the same pattern would be produced by a sphere the size of a golf ball which was quite close to the observer, by a baseball-sized sphere that was further away, or by a basketball-sized sphere still further away. Without other clues, the observer cannot possibly determine which of these stimuli he is presented with, and we would not want to call his incorrect perceptions examples of distortion. Such cases, relatively rare in visual perception, are frequent in international relations. The evidence available to decision-makers is almost always very ambiguous since accurate clues to others' intentions are surrounded by noise[2] and deception. In most cases, no matter how long, deeply, and "objectively" the evidence is analyzed, people can differ in their interpretations, and there are no general rules to indicate who is correct.

The second reason to avoid the label of cognitive distortion is that the distinction between perception and judgment, obscure enough in individual psychology, is almost absent in the making of inferences in international politics. Decision-makers who reject information that contradicts their views—or who develop complex interpretations of it—often do so consciously and explicitly. Since the evidence available contains contradictory information, to make any inferences requires that much information be ignored or given interpretations that will seem tortuous to those who hold a different position.

Indeed, if we consider only the evidence available to a decision-maker at the time of decision, the view later proved incorrect may be supported by as much evidence as the correct one—or even by more. Scholars have often been too unsympathetic with the people who were proved wrong. On closer examination, it is frequently difficult to point to differences between those who were right and those who were wrong with respect to their openness to new information and willingness to modify their views. Winston Churchill, for example, did not open-mindedly view each Nazi action to see if the explanations provided by the appeasers accounted for the data better than his own beliefs. Instead, like Chamberlain, he fitted each bit of ambiguous information into his own hypotheses. That he was correct should not lead us to overlook the fact that his methods of analysis and use of theory to produce cognitive consistency did not basically differ from those of the appeasers.

A consideration of the importance of expectations in influencing perception also indicates that the widespread belief in the prevalence of "wishful thinking" may be incorrect, or at least may be based on inadequate data. The psychological literature on the interaction between affect and perception is immense and cannot be treated here, but it should be noted that phenomena that at first were considered strong evidence for the impact of affect on perception often can be better treated as demonstrating the influence of expectations.[3] Thus, in international relations, cases like the United States' misestimation of the political climate in Cuba in April 1961, which may seem at first glance to have been instances of wishful thinking, may instead be more adequately explained by the theories held by the decision-makers (e.g., Communist governments are unpopular). Of course, desires may have an impact on perception by influencing expectations, but since so many other factors affect expectations, the net influence of desires may not be great.

There is evidence from both psychology[4] and international relations that when expectations and desires clash, expectations seem to be more important. The United States would like to believe that North Vietnam is about to negotiate or that the USSR is ready to give up what the United States believes is its goal of world domination, but ambiguous evidence is seen to confirm the opposite conclusion, which conforms to the United States' expectations. Actors are apt to be especially sensitive to evidence of grave danger if they think they can take action to protect themselves against the menace once it has been detected.

Safeguards

Can anything then be said to scholars and decision-makers other than "Avoid being either too open or too closed, but be especially aware of the latter danger"? Although decision-makers will always be faced with ambiguous and confusing evidence and will be forced to make inferences about others which will often be inaccurate, a number of safeguards may be suggested which could enable them to minimize their errors. First, and most obvious, decision-makers should be aware that they do not make "unbiased" interpretations of each new bit of incoming information, but rather are inevitably heavily influenced by the theories they expect to be verified. They should know that what may appear to them as a self-evident and unambiguous inference often seems so only because of their preexisting beliefs. To someone with a different theory the same data may appear to be unimportant or to support another explanation. Thus many events provide less independent support for the decision-makers' images than they may at first realize. Knowledge of this should lead decision-makers to examine more closely evidence that others believe contradicts their views.

Second, decision-makers should see if their attitudes contain consistent or supporting beliefs that are not logically linked. These may be examples of true psycho-logic. While it is not logically surprising nor is it evidence of psychological pressures to find that people who believe that Russia is aggressive are very suspicious of any Soviet move, other kinds of consistency are more suspect. For example, most people who feel that it is important for the United States to win the war in Vietnam also feel that a meaningful victory is possible. And most people who feel defeat would neither endanger U.S. national security nor be costly in terms of other values also feel that we cannot win. Although there are important logical linkages between the two parts of each of these views (especially through theories of guerrilla warfare), they do not seem strong enough to explain the degree to which the opinions are correlated. Similarly, in Finland in the winter of 1939, those who felt that grave consequences would follow Finnish agreement to give Russia a military base also believed that the Soviets would withdraw their demand if Finland stood firm. And those who felt that concessions would not lead to loss of major values also believed that Russia would fight if need be.[5] In this country, those who favored a nuclear test ban tended to argue that fallout was very harmful, that only limited improvements in technology would flow from further testing, and that a test ban would increase

the chances for peace and security. Those who opposed the test ban were apt to disagree on all three points. This does not mean, of course, that the people holding such sets of supporting views were necessarily wrong in any one element. The Finns who wanted to make concessions to the USSR were probably correct in both parts of their argument. But decision-makers should be suspicious if they hold a position in which elements that are not logically connected support the same conclusion. This condition is psychologically comfortable and makes decisions easier to reach (since competing values do not have to be balanced off against each other). The chances are thus considerable that at least part of the reason why a person holds some of these views is related to psychology and not to the substance of the evidence.

Decision-makers should also be aware that actors who suddenly find themselves having an important shared interest with other actors have a tendency to overestimate the degree of common interest involved. This tendency is especially strong for those actors (e.g., the United States, at least before 1950) whose beliefs about international relations and morality imply that they can cooperate only with "good" states and that with those states there will be no major conflicts. On the other hand, states that have either a tradition of limited cooperation with others (e.g., Britain) or a strongly held theory that differentiates occasional from permanent allies[6] (e.g., the Soviet Union) find it easier to resist this tendency and need not devote special efforts to combating its danger.

A third safeguard for decision-makers would be to make their assumptions, beliefs, and the predictions that follow from them as explicit as possible. An actor should try to determine, before events occur, what evidence would count for and against his theories. By knowing what to expect he would know what to be surprised by, and surprise could indicate to that actor that his beliefs needed reevaluation.[7]

A fourth safeguard is more complex. The decision-maker should try to prevent individuals and organizations from letting their main task, political future, and identity become tied to specific theories and images of other actors.[8] If this occurs, subgoals originally sought for their contribution to higher ends will take on value of their own, and information indicating possible alternative routes to the original goals will not be carefully considered. For example, the U.S. Forest Service was unable to carry out its original purpose as effectively when it began to see its distinctive competence not in promoting the best use of lands and forests but rather in preventing all types of forest fires.[9]

Organizations that claim to be unbiased may not realize the extent to which their definition of their role has become involved with certain beliefs about the world. Allen Dulles is a victim of this lack of understanding when he says, "I grant that we are all creatures of prejudice, including CIA officials, but by entrusting intelligence coordination to our central intelligence service, which is excluded from policy-making and is married to no particular military hardware, we can avoid, to the greatest possible extent, the bending of facts obtained through intelligence to suit a particular occupational viewpoint."[10] This statement overlooks the fact that the CIA has developed a certain view of international relations and of the cold war which maximizes the importance of its information-gathering, espionage, and subversive activities. Since the CIA would lose its unique place in the government if it were decided that the "back alleys" of world politics were no longer vital to U.S. security, it is not surprising that the organization interprets information in a way that stresses the continued need for its techniques.

Fifth, decision-makers should realize the validity and implications of Roberta Wohlstetter's argument that "a willingness to play with material from different angles and in the context of unpopular as well as popular hypotheses is an essential ingredient of a good detective, whether the end is the solution of a crime or an intelligence estimate."[11] However, it is often difficult, psychologically and politically, for any one person to do this. Since a decision-maker usually cannot get "unbiased" treatments of data, he should instead seek to structure conflicting biases into the decision-making process. The decision-maker, in other words, should have devil's advocates around. Just as, as Neustadt points out,[12] the decision-maker will want to create conflicts among his subordinates in order to make appropriate choices, so he will also want to ensure that incoming information is examined from many different perspectives with many different hypotheses in mind. To some extent this kind of examination will be done automatically through the divergence of goals, training, experience, and information that exists in any large organization. But in many cases this divergence will not be sufficient. The views of those analyzing the data will still be too homogeneous, and the decision-maker will have to go out of his way not only to cultivate but to create differing viewpoints.

While all that would be needed would be to have some people examining the data trying to validate unpopular hypotheses, it would probably be more effective if they actually believed and had a stake in the views they were trying to support. If in 1941 someone had had the task of proving the view that Japan would attack Pearl Harbor, the government might have been less surprised by the attack. And only a person who was out to show that Russia would take objectively great risks would have been apt to note that several ships with especially large hatches going to Cuba were riding high in the water, indicating the presence of a bulky but light cargo that was not likely to be anything other than strategic missiles. And many people who doubt the wisdom of the administration's Vietnam policy would be somewhat reassured if there were people in the government who searched the statements and actions of both sides in an effort to prove that North Vietnam was willing to negotiate and that the official interpretation of such moves as the Communist activities during the Têt truce of 1967 was incorrect.

Of course all these safeguards involve costs. They would divert resources from other tasks and would increase internal dissension. Determining whether these costs would be worth the gains would depend on a detailed analysis of how the suggested safeguards might be implemented. Even if they were adopted by a government, of course, they would not eliminate the chance of misperception. However, the safeguards would make it more likely that national decision-makers would make conscious choices about the way data were interpreted rather than merely assuming that they can be seen in only one way and can mean only one thing. Statesmen would thus be reminded of alternative images of others just as they are constantly reminded of alternative policies.

These safeguards are partly based on Hypothesis 3: actors can more easily assimilate into their established image of another actor information contradicting that image if the information is transmitted and considered bit by bit than if it comes all at once. In the former case, each piece of discrepant data can be coped with as it arrives and each of the conflicts with the prevailing view will be small enough to go unnoticed, to be dismissed as unimportant, or to necessitate at most a slight modification of the image (e.g., addition of exceptions to the rule). When the information arrives in a block, the contradiction between it and the prevailing view is apt to be much clearer and the probability of major cognitive reorganization will be higher.

Sources of Concepts

An actor's perceptual thresholds—and thus the images that ambiguous information is apt to produce—are influenced by what he has experienced and learned about.[13] If one actor is to perceive that another fits in a given category he must first have, or develop, a concept for that category. We can usefully distinguish three levels at which a concept can be present or absent. First, the concept can be completely missing. The actor's cognitive structure may not include anything corresponding to the phenomenon he is encountering. This situation can occur not only in science fiction, but also in a world of rapid change or in the meeting of two dissimilar systems. Thus China's image of the Western world was extremely inaccurate in the mid-nineteenth century, her learning was very slow, and her responses were woefully inadequate. The West was spared a similar struggle only because it had the power to reshape the system it encountered. Once the actor clearly sees one instance of the new phenomenon, he is apt to recognize it much more quickly in the future.[14] Second, the actor can know about a concept but not believe that it reflects an actual phenomenon. Thus Communist and Western decision-makers are each aware of the other's explanation of how his system functions, but do not think that the concept corresponds to reality. Communist elites, furthermore, deny that anything *could* correspond to the democracies' description of themselves. Third, the actor may hold a concept, but not believe that another actor fills it at the present moment. Thus the British and French statesmen of the 1930's held a concept of states with unlimited ambitions. They realized that Napoleons were possible, but they did not think Hitler belonged in that category. Hypothesis 4 distinguishes these three cases: misperception is most difficult to correct in the case of a missing concept and least difficult to correct in the case of a recognized but presumably unfilled concept. All other things being equal (e.g., the degree to which the concept is central to the actor's cognitive structure), the first case requires more cognitive reorganization than does the second, and the second requires more reorganization than the third.

However, this hypothesis does not mean that learning will necessarily be slowest in the first case, for if the phenomena are totally new the actor may make such grossly inappropriate responses that he will quickly acquire information clearly indicating that he is faced with something he does not understand. And the sooner the actor realizes that things are not—or may not be—what they seem, the sooner he is apt to correct his image.[15]

Three main sources contribute to decision-makers' concepts of international relations and of other states and influence the level of their perceptual thresholds for various phenomena. First, an actor's beliefs about his own domestic political system are apt to be important. In some cases, like that of the USSR, the decision-makers' concepts are tied to an ideology that explicitly provides a frame of reference for viewing foreign affairs. Even where this is not the case, experience with his own system will partly determine what the actor is familiar with and what he is apt to perceive in others. Louis Hartz claims, "It is the absence of the experience of social revolution which is at the heart of the whole American dilemma. . . . In a whole series of specific ways it enters into our difficulty of communication with the rest of the world. We find it difficult to understand Europe's 'social question'. . . . We are not familiar with the deeper social struggles of Asia and hence tend to interpret even reactionary regimes as 'democratic.'"[16] Similarly, George Kennan argues that in World War I the Allied powers, and especially America, could not understand the bitterness and violence of others' internal conflicts: ". . . The inability of the Allied statesmen to picture to themselves the passions of the Russian civil war [was partly caused by the fact that] we represent . . . a society in which the manifestations of evil have been carefully buried and sublimated in the social behavior of people, as in their very consciousness. For this reason, probably, despite our widely traveled and outwardly cosmopolitan lives, the mainsprings of political behavior in such a country as Russia tend to remain concealed from our vision."[17]

Second, concepts will be supplied by the actor's previous experiences. An experiment from another field illustrates this. Dearborn and Simon presented business executives from various divisions

(e.g., sales, accounting, production) with the same hypothetical data and asked them for an analysis and recommendations from the standpoint of what would be best for the company as a whole. The executives' views heavily reflected their departmental perspectives.[18] William W. Kaufmann shows how the perceptions of Ambassador Joseph Kennedy were affected by his past: "As befitted a former chairman of the Securities Exchange and Maritime Commissions, his primary interest lay in economic matters. . . . The revolutionary character of the Nazi regime was not a phenomenon that he could easily grasp. . . . It was far simpler, and more in accord with his own premises, to explain German aggressiveness in economic terms. The Third Reich was dissatisfied, authoritarian, and expansive largely because her economy was unsound."[19] Similarly it has been argued that Chamberlain was slow to recognize Hitler's intentions partly because of the limiting nature of his personal background and business experiences. The impact of training and experience seems to be demonstrated when the background of the appeasers is compared to that of their opponents. One difference stands out: "A substantially higher percentage of the anti-appeasers (irrespective of class origins) had the kind of knowledge which comes from close acquaintance, mainly professional, with foreign affairs."[20] Since members of the diplomatic corps are responsible for meeting threats to the nation's security before these grow to major proportions and since they have learned about cases in which aggressive states were not recognized as such until very late, they may be prone to interpret ambiguous data as showing that others are aggressive. It should be stressed that we cannot say that the professionals of the 1930s were more apt to make accurate judgments of other states. Rather, they may have been more sensitive to the chance that others were aggressive. They would then rarely take an aggressor for a status-quo power, but would more often make the opposite error. Thus in the years before World War I the permanent officials in the British Foreign Office overestimated German aggressiveness.[21]

A parallel demonstration in psychology of the impact of training on perception is presented by an experiment in which ambiguous pictures were shown to both advanced and beginning police-administration students. The advanced group perceived more violence in the pictures than did the beginners. The probable explanation is that "the law enforcer may come to accept crime as a familiar personal experience, one which he himself is not surprised to encounter. The acceptance of crime as a familiar experience in turn increases the ability or readiness to perceive violence where clues to it are potentially available."[22] This experiment lends weight to the view that the British diplomats' sensitivity to aggressive states was not totally a product of personnel selection procedures.

A third source of concepts, which frequently will be the most directly relevant to a decision-maker's perception of international relations, is international history. As Henry Kissinger points out, one reason why statesmen were so slow to recognize the threat posed by Napoleon was that previous events had accustomed them only to actors who wanted to modify the existing system, not overthrow it.[23] The other side of the coin is even more striking: historical traumas can heavily influence future perceptions. They can either establish a state's image of the other state involved or can be used as analogies. An example of the former case is provided by the fact that for at least ten years after the Franco-Prussian War most of Europe's statesmen felt that Bismarck had aggressive plans when in fact his main goal was to protect the status quo. Of course the evidence was ambiguous. The post-1871 Bismarckian maneuvers, which were designed to keep peace, looked not unlike the pre-1871 maneuvers designed to set the stage for war. But that the post-1871 maneuvers were seen as indicating aggressive plans is largely attributable to the impact of Bismarck's earlier actions on the statesmen's image of him.

A state's previous unfortunate experience with a type of danger can sensitize it to other examples of that danger. While this sensitivity may lead the state to avoid the mistake it committed in the past, it may also lead it mistakenly to believe that the present situation is like the past one. Santayana's maxim could be turned around: "Those who remember the past are condemned to make the opposite mistakes." As Paul Kecskemeti shows, both defenders and critics of the unconditional surrender plan of the Second World War thought in terms of the conditions of World War I.[24] Annette Baker Fox found that the Scandinavian countries' neutrality policies in World War II were strongly influenced by their experiences in the previous war, even though vital aspects of the two situations were different. Thus "Norway's success [during the First World War] in remaining non-belligerent though pro-Allied gave the Norwegians confidence that their country could again stay out of war."[25] And the lesson drawn from the unfortunate results of this policy was an important factor in Norway's decision to join NATO.

The application of the Munich analogy to various contemporary events has been much commented on, and I do not wish to argue the substantive points at stake. But it seems clear that the probabilities that any state is facing an aggressor who has to be met by force are not altered by the career of Hitler and the history of the 1930s. Similarly the probability of an aggressor's announcing his plans is not increased (if anything, it is decreased) by the fact that Hitler wrote *Mein Kampf.* Yet decision-makers are more sensitive to these possibilities, and thus more apt to perceive ambiguous evidence as indicating they apply to a given case, than they would have been had there been no Nazi Germany.

Historical analogies often precede, rather than follow, a careful analysis of a situation (e.g., Truman's initial reaction to the news of the invasion of South Korea was to think of the Japanese invasion of Manchuria). Noting this precedence, however, does not show us which of many analogies will come to a decision-maker's mind. Truman could have thought of nineteenth-century European wars that were of no interest to the United States. Several factors having nothing to do with the event under consideration influence what analogies a decision-maker is apt to make. One factor is the number of cases similar to the analogy with which the decision-maker is familiar. Another is the importance of the past event to the political system of which the decision-maker is a part. The more times such an event occurred and the greater its consequences were, the more a decision-maker will be sensitive to the particular danger involved and the more he will be apt to see ambiguous stimuli as indicating another instance of this kind of event. A third factor is the degree of the decision-maker's personal involvement in the past case—in time, energy, ego, and position. The last-mentioned variable will affect not only the event's impact on the decision-maker's cognitive structure, but also the way he perceives the event and the lesson he draws. Someone who was involved in getting troops into South Korea after the attack will remember the Korean War differently from someone who was involved in considering the possible use of nuclear weapons or in deciding what messages should be sent to the Chinese. Greater personal involvement will usually give the event greater impact, especially if the decision-maker's own views were validated by the event. One need not accept a total application of learning theory to nations to believe that "nothing fails like success."[26] It also seems likely that if many critics argued at the time that the decision-maker was wrong, he will be even more apt to see other situations in terms of the original event. For example, because Anthony Eden left the government on account of his views and was later shown to have been correct, he probably was more apt to see as Hitlers other leaders with whom he had conflicts (e.g., Nasser). A fourth factor is the degree to which the analogy is compatible with the rest of his belief system. A fifth is the absence of alternative concepts and analogies. Individuals and states vary in the amount of direct or indirect political experience they have had which can provide different ways of interpreting data. Decision-makers who are aware of multiple possibilities of states' intentions may be less likely to seize on an analogy prematurely. The perception of citizens of nations like the United States which have relatively little history of international politics may be more apt to be heavily influenced by the few major international events that have been important to their country.

The first three factors indicate that an event is more apt to shape present perceptions if it occurred in the recent rather than the remote past. If it occurred recently, the statesman will then know about it at first hand even if he was not involved in the making of policy at the time. Thus if generals are prepared to fight the last war, diplomats may be prepared to avoid the last war. Part of the Anglo-French reaction to Hitler can be explained by the prevailing beliefs that the First World War was to a large extent caused by misunderstandings and could have been avoided by farsighted and nonbelligerent diplomacy. And part of the Western perception of Russia and China can be explained by the view that appeasement was an inappropriate response to Hitler.[27]

The Evoked Set

The way people perceive data is influenced not only by their cognitive structure and theories about other actors but also by what they are concerned with at the time they receive the information. Information is evaluated in light of the small part of the person's memory that is presently active—the "evoked set." My perceptions of the dark streets I pass walking home from the movies will be different if the film I saw had dealt with spies than if it had been a comedy. If I am working on aiding a country's education system and I hear someone talk about the need for economic development in that state, I am apt to think he is concerned with education, whereas if I had been working on, say, trying to achieve political stability in that country, I would have placed his remarks in that framework.[28]

Thus Hypothesis 5 states that when messages are sent from a different background of concerns and information than is possessed by the receiver, misunderstanding is likely. Person A and person B will read the same message quite differently if A has seen several related messages that B does not know about. This difference will be compounded if, as is frequently the case, A and B each assume that the other has the same background he does. This means that misperception can occur even when deception is neither intended nor expected. Thus Roberta Wohlstetter found not only that different parts of the United States government had different perceptions of data about Japan's intentions and messages partly because they saw the incoming information in very different contexts, but also that officers in the field misunderstood warnings from Washington: "Washington advised General Short [in Pearl Harbor] on November 27 to expect 'hostile action' at any moment, by which it meant 'attack on American possessions from without,' but General Short understood this phrase to mean 'sabotage.'"[29] Washington did not realize the extent to which Pearl Harbor considered the danger of sabotage to be primary, and furthermore it incorrectly believed that General Short had received the intercepts of the secret Japanese diplomatic messages available in Washington which indicated that surprise attack was a distinct possibility. Another implication of this hypothesis is that if important information is known to only part of the government of state A and part of the government of state B, international messages may be misunderstood by those parts of the receiver's government that do not match, in the information they have, the part of the sender's government that dispatched the message.[30]

Two additional hypotheses can be drawn from the problems of those sending messages. Hypothesis 6 states that when people spend a great deal of time drawing up a plan or making a decision, they tend to think that the message about it they wish to convey will be clear to the receiver.[31] Since they are aware of what is to them the important pattern in their actions, they often feel that the pattern will be equally obvious to others, and they overlook the degree to which the message is apparent to them only because they know what to look for. Those who have not participated in the endless meetings may not understand what information the sender is trying to convey. George Quester has shown how the German and, to a lesser extent, the British desire to maintain target limits on bombing in the first eighteen months of World War II was undermined partly by the fact that each side knew the limits it was seeking and its own reasons for any apparent "exceptions" (e.g., the German attack on Rotterdam) and incorrectly felt that these limits and reasons were equally clear to the other side.[32]

Hypothesis 7 holds that actors often do not realize that actions intended to project a given image may not have the desired effect because the actions themselves do not turn out as planned. Thus even without appreciable impact of different cognitive structures and backgrounds, an action may convey an unwanted message. For example, a country's representatives may not follow instructions and so may give others impressions contrary to those the home government wished to convey. The efforts of Washington and Berlin to settle their dispute over Samoa in the late 1880s were complicated by the provocative behavior of their agents on the spot. These agents not only increased the intensity of the local conflict, but led the decision-makers to become more suspicious of the other state because they tended to assume that their agents were obeying instructions and that the actions of the other side represented official policy. In such cases both sides will believe that the other is reading hostility into a policy of theirs which is friendly. Similarly, Quester's study shows that the attempt to limit bombing referred to above failed partly because neither side was able to bomb as accurately as it thought it could and thus did not realize the physical effects of its actions.[33]

Further Hypotheses from the Perspective of the Perceiver

From the perspective of the perceiver several other hypotheses seem to hold. Hypothesis 8 is that there is an overall tendency for decision-makers to see other states as more hostile than they are.[34] There seem to be more cases of statesmen incorrectly believing others are planning major acts against their interest than of statesmen being lulled by a potential aggressor. There are many reasons for this which are too complex to be treated here (e.g., some parts of the bureaucracy feel it is their responsibility to be suspicious of all other states; decision-makers often feel they are "playing it safe" to believe and act as though the other state were hostile in questionable cases; and often, when people do not feel they are a threat to others, they find it difficult to believe that others may see them as a threat). It should be noted, however, that decision-makers whose perceptions are described by this hypothesis would not necessarily further their own values by trying to correct for this tendency. The values of possible outcomes as well as their probabilities must be considered, and it may be that the probability of an unnecessary arms-tension cycle arising out of misperceptions, multiplied by the costs of such a cycle, may seem less to decision-makers than the probability of incorrectly believing another state is friendly, multiplied by the costs of this eventuality.

Hypothesis 9 states that actors tend to see the behavior of others as more centralized, disciplined, and coordinated than it is. This hypothesis holds true in related ways. Frequently, too many complex events are squeezed into a perceived pattern. Actors are hesitant to admit or even see that particular incidents cannot be explained by their theories.[35] Those events not caused by factors that are important parts of the perceiver's image are often seen as though they were. Further, actors see others as more internally united than they in fact are and generally overestimate the degree to which others are following a coherent policy. The degree to which the other side's policies are the product of internal bargaining,[36] internal misunderstandings, or subordinates' not following instructions is underestimated. This is the case partly because actors tend to be unfamiliar with the details of another state's policy-making processes. Seeing only the finished product, they find it simpler to try to construct a rational explanation for the policies, even though they know that such an analysis could not explain their own policies.[37]

Familiarity also accounts for Hypothesis 10: because a state gets most of its information about the other state's policies from the other's foreign office, it tends to take the foreign office's position for the stand of the other government as a whole. In many cases this perception will be an accurate one, but when the other government is divided or when the other foreign office is acting without specific authorization, misperception may result. For example, part of the reason why in 1918 Allied governments incorrectly thought "that the Japanese were preparing to take action [in Siberia], if need be, with agreement with the British and French alone, disregarding the absence of American consent,"[38] was that Allied ambassadors had talked mostly with Foreign Minister Motono, who was among the minority of the Japanese favoring this policy. Similarly, America's NATO allies may have gained an inaccurate picture of the degree to which the American government was committed to the MLF because they had greatest contact with parts of the government that strongly favored the MLF. And states that tried to get information about Nazi foreign policy from German diplomats were often misled because these officials were generally ignorant of or out of sympathy with Hitler's plans. The Germans and the Japanese sometimes purposely misinformed their own ambassadors in order to deceive their enemies more effectively.

Hypothesis 11 states that actors tend to overestimate the degree to which others are acting in response to what they themselves do when the others behave in accordance with the actor's desires; but when the behavior of the other is undesired, it is usually seen as derived from internal forces. If the *effect* of another's action is to injure or threaten the first side, the first side is apt to believe that such was the other's *purpose*. An example of the first part of the hypothesis is provided by Kennan's account of the activities of official and unofficial American representatives who protested to the new Bolshevik government against several of its actions. When the Soviets changed their position, these representatives felt it was largely because of their influence.[39] This sort of interpretation can be explained not only by the fact that it is gratifying to the individual making it, but also, taking the other side of the coin mentioned in Hypothesis 9, by the fact that the actor is most familiar with his own input into the other's decision and has less knowledge of other influences. The second part of Hypothesis 11 is illustrated by the tendency of actors to believe that the hostile behavior of others is to be explained by the other side's motives and not by its reaction to the first side. Thus Chamberlain did not see that Hitler's behavior was related in part to his belief that the British were weak. More common is the failure to see that the other side is reacting out of fear of the first side, which can lead to self-fulfilling prophecies and spirals of misperception and hostility.

This difficulty is often compounded by an implication of Hypothesis 12: when actors have intentions that they do not try to conceal from others, they tend to assume that others accurately perceive these intentions. Only rarely do they believe that others may be reacting to a much less favorable image of themselves than they think they are projecting.[40]

For state A to understand how state B perceives A's policy is often difficult because such understanding may involve a conflict with A's image of itself. Raymond Sontag argues that Anglo-German relations before World War I deteriorated partly because "the British did not like to think of themselves as selfish, or unwilling to tolerate 'legitimate' German expansion. The Germans did not like to think of themselves as aggressive, or unwilling to recognize 'legitimate' British vested interest."[41]

Hypothesis 13 suggests that if it is hard for an actor to believe that the other can see him as a menace, it is often even harder for him to see that issues important to him are not important to others. While he may know that another actor is on an opposing team, it may be more difficult for him to realize that the other is playing an entirely different game. This is especially true when the game he is playing seems vital to him.[42]

The final hypothesis, Hypothesis 14, is as follows: actors tend to overlook the fact that evidence consistent with their theories may also be consistent with other views. When choosing between two theories we have to pay attention only to data that cannot be accounted for by one of the theories. But it is common to find people claiming as proof of their theories data that could also support alternative views. This phenomenon is related to the point made earlier that any single bit of information can be interpreted only within a framework of hypotheses and theories. And while it is true that "we may without a vicious circularity accept some datum as a fact because it conforms to the very law for which it counts as another confirming instance, and reject an allegation of fact because it is already excluded by law,"[43] we should be careful lest we forget that a piece of information seems in many cases to confirm a certain hypothesis only because we already believe that hypothesis to be correct and that the information can with as much validity support a different hypothesis. For example, one of the reasons why the German attack on Norway took both that country and England by surprise, even though they had detected German ships moving toward Norway, was that they expected not an attack but an attempt by the Germans to break through the British blockade and reach the Atlantic. The initial course of the ships was consistent with either plan, but the British and Norwegians took this course to mean that their predictions were being borne out.[44] This is not to imply, that the interpretation made was foolish, but only that the decision-makers should have been aware that the evidence was also consistent with an invasion and should have had a bit less confidence in their views.

The longer the ships would have to travel the same route whether they were going to one or another of two destinations, the more information would be needed to determine their plans. Taken as a metaphor, this incident applies generally to the treatment of evidence. Thus as long as Hitler made demands for control only of ethnically German areas, his actions could be explained either by the hypothesis that he had unlimited ambitions or by the hypothesis that he wanted to unite all the Germans. But actions against non-Germans (e.g., the takeover of Czechoslovakia in March 1938) could not be accounted for by the latter hypothesis. And it was this action that convinced the appeasers that Hitler had to be stopped. It is interesting to speculate on what the British reaction would have been had Hitler left Czechoslovakia alone for a while and instead made demands on Poland similar to those he eventually made in the summer of 1939. The two paths would then still not have diverged, and further misperception could have occurred.

NOTES

1. Floyd Allport, *Theories of Perception and the Concept of Structure* (New York 1955), 382; Ole Holsti, "Cognitive Dynamics and Images of the Enemy," in David Finlay, Ole Holsti, and Richard Fagen, *Enemies in Politics* (Chicago 1967), 70.

2. For a use of this concept in political communication, see Roberta Wohlstetter, *Pearl Harbor* (Stanford 1962).

3. See, for example, Donald Campbell, "Systematic Error on the Part of Human Links in Communications Systems," *Information and Control*, 1 (1958), 346–50; and Leo Postman, "The Experimental Analysis of Motivational Factors in Perception," in Judson S. Brown, ed., *Current Theory and Research in Motivation* (Lincoln, Neb., 1953), 59–108.

4. Dale Wyatt and Donald Campbell, "A Study of Interviewer Bias as Related to Interviewer's Expectations and Own Opinions," *International Journal of Opinion and Attitude Research*, IV (Spring 1950), 77–83.

5. Max Jacobson, *The Diplomacy of the Winter War* (Cambridge, MA, 1961), 136–39.

6. Raymond Aron, *Peace and War* (Garden City 1966), 29.

7. [Thomas] Kuhn, *The Structure of Scientific Revolution* [(Chicago 1964)], 65.

8. See Philip Selznick, *Leadership in Administration* (Evanston 1957).

9. Ashley Schiff, *Fire and Water: Scientific Heresy in the Forest Service* (Cambridge, MA, 1962).

10. *The Craft of Intelligence* (New York 1963), 53.

11. P. 302. See Beveridge, 93, for a discussion of the idea that the scientist should keep in mind as many hypotheses as possible when conducting and analyzing experiments.

12. *Presidential Power* (New York 1960).

13. Most psychologists argue that this influence also holds for perception of shapes. For data showing that people in different societies differ in respect to their predisposition to experience certain optical illusions and for a convincing argument that this difference can be explained by the societies' different physical environments, which have led their people to develop different patterns of drawing inferences from ambiguous visual cues, see Marshall Segall, Donald Campbell, and Melville Herskovits, *The Influence of Culture on Visual Perceptions* (Indianapolis 1966).

14. Thus when Bruner and Postman's subjects first were presented with incongruous playing cards (i.e., cards in which symbols and colors of the suits were not matching, producing red spades or black diamonds), long exposure times were necessary for correct identification. But once a subject correctly perceived the card and added this type of card to his repertoire of categories, he was able to identify other incongruous cards much more quickly. For an analogous example—in this case, changes in the analysis of aerial reconnaissance photographs of an enemy's secret weapons-testing facilities produced by the belief that a previously unknown object may he present—see David Irving, *The Mare's Nest* (Boston 1964), 66–67, 274–75.

15. [Jerome Bruner and Leo Postman, "On the Perceptions of Incongruity: A Paradigm," in Jerome Bruner and David Krech, eds., *Perception and Personality* (Durham, NC, 1949)].

16. *The Liberal Tradition in America* (New York 1955), 306.

17. *Russia and the West Under Lenin and Stalin* (New York 1962), 142–43.

18. DeWitt Dearborn and Herbert Simon, "Selective Perception: A Note on the Departmental Identification of Executives," *Sociometry*, XXI (June 1958), 140–44.

19. "Two American Ambassadors: Bullitt and Kennedy," in [Gordon Craig and Felix Gilbert, eds., *The Diplomats*, Vol. 3 (New York 1963)], 358–59.

20. [Donald Lammers, *Explaining Munich* (Stanford 1966)], 15.

21. George Monger, *The End of Isolation* (London 1963).

22. Hans Toch and Richard Schulte, "Readiness to Perceive Violence as a Result of Police Training," *British Journal of Psychology*, LII (November 1961), 392 (original italics omitted). It should be stressed that one cannot say whether or not the advanced police students perceived the pictures "accurately." The point is that their training predisposed them to see violence in ambiguous situations. * * * For an experiment showing that training can lead people to "recognize" an expected stimulus even when that stimulus is in fact not shown, see Israel Goldiamond and William F. Hawkins, "Vexierversuch: The Log Relationship Between Word-Frequency and Recognition Obtained in the Absence of Stimulus Words," *Journal of Experimental Psychology*, LVI (December 1958), 457–63.

23. *A World Restored* (New York 1964), 2–3.

24. *Strategic Surrender* (New York 1964), 215–41.

25. *The Power of Small States* (Chicago 1959), 81.

26. William Inge, *Outspoken Essays*, First Series (London 1923), 88.

27. Of course, analogies themselves are not "unmoved movers." The interpretation of past events is not automatic and is informed by general views of international relations and complex judgments. And just as beliefs about the past influence the present, views about the present influence interpretations of history. It is difficult to determine the degree to which the United States' interpretation of the reasons it went to war in 1917 influenced American foreign policy in the 1920s and 1930s and how much the isolationism of that period influenced the histories of the war.

28. For some psychological experiments on this subject, see Jerome Bruner and A. Leigh Minturn, "Perceptual Identification and Perceptual Organization," *Journal of General Psychology*, LIII (July 1955), 22–28; Seymour Feshbach and Robert Singer, "The Effects of Fear Arousal and Suppression of Fear Upon Social Perception," *Journal of Abnormal and Social Psychology*, LV (November 1957), 283–88; and Elsa Sippoal, "A Group Study of Some Effects of Preparatory Sets," *Psychology Monographs*, XLVI, No. 210 (1935), 27–28. For a general discussion of the importance of the perceiver's evoked set, see Postman, 87.

29. Pp. 73–74.

30. For example, Roger Hilsman points out, "Those who knew of the peripheral reconnaissance flights that probed Soviet air defenses during the Eisenhower administration and the U-2 flights over the Soviet Union itself . . . were better able to understand some of the things the Soviets were saying and doing than people who did not know of these activities" (*To Move a Nation* [Garden City 1967], 66). But it is also possible that those who knew about the U-2 flights at times misinterpreted Soviet messages by incorrectly believing that the sender was influenced by, or at least knew of, these flights.

31. I am grateful to Thomas Schelling for discussion on this point.

32. *Deterrence Before Hiroshima* (New York 1966), 105–22.

33. Ibid.

34. For a slightly different formulation of this view, see [Ole Holsti, "Cognitive Dynamics and Images of the Enemy," in David Finlay, Ole Holsti, and Richard Fagen, *Enemies in Politics* (Chicago 1967)], 27.

35. The Soviets consciously hold an extreme version of this view and seem to believe that nothing is accidental. See the discussion in Nathan Leites, *A Study of Bolshevism* (Glencoe 1953), 67–73.

36. A. W. Marshall criticizes Western explanations of Soviet military posture for failing to take this into account. See his "Problems of Estimating Military Power," a paper presented at the 1966 Annual Meeting of the American Political Science Association, 16.

37. It has also been noted that in labor-management disputes both sides may be apt to believe incorrectly that the other is controlled from above, either from the international union office or from the company's central headquarters (Robert Blake, Herbert Shepard, and Jane Mouton, *Managing Intergroup Conflict in Industry* [Houston 1964], 182). It has been further noted that both Democratic and Republican members of the House tend to see the other party as the one that is more disciplined and united (Charles Clapp, *The Congressman* [Washington 1963], 17–19).

38. George Kennan, *Russia Leaves the War* (New York 1967), 484.

39. Ibid., 404, 408, 500.

40. Herbert Butterfield notes that these assumptions can contribute to the spiral of "Hobbesian fear. . . . You yourself may vividly feel the terrible fear that you have of the other party, but you cannot enter into the other man's counter-fear, or even understand why he should be particularly nervous. For you know that you yourself mean him no harm, and that you want nothing from him save guarantees for your own safety; and it is never possible for you to realize or remember properly that since he cannot see the inside of your mind, he can never have the same assurance of your intentions that you have" (*History and Human Conflict* [London 1951], 20).

41. *European Diplomatic History 1871–1932* (New York 1933), 125. It takes great mental effort to realize that actions which seem only the natural consequence of defending your vital interests can look to others as though you are refusing them any chance of increasing their influence. In rebutting the famous Crowe "balance of power" memorandum of 1907, which justified a policy of "containing" Germany on the grounds that she was a threat to British national security, Sanderson, a former permanent undersecretary in the Foreign Office, wrote, "It has sometimes seemed to me that to a foreigner reading our press the British Empire must appear in the light of some huge giant sprawling all over the globe, with gouty fingers and toes stretching in every direction, which cannot be approached without eliciting a scream" (quoted in Monger, 315). But few other Englishmen could be convinced that others might see them this way.

42. George Kennan makes clear that in 1918 this kind of difficulty was partly responsible for the inability of either the Allies or the new Bolshevik government to understand the motivations of the other

side: "There is . . . nothing in nature more egocentrical than the embattled democracy. . . . It . . . tends to attach to its own cause an absolute value which distorts its own vision of everything else. . . . It will readily be seen that people who have got themselves into this frame of mind have little understanding for the issues of any contest other than the one in which they are involved. The idea of people wasting time and substance on any *other* issue seems to them preposterous" (*Russia and the West*, 11–12).

43. [Abraham Kaplan, *The Conduct of Inquiry* (San Francisco 1964)], 89.

44. Johan Jorgen Hoist, "Surprise, Signals, and Reaction: The Attack on Norway," *Cooperation and Conflict*, No. 1 (1966), 34. The Germans made a similar mistake in November 1942 when they interpreted the presence of an Allied convoy in the Mediterranean as confirming their belief that Malta would be resupplied. They thus were taken by surprise when landings took place in North Africa (William Langer, *Our Vichy Gamble* [New York 1966], 365).

Keren Yarhi-Milo

IN THE EYE OF THE BEHOLDER
How Leaders and Intelligence Communities Assess the Intentions of Adversaries

How do policymakers infer the long-term political intentions of their states' adversaries? This question has important theoretical, historical, and political significance. If British decisionmakers had understood the scope of Nazi Germany's intentions for Europe during the 1930s, the twentieth century might have looked very different. More recently, a Brookings report observes that "[t]he issue of mutual distrust of long-term intentions . . . has become a central concern in U.S.–China relations."[1] Statements by U.S. and Chinese officials confirm this suspicion. U.S. Ambassador to China Gary Locke noted "a concern, a question mark, by people all around the world and governments all around the world as to what China's intentions are."[2] Chinese officials, similarly, have indicated that Beijing regards recent U.S. policies as a "sophisticated ploy to frustrate China's growth."[3]

Current assessments of the threat posed by a rising China—or for that matter, a possibly nuclear-armed Iran, or a resurgent Russia—depend on which indicators observers use to derive predictions about a potential adversary's intentions. Surprisingly, however, little scholarship exists to identify which indicators leaders and the state's intelligence apparatus tasked with estimating threats use to assess intentions. For example, disputes among American analysts over the military capabilities of the Soviet Union dominated

debates on the Soviet threat throughout the Cold War, yet there has been little examination of the extent to which such calculations shaped or reflected U.S. political decisionmakers' assessments of Soviet intentions. Analyzing how signals are filtered and interpreted by the state's decisionmakers and its intelligence apparatus can lead to better understanding of the types of signals that tend to prompt changes in relations with adversaries, as well as help to develop useful advice for policymakers on how to deter or reassure an adversary more effectively.

In this article, I compare two prominent rationalist approaches in international relations theory about how observers can be expected to infer adversaries' political intentions, with a third approach that I develop and term the "selective attention thesis." First, the behavior thesis asserts that observers refer to certain noncapability-based actions—such as the adversary's decision to withdraw from a foreign military intervention or join binding international organizations—to draw conclusions regarding that adversary's intentions. This approach focuses on the role of costly information in influencing state behavior. Actions are considered costly if they require the state to expend significant, unrecoverable resources or if they severely constrain its future decisionmaking. The basic intuition behind this approach is that an action that costs nothing could equally be taken by actors with benign or with malign intentions, and thus it provides no credible information about

From *International Security* 38, No. 1 (Summer 2013): 7–51. Some of the author's notes have been omitted.

the actor's likely plans.[4] Observers should therefore ignore "cheap talk."[5] Second, the capabilities thesis, drawing on insights from realism as well as costly signaling, asserts that states should consider an adversary's military capabilities in assessing its intentions. Of particular importance would be significant changes in armament policies, such as a unilateral reduction in military capabilities. Such changes reveal credible information about an adversary's ability to engage in warfare and thus its intention to do so.[6]

Drawing on insights from psychology, neuroscience, and organizational theory, I develop a third approach, the selective attention thesis. This thesis posits that individual perceptual biases and organizational interests and practices influence which types of indicators observers regard as credible signals of the adversary's intentions. Thus, the thesis predicts differences between a state's political leaders and its intelligence community in their selection of which signals to focus on and how to interpret those signals. In particular, decision-makers often base their interpretations on their own theories, expectations, and needs, sometimes ignoring costly signals and paying more attention to information that, though less costly, is more vivid (i.e., personalized and emotionally involving). The thesis also posits that organizational affiliations and roles matter: intelligence organizations predictably rely on different indicators than civilian decisionmakers do to determine an adversary's intentions. In intelligence organizations, the collection and analysis of data on the adversary's military inventory typically receive priority. Over time, intelligence organizations develop substantial knowledge of these material indicators that they then use to make predictions about an adversary's intentions.

To test the competing theses, I examined * * * U.S. assessments of Soviet intentions under the administration of President Jimmy Carter (a period when détente collapsed) [and] U.S. assessments of Soviet intentions in the years leading to the end of the Cold War during the second administration of President Ronald Reagan. * * * My findings are based on review of more than 30,000 archival documents and intelligence reports, as well as interviews with former decisionmakers and intelligence officials. The cases yield findings more consistent with the selective attention thesis than with either the behavior or capabilities thesis, as I explain in the conclusion.

Before proceeding, it is important to note what lies outside the scope of this study. First, I am concerned primarily with the perceptions of an adversary's long-term political intentions because these are most likely to affect a state's foreign policy and strategic choices. Second, I do not address whether observers correctly identified the intentions of their adversaries. Addressing this question would require that we first establish what the leaders of * * * the Soviet Union during the periods examined here genuinely believed their own intentions to be at the time. Third, elsewhere I address the effects of perceived intentions on the collective policies of the states.[7] Rather, the focus of this article is on the indicators that leaders and intelligence organizations tend to privilege or ignore in their assessments of an adversary's political intentions. * * *

Theories of Intentions and the Problem of Attention

The three theses I outline below provide different explanations as to how observers reach their assessments about the adversary's political intentions. The term "political intentions" refers to beliefs about the foreign policy plans of the adversary with regard to the status quo.[8] I divide assessments of political intentions into three simple categories: expansionist, opportunistic, or status quo.[9] Expansionist adversaries exhibit strong determination to expand their power and influence beyond their territorial boundaries. Opportunistic states desire a favorable change in the distribution of power with either a limited or an unlimited geographical scope, but do not actively seek change. They may have contingent plans to seize opportunities to achieve this objective, but they will not pursue their revisionist goals when the cost of doing so appears high.[10] Status quo powers want only to maintain their relative power position.

The Selective Attention Thesis

Information about intentions can be complex, ambiguous, and potentially deceptive, and thus requires much interpretive work. Cognitive, affective, and organizational practices impede individuals' ability to process this information. To distinguish between signals and noise, individuals use a variety of heuristic inference strategies.[11] These simplified models of reality, however, can have the unintended effect of focusing excessive attention on certain pieces of information and away from others. The selective attention thesis recognizes that individual decisionmakers and bureaucratic organizations, such as an intelligence community, process information differently. The thesis yields two hypotheses: the subjective credibility hypothesis explains the inference process of decisionmakers, and the organizational expertise hypothesis describes that of intelligence organizations.

THE SUBJECTIVE CREDIBILITY HYPOTHESIS

The subjective credibility hypothesis predicts that decisionmakers will not necessarily detect or interpret costly actions as informative signals.[12] This psychology-based theory posits that both the degree of credence given to evidence and the interpretation of evidence deemed credible will depend on a decisionmaker's expectations about the links between the adversary's behavior and its underlying characteristics; his or her own theories about

which signals are indicative of the adversary's type; and the vividness of the information.[13]

First, the attention paid to costly actions hinges on observers' expectations about the adversary.[14] Observers are likely to vary in their prior degree of distrust toward an adversary and the extent to which they believe its intentions are hostile. This variation in decisionmakers' beliefs and expectations affects their selection and reading of signals in predictable ways. Given cognitive assimilation mechanisms and the human tendency to try to maintain cognitive consistency, decisionmakers who already hold relatively more hawkish views about the adversary's intentions when they assume power are less likely to perceive and categorize even costly reassuring actions as credible signals of benign intent. They are likely to reason, for example, that the adversary's actions are intended to deceive observers into believing that it harbors no malign intentions. Or they may believe that the adversary's reassuring signals merely reflect its economic or domestic political interests, and thus should not be seen as signaling more benign foreign policy goals. In contrast, those with relatively less hawkish views of an adversary's intentions are more likely to interpret reassuring signals as conforming with their current beliefs and, therefore, are more likely to see such signals as benign. Hawks are likely to focus on costly actions that indicate malign intentions, because such actions are consistent with their existing beliefs about the adversary's intentions.[15]

Second, decisionmakers' interpretations are also guided by their theories about the relationship between an adversary's behavior and its underlying characteristics. As Robert Jervis points out, different observers will interpret even costly behavior differently, "because some of them saw a certain correlation while others either saw none or believed that the correlation was quite different."[16] If, for instance, a decisionmaker believes in the logic of diversionary war, he or she is likely to pay attention to indicators of an adversary state's domestic social unrest and see them as evidence that its leadership is about to embark on a revisionist foreign policy. Thus, social unrest serves as an index of intention, one that the adversary is unlikely to manipulate to project a false image. Those within the administration who do not share this theory of diversionary war will view social unrest as an unreliable indicator of future intentions.

Third, the subjective credibility hypothesis expects decisionmakers to focus on information that, even if perhaps costless, is vivid. Vividness refers to the "emotional interest of information, the concreteness and imaginability of information, and the sensory, spatial, and temporal proximity of information."[17] One "vivid" indicator that is particularly salient to the issues studied in this article consists of a decisionmaker's impressions from personal interactions with members of the adversary's leadership.[18] Recent work in psychology and political science has shown that our emotional responses in face-to-face meetings shape the certainty of our beliefs and preferences for certain choices.[19] As Eugene Borgida and Richard Nisbett argued, "[T]here may be a kind of 'eyewitness' principle of the weighing of evidence, such that firsthand, sense-impression data is assigned greater validity."[20] Accordingly, information about intentions that is vivid, personalized, and emotionally involving is more likely to be remembered, and hence to be disproportionately available for influencing inferences. Conversely, decisionmakers will be reluctant to rely on evidence that is abstract, colorless, objective, or less tangible—such as measurements of the adversary's weapon inventory or the contents of its doctrinal manuals—even if such evidence could be regarded as extremely reliable. This kind of information is not nearly as engaging as the vivid, salient, and often emotionally laden personal responses that leaders take away from meeting with their opponents.[21]

A few clarifications about the selective attention thesis are in order. First, the importance of prior beliefs in assimilating new information is central to both psychological and some rationalist approaches.[22] In Bayesian learning models, observers evaluating new evidence are not presumed to possess identical prior beliefs. The prediction that distinguishes Bayesian models from biased-learning models concerns whether observers with identical prior beliefs and levels of uncertainty will be similarly affected by new information revealed by costly signals.[23] In contrast, the subjective credibility hypothesis claims that a process of updating might not occur even in the face of costly signals, and that vivid, noncostly actions can also be seen as informative. Further, the concept of Bayesian updating suggests that disconfirming data will always lead to some belief change, or at least to lowered confidence. The subjective credibility hypothesis, however, recognizes that some decisionmakers will not revise their beliefs even when confronted with valuable and costly information for reasons described above, such as a strong confirmation bias, the colorless nature of the information, or incongruity with the decisionmaker's theories. This study also asks a set of questions about the importance of costly actions that Bayesian models tend to ignore: that is, do different observers select different kinds of external indicators to update their beliefs?

THE ORGANIZATIONAL EXPERTISE HYPOTHESIS

The bureaucratic-organizational context in which intelligence analysts operate has specific effects that do not apply to political decisionmakers. As a collective, intelligence organizations tend to analyze their adversary's intentions through the prism of their relative expertise. Intelligence organizations tend to devote most of their resources to the collection, production, and analysis of information about the military inventory of the adversary, which can be known and tracked over time. As Mark

Lowenthal writes, "[T]he regularity and precision that govern each nation's military make it susceptible to intelligence collection."[24] Quantified inventories can also be presented in a quasi-scientific way to decisionmakers.

Over time, the extensive monitoring of the adversary's military inventory creates a kind of narrow-mindedness that influences the inference process. To use Isaiah Berlin's metaphor, extensive monitoring creates hedgehogs: "[T]he intellectually aggressive hedgehogs knew one big thing and sought, under the banner of parsimony, to expand the explanatory power of that big thing to 'cover' new cases."[25] This is not to argue that intelligence organizations know only how to count an adversary's missiles and military divisions. Rather, the organizational expertise hypothesis posits that, because analyzing intentions is one central issue with which intelligence organizations are explicitly tasked, and because there is no straightforward or easy way to predict the adversary's intentions, a state's intelligence apparatus has strong incentives to use the relative expertise that it has, which emphasizes careful empirical analysis of military capabilities. Unlike the capabilities thesis, the organizational expertise hypothesis sees the logic of relying on capabilities as arising from bureaucratic and practical reasons specific to intelligence organizations.[26]

The Capabilities Thesis

The capabilities thesis posits that observers should infer an adversary's intentions based on indexes of its military power. This thesis draws on several realist theories that suggest that a state's intentions reveal, or are at least constrained by, its military capabilities. Two pathways link military power and perceived intentions.[27] First, according to John Mearsheimer's theory of offensive realism, decisionmakers in an anarchic international system must "assume the worst" about adversaries' intentions.[28] How aggressive a state can (or will) be is essentially a function of its power. A second pathway relies on the logic of costly actions, according to which the size of an incremental increase or decrease in an adversary's military capabilities, in combination with how powerful the observing country sees it to be, can serve as a credible signal of aggressive or benign intentions.[29]

Drawing on these insights, the capabilities hypothesis predicts that observers in a state will infer an adversary's intentions from perceived trends in the level of the adversary's military capabilities compared with its own military capabilities. Under conditions of uncertainty about states' intentions, a perception that an adversary is devoting more resources to building up its military capabilities is likely to be seen as a costly signal of hostile intentions. As Charles Glaser puts it, "[A] state's military buildup can change the adversary's beliefs about the state's motives, convincing the adversary that the state is inherently more dangerous than it had previously believed. More specifically, the state's buildup could increase the adversary's assessment of the extent to which it is motivated by the desire to expand for reasons other than security."[30] Conversely, a perception of a freeze or a decrease in the adversary's military capabilities or its investment in them is likely to be seen as a costly and reassuring signal of more benign intentions. At the same time, realists have long emphasized that a state's perception of security or threat depends on how its military power compares with the power of the adversary, that is, on the balance of military power. Thus, in the process of discerning intentions, assessments of the balance of military capabilities are also likely to affect interpretations of benign or hostile intent. For example, if the adversary already enjoys military superiority over the observer, then observers will perceive an increase in the adversary's military capabilities as clear evidence of hostile intentions.

The Behavior Thesis

The behavior thesis posits that certain kinds of noncapability-based actions are also useful in revealing information about political intentions, because undertaking them requires the adversary either to sink costs or to commit itself credibly by tying its own hands. I evaluate the potential causal role of three types of such "costly" actions. The first is a state's decision to join or withdraw from binding international institutions.[31] Some institutions can impose significant costs on states, and they are thus instrumental in allowing other states to discern whether a state has benign or malign intentions.[32] The structural version of the democratic peace, for instance, posits that the creation of democratic domestic institutions—because of their constraining effects, transparency, and ability to generate audience costs—should make it easier for others to recognize a democratic state's benign intentions.[33]

The second costly signal involves foreign interventions in the affairs of weaker states, or withdrawals from such interventions. A state's decision to spill blood and treasure in an effort to change the status quo, for example, is likely to be viewed as a costly, hence credible, signal of hostile intentions.

A third type of behavioral signal involves arms control agreements. Scholars have pointed out that, when offensive and defensive weapons are distinguishable, arms control agreements—especially those that limit offensive deployment and impose effective verification—provide an important and reassuring signal of benign intentions.[34] Cheating or reneging on arms control agreements would lead others to question the intentions of that state. It is important to differentiate indicators such as the signing of arms control agreements as a behavioral signal of intentions from indicators associated with the capabilities thesis. Although both theses ultimately deal with the relationship between a state's military policy and others' assessments of its intentions, they have different predictions. If the capabilities thesis is correct, a change in perceived intentions should occur only when the implementation of the agreement results in an actual decrease in the adversary's capabilities. Policymakers should refer to the actual change in capabilities as the reason for a change in their perceptions of the adversary's intentions. If the behavior thesis is correct, perceptions of intentions should shift when the arms control agreement is signed, and policymakers should refer to the action of signing the agreement as a critical factor. Evidence indicating that changes in assessments of intentions occurring at the time of the signing of a treaty in response to expectations of future shifts in capabilities, or reasoning pointing to both the symbolic and the actual value of a treaty, confirms both theses.

■　■　■

Research Design

To evaluate the selective attention, capabilities, and behavior theses, I examine, first, the perceptions of key decisionmakers and their closest senior advisers on the foreign policy of a particular adversary and, second, the coordinated assessments of the intelligence community.[35] In addition to variation on the dependent variable—perceptions of political intentions—the cases also provide useful variation on the explanatory variables.

To test the propositions offered by the selective attention thesis, I examine how the primary decisionmakers—President Jimmy Carter [and] President Ronald Reagan * * * and their senior advisers—varied in their initial assessments of the enemy. Also, all three key decisionmakers were engaged in personal meetings with the adversary's leadership, albeit to various degrees.

The cases also allow testing of the capabilities thesis, because both the initial balance of capabilities and the magnitude of change in the adversary's capabilities during the period of interaction vary across the cases. Both Cold War cases assume relative equality in military capabilities between the superpowers with a moderate increase (the collapse of détente case) or decrease (the end of the Cold War case) in Soviet capabilities during the interaction period. In contrast, the German military was vastly inferior to the British military, but an unprecedented increase in German military capabilities during the mid-to-late 1930s shifted the balance of power in Germany's favor. Thus, the interwar case should be an easy test case for the capabilities thesis, as the dramatic increase in German military capabilities and the shift in the balance of power during the period should have led observers to focus on this indicator as a signal of intentions.

The cases are also useful in testing the predictions of the behavior thesis. In particular, the end of the Cold War case is an easy test for the behavior thesis, given that the Soviet leader, Mikhail Gorbachev, took a series of extremely costly actions. This should have had a significant reassuring influence on observers' perceptions.

In each case, I subject the evidence to two probes. First, I look for covariance between changes in the independent variables cited in each thesis and changes in the dependent variable of perceptions of intentions. A finding of no correlation between the predictions of a thesis and the time or direction in which perceptions of intentions change is evidence against that thesis. Second, through process tracing, I examine whether decisionmakers or collective intelligence reports explicitly cited the adversary's capabilities or its behavior, for example, as relevant evidence in their assessments of the adversary's intentions. This step provides a further check against mistaking correlation for causation. Third, in each case I test the predictions of the selective attention framework by comparing decisionmakers' assessments with those of the intelligence communities, as well as

by tracing the process by which the selective attention criteria account for the variation among decisionmakers in how they categorized credible signals, and the timing of changes in their perceived intentions.

The Collapse of Détente, 1977–80

Jimmy Carter began his presidency with great optimism about relations with the Soviet Union. But by his last year in office, the U.S.-Soviet détente had collapsed: Carter did not meet with Soviet leaders; he increased the defense budget; he withdrew the Strategic Arms Limitation Talks (SALT) II Treaty from Senate consideration; and he announced the Carter Doctrine, which warned against interference with U.S. interests in the Middle East. In this case, I briefly outline trends in Soviet military capabilities and costly actions during that period that inform the capabilities and behavior theses, respectively. Then I show how the main decisionmakers in the Carter administration—President Jimmy Carter, National Security Adviser Zbigniew Brzezinski, and Secretary of State Cyrus Vance[36]— assessed Soviet intentions in a manner that is most consistent with the subjective credibility hypothesis of the selective attention thesis. This is followed by a discussion of the U.S. intelligence community's assessments which, I argue, are in line with both the capabilities thesis and the selective attention thesis's organizational expertise hypothesis.

The U.S. consensus during this period was that the Soviet Union was building up and modernizing its military capabilities and that the correlation of military forces was shifting in its favor.[37] The Soviets were expanding their already large conventional ground and theater air forces and introducing modern systems that were equal or superior to those of NATO.[38] The deployment of Soviet intermediate-range ballistic missiles in Europe produced a growing concern over the potential threat of Soviet continental strategic superiority.[39] While the United States maintained what it called "asymmetric equivalence" with the Soviet Union,[40] the U.S. defense establishment was especially worried about increases in Soviet nuclear counterforce capability. The Soviets were steadily improving the survivability and flexibility of their strategic forces, which had reached the potential to destroy about four-fifths of the U.S. Minuteman silos by 1980 or 1981.[41] In mid-1979, the National Security Council (NSC) cautioned that the strategic nuclear balance was deteriorating faster than the United States had expected two years earlier, and would get worse into the early 1980s.

The Soviets took two kinds of costly actions that fit the criteria of the behavior thesis. The first was signing the SALT II Treaty in June 1979, which called for reductions in U.S. and Soviet strategic forces to 2,250 in all categories of delivery vehicles.[42] The second was Soviet interventions in crises around the world. The Soviets intervened in twenty-six conflicts during 1975–80.[43] Unlike previous interventions during that period, however, the 1978 Soviet intervention in Ethiopia was direct, not simply through Cuban proxies, and the Soviet invasion of Afghanistan in late 1979 was a full-scale application of Soviet military power. The United States feared that the pattern of Soviet actions would expand beyond the "arc of crisis" to include additional regions and countries more important to U.S. interests. The Soviet invasion of Afghanistan, in particular, significantly intensified this fear, because it was the first direct use of Soviet force beyond the Warsaw Pact nations to restore a pro-Soviet regime. In addition to these two interventions, reports in 1979 that the Soviets had placed a combat brigade in Cuba created a sense of panic in Washington that subsided only when American decisionmakers realized that the brigade had been in Cuba since 1962.[44]

Carter Administration Assessments of Soviet Intentions

In what follows I show that, consistent with the subjective credibility hypothesis derived from the selective attention thesis, Carter and his advisers did not agree on the informative value of Soviet costly actions. Rather, they debated the importance of various indicators in inferring intentions, and interpreted costly Soviet behavior markedly differently from one another. Specifically, their initial beliefs and theories about the Soviet Union affected the degree of credibility that each of the three decisionmakers attached to various Soviet actions.

Prior to becoming national security adviser, Brzezinski had held a more negative impression of the Soviet Union than either Carter or Vance.[45] During their first year in office, Carter and Vance perceived Soviet intentions as, at worst, opportunistic.[46] Brzezinski's private weekly memoranda to Carter reveal that, even though he was more skeptical than the president about Soviet intentions, he, too, was hopeful that the Soviets would remain relatively cooperative.[47] As conflicts in the third world grew in scope, intensity, and importance throughout 1978, however, Brzezinski concluded that the Soviet involvement in Africa was expansionist, not merely opportunistic. In January 1978, he maintained that "either by design or simply as a response to an apparent opportunity, the Soviets have stepped up their efforts to exploit African turbulence to their own advantage."[48] Soon after, he cautioned Carter that the "Soviet leaders may be acting merely in response to an apparent opportunity, or the Soviet actions may be part of a wider strategic design."[49] On February 17, Brzezinski provided Carter with a rare, explicit account of his impressions of Soviet intentions, including a table that divided Soviet behavior into three categories: benign, neutral, and malignant.[50] Brzezinski described Soviet objectives as seeking "selective détente,"[51] and explained that his revised assessments about Soviet intentions "emerge from Soviet behavior and statements since the election."[52] The table is particularly illuminating because it provides no mention of Soviet military capabilities, only of Soviet behavior, although the latter was not confined to Soviet interventionism or costly actions alone. During February and March, Cuban and Soviet forces backed the government of Ethiopia in its effort to expel the defeated Somali army; Brzezinski believed that the Soviet Union was in Ethiopia "because it has a larger design in mind."[53] He reiterated these conclusions in subsequent reports to the president.[54]

In contrast, Secretary of State Vance believed that the Soviet Union's actions in Africa were not "part of a grand Soviet plan, but rather attempts to exploit targets of opportunity,"[55] and that they were "within the bounds of acceptable competition."[56] Alarmed by Carter's growing skepticism about Soviet motivations and objectives, Vance requested a formal review of U.S.–Soviet relations in May 1978. "Many are asking whether this Administration has decided to make a sharp shift in its foreign policy priorities," Vance noted, expressing alarm about the more hawkish Brzezinski's influence on the president's view of the Soviet Union.[57] Indeed, Carter's growing distrust of Soviet intentions, ignited by the Soviet involvement in the Horn of Africa, had become apparent in a series of public statements depicting the Soviets as less trustworthy and calling for the adoption of a harsher U.S. stance.[58] Yet Carter continued to see the Soviet Union's actions in the Horn as opportunistic.[59]

By mid-1978, Brzezinski and Vance found themselves in opposing camps while Carter vacillated. Brzezinski summarized the differences:

One view . . . was that "the Soviets have stomped all over the code of détente." They continue to pursue a selective détente. Their action reflects growing assertiveness in Soviet foreign policy generally. Brezhnev's diminished control permits the natural, historical, dominating impulse of the regime to assert itself with less restraint.

Another view . . . was that the record of Soviet action is much more mixed and has to be considered case-by-case. The Soviets are acting on traditional lines and essentially reacting to U.S. steps.[60]

Convinced by early 1979 that the Soviets were pursuing an expansionist "grand design," Brzezinski continued to press Carter to act more assertively. He wrote to Carter that the recent pattern in Soviet interventions revealed revisionist intentions.[61] Although alarmed, the president continued to reject Brzezinski's calls to "deliberately toughen both the tone and the substance of our foreign policy."[62] The issue of Soviet intentions resurfaced in the fall of 1979 during the uproar over the Soviet brigade in Cuba. Brzezinski saw this as another credible indicator of Soviet expansionist intentions, but Carter and Vance were unpersuaded.[63]

The Soviet invasion of Afghanistan in December 1979 caused Carter to re-evaluate his perceptions of Soviet intentions. On January 20, 1980, he declared that it had made "a more dramatic change in my opinion of what the Soviets' ultimate goals are than anything they've done in the previous time that I've been in office."[64] Carter now viewed the Soviet Union as expansionist, not necessarily because of the financial or political costs incurred by the Soviets, but because the invasion represented a qualitative shift in Soviet behavior. Explaining this shift, Carter adopted Brzezinski's line of reasoning, saying, "[I]t is obvious that the Soviets' actual invasion of a previously nonaligned country, an independent, freedom-loving country, a deeply religious country, with their own massive troops is a radical departure from the policy or actions that the Soviets have pursued since the Second World War."[65] Consequently, he warned that the invasion of Afghanistan was "an extremely serious threat to peace because of the threat of further Soviet expansion into neighboring countries."[66]

The invasion was seen as an informative indicator of intention not solely because it was a "costly" action, but also because of the emotional response it invoked in Carter. Indeed, the reason he saw the invasion as indicative of Soviet intentions can also be explained, as Richard Ned Lebow and Janice Stein point out, by the "egocentric bias" that led Carter to exaggerate the extent to which he, personally, was the target of Soviet actions.[67] In particular, the invasion contradicted the frank rapport and the understanding that he felt he had achieved with Brezhnev during their meeting in June 1979 in Vienna.[68] Indeed, during that summit meeting, Carter spoke of "continuing cooperation and honesty in our discussions," and upon his return he had proudly reported to Congress that "President Brezhnev and I developed a better sense of each other as leaders and as men."[69] Brezhnev's justification for the invasion—which asserted that the Soviet troops were sent in response to requests by the Afghan government—infuriated Carter, as he interpreted it as an "insult to his intelligence."[70] Finally, Brezhnev's betrayal also suggested that the Soviet leader could not be trusted to be a partner for détente. As Carter explained, "[T]his is a deliberate aggression that calls into question détente and the way we have been doing business with the Soviets for the past decade. It raises grave questions about Soviet intentions and destroys any chance of getting the SALT Treaty through the Senate. And that makes the prospects for nuclear war even greater."[71] Carter wrote in his diary, "[T]he Soviet invasion sent a clear indication that they were not to be trusted."[72]

Vance's reactions to and interpretation of the Soviet invasion differed dramatically from Carter's. He did not see the invasion as significant and costly, and thus informative of Soviet intentions. Rather, he considered it an "aberration" from past behavior, and "largely as an expedient reaction to opportunities rather than as a manifestation of a more sustained trend."[73] Vance understood why others might view the invasion as a significant signal of expansionist intentions, but he believed that "the primary motive for the Soviet actions was defensive, [and] that the Soviets do not have long-term regional ambitions beyond Afghanistan."[74] Indeed, Vance continued to view Soviet intentions as opportunistic long after the invasion of Afghanistan.[75]

In sum, the evidence presented provides strong support for the selective attention thesis. The support for the capabilities thesis is weak: the significant Soviet military buildup did not lead all U.S. observers to see Soviet intentions as becoming more hostile throughout this period. More important, none of the decisionmakers referred to the Soviet military buildup in explaining his assessment of Soviet political intentions. Brzezinski's writings rarely discussed the recent Soviet military buildup, even though it would have bolstered the hawkish case.[76] The evidence for the behavior thesis is moderate. Both Carter and Brzezinski used Soviet military interventions to infer political intentions. Yet the behavior thesis does not explain why, unlike Brzezinski, Carter and Vance did not infer hostile or expansionist motives from Soviet involvement in the Horn of Africa; it also does not explain why the invasion of Afghanistan triggered such a dramatic change in Carter's beliefs about Soviet intentions but had no such effect on Vance. Finally, the behavior thesis fails to account for the differences between the decisionmakers' inference processes—which largely relied on assessments of Soviet actions, albeit not necessarily "costly" ones—and the U.S. intelligence community's inference process, which, as described in the next section, largely relied on assessments of Soviet capabilities.

U.S. Intelligence Community Assessments of Soviet Intentions

The bulk of the integrated national intelligence estimates (NIEs) on the Soviet Union throughout the Cold War focused on aspects of the Soviet military arsenal. As Raymond Garthoff stated, "Estimates of Soviet capabilities were the predominant focus of attention and received virtually all of the intelligence collection, analysis, and estimative effort."[77] Former Director of Central Intelligence George Tenet noted that "from the mid-1960s on to the Soviet collapse, we knew roughly how many combat aircraft or warheads the Soviets had, and where. But why did they need that many or that kind? What did they plan to do with them? To this day, Intelligence is always much better at counting heads than divining what is going on inside them. That is, we are very good at gauging the size and location of militaries and weaponry. But for obvious reasons, we can never be as good at figuring out what leaders will do with them."[78]

During the mid-to-late 1970s, various agencies within the U.S. intelligence community held differing views about Soviet intentions. For example, the State Department's Bureau of Intelligence and Research and the Central Intelligence Agency (CIA) saw the Soviets as opportunistic. The military intelligence agencies and the Defense Intelligence Agency (part of the Department of Defense) viewed Soviet intentions as expansionist. The reasoning described in the integrated NIEs shows that all U.S. intelligence agencies viewed measures of Soviet current and projected strategic power as the most important indicator of Soviet political intentions. For example, NIE 11-4-78 estimated that "more assertive Soviet international behavior" was "likely to persist as long as the USSR perceives that Western strength is declining and its own strength is steadily increasing." It judged that "if the new [Soviet] leaders believe the 'correlation of forces' to be favorable, especially if they are less impressed than Brezhnev with U.S. military might and more impressed with their own, they might employ military power even more assertively in pursuit of their global ambitions."[79] The centrality of Soviet capabilities and the balance of capabilities as indicators of intentions also

dominated NIE 11-3/8-79, in which Director of Central Intelligence Stansfield Turner asserted that "as they [the Soviets] see this [military] superiority increase during the next three to five years, they will probably attempt to secure maximum political advantage from their military arsenal in anticipation of U.S. force modernization programs."[80] * * *

Interagency disagreements about Soviet military strength and the evolving correlation of forces shaped readings of Soviet intentions. Agencies that perceived the Soviet Union as highly confident in its power also predicted that Soviet foreign policy would become more aggressive. Agencies that perceived Soviet capabilities as weaker also saw Soviet intentions as less aggressive and Soviet objectives as more moderate.[81] Bureaucratic interests did sometimes influence interpretations of Soviet capabilities and intentions, but whatever the parochial motives of analysts from different agencies and in spite of their disagreements about Soviet intentions, all of the intelligence agencies grounded their estimates of intentions in Soviet capabilities. Furthermore, in stark contrast to the Carter administration's decisionmakers, the intelligence community made almost no references to presumably costly noncapabilities-based actions to support the inferences they were drawing about their political intentions.[82]

In sum, the review of the NIEs on the Soviet Union reveals that unlike Carter, Brzezinski, and Vance, the U.S. intelligence community did not assess Soviet political intentions on the basis of behavioral or vivid indicators, but rather on their reading of Soviet military capabilities. This finding is consistent with both the capabilities thesis and the selective attention thesis's organizational expertise hypothesis. The marked differences between evaluations by the civilian decisionmakers and those of the intelligence community, as well as the substantial number of NIEs dedicated to assessing Soviet military capabilities, provide further support for the selective attention thesis.

The End of the Cold War, 1985–88

During his first term, President Ronald Reagan perceived Soviet intentions as expansionist. His views changed dramatically, however, during his second administration. Following the Moscow summit in May 1988, Reagan asserted that his characterization of the Soviet Union five years earlier as an "evil empire" belonged to "another time, another era."[83] When asked if he could declare the Cold War over, the president responded, "I think right now, of course."[84] This section explores the indicators that President Reagan, Secretary of State George Shultz, and Secretary of Defense Caspar Weinberger used to assess Soviet political intentions during Reagan's second term, and how the U.S. intelligence community analyzed similar indicators to infer Gorbachev's intentions during the same period. The discussion that follows begins with some background information about trends in Soviet capabilities and costly action. This is followed by an analysis of how Reagan and his advisers perceived Soviet intentions. The final section evaluates the inference process that the coordinated assessments of the U.S. intelligence community used to judge Soviet intentions during the same period.

Realist accounts of the end of the Cold War point to the decline in Soviet power relative to that of the United States during the late 1980s.[85] Yet archival documents show that at this time, the U.S. defense establishment estimated that the Soviet Union's military power was growing; that the Soviets were modernizing their strategic force comprehensively;[86] and that the Warsaw Pact had a strong advantage over NATO in almost all categories of forces as a result of its continuing weapons production.[87] In addition, prior to the signing of the Intermediate Nuclear Forces (INF) Treaty, the United States perceived the theater nuclear balance of power as extremely threatening, given the Soviet Union's vigorous modernization and initial deployment of intermediate-range ballistic missiles in Europe. Although the INF Treaty, which took effect in June 1988, substantially limited Soviet medium-range and intermediate-range ballistic missile forces, the U.S. intelligence community believed that it did not diminish the Soviets' ability to wage a nuclear war.[88] Then, in December 1988, Soviet Head of State Mikhail Gorbachev announced a unilateral and substantial reduction in Soviet conventional forces in Eastern Europe. Even so, U.S. perceptions of the balance of capabilities did not change until late 1989, following initial implementation of the Soviet force reductions. The announcement itself did not result in U.S. recognition of any significant diminution of Soviet capabilities in either size or quality.[89]

As for Soviet behavioral signals, Gorbachev's proposals during 1985 and 1986 were not sufficiently "costly."[90] During 1987 and 1988, however, the Soviet Union offered additional and significant reassurances to the United States. Especially costly were the Soviet acceptance of asymmetric reductions in the INF in 1987, the withdrawal of Soviet troops from Afghanistan announced publicly in February 1988,[91] and a series of other actions that Gorbachev undertook throughout 1988 aimed at restructuring the political system in the Soviet Union.[92]

Second Reagan Administration's Assessments of Soviet Intentions

A review of the historical record shows that Reagan, Shultz, and Weinberger disagreed on which Soviet actions they categorized as costly. Their interpretation of signals was shaped by their expectations, theories, and vivid, costless information.

To be sure, all three decisionmakers shared similar hawkish views of the Soviet Union, but they exhibited important differences in outlook. Weinberger held much more hawkish views than Reagan and Shultz at the start of Reagan's second administration.[93] Shultz was far less hawkish and did not believe, prior to 1985, that the Soviet Union desired global domination. Reagan's views were closer to those of Weinberger than Shultz. During his first term, Reagan had repeatedly referred to the Soviet Union as an ideologically motivated power bent on global hegemony.[94] Until mid-1987, Reagan continued to view Soviet intentions as expansionist. In December 1985, Reagan stated both in public and in private his belief that Gorbachev was still dedicated to traditional Soviet goals and that he had yet to see a break from past Soviet behavior.[95] In 1986, although Reagan had begun to view Gorbachev's policies as signaling a positive change in attitude, he still asserted that he had no illusions about the Soviets or their ultimate intentions."[96]

Reagan and Shultz began to gradually reevaluate their perceptions of Gorbachev's intentions during 1987. The Soviet leader's acceptance of the U.S. proposal on INF was a major contributing factor. In 1987 Reagan reflected on his evolving characterization of the Soviet Union: "With regard to the evil empire. I meant it when I said it [in 1983], because under previous leaders they have made it evident that . . . their program was based on expansionism."[97] Still, neither Reagan nor Shultz expected Gorbachev to signal a genuine change in Soviet foreign policy objectives. Reagan wrote, "[I]n the spring of 1987 we were still facing a lot of uncertainty regarding the Soviets. . . . It was evident something was up in the Soviet Union, but we still didn't know what it was."[98]

Two events in the spring of 1988 persuaded Reagan and Shultz of a change in Soviet intentions. First, the initial Soviet withdrawal from Afghanistan in April symbolized to both that the Brezhnev Doctrine was dead.[99] Shultz explained that the dominant perception in the administration was that "if the Soviets left Afghanistan, the Brezhnev Doctrine would be breached, and the principle of 'never letting go' would be violated."[100] In a private conversation with Gorbachev, Reagan acknowledged that the withdrawal "was a tangible step in the right direction," and took note of Gorbachev's statement that "the settlement could serve as a model for ending other regional conflict."[101] The second event occurred during the 19th Communist Party Conference, at which Gorbachev proposed major domestic reforms such as the establishment of competitive elections with secret ballots; term limits for elected officials; separation of powers with an independent judiciary; and provisions for freedom of speech, assembly, conscience, and the press. The proposals signaled to many in the Reagan administration that Gorbachev's domestic reforms were meant to make revolutionary and irreversible changes. Ambassador Jack Matlock described these proposals as "nothing short of revolutionary in the Soviet context," adding that they "provided evidence that Gorbachev was finally prepared to cross the Rubicon and discard the Marxist ideology that had defined and justified the Communist Party dictatorship in the Soviet Union."[102]

Reagan also paid significant attention to some "costless" actions and viewed them as credible signals of changed intentions given their vividness. Reagan repeatedly cited his positive impressions of Gorbachev from their private interactions in four summit meetings as persuading him that Gorbachev was genuinely seeking to reduce U.S.-Soviet tensions.[103] Emphasizing his growing conviction of Gorbachev's trustworthiness,[104] Reagan began increasingly to refer to Gorbachev as a friend who was "very sincere about the progressive ideas that he is introducing there [in the Soviet Union] and the changes that he thinks should be made."[105] * * * The president wrote, "It's clear that there was a chemistry between Gorbachev and me that produced something very close to a friendship. He was a tough, hard bargainer. . . . I liked Gorbachev even though he was a dedicated Communist."[106] * * *

Other members of Reagan's administration noticed the importance of vivid information in shaping his views. Matlock thus notes, "Once he [Reagan] and Shultz started meeting with Gorbachev they relied on their personal impressions and personal instincts." * * * Reagan's personality—specifically his openness to contradictory information, his belief in his power of persuasion, and his emotional intelligence[107]—allowed him to rely heavily on his personal impressions of Gorbachev. As Barbara Farnham puts it, for Reagan, "[p]ersonal experience counted for everything."[108] Reagan's confidants have pointed to his tendency to reduce issues to personalities: "If he liked and trusted someone, he was more prone to give credence to the policies they espoused."[109]

■　■　■

As for the role of Soviet capabilities, both Reagan and Shultz saw a connection between the Soviet Union's capabilities, its actions, and its political intentions. In their eyes, Soviet expansionist conduct during the 1970s occurred at a time when the United States had lost its superiority over the Soviet Union in strategic nuclear weapons.[110] They made it clear, however, that it was Soviet behavior during that period, rather than the Soviet military buildup, that was the decisive evidence of Soviet aggressive intentions. In fact, one of Reagan's favorite quotations was that "nations do not mistrust each other because they are armed; they are armed because they mistrust each other."[111] Reagan similarly acknowledged that the adversary's capabilities by themselves are not good indicators of its intentions; instead they are a by-product of how each state perceives the other's intentions.

■　■　■

In conclusion, the series of Gorbachev's costly actions should make this an easy case for the behavior thesis, yet, the empirical evidence lends only moderate support. While Reagan and Shultz relied on costly behavior signals to infer intentions, they also focused significantly on behavioral actions such as their own personal impressions of Gorbachev. Further, the behavior thesis fails to explain

Weinberger's inference process: the secretary of defense stated explicitly that he did not regard any of Gorbachev's costly actions as credible reassuring indicators of intentions. As a result, his assessments of Soviet intentions did not change at all, even after leaving office. These aspects in the inference processes underscore the subjective nature of credibility. The support for the capabilities thesis is weak. Given the perceived trends in Soviet capabilities described at the beginning of this section, one would have expected the perceived intentions of the Soviet Union to have remained hostile until mid-1988. This thesis, therefore, cannot explain the radical change in Reagan's and Shultz's perceptions, and why the president and his secretary of state rarely focused on the Soviet military arsenal as an indicator that shaped their assessments of Soviet political intentions during the period under examination.

U.S. Intelligence Community's Assessment of Soviet Intentions

The U.S. intelligence community's National Intelligence Estimates focused on markedly different indicators of Soviet intentions from 1985 to 1988 than did Reagan, Shultz, and Weinberger.[112] It gave greatest weight to the Soviet Union's military capabilities in judging Soviet political intentions. The U.S. intelligence community, as is now known, overestimated Soviet strategic forces and defense spending during the 1980s; this overestimation was an important contributing factor to the community's tendency to overstate Soviet hostility.[113]

Intelligence estimates from 1985 to 1987 concluded that Gorbachev was seeking détente with the West to reduce U.S. challenges to Soviet interests and to decrease U.S. defense efforts. His long-term goal was said to be to "preserve and advance the USSR's international influence and its relative military power."[114] Recognition by the Soviet leadership that the correlation of forces would soon shift against the Soviet Union and a relative decline in Soviet economic power were offered as the leading explanations for Gorbachev's cooperative initiatives.[115] A 1985 NIE stated, "Moscow has long believed that arms control must first and foremost protect the capabilities of Soviet military forces relative to their opponents. The Soviets seek to limit U.S. force modernization through both the arms control process and any resulting agreements."[116] A Special NIE in 1986 pointed to Soviet concerns about the Reagan administration's Strategic Defense Initiative as the primary motive behind Gorbachev's pursuit of a détente-like policy vis-à-vis the West. The NIEs portrayed Gorbachev's arms control initiatives as propaganda aimed at bolstering his campaign of deception.[117] The intelligence community's working assumption was that, despite serious economic problems since the mid-1970s, Soviet objectives remained unchanged.[118]

By mid-1988, Reagan's and Shultz's assessments of Soviet intentions had undergone a fundamental change, but the available NIEs indicate that the U.S. intelligence community did not revise its estimates of Soviet objectives until mid-1989.[119] Throughout 1987 and 1988, the community continued to hold that Gorbachev's foreign policy initiatives were merely tactical, and that no significant discontinuity in Soviet traditional goals and expectations could be anticipated.[120] For instance, in describing Gorbachev's "ultimate goal[s]," a late-1987 NIE repeated earlier assertions that Gorbachev was pursuing a clever plan to pursue communism, not through the use of blunt force, but through a deceiving posture of accommodation with the West that was intended to win more friends in the underdeveloped world.[121] Soviet modernization efforts toward greater "war-fighting" capabilities, coupled with calculations as to how economic difficulties would affect the strategic balance of power, were said to provide the most reliable guides to Soviet objectives.[122]

In conclusion, consistent with the expectations of the selective attention thesis's organizational expertise hypothesis, as well as with those of the capabilities thesis, the intelligence community's NIEs inferred Soviet political intentions primarily from its military capabilities. Throughout this period, the community did not update its assessments in response to Gorbachev's costly actions of reassurance, and it rarely used costly Soviet behavior to draw inferences about Soviet foreign policy goals. It saw Gorbachev's policies on arms limitations, for example, as rooted in the need to increase Soviet relative economic capabilities, a task that could be accomplished only by reducing pressure to allocate more resources to defense. Engaging NATO in arms control agreements was merely a ploy to undercut support in the West for NATO's weapons modernization efforts.[123] Thus, the support for the behavior thesis is weak.

Interestingly, the intelligence community's reluctance to revise its estimates of Soviet intentions led to repeated clashes between Director of Central Intelligence Robert Gates and Secretary of State Shultz, the latter saying later that he had little confidence in the community's intelligence reports on the Soviet Union.[124] Nevertheless, intelligence assessments had only limited impact on Reagan and Shultz, who drew conclusions about Soviet intentions largely from their personal impressions and insights from meetings with Gorbachev. As Matlock explains, "They are very experienced people and experienced politicians and it meant much more to them what they were experiencing."[125] Paul Pillar contends that Reagan and his advisers, apart from Shultz, "brushed aside as irrelevant any careful analysis of Soviet intentions, just as Carter and Brzezinski had brushed aside the question of the Soviets' reason for intervening in Afghanistan."[126]

■   ■   ■

In sum, the findings imply that any study on the efficacy of signals that fails to consider how signals are perceived and interpreted may be of little use to policymakers seeking to deter or reassure an adversary. They also suggest that policymakers should not assume that their costly signals will be understood clearly by their state's adversaries. They should not fear that others are necessarily making worst-case assumptions about their intentions on the basis of their military capabilities, but they should be aware that the adversary's intelligence apparatus is likely to view such an indicator as a credible signal of intentions. Decisionmakers' inclination to rely on their own judgments and subjective reading of signals to infer political intentions is pervasive and universal, but these individuals should be wary: getting inside the mind of the adversary is perhaps one of the most difficult tasks facing intelligence organizations, and perhaps most susceptible to bias and bureaucratic interests. * * *

NOTES

1. Kenneth Lieberthal and Wang Jisi, "Addressing U.S.-China Strategic Distrust" (Washington, DC: Brookings Institution, 2012), p. vi.

2. Gary Locke, "China Is a Country of Great Contrasts," National Public Radio, January 18, 2012, http://www.npr.org/2012/01/18/145384412/ambassador-locke-shares-his-impressions-of-china.

3. Jeffrey A. Bader, Obama and China's Rise: An Insider's Account of America's Asia Strategy (Washington, DC: Brookings Institution Press, 2012).

4. In the context of foreign policy intentions, see James D. Fearon, "Signaling Foreign Policy Interests: Tying Hands versus Sinking Costs," Journal of Conflict Resolution, Vol. 41, No. 1 (February 1997), pp. 68–90; Andrew Kydd, Trust and Mistrust in International Relations (Princeton, NJ: Princeton University Press, 2005); and Robert F. Trager, "Diplomatic Calculus in Anarchy: How Communication Matters," American Political Science Review, Vol. 104, No. 2 (May 2010), pp. 347–68.

5. Thomas C. Schelling, The Strategy of Conflict (Cambridge, Mass.: Harvard University Press, 1980); and Fearon, "Signaling Foreign Policy Interests." On when and how "cheap talk" could matter, see Trager, "Diplomatic Calculus in Anarchy"; Joseph Farrell and Robert Gibbons, "Cheap Talk Can Matter in Bargaining," Journal of Economic Theory, Vol. 48, No. 1 (June 1989), pp. 221–37; and Anne E. Sartori, Deterrence by Diplomacy (Princeton, NJ: Princeton University Press, 2005).

6. Charles L. Glaser, Rational Theory of International Politics: The Logic of Competition and Cooperation (Princeton, NJ: Princeton University Press, 2010).

7. For the effects of perceived intentions on policies, see Keren Yarhi-Milo, Knowing [the] Adversary: Leaders, Intelligence, and Assessments of Intentions in International Relations (Princeton, NJ: Princeton University Press, [2014]).

8. Intention should be distinguished from states' motives for keeping or changing the status quo. On motives, see Glaser, Rational Theory of International Politics, pp. 38–39.

9. The scope of the revisionist intentions in expansionist and opportunistic states can be limited or unlimited. For a similar typology, see Keith L. Shimko, Images and Arms Control: Perceptions of the Soviet Union in the Reagan Administration (Ann Arbor: University of Michigan Press, 1991).

10. Douglas Seay, "What Are the Soviets' Objectives in Their Foreign, Military, and Arms Control Policies?" in Lynn Eden and Steven E. Miller, eds., Nuclear Arguments: Understanding the Strategic Nuclear Arms and Arms Control Debates (Ithaca, NY: Cornell University Press, 1989), pp. 47–108; and Robert Jervis, Perception and Misperception in International Politics (Princeton, NJ: Princeton University Press, 1976).

11. Amos Tversky and Daniel Kahneman, "Availability: A Heuristic for Judging Frequency and Probability," Cognitive Psychology, Vol. 5, No. 2 (September 1973), pp. 207–32; and Thomas Gilovich, Dale Griffin, and Daniel Kahneman, eds., Heuristics and Biases: The Psychology of Intuitive Judgment (Cambridge: Cambridge University Press, 2002).

12. Robert Jervis, "Signaling and Perception: Drawing Inferences and Projecting Images," in Kristen Monroe, ed., Political Psychology (Mahwah, NJ: Lawrence Erlbaum, 2002); and Jonathan Mercer, "Emotional Beliefs," International Organization, Vol. 64, No. 1 (January 2010), pp. 1–31.

13. The literature on such biases is vast. For important works and good summaries, see Jervis, Perception and Misperception in International Politics; Ole Holsti, "The Belief System and National Images: A Case Study," Journal of Conflict Resolution, Vol. 6, No. 3 (September 1962), pp. 244–52; and Philip E. Tetlock, "Social Psychology and World Politics," in Susan T. Fiske, Daniel T. Gilbert, and Gardner Lindzey, eds., Handbook of Social Psychology, 4th ed. (New York: McGraw-Hill, 1998), pp. 868–914.

14. Robert Jervis, "Understanding Beliefs," Political Psychology, Vol. 27, No. 5 (October 2006), pp. 641–63.

15. This hypothesis cannot indicate a priori when observers will change their assessments about intentions, but it can predict the possibility of change in perceived intentions relative to those of other observers on the basis of their initial beliefs about the intentions of the adversary.

16. Peer Schouten, "Theory Talk #12: Robert Jervis on Nuclear Weapons, Explaining the Non-Realist Politics of the Bush Administration and U.S. Military Presence in Europe," Theory Talks, January 24, 2008, http://www.theory-talks.org/2008/07/theory-talk-12.html.

17. Richard E. Nisbett and Lee Ross, Human Inference: Strategies and Shortcomings of Social Judgment (Englewood Cliffs, NJ: Prentice Hall, 1980), p. 62.

18. On the importance of personal meetings in inferring leaders' sincerity, see Todd Hall and Keren Yarhi-Milo, "The Personal Touch: Leaders' Impressions, Costly Signaling, and Assessments of Sincerity in International Affairs," International Studies Quarterly, Vol. 56, No. 3 (September 2012), pp. 560–73.

19. See, for example, Mercer, "Emotional Beliefs"; and Rose McDermott, "The Feeling of Rationality: The Meaning of Neuroscientific Advances for Political Science," Perspectives on Politics, Vol. 2, No. 4 (December 2004), pp. 691–706.

20. Borgida and Nisbett, "Differential Impact of Abstract vs. Concrete Information," p. 269.

21. Nisbett and Ross, *Human Inference*, pp. 188–91; Fiske and Taylor, *Social Cognition*, pp. 278–79; Tversky and Kahneman, "Availability"; Kaufmann, "Out of the Lab and into the Archives"; and Rose McDermott, Jonathan Cowden, and Stephen Rosen, "The Role of Hostile Communications in a Simulated Crisis Game," *Peace and Conflict: Journal of Peace Psychology*, Vol. 14, No. 2 (2008), p. 156.

22. For a debate on the role of "common prior beliefs" in bargaining models, see Alastair Smith and Allan Stam, "Bargaining and the Nature of War." *Journal of Conflict Resolution*, Vol. 50, No. 6 (December 2004), pp. 783–813; and Mark Fey and Kristopher W. Ramsay, "The Common Priors Assumption: A Comment on 'Bargaining and the Nature of War,'" *Journal of Conflict Resolution*, Vol. 50, No. 4 (2006), pp. 607–13.

23. Alan Gerber and Donald P. Green, "Rational Learning and Partisan Attitudes," *American Journal of Political Science*, Vol. 42, No. 3 (July 1998), pp. 189–210; and Charles S. Taber and Milton Lodge, "Motivated Skepticism in the Evaluation of Political Beliefs," *American Journal of Political Science*, Vol. 50, No. 3 (July 2006), pp. 755–69.

24. As Mark M. Lowenthal writes, "Deployed conventional and strategic forces . . . are difficult to conceal, as they tend to exist in identifiable garrisons and must exercise from time to time. They also tend to be garrisoned or deployed in large numbers, which makes hiding them or masking them impractical at best." Lowenthal, *Intelligence: From Secrets to Policy* (Washington, DC: CQ Press, 2009), pp. 234–35.

25. Philip E. Tetlock, *Expert Political Judgment: How Good Is It? How Can We Know?* (Princeton, NJ: Princeton University Press, 2005), pp. 20–21.

26. For analyses of how organizations influence information processes, see Martha S. Feldman and James G. March, "Information in Organizations as Signal and Symbol," *Administrative Science Quarterly*, Vol. 26, No. 2 (June 1981), pp. 171–86.

27. A third pathway concerns the offensive or defensive nature of the military capabilities as a signal of intentions. On the little impact that such indicators had on the inference processes of decisionmakers during these periods, see Yarhi-Milo, *Knowing [the] Adversary*.

28. John J. Mearsheimer, *The Tragedy of Great Power Politics* (New York: W. W. Norton, 2001), p. 31.

29. Kydd, *Trust and Mistrust in International Relations;* and Glaser, *Rational Theory of International Politics.*

30. Charles L. Glaser, "The Security Dilemma Revisited," *World Politics*, Vol. 50, No. 1 (October 1997), p. 178.

31. On the role of institutions in signaling intentions, see Robert O. Keohane, *After Hegemony: Cooperation and Discord in the World Political Economy* (Princeton, NJ: Princeton University Press, 1984); G. John Ikenberry, *After Victory: Institutions, Strategic Restraint, and the Rebuilding of Order after Major Wars* (Princeton, NJ: Princeton University Press, 2001); Seth Weinberger, "Institutional Signaling and the Origins of the Cold War," *Security Studies*, Vol. 12, No. 4 (Summer 2003), pp. 80–115.

32. The usefulness of international institutions in revealing information about intentions depends on institutional characteristics such as the nature of enforcement, the effects of veto points on state decision-making, and the institution's effects on member states' domestic political institutions.

33. For a summary of how domestic institutions can be a signal of intentions, see Mark L. Haas, "The United States and the End of the Cold War: Reactions to Shifts in Soviet Power, Policies, or Domestic Politics?" *International Organization*, Vol. 61, No. 1 (Winter 2007), p. 152; and James D. Fearon, "Domestic Political Audiences and the Escalation of International Disputes," *American Political Science Review*, Vol. 88, No. 3 (September 1994), pp. 577–92.

34. Glaser, "The Security Dilemma Revisited"; and Charles L. Glaser, *Analyzing Strategic Nuclear Policy* (Princeton, NJ: Princeton University Press, 1991).

35. For the U.S. cases, I use the declassified National Intelligence Estimates (NIEs) on the Soviet Union. NIEs, which are produced by the National Intelligence Council, are the most authoritative product of the intelligence community. The community regularly assessed Soviet intentions in the 11-4 and 11-8 series of NIEs, supplemented by occasional Special NIEs (SNIEs). In all NIEs, I analyze only those sections that deal with the question of intentions. In the British case, the main focus of the analysis is the coordinated Chiefs of Staff reports and memoranda, because these represent the integrated analysis of all three military service intelligence agencies.

36. On the relationship between the three decisionmakers, see Jerel A. Rosati, *The Carter Administration's Quest for Global Community: Beliefs and Their Impact on Behavior* (Columbia: University of South Carolina Press. 1987); and Betty Glad, *An Outsider in the White House: Jimmy Carter, His Advisors, and the Making of American Foreign Policy* (Ithaca, NY: Cornell University Press, 2009).

37. Zbigniew Brzezinski, memo, "Comprehensive Net Assessment, 1978," p. 8; and Harold Brown, "Report of Secretary of Defense Harold Brown to the Congress on the FY 1979 Budget, FY Authorization Request, and FY 1979–1983 Defense Programs," January 23, 1978, pp. 65–66.

38. Office of Strategic Research, "The Development of Soviet Military Power: Trends since 1965 and Prospects for the 1980s," SR 81-10035X (Washington, DC: National Foreign Research Center, April 1981), pp. xiii–xv.

39. NIE 11-6-78, pp. 2–3.

40. National Security Council (NSC) meeting, June 4, 1979, quoted in Zbigniew Brzezinski, *Power and Principle: Memoirs of the National Security Advisor, 1977–1981* (New York: Farrar, Straus and Giroux, 1983), pp. 334–36. The conventional military balance in Europe was perceived as favoring the Warsaw Pact forces. See National Foreign Assessment Center, "The Balance of Nuclear Forces in Central Europe," SR 78-10004 (Washington, DC: Central Intelligence Agency, January 1978); and "Comprehensive Net Assessment, 1978."

41. NIE 11-3/8-79, pp. 2, 4. Soviet damage-limitation capabilities were, however, still judged to be poor despite a large, ongoing Soviet investment. NIE 11-3/8-78, pp. 5–6, 11. See also Harold Brown, "Report of Secretary of Defense Harold Brown, on the FY 1979 Budget," pp. 65–66; and Harold Brown, "Department of Defense Annual Report, Fiscal Year 1980," January 25, 1979, p. 70.

42. As a result of the Soviet invasion of Afghanistan, Carter decided to table SALT II. NSC Weekly Report 123, December 28, 1979.

43. The Soviet Union had low-level involvement in eleven crises and conducted covert or semi-military activities in thirteen crises, in addition to using direct military force in Ethiopia and Afghanistan.

See International Conflict Behavior Project dataset, http://www
.cidcm.umd.edu/icb/.

44. On the episode of the Soviet brigade in Cuba, see Cyrus R. Vance,
Hard Choices: Critical Years in America's Foreign Policy (New York:
Simon and Schuster, 1983), pp. 360–61; Brzezinski, *Power and
Principle,* p. 347; and NSC Weekly Report 98, May 25, 1979; NSC
Weekly Report 103, July 20, 1979; NSC Weekly Report 104,
July 27, 1979; and NSC Weekly Report 109, September 13, 1979.

45. Rosati, *The Carter Administration's Quest for Global Community*;
Melchiore Laucella, "A Cognitive-Psychodynamic Perspective to
Understanding Secretary of State Cyrus Vance's Worldview," *Presi-
dential Studies Quarterly,* Vol. 34, No. 2 (June 2004), pp. 227–71.

46. See, for example, *Public Papers of the President of the United States*
[hereafter *PPP*] (Washington, DC: Government Printing Office,
June 30, 1977), p. 1198; and *PPP*, December 15, 1977, p. 2119.

47. NSC Weekly Report 18, June 24, 1977.

48. NSC Weekly Report 42, January 13, 1978.

49. Quoted in Brzezinski, *Power and Principle,* p. 181.

50. NSC Weekly Report 47, February 17, 1978.

51. Ibid.

52. NSC Weekly Report 2, February 26, 1977.

53. Zbigniew Brzezinski, memo for the president, "The Soviet Union
and Ethiopia: Implications for U.S. Soviet Relations," March 3,
1978.

54. NSC Weekly Report 55, April 21, 1978; and NSC Weekly Report
57, May 5, 1978.

55. Vance, *Hard Choices,* p. 84.

56. Ibid., p. 101.

57. Vance, memo to President Jimmy Carter, May 29, 1978. Document
released to author under the Freedom of Information Act, July 2007.

58. *PPP*, May 20, 1978, pp. 872, 940; and *PPP*, May 25, 1978, p. 977.
See also Brzezinski, *Power and Principle,* pp. 188–89; and Rich-
ard C. Thornton, *The Carter Years: Toward a New Global Order*
(New York: Paragon House, 1991), p. 185.

59. *PPP*, November 13, 1978, p. 2017.

60. NSC Weekly Report 65, June 30, 1978.

61. NSC Weekly Report 84, January 12, 1979.

62. NSC Weekly Report 109, September 13, 1979.

63. Brzezinski, *Power and Principle,* pp. 347–51.

64. Jimmy Carter, interview, *Meet the Press,* January 20, 1980.
See also Jimmy Carter, *Keeping Faith: Memoirs of a President*
(Fayetteville: University of Arkansas Press, 1995), p. 480; "Message
for Brezhnev from Carter Regarding Afghanistan," December 28,
1979; and Brzezinski, *Power and Principle,* p. 429.

65. *PPP*, January 20, 1980, p. 11. For a similar line of reasoning, see
also pp. 308, 329.

66. *U.S. Department of State Bulletin (DSB)*, Vol. 80, No. 2034 (January 1980).

67. Richard Ned Lebow and Janice Gross Stein, "Afghanistan, Carter,
and Foreign Policy Change: The Limits of Cognitive Models,"
in Dan Caldwell and Timothy J. McKeown, eds., *Diplomacy,
Force, and Leadership: Essays in Honor of Alexander L. George*
(Boulder, CO: Westview, 1993), p. 112.

68. Raymond L. Garthoff, *Détente and Confrontation: American-Soviet
Relations from Nixon to Reagan,* rev. ed. (Washington, DC:
Brookings Institution Press, 1994), p. 1059.

69. Quoted in ibid.

70. Ibid.

71. Hamilton Jordan, *Crisis: The Last Year of the Carter Presidency* (New
York: G. P. Putnam's Sons, 1982), p. 99.

72. Jimmy Carter, *White House Diary* (New York: Farrar, Straus and
Giroux, 2010), p. 383.

73. Ibid. For a similar logic, see Marshall Shulman, memorandum for
Warren Christopher, "Notes on SU/Afghanistan," January 22,
1980; and Vance, *Hard Choices*, p. 388.

74. NSC Weekly Report 134, March 28, 1980.

75. See interviews with Vance and Shulman in Melchiore Laucella,
"Cyrus Vance's Worldview: The Relevance of the Motivated
Perspective," Ph.D. dissertation, Union Institute, 1996.

76. In only a few statements did the decisionmakers link Soviet intentions to the buildup. For example, in a report to Carter, Brzezinski
wrote: "Soviet defense programs are going beyond the needs of
legitimate deterrence and are increasingly pointing towards the
acquisition of something which might approximate a war-fighting
capability. While we do not know why the Soviets are doing this
(intentions?), we do know that their increased capabilities have
consequences for our national security." This statement does not,
however, lend support to the capabilities thesis, as Brzezinski explicitly says that he cannot infer Soviet intentions from these indicators.

77. In this section, I rely in part on interviews I conducted with
William Odom, head of the National Security Agency at the time,
and Fritz Ermarth, Raymond Garthoff, Melvin Goodman, and
Douglas MacEachin, all former CIA analysts of the Soviet Union.
Raymond L. Garthoff, "Estimating Soviet Intentions and
Capabilities," in Gerald K. Haines and Robert E. Leggett, eds.,
Watching the Bear: Essays on CIA's Analysis of the Soviet Union (Washington, DC: Center for the Study of Intelligence Publications,
2003), chap. 5, https://www.cia.gov/library/center-for-the-study-of
-intelligence/csi-publications/books-and-monographs/watching-the
-bear-essays-on-cias-analysis-of-the-soviet-union.

78. "Speeches Delivered at the Conference," in ibid., chap. 8.

79. NIE 11-4-78, p. 6.

80. NIE 11-3/8-79, p. 4.

81. See, for example, NIE 11-4-77; NIE 11-3/8-79; and NIE 11-3/8-80.

82. NIE 11-4-78 made some references to current Soviet actions with
respect to SALT and détente. This line of reasoning, however, was
rarely invoked. NIE 4-1-78, pp. ix, x, 17.

83. Quoted in Raymond L. Garthoff, *The Great Transition:
American-Soviet Relations and the End of the Cold War* (Washington,
DC: Brookings Institution Press, 1994), p. 352.

84. President's news conference, Spaso House, Moscow, *DSB,* June
1988, p. 32.

85. William C. Wohlforth, "Realism and the End of the Cold War,"
International Security, Vol. 19, No. 3 (Winter 1994/95), pp. 91–129.

86. See, for example, NIE 11-3/8-86; NIE 11-3/8-87; and NIE
11-3/8-88.

87. Frank Carlucci, "Annual Report to the President and Congress,
1989" (Washington, DC: Government Printing Office, February 18, 1988), p. 29.

88. NIE 11-3/8-88, p. 5. The Department of Defense reached a similar
conclusion. U.S. Department of Defense, Office of the Secretary of
Defense, "Soviet Military Power" (Washington, DC: U.S.

Department of Defense, 1989), p. 7; and U.S. Department of Defense, Office of the Secretary of Defense, "Soviet Military Power" (Washington, DC: Government Printing Office, 1990), pp. 54–55.

89. National Intelligence Council (NIC), "Status of Soviet Unilateral Withdrawal," M 89-10003 (Washington, DC: NIC, October 1989).

90. Jack F. Matlock, *Reagan and Gorbachev: How the Cold War Ended* (New York: Random House, 2004), pp. 275–76; and Garthoff, *The Great Transition*, p. 334. For an analysis of Gorbachev's costly actions and their effects on perceived intentions, see Haas, "The United States and the End of the Cold War"; and Kydd, *Trust and Mistrust in International Relations.*

91. Soviet Foreign Minister Eduard Shevardnadze informed Shultz of the decision to withdraw from Afghanistan in September 1987. Gorbachev publicly confirmed this decision in February 1988.

92. Some decisionmakers in the United States did recognize the significance of Gorbachev's efforts to institute glasnost (openness, or transparency) within the Soviet Union during 1987. It was only from mid-1988, however, that his actions seemed aimed at fundamental institutional change. Both Shultz and Matlock argue that Gorbachev's actions had not, as of the end of 1987, signified fundamental reforms. George Shultz, *Turmoil and Triumph: My Years as Secretary of State* (New York: Charles Scribner's Sons, 1993), p. 1081; and Matlock, *Reagan and Gorbachev,* pp. 295–96. By mid-1988, however, Reagan had begun to praise Gorbachev for initiating true "democratic reform." He said that Gorbachev's efforts were "cause for shaking the head in wonder," leading him to view Gorbachev as "a serious man seeking serious reform." *DSB,* Vol. 2137 (1988), pp. 37–38.

93. In his comprehensive study on perceptions of the Soviet Union during the Reagan administration, Keith Shimko noted that "Weinberger's views of the Soviet Union were about as hardline as one could get." Shimko, *Images and Arms Control,* p. 233.

94. Ibid., pp. 235–37.

95. See, for example, *DSB,* November 1985, p. 11; and *PPP,* 1985, p. 415.

96. *PPP,* 1986, p. 1369.

97. *PPP,* 1987, pp. 1508–09.

98. Ronald Reagan, *An American Life* (New York: Simon and Schuster, 1990), p. 683.

99. The Brezhnev Doctrine, announced in 1968, asserted the Soviet Union's right to use Warsaw Pact forces to intervene in any Eastern bloc nation that was seen as compromising communist rule and Soviet domination, either by trying to leave the Soviet sphere of influence or even by attempting to moderate Moscow's policies.

100. Shultz, *Turmoil and Triumph,* p. 1086.

101. Transcripts of the Washington Summit, June 1, 1988, 10:05 A.M.–11:20 A.M.; and *PPP,* 1988, pp. 632, 726.

102. Matlock, *Reagan and Gorbachev,* pp. 295–96.

103. Reagan and Gorbachev interacted during four summit meetings: the Geneva Summit (November 1985), the Reykjavik Summit (October 1986), the Washington Summit (December 1987), and the Moscow Summit (May 1988). During these summits, the two held long, private meetings, as a result of which Reagan gained a positive impression of the Soviet leader. Yarhi-Milo, *Knowing* [the] *Adversary.*

104. *PPP,* June 1, 1987, pp. 594–95; *PPP,* June 11, 1987, p. 624; *PPP,* June 12, 1987, pp. 635–36; *PPP,* August 29, 1987, p. 988; and *PPP,* September 16, 1987, p. 1038.

105. *PPP,* May 24, 1988, p. 649.

106. Reagan, *An American Life,* p. 707.

107. For an excellent analysis of Reagan's personality traits that allowed him to revise his beliefs about the Soviet threat, see Barbara Farnham, "Reagan and the Gorbachev Revolution: Perceiving the End of Threat," *Political Science Quarterly,* Vol. 116, No. 2 (Summer 2001), pp. 225–52; and Fred I. Greenstein, "Ronald Reagan, Mikhail Gorbachev, and the End of the Cold War: What Difference Did They Make?" in William C. Wolforth, ed., *Witnesses to the End of the Cold War* (Baltimore, MD: Johns Hopkins University Press, 1996).

108. Farnham, "Reagan and the Gorbachev Revolution," p. 248.

109. "Leadership and the End of the Cold War," in Richard K. Herrmann and Richard Ned Lebow, eds., *Ending the Cold War: Interpretations, Causation, and the Study of International Relations* (Basingstoke, UK: Palgrave Macmillan, 2004), p. 183.

110. *PPP,* 1985, pp. 650, 1287–88.

111. See, for example, Ronald Reagan, speech given at Moscow State University, May 31, 1988; and *DSB,* August 1988.

112. In addition to NIEs, I relied on the interviews that I conducted with Ermath, Garthoff, Goodman, MacEachin, and Odom.

113. The CIA's Office of Soviet Analysis had become increasingly concerned that estimates of projected Soviet strategic weapons systems were inflated. See, for example, MacEachin, memorandum to deputy director for intelligence, "Force Projections," NIE 11-3/8, April 22, 1986.

114. SNIE 11-9-86, p. 4; and NIE 11-18-87, pp. 3–4.

115. NIE 11-3/8-86; NIE 11-8-87; SNIE 11-16-88; and NIE 11-3/8-88.

116. NIE 11-3/8-85, p. 18. This line of reasoning is repeated in NIE 11-16-85, pp. 3–9.

117. See NIE 11-16-85, p. 13; and SNIE 11-8-86, pp. 15–17.

118. NIE 11-3/8-86, pp. 2, 18.

119. In an estimate published five days after the fall of the Berlin Wall, the intelligence community still viewed Warsaw Pact intentions as hostile, and warned of the possibility of an unprovoked attack on Western Europe. NIE 11-14-89, p. iii.

120. "NIE 11-18-87; SNIE, "Soviet Policy during the Next Phase of Arms Control in Europe"; Robert Gates, memorandum, "Gorbachev's Gameplan: The Long View," November 24, 1987; and NIE 11-3-8-88.

121. NIE 11-3/8-88.

122. Ibid. On the INF Treaty, see ibid., p. 6.

123. Shultz, *Turmoil and Triumph,* p. 864. See also "Nomination of Robert M. Gates," p. 481.

124. Author phone interview with Jack Matlock.

125. Paul Pillar, *Intelligence and U.S. Foreign Policy: Iraq, 9/11, and Misguided Reform* (New York: Columbia University Press, 2011), p. 116.

126. Mercer, "Emotional Beliefs," p. 14.

Thomas J. Christensen

FROM *THE CHINA CHALLENGE*
Shaping the Choices of a Rising Power

■ ■ ■

As the leading State Department official focusing on China [from 2006 to 2008], I often testified before congressional committees and congressionally mandated commissions about China's rise and the U.S. response. My message was consistent and reflected a broad consensus in the interagency process: the goal of the United States, its allies, and all like-minded states should not be to contain China but to shape Beijing's choices so as to channel China's nationalist ambitions into cooperation rather than coercion. If we can demonstrate that Chinese nationalist greatness can best be achieved in the new century through participation in global projects, we will have accomplished this strategic goal. * * *

■ ■ ■

China's Rise: Why It Is Real

China's rise in wealth, diplomatic influence, and military power since 1978 is real and it's stunning. For all the scars on his personal political history—from support for the disastrous Great Leap Forward in the late 1950s to the Tiananmen massacre in 1989—Deng Xiaoping will be

From Thomas J. Christensen, *The China Challenge: Shaping the Choices of a Rising Power* (New York: W. W. Norton & Co., 2015). Some of the author's notes have been omitted.

remembered most by historians for launching the program of Reform and Opening. That program pulled hundreds of millions of people out of grinding poverty and allowed China to become a potent international actor for the first time since the first half of the Qing Dynasty, which spanned the mid-seventeenth to the early nineteenth centuries.

Deng's market reforms unleashed the pent-up economic energy of the Chinese people, who had suffered for more than two decades under Mao's postmodern version of Communism. Under Mao, market laws of supply and demand and basic economic concepts such as diminishing returns on investment were dismissed as bourgeois, imperialist myths. Expertise and management skills were valued much less than blind loyalty to Mao and devotion to the bizarre economic model he created in the late 1950s. Mao communized agriculture, localized industry, and commanded unrealistic production targets. He mobilized the population around Utopian Communist economics and radical political activism. His goal was to have China catch up with the Soviet Union and the United States in a short time frame and position the People's Republic of China as the leader of the international Communist movement. But his Great Leap of the 1950s and the Great Proletarian Cultural Revolution of the 1960s led instead to domestic economic disaster, international isolation, and the premature deaths of some forty million Chinese citizens. In the late 1970s Deng Xiaoping would restore market incentives and place an emphasis on skill and practicality rather than ideological purity in professional promotion. Practical control of agricultural land, if not ownership, was taken away from communes and given to farmers. The reform program also injected market-based pricing and incentives into the Chinese economy and opened China up to foreign trade and investment. Officials, engineers, and scientists were chosen for being expert, not "red." The resulting growth brought some three hundred million people—about the size of the U.S. population today—above the threshold of poverty as measured by international organizations: an income of less than one dollar per day.

These results are unprecedented in world history. For the past thirty-six years, China's economy has grown on an average of about 10 percent per annum in real terms (meaning adjusted for inflation). Accordingly, the gross domestic product (GDP) of China has almost doubled every seven years since 1979. And with a Chinese population of 1.3 billion, the economy has moved from one that was poor but still large to one that is now much less poor and truly gargantuan. China's per capita income is still very modest compared to the wealthiest countries of the world, but the change is nonetheless astonishing. Official per capita income rose from $220 USD in 1978 to $4,940 in 2011,[1] and according to some measures using "purchase power parity," China's per capita income was $9,300 in 2012 (an impressive figure, though it is notable that the per capita income of the United States, by comparison, was $50,700).[2] While still a developing country, China surpassed Japan in 2010 to become the world's second largest economy, a feat simply unimaginable in the early years of the reform era. At that time Americans were fretting about the economic recession of the early 1980s and Japan was seen as the great power likely to surpass the United States in the next cycle in the "rise and fall of the great powers," to use Yale professor Paul Kennedy's famous phrase.

The economic reforms have had more than just economic results. The individual citizen's life is incomparably more energetic and free in China today than in the pre-reform period. My first trip to China was in the summer of 1987, the eighth year of the reform era. The anesthetic grip of socialism was still very strong on Chinese society. At midday, cities like Beijing and Shanghai, moving at a slow pace already, ground to a halt as the population rested and often slept for two hours, wherever they might be. This was the *xiuxi* period, a designated siesta for urban Chinese citizens, many of whom still worked in inefficient state-owned work units. By contrast, the energy on the contemporary streets of Beijing and Shanghai is palpable and sometimes overwhelming. Cranes rotate at construction sites in every direction, and one is more likely to find oneself stuck in stultifying traffic at midday than stepping around a slumbering deliveryman sleeping on his bicycle's flatbed. The slowly rolling bicycles of the 1980s urban landscape have been replaced by the twenty-first-century traffic of young professionals in new and relatively sturdy automobiles. In fact, China has become the largest market for new cars in the world and the lifeline of companies like GM facing declining domestic sales.

The government's often impressive efforts to build an infrastructure capable of handling this new burden has kept world-famous equipment companies like Caterpillar in the black despite diminishing demand in wealthier countries. Still, the growth in the new Chinese middle class has outstripped the growth of new roads; epic traffic jams in Chinese cities are a regular occurrence. Beijing now ranks alongside Mexico City as the worst in the world for traffic. In less thoughtful moments, the experienced traveler almost yearns for the slower but more predictable pace of Beijing's bicycle lanes, where coal couriers and relatively unstressed citizens spat out the sand and industrial dust blown downwind from the manufacturing centers and the Gobi desert.

Marketization has had a big impact on personal freedoms in China as well and thus constitutes what the political scientist Harry Harding aptly described as the People's Republic's Second Revolution.[3] In Mao's China, the Party secretaries in charge of state-owned enterprises had a degree of power over the workers that Americans simply cannot imagine. Local Party chiefs had near total control over the lives of their charges from cradle to cremation. They had authority over not only salary and career promotion but also education, health care, housing, retirement, and even permission to marry. Marketization changed this to a large degree by creating both a vibrant private sector outside of the state-owned enterprise system, to which disgruntled workers could escape from meddling Party chiefs, and a new standard of success—market competitiveness—for the state-owned enterprises themselves. The combination meant that Party chiefs in those enterprises needed to focus on something other than micromanaging the personal lives of their workers and could ill afford to alienate their most able staff lest they jump ship to the private sector. The personal individual space created by this process, even space to privately express disappointment with the state itself, moved China very quickly from what Ambassador Jeane Kirkpatrick had categorized in the Cold War as a totalitarian state to what she described as a typical authoritarian one. Nations living under the latter suffer from lack of democracy, free press, freedom of assembly, and often rule of law, but the life of the individual on a day-to-day basis is still much freer than under the ever-present thumb of totalitarianism. Along the same lines, the hope for positive future economic and political change in China is also much greater now than it was in the totalitarian Mao era, and hope for a better future may be one of the most underappreciated human rights of all.

■ ■ ■

This Time Should Be Different: China's Rise in a Globalized World

When great powers rise, there is often real trouble. The examples are both numerous and horrific. Modern German history alone provides a series of demonstrations. The punctuated and violent rise of Bismarck's Prussia and the German successor states helped cause several great power wars in the late nineteenth and early twentieth centuries, including the two most brutal armed conflicts in world history. In Asia, the rise of Japan after the Meiji Restoration also led to several wars from the 1880s to 1945 involving Japan, China, Russia, Great Britain, and the United States.

There have been partial exceptions to what seems like a general rule of international relations. The rise of the United States and the decline of Great Britain as a global leader in the late nineteenth and early twentieth centuries did not lead to conflict between the two democracies. In fact, they would be allied together in two subsequent world wars against a rising Germany, in the Cold War that followed, and ever since. But even in that instance, structural transition was not truly peaceful. As I argued with Columbia professor Richard Betts in 2000, if China handles disputes with its neighbors as poorly as the United States did in the late nineteenth century, East Asia is in for a very rocky ride.[4] Racism under the thin academic patina of social Darwinism and the yellow journalism of a jingoistic press helped spark the Spanish-American war over Cuba, which in turn placed the U.S. military in a costly counterinsurgency war in the Philippines. The ostensible reason for conflict was a nebulous naval incident in Havana Harbor with American casualties that became a national rallying cry for war ("Remember the *Maine,* to hell with Spain!").

It does not take great imagination to see how similar factors could contribute to Chinese belligerence as it pursues expansive maritime claims against rivals like Japan, Vietnam, and the Philippines. Those nations are often treated with derision, condescension, or both in Chinese nationalist circles. The prospect of U.S. intervention in such disputes and in relations across the Taiwan Strait could eventually lead China to mimic another nineteenth-century American concept, the Monroe Doctrine, which sought to prevent further European imperial incursions in the Western Hemisphere. In fact, some U.S. scholars like Princeton's Aaron Friedberg already ascribe to China the goal of "extruding," or expelling, the United States from its regional bases in neighboring countries. Friedberg and others believe China plans to target the United States and its regional allies and security partners with a combination of economic and military coercion and diplomatic persuasion to achieve this goal. In this scenario, either the United States would leave of its own volition, fearing conflict with a rising China or, more likely, would be deprived of regional partners because no Asian actor would want to run the risk of alienating or provoking Beijing by maintaining traditional security ties with the United States.[5]

Friedberg lays out his argument with typical intelligence and care. While I find scant evidence in Chinese strategic writings to support this claim about Beijing's intentions at present, it is definitely a real and dangerous possibility for the future. Avoiding such a turn in Chinese doctrine and ensuring its failure if it were adopted, in that order, should be priority goals for U.S. policy in the region. If such a doctrine were actually adopted by China and proved successful, the decline of American power would be severe indeed. But even a failed attempt by China to expel the United States from the region would likely be fraught with crises and military conflicts. For this reason, University of Chicago professor John Mearsheimer has adopted an even more pessimistic stance than Friedberg, declaring that China's rise cannot be peaceful because it is inevitable that China will pursue what Friedberg calls extrusion, whether such an effort proves successful or not.[6]

Despite these dreary historic precedents and prognostications, there are reasons to be more sanguine that the rise of China can be managed in a way that preserves both American power in East Asia and regional peace and stability. Two related arguments about the destabilizing effects of the rise and fall of great powers predict that China's rise will hurt regional and global stability. I hope to show that both are wrong. The first is a purely structural argument, based in the strategic history of past disasters associated with the rise of new challengers in the international system. The rise of new rivals destabilizes the international system by creating opportunities for territorial expansion and leads to intense spirals of tension among the great powers. The greed and fear created by these shifts in the distribution of great power capabilities result in crises among the great powers that lead to large-scale war and massive suffering.

The second argument is a corollary of the first and has less to do with material power and more to do with the international norms, institutions, and rules of the road. Scholars of institutions like the UN and the International Monetary Fund (IMF) often claim that the international rules and institutions in place at any time were previously set by the leading power at the apex of its hegemony over the system. The more cynical version of this theory suggests that such a hegemonic leader would only set up institutions that disproportionately benefit itself, not the system as a whole. When the leader's power declines in comparison to a rising rival, it is only natural, then, that the up-and-coming rival would want to revise or even overturn the existing rules and create new institutions that disproportionally benefit the rising state. So at the close of World War II, the United States sought the end of European colonial preferences in trade and finance and the creation of free trade regimes and a global financial system. According to the most cynical interpretation, Washington did not do so altruistically to create a more prosperous and stable world but rather because the United States was economically much more competitive than the remaining European great powers after World War II. In the current day, if China wanted to undercut existing international institutions in order to foster new ones that benefited itself more and the United States less, the process of change could damage near-term global cooperation on economics, security matters, humanitarian crises, and environmental problems and thus prove fundamentally destabilizing.

Fortunately, in the case of China's ongoing rise, there are several reasons to doubt these two arguments. The kinds of temptations that led to great power wars during previous power transitions are much less prominent in Asia today than they were in the Western Hemisphere and Asia in the past. Substantial changes in global economics and politics have made the current international system more robust than previous systems. Broader economic trends have made territorial conquest of colonies less tempting, and changes in both economics and weaponry have decreased the need for invasion and conquest of either peer competitors or their smaller allies. Furthermore, the institutions set up by the United States and its allies after World War II were beneficial not just to themselves but to all states willing to open up their economies to a rule-based global order. No country has benefited from that global order more than China, particularly since it joined the World Trade Organization (WTO) in 2001. Since domestic stability is paramount for the CCP [Chinese Communist Party] and the maintenance of that stability depends in large part on economic growth, I can see few reasons why China would intentionally seek conflict with its trade and investment partners or undercut the institutional framework that has enabled its historic economic development.

■   ■   ■

Why Chinese Power Will Not Surpass U.S. Power Anytime Soon

China's rise is real, as discussed [earlier]. And for reasons that will be discussed [later], China's increased military, economic, and political power poses challenges for U.S. national security and regional stability in Asia. But we need not panic. Not only does China have many disincentives for aggression, but it is not likely to catch up or surpass the United States in terms of comprehensive national power anytime soon.

There is a growing chorus that portrays China as being on a clear path to economic, military, and diplomatic supremacy. For example, Martin Jacques predicts China's impending hegemony in the title of his book *When China Rules the World*.[7] * * *

Pessimistic commentators like Jacques * * * ignore too many sources of Chinese weakness and American strength. In addition to viewing trade and investment in the developing world as a realpolitik competition between great powers, a highly questionable proposition, these studies often exaggerate the political leverage enjoyed by countries that are purchasing raw materials. Moreover, there are several negative factors for China's reputation in these areas. China's extractive business practices have led to resentment of Chinese companies, including some high-profile instances of violence in Africa. Democratization in Latin America and Africa has led to a political backlash against China's support for states like Zimbabwe. The Arab Spring in the Middle East has also complicated Beijing's relations with some members of the Arab League as Beijing joins Russia in blocking the international community from pressuring Assad's regime in Syria.

In military matters, China's defense modernization does pose real problems for the United States, but the scope of that newfound military power is often exaggerated by scholars and public officials. Too often these observers approach military net assessments as if they are tallying a sports score, with each country getting a certain number of points for each counted asset. But even though the United States still does well in such a competition with China, numbers are not everything. A more sophisticated analysis would take into account the quality of systems, the quality of personnel, and the wartime experience of the two militaries. Such a study reveals that China is unlikely to have the military wherewithal to become a global peer competitor of the United States for decades to come. Chinese strategic writings, even those not meant for foreign consumption, seem to recognize China's shortcomings. They often refer to the need to develop strategies that overcome China's relative military weakness in comparison to a potential great power foe. While they discuss closing the gap in overall military power, there is almost no sense that such a goal will be achieved anytime soon. It seems then that Americans often give the Chinese higher grades and aspirations than Chinese military officers themselves are willing to accept.

For similar reasons, China is also unlikely to have the wherewithal to deny the United States access to the western Pacific, a goal that the Pentagon believes China is pursuing under the distinctly American concept of "anti-access/area denial" (or A2AD in DoD-speak). As with Friedberg's concept of extrusion, I have seen in my research no Chinese-language equivalent to these terms in authoritative strategic writings. The closest Chinese term is "counterintervention," but this concept has more to do with raising the costs to intervening foreign forces than to physically preventing their entry in the first place. This does not mean that China will not adopt such a strategy of exclusion, only that it currently seems to lack the capability and intention to do so.

◼   ◼   ◼

Assessing Chinese nuclear modernization recalls Cold War–era debates about the role of nuclear weapons in deterring superpower aggression. During the Cold War, hawkish theorists in the United States claimed that there was something called the "stability-instability paradox," meaning that since both the United States and the Soviet Union enjoyed secure nuclear arsenals that could obliterate each other, nuclear weapons, in effect, simply canceled one another out. By this logic, stability at the nuclear level—known as mutually assured destruction (MAD)—allegedly fostered a robust rivalry at the conventional level. The argument ran that a conventionally superior power would know that its conventionally inferior rival would never have a rational reason to escalate to the nuclear level because such escalation would lead to an unacceptably devastating nuclear retaliation. This was a hawkish analysis in Cold War America because it was widely believed that the Soviets and their allies enjoyed conventional superiority over NATO forces in central Europe. U.S. hawks believed that Soviet conventional superiority posed a danger that strategic nuclear weapons could not neutralize because of the stability-instability paradox. So the Soviets might be emboldened by allied weakness unless conventional NATO forces were beefed up and/or bolstered by tactical and theater nuclear weapons that could be used short of a full-scale nuclear war to offset those Soviet conventional advantages.[8]

Less hawkish Cold War critics of this viewpoint, such as Robert Jervis and Thomas Schelling, believed that nuclear deterrence cast a much larger shadow over the behavior of nuclear-armed states than the hawks allowed. They believed that attackers seeking to change the status quo would have to consider the threat of escalation from conventional war to nuclear war. Defenders of the status quo could manipulate what Schelling famously, called the "threat that leaves something to chance": the dangerous prospect that limited, conventional warfare could escalate at "time t+1" in ways such that no one could accurately predict at "time t," and that escalation to the nuclear level could occur as the tensions spiraled. In other words, an actor could not easily exploit its conventional superiority for fear of unleashing an unintended escalatory process that would end in nuclear conflict. That both superpowers deployed tactical and theater nuclear weapons to the European theater bolstered this analysis. Those deployments provided a slippery slope between conventional and nuclear combat that the Soviets could hardly ignore when plotting a conventional attack.[9]

It is important to remember that the U.S. and NATO, while possessing inferior conventional forces, were defending the recognized status quo in western Europe. And one of the underappreciated stabilizing factors in the Cold War was that—with the notable exceptions of volatile areas like West Berlin—the geographic lines between the two ideological camps in Europe were fairly clear and mutually accepted. Schelling and Jervis theorized that this made for relatively stable superpower relations in the Cold War, an analysis consistent with psychological theories developed by Amos Tversky and Nobel laureate Daniel Kahneman. Tversky and Kahneman's work on prospect theory demonstrates that, in general, humans accept higher risks and pay greater costs to defend what they believe to be rightfully theirs than they will to acquire new possessions.[10] Applying these findings to Cold War Europe, Jervis asserted that, even if the United States and NATO could not prevail in a conventional physical struggle with the Soviets and the Warsaw Pact, they could successfully deter the Soviets from invading western Europe by raising the prospect that they would exact unacceptable costs on the Soviets to defend the status quo in this geostrategic game of chicken.[11]

■　■　■

Given the arguments laid out by Jervis and Schelling, one could take comfort in the notion that only a very aggressive China would want to unleash dangerous forces by challenging the status quo in the East Asian region. For reasons laid out [earlier], some new aspects of modern international politics and economics should dissuade Beijing from such brazen adventurism. But one must curb unalloyed optimism because in contemporary East Asia there are many sovereignty disputes, particularly in the maritime domain. Indeed, there is nothing close to a mutually accepted territorial status quo among potential belligerents. China itself has active disputes with many of its neighbors, including U.S. allies and security partners such as Japan, the Philippines, and Taiwan and important nonallied states such as Vietnam, Malaysia, and Brunei.[12] In addition, China has overlapping exclusive economic zones (EEZ) at sea under the UN Convention of the Law of the Sea (UNCLOS) with even more states, including South Korea, another U.S. ally, and Indonesia.

Such disputes are dangerous because all potential belligerents can believe that they are defending sovereign territory and the status quo. There does not need to be a clear aggressor for there to be trouble. Per Tversky and Kahneman's prospect theory, if both sides believe they own the disputed territories, then the game of chicken is much more likely to lead to a head-on collision than if one side is trying to change the status quo.

Such tendencies among individual humans can become even more pronounced for governments, which have to worry about the strategic and domestic political consequences of appearing not to defend the status quo. On strategic grounds, if a nation is willing to back down on an issue related to one's proclaimed sovereign territory, that nation will lose face, thus undermining its positions on other matters. So, in any given dispute, a country like China or Japan, with multiple island disputes, has to worry about the implications for future negotiations not only with the rival disputant but with third-party onlookers (Japan also has island disputes with South Korea

Figure 4.1. South China Sea Territorial Claims

The map outlines the identical claim of the People's Republic of China and the Republic of China (Taiwan) and the claims of the four other nations in the dispute.

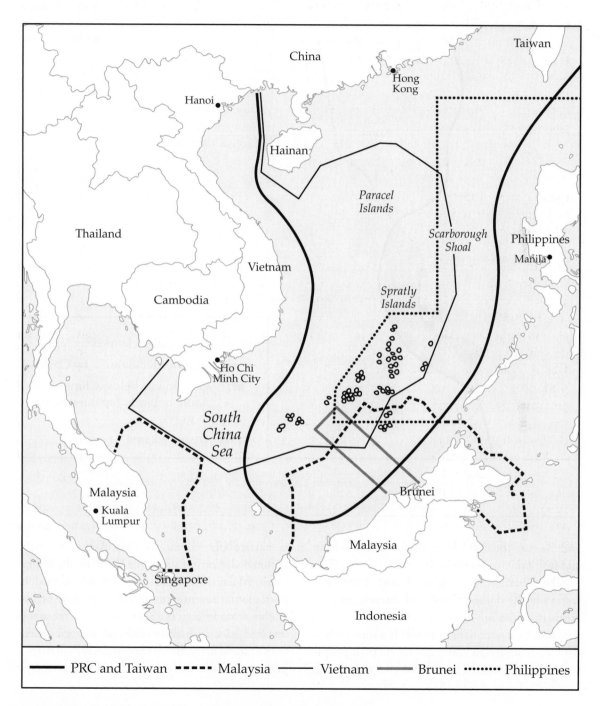

Source: http://www.southchinasea.org/files/2014/09/China-claims-a-big-backyard.png.

Editor: David Rosenberg

Figure 4.2. East China Sea Territorial Claims

The map outlines the overlapping claims of China and Japan in the East China Sea, and the known oil and gas fields in and around those overlapping claims.

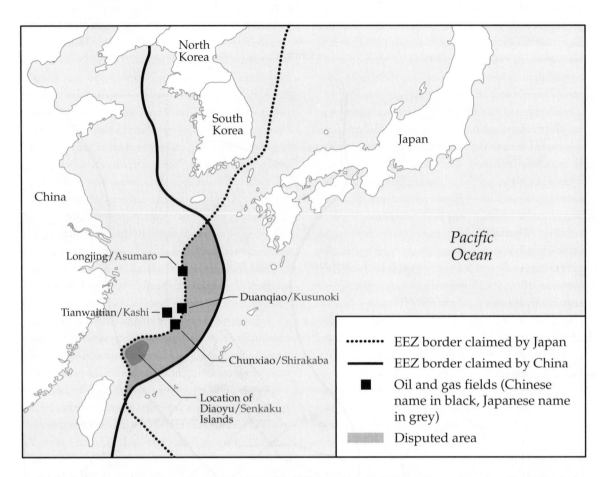

Source: "East China Sea," U.S. Energy Information Administration (EIA), September 25, 2012, http://www.eia.gov/countries/regions-topics .cfm?fips=ECS.

and Russia; the PRC has disputes with Taiwan and four other countries in the South China Sea).

The situation only looks worse when one factors in the domestic political interests of governments, who are loath to look weak on issues that touch on nationalistic pride. If a state fails to defend its sovereign claims, then its own people can hold it to task. This is true everywhere but is particularly salient in East Asia, where the national ideology of states like Vietnam, the Philippines, Malaysia, and China itself are steeped in postcolonial resentment and the narrative of liberation from foreign bullying. When all the actors involved have such emotional and strategic incentives to stand firm, the mix becomes very volatile—perhaps volatile enough that fishing and energy disputes over uninhabited rocks in the East and South China Seas can escalate to shooting wars.

In China, continued Party rule is the top security goal. If there is any doubt about this, please note that the People's Liberation Army is dedicated not to China as a nation but to the Chinese Communist Party. This has always been the case since the days of the revolution, and if the rhetoric of Xi Jinping and the recently selected leadership of the Party is any indication, it is not going to change anytime soon. One major problem for the Party in recent years has been the increase in "mass social incidents" (protests and riots) and the suggestion that Chinese society is increasingly unstable. Before the government stopped publicly discussing the number of such incidents in the middle of the past decade, it was already reporting as many as 87,000 per year.[13] Extrapolating from those trends, some analysts estimate that there are more than 100,000 of these every year in China today; one Chinese academic study in 2010 put the number as high as 180,000.[14] There is little doubt from my many recent trips to China that the public and the government alike are concerned about the long-term stability of China in a way that they have not been since the years immediately following the Tiananmen protests and massacre of 1989. Citizens seem frustrated by official corruption, eminent domain problems related to the fast-paced growth of cities and infrastructure, environmental degradation, and the unbalanced distribution of wealth. Adding to the unease of Chinese elites are uncertainties about the sources of future Chinese economic growth, particularly since the financial crisis called into question the reliability of markets abroad. There is, therefore, a growing consensus that China needs to restructure its economy to become less dependent on trade and investment and to increase the role of domestic consumption, but there is no consensus on how to achieve this transformation or at what pace.[15] All of these changes can create new controversies and dashed expectations, thus sparking new challenges to social and political stability.

Since jettisoning Maoist Communist ideology in the reform period, the nominally Communist CCP has legitimized itself through fast-paced economic growth and by nationalism. It portrays itself as an increasingly capable protector of Chinese interests and national honor. The ways that the CCP has managed domestic dissent in China renders nationalist issues such as Taiwan or other sovereignty disputes particularly delicate. The central government in China has successfully ridden the waves of popular discontent by keeping protests local and small and keeping the protestors out of the Party. The higher authorities have often been able to paint themselves as the solution to local problems by coming in to quell protests, making arrests when necessary, firing and replacing local officials, and paying off some of the aggrieved citizens. Still, the increasing frequency of the protests is alarming to Chinese officials.

One reason potential nationalist humiliation is so worrisome to the central government is that people angry at the state for other reasons can take the opportunity of such a humiliation, to criticize government policies using politically correct slogans fostered for decades by the government's own "patriotic education" campaigns. Take, for example, the urban protests that arose across China over a nationalist issue: Japan's central government had purchased the disputed Senkaku Islands from a private Japanese family in 2012. One angry Chinese man held a placard that read: "Oppose Japan, Oppose America, Oppose Price Inflation!" (*Fan Ri, Fan Mei, Fan Zhangjia!*) In so doing, he was linking a serious domestic concern with protests over international humiliation. Even when the topics of protests appear to remain international in nature, they can have dangerous domestic repercussions for the Chinese economy and political stability. So protestors targeting "Little Japan" (*Xiao Riben*) often call on their Chinese compatriots to boycott

Japanese products (*Dizhi Rihuo!*). But a boycott, if enacted, would severely harm China's own economy. Many products in China bearing Japanese brands are made in-country by Chinese workers in Japanese-invested factories. Many other domestic and international firms operating in China depend on Japanese parts in their transnational production chains. Chinese officials are well aware of the irony. Anti-Japanese protestors in China often carry portraits of Chairman Mao, indirectly criticizing contemporary leaders for their lack of fortitude on the international stage in comparison to Mao.

Popular calls for national action have grown all the more dangerous for the central government as individuals and disgruntled groups around the nation can increasingly communicate through social media. Furthermore, as with most governments and militaries, there is plenty of sincere nationalism within the CCP regime. Protestors in the future then might find sympathetic ears inside the state security mechanism. Moreover, military or civilian elites who are unhappy with their colleagues' lack of fortitude on international issues could stir up popular protest through expanding media channels to pressure more moderate leaders to change policy or, at the extreme, to help drive them from office. In fact, frustration with insufficiently robust resistance to the United States, Japan, and Vietnam, for example, has already been expressed in the mainstream press in China, sometimes by active duty or recently retired military officers. (More broadly, that press, although more open than in earlier decades, is still ultimately controlled by the state.) For these reasons, nationalist humiliation, particularly as it pertains to issues such as Japan or Taiwan independence, is the third rail of Chinese Communist politics.

Of course, China has no regional monopoly on nationalism or domestic political concerns related to foreign policy. Strong strands of postcolonial nationalism run through Filipino, Vietnamese, and Malaysian politics. And citizens in these countries are no less certain than those Chinese protestors that their countries are the rightful owners of disputed islands. Japanese prime ministers have sat atop extremely shaky coalition governments for the past ten years while the Japanese public believes that the Senkaku Islands are rightfully Japanese and that China only became interested in the islands after natural resources were discovered in the seabed around them in the late 1960s. While only a few Japanese rightists seem eager for a fight over the islands, no Japanese leader wants to appear ineffective or weak in the face of Chinese pressure. If all sides are willing to run high risks to avoid humiliation and defend national honor, then coercive diplomatic crises become very dangerous games indeed.

The United States finds itself in the unenviable position of having alliances or security relationships with three of the actors with which China has territorial disputes (Japan, the Philippines, and Taiwan) but no position on any of the sovereignty disputes themselves. In the case of Taiwan, the U.S. legal position on its sovereignty has been "undetermined" since the U.S. decision to enter the Korean War on June 27, 1950. The consistent U.S. government demand since the 1970s has been that the two sides of the Strait should work out their differences peacefully and that each side of the Strait should avoid actions that unilaterally change the status quo in cross-Strait relations without the acquiescence of the other. In general this means that the United States opposes mainland China's use of force or the threat of force to compel Taiwan into unification against the will of the Taiwan people, and it opposes actions by Taiwan that move the island in the direction of permanent legal independence from the broader Chinese nation without the consent of Beijing. In the case of the largely uninhabited islands, rocks, and reefs in the South China Sea (Paracels and Spratlys) disputed by China, Taiwan, the Philippines, Vietnam, Malaysia, and Brunei as well as the case of the uninhabited rocks in the East China Sea disputed by Japan and China (Diaoyu in Chinese and Senkaku in Japanese), the United States takes no position on the sovereignty of the islands, even those claimed by U.S. allies. This is part of a global maritime legal policy in which the United States takes no position on disputed islands but simply insists that disputes be settled peacefully and in accordance with prevailing international law so as not to disturb freedom of navigation. The only partial exception is the Senkakus. In 1971, the United States transferred control of the islands to postwar Japan as part of the reversion of Okinawa. The Americans did this despite the protests of mainland China and Taiwan. The United States never recognized Japan's sovereignty over the Senkaku islands, however, just its administrative control. But it is notable that the United States claims that the islands fall under the purview of Article V of the U.S.–Japan Security Treaty in a way that the United States has never asserted for any of the Filipino claims in the South China Sea.

While Washington enjoys military superiority over China, it is increasingly the case that China enjoys military superiority over most, if not all, of the United States' regional friends and allies. It may be this factor, above all others, that proves China's rise is real. So when, exactly, would the United States choose to intervene in support of its friends and allies? The question is complicated by Washington's status as a non-claimant on the sovereignty issues. For its part, China has somewhat cleverly, if at times clumsily, deployed maritime security forces and civilian ships instead of PLA Navy assets to assert and protect China's claims. This puts the onus of escalation on the other disputant and places Washington in the extremely uncomfortable position of urging restraint on its ally while trying to dissuade China from continued provocations and manipulation of risk. The United States has its own reputational reasons not to appear indifferent or weak in the region, but it also has reputational and other strategic reasons not to allow its weaker allies to drag it into a conflict, especially a conflict over uninhabited rocks!

One can see how the real world of international security politics can diverge sharply from the predictions and concerns of the allegedly "realist" balance-of-power theories. One can also see why a China with inferior conventional and nuclear capabilities in comparison to the United States can still pose serious problems for the United States and its regional friends and allies. Unlike a brute-force struggle for regional or global supremacy, coercive diplomacy is a bargaining process. As Thomas Schelling argued during the Cold War, for coercive diplomacy to work, the target of one's efforts must not only understand the credibility of one's own threat of intervention and punishment but must also be credibly reassured that if it forgoes aggression or some other transgression it will not be punished anyway. Otherwise, it has no incentive to comply with the demands being leveled. So in the context of U.S.–China relations, the United States needs to credibly threaten to defend its own interests and the interests of its allies without at the same time suggesting to Beijing that Washington is preparing the means with which to harm China's security interests regardless of Beijing's behavior. This is no easy task, particularly given the ambiguous nature of the maritime sovereignty disputes. Any U.S. military units capable of intervening in the region could, from a Chinese perspective, also be used to promote revisionist goals at the expense of China. Along the same lines, it is a challenge for China to develop coercive capabilities designed to protect what it sees as legitimate interests without, in the process, appearing to those actors to be threatening, aggressive, and destabilizing.

The combination of ambiguous and contested political claims, geography, and military technology make managing East Asia while China rises a complex task, particularly since there are more than two actors involved. In the Taiwan context, for example, any combination of U.S., Taiwanese, or Japanese military power that could be used to deter China from forcing Taiwan into unification with the mainland against its will might also be used for the purpose of protecting Taiwan's moves toward permanent legal independence from mainland China. Similarly, any combination of PRC coercive capabilities designed to deter Taiwan's unilateral declaration of formal independence from the mainland could also be used to compel unification with the mainland against Taiwan's will. The fact that both Taiwan and the mainland can adopt political initiatives deemed provocative by the other side only makes the headaches in Washington all the greater. The same applies to Japan and the Philippines, formal U.S. allies with whom China has maritime disputes.

The United States needs to balance its deterrence of mainland aggression against the need to reassure China that Washington does not seek to promote provocative policies by its allies nor change its own neutrality policy. The challenges in this may become even more difficult as China's own rise exacerbates tensions with the United States and its neighbors and, along with the discovery of energy resources in the seabeds around the islands, accelerates other claimants' timetables for pursuing and consolidating their claims.

Global Governance: The Biggest Challenge of All

Deterring Chinese aggression toward its neighbors and the United States will be increasingly challenging, but there are many reasons to be hopeful. China has major incentives to avoid unnecessary conflict, and after decades of a global Cold War, the United States government is highly experienced in the practice of coercive diplomacy. But no government has experience tackling the least appreciated challenge: persuading a uniquely large developing country with enormous domestic challenges and a historical chip on its national shoulder to cooperate actively with the international community. For the many reasons already offered, China has an interest in the stability of the current international system, but that does not easily translate into China helping to pay the costs to maintain that system.

Two stark facts underpin this challenge. First, China is by far the most influential developing country in world history. Second, globalization has made the world so interconnected that the behavior of every great power has become very consequential. As a result, China is being asked to do more at present than any developing country has in the past. Moreover, the intensity and diversity of those requests are only going to increase with the continuing rise of China and the deepening of globalization. If China actively tries to block efforts at improved global governance, many international problems will be extremely difficult to solve. But even if China simply tries to lie low and ride free on the efforts of others, we will have great difficulty managing some of the globe's biggest security, economic, environmental and humanitarian problems.

There are a number of reasons why it will be so difficult to convince China to assert itself in the role of responsible stakeholder described by then–Deputy Secretary Robert Zoellick in his thoughtful and influential September 2005 speech. Zoellick correctly argued that China had benefited greatly from the security and prosperity created by a stable, rule-based international economic and political order.[16] But China had contributed a disproportionally small amount to maintain that order. Zoellick recognized that one of the great challenges facing diplomats in the United States, Europe, and Japan was to persuade China to do more to contribute to the global commons. So far the record of this effort is at best mixed, and there are real reasons to be concerned that the other great powers will continue to have a difficult time encouraging China to do more.

The goal here is analysis, not moral judgment. China's postcolonial nationalism often leads Chinese commentators to level over-the-top accusations against the United States and other great powers, suggesting that their entreaties to cooperation have some nefarious intent. But Chinese analysts and officials also make more thoughtful, logical, and compelling arguments for why China should be treated differently than advanced industrial nations. Compared to all other great powers and medium powers, China's per capita GDP is quite small and its social and political challenges incomparably larger than any other great power. China's per capita GDP in 2013 was the same as Ecuador's. Nobody is expecting Ecuadorians to contribute greatly to global governance—not so for the Chinese. While China has the largest holdings of foreign reserves in the world and has run a current account surplus with the developed world for decades, it also has a nascent and underdeveloped social security system at home and more than 100 million people still living in abject poverty. So when, for instance, it is asked to use its foreign exchange reserves on a large scale abroad to prop up economies in Europe, many in China wonder about the social justice in such a proposal. Why should a developing country with the frailest of safety nets bail out rich social democracies with per capita GDPs several times China's simply because those states are now realizing the results of many years of profligate government spending?

China, the world's largest emitter of greenhouse gases, also needs to burn carbon to continue to grow. Developed countries dispersed massive amounts of CO_2 into the atmosphere as they industrialized and have only in the past two or three decades turned their attention to the negative results of that behavior. But the world's most advanced economies have also become much more service-oriented, so the realization comes at a relatively convenient time in their economic histories. Chinese leaders and scholars also correctly point out that those same advanced countries benefit from consuming the cheap products manufactured in China's coastal greenhouse gas belt, often by firms owned in the countries complaining most loudly about Beijing's emissions.

China is a major importer of natural resources and has energy firms that are entering the global marketplace relatively late in the game. Chinese officials and commentators argue that China cannot be so finicky as to turn down oil and gas partnerships with regimes considered unsavory in Washington, Tokyo, and European capitals simply because those partnerships might serve to undercut global humanitarian or non-proliferation efforts. So China does lots of business with perpetrators of mass killings in Sudan, supporters of terrorism and violators of the Nuclear Nonproliferation Treaty in Iran, and other questionable suppliers. Chinese leaders can also point to the long history of close relations between unsavory oil-producing regimes and the United States, Great Britain, and France. With its own authoritarian rule, its recent history of the use of military force against civilians, and its own recent experience with international sanctions and condemnation, Beijing is also predictably less comfortable than the capitals of the advanced liberal democracies with condemning, sanctioning, and intervening in authoritarian regimes in the developing world.

Fortunately, there are solid responses to these Chinese arguments, some of which are accepted by segments of China's elite. All are based in long-term thinking and a recognition that China has benefited and continues to benefit greatly from the economic stability and security of the current international system. Nuclear proliferation, terrorists finding safe haven in poorly governed states, financial instability in its export markets, and potentially catastrophic changes in the global climate would all affect China at least as much as they do any of the advanced democracies. But such a holistic, over-the-horizon approach to current issues is difficult to market in any country, democratic or authoritarian. It is a particularly hard sell in a country like China with very pressing near-term challenges. * * *

Diplomats from the United States and its allies have enjoyed limited success in convincing China to make near-term sacrifices. Such entreaties might appear to be a trap designed to undercut China's overall national power. * * *

* * * [M]any Chinese commentators view Zoellick's challenge to China as a ruse to get China to foot the bill for something that will benefit the United States and other countries much more than China. Rather than accepting Zoellick's arguments that global governance is a shared mission of all the great powers, they wonder why China should "help" the United States with its problems. After all, Washington continues to sell weapons to Taiwan and support Japanese military enhancements. Since Chinese elites are worried about regime stability and personal promotion within the CCP, they are likely more concerned about the domestic political need for near-term job creation at home than the future effects of long-term global warming. * * *

The reality, however, is that those countries have little choice but to foster Chinese activism. China's sheer size and its deep connections to the global economy as both a producer and an importer mean that the world cannot afford to give China a pass. China is the world's largest trader of manufactured goods, one of the world's largest importers of natural resources, the world's largest emitter of greenhouse gases, a close diplomatic and economic partner of several of the world's worst proliferators and failed states, and the holder of the largest reserves of foreign currency. When the other great powers seek cooperation from China on international security and humanitarian, economic, and environmental problems, China can undercut the efforts without even intentionally doing so. It is in this sense that China is too big to fail to pull its weight on global governance.

■   ■   ■

NOTES

1. World Bank, http://data.worldbank.org/indicator/NY.GNP.PCAP.CD.
2. GDP per capita (PPP) in 2012. CIA World Factbook, https://www.cia.gov/library/publications/the-world-factbook/geos/us.html.
3. Harry Harding, *China's Second Revolution: Reform After Mao* (Washington, DC: Brookings Institution, 1987).
4. Richard K. Betts and Thomas J. Christensen, "China: Getting the Questions Right," *The National Interest,* Winter 2000–2001.
5. Aaron L. Friedberg, *A Contest for Supremacy: China, America, and the Struggle for Mastery in Asia* (New York: Norton, 2011).
6. John J. Mearsheimer, "China's Unpeaceful Rise," *Current History,* April 2006.
7. Martin Jacques, *When China Rules the World: The End of the Western World and the Birth of a New Global Order* (New York: Penguin Books, 2009).
8. For the work that originally coined the term "stability-instability paradox," see Glenn Snyder, "The Balance of Power and the Balance of Terror," in *The Balance of Power,* ed. Paul Seabury (San Francisco: Chandler Publishers, 1965), 184–201.
9. See [Robert] Jervis, *The Meaning of the Nuclear Revolution,* [the Prospect of Armageddon (Ithaca, NY: Cornell University Press, 1989),] chapter 3; and Thomas Schelling, *Arms and Influence* (New Haven, CT: Yale University Press, 1967), 18–25.
10. Amos Tversky and Daniel Kahneman, "Prospect Theory: An Analysis of Decision under Risk," *Econometrica* 47, no. 2 (March 1979), 263–91. For interesting applications of the theory to international relations, see Rose McDermott, *Risk Taking in International Relations: Prospect Theory in Post-War American Foreign Policy* (Ann Arbor: University of Michigan Press, 1998); Barbara Farnham, ed., *Avoiding Losses/Taking Risks: Prospect Theory and International Conflict* (Ann Arbor: University of Michigan Press, 1994); and James W. Davis, *Threats and Promises: The Pursuit of International Influence* (Baltimore, MD: Johns Hopkins University Press, 2000), 32–35.
11. Jervis, *The Meaning of the Nuclear Revolution,* 168–73.
12. For a masterful overview of China's historical handling of its sovereignty disputes on land and at sea, see Taylor Fravel, *Strong Borders, Secure Nation: Cooperation and Conflict in China's Territorial Disputes* (Princeton, NJ: Princeton University Press, 2008). For analysis of China's most assertive recent reactions to Japanese and Filipino behavior in the South China Sea and East China Sea, see Taylor Fravel, "China's Island Strategy: 'Redefine the Status Quo,'" *The Diplomat,* November 1, 2012,

http://thediplomat.com/china-power/chinas-island-strategy-redefine-the-status-quo/.

13. See Kevin O'Brien and Rachel E. Stern, "Introduction: Studying Contention in Contemporary China," in *Popular Protests in China,* ed. Kevin O'Brien (Cambridge, MA: Harvard University Press, 2008), 12.

14. Kathrin Hille, "China: Citizens United," *Financial Times,* July 29, 2013, citing the work of Professor Sun Liping of Tsinghua University.

15. For a good summation of the challenges facing the Xi Jinping government, see Bruce Dickson, "Revising Reform: China's New Leaders and the Challenges of Governance," *China: An International Journal* 10, no. 2 (August 2012), 34–51.

16. Robert B. Zoellick, "Whither China: From Membership to Responsibility?" Remarks to the National Committee of U.S–China Relations, New York City, September 21, 2005, http://2001-2009.state.gov/s/d/former/zoellick/rem/53682.htm.

Alastair Iain Johnston

HOW NEW AND ASSERTIVE IS CHINA'S NEW ASSERTIVENESS?

In recent years, it has become increasingly common in U.S. media, pundit, and academic circles to describe the diplomacy of the People's Republic of China (PRC) as newly or increasingly assertive.[1] Some observers have even suggested that this new assertiveness reflects a fundamental shift in Chinese diplomacy away from Beijing's more status quo–oriented behavior of the previous thirty years.[2] Many believe that it reflects a conscious decision by the top leadership in the wake of the 2008–09 financial crisis to be much more proactive in challenging U.S. interests in East Asia and, indeed, elsewhere around the world. The new assertiveness meme has "gone viral" in the U.S. media, the blogosphere, and in scholarly work.

This article argues, however, that the new assertiveness meme underestimates the degree of assertiveness in certain policies in the past, and overestimates the amount of change in China's diplomacy in 2010 and after. Much of China's diplomacy in 2010 fell within the range in foreign policy preferences, diplomatic rhetoric, and foreign policy behavior established in the Jiang Zemin and Hu Jintao eras. Moreover, the claims about a new assertiveness typically do not provide a definition of assertiveness, are unclear about the causal mechanisms behind this shift toward assertiveness, and lack comparative rigor that better contextualizes China's diplomacy in 2010.

From *International Security* 37, no. 4 (Spring 2013): 7–48; *International Security* 41, no.3 (Winter 2016/17): 7–43; with Kai Quek, *International Security* 42, no.3 (Winter 2017/18): 7–36. Some of the author's notes have been omitted.

Why should policymakers and scholars worry about a problematic characterization of Chinese foreign policy? Putting aside the intellectual importance of accurately measuring the dependent variable in the study of a major power's foreign policy, there are two good reasons. First, if it persists, the new assertiveness meme could contribute to an emerging security dilemma in the U.S.-China relationship. "Talk" is consequential for both interstate and intrastate politics during intensifying security dilemmas and strategic rivalries. How adversaries are described reverberates in the domestic politics of both sides.[3] The effect is often the narrowing of public discourse. As public discourse narrows and as conventional wisdoms become habituated, it becomes more difficult for other voices to challenge policy orthodoxies.[4] Similar to the "containment" meme in China,[5] the new assertiveness meme or others similar to it in the United States could, in the future, reduce the range of interpretations of Chinese foreign policy, potentially narrowing policy options available to decisionmakers (assuming this discourse becomes accepted by national security decisionmakers).

Second, the new assertiveness meme may reflect an important but understudied feature of international relations going forward—that is, the speed with which discursive bandwagoning (or herding, to use a different metaphor) in the online media and the pundit blogosphere creates faulty conventional wisdoms. As I show later, a growing literature on the intensive and extensive agenda-setting interaction between the online media and the blogosphere has emerged in U.S. political discourse. The implications of this interactivity for interstate conflict, however, remain unexplored.

The first section of this article reviews examples of PRC assertiveness prior to 2010 to contextualize the emergence of the new assertiveness meme in 2010. The second section looks in more critical detail at several PRC foreign policy actions in 2010 that observers have described as newly assertive. The third section asks why the inaccuracies in the characterization of Chinese diplomacy during this period occurred. I focus, in particular, on the tendency of analysts to select on the dependent variable; on the a historical nature of much of their analysis; and on the generally poor specification of their causal arguments.

Assertiveness before 2010

Beginning in late 2009 and into 2010, U.S. analysts and media started to claim that Chinese rhetoric and behavior had begun to demonstrate substantial change. As evidence of a newly assertive China, they pointed to China's allegedly more assertive diplomacy at the Copenhagen conference on climate change in December 2009; to its angry reaction to U.S. arms sales to Taiwan in January 2010 and to the Dalai Lama's visit in February 2010; to its apparently more expansive claims over the South China Sea in March 2010; to its diplomatic defense of violent actions by the Democratic People's Republic of Korea (DPRK) in March and November 2010; and to its tough response to the Japanese arrest of a Chinese fishing captain in September 2010.[6] * * * The new assertiveness meme took off in the media, pundit, and academic communities. Judging from the sharp spike in [the number of U.S. news articles, English-language blogs, and academic works referencing an "assertive China"] beginning in 2010, if this discourse accurately reflected reality, one would expect there to have been a radical change in Chinese foreign policy.

This perception of a new assertiveness, however, is problematic on two grounds. First, it ignores persistent assertiveness in Chinese foreign policy on sovereignty and territory issues prior to 2010. Second, it misreads many of the specifics of the cases of alleged assertiveness in 2010. Let me turn to the first problem. I take up the second problem in the next section.

There are two requirements for making the claim of a new Chinese assertiveness beginning in 2010: (1) a clear definition and indicators of assertiveness; and (2) evidence that diplomacy displayed a substantially higher value on these indicators in 2010 compared with previous years. Unfortunately, the discourse about a newly assertive China has suffered from a dearth of definitions and valid indicators. Analysts have used a number of synonyms in lieu of a definition: truculent, arrogant, belligerent, hard-line, tough, bullying, militant, and even revolutionary. The implication is that China's diplomacy was notably more threatening, exhibited more hostile preferences, and expressed these preferences in more conflictual language than at any other time after the end of the Cold War (though the newly assertive argument is unclear about the temporal baseline one should use). Today, there is still no consensus definition of "assertive" in the international relations literature on which to draw. Some scholars use assertive to refer to a constructive activism in international life.[7] Others use it to describe imperialistic, nationalistic, or anti-normative behavior.[8] There is no international relations theory that employs a typology of state behavior that includes "assertive" as a category. From usage, however, one can come up with a relatively simple and clearer definition than is implied in most of the commentary, namely, a form of assertive diplomacy that explicitly threatens to impose costs on another actor that are clearly higher than before (e.g., "if you sell weapons to Taiwan, we will harm you in much more costly ways than before"; or "if you let the Dalai

Lama visit, the costs for you will be substantially greater than before").

Given this definition, it is hard to conclude that 2010 saw an unprecedented spike in Chinese assertiveness compared with other periods after the Cold War. One need only recall the massive exercises, including missile firings, that the People's Liberation Army (PLA) held opposite Taiwan in 1995–96 to signal to the United States that the PRC was still involved in the Chinese civil war and that, as a result, Washington could not expect a permanent peace. Or the reaction to the U.S. bombing of China's embassy in Belgrade in 1999, where the Chinese government allowed students to violate international law and to bombard the U.S. embassy with rocks and bottles. Anti-U.S. rhetoric was unrelentingly shrill for several months after the bombing. For instance, through the rest of 1999, out of 447 reports on the embassy bombing in the *People's Daily,* 165 (37 percent) referenced "barbaric" (*yeman*) U.S./NATO behavior. On June 22, 1999, an "observer" piece in the *People's Daily*—representing some, though not all, voices in the Chinese leadership—likened the United States to Nazi Germany.[9] Then, in April 2001, after a midair collision between a U.S. EP-3 surveillance airplane and a Chinese fighter jet compelled the EP-3 to land at a Chinese military airport on Hainan Island, China held the downed U.S. military personnel essentially as hostages for more than a week to extract an apology from the United States for an accident caused by a reckless Chinese pilot. The reported rudeness of Chinese diplomats toward President Barack Obama at the Copenhagen climate change conference in December 2009, as well as other reports about the new arrogance of Chinese diplomats of late, would seem to pale in comparison with these sorts of actions.[10]

These are well-known anecdotes of pre-2010 assertiveness, but a more systematic indicator of assertiveness—the official discourse about issues of sovereignty—also suggests that 2010 does not represent as dramatic a shift as most analysts claim. The sensitivity to challenges to sovereignty is at the heart of much of China's more uncompromising foreign policy positions on territory. Figure 4.3 shows the monthly frequency of articles that reference "sovereignty" (*zhuquan*) in the *People's Daily* from 1990 to 2012, with trends highlighted by a lowess curve.[11] Despite an increase beginning in 2009 and into 2010, the sovereignty discourse did not reach the levels expressed following the 1996 Taiwan Strait crisis; the May 1999 embassy bombing; the EP-3 downing in April 2001; or the anti-Japanese demonstrations of the spring of 2005. The data appear to show that the most recent increase in the frequency of references began in the first half of 2009 partly in response to the Philippines passing a law claiming the Scarborough Shoal (Huangyan Island) as Philippines territory and Malaysia's and Vietnam's submission of their continental shelf claims to the United Nations Commission on the Limitations of the Continental Shelf.[12]

Together, these past examples of Chinese assertiveness and the data on the official sovereignty discourse suggest that 2010 was not a watershed in Chinese diplomacy toward sovereignty and territorial integrity issues. I now turn to the second problem with the conventional wisdom about an assertive China—the misreading of several positions taken by Chinese diplomacy in 2010.

Examples of China's New Assertiveness?

Much of the commentary on China's new assertiveness has centered on seven events that occurred in late 2009 and 2010. Yet if one pays close attention to the carefully crafted linguistic formulae that the Chinese government uses to express authoritative diplomatic positions[13], as well as to the actual foreign policy behavior "on the ground,"

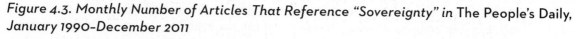

Figure 4.3. Monthly Number of Articles That Reference "Sovereignty" in The People's Daily, *January 1990–December 2011*

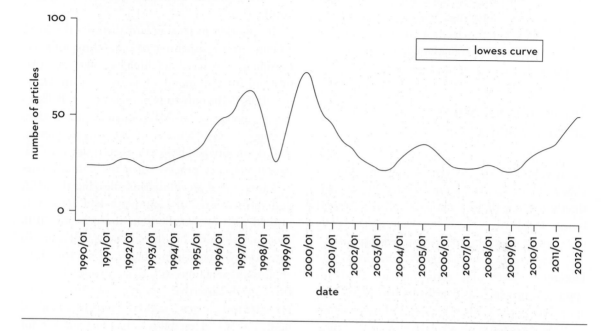

Copenhagen Summit on Climate Change, December 2009

The Copenhagen conference held in December 2009 was aimed at strengthening states' commitments to mitigate climate change. Many analysts pointed to China's behavior at Copenhagen as the first example of an increased level of assertiveness. Some commentators focused on the allegedly rude and in-your-face behavior of some Chinese diplomats as evidence of a new assertiveness.[14] Others, however, saw China's diplomacy at the conference as symptomatic of a more proactive effort by China to resist demands from Europe, the United States, and many developing countries to commit to a timetable for greenhouse gas reductions and to accept monitoring of national performance. This interpretation misreads Chinese diplomacy in Copenhagen (or misuses the term "assertive"). Rather than representing a new assertiveness, the Chinese position in Copenhagen—no commitments on ceilings and timetables and resistance to strict verification of national performance—reflected an enduring position, dating to the early 1990s.[15] In other words, there was virtually no change in Chinese diplomacy at the summit. Chinese diplomacy on this issue was risk averse—avoid any changes in policy and try to prevent outcomes inconsistent with this policy. What had changed was the reaction to China's position. The Chinese Ministry of Foreign Affairs (MFA) was unprepared for the level of activism by the United States and Europe in criticizing China's position on climate change, and it overestimated the unity within the developing world on the issue. In particular, it was unprepared for being singled

there is no obvious pattern of new assertiveness across all these cases.

out so vociferously by various actors as a major part of the global warming problem. In short, it was unprepared for the changing diplomatic alignments on global warming. As a result, some of its prickly diplomacy was likely a conservative backlash to changed diplomatic conditions, not a change in preferences or tactics on the issue.

Taiwan Arms Sales, January 2010

Many analysts characterized Beijing's reaction to U.S. arms sales to Taiwan in January 2010 as distinctly tougher than in the past.[16] This portrayal is too simplistic. China's reaction to the arms sales can be divided into two distinct responses.[17] The first was to the Pentagon's decision in late December 2009 and early January 2010 to approve contracts to U.S. arms industries for sales agreed to by the George W. Bush administration in 2008. This response was relatively mild. Using the basic standard language for a reaction to U.S. arms sales, the MFA denounced the Pentagon's decision as "harming China's national security" and as "interference in internal affairs." In contrast to statements from 2000 to 2008, the MFA moderated its position slightly by omitting the term "crude" (*cubao*) to modify "interference in internal affairs" and omitting "endangering" (*weihai*) to modify "national security."[18] These linguistic choices were most likely designed to signal China's understanding that the Department of Defense announcements were about a Bush administration decision.

Beijing's second response was to a new package of arms sales of about $6.4 billion authorized by the Obama administration in late January 2010. This time the reaction was stronger. In rhetorical terms, the MFA restored the term "crude" to modify "interference" and replaced "harming" with the tougher term "seriously endangering" to modify "national security."[19] Still, the MFA's rhetorical response to the second arms sales decision fell within the boundaries of past public responses to U.S. arms sales to Taiwan dating back to at least 2000.

In addition to its standard rhetoric, the MFA announced the suspension of U.S.-China military-to-military contacts; but China had taken a similar measure after a round of arms sales in October 2008.[20] The only truly new element in Beijing's 2010 response was an MFA statement about sanctioning U.S. companies that sold arms to Taiwan. This possibility had been discussed inside the Chinese interagency process when the United States had announced previous arms sales, but the MFA and the Ministry of Commerce had apparently resisted calls for sanctions in the past. In 2010, though, they agreed to the sanctions language. To date, however, no evidence has emerged that China applied any sanctions to U.S. companies. In short, this "newly assertive" element of the Chinese response to U.S. arms sales to Taiwan was indeed new, and it did establish a baseline marker for future reactions. In practice, however, it was a symbolic element in an overall response within the range of past Chinese reactions.

■ ■ ■

The South China Sea as a "Core Interest," March 2010

In late April 2010, a *New York Times* article cited a single U.S. government source who claimed that during a meeting in March between senior Chinese officials (including State Councillor Dai Bingguo) and two senior U.S. officials (Deputy Secretary of State James Steinberg and National Security Council Asia Director Jeffrey Bader), China had stated for the first time that the South China Sea was a "core interest, on par with Taiwan and Tibet."[21] If true, this would have signaled a major change in China's policy toward the area. It would have been a clear indication that Beijing had dropped the idea of negotiation over maritime disputes in the region, just as there could be no negotiation over the formal status of Taiwan or Tibet. The *New York Times* report spread rapidly through the media and pundit blogosphere in the United States.[22] At a minimum, it was responsible for 36 percent (and almost certainly much more) of the subsequent U.S. media coverage of the "core interest" story through late 2011. In the English-language blogosphere, at least 51 percent of the blogs that referred to China's alleged claim about core interests and the South China Sea were ultimately derived from the *New York Times* story and its single anonymous source.[23] It became conventional wisdom that senior Chinese officials had announced this change in their meeting with Steinberg and Bader.[24]

There is, however, no corroborating evidence that Steinberg and Bader were told that the South China Sea was a "core interest" similar to Taiwan or Tibet. Michael Swaine reports that high-level U.S. officials deny that it was the message they took away from the meeting with Dai Bingguo.[25] My own conversations with relevant U.S. officials confirm Swaine's findings. Bader himself notes in his recent book about Obama's Asia policy that no Chinese official at that meeting said that the South China Sea was a core interest.[26]

The Chinese government was slow to try to control the effects of this story, however. Only in August 2010, when it became clear that the supposed "core interest" statement was producing blowback from other states, did the Chinese government began to counter the story through surrogates in China's academic and media worlds. Some well-connected Chinese academics suggested that Steinberg and Bader might have been told that the islands China occupied in the South China Sea were core interests or that the islands were related to China's territorial integrity, which, in turn, was a core interest. These suggestions would be consistent with long-standing general statements that defending sovereign territory is a core interest.[27]

Regardless, the academics claimed, no senior foreign policy official had said that the entire South China Sea was a core interest similar to Taiwan or Tibet. As part of the subtle pushback, Premier Wen Jiabao repeated a standard list of core Chinese interests—sovereignty, unification, territorial integrity—in a speech to the United Nations in September 2010, a list that pointedly excluded the South China Sea.[28]

The MFA's indirect effort to deny the story was apparently a function of its sensitivity to appearing too soft on territorial issues. As a senior Chinese foreign policy official put it, once the story was out, the MFA could not publicly say that the South China Sea was not a core interest—China does not want to preempt the possibility of making such a declaration. Nor could it state publicly that no senior official had said the South China Sea was a core interest, that the *New York Times* source was wrong. This, too, might have raised the ire of nationalists within the population and the elite.[29] It would seem, then, that the preferred response was to try to counter the story through the media and through closed meetings with governments in the region.

It is likely, then, that the source for this particular story about China's rhetorical new assertiveness was wrong. Nonetheless, it appears that China lost control of the discourse to the foreign media, to the quasi-commercialized media in China, and to the pundit world outside China. To be sure, in 2009 and 2010 China's military and paramilitary presence in the South China Sea was more active than in previous years. Indeed, the South China Sea is perhaps the only example where China's diplomatic rhetoric and practice did shift fairly sharply in a more hard-line direction in this period.[30] As Taylor Fravel points out, however, some of this activity was in response to more proactive diplomacy by other claimants to establish the legal boundaries of their claims in the region.[31] Some of this activity may also have been a function of a decision to begin to assert the extent of China's claims so as to clarify what it can (and will) diplomatically and militarily defend. So even though China's diplomacy on this issue was more active in defending its maritime interests, these interests and preferences concerning its claims were unchanged. The timing of the most recent increase in rhetorical toughness (as measured by references to sovereignty in the *People's Daily*; see Figure 4.3) would be consistent with this assertiveness.

Response to U.S. Deployment of Carrier to the Yellow Sea, July 2010

In response to the DPRK's sinking of the South Korean naval vessel, the *Cheonan*, in March 2010, the United States and the Republic of Korea (ROK) engaged in a series of military deterrence exercises. In early June, the South Korean media reported—evidently based on leaked Pacific Command contingency plans[32]—that the United States was planning to deploy an aircraft carrier to the Yellow Sea to participate in these exercises.[33] China's tough response to these reports contributed to a view in the United States that China was not just ignoring North Korea's provocative actions, but enabling the North by refusing to condemn it and by criticizing U.S. (and ROK) efforts to deter Pyongyang. The Chinese reaction was seen by many as part of Beijing's new assertiveness.

It appears, however, that in this instance, PLA hard-liners were the first to respond to the initial reports that the United States was planning to exercise an aircraft carrier in the Yellow Sea. In late June 2010, the PRC announced it would conduct live-fire exercises in the East China Sea.[34] Whether such an exercise could have been conducted without at least Hu Jintao's approval is doubtful. The rhetorical response, however, seems to have been driven by the PLA.

■   ■   ■

In sum, this particular instance of new assertiveness may have been more a function of inter-bureaucratic conflict and poor coordination than a reflection of a decision by top leaders to be more proactive in diplomatically challenging a U.S. military presence close to China's territory. In essence, the PLA's Ma Xiaotian ended up claiming the Chinese position before the MFA had responded. * * *

Senkaku/Diaoyudao Trawler Incident, September 2010

On September 7, 2010, a Chinese trawler captain ordered his ship to ram Japanese coast guard ships that were trying to chase the trawler away from the Senkaku/Diaoyudao Islands.[35] The crew was sent back to China, but the captain was detained, and Japanese authorities began a legal investigation of his actions. The Chinese government responded with repeated and increasingly tough demands for the captain's release. For the most part, the foreign media defined China's reaction as unprecedentedly assertive.[36]

Chinese leaders believed that Japan was engaging in unusually provocative behavior by refusing to release the captain early on.[37] The Chinese claim that there has been an unwritten norm to release fishermen who violate the twelve-mile limit around the islands, and that past Japanese practice had led China to believe the captain would be released quickly and without publicity.[38] Different Chinese analysts proposed other reasons for Japan's decision to use its domestic legal process to detain and investigate the captain.[39] Some believed it reflected paralysis in Japan's decisionmaking process resulting from the distraction of a leadership contest in the ruling Democratic Party of Japan (DPJ) at the time. Others suggested that the DPJ's unfamiliarity with how previous Japanese governments had handled similar situations was to blame. Still others pointed to a general hardening of Japan's diplomacy on all of its territorial disputes, whether with China in the East China Sea or with Russia over the Northern Islands. * * *

From a crisis management perspective, however, China's official response was systematic and relatively controlled. Over the two-week period after the captain was first detained, the demand for his release moved systematically from the Chinese embassy in Japan to the Foreign Ministry spokesperson to the foreign minister to the state counselor in charge of foreign policy and eventually to Premier Wen Jiabao.

As the demands moved up the chain of command, the Chinese government's language become tougher, escalating from statements about the need to "protect" sovereignty to the need to "defend" sovereignty, and from "dissatisfaction" with the Japanese response to "strong indignation." Wen Jiabao's tone was the harshest. He referred to the islands as "sacred territory" (*shensheng lingtu*), the only time in the crisis that a China official described the islands this way.[40]

As the rhetoric escalated, so did the actions taken to signal Beijing's discontent. These included progressively canceling more and more local and central government-to-government interactions and arresting four Japanese citizens for allegedly photographing military sites. Some observers believe that China's assertiveness was especially evident in two other actions: the demand for compensation and an apology from the Japanese government after the captain had been released; and an embargo on Chinese rare earth exports to Japan.[41] The demand for compensation, however, was perfunctory and clearly aimed at a domestic Chinese audience. The MFA mentioned this demand only once (on September 25) and then promptly dropped it from the official discourse. In this regard, it is hard to see it as a particularly escalatory move.

The rare earth embargo, if true, would constitute a new assertiveness because it threatened to impose much higher costs on a key Japanese economic interest. There have been conflicting reports, however, about how many rare earth exports were delayed, for how long, and by whom. Some reports suggest that Chinese customs officials, anticipating further deterioration in the relationship with Japan, might have taken it upon themselves to slow down export approvals.[42] This seems uncharacteristically proactive for a Chinese bureaucracy, however. Others suggest that the central leadership made an explicit decision to reduce shipments as a warning to Japan, which is possible: the timing of the alleged embargo—reported to have begun on September 21[43]—was the same as that of Wen Jiabao's tough demands in New York. Other reports suggest, however, that little evidence exists that the leadership decided to embargo rare earths, and that Japanese media and some industry experts misinterpreted the rather volatile nature of Chinese rare earth shipments in general. Previous months had seen more dramatic drops in shipments having to do with Japanese demand bumping up against a quota system for exports, yet there was no speculation about embargoes then.[44]

■   ■   ■

For all of China's rhetorical escalation, in some ways Beijing took efforts to control domestic reactions and to prevent large-scale anti-Japanese demonstrations. As the crisis escalated in mid-September and as both sides began to worry about a repeat of the large-scale anti-Japanese violence in 2005 in response to Japan's efforts to obtain a permanent seat on the UN Security Council, the Chinese Communist Party–connected *Global Times* explicitly signaled that 2010 would not be a repeat of 2005. The editorial stated that the violent escalation of 2005 demonstrations was a "road to ruin," that is, too extreme.[45]

Moreover, the government took steps to dampen harsher expressions of anti-Japanese emotion. For example, on or around September 16, about two days before the September 18 anniversary and not long after a Japanese school in Tianjin had been damaged by anti-Japanese vandals, even the *Global Times* stopped all anonymous postings from netizens, shutting down a forum that had seen increasingly racist postings inciting violence against Japanese in China. It appears, too, that the authorities prevented most of the high-profile, hard-line PLA media commentators from writing or talking publicly during the Senkaku/Diaoyudao dustup.[46]

Response to the DPRK Shelling of Yeongpyeong Island, November 2010

On November 23, 2010, the DPRK shelled ROK-held Yeongpyeong Island, killing four military and civilian personnel and wounding several more. The ROK responded by shelling the North Korean batteries. In the wake of the DPRK attack, the U.S. chairman of the Joint Chiefs, Adm. Michael Mullen, bluntly noted that Pyongyang's "reckless behavior" was "enabled by their friends in China."[47] His reference, and that of others, was to China's unwillingness to directly criticize the DPRK after the *Cheonan* sinking and the Yeongpyeong shelling. Some contrasted China's apparent acquiescence to North Korea's provocations in 2010 with the harsh language that Beijing had used to criticize its first nuclear test in 2006.

Although China officially used a particularly pointed term in 2006—flagrant (*hanran*)—to criticize the North Korean test, it also tempered this criticism by noting that all sides should respond coolly, use peaceful means to resolve problems, and avoid actions that would increase tensions.[48] Since then, the Chinese government has employed similar language whenever Pyongyang has engaged in behavior that raises tensions on the Korean Peninsula, including in its 2010 response to the *Cheonan* sinking and the shelling of Yeongpyeong Island.[49] In other words, it was not new language, and for Beijing it embodies the basic principles of crisis management that all sides should follow.

These principles reflect the PRC leadership's preference for preserving the existence of a stable DPRK. One internal assessment of crisis management on the peninsula, written by regional experts at the PLA Academy of Military Sciences, summarized Beijing's concerns: North Korea is an unstable regime that engages in provocative and unpredictable behavior, "walking on the margins of war."[50] Yet war on the peninsula would mean the regime's collapse. This, in turn, would threaten not only China's border security, but also the peaceful international environment necessary for China's economic development, and the existence of a buffer against the United States. Thus North Korea's survival is a question of China's national security.[51] By this logic, Chinese policy should thus focus on minimizing threats to the DPRK's internal stability and preventing shocks to the political and military relationship between the relevant parties. Even though many in China recognized that North Korea's behavior in 2010 was a main source of instability on the peninsula, Beijing believed that, given the regime's fragile condition, it made little sense to add to the pressure on the DPRK, or to publicly humiliate it by endorsing the ROK's version of the *Cheonan* incident.[52] Rather, China appears to have taken a two-pronged approach to resolving the DPRK problem, arguing that the United States should provide security assurances and improve the DPRK's external security environment, while China should be responsible for helping the DPRK reform its economy and open to the outside.[53]

The problem for Beijing was that, in the context of DPRK behavior in 2010, its standard position of all sides avoiding provocative behavior was rightly viewed as taking the DPRK's side. In other words, Beijing's policy prescription for stability on the peninsula had not changed as much as the situation had, leaving China's status quo–oriented policy even more in tension with the preferences of other states.[54]

Summary

These seven major events in Chinese foreign policy in 2010 represent a mixture of new assertiveness (South China Sea), old assertiveness with a twist (the threat to sanction U.S. arms manufacturers that sell to Taiwan); reduced assertiveness (the Dalai Lama visit); probably predictable responses to exogenous shocks (Senkaku/Diaoyudao incident); the continuation of reactive/passive policies in the face of changed and less-hospitable diplomatic circumstances (Copenhagen, DPRK policy); and in one case, empirical inaccuracy (the South China Sea as a core interest claim). In toto, the differences across these cases suggest that there was no across-the-board new assertiveness in Chinese diplomacy in 2010.

Analytical Problems with the New Assertiveness Meme

The argument that China's diplomacy in 2010 was newly assertive contains at least three analytical flaws that have characterized much of the commentary on Chinese foreign policy in the United States and elsewhere—selection on the dependent variable; ahistoricism; and poor causal specification. The first two are general methodological problems that often plague media and pundit analysis on a range of public policy questions; though serious, I do not go into them in detail here. The last deals with problematic empirical

claims associated with causal arguments, the evaluation of which requires critical examination of the available evidence.

Selecting on the Dependent Variable

A common problem in the new assertiveness analyses is that they consider only confirming evidence while ignoring disconfirming examples. The risk here is exaggerating change and discounting continuity. The pundit and media world thus tended to miss a great deal of ongoing cooperative interaction between the United States and China throughout 2010. Examples include the continued growth of U.S. exports to China during the year; the continued high congruence in U.S. and Chinese voting in the UN Security Council;[55] Chinese support for UN Security Council Resolution 1929, which imposed tougher sanctions on the Iranian regime—a move appreciated by the Obama administration;[56] Beijing's abiding by its 2009 agreement with the United States to hold talks with representatives of the Dalai Lama;[57] a Chinese decision to continue the appreciation of the renminbi prior to the Group of Twenty meeting in Toronto in June 2010; Hu Jintao's decision to attend the U.S.-hosted nuclear summit in April 2010 (in the wake of the January 2010 Taiwan arms sales decision, the Chinese had hinted that Hu would not attend the summit); a Chinese decision to pressure the Sudan government to exercise restraint should South Sudan declare independence; and China's more constructive cross-strait policies, in the wake of Ma Ying-jeou's 2008 election as president of the Republic of China, which have contributed to a decline in tensions between China and Taiwan, thus reducing the probability, for the moment, of a U.S. military conflict with the PRC.

■   ■   ■

Problematic Causal Arguments

A third problem with China's newly assertive meme is the poor specification of the causal arguments that observers use to explain this alleged change in diplomacy. The first rule of causal argument concerns timing: any change in the explanatory variable has to occur prior to a change in the variable to be explained. Thus any change in the main explanatory factors had to have been quite quick and acute prior to the new assertiveness of 2010. Was this, in fact, the case? Typically analysts point to four main explanations for China's new assertiveness in 2010.

CHANGE IN THE DISTRIBUTION OF POWER

The first explanation for a newly assertive China is a change in Chinese leaders' perceptions of the distribution of power, whereby they interpreted the 2008 financial crisis as a clear signal of the decline of U.S. power relative to China's. Chinese leaders therefore felt more confident in ignoring Deng Xiaoping's longtime axiom not to treat the United States as an adversary, and in challenging the United States on China's interests. Undoubtedly, such arguments appeared throughout 2009 and 2010 in China, particularly among more nationalistic commentators. Yet there was, and continues to be, an ongoing debate as to how much power has shifted between the United States and China, and what advantages this creates for China.

■   ■   ■

RISING CHINESE NATIONALISM

A second explanation for the new assertiveness is rising Chinese nationalism or anti-Americanism

or both. This is also a problematic explanation. For example, few of the new assertiveness analyses provide indicators of rising nationalism, let alone show a dramatic spike in nationalist sentiment just before 2010. In fact, empirically, the evidence for rising nationalism is mixed and depends on the indicators one uses. Some indicators suggest that the portion of the population with strongly anti-Japanese sentiment is increasing, but the portion of those with strongly anti-American views appears to be steady.[58] Other indicators suggest that, while pride in nation is at high levels (and increasing),[59] uncritical support for the government (a version of "China, love it or leave it") is much lower.[60] The denigration of American lifestyles and culture among the Chinese population appears to remain relatively low compared to criticisms of U.S. foreign policy.[61]

Even if there had been a steep jump in nationalism in 2009, for it to have a causal effect one would have to demonstrate how and why in 2010 Chinese leaders decided to take rising nationalism into greater account when making foreign policy decisions. Proponents of the nationalism argument offer no theory about how popular sentiments are translated into foreign policy. The explanation makes an assumption about the hypersensitivity of the top leadership to nationalist public opinion for which there is almost no systematic evidence as yet. In a political system where there are no electoral costs to ignoring public opinion, it is unclear why China's authoritarian leaders would care much about public views. Nor is it clear that China's top leaders would want public opinion to matter on strategically important questions—they prefer maneuverability, not constraint. One can develop at least four hypotheses for why the regime might be more sensitive to nationalism: (1) the more it fears that anti-foreign protests might turn into anti-CCP protests, the more it tries to head off nationalist protest by co-opting certain hard-line foreign policy rhetoric; (2) the more that political leaders normatively believe that the leadership should respond to the "minds of the people" (*minxin*), the more public opinion will be taken into account; (3) the more intense elite political struggle is, the more likely political competitors will use public opinion as a political tool against opponents; (4) and the more public opinion is emotional and mobilized (e.g., on relations with Japan or perhaps on alleged foreign intervention in China's relations with ethnic minorities), the more likely leaders will take public opinion into account (through one of the first three mechanisms).[62] No one has systematically tested these hypotheses on Chinese foreign policy in 2010.

THE POLITICS OF LEADERSHIP TRANSITION

A third explanation for China's new assertiveness concerns the political succession process leading up to the 18th Party Congress in November 2012. Here the argument is that, for the last few years, Hu Jintao focused on preserving his accomplishments and his political legacy once he left his posts. He was loathe to be seen as weak in foreign policy, especially in the context of a rapidly growing concern about social stability and regime legitimacy. Perceived weakness could encourage elite and mass criticism of the regime, thus undermining his legacy and weakening the CCP's rule. Presumably Hu's successor, Xi Jinping, is also determined not to be seen as weak in foreign policy as he maneuvers to consolidate his power and that of his possible allies.

■ ■ ■

THE POWER OF THE PLA

A fourth explanation for the new assertiveness centers on the possibility that the PLA is playing an increasingly independent role in foreign policy, either by acting with little policy guidance and presenting faits accomplis to the political leadership, or by taking high-profile public positions that political leaders are compelled to accept or, at least, consider seriously. This explanation is even more speculative than the other three. No one really knows the working relationship between the top political leadership and the PLA, as one hears different versions in Beijing.[63]

■ ■ ■

The answer to the question of PLA influence might best be divided, roughly speaking, into operations and strategy. On the one hand, the PLA has a near monopoly of expertise on operational issues and considerable institutional autonomy from other civilian institutions. This means there is limited civilian oversight of PLA operational activities, and whatever CCP monitoring there is depends on the time and expertise of the chair of the Central Military Commission (Hu Jintao in 2010) and his close advisers. When Hu was focused—as he most often appears to have been—on economic problems and political legitimacy issues, the PLA may ultimately have taken actions that were inconsistent with or in tension with China's overall foreign policy goals.[64] This is not a problem unique to the Chinese system—the United States has a considerably larger and more powerful civilian oversight apparatus of U.S. military operations, but even so civilians on the National Security Staff have complained that parts of the Department of Defense are not always as forthcoming about operational details as the civilians would like. In comparison with the United States, the problem facing Chinese civilian leaders may be one of degree not of kind. As in the U.S. case, however, the operational actions of the military are not necessarily a good guide to the more basic foreign policy preferences and intentions of the civilian leadership.

On the other hand, as an institution the PLA is not publicly expressing views on major policy

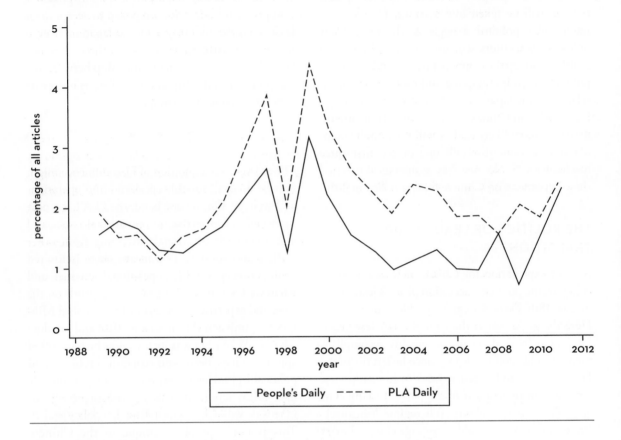

Figure 4.4. Relative Number of Articles That Reference "Sovereignty" (zhuquan)

issues and strategic orientation that are far from the CCP's message. There is a strong correlation between foreign policy rhetoric in the CCP's civilian voice—the *People's Daily*—and its military voice—the *PLA Daily*. As Figure [4.4] shows, articles that reference sovereignty (*zhuquan*) as a percentage of all articles in the *People's Daily* and the *PLA Daily* are closely correlated from year to year ($r = 0.77$, $p = 0.000$).

An anecdotal example of this consistency was the recent, apparently off-the-cuff comments by Deputy Chief of the General Staff Ma Xiaotian. When asked by the press in early June 2012 about the use of force in territorial disputes with the Philippines, he replied that diplomacy was the best method to resolve the issue and that force was a last resort. This was in contrast to PLA-connected pundits who have called for the early use of force to enforce China's claims.[65]

■　■　■

Conclusion

The seven events in Chinese diplomacy in 2010 that observers point to most frequently to support the new assertiveness argument did not constitute an across-the-board new assertiveness or a funda-mental change. Much of the media, pundit, and academic analysis glosses over crucial evidence, decontextualizes Chinese diplomacy, or relies on poorly specified causal arguments. This does not mean there was nothing newly assertive about Chinese diplomacy in this period. As noted, the one area where Beijing's rhetoric and behavior did threaten to impose substantially higher costs on states with disputes with China concerned mari-time claims in the South China Sea. Perhaps trig-gered by more proactive efforts by other claimants to legalize their claims through declarations and actions relating to the United Nations Convention of the Law of the Sea, PRC presence activities have generally increased in the last few years (e.g., more frequent patrols by various maritime-related administrative agencies, more risk-acceptant action to defend Chinese fishing activities, the encourage-ment of tourism, and more vigorous diplomatic pushback against other states' claims). Judging from the responses of other countries in the region, these activities clearly contributed to an escalation of tension in the East Asian maritime space.

Still, one should be cautious about generalizing from these maritime disputes to Chinese foreign policy writ large.

■   ■   ■

In security dilemmas, discourses about Self and Other tend to simplify and to polarize as attribution errors multiply and ingroup-outgroup differentia-tion intensifies.[66] The newly assertive China meme and the problematic analysis on which it is based suggest that the nature of the media-blogosphere interaction may become an important factor in explaining the speed and intensity of future security dilemma dynamics between states, including those between the United States and China.

■   ■   ■

IS CHINESE NATIONALISM RISING?
Evidence from Beijing

"Rising nationalism" has been a major meme in commentary on the development of China's material power since the early 1990s. Indeed, "ris-ing" is one of the most common qualifiers used by analysts to modify the term "Chinese national-ism." It is a common meme in media from around the world, as a search of LexisNexis will attest.[67] It appears in think tank analyses,[68] in statements from the U.S. Department of State, in U.S. Con-gress members' commentary, and in other govern-ment analysis.[69] Some of the earliest references to the meme came after Chinese leaders launched the Patriotic Education Campaign (PEC) in the post-Tiananmen period, in an effort to inoculate China's youth against an alleged Western ideological "peace-ful evolution" strategy.[70] If one searches "rising Chinese nationalism" in Google Scholar, one finds that much of the scholarship on Chinese politics and foreign policy has used the term. In short, among many, if not most, non-Chinese and many Chinese observers, it is largely taken for granted that nationalism in China has been rising since at least the early 1990s. Given the persistence of this empirical claim, one might wonder just how high or extreme nationalism in China can get.

Although little of this commentary defines the term "rising," by usage it seems to mean anything from more intensely felt, to more extreme, to more pervasive within society, to more salient for leaders, to more influential on policy. For the purposes of this article, I focus on rising nationalism in reference to the intensity or degree of nationalism expressed by ordinary citizens. I do not focus on the question of whether Chinese leaders are more sensitive to nationalism (indeed, they could be more sensitive to nationalism even as it declines in intensity or degree). Nor do I examine in detail the question of whether China's leaders have been more intensively promoting nationalism over time. In general, the discourse about rising nationalism, particularly in the media and among pundits, tends to refer more to the intensity of popular nationalism and less to its influence on policy.

The rising nationalism meme is one element in the narrative of a "newly assertive China" that generalizes from China's coercive diplomacy in maritime space to claims that a dissatisfied China is challenging a U.S.-dominated liberal international order writ large.[71] Rising nationalism, in this narrative, constrains the Chinese leadership and helps explain its more militantly realpolitik or noncooperative behaviors, as well as China's more proactive challenges to international "rules of the game."[72] In addition, rising popular nationalism has led many U.S. government officials to worry that the Chinese leadership will engage in diversionary conflict when China's economic growth slows.[73] Thus the rising nationalism meme is an important element of an even larger emerging narrative about a revisionist China.

Using an original time-series survey dataset from Beijing and a range of indicators of nationalism extending back to 1998, I conduct five different tests of the claim about China's rising nationalism. The analysis shows that there has not been a continuously rising level of nationalism among the survey respondents. Indeed, most indicators show a decline in levels of nationalism since around 2009. Moreover, contrary to the conventional wisdom, the data do not show that China's youth express higher levels of nationalism than older generations. Indeed, it is China's older generations that are more nationalistic than its youth. These findings—with due regard for caveats about representativeness—suggest that rising popular nationalism may not be a critically important variable constraining Chinese foreign policy.

The findings from the survey have a number of implications. First, they suggest that China's coercive diplomacy in maritime disputes over the last few years is unlikely to be a driven by rising popular nationalism. A list of more likely explanations includes the search for energy, fishing rights, the organizational interests of the military and of maritime law enforcement, leaders' preferences, elite nationalism, Chinese reactions to actions by other maritime claimants, an emerging U.S.-China security dilemma, and growing naval capabilities. Second, the findings suggest that rising popular nationalism is unlikely to spur Chinese leaders to engage in diversionary conflict in the face of an economic slowdown.[74] On a number of measures, levels of Chinese nationalism have stagnated or dropped since around 2009, even as annual economic growth rates have declined somewhat. Finally, the findings underscore that analysis of Chinese foreign policy has to be more consciously self-critical of the assumptions, conventional wisdoms, and memes that are circulated in the media, among pundits, and in academia. They also confirm that these elements are being rapidly reproduced in an era of digital and social media. Given the implications for stability in U.S.-China relations of the emergence of a "revisionist China" meme in the United States and of a "containing China" meme in China, it is especially important that scholars examine emerging conventional wisdoms and viral memes carefully and with a variety of data and methods.

The article starts with a review of the debate in the academic literature over rising Chinese nationalism and suggests how the heretofore absence of time-series data has limited progress in analysts' understanding of Chinese nationalism. The next section introduces the Beijing Area Study survey, a dataset that provides time-series data on a range of questions that tap into different components of nationalism. I then present five tests for rising nationalism, including the results of questions that are standard in the survey literature on nationalism, questions that tap into ethnocentrist views, and questions that measure hostility toward other countries. I also control for age, given that one element of the rising nationalism meme is the belief that the most extreme expressions come from Chinese youth as a whole. I find that on balance among the survey respondents Chinese nationalism has not been rising continuously over the last decade and a half, and in some measures has declined. Moreover, it is clear that younger respondents are less nationalistic than older ones.

Debates over Rising Nationalism in China

How do we know if Chinese nationalism is rising? We know in part because the media tells us so. As media system dependency theory in sociology and media agenda-setting literature in political science would suggest, the media is one of the main sources of information about international politics for nonspecialists,[75] Yet, often, reporting or analysis that mentions "rising Chinese nationalism" does not provide much, if any, systematic evidence for this claim.[76] * * *

This is not to say that the extant literature on Chinese nationalism is of poor quality. Most scholars working on nationalism in China fully understand the complex content and evolution of modern Chinese nationalism. One only need think of Vanessa Fong's thoughtful anthropological work that uncovered a youth nationalism expressed as a filial, though critical, loyalty to the cause of China's modernization;[77] or William Callahan's careful unpacking of the historical evolution and social construction of memories of humiliation;[78] or Tang Wenfang and Benjamin Darr's innovative comparison of levels of nationalism in China with those in other countries;[79] or Brian Rathbun's rigorous differentiation between patriotism and nationalism;[80] or Peter Gries' creative analysis of letters in the wake of the 1999 U.S. bombing of China's embassy in Belgrade to gauge the genuinely emotional content of youth nationalism;[81] or James Leibold's careful discourse analysis of a revived Han chauvinism among some Chinese youth.[82] Then there are James Reilly and Jessica Chen Weiss, who are leading the way in understanding the scope conditions under which nationalism may affect foreign policy.[83] They focus mainly on the minority of citizens who participate in nationalist demonstrations, rather than on broad trends in popular nationalism per se. But as good as this and other work is at uncovering the subtleties of Chinese nationalism, much of it either accepts the rising nationalism meme or does not study the phenomenon across time.

Testing the Rising Nationalism Claim: The Beijing Area Study

Testing the empirical validity of the rising nationalism meme has three requirements: conceptually valid, consistent, and observable or measurable indicators of nationalism; a metric with which to observe whether nationalism is rising or not; and a starting point, or baseline, against which to observe nationalism over time.[84] The Beijing Area Study (BAS), a more or less regularly administered random sample survey of opinion in the Beijing municipality, meets these requirements for testing the rising nationalism claim. From the late 1990s onward, in up to eleven waves, the study has included questions that are standard in the survey literature on nationalism.[85] * * *

The BAS includes questions that can tap into these three different components of nationalism. First, since 2002 it has asked respondents whether they strongly agreed, somewhat agreed, somewhat disagreed, or strongly disagreed with the following standard statements used in many other nationalism surveys: (1) even if I could choose any other country in the world, I would prefer to be a citizen of China than any other country; (2) in general, China is a better country than most others; and (3) everyone should support their government even when it is wrong.[86] Although distinct, these components are nonetheless correlated.[87]

Second, since 2000 the BAS has asked questions about perceived ethnonational identity differences between Chinese people, on the one hand, and Japanese and Americans, on the other. Specifically, the BAS asks respondents to place Chinese people and members of an out-group (Japanese people and American people) on a 7-point scale anchored by antonyms. The difference between where respondents placed Chinese people and where they placed members of the out-group is a measure of ethnonational identity difference. Identity difference perceptions are proving to be important explanations of policy preferences.[88]

Finally, since 1998 the BAS has measured the level of respondents' amity toward various countries on a 100-degree feeling thermometer, where 0 represents the most extreme cold and hostile feelings and 100 represents the most extreme warm and friendly feelings. The list of countries has included potential adversaries and competitors such as Japan and the United States.

■ ■ ■

What, then, do the BAS data show? In short, the conventional wisdom may overestimate the evidence for rising Chinese nationalism. In four tests for rising nationalism, I find evidence that in some cases levels of nationalism in Beijing today are lower than they were in the early 2000s. In other cases, the levels of nationalism may be somewhat higher today than they were in the early 2000s but are lower than they were in the mid-to-late 2000s. Moreover, as a fifth test suggests, contrary to the conventional wisdom, Chinese youth are less nationalistic than older generations, and by some measures less nationalistic today compared to the early 2000s.

Five Tests of the Rising Nationalism Claim

* * * Test 1: Pride in Nation and Blind Support for the State

* * * The longitudinal data for these measures suggest that there has been no sharp rise in nationalism in China since 2002, the first year the BAS used these measures. As Figure 4.5 indicates, prior to the Beijing Olympic Games in 2008, strong agreement with the statement about preferring to be a citizen of China than of any other country waivered around a stable mean, and the trend line was essentially flat. Strong agreement spikes in 2009, possibly in response to the effects of the 2008 Olympics. Thereafter it drops considerably to levels lower than before 2008. By 2015 the plurality response is no longer "strongly agree" but rather "somewhat agree."

Agreement with the statement that China is better than most other countries is somewhat less extreme, with higher portions choosing the "somewhat" answer (Figure 4.6). As with the first

Figure 4.5. *"I Would Prefer to Be a Citizen of China"*

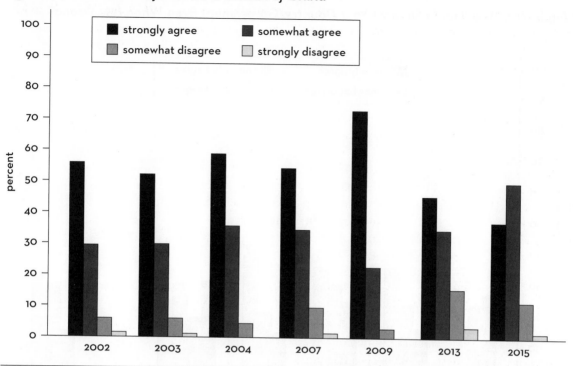

Figure 4.6. *"China Is a Better Country Than Most"*

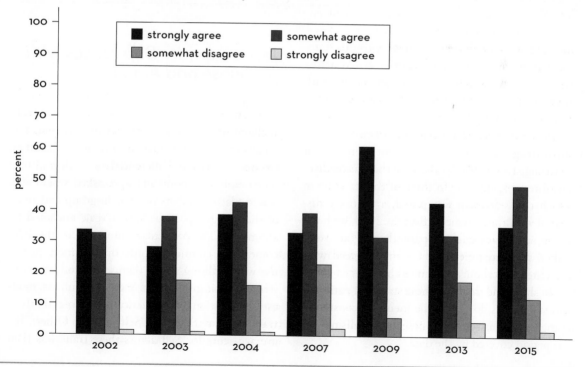

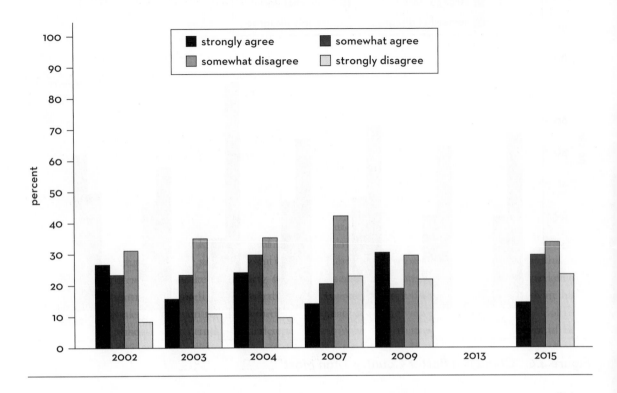

Figure 4.7. "You Should Support Your Country/Government Even When It is Wrong"

measure of nationalism, agreement with this statement prior to the Olympic Games varied across time. There was a peak in strong agreement with the statement in 2009, but by 2013 opinion shifts toward the "somewhat agree" category as well.

As for support for the nativist statement about supporting the country/government even when it is wrong, this is the weakest of the nationalism measures (Figure 4.7). In three of the six years in which this statement was posed, a plurality disagreed with the statement. Even in 2009, with the Olympic Games effect apparently still at work, only a small majority of the sample agreed with the statement, about the same as in 2004.

In short, the trends in these standard nationalism statements do not fit the meme of constantly rising or intensifying Chinese nationalism over the period covered by the data.[89]

Test 2: Identity Differences with Japanese and Americans

The second test of rising Chinese nationalism looks at change in what I call "identity difference scores" across time. The data used in this test are based on Osgood semantic differential procedures.[90] As noted earlier, respondents were asked where they would place members of their in-group and those of the out group on a 7-point scale anchored by antonyms. The particular antonyms in the BAS come from common words that Chinese people use when talking about themselves and others in terms of basic group traits (e.g., peacefulness, modesty, civilization, and sincerity). The scores on these traits were averaged for Self and for Other. The average score for Self across these traits was then subtracted from the average score for Other across these traits. This difference is the identity difference score. The identity difference score taps into the degree to which Chinese people believe that they are different in their essence from Japanese and American people. It captures a deep cognitive structure that influences individuals' policy preferences toward out-groups. * * *

Based on these identity difference scores, the data do not confirm a rapidly or even constantly rising level of Chinese nationalism. The data appear to show that perceptions of identity difference (mean value) peaked in 2009 and declined somewhat after that (though the 95 percent confidence interval in the Japan cases suggest possibly more stasis). There is virtually no difference if one looks at the trends in median values.

Test 3: Are Extreme Views Becoming More Common?

A third test focuses on change in the distribution of these various measures of nationalism. * * *

The data do not support a linear increase in extremist views. * * *

Test 4: Amity and Hostility toward Other Major Powers

A fourth test focuses on the degree of Chinese amity toward other major potential adversary states. * * *

■   ■   ■

Figure 4.8. "I Would Prefer to Be a Citizen of China" and Generation (BAS 2007–15)

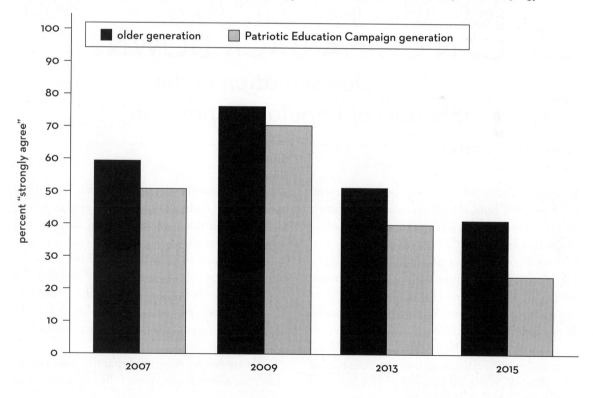

Chinese amity toward Japan and the United States declined from 1998 to around 2009, when it appears that the trend line bottomed out. In fact, there was a slight increase in amity toward the United States from 2009 to 2015, though this change falls within the 95 percent confidence lines.

Test 5: Nationalism and Age

A fifth test focuses on trends in nationalism among Chinese youth. Regardless of whether Chinese nationalism is instrumentally produced from above, spontaneously arises from below, or both, the Chinese Communist Party (CCP) has explicitly tried to promote nationalism among Chinese youth.[91] As a result, analysts from both inside and outside China often claim that rising nationalism is mainly a youth phenomenon, as references to a rising "angry youth" (*fenqing*) generation suggest.

The data show, however, that younger respondents are no more nationalist than older generations. For instance, in reexamining all the BAS statements related to nationalism, I controlled for respondents who were the targets of the Patriotic Education Campaign begun in 1993/94. For convenience, I call them members of the patriotic education generation (PEG). I define the PEG as including those who were fifteen years old in 1993 or younger. As Figure 4.8 shows, from 2007 to 2015 the patriotic education generations were consistently less likely to strongly agree with the three standard nationalism statements compared to older respondents.[92]

■　■　■

CAN CHINA BACK DOWN?
Crisis De-escalation in the Shadow of Popular Opposition

Many pundits and analysts, both inside and outside China, claim that public sentiment is an important driver in China's coercive diplomacy in the East and South China Seas. They argue that China's leadership faces potential domestic instability arising from ethnic unrest, socioeconomic inequality, environmental degradation, and a slowing economy. The regime therefore has an interest in pursuing tough external policies, as variants of diversionary conflict theory might suggest. Moreover, owing to socialization into the "Century of Humiliation" narrative (namely, that China was bullied by stronger imperialist powers from 1840 to 1949), the Chinese public reacts angrily to any hints of government concessions on territory and sovereignty issues. Public opinion, therefore, can create the worst of all worlds for Chinese leaders' ability to control the escalation of conflicts. It explains coercive external behavior that could give rise to militarized crises, but it also limits the regime's options to de-escalate once militarized crises have broken out.

We are not yet convinced that the potential for domestic political unrest can fully explain China's maritime behavior over the last decade. The top leadership exercises considerable control over official media messaging. It sits on a massive coercive apparatus, consisting of internal security services, a paramilitary, and the military. Moreover, it does not face elections. Thus, other factors may be at work as well—among them, a reaction to activities of other contenders in the East and South China Seas that Beijing perceives as challenging its definition of the status quo distribution of territory; an increasingly intense security dilemma with the United States; organizational interests being pushed by China's military; and sensitivity to both elite and mass opinion.[93] The alternative explanations for China's coercive diplomacy have generally not been rigorously tested, and the case for a diversionary conflict argument has yet to be made.[94]

We are not arguing, however, that domestic popular opinion does not constrain the intra-crisis behavior of China's leaders in particular conflicts with particular adversaries.[95] Relations with Japan appear to be particularly susceptible to popular emotions, given how the destructive history of Japanese imperialism in China is emphasized in education and media in China. Were a militarized crisis to break out with Japan over competing claims of ownership of the Diaoyu (in Chinese)/Senkaku (in Japanese) Islands, many analysts suggest that public opinion would limit the regime's options, reducing China's ability to signal intra-crisis restraint. Some senior Chinese officials also worry that public opinion may reduce China's maneuverability in a crisis.[96] From a crisis management perspective, then, it is in the interests of the regime to have flexibility of action.[97] Assuming that Chinese officials' preference against having their hands tied by public opinion in a crisis is more or less genuine, the question for the regime is how to influence public opinion so as to reduce the costs of backing down or making concessions if needed after issuing threats, but without providing incentives to the challenger to push for even more concessions.

More generally, all states in the East Asia region, as well as the United States, have an interest in expanding the political space for Chinese leaders to make concessions. Even advocates of imposing costs on China to curb its coercive diplomacy over maritime disputes should hope that China's leaders pay domestic costs sufficiently low to allow them to back down in a crisis.

Based on an original national-level survey experiment conducted in China in 2015, we ask what kinds of strategies—behavioral and rhetorical—might help minimize the public opinion costs of restraint in a crisis over disputed territory. In the experiment, we developed a real-world scenario in which Japan engages in building structures on disputed islands, and the Chinese leader threatens to respond with force. We then use randomized treatments to gauge changes in support for Chinese leaders under a range of different policies. We find that there are some strategies and reasons that do reduce the public opinion costs from backing down—for example, the threat of economic sanctions instead of the use of force; China's invocation of its peaceful identity; the existence of an offer of mediation by the United Nations; and acknowledgment of the economic costs of war. In our experiment, the one reason for backing down that seemed to have the potential to increase, rather than reduce, public opinion costs was making concessions in the face of U.S. military threats. Our respondents did not react positively to a leader who backed down in the face of these U.S. cost-imposition threats.

These findings about the effects of using different strategies to reduce the public costs of backing down in a crisis have important implications for crisis bargaining, particularly when the purpose is not to prevail outright over an adversary in a crisis but to manage its de-escalation, or when the actors worry that above a certain threshold of violence neither side will want to back down.[98] The standard logic of the audience cost argument suggests that whereas signaling resolve may be easier given audience costs, signaling a genuine desire to de-escalate may be harder.[99] Moreover, it becomes harder as audience costs increase with greater levels of commitment to the conflict.[100] Thus to de-escalate, leaders have to reduce the domestic public opinion costs of bluffing or making concessions. Evidence that different policy actions can reduce these costs by providing the political space needed for concessions suggests that audience costs and the threat of punishment for bluffing may not be as constraining as leaders think.

In sum, our study suggests that Chinese leaders may have more agency in the face of public opinion during a crisis than they themselves may believe. Put differently, our findings suggest that if the Chinese leadership were willing to de-escalate in the early stages of a crisis with Japan over the Diaoyu/Senkaku Islands, there are a number of strategies that would give them the flexibility that they apparently prefer. Our findings suggest that other countries therefore have a general interest in supporting certain de-escalation strategies available to the Chinese leadership. Other countries may have, for example, an interest in encouraging United Nations offers of mediation. They may have an interest in tactfully pointing out the economic costs to China should a crisis with Japan escalate. They may also have an interest in moderating their opposition to a Chinese decision to threaten economic sanctions against Japan, insofar as such a threat allows China's leaders more room to compromise in an immediate crisis. They do not necessarily have an interest, however, in threatening to impose greater military costs on China. Of course, all but the last of these interests are stronger the more tightly the Chinese leadership is constrained by public sentiments, as many pundits and analysts seem to believe.

The article proceeds in four stages. We first discuss the literature on audience costs and the question of how much agency leaders may have to manipulate these costs. We then describe how we designed and implemented the survey experiment in China. Next, we analyze the effects of the various treatment conditions on baseline public opinion costs imposed on a leader who backs down. We conclude with a discussion of the implications of our findings for the theoretical possibilities of leader agency in the face of audience costs. We also offer comments on the tensions between some of these findings and the notion of "cost imposition" by the United States on China for its handling of maritime disputes.

Audience Costs and Leader Agency

Domestic audience costs are the losses in domestic approval suffered by a national leader for backing down after making a threat in an international crisis. According to the standard audience cost argument, the relevant publics are concerned about inconsistencies between their leader's words and deeds, on the one hand, and the implications of these inconsistencies for the country's reputation or honor, on the other. For political leaders, lower levels of approval could redound in the form of losses in influence or difficulties in pushing a particular political agenda.[101] If audience costs increase during a crisis, leaders have less incentive to back down from their threat; hence, as the crisis proceeds, more information about their resolve is revealed. For political leaders, the upside of audience costs is the enhanced credibility of signals. The downside is being pressured by domestic audiences to take escalatory actions.[102]

Over the years, however, critics have raised a number of tough questions about the audience cost argument. Among them are three major critiques that together suggest a lack of realism and thus limited generalizability.[103] First, the survey and experimental evidence for audience costs rests almost exclusively on evidence from American respondents.[104] Thus the generalizability to other countries and political systems is unclear, particularly as regards authoritarian societies where regimes have tried explicitly to socialize their populations into uncritical support for nationalist and sovereignty-centric foreign policies. Second, these respondents are asked to react to underspecified hypothetical scenarios that may or may not matter when they judge the performance of real leaders.[105] Usually the scenario involves an unnamed country invading an unnamed neighbor.

In our view, however, the most fundamental critique is that hypothetical leaders in these experiments have little or no agency and do not act strategically to control audience costs.[106] Most of the audience cost literature assumes that leaders do not have the option of strategically using public rhetoric or nonmilitarized policies to reduce criticisms of their bluffing. Yet it would seem obvious that, in a crisis, rational leaders might want to preserve their flexibility, including the option of backing down with minimal domestic costs to their legitimacy as leaders. In the course of an emerging crisis, leaders may acquire new information about the military, political, economic, or personal costs of following through with their initial public threats. They may want to have the flexibility to negotiate more advantageous outcomes once they have signaled their willingness to use force against an adversary. Yet the audience cost literature generally does not test for the ways in which leaders might use specific policies or framing devices to reduce the domestic costs of concessions or moderation.

To be sure, there are exceptions in the audience cost literature in this regard. Matthew Levendusky and Michael Horowitz show that by merely claiming that s/he has new information, a leader can reduce disapproval rates for backing down.[107]

■   ■   ■

Study Design and Implementation

What factors and framing devices can leaders use to reduce the public political costs imposed on them if they bluff? To explore this and other questions, we fielded an original survey in the second quarter of 2015 that covers all provinces and capital municipalities in mainland China.[108] We developed a scenario based on the existing Sino-Japanese dispute over ownership of the Diaoyu/Senkaku Islands. As far as we are aware, this is the most realistic scenario heretofore used in academic studies of audience costs. In the actual dispute, Tokyo claims sovereignty and exercises administrative control over the islands. Since 2012, when the Japanese government purchased some of the islands from their private owners, China, which also claims sovereignty, has challenged this control by regularly sending government vessels inside the twelve-nautical-mile territorial waters limit.

In our scenario, Japan begins building structures on the disputed islands. From the Chinese perspective, Japan's action is highly provocative because it represents an enhancement of Japan's "actual control" (*shiji kongzhi*) over the islands. We examine support for Chinese leaders under two settings. The first is a control setting, where the leader issues a threat to use force that is ultimately not carried out (a bluff). The second is a treatment setting, where the leader engages in a bluff accompanied by one in a range of specific and plausible economic, political, and strategic actions or conditions.[109] For reasons we explain below, we examine how levels of approval are affected when bluffing is accompanied by a UN mediation offer; when the United States issues deterrent threats; when the leader invokes Chinese people's peaceful identity; when the leader indicates the costs of conflict to China's economic development; and when the leader deploys economic sanctions as an alternative to the use of military force. * * *

The advantage of using a real-world case in which Chinese public opinion has historically been hostile toward Japan is that this should be a hard case for showing the positive effect on approval ratings of different strategies and rationales for backing down.[110] If these strategies and reasons do increase approval rates in the face of strong anti-Japanese sentiment, leaders may have a fair amount of agency in reducing the domestic constraints on their foreign policy options.

In our experiment, the respondents were asked to read about a possible international crisis in the future. To keep our vignette as clean as possible, our experiment used a short vignette that focused solely on the objective facts of the crisis. Respondents were presented with the following crisis scenario: "China and Japan have a long-standing dispute over the sovereignty of a piece of territory. In a recent turn of events, Japan started to install structures on the disputed territory." The dependent variable measures public approval over how the leader handled the crisis.

We randomly assigned our respondents to a control condition or one of six treatments under a between-subjects design.[111] By design, the control and all six treatments have the same crisis scenario—the only difference is in the way the Chinese leader responded to the crisis. The treatments cover a plausible range of options that we might observe in the real world, and we suggest different ways in which these conditions might affect the costs of backing down.

Experimental Conditions

The control condition was a statement indicating that, after threatening military force, the leader backed down (i.e., bluffed). Respondents randomized into the control condition read the following scenario: "The Chinese leader said that if the installation continued, China would take military action. Japan continued to install structures on the disputed territory. In the end, the Chinese leader decided not to take military action against Japan."[112] Meanwhile, respondents randomized into one of the six treatment groups read a similar scenario as in the control condition, except that their scenario included an additional piece of information that encapsulated a particular treatment.

The first treatment involved China's leader backing down after a UN offer to mediate the crisis. We included this scenario for two reasons. First, empirical evidence suggests that third-party mediation may be more successful than bilateral agreements in prolonging agreements over territory.[113] Some scholars have suggested, however, that this success reflects the application of multilateral agreements to easy cases, where the issue at stake is relatively minor. Instead, most states prefer bilateral agreements because the parties—particularly the one with the power or stakes advantage—may be better able to control the outcome. States, therefore, tend to select into bilateral agreements and avoid third-party mediation.[114] In view of this literature, we are interested in whether Chinese respondents are willing to allow third-party mediation for a high-profile territorial dispute such as that over the Diaoyu/Senkaku Islands. Second, precisely because of perceptions of high stakes and the emotional commitments embodied in territorial disputes, third-party mediation may offer "political cover" to leaders who face domestic opposition to making concessions, thus reducing the constraints of domestic opinion.[115] In recent maritime disputes, the Chinese government has explicitly indicated a preference for bilateral negotiations and has opposed-third party involvement, including arbitration from international legal tribunals. The public may be aware of this and indeed may endorse it. Backing down in the face of third-party mediation, therefore, may not reduce the costs from bluffing. On the other hand, the Chinese government and the public treat the United Nations as the most legitimate intergovernmental institution that should be at the center of global order. Thus, offers of UN mediation may be seen by some members of the Chinese public as a viable alternative to bilateral conflict. To the extent that the possibility of UN mediation reduces the costs of backing down over a baseline level, public preferences may be flexible. In our study, respondents randomly assigned to this treatment read that the UN secretary-general had called for peace and had offered mediation. They then read that the Chinese leader decided not to take military action against Japan. We test the following hypothesis: *Compared to the control condition, respondents' approval for leaders will increase if backing down is accompanied by a UN offer to mediate the dispute.*

The second treatment had China's leader backing down in the face of U.S. deterrent threats. We chose this treatment because, given U.S. treaty obligations, it reflects a highly likely U.S. response to a Chinese threat to use force. A straightforward rationalist prediction might be that the domestic costs of backing down should drop in the face of deterrent threats from a stronger actor. That is, audiences should judge that a leader who backs down is doing so because s/he faces higher costs of conflict. This would be a prudent response to deterrent threats from more powerful states. One might therefore expect public approval to increase in the face of such threats. It is also plausible, however, that backing down in the face of U.S. threats could trigger an emotional public response to being bullied by a stronger player, and thus lead to a decrease in public support for a leader. In our study, respondents assigned to this treatment first read that the United States had threatened to intervene militarily if Japan were attacked, and then read that the Chinese leader decided not to use military force against Japan. We test the following mainstream rationalist hypothesis: *Compared to the control condition, respondents' approval for leaders will increase if backing down is done in the context of U.S. deterrent threats.*

The third treatment involved invoking a claim about China's alleged peaceful identity as a reason for not using force. Role theory in social psychology suggests that when people identify themselves as members of a social in-group (e.g., an ethnonational group), they will tend to act in ways consistent with the constitutive norms of that identity.[116] The motivation may be normative; it may have to do with the desire for social-liking through group conformity; or it may be a psychological discomfort from being accused of hypocrisy, among other mechanisms.[117] Role identities vary depending on appropriate social circumstances. In a conflict with the outside world, a role identity likely to resonate with the Chinese population is the claim that the Chinese people are inherently peaceful. Although this exceptionalist claim is empirically unsubstantiated, it is clear that ordinary Chinese people, on average, strongly believe that they as a people are inherently peaceful, certainly much more so than other peoples. For instance, in a survey of Beijing residents conducted in 2015, respondents were asked to assess the essential nature of the Chinese people as a people on a 7-point semantic differential scale anchored by peaceful at one end and warlike at the other. Fifty-four percent of those surveyed put the Chinese people at 1 (peaceful) on the scale, and 80 percent put the Chinese at 1 or 2. In contrast, 59 percent of respondents put the Japanese people as people at 7 (warlike), and 94 percent of respondents put the Japanese at 6 or 7 on the scale. This rhetorical tool is regularly invoked by Chinese leaders when claiming that China's rise does not pose a threat to anyone. Premier Li Keqiang has referred to the ancient Confucian phrase that "peace/harmony is the most valued" as the essence of traditional Chinese culture.[118] Party General Secretary Xi Jinping has noted that the Chinese people are by nature "peace-loving," and that there is "no gene for invasion in the Chinese people's blood."[119]

Role theory suggests that if leaders invoke the peaceful identity of the Chinese people as a reason for not following through with threats of force, the costs of backing down may decline, as respondents support actions that are perceived to be consistent with their "peaceful identity." Survey respondents randomized into this treatment read that the Chinese leader had decided not to take military action against Japan, and had declared that the Chinese people were a peaceful people who would try to resolve the conflict without force. We test the following hypothesis: *Compared to the control condition, respondents' approval for leaders will increase if backing down is accompanied by leaders invoking the Chinese people's "peaceful identity."*

In our fourth treatment, the leader of China invoked the economic costs of military conflict as a reason for not following through with the military threat. Our argument here is that given the importance of economic growth to the material well-being of ordinary citizens and thus for the legitimacy of Communist Party rule, one would expect Chinese leaders and publics alike to worry about the negative impact of military conflict on China's economic development. Japan is an important source of technology and a critical market for Chinese exports. A conflict with Japan might plausibly have severe economic costs, especially if the United States came to Japan's defense. Invoking these costs may reduce the political costs for Chinese leaders of bluffing in a crisis. Respondents in this treatment read that the Chinese leader had decided not to take military action on the grounds that a military conflict would derail China's economic development. This treatment tests the following hypothesis: *Compared to the control condition, respondents' approval for leaders will increase if backing down is accompanied by leaders invoking the costs to China's economic development of a conflict with Japan.*

The fifth treatment had the Chinese leader using economic sanctions instead of military force in reaction to Japan's actions. We chose this treatment because economic sanctions have become a tool of first resort to punish another state for provocative political-military behavior short of major military attacks. Although their effectiveness in eliciting desired responses in the target is open to debate, sanctions can reduce the pressures to escalate militarily in response to provocations while still imposing at least some concrete material costs on the target. China has typically not employed economic sanctions at nearly the same frequency as the United States or Europe, often labeling sanctions as interference in internal affairs. That said, Beijing has used economic pressure against the Philippines over territorial disputes in the South China Sea and against South Korea over the deployment of missile defenses. It has joined UN sanctions against Iran and North Korea, and in 2010 it threatened to impose sanctions on U.S. companies involved in arms sales to Taiwan. Some analysts claim that China may have used export cut-offs in reaction to a dispute with Japan in 2010. The imposition of economic sanctions may reduce the costs of backing down, as such action lowers the risk of major war while still signaling a coercive response. In our study, respondents randomized to this treatment read that the Chinese leader decided not to take military action against Japan, but implemented economic sanctions and boycotts on Japan. With this treatment, we test the following hypothesis: *Compared to the control condition, respondents' approval for leaders will increase if backing down is accompanied by leaders imposing economic sanctions on Japan.*

The sixth treatment involved the Chinese leader issuing a vaguer initial threat in order to retain maneuverability. While decisionmakers sometimes believe that their bargaining power is enhanced by claiming (perhaps even demonstrating) that their options are limited by domestic opinion, they nonetheless often prefer to have freedom of action in crises. Issuing specific ultimatums can be risky because, if rejected, these tend to shine a brighter light on whether the leader escalates or capitulates. Vaguer threats can blur this distinction, making it harder for audiences to observe bluffing and thereby reducing the costs of backing down. A specific ultimatum can also force the other side to respond more aggressively in order to demonstrate its resolve in the face of the threat. For this reason, a major principle of crisis management is to avoid issuing ultimatums. History suggests that leaders frequently frame their threats with some ambiguity.[120] Robert Trager and Lynn Vavreck, in particular, have argued that the more explicit the threat is, the greater the cost of backing down.[121] In our experiment, respondents in this treatment did not read about an explicit threat to Japan to remove the structures on the islands. Rather they read that China's leader had warned Japan that it "must be held fully responsible for the consequences arising therefrom" if Japan did not remove these structures.[122] We therefore test the hypothesis that *compared to the control condition, respondents' approval for leaders will increase if backing down is preceded by ambiguous threats to impose costs on Japan.*

Dependent Variable

We used a two-stage elicitation procedure to construct the dependent variable. Respondents were first asked whether they "approve, disapprove, or neither approve nor disapprove of the way the Chinese leader handled the situation." The first question gives us the raw percentage of respondents who approved (disapproved) of the leader's action. In the second question, respondents who answered "approve" ("disapprove") in the first question were asked how strongly they approve (disapprove). Those who answered "neither approve nor disapprove" were asked if they leaned toward approving or disapproving, or if they leaned neither way. Answers to the two questions generate an approval rating on a 7-point scale from 0 (strong disapproval) to 6 (strong approval). Our results report both the approval rating and the raw percentage of respondents who approved of the leader's action.

The treatment effect is measured based on the difference in public approval in the control condition compared to a specific treatment condition. As all respondents were randomly assigned, the control and treatment groups would be statistically identical across all observed and unobserved characteristics. Because the control and treatment conditions were the same except for the additional sentence that embedded the treatment, any systematic difference in the costs of backing down can be attributed to the treatment variable.

Treatment Results

Figure 4.9 shows that four of the six treatments significantly reduced the public opinion costs a Chinese leader would face for backing down after threatening to prevent Japan from building structures on the Diaoyu/Senkaku Islands. In one treatment (U.S. deterrent threat), the public costs rose rather than decreased, though the significance of that change depends on certain conditions, which we discuss below. In general, though, it appears that U.S. deterrent threats do not create political space for a Chinese leader, in the view of the public. Below we discuss the treatment effects in detail.

UN Mediation Offer (Treatment 1)

The average approval for the leader increased by 11 percentage points under the UN mediation treatment when compared against the control condition, a statistically significant difference ($p < 0.001$).[123] More precisely, the average approval rating (7-point scale from 0 to 6) was higher at 3.70 in the treatment group compared to 3.24 in the control group ($p < 0.001$). As a robustness check, we used ordered logit models to estimate the relationship between public approval and the treatment dummy. The treatment variable, *UN_mediation*, is coded 1 if a respondent was randomly assigned to treatment 1 (UN mediation) and 0 if assigned to the control group.[124]

Taken together, the findings suggest that the Chinese public is amenable to UN offers of

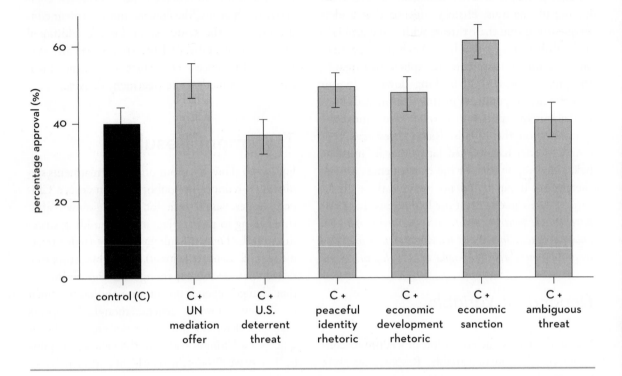

Figure 4.9. Public Approval for Backing Down across Experimental Groups

mediation in a Sino-Japanese conflict scenario; that is, UN mediation may reduce the cost of backing down for Chinese leaders, giving them more flexibility in their actions concerning the Diaoyu/Senkaku Islands.[125]

■　■　■

U.S. Deterrent Warning (Treatment 2)

In our second treatment, approval for the leader fell by 3 percentage points, though the difference is statistically insignificant. ***

This result suggests that respondents may not always be rationally calculating the costs of a potential conflict over the Diaoyu/Senkaku Islands. Both

Chinese officials and citizens widely acknowledge that the United States is militarily more powerful than China. Yet respondents remain generally unforgiving of a leader who backs down in the face of U.S. threats. They are not willing to increase support for concession as leaders rationally calculate the costs of U.S. intervention, contrary to what the standard rationalist inference might suggest.

Peaceful Identity Rhetoric (Treatment 3)

Approval for the leader increased by 9 percentage points under the peaceful identity treatment ($p < 0.01$). ***

This result suggests that Chinese respondents are sensitive to the cueing of the constitutive norms of their role identities. We are not able to ascertain whether a concern about social status, social-liking, or normative considerations are at work. However, the invocation of Chinese identity as uniquely peaceful—an invocation often used by Chinese leaders in their foreign policy statements—appears to lead respondents to reduce the costs on a leader who is bluffing but who nonetheless claims to act consistently with this identity.

Economic Costs Rhetoric (Treatment 4)

Approval for the leader increased by 8 percentage points when respondents read a statement from the leader about the economic development costs to China of a conflict with Japan. * * *

The outcome of this treatment suggests that Chinese respondents will sometimes make material cost-benefit calculations about the wisdom of backing down in a crisis. In this instance, the costs to China's economic development—arguably the most important material benefit the Communist Party leadership has provided ordinary Chinese people—can serve as a persuasive reason for backing down in a crisis with Japan over territory.

Economic Sanctions (Treatment 5)

Public approval for the Chinese leader jumps 21 percentage points if the leader backs down but imposes economic sanctions on Japan. * * *

Respondents appear to believe that punishing Japan economically is a much-preferred alternative to backing down. Many respondents favored sanctions over all other reasons and responses accompanying a decision to back down. In short, if a Chinese leader chose economic sanctions instead, this would best minimize the costs of backing down compared to the bluff base condition.

Ambiguous Threat (Treatment 6)

Approval for the Chinese leader is essentially unchanged under the ambiguous-threat treatment: approval for the leader was 40 percent compared to 39 percent in the control condition. * * *

This result suggests that the historically employed rhetoric used to threaten the use of force is not read by the public as a credible signal that China's leaders are considering military coercion. Apparently, Chinese respondents are not especially familiar with this history, even though, as foreign specialists of China's use of force point out, this particular rhetorical formula clearly connotes "a potential response by force."[126] There is thus an intriguing asymmetry in how foreign experts view the seriousness of this threat and how the Chinese public views the same threat and imposes the political costs thereof.

The Effects of Nationalism and Hawkishness

In an international crisis, such as the one we posit, it is possible that other political and foreign policy attitudes will mediate the degree of approval for a leader who backs down under various conditions. If so, it is in the interests of leaders to mobilize or suppress these attitudes in order to further reduce popular pressure when thinking about backing down in a crisis. * * *

For a measure of nativism, we asked respondents their level of agreement with the following statement: "People should support their own country even if what it does is wrong."[127] We then coded responses using a dummy variable, with 1 for those who strongly agreed or somewhat agreed with the statement and 0 for those who somewhat disagreed or strongly disagreed.

Overall, as one might expect, nativists were not especially convinced by reasons for backing down

Figure 4.10. Treatment Effects for Nativist Nationalists versus Non-nativists

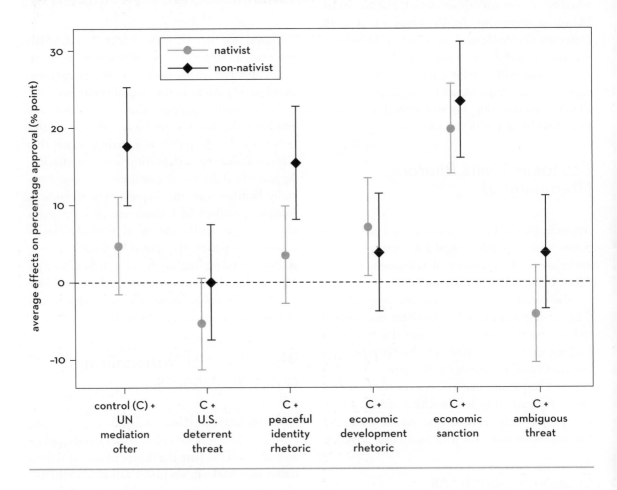

absent any punishment of Japan (see Figure 4.10). When it came to the UN offer of mediation, there was no significant improvement for the nativists in their levels of approval for the leadership over the baseline bluff condition. In contrast, for the non-nativists there was a strong and statistically significant rise in support for the leader.[128] Nativists were also indifferent to the invocation of Chinese people's peaceful role identity; their support for the leader increased slightly but not significantly. In contrast, non-nativists' support for the leadership surged with this treatment.[129] Both nativist and non-nativist support for the Chinese

leader, however, jumped significantly when the leader used economic sanctions to punish Japan.[130]

However, regarding the threat of U.S. intervention, nativists were willing to impose even higher costs on the leadership for backing down in the face of U.S. threats than were non-nativists. Nativists' approval for the leader drops significantly. For non-nativists, there is virtually no difference in approval levels between the control and treatment.[131] * * *

As for hawkishness, we constructed a dummy variable using answers to the following question posing a guns versus butter trade-off: "As a developing country, the government of China has to

Figure 4.11. Treatment Effects for Hawks versus Doves

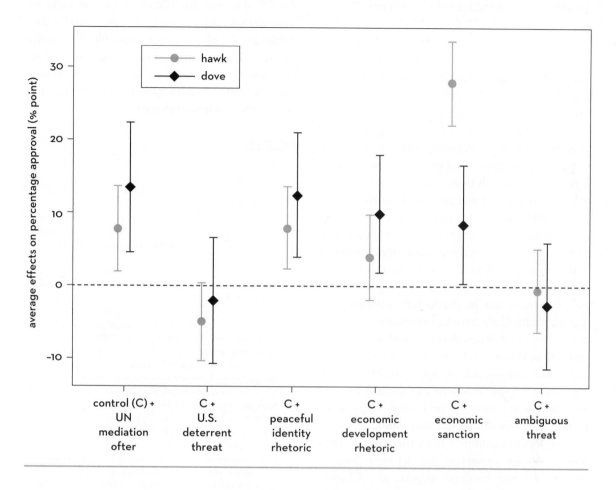

allocate its budget to different areas given limited resources. Some people think that for building a better social welfare system, the government should reduce its spending on national defense. Do you agree with this view?" Those who strongly agreed or somewhat agreed with the statement we labeled "doves"; those who somewhat disagreed or strongly disagreed we labeled "hawks" (see Figure 4.11).

Both doves' and hawks' approval ratings for leaders who back down in the face of UN mediation offers are higher than in the control condition.[132] Interestingly, doves and hawks were also more or less equally convinced by appeals to Chinese role identity as a peaceful people to increase their support for a leader who backs down.[133]

Doves' support increased significantly when the economic costs of military force were invoked by the Chinese leader, whereas hawks were not convinced by this argument.[134] Meanwhile, approval rates from both doves and hawks increased significantly when the leader chose economic sanctions.[135] In the case of U.S. deterrent threats, doves' approval rates did not change compared to the control group. Hawks discounted the costs of greater conflict with the United States, however, and they punished the Chinese leaders for concessions in the face of U.S. threats.[136]

■ ■ ■

Our findings suggest that Chinese leaders have certain diplomatic and practical options for giving themselves more domestic space to pursue concessions in high-stake crises. Our findings also suggest, however, that controlling emotional nativist tendencies, and mobilizing more moderate "butter over guns" or dovish constituencies, may be critical if the regime wants to minimize the public costs of making concessions in a crisis. Mobilizing opinions in a well-calibrated way is obviously not easy to do in an emerging crisis over territorial issues. In the tensions created by nationalist rhetoric and military moves, mobilizing moderate public opinion can be particularly difficult. The regime would likely have to communicate quietly with the United States that it would use rhetoric and actions that give it more room for self-restraint and concessions—such as some combination of symbolic economic sanctions and requests for UN mediation—in return for the United States minimizing its public threats of intervention.

This latter reassurance from the United States appears to be important for Chinese leaders' agency. As our findings suggest, the Chinese public—particularly those segments of the public with nativist and hawkish beliefs—might increase rather than lower the costs for leaders should the latter back down in the face of U.S. military threats, especially highly public ones. This likelihood creates a tension in the arguments some pundits make in Washington for a tougher U.S. deterrence strategy against China in maritime disputes in East Asia. Given our findings, one cannot both argue—as some in Washington do—that popular nationalism constrains the Chinese leadership and that certain cost-imposition strategies (e.g., military deterrent threats) will constrain China's coercive diplomacy. If general deterrence

has failed and China and Japan face a crisis over the Diaoyu/Senkaku Islands, imposing costs for immediate deterrence purposes runs into this contradiction. If public opinion does indeed constrain Chinese leaders, then high-profile immediate deterrent threats are likely to reduce the leadership's flexibility and, in turn, reduce the effectiveness of these deterrent threats.

NOTES

1. For examples of this type of commentary, see Michael Swaine, "Perceptions of an Assertive China," *China Leadership Monitor*, No. 32 (May 2010), p. 10 n 1.

2. Daniel Twining described China's diplomacy as "militant assertiveness." See Twining, "Were U.S.-India Relations Oversold? Part II," *Shadow Government, Foreign Policy*, blog, June 12, 2012, http://shadow.foreignpolicy.com.

3. John A. Vasquez, *The War Puzzle Revisited* (Cambridge: Cambridge University Press, 2009); Ken Booth and Nicholas J. Wheeler, *The Security Dilemma: Fear, Cooperation, and Trust in World Politics* (New York: Palgrave Macmillan, 2008); and William R. Thompson, "Identifying Rivals and Rivalries in World Politics," *International Studies Quarterly*, Vol. 45, No. 4 (December 2001), pp. 557–586.

4. For examples of the literature on discourse and participation, see Pierre Bourdieu, *Language and Symbolic Power* (Cambridge, Mass.: Harvard University Press); Murray Edelman, *Political Language: Words That Succeed and Policies That Fail* (Ann Arbor: University of Michigan Press, 1977); and Ted Hopf, "The Logic of Habit in International Relations," *European Journal of International Relations*, Vol. 16, No. 4 (December 2010), pp. 539–561.

5. Over the past few years, Chinese analysts have increasingly used the term "containment" to characterize U.S. strategy toward China. These analysts claim that the United States wants to prevent China's rise, a view that resonates with deeply held beliefs about the humiliations that China suffered at the hands of stronger modern states in the nineteenth and twentieth centuries. Yet it is hard to find any evidence from official U.S. documents, policymakers' memoirs, or journalist exposés published after 1972 that the containment of China is the national security strategy as determined by U.S. presidents. Thus this particular claim is even more problematic empirically than the newly assertive China meme.

6. See Swaine, "Perceptions of an Assertive China," pp. 2–4.

7. Andrew Hurrell, "Brazil and the New Global Order," *Current History*, February 2010, pp. 60–66.

8. Michael Cox, "Is the United States in Decline—Again? An Essay," *International Affairs*, Vol. 83, No. 4 (July 2007), pp. 643–653; Andrei P. Tsygankov, "Russia's International Assertiveness: What Does It Mean for the West? Problems of Post-Communism," Vol. 55, No. 2 (March/April 2008), pp. 38–55.

9. Guanchajia [Observer], "Fengquan dangjin baquanzhuyi zhao yi zhao lishi zhe mian jinzi" [May we advise today's hegemonism to

look in history's mirror], *Renmin ribao* [People's Daily], June 22, 1999.

10. For a similar point about the history of China's rhetorical assertiveness, see Jeffrey A. Bader, *Obama and China's Rise: An Insider's Account of America's Asia Strategy* (Washington, D.C.: Brookings Institution Press, 2012), p. 80.

11. The lowess (locally weighted least squares) curve is a smoothing technique that fits a regression line to a specified fraction of time-series data. I thank Robert Lee, who graciously allowed me to use the data he collected for his master's thesis. Lee, "Public Opinion and Foreign Policy in the People's Republic of China: An Econometric Analysis," master's thesis, Harvard University, 2012.

12. On China's response to these events, see M. Taylor Fravel, "China's Strategy in the South China Sea," *Contemporary Southeast Asia,* Vol. 33, No. 3 (December 2011), pp. 292–319.

13. On the importance of understanding the hierarchy of authoritative statements in the Chinese system, see Paul H.B. Godwin and Alice Miller, "China's Forbearance Has Limits: Chinese Threat and Retaliation Signaling and Its Implications for a Sino-American Military Confrontation," *China Security Perspectives,* No. 6 (March 2013).

14. Anthony Faiola, Juliet Eilperin, and John Pomfret, "Copenhagen Talks Show U.S., China May Shape Future," *Washington Post,* December 20, 2009; and John Pomfret, "Strident Tone from China Raises Concerns in West," *Washington Post,* January 31, 2010.

15. On the absence of change in China's global warming policy, see Gloria Jean Gong, "What China Wants: China's Climate Change Priorities in a Post-Copenhagen World," *Global Change, Peace, & Security,* Vol. 23, No. 2 (June 2011), pp. 159–175.

16. Australian scholar Ron Huisken describes the Chinese reaction as "fierce." See Huisken, "Taiwan: Is Beijing Testing Obama's Mettle?" *East Asia Forum,* blog, East Asian Bureau of Economic Research, February 24, 2010, http://www.eastasiaforum.org/2010/02/24 /taiwan-is-beijing-testing-obamas-mettle/.

17. For details about these sales, see Alan Romberg, "2010: The Winter of PRC Discontent," *China Leadership Monitor,* No. 31 (February 2010).

18. "Waijiaobu fayanren Jiang Yu jiu Mei dui Tai junshou da jizhe wen" [Foreign Ministry spokesperson Jiang Yu answers journalists' questions about U.S. arms sales to Taiwan] (Beijing: Ministry of Foreign Affairs of the People's Republic of China, January 7, 2010), http:// www.fmprc.gov.cn/mfa_chn/wjdt_611265/fyrbt_611275/t649080 .shtml.

19. "Waijiaobu fubuzhang He Yafei jiu Mei shou Tai wuqi wenti xiang Mei zhu Hua dashi tichu yanzheng jiaoshe" [Vice Foreign Minister He Yafei raises solemn representations to the U.S. ambassador to China on the issue of U.S. arms sales to Taiwan] (Beijing: Ministry of Foreign Affairs of the People's Republic of China, January 30, 2010), http://www.fmprc.gov.cn/mfa_chn/zyxw_602251/t654807.shtml.

20. Michael Wines, "U.S. and China Revive Military Talks," *New York Times,* February 28, 2009.

21. Edward Wong, "Chinese Military Seeks to Extend Its Naval Power," *New York Times,* April 23, 2010.

22. China's Xinhua news agency repeated the claim in Wong's *New York Times* story a few days later. See "Mei mei jianyl Meijun dingqi zai Nanhal yanxi fangzhi Zhongguo kongzhi" [U.S. media proposes that the U.S. military will regularly exercise in the South Sea to prevent China's control], Xinhua news agency, April 28, 2010. Many in the Chinese media and a number of Chinese analysts also assumed the claim to be true, as did pundits throughout East Asia. A number of Asian participants in the PLA organized Xiangshan Forum in October 2010, for instance, prefaced their remarks and questions by noting that China had declared the South China Sea to be a core interest.

23. These figures are based on a search of articles in LexisNexis and of blogs in Google that explicitly used language unique to the *New York Times* article, the phrase "on par with" in particular. Thus, these are conservative figures because they do not include what is likely a large number of articles and blogs that relied on the article but did not use language specific to it.

24. Two slightly different articles (one from *Kyodo* and one in the *Washington Post*) later reported a similar story, though their impact on the U.S. public discourse was more limited. See "China Told US South China Sea Is 'Core Interest'—Kyodo," *BBC Monitoring Asia Pacific,* July 3, 2010; and John Pomfret, "U.S. Takes Tougher Stance with China; Strategy Acknowledges Beijing's Rise in Power but Lays Down Markers," *Washington Post,* July 30, 2010.

25. Michael D. Swaine, "China's Assertive Behavior, Part One: On 'Core Interests,'" *China Leadership Monitor,* No. 34 (2011), p. 8. Secretary of State Hillary Clinton stated publicly that Dai Bingguo told her at the May 2010 Strategic and Economic Dialogue that the South China Sea was a core interest, but Swaine claims there is no evidence of this. Sources I have asked also suggest there is no evidence in the State Department record of such a comment by Dai to Clinton. It is possible Clinton is misremembering or perhaps remembers a memo about the alleged Chinese claim.

26. Bader, *Obama and China's Rise,* p. 77.

27. Author interviews, Beijing, 2010.

28. Wen Jiabao zai di 65 jie Lianda yibanxing bianlun shang de jianghua [Wen Jiabao's speech at the 65th UN General Assembly general debate] (Beijing: Ministry of Foreign Affairs of the People's Republic of China, September 23, 2010).

29. Author interview with a senior Chinese official involved in foreign policymaking, Beijing, June 2011.

30. China's diplomatic and military response to Japan's 2012 purchase of some of the Senkaku/Diaoyu Islands from private owners would also meet the criteria for a new assertiveness in its policy toward maritime disputes.

31. See Fravel, "China's Strategy in the South China Sea"; and Michael D. Swaine and M. Taylor Fravel, "China's Assertive Behavior, Part Two: The Maritime Periphery," *China Leadership Monitor,* No. 35 (Summer 2011).

32. Bader, *Obama and China's Rise,* p. 87.

33. Jung Sung-ki, "Korea-US Naval Drills to Begin in Late June," *Korea Times,* June 6, 2010; and "South Korea, US to Hold Naval Drills 7–10 June," *Yonhap,* June 3, 2010.

34. Michael Sainsbury and Rick Wallace, "China's Navy to Match S Korea–US War Games," *Australian,* June 30, 2010.

35. The islands are called the Senkaku by Japan and the Diaoyu by China. Both countries claim sovereignty over them.

36. Calum MacLeod, "China's Aggressive Posture Stuns Japan; Nation Dishes Out 'Shock and Awe' in Territorial Disputes," *USA Today,* September 28, 2010; Michael Richardson, "Beijing's Arm-Twisting Poses a New Challenge," *Australian Financial Review,* November 24, 2010.

37. Even Obama's top Asia specialist at the time, Ambassador Jeffrey Bader, noted in his analysis of the event that the Japanese did not follow their "usual practice" of sending the boats out of the area. See Bader, *Obama and China's Rise*, p. 106.

38. Author interview with a senior Chinese official involved in foreign policy making, Beijing, June 2011. Past practice also included the quick release of Chinese nationalist activists who were arrested in 2004 while trying to land on the Senkaku/Diaoyudao shortly after Japan started legal proceedings against them. See James Reilly, *Strong Society, Smart State: The Rise of Public Opinion in China's Japan Policy* (New York: Columbia University Press, 2011), pp. 145–146.

39. Author conversations with Chinese international relations specialists, Beijing, 2010.

40. In fact, this term was rarely used to describe the Diaoyudao—it had last been used in the *People's Daily* in the early 1970s.

41. Paul Krugman wrote that China's embargo "shows a Chinese government that is dangerously trigger-happy, willing to wage economic warfare on the slightest provocation." See Krugman, "Rare and Foolish," *New York Times*, October 17, 2010.

42. Author conversations with Chinese International relations specialists and with a senior Chinese foreign policy official, Beijing, 2010–11.

43. Keith Bradsher, "China Restarts Rare Earth Shipments to Japan," *New York Times*, November 20, 2010.

44. "Rare-Earth Furor Overlooks China's 2006 Industrial Policy Signal," *Bloomberg News*, October 21, 2010.

45. "Zhongguo bus hi yi nu jiu shitai de xiangbalao" [China isn't a bumpkin who in a fit of anger loses control], *Huanqiu shibao*, September 16, 2010.

46. Based on an analysis of more than 600 blog posts, op-eds, and media quotes by four of the most prominent PLA commentators (Dal Xu, Han Xudong, Luo Yuan, and Zhang Zhaozhong) between 2007 and 2011, it appears that none of them made any public comments about the Diaoyudao issue during September 2010, whereas they had mentioned it relatively frequently in previous and in subsequent months.

47. Donna Miles, "Mullen: Trilateral Cooperation Best Response to North Korea" (Washington, D.C.: U.S. Department of Defense American Forces Press Service, December 9, 2010).

48. See "Zhonghua Renmin Gonghe Guo Waijiaobu shengming" [Statement by the People's Republic of China Ministry of Foreign Affairs], October 9, 2006. For an account that sees China's DPRK policy as essentially constant, notwithstanding the initial reaction to the 2006 test, see Victor Cha, *The Impossible State: North Korea Past and Future* (New York: HarperCollins, 2012), pp. 329–334.

49. Waijiaobu fayanren Mao Chaoxu jiu Zhong-Han, Zhong-Ri waizhang huiwu youguan qingkuang da jizhe wen [Foreign Ministry spokesperson Mao Chaoxu answers journalists' questions about issues questions about issues related to the Sino-ROK and Sino-Japanese Foreign Ministers meeting], May 15, 2010; and Waijiaobu fayanren Hong Lei juxing lixing jizhehui [Foreign Ministry spokesperson Hong Lei holds regular press meeting], November 25, 2010.

50. Li Xiaodong, Wang Yisheng, and Li Rui, *Chaoxian bandao weiji guanli yanjiu* [Research on Korean Peninsula crisis management] (Beijing: Academy of Military Sciences Press, 2010), p. 85.

51. Ibid., p. 52. See also International Crisis Group, "China and Inter-Korean Clashes in the Yellow Sea," *Asia Report*, No. 200 (January 2011); and Bader, *Obama and China's Rise*, p. 83.

52. See Jonathan D. Pollack, *No Exit: North Korea, Nuclear Weapons, and International Security* (London: Routledge, 2011), pp. 201–203; and Bonnie Glaser, "China's Policy in the Wake of the Second DPRK Nuclear Test," *China Security*, Vol. 5, No. 2 (2009), pp. 1–11. Some Chinese analysts even make a credibility of commitment argument. That is, if China dropped the DPRK as an ally, then it might be harder to play for support from other smaller powers in the developing world. See Lin Jianyi, "Zhong Mei guanxizhongde Chaoxian wenti" [The North Korea issue in Sino-U.S. relations], *Jianbao* [Briefing], No. 22 (Beijing: Chinese Academy of Social Sciences Regional Security Research Center: October/November 2010), p. 2. Interlocutors from Northeast China who specialize in Korean issues noted that the credibility of commitment issue gave the DPRK more leverage over China. This, they said, was a similar phenomenon to the relationship between the United States and its small allies, such as Israel, so the United States ought to understand China's predicament. Author conversations with Jinan University specialists, Changchun, June 2011.

53. Yang Xiyu, "Chao he wenti yu Chaoxian bandao heping tizhi wenti" [The North Korean nuclear problem and the question of a peace system on the Korean Peninsula], *Shijie fazhan yanjiu* [Research in world development], No. 8 (2010). Yang was an important player in the Chinese six-party talks team.

54. On China's reactiveness on the DPRK issue, see Andrew Scobell, "The View from China," in Gilbert Rozman, ed., *Asia at a Tipping Point: Korea, the Rise of China, and the Impact of Leadership Transitions* (Washington, D.C.: Joint U.S.-Korea Academic Studies, 2012), pp. 70–81; and Bader, *Obama and China's Rise*, pp. 37–39.

55. China and the United States voted together 98 percent of the time in 2010 and 97 percent of the time in 2011, continuing the trend toward convergence in voting among the permanent members from previous years. For pre-2010 data, see Joel Wuthnow, "Discord and Collaboration in UN Security Council Negotiations: The Case of China, 1971–2009," paper presented at the annual meeting of the American Political Science Association, Washington, D.C., September 2–5, 2010, p. 35.

56. Bader, *Obama and China's Rise*, p. 117. Similarly, Thomas Christensen, a former Bush administration official in charge of China policy, also thought that China's policy on this score did not fit with the standard "new assertiveness" narrative. Christensen, "The Advantages of an Assertive China: Responding to Beijing's Abrasive Diplomacy," *Foreign Affairs*, Vol. 90, No. 2 (March/April 2011), pp. 54–67. Indeed, on this American "core interest," the State Department cables distributed by Wikileaks reveal evidence of common purpose with China, though some differences in tactics. Wikileaks, "Deputy Secretary Steinberg's September 29, 2009 Conversation with State Councilor Dai Bingguo," http://wikileaks.org/cable/2009/10/09BEIJING2965.html. See also Bader, *Obama and China's Rise*, p. 78.

57. Bader, *Obama and China's Rise*, pp. 74–75. As in the past, the PRC conceded nothing to the Dalai Lama about greater Tibetan autonomy, but an assertive China could have easily broken its commitment on this issue.

58. The Beijing Area Study (BAS), a random sample of people living in the Beijing municipality, includes questions that measure Chinese respondents' perceptions of the warlikeness of Chinese, American, and Japanese as people, and the warlikeness of China, the United States, and Japan as major powers. I define anti-Americans and anti-Japanese as those respondents who believe that the Chinese are maximally different from Americans and Japanese and who also believe there is no difference between Americans and Japanese and their countries. In other words, anti-Americans and anti-Japanese believe Americans and Japanese are, like their countries, maximally warlike. In 2007, 41 percent of respondents could be classified as anti-Japanese; in 2009 this figure increased to 52 percent. In contrast, at 34 percent of the sample, the proportion that fit this definition of anti-American did not change between 2007 and 2009.

59. In 2007, 74 percent of BAS respondents agreed with the statement that "in general China is better than most other countries." In 2009, this figure jumped to 93 percent.

60. According to BAS data, in 2007, 35 percent of respondents agreed that one should support his or her government even if it is wrong; in 2009, this increased to 46 percent, though a majority still disagreed with this statement.

61. Alastair Iain Johnston and Daniela Stockmann, "Chinese Attitudes toward the United States and Americans," in Peter J. Katzenstein and Robert O. Keohane, eds., *Anti-Americanisms in World Politics* (Ithaca, N.Y.: Cornell University Press, 2006), pp. 157–195.

62. For recent research on public opinion and foreign policy in China, see Jessica Chen Weiss, "Autocratic Signaling, Mass Audiences, and Nationalist Protest in China," *International Organization*, Vol. 67, No. 1 (January 2013), pp. 1–35; Reilly, *Strong Society, Smart State;* and Wang Jun, *Wangluo minzuzhuyi yu Zhongguo waijiao* [Cybernationalism and China's diplomacy] (Beijing: China Social Science Press, 2011).

63. For the claim that the PLA is in control of Chinese foreign policy, see Willy Lam, "China's Hawks in Command," *Wall Street Journal,* July 1, 2012. For a careful discussion of this problem, see Michael D. Swaine, "China's Assertive Behavior, Part Three: The Role of the Military in Foreign Policy," *China Leadership Monitor,* No. 36 (January 2012); and Dennis Blasko, "The Role of the PLA," in Chris Ogden, ed., *Handbook of China's Governance and Domestic Politics* (New York: Routledge, 2012).

64. Swaine, "China's Assertive Behavior, Part Three," pp. 8–9.

65. See M. Taylor Fravel, "The PLA and the South China Sea," *China Power, Diplomat,* blog, June 17, 2012, http://thediplomat.com/china-power/pla-and-the-south-china-sea/.

66. For empirical examples that show how perception of difference with outgroups helps to explain competitive or conflictual foreign policy preferences, see Edward Mansfield and Diana Mutz, "Support for Free Trade: Self-Interest, Sociotropic Politics, and Out-Group Anxiety," *International Organization*, Vol. 63, No. 3 (Summer 2009), pp. 425–457; Donald R. Kinder and Cindy D. Kam, *Us against Them: Ethnocentric Foundations of American Opinion* (Chicago: University of Chicago Press, 2009).

67. Along with "rising," a survey of hits across the years in LexisNexis for the word "China" appearing within ten words of "nationalism" finds similar but less commonly used quasi synonyms such as "muscular," "aggressive," "increasing," "whipped up," "heightened,"

"resurgent," "rising tide of," "fanned," "high," "expanding," "neo-," "ebullient," and "growing."

68. See Clive Schofield and Ian Story, *The South China Sea Dispute: Increasing Stakes and Rising Tensions* (Washington, D.C.: Jamestown Foundation 2009), p. 3; Michael Schiffer and Gary Schmitt, "Keeping Tabs on China's Rise" (Muscatine, Iowa: Stanley Foundation, May 2007), www.stanleyfoundation.org/publications/other/SchifferSchmitt07.pdf; Francis Fukuyama, "Re-Envisioning Asia," *Foreign Affairs*, Vol. 84, No. 1 (January/February 2005), http://www.cfr.org/asia-and-pacific/re-envisioning-asia/p7927.

69. "Country Reports on Human Rights Practices: China" (Washington, D.C.: U.S. Department of State, February 23, 2000), http://www.state.gov/j/drl/rls/hrrpt/1999/284.htm. See also Secretary of State Hillary Clinton's remarks on a "new streak of assertive Chinese nationalism." Clinton, "Inaugural Richard C. Holbrooke Lecture on a Broad Vision of U.S.-China Relations in the 21st Century" (Washington, D.C.: U.S. Department of State, 2011), http://www.state.gov/secretary/20092013clinton/rm/2011/01/154653.htm.

70. See, for instance, Thomas L. Friedman, "China's Nationalist Tide," *New York Times*, March 13, 1996.

71. For a preliminary effort to assess whether there is a hegemonic liberal world order that China seeks to challenge, see Alastair Iain Johnston, "China and International Order: Which China? Which Order?" paper presented at the conference "Negotiating the Future: Visions of Global Order," German Institute of Global and Area Studies, Hamburg, Germany, December 3–4, 2015. See also Richard Fontaine and Mira Rapp-Hooper, "How China Sees World Order," *National Interest*, April 20, 2016, http://nationalinterest.org/feature/how-china-sees-world-order-15846.

72. See Robert D. Kaplan, "Eurasia's Coming Anarchy: The Risks of Chinese and Russian Weakness," *Foreign Affairs*, Vol. 95, No. 2 (March/April 2016), https://www.foreignaffairs.com/articles/china/2016-02-15/eurasias-coming-anarchy; Jian Zhang, "China's Growing Assertiveness in the South China Sea: A Strategic Shift?" in Leszek Buszynski and Christopher Roberts, eds., *The South China Sea and Australia's Regional Security Environment*, National Security College Occasional Paper No. 5 (Action: National Security College, Australia National University, September 2013), http://nsc.anu.edu.au/documents/occasional-5.pdf; Michael Yahuda, "China's New Assertiveness in the South China Sea," *Journal of Contemporary China*, Vol. 22, No. 81 (2013), pp. 446–459; Jiang Zongqiang and Hu Xin, "China's Dilemma: Nationalism Could Hijack Policy Response," *Straits Times*, December 8, 2015, http://www.straitstimes.com/opinion/chinas-dilemma-nationalism-could-hijack-policy-response; and Sasa Petricic, "Forget the 'Farce' Bluster, China Received the Tribunal Ruling It Dreaded," *CBC News*, July 12, 2016, http://www.cbc.ca/news/world/south-china-sea-ruling-1.3675714.

73. Author conversations with senior U.S. military officers, August 2015 and April 2016.

74. New research suggests that China has engaged in controlled diversionary conflict in reaction to elite, rather than mass, dissatisfaction with the state of the economy. The regime, however, tries to minimize the destabilizing effect of these actions on relations with other states. See Erin Baggott, "Four Essays in Computational

Approaches to Autocratic Politics," Ph.D. dissertation, Harvard University, 2016.

75. For formative statements, see S.J. Ball-Rokeach and M.L. Defleur, "A Dependency Model of Mass Media Effects," *Communication Research*, Vol. 3, No. 1 (January 1976), pp. 3–21; and Maxwell E. McCombs and Donald L. Shaw, "The Agenda Setting Function of Mass-Media, *Public Opinion Quarterly*, Vol. 36, No. 2 (Summer 1972), pp. 1761–187.

76. The following is based mainly on an analysis of the twenty-eight news media articles and op-eds in LexisNexis from 1996 through to September 2016 that refer to "Chinese nationalism" as "rising."

77. Vanessa Fong, "Filial Nationalism among Chinese Teenagers with Global Identities," *American Ethnologist*, Vol. 31, No. 4 (November 2004), pp. 631–648.

78. William A. Callahan, "History, Identity, and Security: Producing and Consuming Nationalism in China," *Critical Asian Studies*, Vol. 38, No. 2 (2006), pp. 179–208.

79. Tang Wenfang and Benjamin Darr, "Chinese Nationalism and Its Political and Social Origins," *Journal of Contemporary China*, Vol. 21, No. 77 (2012), pp. 811–826.

80. Brian C. Rathbun, "Chinese Attitudes toward Americans and Themselves: Is There a Relationship?" In Alastair Iain Johnston and Shen Mingming, eds., *Perception and Misperception in American and Chinese Views of the Other* (Washington, D.C.: Carnegie Endowment for International Peace, 2015), pp. 9–21.

81. Peter Hayes Gries, "Tears of Rage: Chinese Nationalism and the Belgrade Embassy Bombing," *China Journal*, July 2001, pp. 25–43.

82. James Leibold, "More Than a Category: Han Supremacism on the Chinese Internet," *China Quarterly*, September 2010, pp. 539–559.

83. See James Reilly, *Strong Society, Smart State: The Rise of Public Opinion in China's Japan Policy* (New York: Columbia University Press, 2012); Jessica Chen Weiss, *Powerful Patriots: Nationalist Protest in China's Foreign Relations* (Oxford: Oxford University Press, 2014); Hao Yufan and Lin Su, eds., *Zhongguo waijiao juece: kaifang yu duoyuande shehui yinsu fenxi* [Chinese foreign policy making: Societal forces in Chinese foreign policy making] (Beijing: Chinese Academy of Social Sciences, 2007); and Wang Jun "Wangluo minzuzhuyi yu Zhongguo waijiao" [Internet nationalism and China's diplomacy] (Beijing: Chinese Academy of Social Sciences, 2011).

84. Carlson, "A Flawed Perspective," p. 25.

85. The BAS is administered by the Research Center for Contemporary China at Peking University. It began in 1995 and was modeled on the Detroit Area Study. The survey is mainly focused on attitudes toward city and local governance performance. Over the years, however, it has included some questions about national government performance, consumer confidence, political reform, and foreign policy. Since 1998 I have collaborated with the designers of the BAS in fielding questions about foreign policy and international affairs. From 1995 to 2007, the BAS sampled Beijing residents from the main urban districts, using probability proportional to size sampling procedures. Since 2007 it has used GPS sampling so as to increase the sample size and to include urban and rural registered residents of Beijing and unregistered residents living in the larger municipal area. On BAS sampling, see Hao Hongsheng, "The Sampling Design and Implementation for the 1995 Beijing Area Study," Peking University, 1996; and Pierre F. Landry and Shen Mingming, "Reaching

Migrants in Survey Research: The Use of the Global Positioning System to Reduce Coverage Bias in China," *Political Analysis*, Vol. 13, No. 1 (Winter 2005), pp. 1–22. The BAS data used in this study are freely available from me for academic research purposes. As far as I am aware, the BAS is the only available time-series survey of ordinary Chinese people's views of a range of foreign policy issues such as military spending, foreign aid, trade preferences, amity, and nationalism. The Japanese nongovernmental organization, Genron NPO, has gathered times-series data on Chinese views of Japan. Although the Genron NPO survey includes detailed and useful questions that address the constitutive elements of these views, the primary attitudinal question concerns favorability—a vague concept that is hard to interpret and that does not measure nationalist sentiments. For the Genron NPO studies, see http://www.genron-npo .net/en/opinion_polls/. The Pew Research Center has also asked favorability questions across several years. Its Global Trends and Attitudes survey of Chinese opinion of Japan includes two separate years (2006 and 2016) with questions about stereotypes of the Other (In this case, Japanese people). The stereotype questions, however, do not ask about stereotypes of Self, so it is not possible to generate perceptions of difference and therefore measures of ethnocentrism. See Bruce Stokes, "Hostile Neighbors: China vs. Japan" (Washington, D.C.: Pew Research Center, September 2016), http://www .pewglobal.org/2016/09/13/hostile-neighbors-china-vs-japan/.

86. These types of questions are asked, for example, in all three waves (1995, 2003, and 2013) of the International Social Survey Programme (ISSP) surveys on national identity. For the 2013 survey, see http://www.issp.org/uploads/editor_uploads/files/2013_final .doc, p. 3. The ISSP is widely used in studies of nationalism. In some years, BAS replaced "government" with "country" in the third question. In 2003 we ran a survey experiment to see if there was a difference in responses depending on which term was used. There was no statistically significant difference in the distribution of responses using these two different wordings. The third nationalism question was not asked in 2013. In addition, in 2002 and 2003 the BAS offered a "neutral" option between the "agree" and "disagree" choices. This was removed beginning in 2004. Unless otherwise indicated, reported results exclude "don't knows" and "no answers."

87. In the 2015 BAS data, for instance, there is a strong relationship between desire to be a citizen of China and nativist blind support for the state ($X^2=821.99$ p=0.000, N=2381). There is also a strong association between valuation of China as a country and blind support for the state ($X^2=778.9$ p=0.000, N=2357). Finally, there is a strong association between desire to be a citizen and valuation of China as a country ($X^2=2800$ p=0.000, N=2389). There is also a strong linear relationship between preferring to be a citizen of China and negative perceptions of Japanese (ANOVA F=65.90 p=0.000, N=2040) as well as between the positive valuation of China as a country and negative perceptions of Japanese (ANOVA F=88.01 p=0.000, N=2023)

88. See Edward D. Mansfield and Diana C. Mutz, "Support for Free Trade: Self-Interest, Sociotropic Politics, and Out-Group Anxiety," *International Organization*, Vol. 63, No. 3 (July 2009), pp. 425–457; and Donald R. Kinder and Cindy D. Kam, *Us against Them: Ethnocentric Foundations of American Opinion* (Chicago: University of Chicago Press, 2010). For a summary of the social

neuroscience microfoundations for the link among identity differ- ence, fear, and preferences for relative gains, see Han Dongfang et al., "Nationalism, Ethnocentrism, and Trade Preferences: Find- ings from Beijing," People's University of China, 2015.

89. If one combines the "strongly agree" and "somewhat agree" responses, the variation across time is similar, except that the total percentage that agrees moves slightly higher in the 2015 survey compared with the 2013 survey. This increase, however, is accounted for by a large increase in "somewhat agree" responses over the previ- ous survey, and thus arguably reflects a dilution of nationalism compared to 2013. I find, however, that this kind of aggregation is of limited use, as it assumes that the views represented by "strongly agree" and "somewhat agree" are closer together than, say, the views represented by "somewhat agree" and "somewhat disagree."

90. See Charles E. Osgood, George J. Suci, and Percy H. Tannenbaum, *The Measurement of Meaning* (Urbana: University of Illinois Press, 1957).

91. The Patriotic Education Campaign was launched in the early 1990s in response to the student and worker demonstrations against Communist Party rule in 1989. The campaign was designed to inocu- late Chinese youth against so-called Western values by playing up historical memories of China's past humiliation at the hands of impe- rialists. See Zhao Suisheng, "A State-led Nationalism: The Patriotic Education Campaign in Post-Tiananmen China," *Communist and Post-Communist Studies*, Vol. 31, No. 3 (September 1998), pp. 287–302; Zheng Wang, *Never Forget National Humiliation: Historical Memory in Chinese Politics and Foreign Relations* (New York: Columbia University Press, 2012); and William A. Callahan, *China: The Pessoptimist Nation* (Oxford: Oxford University Press, 2010).

92. To obtain as representative a sample as possible, I used the data including respondents with urban, rural, Beijing, and non-Beijing residency permits, Doing so limits the years for the analysis to 2007–15. In ten of the eleven total comparisons between those who had experienced the PEC and older generations in this time period, the differences between the generations were statistically significant. I also looked at the same data for the pre-2007 period, and the findings are consistent with the later period.

93. For examples of the claim about nationalism and maritime asser- tiveness as well as alternative explanations, see Robert D. Kaplan, "Eurasia's Coming Anarchy: The Risks of Chinese and Russian Weakness," *Foreign Affairs*, Vol. 95, No. 2 (March/April 2016), https://www.foreignaffairs.com/articles/china/2016-02-15/eurasias -coming-anarchy.

94. Jessica L.P. Weeks, *Dictators at War and Peace* (Ithaca, N.Y.: Cornell University Press, 2014); Jessica Chen Weiss, *Powerful Patriots: Nationalist Protest in China's Foreign Relations* (New York: Oxford University Press, 2014). In the audience cost context, cogent critiques maintain that archival evidence does not support the claim that leaders use public concerns about reputation or honor to tie their hands and enhance their bargaining power. See Jack Snyder and Erica D. Borghard, "The Cost of Empty Threats: A Penny, Not a Pound," *American Political Science Review*, Vol. 105, No. 3 (August 2011), pp. 437–456, doi:10.1017/S000305541100027X; and Marc Trachtenberg, "Audience Costs: An Historical Analy- sis," *Security Studies*, Vol. 21, No. 1 (2012), pp. 3–42, doi:10.1080/0 9636412.2012.650590.

95. There is a burgeoning literature on the conditions under which the Chinese regime may be sensitive and responsive to public pressure in domestic politics. See, for example, Chen Jidong, Jennifer Pan, and Xu Yiqing, "Sources of Authoritarian Responsiveness: A Field Experiment in China," *American Journal of Political Science*, Vol. 60, No. 2 (April 2016), pp. 383–400, doi:10.1111/ajps.12207; Greg Distelhorst and Yue Hou, "Constituency Service under Nondemocratic Rule: Evidence from China," *Journal of Politics*, Vol. 79, No. 3 (July 2017), pp. 1024–1040, doi:10.1086/690948;

96. Interviews with senior Chinese officials, 2010–2011. Some of the interviewees have been or could have been in a position to observe and/or advise senior leaders during external political- military crises. In interactions with Chinese government crisis management experts since the mid-2000s, one of the authors has observed a consistent desire to enhance rather than reduce flex- ibility in crises. In crisis management, at least, the preferred strategy is not to tie hands.

97. On the principles of successful crisis management, see Michael Brecher and Jonathan Wilkenfeld, *A Study of Crisis* (Ann Arbor: University of Michigan Press, 1997). Many of these principles relate to the clear signaling of limited intent and of military self- restraint. Thus, in contrast to military conflicts where one or both sides aim to deter the other side and, if that fails, to coerce the other side into capitulation, leaders in a crisis should want flexibil- ity rather than tied hands. On the empirical evidence for leaders' preferences for flexibility and maneuverability in crises, see Snyder and Borghard, "The Cost of Empty Threats," pp. 437–456; and Trachtenberg, "Audience Costs," pp. 3–42.

98. James D. Fearon, "Domestic Political Audiences and the Escala- tion of International Disputes," *American Political Science Review*, Vol. 88, No. 3 (September 1994), p. 577, doi:10.2307/2944796.

99. This standard logic applies to traditional audience costs (type I): the costs of backing down after threatening to fight. The logic does not apply to "type II audience costs": the costs of entering a conflict after promising not to fight. See Kai Quek, "Type II Audience Costs," *Journal of Politics*, Vol. 79, No. 4 (2017), pp. 1438–1443, doi:10.1086/693348; and Jack S. Levy et al., "Backing Out or Backing In? Commitment and Consistency in Audience Costs Theory," *American Journal of Political Science*, Vol. 59, No. 4 (October 2015), pp. 988–1001, doi:10.1111/ ajps.12197.

100. Fearon, "Domestic Political Audiences and the Escalation of International Disputes," p. 580.

101. Christopher Gelpi and Joseph M. Grieco, "Competency Costs in Foreign Affairs: Presidential Performance in International Conflicts and Domestic Legislative Success, 1953–2001," *Ameri- can Journal of Political Science*, Vol. 59, No. 2 (April 2015), pp. 440–456, doi:10.1111/ajps.12169.

102. Fearon, "Domestic Political Audiences and the Escalation of Inter- national Disputes"; Kenneth A. Schultz, *Democracy and Coercive Diplomacy* (New York: Cambridge University Press, 2001); and Branislav L. Slantchev, "Politicians, the Media, and Domestic Audience Costs," *International Studies Quarterly*, Vol. 50, No. 2 (June 2006), pp. 445–477, oi:10.1111/j.1468-2478.2006.00409.x.

103. Another tough question, which is not examined here, is whether the audience costs generated by the signaler are appreciated by the

receiver. Audience costs matter to signaling only insofar as they are perceptible. Recent experimental evidence, however, suggests that a costly signal can be perceived differently depending on whether one is the signaler or receiver. The logic of costly signaling seems to grip the signaler more than it grips the receiver. On the "sender-receiver gap," see Kai Quek, "Are Costly Signals More Credible? Evidence of Sender-Receiver Gaps," *Journal of Politics*, Vol. 78, No. 3 (July 2016), pp. 925–940, doi:10.1086/685751.

104. The published exceptions are those by Graeme A.M. Davies and Robert Johns, who ran a survey experiment using British subjects, and Adam Berinsky, Kai Quek, and Michael Sances, who used a global non-U.S. sample recruited through Amazon.com's Mechanical Turk.

105. Shuhei Kurizaki and Taehee Whang, "Detecting Audience Costs in International Disputes," *International Organization*, Vol. 69, No. 4 (Fall 2015), p. 957, doi:10.1017/S0020818315000211.

106. For this criticism about the lack of agency attributed to leaders by most audience costs studies, see Snyder and Borghard, "The Cost of Empty Threats"; and Trachtenberg, "Audience Costs."

107. Matthew S. Levendusky and Michael C. Horowitz, "When Backing Down Is the Right Decision: Partisanship, New Information, and Audience Costs," *Journal of Politics*, Vol. 74, No. 2 (April 2012), pp. 323–338, doi:10.1017/S002238161100154X.

108. We contracted with a survey company to recruit a constructed target sample matching the census population of Chinese adults (18 years and older) on gender, income, ethnicity, and geography. We embedded the experiment in the survey and fielded the survey over the internet to cover all provinces and capital municipalities of mainland China. The recruited subjects were routed to the survey, which was managed at the researcher end, allowing us full control over the experimental implementation and data collection. Researchers have shown that anonymized online surveys can help to minimize political and social desirability biases, which is particularly important in China. See, for example, Huang Haifeng, "International Knowledge and Domestic Evaluations in a Changing Society: The Case of China," *American Political Science Review*, Vol. 109, No. 3 (August 2015), p. 630, doi:10.1017/S000305541500026X; and Linchiat Chang and Jon A. Krosnick, "Comparing Oral Interviewing with Self-Administered Computerized Questionnaires: An Experiment," *Public Opinion Quarterly*, Vol. 71, No. 1 (Spring 2010), pp. 154–167, doi:10.1093/poq/nfp090. The appendix documents the instrument used in the experiment and compares the sample demographics with the 2010 National Census. We note that research by David Denemark and Andrew Chubb indicates that those in China who acquire information about maritime disputes mainly from the internet tend to be more critical of the government than those who rely on traditional media sources. We did not have a question on information sources about maritime disputes, but we did ask respondents to choose one or more news sources that they had consulted in the previous twenty-four hours. Respondents were free to choose more than one source. About 86 percent indicated that they had looked at news on the internet. Only 31 percent chose newspapers, and 56 percent chose television. In light of Denemark and Chubb's findings, this suggests that our sample may be more critical of the government in their

self-reported responses than a traditional face-to-face or telephone interview survey sample. This possibility, however, has the analytical advantage of creating a harder test for the effects of different treatments used to influence levels of support for the government. See Denemark and Chubb, "Citizen Attitudes towards China's Maritime Territorial Disputes: Traditional Media and Internet Usage as Distinctive Conduits of Political Views in China," *Information, Communication & Society,* Vol. 19, No. 1 (2016) pp. 59–79, doi:10.1080/1369118X.2015.1093527.

109. In a separate study, we conducted a test for the existence of audience costs, comparing approval for a Chinese leader under three conditions: not responding to Japanese construction, issuing a threat to use force and carrying through with that threat, and issuing a threat to use force but backing down in the end. That experiment tested for the external validity of audience costs, given that the vast majority of such tests are based on U.S. respondents. For details about and theoretical implications of the findings, see Kai Quek and Alastair Iain Johnston, "Crisis Management in the Shadow of Audience Costs," paper prepared for the annual meeting of the American Political Science Association, Philadelphia, Pennsylvania, September 3, 2016.

110. According to the Beijing Area Study 2015 wave, a random sample survey of people living in Beijing, the mean level of warmth toward Japan was 31 degrees on a scale of 0–100 degrees, the lowest of nine countries tested. This was significantly lower than even for Vietnam (38 degrees, N = 2,090, $p < 0.001$) and the Philippines (36 degrees, N = 1949, $p < 0.001$), with which China also has territorial disputes, and it was a great deal lower than the mean for the United States (48 degrees, N = 2,299, $p < 0.001$), which many Chinese officials claim is trying to contain China's rise. In another variable using an Osgood semantic differential instrument to measure respondents' perceptions of difference between Chinese and Japanese, the mean score for the Chinese as a people was 1.8 (N = 2571, sd = 1.14) on a scale of 1–7 from peaceful to warlike, whereas the mean score for the Japanese as a people was 5.5 (N = 2,294, sd = 1.75).

111. Each subject is assigned to only one experimental condition.

112. Our vignette follows the same approach used in previous audience cost experiments, without saturating the scenario with extra information such as elite cues and media frames. See, for example, Michael Tomz, "Domestic Audience Costs in International Relations: An Experimental Approach," *International Organization*, Vol. 61, No. 4 (October 2007), pp. 821–840, doi:10.1017/S0020818307070282.

113. Stephen E. Gent and Megan Shannon, "The Effectiveness of International Arbitration and Adjudication: Getting into a Bind," *Journal of Politics,* Vol. 72, No. 2 (April 2010), pp. 366–380, doi:10.1017/S0022381609990788; Stephen E. Gent and Megan Shannon, "Decision Control and the Pursuit of Binding Conflict Management: Choosing the Ties That Bind," *Journal of Conflict Resolution*, Vol. 55, No. 5 (2011), pp. 710–734, doi:10.1177/0022002711408012; and Krista E. Wiegand and Emilia Justyna Powell, "Unexpected Companions: Bilateral Cooperation between States Involved in Territorial Disputes," *Conflict Management and Peace Science*, Vol. 28, No. 3 (2011), pp. 209–229, doi:10.1177/0738894211404792.

114. For discussions of this problem, see George W. Downs, David M. Rocke, and Peter N. Barsoom, "Is the Good News about Compliance Good News about Cooperation?" *International Organization,* Vol. 50, No. 3 (Summer 1996), pp. 379–406, doi:10.1017/S0020818300033427; Jana Von Stein, "Do Treaties Constrain or Screen? Selection Bias and Treaty Compliance," *American Political Science Review,* Vol. 99, No. 4 (November 2005), pp. 611–622, doi:10.1017/S0003055405051919; and Sara McLaughlin Mitchell and Paul R. Hensel, "International Institutions and Compliance with Agreements," *American Journal of Political Science,* Vol. 51, No. 4 (October 2007), pp. 721–737, doi:10.1111/j.1540-5907.2007.00277.x.

115. Kyle C. Beardsley, "Pain, Pressure, and Political Cover: Explaining Mediation Incidence," *Journal of Peace Research,* Vol. 47, No. 4 (2010), pp. 395–406, doi:10.1177/0022343309356384; and Kyle Beardsley and Nigel Lo, "Third-Party Conflict Management and the Willingness to Make Concessions," *Journal of Conflict Resolution,* Vol. 58, No. 2 (2014), pp. 363–392, doi:10.1177/0022002712467932.

116. Rawi Abdelal et al., eds., *Measuring Identity: A Guide for Social Scientists* (New York: Cambridge University Press, 2009).

117. Alastair Iain Johnston, *Social States: China in International Institutions, 1980–2000* (Princeton, N.J.: Princeton University Press, 2008), pp. 79–84.

118. See "Li Keqiang zai Zhong Ma jingji gaoceng luntan fabiao zhuzhi yanjiang" [Li Keqiang gives keynote speech at high-level China-Malaysia economic forum], *Renmin Ribao* [People's Daily], November 24, 2015.

119. "Heping, keqin, wenming de shizi" [Peaceful, amiable, civilized "lion"], *Jiefangjun bao* [People's Liberation Army Daily], December 15, 2014.

120. Thomas C. Schelling, *Arms and Influence* (New Haven, Conn.: Yale University Press, 1966); John Lewis Gaddis, *Strategies of Containment: A Critical Appraisal of Postwar American National Security Policy* (New York: Oxford University Press, 1982); and Snyder and Borghard, "The Cost of Empty Threats."

121. Robert F. Trager and Lynn Vavreck, "The Political Costs of Crisis Bargaining: Presidential Rhetoric and the Role of Party," *American Journal of Political Science,* Vol. 55, No. 3 (July 2011), pp. 526–545, doi:10.1111/j.1540-5907.2011.00521.x.

122. This language replicates the threat that China delivered in the Sino-Indian territorial dispute that escalated after India commenced its "Forward Policy" in November 1961. The Chinese government had also used variations on this language in other crises. See Kai Quek, "Discontinuities in Signaling Behavior upon the Decision for War: An Analysis of China's Prewar Signaling Behavior," *International Relations of the Asia-Pacific,* Vol. 15 (2015), pp. 279–317, especially pp. 315–317, doi:10.1093/irap/Icu023. Most recently, China used similar language in 2012 in response to Japan's nationalization of the Diaoyu/Senkaku Islands. After issuing the threat, China began regular coast guard patrols within twelve nautical miles of the islands, thus, in Japan's view, routinely violating Japanese sovereignty. The warning language, therefore, is historically associated with China's proactive use of military force or paramilitary coercion.

123. Unless stated otherwise, all *p*-values are based on two-tailed tests of proportions comparing the approval percentages or two-tailed *t*-tests comparing the approval rating scores.

124. The model specifications include a baseline model without controls and alternative specifications with controls for respondent demographics. Although the control covariates have no causal interpretations, adding them to the model can reduce disturbance variability.

125. One might wonder if this reflects confidence in Chinese claims of sovereignty over the disputed islands, rather than a preference for third-party mediation. For example, in a survey of Chinese attitudes toward South China Sea territorial disputes, Chubb found that a strong majority of respondents supported asking the UN to mediate the dispute, even though the Chinese government is opposed to this kind of solution. It is unclear, however, whether support for mediation would be anywhere near as high if respondents thought that the mediator might not hand over the islands to China. See Andrew Chubb, "Exploring China's 'Maritime Consciousness': Public Opinion on the South and East China Sea Disputes" (Perth, Australia: Perth USAsia Center, 2014), p. 10, http://perthusasia.edu.au/usac/assets/media/docs/publications/2014_Exploring_Chinas_Maritime_Consciousness_Final.pdf. In our scenario, however, respondents are not being cued to think about whether the UN would determine who owns the disputed islands. Rather, the UN is offering to prevent escalation and to facilitate peaceful management of the dispute. Thus, the respondents' confidence in the rightness of China's sovereignty over the disputed islands should not be motivating their responses to our question.

126. Paul H.B. Godwin and Alice Miller, "China's Forbearance Has Limits: Chinese Threat and Retaliation Signaling and Its Implications for a Sino-American Military Confrontation," *China Security Perspectives,* No. 6 (March 2013), p. 33.

127. This question is a standard one used in studies of nationalism such as the International Social Survey Programme surveys on national identity and the Beijing Area Study surveys. See Alastair Iain Johnston, "Is Chinese Nationalism Rising? Evidence from Beijing," *International Security,* Vol. 41, No. 3 (Winter 2016/17), pp. 7–43, doi:10.1162/ISEC_a_00265.

128. For nativists, $p = 0.11$ (N = 480); for non-nativists, $p = 0.02$ (N = 329). All tests are two-tailed, based on approval scores.

129. For nativists, $p = 0.29$ (N = 486); for non-nativists, $p = 0.01$ (N = 350).

130. For nativists, $p < 0.001$ (N = 487); for non-nativists, $p < 0.001$ (N = 339).

131. For nativists, $p = 0.03$ (N = 494); for non-nativists, $p = 0.79$ (N = 330).

132. For doves, $p = 0.02$ (N = 257); for hawks, $p = 0.09$ (N = 545).

133. For doves, $p = 0.06$ (N = 266); for hawks, $p = 0.05$ (N = 561).

134. For doves, $p = 0.05$ (N = 264); for hawks, $p = 0.46$ (N = 531).

135. For doves, $p = 0.03$ (N = 277); for hawks, $p = 0.001$ (N = 540).

136. For doves, $p = 0.81$ (N = 266); for hawks, $p = 0.02$ (N = 548).

5

THE STATE AND THE TOOLS OF STATECRAFT

States are key actors in international relations, and how they act depends, in part, on domestic political considerations, as explained in Chapter 5 of *Essentials of International Relations*. In a widely cited article, Robert D. Putnam explains the entanglements between international and domestic factors during negotiations, using the metaphor and the language of the two-level game. Negotiators consider not only what the other state wants but also what the domestic constituencies in each state will accept. This approach connects the disciplines of international relations and comparative politics.

Also examining the borders between domestic and international politics is Barry Posen's essay on ethnic conflict and the security dilemma. At the end of the Cold War, many communist regimes collapsed, in some cases leading to the breakdown of the states into anarchy. Some African regimes that had been sustained by communist Russia and Cold War rivalry also collapsed at this time. Posen, a realist international relations scholar, put the theory of the causes of war in international anarchy to the task of explaining the rise of ethnic conflict in postcommunist anarchy. In this piece, he draws on Robert Jervis's seminal article on the security dilemma in anarchy, which is reprinted in Chapter 7.

Robert D. Putnam

DIPLOMACY AND DOMESTIC POLITICS
The Logic of Two-Level Games

Introduction: The Entanglements of Domestic and International Politics

Domestic politics and international relations are often somehow entangled, but our theories have not yet sorted out the puzzling tangle. It is fruitless to debate whether domestic politics really determine international relations, or the reverse. The answer to that question is clearly "Both, sometimes." The more interesting questions are "When?" and "How?" This article offers a theoretical approach to this issue, but I begin with a story that illustrates the puzzle.

One illuminating example of how diplomacy and domestic politics can become entangled culminated at the Bonn summit conference of 1978.[1] In the mid-1970s, a coordinated program of global reflation, led by the "locomotive" economies of the United States, Germany, and Japan, had been proposed to foster Western recovery from the first oil shock.[2] This proposal had received a powerful boost from the incoming Carter administration and was warmly supported by the weaker countries, as well as the Organization for Economic

Co-operation and Development (OECD) and many private economists, who argued that it would overcome international payments imbalances and speed growth all around. On the other hand, the Germans and the Japanese protested that prudent and successful economic managers should not be asked to bail out spendthrifts. Meanwhile, Jimmy Carter's ambitious National Energy Program remained deadlocked in Congress, while Helmut Schmidt led a chorus of complaints about the Americans' uncontrolled appetite for imported oil and their apparent unconcern about the falling dollar. All sides conceded that the world economy was in serious trouble, but it was not clear which was more to blame, tight-fisted German and Japanese fiscal policies or slack-jawed U.S. energy and monetary policies.

At the Bonn summit, however, a comprehensive package deal was approved, the clearest case yet of a summit that left all participants happier than when they arrived. Helmut Schmidt agreed to additional fiscal stimulus, amounting to 1 percent of GNP, Jimmy Carter committed himself to decontrol domestic oil prices by the end of 1980, and Takeo Fukuda pledged new efforts to reach a 7 percent growth rate. Secondary elements in the Bonn accord included French and British acquiescence in the Tokyo Round trade negotiations; Japanese undertakings to foster import growth and restrain exports; and a generic American promise to fight inflation. All in all, the Bonn summit produced a balanced agreement of unparalleled breadth and specificity.

From *International Organization* 42, no. 3 (Summer 1988), 427–60. Some of the author's notes have been omitted.

More remarkably, virtually all parts of the package were actually implemented.

Most observers at the time welcomed the policies agreed to at Bonn, although in retrospect there has been much debate about the economic wisdom of this package deal. However, my concern here is not whether the deal was wise economically, but how it became possible politically. My research suggests, first, that the key governments at Bonn adopted policies different from those that they would have pursued in the absence of international negotiations, but second, that agreement was possible only because a powerful minority within each government actually favored on domestic grounds the policy being demanded internationally.

Within Germany, a political process catalyzed by foreign pressures was surreptitiously orchestrated by expansionists inside the Schmidt government. Contrary to the public mythology, the Bonn deal was not forced on a reluctant or "altruistic" Germany. In fact, officials in the Chancellor's Office and the Economics Ministry, as well as in the Social Democratic party and the trade unions, had argued privately in early 1978 that further stimulus was domestically desirable, particularly in view of the approaching 1980 elections. However, they had little hope of overcoming the opposition of the Finance Ministry, the Free Democratic party (part of the government coalition), and the business and banking community, especially the leadership of the Bundesbank. Publicly, Helmut Schmidt posed as reluctant to the end. Only his closest advisors suspected the truth: that the chancellor "let himself be pushed" into a policy that he privately favored, but would have found costly and perhaps impossible to enact without the summit's package deal.

Analogously, in Japan a coalition of business interests, the Ministry of Trade and Industry (MITI), the Economic Planning Agency, and some expansion-minded politicians within the Liberal Democratic Party pushed for additional domestic stimulus, using U.S. pressure as one of their prime arguments against the stubborn resistance of the Ministry of Finance (MOF). Without internal divisions in Tokyo, it is unlikely that the foreign demands would have been met, but without the external pressure, it is even more unlikely that the expansionists could have overridden the powerful MOF. "Seventy percent foreign pressure, 30 percent internal politics," was the disgruntled judgment of one MOF insider. "Fifty-fifty," guessed an official from MITI.[3]

In the American case, too, internal politicking reinforced, and was reinforced by, the international pressure. During the summit preparations American negotiators occasionally invited their foreign counterparts to put more pressure on the Americans to reduce oil imports. Key economic officials within the administration favored a tougher energy policy, but they were opposed by the president's closest political aides, even after the summit. Moreover, congressional opponents continued to stymie oil price decontrol, as they had under both Nixon and Ford. Finally, in April 1979, the president decided on gradual administrative decontrol, bringing U.S. prices up to world levels by October 1981. His domestic advisors thus won a postponement of this politically costly move until after the 1980 presidential election, but in the end, virtually every one of the pledges made at Bonn was fulfilled. Both proponents and opponents of decontrol agree that the summit commitment was at the center of the administration's heated intramural debate during the winter of 1978–79 and instrumental in the final decision.[4]

In short, the Bonn accord represented genuine international policy coordination. Significant policy changes were pledged and implemented by the key participants. Moreover—although this counterfactual claim is necessarily harder to establish— those policy changes would very probably not have been pursued (certainly not the same scale and within the same time frame) in the absence of the international agreement. Within each country, one faction supported the policy shift being demanded of its country internationally, but that faction was initially outnumbered. Thus, international pressure was a necessary condition for these policy shifts. On the other hand, without domestic resonance, international forces would not have sufficed to produce the accord, no matter how balanced and intellectually persuasive the overall package. In the end, each leader believed that what he was doing was in his nation's interest— and probably in his own political interest, too, even though not all his aides agreed.[5] Yet without the summit accord he probably would not (or could not) have changed policies so easily. In that sense, the Bonn deal successfully meshed domestic and international pressures.

Neither a purely domestic nor a purely international analysis could account for this episode. Interpretations cast in terms either of domestic causes and international effects ("Second Image"[6]) or of international causes and domestic effects ("Second Image Reversed"[7]) would represent merely "partial equilibrium" analyses and would miss an important part of the story, namely, how the domestic politics of several countries became entangled via an international negotiation. The events of 1978 illustrate that we must aim instead for "general equilibrium" theories that account simultaneously for the interaction of domestic and international factors. This article suggests a conceptual framework for understanding how diplomacy and domestic politics interact.

Domestic-International Entanglements: The State of the Art

Much of the existing literature on relations between domestic and international affairs consists either of ad hoc lists of countless "domestic influences" on foreign policy or of generic observations that national and international affairs are somehow "linked."[8]

■ ■ ■

We need to move beyond the mere observation that domestic factors influence international affairs and vice versa, and beyond simple catalogs of instances of such influence, to seek theories that integrate both spheres, accounting for the areas of entanglement between them.

Two-Level Games: A Metaphor for Domestic-International Interactions

Over two decades ago Richard E. Walton and Robert B. McKersie offered a "behavioral theory" of social negotiations that is strikingly applicable to international conflict and cooperation.[9] They pointed out, as all experienced negotiators know, that the unitary-actor assumption is often radically misleading. As Robert Strauss said of the Tokyo Round trade negotiations: "During my tenure as Special Trade Representative, I spent as much time negotiating with domestic constituents (both industry and labor) and members of the U.S. Congress as I did negotiating with our foreign trading partners."[10]

The politics of many international negotiations can usefully be conceived as a two-level game. At the national level, domestic groups pursue their interests by pressuring the government to adopt favorable policies, and politicians seek power by constructing coalitions among those groups. At the international level, national governments seek to maximize their own ability to satisfy domestic pressures, while minimizing the adverse consequences of foreign developments. Neither of the two games can be ignored by central decision-makers, so long as their countries remain interdependent, yet sovereign.

Each national political leader appears at both game boards. Across the international table sit his foreign counterparts, and at his elbows sit diplomats and other international advisors. Around the domestic table behind him sit party and parliamentary figures, spokespersons for domestic agencies, representatives of key interest groups, and the leader's own political advisors. The unusual complexity of this two-level game is that moves that are rational for a player at one board (such as raising energy prices, conceding territory, or limiting auto imports) may be impolitic for that same player at the other board. Nevertheless, there are powerful incentives for consistency between the two games. Players (and kibitzers) will tolerate some differences in rhetoric between the two games, but in the end either energy prices rise or they don't.

The political complexities for the players in this two-level game are staggering. Any key player at the international table who is dissatisfied with the outcome may upset the game board, and conversely, any leader who fails to satisfy his fellow players at the domestic table risks being evicted from his seat. On occasion, however, clever players will spot a move on one board that will trigger realignments on other boards, enabling them to achieve otherwise unattainable objectives. This "two-table" metaphor captures the dynamics of the 1978 negotiations better than any model based on unitary national actors.

* * * Probably the most interesting empirically based theorizing about the connection between domestic and international bargaining is that of Glenn Snyder and Paul Diesing. Though working in the neo-realist tradition with its conventional assumption of unitary actors, they found that, in fully half of the crises they studied, top decision-makers were *not* unified. They concluded that prediction of international outcomes is significantly improved by understanding internal bargaining, especially with respect to minimally acceptable compromises.[11]

Metaphors are not theories, but I am comforted by Max Black's observation that "perhaps every science must start with metaphor and end with algebra; and perhaps without the metaphor there would never have been any algebra."[12] Formal analysis of any game requires well-defined rules, choices, payoffs, players, and information, and even then, many simple two-person, mixed-motive games have no determinate solution. Deriving analytic solutions for two-level games will be a difficult challenge. In what follows I hope to motivate further work on that problem.

Towards a Theory of Ratification: The Importance of "Win-Sets"

Consider the following stylized scenario that might apply to any two-level game. Negotiators representing two organizations meet to reach an agreement between them, subject to the constraint that any tentative agreement must be ratified by their respective organizations. The negotiators might be heads of government representing nations, for example, or labor and management representatives, or party leaders in a multiparty coalition, or a finance minister negotiating with an IMF team, or leaders of a House-Senate conference committee, or ethnic-group leaders in a consociational democracy. For the moment, we shall presume that each side is represented by a single leader or "chief negotiator," and that this individual has no independent policy preferences, but seeks simply to achieve an agreement that will be attractive to his constituents.[13]

It is convenient analytically to decompose the process into two stages:

1. bargaining between the negotiators, leading to a tentative agreement; call that Level I.
2. separate discussions within each group of constituents about whether to ratify the agreement; call that Level II.

This sequential decomposition into a negotiation phase and a ratification phase is useful for purposes of exposition, although it is not descriptively accurate. In practice, expectational effects will be quite important. There are likely to be prior consultations and bargaining at Level II to hammer out an initial position for the Level I negotiations. Conversely, the need for Level II ratification is certain to affect the Level I bargaining. In fact, expectations of rejection at Level II may abort negotiations at Level I without any formal action at Level II. For example, even though both the American and Iranian governments seem to have favored an arms-for-hostages deal, negotiations collapsed as soon as they became public and thus liable to de facto "ratification." In many negotiations, the two-level process may be iterative, as the negotiators try out possible agreements and probe their constituents' views. In more complicated cases, as we shall see later, the constituents' views may themselves evolve in the course of the negotiations. Nevertheless, the requirement that any Level I agreement must, in the end, be ratified at Level II imposes a crucial theoretical link between the two levels.

"Ratification" may entail a formal voting procedure at Level II, such as the constitutionally required two-thirds vote of the U.S. Senate for ratifying treaties, but I use the term generically to refer to any decision-process at Level II that is required to endorse or implement a Level I agreement, whether formally or informally. It is sometimes convenient to think of ratification as a parliamentary function, but that is not essential. The actors at Level II may represent bureaucratic agencies, interest groups, social classes, or even "public opinion." For example, if labor unions in a debtor country withhold necessary cooperation from an austerity program that the government has negotiated with the IMF, Level II ratification of the agreement may be said to have failed; ex ante expectations about that prospect will surely influence the Level I negotiations between the government and the IMF.

Domestic ratification of international agreements might seem peculiar to democracies. As the German Finance Minister recently observed, "The limit of expanded cooperation lies in the fact that we are democracies, and we need to secure electoral majorities at home."[14] However, ratification need not be "democratic" in any normal sense. For example, in 1930 the Meiji Constitution was interpreted as giving a special role to the Japanese military in the ratification of the London Naval Treaty;[15] and during the ratification of any agreement between Catholics and Protestants in Northern Ireland, presumably the IRA would throw its power onto the scales. We need only stipulate that, for purposes of counting "votes" in the ratification process, different forms of political power can be reduced to some common denominator.

The only formal constraint on the ratification process is that since the identical agreement must be ratified by both sides, a preliminary Level I agreement cannot be amended at Level II without reopening the Level I negotiations. In other words, final ratification must be simply "voted" up or down; any modification to the Level I agreement counts as a rejection, unless that modification is approved by all other parties to the agreement.[16] Congresswoman Lynn Martin captured the logic of ratification when explaining her support for the 1986 tax reform bill as it emerged from the conference committee: "As worried as I am about what this bill does, I am even more worried about the current code. The choice today is not between this bill and a perfect bill; the choice is between this bill and the death of tax reform."[17]

Given this set of arrangements, we may define the "win-set" for a given Level II constituency as the set of all possible Level I agreements that would "win"—that is, gain the necessary majority among the constituents—when simply voted up or down.[18] For two quite different reasons, the contours of the Level II win-sets are very important for understanding Level I agreements.

First, **larger win-sets make Level I agreement more likely**, *ceterls paribus*.[19] By definition, any successful agreement must fall within the Level II win-sets of each of the parties to the accord. Thus, agreement is possible only if those win-sets overlap, and the larger each win-set, the more likely they are to overlap. Conversely, the smaller the win-sets, the greater the risk that the negotiations will break down. For example, during the prolonged pre-war Anglo-Argentine negotiations over the Falklands/Malvinas, several tentative agreements were rejected in one capital or the other for domestic political reasons; when it became clear that the initial British and Argentine win-sets did not overlap at all, war became virtually inevitable.[20]

■   ■   ■

The second reason why win-set size is important is that **the relative size of the respective Level II win-sets will affect the distribution of the joint gains from the international bargain**. The larger the perceived win-set of a negotiator, the more he can be "pushed around" by the other Level I negotiators. Conversely, a small domestic win-set can be a bargaining advantage: "I'd like to accept your proposal, but I could never get it accepted at home." Lamenting the domestic constraints under which one must operate is (in the words of one experienced British diplomat) "the natural thing to say at the beginning of a tough negotiation."[21]

This general principle was, of course, first noted by Thomas Schelling nearly thirty years ago:

> The power of a negotiator often rests on a manifest inability to make concessions and meet demands. . . . When the United States

Government negotiates with other governments . . . if the executive branch negotiates under legislative authority, with its position constrained by law, . . . then the executive branch has a firm position that is visible to its negotiating partners. . . . [Of course, strategies such as this] run the risk of establishing an immovable position that goes beyond the ability of the other to concede, and thereby provoke the likelihood of stalemate or breakdown.[22]

Writing from a strategist's point of view, Schelling stressed ways in which win-sets may be manipulated, but even when the win-set itself is beyond the negotiator's control, he may exploit its leverage. A Third World leader whose domestic position is relatively weak (Argentina's Alfonsin?) should be able to drive a better bargain with his international creditors, other things being equal, than one whose domestic standing is more solid (Mexico's de la Madrid?).[23] The difficulties of winning congressional ratification are often exploited by American negotiators. During the negotiation of the Panama Canal Treaty, for example, "the Secretary of State warned the Panamanians several times . . . that the new treaty would have to be acceptable to at least sixty-seven senators," and "Carter, in a personal letter to Torrijos, warned that further concessions by the United States would seriously threaten chances for Senate ratification."[24] Precisely to forestall such tactics, opponents may demand that a negotiator ensure himself "negotiating room" at Level II before opening the Level I negotiations.

■   ■   ■

Determinants of the Win-Set

It is important to understand what circumstances affect win-set size. Three sets of factors are especially important:

- Level II preferences and coalitions
- Level II institutions
- Level I negotiators' strategies

Let us consider each in turn.

1. *The size of the win-set depends on the distribution of power, preferences, and possible coalitions among Level II constituents.*

Any testable two-level theory of international negotiation must be rooted in a theory of domestic politics, that is, a theory about the power and preferences of the major actors at Level II. This is not the occasion for even a cursory evaluation of the relevant alternatives, except to note that the two-level conceptual framework could in principle be married to such diverse perspectives as Marxism, interest group pluralism, bureaucratic politics, and neo-corporatism. For example, arms negotiations might be interpreted in terms of a bureaucratic politics model of Level II politicking, while class analysis or neo-corporatism might be appropriate for analyzing international macroeconomic coordination.

Abstracting from the details of Level II politics, however, it is possible to sketch certain principles that govern the size of the win-sets. For example, the lower the cost of "no-agreement" to constituents, the smaller the win-set.[25] Recall that ratification pits the proposed agreement, *not* against an array of other (possibly attractive) alternatives, but only against "no-agreement."[26] No-agreement often represents the status quo, although in some cases no-agreement may in fact lead to a worsening situation; that might be a reasonable description of the failed ratification of the Versailles Treaty.

Some constituents may face low costs from no-agreement, and others high costs, and the former will be more skeptical of Level I agreements than the latter. * * * The size of the win-set (and thus the negotiating room of the Level I negotiator) depends on the relative size of the "isolationist" forces (who oppose international cooperation in general) and the "internationalists" (who offer "all-purpose" support). All-purpose support for international agreements is probably greater in smaller, more dependent countries with more open economies, as compared to more self-sufficient countries, like the United States, for most of whose citizens the costs of no-agreement are generally lower. *Ceteris paribus*, more self-sufficient states with smaller win-sets should make fewer international agreements and drive harder bargains in those that they do make.

In some cases, evaluation of no-agreement may be the *only* significant disagreement among the Level II constituents, because their interests are relatively homogeneous. For example, if oil imports are to be limited by an agreement among the consuming nations—the sort of accord sought at the Tokyo summit of 1979, for example—then presumably every constituent would prefer to maximize his nation's share of the available supply, although some constituents may be more reluctant than others to push too hard, for fear of losing the agreement entirely. * * * Other international examples in which domestic interests are relatively homogeneous except for the evaluation or no-agreement might include the SALT talks, the Panama Canal Treaty negotiations, and the Arab-Israeli conflict. A negotiator is unlikely to face criticism at home that a proposed agreement reduces the opponents' arms too much, offers too little compensation for foreign concessions, or contains too few security guarantees for the other side, although in each case opinions may differ on how much to risk a negotiating deadlock in order to achieve these objectives.

The distinctive nature of such "homogeneous" issues is thrown into sharp relief by contrasting them to cases in which constituents' preferences are more heterogeneous, so that any Level I agreement bears unevenly on them. Thus, an internationally coordinated reflation may encounter domestic opposition *both* from those who think it goes too far (bankers, for example) *and* from those who think it does not go far enough (unions, for example). In 1919, some Americans opposed the Versailles Treaty because it was too harsh on the defeated powers and others because it was too lenient.[27] Such patterns are even more common, as we shall shortly see, where the negotiation involves multiple issues, such as an arms agreement that involves tradeoffs between seaborne and airborne weapons, or a labor agreement that involves tradeoffs between take-home pay and pensions. (Walton and McKersie term these "factional" conflicts, because the negotiator is caught between contending factions within his own organization.)

The problems facing Level I negotiators dealing with a *homogeneous* (or "boundary") conflict are quite different from those facing negotiators dealing with a *heterogeneous* (or "factional") conflict. In the former case, the more the negotiator can win at Level I—the higher his national oil allocation, the deeper the cuts in Soviet throw-weight, the lower the rent he promises for the Canal, and so on—the better his odds of winning ratification. In such cases, the negotiator may use the implicit threat from his own hawks to maximize his gains (or minimize his losses) at Level I, as Carter and Vance did in dealing with the Panamanians. Glancing over his shoulder at Level II, the negotiator's main problem in a homogeneous conflict is to manage the discrepancy between his constituents' expectations and the negotiable outcome. Neither negotiator is likely to find much sympathy for the enemy's demands among his own constituents, nor much support for his constituents' positions in the enemy camp. The effect of domestic division, embodied in hard-line opposition from hawks, is to raise the risk of involuntary defection and thus to impede agreement at Level I. The common belief that domestic politics is inimical to international cooperation no doubt derives from such cases.

The task of a negotiator grappling instead with a heterogeneous conflict is more complicated, but potentially more interesting. Seeking to maximize the chances of ratification, he cannot follow a simple "the more, the better" rule of thumb; imposing more severe reparations on the Germans in 1919 would have gained some votes at Level II but lost others, as would hastening the decontrol of domestic oil prices in 1978. In some cases, these lines of cleavage within the Level II constituencies will cut across the Level I division, and the Level I negotiator may find silent allies at his opponent's domestic table. German labor unions might welcome foreign pressure on their own government to adopt a more expansive fiscal policy, and Italian bankers might welcome international demands for a more austere Italian monetary policy. Thus transnational alignments may emerge, tacit or explicit, in which domestic interests pressure their respective governments to adopt mutually supportive policies. This is, of course, my interpretation of the 1978 Bonn summit accord.

In such cases, domestic divisions may actually improve the prospects for international cooperation. * * *

Thus far we have implicitly assumed that all eligible constituents will participate in the ratification process. In fact, however, participation rates vary across groups and across issues, and this variation often has implications for the size of the win-set. For example, when the costs and/or benefits of a proposed agreement are relatively concentrated, it is reasonable to expect that those constituents whose interests are most affected will exert special influence on the ratification process.[28] One reason why Level II games are more important for trade negotiations than in monetary matters is that the "abstention rate" is higher on international monetary issues than on trade issues.[29]

The composition of the active Level II constituency (and hence the character of the win-set) also varies with the politicization of the issue. Politicization often activates groups who are less worried about the costs of no-agreement, thus reducing the effective win-set. For example, politicization of the Panama Canal issue seems to have reduced the negotiating flexibility on both sides of the diplomatic table.[30] This is one reason why most professional diplomats emphasize the value of secrecy to successful negotiations. However, Woodrow Wilson's transcontinental tour in 1919 reflected the opposite calculation, namely, that by expanding the active constituency he could ensure ratification of the Versailles Treaty, although in the end this strategy proved fruitless.[31]

Another important restriction of our discussion thus far has been the assumption that the negotiations involve only one issue. Relaxing this assumption has powerful consequences for the play at both levels.[32] Various groups at Level II are likely to have quite different preferences on the several issues involved in a multi-issue negotiation. As a general rule, the group with the greatest interest in a specific issue is also likely to hold the most extreme position on that issue. In the Law of the Sea negotiations, for example, the Defense Department felt most strongly about sea-lanes, the Department of the Interior about sea-bed mining rights, and so on.[33] If each group is allowed to fix the Level I negotiating position for "its" issue, the resulting package is almost sure to be "non-negotiable" (that is, non-ratifiable in opposing capitals).[34]

Thus, the chief negotiator is faced with tradeoffs across different issues: how much to yield on mining rights in order to get sea-lane protection, how much to yield on citrus exports to get a better deal on beef, and so on. * * * The central point is simple: the possibility of package deals opens up a rich array of strategic alternatives for negotiators in a two-level game.

One kind of issue linkage is absolutely crucial to understanding how domestic and international politics can become entangled.[35] Suppose that a majority of constituents at Level II oppose a given policy (say, oil price decontrol), but that some members of that majority would be willing to

switch their vote on that issue in return for more jobs (say, in export industries). If bargaining is limited to Level II, that tradeoff is not technically feasible, but if the chief negotiator can broker an international deal that delivers more jobs (say, via faster growth abroad), he can, in effect, overturn the initial outcome at the domestic table. Such a transnational issue linkage was a crucial element in the 1978 Bonn accord.

Note that this strategy works not by changing the preferences of any domestic constituents, but rather by creating a policy option (such as faster export growth) that was previously beyond domestic control. Hence, I refer to this type of issue linkage at Level I that alters the feasible outcomes at Level II as *synergistic linkage*. For example, "in the Tokyo Round . . . nations used negotiation to achieve internal reform in situations where constituency pressures would otherwise prevent action without the pressure (and tradeoff benefits) that an external partner could provide."[36] Economic interdependence multiplies the opportunities for altering domestic coalitions (and thus policy outcomes) by expanding the set of feasible alternatives in this way—in effect, creating political entanglements across national boundaries. Thus, we should expect synergistic linkage (which is, by definition, explicable only in terms of two-level analysis) to become more frequent as interdependence grows.

2. *The size of the win-set depends on the Level II political institutions.*

Ratification procedures clearly affect the size of the win-set. For example, if a two-thirds vote is required for ratification, the win-set will almost certainly be smaller than if only a simple majority is required. As one experienced observer has written: "Under the Constitution, thirty-four of the one hundred senators can block ratification of any treaty. This is an unhappy and unique feature of our democracy. Because of the effective veto power of a small group, many worthy agreements have been rejected, and many treaties are never considered for ratification."[37] As noted earlier, the U.S. separation of powers imposes a tighter constraint on the American win-set than is true in many other countries. This increases the bargaining power of American negotiators, but it also reduces the scope for international cooperation. It raises the odds for involuntary defection and makes potential partners warier about dealing with the Americans.

■ ■ ■

Not all significant ratification practices are formalized; for example, the Japanese propensity for seeking the broadest possible domestic consensus before acting constricts the Japanese win-set, as contrasted with majoritarian political cultures. Other domestic political practices, too, can affect the size of the win-set. Strong discipline within the governing party, for example, increases the win-set by widening the range of agreements for which the Level I negotiator can expect to receive backing. For example, in the 1986 House-Senate conference committee on tax reform, the final bill was closer to the Senate version, despite (or rather, *because of*) Congressman Rostenkowski's greater control of his delegation, which increased the House win-set. Conversely, a weakening of party discipline across the major Western nations would, *ceteris paribus*, reduce the scope for international cooperation.

The recent discussion of "state strength" and "state autonomy" is relevant here. The greater the autonomy of central decision-makers from their Level II constituents, the larger their win-set and thus the greater the likelihood of achieving international agreement. For example, central bank insulation from domestic political pressures in effect increases the win-set and thus the odds for international monetary cooperation; recent proposals for an enhanced role for central bankers in international policy coordination rest on this point.[38] However, two-level analysis also implies

that, *ceteris paribus*, the stronger a state is in terms of autonomy from domestic pressures, the weaker its relative bargaining position internationally. For example, diplomats representing an entrenched dictatorship are less able than representatives of a democracy to claim credibly that domestic pressures preclude some disadvantageous deal.[39] This is yet another facet of the disconcerting ambiguity of the notion of "state strength."

■ ■ ■

3. *The size of the win-set depends on the strategies of the Level I negotiators.*

Each Level I negotiator has an unequivocal interest in maximizing the other side's win-set, but with respect to his own win-set, his motives are mixed. The larger his win-set, the more easily he can conclude an agreement, but also the weaker his bargaining position vis-à-vis the other negotiator. This fact often poses a tactical dilemma. For example, one effective way to demonstrate commitment to a given position in Level I bargaining is to rally support from one's constituents (for example, holding a strike vote, talking about a "missile gap," or denouncing "unfair trading practices" abroad). On the other hand, such tactics may have irreversible effects on constituents' attitudes, hampering subsequent ratification of a compromise agreement.[40] Conversely, preliminary consultations at home, aimed at "softening up" one's constituents in anticipation of a ratification struggle, can undercut a negotiator's ability to project an implacable image abroad.

Nevertheless, disregarding these dilemmas for the moment and assuming that a negotiator wishes to expand his win-set in order to encourage ratification of an agreement, he may exploit both conventional side-payments and generic "good will." The use of side-payments to attract marginal supporters is, of course, quite familiar in game theory, as well as in practical politics. For example, the Carter White House offered many inducements (such as public works projects) to help persuade wavering Senators to ratify the Panama Canal Treaty.[41] In a two-level game the side-payments may come from unrelated domestic sources, as in this case, or they may be received as part of the international negotiation.

The role of side-payments in international negotiations is well known. However, the two-level approach emphasizes that the value of an international side-payment should be calculated in terms of its marginal contribution to the likelihood of ratification, rather than in terms of its overall value to the recipient nation. What counts at Level II is not total national costs and benefits, but their *incidence, relative to existing coalitions and proto-coalitioins.* An across-the-board trade concession (or still worse, a concession on a product of interest to a committed free-trade congressman) is less effective than a concession (even one of lesser intrinsic value) that tips the balance with a swing voter. Conversely, trade retaliation should be targeted, neither at free-traders nor at confirmed protectionists, but at the uncommitted.

An experienced negotiator familiar with the respective domestic tables should be able to maximize the cost-effectiveness (to him and his constituents) of the concessions that he must make to ensure ratification abroad, as well as the cost-effectiveness of his own demands and threats, by targeting his initiatives with an eye to their Level II incidence, both at home and abroad. In this endeavor Level I negotiators are often in collusion, since each has an interest in helping the other to get the final deal ratified. In effect, they are moving jointly towards points of tangency between their respective political indifference curves. The empirical frequency of such targeting in trade negotiations and trade wars, as well as in other international negotiations, would be a crucial test of the relative merits of conventional unitary-actor

analysis and the two-level approach proposed here.[42]

In addition to the use of specific side-payments, a chief negotiator whose political standing at home is high can more easily win ratification of his foreign initiatives. Although generic good will cannot guarantee ratification, as Woodrow Wilson discovered, it is useful in expanding the win-set and thus fostering Level I agreement, for it constitutes a kind of "all-purpose glue" for his supporting coalition. * * *

Note that each Level I negotiator has a strong interest in the popularity of his opposite number, since Party A's popularity increases the size of his win-set, and thus increases both the odds of success and the relative bargaining leverage of Party B. Thus, negotiators should normally be expected to try to reinforce one another's standing with their respective constituents.

Partly for this reason and partly because of media attention, participation on the world stage normally gives a head of government a special advantage vis-à-vis his or her domestic opposition. Thus, although international policy coordination is hampered by high transaction costs, heads of government may also reap what we might term "transaction benefits." Indeed, the recent evolution of Western summitry, which has placed greater emphasis on publicity than on substance, seems designed to appropriate these "transaction benefits" without actually seeking the sort of agreements that might entail transaction costs.[43]

Higher status negotiators are likely to dispose of more side-payments and more "good will" at home, and hence foreigners prefer to negotiate with a head of government than with a lower official. In purely distributive terms, a nation might have a bargaining advantage if its chief negotiator were a mere clerk. Diplomats are acting rationally, not merely symbolically, when they refuse to negotiate with a counterpart of inferior rank. America's negotiating partners have reason for concern whenever the American president is domestically weakened.

Uncertainty and Bargaining Tactics

Level I negotiators are often badly misinformed about Level II politics, particularly on the opposing side. In 1978, the Bonn negotiators were usually wrong in their assessments of domestic politics abroad; for example, most American officials did not appreciate the complex domestic game that Chancellor Schmidt was playing over the issue of German reflation. Similarly, Snyder and Diesing report that "decision makers in our cases only occasionally attempted such assessments, and when they tried they did pretty miserably. . . . Governments generally do not do well in analyzing each other's internal politics in crises [and, I would add, in normal times], and indeed it is inherently difficult."[44] Relaxing the assumption of perfect information to allow for uncertainty has many implications for our understanding of two-level games. Let me illustrate a few of these implications.

Uncertainty about the size of a win-set can be both a bargaining device and a stumbling block in two-level negotiation. In purely distributive Level I bargaining, negotiators have an incentive to understate their own win-sets. Since each negotiator is likely to know more about his own Level II than his opponent does, the claim has some plausibility. * * *

On the other hand, uncertainty about the opponent's win-set increases one's concern about the risk of involuntary defection. Deals can only be struck if each negotiator is convinced that the proposed deal lies within his opposite number's win-set and thus will be ratified. Uncertainty about party A's ratification lowers the expected value of the agreement to party B, and thus party B will demand more generous side-payments from party A than would be needed under conditions of certainty. In fact, party B has an incentive to feign doubt about party A's ability to deliver, precisely in order to extract a more generous offer.[45]

Thus, a utility-maximizing negotiator must seek to convince his opposite number that his own win-set is "kinky," that is, that the proposed deal is certain to be ratified, but that a deal slightly more favorable to the opponent is unlikely to be ratified. * * *

The analysis of two-level games offers many illustrations of Zartman's observation that all negotiation involves "the controlled exchange of partial information."[46]

Restructuring and Reverberation

Formally speaking, game-theoretic analysis requires that the structure of issues and payoffs be specified in advance. In reality, however, much of what happens in any bargaining situation involves attempts by the players to restructure the game and to alter one another's perceptions of the costs of no-agreement and the benefits of proposed agreements. Such tactics are more difficult in two-level games than in conventional negotiations, because it is harder to reach constituents on the other side with persuasive messages. Nevertheless, governments do seek to expand one another's win-sets. Much ambassadorial activity—wooing opinion leaders, establishing contact with opposition parties, offering foreign aid to a friendly, but unstable government, and so on—has precisely this function. When Japanese officials visit Capitol Hill, or British diplomats lobby Irish-American leaders, they are seeking to relax domestic constraints that might otherwise prevent the administration from cooperating with their governments.

■ ■ ■

In some instances, perhaps even unintentionally, international pressures "reverberate" within domestic politics, tipping the domestic balance and thus influencing the international negotiations. Exactly this kind of reverberation characterized the 1978 summit negotiations. Dieter Hiss, the German sherpa and one of those who believed that a stimulus program was in Germany's own interest, later wrote that summits change national policy

> only insofar as they mobilize and/or change public opinion and the attitude of political groups. . . . Often that is enough, if the balance of opinion is shifted, providing a bare majority for the previously stymied actions of a strong minority. . . . No country violates its own interests, but certainly the definition of its interests can change through a summit with its possible tradeoffs and give-and-take.[47]

From the point of view of orthodox social-choice theory, reverberation is problematic, for it implies a certain interconnectedness among the utility functions of independent actors, albeit across different levels of the game. Two rationales may be offered to explain reverberation among utility-maximizing egoists. First, in a complex, interdependent, but often unfriendly world, offending foreigners may be costly in the long run. "To get along, go along" may be a rational maxim. This rationale is likely to be more common the more dependent (or interdependent) a nation, and it is likely to be more persuasive to Level II actors who are more exposed internationally, such as multinational corporations and international banks.

A second rationale takes into account cognitive factors and uncertainty. It would be a mistake for political scientists to mimic most economists' disregard for the suasive element in negotiations.[48] Given the pervasive uncertainty that surrounds many international issues, messages from abroad can change minds, move the undecided, and hearten those in the domestic minority. * * *

Suasive reverberation is more likely among countries with close relations and is probably more frequent in economic than in political–military negotiations. Communiqués from the Western summits are often cited by participants to domestic audiences as a way of legitimizing their policies. After one such statement by Chancellor Schmidt, one of his aides privately characterized the argument as "not intellectually valid, but politically useful." Conversely, it is widely believed by summit participants that a declaration contrary to a government's current policy could be used profitably by its opponents. Recent congressional proposals to ensure greater domestic publicity for international commentary on national economic policies (including hitherto confidential IMF recommendations) turn on the idea that reverberation might increase international cooperation.[49]

Reverberation as discussed thus far implies that international pressure expands the domestic win-set and facilitates agreement. However, reverberation can also be negative, in the sense that foreign pressure may create a domestic backlash. Negative reverberation is probably less common empirically than positive reverberation, simply because foreigners are likely to forgo public pressure if it is recognized to be counterproductive. Cognitive balance theory suggests that international pressure is more likely to reverberate negatively if its source is generally viewed by domestic audiences as an adversary rather than an ally. Nevertheless, predicting the precise effect of foreign pressure is admittedly difficult, although empirically, reverberation seems to occur frequently in two-level games.

■   ■   ■

The Role of the Chief Negotiator

In the stylized model of two-level negotiations outlined here, the chief negotiator is the only formal link between Level I and Level II. Thus far, I have assumed that the chief negotiator has no independent policy views, but acts merely as an honest broker, or rather as an agent on behalf of his constituents. That assumption powerfully simplifies the analysis of two-level games. However, as principal-agent theory reminds us, this assumption is unrealistic.[50] Empirically, the preferences of the chief negotiator may well diverge from those of his constituents. Two-level negotiations are costly and risky for the chief negotiator, and they often interfere with his other priorities, so it is reasonable to ask what is in it for him.

The motives of the chief negotiator include:

1. Enhancing his standing in the Level II game by increasing his political resources or by minimizing potential losses. * * *
2. Shifting the balance of power at Level II in favor of domestic policies that he prefers for exogenous reasons. International negotiations sometimes enable government leaders to do what they privately wish to do, but are powerless to do domestically. * * *
3. To pursue his own conception of the national interest in the international context. * * *

It is reasonable to presume, at least in the international case of two-level bargaining, that the chief negotiator will normally give primacy to his domestic calculus, if a choice must be made, not least because his own incumbency often depends on his standing at Level II. Hence, he is more likely to present an international agreement for ratification, the less of his own political capital he expects to have to invest to win approval, and the greater the likely political returns from a ratified agreement.

This expanded conception of the role of the chief negotiator implies that he has, in effect, a veto over possible agreements. Even if a proposed deal lies within his Level II win-set, that deal is unlikely to be struck if he opposes it.[51] Since this proviso applies on both sides of the Level I table,

the actual international bargaining set may be narrower—perhaps much narrower—than the overlap between the Level II win-sets. Empirically, this additional constraint is often crucial to the outcome of two-level games. One momentous example is the fate of the Versailles Treaty. The best evidence suggests, first, that perhaps 80 percent of the American public *and* of the Senate in 1919 favored ratification of the treaty, if certain reservations were attached, and second, that those reservations were acceptable to the other key signatories, especially Britain and France. In effect, it was Wilson himself who vetoed this otherwise ratifiable package, telling the dismayed French Ambassador, "I shall consent to nothing."[52]

Yet another constraint on successful two-level negotiation derives from the leader's existing domestic coalition. Any political entrepreneur has a fixed investment in a particular pattern of policy positions and a particular supporting coalition. If a proposed international deal threatens that investment, or if ratification would require him to construct a different coalition, the chief negotiator will be reluctant to endorse it, even if (judged abstractly) it could be ratified. Politicians may be willing to risk a few of their normal supporters in the cause of ratifying an international agreement, but the greater the potential loss, the greater their reluctance.

In effect, the fixed costs of coalition-building thus imply this constraint on the win-set: How great a realignment of prevailing coalitions at Level II would be required to ratify a particular proposal? For example, a trade deal may expand export opportunities for Silicon Valley, but harm Aliquippa. This is fine for a chief negotiator (for example, Reagan?) who can easily add Northern California yuppies to his support coalition and who has no hope of winning Aliquippa steelworkers anyhow. But a different chief negotiator with a different support coalition (for example, Mondale?) might find it costly or even impossible to convert the gains from the same agreement into politically usable form. * * *

Relaxing the assumption that the chief negotiator is merely an honest broker, negotiating on behalf of his constituents, opens the possibility that the constituents may be more eager for an agreement (or more worried about "no-agreement") than he is. Empirical instances are not hard to find: in early 1987, European publics were readier to accept Gorbachev's "double-zero" arms control proposal than European leaders, just as in the early 1970s the American public (or at least the politically active public) was more eager for a negotiated end to the Vietnam War than was the Nixon administration. As a rule, the negotiator retains a veto over any proposed agreement in such cases. However, if the negotiator's own domestic standing (or indeed, his incumbency) would be threatened if he were to reject an agreement that falls within his Level II win-set, and if this is known to all parties, then the other side at Level I gains considerable leverage. Domestic U.S. discontent about the Vietnam War clearly affected the agreement reached at the Paris talks.[53] Conversely, if the constituents are (believed to be) hard-line, then a leader's domestic weakness becomes a diplomatic asset. * * *

■   ■   ■

Conclusion

The most portentous development in the fields of comparative politics and international relations in recent years is the dawning recognition among practitioners in each field of the need to take into account entanglements between the two. Empirical illustrations of reciprocal influence between domestic and international affairs abound. What we need now are concepts and theories that will help us organize and extend our empirical observations.

Analysis in terms of two-level games offers a promising response to this challenge. Unlike state-centric theories, the two-level approach recognizes

the inevitability of domestic conflict about what the "national interest" requires. Unlike the "Second Image" or the "Second Image Reversed," the two-level approach recognizes that central decision-makers strive to reconcile domestic and international imperatives simultaneously. As we have seen, statesmen in this predicament face distinctive strategic opportunities and strategic dilemmas.

This theoretical approach highlights several significant features of the links between diplomacy and domestic politics, including:

- the important distinction between voluntary and involuntary defection from international agreements;
- the contrast between issues on which domestic interests are homogeneous, simply pitting hawks against doves, and issues on which domestic interests are more heterogeneous, so that domestic cleavage may actually foster international cooperation;
- the possibility of synergistic issue linkage, in which strategic moves at one game-table facilitate unexpected coalitions at the second table;
- the paradoxical fact that institutional arrangements which strengthen decision-makers at home may weaken their international bargaining position, and vice versa;
- the importance of targeting international threats, offers, and side-payments with an eye towards their domestic incidence at home and abroad;
- the strategic uses of uncertainty about domestic politics, and the special utility of "kinky win-sets";
- the potential reverberation of international pressures within the domestic arena;
- the divergences of interest between a national leader and those on whose behalf he is negotiating, and in particular, the international implications of his fixed investments in domestic politics.

Two-level games seem a ubiquitous feature of social life, from Western economic summitry to diplomacy in the Balkans and from coalition politics in Sri Lanka to legislative maneuvering on Capitol Hill. Far-ranging empirical research is needed now to test and deepen our understanding of how such games are played.

NOTES

1. The following account is drawn from Robert D. Putnam and C. Randall Henning, "The Bonn Summit of 1978: How Does International Economic Policy Coordination Actually Work?" *Brookings Discussion Papers in International Economics*, no. 53 (Washington, DC: Brookings Institution, October 1986), and Robert D. Putnam and Nicholas Bayne, *Hanging Together: Cooperation and Conflict in the Seven-Power Summits*, rev. ed. (Cambridge, MA: Harvard University Press, 1987), pp. 62–94.

2. Among interdependent economies, most economists believe, policies can often be more effective if they are internationally coordinated. For relevant citations, see Putnam and Bayne, *Hanging Together*, p. 24.

3. For a comprehensive account of the Japanese story, see I. M. Destler and Hisao Mlisuyu, "Locomotives on Different Tracks; Macroeconomic Diplomacy, 1977–1979," in I. M. Destler and Hideo Sato, eds., *Coping with U.S.-Japanese Economic Conflicts* (Lexington, MA: Heath, 1982).

4. For an excellent account of U.S. energy policy during this period, see G. John Ikenberry, "Market Solutions for State Problems: The International and Domestic Politics of American Oil Decontrol," *International Organization* 42 (Winter 1988).

5. It is not clear whether Jimmy Carter fully understood the domestic implications of his Bonn pledge at the time. See Putnam and Henning, "The Bonn Summit," and Ikenberry, "Market Solutions for State Problems."

6. Kenneth N. Waltz, *Man, the State, and War: A Theoretical Analysis* (New York: Columbia University Press, 1959).

7. Peter Gourevitch, "The Second Image Reversed: The International Sources of Domestic Politics," *International Organization* 32 (Autumn 1978), pp. 881–911.

8. I am indebted to Stephen Haggard for enlightening discussions about domestic influences on international relations.

9. Richard E. Walton and Robert B. McKersie, *A Behavioral Theory of Labor Negotiations: An Analysis of a Social Interaction System* (New York: McGraw-Hill, 1965).

10. Robert S. Strauss, "Foreword," in Joan E. Twiggs, *The Tokyo Round of Multilateral Trade Negotiations: A Case Study in Building Domestic Support for Diplomacy* (Washington, DC: Georgetown University Institute for the Study of Diplomacy, 1987), p. vii. Former Secretary of Labor John Dunlop is said to have remarked that "bilateral negotiations usually require three agreements—one across the [t]able and one on each side of the table," as cited in Howard Raiffa, *The Art and Science of Negotiation* (Cambridge, MA: Harvard University Press, 1982), p. 166.

11. Glenn H. Snyder and Paul Diesing, *Conflict Among Nations: Bargaining, Decision Making, and System Structure in International Crises* (Princeton: Princeton University Press, 1977), pp. 510–25.

12. Max Black, *Models and Metaphors* (Ithaca, NY: Cornell University Press, 1962), p. 242, as cited in Duncan Snidal, "The Game Theory of International Politics," *World Politics* 38 (October 1985), p. 36n.

13. To avoid unnecessary complexity, my argument throughout is phrased in terms of a single chief negotiator, although in many cases some of his responsibilities may be delegated to aides. Later in this article I relax the assumption that the negotiator has no independent preferences.

14. Gerhardt Stoltenberg, *Wall Street Journal Europe*, 2 October 1986, as cited in C. Randall Henning, *Macroeconomic Diplomacy in the 1980s: Domestic Politics and International Conflict Among the United States, Japan, and Europe*, Atlantic Paper No. 65 (New York: Croom Helm, for the Atlantic Institute for International Affairs, 1987), p. 1.

15. Ito Takashi, "Conflicts and Coalition in Japan, 1930: Political Groups and the London Naval Disarmament Conference," in Sven Groennings et al., eds., *The Study of Coalition Behavior* (New York: Holt, Rinehart, & Winston, 1970); Kobayashi Tatsuo, "The London Naval Treaty, 1930," in James W. Morley, ed., *Japan Erupts: The London Naval Conference and the Manchurian Incident, 1928–1932* (New York: Columbia University Press, 1984), pp. 11–117. I am indebted to William Jarosz for this example.

16. This stipulation is, in fact, characteristic of most real-world ratification procedures, such as House and Senate action on conference committee reports, although it is somewhat violated by the occasional practice of appending "reservations" to the ratification of treaties.

17. *New York Times*, 26 September 1986.

18. For the conception of win-set, see Kenneth A. Shepsle and Barry R. Weingast, "The Institutional Foundations of Committee Power," *American Political Science Review* 81 (March 1987), pp. 85–104. I am indebted to Professor Shepsle for much help on this topic.

19. To avoid tedium, I do not repeat the "other things being equal" proviso in each of the propositions that follow. Under some circumstances an expanded win-set might actually make practicable some outcome that could trigger a dilemma of collective action. See Vincent P. Crawford, "A Theory of Disagreement in Bargaining," *Econometrica* 50 (May 1982), pp. 607–37.

20. The Sunday Times Insight Team, *The Falklands War* (London: Sphere, 1982); Max Hastings and Simon Jenkins, *The Battle for the Falklands* (New York: Norton, 1984); Alejandro Dabai and Luis Lorenzano, *Argentina: The Malvinas and the End of Military Rule* (London: Verso, 1984). I am indebted to Louise Richardson for these citations.

21. Geoffrey W. Harrison, in John C. Campbell, ed., *Successful Negotiation: Trieste 1954* (Princeton: Princeton University Press, 1976), p. 62.

22. Thomas C. Schelling, *The Strategy of Conflict* (Cambridge, MA: Harvard University Press, 1960), pp. 19–28.

23. I am grateful to Lara Putnam for this example. For supporting evidence, see Robert R. Kaufman, "Democratic and Authoritarian

Responses to the Debt Issue: Argentina, Brazil, Mexico," *International Organization* 39 (Summer 1985), pp. 473–503.

24. W. Mark Habeeb and I. William Zartman, *The Panama Canal Negotiations* (Washington, DC: Johns Hopkins Foreign Policy Institute, 1986), pp. 40, 42.

25. Thomas Romer and Howard Rosenthal, "Political Resource Allocation, Controlled Agendas, and the Status Quo," *Public Choice* 33 (no. 4, 1978), pp. 27–44.

26. In more formal treatments, the no-agreement outcome is called the "reversion point." A given constituent's evaluation of no-agreement corresponds to what Raiffa terms a seller's "walk-away price," that is, the price below which he would prefer "no deal." (Raiffa, *Art and Science of Negotiation*.) No-agreement is equivalent to what Snyder and Diesing term "breakdown," or the expected cost of war. (Snyder and Diesing, *Conflict Among Nations*.)

27. Thomas A. Bailey, *Woodrow Wilson and the Great Betrayal* (New York: Macmillan, 1945), pp. 16–37.

28. See James Q. Wilson, *Political Organization* (New York: Basic Books, 1975) on how the politics of an issue are affected by whether the costs and the benefits are concentrated or diffuse.

29. Another factor fostering abstention is the greater complexity and opacity of monetary issues; as Gilbert R. Winham ("Complexity in International Negotiation," in Daniel Druckman, ed., *Negotiations: A Social-Psychological Perspective* [Beverly Hills: Sage, 1977], p. 363) observes, "complexity can strengthen the hand of a negotiator vis-à-vis the organization he represents."

30. Habeeb and Zariman, *Panama Canal Negotiations*.

31. Bailey, *Wilson and the Great Betrayal*.

32. I am grateful to Ernst B. Haas and Robert O. Keohane for helpful advice on this point.

33. Ann L. Hollick, *U.S. Foreign Policy and the Law of the Sea* (Princeton: Princeton University Press, 1981), especially pp. 208–37, and James K. Sebenius, *Negotiating the Law of the Sea* (Cambridge, MA: Harvard University Press, 1984), especially pp. 74–78.

34. Raiffa, *Art and Science of Negotiation*, p. 175.

35. I am grateful to Henry Brady for clarifying this point for me.

36. Gilbert R. Winham, "The Relevance of Clausewitz to a Theory of International Negotiation," prepared for delivery at the 1987 annual meeting of the American Political Science Association.

37. Jimmy Carter, *Keeping Faith: Memoirs of a President* (New York: Bantam Books, 1982), p. 225.

38. Michael Artis and Sylvia Ostry, *International Economic Policy Coordination*, Chatham House Papers: 30 (London: Routledge & Kegan Paul, 1986), pp. 75–76. Of course, whether this is desirable in terms of democratic values is quite another matter.

39. Schelling, *Strategy of Conflict*, p. 28.

40. Walton and McKersie, *A Behavioral Theory of Labor Negotiations*, p. 345.

41. Carter, *Keeping Faith*, p. 172. See also Raiffa, *Art and Science of Negotiation*, p. 183.

42. The strategic significance of targeting at Level II is illustrated in John Conybeare, "Trade Wars: A Comparative Study of Anglo-Hanse, Franco-Italian, and Hawley-Smoot Conflicts," *World Politics* 38 (October 1985), p. 157. Retaliation in the Anglo-Hanse trade wars did not have the intended deterrent effect, because it was not (and perhaps could not have been) targeted at the crucial members of the opposing Level II coalition. Compare Snyder and Diesing, *Conflict Among Nations*, p. 552: "If one faces a coercive opponent, but the opponent's majority coalition includes a few wavering members inclined to compromise, a compromise proposal that suits their views may cause their defection and the formation of a different majority coalition. Or if the opponent's strategy is accommodative, based on a tenuous soft-line coalition, one knows that care is required in implementing one's own coercive strategy to avoid the opposite kind of shift in the other state."

43. Transaction benefits may be enhanced if a substantive agreement is reached, although sometimes leaders can benefit domestically by loudly rejecting a proffered international deal.

44. Snyder and Diesing, *Conflict Among Nations*, pp. 516, 522–23. Analogous misperceptions in Anglo-American diplomacy are the focus of Richard E. Neustadt, *Alliance Politics* (New York: Columbia University Press, 1970).

45. I am grateful to Robert O. Keohane for pointing out the impact of uncertainty on the expected value of proposals.

46. William Zartman, *The 50% Solution* (Garden City, NJ: Anchor Books, 1976), p. 14. The present analysis assumes that constituents are myopic about the other side's Level II, an assumption that is not unrealistic empirically. However, a fully informed constituent would consider the preferences of key players on the other side, for if the current proposal lies well within the other side's win-set, then it would be rational for the constituent to vote against it, hoping for a second-round proposal that was more favorable to him and still ratifiable abroad; this might be a reasonable interpretation of Senator Lodge's position in 1919 (Bailey, *Wilson and the Great Betrayal*). Consideration of such strategic voting at Level II is beyond the scope of this article.

47. Dieter Hiss, "Weitwirtschaftsgipfel: Betrachtungen eines Insiders [World Economic Summit: Observations of an Insider]," in Joachim Frohn and Reiner Staeglin, eds., *Empirische Wirtschaftsforschung* (Berlin: Duncker and Humblot, 1980), pp. 286–87.

48. On cognitive and communications explanations of international cooperation, see, for example, Ernst B. Haas, "Why Collaborate? Issue-Linkage and International Regimes," *World Politics* 32 (April 1980), pp. 357–405; Richard N. Cooper, "International Cooperation in Public Health as a Prologue to Macroeconomic Cooperation," *Brookings Discussion Papers in International Economics* 44 (Washington, DC: Brookings Institution, 1986); and Zartman, *50% Solution*, especially Part 4.

49. Henning, *Macroeconomic Diplomacy in the 1980s*, pp. 62–63.

50. For overviews of this literature, see Terry M. Moe, "The New Economics of Organization," *American Journal of Political Science* 28 (November 1984), pp. 739–77; John W. Prati and Richard J. Zeckhauser, eds., *Principals and Agents: The Structure of Business* (Boston, MA: Harvard Business School Press, 1985); and Barry M. Mitnick, "The Theory of Agency and Organizational Analysis," prepared for delivery at the 1986 annual meeting of the American Political Science Association. This literature is only indirectly relevant to our concerns here, for it has not yet adequately addressed the problems posed by multiple principals (or constituents, in our terms). For one highly formal approach to

the problem of multiple principals, see R. Douglas Bernheim and Michael D. Whinston, "Common Agency," *Econometrica* 54 (July 1986), pp. 923–42.

51. This power of the chief negotiator is analogous to what Shepsle and Weingast term the "penultimate" or "ex post veto" power of the members of a Senate-House conference committee. (Shepsle and Weingast, "Institutional Foundations of Committee Power.")

52. Bailey, *Wilson and the Great Betrayal*, quotation at p. 15.

53. I. William Zartman, "Reality, Image, and Detail: The Paris Negotiations, 1969–1973," in Zartman, *50% Solution*, pp. 372–98.

Barry R. Posen

THE SECURITY DILEMMA AND ETHNIC CONFLICT

The end of the Cold War has been accompanied by the emergence of nationalist, ethnic and religious conflict in Eurasia. However, the risks and intensity of these conflicts have varied from region to region: Ukrainians and Russians are still getting along relatively well; Serbs and Slovenians had a short, sharp clash; Serbs, Croats and Bosnian Muslims have waged open warfare; and Armenians and Azeris seem destined to fight a slow-motion attrition war. The claim that newly released, age-old antipathies account for this violence fails to explain the considerable variance in observable intergroup relations.

The purpose of this article is to apply a basic concept from the realist tradition of international relations theory, 'the security dilemma', to the special conditions that arise when proximate groups of people suddenly find themselves newly responsible for their own security. A group suddenly compelled to provide its own protection must ask the following questions about any neighbouring group: is it a threat? How much of a threat? Will the threat grow or diminish over time? Is there anything that must be done immediately? The answers to these questions strongly influence the chances for war.

This article assesses the factors that could produce an intense security dilemma when imperial order breaks down, thus producing an early resort to violence. The security dilemma is then employed to analyse * * * the break-up of Yugoslavia * * * to illustrate its utility. Finally, some actions are suggested to ameliorate the tendency towards violence.

The Security Dilemma

The collapse of imperial regimes can be profitably viewed as a problem of 'emerging anarchy'. The longest standing and most useful school of international relations theory—realism—explicitly addresses the consequences of anarchy—the absence of a sovereign—for political relations among states.[1] In areas such as the former Soviet Union and Yugoslavia, 'sovereigns' have disappeared. They leave in their wake a host of groups—ethnic, religious, cultural—of greater or lesser cohesion. These groups must pay attention to the first thing that states have historically addressed—the problem of security—even though many of these groups still lack many of the attributes of statehood.

Realist theory contends that the condition of anarchy makes security the first concern of states. It can be otherwise only if these political organizations do not care about their survival as independent entities. As long as some do care, there will be competition for the key to security—power. The competition will often continue to a point at which the competing entities have amassed more power than needed for security and, thus, consequently begin to threaten others. Those threatened will respond in turn.

From *Survival* 35, no. 1 (Spring 1993): 27–47. Some of the author's notes have been omitted.

Relative power is difficult to measure and is often subjectively appraised; what seems sufficient to one state's defence will seem, and will often be, offensive to its neighbours. Because neighbours wish to remain autonomous and secure, they will react by trying to strengthen their own positions. States can trigger these reactions even if they have no expansionist inclinations. This is the security dilemma: what one does to enhance one's own security causes reactions that, in the end, can make one less secure. Cooperation among states to mute these competitions can be difficult because someone else's 'cheating' may leave one in a militarily weakened position. All fear betrayal.

Often statesmen do not recognize that this problem exists: they do not empathize with their neighbours; they are unaware that their own actions can seem threatening. Often it does not matter if they know of this problem. The nature of their situation compels them to take the steps they do.

The security dilemma is particularly intense when two conditions hold. First, when offensive and defensive military forces are more or less identical, states cannot signal their defensive intent—that is, their limited objectives—by the kinds of military forces they choose to deploy. Any forces on hand are suitable for offensive campaigns. For example, many believe that armoured forces are the best means of defence against an attack by armoured forces. However, because armour has a great deal of offensive potential, states so outfitted cannot distinguish one another's intentions. They must assume the worst because the worst is possible.

A second condition arises from the effectiveness of the offence versus the defence. If offensive operations are more effective than defensive operations, states will choose the offensive if they wish to survive. This may encourage pre-emptive war in the event of a political crisis because the perceived superiority of the offensive creates incentives to strike first whenever war appears likely. In addition, in the situation in which offensive capability is strong, a modest superiority in numbers will appear to provide greatly increased prospects for military success. Thus, the offensive advantage can cause preventive war if a state achieves a military advantage, however fleeting.

The barriers to cooperation inherent in international politics provide clues to the problems that arise as central authority collapses in multi-ethnic empires. The security dilemma affects relations among these groups, just as it affects relations among states. Indeed, because these groups have the added problem of building new state structures from the wreckage of old empires, they are doubly vulnerable.

Here it is argued that the process of imperial collapse produces conditions that make offensive and defensive capabilities indistinguishable and make the offence superior to the defence. In addition, uneven progress in the formation of state structures will create windows of opportunity and vulnerability. These factors have a powerful influence on the prospects for conflict, regardless of the internal politics of the groups emerging from old empires. Analysts inclined to the view that most of the trouble lies elsewhere, either in the specific nature of group identities or in the short-term incentives for new leaders to 'play the nationalist card' to secure their power, need to understand the security dilemma and its consequences. Across the board, these strategic problems show that very little nationalist rabble-rousing or nationalistic combativeness is required to generate very dangerous situations.

The Indistinguishability of Offence and Defence

Newly independent groups must first determine whether neighbouring groups are a threat. They will examine one another's military capabilities to do so. Because the weaponry available to these groups will often be quite rudimentary, their offensive military capabilities will be as much a function of the quantity and commitment of the soldiers they can mobilize as the particular characteristics of the weapons they control. Thus, each group will have to assess the other's offensive military potential in terms of its cohesion and its past military record.

The nature of military technology and organization is usually taken to be the main factor affecting the distinguishability of offence and defence. Yet, clear distinctions between offensive and defensive capabilities are historically rare, and they are particularly difficult to make in the realm of land warfare. For example, the force structures of armed neutrals such as Finland, Sweden and Switzerland are often categorized as defensive. These countries rely more heavily on infantry, which is thought to have weak offensive potential, than on tanks and other mechanized weaponry, which are thought to have strong offensive potential. However, their weak offensive capabilities have also been a function of the massive military power of what used to be their most plausible adversary, the former Soviet Union. Against states of similar size, similarly armed, all three countries would have considerable offensive capabilities—particularly if their infantries were extraordinarily motivated—as German and French infantry were at the outset of World War I, as Chinese and North Vietnamese infantry were against the Americans and as Iran's infantry was against the Iraqis.

Ever since the French Revolution put the first politically motivated mass armies into the field, strong national identity has been understood by both scholars and practitioners to be a key ingredient of the combat power of armies.[2] A group identity helps the individual members cooperate to achieve their purposes. When humans can readily cooperate, the whole exceeds the sum of the parts, creating a unit stronger relative to those groups with a weaker identity. Thus, the 'groupness' of the ethnic, religious, cultural and linguistic collectivities that emerge from collapsed empires gives each of them an inherent offensive military power.

The military capabilities available to newly independent groups will often be less sophisticated; infantry-based armies will be easy to organize, augmented by whatever heavier equipment is inherited or seized from the old regime. Their offensive potential will be stronger the more cohesive their sponsoring group appears to be. Particularly in the close quarters in which these groups often find themselves, the combination of infantry-based, or quasi-mechanized, ground forces with strong group solidarity is likely to encourage groups to fear each other. Their capabilities will appear offensive.

The solidarity of the opposing group will strongly influence how each group assesses the magnitude of the military threat of the others. In general, however, it is quite difficult to perform such assessments. One expects these groups to be 'exclusive' and, hence, defensive. Frenchmen generally do not want to turn Germans into Frenchmen, or the reverse. Nevertheless, the drive for security in one group can be so great that it produces near-genocidal behaviour towards neighbouring groups. Because so much conflict has been identified with 'group' identity throughout history, those who emerge as the leaders of any group and who confront the task of self-defence for the first time will be sceptical that the strong group identity of others is benign.

What methods are available to a newly independent group to assess the offensive implications of another's sense of identity?[3] The main mechanism that they will use is history: how did other groups behave the last time they were unconstrained? Is there a record of offensive military activity by the other? Unfortunately, the conditions under which this assessment occurs suggest that these groups are more likely to assume that their neighbours are dangerous than not.

The reason is that the historical reviews that new groups undertake rarely meet the scholarly standards that modern history and social science hold as norms (or at least as ideals) in the West.

First, the recently departed multi-ethnic empires probably suppressed or manipulated the facts of previous rivalries to reinforce their own rule; the previous regimes in the Soviet Union and Yugoslavia lacked any systemic commitment to truth in historical scholarship. Second, the members of these various groups no doubt did not forget the record of their old rivalries; it was preserved in oral history. This history was undoubtedly magnified in the telling and was seldom subjected to critical appraisal. Third, because their history is mostly oral, each group has a difficult time divining another's view of the past. Fourth, as central authority begins to collapse and local politicians begin to struggle for power, they will begin to write down their versions of history in political speeches. Yet, because the purpose of speeches is domestic political mobilization, these stories are likely to be emotionally charged.

The result is a worst-case analysis. Unless proven otherwise, one group is likely to assume that another group's sense of identity, and the cohesion that it produces, is a danger. Proving it to be otherwise is likely to be very difficult. Because the cohesion of one's own group is an essential means of defence against the possible depredations of neighbours, efforts to reinforce cohesion are likely to be undertaken. Propagandists are put to work writing a politicized history of the group, and the mass media are directed to disseminate that history. The media may either willingly, or under compulsion, report unfolding events in terms that magnify the threat to the group. As neighbouring groups observe this, they do the same.

In sum, the military capability of groups will often be dependent on their cohesion, rather than their meagre military assets. This cohesion is a threat in its own right because it can provide the emotional power for infantry armies to take the offensive. An historical record of large-scale armed clashes, much less wholesale mistreatment of unarmed civilians, however subjective, will further the tendency for groups to see other groups as threats. They will all simultaneously 'arm'— militarily and ideologically—against each other.

The Superiority of Offensive over Defensive Action

Two factors have generally been seen as affecting the superiority of offensive over defensive action—technology and geography. Technology is usually treated as a universal variable, which affects the military capabilities of all the states in a given competition. Geography is a situational variable, which makes offence particularly appealing to specific states for specific reasons. This is what matters most when empires collapse.

In the rare historical cases in which technology has clearly determined the offence–defence balance, such as World War I, soldiers and statesmen have often failed to appreciate its impact. Thus, technology need not be examined further, with one exception: nuclear weapons. If a group inherits a nuclear deterrent, and its neighbours do as well, 'groupness' is not likely to affect the security dilemma with as much intensity as would be the case in non-nuclear cases. Because group solidarity would not contribute to the ability of either side to mount a counterforce nuclear attack, nationalism is less important from a military standpoint in a nuclear relationship.

Political geography will frequently create an 'offence-dominant world' when empires collapse. Some groups will have greater offensive capabilities because they will effectively surround some or all of the other groups. These other groups may be forced to adopt offensive strategies to break the ring of encirclement. Islands of one group's population are often stranded in a sea of another. Where one territorially concentrated group has 'islands' of settlement of its members distributed across the nominal territory of another group (irredenta), the protection of these islands in the event of hostile action can seem extremely difficult. These islands may not be able to help one another; they may be subject to blockade and siege, and by virtue of their numbers relative to the surrounding population and because of topography, they may be militarily indefensible. Thus, the brethren of the stranded group may come to believe that only rapid offensive military action can save their irredenta from a horrible fate.[4]

The geographic factor is a variable, not a constant. Islands of population can be quite large, economically autonomous and militarily defensible. Alternatively, they can have large numbers of nearby brethren who form a powerful state, which could rescue them in the event of trouble. Potentially, hostile groups could have islands of another group's people within their states; these islands could serve as hostages. Alternatively, the brethren of the 'island' group could deploy nuclear weapons and thus punish the surrounding group if they misbehave. In short, it might be possible to defend irredenta without attacking or to deter would-be aggressors by threatening to retaliate in one way or another.

Isolated ethnic groups—ethnic islands—can produce incentives for preventive war. Theorists argue that perceived offensive advantages make preventive war more attractive: if one side has an advantage that will not be present later and if security can best be achieved by offensive military action in any case, then leaders will be inclined to attack during this 'window of opportunity'.[5] For example, if a surrounding population will ultimately be able to fend off relief attacks from the home territory of an island group's brethren, but is currently weak, then the brethren will be inclined to attack sooner rather than later.

In disputes among groups interspersed in the same territory, another kind of offensive advantage exists—a tactical offensive advantage. Often the goal of the disputants is to create ever-growing areas of homogeneous population for their brethren. Therefore, the other group's population must be induced to leave. The Serbs have introduced the term 'ethnic cleansing' to describe this objective, a term redolent with the horrors of 50 years earlier. The offence has tremendous tactical military advantages in operations such as these. Small military forces directed against unarmed or poorly armed civilians can generate tremendous terror. This has always been true, of course, but even simple modern weapons, such as machine guns and mortars, increase the havoc that small bands of fanatics can wreak against the defenceless: Consequently, small bands of each group have an incentive to attack the towns of the other in the hopes of driving the people away.[6] This is often quite successful, as the vast populations of war refugees in the world today attest.

The vulnerability of civilians makes it possible for small bands of fanatics to initiate conflict. Because they are small and fanatical, these bands are hard to control. (This allows the political leadership of the group to deny responsibility for the actions those bands take.) These activities produce disproportionate political results among the opposing group—magnifying initial fears by confirming them. The presence or absence of small gangs of fanatics is thus itself a key determinant of the ability of groups to avoid war as central political authority erodes. Although almost every society produces small numbers of people willing to engage in violence at any given moment, the rapid emergence of organized bands of particularly violent individuals is a sure sign of trouble.

The characteristic behaviour of international organizations, especially the United Nations (UN), reinforces the incentives for offensive action. Thus far, the UN has proven itself unable to anticipate conflict and provide the credible security guarantees that would mitigate the security dilemma. Once there is politically salient trouble in an area, the UN may try to intervene to 'keep the peace'. However, the conditions under which peacekeeping is attempted are favourable to the party that has had the most military success. As a general rule, the UN does not make peace: it negotiates cease-fires. Two parties in dispute generally agree to a cease-fire only because one is successful and happy with its gains, while the other has lost, but fears even worse to come. Alternatively, the two sides have fought to a bloody stalemate and would like to rest. The UN thus protects, and to some extent legitimates, the military gains of the winning side, or gives both a respite to recover. This approach by the international community to intervention in ethnic conflict, helps create an incentive for offensive military operations.

Windows of Vulnerability and Opportunity

Where central authority has recently collapsed, the groups emerging from an old empire must calculate their power relative to each other at the time of collapse and make a guess about their relative power in the future. Such calculations must account for a variety of factors. Objectively, only one side can be better off. However, the complexity of these situations makes it possible for many competing groups to believe that their prospects in a war would be better earlier, rather than later. In addition, if the geographic situation creates incentives of the kind discussed earlier, the temptation to capitalize on these windows of opportunity may be great. These windows may also prove tempting to those who wish to expand for other reasons.

The relative rate of state formation strongly influences the incentives for preventive war. When central authority has collapsed or is collapsing, the groups emerging from the political rubble will try to form their own states. These groups must choose leaders, set up bureaucracies to collect taxes and provide services, organize police forces for internal security and organize military forces for external security. The material remnants of the old state (especially weaponry, foreign currency reserves, raw material stocks and industrial capabilities) will be unevenly distributed across the territories of the old empire. Some groups may have had a privileged position in the old system. Others will be less well placed.

The states formed by these groups will thus vary greatly in their strength. This will provide immediate military advantages to those who are further along in the process of state formation. If those with greater advantages expect to remain in that position by virtue of their superior numbers, then they may see no window of opportunity. However, if they expect their advantage to wane or disappear, then they will have an incentive to solve outstanding issues while they are much stronger than the opposition.

This power differential may create incentives for preventive expropriation, which can generate a spiral of action and reaction. With military resources unevenly distributed and perhaps artificially scarce for some due to arms embargoes, cash shortages or constrained access to the outside world, small caches of armaments assume large importance. Any military depot will be a tempting target, especially for the poorly armed. Better armed groups also have a strong incentive to seize these weapons because this would increase their margin of superiority.

In addition, it matters whether or not the old regime imposed military conscription on all groups in society. Conscription makes arms theft quite easy because hijackers know what to look for and how to move it. Gains are highly cumulative because each side can quickly integrate whatever it steals into its existing forces. High cumulativity of conquered resources has often motivated states in the past to initiate preventive military actions.

Expectations about outside intervention will also affect preventive war calculations. Historically, this usually meant expectations about the intervention of allies on one side or the other, and the value of such allies. Allies may be explicit or tacit. A group may expect itself or another to find friends abroad. It may calculate that the other group's natural allies are temporarily preoccupied, or a group may calculate that it or its adversary has many other adversaries who will attack in the event of conflict. The greater the number of potential allies for all groups, the more complex this calculation will be and the greater the chance for error. Thus, two opposing groups could both think that the expected behaviour of others makes them stronger in the short term.

A broader window-of-opportunity problem has been created by the large number of crises and conflicts that have been precipitated by the end of the Cold War. The electronic media provide free global strategic intelligence about these problems to anyone for the price of a shortwave radio, much less a satellite dish. Middle and great powers, and international organizations, are able to deal with only a small number of crises simultaneously. States that wish to initiate offensive military actions, but fear outside opposition, may move quickly if they learn that international organizations and great powers are preoccupied momentarily with other problems.

Croats and Serbs

Viewed through the lens of the security dilemma, the early stages of Yugoslavia's disintegration were strongly influenced by the following factors. First, the parties identified the re-emerging identities of the others as offensive threats. The last time these groups were free of constraint, during World War II, they slaughtered one another with abandon. In addition, the Yugoslav military system trained most men for war and distributed infantry armament widely across the country. Second, the offensive appeared to have the advantage, particularly against Serbs 'marooned' in Croatian and Muslim territory. Third, the new republics were not equally powerful. Their power assets varied in terms of people and economic resources; access to the wealth and military assets of the previous regime; access to external allies; and possible outside

enemies. Preventive war incentives were consequently high. Fourth, small bands of fanatics soon appeared on the scene. Indeed, the political and military history of the region stressed the role of small, violent, committed groups; the resistance to the Turks; the Ustashe in the 1930s; and the Ustashe state and Serbian Chetniks during World War II.

Serbs and Croats both have a terrifying oral history of each other's behaviour. This history goes back hundreds of years, although the intense Croat–Serb conflict is only about 125 years old. The history of the region is quite warlike: the area was the frontier of the Hapsburg and Turkish empires, and Croatia had been an integral part of the military apparatus of the Hapsburg empire. The imposition of harsh Hungarian rule in Croatia in 1868; the Hungarian divide-and-conquer strategy that pitted Croats and Serbs in Croatia against each other; the rise of the independent Serbian nation-state out of the Ottoman empire, formally recognized in Europe in 1878; and Serbian pretensions to speak for all south Slavs were the main origins of the Croat–Serb conflict. When Yugoslavia was formed after World War I, the Croats had a very different vision of the new state than the Serbs. They hoped for a confederal system, while the Serbs planned to develop a centralized nation-state.[7] The Croats did not perceive themselves to be treated fairly under this arrangement, and this helped stimulate the development of a violent resistance movement, the Ustashe, which collaborated with the Fascist powers during the 1930s.

The Serbs had some reasons for assuming the worst about the existence of an independent Croatian state, given Croatian behaviour during World War II. Ustashe leadership was established in Croatia by Nazi Germany. The Serbs, both communist and non-communist, fought the Axis forces, including the Croats, and each other. (Some Croats also fought in Josef Tito's communist partisan movement against the Nazis.) Roughly a million people died in the fighting—some 5.9%

of Yugoslavia's pre-war population.[8] The Croats behaved with extraordinary brutality towards the Serbs, who suffered nearly 500,000 dead, more than twice as many dead as the Croats.[9] (Obviously, the Germans were responsible for many Serbian deaths as well.) Most of these were not killed in battle; they were civilians murdered in large-scale terrorist raids.

The Croats themselves suffered some 200,000 dead in World War II, which suggests that depredations were inflicted on many sides. (The non-communist, 'nationalist' Chetniks were among the most aggressive killers of Croats, which helps explain why the new Croatian republic is worried by the nationalist rhetoric of the new Serbian republic.) Having lived in a pre- and post-war Yugoslavia largely dominated by Serbs, the Croats had reason to suspect that the demise of the Yugoslavian Communist Party would be followed by a Serbian bid for hegemony. In 1971, the Croatian Communist Party had been purged of leaders who had favoured greater autonomy. In addition, the historical record of the Serbs during the past 200 years is one of regular efforts to establish an ever larger centralized Serbian national state on the Balkan Peninsula. Thus, Croats had sufficient reason to fear the Serbs.

Serbs in Croatia were scattered in a number of vulnerable islands; they could only be 'rescued' by offensive action from Serbia. Such a rescue, of course, would have been enormously complicated by an independent Bosnia, which in part explains the Serbian war there. In addition, Serbia could not count on maintaining absolute military superiority over the Croats forever: almost twice as many Serbs as Croats inhabit the territory of what was once Yugoslavia, but Croatia is slightly wealthier than Serbia.[10] Croatia also has some natural allies within former Yugoslavia, especially Bosnian Muslims, and seemed somewhat more adept at winning allies abroad. As Croatia adopted the trappings of statehood and achieved international recognition, its military power was expected to grow. From the Serbian point of view, Serbs in Croatia were insecure and expected to become more so as time went by.

From a military point of view, the Croats probably would have been better off postponing their secession until after they had made additional military preparations. However, their experience in 1971, more recent political developments and the military preparations of the Yugoslav army probably convinced them that the Serbs were about to strike and that the Croatian leadership would be rounded up and imprisoned or killed if they did not act quickly.

Each side not only had to assess the other's capabilities, but also its intentions, and there were plenty of signals of malign intent. Between 1987 and 1990, Slobodan Milosevic ended the administrative autonomy within Serbia that had been granted to Kosovo and Vojvodina in the 1974 constitution.[11] In August 1990, Serbs in the Dalmatia region of Croatia held a cultural autonomy referendum, which they defended with armed roadblocks against expected Croatian interference.[12] By October, the Yugoslav army began to impound all of the heavy weapons stored in Croatia for the use of the territorial defence forces, thus securing a vast military advantage over the nascent armed forces of the republic.[13] The Serbian window of opportunity, already large, grew larger. The Croats accelerated their own military preparations.

It is difficult to tell just how much interference the Croats planned, if any, in the referendum in Dalmatia. However, Croatia had stoked the fires of Serbian secessionism with a series of ominous rulings. In the spring of 1990, Serbs in Croatia were redefined as a minority, rather than a constituent nation, and were asked to take a loyalty oath. Serbian police were to be replaced with Croats, as were some local Serbian officials. No offer of cultural autonomy was made at the time. These Croatian policies undoubtedly intensified Serbian fears about the future and further tempted them to exploit their military superiority.

It appears that the Croats overestimated the reliability and influence of the Federal Republic of Germany as an ally due to some combination of World War II history, the widespread misperception created by the European media and by Western political leaders of Germany's near-superpower status, the presumed influence of the large Croatian émigré community in Germany and Germany's own diplomacy, which was quite favourable to Croatia even before its June 1991 declaration of independence.[14] These considerations may have encouraged Croatia to secede. Conversely, Serbian propaganda was quick to stress the German–Croatian connection and to speculate on future German ambitions in the Balkans.[15] Fair or not, this prospect would have had an impact on Serbia's preventive war calculus.

■   ■   ■

Conclusion

Three main conclusions follow from the preceding analysis. First, the security dilemma and realist international relations theory more generally have considerable ability to explain and predict the probability and intensity of military conflict among groups emerging from the wreckage of empires.

Second, the security dilemma suggests that the risks associated with these conflicts are quite high. Several of the causes of conflict and war highlighted by the security dilemma operate with considerable intensity among the groups emerging from empires. The kind of military power that these groups can initially develop and their competing versions of history will often produce mutual fear and competition. Settlement patterns, in conjunction with unequal and shifting power, will often produce incentives for preventive war. The cumulative effect of conquered resources will encourage preventive grabs of military equipment and other assets.

Finally, if outsiders wish to understand and perhaps reduce the odds of conflict, they must assess the local groups' strategic view of their situation. Which groups fear for their physical security and why? What military options are open to them? By making these groups feel less threatened and by reducing the salience of windows of opportunity, the odds of conflict may be reduced.

Because the international political system as a whole remains a self-help system, it will be difficult to act on such calculations. Outsiders rarely have major material or security interests at stake in regional disputes. It is difficult for international institutions to threaten credibly in advance to intervene, on humanitarian grounds, to protect groups that fear for the future. Vague humanitarian commitments will not make vulnerable groups feel safe and will probably not deter those who wish to repress them. In some cases, however, such commitments may be credible because the conflict has real security implications for powerful outside actors.

Groups drifting into conflict should be encouraged to discuss their individual histories of mutual relations. Competing versions of history should be reconciled if possible. Domestic policies that raise bitter memories of perceived past injustices or depredations should be examined. This exercise need not be managed by an international political institution; non-governmental organizations could play a role. Discussions about regional history would be an intelligent use of the resources of many foundations. A few conferences will not, of course, easily undo generations of hateful, politicized history, bolstered by reams of more recent propaganda. The exercise would cost little and, therefore, should be tried.

In some cases, outside powers could threaten not to act; this would discourage some kinds of aggressive behaviour. For example, outside powers could make clear that if a new state abuses a minority and then gets itself into a war with that minority and its allies, the abuser will find little sympathy abroad if it begins to lose. To accomplish this, however, outside powers must have a way of detecting mistreatment of minorities.

In other cases, it may be reasonable for outside powers to provide material resources, including armaments, to help groups protect themselves. However, this kind of hard-bitten policy is politically difficult for liberal democratic governments now dominating world politics to pursue, even on humanitarian grounds. In addition, it is an admittedly complicated game in its own right because it is difficult to determine the amount and type of military assistance needed to produce effective defensive forces, but not offensive capabilities. Nevertheless, considerable diplomatic leverage may be attained by the threat to supply armaments to one side or the other.

■   ■   ■

It will frequently prove impossible, however, to arrange military assets, external political commitments and political expectations so that all neighbouring groups are relatively secure and perceive themselves as such. War is then likely. These wars will confirm and intensify all the fears that led to their initiation. Their brutality will tempt outsiders to intervene, but peace efforts originating from the outside will be unsuccessful if they do not realistically address the fears that triggered the conflicts initially. In most cases, this will require a willingness to commit large numbers of troops and substantial amounts of military equipment to troubled areas for a very long time.

NOTES

1. The following realist literature is essential for those interested in the analysis of ethnic conflict: Kenneth Waltz, *Theory of International Politics* (Reading, MA: Addison Wesley, 1979), Chapters 6 and 8; Robert Jervis, 'Cooperation under the security dilemma', *World Politics*, no. 2, January 1978, pp. 167–213; Robert Jervis, *Perception and Misperception in International Politics* (Princeton, NJ: Princeton University Press, 1976), Chapter 3; Thomas C. Schelling, *Arms and*

Influence (New Haven, CT: Yale University Press, 1966, 1976), Chapters 1 and 6.

2. See Carl Von Clausewitz, *On War* (Princeton, NJ: Princeton University Press, 1984), pp. 591–92; Robert Gilpin, 'The Richness of the Tradition of Political Realism', in Robert E. Keohane, *Neorealism and Its Critics* (New York: Columbia University Press, 1986), pp. 300–21, especially pp. 304–308.

3. This problem shades into an assessment of 'intentions', another very difficult problem for states in international politics. This issue is treated as a capabilities problem because the emergence of anarchy forces leaders to focus on military potential, rather than on intentions. Under these conditions, every group will ask whether neighbouring groups have the cohesion, morale and martial spirit to take the offensive if their leaders call on them to do so.

4. It is plausible that the surrounding population will view irredenta in their midst as an offensive threat by the outside group. They may be perceived as a 'fifth column', that must be controlled, repressed or even expelled.

5. See Stephen Van Evera, 'The cult of the offensive and the origins of the First World War', *International Security*, vol. 9, no. 1, Summer 1984, pp. 58–107.

6. Why do they not go to the defence of their own, rather than attack the other? Here, it is hypothesized that such groups are scarce relative to the number of target towns and villages, so they cannot 'defend' their own with any great confidence.

7. James Gow, 'Deconstructing Yugoslavia', *Survival*, vol. 33, no. 4, July/August 1991, p. 292; J.B. Hoptner, *Yugoslavia in Crisis 1934–1941* (New York: Columbia University Press, 1962), pp. 1–9.

8. Ivo Banac, 'Political change and national diversity', *Daedalus*, vol. 119, no. 1, Winter 1990, pp. 145–150, estimates that 487,000 Serbs, 207,000 Croats, 86,000 Bosnian Muslims and 60,000 Jews died in Yugoslavia during the war.

9. Aleksa Djilas, *The Contested Country* (Cambridge, MA: Harvard University Press, 1991), pp. 103–28. See especially, Chapter 4, 'The National State and Genocide: The Ustasha Movement, 1929–1945', especially pp. 120–27, which vividly describes large-scale Croatian murders of Serbs, as well as Jews and Gypsies; however, Djilas does not explain how 200,000 Croats also died.

10. See Sabrina Ramet, *Nationalism and Federalism in Yugoslavia 1962–1991* (Bloomington, IN: Indiana University Press, 2nd ed., 1992), Appendix 2, p. 286.

11. Gow, *op. cit.* in note 7, p. 294. Vojvodina contains the only petroleum and gas in Yugoslavia proximate to Serbia, so this act probably had a strategic motive; see Central Intelligence Agency, *Atlas of Eastern Europe* (Washington, DC: US Government Printing Office, August 1990), p. 10.

12. International Institute for Strategic Studies, *Strategic Survey 1990–1991,* (London: Brassey's for the IISS, 1991), p. 167.

13. Gow, *op. cit.* in note 7, p. 299.

14. See John Newhouse, 'The diplomatic round', *The New Yorker*, 24 August 1992, especially p. 63. See also John Zametica, *The Yugoslav Conflict*, Adelphi Paper 270 (London: Brassey's for the IISS, 1992), pp. 63–65.

15. Ramet, *op. cit.* in note 10, p. 265.

6 WAR AND SECURITY

Warfare and military intervention continue to be central problems of international relations. Two of the readings in this section address a core issue: the relationship between the use of force and politics. Excerpts from classic books by Carl von Clausewitz, *On War* (originally published in the 1830s), and Thomas C. Schelling, *Arms and Influence* (1966), remind us that warfare is not simply an exercise of brute force; war needs to be understood as a continuation of political bargaining. In the most influential treatise on warfare ever written, Prussian general Clausewitz reminded the generation that followed the devastating Napoleonic Wars that armed conflict should not be considered a blind, all-out struggle governed by the logic of military operations. Rather, he said, the conduct of war had to be subordinated to its political objectives.

These ideas resonated strongly with American strategic thinkers of Schelling's era, who worried that military plans for total nuclear war would outstrip the ability of political leaders to control them. Schelling, a Harvard professor who also advised the U.S. Air Force on its nuclear weapons strategy, explained that political bargaining and risk-taking, not military victory, lay at the heart of the use and threat of force in the nuclear era. Erica Borghard and Shawn Lonergan apply Schelling's ideas to an analysis of the contemporary problem of cyber conflict.

James D. Fearon's 1995 article, "Rationalist Explanations for War," explores the puzzle of why two rational states would ever fight a costly war rather than settle their dispute more cheaply through peaceful bargaining. He shows that three problems can hinder the achievement of bargains that would benefit both sides: first, states may have private information (such as their military capabilities) that leads the sides to make different estimates as to who would prevail in a fight; second, side A may be unable to convince side B that it would live up to their bargain in the future; third, it may be impossible to divide up the stakes that lie at the heart of the dispute.

The advent of nuclear weapons has led to a lively debate over the relationship between nuclear proliferation and international system stability. The debate has been fueled by the emergence of nuclear states in South Asia and fears over nuclearization in both Iran and North Korea. Kenneth N. Waltz takes a contrarian position in this debate: a nuclear Iran would lead to a more stable Middle East. He derives this from his long-held, theoretically grounded view that "when it comes to nuclear weapons, now as ever, more may be better." For those who doubt that a democratic people would support a nuclear attack on civilians, Scott Sagan and Benjamin Valentino present some sobering survey research showing that the high historical public support for the atomic attack on Hiroshima in World War II may be echoed in attitudes toward scenarios for a hypothetical future war between the United States and Iran.

While terrorism has long been used as a means of achieving political objectives, the attention of the international community has been drawn to this phenomenon following the September 11, 2001, attacks. Virginia Page Fortna brings an exemplary research design to bear on the latter question in "Do Terrorists Win?"

Carl von Clausewitz

WAR AS AN INSTRUMENT OF POLICY

■ ■ ■

* * * *War is only a part of political intercourse, therefore by no means an independent thing in itself.*

We know, certainly, that War is only called forth through the political intercourse of Governments and Nations; but in general it is supposed that such intercourse is broken off by War, and that a totally different state of things ensues, subject to no laws but its own.

We maintain, on the contrary, that War is nothing but a continuation of political intercourse, with a mixture of other means. We say mixed with other means in order thereby to maintain at the same time that this political intercourse does not cease by the War itself, is not changed into something quite different, but that, in its essence, it continues to exist, whatever may be the form of the means which it uses, and that the chief lines on which the events of the War progress, and to which they are attached, are only the general features of policy which run all through the War until peace takes place. And how can we conceive it to be otherwise? Does the cessation of diplomatic notes stop the political relations between different Nations and Governments? Is not War merely another kind of writing and language for political thoughts? It has certainly a grammar of its own, but its logic is not peculiar to itself.

Accordingly, War can never be separated from political intercourse, and if, in the consideration of the matter, this is done in any way, all the threads of the different relations are, to a certain extent, broken, and we have before us a senseless thing without an object.

This kind of idea would be indispensable even if War was perfect War, the perfectly unbridled element of hostility, for all the circumstances on which it rests, and which determine its leading features, viz. our own power, the enemy's power, Allies on both sides, the characteristics of the people and their Governments respectively, etc.— are they not of a political nature, and are they not so intimately connected with the whole political intercourse that it is impossible to separate them? But this view is doubly indispensable if we reflect that real War is no such consistent effort tending to an extreme, as it should be according to the abstract idea, but a half-and-half thing, a contradiction in itself; that, as such, it cannot follow its own laws, but must be looked upon as a part of another whole—and this whole is policy.

Policy in making use of War avoids all those rigorous conclusions which proceed from its nature; it troubles itself little about final possibilities, confining its attention to immediate probabilities. If such uncertainty in the whole action ensues therefrom, if it thereby becomes a sort of game, the policy of each Cabinet places its confidence in the belief that in this game it will surpass its neighbour in skill and sharp-sightedness.

Thus policy makes out of the all-overpowering element of War a mere instrument, changes the tremendous battle-sword, which should be lifted with both hands and the whole power of the body

From Carl von Clausewitz, *On War* (Harmondsworth: Penguin Books, 1968), Bk. 5, Chap. 6. The author's notes have been omitted.

to strike once for all, into a light handy weapon, which is even sometimes nothing more than a rapier to exchange thrusts and feints and parries.

Thus the contradictions in which man, naturally timid, becomes involved by War may be solved, if we choose to accept this as a solution.

If War belongs to policy, it will naturally take its character from thence. If policy is grand and powerful, so also will be the War, and this may be carried to the point at which War attains to *its absolute form.*

In this way of viewing the subject, therefore, we need not shut out of sight the absolute form of War, we rather keep it continually in view in the background.

Only through this kind of view War recovers unity; only by it can we see all Wars as things of *one* kind; and it is only through it that the judgement can obtain the true and perfect basis and point of view from which great plans may be traced out and determined upon.

It is true the political element does not sink deep into the details of War. Vedettes are not planted, patrols do not make their rounds from political considerations; but small as is its influence in this respect, it is great in the formation of a plan for a whole War, or a campaign, and often even for a battle.

For this reason we were in no hurry to establish this view at the commencement. While engaged with particulars, it would have given us little help, and, on the other hand, would have distracted our attention to a certain extent; in the plan of a War or campaign it is indispensable.

There is, upon the whole, nothing more important in life than to find out the right point of view from which things should be looked at and judged of, and then to keep to that point; for we can only apprehend the mass of events in their unity from *one* standpoint; and it is only the keeping to one point of view that guards us from inconsistency.

If, therefore, in drawing up a plan of a War, it is not allowable to have a two-fold or three-fold point of view, from which things may be looked at, now with the eye of a soldier, then with that of an administrator, and then again with that of a politician, etc., then the next question is, whether *policy* is necessarily paramount and everything else subordinate to it.

That policy unites in itself, and reconciles all the interests of internal administrations, even those of humanity, and whatever else are rational subjects of consideration is presupposed, for it is nothing in itself, except a mere representative and exponent of all these interests towards other States. That policy may take a false direction, and may promote unfairly the ambitious ends, the private interests, the vanity of rulers, does not concern us here; for, under no circumstances can the Art of War be regarded as its preceptor, and we can only look at policy here as the representative of the interests generally of the whole community.

The only question, therefore, is whether in framing plans for a War the political point of view should give way to the purely military (if such a point is conceivable), that is to say, should disappear altogether, or subordinate itself to it, or whether the political is to remain the ruling point of view and the military to be considered subordinate to it.

That the political point of view should end completely when War begins is only conceivable in contests which are Wars of life and death, from pure hatred: as Wars are in reality, they are, as we before said, only the expressions or manifestations of policy itself. The subordination of the political point of view to the military would be contrary to common sense, for policy has declared the War; it is the intelligent faculty, War only the instrument, and not the reverse. The subordination of the military point of view to the political is, therefore, the only thing which is possible.

If we reflect on the nature of real War, and call to mind what has been said, *that every War should be viewed above all things according to the probability of its character, and its leading features as they are to be deduced from the political forces and proportions,* and that often—indeed we may safely affirm, in our days, *almost* always—War is to be regarded as an organic whole, from which the single branches are not to be separated, in which therefore every individual activity flows into the whole, and also has its origin in the idea of this whole, then it becomes certain and palpable to us that the superior standpoint for the conduct of the War, from which its leading lines must proceed, can be no other than that of policy.

From this point of view the plans come, as it were, out of a cast; the apprehension of them and the judgement upon them become easier and more natural, our convictions respecting them gain in force, motives are more satisfying and history more intelligible.

At all events from this point of view there is no longer in the nature of things a necessary conflict between the political and military interests, and where it appears it is therefore to be regarded as imperfect knowledge only. That policy makes demands on the War which it cannot respond to, would be contrary to the supposition that it knows the instrument which it is going to use, therefore, contrary to a natural and indispensable supposition. But if policy judges correctly of the march of military events, it is entirely its affair to determine what are the events and what the direction of events most favourable to the ultimate and great end of the War.

In one word, the Art of War in its highest point of view is policy, but, no doubt, a policy which fights battles instead of writing notes.

According to this view, to leave a great military enterprise or the plan for one, to *a purely military judgement and decision* is a distinction which cannot be allowed, and is even prejudicial; indeed, it is an irrational proceeding to consult professional soldiers on the plan of a War, that they may give a *purely military opinion* upon what the Cabinet ought to do; but still more absurd is the demand of Theorists that a statement of the available means of War should be laid before the General, that he may draw out a purely military plan for the War or for a campaign in accordance with those means. Experience in general also teaches us that notwithstanding the multifarious branches and scientific character of military art in the present day, still the leading outlines of a War are always determined by the Cabinet, that is, if we would use technical language, by a political not a military organ.

This is perfectly natural. None of the principal plans which are required for a War can be made without an insight into the political relations; and, in reality, when people speak, as they often do, of the prejudicial influence of policy on the conduct of a War, they say in reality something very different to what they intend. It is not this influence but the policy itself which should be found fault with. If policy is right, that is, if it succeeds in hitting the object, then it can only act with advantage on the War. If this influence of policy causes a divergence from the object, the cause is only to be looked for in a mistaken policy.

It is only when policy promises itself a wrong effect from certain military means and measures, an effect opposed to their nature, that it can exercise a prejudicial effect on War by the course it prescribes. Just as a person in a language with which he is not conversant sometimes says what he does not intend, so policy, when intending right, may often order things which do not tally with its own views.

This has happened times without end, and it shows that a certain knowledge of the nature of War is essential to the management of political intercourse.

But before going further, we must guard ourselves against a false interpretation of which this is very susceptible. We are far from holding the opinion that a War Minister smothered in official papers, a scientific engineer, or even a soldier who has been well tried in the field, would, any of them, necessarily make the best Minister of State where the Sovereign does not act for himself; or, in other words, we do not mean to say that this acquaintance with the nature of War is the principal qualification for a War Minister; elevation, superiority of mind, strength of character, these are the principal qualifications which he must possess; a knowledge of War may be supplied in one way or the other. * * *

■   ■   ■

We shall now conclude with some reflections derived from history.

In the last decade of the past century, when that remarkable change in the Art of War in Europe took place by which the best Armies found that a part of their method of War had become utterly unserviceable, and events were brought about of a magnitude far beyond what any one had any previous conception of, it certainly appeared that a false calculation of everything was to be laid to the charge of the Art of War. * * *

■   ■   ■

But is it true that the real surprise by which men's minds were seized was confined to the conduct of War, and did not rather relate to policy itself? That is: Did the ill success proceed from the influence of policy on the War, or from a wrong policy itself?

The prodigious effects of the French Revolution abroad were evidently brought about much less through new methods and views introduced by the French in the conduct of War than through the changes which it wrought in state-craft and civil administration, in the character of Governments, in the condition of the people, etc. That other Governments took a mistaken view of all these things; that they endeavoured, with their ordinary means, to hold their own against forces of a novel kind and overwhelming in strength—all that was a blunder in policy.

Would it have been possible to perceive and mend this error by a scheme for the War from a purely military point of view? Impossible. For if

there had been a philosophical strategist, who merely from the nature of the hostile elements had foreseen all the consequences, and prophesied remote possibilities, still it would have been practically impossible to have turned such wisdom to account.

If policy had risen to a just appreciation of the forces which had sprung up in France, and of the new relations in the political state of Europe, it might have foreseen the consequences which must follow in respect to the great features of War, and it was only in this way that it could arrive at a correct view of the extent of the means required as well as of the best use to make of those means.

We may therefore say, that the twenty years' victories of the Revolution are chiefly to be ascribed to the erroneous policy of the Governments by which it was opposed.

It is true these errors first displayed themselves in the War, and the events of the War completely disappointed the expectations which policy entertained. But this did not take place because policy neglected to consult its military advisers. That Art of War in which the politician of the day could believe, namely, that derived from the reality of War at that time, that which belonged to the policy of the day, that familiar instrument which policy had hitherto used—*that* Art of War, I say, was naturally involved in the error of policy, and therefore could not teach it anything better. It is true that War itself underwent important alterations both in its nature and forms, which brought it nearer to its absolute form; but these changes were not brought about because the French Government had, to a certain extent, delivered itself from the leading-strings of policy; they arose from an altered policy, produced by the French Revolution, not only in France, but over the rest of Europe as well. This policy had called forth other means and other powers, by which it became possible to conduct War with a degree of energy which could not have been thought of otherwise.

Therefore, the actual changes in the Art of War are a consequence of alterations in policy; and, so far from being an argument for the possible separation of the two, they are, on the contrary, very strong evidence of the intimacy of their connexion.

Therefore, once more: War is an instrument of policy; it must necessarily bear its character, it must measure with its scale: the conduct of War, in its great features, is therefore policy itself, which takes up the sword in place of the pen, but does not on that account cease to think according to its own laws.

Thomas C. Schelling
THE DIPLOMACY OF VIOLENCE

The usual distinction between diplomacy and force is not merely in the instruments, words or bullets, but in the relation between adversaries—in the interplay of motives and the role of communication, understandings, compromise, and restraint. Diplomacy is bargaining: it seeks outcomes that, though not ideal for either party, are better for both than some of the alternatives. In diplomacy each party somewhat controls what the other wants, and can get more by compromise, exchange, or collaboration than by taking things in his own hands and ignoring the other's wishes. The bargaining can be polite or rude, entail threats as well as offers, assume a status quo or ignore all rights and privileges, and assume mistrust rather than trust. But whether polite or impolite, constructive or aggressive, respectful or vicious, whether it occurs among friends or antagonists and whether or not there is a basis for trust and goodwill, there must be some common interest, if only in the avoidance of mutual damage, and an awareness of the need to make the other party prefer an outcome acceptable to oneself.

With enough military force a country may not need to bargain. Some things a country wants it can take, and some things it has it can keep, by sheer strength, skill and ingenuity. It can do this *forcibly*, accommodating only to opposing strength, skill, and ingenuity and without trying to appeal to an enemy's wishes. Forcibly a country can repel and expel, penetrate and occupy, seize, exterminate, disarm and disable, confine, deny access, and directly frustrate intrusion or attack. It can, that is, if it has enough strength. "Enough" depends on how much an opponent has.

There is something else, though, that force can do. It is less military, less heroic, less impersonal, and less unilateral; it is uglier, and has received less attention in Western military strategy. In addition to seizing and holding, disarming and confining, penetrating and obstructing, and all that, military force can be used *to hurt*. In addition to taking and protecting things of value it can *destroy* value. In addition to weakening an enemy militarily it can cause an enemy plain suffering.

Pain and shock, loss and grief, privation and horror are always in some degree, sometimes in terrible degree, among the results of warfare; but in traditional military science they are incidental, they are not the object. If violence can be done incidentally, though, it can also be done purposely. The power to hurt can be counted among the most impressive attributes of military force.

Hurting, unlike forcible seizure or self-defense, is not unconcerned with the interest of others. It is measured in the suffering it can cause and the victims' motivation to avoid it. Forcible action will work against weeds or floods as well as against armies, but suffering requires a victim that can feel pain or has something to lose. To inflict suffering gains nothing and saves nothing directly; it can only make people behave to avoid it. The only purpose, unless sport or revenge, must be to influence somebody's behavior, to coerce his decision or choice. To be coercive, violence has to be anticipated. And it has to be avoidable by accommodation. The power to hurt is bargaining power. To exploit it is diplomacy—vicious diplomacy, but diplomacy.

The Contrast of Brute Force with Coercion

There is a difference between taking what you want and making someone give it to you, between fending off assault and making someone afraid to assault you, between holding what people are trying to take and making them afraid to take it, between losing what someone can forcibly take and giving it up to avoid risk or damage. It is the difference between defense and deterrence, between brute force and intimidation, between conquest and blackmail, between action and threats. It is the difference between the unilateral, "undiplomatic" recourse to strength, and coercive diplomacy based on the power to hurt.

The contrasts are several. The purely "military" or "undiplomatic" recourse to forcible action is concerned with enemy strength, not enemy interests; the coercive use of the power to hurt, though, is the very exploitation of enemy wants and fears. And brute strength is usually measured relative to enemy strength, the one directly opposing the other, while the power to hurt is typically not reduced by the enemy's power to hurt in return. Opposing strengths may cancel each other, pain and grief do not. The willingness to hurt, the credibility of a threat, and the ability to exploit the power to hurt will indeed depend on how much the adversary can hurt in return; but there is little or nothing about an adversary's pain or grief that directly reduces one's own. Two sides cannot both overcome each other with superior strength; they may both be able to hurt each other. With strength they can dispute objects of value; with sheer violence they can destroy them.

And brute force succeeds when it is used, whereas the power to hurt is most successful when held in reserve. It is the *threat* of damage, or of more damage to come, that can make someone yield or comply. It is *latent* violence that can influence someone's choice—violence that can still be withheld or inflicted, or that a victim believes can be withheld or inflicted. The threat of pain tries to structure someone's motives, while brute force tries to overcome his strength. Unhappily, the power to hurt is often communicated by some performance of it. Whether it is sheer terroristic violence to induce an irrational response, or cool premeditated violence to persuade somebody that you mean it and may do it again, it is not the pain and damage itself but its influence on somebody's behavior that matters. It is the expectation of *more* violence that gets the wanted behavior, if the power to hurt can get it at all.

To exploit a capacity for hurting and inflicting damage one needs to know what an adversary treasures and what scares him and one needs the adversary to understand what behavior of his will cause the violence to be inflicted and what will cause it to be withheld. The victim has to know what is wanted, and he may have to be assured of what is not wanted. The pain and suffering have to appear *contingent* on his behavior; it is not alone the threat that is effective—the threat of pain or loss if he fails to comply—but the corresponding assurance, possibly an implicit one, that he can avoid the pain or loss if he does comply. The prospect of certain death may stun him, but it gives him no choice.

Coercion by threat of damage also requires that our interests and our opponent's not be absolutely opposed. If his pain were our greatest delight and our satisfaction his greatest woe, we would just proceed to hurt and to frustrate each other. It is when his pain gives us little or no satisfaction compared with what he can do for us, and the action or inaction that satisfies us costs him less than the pain we can cause, that there is room for coercion. Coercion requires finding a bargain, arranging for him to be better off doing what we want—worse off not doing what we want—when he takes the threatened penalty into account.

It is this capacity for pure damage, pure violence, that is usually associated with the most vicious labor disputes, with racial disorders, with civil uprisings and their suppression, with racketeering. It is also the power to hurt rather than brute force that we use in dealing with criminals; we hurt them afterward, or threaten to, for their misdeeds rather than protect ourselves with cordons of electric wires, masonry walls, and armed guards. Jail, of course, can be either forcible restraint or threatened privation; if the object is to keep criminals out of mischief by confinement, success is measured by how many of them are gotten behind bars, but if the object is to *threaten* privation, success will be measured by how few have to be put behind bars and success then depends on the subject's understanding of the consequences. Pure damage is what a car threatens when it tries to hog the road or to keep its rightful share, or to go first through an intersection. A tank or a bulldozer can force its way regardless of others' wishes; the rest of us have to threaten damage, usually mutual damage, hoping the other driver values his car or his limbs enough to give way, hoping he sees us, and hoping he is in control of his own car. The threat of pure damage will not work against an unmanned vehicle.

This difference between coercion and brute force is as often in the intent as in the instrument. To hunt down Comanches and to exterminate them was brute force; to raid their villages to make them behave was coercive diplomacy, based on the power to hurt. The pain and loss to the Indians might have looked much the same one way as the other; the difference was one of purpose and effect. If Indians were killed because they were in the way, or somebody wanted their land, or the authorities despaired of making them behave and could not confine them and decided to exterminate them, that was pure unilateral force. If *some* Indians were killed to make *other* Indians behave, that was coercive violence—or intended to be, whether or not it was effective. The Germans at Verdun perceived themselves to be chewing up hundreds of thousands of French soldiers in a gruesome "meatgrinder." If the purpose was to eliminate a military

obstacle—the French infantryman, viewed as a military "asset" rather than as a warm human being—the offensive at Verdun was a unilateral exercise of military force. If instead the object was to make the loss of young men—not of impersonal "effectives," but of sons, husbands, fathers, and the pride of French manhood—so anguishing as to be unendurable, to make surrender a welcome relief and to spoil the foretaste of an Allied victory, then it was an exercise in coercion, in applied violence, intended to offer relief upon accommodation. And of course, since any use of force tends to be brutal, thoughtless, vengeful, or plain obstinate, the motives themselves can be mixed and confused. The fact that heroism and brutality can be either coercive diplomacy or a contest in pure strength does not promise that the distinction will be made, and the strategies enlightened by the distinction, every time some vicious enterprise gets launched.

The contrast between brute force and coercion is illustrated by two alternative strategies attributed to Genghis Khan. Early in his career he pursued the war creed of the Mongols: the vanquished can never be the friends of the victors, their death is necessary for the victor's safety. This was the unilateral extermination of a menace or a liability. The turning point of his career, according to Lynn Montross, came later when he discovered how to use his power to hurt for diplomatic ends. "The great Khan, who was not inhibited by the usual mercies, conceived the plan of forcing captives—women, children, aged fathers, favorite sons—to march ahead of his army as the first potential victims of resistance."[1] Live captives have often proved more valuable than enemy dead; and the technique discovered by the Khan in his maturity remains contemporary. North Koreans and Chinese were reported to have quartered prisoners of war near strategic targets to inhibit bombing attacks by United Nations aircraft. Hostages represent the power to hurt in its purest form.

Coercive Violence in Warfare

This distinction between the power to hurt and the power to seize or hold forcibly is important in modern war, both big war and little war, hypothetical war and real war. For many years the Greeks and the Turks on Cyprus could hurt each other indefinitely but neither could quite take or hold forcibly what they wanted or protect themselves from violence by physical means. The Jews in Palestine could not expel the British in the late 1940s but they could cause pain and fear and frustration through terrorism, and eventually influence somebody's decision. The brutal war in Algeria was more a contest in pure violence than in military strength; the question was who would first find the pain and degradation unendurable. The French troops preferred—indeed they continually tried—to make it a contest of strength, to pit military force against the nationalists' capacity for terror, to exterminate or disable the nationalists and to screen off the nationalists from the victims of their violence. But because in civil war terrorists commonly have access to victims by sheer physical propinquity, the victims and their properties could not be forcibly defended and in the end the French troops themselves resorted, unsuccessfully, to a war of pain.

Nobody believes that the Russians can take Hawaii from us, or New York, or Chicago, but nobody doubts that they might destroy people and buildings in Hawaii, Chicago, or New York. Whether the Russians can conquer West Germany in any meaningful sense is questionable; whether they can hurt it terribly is not doubted. That the United States can destroy a large part of Russia is universally taken for granted; that the United States can keep from being badly hurt, even devastated, in return, or can keep Western Europe from being devastated while itself destroying Russia, is at best arguable; and it is virtually out of the question that we could conquer Russia territorially and use its economic assets unless it were by threatening disaster and inducing compliance. It is the power to hurt, not military strength in the traditional sense, that inheres in our most impressive military capabilities at the present time [1966]. We have a Department of *Defense* but emphasize *retaliation*—"to return evil for evil" (synonyms: requital, reprisal, revenge, vengeance, retribution). And it is pain and violence, not force in the traditional sense, that inheres also in some of the least impressive military capabilities of the present time—the plastic bomb, the terrorist's bullet, the burnt crops, and the tortured farmer.

War appears to be, or threatens to be, not so much a contest of strength as one of endurance, nerve, obstinacy, and pain. It appears to be, and threatens to be, not so much a contest of military strength as a bargaining process—dirty, extortionate, and often quite reluctant bargaining on one side or both—nevertheless a bargaining process.

The difference cannot quite be expressed as one between the *use* of force and the *threat* of force. The actions involved in forcible accomplishment, on the one hand, and in fulfilling a threat, on the other, can be quite different. Sometimes the most effective direct action inflicts enough cost or pain on the enemy to serve as a threat, sometimes not. The United States threatens the Soviet Union with virtual destruction of its society in the event of a surprise attack on the United States; a hundred million deaths are awesome as pure damage, but they are useless in stopping the Soviet attack—especially if the threat is to do it all afterward anyway. So it is worth while to keep the concepts distinct—to distinguish forcible action from the threat of pain—recognizing that some actions serve as both a means of forcible accomplishment and a means of inflicting pure damage, some do not. Hostages tend to entail almost pure pain and damage, as do all forms of reprisal after the fact. Some modes of self-defense may exact so little in blood or treasure as to entail negligible violence; and some forcible actions entail so much violence that their threat can be effective by itself.

The power to hurt, though it can usually accomplish nothing directly, is potentially more versatile than a straightforward capacity for forcible accomplishment. By force alone we cannot even lead a horse to water—we have to drag him—much less make him drink. Any affirmative action, any collaboration, almost anything but physical exclusion, expulsion, or extermination, requires that an opponent or a victim *do* something, even if only to stop or get out. The threat of pain and damage may make him want to do it, and anything he can do is potentially susceptible to inducement. Brute force can only accomplish what requires no collaboration. The principle is illustrated by a technique of unarmed combat: one can disable a man by various stunning, fracturing, or killing blows, but to take him to jail one has to exploit the man's own efforts. "Come-along" holds are those that threaten pain or disablement, giving relief as long as the victim complies, giving him the option of using his own legs to get to jail.

We have to keep in mind, though, that what is pure pain, or the threat of it, at one level of decision can be equivalent to brute force at another level. Churchill was worried, during the early bombing raids on London in 1940, that Londoners might panic. Against people the bombs were pure violence, to induce their undisciplined evasion; to Churchill and the government, the bombs were a cause of inefficiency, whether they spoiled transport and made people late to work or scared people and made them afraid to work. Churchill's decisions were not going to be coerced by the fear of a few casualties. Similarly on the battlefield: tactics that frighten soldiers so that they run, duck their heads, or lay down their arms and surrender represent coercion based on the power to hurt; to the top command, which is frustrated but not coerced, such tactics are part of the contest in military discipline and strength.

The fact that violence—pure pain and damage—can be used or threatened to coerce and to deter, to intimidate and to blackmail, to demoralize and to paralyze, in a conscious process of dirty bargaining, does not by any means imply that violence is not often wanton and meaningless or, even when purposive, in danger of getting out of hand. Ancient wars were often quite "total" for the loser, the men being put to death, the women sold as slaves, the boys castrated, the cattle slaughtered, and the buildings leveled, for the sake of revenge, justice, personal gain, or merely custom. If an enemy bombs a city, by design or by carelessness, we usually bomb his if we can. In the excitement and fatigue of warfare, revenge is one of the few satisfactions that can be savored; and justice can often be construed to demand the enemy's punishment, even if it is delivered with more enthusiasm than justice requires. When Jerusalem fell to the Crusaders in 1099 the ensuing slaughter was one of the bloodiest in military chronicles. "The men of the West literally waded in gore, their march to the church of the Holy Sepulcher being gruesomely likened to 'treading out the wine press'. . . . ," reports Montross (p. 138), who observes that these excesses usually came at the climax of the capture of a fortified post or city. "For long the assailants have endured more punishment than they were able to inflict; then once the walls are breached, pent up emotions find an outlet in murder, rape and plunder, which discipline is powerless to prevent." The same occurred when Tyre fell to Alexander after a painful siege, and the phenomenon was not unknown on Pacific islands in the Second World War. Pure violence, like fire, can be harnessed to a purpose; that does not mean that behind every holocaust is a shrewd intention successfully fulfilled.

But if the occurrence of violence does not always bespeak a shrewd purpose, the absence of pain and destruction is no sign that violence was idle. Violence is most purposive and most successful when it is threatened and not used. Successful threats are those that do not have to be carried out. By European standards, Denmark was virtually unharmed in the Second World War; it was violence that made the Danes submit. Withheld violence—successfully threatened violence—can look clean, even merciful. The fact that a kidnap victim is returned unharmed, against receipt of ample ransom, does not make kidnapping a nonviolent enterprise. * * *

■ ■ ■

The Strategic Role of Pain and Damage

Pure violence, nonmilitary violence, appears most conspicuously in relations between unequal countries, where there is no substantial military challenge and the outcome of military engagement is not in question. Hitler could make his threats contemptuously and brutally against Austria; he could make them, if he wished, in a more refined way against Denmark. It is noteworthy that it was Hitler, not his generals, who used this kind of language; proud military establishments do not like to think of themselves as extortionists. Their favorite job is to deliver victory, to dispose of opposing military force and to leave most of the civilian violence to politics and diplomacy. But if there is no room for doubt how a contest in strength will come out, it may be possible to bypass the military stage altogether and to proceed at once to the coercive bargaining.

A typical confrontation of unequal forces occurs at the *end* of a war, between victor and vanquished. Where Austria was vulnerable before a shot was fired, France was vulnerable after its military shield had collapsed in 1940. Surrender negotiations are the place where the threat of civil violence can come to the fore. Surrender negotiations are often so one-sided, or the potential violence so unmistakable, that bargaining succeeds and the violence remains in reserve. But the fact that most of the actual damage was done during the military stage of the war, prior to victory and defeat, does not mean that violence was idle in the aftermath, only that it was latent and the threat of it successful.

Indeed, victory is often but a prerequisite to the exploitation of the power to hurt. When Xenophon was fighting in Asia Minor under Persian leadership, it took military strength to disperse enemy soldiers and occupy their lands; but land was not what the victor wanted, nor was victory for its own sake.

> Next day the Persian leader burned the villages to the ground, not leaving a single house standing, so as to strike terror into the other tribes to show them what would happen if they did not give in. . . . He sent some of the prisoners into the hills and told them to say that if the inhabitants did not come down and settle in their houses to submit to him, he would burn up their villages too and destroy their crops, and they would die of hunger.[2]

Military victory was but the *price of admission*. The payoff depended upon the successful threat of violence.

■ ■ ■

The Nuclear Contribution to Terror and Violence

Man has, it is said, for the first time in history enough military power to eliminate his species from the earth, weapons against which there is no conceivable defense. War has become, it is said, so destructive and terrible that it ceases to be an instrument of national power. "For the first time in human history," says Max Lerner in a book whose title, *The Age of Overkill,* conveys the point, "men have bottled up a power . . . which they have thus far not dared to use."[3] And Soviet military authorities, whose party dislikes having to accommodate an entire theory of history to a single technological event, have had to reexamine a set of principles that had been given the embarrassing name of "permanently operating factors" in warfare. Indeed, our era is epitomized by words like "the first time in human history," and by the abdication of what was "permanent."

For dramatic impact these statements are splendid. Some of them display a tendency, not at all necessary, to belittle the catastrophe of earlier wars. They may exaggerate the historical novelty of deterrence and the balance of terror. More important, they do not help to identify just what is new about war when so much destructive energy can be packed in warheads at a price that permits advanced countries to have them in large numbers. Nuclear warheads are incomparably more devastating than anything packaged before. What does that imply about war?

It is not true that for the first time in history man has the capability to destroy a large fraction, even the major part, of the human race. Japan was defenseless by August 1945. With a combination of bombing and blockade, eventually invasion, and if necessary the deliberate spread of disease, the United States could probably have exterminated the population of the Japanese islands without nuclear weapons. It would have been a gruesome, expensive, and mortifying campaign; it would have taken time and demanded persistence. But we had the economic and technical capacity to do it; and, together with the Russians or without them, we could have done the same in many populous parts of the world. Against defenseless people there is not much that nuclear weapons can do that cannot be done with an ice pick. And it would not have strained our Gross National Product to do it with ice picks.

It is a grisly thing to talk about. We did not do it and it is not imaginable that we would have done it. We had no reason; if we had had a reason, we would not have the persistence of purpose,

once the fury of war had been dissipated in victory and we had taken on the task of executioner. If we and our enemies might do such a thing to each other now, and to others as well, it is not because nuclear weapons have for the first time made it feasible.

■　　■　　■

* * * In the past it has usually been the victors who could do what they pleased to the enemy. War has often been "total war" for the loser. With deadly monotony the Persians, Greeks, or Romans "put to death all men of military age, and sold the women and children into slavery," leaving the defeated territory nothing but its name until new settlers arrived sometime later. But the defeated could not do the same to their victors. The boys could be castrated and sold only after the war had been won, and only on the side that lost it. The power to hurt could be brought to bear only after military strength had achieved victory. The same sequence characterized the great wars of this century; for reasons of technology and geography, military force has usually had to penetrate, to exhaust, or to collapse opposing military force—to achieve military victory—before it could be brought to bear on the enemy nation itself. The Allies in World War I could not inflict coercive pain and suffering directly on the Germans in a decisive way until they could defeat the German army; and the Germans could not coerce the French people with bayonets unless they first beat the Allied troops that stood in their way. With two-dimensional warfare, there is a tendency for troops to confront each other, shielding their own lands while attempting to press into each other's. Small penetrations could not do major damage to the people; large penetrations were so destructive of military organization that they usually ended the military phase of the war.

Nuclear weapons make it possible to do monstrous violence to the enemy without first achieving victory. With nuclear weapons and today's means of delivery, one expects to penetrate an enemy homeland without first collapsing his military force. What nuclear weapons have done, or appear to do, is to promote this kind of warfare to first place. Nuclear weapons threaten to make war less military, and are responsible for the lowered status of "military victory" at the present time. *Victory is no longer a prerequisite for hurting the enemy.* And it is no assurance against being terribly hurt. One need not wait until he has won the war before inflicting "unendurable" damages on his enemy. One need not wait until he has lost the war. There was a time when the assurance of victory—false or genuine assurance—could make national leaders not just willing but sometimes enthusiastic about war. Not now.

Not only *can* nuclear weapons hurt the enemy before the war has been won, and perhaps hurt decisively enough to make the military engagement academic, but it is widely assumed that in a major war that is *all* they can do. Major war is often discussed as though it would be only a contest in national destruction. If this is indeed the case—if the destruction of cities and their populations has become, with nuclear weapons, the primary object in an all-out war—the sequence of war has been reversed. Instead of destroying enemy forces as a prelude to imposing one's will on the enemy nation, one would have to destroy the nation as a means or a prelude to destroying the enemy forces. If one cannot disable enemy forces without virtually destroying the country, the victor does not even have the option of sparing the conquered nation. He has already destroyed it. Even with blockade and strategic bombing it could be supposed that a country would be defeated before it was destroyed, or would elect surrender before annihilation had gone far. In the Civil War it could be hoped that the South would become too weak to fight before it became too weak to survive. For "all-out" war, nuclear weapons threaten to reverse this sequence.

So nuclear weapons do make a difference, marking an epoch in warfare. The difference is not just in the amount of destruction that can be accomplished but in the role of destruction and in the decision process. Nuclear weapons can change the speed of events, the control of events, the sequence of events, the relation of victor to vanquished, and the relation of homeland to fighting front. Deterrence rests today on the threat of pain and extinction, not just on the threat of military defeat. We may argue about the wisdom of announcing "unconditional surrender" as an aim in the last major war, but seem to expect "unconditional destruction" as a matter of course in another one.

Something like the same destruction always *could* be done. With nuclear weapons there is an expectation that it *would* be done. It is not "overkill" that is new; the American army surely had enough 30 caliber bullets to kill everybody in the world in 1945, or if it did not it could have bought them without any strain. What is new is plain "kill"—the idea that major war might be just a contest in the killing of countries, or not even a contest but just two parallel exercises in devastation.

That is the difference nuclear weapons make. At least they *may* make that difference. They also may not. If the weapons themselves are vulnerable to attack, or the machines that carry them, a successful surprise might eliminate the opponent's means of retribution. That an enormous explosion can be packaged in a single bomb does not by itself guarantee that the victor will receive deadly punishment. Two gunfighters facing each other in a Western town had an unquestioned capacity to kill one another; that did not guarantee that both would die in a gunfight—only the slower of the two. Less deadly weapons, permitting an injured one to shoot back before he died, might have been more conducive to a restraining balance of terror, or of caution. The very efficiency of nuclear weapons could make them ideal for starting war, if they can suddenly eliminate the enemy's capability to shoot back.

And there is a contrary possibility: that nuclear weapons are not vulnerable to attack and prove not to be terribly effective against each other, posing no need to shoot them quickly for fear they will be destroyed before they are launched, and with no task available but the systematic destruction of the enemy country and no necessary reason to do it fast rather than slowly. Imagine that nuclear destruction *had* to go slowly—that the bombs could be dropped only one per day. The prospect would look very different, something like the most terroristic guerilla warfare on a massive scale. It happens that nuclear war does not have to go slowly; but it may also not have to go speedily. The mere existence of nuclear weapons does not itself determine that everything must go off in a blinding flash, any more than that it must go slowly. Nuclear weapons do not simplify things quite that much.

■   ■   ■

War no longer looks like just a contest of strength. War and the brink of war are more a contest of nerve and risk-taking, of pain and endurance. Small wars embody the threat of a larger war; they are not just military engagements but "crisis diplomacy." The threat of war has always been somewhere underneath international diplomacy, but for Americans it is now much nearer the surface. Like the threat of a strike in industrial relations, the threat of divorce in a family dispute, or the threat of bolting the party at a political convention, the threat of violence continuously circumscribes international politics. Neither strength nor goodwill procures immunity.

Military strategy can no longer be thought of, as it could for some countries in some eras, as the science of military victory. It is now equally, if not more, the art of coercion, of intimidation and deterrence. The instruments of war are more punitive than acquisitive. Military strategy, whether we like it or not, has become the diplomacy of violence.

NOTES

1. Lynn Montross, *War Through the Ages* (3d ed. New York, Harper and Brothers, 1960), p. 146.
2. Xenophon, *The Persian Expedition*, Rex Warner, transl. (Baltimore, Penguin Books, 1949), p. 272. "The 'rational' goal of the threat of violence," says H. L. Nieburg, "is an accommodation of interests, not the provocation of actual violence. Similarly the 'rational' goal of actual violence is demonstration of the will and capability of action, establishing a measure of the credibility of future threats, not the exhaustion of that capability in unlimited conflict." "Uses of Violence," *Journal of Conflict Resolution*, 7 (1963), 44.
3. New York, Simon and Schuster, 1962, p. 47.

James D. Fearon

RATIONALIST EXPLANATIONS
FOR WAR

The central puzzle about war, and also the main reason we study it, is that wars are costly but nonetheless wars recur. Scholars have attempted to resolve the puzzle with three types of argument. First, one can argue that people (and state leaders in particular) are sometimes or always irrational. They are subject to biases and pathologies that lead them to neglect the costs of war or to misunderstand how their actions will produce it. Second, one can argue that the leaders who order war enjoy its benefits but do not pay the costs, which are suffered by soldiers and citizens. Third, one can argue that even rational leaders who consider the risks and costs of war may end up fighting nonetheless.

This article focuses on arguments of the third sort, which I will call rationalist explanations.[1] Rationalist explanations abound in the literature on international conflict, assuming a great variety of specific forms. Moreover, for at least two reasons many scholars have given rationalist explanations a certain pride of place. First, historians and political scientists who have studied the origins of particular wars often have concluded that war can be a rational alternative for leaders who are acting in their states' interest—they find that the expected benefits of war sometimes outweigh the expected costs, however unfortunate this may be. Second, the

dominant paradigm in international relations theory, neorealism, is thought to advance or even to depend on rationalist arguments about the causes of war. Indeed, if no rationalist explanation for war is theoretically or empirically tenable, then neither is neorealism. The causes of war would then lie in the defects of human nature or particular states rather than in the international system, as argued by neorealists. What I refer to here as "rationalist explanations for war" could just as well be called "neorealist explanations."[2]

This article attempts to provide a clear statement of what a rationalist explanation for war is and to characterize the full set of rationalist explanations that are both theoretically coherent and empirically plausible. It should be obvious that this theoretical exercise must take place prior to testing rationalist explanations against alternatives—we cannot perform such tests unless we know what a rationalist explanation really is. Arguably, the exercise is also foundational for neorealism. Despite its prominence, neorealist theory lacks a clearly stated and fully conceived explanation for war. As I will argue below, it is not enough to say that under anarchy nothing stops states from using force, or that anarchy forces states to rely on self-help, which engenders mutual suspicion and (through spirals or the security dilemma) armed conflict. Neither do diverse references to miscalculation, deterrence failure because of inadequate forces or incredible threats, preventive and preemptive considerations, or free-riding in alliances amount to theoretically coherent rationalist explanations for war.

From *International Organization* 49, no. 3 (Summer 1995), 379–410. Bracketed editorial insertions are the editor's and three asterisks (***) are used to mark places where technical material has been omitted. Some notes and a technical appendix have been omitted.

My main argument is that on close inspection none of the principal rationalist arguments advanced in the literature holds up as an explanation because none addresses or adequately resolves the central puzzle, namely, that war is costly and risky, so rational states should have incentives to locate negotiated settlements that all would prefer to the gamble of war. The common flaw of the standard rationalist arguments is that they fail either to address or to explain adequately what prevents leaders from reaching *ex ante* (prewar) bargains that would avoid the costs and risks of fighting. A coherent rationalist explanation for war must do more than give reasons why armed conflict might appear an attractive option to a rational leader under some circumstances—it must show why states are unable to locate an alternative outcome that both would prefer to a fight.

To summarize what follows, the article will consider five rationalist arguments accepted as tenable in the literature on the causes of war. Discussed at length below, these arguments are given the following labels: (1) anarchy; (2) expected benefits greater than expected costs; (3) rational preventive war; (4) rational miscalculation due to lack of information; and (5) rational miscalculation or disagreement about relative power. I argue that the first three arguments simply do not address the question of what prevents state leaders from bargaining to a settlement that would avoid the costs of fighting. The fourth and fifth arguments do address the question, holding that rational leaders may miss a superior negotiated settlement when lack of information leads them to miscalculate relative power or resolve. However, as typically stated, neither argument explains what prevents rational leaders from using diplomacy or other forms of communication to avoid such costly miscalculations.

If these standard arguments do not resolve the puzzle on rationalist terms, what does? I propose that there are three defensible answers, which take the form of general mechanisms, or causal logics, that operate in a variety of more specific international contexts.[3] In the first mechanism, rational leaders may be unable to locate a mutually preferable negotiated settlement due to *private information* about relative capabilities or resolve and *incentives to misrepresent* such information. Leaders know things about their military capabilities and willingness to fight that other states do not know, and in bargaining situations they can have incentives to misrepresent such private information in order to gain a better deal. I show that given these incentives, communication may not allow rational leaders to clarify relative power or resolve without generating a real risk of war. This is not simply a matter of miscalculation due to poor information but rather of specific strategic dynamics that result from the combination of asymmetric information and incentives to dissemble.

Second, rationally led states may be unable to arrange a settlement that both would prefer to war due to *commitment problems,* situations in which mutually preferable bargains are unattainable because one or more states would have an incentive to renege on the terms. While anarchy (understood as the absence of an authority capable of policing agreements) is routinely cited as a cause of war in the literature, it is difficult to find explanations for exactly why the inability to make commitments should imply that war will sometimes occur. That is, what are the specific, empirically identifiable mechanisms by which the inability to commit makes it impossible for states to strike deals that would avoid the costs of war? I identify three such specific mechanisms, arguing in particular that preventive war between rational states stems from a commitment problem rather than from differential power growth per se.

The third sort of rationalist explanation I find less compelling than the first two, although it is logically tenable. States might be unable to locate a peaceful settlement both prefer due to *issue indivisibilities.* Perhaps some issues, by their very natures, simply will not admit compromise.

Though neither example is wholly convincing, issues that might exhibit indivisibility include abortion in domestic politics and the problem of which prince sits on the throne of, say, Spain, in eighteenth- or nineteenth-century international politics. Issue indivisibility could in principle make war rational for the obvious reason that if the issue allows only a finite number of resolutions, it might be that none falls within the range that both prefer to fighting. However, the issues over which states bargain typically are complex and multidimensional; side-payments or linkages with other issues typically are possible; and in principle states could alternate or randomize among a fixed number of possible solutions to a dispute. War-prone international issues may often be *effectively* indivisible, but the cause of this indivisibility lies in domestic political and other mechanisms rather than in the nature of the issues themselves.

In the first section of the article I discuss the puzzle posed by the fact that war is costly. Using a simple formalization of the bargaining problem faced by states in conflict, I show that under very broad conditions bargains will exist that genuinely rational states would prefer to a risky and costly fight. The second section argues that rational miscalculations of relative power and resolve must be due to private information and then considers how war may result from the combination of private information and incentives to misrepresent that information in bargaining. In the third section, I discuss commitment problems as the second class of defensible rationalist explanations for war. Throughout, I specify theoretical arguments with simple game-theoretic representations and assess plausibility with historical examples.

Before beginning, I should make it clear that I am not presenting either commitment problems or private information and incentives to misrepresent as wholly novel explanations for war that are proposed here for the first time. The literature on

the causes of war is massive, and these ideas, mixed with myriad others, can be found in it in various guises. The main theoretical task facing students of war is not to add to the already long list of arguments and conjectures but instead to take apart and reassemble these diverse arguments into a coherent theory fit for guiding empirical research. Toward this end, I am arguing that when one looks carefully at the problem of explaining how war could occur between genuinely rational, unitary states, one finds that there are really only two ways to do it. The diverse rationalist or neorealist explanations commonly found in the literature fail for two reasons. First, many do not even address the relevant question—what prevents states from locating a bargain both sides would prefer to a fight? They do not address the question because it is widely but incorrectly assumed that rational states can face a situation of deadlock, wherein no agreements exist that both sides would prefer to a war.[4] Second, the rationalist arguments that do address the question—such as (4) and (5) above—do not go far enough in answering it. When fully developed, they prove to be one of the two major mechanisms developed here, namely, either a commitment problem or a problem arising from private information and incentives to misrepresent. These two mechanisms, I will argue, provide the foundations for a rationalist or neorealist theory of war.

The Puzzle

Most historians and political scientists who study war dismiss as naive the view that all wars must be unwanted because they entail destruction and suffering. Instead, most agree that while a few wars may have been unwanted by the leaders who brought them about—World War I is sometimes given as an example—many or perhaps most wars were simply wanted. The leaders involved viewed war as a costly but worthwhile gamble.[5]

Moreover, many scholars believe that wanted wars are easily explained from a rationalist perspective. Wanted wars are thought to be Pareto-efficient—they occur when no negotiated settlements exist that both sides would prefer to the gamble of military conflict. Conventional wisdom holds that while this situation may be tragic, it is entirely possible between states led by rational leaders who consider the costs and risks of fighting. Unwanted wars, which take place despite the existence of settlements both sides preferred to conflict, are thought to pose more of a puzzle, but one that is resolvable and also fairly rare.

The conventional distinction between wanted and unwanted wars misunderstands the puzzle posed by war. The reason is that the standard conception does not distinguish between two types of efficiency—*ex ante* and *ex post*. As long as both sides suffer some costs for fighting, then war is always inefficient *ex post*—both sides would have been better off if they could have achieved the same final resolution without suffering the costs (or by paying lower costs). This is true even if the costs of fighting are small, or if one or both sides viewed the potential benefits as greater than the costs, since there are still costs. Unless states enjoy the activity of fighting for its own sake, as a consumption good, then war is inefficient *ex post*.

From a rationalist perspective, the central puzzle about war is precisely this *ex post* inefficiency. Before fighting, both sides know that war will entail some costs, and even if they expect offsetting benefits they still have an incentive to avoid the costs. The central question, then, is what prevents states in a dispute from reaching an *ex ante* agreement that avoids the costs they know will be paid *ex post* if they go to war? Giving a rationalist explanation for war amounts to answering this question.

Three of the most common and widely employed rationalist arguments in the literature do not directly address or answer the question. These are arguments from anarchy, preventive war, and positive expected utility.

Anarchy

Since Kenneth Waltz's influential *Man, the State, and War,* the anarchical nature of the international realm is routinely cited as a root cause of or explanation for the recurrence of war. Waltz argued that under anarchy, without a supranational authority to make and enforce law, "war occurs because there is nothing to prevent it. . . . Among states as among men there is no automatic adjustment of interests. In the absence of a supreme authority there is then the constant possibility that conflicts will be settled by force."[6]

The argument focuses our attention on a fundamental difference between domestic and international politics. Within a well-ordered state, organized violence as a strategy is ruled out—or at least made very dangerous—by the potential reprisals of a central government. In international relations, by contrast, no agency exists that can credibly threaten reprisal for the use of force to settle disputes.[7] The claim is that without such a credible threat, war will sometimes appear the best option for states that have conflicting interests.

While I do not doubt that the condition of anarchy accounts for major differences between domestic and international politics, and that anarchy encourages both fear of and opportunities for military conflict, the standard framing of the argument is not enough to explain why wars occur and recur. Under anarchy, nothing stops states from using force if they wish. But if using force is a costly option regardless of the outcome, then why is it ever employed? How exactly does the lack of a central authority prevent states from negotiating agreements both sides would prefer to fighting? As it is typically stated, the argument that anarchy provides a rationalist explanation for war does not address this question and so does not solve the problem posed by war's *ex post* inefficiency.

Neither, it should be added, do related arguments invoking the security dilemma, the fact that under anarchy one state's efforts to make itself more secure can have the undesired but unavoidable effect of making another state less secure.[8] By itself this fact says nothing about the availability or feasibility of peaceful bargains that would avoid the costs of war. More elaborate arguments are required, and those that are typically given do not envision bargaining and do not address the puzzle of costs. Consider, for instance, a spiral scenario in which an insecure state increases its arms, rendering another so insecure that it decides to attack. If the first state anticipated the reaction producing war, then by itself this is a deadlock argument; I argue against these below. If the first state did not anticipate war and did not want it, then the problem would seem to be miscalculation rather than anarchy, and we need to know why signaling and bargaining could not have solved it. As Robert Jervis has argued, anarchy and the security dilemma may well foster arms races and territorial competition.[9] But with the exception of occasional references to the preemptive war problem, the standard security dilemma arguments do not explicitly address the question of why the inability to make commitments should necessarily make for war between rational states.[10]

Below I will argue that anarchy is indeed implicated as a cause of specific sorts of military conflict (e.g., preventive and preemptive war and in some cases war over strategic territory). In contrast to the standard arguments, however, showing how anarchy figures in a coherent rationalist explanation entails describing the specific mechanism by which states' inability to write enforceable contracts makes peaceful bargains both sides would prefer unattainable.

Preventive War

It frequently is argued that if a declining power expects it might be attacked by a rising power in the future, then a preventive war in the present may be rational. Typically, however, preventive war arguments do not consider whether the rising and declining powers could construct a bargain, perhaps across time, that would leave both sides better off than a costly and risky preventive war would.[11] The incentives for such a deal surely exist. The rising state should not want to be attacked while it is relatively weak, so what stops it from offering concessions in the present and the future that would make the declining state prefer not to attack? Also, if war is inefficient and bargains both sides prefer to a fight will exist, why should the declining power rationally fear being attacked in the future? The standard argument supposes that an anticipated shift in the balance of power can by itself be enough to make war rational, but this is not so.

Positive Expected Utility

Perhaps the most common informal rationalist explanation found in the literature is that war may occur when two states each estimate that the expected benefits of fighting outweigh the expected costs. As Bruce Bueno de Mesquita argued in an influential formalization of this claim, war can be rational if both sides have positive expected utility for fighting; that is, if the expected utility of war (expected benefits less costs) is greater than the expected utility of remaining at peace.[12]

Informal versions of the expected utility argument typically fail to address the question of how or under what conditions it can be possible for two states both to prefer the costly gamble of war to any negotiated settlement. Formal versions have tended to avoid the question by making various restrictive and sometimes nonrationalist assumptions. To support these claims, I need to be more precise about the expected utility argument.

When Will There Exist Bargains Both Sides Prefer to War?

This section considers the question of whether and when two rationally led states could both prefer war to any negotiated settlement.

Consider two states, A and B, who have preferences over a set of issues represented by the interval $X = [0, 1]$. State A prefers issue resolutions closer to 1, while B prefers outcomes closer to 0.* * * For concreteness we might think of x as representing the proportion of all territory between A and B that is controlled by A. [Thus, a point X in the interval represents the situation where state A controls all the territory from ϕ to X, while state B controls all the territory from X to 1.][13]

In order to say whether the set X contains negotiated settlements that both sides would prefer to conflict, it must be possible to say how the states evaluate the military option versus those outcomes. Almost all analysts of war have stressed that war is a gamble whose outcome may be determined by random or otherwise unforeseeable events.[14] As Bueno de Mesquita argued, this makes expected utility a natural candidate.[15] Suppose that if the states fight a war, state A prevails with probability $p \in [0, 1]$, and that the winner gets to choose its favorite outcome in the issue space. * * * [Thus, A's expected utility for war is $p - c$, since A gets all the territory, which is worth 1, with probability p, loses everything with probability $1 - p$, and pays a cost for fighting c_A in either event.] Similarly, state B's expected utility for war will be $1 - p - c_B$. Since we are considering rationalist theories for war, we assume that c_A and c_B are both positive. War is thus represented as a costly lottery.[16] * * *

We can now answer the question posed above. The following result is easily demonstrated: given the assumptions stated in the last two paragraphs, there always exists a set of negotiated settlements that both sides prefer to fighting. * * *

[For example, in the special case where each state's value for an additional increment of territory is constant, the two states will both prefer any division of territory in the range from $p - c_A$ to $p + c_B$ over fighting a war. This interval represents the bargaining range, with $p - c_A$ and $p + c_B$ as the reservation levels that delimit it. This case of "risk neutral" states is depicted in Figure 6.1.]

This simple but important result is worth belaboring with some intuition. Suppose that two people (or states) are bargaining over the division of $100—if they can agree on a split they can keep what they agree to. However, in contrast to the usual economic scenarios, in this international relations example the players also have an outside option.[17] For a price of $20, they can go to war, in which case each player has a 50-percent chance of winning the whole $100. This implies that the expected value of the war option is $30 (0.5 · 100 + 0.5 · 0 − 20) for each side, so that if the players are risk-neutral, then neither should be willing to accept less than $30 in the bargaining. But notice that there is still a range of peaceful, bargained outcomes from ($31, $69) to ($69, $31) that make both sides strictly better off than the war option. Risk aversion will tend to increase the range yet further; indeed, even if the leaders pay no costs for war, a set of agreements both sides prefer to a fight will still exist provided both are risk-averse over the issues. In effect, the costs and risks of fighting open up a "wedge" of bargained solutions that risk-neutral or risk-averse states will prefer to the gamble of conflict. The existence of this *ex ante* bargaining range derives from the fact that war is inefficient *ex post*.

Three substantive assumptions are needed for the result, none of which seems particularly strong. First, the states know that there is some true probability p that one state would win in a military contest. As discussed below, it could be that the states have conflicting estimates of the likelihood of victory, and if both sides are optimistic about their chances this can obscure the bargaining range.

Figure 6.1. The Bargaining Range

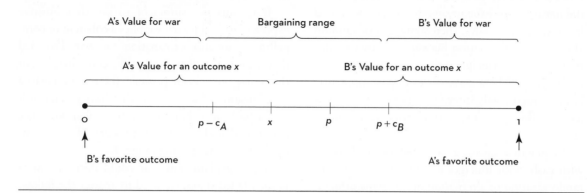

But even if the states have private and conflicting estimates of what would happen in a war, if they are rational, they should know that there can be only one true probability that one or the other will prevail (perhaps different from their own estimate). Thus rational states should know that there must in fact exist a set of agreements all prefer to a fight.

Second, it is assumed that the states are risk-averse or risk-neutral over the issues. Because risk attitude is defined relative to an underlying metric (such as money in economics), the substantive meaning of this assumption depends on the bargaining context. Loosely, it says that the states prefer a fifty-fifty split or share of whatever is at issue (in whatever metric it comes, if any) to a fifty-fifty chance at all or nothing, where this refers to the value of winning or losing a war. In effect, the assumption means that leaders do not like gambling when the downside risk is losing at war, which seems plausible given the presumption that state leaders normally wish to retain territory and power. A risk-acceptant leader is analogous to a compulsive gambler—willing to accept a sequence of gambles that has the expected outcome of eliminating the state and regime. Even if we admitted such a leader as rational, it seems doubtful that many have held such preferences (Hitler being a possible exception).

Finally, it was assumed that a continuous range of peaceful settlements (from 0 to 1) exists. In other words, the issues in dispute are perfectly divisible, so that there are always feasible bargains between the states' reservation levels $p - c_A$ and $p + c_B$. This third assumption immediately suggests a tenable rationalist explanation for war. Perhaps something about the nature of some international issues, such as which successor will sit on a throne, does not admit finely graded divisions and compromise. If so, then small costs for fighting and bad luck may make for rational war over such issues.

But we would immediately like to know what about the nature of an issue makes it impossible to divide up. On more thought, this seems empirically implausible. In the first place, most issues states negotiate over are quite complex—they have many dimensions of concern and allow many possible settlements. Second, if states can simply pay each other sums of money or goods (which they can, in principle), or make linkages with other issues, then this should have the effect of making any issues in dispute perfectly divisible. Before the age of nationalism, princes often bought, sold, and partitioned land.[18] In the nineteenth century the United States purchased the Louisiana Territory from France, and Alaska from Russia, and as late as 1898 President McKinley explored the possibility of buying Cuba from Spain in order to avoid a war over it.[19] Third, if something about the nature of an issue means that it can be settled in only, say, two ways, then some sort of random allocation or alternation between the two resolutions could in principle serve to create intermediate bargains. Mafia dons, for example, apparently have avoided costly internal wars by using lotteries to allocate construction contracts among families.[20]

In practice, creating intermediate settlements with cash, with linkages to other issues, or with randomization or alternation often seems difficult or impossible for states engaged in a dispute. For example, the immediate issue that gave rise to the Franco–Prussian war was a dispute over which prince would take the Spanish throne. It doubtless occurred to no one to propose that the two candidates alternate year by year, or three years for the Hapsburg and one for the Hohenzollern, or whatever. In this case as in many others, the issue could in principle have been made more continuous and was not for other reasons—here, alternating kings would have violated so many conventions and norms as to have been domestically unworkable. To give a more realistic example, nineteenth- and twentieth-century leaders cannot divide up and trade territory in international negotiations as easily as could rulers in the seventeenth and eighteenth centuries, due in part to domestic political consequences of the rise of nationalism; contrast, for example, the Congress of Vienna with the negotiations following World War I.

So in principle the indivisibility of the issues that are the subject of international bargaining can provide a coherent rationalist explanation for war. However, the real question in such cases is what prevents leaders from creating intermediate settlements, and the answer is likely to be other mechanisms (often domestic political) rather than the nature of the issues themselves.[21] Both the intrinsic complexity and richness of most matters over which states negotiate and the availability of linkages and side-payments suggest that intermediate bargains typically will exist.

It is thus not sufficient to say that positive expected utility by itself supplies a coherent or compelling rationalist explanation for war. Provided that the issues in dispute are sufficiently divisible, or that side-payments are possible, there should exist a set of negotiated agreements that have greater utility for both sides than the gamble of war does. The reason is that the *ex post* inefficiency of war opens up an *ex ante* bargaining range.

So, to explain how war could occur between rationally led states, we need to answer the following question. Given the existence of an *ex ante* bargaining range, why might states fail either to locate or to agree on an outcome in this range, so avoiding the costs and risks of war?

War Due to Private Information and Incentives to Misrepresent

Two commonly employed rationalist explanations in the literature directly address the preceding question. Both turn on the claim that war can be and often is the product of rational miscalculation. One explanation holds that a state's leaders may rationally overestimate their chance of military victory against an adversary, so producing a disagreement about relative power that only war can resolve. The other argues that rationally led states may lack information about an adversary's willingness to fight over some interest and so may challenge in the mistaken belief that war will not follow.

In this section I argue that while these ideas point toward a tenable rationalist explanation for war, neither goes far enough and neither works by itself. Both neglect the fact that states can in principle communicate with each other and so avoid a costly miscalculation of relative power or will. The cause of war cannot be simply lack of information, but whatever it is that prevents its disclosure. I argue that the fact that states have incentives to misrepresent their positions is crucial here, explaining on rationalist terms why diplomacy may not allow rational states to clarify disagreements about relative power or to avoid the miscalculation of resolve.

The mainstream international relations literature recognizes the existence of both private information and incentives to misrepresent, but typically views them as background conditions to be taken for granted rather than as key elements of an explanation of how rationally led states might end up at war. For example, Jack Levy's impressive review of the literature on the causes of war contains nothing on the role of incentives to misrepresent and discusses private information largely in the context of misperceptions of other states' intentions (which are linked to psychological biases). This is an accurate reflection of where these factors stand in the mainstream literature.[22]

Disagreements about Relative Power

Geoffrey Blainey's well-known and often-cited argument is that "wars usually begin when two nations disagree on their relative strength."[23] It is easy to see how a disagreement about relative strength—understood as conflicting estimates of the likelihood of military victory—can eliminate any *ex ante* bargaining range. Recall the example given above, where two states bargain over the division of $100, and each has the outside option of going to war. If each expects that it surely would prevail at war, then each side's expected value for the war option is $80 ($1 \cdot 100 + 0 \cdot 0 - 20$). So given these expectations, neither side will accept less than $80 in the bargaining, implying that no negotiated outcome is mutually preferred to war. More generally, suppose that state A expects to win with probability p, state B expects to win

with probability r, and p and r sum to greater than one. Such conflicting expectations will certainly shrink and could eliminate any *ex ante* bargaining range.

But how could rationally led states have conflicting expectations about the likely outcome of military conflict? In the extreme case, how could both sides rationally expect to win? The literature barely addresses this question in explicit terms. Blainey, whom the literature views as advancing a rationalist explanation for war, in fact explains disagreements about relative power as a consequence of human *ir*rationality. He says that mutual optimism about victory in war is the product of "moods which cannot be grounded in fact" and which "permeate what appear to be rational assessments of the relative military strength of two contending powers." Mutual optimism is said to result from a "process by which nations evade reality," which hardly sounds like a rationalist explanation.[24]

Conflicting expectations about the likely outcome of military conflict may be explained in three ways. First, as Blainey suggests, emotional commitments could irrationally bias leaders' military estimates. They might, for instance, come to believe nationalist rhetoric holding that their soldiers are more courageous and spirited than those of the adversary.[25] Second, the world is a very complex place, and for this reason military analysts in different states could reach different conclusions about the likely impact of different technologies, doctrines, and tactics on the expected course of battle. Third, state leaders might have private information about militarily relevant factors—military capabilities, strategy, and tactics; the population's willingness to prosecute a long war; or third-state intentions. If a state has superior (and so private) information about any such factor, then its estimate of the probable course of battle may differ from that of an adversary.

Under a strict but standard definition of rationality, only the third explanation qualifies as an account of how rationally led states could have conflicting estimates of the probability of winning in war. As argued by John Harsanyi, if two rational agents have the same information about an uncertain event, then they should have the same beliefs about its likely outcome.[26] The claim is that given identical information, truly rational agents should reason to the same conclusions about the probability of one uncertain outcome or another. Conflicting estimates should occur only if the agents have different (and so necessarily private) information.[27]

It follows that the second explanation for disagreements about relative power listed above—the complexity of the world—is not a rationalist account. Instead, it is an account that explains conflicting military estimates as a consequence of bounded rationality. In this view, leaders or military analysts with the same information about military technology, strategy, political will, etc., might reason to different conclusions about the likely course of a war because of differential ability to cope with complexity of the problem. This is entirely plausible, but it is a bounded rationality explanation rather than a fully rationalist one.[28]

The rationalist account of how disagreements about the probability of winning might arise also seems empirically plausible. States certainly have private information about factors affecting the likely course of battle—for example, they jealously guard military secrets and often have superior information about what an ally will or will not fight for. Nonetheless, while private information about militarily relevant capabilities provides a first step, it does not provide a coherent rationalist explanation for war. The problem is that even if leaders have such private information, they should understand that their own estimates based on this information are suspect because they do not know the other side's private information. In principle, both sides could gain by sharing information, which would yield a consensus military estimate (absent bounded rationality). And, as shown above, doing so could not help but reveal bargains that both would prefer to a fight.[29]

So the question of how rationally led states can disagree about relative power devolves to the question of what prevents states from sharing private information about factors that might affect the course of battle. Before turning to this question, I will consider the second common explanation for how a rational miscalculation may produce war.

War Due to the Miscalculation of an Opponent's Willingness to Fight

Many wars have been given the following so-called rationalist explanation: state A transgressed some interest of state B in the erroneous belief that B would not fight a war over the matter. Though rationally led, state A lacked information about B's willingness to fight and simply happened to guess wrong, causing a war. Thus, some say that Germany miscalculated Russian and/or British willingness to fight in 1914; Hitler miscalculated Britain and France's willingness to resist his drive to the east; Japanese leaders in 1941 miscalculated U.S. willingness to fight a long war over control in the South Pacific; North Korea miscalculated U.S. willingness to defend South Korea; the United States miscalculated China's willingness to defend North Korea; and so on. In each case, the argument would hold that lack of information led a more-or-less rational actor to guess wrong about the extent of the bargaining range.

Blainey has argued that if states agree on relative power they are very unlikely to go to war against each other.[30] It is worth pointing out that in the preceding argument, war can occur despite complete agreement on relative power across states. To show how and for later use, I will introduce a simple model of international bargaining. As in the empirical examples just mentioned, in the model one state unilaterally chooses some revision of the status quo. The second state can then either acquiesce to the revision or can go to war to reverse it.

Formally, suppose there is a status quo resolution of the issues [represented as number q between 0 and 1] and that state A has the opportunity to choose any outcome x [between 0 and 1], presenting state B with a fait accompli. On observing what state A did (which might be nothing, i.e., $x = q$), state B can choose whether to go to war or to acquiesce to A's revision of the status quo.

If neither state has any private information, so that all payoffs are common knowledge, state A does best to push the outcome just up to B's reservation level $p + c_B$, which makes B just willing to acquiesce rather than go to war. With complete information, then, the states avoid the inefficient outcome of war.[31] On the other hand, if state B has private information about either its capabilities (which affect p) or its value for the issues at stake relative to the costs of conflict (c_B), then state A may not know whether a particular "demand" x will yield war or peace. Lacking this information, state A faces a trade-off in deciding whether and how much territory to "grab": The larger the grab, the greater the risk of war, but the better off A will be if state B acquiesces.

Suppose, for example, that A and B share a common estimate of p—they agree about relative power—but that A is unsure about B's costs for fighting. Under very broad conditions, if A cannot learn B's private information and if A's own costs are not too large, then state A's optimal grab produces a positive chance of war. Intuitively, if A is not too fearful of the costs of war relative to what might be gained in bargaining, it will run some risk of war in hopes of gaining on the ground. So Blainey's suggestion that a disagreement about relative power is necessary for war is incorrect—all that is necessary is that the states in dispute be unable to locate or agree on some outcome in the bargaining range. Since the bargaining range is determined not just by relative power but also by states' values for the issues at stake relative to the costs of fighting, uncertainty

about the latter can (and apparently does) produce war.

Once again, it is entirely plausible that state leaders have private information about their value for various international interests relative to their costs of fighting over them.[32] Thus it seems we have a second tenable rationalist explanation for war, again based on the concept of private information. But as in the case of disagreements about relative power, the explanation fails as given because it does not explain why states cannot avoid miscalculating a potential opponent's willingness to fight. In the model, why cannot state A simply ask state B whether it would fight rather than acquiesce to a particular demand? To give a concrete example, why did German leaders in 1914 not simply ask their British and Russian counterparts what they would do if Austria were to attack Serbia? If they could have done so and if the answers could have been believed, the Germans might not have miscalculated concerning Russian and, more importantly, British willingness to fight. In consequence they might have avoided the horrendous costs of World War I.

To recap, I have argued that in a rationalist framework, disagreements about relative power and uncertainty about a potential opponent's willingness to fight must have the same source: leaders' private information about factors affecting the likely course of a war or their resolve to fight over specific interests. In order to avoid war's *ex post* inefficiency, leaders have incentives to share any such private information, which would have the effect of revealing peaceful settlements that lie within the bargaining range. So, to explain how war could occur between states led by rational leaders who consider the costs of fighting, we need to explain what would prevent them from sharing such private information.

Incentives to Misrepresent in Bargaining

Prewar bargaining may fail to locate an outcome in the bargaining range because of strategic incentives to withhold or misrepresent private information. While states have an incentive to avoid the costs of war, they also wish to obtain a favorable resolution of the issues. This latter desire can give them an incentive to exaggerate their true willingness or capability to fight, if by doing so they might deter future challenges or persuade the other side to make concessions. States can also have an incentive to conceal their capabilities or resolve, if they are concerned that revelation would make them militarily (and hence politically) vulnerable or would reduce the chances for a successful first strike. Similarly, states may conceal their true willingness to fight in order to avoid appearing as the aggressor.

Combined with the fact of private information, these various incentives to misrepresent can explain why even rational leaders may be unable to avoid the miscalculations of relative will and power that can cause war. This section first considers why this is so theoretically and then discusses two empirical examples.

A drawback of the simple bargaining model given above was that state B had no opportunity to try to communicate its willingness to fight to state A. It is easy to imagine that if communication were possible—say, if B could announce what interests in X it considered vital enough to fight over—this might at least lower the chance of war by miscalculation. To check this, we give state B an initial opportunity to make a foreign policy announcement f, which can be any statement about its foreign policy or what it considers to be vital or peripheral interests. (Assume as before that A is uncertain about B's capabilities or costs for fighting.)

If the announcement itself has no effect on either side's payoffs, then it can be shown that in any equilibrium in which state A does not choose randomly among demands, A will make the same demand regardless of what state B says, and the *ex ante* risk of war will remain the same as in the game without communication by state B. To gain an intuition for these results, suppose that A conditioned its behavior on f, grabbing more or less depending on what B announced. Then regardless of B's true willingness to fight, B does best to make the announcement that leads to the smallest grab by A—that is, B has an incentive to misrepresent its actual willingness to resist. But then A learns nothing from the announcement.[33]

This conclusion is slightly altered if the leaders of B can render the announcement f costly to make.[34] In practice, five common methods include building weapons, mobilizing troops, signing alliance treaties, supporting troops in a foreign land, and creating domestic political costs that would be paid if the announcement proves false. Of course, signaling by means of domestic political audience costs lies outside a purely unitary rational-actor framework, since this presumes a state run by an agent on behalf of a principal (the "audience") rather than a unitary state with a perfectly secure leadership. In the latter case, leaders may be able to make foreign policy announcements credible only by engaging an international reputation, taking financially costly mobilization measures, or bearing the costs and risks of limited military engagements.[35]

Even when the signal is costly, however, this will not in general completely eliminate all risk of war by miscalculation—indeed, it may even increase it. The reason concerns the nature of the signals that states have incentives to send. To be genuinely informative about a state's actual willingness or ability to fight, a signal must be costly in such a way that a state with lesser resolve or capability might not wish to send it. Actions that generate a real risk of war—for example, troop mobilizations that engage a leadership's reputation before international or domestic audiences—can easily satisfy this constraint, since states with high resolve are less fearful of taking them. In other words, a rational state may choose to run a real risk of (inefficient) war in order to signal that it will fight if not given a good deal in bargaining.[36]

The July crisis of World War I provides several examples of how incentives to misrepresent can make miscalculations of resolve hard to dispel. Soon after German leaders secretly endorsed Austrian plans to crush Serbia, they received both direct and indirect verbal indications from St. Petersburg that Russia would fight rather than acquiesce.[37] For example, on 21 July, the Russian Foreign Minister told the German ambassador that "Russia would not be able to tolerate Austria-Hungary's using threatening language to Serbia or taking military measures."[38] Such verbal statements had little effect on German leaders' beliefs, however, since they knew Russian leaders had a strategic incentive to misrepresent. On 18 July in a cable explaining Berlin's policy to Ambassador Lichnowsky in London, Secretary of State Jagow wrote that "there is certain to be some blustering in St. Petersburg."[39] Similarly, when on 26 July Lichnowsky began to report that Britain might join with France and Russia in the event of war, German Chancellor Bethmann Hollweg told his personal assistant of the "danger that France and England will commit their support to Russia in order not to alienate it, perhaps without really believing that for us mobilization means war, thinking of it as a bluff which they answer with a counterbluff."[40]

At the same time, the Chancellor had an incentive to misrepresent the strength and nature of German support for Austria's plans. Bethmann correctly anticipated that revealing this information would make Germany appear the aggressor, which might undermine Social Democratic support for his policies in Germany as well as turn British public opinion more solidly against his state.[41] This incentive led the Chancellor to avoid making direct or pointed inquiries about England's attitude in case of war. The incentive also led him to pretend to go along with the British Foreign Secretary's proposals for a conference to mediate the dispute.[42] In consequence, Lord Grey may not have grasped the need for a stronger warning to Germany until fairly late in the crisis (on 29 July), by which time diplomatic and military actions had made backing off more difficult for both Austria and Germany.

In July 1914, incentives to misrepresent private information fostered and supported miscalculations of willingness to fight. Miscalculations of relative power can arise from this same source. On the one hand, states at times have an incentive to exaggerate their capabilities in an attempt to do better in bargaining. On the other hand, they can also have the well-known incentive to withhold information about capabilities and strategy. Presumably because of the strongly zero-sum aspect of military engagements, a state that has superior knowledge of an adversary's war plans may do better in war and thus in prewar bargaining—hence, states rarely publicize war plans. While the theoretical logic has not been worked out, it seems plausible that states' incentives to conceal information about capabilities and strategy could help explain some disagreements about relative power.

The 1904 war between Japan and Russia serves to illustrate this scenario. On the eve of the war, Russian leaders believed that their military could almost certainly defeat Japan.[43] In this conviction they differed little from the view of most European observers. By contrast, at the imperial council of 4 February that decided for war, the Japanese chief of staff estimated a fifty-fifty chance of prevailing, if their attack began immediately.[44] Thus Japanese and Russian leaders disagreed about relative power—their estimates of the likelihood of victory summed to greater than 1.

Moreover, historical accounts implicate this disagreement as a major cause of the war: Russia's refusal to compromise despite repeated offers by the Japanese was motivated in large measure by their belief that Japan would not dare attack them. The Japanese Cabinet finally decided for war after the Tsar and his advisers failed to make any real compromises over Korea or Manchuria in a series of proposals exchanged in 1903. The Tsar and his top advisers were hardly eager to fight, not because they expected to lose but because they saw an Asian war as a costly diversion of resources to the wrong theater.[45] Nonetheless, they refused to make concessions from what they viewed as a position of great military strength. They believed that Japan would have to settle for less, given its relative military weakness.[46]

The disagreement arose in substantial part from Japanese private information about their military capabilities and how they compared with Russia's. A far superior intelligence service had provided the Japanese military with a clear picture of Russian strengths and weaknesses in Northeast Asia and enabled them to develop an effective offensive strategy. According to John Albert White, due to this intelligence "the Japanese government apparently faced the war with a far more accurate conception of their task than their enemy had."[47] In addition, compared with the Russians or indeed with any European power, Japanese leaders had much better knowledge of the fighting ability of the relatively untested Japanese army and of the effect of the reforms, training, and capital development of the previous decade.[48]

If by communicating this private information the Japanese could have led the Russians to see that their chances of victory were smaller than expected, they might have done so. Almost all historians who have carefully examined the case agree that the Japanese government was not bent on war for its own sake—they were willing to compromise if the Russians would as well.[49] However, it was unthinkable for the Japanese to reveal such information or convince the Russians even if they did. In the first place, the Japanese could not simply make announcements about the quality of their forces, since the Russians would have had no

reason to believe them. Second, explaining how they planned to win a war might seriously compromise any such attempt by changing the likelihood that they would win; there is a trade-off between revealing information about resolve or capabilities to influence bargaining and reducing the advantages of a first strike.

In sum, the combination of private information about relative power or will and the strategic incentive to misrepresent these afford a tenable rationalist explanation for war. While states always have incentives to locate a peaceful bargain cheaper than war, they also always have incentives to do well in the bargaining. Given the fact of private information about capabilities or resolve, these incentives mean that states cannot always use quiet diplomatic conversations to discover mutually preferable settlements. It may be that the only way to surmount this barrier to communication is to take actions that produce a real risk of inefficient war.

This general mechanism operates in at least two other empirically important ways to produce conflict in specific circumstances. First, private information about the costs of fighting or the value leaders place on international interests can give them an incentive to cultivate a reputation for having lower costs or more far-flung vital interests than they actually do. If cutting a deal in one dispute would lead other states to conclude the leader's costs for using force are high, then the leader might choose a costly war rather than suffer the depredations that might follow from making concessions. The U.S. interventions in Korea and Vietnam are sometimes explained in these terms, and states surely have worried about such inferences drawn by other states for a long time.[50] The same logic operates when a small state or group (for example, Finland or the Chechens) chooses to fight a losing war against a larger one (for example, the Soviet Union or Russia) in order to develop a reputation for being hard to subjugate. In both cases, states employ war itself as a costly signal of privately known and otherwise unverifiable information about willingness to fight.

Second, since incentives to misrepresent military strength can undermine diplomatic signaling, states may be forced to use war as a credible means to reveal private information about their military capabilities. Thus, a rising state may seek out armed conflict in order to demonstrate that it is more powerful than others realize, while a state in apparent decline may fight in hope of revealing that its capabilities remain better than most believe. In both instances, the inefficient outcome of war derives from the fact that states have private information about their capabilities and a strategic incentive to misrepresent it to other states.

War as a Consequence of Commitment Problems

This section considers a second and quite different rationalist mechanism by which war may occur even though the states in dispute share the same assessment of the bargaining range. Even if private information and incentives to misrepresent it do not tempt states into a risky process of discovery or foster costly investments in reputation, states may be unable to settle on an efficient bargained outcome when for structural reasons they cannot trust each other to uphold the deal.

In this class of explanations, the structural condition of anarchy reemerges as a major factor, although for nonstandard reasons. In the conventional argument, anarchy matters because no hegemonic power exists to threaten states with "jail" if they use force. Without this threat, states become suspicious and worried about other states' intentions; they engage in self-help by building weapons; and somehow uncertainty-plus-weapons leads them ultimately to attack each other (the security dilemma or spiral model). Below, I show that anarchy does indeed matter but for more specific

reasons and in more specific contexts. Anarchy matters when an unfortunate combination of state preferences and opportunities for action imply that one or both sides in a dispute have incentives to renege on peaceful bargains which, if they were enforceable, would be mutually preferred to war. I will consider three such unfortunate situations that can claim some empirical plausibility.

It should be stressed that in standard security dilemma and spiral model arguments the suspicions and lack of trust engendered by anarchy are understood to originate either from states' inability to observe each other's motivations (that is, from private information about greed or desire for conquest) or from the knowledge that motivations can change.[51] By contrast, in the arguments given below, states have no private information and motivations never change; thus states understand each other's motivations perfectly. This is not to argue that private information about the value a leadership places on expansion is unimportant in international politics—it surely is. Indeed, private information about motivation and various incentives to misrepresent it might exacerbate any of the three specific commitment problems discussed below. However, when they do so this is a matter of an interaction between informational and commitment problems rather than of anarchy per se. Our first task should be to isolate and specify the mechanisms by which anarchy itself might cause war.

Preemptive War and Offensive Advantages

Consider the problem faced by two gunslingers with the following preferences. Each would most prefer to kill the other by stealth, facing no risk of retaliation, but each prefers that both live in peace to a gunfight in which each risks death. There is a bargain here that both sides prefer to "war"—namely, that each leaves the other alone—but without the enforcement capabilities of a third party, such as an effective sheriff, they may not be able to attain it. Given their preferences, neither person can credibly commit not to defect from the bargain by trying to shoot the other in the back. Note that no matter how far the shadow of the future extends, iteration (or repeat play) will not make cooperation possible in strategic situations of this sort. Because being the "sucker" here may mean being permanently eliminated, strategies of conditional cooperation such as tit-for-tat are infeasible.[52] Thus, if we can find a plausible analogy in international relations, this example might afford a coherent rationalist explanation for war.

Preemptive war scenarios provide the analogy. If geography or military technology happened to create large first-strike or offensive advantages, then states might face the same problem as the gunslingers. To demonstrate this theoretically, I consider how offensive advantages affect the bargaining range between two states engaged in a dispute.

There are at least three ways of interpreting offensive advantages in a formal context. First, an offensive advantage might mean that a state's odds of winning are better if it attacks rather than defends. Second, an offensive advantage might mean that the costs of fighting are lower for an attacking state than for a defending state. It can be shown that no commitment problem operates in this second case, although lowering the costs of war for attackers does narrow the de facto bargaining range. Third, offensive advantages might mean that military technology and doctrine increase the variance of battlefield outcomes. That is, technology and doctrine might make total victory or total defeat more likely, while rendering stalemate and small territorial changes less likely. In this case, offensive advantages can actually reduce the expected utility of war for both sides, thus increasing the bargaining range and perhaps making war less rather than more likely. Intuitively, if states care most of all about security (understood as survival), then offensive advantages make war less safe by increasing the risk of total defeat.[53]

A commitment problem of the sort faced by the gunslingers arises only under the first interpretation, in which "offensive advantage" refers to an increase in a state's military prospects if it attacks rather than defends. To demonstrate this, let p_f be the probability that state A wins a war if A attacks; p_s the probability that A wins if A strikes second or defends; and p the chance that A wins if both states mobilize and attack at the same time. Thus, an offensive advantage exists when $p_f > p > p_s$.

Since states can always choose to attack if they wish, a peaceful resolution of the issues is feasible only if neither side has an incentive to defect unilaterally by attacking. * * * [It is easy to show that there will exist stable outcomes both sides prefer to conflict only if there is a de facto bargaining range represented by issue resolutions between $p_f - c_A$ and $p_s + c_B$. One end of the range is determined by A's value for attacking with a first strike advantage, and the other by B's.]

Notice that as p_f increases above p, and p_s decreases below it, this interval shrinks and may even disappear. Thus, first-strike advantages narrow the de facto bargaining range, while second-strike (or defensive) advantages increase it. The reason is that when first-strike advantages are large, both states must be given more from the peacetime bargain in order to allay the greater temptation of unilateral attack.

In the extreme case, [if the first-strike advantage is sufficiently large relative to the total costs of fighting,] no self-enforcing peaceful outcomes exist [$p_f - c_A$ is greater than $p_s + c_B$]. This does not mean that no bargains exist that both sides would prefer to war. Since by definition both states cannot enjoy the advantage of going first, agreements that both sides prefer to fighting are always available in principle. The problem is that under anarchy, large enough first-strike incentives (relative to cost-benefit ratios) can make all of these agreements unenforceable and incredible as bargains.

Does this prisoners' dilemma logic provide an empirically plausible explanation for war? Though I lack the space to develop the point, I would argue that first-strike and offensive advantages probably are an important factor making war more likely in a few cases, but not because they make mobilization and attack a dominant strategy, as in the extreme case above. In the pure preemptive war scenario leaders reason as follows: "The first-strike advantage is so great that regardless of how we resolve any diplomatic issues between us, one side will always want to attack the other in an effort to gain the (huge) advantage of going first." But even in July 1914, a case in which European leaders apparently held extreme views about the advantage of striking first, we do not find leaders thinking in these terms.[54] It would be rather surprising if they did, since they had all lived at peace but with the same military technology prior to July 1914. Moreover, in the crisis itself military first-strike advantages did not become a concern until quite late, and right to the end competed with significant political (and so strategic) disadvantages to striking first.[55]

Rather than completely eliminating enforceable bargains and so causing war, it seems more plausible that first-strike and offensive advantages exacerbate other causes of war by narrowing the bargaining range. If for whatever reason the issues in dispute are hard to divide up, then war will be more likely the smaller the set of enforceable agreements both sides prefer to a fight. Alternatively, the problems posed by private information and incentives to misrepresent may be more intractable when the de facto bargaining range is small.[56] For example, in 1914 large perceived first-strike advantages meant that relatively few costly signals of intent were sufficient to commit both sides to war (chiefly, for Germany/Austria and Russia). Had leaders thought defense had the advantage, the set of enforceable agreements both would have preferred would have been larger, and this may have made costly signaling less likely to have destroyed the bargaining range.

I should note that scholars have sometimes portrayed the preemptive war problem differently, assuming that neither state would want to attack unilaterally but that each would want to attack if the other was expected to also. This is a coordination problem known as "stag hunt" that would seem easily resolved by communication. At any rate, it seems farfetched to think that small numbers of states (typically dyads) would have trouble reaching the efficient solution here, if coordination were really the only problem.[57]

Preventive War as a Commitment Problem

Empirically, preventive motivations seem more prevalent and important than preemptive concerns. In his diplomatic history of Europe from 1848 to 1918, A.J.P. Taylor argued that "every war between the Great Powers [in this period] started as a preventive war, not a war of conquest."[58] In this subsection I argue that within a rationalist framework, preventive war is properly understood as arising from a commitment problem occasioned by anarchy and briefly discuss some empirical implications of this view.[59]

The theoretical framework used above is readily adapted for an analysis of the preventive war problem. Whatever their details, preventive war arguments are necessarily dynamic—they picture state leaders who think about what may happen in the future. So, we must modify the bargaining model to make it dynamic as well. Suppose state A will have the opportunity to choose the resolution of the issues in each of an infinite number of successive periods. For periods $t = 1, 2, \ldots$, state A can attempt a fait accompli to revise the status quo, choosing a demand x_t. On seeing the demand x_t, state B can either acquiesce or go to war, which state A is assumed to win with probability p_t. * * *

This model extends the one-period bargaining game considered above to an infinite-horizon case in which military power can vary over time. An important observation about the multiperiod model is that war remains a strictly inefficient outcome. * * * It is straightforward to show that there will always exist peaceful settlements in X such that both states would prefer to see one of these settlements implemented in every period from t forward rather than go to war.[60]

The strategic dilemma is that without some third party capable of guaranteeing agreements, state A may not be able to commit itself to future foreign policy behavior that makes B prefer not to attack at some point. Consider the simple case in which A's chance of winning a war begins at p_1 and then will increase to $p_2 > p_1$ in the next period, where it will remain for all subsequent periods. Under anarchy, state A cannot commit itself not to exploit the greater bargaining leverage it will have starting in the second period. * * * [At that time, A will choose a resolution of the issues that makes state B just willing to acquiesce, given the new distribution of military power. This means that in the first period, when state B is still relatively strong, B is choosing between going to war and acquiescing to A's first period demand, which gives it some value today plus the issue equivalent of fighting a war at a disadvantage in the next period. The most state A could possibly do for B in the first period would be to cede B's most preferred outcome ($x_1 = 0$). However, if the change in relative military power is large enough, this concession can still be too small to make accepting it worthwhile for state B. B may prefer to "lock in" what it gets from war when it is relatively strong, to one period of concessions followed by a significantly worse deal when it is militarily weaker. In sum,] if B's expected decline in military power is too large relative to B's costs for war, then state A's inability to commit to restrain its foreign policy demands after it gains power makes preventive attack rational for state B.[61] Note also that A's commitment problem meshes with a parallel problem facing B. If B could commit to fight in

the second period rather than accept the rising state's increased demands, then B's bargaining power would not fall in the second period, so that preventive war would be unnecessary in the first.

Several points about this rationalist analysis of preventive war are worth stressing. First, preventive war occurs here despite (and in fact partially because of) the states' agreement about relative power. Preventive war is thus another area where Blainey's argument misleads. Second, contrary to the standard formulation, the declining state attacks not because it fears being attacked in the future but because it fears the peace it will have to accept after the rival has grown stronger. To illustrate, even if Iraq had moved from Kuwait to the conquest of Saudi Arabia, invasion of the United States would not have followed. Instead, the war for Kuwait aimed to prevent the development of an oil hegemon that would have had considerable bargaining leverage due to U.S. reliance on oil.[62]

Third, while preventive war arises here from states' inability to trust each other to keep to a bargain, the lack of trust is not due to states' uncertainty about present or future motivations, as in typical security-dilemma and spiral-model accounts. In my argument, states understand each other's motivations perfectly well—there is no private information—and they further understand that each would like to avoid the costs of war—they are not ineluctably greedy. Lack of trust arises here from the situation, a structure of preferences and opportunities, that gives one party an incentive to renege. For example, regardless of expectations about Saddam Hussein's future motivation or intentions, one could predict with some confidence that decreased competition among sellers of oil would have led to higher prices. My claim is not that uncertainty about intentions is unimportant in such situations—it surely is—but that commitment and informational problems are distinct mechanisms and that a rationalist preventive war argument turns crucially on a commitment problem.

Finally, the commitment problem behind preventive war may be undermined if the determinants of military power can reliably be transferred between states. In the model, the rising state can actually have an incentive to transfer away or otherwise limit the sources of its new strength, since by doing so it may avoid being attacked. While such transfers might seem implausible from a realist perspective, the practice of "compensation" in classical balance-of-power politics may be understood in exactly these terms: states that gained territory by war or other means were expected to (and sometimes did) allow compensating gains in order to reduce the incentive for preventive war against them.[63]

Preventive motivations figured in the origins of World War I and are useful to illustrate these points. One of the reasons that German leaders were willing to run serious risks of global conflict in 1914 was that they feared the consequences of further growth of Russian military power, which appeared to them to be on a dangerous upward trajectory.[64] Even if the increase in Russian power had not led Russia to attack Austria and Germany at some point in the future—war still being a costly option—greater Russian power would have allowed St. Petersburg to pursue a more aggressive foreign policy in the Balkans and the Near East, where Austria and Russia had conflicting interests. Austrian and German leaders greatly feared the consequences of such a (pro-Slav) Russian foreign policy for the domestic stability of the Austro-Hungarian Empire, thus giving them incentives for a preventive attack on Russia.[65]

By the argument made above, the states should in principle have had incentives to cut a multiperiod deal both sides would have preferred to preventive war. For example, fearing preventive attack by Austria and Germany, Russian leaders might have wished to have committed themselves not to push so hard in the Balkans as to endanger the Dual Monarchy. But such a deal would be so obviously unenforceable as to not be worth proposing.

Leaving aside the serious monitoring difficulties, once Russia had become stronger militarily, Austria would have no choice but to acquiesce to a somewhat more aggressive Russian policy in the Balkans. And so Russia would be drawn to pursue it, regardless of its overall motivation or desire for conquest of Austria-Hungary.

While German leaders in July 1914 were willing to accept a very serious risk that Russia might go to war in support of Serbia, they seem to have hoped at the start of the crisis that Russia would accept the Austrian demarche.[66] Thus, it is hard to argue that the preventive logic itself produced the war. Rather, as is probably true for other cases in which these concerns appear, the preventive logic may have made war more likely in combination with other causes, such as private information, by making Berlin much more willing to risk war.[67] How preventive concerns impinge on international bargaining with private information is an important topic for future research.

Commitment, Strategic Territory, and the Problem of Appeasement

The objects over which states bargain frequently are themselves sources of military power. Territory is the most important example, since it may provide economic resources that can be used for the military or be strategically located, meaning that its control greatly increases a state's chances for successful attack or defense. Territory is probably also the main issue over which states fight wars.[68]

In international bargaining on issues with this property, a commitment problem can operate that makes mutually preferable negotiated solutions unattainable. The problem is similar to that underlying preventive war. Here, both sides might prefer some package of territorial concessions to a fight, but if the territory in question is strategically vital or economically important, its transfer could radically increase one side's future bargaining leverage (think of the Golan Heights). In principle, one state might prefer war to the status quo but be unable to commit not to exploit the large increase in bargaining leverage it would gain from limited territorial concessions. Thus the other state might prefer war to limited concessions (appeasement), so it might appear that the issues in dispute were indivisible. But the underlying cause of war in this instance is not indivisibility per se but rather the inability of states to make credible commitments under anarchy.[69]

As an example, the 1939 Winter War between Finland and the Soviet Union followed on the refusal of the Finnish government to cede some tiny islands in the Gulf of Finland that Stalin seems to have viewed as necessary for the defense of Leningrad in the event of a European war. One of the main reasons the Finns were so reluctant to grant these concessions was that they believed they could not trust Stalin not to use these advantages to pressure Finland for more in the future. So it is possible that Stalin's inability to commit himself not to attempt to carry out in Finland the program he had just applied in the Baltic states may have led or contributed to a costly war both sides clearly wished to avoid.[70]

Conclusion

The article has developed two major claims. First, under broad conditions the fact that fighting is costly and risky implies that there should exist negotiated agreements that rationally led states in dispute would prefer to war. This claim runs directly counter to the conventional view that rational states can and often do face a situation of deadlock, in which war occurs because no mutually preferable bargain exists.

Second, essentially two mechanisms, or causal logics, explain why rationally led states are sometimes unable to locate or agree on such a bargain:

(1) the combination of private information about resolve or capability and incentives to misrepresent these, and (2) states' inability, in specific circumstances, to commit to uphold a deal. Historical examples were intended to suggest that both mechanisms can claim empirical relevance.

I conclude by anticipating two criticisms. First, I am not saying that explanations for war based on irrationality or "pathological" domestic politics are less empirically relevant. Doubtless they are important, but we cannot say how so or in what measure if we have not clearly specified the causal mechanisms making for war in the "ideal" case of rational unitary states. In fact, a better understanding of what the assumption of rationality really implies for explaining war may actually raise our estimate of the importance of particular irrational and second-image factors.

For example, once the distinction is made clear, bounded rationality may appear a more important cause of disagreements about relative power than private information about military capabilities. If private information about capabilities was often a major factor influencing the odds of victory, then we would expect rational leaders to update their war estimates during international crises; a tough bargaining stand by an adversary would signal that the adversary was militarily stronger than expected. Diplomatic records should then contain evidence of leaders reasoning as follows: "The fact that the other side is not backing down means that we are probably less likely to win at war than we initially thought." I do not know of a single clear instance of this sort of updating in any international crisis, even though updating about an opponent's resolve, or willingness to fight, is very common.

Second, one might argue that since both anarchy and private information plus incentives to misrepresent are constant features of international politics, neither can explain why states fail to strike a bargain preferable to war in one instance but not another. This argument is correct. But the task of specifying the causal mechanisms that explain the occurrence of war must precede the identification of factors that lead the mechanisms to produce one outcome rather than another in particular settings. That is, specific models in which commitment or information problems operate allow one to analyze how different variables (such as power shifts and cost-benefit ratios in the preventive war model) make for war in some cases rather than others.

This is the sense in which these two general mechanisms provide the foundations for a coherent rationalist or neorealist theory of war. A neorealist explanation for war shows how war could occur given the assumption of rational and unitary ("billiard ball") states, the assumption made throughout this article. Consider any particular factor argued in the literature to be a cause of war under this assumption—for example, a failure to balance power, offensive advantages, multipolarity, or shifts in relative power. My claim is that showing how any such factor could cause war between rational states requires showing how the factor can occasion an unresolvable commitment or information problem in specific empirical circumstances. Short of this, the central puzzle posed by war, its costs, has not been addressed.

NOTES

1. Of course, arguments of the second sort may and often do presume rational behavior by individual leaders; that is, war may be rational for civilian or military leaders if they will enjoy various benefits of war without suffering costs imposed on the population. While I believe that "second-image" mechanisms of this sort are very important empirically, I do not explore them here. A more accurate label for the subject of the article might be "rational unitary-actor explanations," but this is cumbersome.

2. For the founding work of neorealism, see Kenneth Waltz, *Theory of International Politics* (Reading, MA: Addison-Wesley, 1979). For examples of theorizing along these lines, see Robert Jervis, "Cooperation Under the Security Dilemma," *World Politics* 30 (January 1978), pp. 167–214; Stephen Walt, *The Origins of Alliances* (Ithaca, NY: Cornell University Press, 1987); John J. Mearsheimer, "Back to the Future: Instability in Europe After the Cold War," *International Security* 15 (Summer 1990), pp. 5–56; and Charles Glaser, "Realists as Optimists: Cooperation as Self-Help," *International Security* 19 (Winter 1994/95), pp. 50–90.

3. The sense of "mechanism" is similar to that proposed by Elster, although somewhat broader. See Jon Elster, *Political Psychology* (Cambridge: Cambridge University Press, 1993), pp. 1–7; and Jon Elster, *Nuts and Bolts for the Social Sciences* (Cambridge: Cambridge University Press, 1989), chap. 1.

4. For an influential example of this common assumption see Glenn Snyder and Paul Diesing, *Conflict among Nations* (Princeton, NJ: Princeton University Press, 1977).

5. See, for examples, Geoffry Blainey, *The Causes of War* (New York: Free Press, 1973); Michael Howard, *The Causes of Wars* (Cambridge, MA: Harvard University Press, 1983), especially chap. 1; and Arthur Stein, *Why Nations Cooperate: Circumstance and Choice in International Relations* (Ithaca, NY: Cornell University Press, 1990), pp. 60–64. Even the case of World War I is contested; an important historical school argues that this was a wanted war. See Fritz Fisher, *Germany's Aims in the First World War* (New York: Norton, 1967).

6. The quotation is drawn from Kenneth Waltz, *Man, the State, and War: A Theoretical Analysis* (New York: Columbia University Press, 1959), p. 188.

7. For a careful analysis and critique of this standard argument on the difference between the international and domestic arenas, see R. Harrison Wagner, "The Causes of Peace," in Roy A. Licklider, ed., *Stopping the Killing: How Civil Wars End* (New York: New York University Press, 1993), pp. 235–68 and especially pp. 251–57.

8. See John H. Herz, "Idealist Internationalism and the Security Dilemma," *World Politics* 2 (January 1950), pp. 157–80; and Jervis, "Cooperation Under the Security Dilemma." Anarchy is implicated in the security dilemma externality by the following logic: but for anarchy, states could commit to use weapons only for nonthreatening, defensive purposes.

9. Jervis, "Cooperation under the Security Dilemma."

10. For an analysis of the security dilemma that takes into account signaling, see Andrew Kydd, "The Security Dilemma, Game Theory, and World War I," paper presented at the annual meeting of the American Political Science Association, Washington, DC, 2–5 September 1993.

11. The most developed exception I know of is found in Stephen Van Evera, "Causes of War," Ph.D. diss., University of California, Berkeley, 1984, pp. 61–64.

12. See Bruce Bueno de Mesquita, *The War Trap* (New Haven, CT: Yale University Press, 1981), and "The War Trap Revisited: A Revised Expected Utility Model," *American Political Science Review* 79 (March 1985), pp. 157–76. For a generalization that introduces the idea of a bargaining range, see James D. Morrow, "A Continuous-Outcome Expected Utility Theory of War," *Journal of Conflict Resolution* 29 (September 1985), pp. 473–502. Informal versions of the expected utility argument are everywhere. For example, Waltz's statement that "A state will use force to attain its goals if, after assessing the prospects for success, it values those goals more than it values the pleasures of peace" appears in different ways in a great many works on war. See Waltz, *Man, the State, and War*, p. 60.

13. Let the states' utilities for the outcome $x \in X$ be $u_A(x)$ and $u_B(1-x)$, and assume for now that $u_A(\cdot)$ and $u_B(\cdot)$ are continuous, increasing,

and weakly concave (that is, risk-neutral or risk-averse). Without losing any generality, we can set $u_i(1)=1$ and $u_i(0)=0$ for both states ($i=A, B$).

14. See, for classic examples, Thucydides, *The Peloponnesian War* (New York: Modern Library, 1951), pp. 45 and 48; and Carl von Clausewitz, *On War* (Princeton, NJ: Princeton University Press, 1984), p. 85.

15. Bueno de Mesquita, *The War Trap.*

16. Note that in this formulation the terms c_A and c_B capture not only the states' values for the costs of war but also the value they place on winning or losing on the issues at stake. That is, c_A reflects state A's costs for war relative to any possible benefits. For example, if the two states see little to gain from winning a war against each other, then c_A and c_B would be large even if neither side expected to suffer much damage in a war.

17. On the theory of bargaining with outside options, see Martin J. Osborne and Ariel Rubinstein, *Bargaining and Markets* (New York: Academic Press, 1990), chap. 3; Motty Perry, "An Example of Price Formation in Bilateral Situations," *Econometrica* 50 (March 1986), pp. 313–21; and Robert Powell, "Bargaining in the Shadow of Power" (University of California, Berkeley, 1993, mimeographed). See also the analyses in R. Harrison Wagner, "Peace, War, and the Balance of Power," *American Political Science Review* 88 (September 1994), pp. 593–607; and Wagner, "The Causes of Peace."

18. See, for example, Evan Luard, *War in International Society* (New Haven, CT: Yale University Press, 1992), p. 191. Schroeder notes that "patronage, bribes, and corruption" were "a major element" of eighteenth-century international relations. See Paul Schroeder, *The Transformation of European Politics, 1763–1848* (Oxford: Oxford University Press, 1994), p. 579.

19. On Cuba, see Ernest May, *Imperial Democracy* (New York: Harper and Row, 1961), pp. 149–50. On the Louisiana Purchase, military threats raised in the U.S. Senate apparently made Napoleon more eager to negotiate the sale. See E. Wilson Lyon, *Louisiana in French Diplomacy* (Norman: University of Oklahoma Press, 1934), pp. 179 and 214ff.

20. Diego Gambetta, *The Sicilian Mafia: The Business of Private Protection* (Cambridge, MA: Harvard University Press, 1993), p. 214.

21. In one of the only articles on this problem, Morrow proposes a private information explanation for states' failures to link issues in many disputes. See James D. Morrow, "Signaling Difficulties with Linkage in Crisis Bargaining," *International Studies Quarterly* 36 (June 1992), pp. 153–72.

22. See Jack Levy, "The Causes of War: A Review of Theories and Evidence," in Philip E. Tetlock et al., eds., *Behavior, Society, and Nuclear War,* vol. 1 (Oxford: Oxford University Press, 1989), pp. 209–333. Recent work using limited-information game theory to analyze crisis bargaining places the strategic consequences of private information at the center of the analysis. See, for examples, Bruce Bueno de Mesquita and David Lalman, *War and Reason* (New Haven, CT: Yale University Press, 1992); James D. Fearon, "Domestic Political Audiences and the Escalation of International Disputes," *American Political Science Review* 88 (September 1994), pp. 577–92; James D. Morrow, "Capabilities, Uncertainty, and Resolve: A Limited Information Model of Crisis Bargaining,"

American Journal of Political Science 33 (November 1989), pp. 941–72; Barry Nalebuff, "Brinkmanship and Nuclear Deterrence: The Neutrality of Escalation," *Conflict Management and Peace Science* 9 (Spring 1986), pp. 19–30; and Robert Powell, *Nuclear Deterrence Theory: The Problem of Credibility* (Cambridge: Cambridge University Press, 1990).

23. Blainey, *The Causes of War,* p. 246.

24. Ibid., p. 54. Blainey also blames patriotic and nationalistic fervor, leaders' (irrational) tendency to surround themselves with yes-men, and crowd psychology.

25. See Ralph K. White, *Nobody Wanted War: Misperception in Vietnam and Other Wars* (New York: Doubleday/Anchor), chap. 7; Blainey, *The Causes of War,* p. 54; and Richard Ned Lebow, *Between Peace and War: The Nature of International Crises* (Baltimore, MD: Johns Hopkins University Press, 1981), p. 247.

26. John C. Harsanyi, "Games with Incomplete Information Played by 'Bayesian' Players, Part III," *Management Science* 14 (March 1968), pp. 486–502.

27. Aumann observed an interesting implication of this doctrine: genuinely rational agents cannot "agree to disagree," in the sense that it cannot be commonly known that they are rational and that they hold different estimates of the likelihood of some uncertain event. See Robert Aumann, "Agreeing to Disagree," *The Annals of Statistics* 4 (November 1976), pp. 1236–39. Emerson Niou, Peter Ordeshook, and Gregory Rose note that this implies that rational states cannot agree to disagree about the probability that one or the other would win in a war in *The Balance of Power: Stability in the International System* (Cambridge: Cambridge University Press, 1989), p. 59.

28. On bounded rationality, see Herbert A. Simon, "A Behavioral Model of Rational Choice," *Quarterly Journal of Economics* 69 (February 1955), pp. 99–118.

29. This analysis runs exactly parallel to work in law and economics on pretrial bargaining in legal disputes. Early studies explained costly litigation as resulting from divergent expectations about the likely trial outcome, while in more recent work such expectations derive from private information about the strength of one's case. For a review and references, see Robert D. Cooter and Daniel L. Rubinfeld, "Economic Analysis of Legal Disputes and Their Resolution," *Journal of Economic Literature* 27 (September 1989), pp. 1067–97.

30. Blainey, *The Causes of War.*

31. This take-it-or-leave-it model of international bargaining is proposed and analyzed under conditions of both complete and incomplete information in James D. Fearon, "Threats to Use Force: The Role of Costly Signals in International Crises," Ph.D. diss., University of California, Berkeley, 1992, chap. 1. Similar results for more elaborate bargaining structures are given in my own work in progress. See James D. Fearon, "Game-Theoretic Models of International Bargaining: An Overview," University of Chicago, 1995. Powell has analyzed an alternative model in which both sides must agree if the status quo is to be revised. See Powell, "Bargaining in the Shadow of Power."

32. For examples and discussion on this point, see Fearon, "Threats to Use Force," chap. 3.

33. * * * Cheap talk announcements can affect outcomes in some bargaining contexts. For an example from economics, see Joseph

Farrell and Robert Gibbons, "Cheap Talk Can Matter in Bargaining," *Journal of Economic Theory* 48 (June 1989), pp. 221–37. These authors show how cheap talk might credibly signal a willingness to negotiate seriously that then affects subsequent terms of trade. For an example from international relations, see James D. Morrow, "Modeling the Forms of International Cooperation: Distribution Versus Information," *International Organization* 48 (Summer 1994), pp. 387–423.

34. The conclusion is likewise altered if the possibility of repeated interactions in sufficiently similar contexts is great enough that reputation building can be supported.

35. On signaling costs in crises and audience costs in particular, see Fearon, "Threats to Use Force," and "Domestic Political Audiences and the Escalation of International Disputes." For an excellent analysis of international signaling in general, see Robert Jervis, *The Logic of Images in International Relations* (Princeton, NJ: Princeton University Press, 1970).

36. For developed models that make this point, see James Fearon, "Deterrence and the Spiral Model: The Role of Costly Signals in Crisis Bargaining," paper presented at the annual meeting of the American Political Science Association, 30 August–2 September 1990, San Francisco, Calif.; Fearon, "Domestic Political Audiences and the Escalation of International Disputes"; Morrow, "Capabilities, Uncertainty, and Resolve"; Nalebuff, "Brinkmanship and Nuclear Deterrence"; and Powell, *Nuclear Deterrence Theory.*

37. Luigi Albertini, *The Origins of the War of 1914*, vol. 2 (London: Oxford University Press, 1953), pp. 183–87.

38. Ibid., p. 187.

39. Ibid., p. 158. For the full text of the cable, see Karl Kautsky, comp., *German Documents Relating to the Outbreak of the World War* (New York: Oxford University Press, 1924), doc. no. 71, p. 130.

40. Konrad Jarausch, "The Illusion of Limited War: Chancellor Bethmann Hollweg's Calculated Risk," *Central European History* 2 (March 1969), pp. 48–76. The quotation is drawn from p. 65.

41. See L. C. F. Turner, *Origins of the First World War* (New York: Norton, 1970), p. 101; and Jarausch, "The Illusion of Limited War," p. 63. Trachtenberg writes that "one of Bethmann's basic goals was for Germany to avoid coming across as the aggressor." See Marc Trachtenberg, *History and Strategy* (Princeton, NJ: Princeton University Press, 1991), p. 90.

42. Albertini concludes that "on the evening of the 27th all the Chancellor sought to do was to throw dust in the eyes of Grey and lead him to believe that Berlin was seriously trying to avert a conflict, that if war broke out it would be Russia's fault and that England could therefore remain neutral." See Albertini, *The Origins of the War of 1914*, vol. 1, pp. 444–45. See also Turner, *Origins of the First World War*, p. 99.

43. See J. A. White, *The Diplomacy of the Russo–Japanese War* (Princeton, NJ: Princeton University Press, 1964), pp. 142–43; and Ian Nish, *The Origins of the Russo–Japanese War* (London: Longman, 1985), pp. 241–42.

44. J. N. Westwood, *Russia against Japan, 1904–5: A New Look at the Russo–Japanese War* (Albany: State University of New York Press, 1986), p. 22. Estimates varied within the Japanese leadership, but with the exception of junior-level officers, few seem to have been highly confident of victory. For example, as the decision for war was taken the Japanese navy requested a two-week delay to allow it to even the odds at sea. See Nish, *The Origins of the Russo–Japanese War*, pp. 197–200 and 206–7.

45. See, for example, David Walder, *The Short Victorious War: The Russo–Japanese Conflict, 1904–5* (London: Hutchinson, 1973), pp. 53–56; and Nish, *The Origins of the Russo–Japanese War*, p. 253.

46. See White, *The Diplomacy of the Russo–Japanese War*, chaps. 6–8; Nish, *The Origins of the Russo–Japanese War*, p. 241; and Lebow, *Between Peace and War*, pp. 244–46.

47. White, *The Diplomacy of the Russo–Japanese War*, p. 139. Nish writes that "many Russians certainly took a view of [the Japanese military] which was derisory in comparison with themselves. It may be that this derived from a deliberate policy of secrecy and concealment which the Japanese army applied because of the historic coolness between the two countries." See Nish, *The Origins of the Russo–Japanese War*, p. 241.

48. The British were the major exception, who as recent allies of Japan had better knowledge of its capabilities and level of organization. See Nish, *The Origins of the Russo–Japanese War*, p. 241.

49. See, for example, William Langer, "The Origins of the Russo–Japanese War," in Carl Schorske and Elizabeth Schorske, eds., *Explorations in Crisis* (Cambridge, MA: Harvard University Press, 1969), p. 44.

50. For some examples, see Fearon, "Threats to Use Force," chap. 3. For a formal version of reputational dynamics due to private information, see Barry Nalebuff, "Rational Deterrence in an Imperfect World," *World Politics* 43 (April 1991), pp. 313–35.

51. See, for examples, Robert Jervis, *Perception and Misperception in International Politics* (Princeton, NJ: Princeton University Press, 1976), pp. 62–67; Barry Posen, *The Sources of Military Doctrine* (Ithaca, NY: Cornell University Press, 1984), pp. 16–17; and Charles Glaser, "The Political Consequences of Military Strategy," *World Politics* 44 (July 1992), p. 506.

52. For dynamic game models that demonstrate this, see Robert Powell, "Absolute and Relative Gains in International Relations Theory," *American Political Science Review* 85 (December 1991), pp. 1303–20; and James D. Fearon, "Cooperation and Bargaining Under Anarchy," (University of Chicago, 1994, mimeographed). On tit-for-tat and the impact of the shadow of the future, see Robert Axelrod, *The Evolution of Cooperation* (New York: Basic Books, 1984); and Kenneth Oye, ed., *Cooperation under Anarchy* (Princeton, NJ: Princeton University Press, 1986).

53. This argument about military variance runs counter to the usual hypothesis that offensive advantages foster war. For a discussion and an empirical assessment, see James D. Fearon, "Offensive Advantages and War since 1648," paper presented at the annual meeting of the International Studies Association, 21–25 February 1995. On the offense–defense balance and war, see Jervis, "Cooperation under the Security Dilemma"; and Van Evera, "Causes of War," chap. 3.

54. For the argument about leaders' views on first-strike advantages in 1914, see Stephen Van Evera, "The Cult of the Offensive and the Origins of the First World War," *International Security* 9 (Summer 1984), pp. 58–107.

55. See, for example, Trachtenberg, *History and Strategy*, p. 90.

56. This is suggested by results in Roger Myerson and Mark Satterthwaite, "Efficient Mechanisms for Bilateral Trading," *Journal of Economic Theory* 29 (April 1983), pp. 265–81.

57. Schelling suggested that efficient coordination in stag hunt–like preemption problems might be prevented by a rational dynamic of "reciprocal fear of surprise attack." See Thomas Schelling, *The Strategy of Conflict* (Cambridge, MA: Harvard University Press, 1960), chap. 9. Powell has argued that no such dynamic exists between rational adversaries. See Robert Powell, "Crisis Stability in the Nuclear Age," *American Political Science Review* 83 (March 1989), pp. 61–76.

58. Taylor, *The Struggle for Mastery in Europe, 1848–1918* (London: Oxford University Press, 1954), p. 166. Carr held a similar view: "The most serious wars are fought in order to make one's own country militarily stronger or, more often, to prevent another country from becoming militarily stronger." See E. H. Carr, *The Twenty Years' Crisis, 1919–1939* (New York: Harper and Row, 1964), pp. 111–12.

59. To my knowledge, Van Evera is the only scholar whose treatment of preventive war analyzes at some length how issues of credible commitment intervene. The issue is raised by both Snyder and Levy. See Van Evera, "Causes of War," pp. 62–64; Jack Snyder, "Perceptions of the Security Dilemma in 1914," in Robert Jervis, Richard Ned Lebow, and Janice Gross Stein, eds., *Psychology and Deterrence* (Baltimore, MD: Johns Hopkins University Press, 1985), p. 160; and Jack Levy, "Declining Power and the Preventive Motivation for War," *World Politics* 40 (October 1987), p. 96.

60. If the states go to war in period t, expected payoffs from period t on are $(p_t/(1-\delta)) - c_A$ for state A and $((1 - p_t)/(1-\delta)) - c_B$ for state B [where δ is the time discount factor that both states apply to payoffs to be received in the next period].

61. The formal condition for preventive war is δ
$$p_2 - p_1 > c_B (1 - \delta)^2.$$

62. According to Hiro, President Bush's main concern at the first National Security Council meeting following the invasion of Kuwait was the potential increase in Iraq's economic leverage and its likely influence on an "already gloomy" U.S. economy.

See Dilip Hiro, *Desert Shield to Desert Storm: The Second Gulf War* (London: Harper-Collins, 1992), p. 108.

63. On compensation, see Edward V. Gulick, *Europe's Classical Balance of Power* (New York: Norton, 1955), pp. 70–72; and Paul W. Schroeder, *The Transformation of European Politics, 1763–1848*, pp. 6–7.

64. See Trachtenberg, *History and Strategy*, pp. 56–59; Albertini, *The Origins of the War of 1914*, vol. 2, pp. 129–30; Turner, *Origins of the First World War*, chap. 4; James Joll, *The Origins of the First World War* (London: Longman, 1984), p. 87; and Van Evera, "The Cult of the Offensive and the Origins of the First World War," pp. 79–85.

65. Samuel Williamson, "The Origins of World War I," *Journal of Interdisciplinary History* (Spring 1988), pp. 795–818 and pp. 797–805 in particular; and D. C. B. Lieven, *Russia and the Origins of the First World War* (New York: St. Martins, 1983), pp. 38–49.

66. Jack S. Levy, "Preferences, Constraints, and Choices in July 1914," *International Security* 15 (Winter 1990/91), pp. 234–36.

67. Levy argues that preventive considerations are rarely themselves sufficient to cause war. See Levy, "Declining Power and the Preventive Motivation for War."

68. See, for example, Kalevi J. Holsti, *Peace and War: Armed Conflicts and International Order, 1648–1989* (Cambridge: Cambridge University Press, 1991); and John Vasquez, *The War Puzzle* (Cambridge: Cambridge University Press, 1993).

69. The argument is formalized in work in progress by the author, where it is shown that the conditions under which war will occur are restrictive: the states must be unable to continuously adjust the odds of victory by dividing up and trading the land. In other words, the smallest feasible territorial transfer must produce a discontinuously large change in a state's military chances for war to be possible. See also Wagner, "Peace, War, and the Balance of Power," p. 598, on this commitment problem.

70. See Max Jakobson, *The Diplomacy of the Winter War: An Account of the Russo-Finnish Conflict, 1939–1940* (Cambridge, MA: Harvard University Press, 1961), pp. 135–39; and Van Evera, "Causes of War," p. 63. Private information and incentives to misrepresent also caused problems in the bargaining here. See Fearon, "Threats to Use Force," chap. 3.

Kenneth N. Waltz

WHY IRAN SHOULD GET THE BOMB
Nuclear Balancing Would Mean Stability

The past several months have witnessed a heated debate over the best way for the United States and Israel to respond to Iran's nuclear activities. As the argument has raged, the United States has tightened its already robust sanctions regime against the Islamic Republic, and the European Union announced in January that it will begin an embargo on Iranian oil on July 1. Although the United States, the EU, and Iran have recently returned to the negotiating table, a palpable sense of crisis still looms.

It should not. Most U.S., European, and Israeli commentators and policymakers warn that a nuclear-armed Iran would be the worst possible outcome of the current standoff. In fact, it would probably be the best possible result: the one most likely to restore stability to the Middle East.

Power Begs to Be Balanced

The crisis over Iran's nuclear program could end in three different ways. First, diplomacy coupled with serious sanctions could convince Iran to abandon its pursuit of a nuclear weapon. But this outcome is unlikely: the historical record indicates that a country bent on acquiring nuclear weapons can rarely be dissuaded from doing so. Punishing a state through economic sanctions does not inexorably derail its nuclear program. Take North

From *Foreign Affairs* 91, no. 4 (July/August 2012), 2–5.

Korea, which succeeded in building its weapons despite countless rounds of sanctions and UN Security Council resolutions. If Tehran determines that its security depends on possessing nuclear weapons, sanctions are unlikely to change its mind. In fact, adding still more sanctions now could make Iran feel even more vulnerable, giving it still more reason to seek the protection of the ultimate deterrent.

The second possible outcome is that Iran stops short of testing a nuclear weapon but develops a breakout capability, the capacity to build and test one quite quickly. Iran would not be the first country to acquire a sophisticated nuclear program without building an actual bomb. Japan, for instance, maintains a vast civilian nuclear infrastructure. Experts believe that it could produce a nuclear weapon on short notice.

Such a breakout capability might satisfy the domestic political needs of Iran's rulers by assuring hard-liners that they can enjoy all the benefits of having a bomb (such as greater security) without the downsides (such as international isolation and condemnation). The problem is that a breakout capability might not work as intended.

The United States and its European allies are primarily concerned with weaponization, so they might accept a scenario in which Iran stops short of a nuclear weapon. Israel, however, has made it clear that it views a significant Iranian enrichment capacity alone as an unacceptable threat. It is possible, then, that a verifiable commitment from Iran to stop short of a weapon could appease major Western powers but leave the Israelis unsatisfied. Israel would be less intimidated by a virtual nuclear weapon than it would be by an actual one and therefore would likely continue its risky efforts at subverting Iran's nuclear program through sabotage and assassination—which could lead Iran to conclude that a breakout capability is an insufficient deterrent, after all, and that only weaponization can provide it with the security it seeks.

The third possible outcome of the standoff is that Iran continues its current course and publicly goes nuclear by testing a weapon. U.S. and Israeli officials have declared that outcome unacceptable, arguing that a nuclear Iran is a uniquely terrifying prospect, even an existential threat. Such language is typical of major powers, which have historically gotten riled up whenever another country has begun to develop a nuclear weapon of its own. Yet so far, every time another country has managed to shoulder its way into the nuclear club, the other members have always changed tack and decided to live with it. In fact, by reducing imbalances in military power, new nuclear states generally produce more regional and international stability, not less.

Israel's regional nuclear monopoly, which has proved remarkably durable for the past four decades, has long fueled instability in the Middle East. In no other region of the world does a lone, unchecked nuclear state exist. It is Israel's nuclear arsenal, not Iran's desire for one, that has contributed most to the current crisis. Power, after all, begs to be balanced. What is surprising about the Israeli case is that it has taken so long for a potential balancer to emerge.

Of course, it is easy to understand why Israel wants to remain the sole nuclear power in the region and why it is willing to use force to secure that status. In 1981, Israel bombed Iraq to prevent a challenge to its nuclear monopoly. It did the same to Syria in 2007 and is now considering similar action against Iran. But the very acts that have allowed Israel to maintain its nuclear edge in the short term have prolonged an imbalance that is unsustainable in the long term. Israel's proven ability to strike potential nuclear rivals with impunity has inevitably made its enemies anxious to develop the means to prevent Israel from doing so again. In this way, the current tensions are best viewed not as the early stages of a relatively recent Iranian nuclear crisis but rather as the final stages of a decades-long Middle East nuclear crisis that will end only when a balance of military power is restored.

Unfounded Fears

One reason the danger of a nuclear Iran has been grossly exaggerated is that the debate surrounding it has been distorted by misplaced worries and fundamental misunderstandings of how states generally behave in the international system. The first prominent concern, which undergirds many others, is that the Iranian regime is innately irrational. Despite a widespread belief to the contrary, Iranian policy is made not by "mad mullahs" but by perfectly sane ayatollahs who want to survive just like any other leaders. Although Iran's leaders indulge in inflammatory and hateful rhetoric, they show no propensity for self-destruction. It would be a grave error for policymakers in the United States and Israel to assume otherwise.

Yet that is precisely what many U.S. and Israeli officials and analysts have done. Portraying Iran as irrational has allowed them to argue that the logic of nuclear deterrence does not apply to the Islamic Republic. If Iran acquired a nuclear weapon, they warn, it would not hesitate to use it in a first strike against Israel, even though doing so would invite massive retaliation and risk destroying everything the Iranian regime holds dear.

Although it is impossible to be certain of Iranian intentions, it is far more likely that if Iran desires nuclear weapons, it is for the purpose of providing for its own security, not to improve its offensive capabilities (or destroy itself). Iran may be intransigent at the negotiating table and defiant in the face of sanctions, but it still acts to secure its own preservation. Iran's leaders did not, for example, attempt to close the Strait of Hormuz despite issuing blustery warnings that they might do so after the EU announced its planned oil embargo in January. The Iranian regime clearly concluded that it did not want to provoke what would surely have been a swift and devastating American response to such a move.

Nevertheless, even some observers and policymakers who accept that the Iranian regime is rational still worry that a nuclear weapon would embolden it, providing Tehran with a shield that would allow it to act more aggressively and increase its support for terrorism. Some analysts even fear that Iran would directly provide terrorists with nuclear arms. The problem with these concerns is that they contradict the record of every other nuclear weapons state going back to 1945. History shows that when countries acquire the bomb, they feel increasingly vulnerable and become acutely aware that their nuclear weapons make them a potential target in the eyes of major powers. This awareness discourages nuclear states from bold and aggressive action. Maoist China, for example, became much less bellicose after acquiring nuclear weapons in 1964, and India and Pakistan have both become more cautious since going nuclear. There is little reason to believe Iran would break this mold.

As for the risk of a handoff to terrorists, no country could transfer nuclear weapons without running a high risk of being found out. U.S. surveillance capabilities would pose a serious obstacle, as would the United States' impressive and growing ability to identify the source of fissile material. Moreover, countries can never entirely control or even predict the behavior of the terrorist groups they sponsor. Once a country such as Iran acquires a nuclear capability, it will have every reason to maintain full control over its arsenal. After all, building a bomb is costly and dangerous. It would make little sense to transfer the product of that investment to parties that cannot be trusted or managed.

Another oft-touted worry is that if Iran obtains the bomb, other states in the region will follow suit, leading to a nuclear arms race in the Middle East. But the nuclear age is now almost 70 years old, and so far, fears of proliferation have proved to be unfounded. Properly defined, the term "proliferation" means a rapid and uncontrolled spread. Nothing like that has occurred; in fact, since 1970, there has been a marked slowdown in the emergence of nuclear states. There is no reason to expect that this pattern will change now. Should Iran become the second Middle Eastern nuclear power since 1945, it would hardly signal the start of a landslide. When Israel acquired the bomb in the 1960s, it was at war with many of its neighbors. Its nuclear arms were a much bigger threat to the Arab world than Iran's program is today. If an atomic Israel did not trigger an arms race then, there is no reason a nuclear Iran should now.

Rest Assured

In 1991, the historical rivals India and Pakistan signed a treaty agreeing not to target each other's nuclear facilities. They realized that far more worrisome than their adversary's nuclear deterrent was the instability produced by challenges to it. Since then, even in the face of high tensions and risky provocations, the two countries have kept the peace. Israel and Iran would do well to consider this precedent. If Iran goes nuclear, Israel and Iran will deter each other, as nuclear powers always have. There has never been a full-scale war between two nuclear-armed states. Once Iran crosses the nuclear threshold, deterrence will apply, even if the Iranian arsenal is relatively small. No other country in the region will have an incentive to acquire its own nuclear capability, and the current crisis will finally dissipate, leading to a Middle East that is more stable than it is today.

For that reason, the United States and its allies need not take such pains to prevent the Iranians from developing a nuclear weapon. Diplomacy between Iran and the major powers should continue, because open lines of communication will make the Western countries feel better able to live with a nuclear Iran. But the current sanctions on Iran can be dropped: they primarily harm ordinary Iranians, with little purpose.

Most important, policymakers and citizens in the Arab world, Europe, Israel, and the United States should take comfort from the fact that history has shown that where nuclear capabilities emerge, so, too, does stability. When it comes to nuclear weapons, now as ever, more may be better.

Scott D. Sagan and Benjamin A. Valentino

REVISITING HIROSHIMA IN IRAN
What Americans Really Think about Using Nuclear Weapons and Killing Noncombatants

In August 1945, 85 percent of the U.S. public told pollsters that they approved of President Harry Truman's decision to drop two atomic bombs on Hiroshima and Nagasaki.[1] In the more than seven decades since that time, however, U.S. public approval of the decision to use nuclear weapons against Japan has declined significantly. Seventy years after the end of the World War II, a majority of Americans no longer approved of Truman's decision: a 2015 poll found that only 46 percent of Americans still viewed the atomic bombing of Japan as "the right thing to do."[2]

What accounts for this apparent decline in U.S. public support for using nuclear weapons and what is its significance? The answers to these questions are of more than just historical interest, for they can provide insights into whether the U.S. public would be a constraint against or a goad to encouraging a president to use nuclear weapons in international crises or conflicts in the future. The answers to these questions also help scholars and policymakers understand how Americans think about killing foreign civilians in war and how well they have internalized the principles of just war doctrine, such as noncombatant immunity, proportionality, and risk acceptance.

An initial review of U.S. public opinion on the decision to drop the bomb provides both a vivid reminder of the depth of hostility that

Americans felt toward Japan in 1945 and a strong sense of declining support for the use of nuclear weapons since then. A University of Chicago National Opinion Research Center poll administered in September 1945 found that 44 percent of the public said the United States should have dropped the bombs "one city at [a] time"; 26 percent said that it should have dropped the bomb "where [there were] no people"; 23 percent said the United States should have "wiped out [all Japanese] cities"; and only 4 percent said they would have "refused to use" the bomb.[3] A Roper poll published later that year in *Fortune* magazine similarly found that just 4.5 percent of the U.S. public believed that the United States should not have used atomic bombs at all; 13.8 percent believed that it should have first dropped a bomb on an unpopulated area; 53.5 percent maintained that it should have used the two bombs on two cities, as it did; and 22.7 percent believed that it should have dropped more bombs before Japan had the chance to surrender.[4]

Although the percentage of Americans approving of Truman's decision has fluctuated over time—in part because of the varied wording of survey questions, and whether alternatives to "approve" or "not approve" response categories were included in the polls—U.S. public support for dropping the bombs on Hiroshima and Nagasaki has been on a downward trajectory. For example, Harris polls in 1971 and 1982 found that 64 percent and 63 percent of Americans, respectively, deemed it

From *International Security* 42, no. 1 (Summer 2017): 41–79.
Some of the authors' notes have been omitted.

Table 6.1. 2015 Replication of the Roper/Fortune 1945 Poll

Polling in the United States on the Use of Atomic Bombs on Japan

POLLING QUESTION: "WHICH OF THESE COMES CLOSEST TO DESCRIBING HOW YOU FEEL ABOUT OUR USE OF THE ATOMIC BOMB?"	ELMO ROPER "ATOMIC BOMB" POLL (NOVEMBER 30, 1945)	ROPER 1945 POLL REPLICATION (JULY 30, 2015)
"We should not have used any atomic bombs at all."	4.5%	14.4%
"We should have dropped one first on some unpopulated region, to show the Japanese its [atomic bombs'] power, and dropped the second one on a city only if they hadn't surrendered after the first one."	13.8%	31.6%
"We should have used the two bombs on cities, just as we did."	53.5%	28.5%
"We should have quickly used many more of them before Japan had a chance to surrender."	22.7%	2.9%
"Don't know."	5.5%	22.7%

Source: "The Fortune Survey," *Fortune*, November 30, 1945, reprinted in "The Quarter's Poll," *Public Opinion Quarterly*, Vol. 9, No. 4 (Winter, 1945/46), p. 530; and "Japan 1945 Poll Replication" (Redwood City, Calif.: YouGov, July 30, 2015).

"necessary and proper" to drop the atomic bombs on Japan. In contrast, a 1998 Roper poll found that only 47 percent thought that dropping the bombs was "a right thing," 26 percent said that it was "a wrong thing," and 22 percent were somewhere between the two extremes.[5] Polls conducted by the Associated Press in March and July 2005 showed that, respectively, 47 percent and 48 percent of the public "approved" of the dropping of atomic bombs on Hiroshima and Nagasaki.[6]

The downward trend has continued in recent years. Indeed, when we replicated the 1945 Roper poll in a July 2015 poll (Table 6.1), both of which included a "demonstration strike" option, we found that in 2015 less than 30 percent of the U.S. public supported dropping the two bombs (down from 53.5 percent in 1945), whereas 31.6 percent said they preferred the demonstration strike (up from 13.8 percent in 1945). The percentage of Americans who felt that the United States should not have used any atomic bombs more than tripled from 1945 to 2015, and the percentage of Americans who felt that it should have used more bombs before Japan had a chance to surrender dropped from 22.7 percent in 1945 to less than 3 percent seventy years later.[7]

Unlike these polls, which examined support for the use of the atomic bombs against Japan in 1945, other polls have focused on U.S. attitudes about contemporary conditions in which the United States might use nuclear weapons. The evidence here also suggests a general decline in support for using nuclear weapons. In 1949, for example, only 20 percent of the U.S. public agreed that "the United States should pledge that we will never use the atomic bomb in warfare until some other nation has used it on us first."[8] In contrast, a 2010 Chicago Council on Global Affairs survey found that 57 percent of the public agreed that "the U.S. should only use nuclear weapons in response to a nuclear attack by another nation" and that 20 percent agreed that "the U.S. should never use nuclear weapons under any circumstances."[9]

Many scholars and policymakers—following the lead of Nina Tannenwald in her important book *The Nuclear Taboo*—have pointed to the decline in U.S. public support for using nuclear weapons as evidence of the gradual emergence of an ethical norm, a taboo, against the first use of nuclear weapons.[10] Other scholars—most prominently, Steven Pinker, Neta Crawford, and Ward Thomas—have contended that the decline in support for using nuclear weapons is part of a much larger "humanitarian revolution" among the public, which has led to a broad acceptance of the just war doctrine principle of noncombatant immunity.[11] A third school of thought—featured most prominently in the work of Alexander Downes, Daryl Press, Scott Sagan, and Benjamin Valentino—has argued that the U.S. public has internalized neither the nuclear taboo nor a noncombatant immunity norm. These scholars contend that Americans appear to be willing both to support the use of whatever weaponry is deemed most effective militarily and to kill foreign civilians on a massive scale whenever such attacks are considered useful to defend critical U.S. national security interests and protect the lives of significant numbers of U.S. military personnel.[12]

In this article, we address these debates about U.S. public opinion concerning nuclear use and noncombatant immunity. We argue that the previous polls showing a decline in support for the atomic bombings in 1945 and contemporary uses of nuclear weapons are a misleading guide to understanding the real views of the American public about the use of nuclear weapons and the killing of noncombatants. Such polls failed to place respondents into a mind-set in which they are forced to make a trade-off between risking U.S. soldiers' lives (if the United States does not use nuclear weapons) and killing foreign noncombatants (if the United States does use nuclear weapons). Yet, precisely this type of trade-off was at the heart of Truman's decision in 1945; and scenarios that entail this kind of trade-off are arguably among the most realistic and serious conditions in which a president and the public would be forced to contemplate the use of nuclear weapons in the future.

The first section of the article reviews the three main schools of thought about public attitudes toward the use of nuclear weapons and the killing of foreign noncombatants. The second section presents the findings from a survey experiment conducted in July 2015 in which a representative sample of the U.S. public was asked about a contemporary, hypothetical scenario designed to replicate the 1945 decision—the use of a nuclear weapon against a city in Iran in an attempt to end a war that the Iranian government had started in response to the imposition of U.S. economic sanctions. This type of thought experiment obviously cannot re-create the depth of urgency and emotion that many Americans felt in 1945. As such, it constitutes a conservative test of the public's willingness to use nuclear weapons and target large numbers of noncombatants in a war.

The findings demonstrate that, contrary to the nuclear taboo thesis, a clear majority of Americans would approve of using nuclear weapons first against the civilian population of a nonnuclear-armed adversary, killing 2 million Iranian civilians, if they believed that such use would save the lives of 20,000 U.S. soldiers. In addition, contrary to the noncombatant immunity norm thesis, an even larger percentage of Americans would approve of a conventional bombing attack designed to kill 100,000 Iranian civilians in the effort to intimidate Iran into surrendering (see Table 6.2).

The third section of the article analyzes the reasons why so many Americans in our scenarios approved of using nuclear weapons. We present demographic data on the key characteristics of the supporters of nuclear use and demonstrate how our survey respondents explained their preferences about whether or not to use nuclear weapons. Here we present some novel findings showing that women support nuclear weapons use and violations of noncombatant immunity no less (and in some cases more) than male respondents. We also provide insights into how a belief in retribution and an ability to assign culpability retrospectively to foreign civilians allows individuals to rationalize the killing of foreign noncombatants. In the fourth section, we present the results of a related survey experiment constructed to determine whether Americans would support a diplomatic compromise in a war with Iran to avoid either the killing of U.S. soldiers or the killing of foreign noncombatants. In the concluding section, we outline a future research agenda to further understand these phenomena and present the implications of our findings for debates about just war doctrine and the risk of the use of nuclear weapons in future conflicts.

The Nuclear Taboo, Noncombatants, and Military Effectiveness

There are three main schools of thought about U.S. public opinion and the use of nuclear weapons against civilian targets. The first theory, advanced most clearly in the work of Nina Tannenwald, is that over time both U.S. leaders and the public have internalized a belief in a "nuclear taboo." According to Tannenwald, "The taboo is not the behavior (of non-use) itself but rather the normative belief about the behavior . . . a shared expectation about behavior, a standard of right and wrong."[13] Tannenwald insists that "leaders and publics have come to view this phenomenon not simply as a rule of prudence but as a taboo, with an explicit normative aspect, a sense of obligation attached to it."[14]

For Tannenwald, and many others, decreasing public support over time for dropping the atomic bombs in 1945 is clear evidence that a nuclear taboo exists. Tannenwald, for example, has argued that "the public's changing interpretation of the correctness of Hiroshima and Nagasaki over the years is perhaps explicable in the terms of a general delegitimation of nuclear weapons."[15] * * *

The nuclear taboo literature has shown that some U.S. leaders, during specific crises or wars, have felt that they were constrained by public opposition to the United States initiating the use of

Table 6.2. Iran Bombing Conditions

EXPECTED U.S. FATALITIES IN GROUND ASSAULT	EXPECTED IRANIAN FATALITIES IN AIR ATTACK
20,000 U.S. troops dead	100,000 Iranian civilians dead in nuclear attack
20,000 U.S. troops dead	2,000,000 Iranian civilians dead in nuclear attack
20,000 U.S. troops dead	100,000 Iranian civilians dead in conventional bombing attack

nuclear weapons. Tannenwald, for example, notes that Secretary of State John Foster Dulles commented in a 1953 National Security Council discussion about nuclear use in Korea that the public believed there to be a "moral problem" with these weapons and suggested that the Dwight Eisenhower administration actively "break down this false distinction" so that nuclear weapons would be viewed "as simply another weapon in our arsenal."[16] William Burr and Jeffrey Kimball, and Scott Sagan and Jeremi Suri, have similarly demonstrated that President Richard Nixon felt constrained in his ability even to threaten to use nuclear weapons against North Vietnam, as part of his "madman theory" of nuclear coercion, and therefore had to resort to a "secret" (and less effective) nuclear alert in October 1969.[17]

Still, a number of weaknesses of the existing tests of the nuclear taboo thesis are worth noting. First, although there is historical evidence that some U.S. presidents felt constrained by U.S. public opinion in particular crises or conflicts, scholars have not systematically studied contemporary public opinion polls on nuclear weapons use in those periods. Thus, we do not know if these leaders' perceptions of public opposition were accurate. Second, polls showing declining support for the bombing of Hiroshima and Nagasaki do not tell us whether the decrease in support reflects changes in the U.S. public's attitudes toward using nuclear weapons or changes in attitudes toward Japan and increasing temporal distance from the pressures of the war. It was much easier for Americans to support using nuclear weapons against an adversary in a brutal war in 1945 than it is to imagine using such weapons today against Japan, one of the United States' closest allies. In addition, these polls rarely specified the known or expected numbers of civilians killed in atomic bombing attacks or whether they were targeted intentionally. Consequently, it was up to the respondents and their knowledge of the past to judge whether the use of nuclear weapons conformed with the principle of noncombatant immunity or proportionality (whether the costs of civilian deaths were proportionate to the benefits gained). And most important, existing polls have not forced survey respondents to contemplate the trade-off between the use of nuclear weapons, including the resulting loss of civilian lives in the adversary's nation, and the use of U.S. ground troops in an invasion and the resulting loss of American soldiers' lives.

The Noncombatant Immunity Norm

A second school of thought argues that an even broader norm has constrained the conduct of war in recent years. Proponents of this view assert that a phenomenon that Steven Pinker has called "the Humanitarian Revolution" has led to a deeply embedded and widely held norm against killing noncombatants, regardless of the choice of weapon. Pinker argues that the strengthening of "the better angels of our nature . . . can be credited for declines in violence."[18] He contrasts the common popularity of cruel criminal punishments and the brutality of soldiers in war in the past to more civilized norms today and suggests that both rational choice and emotional development have been at play: "The expansion of empathy may help explain why people today abjure cruel punishments and think more about the human costs of war. . . . The decline of violence may owe something to an expansion of empathy, but it also owes much to harder-boiled faculties like prudence, reason, fairness, self-control, norms and taboos, and conceptions of human rights."[19] For Pinker, "The nuclear taboo emerged only gradually. . . . It began to sink in that the weapons' destructive capacity was of a different order from anything in history, that they violated any conception of proportionality in the waging of war."[20] * * *

Winning the War and Saving U.S. Troops

A third school of thought maintains that the American people have internalized neither a nuclear taboo nor an unconditional norm supporting the principle of noncombatant immunity. Instead, scholars in this school argue that concerns about winning wars and the desire to minimize the loss of lives of their nation's soldiers dominate public opinion about military operations. Alexander Downes, for example, examined all known cases of "civilian victimization" in interstate war from 1816 to 2003, defining civilian victimization as "a military strategy in which civilians are either targeted intentionally or force is used indiscriminately" and that produces at least 50,000 noncombatant deaths.[21] Drawing on quantitative data and historical case studies, he concludes that "states—including democracies—tend to prize victory and preserving the lives of their own people above humanity in warfare: desperation overrides moral inhibitions against killing noncombatants."[22] Indeed, contrary to theories that emphasize that authoritarian regimes are more likely to target and kill foreign noncombatants, Downes found that electoral pressures on leaders in democracies make them "somewhat more likely than nondemocracies to target civilians."[23]

Downes's work has three limitations, however, that reduce the applicability of its insights to the specific questions we explore here. First, Downes did not directly assess public support or lack of support for mass killings, leaving open the possibility that democratic leaders incorrectly assumed that public support for violence against foreign civilians was high. Second, his research included both cases in which the killing of civilians was intentional and cases in which it occurred as a result of collateral damage, which limits the degree to which his findings can be said to measure support or rejection of the principle of noncombatant immunity. Third, all

of Downes's main case studies focus on events that occurred in the first half of the twentieth century, before many scholars believed that the nuclear taboo and norms of noncombatant immunity were firmly established.

A second major contribution to this school of thought is Christopher Gelpi, Peter Feaver, and Jason Reifler's 2009 study, *Paying the Human Costs of War: American Public Opinion and Casualties in Military Conflicts*, which focuses primarily on how changes in real or estimated U.S. military casualties over time influence public support for ongoing or potential U.S. wars.[24] Although their book does not investigate potential nuclear-weapons-use scenarios, it does include a brief analysis of how expected civilian casualties in an enemy country might influence U.S. public support for starting a war. They acknowledge that there is often an "unavoidable trade-off between *their* civilian casualties and *our* military casualties" and therefore ask "how does the public weigh that trade-off and what, to use an infelicitous metaphor from economics, is the exchange rate?"[25]

Gelpi, Feaver, and Reifler conducted an original survey experiment measuring U.S. public support for an attack on North Korea to destroy its nuclear program. They found, unsurprisingly, that support for an attack was higher (60 percent) when no casualty estimates were mentioned, but dropped (by sixteen percentage points to 44 percent) when the survey informed participants that the attack would result in 2,000 U.S. military fatalities. Surprisingly, however, when a separate sample of the public was given a scenario that estimated that 2,000 North Korean civilians would be killed in the U.S. attack, an almost identical drop in U.S. public support for the attack was recorded. This finding could suggest that the U.S. public holds a cosmopolitan view about justice in war: that all human life has equal moral worth and therefore the lives of North Korea civilians should be valued as highly as the lives of U.S. soldiers.[26] Alternatively, because the experiments drew on separate representative samples of the U.S. public, the result could simply reveal that there is a significant drop in support for starting an attack whenever any casualties—U.S. military, enemy civilians, or allied civilians—are mentioned.[27] Moreover, the experiment did not include a condition in which the same respondents were asked about a direct trade-off between killing U.S. soldiers and killing North Korean civilians, nor did it ask respondents to consider the intentional targeting of North Korean civilians. All respondents, however, were asked: "In general, how would you rate the importance of limiting American military deaths as compared to limiting foreign civilian deaths? Is limiting U.S. military deaths much more important, somewhat more important, about equally important, somewhat less important, or much less important than limiting foreign civilian deaths?" Gelpi, Feaver, and Reifler report that 52 percent of the respondents answered "much more" or "somewhat more important"; 38 percent answered "about equally important"; and 6 percent said "somewhat less" or "much less important."[28]

The third example of this school of thought is the 2012 study by Daryl Press, Scott Sagan, and Benjamin Valentino, which utilizes a set of survey experiments to examine the degree to which the U.S. public has an aversion to using nuclear weapons. Their study demonstrated that a majority of the U.S. public based their preferences about the choice of weapons not on whether the weapon was nuclear or conventional, but rather on its relative effectiveness in destroying the target. When presented with a hypothetical scenario in which U.S. intelligence agencies informed the president that al-Qaida was suspected of building a nuclear weapon in a remote site in Syria, 18.9 percent preferred a nuclear attack, and 47.9 percent said they would approve of using nuclear weapons if the president had decided to do so, even when nuclear weapons were deemed to be of equal effectiveness to conventional weapons. When nuclear weapons were deemed to be twice as effective in destroying the target, however, 51.4 percent of the public preferred

a nuclear strike and approval ratings increased to 77.2 percent.[29] Moreover, the majority of respondents who opposed using nuclear weapons reported that they did so primarily for fear of setting a precedent that might encourage the use of such weapons in the future against the United States or its allies, not because of moral concerns. Press, Sagan, and Valentino conclude, "[F]or most Americans, the inhibitions against using nuclear weapons are relatively weak and decidedly not subject to a taboo."[30]

There were three limitations, however, of the Press, Sagan, and Valentino study. First, to measure the strength of the nuclear taboo per se (and avoid conflating the taboo with an aversion to killing large numbers of civilians), the experiment held the number of expected fatalities in the attack constant and relatively low, at 1,000 noncombatants killed. Although the results showed that most Americans were willing to use nuclear weapons against a terrorist target, the study could not assess the degree to which that support would drop if larger numbers of civilians in Syria had been expected to be killed in the attack.[31] Second, the nature of the enemy—in particular, a terrorist organization that had attacked the United States—may have influenced the public support for the U.S. nuclear attack. Many Americans may have been willing to use nuclear weapons against al-Qaida, but the study did not examine whether they would be willing to use nuclear weapons against a foreign state, as the United States did in World War II. * * *

Hiroshima in Iran Experiments

To test the alternative theories concerning U.S. public opinion, nuclear weapons use, and noncombatant immunity, we designed a set of survey experiments focused on a contemporary conflict with Iran.[32] The experiments asked subjects to consider a scenario in which Iran attacked the United

States first and in which the president was presented with two options: (1) to send ground troops to capture Tehran, which would lead to large-scale U.S. military fatalities; or (2) to attack a major Iranian city, deliberately killing civilians, in the effort to shock the Iranian government into accepting unconditional surrender. The three theoretical approaches described above lead to different hypotheses about how a representative sample of the U.S. public would respond if asked about the potential first use of nuclear weapons against Iran, a country that Americans have negative feelings about today.[33] Tannenwald argues that the nuclear taboo has "qualities such as absoluteness, unthinkingness, and taken-for-grantedness."[34] If the nuclear taboo thesis is correct, therefore, the majority of Americans should oppose the hypothetical U.S. nuclear attack against Iran. If Pinker, Ward, and Crawford are correct and the U.S. public has deeply internalized the noncombatant immunity norm, then the majority of Americans should also oppose the use of both nuclear and conventional bombing when it is designed to kill a large number of Iranian civilians. If the arguments that Americans prioritize winning the war and saving the lives of U.S. soldiers are valid, however, the majority of Americans should support the use of nuclear weapons or conventional weapons against Iranian civilians in the scenarios described in the survey experiment. If this final thesis is correct, moreover, it suggests that there has been relatively little change in U.S. public opinion about using nuclear weapons or killing noncombatants since 1945.

We contracted a leading political polling firm, YouGov, to administer our survey experiments to a sample of U.S. citizens older than 18. The polling was conducted from July 23 to July 30, 2015, among 780 respondents selected from individuals who registered to participate in YouGov internet surveys, with the data weighted by YouGov to reflect the demographic composition of the U.S. public. * * *

Experiment Design

Unlike public opinion polls that inquire about actual wars, a survey experiment allows us to construct hypothetical scenarios in which we can hold relevant facts about the war constant (e.g., the causes of the war or the identity of the enemy) while varying only one aspect of the conflict (e.g., the number of noncombatants killed or the kind of weapons used). This design enables us to isolate the effects of different levels of expected noncombatant deaths and the effects of conventional versus nuclear bombing on the U.S. public's approval of attacks.

All the stories used in our experiments are presented in the online appendix.[35] Each respondent read a mock news article that reported that the United States had placed severe sanctions on Iran in response to allegations that the Tehran government had been caught violating the terms of the 2015 Joint Comprehensive Plan of Action (colloquially known as the Iran Nuclear Deal). In response, Iran attacked a U.S. aircraft carrier in the Persian Gulf, killing 2,403 military personnel (the same number killed in the Pearl Harbor attack, though that is not mentioned in the story). As described in the mock news story, "U.S. forces retaliated immediately with large-scale airstrikes that destroyed all of Iran's nuclear infrastructure, air defenses, and all Iranian Air Force bases and planes. When Iran rejected the United States' demand for the 'immediate and unconditional surrender' of the Iranian government, the President ordered a ground invasion by U.S. Marines and Army forces designed to destroy the Iranian military and replace the government in Iran." The story then reported that the invasion eventually stalled after several months of fighting and 10,000 U.S. military fatalities.

Subjects next read that the Joint Chiefs of Staff had presented the president with two options to end the war. The first option was to continue the land invasion to capture Tehran and compel the Iranian government to surrender. The second option was to "shock" the Iranian government into accepting unconditional surrender by dropping a single nuclear weapon on Mashhad, Iran's second-largest city. The article stated that a weapon would be targeted "directly on Mashhad . . . in the effort to undermine civilian support for the war and pressure the Iranian government to surrender." Thus, it was clear that the bombing was a direct violation of the principle of noncombatant immunity and had no military target. Holding the estimated number of U.S. military fatalities in a continued ground invasion at 20,000, we varied the number of Iranian noncombatants expected to be killed in the attack on Mashhad from 100,000 to 2 million to measure the degree to which the U.S. public would be willing to use nuclear weapons and violate the principle of distinction (or noncombatant immunity) in a scenario similar to the Pacific War in 1945. We also included a third condition in which 100,000 Iranian noncombatants were estimated to be killed in a conventional bombing attack. The purpose of this condition was to determine how the use of nuclear versus conventional bombing would affect U.S. public attitudes about targeting large numbers of noncombatants. This condition thus provides a direct measure of the depth of the public's support for the noncombatant immunity norm compared to its aversion toward the use of nuclear weapons. * * *

For each of these scenarios, we posed the following questions to respondents: "Given the facts described in the article, if you had to choose between launching the strike against the Iranian city or continuing the ground war against Iran, which option would you prefer?" and "Regardless of which option you preferred, if the United States decided to conduct the strike against the Iranian city, how much would you approve or disapprove of that decision?" * * *

Support for Nuclear and Conventional Air Strikes

As shown in Figure 6.2, a majority of the U.S. public indicated that they would approve the bombing of Mashhad across all three conditions (columns B, D, and F). Indeed, Americans explicitly preferred the air-strike option against Mashhad to the ground assault on Tehran in two of the three conditions (columns A and E). Only in the condition in which 2 million Iranian civilians would be killed did a slight majority (52.3 percent) prefer the ground attack: the preference for a nuclear strike against Iranian civilians drops from 55.6 percent (column A) to 47.7 percent (column C) when the number of expected Iranian civilian fatalities rises from 100,000 to 2 million. Although this difference is not statistically significant, it suggests that there may be some degree of aversion to killing extremely large numbers of civilians. Approval rates, however, remain higher, at close to 60 percent, in both conditions (as seen in column B and D).

The percentage of Americans who approved of the bombing attack against Mashhad remained relatively stable regardless of whether conventional or nuclear weapons were used, and regardless of whether the attack was estimated to kill 100,000 or 2 million civilians. The absence of statistically significant differences in these latter results across different conditions is precisely what is substantively and politically significant. That nearly 60 percent of the U.S. public would approve of a nuclear attack on Iran that would kill 2 million civilians suggests that the decreasing level of support found in recent polls about Truman's decision to drop the bombs in 1945 is a misleading guide to public opinion about nuclear use today.

That approval ratings were higher than preference ratings in both of our nuclear survey conditions (the difference was only statistically significant

Figure 6.2. U.S. Public Opinion on Bombing Iran

Question 1 (A, C, E) : "Given the facts described in the article, if you had to choose between launching the strike against the Iranian city or continuing the ground war against Iran, which option would you prefer?"

Question 2 (B, C, F) : "Regardless of which option you preferred, if the United States decided to conduct the strike against the Iranian city, how much would you approve or disapprove of that decision?"

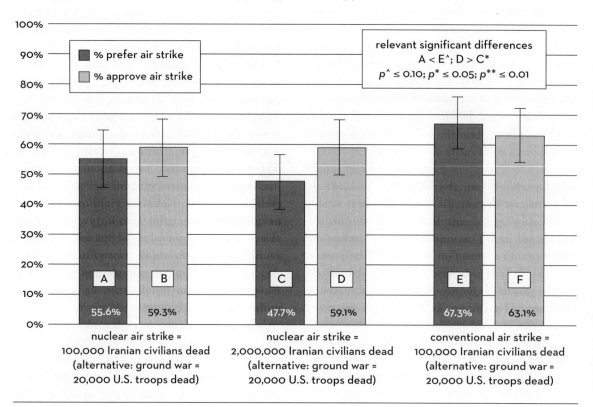

in the 2 million Iranian deaths condition, columns C and D) suggests that there may be a small "rally around the bomb" effect, like the common "rally around the flag" phenomenon seen after most U.S. decisions to use military force.[36] Some Americans are willing to approve of a presidential decision to use nuclear weapons even in situations in which they did not personally prefer a nuclear response. These results do not appear to be influenced by the perception that the more destructive

attack would likely be more effective. When we asked a follow-up question about whether the air strike was likely to lead to unconditional surrender, the percentages of respondents who answered positively were statistically indistinguishable across all conditions.

The conventional bombing scenario also produced noteworthy results. In column E, 67.3 percent of respondents preferred the conventional bombing attack that deliberately killed 100,000

Iranians, an increase of 11.7 percent from the percentage of respondents who preferred the nuclear attack in column A ($p = 0.07$). This result suggests that although these Americans may have been influenced by an aversion to using nuclear weapons against civilians, they were not averse to intentionally killing civilians with conventional weapons. That such a large majority of respondents preferred a conventional bombing attack on a city that would kill 100,000 civilians over a ground assault that would kill 20,000 U.S. soldiers is strong evidence against the theory that a robust noncombatant immunity norm has been internalized by the U.S. public today.

To explore the reasons why some Americans are more willing to use conventional weapons than nuclear weapons, we asked all of our subjects two additional questions. First, "Regardless of which option you preferred, how ethical or unethical do you think it would be if the United States decided to conduct the strike against the Iranian city in the situation described in the article?" Second, subjects were asked whether they agreed or disagreed with the statement that "launching the strike against the Iranian city would set a precedent that would encourage our adversaries to launch similar attacks against America or our allies in the future." Our results indicate that a combination of normative and practical concerns help explain the higher support for the conventional air strike. Among those who opposed the nuclear strike, 65.1 percent judged it unethical. Among those who opposed the conventional strike, however, the percentage that judged it immoral declined only slightly, to 61.6 percent (the difference was not statistically significant). This suggests that anti-nuclear norms add little to the aversion to killing civilians. A larger percentage of those opposed to the strike, however, agreed that it would set a bad precedent both in the nuclear condition (76.1 percent) and in the conventional condition (76.8 percent).[37]

Explaining U.S. Public Support for the Use of Nuclear Weapons

The main conclusions of these survey experiments are clear. The majority of the U.S. public has not internalized either a belief in the nuclear taboo or a strong noncombatant immunity norm. When faced with realistic scenarios in which they are forced to contemplate a trade-off between sacrificing a large number of U.S. troops in combat or deliberately killing even larger numbers of foreign noncombatants, the majority of respondents approve of killing civilians in an effort to end the war. Protecting the lives of U.S. troops was a higher priority than preventing the use of a nuclear weapon or avoiding the large-scale conventional bombing of an Iranian city.[38] * * *

Polling evidence from World War II suggests that U.S. public support for killing enemy civilians on a large scale with chemical weapons increased when subjects were cued that using such weapons would save the lives of U.S. soldiers. In September 1944, for example, only 23 percent of the U.S. public said they would approve of "using poison gas against Japanese cities" if it meant "an earlier end of the war in the Pacific"; yet support surged to 40 percent in a June 1945 poll in which the prompt stated that a poison gas attack "against the Japanese" might "reduce the number of U.S. soldiers killed or wounded."[39] * * *

■   ■   ■

Women and War

The finding that women were no less willing than men to support using nuclear weapons or conventional weapons in a manner that violated noncombatant immunity principles was particularly surprising. Women have been found to be

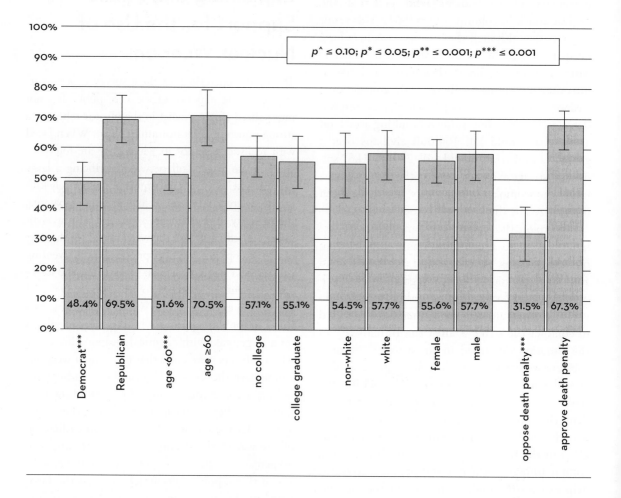

Figure 6.3. Preference of the U.S. Public for Air Strike by Demographic Subgroup

$p^{\wedge} \leq 0.10; p^{*} \leq 0.05; p^{**} \leq 0.001; p^{***} \leq 0.001$

Democrat***	Republican	age <60***	age ≥60	no college	college graduate	non-white	white	female	male	oppose death penalty***	approve death penalty
48.4%	69.5%	51.6%	70.5%	57.1%	55.1%	54.5%	57.7%	55.6%	57.7%	31.5%	67.3%

less hawkish than men in most studies on the effect of gender on support for going to war or using nuclear weapons. Lisa Brandes's 1994 study examined all polls from 1945 to 1988 regarding support for the use of nuclear weapons and found an average 9.1 percent "gender gap" between women and men regarding approval of U.S. nuclear weapons use.[40] Richard Eichenberg's broader 2003 study analyzed 486 surveys conducted from 1990 to 2003 and found that women are less supportive of the use of military force in general and that the gender gap between men and women concerning support for a war increases when likely or current U.S. military casualties are mentioned in the polling questions.[41] A rare finding to the contrary is reported in Deborah Brooks and Benjamin Valentino's 2011 study, which demonstrated that U.S. women are more hawkish than men in supporting the use of military force in two scenarios: when the war was described as a humanitarian intervention and when it had the support of a multinational organization, such as the United Nations, rather than when it was the product of a unilateral national decision.[42]

We therefore disaggregated our respondents by gender to examine how male and female preferences for the air strike varied across our three scenarios. Our findings demonstrate that women were no less, or even more, hawkish than men regarding their support for killing large numbers of foreign civilians to avoid the deaths of U.S. soldiers. Female respondents supported using the atomic bomb at virtually the same percentages (55.9 percent in column B, 54.3 percent in column D) regardless of whether 100,000 or 2 million Iranian noncombatants were killed. That a higher percentage of U.S. women (54.3 percent, column D) preferred the atomic attack that killed 2 million Iranians than did U.S. men (39.8 percent, column C) is particularly surprising, although given the relatively small cell sizes resulting from dividing our sample in two, this difference is not significant at conventional levels ($p = 0.128$). In addition, women's support for the air strike, unlike men's, did not increase significantly in the conventional condition. The interaction between gender and nuclear/conventional conditions, however, was only marginally significant ($p = 0.079$). Nevertheless, this finding provides some suggestive and surprising evidence that the aversion to nuclear weapons use may be stronger among men than women.

This finding about gender also provides another example of historical resonance, for it shines a new light on American public opinion during World War II. The approval rate in August 1945 for dropping the atomic bombs on Japan among U.S. women (83 percent) was virtually identical to that of American men (86 percent).[43] * * *

Rationaliztion and Retribution

* * * In an open-ended question, we asked respondents to write down the single most important reason they supported the air strike. The results revealed that utilitarian calculations about saving U.S. lives and ending the war promptly, as well as

assigning culpability retrospectively, may have motivated subjects' preference for the air strike. The majority of respondents in all three conditions who supported the bombing attack cited saving American lives or ending the war quickly as the reason for their support. That was not unexpected. What was surprising was the number of Americans who suggested that Iranian civilians were somehow culpable or were less than human. Justifications for the atomic attack that killed 100,000 Iranians included: "Hate the thought of being the only nation again to launch a nuclear strike, but they started it and we have lost enough lives"; and "Iran lied again about their nuclear facilities, launched an attack on an American warship that killed and hurt 4,000 Americans, and nothing short of complete and total victory over the lying savages would be acceptable to me." Justifications for killing 2 million noncombatants included: "They were dancing in the streets and partying in favor of what happened to the twin towers"; "They hate us and they will violate any agreement"; "Islam is a religion of fanatics [and] they need to be taught a lesson"; "Air strike would wipe out any military opponents who will be hiding among civilians"; and "Kill the cockroaches." Answers given by those who voted for the conventional attack that was estimated to kill 100,000 Iranian civilians included: "The article said that Iran attacked the U.S. ship first. The U.S. is not the aggressor here"; "Iran is ruled by radicals who have no regard for innocent life"; and "My first choice would be to decapitate the snake—wipe out the capital—wipe it clean—every living thing."

■ ■ ■

Conclusion

The novel survey experiments described in this article, by re-creating the trade-off between an atomic attack and the risk to the lives of U.S. soldiers that the United States faced at the end of World War II, produced many surprising findings.

The U.S. public's willingness to use nuclear weapons and deliberately kill foreign civilians has not changed as much since 1945 as many scholars have assumed. Contrary to the nuclear taboo thesis, a majority of Americans are willing to support the use of a nuclear weapon against an Iranian city killing 100,000 civilians. Contrary to the theory that Americans accept the noncombatant immunity norm, an even larger percentage of the U.S. public was willing to kill 100,000 Iranian civilians with conventional weapons. Women are as hawkish as men and, in some scenarios, are even more willing to support the use of nuclear weapons. Belief in the value of retribution is strongly related to support for using nuclear weapons, and a large majority of those who favor the use of nuclear weapons against Iran stated that the Iranian people bore some of the responsibility for that attack because they had not overthrown their government. * * *

Past surveys that show a very substantial decline in U.S. public support for the 1945 dropping of the atomic bombs are a misleading guide to how the public would react if placed in similar wartime circumstances in the future. It is fortunate that the United States has not faced wartime conditions in the nuclear era in which U.S. political leaders and the public had to contemplate such grave trade-offs.[44] Today, as in 1945, the U.S. public is unlikely to serve as a serious constraint on any president who might consider using nuclear weapons in the crucible of war.

NOTES

1. David W. Moore, "Majority Supports Use of Atomic Bomb on Japan in WWII," *Gallup*, August 5, 2005, http://www.gallup.com/poll/17677/majority-supports-use-atomic-bomb-japan-wwii.aspx.

2. Peter Moore, "A-Bomb Legacy: Most Americans Negative about the Invention of Nuclear Weapons" (Redwood City, Calif.: YouGov, July 22, 2015), https://today.yougov.com/news/2015/07/22/a-bomb-legacy/.

3. "Survey by National Opinion Research Center, September, 1945," conducted by the National Opinion Research Center, University of Chicago (1945; Ithaca, N.Y.: iPoll, Roper Center for Public Opinion Research, Cornell University, n.d.).

4. "The Fortune Survey," *Fortune*, November 30, 1945, reprinted in "The Quarter's Poll," *Public Opinion Quarterly*, Vol. 9, No. 4 (Winter, 1945/46), p. 530, doi:10.1086/265765.

5. Louis Harris, "The American View of Japan and the Japanese: A Sharp Decline in Racism but Memories of WWII Still Linger," *Harris Survey*, April 19, 1982, http://media.theharrispoll.com/documents/Harris-Interactive-Poll-Research-THE-AMERICAN-VIEW-OF-JAPAN-AND-THE-JAPANESE-A-SHAR-1982-04.pdf; and Carl Brown, "Public Opinion about Using Nuclear Weapons" (Ithaca, N.Y.: Roper Center for Public Opinion Research, Cornell University, n.d.), http://ropercenter.cornell.edu/public-opinion-using-nuclear-weapons/.

6. Ipsos Public Affairs, "The Associated Press Poll," Associated Press, March 24, 2005, http://surveys.ap.org/data/Ipsos/national/2005/2005-03-23%20AP%20Topline%20results.pdf; and Ipsos Public Affairs, "Associated Press World War II/Japan Study," Associated Press, July 12, 2005, http://surveys.ap.org/data/Ipsos/national/2005/2005-07-11%20AP%20_World%20War%2011_%20topline%20results.pdf.

7. We do not know, however, what percentage of respondents who preferred a demonstration strike would have supported the attacks on Hiroshima and Nagasaki had the demonstration strike failed to cause the Japanese government to surrender.

8. George H. Gallup, ed., *The Gallup Poll: Public Opinion, 1935–1971*, Vol. 1: *1935–1948* (New York: Random House, 1972), p. 839.

9. Chicago Council on Global Affairs, "Global Views 2010" (Chicago: Chicago Council on Global Affairs, September 22, 2010), pp. 99–100, https://www.thechicagocouncil.org/sites/default/files/Global%20Views%202010_USTopline.pdf.

10. Nina Tannenwald, *The Nuclear Taboo: The United States and the Non-Use of Nuclear Weapons since 1945* (New York: Cambridge University Press, 2007).

11. See Steven Pinker, *The Better Angels of Our Nature: Why Violence Has Declined* (New York: Viking, 2011); Neta C. Crawford, *Accountability for Killing: Moral Accountability for Collateral Damage in America's Post-9/11 Wars* (New York: Oxford University Press, 2013); Neta C. Crawford, "Targeting Civilians and U.S. Strategic Bombing Norms: *Plus ça change, plus c'est la même chose?*" in Matthew Evangelista and Henry Shue, eds., *The American Way of Bombing: Changing Ethical and Legal Norms, from Flying Fortresses to Drones* (Ithaca, N.Y.: Cornell University Press, 2014), pp. 64–86; and Ward Thomas, *The Ethics of Destruction: Norms and Force in International Relations* (Ithaca, N.Y.: Cornell University Press, 2001).

12. See Alexander B. Downes, *Targeting Civilians in War* (Ithaca, N.Y.: Cornell University Press, 2008); and Daryl G. Press, Scott D. Sagan, and Benjamin A. Valentino, "Atomic Aversion: Experimental Evidence on Taboos, Traditions, and the Non-Use of Nuclear Weapons," *American Political Science Review*, Vol. 107, No. 1 (February 2013), pp. 188–206, doi:10.1017/S0003055412000597.

13. Tannenwald, *The Nuclear Taboo*, p. 10. For the alternative view that the non-use of nuclear weapons is caused by U.S. leaders' concerns about setting a precedent that might lead to future nuclear weapons use by others, see T.V. Paul, *The Tradition of Non-Use of Nuclear Weapons* (Stanford, Calif.: Stanford University Press, 2009); and Scott D. Sagan, "Realist Perspectives on Ethical Norms and Weapons

of Mass Destruction," in Sohail H. Hashmi and Steven P. Lee, eds., *Ethics and Weapons of Mass Destruction: Religious and Secular Perspectives* (Cambridge: Cambridge University Press, 2004), pp. 73–95.

14. Tannenwald, *The Nuclear Taboo*, p. 14.

15. Ibid., p. 374. See also Beatrice Heuser, *The Bomb: Nuclear Weapons in Their Historic, Strategic, and Ethical Context* (London: Longmans, 2000).

16. NSC meeting, February 11, 1953, *Foreign Relations of the United States (FRUS), 1952–54*, Vol. 15, Part 1: *Korea* (Washington, D.C.: Government Printing Office [GPO], 1984), p. 770, quoted in Nina Tannenwald, "The Nuclear Taboo: The United States and the Normative Basis of Nuclear Non-Use," *International Organization*, Vol. 53, No. 3 (Summer 1999), pp. 448–449, https://doi.org/10.1162/002081899550959.

17. William Burr and Jeffrey P. Kimball, *Nixon's Nuclear Specter: The Secret Alert of 1969, Madman Diplomacy, and the Vietnam War* (Lawrence: University of Kansas Press, 2015); and Scott D. Sagan and Jeremi Suri, "The Madman Nuclear Alert: Secrecy, Signaling, and Safety in October 1969," *International Security*, Vol. 27, No. 4 (Spring 2003), pp. 150–183, doi:10.1162/016228803321951126.

18. Pinker, *The Better Angels of Our Nature*, p. 573.

19. Ibid., p. 572. For analyses of the evolution of the definitions of combatant and noncombatant, see Helen M. Kinsella, *The Image before the Weapon: A Critical History of the Distinction between Combatant and Noncombatant* (Ithaca, N.Y.: Cornell University Press, 2011); and Sahr Conway-Lanz, *Collateral Damage: Americans, Noncombatant Immunity, and Atrocity after World War II* (New York: Routledge, 2006).

20. Pinker, *The Better Angels of Our Nature*, pp. 270–271.

21. Downes, *Targeting Civilians in War*, p. 44.

22. Ibid., pp. 3–4.

23. Ibid., p. 3.

24. Christopher Gelpi, Peter D. Feaver, and Jason Reifler, *Paying the Human Costs of War: American Public Opinion and Casualties in Military Conflicts* (Princeton, N.J.: Princeton University Press, 2009), p. 255 (emphasis in the original).

25. Ibid., p. 256.

26. See Cécile Fabre, *Cosmopolitan War* (Oxford: Oxford University Press, 2012).

27. Gelpi, Feaver, and Reifler, *Paying the Human Costs of War*, p. 256.

28. Ibid., p. 257.

29. Press, Sagan, and Valentino, "Atomic Aversion," p. 199.

30. Ibid., p. 202.

31. In another experiment dealing with a U.S. attack on an al-Qaida nuclear weapons development facility in Syria, however, Press, Sagan, and Valentino found that 52 percent of the American public was willing to approve of a nuclear strike that killed 25,000 foreign noncombatants. See ibid.

32. For prominent examples of the use of survey experiments in international relations, see Michael Tomz, "Domestic Audience Costs in International Relations: An Experimental Approach," *International Organization*, Vol. 61, No. 4 (Fall 2007), pp. 821–840, doi:10.1017/S0020818307070282; and Joshua D. Kertzer et al., "Moral Support: How Moral Values Shape Foreign Policy Attitudes," *Journal of Politics*, Vol. 76, No. 3 (July 2014), pp. 825–840, doi:10.1017/S0022381614000073.

33. A Pew poll administered in April 2015, two months prior to our survey, found that 76 percent of Americans held very or somewhat unfavorable opinions of Iran. Only 14 percent held favorable or somewhat favorable views. See "Pew Global Attitudes Project Poll, April 2015" (Washington, D.C.: Pew Global Attitudes Project, 2015).

34. Tannenwald, *The Nuclear Taboo*, p. 11.

35. See doi:10.7910/DVN/9XHAPW/.

36. See Gelpi, Feaver, and Reifler, *Paying the Human Costs of War*, pp. 9–10, 236.

37. The nearly 13-percentage-point difference between those citing ethical or precedential reasons for opposing the strike in the nuclear scenario versus those doing so in the conventional scenario was not statistically significant ($p=0.14$), however, possibly because the small numbers of subjects who opposed the strike reduced the statistical power of our difference of means tests.

38. In related work focusing on U.S. public opinion on the use of conventional weapons in Afghanistan, we directly measured the public's willingness to accept foreign civilian casualties if doing so would decrease U.S. military casualties. We found that the public was extremely sensitive to U.S. military losses. Holding the probability of successfully completing the mission constant, we found that a slight majority of the public was willing to accept the deaths of 5 U.S. troops if those deaths would avert the deaths of 200 foreign civilians. Nearly three-quarters of Americans opposed the mission, however, if it would cost 40 U.S. military lives to avert the deaths of 200 foreign civilians. See Scott D. Sagan and Benjamin A. Valentino, "Just a War Theory? American Public Opinion on Ethics in Military Combat," Stanford University and Dartmouth College, 2017.

39. Gallup, *The Gallup Poll: Public Opinion, 1935–1971*, Vol. 1, pp. 521–522. It is important to note, however, that these polls were conducted at different times during the war, and that the brutality of the campaign in the Pacific, especially the large numbers of Americans killed during the fighting in early 1945, likely also influenced the increased support for using poison gas by the summer of 1945 as compared to September 1944.

40. Lisa Brandes, "Public Opinion, International Security, and Gender: The United States and Great Britain since 1945," Ph.D. dissertation, Yale University, 1994, p. 166.

41. Richard C. Eichenberg, "Gender Differences in Public Attitudes toward the Use of Force by the United States, 1990–2003," *International Security*, Vol. 28, No. 1 (Summer 2003), pp. 111–112, doi:10.1162/016228803322427992. See also Dan Reiter, "The Positivist Study of Gender and International Relations," *Journal of Conflict Resolution*, Vol. 59, No. 7 (October 2015), pp. 1301–1326, doi:10.1177/0022002714560351.

42. Deborah Jordan Brooks and Benjamin A. Valentino, "A War of One's Own: Understanding the Gender Gap in Support for War," *Public Opinion Quarterly*, Vol. 75, No. 2 (Summer 2011), pp. 270–286, doi:10.1093/poq/nfr005.

43. Hadley Cantril and Mildred B. Strunk, *Public Opinion, 1935–46* (Princeton, N.J.: Princeton University Press, 1951), p. 20.

44. For further discussion of this issue, see Benjamin A. Valentino, "Moral Character or Character of War? American Public Opinion on Targeting of Civilians in Time of War," *Daedalus*, Vol. 145, No. 4 (Fall 2016), pp. 127–138, doi:10.1162/DAED_a_00417.

Virginia Page Fortna

DO TERRORISTS WIN?
Rebels' Use of Terrorism and Civil War Outcomes

■ ■ ■

How effective is terrorism? This question has generated lively scholarly debate and is of obvious importance to policymakers. However, most existing studies of terrorism are not well equipped to answer this question for a simple reason—they lack an appropriate comparison. Few studies of terrorism have compared conflicts in which terrorism is used with those in which it is not. This article examines the outcomes of civil wars to assess whether rebel groups that use terrorism fare better than those who eschew this tactic.[1] I argue that terrorism is not a particularly effective tactic for winning outright, nor for obtaining concessions at the bargaining table. On balance, terrorists undermine rather than enhance their military effectiveness by attacking civilians indiscriminately. If it does not help rebels achieve their ultimate political goals, one might reasonably ask why rebels ever employ terrorism? A second finding of this research provides a possible answer. Wars in which terrorism is used last longer than others, suggesting that terrorism enhances rebel organizations' survival. Rebels thus appear to face a dilemma: what helps them survive comes at the expense of the larger political goals for which they ostensibly fight.

In the next section I review the literature and debate over the effectiveness of terrorism and argue that civil wars provide a fruitful testing ground for evaluating the relative success of terrorism. I then present definitions and explain how "terrorist" rebel groups are distinguished from others, as well as how I use war outcomes to gauge "success." Next I examine the strategic uses of terrorism to evaluate theoretically its advantages and disadvantages, and to generate hypotheses about its effects on war outcomes. In the following section I discuss how selection effects and endogeneity issues affect this study. After describing the data, I turn to empirical findings. * * * The data support hypotheses that although civil wars involving terrorism last longer than other wars, terrorist rebel groups are less likely than those who eschew terrorism to achieve outright victory or concessions at the negotiating table. Terrorism may be somewhat less ineffective against democracies, but even in this context, terrorists do not win.

State of the Debate

A number of authors have argued that terrorism works. Pape, for example, argues that suicide terrorism is on the rise because terrorists have learned that it pays, generating "gains for the terrorists' political cause" about half the time.[2] Similarly, Kydd and Walter argue that terrorism

From *International Organization* 69 (Summer 2015): 519–56.
Some of the author's notes have been omitted.

more generally "is a form of costly signaling" and that "terrorism often works."[3] Thomas argues that terrorism gives rebels the "power to hurt," inducing governments to negotiate and make concessions.[4] Some scholars suggest that although terrorism can sometimes backfire and effects may be nonlinear, it is, on balance, effective.[5]

Others, however, maintain that terrorism is not particularly effective. Abrahms argues that the prevailing view of terrorism as a potent coercive strategy rests on scant empirical footing, and that campaigns of violence that primarily target civilians almost never succeed.[6] Jones and Libicki conclude that "there is rarely a causal link between the use of terrorism and the achievement of [group] goals."[7] Merari and Cronin both argue that, although terrorist groups may achieve partial or tactical (for example, recruitment) objectives, they almost never achieve their strategic goals in full.[8]

Some of this debate hinges on what one counts as success: only full achievement of the group's goals, or any political concession, or achievement of intermediate goals meant eventually to help a group achieve its goals?—an issue I return to below.[9] Whether terrorism is considered effective also depends on what the chances of success, however defined, are if terrorism is not used. Not surprisingly, terrorists achieve higher levels of success when groups have limited objectives that do not impinge on the core interests of the target state.[10] So perhaps terrorism only "works" when achieving political change is relatively easy. Success rates cannot be judged without some sort of context.

Claims that terrorism "works" or "does not work" reflect a causal argument; that terrorism leads, or does not lead, to political change in favor of the group using it. Implicit in any causal argument is an argument about variation: using terrorism leads to more change (or no more change) than not using terrorism. But few empirical studies examine variation on the independent variable; most look only at terrorist organizations, with no comparison with otherwise similar groups that do not use terrorism.[11]

I use data on civil wars to introduce variation. Civil wars represent a universe of cases in which a group has a serious enough perceived grievance against the state to launch a violent rebellion in which some groups choose to use terrorism as part of their repertoire of tactics whereas others do not. Data on civil wars are relatively well developed, allowing me to explore and control for a number of factors that are likely to affect both this tactical choice and the outcome I wish to explain.

The study of terrorism and the study of civil wars have generally proceeded in isolation from one another.[12] However, if one thinks of prominent cases such as the LTTE in Sri Lanka, the PLO or Hamas in Palestine, the IRA in Northern Ireland, the PKK in Turkey, or the MNLF and MILF in the Philippines, it is clear that much terrorism takes place in the context of civil war. Indeed, the vast majority—75 to 85 percent by most estimates—of all terrorism is domestic.[13] This article merges insights from the two literatures.

This raises the thorny question of the definition of terrorism, however, because some scholars maintain that in the Venn diagram of political violence, terrorism and civil war do not overlap, whereas for others they overlap completely.

Definitions

"Terrorist" Rebel Groups

Defining terrorism is notoriously difficult; as the cliché goes, one person's terrorist is another's freedom fighter, and this is particularly true in the context of civil wars. Because it is such a loaded term, its definition is highly contested.[14] I define *terrorist rebel groups* as those who employ a systematic campaign of indiscriminate violence against public civilian targets to influence a wider audience. The ultimate aim of this type of violence is to coerce the government to make political concessions, up to and including conceding outright defeat. This definition allows for distinctions among rebel groups and does not include in the definition other variables whose relationship to terrorism I wish to examine.[15]

For many scholars of terrorism, though by no means all,[16] a defining characteristic of terrorism is that it deliberately attacks civilians.[17] This distinguishes terrorism from "normal" rebel attacks on military targets. However, civilian targeting is ubiquitous; almost all rebel groups (and almost all governments involved in civil wars) target individuals as a form of "control" to force cooperation and deter civilians from providing aid to the opponents.[18] Violence against civilians is thus too broad a criterion by itself to distinguish terrorist rebel groups from others. Moreover, this type of selective violence against civilians to punish or deter collaboration with the other side is not what most people think of when they think of "terrorism."

By narrowing the definition to deliberately indiscriminate violence, I exclude this more common form of violence and focus on that which makes terrorism so terrifying: its randomness; and so outrageous: the intentional targeting of innocent civilians (as opposed to collaborators). This definition also captures what the literature often refers to as the "symbolic" nature of terrorism: that it aims not to influence the victims of the violence but to send a political message to a wider audience.[19] Stanton distinguishes strategies of "coercion" from the above-mentioned control by focusing on "the use of violence as a means of forcing the opponent to take a particular desired action—to agree to negotiations, to reduce its war aims, to make concessions, to surrender." This strategy is "intended not to coerce civilians themselves, but to coerce *the opponent* into making concessions."[20] An attack on a public market, for example, is intended to influence the government, not shoppers.

Stanton's strategies of "destabilization" and "cleansing," which she distinguishes from coercion, also sound like terrorism to some degree. These involve attacks on civilians intended to destabilize a country or to force people to flee by terrorizing the population. However, Stanton's operational coding of these strategies involve massacres and "scorched earth" campaigns (burning homes and crops), which, although terrifying to their victims are farther from our intuitive understanding of terrorism than the indiscriminate attacks she codes under coercion.[21] Thus, not all who "terrify" a population are "terrorist" as I use the term here—groups such as the RUF in Sierra Leone or the Lord's Resistance Army in Uganda are not coded as terrorist under my definition, for example. Some terrorist groups (such as the FMLN or the IRA, depending on one's political leanings) might thus be considered morally preferable to some nonterrorist groups.[22] Indeed, it is important not to let judgments of the morality of a group's cause influence the use of the term *terrorism*.

War Outcomes and Relative Success

Civil wars end in one of four ways: either the government or the rebels win outright, or they reach a peace agreement of some sort, or the rebellion peters out. These possibilities can be thought of as representing a continuum of success for the rebel group. Government victory and rebel victory obviously lie at opposite ends of this continuum, as depicted in Figure 6.4. Peace agreements represent a second-best outcome from the rebels' perspective. Agreements entail concessions and compromise by both sides, but since rebels fight to change the status quo, whereas governments fight to maintain it, government concessions represent at least partial political victory for rebels. Moreover, agreements require the government to accept rebels as legitimate negotiating partners, itself a significant concession. Indeed,

Figure 6.4. A Continuum of Rebel Political Success

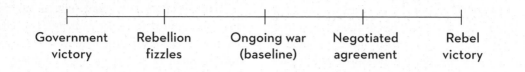

| Government victory | Rebellion fizzles | Ongoing war (baseline) | Negotiated agreement | Rebel victory |

many civil wars coded as ending in an agreement could easily be considered rebel victories in political if not military terms. For example, the peace agreement between South Africa and the ANC represented the fulfillment of that group's primary goal, the end of apartheid.[23]

Second worst from the rebels' perspective are wars that end when a formerly full-scale rebellion fizzles out with violence ending or dropping to such low levels that the conflict is no longer considered ongoing. Although the rebel group may still exist, it is not causing much trouble at this low level of violence. Most rebellions in this category have been largely defeated, though not eliminated outright.[24] Examples include Sendero Luminoso in Peru, which ended its fight after the capture of its leader; and the MQM in Pakistan, which "decided to pursue a peaceful strategy rather than a violent one" after the Pakistani military dealt "a serious blow to the militants."[25]

Scholars in the effectiveness debate differ on how to treat conflicts that have not yet ended. Should ongoing conflict count as failure because rebels have not yet achieved their goals,[26] or success because they have avoided defeat?[27] In relation to a group's ultimate political objectives, one can treat ongoing conflict as a baseline category of intermediate success; neither side has been able to defeat the other, no significant concessions have been agreed to, and the rebels continue to inflict pain on the country. However, rebel groups are organizations, and as such they seek to survive.[28] Ongoing war therefore represents success on that dimension. As I shall show, the goals of political change and organizational survival may be in tension.

Advantages and Disadvantages of Terrorism

Terrorism has both advantages and disadvantages. I argue that the advantages tend to help rebels survive rather than to win, whereas the disadvantages make it harder for terrorists to achieve political concessions or to win outright. Much of the literature considers the usefulness of terrorism in isolation. The implicit comparison is thus effectiveness relative to doing nothing. But how effective is terrorism relative to other tactics a rebel organization could employ? All rebel groups attack military targets; terrorist rebel groups, as defined here, are distinguished by the fact that they also purposively attack civilians indiscriminately to influence a wider audience.[29]

There are several potential audiences to consider. The primary audience is the government, which rebels hope to induce to make concessions or to give up the fight. There are also secondary audiences, those whose support rebels attempt to win, and those rebels hope to induce to put pressure on the government. Within the country, there is an "aggrieved" population on whose behalf the rebel organization claims to fight.[30] There are also civilians on the other side of the conflict—those who support the government or generally consent to be governed by it. For lack of a better term, I refer to this group as the "mainstream." It includes both those who benefit from and support the state and its use of violence against the rebel group and "fence-sitters." Finally, there are international audiences—particularly those (great or regional powers, neighboring states, relevant diasporas) in a position to aid or pressure either side of the conflict.

Terrorism has obvious disadvantages as a military tactic. Attacking civilians indiscriminately in public places is not useful for taking or holding territory or the capital. It is thus much less effective than other tactics for winning outright. Unlike attacks on the government's military forces, or even other types of attacks on civilians (such as ethnic cleansing of territory, or attacks to prevent collaboration with the enemy), indiscriminate attacks on public targets such as markets or buses have no direct military value.

The terrorism literature identifies a number of less direct ways through which it is thought to "work." These include (1) attrition, (2) advertising the cause, (3) provocation, (4) outbidding, and (5) spoiling.[31] Of these, attrition is arguably the most important because it entails the most direct (or least indirect) link between rebel actions and the achievement of political goals. The other strategies aim at intermediate goals, including mobilizing support, and/or preserving organizational survival, often in competition among groups claiming to represent the same aggrieved population. I discuss each of these strategies in turn, considering both the advantages and disadvantages of terrorism for the rebels' larger military effort.[32]

Attrition

Terrorism is used as part of an attrition strategy, meant to inflict pain on the other side so as to undermine the adversary's will, rather than its capacity, to fight.[33] However, terrorist attacks are not the only way to fight a war of attrition. Insurgency or guerrilla warfare tactics classically employ hit-and-run attacks to dog the adversary's forces and undermine its will to continue the fight. Unlike other forms of insurgency, terrorism, by definition, does not target military forces,

and thus does not degrade the government's military capacity.

Terrorist attacks do entail some advantages in their sheer ability to inflict pain in a cost-effective manner. It is less costly (in material terms) to attack "soft" civilian targets than "hard" military ones. Because terrorism attacks targets that are inherently hard to defend, preventing every single attack is difficult. As Condoleezza Rice described counterterrorism efforts (paraphrasing the IRA): "They only have to be right once. We have to be right 100 percent of the time."[34] It takes relatively few people to organize and carry out a terrorist attack, making full elimination of terrorist groups difficult; mere remnants can continue to inflict damage.

Terrorism is also a relatively cheap way to impose costs on civilians such that the mainstream population pressures its government to give in to terrorist demands. There is some evidence that this can be effective, up to a point,[35] perhaps particularly so in democracies (see hypothesis 4). However, terrorism can also induce pressure on the government not to concede by rallying the mainstream population around the flag. Moreover, many governments have a stated policy never to negotiate with terrorists. This is often observed only in the breach, and governments are always reluctant to negotiate with and grant concessions to any rebel group. The rhetoric of nonnegotiation with terrorists can nonetheless make it especially politically difficult to do so.

Terrorism is also thought to be a communication device, meant to signal strength and resolve, to convince the opponent that the war of attrition will be long and costly.[36] Compared with not attacking at all, terrorism may indeed be effective as a costly signal, but compared with attacks against the military, the effectiveness of terrorism as a signal of resolve is unclear at best, whereas terrorism signals weakness rather than strength.

Terrorism signals a willingness to use extreme tactics that violate widely held norms and this may be interpreted as a signal of resolve. However, extremism and resolve are not necessarily the same thing. Willingness to attack civilians signals willingness to impose these costs in the future. To the extent that the government cares more about the loss of civilian life than the loss of soldiers' lives, this may provide a signaling advantage to terrorist tactics.

There are also downsides to sending such signals, however. By deliberately violating the norm against targeting noncombatants, terrorists place themselves beyond the pale, painting themselves as untrustworthy—likely to break their promises rather than abide by a negotiated agreement.[37] The targets of terrorism may also infer from the extreme nature of the tactics used that the groups' demands are also extreme; that terrorists seek to destroy their society.[38] Opponents will therefore view negotiations as an act of appeasement. Use of extreme tactics may credibly signal resolve to carry on the fight, but it undermines the credibility of promises to reward concessions with peace.

Terrorism can also make it harder for rebels to accept concessions. Terrorist rebel groups may be particularly suspicious of the government in any potential negotiations to end the conflict. This may be, in part, because of a selection effect if only particularly hardline groups choose terrorist tactics. But it could also be induced by this choice. Having committed terrorist attacks, rebels may not believe that they will be accepted into a peaceful postwar political order.[39] Government promises of amnesty or of a power-sharing role for rebels may therefore not be credible to terrorist rebel groups. Mistrust and problems of credible commitment plague all civil wars,[40] but terrorism makes them even worse. For a number of reasons, then, signaling extremism can make one's would-be negotiating partner less, rather than more, willing to make political concessions.

As a signal of strength, moreover, terrorist attacks are clearly inferior. Despite the empirical (non)finding presented shortly, the deeply embedded conventional wisdom is that terrorism is a "weapon of the weak." To be credible, signals have to be costly. Precisely because it is less costly to attack "soft" civilian targets than hardened military ones, terrorism signals military impotence rather than strength.

In sum, terrorism is a cheap way to inflict costs in a war of attrition, and is hard to eliminate fully, fostering organizational survival. On the other hand, it creates pressures on the government not to concede, and its very affordability undermines its value as a credible signal.

Rebellion, particularly insurgency or guerrilla warfare, as Mao famously stressed, requires a supportive population.[41] Though Mao would disagree, the terrorism literature generally maintains that terrorism is a strategy used to mobilize support.[42] Do indiscriminate attacks on civilians enhance or undermine popular support?[43]

Advertising the Cause

One way terrorism is thought to mobilize support is by publicizing grievances—"propaganda of the deed"—to put the cause on the political agenda.[44] Because they are more outrageous, terrorist attacks usually generate more publicity than attacks against the military. This attention can create a sense of urgency about resolving a political issue.

At whom is such a strategy aimed? Publicizing grievances probably plays less of a role in situations that have escalated to the level of civil war than in lower-level conflicts. In civil wars, both the aggrieved and the mainstream population are already aware of the grievances. Terrorism can, however, publicize grievances to international audiences; or in some conflicts over secession or autonomy, to advertise the plight of an aggrieved population whose lives are quite remote to citizens in other parts of the country.

The disadvantages of targeting civilians to generate their support are obvious. Those who see such attacks as justified given their view of the righteousness of the cause, are those most likely already to support the rebellion. Terrorism "preaches to the choir." Those potential supporters who remain to be mobilized—less radical or politicized members of the aggrieved population, "fence-sitters," and the international community—are more likely to feel revulsion at the taking of innocent life.[45] Moreover, as Abrahms argues, the publicity gained by terrorism often focuses on the "senseless" or irrational nature of the violence rather than the grievances or demands the terrorist group wishes to make.[46] In the battle for legitimacy and "hearts and minds," terrorism is counterproductive.[47]

Provocation

The literature also suggests that terrorism can be used to mobilize support by provoking the state to overreact.[48] This strategy hopes to induce the government to crack down on the aggrieved population, creating new grievances and exacerbating old ones, causing an increase in support for the rebel organization. Because they violate norms of warfare, terrorist attacks may be more likely than attacks on military targets to provoke an overreaction. However, using terrorism for this purpose is risky for two reasons. First, successful provocation requires that the aggrieved will blame the government for the crackdown, rather than the rebel group that provoked it.[49] Second, by attacking civilians, terrorist attacks make it easier for the government to justify—both domestically and internationally—draconian measures to crush the rebellion. The opprobrium directed against a government that employs extreme measures will be lower when it is fighting a terrorist rebel group than a nonterrorist rebel group.[50] For provocation to work, the rebels must be able to goad the government into a "middling level of brutality."[51] A government strongly committed to human rights is difficult to provoke, whereas one willing to employ extreme brutality in its fight will be able to wipe out the rebels and the constituency they claim to represent.[52] In this Goldilocks equation, terrorism may induce governments to move from "too soft" to "just right," but can also make governments "too hard," allowing them to justify measures to crush the rebels rather than creating a backlash of support in their favor.

Outbidding

Terrorism is thought useful as a means of competing with other rival groups that claim to represent the same aggrieved population. Outbidding is intended to mobilize popular support for a group by demonstrating commitment to the cause and ability to fight for the interests of the aggrieved.[53] But why should the aggrieved population support groups that use terrorism over those who do not? Kydd and Walter respond that it is advantageous to be represented by an agent who will drive a harder bargain than oneself, and extreme tactics signal a tougher negotiating stance.[54] This argument discounts the cost of continued conflict to the aggrieved population, however. Supporting a group whose reservation price is higher than one's own by definition rules out settlements one would prefer to ongoing conflict. If one fears the government will never compromise (Kydd and Walter's second answer), then one should prefer not a more extreme agent, but a militarily more competent one. Given that terrorism signals military weakness rather than strength, it is unclear how attacking civilians rather than military targets might win political support.[55] Although competition among groups and factions is undoubtedly an important motive for rebel behavior, it is questionable how terrorism serves these competitive purposes better than other tactics.

Spoiling

Spoiling is another manifestation of competition among rebel groups. It occurs when a more extreme group is threatened by the prospect of peace between the government and a more moderate group. By launching a terrorist attack and inducing doubt about the moderates' ability or willingness to control terrorism, extremists can derail peace.[56] This can help ensure the survival of an extremist group that might otherwise become obsolete in the face of peace. Spoilers presumably hope for an eventual outcome more favorable to their cause than the one moderates were willing to accept, but spoiling does nothing to ensure this more favorable outcome rather than a less favorable one. Terrorism driven by spoiling thus contributes to survival but does nothing to help a group achieve its political goals.

Hypotheses

This evaluation of the pros and cons of terrorism relative not to inaction but to other types of attacks (notably attacks on military targets), leads to several hypotheses. On balance, terrorism generally undermines military effectiveness. It has no direct value for winning the war outright; it does not degrade the government's military capability, nor can it be used to take and hold territory. It is a cheap way to inflict costs on the enemy and may help signal resolve, but its low cost also signals weakness. It may help advertise the cause, but it also drives potential supporters away. It can provoke a government into self-destructive overreaction, but it can also help the government justify draconian measures in their fight against rebels.

H1:   Terrorist rebels are less likely than nonterrorist rebels to achieve military victory.

Terrorism also makes the second-best outcome for rebels less likely. Governments will grant fewer concessions to a less militarily effective opponent. Moreover, rebels' use of extreme tactics makes it harder for the government to negotiate an agreement and exacerbates the problems of trust and credible commitment that plague all civil wars.

H2:   Rebels using terrorism are less likely than those who eschew terrorism to achieve negotiated settlements.

There are, however, some advantages to terrorism for organizational survival. Terrorist rebel groups are hard to eliminate entirely, and spoiling can prevent peace with more moderate groups from making extremist groups obsolete. For both these reasons, and because terrorism prevents negotiated settlements that would otherwise end the war more quickly, terrorism should increase civil war duration.

H3:   Wars involving terrorist rebels are likely to last longer than those involving nonterrorist rebels.

I argue that terrorism is, on balance, ineffective for achieving political goals. But there are several reasons to think that terrorism might be relatively more effective against democracies than against autocracies. First, democratic governments are likely more sensitive to civilian loss of life.[57] If terrorism works by inflicting pain on civilians who then pressure their government to make concessions, then it stands to reason that the more accountable the government is to popular pressure, the more likely this strategy will work.

Second, democracies are thought to have trouble repressing or preventing and policing terrorist groups.[58] Because they start on the "soft" end of the spectrum, democracies should be more likely provoked into the "just right" level of brutality discussed earlier, whereas nondemocracies will be provoked into a response that is "too hard" and that brutally but effectively represses rebellion.

Terrorism may also be less likely to backfire by undermining support among the aggrieved when its victims are seen as "complicitous" in government policy because they have voted the government into power in democratic elections.[59]

H4: *Terrorism will be more effective against demo-cratic governments than against nondemocratic governments.*

Selection and Potential Confounders

Because I look at the use of terrorism only in the context of civil wars, this study does not cover all terrorist organizations, raising issues of selection bias. The analysis excludes transnational terrorist groups that attack primarily across borders rather than in their home state.[60] It also excludes organizations involved in conflicts that do not meet the standard 1,000 battle death threshold of a civil war.[61] The smallest and weakest groups are thus excluded.[62] Focusing on the deadliest groups is defensible on policy grounds and is necessary for empirical comparison with nonterrorist groups. It does, however, limit generalizability because I evaluate terrorism by only groups capable of mounting civil war, not terrorism relative to other options for those without this capability. The notion that terrorism is used only by those with no other option is belied, however, by the terrorist rebel groups examined in this study, who by definition can mount a civil war.

The selection of organizations involved in civil wars likely overrepresents ethno-nationalist organizations, which are more likely to have clear political or territorial goals that are more easily negotiable than the goals of other types of terrorist organizations.[63] The data used here also exclude coups,[64] which are quite unlikely to involve terrorism and which may be more often successful than other types of rebellion. All of these selection issues bias the study toward finding terrorism successful, and against my own argument.

The temporal bounds of the data used in this study (post-1989) do not cover the era of decolonization, and therefore exclude a set of highly successful rebellions; virtually all of these cases led to independence. Some notable cases of terrorist success (for example, Algeria) are thus omitted. If terrorism was used disproportionally in anticolonial wars of this era (an open empirical question), excluding this era will bias the results away from finding terrorism effective. On the other hand, anticolonial struggles enjoyed particular legitimacy; relationships in that era may not apply to more recent conflicts.

Arguably more important as a concern than selection bias are the thorny issues of endogeneity and spuriousness for although terrorism inflicts random violence, it is not a tactic chosen at random. To assess its effectiveness accurately, I must therefore pay particular attention to any variables that might affect both the use of terrorism and the outcome of the war. The literature on the causes of terrorism, particularly on why terrorism appears in some places rather than others, suggests several potential confounders. I explore the relationships between these factors and the use of terrorism in greater depth elsewhere, but I discuss them briefly here.[65]

The most obvious potential confounding variable is the strength of the rebel group relative to the government. If, as is commonly asserted, terrorism is a "weapon of the weak,"[66] failure to take this into account will make terrorism look less effective than it really is.

The relationship between democracy and terrorism has generated significant theoretical and empirical debate.[67] Many see a positive relationship between democracy and terrorism, in part because terrorism is thought to be more effective against democracies, as discussed earlier.

Terrorism is also thought to be a tactic used by groups with particularly extreme aims. This argument is often tautological: groups that use extreme tactics such as terrorism are considered extremist, therefore extremist groups use terrorism. But it is possible to assess group aims independent of their tactics by focusing on how far rebels' stated aims are from the status quo. I argue elsewhere that in wars over a particular region, secessionist rebels can be considered more extreme than those fighting for autonomy, whereas in wars over control of the state, those who seek to transform society in fundamental ways (for example, by instituting Sharia in a secular state, or communism in a capitalist state, or vice versa) are more extreme than those merely engaged in a power struggle to take the reins of power (the fight between Lissouba and Sassou Nguesso in Congo–Brazzaville is a good example).[68]

Secessionist aims are particularly important to consider because scholars such as Pape and Stanton suggest that terrorism should be especially likely in secessionist conflicts.[69] Fazal suggests just the opposite, however; because separatists desire to become accepted members of the international system, they have incentives to avoid targeting civilians indiscriminately.[70] Scholars have also noted links between religious conflict and terrorism,[71] and between population and/or gross domestic product (GDP) per capita and terrorism.[72] Terrorism as defined here may be less likely in Africa than elsewhere,[73] and may be more likely where rebels do not have the advantage of rough terrain that enables other forms of insurgency.[74] The outbidding argument suggests that terrorism is more likely when there are several rebel groups active as part of the same struggle.[75]

This set of variables by no means exhausts the list of factors that might make rebel groups more likely to choose terrorism—this is obviously an important questions in its own right. For the purposes of this article, however, my focus is on

variables that likely also affect the outcome of war, and whose omission could thus lead to spurious findings about the effectiveness of terrorism.[76]

The Data

The data analyzed here consist of 104 rebel groups involved in full-scale civil wars active between 1989 and 2004. Much of the data come from Cunningham, Gleditsch, and Salehyan's Non-State Actor data set (hereafter CGS),[77] which builds on and expands the well-known Uppsala-PRIO Armed Conflict Data (hereafter UCDP)[78] by identifying each nonstate (or rebel) actor.[79] These data are particularly useful for several reasons. First, the unit of analysis is the government-rebel group dyad, rather than the conflict as is common in many data sets on civil war. Second, the relative strength of the government and each rebel group is coded. The CGS data are time varying, allowing for variables that change over the course of the conflict, for example, changes in the relative strength of the actors, or changes in democracy or economic variables.

The dependent variable is war outcome for each dyad, covering the five possibilities discussed here: government victory, rebel victory, agreement (including peace agreements and ceasefire agreements), wars that fizzle out to "low or no activity" by dropping below twenty-five battle deaths per year, and ongoing conflicts. Outcomes data are from UCDP through 2003; I updated through 2009 and corrected a few cases based on case-specific research.[80]

The measure of the main independent variable, whether a rebel group uses terrorist tactics, comes from Stanton's coding of "high casualty terrorism," a measure of a group's systematic use of "small-scale bombs . . . to attack unambiguously civilian targets" excluding attacks on infrastructure (for example, power stations, pipelines, bridges) which impose costs on civilians, but in which casualties are rare.[81] I use this more restrictive, high-casualty-only measure of terrorism because it best captures the deliberate and indiscriminate killing of civilians on which my definition and theory focus. Of the 104 eases examined here, twenty-four (23 percent) use high-casualty terrorism.

This measure captures groups generally classified as "terrorist" by other sources, such as the LTTE in Sri Lanka, the Taliban in Afghanistan (after 2003), the FARC in Colombia, the Provisional IRA in Northern Ireland, and so on. One advantage of Stanton's data over databases more commonly used in the terrorism literature is that this minimizes some of the well-known geographical biases in the terrorism data, particularly their overrepresentation of terrorism in Western democracies and underrepresentation or spotty coverage of groups in Africa and other strategically less important (to the US) places. The main disadvantage of this measure is that it is limited to full-scale civil wars active between 1989 and 2004, thus providing the bounds of the empirical analysis. Merging the Stanton and time varying CGS data yields 104 cases and 566 observations over time.[82] * * *

Stanton found surprisingly little variation over time within conflicts in the types of strategies rebels and governments used in terms of targeting civilians. With very few exceptions, groups that used terrorism did so throughout the conflict, whereas those who eschewed the tactic early on continued to avoid it later.[83] This in itself is quite interesting, and suggests that rebel organizations' choices about using terrorism are remarkably "sticky."

The CGS data include a five-point indicator of rebel group strength relative to the government, ranging from much weaker to much stronger. This variable summarizes assessments of the rebel group's ability to mobilize supporters, arms procurement ability, and fighting capacity, which Cunningham and colleagues argue capture the rebel group's ability to target government forces, or "offensive strength."[84] To capture the effects of war aims, I include two dummy variables. The first marks whether the group seeks full independence and is taken from Coggins's data on secessionist movements.[85] The second differentiates among groups fighting for control of the center, marking those who aim to transform society in fundamental ways. This I coded myself, based on case descriptions in the CGS data coding notes, Minorities at Risk (MAR), START's Terrorist Organization Profiles (TOPs), UCDP's case summaries, and case-specific sources.[86] Together, the independence and transform society dummy variables can be compared with an omitted category of relatively "moderate" rebels who aim either for autonomy, or who are engaged in power struggles at the top without a desire to transform society.[87] Because this is a newly coded variable, Figures 6.5 and 6.6 provide information about its relationship with both terrorism and war outcomes, respectively. From this bivariate look at the data, we see that moderate rebels appear to be less likely to use terrorism and more likely to succeed, making inclusion of this variable particularly important to avoid spuriousness.

■   ■   ■

Which Groups Use Terrorism?

Before turning to tests of the hypotheses, I take a brief detour to address the issue of spuriousness, examining the effects of potentially confounding variables on the use of terrorism. Of the rebel groups examined in this study, fewer than a quarter used terrorism as a tactic in their fight against the government, whereas the rest did not. What accounts for this variation? [The data, not shown in this excerpt,] shows the results of logistic analysis with terrorist rebel group as the dependent variable.

Figure 6.5. War Aims and Percent Terrorist

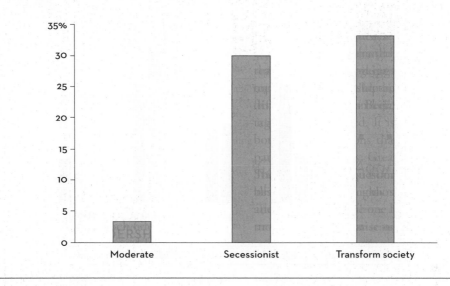

* * * Analysis of terrorism as the dependent variable, rather than the independent variable as it is in the rest of the article, suggests that terrorism is most likely in civil wars in democracies, where rebels face governments representing a different religion, and is seldom seen in Africa (indeed in the data used in this study, there are no cases of high-casualty terrorism by African rebel groups).[88]

Given how deeply entrenched it is, the conventional wisdom that terrorism is more likely to be used by weaker groups receives surprisingly weak support. The relationship between relative strength and terrorism is negative, but it is never statistically significant.[89] I also find that the apparent link between a group's war aims and its use of terrorism seen in Figure 6.5 disappears once other variables are controlled for. Those fighting for secession are, if anything, less likely to use terrorism, whereas those aiming to transform society appear more likely to do so, but neither effect is significant. Together, these findings indicate that the extremity of a group's aims are not necessarily associated with the extremity of its tactics. * * *

Do Terrorist Rebels Win? The Effects of Terrorism on War Outcomes

Figure 6.7 shows the percentage of terrorist and nonterrorist rebellions ending in each outcome. Although these bivariate relationships obviously do not yet take into account potentially confounding variables, the figures do suggest preliminary support for H1 to H3. Most tellingly, of the groups examined here none of those that deliberately killed large numbers of civilians through terrorist attacks won its fight outright.[90] Peace agreements, which I argue represent significant concessions to the rebel cause, are also much less frequent when rebels use terrorism. Meanwhile, government victories and wars ending through low or no activity are slightly more common in civil wars involving terrorism. Wars in which rebels used terror were much more likely to be ongoing as of 2009 than were wars with nonterrorist rebels, suggesting that terrorism makes wars particularly difficult to terminate.

Figure 6.6. War Aims and Percent in Each War Outcome

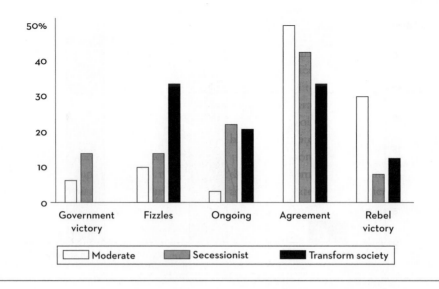

* * * Figure 6.8 depict[s] the survival function for wars in which terrorism is and is not used.[91] As expected, civil wars in which rebels use terrorism last longer than those in which rebels do not; terrorism contributes to organizational survival.

■   ■   ■

The basic pattern in the bivariate analysis represented in Figure 6.7 generally holds, even when potential confounders are controlled for. Although there is no significant difference between ongoing war (the omitted baseline category) and rebel defeat or wars that fizzle out, the "good" outcomes for rebels—peace agreements and rebel victory—are both significantly less likely, relative to ongoing war, when rebels employ terrorism as a tactic, supporting H1 and H2. * * * The predicted probability of a war ending in an agreement is 6.6 percent for rebels that do not resort to terrorism, but only 1 percent for those who do. The predicted probability of a rebel victory is low for all rebellions, but drops from 3.4 to 0 percent for those who employ terrorism.

I also test these hypotheses with a competing risks model. * * * This analysis indicates that the use of terrorism increases the risk of government defeat by more than four times. Unlike the multinomial logit results, this effect is statistically significant. Terrorism has no appreciable effect on the likelihood of war fizzling out. Meanwhile, the use of terrorism reduces the likelihood that rebels reach a negotiated agreement by 80 percent, and given that there are no cases of rebel victories by terrorist rebels, the competing risks model predicts that terrorism reduces the chance of a rebel victory to zero; both results easily pass tests of statistical significance. In other words, I again find strong support for H1 and H2.

■   ■   ■

Figure 6.9 shows the results of the competing risks analysis graphically, plotting the cumulative incidence rate of each outcome over time for terrorist and nonterrorist rebels, holding other variables at their mean or modal values. As can

Figure 6.7. Terrorism and Percent in Each War Outcome

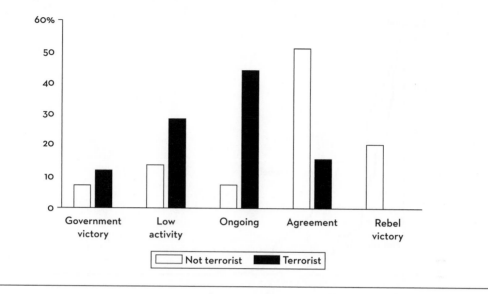

be seen, the incidence of the best outcomes for rebels, negotiated agreement and rebel victory, are lower for those who resort to terrorism, whereas the worst outcome, government victory, is higher for terrorist rebels. In sum, rebel groups who deliberately and indiscriminately kill civilians are, all else equal, much less likely to win outright or to achieve concessions in the form of an agreement than are nonterrorist rebel groups, but are no less likely to fizzle out or be defeated rather than to live to fight another day.

I turn, finally, to analysis of the relative effects of terrorism against democratic and nondemocratic governments. An initial look at the cases is consistent with H4; of the terrorist rebel groups that succeeded in reaching a negotiated agreement, three out of four fought democratic governments.[92] * * *

■   ■   ■

[However,] I find only mixed support for H4 overall. The negative effects of terrorism are smaller against democracies, but not always significantly so.

Terrorist rebels may be somewhat more likely to succeed against democratic governments than non-democratic governments, but they are still less likely to succeed than rebels who do not use terrorism.

Conclusion

Research on terrorism has exploded since 2001 for obvious reasons. However, the ability of this literature to answer fundamental questions has been hampered by a lack of variation on the phenomenon. This project uses variation within civil wars, namely the fact that some rebel groups use terrorism whereas others do not, to help resolve the debate about the effectiveness of terrorism.

I argue that when it comes to achieving a rebel group's political goals, the disadvantages of terrorism generally outweigh its advantages. It is a cheap way to inflict pain on the other side, and terrorist groups are hard to eliminate completely, but it is useless for taking or holding territory. It may help signal commitment to a cause, but because it is

Figure 6.8. Terrorism and the Duration of War

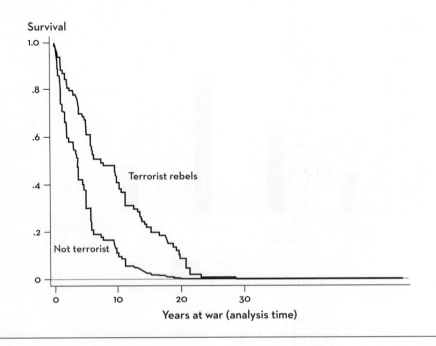

cheap, it signals weakness rather than strength. It may be useful for provoking an overreaction by the government, but it also helps justify draconian measures to crush the rebellion. Its outrageous nature may help bring attention to a cause, but it also undermines legitimacy and alienates potential supporters. Terrorism may help achieve tactical results, but these apparently do not translate into strategic success. It may also be useful at lower levels of conflict or for groups that do not have the ability to wage full-scale war (a question I cannot yet address with available data). Empirically, I find much more support for the argument that terrorism is likely to backfire than for the notion that it is effective. Rebels who use terrorism do not win outright, and they are less likely to achieve concessions in a negotiated outcome. This negative effect may be somewhat attenuated when rebels fight against democracies rather than autocracies. But even in democratic states, terrorist rebel groups do not achieve victory and are unlikely to obtain concessions at the

negotiating table. The short answer to the question "Do terrorist rebels win?" is "No."

If terrorism is so ineffective, one might reasonably ask why rebel groups use it, especially rebels who are not fighting democratic governments.[93] The answer may lie in the finding that civil wars in which terrorism is used last significantly longer than others. The use of terrorism contributes to rebels' organizational survival. Rebels thus appear to face a dilemma—using terrorism as a tactic is good for the immediate goal of survival, but comes at the expense of the long-term political goals for which they are, ultimately (or ostensibly) fighting.

This study begins to shed light on the causes of terrorism, as well as its effects. I examine this question only briefly in this article, focusing on variables that might also affect war outcomes, to avoid spurious results. The results are intriguing, however. They cast doubt on the conventional wisdom that terrorism is a "weapon of the weak." Among rebels fighting full-fledged civil wars, there is surprisingly

Figure 6.9. Terrorism and War Outcomes (Competing Risks)

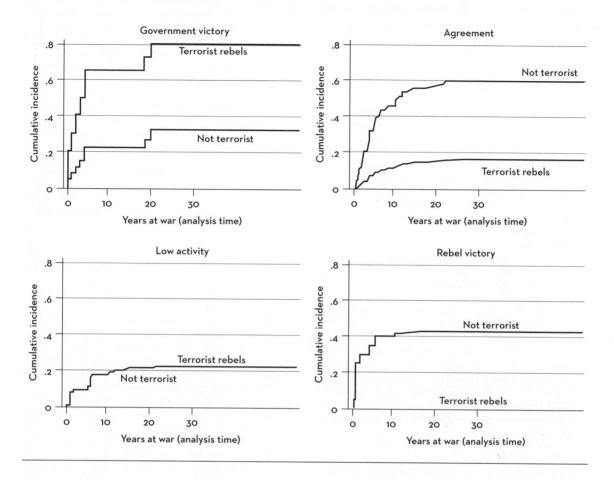

little evidence that weaker groups are more likely to use terrorism than stronger ones. Nor is terrorism more likely, again contrary to conventional wisdom, in secessionist wars, or when rebels profess extreme aims. Terrorism is more likely, however, in civil wars in democracies, as many have argued, and where religion divides rebels from the government they fight. It is much less likely to be used in Africa, a finding that remains to be explained theoretically. Expanding the analysis of why some groups turn to terrorism whereas others do not is an obvious avenue for further research.

Extensions of this study to further our understanding both of where terrorism arises, and how

successful it is, will require new data. Data are currently available for only a relatively short period (1989–2004) and for full-fledged civil wars. Extending the analysis temporally before the end of the Cold War and to include more recent conflicts, and especially to lower level conflicts will strengthen the analysis, and in particular allow fuller testing, for example, of the notion that terrorism is a "weapon of the weak." Further research is also needed to establish how rebel groups navigate the tradeoff between organizational survival and political efficacy.

In the meantime, the empirical evidence presented in this study suggests that terrorism is likely to be a persistent problem—elongating the destruction and suffering that civil wars entail—but not a potent force for political change. Terrorism may help rebel groups survive, but it does not help them get what they want politically.

NOTES

1. This study examines only rebels' use of terrorism, not governments' use of such tactics (state terrorism), thus sidestepping the question of whether the definition of terrorism should be limited to nonstate actors.

2. Pape 2003, 351. Pape is ambiguous on whether his argument applies to terrorism more broadly, arguing that suicide terrorism is to terrorism as lung cancer is to cancer—a particularly virulent strain. Author discussion with Pape, 11 November 2010; and Pape and Feldman 2010.

3. Kydd and Walter 2006, 49–50.

4. Thomas 2014, 807–9.

5. See Bueno de Mesquita and Dickson 2007; Gould and Klor 2010; and Wood and Kathman 2014.

6. See Abrahms 2005, 2006, 43, and 2012.

7. Jones and Libicki 2008, 32–33.

8. See Merari 1993, 238–39; and Cronin 2009, 11. See also Acosta 2014.

9. See Krause 2013.

10. See Jones and Libicki 2008, 34; Abrahms 2006, 53–54; and Pape 2003, 355.

11. Wood and Kathman 2014; and Thomas 2014 are exceptions. Abrahms's work is a partial exception, however because he examines only groups designated as "foreign terrorist organizations" by the U.S. State Department, variation on the independent variable is truncated.

12. Exceptions include Sambanis 2008; Findley and Young 2012a; and Boulden 2009.

13. See Enders, Sandler, and Gaibulloev 2011, 323; LaFree and Dugan 2007, 187; and Asal and Rethemeyer 2008a, 447.

14. McCormick 2003, 473. For a good discussion of definitions, see Merari 1993.

15. Some draw a distinction, often based on group size or strength or even the regime type of the opponent, between terrorism and guerrilla warfare or insurgency. These definitions exclude all rebel groups, and preclude the examination of the relationship, for example, between terrorism and group strength. See Schmid and Jongman 1988, especially 13–18; Silke 1996; Cronin 2006, 31–32; and Sambanis 2008.

16. Many definitions in the literature are so broad as arguably to encompass all rebel groups in all civil wars. Indeed, much of the terrorism literature could easily substitute *rebellion* or *insurgency* for *terrorism*. See, for example, Hoffman 2006, 40.

17. Cronin 2003, 32–33.

18. See Stanton 2009, 31. Kydd and Walter 2006, 66–69, refer to this as "intimidation." See also Kalyvas 2006.

19. See Crenshaw 1981, 379; and McCormick 2003, 474.

20. See Stanton 2009, 34–35, emphasis in the original. In more recent work, Stanton refers to this strategy as "terrorism." Stanton 2013.

21. Ibid., 8–9, 90–93. Some of the groups that engage in these strategies also engage in coercion (Stanton's strategies are not mutually exclusive), so are captured under my definition in any case. Investigating the causes and effectiveness of these other types of strategies of violence against civilians is beyond the scope of this article.

22. On the relative morality of terrorism, see Crenshaw 1983, 3; and Merari 1993, 227–31.

23. Some agreements are reached when rebels are largely defeated (for example, the RUF in Sierra Leone), but in the vast majority of cases, agreements represent political gains for the rebels. Terrorism is also sometimes used to prevent agreements between the government and another more moderate group (see my discussion on spoiling). Kydd and Walter 2002. However, an agreement represents a relatively successful outcome for the group that negotiates it.

24. Some conflicts admittedly fizzle out because rebel demands have been partially met (for example, de facto autonomy for Kurds in Iraq after the Persian Gulf War). However, in most low/no activity cases, rebels were all but defeated militarily, making this category a reasonable proxy.

25. Cunningham, Gleditsch, and Salehyan 2009b, 350.

26. Abrahms 2006.

27. Jones and Libicki 2008.

28. See Wilson 1974, 10; and Acosta 2014.

29. Terrorist groups may also attack civilians in other more discriminating ways, as discussed earlier (for example, to punish collaboration with the enemy). Groups that attack only civilians and no military targets do not reach the threshold of civil war—on selection effects, see section on selection effects.

30. Bueno de Mesquita and Dickson 2007, 369.

31. See Kydd and Walter 2006; Thornton 1964; and Crenshaw 1981 and 2011. Kydd and Walter also discuss intimidation, which as I explained is not considered terrorism in this study.

32. See also Goodwin 2006, especially 2038.

33. See Pape 2003, 346; and Kydd and Walter 2006. See also Arreguín-Toft 2001, especially 105.

34. Quoted in Nina Easton, "Condi: The Should-Be Face of the GOP," *Fortune* (Internet ed.), 22 September 2009.

35. Gould and Klor 2010.

36. See Kydd and Walter 2006, 59–60; Merari 1993; and Wood and Kathman 2014.

37. Bapat 2006, 214.

38. Abrahms 2012, 22.

39. This can make terrorism a self-perpetuating tactic. Laitin and Shapiro 2008, 222–23.

40. Walter 2002.

41. Mao 1937. See also Arreguín-Toft 2001, 104.

42. See, for example, Pape 2003; Bueno de Mesquita and Dickson 2007; and DeNardo 1985.

43. To my knowledge, there is no empirical work supporting the contention that terrorism mobilizes support more effectively than other forms of resistance.

44. See Crenshaw 2011, 118; and Thornton 1964, 82–83.

45. The international reaction may be particularly pronounced after 11 September 2001 and the US-led strengthening of the norm against terrorism.

46. Abrahms 2012, 21.

47. Cronin 2009, 93. Stephan and Chenoweth 2008 argue that violence in general decreases legitimacy and discourages broad-based participation.

48. See Kydd and Walter 2006, especially 69–72; Lake 2002; and Crenshaw 2011, 119.

49. Bueno de Mesquita and Dickson suggest that the aggrieved cannot credibly threaten to punish "extremists" for provoking the government's crackdown because the crackdown itself (by diminishing economic opportunities) makes the population inclined toward direct struggle. Bueno de Mesquita and Dickson 2007, 375. But why should the population react to diminished opportunities brought on by the conflict by choosing to continue it, rather than settle?

50. Hence the attempt by almost all governments to label rebels as "terrorists" whether they employ terrorist tactics or not.

51. Kydd and Walter 2006, 70.

52. Arreguín-Toft 2001, 109.

53. Bloom 2005.

54. Kydd and Walter 2006.

55. Terrorist attacks are likely to signal lack of popular support to the aggrieved, rather than strength. Laitin and Shapiro 2008, 216.

56. Kydd and Walter 2002.

57. See Stanton 2009; and Heger 2010.

58. See Cronin 2006, 31; Crenshaw 1981, 383; Pape 2003, 349–50; and Eubank and Weinberg 1994. But see also Lyall 2010.

59. Goodwin 2006, 2027.

60. It is not clear what the equivalent nonterrorist actors would be for a comparison with transnational terrorist groups.

61. Battle deaths exclude civilian deaths, so this could in theory exclude highly lethal terrorist groups that did not also engage in significant attacks on military targets. I checked the Global Terrorism Database to ensure that no domestic terrorist group responsible for 1,000 deaths was omitted from the study. LaFree and Dugan 2007.

62. In some terrorism databases, the majority of "terrorist" groups have never killed anyone. See Asal and Rethemeyer 2008b; and Sánchez-Cuenca and de la Calle 2009, 35.

63. Cronin 2003, 39–40.

64. Cunningham, Gleditsch, and Salehyan 2009a.

65. Fortna 2014.

66. Among many examples, see Crenshaw 1981, 387; McCormick 2003, 483; Merari 1993, 231; Pape 2003, 349; Sánchez-Cuenca and de la Calle 2009; and DeNardo 1985, 230. Little empirical work has tested this conventional wisdom directly, however. The few existing studies come to contradictory conclusions. See Stanton 2009 and 2013; Goodwin 2006; and Metelits 2010.

67. For a good overview, see Chenoweth 2010 and 2013.

68. Fortna 2014.

69. See Pape 2005, 23; and Stanton 2009, especially chapter 5.

70. Fazal 2013.

71. See Pape 2005, 22; Svensson 2007; Asal and Rethemeyer 2008a; Stanton 2013; and Satana, Inman, and Birnir 2013.

72. See Chenoweth 2010; Sánchez-Cuenca and de la Calle 2009; Burgoon 2006; Li and Schaub 2004; and Abadie 2006.

73. Boulden 2009, 13.

74. Laitin and Shapiro 2008, 213.

75. See Lawrence 2010; Bloom 2005; and Nemeth 2014. But see also Findley and Young 2012b; and Stanton 2009, 232–33.

76. On the relationship between these variables and war outcomes, see Cunningham, Gleditsch, and Salehyan 2009a; DeRouen and Sobek 2004; Fortna 2008; Balch-Lindsay, Enterline, and Joyce 2008; and Mason, Weingarten, and Fett 1999.

77. Cunningham, Gleditsch, and Salehyan 2009a, version 2.4.

78. See Gleditsch et al. 2002.

79. Note that although the overall conflict must reach the 1,000 battle death threshold, it is not the case that each rebel group/government dyad included in this study reaches this threshold.

80. For example, I updated Sri Lanka versus LTTE to reflect the government victory in 2009. This updating introduces possible inconsistencies since some variables are coded only through 2003. I also recoded cases in which a peace agreement was reached shortly after UCDP codes a war as terminated in low activity (for example, the Good Friday Agreement settling the Northern Ireland conflict). This change improves the outcomes for two terrorist rebel groups (Provisional IRA and the MNLF in the Philippines) thus working against the argument made here. I also corrected two clearly miscoded cases: Burundi versus CNDD, and UK versus Real IRA. Cases affected by these changes are dropped in robustness tests.

81. Stanton 2013, 1014–15. For further discussion, see also Stanton 2009. In some cases, Stanton's coding for a single case was applicable to more than one dyad in the CGS data (for example, Stanton codes Fatah and Hamas together in a single conflict against Israel).

82. Because thirty-four cases involve wars that began before 1989, there are another 449 observations in the data that are used for some robustness checks.

83. The PKK turned to terrorism after 1993 (a shift reflected in the time-varying data used here). The MILF (Philippines) did so after 1986 (before the start of the data). E-mail correspondence with Stanton, 25 July 2008. The Taliban did not use terrorism in its fight against the Rabbani government of Afghanistan in the 1990s, but used terrorism against the Karzai government and its Western backers in the 2000s. These are treated as separate conflicts here.

84. Cunningham, Gleditsch, and Salehyan 2009a, 574–75.

85. Coggins 2011.

86. See Minorities at Risk Project 2009; National Consortium for the Study of Terrorism and Responses to Terrorism 2008; and Uppsala Conflict Data Program 2012. Detailed coding notes available from the author.

87. This moderate category is dominated by power struggle cases, of which there are twenty-three, because there are only a handful (five) of cases of rebel groups fighting for autonomy only.

88. More recent use of terrorism in Nigeria and Somalia may, unfortunately, temper this finding.

89. This could be the result of selection effects; this analysis covers only the strongest opposition groups, those involved in full-scale civil

wars. However, among these relatively strong groups, it is clearly not the case that only weak groups resort to terrorism.

90. See Fortna 2014.
91. Nor have any of the cases of terrorist rebel groups that were ongoing as of 2010 ended in rebel victory since then (at least as of this writing [January 2015]).
92. These include Fatah versus Israel, IRA versus the UK, and the MNLF versus Philippines (all in 1993). The only case of an agreement with terrorist rebels in a nondemocracy is the CPN-M/UPF versus Nepal in 2003.
93. Forty-two percent of the rebels who use terrorism were engaged in civil war in a nondemocratic state (measured in the year the war started).

■　■　■

REFERENCES

Abadie, Alberto. 2006. Poverty, Political Freedom, and the Roots of Terrorism. *American Economic Review* 96 (2):50–56.

Abrahms, Max. 2005. Review of *Dying to Win: The Strategic Logic of Suicide Terrorism* by Robert A. Pape. *Middle East Policy* 12 (4):176–78.

———. 2006. Why Terrorism Does Not Work. *International Security* 31 (2):42–78.

———. 2012. The Political Effectiveness of Terrorism Revisited. *Comparative Political Studies* 45 (3): 366–93.

Acosta, Benjamin. 2014. Live to Win Another Day: Why Many Militant Organizations Survive yet Few Succeed. *Studies in Conflict and Terrorism* 37 (2):135–61.

Arreguín-Toft, Ivan. 2001. How the Weak Win Wars: A Theory of Asymmetric Conflict. *International Security* 26 (1):93–128.

Asal, Victor, and R. Karl Rethemeyer. 2008a. The Nature of the Beast: Organizational Structures and the Lethality of Terrorist Attacks. *Journal of Politics* 70 (2):437–49.

———. 2008b. Dilettantes, Ideologues, and the Weak: Terrorists Who Don't Kill. *Conflict Management and Peace Science* 25 (3):244–63.

Balch-Lindsay, Dylan, Andrew J. Enterline, and Kyle A. Joyce. 2008. Third-Party Intervention and the Civil War Process. *Journal of Peace Research* 45 (3):345–63.

Bapat, Navin A. 2006. State Bargaining with Transnational Terrorist Groups. *International Studies Quarterly* 50 (1):213–29.

Bloom, Mia. 2005. *Dying to Kill: The Allure of Suicide Terror*. New York: Columbia University Press.

Boulden, Jane. 2009. Terrorism and Civil Wars. *Civil Wars* 11 (1):5–21.

Bueno de Mesquita, Ethan, and Eric S. Dickson. 2007. The Propaganda of the Deed: Terrorism, Counterterrorism, and Mobilization. *American Journal of Political Science* 51 (2):364–81.

Burgoon, Brian. 2006. On Welfare and Terror: Social Welfare Policies and Political-Economic Roots of Terrorism. *Journal of Conflict Resolution* 50 (2):176–203.

Chenoweth, Erica. 2010. Democratic Competition and Terrorist Activity. *Journal of Politics* 72 (1):16–30.

———. 2013. Terrorism and Democracy. *Annual Review of Political Science* 16:355–78.

Coggins, Bridget. 2011. Friends in High Places: International Politics and the Emergence of States from Secessionism. *International Organization* 65 (3):433–67.

Crenshaw, Martha. 1981. The Causes of Terrorism. *Comparative Politics* 13 (4):379–99.

———. 1983. *Terrorism, Legitimacy, and Power: The Consequences of Political Violence*. Middletown, CT: Wesleyan University Press.

———. 2011. *Explaining Terrorism: Causes, Processes, and Consequences*. New York: Routledge.

Cronin, Audrey K. 2003. Behind the Curve: Globalization and International Terrorism. *International Security* 27 (3):30–58.

———. 2006. How al-Qaida Ends: The Decline and Demise of Terrorist Groups. *International Security* 31 (1):7–48.

———. 2009. *How Terrorism Ends: Understanding the Decline and Demise of Terrorist Campaigns*. Princeton, NJ: Princeton University Press.

Cunningham, David E., Kristian Skrede Gleditsch, and Idean Salehyan. 2009a. It Takes Two: A Dyadic Analysis of Civil War Duration and Outcome. *Journal of Conflict Resolution* 53 (4):570–97. Data available at http://privatewww.essex.ac.uk/~ksg/eacd.html Version 2.4. Accessed 13 January 2010.

———. 2009b. Data Coding Notes. Available at http://jcr.sagepub.com /content/53/4/570/suppl/DC1. Accessed 25 January 2010.

DeNardo, James. 1985. *Power in Numbers: The Political Strategy of Protest and Rebellion*. Princeton, NJ: Princeton University Press.

DeRouen, Karl, and David Sobek. 2004. The Dynamics of Civil War Duration and Outcome. *Journal of Peace Research* 41 (3):303–20.

Dow, Jay K., and James W. Endersby. 2004. Multinomial Probit and Multinomial Logit: A Comparison of Choice Models for Voting Research. *Electoral Studies* 23 (1):107–22.

Enders, Walter, Todd Sandler, and Khusrav Gaibulloev. 2011. Domestic Versus Transnational Terrorism: Data, Decomposition, and Dynamics. *Journal of Peace Research* 48 (3):319–37.

Eubank, William L., and Leonard Weinberg. 1994. Does Democracy Encourage Terrorism? *Terrorism and Political Violence* 6 (4):417–63.

Fazal, Tanisha M. 2013. Secessionism and Civilian Targeting. Paper presented at the 2013 Annual Meeting of the American Political Science Association, August, Chicago.

Findley, Michael G., and Joseph K. Young. 2012a. Terrorism and Civil War: A Spatial and Temporal Approach to a Conceptual Problem. *Perspectives on Politics* 10 (2):285–305.

———. 2012b. More Combatant Groups, More Terror? Empirical Tests of an Outbidding Logic. *Terrorism and Political Violence* 24 (5):706–21.

Fortna, Virginia Page. 2008. *Does Peacekeeping Work? Shaping Belligerents' Choices after Civil War*. Princeton, NJ: Princeton University Press.

———. 2014. Choosing Terror: Rebels' Use of Terrorism in Internal Armed Conflict, 1970–2010. Unpublished manuscript, Columbia University, New York.

Gleditsch, Nils P., Peter Wallensteen, Mikael Eriksson, Margareta Sollenberg, and Hoavard Strand. 2002. Armed Conflict 1946–2001: A New Dataset. *Journal of Peace Research* 39 (5):615–37. Data available at http://www.pcr.uu.se/research/ucdp/datasets /ucdp_prio_armed_conflict_dataset/. Accessed 1 April 2010.

Goodwin, Jeff. 2006. A Theory of Categorical Terrorism. *Social Forces* 84 (4):2027–46.

Gould, Eric D., and Esteban F. Klor. 2010. Does Terrorism Work? *Quarterly Journal of Economics* 125 (4):1459–510.

Heger, Lindsay L. 2010. In the Crosshairs: Explaining Violence Against Civilians. PhD diss., University of California, San Diego.

Hoffman, Bruce. 2006. *Inside Terrorism.* New York: Columbia University Press.

Jones, Seth G., and Martin C. Libicki. 2008. *How Terrorist Groups End: Lessons for Countering al Qa'ida.* Santa Monica, CA: Rand Corporation.

Kalyvas, Stathis N. 2006. *The Logic of Violence in Civil War.* New York: Cambridge University Press.

Krause, Peter. 2013. The Political Effectiveness of Non-State Violence: A Two-Level Framework to Transform a Deceptive Debate. *Security Studies* 22 (2):259–94.

Kydd, Andrew H., and Barbara F. Walter. 2002. Sabotaging the Peace: The Politics of Extremist Violence. *International Organization* 56 (2):263–96.

———. 2006. The Strategies of Terrorism. *International Security* 31 (1):49–80.

LaFree, Gary, and Laura Dugan. 2007. Introducing the Global Terrorism Database. *Terrorism and Political Violence* 19 (2):181–204.

Laitin, David D., and Jacob N. Shapiro. 2008. The Political, Economic, and Organizational Sources of Terrorism. In *Terrorism, Economic Development, and Political Openness,* edited by Philip Keefer and Norman Loayza, 209–32. New York: Cambridge University Press.

Lake, David A. 2002. Rational Extremism: Understanding Terrorism in the Twenty-First Century. *Dialogue IO* 1 (1):15–29.

Lawrence, Adria S. 2010. Triggering Nationalist Violence: Competition and Conflict in Uprisings Against Colonial Rule. *International Security* 35 (2):88–122.

Li, Quan, and Drew Schaub. 2004. Economic Globalization and Transnational Terrorism: A Pooled Time-Series Analysis. *Journal of Conflict Resolution* 48 (2):230–58.

Lyall, Jason. 2010. Do Democracies Make Inferior Counterinsurgents? Reassessing Democracy's Impact on War Outcomes and Duration. *International Organization* 64 (1):167–92.

Mao, Tse-Tung. 1961 [1937]. *On Guerrilla Warfare.* Translated by Samuel B. Griffith. New York: Praeger.

Mason, T. David, Joseph P. Weingarten, and Patrick J. Fett. 1999. Win, Lose, or Draw: Predicting the Outcome of Civil Wars. *Political Research Quarterly* 52 (2):239–68.

McCormick, Gordon H. 2003. Terrorist Decision Making. *Annual Review of Political Science* 6:473–507.

Merari, Ariel. 1993. Terrorism as a Strategy of Insurgency. *Terrorism and Political Violence* 5 (4):213–51.

Metelits, Claire. 2010. *Inside Insurgency: Violence, Civilians, and Revolutionary Group Behavior.* New York: New York University Press.

Minorities at Risk Project. 2009. Minorities at Risk Dataset: "Minority Group Assessments" and "Chronologies." College Park, MD: Center for International Development and Conflict Management. Available at http://www.cidcm.umd.edu/mar/data.asp. Accessed 29 November 2012.

National Consortium for the Study of Terrorism and Responses to Terrorism (START). 2008. Terrorist Organization Profiles (TOPs). Available at http://www.start.umd.edu/start/data_collections/tops/. Accessed 29 November 2012.

Nemeth, Stephen. 2014. The Effect of Competition on Terrorist Group Operations. *Journal of Conflict Resolution* 58 (2):336–62.

Pape, Robert A. 2003. The Strategic Logic of Suicide Terrorism. *American Political Science Review* 97 (3): 343–61.

———. 2005. *Dying to Win: The Strategic Logic of Suicide Terrorism.* New York: Random House.

Pape, Robert A., and James K. Feldman. 2010. *Cutting the Fuse: The Explosion of Suicide Terrorism and How to Stop It.* Chicago: University of Chicago Press.

Sambanis, Nicholas, 2008. Terrorism and Civil War. In *Terrorism, Economic Development, and Political Openness,* edited by Philip Keefer and Norman Loayza, 174–208. Cambridge, UK: Cambridge University Press.

Sánchez-Cuenca, Ignacio, and Luis de la Calle. 2009. Domestic Terrorism: The Hidden Side of Political Violence. *Annual Review of Political Science* 12:31–49.

Satana, Nil S., Molly Inman, and Johanna K. Birnir. 2013. Religion, Government Coalitions, and Terrorism. *Terrorism and Political Violence* 25 (1):29–52.

Schmid, Alex P., and Albert J. Jongman. 1988. *Political Terrorism: A New Guide to Actors, Authors, Concepts, Data Bases, Theories, and Literature.* Rev. ed. Amsterdam: North Holland.

Silke, Andrew. 1996. Terrorism and the Blind Man's Elephant. *Terrorism and Political Violence* 8 (3):12–28.

Stanton, Jessica A. 2009. Strategies of Violence and Restraint in Civil War. PhD diss., Department of Political Science, Columbia University, New York.

———. 2013. Terrorism in the Context of Civil War. *Journal of Politics* 75 (4):1009–22.

Stephan, Maria J., and Erica Chenoweth. 2008. Why Civil Resistance Works: The Strategic Logic of Nonviolent Conflict. *International Security* 33 (1):7–44.

Svensson, Isak. 2007. Fighting with Faith: Religion and Conflict Resolution in Civil Wars. *Journal of Conflict Resolution* 51 (6):930–49.

Thomas, Jakana. 2014. Rewarding Bad Behavior: How Governments Respond to Terrorism in Civil War. *American Journal of Political Science* 58 (4):804–18.

Thornton, Thomas P. 1964. Terror as a Weapon of Political Agitation. In *Internal War: Problems and Approaches,* edited by Harry Eckstein, 71–99. London: Free Press.

Uppsala Conflict Data Program. 2012. UCDP Conflict Encyclopedia. Uppsala, Sweden: Uppsala University. Available at www.ucdp.uu.se/database. Accessed 29 November 2012.

Walter, Barbara F. 2002. *Committing to Peace: The Successful Settlement of Civil Wars.* Princeton, NJ: Princeton University Press.

Wilson, James Q. 1974. *Political Organizations.* Princeton, NJ: Princeton University Press.

Wood, Reed M., and Jacob D. Kathman. 2014. Too Much of a Bad Thing? Civilian Victimization and Bargaining in Civil War. *British Journal of Political Science* 44 (3):1–22.

Erica D. Borghard and Shawn W. Lonergan

THE LOGIC OF COERCION IN CYBERSPACE

Cyberspace has definitively emerged as the latest frontier of militarized interactions between nation-states. Governments, as they are wont to do in an anarchic international system, have already invested considerable resources to develop offensive and defensive military capabilities in cyberspace. It remains to be seen, however, how and to what extent these tools can be employed to achieve desired political objectives. Put simply, what is the logic of coercion in cyberspace? Can governments use cyber power to deter state adversaries from taking undesirable actions or compel them to bend to their wills and, if so, how and under what conditions?[1] This analysis draws on the large corpus of coercion theory to assess the extent to which existing frameworks can shed light on the dynamics of coercion in cyberspace. The article proceeds as follows. First, we outline the theoretical logic of coercion theory and identify the factors necessary for successful coercion. Each element of coercion is immediately followed by a discussion of how it applies to the cyber domain and an assessment of how the particularities of the domain reflect on the requirements of successful coercion. We demonstrate that, based on current capabilities, cyber power has limited effectiveness as an independent tool of coercion. Second, we explore the extent to which cyber power could be used as part of a warfighting strategy to target an adversary's ability or willingness to resist and suggest which

strategies are likely to be more versus less effective.[2] We assert that, based on current capabilities, attrition, denial, and decapitation strategies are most likely to be effective in cyberspace. Finally, we conclude with recommendations for policymaking and further research.

Coercion Theory

As Thomas C. Schelling so eloquently articulated, coercion is fundamentally about affecting an adversary's behavior using the threat or limited application of military force; "[i]t is the *threat* of damage, or of more damage to come, that can make someone yield or comply."[3] Coercion involves producing a desired behavior or outcome on the part of an adversary by forcing her to confront a cost–benefit calculus, such that the adversary believes it is less costly to concede to the threatener's preferred course of (in)action than to defy the latter's demands.[4] Coercion is distinct from brute force. In the latter case, one state defeats another militarily and then imposes a political settlement on the defeated power; in the former case, the target of coercion retains the military capacity to resist or concede, and the coercer seeks to achieve a political settlement short of full-scale war by manipulating the cost–benefit calculus of the target state.[5] While coercion has always been a fundamental element of the exercise of state power, the advent of nuclear weapons and mutual assured destruction has made coercion even more critical. As Schelling explains, the prospect of

From *Security Studies* 26, no. 3 (2017): 452–81. Some of the authors' notes have been omitted.

civilization-ending nuclear warfare, coupled with advances in technology making it possible to target an enemy's population centers and hold its society at risk without first defeating its armed forces, has turned statecraft into the diplomacy of violence.[6] The significance of coercion for interstate relations has not decreased with the advent of cyber warfare; if anything, it has increased. Indeed, like nuclear weapons, cyber weapons enable governments to target adversary populations while bypassing the latter's military forces. For example, cyber weapons could be employed to target a state's critical infrastructure to render key pieces of a state's military systems inoperable at decisive times, as was allegedly the case when Syrian air defense systems failed to respond to an Israeli bombing operation against a purported Syrian nuclear enrichment facility in 2007.[7]

Notwithstanding the central role coercion plays in states' strategies, successful coercion—both its deterrent and compellent varieties—is difficult to achieve.[8] There is a large body of empirical literature that assesses the reasons for failed coercion, particularly focusing on examples of failed coercion in American foreign policy during the Vietnam War and through the use of air power in the post–Cold War international system.[9] In general, using the threat or limited application of military force to affect an adversary's behavior is difficult to accomplish because there are many factors that are necessary conditions for successful coercion, some of which are in tension with others. Moreover, if coercion is difficult to achieve through the threat or use of conventional military power, we argue that it is even more challenging in cyberspace. The literature on coercion suggests that four fundamental conditions must be met for coercion to succeed: the coercive threat must be clearly communicated; it must be linked to a cost–benefit calculus such that the target's costs of conceding are less than the costs of not complying; it must be credible; and there must be an element of reassurance.[10]

Communication

The essence of successful coercion is clear communication.[11] The target of a coercive threat has to know precisely the behavior in which the coercing state wants the target state to engage (or refrain from engaging), the timeframe in which the coercing state expects the target to comply, and the costs associated with cooperation versus defection. The target state must understand "what behavior of his will cause the violence to be inflicted and what will cause it to be withheld."[12] Ideally, coercion takes the form of an ultimatum: if State B does not do action X within timeframe Y, State A will take specified action Z. However, in the vast majority of international crises, political leaders default to ambiguity, rather than clarity, of threats; leaders often prefer to retain flexibility to escape from costly or imprudent commitments or be adaptive in their responses to an adversary's behavior, especially if they lack domestic political support.[13] The fundamental fact of anarchy complicates clear communication because it leads to poor, fragmentary information and creates incentives to misrepresent private information—indeed, this is a cause of war.[14] Beyond incentives for strategic ambiguity, clear signaling is complicated by misperceptions stemming from both cultural differences and cognitive limitations.[15] Insights from cognitive psychology have demonstrated that recipients of a signal tend to fit incoming information into preexisting beliefs, interpret signals based on implicit theories about their meaning, prefer simplicity over complexity, and are influenced by motivated biases.[16] Put simply, signaling often fails "because the perceiver does not understand what message the actor is trying to communicate."[17] Communication is facilitated when actors can agree on a shared meaning of a particular type or vehicle of signaling (such as diplomatic language). In the case of diplomatic language, for example, clarity is easier to achieve because "both the signaler and the perceiver agree as to the message that the former is trying to convey."[18]

Communication in Cyberspace

Understanding intent is exceptionally difficult in the cyber domain. Many scholars and US government-sponsored studies have noted that cyber operations create a high probability of misunderstanding the coercing state's intentions.[19] Unlike diplomatic channels, in cyberspace there is no agreed-upon language that guides policymakers to a common understanding that helps divine the meaning behind a cyber signal. Moreover, in cyberspace, most operations are interactions between humans and machines facilitated by code for which there are few, if any, norms governing the exchange.[20] That many high-level decision makers lack even a basic understanding of the cyber domain and, therefore, are likely to be intellectually unprepared during a time of crisis, compounds this uncertainty. Furthermore, the signaler may be uncertain about what kind of cyber tool she should select to communicate in cyberspace because the actual effects of a cyber attack may be unpredictable ex ante—even to the signaler.

Signaling in cyberspace is the most problematic of all the domains (land, sea, air, space, and cyber) because the signal may go unrealized. In other words, in cyberspace only the initiator may perceive the engagement.[21] Moreover, even if a target state realizes it has been attacked, it is difficult to infer the intent behind a cyber signal based solely on an observed incursion. This ambiguity has the potential to trigger unintended escalation because it is difficult to distinguish between hostile and benign intentions when an outside actor is perceived to have accessed a critical system.[22] In a hypothetical example, Japan may have an intelligence requirement to monitor the uranium enrichment efforts of North Korea. However, Japan's access to a network at a North Korean enrichment facility does not necessarily suggest that it intends to destroy North Korea's nuclear ambitions through cyber means; Japan could simply be monitoring the program to meet its own defensive requirements, which is widely accepted by international convention to be a necessary state practice.[23] Actors could exploit this uncertainty to their advantage, but it may also lead to unintended conflict.[24] Herbert Lin notes this ambiguity in cyberspace and concludes that the cyber domain presents an increased risk of accidental escalation: "In the absence of direct contact with those conducting such operations—sometimes even in the presence of such contact—determining intent is likely to be difficult and may rest heavily on inferences made on the basis of whatever attribution is possible. Thus, attempts to send signals to an adversary through limited and constrained military actions—problematic even in kinetic warfare—are likely to be even more problematic when cyber attacks are involved."[25]

Attribution problems complicate effective communication in cyberspace because they create problems for both target and initiator. From the perspective of the target state, a fundamental impediment to deciphering the intent behind a cyber signal is the difficulty of identifying the actor who sent it. This presents a challenge to policymakers because, if a cyber action is uncovered, the true meaning of the signal may not be ascertained without attribution. While some actions in themselves may send a clear signal without attribution, typically the identity of the signaling state is critical for coercion to succeed. For instance, in the prior scenario we assumed North Korea attributed the cyber incursion to Japan. However, what if North Korea were unable to attribute the access to Japan and had to surmise the intent of the incursion devoid of attribution? The spectrum of possible motivations of such an incursion ranges from a preparation for a preemptive attack from a rival such as Japan or the United States on one end of the spectrum, to a benign case of espionage from an ally such as China on the other. In this hypothetical case, not only is the signal obfuscated because intent cannot be deduced without attribution, but North Korea also does not know what is an appropriate response and against whom to respond. If these conditions are not met, coercion is by definition not possible.

There are, however, several methods to assign attribution following a cyber incursion.[26] The easiest ascription approach is when the perpetrator publically accepts responsibility for the action and the target state believes that the self-identified attacker possessed both the capability and motivation to carry it out. Another attribution technique mandates that the target state had access to the attacker's network from which the incursion originated and either witnessed the operation in real time or recorded it. This second method is difficult because it requires that the target state had access to the specific network from which the aggressor initiated an attack; that they observed the onslaught developing in real time and intentionally refrained from establishing tailored defenses or engaging in a preemptive attack to block the assault; or that that they had complete intelligence collection of all cyber operations from the adversary's network, which is typically technically difficult to consistently collect. However, in some instances governments may decide that the intelligence value of maintaining access outweighs the likely damage from the attack. Another attribution method is when sensors placed either at Internet service providers or key nodes in the Internet run algorithms that analyze raw data flows and scan for anomalies and variants of known attack signatures. However, the real-time use of such technology is still in a nascent stage and there is currently no guarantee that, once detected, the source of the malware could be traced back to the true originator.[27] The final method of assigning attribution occurs when the signature of the attack (the coding) is so unique that it could be traced to a specific actor or threat network. Yet, this method heightens the risk of falling victim to deceptive techniques, such as embedding remarks in a foreign language of a noninvolved party, which may confound forensic experts seeking to assign attribution. Recently, however, there have been advances in signature recognition software designed to scour millions of lines of code to compile unique profiles of the developers.[28] Moreover, from the target's perspective, even if she is able to successfully attribute an attack to a particular actor, she may be hesitant to reveal her ability to do so because it would likely require going public with valuable information that could compromise her own capabilities and accesses. For instance, the United States' decision to quickly attribute the Sony hack in late 2014 to North Korea likely revealed and compromised American accesses to other governments' cyber infrastructure.

Attribution issues create problems not only for the target state attempting to infer the intent behind a signal, but also for the coercing state seeking to send a clear signal. The conventional wisdom on cyber operations posits that states typically seek to avoid attribution when conducting cyber exploitation and espionage operations. However, coercion in cyberspace requires attribution to be effective. A coercing state may employ several methods to ensure attribution. First, a state could couple the action in cyberspace with a formal diplomatic message, elucidating the meaning the signal (the cyber attack) was intended to convey.[29] Coupling a cyber operation with a diplomatic message may be the least costly method to ensure ascription for the coercer, but it must also be credible. This technique was observed in March 2016 when Secretary of Defense Ashton Carter, in a formal public statement, acknowledged that the United States conducted a cyber attack against the Islamic State of Iraq and Syria's command and control systems in Mosul, Iraq.[30] However, a coercing state must ensure that the target believes its self-declared attribution. This could present a problem for the coercing state if, in order to demonstrate that it was the one sending a signal, it had to reveal capabilities and accesses that it may prefer to keep private. Second, if coupling is not an available avenue, some have postulated several technical methods to ensure attribution, such as embedding unique signatures in code.[31] This type of ascription technique demands that some trace of the cyber operation remain on the target's machines.

This suggests that simply gaining access to a network and conducting cyber espionage is not sufficient to send a coercive signal in cyberspace—even if such accesses may be necessary to support a coercive signal.[32] While much of the discussion in the public domain conflates cyber espionage and cyber military operations, these are in fact distinct, just as they are in conventional domains. All forms of espionage, whether conducted in cyberspace or elsewhere, are fundamentally about collecting private information against another actor. Conversely, to be coercive, a cyber signal must be attributable and aim to disrupt, deny, degrade, and/or destroy data resident on computers and computer networks, or the systems themselves.

Cost-Benefit Calculus

Coercion theory assumes that states are rational actors who make cost–benefit calculations when determining how to respond to threats and inducements posed by other actors in the international system. The benefit side of the calculus involves how much the adversary values a particular course of action, while the cost side entails the price she anticipates paying in order to carry it out.[33] Coercion, put simply, forces the target state to choose between "making concessions or suffering the consequences."[34] Therefore, to be effective, a coercing state must issue a threat such that the target perceives it to be more costly to suffer those

consequences than to concede.[35] To succeed, the coercer must know what the target state values and, therefore, what it can hold at risk to get the target to comply. * * * More important than an objective measure of costs versus benefits, however, is how the adversary perceives them, which stems from "the magnitude of the dangers and profits the adversary sees ahead for a given path and the probability of their occurrence."[36] At its core, therefore, coercion is the manipulation of the target's perceptions of the cost–benefit balance of a particular course of action.[37]

Affecting an adversary's cost–benefit calculus may seem deceptively simple; in practice, it could fail across multiple dimensions. Coercion could fail because the target does not understand what the adversary values and, therefore, does not know how to appropriately tilt the cost–benefit calculus. This could stem from poor intelligence or, more fundamentally, from the fact that leaders are not always rational, utility-maximizing economic individuals. It may be difficult to quantify what a target state values if it involves something intangible (such as prestige) and, therefore, hard to assign a numerical value to the cost a coercer must threaten to impose to achieve a desired behavior. Relatedly, coercion could fail because states are not unitary actors and, therefore, there may be domestic political or bureaucratic organizational considerations that factor into what a target state values, how it perceives costs versus benefits, and acceptable levels of risk that the coercing state does not take into account. Moreover, even if the coercer knew what the adversary values, it could be politically difficult to make a sufficiently costly threat. Finally, coercion could fail due to cognitive limitations on the part of the target. Insights gleaned from prospect theory, for instance, have illustrated that individuals often fail to make rational, cost–benefit calculations when assessing risk (such as being more averse to losses than gains) and misunderstand sunk costs.[38]

Cost-Benefit Calculus in Cyberspace

In cyberspace, the state issuing a coercive threat must calculate what target to go after and the effect it seeks to deliver against it. Similarly, the target must also calculate whether it can absorb the cost and, if so, whether the coercer can ratchet up the cost to the target while avoiding too much cost itself. There are several categories of targets a state may consider attacking in cyberspace to coerce another state. Generally speaking, the class of target that inflicts the highest level of cost, a state's critical infrastructure, is typically the hardest to gain access to due to the technical complexities stemming from custom, tailored uses and advanced physical and virtual defensive measures commonly emplaced around these vital capabilities. The United States Department of Homeland Security has defined these crucial nodes as ". . . systems and assets, whether physical or virtual, so vital that the incapacity or destruction of such may have a debilitating impact on the security, economy, public health or safety, environment, or any combination of these matters."[39] This category includes critical infrastructure that is essential for everything from the safeguarding of nuclear regulatory systems to gas pipelines, and control systems that enable communication systems to work.[40] In the United States, many of these critical systems are run by private industry, but in states with parastatal enterprises (such as China), they remain centrally controlled by the government. Not all pieces of critical infrastructure, however, are universally valued across states. For instance, diverging state opinions over the ideal relationship between the citizen and the Internet has changed what states may consider critical infrastructure. Indeed, one accomplished Chinese academic with senior-level party connections noted to the authors that their "Great Fire Wall," which restricts citizen access to Western media sources, is considered part of China's critical infrastructure.[41] In this case, attacking a vital node that the state links to regime stability would be significantly costlier for China than the destruction of other types of critical infrastructure. Similarly, the recent hack of the US Democratic National Committee, allegedly committed by Russia or Russian-sponsored groups, is an example of how a state could target a critical component of a democratic regime—its electoral system.[42] This creates the potential for unintended escalation dynamics if the coercing state did not accurately calculate the extent to which the target values its electoral process.

Military capabilities may also be targeted by cyber attacks. These targets include everything from software running on advanced avionic platforms, to air defense assets, communication systems, and satellites tied into the Global Positioning System (GPS). Setting one's cyber sights on these military systems is similar in terms of costliness to targeting civilian critical infrastructure in that both are custom engineered and are typically difficult to gain access to and, therefore, mandate a highly tailored capability to exploit. Additionally, given that military systems are designed to be used during times of conflict, they tend to be more secure than civilian infrastructure because they are created with the expectation that they may be attacked via cyber means and, therefore, there is a greater emphasis placed on survivability and resilience early on in the development cycle.

From the target's perspective, attacks against critical national infrastructure and military capabilities are the most costly types of attacks, precisely because governments rely on these to survive in the international system and perform their basic functions. Coercing states may also choose to target the corporate sector of another state, depending on permissibility allowed by its own domestic legal regimes. Targets could include the online banking ability of a particular bank, the network of a leading defense contractor, or consumer information held by retailers. There is variation in terms of the cost to a coercer of targeting a particular company or sector of the economy, and this variation is largely a function of the resiliency and defenses that private actors choose to incorporate into their networks and systems. However, in terms of the perceived cost to the target state, generally speaking, cyber attacks against a private company are of a lower magnitude than attacks against critical national infrastructure and military capability, including command and control capabilities. Therefore, these kinds of attacks would only be useful to coerce a target state into conceding on relatively minor issues, if at all. This is analogous to conventional domains—dropping ordnance on a Walmart is fundamentally different from dropping ordnance on a communications node. However, there are two important caveats to this analysis. First, there may be some reputational costs a target may incur if attacks against certain private sectors actors are perceived to undermine the legitimacy of the regime. Second, there is likely to be important variation stemming from regime type, because some kleptocratic states may rely on the support of key industries or even companies to maintain regime stability. In these cases, attacks against business or industry may be comparable in terms of perceived cost to attacks against critical national infrastructure.

Regardless of the nature of the target, when sending a coercive signal in cyberspace, a policymaker must decide if she wants to produce a disruptive or destructive effect, the most salient distinction in the domain. Thus, a policymaker employing cyber attacks as a coercive instrument of state power must make a calculation of what effect is necessary to achieve the desired outcome. Destructive cyber attacks take two forms: the rare cyber attacks that generate an effect felt in the physical world, and the more common destruction of digital information, which can be almost as dire

as a physical attack for many pieces of infrastructure. Disruptive attacks, conversely, seek to operationally diminish a system to the point that a user lacks confidence in its ability to perform some function. The latter may be more appealing to a coercing government because disruptive attacks enable functionality of the affected system to be restored once the attack is ceased and, thus, may aid in reassuring the target state, as will be discussed in a later section. Notwithstanding the above discussion, states may be unable to perfectly tailor a cyber signal to affect a target's cost–benefit calculus. In other words, the technical complexities of certain types of costly operations may force less capable states into sending less costly signals that don't sufficiently alter the target's calculations. Governments may find cheap, fast, and easy cyber operations appealing even when they are less effective for the purposes of coercion. Put simply, governments may hit what they can get, rather than the optimal target to coerce another state.

Credibility

Beyond being costly, a coercer's threat must be credible—the target must believe that the coercer will actually carry it out. A threat is credible if it is in a state's interests to carry it out and if that state has both the capability and the resolve, or political will, to do so.[43] * * * A target may doubt a coercer's resolve because it doesn't believe that it is in the latter's interests to carry out the threat (this was particularly important in the context of nuclear deterrence); or because it doubts that the leader has sufficient domestic political support to carry out the threat;[44] or because the coercer has not established a reputation for carrying out past threats.[45] How individuals actually assess credibility, however, is poorly understood.[46]

Because credibility is difficult to convey but essential for coercion, states attempt to enhance the credibility of their threats by making them costly—through sending costly signals. James D. Fearon asserts that, "to be credible, a threat must have some cost or risk attached to it that might discourage an unresolved state from making it."[47] That's because talk is cheap: "words are cheap, not inherently credible when they emanate from an adversary, and sometimes too intimate a mode of expression."[48] There are two mechanisms states can employ to generate costly and, therefore, credible signals. First, states can tie their hands, limiting their choices and increasing the costs of backing down in the event the target of coercion does not comply with the terms of the threat. Second, states can sink costs, taking actions that are costly up front, such as mobilizing troops.[49] Using a similar framework, Robert Jervis describes how states can use indices to generate costly signals. Indices are "behaviors (either verbal or nonverbal) that the perceiver believes are inextricably linked to a characteristic that helps predict what the actor will do in the future."[50] Democracies, it has been argued, may have an advantage in costly signaling because they can more easily tie their hands through incurring audience costs.[51] Generating costly signals does not come without risks—indeed, costly signaling, paradoxically, is designed to increase the risk of war through locking in coercers to the use of force in order to (hopefully) avoid it.[52] Furthermore, there are myriad reasons states may seek to avoid a perfectly committing threat through sending an unambiguous costly signal, as previously noted.

Credibility in Cyberspace

* * * Credibility in cyberspace could be established via two mechanisms. First, establishing indices could create a venue for states to better communicate and demonstrate capability. However, indices of cyber power do not yet exist and are likely to be difficult to form. Therefore, at present, credibility is most likely to be inferred through costly signaling.

Cyber Power Indices

Establishing indices of cyber power contributes to the credibility of threats in cyberspace because it helps ascertain a state's capability.[53] Perfect information of another state's cyber capabilities does not exist; therefore, indices facilitate a state's assessment of another state's ability to carry out threats. In cyberspace, these indices include budgets, growing and training cyber forces, establishing commands, and advertising participation in major cyber exercises.[54] When assessing capabilities in cyberspace, it is also critical to analyze how the latter would be employed. In particular, states in this domain may feel less constrained by international laws and norms (or even the threat of assured retaliation because, as this analysis demonstrates, these threats are difficult to credibly convey). This is because actors in the cyber domain tend to prefer to obfuscate their identities, leading some state actors to be more willing to act in ways that they would not otherwise be willing to on a battlefield or via formal diplomatic channels.

Estimating the capability of a cyberspace actor is a conundrum that has challenged scholars because the opaque nature of the domain confounds measurement efforts.[55] In the nuclear and chemical warfare arenas, there are methods to estimate the stockpiles of arms a nation holds and for which there exist treaties, accords, and international oversight institutions that monitor and limit the quantities of these weapons. However, in the cyber world there is no measure of relative strength; one cannot simply count the number of cyber tools the way one can count the number of warheads or the pounds of poison gas a country possesses. This is because offensive cyber capabilities are not universally lethal. A shroud of secrecy surrounds a nation-state's cyber capability and, therefore, creates a situation of imperfect information from which a policymaker must judge another state's actions and intent. Unlike in the conventional or nuclear realms, where states can reveal their capabilities to bolster credibility (or where the technology necessitates public tests to assess their effectiveness, such as nuclear tests), in the cyber realm states typically prefer to—and can—keep capabilities secret because revealing them would enable adversaries to defend against them and render the capabilities impotent. In other words, it is harder for states to reveal private information in cyberspace to enhance the credibility of their threats. Moreover, governments face unique difficulties deriving intent based on observed capabilities because many states in the cyber domain find themselves coercing with the weapons they have, rather than the ones they may want or need. In other words, there may be a large gap between capabilities and intent. A distinction should be made here between what a state can measure about its own cyber capabilities and what its adversaries can assess. Measuring a rival's military strength has always been more difficult than introspective assessment due to military secrecy. However, the difference in cyberspace is that self-assessments of cyber capabilities (at least currently) also happen to be much harder to conduct because effective metrics have yet to be devised. This, in turn, makes assessing another state's cyber-military might even more difficult than for other domains and types of weapons.

Furthermore, measures of cyber power include factors beyond raw estimates of the size of cyber forces. While human capital and skill levels are important contributors to capability in the conventional domain, they are arguably even more vital in the cyber domain. Simply counting the number of cyber forces that a country may openly report as an assessment of cyber power does not take into account the differences in skill levels and a state's relative depth of cyber operations. A lack of homogeneity of material resources and technically proficient human capital across states means that one cannot precisely compare cyber capabilities between states. Comparing quantities of cyber forces is akin to comparing quantities of ships in a navy without distinguishing between tugboats and aircraft carriers. Regime type also factors into capabilities. Some states, such as Russia and China, place a greater emphasis on developing cyber forces to monitor their citizenry to detect unrest and preserve regime stability. From a technical standpoint, these operations are markedly different from conducting a destructive cyber attack against a state adversary. Democratic states have the advantage of devoting fewer cyber resources to population monitoring and, therefore, are freer to invest in adversary-centric capabilities.[56] Finally, what matters for capability in cyberspace is having the right operator, armed with the right capability, with access to a vulnerable target, rather than a numerical advantage. Capability and access imply that, regardless of how skilled an individual operator is, she will always be constrained by the cyber tools with which she has been equipped.

Cyber Operations as Costly Signals

In order to bolster the credibility of a threat, states often engage in costly signaling that ranges from national leaders' threats and troop mobilizations, to onshore trip wires, to the movement of aircraft carriers during times of crises.[57] All of these serve to demonstrate a state's capability and willingness to follow through with the terms of a threat. The greater the cost to the initiating state of producing a given signal, ceteris paribus, the more effective the signal is as an indication of the initiating state's resolve. Therefore, leaders could use cyber operations to convey their commitment to a particular course of action if they are sufficiently costly to produce.[58] Not all cyber operations are equally costly for the coercing state, however. Some operations are resource intensive, whereas other types of operations, such as a Distributed Denial of Service (DDoS) attacks and website defacements, can be conducted using minimal resources. In this regard, it is help-ful to conceptualize interstate cyber signaling as existing along a spectrum where the greater the resource requirements, the costlier the signal is to produce, and the more resolve it demonstrates.

States can send signals via five broad categories of cyber attacks that are increasingly costly. The cheapest way to attack another entity is to conduct a DDoS attack. This is an operation where multi-ple compromised systems are directed by a central computer to flood another computer with informa-tion requests. When enough compromised com-puters are connected together they act as one botnet (a network of enslaved information technol-ogy devices that can be centrally controlled) and, if the network is large enough, it may overwhelm the processing capabilities of the intended target and force it to shut down. Examples of this include the alleged Iranian-based DDoS attacks against the US financial sector in 2013, which took down the retail pages of over twenty-six corporations over a four-month time span.[59] These operations are on the far left of the spectrum because they are not inherently expensive to conduct (even though they may force the target to absorb high costs). The cur-rent going rate for a 24-hour DDoS attack is approximately $400–800 USD on the black mar-ket, depending on the size of the botnet being employed.[60] Furthermore, these operations are access agnostic in that, in order to conduct the operation, the attacker does not have to be pre-positioned with a back door into the target's net-work to facilitate the attack.

To send a costlier signal, a state could engage in operations designed to hack user accounts, including email and social media accounts. These are slightly costlier than DDoS attacks because they involve acquiring the credentials of an indi-vidual with access to the specific target (unless, in the unlikely scenario, the perpetrator can guess the target account's password). A well-known example of this is the 2013 hack of the Associated Press's Twitter feed, where hackers tweeted that there were two explosions in the White House and that the president was injured, prompting volatility in the stock market.[61]

Website defacement represents an additional level of cost for several reasons. First, it requires a minimal level of knowledge of webpage design coding. Second, website defacements involve deliv-ering an effect to produce the observed defacement or redirection. Third, it is dependent on gaining access to the website administrator's account. Nota-ble examples include the defacement of the United States Army's official website in 2015 and the Syr-ian Electronic Army's hack of a *Washington Post* website in 2015.[62]

Even more costly is gaining privileged access to internal networks for the purposes of data theft. This is more difficult than gaining access to a typi-cal end user's account because it often relies on gaining access to internal systems and data reposi-tories to which end users typically lack access. Most companies limit privileged accesses of this nature and compartmentalize this kind of information due to the potential consequences of a breach per-petrated against even a single actor with such extraordinary accesses (or by the actor herself). There is also an element of scale in these types of cases because attackers can acquire large amounts of private information, such as the contents of cor-porate email servers, billing records, personally identifiable information, and confidential informa-tion and documents pertaining to corporate strat-egy and development efforts. Two well-publicized examples of this kind of attack include the hack of the Department of Defense's Office of Personnel Management in 2015, allegedly committed by China, which compromised the personal informa-tion of nearly twenty-two million federal employ-ees and their friends and family; and the 2014 attack against Sony Picture Entertainment, attrib-uted by the US government to North Korea, which released embarrassing corporate communications, policies, and personally identifiable information of employees.[63]

The costliest type of signaling is a cyber attack that requires gaining access to well-defended or closed networks and seeks to disrupt or destroy key systems. Within this category, there is wide variation in the resources required to conduct these operations. The cost depends on the complexity of the attack and the relative difficulty of gaining access to the targeted systems. Since these types of operations disrupt or destroy data, they require customized tools that will produce the desired effect once inside the network. Furthermore, transacting in what is often a well-defended, restricted area is difficult not only because of the code-based language of exchange, but also because gaining access to closed and defended networks requires a significant investment of materiel resources and human capital. This investment includes not only the development of cyber tools to gain access to specific systems, but also the development of capabilities to exfiltrate information resident on the system and/or, more invasively, to completely subjugate the targeted machine. This investment extends beyond the development of cyber arms; it also requires extensive testing against a mockup of the intended target for both the developer and eventual cyber operator. The combination of technical knowhow with financial resources severely limits the number of states that can be called genuine cyber powers—particularly since such investments may be long-term commitments without guaranteed successful outcomes. Indeed, some cyber operations may take years from the time the concept is conceived until the operation is implemented. Operations that involve gaining access to hardened systems that use closed networks not connected to the open Internet, such as the Stuxnet attack against Iran to delay its uranium enrichment program, are significantly costly. In the case of Stuxnet, custom-engineered cyber capabilities containing over fifteen thousand lines of code were required to manipulate Iran's customized Supervisory Control and Data Acquisition (SCADA) systems; this would certainly be costlier than a cyber attack that simply deleted information from servers to which an actor had gained access.[64] In this example, the Stuxnet attack would be significantly more costly to conduct than the 2012 Saudi Aramco breach, which destroyed data resident on over thirty thousand corporate computers, due to the time, material, and personnel requirements that would be mandated by the former compared to the later. Finally, this category of cyber attacks could require incurring the additional cost of gaining physical access to a network, particularly if it is closed, through using human operators.[65]

Operating militarily in cyberspace requires a skill set that is not uniformly distributed across all states and takes years to develop. Moreover, unlike traditional means of signaling, sending a signal via cyberspace is uniquely costly because, once an attack capability is used, it often cannot be used again. While it may be possible to replicate a capability, as already noted, there is little universality of cyber capabilities. Most critical targets are unique, and potential victims can prevent exploitation once the threat signature has been identified and incorporated into their defenses, which also compounds the difficulty of a sustained assault. Furthermore, once these tools are deployed they have a limited lifespan as routine defensive techniques and vulnerability patching may render a tool that took years to develop obsolete within seconds of employment.

Governments can also generate costly signals through manipulating the shared risk of war. This concept was championed by Schelling, who submits that credibility can be enhanced by exhibiting risky behavior, particularly during times of crisis.[66] States can demonstrate resolve through acting in a manner that increases the risk of war and/or increases political costs to the party issuing the threat, but falls short of initiating an attack. For instance, a state can raise the alert status of its forces or move naval fleets into close proximity of an area of hostiles. Neither of these signals is inherently costly; however, during a time of increased tension, such maneuvers increase the likelihood of war due to the potential misperception of intent and miscalculation. Furthermore, leaders can generate political costs through tying hands. In other words, politicians that are subjected to electoral sanctioning may generate self-imposed reputational costs by committing themselves to a course of action, which could put their political future in jeopardy if they waiver from it.[67]

In cyberspace, risk generation occurs by acting in overt ways that ensure the receiver perceives the signal, but falls short of a cyber attack. These types of actions include actively scanning networks, pinging pieces of key infrastructure, and perhaps even deploying beacons on compromised infrastructure. These operations can increase the risk of war because their intent cannot be surmised and could be interpreted as a precursory step to offensive cyber operations. However, these operations generate tradeoffs between intelligence collection and coercion strategies that policymakers should take into account.

Reassurance

Finally, to succeed, a coercive threat must have an element of reassurance, such that the target is made to believe that compliance with the terms of the threat will ensure the coercer does not mete out the threatened punishment regardless.[68] In other words, "the pain and suffering have to appear contingent on his behavior; it is not alone the threat that is effective—the threat of pain or loss if he fails to comply—but the corresponding assurance, possibly an implicit one, that he can avoid the pain or loss if he does comply."[69] Related to reassurance, Schelling also describes the importance of saving face—leaving a backdoor that enables that adversary to back down without paying too high a price in its own reputation and integrity. Coercers should therefore deliver the threat in a way that

"decouple[s] an adversary's prestige and reputation from a dispute."[70]

Reassurance is also a difficult aspect of coercion. Todd S. Sechser argues that great powers encounter problems reassuring weaker states that are the targets of compellent threats because the very military capability that enhances the credibility of the stronger state's coercive threat makes it more difficult for the target to believe that the stronger state won't simply make more demands following the former's compliance with the initial threat.[71] This sheds light on the inherent tension between the actions that enhance credibility versus those that buttress reassurance; the more a target believes the coercer will actually carry out a threat (credibility), the less likely the target believes the coercer will refrain from doing so in the event she complies (reassurance). * * *

Reassurance in Cyberspace

Assuring a target state that, once it capitulates to the aggressor's demands, the punishment will cease is perhaps the greatest obstacle to successful coercion in cyberspace. Effective command and control of a cyber attack are essential for reassurance. However, this is often exceedingly difficult in cyberspace depending on how and by whom an attack is carried out. For instance, 128 distinct cyber attacks were recorded against Estonian websites during May 2007 in response to the Estonian government's decision to relocate a Soviet-era war monument.[72] Since these assaults lacked a centralized controller, it would have been difficult for a unitary actor to provide the Estonian government with a credible assurance that the attacks would cease if the statue were returned to its original location (if we can assume this was the objective of the attacks). Furthermore, many states choose to employ cyber proxies to conduct cyber operations because they may not have the means to conduct the operation themselves or desire plausible deniability. Proxies may not act in the way a government desires depending on the proxy's incentives for participating in the attack and a government's ability to incentivize good behavior.[73] Furthermore, once the attack tool is released, it may be exceedingly difficult to stop. For instance, the Stuxnet computer virus was presumably never intended to propagate beyond Iranian nuclear centrifuges, but it infected over 100,000 computers worldwide before it could be stopped.[74] Due to the technical complexities of cyber capabilities and the collective action issues that may surround command and control of a cyber attack, a rational actor would be wise to second guess a reassurance that an assault will stop in exchange for submission.

A unique paradox occurs as an implication of this analysis. The ideal means to reassure a target is to engage in a disruptive cyber attack. Disruptive attacks are easily reversible and can, therefore, be credibly revoked if a target complies with a coercer's demands. However, disruptive attacks are not particularly costly and, therefore, are less credible than a destructive attack. A destructive attack can deliver an immediate effect, and it also generates irreversible costs to the target that can increase over time. Together, this implies that a coercive cyber attack that both reassures and maximizes costs for the target may be unachievable.

Assessing Warfighting Strategies in Cyberspace[75]

As the above discussion illustrates, cyber power is not an ideal independent tool of coercion. Nevertheless, governments may still choose to use cyber power to pursue warfighting strategies aimed at eroding a target's ability or willingness to resist due to the perceived ease or cost effectiveness of conducting cyber operations as opposed to conventional ones, particularly under conditions of conventional asymmetry—as well as their destructive nature in many cases.[76] * * *

Viable and Effective Strategies

Currently, we argue that there are three warfighting strategies that are likely to succeed using cyber power: attrition, denial, and decapitation. We claim that governments are most likely to achieve desired objectives using these strategies because the technical requirements and capabilities for carrying out these operations in cyberspace exist and because they can generate sufficient costs (in theory) to force a target government to concede. However, it is imperative to note that this discussion remains theoretical and its efficacy in practice is highly context dependent—whether a given government will concede to the demands of a coercing state will depend on the particular cost–benefit calculus it makes for a specific situation. While attrition, denial, and decapitation have different logics, what unites them is their discrete military application—these strategies are generally employed against military targets—and they are most likely to be successful when coupled with conventional military operations and/or diplomacy. In other words, the use of cyber power to undermine a government's ability or willingness to resist is not as effective in isolation from other instruments of state power.

ATTRITION

Attrition strategies seek to erode the adversary's military capability such that the target can no longer resist. Within the cyber domain, this strategy could include attacks that both degrade and destroy government or private networks and systems, depending on the latter's military utility. In cyberspace, the successful application of an attrition strategy would force a target to abandon a network or system through destroying it or building up a user's mistrust in it such that the target is forced to abandon its operation. A notable attribute of attrition strategies is that they seek to exhaust a target state's resources as it is forced to dedicate assets to protect or replicate capabilities in different and more secure manners. In particular, cyber raiding—targeting an enemy in its weakest areas—is a common tactic of attrition, where data is the equivalent of an enemy's provisions. Conventionally, raiding refers to stealing or destroying an enemy's provisions or equipment. These forays are commonly conducted behind an adversary's lines and are directed against their supply convoys and depots. In cyberspace, destroying or corrupting servers that handle military plans, air or ship tasking orders, or even defense developmental efforts, can prevent certain actions from occurring at the time they are urgently needed. More importantly, if they persist they will eventually erode a state's confidence in its networks and the data resident on them. It is difficult, if not impossible, to destroy a state's militarily capabilities through the exercise of cyber power alone. However, it is theoretically possible to force a state to suffer the gradual erosion of its capabilities—especially of its confidence in them—as vulnerable targets are attacked and as governments are forced to divert considerable resources to investigating and repairing them until the cost of continued resistance becomes unbearable.

DENIAL

A denial strategy involves increasing the costs to an adversary such that achieving a military objective—such as taking a piece of territory—becomes prohibitive or impossible.[77] As such, it could involve both a defensive component (increasing one's own defenses such that an adversary cannot go on the offense without incurring significant costs), as well as an offensive one (actively taking out enemy capabilities to deny the adversary the ability to achieve an objective).[78] In cyberspace, the targets of denial strategies mirror those of traditional domains of warfare, except that the effect achieved is delivered via a cyber operation. An adversary's Integrated Air Defense Systems (IADS), command and control apparatuses, and air traffic control systems are all examples of legitimate targets for a state pursuing a denial strategy. An example of using cyber means (coupled, in this case, with conventional military power) to target an adversary's air defense systems is the alleged 2007 Israeli air attack against Syria's nuclear facilities.[79] Unlike conventional approaches to denial, in cyberspace, due to the increasing reliance of embedded technology in many modern battlefield systems, the surface from which these systems can be attacked has significantly increased. For instance, in conventional warfare the only way to remove tanks from a battlefield is to destroy them piecemeal from the air or ground. However, theoretically, it may be possible in the not too distant future (if not already) to use a cyber attack to render entire fleets of weapon systems inert at a critical moment. This concern has already been realized by many policymakers and is evident in the discussion over Chinese cyber espionage of the research and development of the Joint Strike Fighter.[80] On the other hand, the length of the timeframe under consideration could affect assessments of the potential costliness of denial strategies in cyberspace. For instance, cyber instruments could be used to disable, rather than destroy, an adversary's weapons systems or command and control, rendering an attack costly in the short term but less costly than the ostensibly permanent destruction of those systems through conventional means.[81]

Decapitation

Decapitation strategies seek to achieve strategic paralysis by targeting command and control centers, leadership, critical economic nodes, and key weapons systems.[81] Currently, it is technically possible to use cyber attacks to shut down a command and control node. However, given that most states employ secondary and tertiary redundant systems (for example, analogue or even courier-based communication), as well as separate communication networks (for example, multiple classified and unclassified networks), the impact of this type of operation could be short lived. Nevertheless, successfully targeting a critical command and control node, such as the US government's Secure Internet Protocol Router Network (SIPRNET) or Joint Worldwide Intelligence Communications System (JWICS), would have immediate and significant material and psychological effects. Therefore, governments should either take into account temporal limitations when targeting command and control networks, or ensure that they also target all additional means of adversary communication. Conventional military operations that target command and control facilities can wipe out entire communications networks, for example, through dropping ordnance on a facility. In contrast, cyber operations can typically target a single or limited number of communications nodes or networks due to the compartmentalized nature of each network. This would therefore require multiple distinct cyber operations to achieve near-complete command and control paralysis. Furthermore, even if cyber attacks could be used to successfully target a government's primary communications networks, backup systems would likely need to be defeated through traditional forms of electronic warfare or conventional operations (for example, jamming transmissions, capturing curriers, or cutting telephone lines or undersea cables). Altogether, this analysis implies that one is more likely to observe decapitation strategies employed at lower echelons of command, such as troops in the field, where there are typically fewer redundant systems, or against less-capable state adversaries.

Viable and Ineffective Strategies

Warfighting strategies in cyberspace can be technically viable but ineffective because they cannot force the adversary to incur sufficiently high costs to prompt a change in her behavior. Much of the activity that currently occurs in cyberspace falls into this category—actors can harass, annoy, or otherwise inconvenience each other. Indeed, those who claim that the threat of a cyber Armageddon is exaggerated focus on these kinds of cyber attacks.[82]

INTIMIDATION

An intimidation strategy is designed to directly address a state's domestic audiences and sometimes, national policymakers. Actions as part of an intimidation strategy do not cause significant damage and are typically tailored to undermine a government's legitimacy or convince domestic audiences that the government is powerless, prompting a loss of confidence by the public.[83] In cyberspace, intimidation typically takes the form of website defacement and email spamming campaigns. While these operations are technically easy to conduct because they involve fewer resources and a lower skill set compared to other types of operations, they cause minimal cost to the recipient. The effect these attacks produce is typically perceived as an annoyance, rather than a strategic message, because these types of attacks are fairly common and easy from which to recover. Therefore, they are unlikely to be sufficiently costly to force targeted governments to change their behavior. Indeed, observed intimidation strategies, such as the 2008 defacements of Georgian government websites portraying President Mikheil Saakashvili as Adolf Hitler, have had no real effect.[84]

Nonviable and Ineffective Strategies

The two paradigmatic strategies of traditional coercion that currently have the least utility in cyberspace are punishment and risk. While there has been considerable brouhaha in public and even government spheres regarding the potentially dire consequences of a "World War 3.0" or a "cyber Pearl Harbor," these are largely unrealistic given the current state of the domain.[85] However, as we will describe below, changes in modern societies' interconnectivity and reliance on automated systems, as well as advances in military cyber technologies, could change the value of these strategies.[86]

PUNISHMENT

Originally stemming from the work of Giulio Douhet, an Italian general and early proponent of the strategic use of air power, punishment strategies are designed to inflict sudden, large-scale pain and devastation on an adversary's civilian population until the panic-stricken citizenry demands an end to the war.[87] Indeed, Douhet envisioned that a single successful air raid on an enemy's population center could " . . . spread terror through the nation and quickly break down [a state's] material and moral resistance."[88] This concept was further refined by Schelling and modern coercion theorists, who applied it to the strategic use of nuclear weapons; holding an adversary's population at risk of extreme destruction is the foundation of modern deterrence theory.[89]

In theory, inflicting punishment in cyberspace would involve the use of cyber power to cause virtual and physical damage to civilian infrastructure and population centers. This could entail attacks against essential services, such as water treatment facilities, transportation, air traffic control systems, nuclear power plants, electrical grids, food safety systems, waste management systems, etc. However, in practice, there are two critical elements of punishment that cannot be sustained given the current nature of the cyber domain: first, the immediate and sudden nature of an attack; and second, the scale and scope of the pain. Put simply, governments cannot kill a lot of people in a very short period of time using cyber weapons; the magnitude of the pain states are currently capable of inflicting via the cyber domain alone is hardly comparable to the devastation wrought by conventional or nuclear attacks against cities. Access requirements and the customized nature of cyber capabilities render it nearly impossible to launch a time-dependent, highly coordinated cyber campaign of the scale required to inflict severe costs on enemy populations. The scope is also nearly impossible to achieve because it would require an extraordinarily large number of discrete and distinct cyber attacks. As discussed in prior sections, there is limited universal lethality of cyber weapons, which means that governments would have to develop unique accesses and distinct tools for each targeted system. Moreover, there is no guarantee that an effect can be delivered as planned. Additionally, it is difficult to envision a government entity being able to sustain a cyber assault against multiple key pieces of infrastructure in order to push a society to a breaking point before the target moves to mitigate the onslaught through preestablished redundant mechanisms and/or cyber or kinetic military operations.

MANIPULATION OF RISK

Punishment and risk are fundamentally related—both involve targeting an adversary's population centers to force the government to concede to the coercer's demands. However, unlike punishment strategies that call for immediate and decisive destruction, risk strategies entail gradually escalating the intensity and scope of attacks against civilian targets.[90] There is a critical psychological element to the manipulation of risk in that what drives concessions is the threat and prospect of future pain. This requires that the coercing state can sustain and ratchet up an assault over time.

Like punishment, the manipulation of risk does not translate well into cyberspace. Carrying out a comprehensive, tiered cyber campaign plan to create the ratcheting effect of punishment that Schelling proscribes is exceedingly difficult for reasons already articulated. To wit, this would require a significant planning effort and mandate a costly access and capability development program. Furthermore, risk strategies do not rely upon the sudden and intense destruction that are envisioned by punishment strategies, but instead are designed to be employed over time. In order to be effective, the attack would have to be maintained against an adversary that would likely be active in trying to stop or mitigate the effects of the onslaught. Presumably, if a state is at the technical level where it is susceptible to large-scale cyber attacks, it also has the wherewithal to defend against them over time. Finally, the effective employment of a risk strategy in cyberspace would require an impossibly high level of control by the coercing government over the cyber tools it would employ against an adversary. According to Schelling, risk is most likely to succeed when an action, "once initiated, causes minimal harm if compliance is forthcoming and great harm if compliance is not forthcoming, is consistent with the time schedule of feasible compliance, is beyond recall once initiated, and cannot be stopped by the party that started it but *automatically* stops upon compliance, with all this fully understood by the adversary."[91] Indeed, the risks of using cyber power—effects getting beyond the control of the initiating state in unanticipated and potentially undesirable ways—are precisely the opposite of the calibrated manipulation of risk Schelling envisions.

Future Trends in Viability and Effectiveness

The negligible utility of punishment and risk strategies rests on the current state of technology and the dependence (and, therefore, vulnerability) of modern societies on cyber-enabled essential services. Changes along either of these dimensions—technical viability and/or the costs that can be imposed on civilian populations—would alter the feasibility and effectiveness of these strategies. For instance, the dawn of the "Internet of Things" (a concept that depicts a not-too-distant future where everything from an individual's toaster and refrigerator to a city's garbage collection and other essential services are automated and connected to the Internet) could make it possible for governments to impose high and devastating costs on society through cyber means.[92] Moreover, it is conceivable that, as societies remove human redundancy through increased automation and become more dependent on interconnected networks of services, punishment and risk strategies could become more effective as the attack surface expands and more targets become vulnerable to a cyber attack.

Additionally, punishment and risk strategies could become more viable due to better investment in human capital, decreasing costs of planning and conducting large-scale cyber campaigns, increased government spending on developing cyber capabilities, and gaining and maintaining accesses to potential target sets, and the unknown unknowns of potentially disruptive technological innovations that make these attacks easier.

Strategic Implications of the Coercive Use of Cyber Power

This analysis explores the applicability of traditional theories of coercion to the cyber domain. We identify four key elements of coercion—communication, cost–benefit calculus, credibility, and reassurance—and assess how each manifests itself in cyberspace. We then analyze the utility of various warfighting strategies that seek to undermine an adversary's ability and/or willingness to resist and find that, based on the current state of the field, only three—attrition, denial, and decapitation—are likely to be useful for aspiring coercers in cyberspace. However, even these strategies are most useful in conjunction with conventional instruments of power and/or diplomacy; cyber power is rarely, if ever, independently decisive. For policymakers, this suggests that, especially if a coercing state has an asymmetrical advantage in other elements of national power, using cyber power to enable espionage, sabotage, and other shaping operations to support a cross-domain coercive strategy may be a more effective use of cyber capabilities than employing it as an independent instrument of state power.

This framework also highlights the importance of indices and developing an understanding of another state's intentions in cyberspace due to the high risk of misperception, which can lead to unintended outcomes and inadvertent escalation. A policy implication of this is that states should focus intelligence-collection efforts on developing an advanced understanding of the cyber capabilities and aspirations of potential adversaries. In addition to indices, states may also send signals through the use of cyber attacks. However, since neither of these signaling mechanisms is inherently clear, the most likely way to convey the intent behind an action in cyberspace is to ensure attribution and couple the

event with a diplomatic message or place it within the context of a conventional military operation. Furthermore, for cyber power to be an effective coercive tool, the target needs to believe that an attack will cease once she complies with the coercer's demands. This would require assurances that would have to come via established means that often do not yet exist. Providing a credible reassurance is difficult because many types of cyber attacks, such as DDoS attacks, can come from numerous users and make it difficult for the threatening state to credibly demonstrate it exerts control over a decentralized network of attackers. This leads to a paradox in which the type of cyber attack that is most likely to aid in reassuring a victim may also not be able to generate the punishment that would be necessary for capitulation.

Cyber power can be used as a coercive instrument of state power but, once the theory of coercion meets the reality of cyber operations, many attractive targets may become too costly and out of reach for a state to attack in a timely manner. Therefore, governments are more likely to pursue coercive strategies that allow for a wide variety of targets that are more easily accessible than hardened critical infrastructure. In other words, long development timelines and access constraints often mean that policymakers cannot attack their ideal target(s) in a timely manner and, therefore, are more likely to pursue warfighting strategies that do not necessitate sudden and intense devastation but, rather, inflict costs against vulnerable public and private interests. Given current levels of dependency on technology, this type of attack would provide damaging, but limited, effects. This has unique and potentially troubling implications. Since the end of the Second World War, many states have sought to limit their coercive attacks to key pieces of government and military infrastructure out of ethical and legal concerns surrounding targeting civilian infrastructure (and due to the domestic and international political costs of doing so). However, given that in cyberspace much of the vulnerable infrastructure is owned by private industry, policy-makers may reevaluate norms against targeting these systems as they pursue attrition, denial, or decapitation strategies. Cyber warfighting strategies that intentionally target civilian infrastructure, such as punishment and risk, are currently nonviable and ineffective. However, as technology evolves and the Internet of Things makes societies both more interconnected and vulnerable, states may find strategies that explicitly aim to wreak havoc on civilian populations more effective. Together, this suggests that, at the domestic level, governments should strive to continue to build resiliency into civilian networks and, at the international level, norms governing appropriate targeting in the cyber domain are urgently needed.

NOTES

1. Thomas C. Schelling makes the important distinction between compellence and deterrence. The former involves the threat or limited application of force to change an adversary's behavior, while the latter involves the threat of force (or pain, in Schelling's parlance), to preserve the status quo. See Thomas C. Schelling, *The Strategy of Conflict* (Cambridge, MA: Harvard University Press, 1960) and idem., *Arms and Influence* (New Haven, CT: Yale University Press, 2008), 69–86. Robert J. Art elaborates on this concept. See Robert J. Art, "To What Ends Military Power?" *International Security* 4, no. 4 (Spring 1980): 3–35.

2. The authors are grateful to Jack Snyder for pointing out the distinction between coercion and warfighting strategies.

3. Schelling, *Arms and Influence,* 3. Emphasis in the original. Alexander L. George et al. also emphasize that coercion can involve both the threat or limited application of military power. See Alexander L. George, David K. Hall, and William R. Simons, eds., *The Limits of Coercive Diplomacy: Laos, Cuba, Vietnam* (Boston: Little, Brown and Company, 1971), 2, 18. Lawrence Freedman distinguishes between coercion, as defined by Schelling, and "strategic coercion," which is "the deliberate and purposive use of overt threats to influence another's strategic choices." See Lawrence Freedman, "Strategic Coercion," in *Strategic Coercion: Concepts and Cases,* ed. Lawrence Freedman (Oxford: Oxford University Press, 1998), 15.

4. Robert A. Pape, *Bombing to Win: Air Power and Coercion in War* (Ithaca, NY: Cornell University Press, 1996), 4. It is important to note, however, that Pape's reference to coercion in this context is distinct from deterrence; Schelling uses the umbrella term "coercion" to refer to both compellence and deterrence. See also Daniel L. Byman and Matthew Waxman, *The Dynamics of Coercion: American Foreign Policy and the Limits of Military Might* (Cambridge: Cambridge University Press, 2002), 3.

5. Schelling, *Arms and Influence,* 2–6. Pape, *Bombing to Win,* 13.

6. Schelling, *Arms and Influence,* 18–34. Schelling links technological advances in the power to hurt with the increased "importance of war and threats of war as techniques of influence, not of destruction; of coercion and deterrence, not of conquest and defense; of bargaining and intimidation," 33.

7. Richard A. Clarke and Robert K. Knake, *Cyber War: The Next Threat to National Security and What to Do About It* (New York: Ecco, 2012), 1–8.

8. It is widely accepted that deterrence may be easier to achieve, but harder for social scientists to observe due its negative object (for example, we only observe deterrence failures). Conversely, compellence is easy to observe but more difficult to achieve for precisely the same reason—there are reputational costs associated with being seen to back down and concede to an adversary's demands. Leaders who are successfully deterred could point to a variety of reasons they chose to not alter the status quo without losing face. See the discussion in Schelling, *Arms and Influence,* 74–75; Robert J. Art, "Coercive Diplomacy: What Do We Know?" in *The United States and Coercive Diplomacy,* ed. Robert J. Art and Patrick M. Cronin (Washington, DC: United States Institute of Peace Press, 2003), 361–62.

9. See, for example, Pape, *Bombing to Win*; Todd S. Sechser, "Goliath's Curse: Coercive Threats and Asymmetric Power," *International Organization* 64, no. 4 (October 2010): 627–60; Wallace J. Thies, *When Governments Collide: Coercion and Diplomacy in the Vietnam Conflict, 1964–1968* (Berkeley: University of California Press, 1980); Alexander L. George, *Forceful Persuasion: Coercive Diplomacy as an Alternative to War* (Washington, DC: United States Institute of Peace Press, 1991); Art, "Coercive Diplomacy," Alexander L. George and William E. Simons, eds., *The Limits of Coercive Diplomacy,* 2nd ed. (Boulder, CO: Westview Press, 1990); Byman and Waxman, *Dynamics of Coercion*; Thomas J. Christensen, *Worse Than a Monolith: Alliance Politics and Problems of Coercive Diplomacy in Asia* (Princeton, NJ: Princeton University Press, 2011).

10. Of course, this is not an exhaustive list of all of the factors that contribute to successful coercion. For example, George and Simons identify nine conditions that favor coercive diplomacy: clarity of objective, strong motivation, asymmetry of motivation, sense of urgency, strong leadership, domestic support, international support, fear of unacceptable escalation, and clarity of terms. See George and Simons, eds., *Limits of Coercive Diplomacy,* 279–91. However, we propose that these various lists and factors could be grouped into the four main conditions identified above.

11. However, it is important to note a caveat that, in some instances, sending ambiguous signals can be advantageous for the purposes of coercion. Particularly in the context of nuclear bargaining, the threat that leaves something to chance—precisely because the risk of nuclear war generates extraordinary costs—may help a coercing state. See Schelling, *Strategy of Conflict,* chap. 8.

12. Idem., *Arms and Influence,* 3–4.

13. Jack Snyder and Erica D. Borghard, "The Cost of Empty Threats: A Penny, Not a Pound," *American Political Science Review* 105, no. 3 (August 2011): 429; Robert Jervis, "Deterrence Theory Revisited," *World Politics* 31, no. 2 (January 1979): 303; Richard Ned Lebow, *Between Peace and War: The Nature of International Crises*

(Baltimore, MD: Johns Hopkins University Press, 1981), 29–27; Glen H. Synder and Paul Diesing, *Conflict Among Nations: Bargaining, Decision Making, and System Structure in International Crises* (Princeton, NJ: Princeton University Press, 1977), 213–15, 220. Even Schelling acknowledges that "most commitments are ultimately ambiguous in detail," *Arms and Influence,* 67.

14. Freedman, "Strategic Coercion," 18; James D. Fearon, "Rationalist Explanations for War," *International Organization* 49, no. 3 (Summer 1995): 379–414.

15. Robert Jervis, *Perception and Misperception in International Politics* (Princeton, NJ: Princeton University Press, 1976).

16. Ibid., 117–202. Robert Jervis, "Signaling and Perception: Drawing Inferences and Projecting Images," in *Political Psychology,* ed. Kristen Renwick Monroe (Mahwah, NJ: Lawrence Erlbaum Associates, 2002), 306–8. See also Robert Jervis, *The Logic of Images in International Relations* (New York: Columbia University Press, 1970).

17. Jervis, "Signaling and Perception," 304.

18. Ibid., 300.

19. For further reference, see Andru E. Wall, "Demystifying the Title 10-Title 50 Debate: Distinguishing Military Operations, Intelligence Activities & Covert Action," *Harvard National Security Journal* 3 (December 2011): 85–142.

20. For more on norms and international law as they pertain to the cyber domain, see Catherine Lotrionte, "A Better Defense: Examining the United States' New Norms-Based Approach to Cyber Deterrence," *Georgetown Journal of International Affairs* 8, no. 10 (April 2014): 75–88; Martha Finnemore, "Cultivating International Cyber Norms," in *America's Cyber Future: Security and Prosperity in the Information Age,* ed. Kristin M. Lord and Travis Sharp (Washington, DC: Center for a New American Security, 2011).

21. For instance, it is easy to imagine how a single signal could get lost in the over eighty-eight thousand petabytes of IP traffic that are estimated to transverse the Internet per month.

22. For further discussion of risks surrounding the ambiguity of intent in cyberspace, see Shawn W. Lonergan, "Cooperation under the Cybersecurity Dilemma," in *Confronting Inequality: Wealth, Rights, and Power,* ed. Hugh Liebert, Thomas Sherlock, and Cole Pinheiro (New York: Sloan, 2016).

23. Geoffrey B. Demarest, "Espionage in International Law," *Denver Journal of International Law and Policy* 24 (1995): 321–48.

24. Jervis, *Logic of Images in International Relations,* 86–87.

25. Herbert Lin, "Escalation Dynamics and Conflict Termination in Cyberspace," *Strategic Studies Quarterly* 47 (2012): 57.

26. For further reference on attribution, see Thomas Rid and Ben Buchanan, "Attributing Cyber Attacks," *Journal of Strategic Studies* 38, no. 1–2 (2015): 4–37; Jon R. Lindsay, "Tipping the Scales: The Attribution Problem and the Feasibility of Deterrence against Cyberattack," *Journal of Cybersecurity* 1, no. 1 (2015): 1–15.

27. Gerhard Munz and Georg Carle, "Real-Time Analysis of Flow Data for Network Attack Detection" (paper presented at the 10th IFIP/IEEE International Symposium on Integrated Network Management, Munich, Germany, 21 May 2007).

28. Developing unique signatures of attackers and code developers is becoming more common as exploits become increasingly

sophisticated and threat data is shared among cyber security practitioners. Leon Panetta, "Remarks by Secretary Panetta on Cybersecurity to the Business Executives for National Security, New York City," 11 October 2012, http://archive.defense.gov/transcripts /transcript.aspx?transcriptid=5136. For a review of Panetta's speech, see Jack Goldsmith, "The Significance of Panetta's Cyber Speech and the Persistent Difficulty of Deterring Cyberattacks," *Lawfare,* 15 October 2012.

29. Jervis, *The Logic of Images in International Relations,* 139–44.

30. Damian Paletta and Felicia Schwartz, "Pentagon Deploys Cyberweapons against Islamic State," *Wall Street Journal,* 29 February 2016.

31. Goldsmith, "Panetta's Cyber Speech."

32. This, of course, creates something of a paradox for a coercing state because it may need to gain prior access to a system or network (which requires obfuscation and avoiding attribution) to send a subsequently attributable coercive signal. The one caveat to this is that cyber espionage could be used to conduct a data breach of sensitive information that can later be released to embarrass or otherwise intimidate some actor.

33. Byman and Waxman, *Dynamics of Coercion,* 11.

34. Pape, *Bombing to Win,* 12.

35. Byman and Waxman, *Dynamics of Coercion,* 10. Pape, *Bombing to Win,* 15–16.

36. Byman and Waxman, *Dynamics of Coercion,* 11.

37. George, *Forceful Persuasion,* 11–14. George also points out that the more expansive or extreme the demands of the coercing state are, the costlier the threat must be to secure compliance.

38. Byman and Waxman, *Dynamics of Coercion,* 10–14. Schelling, *Arms and Influence,* 86. Jack S. Levy, "Prospect Theory, Rational Choice, and International Relations," *International Studies Quarterly* 41, no. 1 (March 1997): 87–112.

39. "National Infrastructure Protection Plan: Partnering to Enhance Protection and Resiliency," *Department of Homeland Security,* 2009, https://www.dhs.gov/xlibrary/assets/NIPP_Plan.pdf.

40. Control systems are defined as, "Computer-based systems used within many infrastructure and industries to monitor and control sensitive processes and physical functions. These systems typically collect measurement and operational data from the field, process and display the information, and relay control commands to local or remote equipment or human-machine interfaces (operators)," ibid., 109.

41. Professor at Peking University, Beijing, China, in discussion with the authors, 17 June 2015.

42. David E. Sanger and Eric Schmitt, "Spy Agency Consensus Grows That Russia Hacked D.N.C.," *New York Times,* 26 July 2016.

43. Schelling, *Arms and Influence,* 36.

44. Randall L. Schweller, *Unanswered Threats: Political Constraints on the Balance of Power* (Princeton, NJ: Princeton University Press, 2008).

45. Schelling asserts that a country's image—others' expectations about how it is likely to behave—is "one of the few things worth fighting for." This is due to what Schelling describes as the interdependence of threats. See Schelling, *Arms and Influence,* 124, 55–59. Also see Herman Kahn, *On Thermonuclear War* (Princeton, NJ: Princeton University Press, 1960), 566. For a critique of the importance of

having a reputation for resolve, see Jonathan Mercer, *Reputation and International Politics* (Ithaca, NY: Cornell University Press, 1996).

46. Robert Jervis, "Deterrence and Perception," *International Security* 7, no. 3 (Winter 1982–1983): 9.

47. James D. Fearon, "Signaling Foreign Policy Interests: Tying Hands Versus Sinking Costs," *Journal of Conflict Resolution* 41, no. 1 (February 1997): 69.

48. Schelling, *Arms and Influence,* 150.

49. Fearon, "Signaling Foreign Policy Interests," 70. Schelling also refers to these dynamics in his discussion of commitment through the use of bridge burning, trip wire forces, plate glass windows, and engaging a nation's honor and prestige through public commitments. Schelling, *Arms and Influence,* 44–49.

50. Jervis, "Signaling and Perception," 300.

51. The idea that democracies have an advantage in costly signaling has been the conventional wisdom in the literature, although Jessica L. Weeks argues that autocratic regimes are also capable of generating audience costs. Jessica L. Weeks, "Autocratic Audience Costs: Regime Type and Signaling Resolve," *International Organization* 62, no. 1 (Winter 2008): 35–64. For a different critique of audience costs logic, see Snyder and Borghard, "The Cost of Empty Threats."

52. Fearon, "Signaling Foreign Policy Interests," 82–83.

53. Robert Jervis, *The Logic of Images in International Relations,* 26–28.

54. It general sense, it may be easier for democracies to showcase their level of cyber power due to greater institutionalized transparency over military organizations and budgets compared to authoritarian regimes.

55. For example, see H. J. Seo, Yoon-Cheol Choy, and SoonJa Hong, "A Study on the Methodology to Evaluate the Level of Nation's Capability for Cyber War" (paper presented at the 12th Annual International Workshop on Information Security Applications, Korea, August 2011).

56. Authoritarian states have gone to extensive efforts to institute hierarchies in their Internet infrastructure so that they can keep their citizens from accessing material that they deem may threaten regime stability. However, the West has pursued a free and open Internet that is largely devoid of state censorship. These conflicting visions for the Internet was evident in the 2012 breakdown of the United Nation's International Telecommunications Union's World Conference on International Communication (WCIT) when, in the wake of Arab Spring, many Middle Eastern states joined a voting bloc led by China and Russia to press for a treaty that limited the openness of the Internet and removed protections on free speech and human rights. In response, Canada, the United States, and many European states refused to ratify the treaty. This divide has given rise to extensive debates about Internet governance, state sovereignty in cyberspace, and the "Balkanization" of the Internet. See James D. Fielder, "The Internet and Dissent in Authoritarian State," in *Conflict and Cooperation in Cyberspace: The Challenge to National Security,* ed. Panayotis A. Yannakogeorgos and Adam B. Lowther (Boca Raton, FL: Taylor and Francis, 2014); Stephen K. Gourley, "Cyber Sovereignty," in *Conflict and Cooperation in Cyberspace*; Michael N. Schmitt, ed., *Tallinn Manual on the International Law Applicable to Cyber Warfare* (Cambridge: Cambridge University Press, 2013); Dana Polatin-Reuben and Joss Wright, "An Internet with Brics Characteristics: Data Sovereignty and the Balkanisation of the Internet" (paper presented at the 4th USENIX Workshop on Free and Open Communications on the Internet, San Diego, CA, 18 August 2014).

57. Fearon, "Signaling Foreign Policy Interests." Schelling, *Arms and Influence.* Christian Le Mière, "The Return of Gunboat Diplomacy," *Survival* 53, no. 5 (October–November 2011): 53–68.

58. Though nonstate actors may engage in these activities, the scope of this article is limited to state-to-state exchanges. Furthermore, while Fearon discusses both tying hands and sinking costs as mechanisms for generating costly signals, we focus on cyber operations as sunk costs because the tying hands logic is a poor fit for the cyber domain. The only likely allegory to tying hands in cyberspace is the ability, in some instances, to create automaticity by initiating an autonomous offensive cyber response.

59. Deloitte CIO Journal, "DDoS Attacks on U.S. Banks: Worst Yet to Come?" *Wall Street Journal,* 19 February 2013.

60. Data comes from black markets accessed on the Dark Net on 17 March 2016. We are grateful to "BillyBear" for his assistance with this.

61. David Jackson, "AP Twitter Feed Hacked; No Attack at White House," *USA Today,* 23 April 2013.

62. Polly Mosendz, "Syrian Electronic Army Claims to Have Hacked US Army Website," *Newsweek,* 8 June 2015. Brain Fung, "The Syrian Electronic Army Just Hacked the *Washington Post,* Again," *Washington Post,* 14 May 2015.

63. Julie Hirschfeld Davis, "Hacking of Government Computers Exposed 21.5 Million People," *New York Times,* 9 July 2015. David E. Sanger and Nicole Perlroth, "U.S. Said to Find North Korea Ordered Cyberattack on Sony" *New York Times,* 17 December 2014.

64. Langner, "Stuxnet's Secret Twin." Eric Oliver, "Stuxnet: A Case Study in Cyberwarfare," in *Conflict and Cooperation in Cyberspace.* Jon R. Lindsay, "Stuxnet and the Limits of Cyber Warfare," *Security Studies* 22, no. 3 (July–September 2013): 365–404.

65. Owens, Dam, and Lin, eds., *Cyberattack Capabilities,* 83–89.

66. Schelling, *Arms and Influence,* chap. 3.

67. Fearon, "Signaling Foreign Policy Interests." For an alternative point of view, see Snyder and Borghard, "The Cost of Empty Threats."

68. For a broader discussion of assurance strategies, see Jeffrey W. Knopf, "Varieties of Assurance," *Journal of Strategic Studies* 35, no. 3 (April 2002): 375–399.

69. Schelling, *Arms and Influence,* 4.

70. Ibid., 125.

71. Sechser, "Goliath's Curse."

72. Andreas Schmidt, "The Estonian Cyberattacks," in *A Fierce Domain: Conflict in Cyberspace, 1986 to 2012,* ed. Jason Healey (Vienna, VA: Cyber Conflict Studies Association, 2013), 182.

73. For further reference, see Erica D. Borghard and Shawn W. Lonergan, "Can States Calculate the Risks of Using Cyber Proxies?" *Orbis* 60, no. 3 (Summer 2016): 395–416.

74. Kim Zetter, "Report: Obama Ordered Stuxnet to Continue After Bug Caused It to Spread Wildly," *Wired,* 1 June 2012.

75. For further discussion of the likely impact of cyber on strategy in general, see Joseph S. Nye, Jr., "Nuclear Lessons for Cyber Security?" *Strategic Studies Quarterly* (Winter 2011): 18–36.

76. Anti-Access/Area-Denial strategies currently pursed by states to thwart the movement and maneuver of conventionally superior militaries in a theater of operations typically contain a strong element of cyber power. See, for example, Erica D. Borghard and Shawn W. Lonergan, "Will Air-Sea Battle Be 'Sunk' by Cyberwarriors?" *National Interest,* 8 December 2014.

77. Robert Pape defines coercion by denial as "using military means to prevent the target from attaining its political objectives or territorial goals." *Bombing to Win,* 13.

78. Byman and Waxman, *Dynamics of Coercion,* 78–82.

79. Clarke and Knake, *Cyber War,* 1–8.

80. David E. Sanger, "With Spy Charges, U.S. Draws a Line That Few Others Recognize," *New York Times,* 19 May 2014.

81. Pape, *Bombing to Win,* 79.

82. Thomas Rid, *Cyber War Will Not Take Place* (Oxford: Oxford University Press, 2013), xiv–xv.

83. Andrew H. Kydd, and Barbara F. Walter, "The Strategies of Terrorism," *International Security* 31, no. 1 (Summer 2006): 66.

84. Jeffrey Carr, *Inside Cyber Warfare,* 2nd ed. (Sebastopol, CA: O'Reilly, 2012), 183–84. Andreas Hagen, "The Russo-Georgian War 2008," *A Fierce Domain,* ed. Healy. Ronald J. Deibert,
Rafal Rohozinski, and Masashi Crete–Nishihata, "Cyclones in Cyberspace: Information Shaping and Denial in the 2008 Russia–Georgia War," *Security Dialogue* 43, no. 1 (February 2012): 3–24.

85. See Michael Joseph Gross, "World War 3.0," *Vanity Fair,* 30 March 2012; Erik Gartzke, "The Myth of Cyberwar: Bringing War in Cyberspace Back Down to Earth," *International Security* 38, no. 2 (Fall 2013): 41–73.

86. The utility of punishment or risk strategies in general is beyond the scope of this discussion.

87. Giulio Douhet, *The Command of the Air,* trans. Dino Ferrari (New York: Coward-McCann, 1942), 57–58.

88. Ibid., 57.

89. Beyond Schelling, see, for instance, Patrick M. Morgan, *Deterrence: A Conceptual Analysis* (Beverly Hills, CA: Sage Publications, 1977); Robert Powell, *Nuclear Deterrence Theory: The Search for Credibility* (Cambridge: Cambridge University Press, 1990); Kahn, *On Thermonuclear War.*

90. Schelling, *Arms and Influence,* 3. Also see Pape's discussion of manipulation of risk in *Bombing to Win,* 66–69.

91. Schelling, *Arms and Influence,* 89. Italics in the original.

92. Jayavardhana Gubbi et al., "Internet of Things (IoT): A Vision, Architectural Elements, and Future Directions," *Future Generation Computer Systems* 29, no. 4 (September 2013): 1645–60.

7 INTERNATIONAL COOPERATION AND INTERNATIONAL LAW

Cooperation is a central facet of states' interactions in the international system today, and states often comply with international law. This occurs even though the international system is anarchic and states that cooperate can be exploited by others. There is no world government or world police to enforce international law, to make states cooperate with one another, or to protect states from coercion by other states. This raises an interesting question that many scholars have sought to address: If no one is making them do so, why do states often follow international law and cooperate despite the fact that this makes them vulnerable to exploitation and coercion by other states? The works in this chapter tackle this question from a variety of approaches.

In his article "Cooperation under the Security Dilemma," Robert Jervis uses the game-theoretic framework of the prisoner's dilemma to identify conditions that can help ameliorate the impact of anarchy and assuage states' fear of being exploited or coerced. He shows that dynamics among states can foster cooperation if they increase the gains of mutual cooperation and decrease the costs of cooperating when others do not, if they decrease the gains of taking advantage of cooperation by others and increase the costs of mutual noncooperation, or if they increase each side's expectation that the others will cooperate.

Robert Axelrod and Robert Keohane, in their article "Achieving Cooperation under Anarchy: Strategies and Institutions," also use the prisoner's dilemma to address the question of cooperation, identifying more specific factors that can help states overcome the problem. They highlight the fact that states can have shared interests, that the shadow of the future can be long, and that more than just two states are often involved. All of these factors help to assuage the prisoner's dilemma and foster cooperation.

The other two works address the question of why states often comply with international law. In "International Law: A Compliance-Based Theory," Andrew Guzman provides an overview of the various theories in the traditional legal literature and international relations literature that seek to explain why states comply. Focusing on human rights law in particular, Harold Koh presents a theory in his article "How Is International Human Rights Law Enforced?" about what he calls a "transnational legal process" which can drive compliance. This process involves interactions through which global norms of international human rights law are debated, interpreted, and then internalized in states' domestic legal systems. This internalization is sporadic, however, which is why compliance is not absolute.

Robert Jervis

COOPERATION UNDER THE SECURITY DILEMMA

I. Anarchy and the Security Dilemma

The lack of an international sovereign not only permits wars to occur, but also makes it difficult for states that are satisfied with the status quo to arrive at goals that they recognize as being in their common interest. Because there are no institutions or authorities that can make and enforce international laws, the policies of cooperation that will bring mutual rewards if others cooperate may bring disaster if they do not. Because states are aware of this, anarchy encourages behavior that leaves all concerned worse off than they could be, even in the extreme case in which all states would like to freeze the status quo. This is true of the men in Rousseau's "Stag Hunt." If they cooperate to trap the stag, they will all eat well. But if one person defects to chase a rabbit—which he likes less than stag—none of the others will get anything. Thus, all actors have the same preference order, and there is a solution that gives each his first choice: (1) cooperate and trap the stag (the international analogue being cooperation and disarmament); (2) chase a rabbit while others remain at their posts (maintain a high level of arms while others are disarmed); (3) all chase rabbits (arms competition and high risk of war); and (4) stay at the original position while another chases a rabbit (being disarmed while others are armed). Unless

From *World Politics* 30, no. 2 (Jan. 1978): 167–214. Some of the author's notes have been omitted.

each person thinks that the others will cooperate, he himself will not. And why might he fear that any other person would do something that would sacrifice his own first choice? The other might not understand the situation, or might not be able to control his impulses if he saw a rabbit, or might fear that some other member of the group is unreliable. If the person voices any of these suspicions, others are more likely to fear that he will defect, thus making them more likely to defect, thus making it more rational for him to defect. Of course in this simple case—and in many that are more realistic—there are a number of arrangements that could permit cooperation. But the main point remains: although actors may know that they seek a common goal, they may not be able to reach it.

Even when there is a solution that is everyone's first choice, the international case is characterized by three difficulties not present in the Stag Hunt. First, to the incentives to defect given above must be added the potent fear that even if the other state now supports the status quo, it may become dissatisfied later. No matter how much decision makers are committed to the status quo, they cannot bind themselves and their successors to the same path. Minds can be changed, new leaders can come to power, values can shift, new opportunities and dangers can arise.

The second problem arises from a possible solution. In order to protect their possessions, states often seek to control resources or land outside their own territory. Countries that are not self-sufficient must try to assure that the necessary supplies will continue to flow in wartime. This was part of the explanation for Japan's drive into China and Southeast Asia before World War II. If there were an international authority that could guarantee access, this motive for control would disappear. But since there is not, even a state that would prefer the status quo to increasing its area of control may pursue the latter policy.

When there are believed to be tight linkages between domestic and foreign policy or between the domestic politics of two states, the quest for security may drive states to interfere pre-emptively in the domestic politics of others in order to provide an ideological buffer zone. * * *

More frequently, the concern is with direct attack. In order to protect themselves, states seek to control, or at least to neutralize, areas on their borders. But attempts to establish buffer zones can alarm others who have stakes there, who fear that undesirable precedents will be set, or who believe that their own vulnerability will be increased. When buffers are sought in areas empty of great powers, expansion tends to feed on itself in order to protect what is acquired. * * *

Though this process is most clearly visible when it involves territorial expansion, it often operates with the increase of less tangible power and influence. The expansion of power usually brings with it an expansion of responsibilities and commitments; to meet them, still greater power is required. The state will take many positions that are subject to challenge. It will be involved with a wide range of controversial issues unrelated to its core values. And retreats that would be seen as normal if made by a small power would be taken as an index of weakness inviting predation if made by a large one.

The third problem present in international politics but not in the Stag Hunt is the security dilemma: many of the means by which a state tries to increase its security decrease the security of others. In domestic society, there are several ways to increase the safety of one's person and property without endangering others. One can move to a safer neighborhood, put bars on the windows, avoid dark streets, and keep a distance from suspicious-looking characters. Of course these measures are not convenient, cheap, or certain of success. But no one save criminals need be alarmed if a person takes them. In international politics, however, one state's gain in security often inadvertently threatens others. In explaining British policy on naval disarmament in the interwar period to the Japanese, Ramsey MacDonald said that "Nobody wanted Japan to be insecure."[1] But the problem was not with British desires, but with the consequences of her policy. In earlier periods, too, Britain had needed a navy large enough to keep the shipping lanes open. But such a navy could not avoid being a menace to any other state with a coast that could be raided, trade that could be interdicted, or colonies that could be isolated. When Germany started building a powerful navy before World War I, Britain objected that it could only be an offensive weapon aimed at her. As Sir Edward Grey, the Foreign Secretary, put it to King Edward VII: "If the German Fleet ever becomes superior to ours, the German Army can conquer this country. There is no corresponding risk of this kind to Germany; for however superior our Fleet was, no naval victory could bring us any nearer to Berlin." The English position was half correct: Germany's navy was an anti-British instrument. But the British often overlooked what the Germans knew full well: "in every quarrel with England, German colonies and trade were . . . hostages for England to take." Thus, whether she intended it or not, the British Navy constituted an important instrument of coercion.[2]

II. What Makes Cooperation More Likely?

Given this gloomy picture, the obvious question is, why are we not all dead? Or, to put it less starkly,

Figure 7.1. Stag Hunt and Prisoner's Dilemma

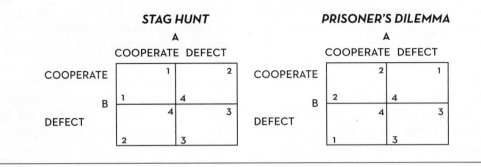

what kinds of variables ameliorate the impact of anarchy and the security dilemma? The working of several can be seen in terms of the Stag Hunt or repeated plays of the Prisoner's Dilemma.[3] The Prisoner's Dilemma differs from the Stag Hunt in that there is no solution that is in the best interests of all the participants; there are offensive as well as defensive incentives to defect from the coalition with the others; and, if the game is to be played only once, the only rational response is to defect [Figure 7.1]. But if the game is repeated indefinitely, the latter characteristic no longer holds and we can analyze the game in terms similar to those applied to the Stag Hunt. It would be in the interest of each actor to have others deprived of the power to defect; each would be willing to sacrifice this ability if others were similarly restrained. But if the others are not, then it is in the actor's interest to retain the power to defect.[4] The game theory matrices for these two situations are given [above], with the numbers in the boxes being the order of the actor's preferences.

We can see the logical possibilities by rephrasing our question: "Given either of the above situations, what makes it more or less likely that the players will cooperate and arrive at CC?" The chances of achieving this outcome will be increased by: (1) anything that increases incentives to cooperate by increasing the gains of mutual cooperation (CC) and/or decreasing the costs the actor will pay

if he cooperates and the other does not (CD); (2) anything that decreases the incentives for defecting by decreasing the gains of taking advantage of the other (DC) and/or increasing the costs of mutual noncooperation (DD); (3) anything that increases each side's expectation that the other will cooperate.[5]

The Costs of Being Exploited (CD)

The fear of being exploited (that is, the cost of CD) most strongly drives the security dilemma; one of the main reasons why international life is not more nasty, brutish, and short is that states are not as vulnerable as men are in a state of nature. People are easy to kill, but as Adam Smith replied to a friend who feared that the Napoleonic Wars would ruin England, "Sir, there is a great deal of ruin in a nation."[6] The easier it is to destroy a state, the greater the reason for it either to join a larger and more secure unit, or else to be especially suspicious of others, to require a large army, and, if conditions are favorable, to attack at the slightest provocation rather than wait to be attacked. If the failure to eat that day—be it venison or rabbit—means that he will starve, a person is likely to defect in the Stag Hunt even if he really likes venison and has a high level of trust in his colleagues.

(Defection is especially likely if the others are also starving or if they know that he is.) By contrast, if the costs of CD are lower, if people are well-fed or states are resilient, they can afford to take a more relaxed view of threats.

A relatively low cost of CD has the effect of transforming the game from one in which both players make their choices simultaneously to one in which an actor can make his choice after the other has moved. He will not have to defect out of fear that the other will, but can wait to see what the other will do. States that can afford to be cheated in a bargain or that cannot be destroyed by a surprise attack can more easily trust others and need not act at the first, and ambiguous, sign of menace. Because they have a margin of time and error, they need not match, or more than match, any others' arms in peacetime. They can mobilize in the prewar period or even at the start of the war itself, and still survive. For example, those who opposed a crash program to develop the H-bomb felt that the U.S. margin of safety was large enough so that even if Russia managed to gain a lead in the race, America would not be endangered. The program's advocates disagreed: "If we let the Russians get the super first, catastrophe becomes all but certain."[7]

When the costs of CD are tolerable, not only is security easier to attain but, what is even more important here, the relatively low level of arms and relatively passive foreign policy that a status-quo power will be able to adopt are less likely to threaten others. Thus it is easier for status-quo states to act on their common interests if they are hard to conquer. All other things being equal, a world of small states will feel the effects of anarchy much more than a world of large ones. Defensible borders, large size, and protection against sudden attack not only aid the state, but facilitate cooperation that can benefit all states.

Of course, if one state gains invulnerability by being more powerful than most others, the problem will remain because its security provides a base from which it can exploit others. When the price a state will pay for DD is low, it leaves others with few hostages for its good behavior. Others who are more vulnerable will grow apprehensive, which will lead them to acquire more arms and will reduce the chances of cooperation. The best situation is one in which a state will not suffer greatly if others exploit it, for example, by cheating on an arms control agreement (that is, the costs of CD are low); but it will pay a high long-run price if cooperation with the others breaks down—for example, if agreements cease functioning or if there is a long war (that is, the costs of DD are high). The state's invulnerability is then mostly passive; it provides some protection, but it cannot be used to menace others. As we will discuss below, this situation is approximated when it is easier for states to defend themselves than to attack others, or when mutual deterrence obtains because neither side can protect itself.

The differences between highly vulnerable and less vulnerable states are illustrated by the contrasting policies of Britain and Austria after the Napoleonic Wars. Britain's geographic isolation and political stability allowed her to take a fairly relaxed view of disturbances on the Continent. Minor wars and small changes in territory or in the distribution of power did not affect her vital interests. An adversary who was out to overthrow the system could be stopped after he had made his intentions clear. And revolutions within other states were no menace, since they would not set off unrest within England. Austria, surrounded by strong powers, was not so fortunate; her policy had to be more closely attuned to all conflicts. By the time an aggressor-state had clearly shown its colors, Austria would be gravely threatened. And foreign revolutions, be they democratic or nationalistic, would encourage groups in Austria to upset the existing order. So it is not surprising that Metternich propounded the doctrine summarized earlier, which defended Austria's right to interfere in the internal affairs of others, and that

British leaders rejected this view. Similarly, Austria wanted the Congress system to be a relatively tight one, regulating most disputes. The British favored a less centralized system. In other words, in order to protect herself, Austria had either to threaten or to harm others, whereas Britain did not. For Austria and her neighbors the security dilemma was acute; for Britain it was not.

The ultimate cost of CD is of course loss of sovereignty. This cost can vary from situation to situation. The lower it is (for instance, because the two states have compatible ideologies, are similar ethnically, have a common culture, or because the citizens of the losing state expect economic benefits), the less the impact of the security dilemma; the greater the costs, the greater the impact of the dilemma. Here is another reason why extreme differences in values and ideologies exacerbate international conflict.

■   ■   ■

SUBJECTIVE SECURITY DEMANDS

Decision makers act in terms of the vulnerability they feel, which can differ from the actual situation; we must therefore examine the decision makers' subjective security requirements. Two dimensions are involved. First, even if they agree about the objective situation, people can differ about how much security they desire—or, to put it more precisely, about the price they are willing to pay to gain increments of security. The more states value their security above all else (that is, see a prohibitively high cost in CD), the more they are likely to be sensitive to even minimal threats, and to demand high levels of arms. And if arms are positively valued because of pressures from a military-industrial complex, it will be especially hard for status-quo powers to cooperate. By contrast, the security dilemma will not operate as strongly when pressing domestic concerns increase the opportunity costs of armaments. In this case, the net advantage of exploiting the other (DC)

will be less, and the costs of arms races (that is, one aspect of DD) will be greater; therefore the state will behave as though it were relatively invulnerable.

The second aspect of subjective security is the perception of threat (that is, the estimate of whether the other will cooperate). A state that is predisposed to see either a specific other state as an adversary, or others in general as a menace, will react more strongly and more quickly than a state that sees its environment as benign. Indeed, when a state believes that another not only is not likely to be an adversary, but has sufficient interests in common with it to be an ally, then it will actually welcome an increase in the other's power.

■   ■   ■

Geography, Commitments, Beliefs, and Security through Expansion

* * * Situations vary in the ease or difficulty with which all states can simultaneously achieve a high degree of security. The influence of military technology on this variable is the subject of the next section. Here we want to treat the impact of beliefs, geography, and commitments (many of which can be considered to be modifications of geography, since they bind states to defend areas outside their homelands). In the crowded continent of Europe, security requirements were hard to mesh. Being surrounded by powerful states, Germany's problem—or the problem created by Germany—was always great and was even worse when her relations with both France and Russia were bad, such as before World War I. In that case, even a status-quo Germany, if she could not change the political situation, would almost have been forced to adopt something like the Schlieffen Plan. Because she could not hold off both of her enemies, she had to be prepared to defeat one quickly and then deal

with the other in a more leisurely fashion. If France or Russia stayed out of a war between the other state and Germany, they would allow Germany to dominate the Continent (even if that was not Germany's aim). They therefore had to deny Germany this ability, thus making Germany less secure. Although Germany's arrogant and erratic behavior, coupled with the desire for an unreasonably high level of security (which amounted to the desire to escape from her geographic plight), compounded the problem, even wise German statesmen would have been hard put to gain a high degree of security without alarming their neighbors.

■ ■ ■

III. Offense, Defense, and the Security Dilemma

Another approach starts with the central point of the security dilemma—that an increase in one state's security decreases the security of others—and examines the conditions under which this proposition holds. Two crucial variables are involved: whether defensive weapons and policies can be distinguished from offensive ones, and whether the defense or the offense has the advantage. The definitions are not always clear, and many cases are difficult to judge, but these two variables shed a great deal of light on the question of whether status-quo powers will adopt compatible security policies. All the variables discussed so far leave the heart of the problem untouched. But when defensive weapons differ from offensive ones, it is possible for a state to make itself more secure without making others less secure. And when the defense has the advantage over the offense, a large increase in one state's security only slightly decreases the security of the others, and status-quo powers can all enjoy a high level of security and largely escape from the state of nature.

Offense-Defense Balance

When we say that the offense has the advantage, we simply mean that it is easier to destroy the other's army and take its territory than it is to defend one's own. When the defense has the advantage, it is easier to protect and to hold than it is to move forward, destroy, and take. If effective defenses can be erected quickly, an attacker may be able to keep territory he has taken in an initial victory. Thus, the dominance of the defense made it very hard for Britain and France to push Germany out of France in World War I. But when superior defenses are difficult for an aggressor to improvise on the battlefield and must be constructed during peacetime, they provide no direct assistance to him.

The security dilemma is at its most vicious when commitments, strategy, or technology dictate that the only route to security lies through expansion. Status-quo powers must then act like aggressors; the fact that they would gladly agree to forego the opportunity for expansion in return for guarantees for their security has no implications for their behavior. Even if expansion is not sought as a goal in itself, there will be quick and drastic changes in the distribution of territory and influence. Conversely, when the defense has the advantage, status-quo states can make themselves more secure without gravely endangering others.[8] Indeed, if the defense has enough of an advantage and if the states are of roughly equal size, not only will the security dilemma cease to inhibit status-quo states from cooperating, but aggression will be next to impossible, thus rendering international anarchy relatively unimportant. If states cannot conquer each other, then the lack of sovereignty, although it presents problems of collective goods in a number of areas, no longer forces states to devote their primary attention to self-preservation. Although, if force were not usable, there would be fewer restraints on the use of nonmilitary instruments, these are rarely powerful enough to threaten the vital interests of a major state.

Two questions of the offense-defense balance can be separated. First, does the state have to spend more or less than one dollar on defensive forces to offset each dollar spent by the other side on forces that could be used to attack? If the state has one dollar to spend on increasing its security, should it put it into offensive or defensive forces? Second, with a given inventory of forces, is it better to attack or to defend? Is there an incentive to strike first or to absorb the other's blow? These two aspects are often linked: if each dollar spent on offense can overcome each dollar spent on defense, and if both sides have the same defense budgets, then both are likely to build offensive forces and find it attractive to attack rather than to wait for the adversary to strike.

These aspects affect the security dilemma in different ways. The first has its greatest impact on arms races. If the defense has the advantage, and if the status-quo powers have reasonable subjective security requirements, they can probably avoid an arms race. Although an increase in one side's arms and security will still decrease the other's security, the former's increase will be larger than the latter's decrease. So if one side increases its arms, the other can bring its security back up to its previous level by adding a smaller amount to its forces. And if the first side reacts to this change, its increase will also be smaller than the stimulus that produced it. Thus a stable equilibrium will be reached. Shifting from dynamics to statics, each side can be quite secure with forces roughly equal to those of the other. Indeed, if the defense is much more potent than the offense, each side can be willing to have forces much smaller than the other's, and can be indifferent to a wide range of the other's defense policies.

The second aspect—whether it is better to attack or to defend—influences short-run stability. When the offense has the advantage, a state's reaction to international tension will increase the chances of war. The incentives for pre-emption and the "reciprocal fear of surprise attack" in this situation have been made clear by analyses of the dangers that exist when two countries have first-strike capabilities.[9] There is no way for the state to increase its security without menacing, or even attacking, the other. Even Bismarck, who once called preventive war "committing suicide from fear of death," said that "no government, if it regards war as inevitable even if it does not want it, would be so foolish as to leave to the enemy the choice of time and occasion and to wait for the moment which is most convenient for the enemy."[10] In another arena, the same dilemma applies to the policeman in a dark alley confronting a suspected criminal who appears to be holding a weapon. Though racism may indeed be present, the security dilemma can account for many of the tragic shootings of innocent people in the ghettos.

Beliefs about the course of a war in which the offense has the advantage further deepen the security dilemma. When there are incentives to strike first, a successful attack will usually so weaken the other side that victory will be relatively quick, bloodless, and decisive. It is in these periods when conquest is possible and attractive that states consolidate power internally—for instance, by destroying the feudal barons—and expand externally. There are several consequences that decrease the chance of cooperation among status-quo states. First, war will be profitable for the winner. The costs will be low and the benefits high. Of course, losers will suffer; the fear of losing could induce states to try to form stable cooperative arrangements, but the temptation of victory will make this particularly difficult. Second, because wars are expected to be both frequent and short, there will be incentives for high levels of arms, and quick and strong reaction to the other's increases in arms. The state cannot afford to wait until there is unambiguous evidence that the other is building new weapons. Even large states that have faith in their economic strength cannot wait, because the war will be over before their products can reach the army. Third, when wars are quick, states will have to recruit allies in advance.[11] Without the opportunity for bargaining and re-alignments during the opening stages of hostilities, peacetime diplomacy loses a degree of the fluidity that facilitates balance-of-power policies. Because alliances must be secured during peacetime, the international system is more likely to become bipo-lar. It is hard to say whether war therefore becomes more or less likely, but this bipolarity increases ten-sion between the two camps and makes it harder for status-quo states to gain the benefits of coopera-tion. Fourth, if wars are frequent, statesmen's per-ceptual thresholds will be adjusted accordingly and they will be quick to perceive ambiguous evidence as indicating that others are aggressive. Thus, there will be more cases of status-quo powers arming against each other in the incorrect belief that the other is hostile.

When the defense has the advantage, all the foregoing is reversed. The state that fears attack does not pre-empt—since that would be a waste-ful use of its military resources—but rather pre-pares to receive an attack. Doing so does not decrease the security of others, and several states can do it simultaneously; the situation will there-fore be stable, and status-quo powers will be able to cooperate. * * *

More is involved than short-run dynamics. When the defense is dominant, wars are likely to become stalemates and can be won only at enor-mous cost. Relatively small and weak states can hold off larger and stronger ones, or can deter attack by raising the costs of conquest to an unac-ceptable level. States then approach equality in what they can do to each other. Like the .45-caliber pistol in the American West, fortifications were the "great equalizer" in some periods. Changes in the status quo are less frequent and cooperation is more common wherever the security dilemma is thereby reduced.

Many of these arguments can be illustrated by the major powers' policies in the periods preceding the two world wars. Bismarck's wars surprised statesmen by showing that the offense had the advantage, and by being quick, relatively cheap, and quite decisive. Falling into a common error, observers projected this pattern into the future. The resulting expectations had several effects. First, states sought semi-permanent allies. In the early stages of the Franco-Prussian War, Napoleon III had thought that there would be plenty of time to recruit Austria to his side. Now, others were not going to repeat this mistake. Sec-ond, defense budgets were high and reacted quite sharply to increases on the other side. * * * Third, most decision makers thought that the next Euro-pean war would not cost much blood and trea-sure.[12] That is one reason why war was generally seen as inevitable and why mass opinion was so bellicose. Fourth, once war seemed likely, there were strong pressures to pre-empt. Both sides believed that whoever moved first could penetrate the other deep enough to disrupt mobilization and thus gain an insurmountable advantage. (There was no such belief about the use of naval forces. Although Churchill made an ill-advised speech saying that if German ships "do not come out and fight in time of war they will be dug out like rats in a hole,"[13] everyone knew that submarines, mines, and coastal fortifications made this impossible. So at the start of the war each navy prepared to defend itself rather than attack, and the short-run destabi-lizing forces that launched the armies toward each other did not operate.)[14] Furthermore, each side knew that the other saw the situation the same way, thus increasing the perceived danger that the other would attack, and giving each added reasons to pre-cipitate a war if conditions seemed favorable. In the long and the short run, there were thus both offen-sive and defensive incentives to strike. This situa-tion casts light on the common question about German motives in 1914: "Did Germany unleash the war deliberately to become a world power or did she support Austria merely to defend a weakening ally," thereby protecting her own position?[15] To some extent, this question is misleading. Because of the perceived advantage of the offense, war was seen as the best route both to gaining expansion and to avoiding drastic loss of influence. There seemed to be no way for Germany merely to retain and safeguard her existing position.

Of course the war showed these beliefs to have been wrong on all points. Trenches and machine guns gave the defense an overwhelming advantage. The fighting became deadlocked and produced horrendous casualties. It made no sense for the combatants to bleed themselves to death. If they had known the power of the defense beforehand, they would have rushed for their own trenches rather than for the enemy's territory. Each side could have done this without increasing the other's incentives to strike. War might have broken out anyway, * * * but at least the pressures of time and the fear of allowing the other to get the first blow would not have contributed to this end. And, had both sides known the costs of the war, they would have negotiated much more seriously. The obvious question is why the states did not seek a negotiated settlement as soon as the shape of the war became clear. Schlieffen had said that if his plan failed, peace should be sought.[16] The answer is complex, uncertain, and largely outside of the scope of our concerns. But part of the reason was the hope and sometimes the expectation that breakthroughs could be made and the dominance of the offensive restored. Without that hope, the political and psychological pressures to fight to a decisive victory might have been overcome.

The politics of the interwar period were shaped by the memories of the previous conflict and the belief that any future war would resemble it. Political and military lessons reinforced each other in ameliorating the security dilemma. Because it was believed that the First World War had been a mistake that could have been avoided by skillful conciliation, both Britain and, to a lesser extent, France were highly sensitive to the possibility that interwar Germany was not a real threat to peace,

and alert to the danger that reacting quickly and strongly to her arms could create unnecessary conflict. And because Britain and France expected the defense to continue to dominate, they concluded that it was safe to adopt a more relaxed and nonthreatening military posture.[17] Britain also felt less need to maintain tight alliance bonds. The Allies' military posture then constituted only a slight danger to Germany; had the latter been content with the status quo, it would have been easy for both sides to have felt secure behind their lines of fortifications. Of course the Germans were not content, so it is not surprising that they devoted their money and attention to finding ways out of a defense-dominated stalemate. *Blitzkrieg* tactics were necessary if they were to use force to change the status quo.

The initial stages of the war on the Western Front also contrasted with the First World War. Only with the new air arm were there any incentives to strike first, and these forces were too weak to carry out the grandiose plans that had been both dreamed and feared. The armies, still the main instrument, rushed to defensive positions. Perhaps the allies could have successfully attacked while the Germans were occupied in Poland.[18] But belief in the defense was so great that this was never seriously contemplated. Three months after the start of the war, the French Prime Minister summed up the view held by almost everyone but Hitler: on the Western Front there is "deadlock. Two Forces of equal strength and the one that attacks seeing such enormous casualties that it cannot move without endangering the continuation of the war or of the aftermath."[19] The Allies were caught in a dilemma they never fully recognized, let alone solved. On the one hand, they had very high war aims; although unconditional surrender had not yet been adopted, the British had decided from the start that the removal of Hitler was a necessary condition for peace.[20] On the other hand, there were no realistic plans or instruments for allowing the Allies to impose their will on the other side. The British Chief of the Imperial General Staff noted, "The French have no intention of carrying out an offensive for years, if at all"; the British were only slightly bolder.[21] So the Allies looked to a long war that would wear the Germans down, cause civilian suffering through shortages, and eventually undermine Hitler. There was little analysis to support this view—and indeed it probably was not supportable—but as long as the defense was dominant and the numbers on each side relatively equal, what else could the Allies do?

To summarize, the security dilemma was much less powerful after World War I than it had been before. In the later period, the expected power of the defense allowed status-quo states to pursue compatible security policies and avoid arms races. Furthermore, high tension and fear of war did not set off short-run dynamics by which each state, trying to increase its security, inadvertently acted to make war more likely. The expected high costs of war, however, led the Allies to believe that no sane German leader would run the risks entailed in an attempt to dominate the Continent, and discouraged them from risking war themselves.

TECHNOLOGY AND GEOGRAPHY

Technology and geography are the two main factors that determine whether the offense or the defense has the advantage. As Brodie notes, "On the tactical level, as a rule, few physical factors favor the attacker but many favor the defender. The defender usually has the advantage of cover. He characteristically fires from behind some form of shelter while his opponent crosses open ground."[22] Anything that increases the amount of ground the attacker has to cross, or impedes his progress across it, or makes him more vulnerable while crossing, increases the advantage accruing to the defense. When states are separated by barriers that produce these effects, the security dilemma is eased, since both can have forces adequate for defense without being able to attack. * * *

Oceans, large rivers, and mountain ranges serve the same function as buffer zones. Being hard to cross, they allow defense against superior numbers. The defender has merely to stay on his side of the barrier and so can utilize all the men he can bring up to it. The attacker's men, however, can cross only a few at a time, and they are very vulnerable when doing so. If all states were self-sufficient islands, anarchy would be much less of a problem. A small investment in shore defenses and a small army would be sufficient to repel invasion. Only very weak states would be vulnerable, and only very large ones could menace others. As noted above, the United States, and to a lesser extent Great Britain, have partly been able to escape from the state of nature because their geographical positions approximated this ideal.

Although geography cannot be changed to conform to borders, borders can and do change to conform to geography. Borders across which an attack is easy tend to be unstable. States living within them are likely to expand or be absorbed. Frequent wars are almost inevitable since attacking will often seem the best way to protect what one has. This process will stop, or at least slow down, when the state's borders reach—by expansion or contraction—a line of natural obstacles. Security without attack will then be possible. Furthermore, these lines constitute salient solutions to bargaining problems and, to the extent that they are barriers to migration, are likely to divide ethnic groups, thereby raising the costs and lowering the incentives for conquest.

Attachment to one's state and its land reinforce one quasi-geographical aid to the defense. Conquest usually becomes more difficult the deeper the attacker pushes into the other's territory. Nationalism spurs the defenders to fight harder; advancing not only lengthens the attacker's supply lines, but takes him through unfamiliar and often devastated lands that require troops for garrison duty. These stabilizing dynamics will not operate, however, if the defender's war materiel is situated near its borders, or if the people do not care about their state, but only about being on the winning side. * * *

■   ■   ■

The other major determinant of the offense-defense balance is technology. When weapons are highly vulnerable, they must be employed before they are attacked. Others can remain quite invulnerable in their bases. The former characteristics are embodied in unprotected missiles and many kinds of bombers. (It should be noted that it is not vulnerability *per se* that is crucial, but the location of the vulnerability. Bombers and missiles that are easy to destroy only after having been launched toward their targets do not create destabilizing dynamics.) Incentives to strike first are usually absent for naval forces that are threatened by a naval attack. Like missiles in hardened silos, they are usually well protected when in their bases. Both sides can then simultaneously be prepared to defend themselves successfully.

In ground warfare under some conditions, forts, trenches, and small groups of men in prepared positions can hold off large numbers of attackers. * * *

■   ■   ■

Concerning nuclear weapons, it is generally agreed that defense is impossible—a triumph not of the offense, but of deterrence. Attack makes no sense, not because it can be beaten off, but because the attacker will be destroyed in turn. In terms of the questions under consideration here, the result is the equivalent of the primacy of the defense. First, security is relatively cheap. Less than one percent of the GNP is devoted to deterring a direct attack on the United States; most of it is spent on acquiring redundant systems to provide a lot of insurance against the worst conceivable contingencies. Second, both sides can simultaneously

gain security in the form of second-strike capability. Third, and related to the foregoing, second-strike capability can be maintained in the face of wide variations in the other side's military posture. There is no purely military reason why each side has to react quickly and strongly to the other's increases in arms. Any spending that the other devotes to trying to achieve first-strike capability can be neutralized by the state's spending much smaller sums on protecting its second-strike capability. Fourth, there are no incentives to strike first in a crisis.

■   ■   ■

Offense-Defense Differentiation

The other major variable that affects how strongly the security dilemma operates is whether weapons and policies that protect the state also provide the capability for attack. If they do not, the basic postulate of the security dilemma no longer applies. A state can increase its own security without decreasing that of others. The advantage of the defense can only ameliorate the security dilemma. A differentiation between offensive and defensive stances comes close to abolishing it. Such differentiation does not mean, however, that all security problems will be abolished. If the offense has the advantage, conquest and aggression will still be possible. And if the offense's advantage is great enough, status-quo powers may find it too expensive to protect themselves by defensive forces and decide to procure offensive weapons even though this will menace others. Furthermore, states will still have to worry that even if the other's military posture shows that it is peaceful now, it may develop aggressive intentions in the future.

Assuming that the defense is at least as potent as the offense, the differentiation between them allows status-quo states to behave in ways that are clearly different from those of aggressors. Three beneficial consequences follow. First, status-quo powers can identify each other, thus laying the foundations for cooperation. Conflicts growing out of the mistaken belief that the other side is expansionist will be less frequent. Second, status-quo states will obtain advance warning when others plan aggression. Before a state can attack, it has to develop and deploy offensive weapons. If procurement of these weapons cannot be disguised and takes a fair amount of time, as it almost always does, a status-quo state will have the time to take countermeasures. It need not maintain a high level of defensive arms as long as its potential adversaries are adopting a peaceful posture. * * *

■   ■   ■

* * * [I]f all states support the status quo, an obvious arms control agreement is a ban on weapons that are useful for attacking. As President Roosevelt put it in his message to the Geneva Disarmament Conference in 1933: "If all nations will agree wholly to eliminate from possession and use the weapons which make possible a successful attack, defenses automatically will become impregnable, and the frontiers and independence of every nation will become secure."[23] The fact that such treaties have been rare * * * shows either that states are not always willing to guarantee the security of others, or that it is hard to distinguish offensive from defensive weapons.

■   ■   ■

IV. Four Worlds

The two variables we have been discussing—whether the offense or the defense has the advantage, and whether offensive postures can be distinguished from defensive ones—can be combined to yield four possible worlds.

The first world is the worst for status-quo states. There is no way to get security without menacing others, and security through defense is terribly difficult to obtain. Because offensive and defensive postures are the same, status-quo states acquire the same kind of arms that are sought by aggressors. And because the offense has the advantage over the defense, attacking is the best route to protecting what you have; status-quo states will therefore behave like aggressors. The situation will be unstable. Arms races are likely. Incentives to strike first will turn crises into wars. Decisive victories and conquests will be common. States will grow and shrink rapidly, and it will be hard for any state to maintain its size and influence without trying to increase them. Cooperation among status-quo powers will be extremely hard to achieve.

There are no cases that totally fit this picture, but it bears more than a passing resemblance to Europe before World War I. Britain and Germany, although in many respects natural allies, ended up as enemies. Of course much of the explanation lies in Germany's ill-chosen policy. And from the perspective of our theory, the powers' ability to avoid war in a series of earlier crises cannot be easily explained. Nevertheless, much of the behavior in this period was the product of technology and beliefs that magnified the security dilemma. Decision makers thought that the offense had a big advantage and saw little difference between offensive and defensive military postures. The era was characterized by arms races. And once war seemed likely, mobilization races created powerful incentives to strike first.

In the nuclear era, the first world would be one in which each side relied on vulnerable weapons that were aimed at similar forces and each side understood the situation. In this case, the incentives to strike first would be very high—so high that status-quo powers as well as aggressors would be sorely tempted to pre-empt. And since the forces could be used to change the status quo as well as to preserve it, there would be no way for both sides to increase their security simultaneously. Now the familiar logic of deterrence leads both sides to see the dangers in this world.

Figure 7.2. The Security Dilemma

	Offense Has the Advantage	Defense Has the Advantage
Offensive Posture Not Distinguishable from Defensive One	1 Doubly dangerous.	2 Security dilemma, but security requirements may be compatible.
Offensive Posture Distinguishable from Defensive One	3 No security dilemma, but aggression possible. Status-quo states can follow different policy than aggressors. Warning given.	4 Doubly stable.

Indeed, the new understanding of this situation was one reason why vulnerable bombers and missiles were replaced. Ironically, the 1950s would have been more hazardous if the decision makers had been aware of the dangers of their posture and had therefore felt greater pressure to strike first. This situation could be recreated if both sides were to rely on MIRVed ICBMs.

In the second world, the security dilemma operates because offensive and defensive postures cannot be distinguished; but it does not operate as strongly as in the first world because the defense has the advantage, and so an increment in one side's strength increases its security more than it decreases the other's. So, if both sides have reasonable subjective security requirements, are of roughly equal power, and the variables discussed earlier are favorable, it is quite likely that status-quo states can adopt compatible security policies. * * *

This world is the one that comes closest to matching most periods in history. Attacking is usually harder than defending because of the strength of fortifications and obstacles. But purely defensive postures are rarely possible because fortifications are usually supplemented by armies and mobile guns which can support an attack. In the nuclear era, this world would be one in which both sides relied on relatively invulnerable ICBMs and believed that limited nuclear war was impossible. * * *

In the third world there may be no security dilemma, but there are security problems. Because states can procure defensive systems that do not threaten others, the dilemma need not operate. But because the offense has the advantage, aggression is possible, and perhaps easy. If the offense has enough of an advantage, even a status-quo state may take the initiative rather than risk being attacked and defeated. If the offense has less of an advantage, stability and cooperation are likely because the status-quo states will procure defensive forces. They need not react to others who are similarly armed, but can wait for the warning they would receive if others started to deploy offensive weapons. But each state will have to watch the others carefully, and there is room for false suspicions. The costliness of the defense and the allure of the offense can lead to unnecessary mistrust, hostility, and war, unless some of the variables discussed earlier are operating to restrain defection.

■　■　■

The fourth world is doubly safe. The differentiation between offensive and defensive systems permits a way out of the security dilemma; the advantage of the defense disposes of the problems discussed in the previous paragraphs. There is no reason for a status-quo power to be tempted to procure offensive forces, and aggressors give notice of their intentions by the posture they adopt. Indeed, if the advantage of the defense is great enough, there are no security problems. The loss of the ultimate form of the power to alter the status quo would allow greater scope for the exercise of non-military means and probably would tend to freeze the distribution of values.

■　■　■

NOTES

1. Quoted in Gerald Wheeler, *Prelude to Pearl Harbor* (Columbia: University of Missouri Press 1963), 167.
2. Quoted in Leonard Wainstein, "The Dreadnought Gap," in Robert Art and Kenneth Waltz, eds., *The Use of Force* (Boston: Little, Brown 1971), 155. * * *
3. In another article, Jervis says: "International politics sometimes resembles what is called a Prisoner's Dilemma (PD). In this scenario, two men have been caught red-handed committing a minor crime. The district attorney knows that they are also guilty of a much more serious offense. He tells each of them separately that if he confesses and squeals on his buddy, he will go free and the former colleague will go to jail for thirty years. If both of them refuse to give any information, they will be prosecuted for the minor crime and be jailed for thirty days; if they both squeal, plea-bargaining will get them ten years. In other words, as long as each criminal cares only about himself, he will confess to the more serious crime no matter what he thinks his colleague will do. If he confesses and his buddy does not, he will get the best possible outcome (freedom); if he confesses and his buddy also does so, the outcome will not be good (ten years in jail), but it will be better than keeping silent and going to jail for thirty years. Since both can see this, both will confess. Paradoxically, if they had both been irrational and kept quiet, they would have gone to jail for only a month." (Robert Jervis, "A Political Science Perspective on the Balance of Power and the Concert," *American Historical Review* 97, no. 3 (June 1992): 720.)
4. Experimental evidence for this proposition is summarized in James Tedeschi, Barry Schlenker, and Thomas Bonoma, *Conflict, Power, and Games* (Chicago: Aldine 1973), 135–41.
5. The results of Prisoner's Dilemma games played in the labouratory support this argument. See Anatol Rapoport and Albert Chammah, *Prisoner's Dilemma* (Ann Arbor: University of Michigan Press 1965), 33–50. Also see Robert Axelrod, *Conflict of Interest* (Chicago: Markham 1970), 60–70.
6. Quoted in Bernard Brodie, *Strategy in the Missile Age* (Princeton: Princeton University Press 1959), 6.
7. Herbert York, *The Advisors: Oppenheimer, Teller, and the Superbomb* (San Francisco: Freeman 1976), 56–60.
8. Thus, when Wolfers [*Discord and Collaboration* (Baltimore: Johns Hopkins Press 1962),] 126, argues that a status-quo state that settles for rough equality of power with its adversary, rather than seeking preponderance, may be able to convince the other to reciprocate by showing that it wants only to protect itself, not menace the other, he assumes that the defense has an advantage.
9. Schelling, [*The Strategy of Conflict* (New York: Oxford University Press 1963),] chap. 9.
10. Quoted in Fritz Fischer, *War of Illusions* (New York: Norton 1975), 377, 461.
11. George Quester, *Offense and Defense in the International System* (New York: John Wiley 1977), 105–06; Sontag [*European Diplomatic History, 1871–1932* (New York: Appleton-Century-Crofts 1933)], 4–5.
12. Some were not so optimistic. Gray's remark is well-known: "The lamps are going out all over Europe; we shall not see them lit again in our life-time." The German Prime Minister, Bethmann Hollweg, also feared the consequences of the war. But the controlling view was that it would certainly pay for the winner.
13. Quoted in Martin Gilbert, *Winston S. Churchill*, III, *The Challenge of War, 1914–1916* (Boston: Houghton Mifflin 1971), 84.
14. Quester (fn. 33), 98–99. Robert Art, *The Influence of Foreign Policy on Seapower*, II (Beverly Hills: Sage Professional Papers in International Studies Series 1973), 14–18, 26–28.
15. Konrad Jarausch, "The Illusion of Limited War: Chancellor Bethmann Hollweg's Calculated Risk, July 1914," *Central European History*, II (March 1969), 50.
16. Brodie (fn. 6), 58.
17. President Roosevelt and the American delegates to the League of Nations Disarmament Conference maintained that the tank and mobile heavy artillery had re-established the dominance of the offensive, thus making disarmament more urgent (Boggs, [*Attempts to Define and. Limit "Aggressive" Armament in Diplomacy and Strategy* (Columbia: University of Missouri Studies, XVI, No. 1, 1941)], pp. 31, 108), but this was a minority position and may not even have been believed by the Americans. The reduced prestige and influence of the military, and the high pressures to cut government spending throughout this period also contributed to the lowering of defense budgets.

18. Jon Kimche, *The Unfought Battle* (New York: Stein 1968); Nicholas William Bethell, *The War Hitler Won: The Fall of Poland, September 1939* (New York: Holt 1972); Alan Alexandroff and Richard Rosecrance, "Deterrence in 1939," *World Politics,* XXIX (April 1977), 404–24.

19. Roderick Macleod and Denis Kelly, eds., *Time Unguarded: The Ironside Diaries, 1937–1940* (New York: McKay 1962), 173.

20. For a short time, as France was falling, the British Cabinet did discuss reaching a negotiated peace with Hitler. The official history ignores this, but it is covered in P.M.H. Bell, *A Certain Eventuality* (Farnborough, England: Saxon House 1974), 40–48.

21. Macleod and Kelly (fn. 19), 174. In flat contradiction to common sense and almost everything they believed about modern warfare, the Allies planned an expedition to Scandinavia to cut the supply of iron ore to Germany and to aid Finland against the Russians. But the dominant mood was the one described above.

22. Brodie (fn. 6), 179.

23. Quoted in Merze Tate, *The United States and Armaments* (Cambridge: Harvard University Press 1948), 108.

Robert Axelrod and Robert O. Keohane

ACHIEVING COOPERATION UNDER ANARCHY
Strategies and Institutions

Achieving cooperation is difficult in world politics. There is no common government to enforce rules, and by the standards of domestic society, international institutions are weak. Cheating and deception are endemic. Yet, as the articles in this symposium have shown, cooperation is sometimes attained. World politics is not a homogeneous state of war: cooperation varies among issues and over time.

Before trying to draw conclusions about the factors that promote cooperation under anarchy, let us recall the definitions of these key terms. Cooperation is not equivalent to harmony. Harmony requires complete identity of interests, but cooperation can only take place in situations that contain a mixture of conflicting and complementary interests. In such situations, cooperation occurs when actors adjust their behavior to the actual or anticipated preferences of others. Cooperation, thus defined, is not necessarily good from a moral point of view.

Anarchy also needs to be defined clearly. As used here, the term refers to a lack of common government in world politics, not to a denial that an international society—albeit a fragmented one—exists. Clearly, many international relationships continue over time, and engender stable expectations about behavior. To say that world politics is anarchic does not imply that it entirely lacks organization. Relationships among actors may be

carefully structured in some issue-areas, even though they remain loose in others. Likewise, some issues may be closely linked through the operation of institutions while the boundaries of other issues, as well as the norms and principles to be followed, are subject to dispute. Anarchy, defined as lack of common government, remains a constant; but the degree to which interactions are structured, and the means by which they are structured, vary.

It has often been noted that military-security issues display more of the characteristics associated with anarchy than do political-economic ones. Charles Lipson, for instance, has recently observed that political-economic relationships are typically more institutionalized than military-security ones.[1] This does not mean, however, that analysis of these two sets of issues requires two separate analytical frameworks. Indeed, one of the major purposes of the present collection is to show that a single framework can throw light on both.

The case studies in this symposium have shown that the three dimensions discussed in the introduction—mutuality of interest, the shadow of the future, and the number of players—help us to understand the success and failure of attempts at cooperation in both military-security and political-economic relations. Section I of this essay synthesizes some of the findings of these case studies, and thereby helps to specify some of the most important ways in which these three factors affect world politics. It deals with issues in isolation from one another, as separate games or as a series of games,

From *World Politics* 38, no. 1 (October 1985): 226–54.

in order to clarify some basic analytic points. In this section, we follow the lead of game theorists, who have tried to avoid complicating their models with extraneous material in order to reach interesting conclusions. If the problem is a small event, such as a duel between two airplanes, our analysis of it may not depend on knowledge of the context (e.g., the purpose of the war). If the issue is of very high salience to participants, such as the 1914 crisis or the Cuban missile crisis, the extraneous issues (such as tariffs, or pollution of the Caribbean) may be so insignificant that they can be ignored. Either way, the strategy of focusing only on the central interaction is clearly justified.

Yet if the issue is neither isolated nor all-consuming, the context within which it takes place may have a decisive impact on its politics and its outcomes. As the case studies illustrate, world politics includes a rich variety of contexts. Issues arise against distinctive backgrounds of past experience; they are linked to other issues being dealt with simultaneously by the same actors; and they are viewed by participants through the prisms of their expectations about the future. To ignore the effects of context would be to overlook many of the most interesting questions raised by a game-theoretic perspective on the problem of cooperation.

In Section II, we therefore consider the context of issues; in so doing, we move outward from the three dimensions on which this collection focuses toward broader considerations, including linkages among issues, multilevel games, complications encountered by strategies of reciprocity in complex situations, and the role of international institutions. Analysis of the context of games leads us to regard context as malleable: not only can actors in world politics pursue different strategies within an established context of interaction, they may also seek to alter that context through building institutions embodying particular principles, norms, rules, or procedures for the conduct of international relations. In the conclusion, we will

argue that a contextual approach to strategy—by leading us to see the importance of international institutions—helps us to forge necessary links between game-theoretic arguments and theories about international regimes.

The Effects of Structure on Cooperation

Three situational dimensions affect the propensity of actors to cooperate: mutuality of interest, the shadow of the future, and the number of actors.

Payoff Structure: Mutual and Conflicting Preferences

It is well established that the payoff structure for a game affects the level of cooperation. For comparisons within a given type of game, this idea was first formalized by Axelrod, who established a measure of conflict of interest for specific games, including Prisoners' Dilemma.[2] Experimental evidence demonstrated that the greater the conflict of interest between the players, the greater the likelihood that the players would in fact choose to defect. Jervis has elaborated on these theories and shown that different types of games, such as Stag Hunt and Chicken, have different potentials for cooperation.[3] He has also applied his strategic analysis to historical and contemporary problems related to the security dilemma. His work clearly indicates that international cooperation is much easier to achieve in some game settings than in others.

Payoff structures often depend on events that take place outside of the control of the actors. The economic depressions of 1873–1896 and of the early 1930s stimulated demands for protection by firms and individuals in distress, and therefore reduced the incentives of governments to cooperate with one another. The weakness and vacillation of the British and French governments before 1939 reduced the potential value of anti-German alliances with those countries for the Soviet Union, making a Nazi-Soviet pact seem relatively more attractive.

This is obvious enough. Slightly less obvious is another point about mutuality of interests: the payoff structure that determines mutuality of interests is not based simply upon objective factors, but is grounded upon the actors' perceptions of their own interests. Perceptions define interests. Therefore, to understand the degree of mutuality of interests (or to enhance this mutuality) we must understand the process by which interests are perceived and preferences determined.

One way to understand this process is to see it as involving a change in payoffs, so that a game such as Prisoners' Dilemma becomes either more or less conflictual. To start with, Prisoners' Dilemma is a game in which both players have an incentive to defect no matter whether the other player cooperates or defects. If the other player *cooperates*, the first player prefers to defect: $DC > CC$. On the other hand, if the other player *defects*, the first player still prefers to defect: $DD > CD$. The dilemma is that, if both defect, both do worse than if both had cooperated: $CC > DD$. Thus, Prisoners' Dilemma has a preference ordering for both players of $DC > CC > DD > CD$.[4]

Now consider a shift in the preferences of both players, so that mutual cooperation is preferred to unilateral defection. This makes the preference ordering $CC > DC > DD > CD$, which is a less conflictual game called Stag Hunt.

Jervis's study of the shift from balance-of-power systems to concerts suggests that after world wars, the payoff matrix for the victors may temporarily be one of Stag Hunt: fighting together results in a short-lived preference for staying together. After a war against a hegemonic power, the other great powers often perceive a mutual interest in continuing to work together in order to ensure that the defeated would-be hegemon does not rise

again. They may even feel empathy for one another, and take an interest in each other's welfare. These perceptions seem to have substantial momentum, both among the mass public and in the bureaucracy. Yet, the cooperation that ensues is subject to fairly easy disruption. As recovery from the war proceeds, one or both parties may come to value cooperation less and relative gains more. And if one side believes that its counterpart prefers to defect, its own preference will shift to defection in order to avoid the worst payoff, CD.

Actors can also move from Prisoners' Dilemma to more conflictual games. If both players come to believe that mutual cooperation is worse than mutual defection, the game becomes Deadlock, with both sides having preferences of $DC > DD > CC > CD$. Since the dominant strategy of each player is to defect regardless of what the other does, the likely outcome is DD. Players in Deadlock, unlike those in Prisoners' Dilemma, will not benefit from repeated plays since mutual cooperation is not preferred to mutual defection.

Kenneth Oye provides a fine example of the movement from Prisoners' Dilemma to Deadlock in his essay on monetary diplomacy in the 1930s, in this collection. Shifts in beliefs, not only about international regimes, but particularly about desirable economic policy, led leaders such as Franklin D. Roosevelt to prefer unilateral, uncoordinated action to international cooperation on the terms that appeared feasible. Oye argues that the early 1930s do not mark a failure of coordination where common interests existed (as in Prisoners' Dilemma); rather, they indicate the decay of these common interests, as perceived by participants. In their essay, Downs, Rocke, and Siverson argue that arms races are often games of Deadlock rather than Prisoners' Dilemma, making them much more difficult to resolve.

Beliefs are as important in the military area as in economics. Consider, for example, Van Evera's study of the beliefs leading to World War I. By 1914, what Van Evera labels "the cult of the offensive" was universally accepted in the major European countries. It was a congenial doctrine for military elites everywhere, since it magnified the role of the military and reduced that of the diplomats. It also happened to be disastrously wrong, since its adherents failed to appreciate the overwhelming advantage that recent technological change had given to the defensive (in what was soon to become trench warfare), and overlooked the experiences of the American Civil War and the Russo-Japanese War.

Gripped by this cult of the offensive, European leaders sought to gain safer borders by expanding national territories, and took more seriously the possibility of successful aggressive war; hence Germany and (to a lesser extent) other European powers adopted expansionist policies that brought them into collision with one another. European leaders also felt greater compulsion to mobilize and strike first in a crisis, since the penalty of moving late would be greater in an offense-dominant world; this compulsion then fueled the spiral of mobilization and countermobilization that drove the July 1914 crisis out of control. Had Europeans recognized the actual power of the defense, expansionism would have lost much of its appeal, and the compulsion to mobilize and countermobilize would have diminished. Put differently, the European payoff structure actually would have rewarded cooperation; but Europeans perceived a payoff structure that rewarded *non*cooperation, and responded accordingly. Beliefs, not realities, governed conduct.

The case of 1914 also illustrates a point made above: subjective interpretations by one side become objective reality for the other side. When a European state adopted expansionist policies, those nearby found themselves with an expansionist neighbor, and had to adjust accordingly. For instance, Germany's expansionism, though largely based on illusions, led to a genuine change in Russia's environment. Russia adopted its inflexible war plan (which required mobilization against

Germany as well as against Austria) partly because the Russians feared that Germany would strike into Russia's northern territories once the Russian armies were embroiled with Austria. Thus the Russian calculus was importantly affected by Russia's image of German intent, and Russia was driven to bellicose measures by fear of German bellicosity. German expansionism was premised largely on illusions, but for Russia this expansionism was a real danger that required a response.

This discussion of payoff structures should make it clear that the contributors to this volume do not assume that Prisoners' Dilemmas are typical of world politics. More powerful actors often face less powerful ones, yielding asymmetric payoff matrices. Furthermore, even symmetrical games can take a variety of forms, as illustrated by Stag Hunt, Chicken, and Deadlock. What is important for our purposes is not to focus exclusively on Prisoners' Dilemma *per se*, but to emphasize the fundamental problem that it (along with Stag Hunt and Chicken) illustrates. In these games, myopic pursuit of self-interest can be disastrous. Yet both sides can potentially benefit from cooperation—if they can only achieve it. Thus, choices of strategies and variations in institutions are particularly important, and the scope for the exercise of intelligence is considerable.

Our review of payoff structures also illustrates one of the major themes of this collection of essays: that political-economic and military-security issues can be analyzed with the same analytical framework. Admittedly, economic issues usually seem to exhibit less conflictual payoff structures than do those of military security. Coordination among bankers, as described by Lipson, has been more extensive and successful than most arms control negotiations, as analyzed by Downs and his colleagues; and the patterns of trade conflict and cooperation described by Conybeare are hardly as conflictual as Van Evera's story of World War I. On the other hand, the great power concerts discussed by Jervis, as well as several of the arms control negotiations, were more cooperative than the trade and monetary measures of 1930–1933 delineated in Oye's essay. And postwar economic relations between the United States and Japan have been more conflictual than military-security relations. As an empirical matter, military issues may more often have payoff structures involving a great deal of conflict of interest; but there is no theoretical reason to believe that this must always be the case.[5]

The Shadow of the Future

In Prisoners' Dilemma, concern about the future helps to promote cooperation. The more future payoffs are valued relative to current payoffs, the less the incentive to defect today—since the other side is likely to retaliate tomorrow.[6] The cases discussed in the present essays support this argument, and identify specific factors that help to make the shadow of the future an effective promoter of cooperation. These factors include:

1. long time horizons;
2. regularity of stakes;
3. reliability of information about the others' actions;
4. quick feedback about changes in the others' actions.

The dimension of the shadow of the future seems to differentiate military from economic issues more sharply than does the dimension of payoffs. Indeed, its four components can be used to analyze some of the reasons why issues of international political economy may be settled more cooperatively than issues of international security, even when the underlying payoff matrices are similar—for example, when Prisoners' Dilemma applies. Most important is a combination of the first two factors: long time horizons and regularity of stakes. In economic relations, actors have to expect that their relationships will continue over an indefinite period of time; that is, the games they play with each other will be iterated. Typically, neither side in an economic interaction can eliminate the other, or change the nature of the game decisively in a single move. In security affairs, by contrast, the possibility of a successful preemptive war can sometimes be a tempting occasion for the rational timing of surprise.[7] Another way to put this is that, in the international political economy, retaliation for defection will almost always be possible; therefore a rational player, considering defection, has to consider its probability and its potential consequences. In security affairs, it may be possible to limit or destroy the opponent's capacity for effective retaliation.

To illustrate this point, let us compare the case of 1914 with contemporary international debt negotiations. In 1914, some Germans, imbued with the cult of the offensive, thought that a continental war would permanently solve Germany's security problems by restructuring power and territorial relations in Europe. For these German leaders, the temptation to defect was huge, largely because the shadow of the future seemed so small. Indeed, it seemed that future retaliation could be prevented, or rendered ineffective, by decisive German action. Moreover, in the opening move of a war the stakes would be far greater than usual because of the value of preempting before the other side was fully mobilized. This perceived irregularity in the stakes further undercut the potential for sustained cooperation based upon reciprocity.

By contrast, contemporary negotiations among banks, and between banks and debtor countries, are heavily affected by the shadow of the future. That is not to say that the stakes of each game are the same; indeed, there are great discontinuities since deadlines for rescheduling take on importance for regulators, banks, and the reputations of borrowers. But the banks know that they will be dealing both with the debtor countries and with one another again and again. Continuing interbank relationships imply, as Lipson points out, that small banks will think twice before double crossing large banks by refusing to participate in rescheduling. This is particularly true if the small banks are closely tied, in a variety of ways, to the large banks. Continuing relations between banks and debtor countries give the banks incentives to cooperate with the debtor countries, not merely in order to facilitate debt servicing on loans already made, but to stay in their good graces—looking toward a more prosperous future. The fact that Argentina, Brazil, and Mexico are so large, and are perceived to be potentially wealthy, is a significant bargaining asset for them now, since it increases the banks' expected profits from future lending, and therefore enlarges the shadow of the future. Indeed, if these governments could credibly promise to favor, in the future, banks that help them now, and to punish or ignore those that defect in these critical times, they could further improve their bargaining positions; but, as sovereign governments whose leaders will be different in the future, they cannot effectively do so.

Reliability of information about the others' actions and promptness of feedback are also important in affecting the shadow of the future, although they do not seem to differentiate military-security from political-economic issues so clearly. Because of the absence of military secrecy, actors may sometimes have more reliable information on political-economic than on military-security issues. Banks thrive on differential access to information, and therefore hold it closely. Furthermore, since the systemic effects of political-economic actions are often difficult to judge, and "cheating at the margin" is frequently easy, feedback between policy and results may be slow. For instance, the distribution of benefits from the Tokyo Round of trade negotiations is still a matter of conjecture and political contention rather than economic knowledge. By contrast, the superpowers publish lists of the precise number of missiles in each other's inventories, and we can assume that information about the effect of a military action by either side—short

of a devastating surprise attack that would destroy command and control facilities—would be communicated almost immediately to the leaders of both states.

The length of the shadow of the future, like the character of payoff structures, is not necessarily dictated by the objective attributes of a situation. On the contrary, as we have just seen, expectations are important. International institutions may therefore be significant, since institutions embody, and affect, actors' expectations.[8] Thus institutions can alter the extent to which governments expect their present actions to affect the behavior of others on future issues. The principles and rules of international regimes make governments concerned about precedents, increasing the likelihood that they will attempt to punish defectors. In this way, international regimes help to link the future with the present. That is as true of arms control agreements, in which willingness to make future agreements depends on others' compliance with previous arrangements, as it is in the General Agreement on Tariffs and Trade, which embodies norms and rules against which the behavior of members can be judged. By sanctioning retaliation for those who violate rules, regimes create expectations that a given violation will be treated not as an isolated case but as one in a series of interrelated actions.

Number of Actors: Sanctioning Problems

The ability of governments to cooperate in a mixed-motive game is affected not only by the payoff structure and the shadow of the future, but also by the number of players in the game and by how their relationships are structured. Axelrod has shown that reciprocity can be an effective strategy to induce cooperation among self-interested players in the iterated, bilateral Prisoners' Dilemma, where the values of each actor's options are clearly specified.[9] However, effective reciprocity depends on three conditions: (1) players can identify defectors; (2) they are able to focus retaliation on defectors; and (3) they have sufficient long-run incentives to punish defectors. When there are many actors, these conditions are often more difficult to satisfy. In such situations, it may be impossible to identify, much less to punish, defection; even if it is possible, none of the cooperators may have an incentive to play the role of policeman. Each cooperator may seek to be a free-rider on the willingness of others to enforce the rules.

We may call the difficulty of preventing defection through decentralized retaliation the "sanctioning problem." Its first form, the inability to identify defectors, is illustrated by the terrorist bombings against American installations in Lebanon in 1983. The United States did not know, at the time the bombings took place, who was responsible. The only state that could plausibly have been held responsible was Syria; but since the Syrians denied responsibility, retaliation against Damascus could have spread and deepened the conflict without punishing the terrorist groups themselves. The issue of identifying defectors is one aspect of a fundamental problem besetting efforts to cooperate in world politics: acquiring, in a timely fashion, adequate amounts of high-quality information. In order to maintain cooperation in games that reward unreciprocated defection, such as Prisoners' Dilemma, governments must have confidence in their ability to monitor their counterparts' actions sufficiently well to enable them to respond effectively to betrayal. As Lipson has pointed out, the greater perils of betrayal (to the side that is betrayed) in military-security than in political-economic relations put more severe demands on gathering information in the former than in the latter area.[10]

The second form of the sanctioning problem occurs when players are unable to focus retaliation on defectors. This difficulty is illustrated by Conybeare's analysis of the Anglo-Hanse trade wars. The Hanseatic League was unable to punish English privateers for their depredations, and instead retaliated against English merchants in Hanseatic towns. This produced escalation rather than cooperation.

The third form of the sanctioning problem arises when some members of a group lack incentives to punish defectors. This obstacle to cooperation often arises where there are many actors, some of which fail to cooperate in the common effort to achieve some collective good. Oye observes that although British devaluation in 1931 hurt other countries, no single government had the incentive to devote its own resources to bring about a revision of British policy. This form of the sanctioning problem—lack of incentives to punish defectors—also arose in the debt negotiations of the 1980s. To prevent default, it was necessary to arrange rescheduling agreements involving additional bank lending. Smaller banks were tempted to refuse to provide new funds. Only the fact that the large banks had strong incentives to put pressure on smaller ones to ante up prevented rescheduling agreements from unravelling "like a cheap sweater."

When sanctioning problems are severe, cooperation is in danger of collapsing. One way to bolster it is to restructure the situation so that sanctioning becomes more feasible. Sometimes this is done unilaterally. Oye points out that external benefits or costs may be "privatizable"; that is, changes can be made in the situation so that the benefits and costs of one's actions are directed specifically at those with whom one has negotiated. He argues that in the early 1930s Britain eventually succeeded in privatizing its international currency relationships by adopting exchange controls and attaching conditions, negotiated bilaterally, to new loans. This transformation of the game permitted a modest revival of international lending, based not on open access to British capital markets but on bilateral reciprocity.

As our examples indicate, sanctioning problems can occur both in the international political economy and on military-security issues. They tend to be more severe on military-security than on political-economy issues, due to the high costs of punishing defections, the difficulties of monitoring behavior, and the stringent demands for information that are imposed when successful defection can dramatically shorten the shadow of the future. But since sanctioning problems occur on both types of issues, issue-area alone cannot account for their incidence or severity. To explain the incidence and severity of sanctioning problems, we need to focus on the conditions that determine whether defection can be prevented through decentralized retaliation: the ease of identifying sources of action, the ability of governments to focus retaliation or reward on particular targets, and the incentives that exist for members of a group to punish defectors.

While the likelihood that these problems will arise may be enhanced by an increase in the number of actors involved, difficulties may also appear on issues that seem at first glance to be strictly bilateral. Consider, for instance, the example of 1914. In the Balkan crisis, Austria sought to impose sanctions against Serbia for its support of revolutionaries who tried to destroy the ethnically heterogeneous Austro-Hungarian empire. But sanctions against Serbia implied punishment for Russia, Serbia's ally, since Russian leaders were averse to accepting another Balkan setback. Russian mobilization, however, could not be directed solely against Austria, since Russia only had plans for general mobilization.[11] Thus, neither Austria nor Russia was able to focus retaliation on the defector; the actions of both helped to spread rather than to contain the crisis. With more clever and moderate leadership, Austria might have found a way to punish Serbia without threatening Russia. And a detailed plan for mobilization only against Austria could have provided Russia with a more precisely directed measure to retaliate against Austria's ultimatum to Serbia.

Privatization is not the only way to maintain cooperation. Moreover, as some of our examples indicate, it can be difficult to achieve. Another way to resolve sanctioning problems is to construct international regimes to provide standards against which actions can be measured, and to assign responsibility for applying sanctions. Regimes provide information about actors' compliance; they facilitate the development and maintenance of reputations; they can be incorporated into actors' rules of thumb for responding to others' actions; and they may even apportion responsibility for decentralized enforcement of rules.[12]

Charles Lipson's discussion of the international lending regime that has been constructed by bankers reveals how regimes can promote cooperation even when there are many actors, no dominant power, and no world central bank. Creditor committees were established under the leadership of large money-center banks. Each money-center bank then took responsibility for a number of relatively large regional banks, which in turn were assigned similar responsibilities for smaller banks.[13] As a result, a hierarchy of banks was created, isolating smaller banks from one another and establishing responsibility for enforcing sanctions. Small banks displaying tendencies toward defection were threatened with being outside the flow of information in the future and, implicitly, with not being offered participation in lucrative future loans. This informal hierarchy, of course, was reinforced by the presence of the U.S. Federal Reserve System looming in the background: stories, whether apocryphal or not, of small bankers being told to "cough up" by high officials of the Fed circulated in banking circles during the early 1980s. It would have taken a bold president of a small bank to ignore both the banking hierarchy and the danger of arousing the Fed's wrath by not participating in a rescheduling.

This reference to the role of institutions in transforming N-person games into collections of two-person games suggests once again the importance of the context within which games are played. In isolation, the basic concepts discussed in the introduction—payoff structures, iteration, and the number of players—provide only a framework for analysis. They take on greater significance, as well as complexity, when they are viewed within the broader context of other issues, other games, and the institutions that affect the course of world politics. We now turn to the question of how the context of interaction affects political behavior and outcomes.

The Context of Interaction

Whether cooperation can take place without central guidance depends not merely on the three game-theoretic dimensions we have emphasized so far, but also on the context within which interaction takes place. Context may, of course, mean many different things. Any interaction takes place within the context of norms that are shared, often implicitly, by the participants. John Ruggie has written of the "deep structure" of sovereignty in world politics,[14] and also of the way in which shifting values and norms of state intervention in society—the emergence and legitimation of the welfare state—affected the world political economy between 1914 and 1945. International political-economic bargaining was fundamentally changed by the shift, during this period, from laissez-faire liberalism as a norm to what Ruggie calls "embedded liberalism."[15]

Interactions also take place within the context of institutions. Robert Keohane has argued elsewhere that even if one adopts the assumption that states are rational and self-interested actors, institutions can be shown to be important in world politics.[16] Institutions alter the payoff structures facing actors, they may lengthen the shadow of the future, and they may enable N-person games to be broken down into games with smaller numbers of actors.

Using the game-theoretic perspective of this symposium, another way of looking at context may be especially revealing. This aspect has to do with what we call multilevel games. In such situations, different games affect one another, so that their outcomes become mutually contingent. Three such situations are particularly important for world politics: issue-linkage, domestic-international connections, and incompatibilities between games among different sets of actors. After considering these situations, we will turn to the implications of these multilevel games for the efficacy of a strategy of reciprocity in fostering cooperation.

Multilevel Games

Issue-linkage. Most issues are linked to other issues. This means that games being played on different issues—different "chessboards," in Stanley Hoffmann's phrase[17]—affect one another. Connections between games become important when issues are linked.

Issue-linkage in this sense involves attempts to gain additional bargaining leverage by making one's own behavior on a given issue contingent on others' actions toward other issues.[18] Issue-linkage may be employed by powerful states seeking to use resources from one issue-area to affect the behavior of others elsewhere; or it may be employed by outsiders, attempting to break into what could otherwise be a closed game. Linkage can be beneficial to both sides in a negotiation, and can facilitate agreements that might not otherwise be possible.[19] Actors' resources may differ, so that it makes sense to trade one for the other: the United States, for instance, may provide economic aid to Egypt in exchange for Egyptian support for American policy in the Middle East. Furthermore, different players may have preferences of different intensities: thus, in a log-rolling game, each party trades its "vote," or policy position, on an issue it values less highly for the other's vote on one it values more highly.

The outstanding example of a successful bargaining linkage in our case studies is that of the

Washington Naval Treaty of 1922. As Downs, Rocke, and Siverson show, these arms control negotiations were successful in part because they linked bargaining over arms with bargaining over other issues. As part of an agreement to limit battleship construction, Japan gave Britain and the United States guarantees regarding trade in China and limitations of fortification on certain Pacific islands; Japan received legal recognition of its right to certain territory taken from Germany after World War I. Bringing these issues into the negotiations to limit the building of battleships helped to make cooperation possible, not only on these specific issues but on the whole package.

Of course, not all issue-linkages promote agreement, any more than each exercise of power can be expected to lead to cooperation. Oye has distinguished between "backscratching," which he regards as welfare-enhancing, and "blackmailing," which may reduce welfare levels.[20] The "backscratcher" merely offers, in return for compensation, to refrain from acting in what would otherwise be its own best interest. For instance, a debtor country, unable to make its payments on time without facing severe hardship or political revolution, may offer to continue servicing its debts only if compensated with new loans and an easier payment schedule. If this offer is rejected, the debtor does what it would have done without the offer: it defaults.

Backscratching entails a promise. Blackmailing, by contrast, implies a threat. As Schelling has pointed out, "the difference is that a promise is costly when it succeeds, and a threat is costly when it fails."[21] Blackmailers threaten to act against their own interests unless compensated. Thus, a debtor country that would be hurt by defaulting may nevertheless threaten to do so unless compensation is offered. This threat, if carried out, would leave both the debtor (the blackmailer, in this case) and its creditors worse off than if it had merely acted in its own interest without bargaining at all. If the

blackmailing strategy works, on the other hand, the effect will be to transfer resources from the creditors to the debtor, an action that will not necessarily improve overall welfare.

Although it may be difficult to differentiate between backscratching and blackmailing in practice, the distinction helps us to recognize that issue-linkages have dangers as well as opportunities. One side may demand so much of the other in other areas that cooperation will not take place even in the area of shared interests. This accusation is frequently made against Henry Kissinger's version of linkage. Kissinger insisted that the Soviets exercise great restraint in the Third World in return for American cooperation on arms control.[22] In Oye's terms, Kissinger was trying to "blackmail" the Soviets by threatening to act against the United States' own interests (delay arms control) unless the Soviets compensated the United States with unilateral restraint.[23]

The most intriguing point about linkage that is highlighted by the case studies is the existence of what could be called "contextual" issue-linkage. In such a situation, a given bargain is placed within the context of a more important long-term relationship in such a way that the long-term relationship affects the outcome of the particular bargaining process. Two cases of contextual issue-linkage show that this form can often work to reduce conflict even without affecting the preferences of the participants on the specific issues being discussed. Oye notes that in 1936, the United States, Britain, and France were able to reach an agreement on international monetary reform because of the common security concern over a rising Nazi Germany. And as Downs and his colleagues point out, by far the most important cause of cooperation in arms races that ended peacefully has been the activity of a third power. For example, the Anglo-French naval arms race of 1852–1853 was resolved when the two states formed an alliance in order to fight the Russians in the Crimean War.

International relations and domestic politics. Similar analytic questions arise in considering connections between international relations and domestic politics. Arms control negotiations involve not merely bargaining between governments, but within societies as well; the Carter administration was able to resolve the SALT II game with the Soviet Union, but not with the U.S. Senate. Trade issues typically also involve both international and domestic games. In the Tokyo Round, the same Carter administration—with a different responsible party, Robert Strauss—was able to mesh international and domestic games, playing them simultaneously rather than sequentially (international first), as had been done on some issues in the Kennedy Round a decade earlier. The result in this case was that the Tokyo Round trade agreements with other countries were all ratified overwhelmingly by Congress, in contrast to the rejection of some of the international agreements made in the Kennedy Round.[24]

Such domestic-international connections are commonplace. Frequently, the incentives provided by domestic bargaining games inhibit effective foreign policy and may exacerbate international conflict. A well-known case is that of American decision making during the early months of the Korean War. General MacArthur was such a formidable figure in American politics that even his military superiors were reluctant to challenge his judgment in marching toward the Yalu River in the fall of 1950; yet this maneuver was so questionable that, if it had not been for the domestic political games taking place, serious reservations would have been expressed in the Pentagon and the White House.[25]

Another type of domestic-international linkage is discussed by Conybeare in this collection. During the 15th century, the Hanseatic League responded to naval setbacks at the hands of Britain by financing and equipping Edward IV, who, upon defeating the Lancastrians in the War of the Roses, signed a treaty that was one-sidedly favorable to the Hanse's trading interests. By intervening in British domestic politics, the Hanse was thus able to triumph despite military weakness. This technique—intervening in a domestic political game as compensation for weakness at the international level—has recently been employed in more subtle ways by small powers with strong interests in American foreign policy.[26]

Compatibilities and incompatibilities among games. Many different games take place in world politics, involving different but overlapping sets of actors. Sometimes the existence of more than one game makes it easier to attain cooperation, but related games may also create difficulties for one another. That is, games in world politics can be compatible or incompatible with each other.

One example of a set of compatible games is provided by cooperation in international economic negotiations among the major industrialized countries. After World War II, such cooperation was facilitated by the fact that these countries were military allies. In contrast to Britain's situation in the 19th century, America's ability to persuade other major trading states to accept the rules that it preferred was greatly enhanced by the fact that in the military-political game the United States was a senior partner, rather than an adversary, of the other major actors in the world economy. To take another example: Lipson's analysis of debt negotiations suggests that the negotiating game among large banks was rendered compatible with games between large and small banks by structuring the situation so that small banks could not coordinate with each other. That is, two sets of negotiations were made compatible by precluding a third one.

The case of 1914 illustrates the problem of incompatibility among games. In non-crisis periods, loyalty within an alliance was compatible with friendly relations across alliances. But when the 1914 crisis occurred, loyalty within an alliance—such as Germany's support for Austria, Russia's for Serbia, and France's for Russia—implied defection across alliances. The increased cooperativeness of intra-alliance games destroyed broader patterns of cooperation.

In the contemporary international political economy, problems of incompatibility may also arise. For instance, negotiations on questions such as tariffs or energy policies are most likely to yield positive results for the advanced industrialized countries when only a few major players are involved in the initial negotiation. Friction with others, however, especially the less developed countries, may produce conflict on a larger scale. Or, to take a different example from the politics of international debt, close and explicit collaboration among debtor countries could, some fear, disrupt relations between debtor governments and banks in the richer countries.

The contrast between the fate of Soviet-American arms control in the 1970s and the Tokyo Round of trade negotiations illustrates the importance of multilevel games. In the face of linkages to other contentious issues, complex domestic political games, and a lack of reinforcement between political-economic and military-security games, even shared interests, a long shadow of the future, and bilateralism may be insufficient to promote cooperation. If the interaction happens to be an iterated game of Chicken, the problem is even worse because each player has a strong incentive to avoid cooperation in the short run in order to develop a reputation for firmness in the long run. Conversely, even when there are quite severe conflicts of interest, these may be overshadowed by more important mutual interests, perhaps institutionalized in organizations such as NATO. Once again, it is not sufficient to analyze a particular situation in isolation from its political context. We must also analyze the patterns of expectations, and the institutions created by human beings, within which particular negotiations are located and in the light of which they are interpreted by participants.

Reciprocity as a Strategy in Multilevel Games

Robert Axelrod has employed computer tournaments and theoretical analysis of the iterated, two-player Prisoners' Dilemma to show that a strategy based on reciprocity—such as Tit-for-Tat—can be remarkably effective in promoting cooperation.[27] Even among pure egoists, cooperation can "emerge" if a small initial cluster of potential cooperators exists.

This argument suggests that governments may have incentives to practice reciprocity in a variety of situations that are characterized by mixtures of conflicting and complementary interests—that is, in certain non–zero-sum games. Evidence for this proposition is established best for the particular case of Prisoners' Dilemma. Axelrod's theory suggests that in this game a strategy based on reciprocity can yield relatively high payoffs against a variety of other strategies. Furthermore, such a strategy helps the whole community by punishing players who use uncooperative strategies. When payoff structures are those of Prisoners' Dilemma, therefore, we can expect practitioners of reciprocity to attempt to institutionalize it as a general practice, so that they will benefit from others' use of the strategy as well as their own.

As we have noted above, not every situation in which conflict or cooperation may occur can be categorized as Prisoners' Dilemma. Games such as Chicken and Stag Hunt are also significant. Evidence on these cases is not as extensive as on Prisoners' Dilemma. Yet, as Oye's introduction points out, there are good reasons to believe that reciprocity is an attractive strategy in a variety of non–zero-sum situations. The key conditions for the successful operation of reciprocity are that mutual cooperation can yield better results than mutual defection, but that temptations for defection also exist. In such situations, reciprocity may permit extensive cooperation without making cooperative participants inordinately vulnerable to exploitation by others. Furthermore, it may deter uncooperative actions.[28]

It is not surprising, therefore, that reciprocity is a popular strategy for practical negotiators as well as for analysts in the laboratory. Oye's analysis of monetary politics in the 1930s reveals that Britain developed such a strategy in its relations with the Scandinavian countries. Contemporary discussions of international trade provide another case in point. U.S. officials have frequently defended reciprocity in trade relations on the grounds that pursuit of this strategy would deter discrimination against American products by other countries, and that relaxation of reciprocity would invite retaliation by others. Even observers skeptical about reciprocity often agree. In a policy-oriented article critical of current proposals that the United States should practice "aggressive reciprocity" in trade negotiations, William Cline argues that such action is rendered less effective by a high probability of foreign counter-retaliation.[29] In Axelrod's terms, Tit-for-Tat (which begins by cooperating and then retaliates once for each defection by the other player) discourages exploitative strategies— "aggressive reciprocity."

Thus, the applicability of Tit-for-Tat does not seem to be limited to Prisoners' Dilemma. Yet it is not a perfect strategy. In the first place, it can perpetuate conflict through an "echo effect": "if the other player defects once, Tit-for-Tat will respond with a defection, and then if the other player does the same in response, the result would be an unending echo of alternating defections."[30] In real-world politics as well as in the laboratory, reciprocity can lead to feuds as well as to cooperation, particularly when players have different perceptions of past outcomes.[31] Soviet-American détente collapsed partly because each side concluded that the other was not practicing reciprocity, but was, on the contrary, taking unilateral advantage of its own restraint.[32] Second, even when many shared interests exist and judgments of equivalence are not distorted,

reciprocity may lead to deadlock. John W. Evans has pointed out that in tariff negotiations conducted according to the principle of reciprocity, potential concessions may become "bargaining chips" to be hoarded: "Tariffs that have no intrinsic economic value for a country that maintains them have acquired value because of the insistence of other countries on reciprocity in the bargaining process." As a result, "tariff levels may be maintained in spite of the fact that a lower level would raise the country's real income."[33] Third, when several actors negotiate separately and sequentially over issues that are substantively interdependent, subsequent bargains may call previous agreements into question by altering the value of concessions that have been made. This "issue interdependence problem" bedeviled trade negotiations under the conditional most-favored-nation clause prior to the institution of multilateral trade negotiations after World War II. Conditional most-favored-nation treatment permitted discrimination among suppliers. Later agreements between an importer and other suppliers therefore eroded the value of earlier concessions. This led to complex, acrimonious, and frustrating patterns of bargaining.[34]

Despite these difficulties, reciprocity remains a valuable strategy for decentralized enforcement of cooperative agreements. Players who are aware of the problems of echo effects, bargaining deadlocks, and issue interdependence can compensate for these pitfalls. Axelrod observes that a better strategy than Tit-for-Tat "might be to return only nine-tenths of a tit for a tat."[35] The Tokyo Round dealt with the deadlock problem by beginning negotiations not on the basis of current tariff rates, but rather on the basis of a formula for hypothetical large across-the-board tariff cuts, with provisions for withdrawing offers on sensitive products, or if adequate compensation was not received. The problem of issue interdependence was dealt with in the trade area through multilateralization of tariff negotiations and adoption of unconditional most-favored-nation treatment.

These difficulties in applying reciprocity, and the responses of players to them, illustrate the significance of the institutions within which reciprocity is practiced. As noted above, multilateral trade negotiations are a case in point. In the military-security area, reciprocity has also been institutionalized. For example, stationing of American troops in Europe is linked to purchases of American military equipment by European governments. NATO as an institution has helped member governments achieve a variety of such reciprocal arrangements.

The debt negotiations discussed by Lipson also illustrate how reciprocity can be institutionalized in an N-person game. First, the major actors are identified, and bilateral negotiations take place between them or their agents. The I.M.F. and committees of banks negotiate with debtor countries. At a second stage, smaller banks are given the opportunity to adhere to these bargains, but not to influence their terms. At this stage, emphasis is placed on reciprocity at a different level: although the smaller actors have the potential to act as free-riders, efforts are made to ensure that they have incentives not to do so for fear that they may suffer in a larger game. Small banks face the threat of being excluded from crucial relationships with big banks, and from future lending consortia, if they fail to provide funds for rescheduling loans. As in the other cases described above, strategies of reciprocity for debt rescheduling are adapted creatively to avoid the problems of issue-interdependence that arise when there are many actors.

Conclusion

The Importance of Perception

The contributors to *Cooperation under Anarchy* did not specifically set out to explore the role of perception in decision making, but the importance of perception has kept asserting itself. The significance of perception, including beliefs and cognition, will come as no surprise to students of international politics.[36] Yet it is worth pointing out once again that decision making in ambiguous settings is heavily influenced by the ways in which the actors think about their problem.

While this point has been made in laboratory studies many times,[37] there is an important twist in international politics that does not get sufficient attention from the psychologists who study decision making in the laboratory. Leaders of one state live far away from the leaders of other states. They are far away not only in space, but also in their cognitive framework: their tacit assumptions differ about what is important, what needs to be done, and who bears the responsibility for change. Put simply, those acting on behalf of states often do not appreciate how their own actions will affect others and how they will be interpreted by others. As Van Evera concludes from his study of World War I, preventing that war would have required dispelling extensive misperceptions that were prevalent in Europe before 1914.

Other striking examples of the importance of perception also come from the security area. For example, Downs, Rocke, and Siverson have found that even when nations in arms races built defensive rather than offensive weapons, it was usually done not to defuse the arms race, but simply because they believed that such weapons offered the greatest amount of security per dollar. Even more to the point is that many arms races were started or accelerated without serious appreciation of the consequences. For example, when the Soviet leaders deliberately exaggerated their bomber strength in 1955 and their ICBM capabilities several years later, they did so for short-term political advantages; there is no evidence that they fully appreciated the long-term consequences that would follow when the United States geared up to take the threat seriously. In general, Downs, Rocke, and Siverson find that arms races are not often perceived as the result of actions chosen by others. In the events leading to the outbreak of war, national leaders may completely misunderstand the consequences of their acts. Van Evera notes, for example, that in 1914 the Russian government did not realize that Russia's mobilization would lead directly to Germany's mobilization, and to war. Another example of the impact of biased interpretations of events is provided by Jervis in his discussion of the decay of great-power concerts, which were undermined by divergent views of which side had made greater concessions to maintain cooperation.

While security issues provide the most dramatic examples, governments may be no better at understanding how their actions in the realm of political economy will be seen by others. Conybeare's study shows that trade wars have sometimes begun when states held mistaken beliefs that other countries would be reluctant to raise tariffs on imported food in retaliation for new tariffs placed on their exported manufactured goods. Trade wars have begun when states had exaggerated expectations about the tolerance of others for attempts at minor exploitation in widely accepted terms of trade.

Groping toward New Institutions and Norms

Our project began with a set of hypotheses about how specific features of an international setting would affect the chances for the development of cooperation. Factors included were mutuality of interests, the shadow of the future, and the number of actors. These hypotheses have been supported by a broad set of cases that began in the 14th century, and covered trade disputes, monetary policy, and debt rescheduling as well as arms races, the outbreak of war, and diplomatic concerts. The three factors did, in fact, help to account for both cooperation and conflict.

We also discovered something else: over and over again we observed that the actors were not satisfied with simply selecting strategies based upon the situation in which they found themselves. In many cases we saw deliberate efforts to change the very structure of the situation by changing the context in which each of them would be acting. Decision makers themselves perceived (more or less consciously) that some aspects of the situations they faced tended to make cooperation difficult. So they worked to alter these background conditions. Among the problems they encountered were the following:

1. how to provide incentives for cooperation so that cooperation would be rewarded over the long run, and defection punished;
2. how to monitor behavior so that cooperators and defectors could be identified;
3. how to focus rewards on cooperators and retaliation on defectors;
4. how to link issues with one another in productive rather than self-defeating ways and, more generally, how to play multilevel games without tripping over their own strategies.

A fundamental strategic concept in attaining these objectives is that of reciprocity. Cooperation in world politics seems to be attained best not by providing benefits unilaterally to others, but by conditional cooperation. Yet reciprocity encounters many problems in practice. As Axelrod has demonstrated, and as Van Evera's discussion of 1914 illustrates, payoff structures in the strategic setting may be so malign that Tit-for-Tat cannot work. Reciprocity requires the ability to recognize and retaliate against a defection. And retaliation can spread acrimoniously.

Actors in world politics seek to deal with problems of reciprocity in part through the exercise of power. Powerful actors structure relationships so that countries committed to a given order can deal effectively with those that have lower levels of commitment. This is done by establishing hierarchies, as one would expect from Herbert Simon's assertion that complex systems will be hierarchic in character.[38] In the present symposium, the construction of hierarchy for the sake of cooperation is best illustrated by Lipson's discussion of interbank networks to facilitate rescheduling of Third World debts; but it is also evident in Jervis's discussion of great-power concerts.

Another way to facilitate cooperation is to establish international regimes. Regimes can be defined as "sets of implicit or explicit principles, norms, rules, and decision-making procedures around which actors' expectations converge in a given area of international relations."[39] International regimes have been extensive in the post-1945 international political economy, as illustrated by the international trade regime (centered on the GATT) and the international monetary regime (including the I.M.F. as well as other organizations and networks).[40] Since the use of power can facilitate the construction of regimes, this approach should be seen as complementary to, rather than in contradiction with, an emphasis on hierarchical authority. Regimes do not enforce rules in a hierarchical sense, but they do change patterns of transaction costs and provide information to participants, so that uncertainty is reduced. Jervis argues that the Concert of Europe helped to facilitate cooperation by making it easier for governments to understand one another. Lipson shows how, in the regime for debt rescheduling, the control of information is used to faciliate cooperation on terms favored by the big banks. He also indicates that one weapon in the hands of those banks is their ability to structure transaction costs: the costs of negotiations involving major money-center banks are reduced while the costs of coordinating resistance by small banks are not. Conybeare's analysis implies that if England and the Hanseatic League had been able to form an international trade regime, they might have been able to make mutually advantageous bargains and to discipline some of their more unruly constituents.

International regimes do not substitute for reciprocity; rather, they reinforce and institutionalize it. Regimes incorporating the norm of reciprocity delegitimize defection and thereby make it more costly. Insofar as they specify precisely what reciprocity means in the relevant issue-area, they make it easier to establish a reputation for practicing reciprocity consistently. Such reputations may become important assets, precisely because others will be more willing to make agreements with governments that can be expected to respond to cooperation with cooperation. Of course, compliance is difficult to assure; and international regimes almost never have the power to enforce rules. Nevertheless, since governments with good reputations can more easily make agreements than governments with bad ones, international regimes can help to facilitate cooperation by making it both easier and more desirable to acquire a good reputation.[41]

International regimes may also help to develop new norms, as Ruggie has argued.[42] Yet few such examples are evident in the cases discussed in this volume. The great-power concerts discussed by Jervis embodied new norms, but these did not last long; and the new norms of the 1930s monetary system described by Oye were largely uncooperative and connected with the breakdown rather than the institutionalization of a regime. Major banks today are trying mightily to strengthen norms of repayment (for debtors) and of relending (for banks), but it is not at all clear that this will be successful. Better examples of creating norms may be provided by the evolution of thinking on chemical and biological warfare, and by the development, under GATT, of norms of nondiscrimination—which are now, as we have seen, under pressure. Evidently, it is difficult to develop new norms, and they often decay in reaction to conspicuous violations.

Establishing hierarchies, setting up international regimes, and attempting to gain acceptance for new norms are all attempts to change the context within which actors operate by changing the very structure of their interaction. It is important to notice that these efforts have usually not been examples of forward-looking rationality. Rather, they have been experimental, trial-and-error efforts to improve the current situation based upon recent experience. Like other forms of trial-and-error experimentation, they have not always worked. Indeed, it is instructive to enumerate the variety of ways in which such experiments can fail.

1. The most important source of failure is that efforts to restructure the relationships may never get off the ground. As Downs, Rocke, and Siverson note, there was an active peace movement in the years before 1914, and World War I was preceded by a series of conferences designed to secure arms control and strengthen international law; but these efforts did not significantly affect the nature of world politics. Similarly, the shakiness of monetary arrangements in the 1920s was perceived by many of the participants, but conferences to deal with these weaknesses, such as that at Genoa in 1922, failed to cope with them effectively. The great-power concerts discussed by Jervis seemed to get somewhat farther, but were never sufficiently institutionalized to have much prospect of longevity.

2. Some agreements are instituted, but turn out to be self-contradictory. We have noted that sequential bilateral negotiations under conditional most-favored-nation treatment may lead to a problem of infinite regress: each bargain tends to require the renegotiation of many others. Bilateral arms control agreements, whose restraints could encourage third parties to increase their armaments in order to catch up with the major powers, face a similar difficulty.

3. Even successful arrangements are subject to decay. Decay can result from actors' attempts to find loopholes in established rules. The very success of GATT in reducing tariff rates contributed to an expansion of nontariff barriers; and efforts to evade those barriers led to their progressive extension and tightening.[43] Likewise, successful cooperation in the area of security may lead governments to believe that their partners' cooperation is not based on reciprocity but is unconditional. Insofar as this belief is incorrect, discord may ensue.

4. In some cases, changes that have nothing to do with the arrangements make them obsolete. Thus the international debt regime in place before the crisis of August 1982 was manifestly ill-equipped to handle a situation in which most Third World debts had to be rescheduled. In this instance, the old regime was adapted to meet new needs. The Depression of the 1930s made the monetary orthodoxy of the gold exchange standard obsolete. Indeed, Oye argues that the cooperative international monetary arrangements of the 1920s hindered attempts at monetary cooperation during the 1930s. The collapse of the old regime was a necessary condition for creation of a new one.

Eventually, any institution is likely to become obsolete. The question is under what conditions international institutions—broadly defined as "recognized patterns of practice around which expectations converge"[44]—facilitate significant amounts of cooperation for a period of time. Clearly, such institutions can change the incentives for countries affected by them, and can in turn affect the strategic choices governments make in their own self-interest.

This interaction between incentives and institutions suggests the importance of linking the upward-looking theory of strategy with the downward-looking theory of regimes. The strategic approach is upward-looking in that it examines what individual actors will choose to do, and derives consequences for the entire system based on these choices. Most of the analysis in this volume has followed this upward-looking approach. On the other hand, much regime analysis has been downward-looking in that it examines the implications, for actors, of the way the entire system is organized. Some recent work has attempted to combine these two approaches,[45] but it has not yet been done in either a formally rigorous or an empirically comprehensive way.

The experimental groping by policy makers does not necessarily lead to stronger and ever more complex ways of achieving cooperation. The process proceeds by fits and starts. The success of each step is uncertain, and there is always danger that prior achievements will come unstuck. New experiments are often tried only under obvious pressure of events (as in debt rescheduling). And they are often dependent upon the active leadership of a few individuals or states who feel a serious need for change and who have the greatest resources.

The essays in this collection show that we are beginning to understand the structural conditions that affect strategic choices leading to cooperation or discord. These factors are mutuality of interest, the shadow of the future, and the number of actors. Over a wide range of historical cases, these three dimensions of situations do help account for the emergence, or nonemergence, of cooperation under anarchy.

But in the course of this collective research we have also found that states are often dissatisfied with the structure of their own environment. We have seen that governments have often tried to transform the structures within which they operate so as to make it possible for the countries involved to work together productively. Some of these experiments have been successful, others have been stillborn, and still others have collapsed before fully realizing the dreams of their founders. We understand the functions performed by international regimes, and how they affect strategies pursued by governments, better than we did a number of years ago. What we need now are theories that account for (1) when experiments to restructure the international environment are tried, and (2) whether a particular

experiment is likely to succeed. Even within a world of independent states that are jealously guarding their sovereignty and protecting their power, room exists for new and better arrangements to achieve mutually satisfactory outcomes, in terms both of economic welfare and military security.

This does not mean that all endeavors to promote international cooperation will yield good results. Cooperation can be designed to help a few at the expense of the rest; and it can accentuate as well as alleviate injustice in an imperfect world. Yet the consequences of failure to cooperate—from warfare to the intensification of depressions—make us believe that more cooperation is often better than less. If governments are prepared to grope their way toward a better-coordinated future, scholars should be prepared to study the process. And, in a world where states have often been dissatisfied with international anarchy, scholars should be prepared to advance the learning process—so that despite the reality of anarchy, beneficial forms of international cooperation can be promoted.

NOTES

1. Lipson, "International Cooperation in Economic and Security Affairs," *World Politics* 37 (October 1984), 1–23.

2. Robert Axelrod, "Conflict of Interest: An Axiomatic Approach," *Journal of Conflict Resolution* II (March 1967), 87–99; and *Conflict of Interest: A Theory of Divergent Goals with Applications to Politics* (Chicago: Markham, 1970).

3. Robert Jervis, "Cooperation under the Security Dilemma," *World Politics* 30 (January 1978), 167–214.

4. The definition of Prisoners' Dilemma also includes one additional restriction: CC > (DC + CD)/2. This is to ensure that it is better to have mutual cooperation than to have an even chance of being the exploiter or the exploited.

5. For an earlier discussion of contemporary events, using a common analytical framework to examine both economic and security relations, see Oye, "The Domain of Choice," in Kenneth A. Oye, Donald Rothchild, and Robert J. Lieber, eds., *Eagle Entangled: U.S. Foreign Policy in a Complex World* (New York: Longman, 1979), 3–33.

6. Robert Axelrod, *The Evolution of Cooperation* (New York: Basic Books, 1984).

7. Robert Axelrod, "The Rational Timing of Surprise," *World Politics* 31 (January 1979), 228–46.

8. Stephen D. Krasner, ed., *International Regimes* (Ithaca, NY: Cornell University Press, 1983); Robert O. Keohane, *After*

Hegemony: Cooperation and Discord in the World Political Economy (Princeton: Princeton University Press, 1984).

9. Axelrod (fn. 6).

10. Lipson (fn. 1).

11. Robert E. Osgood and Robert W. Tucker, *Force, Order and Justice* (Baltimore: Johns Hopkins University Press, 1967), esp. chap. 2, "The Expansion of Force."

12. Keohane (fn. 8), 49–132.

13. Lipson, "Bankers' Dilemmas," in this collection, 200–225.

14. John G. Ruggie, "Continuity and Transformation in the World Polity: Toward a Neorealist Synthesis," *World Politics* 35 (January 1983), 261–85.

15. John G. Ruggie, "International Regimes, Transactions and Change: Embedded Liberalism in the Postwar Economic Order," *International Organization* 36 (Spring 1982), 379–416, reprinted in Krasner (fn. 8), 195–231; Fred Hirsch, "The Ideological Underlay of Inflation," in John Goldthorpe and Fred Hirsch, eds., *The Political Economy of Inflation* (London: Martin Robertson, 1978), 263–84.

16. Keohane (fn. 8).

17. Stanley Hoffmann, "International Organization and the International System," *International Organization* 24 (Summer 1970), 389–413.

18. Ernst B. Haas refers to this as "tactical" issue-linkage, contrasting it with "substantive" issue-linkage resulting from causal knowledge. See Haas, "Why Collaborate? Issue-linkage and International Regimes," *World Politics* 32 (April 1980), 357–405, at 372. For a sophisticated analysis of tactical issue-linkage, see Michael McGinnis, "Issue Linkage and the Evolution of International Cooperation," *Journal of Conflict Resolution* [30 (March 1986), 141–70].

19. Robert E. Tollison and Thomas D. Willett, "An Economic Theory of Mutually Advantageous Issue Linkage in International Negotiations," *International Organization* 33 (Fall 1979), 425–49.

20. Oye (fn. 5).

21. Thomas C. Schelling, *The Strategy of Conflict* (New York: Oxford University Press, 1960), 177.

22. George W. Breslauer, "Why Détente Failed: An Interpretation," in Alexander L. George and others, *Managing U.S.-Soviet Rivalry: Problems of Crisis Prevention* (Boulder, CO: Westview Press, 1983), 319–40; John L. Gaddis, "The Rise, Fall and Future of Détente," *Foreign Affairs* 62 (Winter 1983/84), 354–77; Stanley Hoffmann, "Détente," in Joseph S. Nye, ed., *The Making of America's Soviet Policy* (New Haven: Yale University Press for the Council on Foreign Relations, 1984), 231–64.

23. Oye (fn. 5), 17.

24. Gilbert Winham, "Robert Strauss, the MTN, and the Control of Faction," *Journal of World Trade Law* 14 (September–October 1980).

25. Alexander George and Richard Smoke, *Deterrence in American Foreign Policy* (New York: Columbia University Press, 1974).

26. Robert O. Keohane, "The Big Influence of Small Allies," *Foreign Policy*, No. 2 (Spring 1971), 161–82.

27. Axelrod (fn. 6).

28. Consider the example of Stag Hunt, defined by the preference ordering of both players as CC > DC > DD > CD. If Player *A* is credibly committed to a strategy of reciprocity, beginning with cooperation, *B*'s incentives to cooperate are enhanced. *A*'s commitment to cooperate ensures that *B* will not be double-crossed (which would leave *B* with the worst payoff). Furthermore, *A*'s commitment to retaliate against defection ensures that any defection by *B* would lead, after the first move, not to *B*'s second-best outcome (DC), but to its third-best outcome (DD). The game of Chicken provides another appropriate case in point. In Chicken, mutual cooperation is only the second-best outcome for both players, but mutual defection is worst for both. Thus, DC > CC > CD > DD. A credible strategy of reciprocity by Player *A* in Chicken ensures *B* of its second-best outcome if it cooperates, and guarantees that continual defection will in the long run provide it with its worst payoff. Assuming that *B*'s shadow of the future is sufficiently long, it should respond to *A*'s strategy of reciprocity by cooperating.

29. Cline, "'Reciprocity': A New Approach to World Trade Policy?" Institute for International Economics, Policy Analyses in International Economics 2 (Washington: September 1982), 25.

30. Axelrod (fn. 6), 176.

31. For an analysis of the spiral mode of conflict, see Robert Jervis, *Perception and Misperception in International Politics* (Princeton, NJ: Princeton University Press, 1976), esp. 58–113.

32. See references cited in fn. 22.

33. Evans, *The Kennedy Round in American Trade Policy: The Twilight of the GATT?* (Cambridge: Harvard University Press, 1971), 31–32.

34. See Robert O. Keohane, "Reciprocity in International Relations," *International Organization* 40 (Winter 1986).

35. Axelrod (fn. 6), 138.

36. Jervis (fn. 31).

37. For example, Amos Tversky and Daniel Kahneman, "Judgment under Uncertainty: Heuristics and Biases," *Science* 185 (September 1974), 1124–31; Richard Nisbet and Lee Ross, *Human Inference: Strategies and Shortcomings of Social Judgment* (Englewood Cliffs, NJ: Prentice–Hall, 1980).

38. Simon, *The Sciences of the Artificial* (Cambridge: MIT Press, 2d ed. 1982), chap. 4, "The Architecture of Complexity," p. 99.

39. Krasner (fn. 8), 3.

40. Keohane (fn. 8), chaps. 8–9.

41. *Ibid.*, esp. chaps. 5–7.

42. Ruggie (fn. 15).

43. Vinod Aggarwal, "The Unraveling of the Multi-Fiber Arrangement, 1981: An Examination of Regime Change," *International Organization* 37 (Autumn 1983), 617–46; David B. Yoffie, *Power and Protectionism: Strategies of the Newly Industrializing Countries* (New York: Columbia University Press, 1983).

44. Oran R. Young, "Regime Dynamics: The Rise and Fall of International Regimes," *International Organization* 36 (Spring 1982), 277–98; reprinted in Krasner (fn. 8), 93–114.

45. In *After Hegemony* (fn. 8), Robert Keohane has sought to show how game theory (which is "upward-looking") can be combined fruitfully with the "downward-looking" theories of public goods and market failure to develop a functional theory of international regimes. But he has not formalized his theory, and has applied it only to the post–World War II international political economy.

Andrew T. Guzman

INTERNATIONAL LAW
A Compliance-Based Theory

Introduction

Legal scholarship lacks a satisfactory theory of why and when states comply with international law. Most scholars and practitioners of international law believe that international law matters, by which they mean it affects the behavior of states.[1] Furthermore, this view coincides with empirical evidence on the relevance of international law.[2] Nevertheless, the theories advanced by legal scholars are considered flawed because they are difficult to reconcile with modern international relations theory, rely heavily on axiomatic claims about national behavior, and lack a coherent theory of compliance with international law.[3] The absence of a coherent compliance theory may explain why most conventional international law scholarship assumes that there is compliance but fails to ask why.[4] Yet, the failure to understand the compliance decision is troubling because compliance is one of the most central questions in international law. Indeed, the absence of an explanation for why states obey international law in some instances but not others threatens to undermine the very foundations of the discipline.

Without an understanding of the counection between international law and state actions, scholars cannot hope to provide useful policy advice with respect to international law. Improving the functioning of the international legal system and developing a workable theory of international legal

and regulatory cooperation also require a coherent theory of compliance with international law. At present, the best theories relevant to international law and compliance come not from legal scholarship, but from international relations scholarship.[5] The scholars developing these theories, however, are often skeptical of international law's relevance to the international system,[6] or ignore international law altogether.[7]

This article draws on international relations theory to develop a better theory of compliance with international law. Unlike traditional international law scholarship, the theory developed here explains compliance using a model of rational, self-interested states. It argues that compliance occurs due to state concern about both reputational and direct sanctions triggered by violations of the law. This theory explains not only why nations comply, but also why and when they violate international law. Furthermore, this article responds to the argument that international law is merely epiphenomenal by constructing a model of rational, self-interested states in which international law does, in fact, matter. * * *

■ ■ ■

Existing Theories of International Law

Compliance is central to international law's role in regulating the interaction of nations. Absent an incentive toward compliance, resources devoted to

From *California Law Review* 90 (2002): 1823–86. Some of the author's notes have been omitted.

the creation and maintenance of international legal structures are wasted, and the study of international law is a futile endeavor. Despite the fundamental importance of the compliance question, however, the legal academy has failed to develop a satisfactory theory to explain it. This part presents the most prominent attempts in the international law literature to explain compliance. It also presents theories from international relations that have filtered into the international law literature, including the institutionalist theory upon which this article builds.[8]

Traditional Legal Theories

THE MANAGERIAL MODEL

Chayes and Chayes have provided the most satisfying of the traditional legal theories of international law and compliance.[9] They argue that the "enforcement model" of compliance, in which compliance is achieved through coercive mechanisms such as sanctions, should be replaced with a "managerial model," which relies primarily on "a cooperative, problem-solving approach."[10] Chayes and Chayes claim that the general propensity of states to comply with international law is the product of three factors. First, compliance avoids the need to recalculate the costs and benefits of a decision, saving transaction costs for complying states and generating an efficiency-based rationale for compliance.[11] Second, they argue that treaties are consent-based instruments that serve the interests of the participating states.[12] Finally, they contend that a general norm of compliance furthers state compliance in any particular instance.[13] Although the managerial model presents a thoughtful and useful account of a certain class of treaties, it fails to describe many other types of international agreements. Specifically, it provides a satisfying account of agreements designed to resolve coordination problems, but it does not explain how international law works in other situations.

In the case of coordination problems, once the parties have agreed on a certain set of behaviors, neither party has an incentive to deviate from the agreement, and compliance is the expected outcome even in the absence of enforcement. Because there is no incentive to cheat, there is no need to focus on enforcement. Resources are better directed at managerial issues, including transparency,[14] dispute settlement,[15] and capacity building,[16] which all assist coordination efforts. Thus, at least in the narrow class of international agreements that involve coordination games, the managerial model successfully explains state compliance with international law.

When considering the use of international law beyond coordination games, however, the managerial model is less useful. To see why this is so, consider each of the three factors said to generate compliance.[17] First, the managerial model focuses on transaction costs saved through compliance with international law. Although states save some costs through a rule of compliance, these costs are not likely to be large and, in any event, there are many other strategies that can lead to similar cost savings. A better strategy from the state's perspective would be to make its compliance decisions based on whatever information it has without any presumption in favor of or against compliance. This would maximize the probability of making the appropriate choice while avoiding transaction costs.[18]

The second explanation for compliance is the consent-based theory. [T]he consent theory cannot explain why the existence of an international legal obligation would influence state behavior.

Finally, Chayes and Chayes argue that a compliance norm causes decision-makers to comply not out of fear of sanctions, but rather because the norm itself generates compliance pull. The claim that a norm exists in favor of compliance and that such a norm improves compliance, however, is little more than an assertion that nations comply with the law. After all, why should we think that the presiding norm is one of compliance rather than one of ignoring legal commitments, or perhaps a norm of pursuing the narrow self-interest of the nation or its leaders? Furthermore, observing that a norm generates compliance does not offer an explanation for compliance since we have no theory of why norms operate as a force for compliance. Without a theoretical framework, the norms argument is not helpful in understanding state behavior.

Consider, for example, the managerial model's claim that while dispute resolution is a useful tool that may enhance compliance, it need not be mandatory and, furthermore, a failure to comply need not result in binding sanctions. Underlying this view of dispute resolution is the belief that a failure to comply is the result of a mistake or a lack of communication. Dispute resolution, then, need only serve as a forum where states share information and clarify their expectations. In fact, more can be said under the managerial model. Because states are, by assumption, cooperative, there is no need for binding law of any kind. Simple statements of interest and intent, without any notion of commitment, are sufficient to resolve most coordination games. Therefore international law as conceived by this model need not be binding or irrevocable. It is precisely because states do not have to be compelled to act in a particular way that dispute resolution does not have to be compulsory or backed by sanctions.

When a state violates the law because the law is contrary to its interests, however, the managerial model breaks down. When the states' interests are at odds, as is true in instances of intentional violation, the states conduct negotiations "in the shadow" of potential sanctions. In the absence of such sanctions the offending party has no incentive to accept a negotiated solution that involves any punishment or constraint on future behavior. This, in turn, implies that the law provides no incentive to comply. If one makes dispute resolution mandatory, on the other hand, and provides some form of sanction for a failure to comply with the ruling, it is possible to increase compliance even outside of coordination games.

The managerial model, then, is a useful but incomplete model of compliance. As long as one is only interested in coordination games, it provides a good guide to compliance and national behavior. If one seeks to understand situations where states make agreements that call upon them to act against their own interests in exchange for concessions from other states, a different model is needed. Part II of this article advances such a model.

CONSENT AND TREATIES

An alternative theory of the relevance of international law, and probably the most commonly held rationale for the relevance of international law to national conduct, especially in the context of treaties, is based on the notion of consent.[19] The consent-based theory begins with the claim that states are not subject to any obligation to which they did not consent.[20] The second, and more problematic, step in the consent-based theory invokes the oft-repeated statement that states should obey treaties.[21] Based on this reasoning, proponents of consent-based theories argue that a state's consent generates a legal obligation which leads to compliance.

The consent-based arguments are logically flawed because they confuse a (possibly) necessary condition for states to be bound with a sufficient condition. In other words, the consent-based theory only observes that states are not bound to international agreements unless they consent to them. This initial presumption, even if assumed to be correct,[22] does not lead to the conclusion that consent is enough to bind a state. Consent, by itself, does not provide states with an incentive to obey the law. The standard rendition of consent-based theories fails to address this point. Rather, advocates of the theory simply recite the maxim that "treaties are to be obeyed."[23] This statement, however, either is devoid of content or assumes the conclusion. If the statement is read to mean that treaties should be obeyed, as a normative matter, it says nothing about how states will actually behave. If, on the other hand, it is read to mean that states do, in fact, obey treaties, then it is simply assuming compliance without explaining it.

LEGITIMACY THEORY

Thomas Franck has advanced a general theory of international law that has come to be known as legitimacy theory.[24] The fundamental premise underlying legitimacy theory is that states obey rules perceived to have "come into being in accordance with the right process." Franck argues that four factors determine whether a state complies with international obligations: determinacy, symbolic validation, coherence, and adherence. Where these four factors are present, legitimacy theory predicts a strong pressure toward compliance, and where they are absent, it predicts a very limited impetus in that direction. In the end, however, Franck's legitimacy theory takes the inquiry no further than does consent theory.

Legitimacy theory leaves too many of the central questions regarding compliance and national behavior in the black box of "legitimacy" without explaining why states do or should care about legitimacy. For instance, the claim that nations violate international rules because of the "perceived lack of legitimacy of the actual or proposed rules themselves and of the rule-making and rule-applying institutions of the international system" simply begs the question. Why should we expect nations to honor rules that enjoy legitimacy while ignoring others? In any event, the claim that legitimacy is the driving force behind compliance is an assertion, rather than the result of a theoretical framework or empirical study.

Accordingly, legitimacy theory fails for the same reason that the consent-based theory fails: neither provides a model of compliance so much as an assertion that nations obey the law. Franck's theory fails to explain why "legitimacy" leads to compliance, why the four factors are important, how they interact with other measures of a nation's self-interest, and why states violate laws with which they had previously complied.

TRANSNATIONAL LEGAL PROCESS

Professor Harold Koh has advanced another theory of international law, termed transnational legal process. The theory focuses on how public and private actors interact in various fora, on both domestic and international levels, to make, interpret, enforce, and internalize rules of transnational law.[25] Transnational legal process looks to a wide set of decision-makers to explain conduct, including multinational corporations, nongovernmental organizations, international organizations, private individuals, and others. Koh argues that as transnational entities—including both state and nonstate actors—interact, patterns of behavior and norms emerge and are internalized, leading to their incorporation within the domestic legal institutions of states and, in turn, compliance.[26]

The claim that domestic legal institutions play a critical role in international law is certainly correct. The claim that domestic institutions somehow internalize transnational legal norms and thereby cause compliance is problematic. Transnational legal process theory provides no explanation for why or how certain legal norms are internalized. Even if one assumes, as does Professor Koh, that international legal norms are internalized, one would expect domestic legal norms—in particular, the norm of pursuing the interests of domestic decision-makers—to be internalized more readily. When international legal norms are at odds with the self-interest of the state, it is difficult for transnational legal process theory to explain why international norms would triumph. Moreover, if domestic concerns triumph, then the internalization of international legal norms has no apparent impact on outcomes.

In addition, Koh appears to assume that repeated interaction leads to the internalization of norms that are consistent with international law, but this assumption is not explained. It seems equally plausible that the internalized norms are unrelated to international law. For example, rather than internalizing norms of international law, transnational actors might internalize the norm that powerful nations triumph over weaker nations, or that economic influence resolves international disputes.

Without an understanding of why domestic actors internalize norms of compliance in the international arena, and a theory of why this internalization tends toward compliance, the theory lacks force. Like the consent-based and legitimacy theories, the transnational legal process theory is ultimately founded on the unsupported assumption that states obey the law. It differs from prior theories in that it considers the relevant unit of analysis to be individuals and interest groups rather than the state, but it still fails to ask why these actors follow international law. Without a more complete theory of why these actors follow the law, the theory remains unsatisfactory.

International Relations Theories

Although traditional approaches to legal scholarship remain common, a new approach challenging the traditional methodology has emerged. This approach comes primarily from political science and the theory of international relations, though it also has roots in the economics literature. While a detailed taxonomy and review of the international relations literature is beyond this article's scope, this section offers a thumbnail sketch of the three most relevant schools of thought: neorealist theory, institutionalist theory, and liberal theory.[27]

NEOREALISTS

Neorealist theory, an outgrowth of classical realism,[28] treats states as unitary actors and as the relevant unit in international relations. According to neorealist theory, international cooperation will exist with respect to a particular issue only when it is in the interest of the affected states.[29] Neorealists posit that states primarily seek power and security, and international relations are largely driven by power.[30]

Some scholars conclude that international law has little or no independent impact on the behavior of states.[31] By this view, compliance with international law is explained as a coincidence between international law—whose content, in any event, is said to be largely controlled by powerful states—and the self-interest of nations.[32] International law, therefore, is simply an epiphenomenon.

Criticisms of neorealism can be found in the international relations literature.[33] For present purposes, it is sufficient to simply identify some of the difficulties with adopting a realist perspective on international law. Foremost among the problems for the neorealist conclusion that international law is irrelevant is the difficulty of reconciling it with the observation that a great deal of time, energy, and money are spent in the creation of international law. For example, the Uruguay Round negotiations, leading to the establishment of the World Trade Organization ("WTO"), lasted eight years, consumed enormous resources, and affected the political fortunes of governments around the world.

If neorealists are correct that international law does not matter, why did states devote so many resources to these negotiations? Just as rational individuals would not expend resources to complete a contract that has no effect on behavior, there is no reason to think that states would spend resources to complete treaties and other agreements that have no impact on states' behavior. Nor would states (or nonstate actors) expend resources to influence the status of CIL, as has been done in such fields as foreign investment,[34] human rights,[35] and environmental law,[36] if such efforts would have no impact.

Other observations also undermine the conclusion that international law is irrelevant. For instance, when states claim that an international law has been violated (though it is not clear why anyone would even bother to make such a claim), their accused states would have no reason to proclaim its innocence or expend resources fighting to exonerate themselves, as they so often do.[37] Furthermore, the existence of international dispute-resolution procedures cannot be explained if international law does not matter. A final problem for the neorealist camp is that empirical and anecdotal evidence has begun to emerge indicating that international law does, indeed, influence state behavior.[38]

LIBERAL THEORY

A second international relations theory, known as liberal theory,[39] focuses on interest-group dynamics within each state. Liberal theory begins with the assumption that the key actors in international relations are individuals and private groups, rather than states. Accordingly, the theory is interested in the particulars of domestic politics in addition to the interaction of states. A focus on subnational entities leads to the study of institutions such as courts, legislatures, and administrative agencies.[40]

Liberal theory of international law is hampered by the complexity of a model that rejects the assumption of unitary state actors. An examination of compliance within a liberal framework is really an examination of the domestic politics of countries that might lead to a decision to comply with international law. The problem is that interactions among domestic interest groups are unpredictable, and the results may not be stable over time. Because of the complexity of interest-group politics, it is difficult to generate predictions about how nations behave.[41] The problem with liberal theory, then, is that it is overly complex. Because it is better suited to positive accounts of behavior rather than to predictions, it does not lead to a general model of compliance.

INSTITUTIONALIST THEORY

The third important category of international relations theories is institutionalism.[42] Like neorealism, institutionalism views states as the primary international actors and treats them as rational unitary agents interacting in an anarchical world.[43]

Unlike neorealists, however, institutionalists believe that international cooperation is possible, and that international institutions can play a role in facilitating that cooperation. Specifically, institutionalists argue that institutions can reduce verification costs in international affairs, reduce the cost of punishing cheaters, and increase the repeated nature of interaction, all of which make cooperation more likely.[44]

THEORETICAL APPROACH OF THIS ARTICLE

This article draws upon the institutionalist tradition of international relations to develop a model of compliance with international law.[45] Using a repeated-game model of national behavior, it demonstrates that international law can affect the behavior of states. Consistent with both neorealism and institutionalism, it assumes that states are independent and that they act only in their own self-interest. Unlike most institutionalist discussions of international law, however, treaties do not represent the exclusive focus of the article.[46]

While this article does not adopt a liberal approach, it is not in conflict with that school. Rather, this theory of compliance complements liberal theory. This article assumes, without specifying the particular goals of each state, that states are unitary actors engaged in the pursuit of national goals. Liberal theory is one way of studying these goals. Thus, one can view liberal theory as a methodology whose output—the policy desires of states—is an input for the theory of compliance presented here.

A Theory of Compliance

At a minimum, a sound theory of compliance must explain both (1) instances of compliance with international law and (2) instances of violation. As discussed in the previous part, traditional legal theories of compliance have been unable to provide a constructive theoretical framework for compliance, in part because they cannot explain instances of violation. Neorealists, on the other hand, argue that international law has no effect on national behavior; explaining breach but not compliance.

This part presents a theoretical model of compliance that explains both how international law can affect state behavior and why states sometimes violate that law. * * *

With respect to government behavior, the model makes standard assumptions about states: they are rational, they act in their own self-interest, and they are aware of the impact of international law on behavior.[47] Although it is assumed that states act in a self-interested fashion, no assumption is made regarding the way in which states identify their self-interest. The traditional way of modeling state interest assumes that the government pursues the public interest. Public-choice theory, an alternative approach, views government decisions as the product of interest-group politics and argues that these decisions will not, in general, lead to behavior that is consistent with the national interest. Under this public-choice view, decision-makers are modeled as individuals pursuing their own objectives rather than as faithful agents of their constituencies.[48] The advantage of a public-choice approach is its ability to provide a positive account of government activity that is difficult to explain through more traditional models of government behavior. The difficulty in applying public choice to normative analysis, however, is that the outcome of interest-group politics is very difficult to predict.[49] For the purposes of this article, it is not necessary to choose between the public-interest and public-choice models because the article does not attempt to model the process by which states determine their national goals. Rather, this theory takes national goals as given, and the model explains the conditions under which the pursuit of such goals leads to compliance with international law. For this reason, the article can accommodate both theories of government behavior.

A Theory of the Irrelevance of International Law

The first step in understanding this article's theory of compliance is to understand the theory of the irrelevance of international law. As shown below, the simplest rational-actor model of country behavior leads to the conclusion that international law does not matter. Once that basic model is understood, it is possible to identify the assumptions that generate the irrelevance result and then relax those assumptions to develop a model of compliance in which international law matters.

The most basic model of country behavior is a one-shot game in which states decide whether or not to comply with a particular rule of international law.[50] For concreteness, suppose that two countries have agreed to a ban on satellite-based weapons and the decision at hand is whether or not to comply with that agreement. Assume that (1) each country is better off if it violates the agreement while the other country complies, and (2) both are better off if they both comply than if they both violate. This game [is] a simple prisoner's dilemma, and the well-known equilibrium is for both countries to violate their international obligation.

If this game is a fair representation of international relations, we would expect to see a world of chaos in which cooperation and compliance with international law are nonexistent. Such an observation is clearly at odds with what we observe.[51]

Though international law scholars have cited the widespread compliance with international commitments as evidence that international law matters,[52] a simple extension of the above model shows that a high level of compliance need not imply that international law affects national behavior. Adding an additional round to the game explains how countries can regularly act in a manner consistent with their international obligations even if those obligations have no impact on state behavior. In an extension of the above model, the game is unchanged, but represents only a portion of a larger game. In the larger game, there is an initial period in which the state of nature is determined. Assume that there are two possible states of nature labeled "good" and "bad." * * * [T]he [prior] discussion represent[s] the bad state of nature. In the satellite-based weapons treaty example given above, the bad state of nature corresponds to a situation in which the parties have an incentive to develop space-based weapons in spite of their treaty obligations.

The good state of nature * * * corresponds to the situation in which the parties have an incentive to comply with treaty provisions independent of their international obligations. Suppose that the technology for the construction of a satellite-based weapons system is too primitive to make the system effective and that the cost is prohibitive, making it a poor use of government resources. In this situation, neither party would develop satellite-based weapons, even in the absence of an international agreement.

If both countries violate the treaty, they are both worse off because they would have expended resources on an unreliable system. If [one] violates the treaty, that country is worse off as a result of the expended resources, and [the other] also suffers a loss because even an unreliable weapons system in the hands of a potential enemy is undesirable. If both comply with the treaty, however, both enjoy the maximum possible payoff. * * * [E]ach country is better off if it complies with the treaty, regardless of the action taken by the other party.

Combining the good and bad outcomes yields a theory of national behavior consistent with the observation that countries obey their international obligations much of the time. Further, the analysis is also consistent with the view that international law does not matter. At times, a state's behavior happens to coincide with its international obligations, as in the example of states choosing not to develop satellite-based weapons because the technology is inadequate. At other times, states violate their obligations, as in the example of states choosing to develop such weapons despite the presence of a treaty. In neither case does the existence of an international agreement affect behavior.

This model in which international law is irrelevant has been advanced by the neorealist school in international relations.[53] Though it is simple and elegant, and may explain instances of both observed compliance with international obligations and violations thereof, this theory cannot explain other observed behavior. It cannot explain, for example, why countries enter into treaties in the first place. The negotiation of international treaties and other agreements consumes resources that a state could use in other ways. If international law does not have any impact on behavior, there is no reason for a country to waste resources on international legal conventions and negotiations. Similarly, this simple model is unable to explain why countries invest resources to demonstrate that they are in compliance with international law; if the model is correct that international law has no impact on behavior, countries should ignore it. What we observe, however, are attempts by countries to justify their actions under international law. The model also fails to explain the existence of international law dispute-resolution processes to which nations sometimes submit their disputes. If international law does not matter, there is no reason for such procedures. Finally, the theory is contradicted by empirical data suggesting that international law does, indeed, influence state behavior.[54]

In a finitely repeated prisoner's dilemma like the one presented above, the irrelevance of international law is inevitable. By adopting a finitely repeated game, one ensures that the equilibrium in a prisoner's dilemma context is noncooperative behavior ("defection"). This amounts to an assumption that cooperation will fail and that international law does not matter.

A Theory of the Relevance of International Law

In a domestic setting, even one-shot prisoner's dilemmas can yield the cooperative outcome through the use of contract. Suppose, for example, that two individuals agree to swap vacation homes for the summer. They each agree to care for the other's home, including the performance of certain regular maintenance chores. While on vacation, however, maintenance is time consuming, expensive, and boring, so there is an incentive to avoid it. The standard prisoner's dilemma model predicts that neither party will honor their promise to care for the other's home. Despite this tendency towards shirking, if their agreement is legally enforceable, a shirking party must pay damages which, if high enough, will induce the parties to carry out the promised maintenance. Law * * * solves the prisoner's dilemma by imposing a penalty against the shirking party. To change the equilibrium, the penalty must [be costly] enough to make cooperation [the] dominant strategy for each party.

Just as compliance with promises at the domestic level requires the existence of damages, a model of compliance with international law requires a mechanism through which nations that violate an agreement are sanctioned. The finitely repeated game of the previous section can generate a model of effective international law only if there exists an entity that can sanction those who violate international law, much like courts sanction domestic violations. Those who argue that international law

has little or no impact on national behavior, therefore, are implicitly claiming that the existing penalties for violations of international law are insufficient to change the equilibrium of the game. As mentioned, the use of a finitely repeated game without a coercive compliance mechanism is equivalent to assuming that result.

To generate a model in which international law matters, then, it is necessary to identify a mechanism through which violations are sanctioned. Even those who believe that international law plays an important role in regulating conduct in the international community must concede that there is, at best, a weak system of meting out punishments for violations of law.[55] Nevertheless, a sound model of international law must turn on the impact of sanctions. It is important to note, however, that the term "sanction" must encompass more than just direct punishments resulting from a failure to live up to one's international obligations. Sanctions include all costs associated with such a failure, including punishment or retaliation by other states, and reputational costs that affect a state's ability to make commitments in the future.

To take the role of reputation into account, it is useful to remember one of the most basic elements of contract theory: in the absence of transaction costs, parties to a contract will negotiate to the most efficient outcome.[56] This implies that the best possible rule, both for individuals in the domestic context and for states in the international context, is one in which the parties have complete freedom of contract, including the ability to make irrevocable commitments. In the domestic setting, the power to commit oneself exists because the courts stand ready to enforce contracts. In the international setting, states must rely on the imperfect system of international sanctions and reputational effects. Although states are not able to make fully irrevocable commitments, the greater a state's ability to commit itself, the better off it is.

The model of international law presented in this article is an infinitely repeated game that operates as follows. Any given international obligation is modeled as a two-stage game. In the first stage, states negotiate over the content of the law and the level of commitment. In the second stage, states decide whether or not to comply with their international obligations. International law affects a state's self-interest, and thus its compliance decision, in two ways. First, it can lead to the imposition of direct sanctions such as trade, military, or diplomatic sanctions. Second, it can lead to a loss of reputational capital in the international arena. If the direct and reputational costs of violating international law are outweighed by the benefits thereof, a state will violate that law.

In the first period, states decide whether or not to enter into a legal obligation. For present purposes, an obligation is defined as a promise to other states; it could be a treaty, an informal agreement, or any other form of promise. If no promise is made, the state is free to engage in whatever conduct it chooses in the second period without suffering any sanction.[57]

The second period reveals the state of the world. In the "good" state, the interests of the relevant countries converge and those that comply with the agreement [are better off] than if they had violated the agreement. As a result, all countries comply in this period and in each period thereafter.[58] In the good state, then, countries behave in the same way whether there is an agreement or not, and international law does not affect the behavior of states. If the countries find themselves in the "bad" state, however, they face a prisoner's dilemma. * * * This is the realist [argument], which leads to the conclusion that international law has no effect.

Reputation, however, can alter the above equilibrium. For simplicity, begin by assuming that countries will only enter into agreements with countries that have a good reputation.[59] A good reputation is maintained as long as a country honors all of its previous international commitments. * * * If the state violates its commitment while the other country complies, [this] "cheating" carries with it

a reputational sanction. * * * [A] country will [thus] comply with its international obligation even when it would not have done so in the absence of that obligation * * * in order to avoid the reputational loss that would come with a violation of international law.

Reputation, therefore, causes future relationships to be affected by today's actions. Accounting for reputational effects, a decision to violate international law will increase today's payoff but reduce tomorrow's. This explains not only why nations comply with international law despite the weakness of existing enforcement mechanisms, but also why they sometimes choose to violate the law. The existence of a reputational effect impacts country incentives, but in some instances that impact will be insufficient to alter country behavior. So, unlike some existing theories of international law, this model reconciles the claim that international law affects behavior with the fact that the law is not always followed.

In the absence of other enforcement mechanisms, then, a state's commitment is only as strong as its reputation. When entering into an international commitment, a country offers its reputation for living up to its commitments as a form of collateral.[60] The value of that collateral, of course, varies from country to country and may also vary depending on the identity of the country on the other side of the agreement. Thus, for example, a treaty between Canada and the United States benefits from a high level of reputation and trust. The two countries have a long history of cooperative dealings, and to violate a promise would have a negative effect on many other interactions. A treaty between the United States and Iraq, on the other hand, would enjoy a much lower level of reputational collateral. Iraq and Saddam Hussein are not considered reliable treaty partners, in large part because of earlier violations of international legal commitments.

Because a country's reputation has value and provides that country with benefits, a country will hesitate before compromising that reputation.[61] A country that develops a reputation for compliance with international obligations signals to other countries that it is cooperative. This allows the state to enjoy long-term relationships with other cooperative states, provides a greater ability to make binding promises, and reduces the perceived need for monitoring and verification. On the other hand, failure to live up to one's commitments harms one's reputation and makes future commitments less credible.[62] As a result, potential partners are less willing to offer concessions in exchange for a promised course of action.

It is worth noting that the development of a strong reputation for compliance with international agreements is itself subject to a cost-benefit analysis by nations. If a country suffers a loss of reputation, it must rebuild its reputation by demonstrating a pattern of compliance with international law. If a country's reputation is sufficiently tarnished, of course, attempts to rebuild it may not be worthwhile. The development and destruction of a reputation occur over longer periods of time than do individual decisions regarding compliance with an obligation, but they are nevertheless the result of government decisions.

Nothing in the theory advanced in this article suggests that all countries will want to preserve a reputation for honoring their commitments. Countries that decide against developing a strong reputation for compliance with international obligations choose short-term benefits over long-term gains. Those countries are more likely to ignore international commitments and, as a result, are less likely to find partners willing to rely on such commitments. In the extreme case, a country has zero reputational capital, and international law acts as an independent force only to the extent that it generates direct sanctions.

Finally, when examined in all its dimensions, reputation need not always be a force toward compliance with international law. Nations prefer a reputation for compliance with international law so that they are able to make credible commitments in the future, but they are also concerned about other aspects of their reputation. A reputation of siding with allies can be valuable, as can a reputation for toughness. During the Cold War, for example, the United States sought to establish a reputation for adherence to a policy of containment of communism. Such forces can provide incentives either for or against compliance, depending on the circumstances. This observation does nothing to undermine the theory being advanced here, which seeks to isolate that aspect of reputation that is linked to compliance.

An Application of the Model: Bilateral Investment Treaties

The reputational theory of international law can be applied to a wide range of state behavior. For reasons discussed below, it predicts that international law will have a greater impact on economic matters than on military and security matters. To illustrate how the theory can be applied to a specific topic, this section discusses bilateral investment treaties ("BITs") and their effect on country behavior.[63]

Consider a country that has signed a BIT in which it promises not to expropriate foreign investment.[64] Assume for the purposes of this example that the country makes this promise because doing so increases the flow of foreign direct investment into the country.[65] Even after making the promise, of course, the country could choose to expropriate the local assets of foreign firms. Assume that the available assets have a total value of $100 million to the country. This potential gain of $100 million must be weighed against the cost of an expropriation, which includes several components. First, the violating country loses the benefits currently being provided by foreign firms, including tax revenues, technological transfers, employment, and so on.[66] Suppose that this loss amounts to $40 million.[67]

Second, the country is likely to suffer a reputational loss in the eyes of foreign investors. The act of expropriation signals a willingness to seize the assets of foreigners and reduces the attractiveness of the country to potential investors. Assume this translates into a loss of future investment, which the country values at $40 million. Finally, the country will suffer a loss of reputational capital with respect to other countries. Potential treaty partners will view the country as a less reliable partner and will be less willing to enter into future agreements. Assume that this loss is equivalent to $30 million. Taken together, then, the total cost[68] of the expropriation will be $110 million.

In deciding whether or not to violate its international commitment, a country compares the total costs of doing so to the total benefits. Using the numbers given above, it is clear that the country would prefer to honor its commitment. A violation of the treaty would impose a loss of $110 million and yield a gain of only $100 million—a net loss of $10 million. Notice also that the outcome can change as a result of international law. In the absence of a legal obligation, the expropriating country would not suffer a $30 million reputational loss in the eyes of other states, so its total loss from the expropriation would be no more than $80 million. Because the benefits from expropriation are $100 million, the expropriation would cause a net gain absent the international commitment.[69] This example demonstrates that a reputational loss can affect decisions even when the loss is considerably less than the total potential gains from the action. This is so because there will typically be other costs that the country must consider. This simply illustrates that the reputational consequences of an action can alter the outcome if they are large enough to tip the balance of costs and benefits in favor of compliance.

If we make different assumptions about the numbers, of course, we can generate different results. For example, if the gain from expropriation is $200 million while the other numbers are unchanged, the country will choose to expropriate, even if doing so is a violation of international law.

■   ■   ■

The Level of Commitment

The above discussion demonstrates that a model of rational states is consistent with the existence of international law. This result is important because, just as the ability to bind oneself through contract is valuable to private parties, the ability to commit to a particular action is valuable to states. A state's ability to signal its commitment more credibly through an international agreement, whether a treaty or other form of promise, increases welfare because it allows that state to enter into a broader range of potential agreements. In other words, the ability to make credible commitments makes states better off.[70]

■   ■   ■

Having the ability either to commit or not commit is valuable, then, but the ability to choose from a range of commitment levels is even more valuable. By varying the form of its promise, a state can choose its level of commitment and signal that commitment to other states.[71] Suppose that a country is willing to share certain information regarding Internet-fraud schemes in exchange for a reciprocal promise of information sharing. The state may be concerned, however, that privacy issues will arise, become important to its citizens, and force the state to end the practice of sharing information. The treaty could expressly address this contingency, but the state may also be worried that other unanticipated or unforeseeable developments will make the country want to violate its promise. In this example, because violating a treaty carries reputational costs, a treaty may represent an excessive commitment. However, simply refusing to enter into any agreement frustrates the country's initial goal. The best solution, then, may be an intermediate level of commitment, which could take the form, for example, of an "accord" that falls short of a treaty but that specifies the commitments of each state.[72]

It is possible to identify at least two dimensions along which international agreements can range in order to adjust the level of commitment: (1) the formality of the commitment and (2) the clarity of the agreement. When possible, countries that wish to increase the level of commitment prefer more formal and detailed agreements. For example, trade negotiations often feature schedules of commitments that provide a precise enumeration of commitments and obligations. At the other extreme, vague statements regarding national intent lead to relatively low levels of commitment, in part because it is difficult to determine when a country has violated the agreement.[73]

The ability to modulate the level of obligation should not be mistaken for a system of truly enforceable promises. By choosing one form of international agreement over another, countries are varying the reputational stake that they have in the obligation. A violation will impose a higher reputational cost in the case of a treaty than it will in the case of a nonbinding agreement. In neither case should one conclude that the country cannot turn away from its obligation. The strength of reputation remains limited, and even the strongest commitments will sometimes be ignored. On the other hand, it is a mistake to discount the importance of reputation altogether. As discussed earlier, a reputation for compliance with agreements is valuable to a country, so countries will only compromise that reputation if they receive something else of higher value in exchange.[74]

International Law and Coordination

When states cooperate to resolve straightforward coordination games, it is fair to say that international law plays a limited role. Imagine, for example, that two countries wish to shut down an international organized crime syndicate. By cooperating, the countries stand a good chance of success * * *. A single country acting alone stands little chance of succeeding. * * * [A] state that ignores the syndicate while the other state pursues it can divert resources to other concerns while still enjoying some chance that the syndicate will be hampered. * * * Finally, both countries could ignore the syndicate and endure the associated crime, which will free resources to combat other problems. * * *

In equilibrium, the countries will reach an agreement in which each promises to pursue the syndicate. Once they reach such an agreement, neither country has an incentive to violate its commitment, and no threat of sanction is needed to achieve cooperation. Furthermore, the form of the agreement is not terribly important. The countries could sign a treaty agreeing to pursue the crime syndicate, but a treaty is not necessary. It would be equally effective to reach an informal agreement between the countries or between the relevant law-enforcement agencies. In fact, a similar outcome could be reached without any agreement between the parties. Because this game is resolved through simple coordination and without the need for sanctions, one can question whether this is an example of international law at all.[75] Although international law may serve to focus the interaction on a single outcome where several equilibria exist, it does little else.

If one adopts a more realistic model of a coordination game, however, international law can play a significant role. There are at least two extensions of the simple coordination game that make international law relevant. First, the parties may not know one another's payoffs with certainty. In that situation, * * * the countries may not be certain that coordination is sufficient to ensure the desirable outcome. * * *

Such mistaken beliefs will affect a country's decision to enter into a legal agreement to combat the syndicate. If Country 1 believes that [it is possible that Country 2 might prefer to ignore the syndicate if Country 1 pursues it], Country 1 will not expect mere coordination to be sufficient to ensure that both countries pursue the syndicate. As a result, Country 1 will not pursue the syndicate unless it has some assurance that Country 2 will do the same. If the parties sign a treaty pledging to pursue the crime syndicate, the reputational cost of a failure to do so may be enough to make Country 2's promise credible to Country 1. If so, both countries will sign the treaty and pursue the syndicate. The lesson here is that if the payoffs are not common knowledge, international law may help achieve the value-maximizing outcome in a coordination game.

A second extension of the basic coordination game recognizes that circumstances change over time. Imagine, for example, that in the first period everybody expects that in the second period the crime syndicate will concentrate its operations in one state. Once the syndicate has turned its focus to one of the countries, the other has no incentive to pursue it. Nobody knows, however, which state will face a growth in activity and which will witness a decline. Because neither state is likely to succeed in controlling the syndicate alone, both are willing to commit to a cooperative effort to defeat the syndicate in the future rather than risk being the focus of its activity.

In this example, both states are better off ex ante if they are able to commit to a joint crime-fighting effort, but once the uncertainty is resolved, one state will have an incentive to ignore the syndicate. Both states, therefore, prefer to commit to working together in period one, but once the uncertainty is

resolved, one of them will have an incentive to ignore that commitment.

■ ■ ■

The point here is that although international law has little role to play in a pure coordination game, the dynamics of international relations may cause countries to enter into formal agreements even when they appear to face a simple coordination game. Incomplete information and changes in circumstances can turn a coordination game into a game in which the ability to commit to a particular course of action has value. Even when the game at hand appears to be a coordination game, therefore, there may be reasons to make use of international law and the ability to pledge reputational capital.

Violation and Compliance

An important benefit of a rational-actor model of international law is its ability to provide predictions about when countries will choose to violate international legal obligations. The decision to honor or breach a promise made to another state imposes costs and benefits upon the promising country and its decision-makers. The model assumes that decision-makers behave in such a way as to maximize the payoffs that result from their actions. Thus, where the benefits of breach outweigh its costs, a country is expected to violate its agreements with other states. International law succeeds when it alters a state's payoffs in such a way as to achieve compliance with an agreement when, in the absence of such law, states would behave differently. In other words, international law succeeds when promises made by states generate some compliance pull. On the other hand, even when international law affects a state's payoffs, the costs of compliance will sometimes outweigh the benefits. This part considers why and when states violate their international commitments, some of the factors that influence the magnitude of reputational sanctions, the role of direct sanctions, and when sanctions are most likely to be effective in encouraging compliance.

Reputational Sanctions

To generate predictions about state behavior, one must have a theory about the magnitude of the reputational loss resulting from violations of law.[76] It seems clear that the reputational impact of a violation of international law varies depending on the nature of the violation. For example, a failure to comply with a minor international obligation that is a result of oversight or human error and that is promptly corrected without damage to other states is unlikely to have a major reputational impact. In contrast, an egregious and intentional violation, such as support of terrorist activities against another state, is likely to have a profound impact on a nation's reputation.[77]

A list of factors that influence the reputational impact of a violation, therefore, should include (1) the severity of the violation, (2) the reasons for the violation, (3) the extent to which other states know of the violation, and (4) the clarity of the commitment and the violation.[78] * * *

SEVERITY OF THE VIOLATION

The reputational consequence of a violation is most obviously affected by the severity of that violation. A minor technical violation will have a small impact compared to a major violation of an international obligation.[79] Related to the severity of the violation is the magnitude of the harm suffered by other states. A violation that causes substantial and widespread harm does greater damage to a state's reputation than does a "victimless" violation or one that imposes only slight harms.

REASONS FOR THE VIOLATION

The reason for a violation of international law may also alter the magnitude of the resulting reputational loss. When entering into an agreement, states hope that their counterparty will honor its obligations. They also recognize, however, that compliance with international obligations is imperfect and that violations occur. It is understood that under certain conditions a state will choose to ignore its obligations. For example, violation of a human-rights treaty is viewed in a different light when it takes place under conditions of great national crisis than if the violation occurs during a period of normalcy.[80] A state that breaches such a treaty in time of crisis may be able to retain a reputation for compliance with treaties during normal times. When normalcy returns, and the state seeks to participate in further human-rights negotiations, its reputation may not be unduly compromised.

KNOWLEDGE OF THE VIOLATION

The extent to which a violation is known by the relevant players affects the reputational consequences of the violation. Obviously, if a violation takes place, but no other state has knowledge of it, there is no reputational loss. The reputational consequences will also be less if only a small number of countries know of the violation. * * * This represents part of the reason why states expend resources to deny alleged violations of international law. To the extent that the accused party is able to convince others that it has done nothing wrong, the reputational harm is reduced.

CLARITY OF THE INTERNATIONAL OBLIGATION AND ITS VIOLATION

An issue closely related to the question of states' awareness of a violation of international law is the matter of clarity. The clarity of both the international obligation and its violation are important because a failure to live up to an international obligation triggers a reputational loss. The reputational consequences are most severe when the obligation is clear and the violation is unambiguous. As the uncertainty of an obligation increases, the reputational cost from a violation decreases.

The inverse relationship between the reputational cost of a violation and the certainty of that violation may explain why battles over the content of CIL are fought. If the existence of a rule of customary law is in doubt, the reputational cost of a violation will be smaller. * * *

■   ■   ■

REGIME CHANGES

The above discussion treats each state as an entity that would be permanently tainted by a violation of international law. Because the passage of time reduces the reputational consequences of any particular act, and because a state may be able to neutralize the reputational consequences of prior actions through a change in leadership, this notion of "permanent taint" is clearly an overstatement. * * *

The ability of a new regime to avoid the reputational stigma of past state-sponsored actions will depend a great deal on the particular circumstances of the case. If the new administration is perceived to be ideologically similar to prior ones, it will probably be difficult to shed a negative reputation. In addition, if the former regime is likely to regain power in the near future, its reputation will continue to affect the behavior of other states.

Direct Sanctions

Up to this point, this article has focused on the reputational impact of violations of international law, which is a markedly different approach from the way one ordinarily studies domestic rules. In the domestic setting, state-imposed sanctions receive the primary focus, while reputational effects, if any, are normally considered secondary. The weakness of direct sanctions in the international arena, however, makes reputational sanctions more important. That is not to say that direct sanctions are irrelevant. In certain instances they can have an important impact on a country's incentives and behavior.

If states face direct sanctions for violations of international law, optimal compliance is more likely because reputational sanctions are generally, though not always, weaker than optimal sanctions. Just as compliance with a contract is not always optimal, 100% compliance with international law is not the optimal level of compliance. Like individuals entering into contracts, states entering into agreements are unable to anticipate all possible situations in their agreements, and in certain circumstances the total costs associated with compliance outweigh the costs of violation. Violation of the law is preferable in these cases. This point is understood in contract law, where it is well established that expectation damages encourage "efficient breach."[81] The same result holds in international law. When the total benefits of a violation of international law outweigh the benefits of performance, it is preferable that there be a violation. Consequently, a regime under which violations of international law trigger expectation damages will lead to violations only when they are efficient. In other words, expectation damages lead to optimal levels of deterrence.

Although direct sanctions could take a variety of forms, they most commonly consist of retaliatory measures taken by one or more states against a violator. For example, following the enactment of the Hawley-Smoot Tariff Act of 1930, which increased U.S. tariffs dramatically, other countries retaliated with tariff increases of their own.[82]

In some cases, direct retaliation takes the form of a decision by the complying state to terminate its own compliance with the underlying agreement. These types of retaliation often have the advantage of imposing a cost on the offending state and being in the interest of the complying state. Whether a complying country will resort to this form of retaliation as opposed to another will be relevant to a country's decision to violate the agreement in the first place. Indeed, in some cases the threat of such retaliation will be enough to prevent a violation. In many cases, however, the simple abrogation of the treaty will not be enough to prevent a violation and, more importantly, will not be an optimal sanction. * * *

The inadequacy of withdrawal of one's own compliance may lead states to impose other sanctions intended to punish the offending state. * * *

There are two important problems with the imposition of this sort of penalty. First, without a dispute-settlement procedure, it is difficult to distinguish appropriate sanctions from inappropriate ones. While it is true that punitive sanctions have the potential to be used as optimal sanctions, they generally are not imposed by neutral third parties but unilaterally by injured states. There is, therefore, the risk that the sanctions will be excessive and will overdeter. Second, the imposition of these sanctions imposes costs on both sanctioned and sanctioning states. For instance, the embargo on Iraqi oil has certainly hurt Iraq, but it has also hurt countries participating in the embargo by reducing the number of potential suppliers of oil. Because imposing a sanction inflicts costs on a sanctioning country, the incentive to impose optimal sanctions is often weak, leading to penalties that may be too lenient.

Despite their shortcomings, punitive sanctions should not be dismissed too quickly, especially when compared to the alternative international mechanisms for compliance. In some situations it is possible to have such sanctions imposed and, as a result, to provide more efficient incentives to states.

When Will Sanctions Work Best?

Recognizing the incentive effects of a direct sanction allows us to understand when sanctions are most likely to be imposed and work in an optimal manner. This section addresses two dimensions along which the effectiveness of a sanction—whether direct, reputational, or both—is likely to vary: (1) bilateral versus multilateral sanctions, and (2) sanctions in ongoing versus short-term relationships.

BILATERAL VS. MULTILATERAL SANCTIONS

Within a bilateral relationship, sanctions signal a willingness to punish illegal conduct. Because many of the factors that determine a country's willingness to impose a sanction, including the relative power of the two countries, the frequency of their interactions, and the general state of relations between the states, are slow to change in a bilateral relationship, a reputation for punishing violations is valuable, relatively easy to establish, and relatively easy to maintain. It is valuable because it yields benefits in a wide range of interactions. Such a reputation is easy to establish and maintain because the sanctioning party enjoys the full benefits of the sanction in the form of greater compliance by the would-be violator. It is, therefore, more likely to be worth the cost of establishing such a reputation. These factors make sanctions a relatively attractive strategy in a bilateral relationship.

The use of sanctions is much more difficult in the multilateral context. Faced with a violation, all countries have an incentive to free ride on the sanctioning efforts of others. A country that imposes a sanction gains only a portion of the benefits from that act. Other nonsanctioning members of the group also benefit. Since all countries have an incentive to free ride, one would expect too little use of sanctions in a multilateral environment. This may explain why international sanctions are often considered ineffective. * * *

COMPLEX, ONGOING RELATIONSHIPS VS. SIMPLE, SHORT-TERM RELATIONSHIPS

The role of reputation implies that international law is more powerful in complex, multifaceted relationships than in simple, one-dimensional ones. In a complex, ongoing relationship, individual interactions between countries are normally of modest value compared to the accumulated reputational capital and goodwill that exists.[83] Examples of such ongoing bilateral relationships include those between Canada and the United States, France and Germany, and the United States and Japan.

When states interact in many different ways, a reputational loss to one of those countries can be more costly than it would be in a one-time interaction.[84] It may be something of a fiction to imagine a one-time interaction among states in the modern world. For expositional purposes, however, it is convenient to assume that states can have such a relationship. The point that emerges from the analysis is not limited to simple one-shot interactions versus complex ongoing ones. The more complex a relationship, and the more the parties expect a close relationship in the future, the greater the effect of international law.[85] * * *

Countries engaged in ongoing interactions and facing a high cost for violations of international law have a great deal to gain from a system in which they are able to select from a menu of commitment levels. By adjusting their level of commitment, states are able to signal their willingness to honor their promises and can control the amount of reputational capital they stake as collateral. This flexibility allows states that enjoy a high level of mutual trust to enter into agreements that come with only low levels of commitment. Without the ability to modulate the level of reputational capital pledged, states would sometimes choose to make no deal at all rather than accept an obligation that they may not keep. * * *

Acceptance of Sanctions

States that violate an international obligation can, under certain conditions, be induced to accept a sanction voluntarily. If states are willing to submit to a penalty, it is possible to make the sanction much more effective. Rather than simply imposing a reputational sanction plus whatever direct sanctions are available, the punishment can be tailored to the precise violation. The benefits of such a system include the opportunity to resolve disputes through arbitration or some other form of dispute resolution, a lower cost to complaining states than is the case with retaliatory sanctions, the ability to adopt optimal sanctions, and the potential to choose sanctions that are less disruptive to the international community.

A state will submit to punishment when the costs of that punishment are exceeded by the costs of a failure to accept the punishment. Thus, for example, countries that have signed a BIT are typically willing to submit to arbitration to resolve disputes with investors because a failure to do so may lead to a cancellation of the relevant BIT (and perhaps other BITs) and such cancellation would be more costly than the sanction imposed by the dispute-settlement process.[86] Within the WTO, a state that violates its obligations is expected to voluntarily bring its conduct into conformity with WTO obligations. If it fails to do so, the parties to the dispute are to negotiate an appropriate compensation for the injured party.[87] Finally, if these efforts fail, the injured party can seek authority from the dispute settlement body to impose retaliatory measures. The offending party is expected to accept the imposition of these measures.[88] Similarly, within the European Union, states that lose decisions before the European Court of Justice comply with those rulings partly because a failure to do so imposes too great a risk for the success of the European Union and the place of the country within the Union.

More generally, a country is likely to accept established procedures for dealing with violations of international law when it faces a severe sanction, such as expulsion from a treaty or organization, for a failure to accept punishment; when the consequences of a failure to accept punishment impose large costs on the country, such as actions that risk tearing down the European Union; and when a failure to accept punishment imposes large reputational costs, such as a reputation for ignoring established dispute-resolution procedures.[89]

If states submit disputes to some form of dispute resolution and agree to abide by the sanctions that are handed down, it becomes possible to construct a more effective and efficient set of rules. In particular, it is possible to specify sanctions that are consistent with sound contract principles, the most prominent of which is expectation damages. If countries accept sanctions handed down by a dispute-settlement procedure, a system of expectation damages can be established within the international legal system. As in the domestic context, this will lead to breach if and only if breach is efficient.

Rethinking International Law

Up to this point, this article has focused on developing a more complete theory of compliance with international law. This part uses the theory to take a fresh look at the traditional sources of international law: treaties and CIL. It argues that the current approach to "soft law" must be changed. It then demonstrates that many of the topics upon which international law has focused the most attention are precisely the areas where international law is least likely to influence state behavior. This part closes by exploring the implications of this conclusion, including the need to redirect some of the energies and resources of both states and international law scholars.

Rethinking Treaties

The most formal and reliable international commitment is a treaty.[90] Aside from signaling a high level of commitment by a state, treaties offer several advantages to states: (1) treaties represent clear and well-defined obligations of states; (2) treaties can provide for explicit dispute resolution; and (3) treaties define rules for accession to and exit from their terms. In addition, third parties can observe their content with relative ease. Treaties can also provide for sanctions, the most obvious of which are the ability of complying states to cancel the treaty if it is violated, the potential for a sanction imposed by the treaty itself, and the reputational impact of violations. States agree to an elevated level of commitment in a treaty to obtain an elevated level of commitment from others.[91] A treaty, therefore, should be viewed as a contractual commitment by a group of states. Using treaties, states can increase one another's reputational stakes and thereby increase the costs of breach.[92]

Within traditional international law, all treaties are considered equivalent in the sense that they are all binding.[93] Nevertheless, they are sometimes violated. A major failing of traditional accounts of international law is their inability to explain such violations. When viewed through the lens of the reputational model presented in this article, it is clear that not all treaties have the same impact on national incentives or the same chance of influencing a country's behavior. Without a theory of compliance, it is impossible to consider the circumstances under which violations take place or to develop strategies to improve the compliance pull of a treaty.

At least two dimensions are critical to an understanding of treaty compliance. The first is the reputational impact of a violation, which has already been discussed. The second dimension is the cost of compliance, which is informed by the subject matter of the treaty. Treaties that implicate critical issues of national security and other issues of central importance to states are less likely to succeed in tipping the scales in favor of compliance. These treaties implicate issues of profound national importance, and it is unlikely that reputation will be enough to change a country's course of action from violation to compliance. In other words, the decision of whether to act in accordance with the treaty will most likely be made based on costs and benefits that have nothing to do with international law.[94]

Rethinking Customary International Law

CIL is the second form of international law recognized by traditional scholars. Unlike treaties, however, CIL is not the product of explicit bargaining and formal ratification. Under the traditional interpretation, it arises instead from widespread state practice and opinio juris—a sense of legal obligation.[95] The theory advanced in this article suggests that the standard understanding of CIL needs to be rethought. * * *

* * * First, there is no agreement on how widespread a custom must be in order to satisfy the state practice requirement; indeed, there is not even a consensus on what counts as state practice. Among the instruments that are sometimes considered evidence of state practice are treaties (both bilateral and multilateral), national laws, and governmental statements of policy.[96] The required duration of the state practice is similarly difficult to pin down. Related to the question of duration is the question of continuity. It is difficult to know if a single act, inconsistent with the practice, is enough to

undermine that practice. If it is not, there is no agreement on how much discontinuity is enough. Second, the opinio juris requirement fares no better as a theoretical matter than does the state practice requirement. Professor D'Amato refers to the circularity of opinio juris as its "fatal defect": "How can Custom create law if its psychological component requires action in conscious accordance with preexisting law?"[97] The lack of a sound theoretical foundation for CIL makes it difficult to identify how CIL comes into being and how it changes over time.[98] Furthermore, violations of CIL are difficult to identify because the rules themselves are often vague. Without some formal legal instrument to define the obligation, the scope of the law is hard to know. And even when violations take place and are unambiguous, they can sometimes be justified through the use of the "persistent objector" exception to CIL.[99]

The problems with CIL have led many to question whether it exists at all as a relevant force in international law.[100] Among the recent critics of CIL are Professors Goldsmith and Posner, who have advanced what is essentially the realist model presented in Part II.A[101] and concluded that CIL is irrelevant to state behavior.[102] They recognize the potential for reputation to affect compliance, but express deep skepticism about its role,[103] suggesting that other domestic interests trump reputational concerns.[104] At their most controversial, Goldsmith and Posner assert that "[t]he faulty premise is that CIL—either the traditional or the new—influences national behavior."[105] When they claim CIL is irrelevant to national conduct, however, they go beyond what either the theory or the evidence suggests. As the general theory advanced in this article suggests, CIL may influence state behavior through both reputational and direct sanctions.[106] Even if direct sanctions are weak—as they surely are with respect to CIL—reputational sanctions may be enough to generate compliance.

An alternative interpretation of CIL, one that addresses the theoretical difficulties with the traditional approach without denying the existence of CIL, is suggested by the theory advanced in this article. CIL represents a form of legal obligation that countries have toward one another, even without explicit agreement. * * *

The discussion suggests a new definition of CIL: CIL consists of legal norms whose violation will harm a country's reputation as a law-abiding state.[107] Compare this definition to the traditional one. The practice requirement, present in traditional accounts of CIL, is not an explicit factor under a reputational account of international law. The practice requirement becomes important indirectly, however, if it causes a particular norm to be seen as an obligation.

Unlike the traditional concept of opinion juris, what matters under the theory advanced in this article is that countries other than the offending state believe that there is such an obligation. That is, a state faces a norm of CIL if other states believe that the state has such an obligation and if those other states will view a failure to honor that obligation as a violation. Only under these circumstances will a violation by the state lead to a reputational loss. If, for example, respect for the principles of diplomatic immunity is considered a legal obligation, then a violation of those rules will be viewed by other states (or perhaps only the offended state) in a negative light. This will cause those states to doubt the reliability of the offending state, making them less prone to trust it in the future. * * *

Unfortunately, we simply do not know how much reputational capital is at stake with respect to CIL. It is clear that CIL is weaker than treaties in part because CIL is typically not clearly specified, making its boundaries ambiguous. There is often debate about whether a particular norm of CIL exists at all, and countries normally have not consented to CIL in an explicit way, making their commitment to it uncertain. For all of these reasons, the possibility that CIL is so weak as to be negligible cannot be dismissed until some form of empirical evidence becomes available.

Regardless of the empirical importance of CIL as a category, the reputational model provides a more satisfactory framework within which to view CIL than does the realist model. Under a realist model, one must either treat all international law as irrelevant—a position that is, to my knowledge, not advocated by any legal scholar—or treat CIL as different in kind from other forms of international obligation. The latter option leads to an awkward framework in which each form of international obligation is explained through a separate theory, making it difficult to consider the many different forms of obligation together. The realist theory also fails to explain behavior in those circumstances in which CIL does seem to matter, such as diplomatic immunity. The reputational model, on the other hand, views the many different forms of international agreement as points on a spectrum. CIL is perhaps the weakest form of international law, but it is nevertheless part of the general framework. As the level of state commitment increases, the reputational stake is raised and the commitment becomes more credible. This theory explains not only CIL, but all forms of international commitment. It also explains why nations choose one form of commitment over others and why states expend resources in order to comply, or appear to comply, with their commitments.

Rethinking International Law

The previous section proposed a new definition of CIL that turns on the question of whether a state is perceived, by other states, to have a legal obligation and whether a failure to live up to that obligation harms the state's reputation. This section proposes a broadening of the definition of international law to more explicitly include obligations that are neither treaties nor CIL.

In domestic law, it makes sense to use the term "law" to distinguish obligations that are legally enforceable from those that are not. When using "law" in the international context, however, analogies to domestic contract law are difficult. In particular, it makes no sense to restrict the use of "law" to obligations that are legally enforceable because most international legal obligations exist without any sort of formal enforcement mechanism. The associated conclusion that very little of international law qualifies as law, however, does nothing to help us understand the operation of international law. A vocabulary is needed to distinguish those obligations of states that affect incentives and behavior, and the term law seems to be sufficient for that purpose.

SOFT LAW

The classical usage of "international law" refers only to treaties and CIL. This definition excludes promises made by states through instruments that fall short of full-scale treaties, such as memoranda of understanding, executive agreements, nonbinding treaties, joint declarations, final communiqués, agreements pursuant to legislation, and so on. The place of such commitments, sometimes referred to as "soft law," within the framework of international law is uncertain.[108] What is clear is that traditional international law scholarship considers soft law less "law" than the "hard law" of treaties and custom. The focus of international legal scholars is often exclusively on treaties and custom, as if soft law either does not exist or has no impact.[109] Although only occasionally stated explicitly, the general presumption appears to be that soft law is less binding than the traditional sources of international law, and states are accordingly less likely to comply.[110] * * *

Like treaties, nonbinding agreements benefit from a high degree of clarity and are often drafted by specialists with deep technical knowledge. Because these agreements are not treaties, they are often relatively easy to change and can be concluded more quickly and with less attention. Unlike treaties, however, they do not represent a complete pledge of a nation's reputational capital. The agreements are made with an understanding that they represent a level of commitment that falls below that of a treaty. The violation of such an agreement, therefore, carries a less severe reputational penalty than does the violation of a treaty.

That said, a failure to honor the terms of such an agreement is not costless. The reputational costs imposed on violations of nonbinding agreements can take two forms. First, there is the reputational loss to the country itself. A state that routinely ignores promises that fall short of treaties will find that it cannot extract concessions in exchange for such promises. Second, an additional reputational cost is present when the agreement in question is negotiated and agreed to by government ministers or other agents of the state. If their countries do not honor the commitments, these individuals will be handicapped in their future attempts to enter into such agreements.

■ · ■ ■

A FUNCTIONAL DEFINITION OF INTERNATIONAL LAW

Under the theory advanced in this article, the difference between the traditional sources of international law and those promises made by states that have not been viewed as "law" is one of degree. Agreements among states lie on a spectrum of commitment. The same reputational issues influence such promises regardless of the form in which they are made, but the magnitude of the reputational effect varies with the level of commitment.

■ ■ ■

The central question of interest in this article is whether the practice of making an international commitment alters the behavior of countries. It is tempting, therefore, to define international law in an outcome-based fashion by applying the label of international law to those international obligations that change behavior and denying it to obligations that do not. A definition of this sort, however, ignores the fact that laws—even domestic laws—can only alter the incentives of actors. The law itself cannot determine outcomes. For example, a law against speeding is no less a law when people speed. It is a law because it increases the expected cost of speeding. * * *

The definition of international law, therefore, should turn on the impact of a promise on national incentives. With that in mind, this article defines international law as those promises and obligations that make it materially more likely that a state will behave in a manner consistent with those promises and obligations than would otherwise be the case. In some instances this change in incentives will affect outcomes. In other cases, however, it will not.

The proposed functional definition of international law reflects the fact that international obligation comes in many different forms, with varying levels of compliance pull. This is a significant departure from the conventional view of international law, which simply declares law to be binding. The new theory recognizes that the discrete categories of treaties, CIL, and soft law, though perhaps useful, do not themselves define international law or represent the only possible levels of commitment. Rather, they are attempts to describe the spectrum of commitment from which states choose the level that suits their purposes at any given time.

■ ■ ■ ■

Conclusion

This article hopes to achieve several goals. First, it lays out a theory of international law and compliance that explains how national behavior is influenced by international law. It does so within the framework of a rational actor model in which states value a reputation for compliance with international obligations. Along with the possibility of

direct sanctions, reputation provides an incentive for states to comply with their obligations. By developing and preserving a good reputation, states are able to extract greater concessions for future promises.

Because the magnitude of reputational sanctions is limited, the article points out that they will not always provide sufficient incentive for nations to comply with the law. This explains why one sees violations of international law in some instances. It also suggests that scholars of international law should keep the limits of that law in mind. In particular, it is unlikely that international law can influence decisions of fundamental importance to the state with any frequency. Where individual decisions have a more modest impact, however—a situation that arises frequently in, for example, the world of international economic and regulatory cooperation—international law may be able to alter outcomes more frequently. * * *

Taken seriously, a reputational model of compliance leads to important changes in the way we view international law. It forces us to reject the classical definition of international law, which considers only treaties and CIL to be law. Instead, it leads us to a more functional definition, which considers any international promise or commitment that has a substantial influence on national incentives to be law. It also forces us to recognize in an explicit way that not all international law is created equal. Some obligations are more binding than others, and states choose the level of their commitments against this background fact. We can no longer be satisfied with the simple conclusion that "treaties are to be obeyed."[111]

Above all, the theory advanced in this article offers a more realistic and compelling model of international law—one in which both instances of compliance and instances of violation can be understood, in which the full spectrum of agreements negotiated by states is explained, and in which the role of international law can be understood within a model of self-interested states.

NOTES

1. *See* Louis Henkin, How Nations Behave: Law and Foreign Policy 46–48 (1979); Abram H. Chayes & Antonia Chayes, *On Compliance*, 47 Int'l Org. 175, 176 (1993).

2. *See* Beth A. Simmons, *Money and the Law: Why Comply with the Public International Law of Money?*, 25 Yale J. Int'l L. 323 (2000).

3. *See* Jeffrey L. Dunoff & Joel P. Trachtman, *Economic Analysis of International Law*, 24 Yale J. Int'l L. 1, 28 (1999) ("Past efforts to identify an underlying structure for the law of treaties have proven unsatisfactory."); Harold Hongju Koh, *Why Do Nations Obey International Law?*, 106 Yale L.J. 2599 (1997); John K. Setear, *An Iterative Perspective on Treaties: A Synthesis of International Relations Theory and International Law*, Harv. Int'l L.J. 139, 147 (1996) (criticizing two theoretical justifications for the law of treaties).

4. *See, e.g.*, Abram Chayes & Antonia Handler Chayes, The New Sovereignty: Compliance with International Regulatory Agreements 3 (1995) ("[F]oreign policy practitioners operate on the assumption of a general propensity of states to comply with international obligations.").

5. The most prominent interdisciplinary articles include Kenneth W. Abbott, *Modern International Relations Theory: A Prospectus for International Lawyers*, 14 Yale J. Int'l L. 335 (1989) [hereinafter Abbott, *Prospectus*]; Kenneth W. Abbott, *International Relations Theory, International Law, and the Regime Governing Atrocities in Internal Conflicts*, 93 Am. J. Int'l L. 361 (1999) [hereinafter Abbott, *Atrocities*]; Dunoff & Trachtman, *supra* note 3; Jack L. Goldsmith & Eric A. Posner, *A Theory of Customary International Law*, 66 U. Chi. L. Rev. 1113 (1999); Koh, *supra* note 3; Kal Raustiala & Anne-Marie Slaughter, *International Law, International Relations and Compliance, in* The Handbook of International Relations 28 (Walter Carlsnaes et al. eds., 2002); John K. Setear, *Responses to Breach of a Treaty and Rationalist International Relations Theory: The Rules of Release and Remediation in the Law of Treaties and the Law of State Responsibility*, 83 Va. L. Rev. 1 (1997); Setear, *supra* note 3; Anne-Marie Slaughter, *International Law and International Relations*, 285 Recueil des Cours 9 (2000); Anne-Marie Slaughter et al., *International Law and International Relations Theory: A New Generation of Interdisciplinary Scholarship*, 92 Am. J. Int'l L. 367 (1998); Anne-Marie Slaughter Burley, *International Law and International Relations Theory: A Dual Agenda*, 87 Am. J. Int'l L. 205 (1993); Edwin M. Smith, *Understanding Dynamic Obligations: Arms Control Agreements*, 64 S. Cal. L. Rev. 1549 (1991).

6. *See* George W. Downs et al., *Is the Good News About Compliance Good News About Cooperation?*, 50 Int'l Org. 379 (1996).

7. *See* Michael Byers, Custom, Power and the Power of Rules: International Relations and Customary International Law 8 (1999) ("International relations scholars have traditionally had little time for such questions. Instead, they have regarded international law as something of an epiphenomenon, with rules of international law being dependent on power, subject to short-term alteration by power-applying States, and therefore of little relevance to how States actually behave.").

8. For a discussion of the compliance literature that addresses both the legal and political science debate, see Raustiala & Slaughter, *supra* note 5.

9. *See* Chayes & Chayes, *supra* note 4.

10. *Id.* at 3.

11. *See id.* at 4.

12. *See id.* at 7. Chayes and Chayes note:

    [I]f the agreement is well designed—sensible, comprehensible, and with a practical eye to probable patterns of conduct and interaction—compliance problems and enforcement issues are likely to be manageable. If issues of noncompliance and enforcement are endemic, the real problem is likely to be that the negotiating process did not succeed in incorporating a broad enough range of the parties interests.

    Id. at 7.

13. *See id.* at 8 ("The existence of legal obligation, for most actors in most situations, translates into a presumption of compliance, in the absence of strong countervailing circumstances. So it is with states. . . . The norm [of compliance] is itself a 'reason for action' and thus becomes an independent basis for conforming behavior.").

14. *See id.* at 135–53.

15. *See id.* at 201–25.

16. *See id.* at 197–201.

17. *See supra* notes 10–13 and accompanying text.

18. Other strategies would be better still. The best strategy is to invest in information gathering until the marginal cost of additional information equals the information's marginal benefit in terms of its effect on the probability of making the correct choice and the cost of a mistake. Once a state gathers the optimal amount of information, it could base the decision on that information without a presumption in favor of compliance.

19. *See* Setear, *supra* note 3, at 156; Smith, *supra* note 5, at 1565–66. Though most frequently discussed in the context of treaties, the use of consent as an explanation for the binding character of international law is also present in discussions of CIL. *See* Byers, *supra* note 7, at 7; M. O. Chibundu, *Making Customary International Law Through Municipal Adjudication: A Structural Inquiry*, 39 Va. J. Int'l L. 1069, 1122 (1999).

20. "The rules binding upon states therefore emanate from their own free will. . . . Restrictions upon the independence of states cannot therefore be presumed." *S.S. Lotus Case*, 1927 P.C.I.J. (ser. A) No. 10, at 18; *see also* Louis Henkin, *International Law: Politics, Values and Functions*, 216 Recueil Des Cours D'Academie de Droit Int'l 9, 27 (1989) ("[A] state is not subject to any external authority unless it has voluntarily consented to such authority.").

21. *See* Vienna Convention on the Law of Treaties, May 23, 1969, art. 26, 1155 U.N.T.S. 331 ("Every treaty in force is binding upon the parties to it and must be performed by them in good faith."); Chayes & Chayes, *supra* note 1, at 185 ("It is often said that the fundamental norm of international law is *pacta sunt servanda* (treaties are to be obeyed).") (footnote omitted).

22. I will argue below that it is not quite accurate. (discussing how states can be "bound" by informal agreements, custom, and practice).

23. *See* Chayes & Chayes, *supra* note 1, at 185.

24. Thomas M. Franck, Fairness in International Law and Institutions (1995) [hereinafter Franck, Fairness].

25. *See* Harold H. Koh, *Transnational Legal Process*, 75 Neb. L. Rev. 181, 183–84 (1996) [hereinafter Koh, *Legal Process*]; Koh, *supra* note 3.

26. *See* Koh, *Legal Process, supra* note 25, at 204 ("It is through this repeated process of interaction and internalization that international law acquires its 'stickiness,' that nation-states acquire their identity, and that nations define promoting the rule of international law as part of their national self-interest.").

27. *See* Abbott, *Prospectus, supra* note 5.

28. For a discussion of classical realism, see Edward H. Carr, The Twenty Years' Crisis 1919–1939 (1962); George F. Kennan, American Diplomacy 1900–1950 (1951); Hans J. Morgenthau, Politics Among Nations: The Struggle for Power and Peace (1948); Hans J. Morgenthau, *Positivism, Functionalism, and International Law*, 34 Am. J. Int'l L. 260 (1940).

29. *See* Joseph M. Grieco, *Anarchy and the Limits of Cooperation: A Realist Critique of the Newest Liberal Institutionalism*, 42 Int'l Org. 485 (1988).

30. *See id.*

31. *See* Robert H. Bork, *The Limits of "International Law"*, 18 Nat'l Int. 3 (1989–90); Francis A. Boyle, *The Irrelevance of International Law: The Schism Between International Law and International Politics*, 10 Cal. W. Int'l L.J. 193 (1980).

32. *See* Stephen D. Krasner, Sovereignty: Organized Hypocrisy (1999); Abbott, *Atrocities, supra* note 5, at 364–65; Slaughter Burley, *supra* note 5, at 217 ("For Waltz, norms of any sort, qua norms, lacked independent causal force."). Hans Morgenthau, one of the great realists, conceded that international law is generally observed, but considered this to be the result of either power relations or convergent interests. *See* Beth A. Simmons, *Compliance with International* Agreements, I Ann. Rev. Pol. Sci. 75, 79 (1998); *see also* Morgenthau, *supra* note 28; Morgenthau, *supra* note 28.

33. For a detailed discussion of the problems with neorealism, see Neorealism and Its Critics (Robert O. Keohane ed., 1986).

34. *See* Andrew T. Guzman, *Why LDCs Sign Treaties that Hurt Them: Explaining the Popularity of Bilateral Investment Treaties*, 38 Va. J. Int'l L. 639, 644–51 (1998).

35. Frank Newman & David Weissbrodt, International Human Rights: Law, Policy, and Process 18 (2d ed. 1996).

36. *See* The Implementation and Effectiveness of International Environmental Commitments: Theory and Practice (David G. Victor et al. eds., 1998).

37. *See* Henkin, *supra* note 1, at 43 ("While nations, generally, still deny that they are violating international law, often the denial merely falsifies the facts.").

38. *See, e.g.*, Ronald B. Mitchell, *Compliance with International Treaties: Lessons from Intentional Oil Pollution*, 37 Env't 10 (1995); Stephen M. Schwebel, *Commentary, in* Compliance with Judgments of International Courts 39, 39 (M.K. Bulterman & M. Kuijer eds., 1996) (arguing that states tend to comply with the decisions of international tribunals); Simmons, *supra* note 2, at 325 (presenting an empirical study of state compliance with International Monetary Fund obligations and concluding that "international law has a significant impact on governments' behavior.").

39. *See* Andrew Moravcsik, *Taking Preferences Seriously: A Liberal Theory of International Politics*, 51 Int'l Org. 513 (1997); Anne-Marie Slaughter, *International Law in a World of Liberal States*, 6 Eur. J. Int'l L. 503 (1995) [hereinafter Slaughter, *Liberal States*]; Anne-Marie Slaughter, The Liberal Agenda for Peace: International Relations Theory and the Future of the United Nations, 4 Transnat'l L. & Contemp. Probs. 377 (1995) [hereinafter Slaughter, *Liberal Agenda*]. For a version of liberal theory in the legal literature, see Koh, *Legal Process, supra* note 25, at 183–84 (1994); Koh, *supra* note 3.

40. *See* Laurence R. Helfer & Anne-Marie Slaughter, *Toward a Theory of Effective Supranational Adjudication*, 107 Yale L.J. 273 (1997).

41. *See* Robert O. Keohane, After Hegemony: Cooperation and Discord in the World Political Economy 25 (1984) ("Parsimonious theory, even as a partial 'first cut,' becomes impossible if one starts analysis [at the subnational level], amidst a confusing plethora of seemingly relevant facts."). It should, however, be noted that liberal theorists are attempting to generate general theoretical claims despite the challenge of doing so within a liberal model. *See* Helfer & Slaughter, *supra* note 40.

42. *See* Abbott, *Atrocities, supra* note 5, at 365. Among the important and useful institutionalist contributions are Duncan Snidal, *The Game Theory of International Politics*, 38 World Pol. 25 (1985) [hereinafter Snidal, *Game Theory*]; Duncan Snidal, *The Limits of Hegemonic Stability Theory*, 39 Int'l Org. 579 (1985); Duncan Snidal, *Coordination Versus Prisoners' Dilemma: Implications for International Cooperation and Regimes*, 79 Am. Pol. Sci. Rev. 923 (1985) [hereinafter Snidal, *Prisoners' Dilemma*]; Arthur A. Stein, *Coordination and Collaboration: Regimes in an Anarchic World*, 36 Int'l Org. 299 (1982); Robert Jervis, *Cooperation Under the Security Dilemma*, 30 World Pol. 167 (1978); Robert Jervis, *Security Regimes*, 36 Int'l Org. 357 (1982); Kenneth A. Oye, *Explaining Cooperation Under Anarchy: Hypotheses and Strategies*, 38 World Pol. 1 (1985); Cooperation Under Anarchy (Kenneth A. Oye ed., 1986); Stephan Haggard & Beth A. Simmons, *Theories of International Regimes*, 41 Int'l Org. 491 (1987).

43. *See* Robert Axelrod, The Evolution of Cooperation 3 (1984); Robert Axelrod & Robert O. Keohane, *Achieving Cooperation Under Anarchy: Strategies and Institutions*, 38 World Pol. 226, 226 (1985). Many, and perhaps most, institutionalists recognize that state decisions are the product of a domestic political process in which different interests compete for influence. Nevertheless, as I do in this Article, institutionalists usually model the state as a single actor to simplify the analysis. *See* Abbott, *Atrocities, supra* note 5, at 365.

44. *See* Keohane, *supra* note 41, at 246.

45. The most important prior work with a similar approach is that of Robert Keohane, especially Keohane, *supra* note 41.

46. *See* Abbott, *Atrocities, supra* note 5, at 366 ("In practice, though, institutionalist scholarship focuses on treaties.").

47. *See* Keohane, *supra* note 41, at 27; Abbott, *Prospectus, supra* note 5, at 349.

48. *See* Daniel A. Farber & Philip F. Frickey, Law & Public Choice: A Critical Introduction 17 (1991); Michael E. Levine & Jennifer L. Forrence, *Regulatory Capture, Public Interest, and the Public Agenda: Toward a Synthesis*, 6 J.L. Econ. & Org. 167, 169 (1990).

49. *See* Abbott, *Prospectus, supra* note 5.

50. The basics of game theory are available in many other sources, and they will not be repeated here. For relevant discussions in the context of international law, see Setear, *supra* note 3; Abbott, *Prospectus, supra* note 5; Goldsmith & Posner, *supra* note 5. For more comprehensive presentations of game theory, see Douglas G. Baird et al., Game Theory and the Law (1994); Eric Rasmusen, Games and Information: An Introduction to Game Theory (1989); Drew Fudenberg & Jean Tirole, Game Theory (1991).

51. In the famous words of Henkin, "almost all nations observe almost all principles of international law and almost all of their obligations almost all of the time." *See* Henkin, supra note 37, at 47.

52. *Id.*

53. *See supra* note 31.

54. *See supra* note 38.

55. That said, it would be a mistake to completely disregard the existing set of sanctions altogether. *See* Lori Fisler Damrosch, *Enforcing International Law Through Non-Forcible Measures*, 269 Recueil des Cours 9, 19–22 (1997) (outlining the enforcement mechanisms that currently exist).

56. *See* A. Mitchell Polinsky, An Introduction to Law and Economics 31 (2d ed. 1989).

57. State behavior may provoke reaction from other states even in the absence of a legal commitment. These may be sanctions for the failure to honor an implicit commitment, or they may be a response motivated by some other, nonlegal concerns.

58. For simplicity, it is assumed that the state of the world does not change after the first period.

59. For the moment it is assumed that countries have either a good reputation or a bad one. This is done to clarify the exposition and is not necessary for the theory, and the paper discusses *infra* both how reputation can vary along a spectrum and how a country's reputation may differ from one subject matter to another.

60. *See* Keohane, *supra* note 41, at 26 ("International regimes alter the information available to governments and the opportunities open to them; commitments made to support such institutions can only be broken at a cost to reputation. International regimes therefore change the calculations of advantage that governments make.").

61. *See* Simmons, *supra* note 2, at 325 ("Governments comply with their legal commitments largely to preserve their reputation. . . .").

62. *See* Andrew T. Guzman, *The Cost of Credibility: Explaining Resistance to Interstate Dispute Resolution Mechanisms*, 31 J. Leg. Stud. 303, 311 (2002).

63. For a detailed discussion of BITs, see Guzman, *supra* note 34, at 654–58; Kenneth J. Vandevelde, *U.S. Bilateral Investment Treaties: The Second Wave*, 14 Mich. J. Int'l L. 621 (1993).

64. Other examples could obviously be chosen here. BITs are selected because the costs and benefits are more easily understood and evaluated in the context of such treaties than in many other examples. It is important to note, however, that difficulties expressing costs and benefits in dollar terms do not represent a problem for the theory presented.

65. The expropriation of foreign-owned assets occurred numerous times in the twentieth century. Some examples include: the Mexican expropriation of agrarian and oil properties between 1915 and 1940; the Soviet expropriations following the Russian revolution; the Egyptian expropriations that led to the Suez crisis; Cuban expropriations following the rise to power of Fidel Castro; the taking of partial ownership in copper mines in Chile in 1971; and expropriations by Iran following the fall of the Shah. *See* Charles Lipson, Standing Guard, Protecting Foreign Capital in the Nineteenth and Twentieth Centuries (1985); F. N. Burton & Hisashi Inoue, *Expropriations of Foreign-Owned Firms in Developing Countries*, 18 J. World Trade L. 396 (1984); Detlev F. Vagts, *Foreign Investment Risk Reconsidered: The View from the 1980s*, 2 Foreign Inv. L.J. 1 (1987).

66. It is true that the expropriating country may be able to generate some of these benefits by continuing to operate the expropriated firms. Unless the government can operate the firms as efficiently and introduce the innovations as quickly as the former owners could, however, the expropriation involves some loss.

67. All of the costs and benefits in this example should be treated as the present discounted value of the lost future stream of revenue.

68. Notice that only a portion of the above costs can be attributed to international law. Some benefits are lost due to existing foreign firms that either stop operating or operate less efficiently after expropriation, but are not affected by the country's legal commitments. In the eyes of other states, the reputational loss results from a violation of an international obligation. The country's act of expropriation in the face of a treaty expressly promising not to do so demonstrates that country's willingness to violate international commitments. Other countries will take this into account when dealing with the country. Finally, the reaction of potential foreign investors is partially, though not entirely, a function of the existence of international law. Even in the absence of an international legal commitment (putting aside, for simplicity, the fact that there may be a rule of CIL that prohibits expropriation without full compensation), a decision to expropriate will have a chilling effect on future investments. To the extent that investors view the legal obligation contained in the BIT as a credible commitment, however, the country becomes more attractive to investors and may enjoy higher levels of investment. If expropriation undermines this confidence, a portion of the lost investment can be attributed to a reputational effect resulting from the violation of international law.

69. Strictly speaking, one should include the fact that the BIT caused an increase in investment—meaning that absent a BIT, the country would have less investment to begin with, reducing the attractiveness of expropriation. This detail can easily be added to the above example without changing the results. It is omitted only for simplicity.

70. The value of a good reputation for states can be compared to the value of a high bond rating. Just as a good rating increases investor confidence and, therefore, allows the firm to raise money more cheaply, a strong reputation increases the confidence of counterparties to an international agreement, allowing a state to extract more in exchange for its own promises.

71. *See* Charles Lipson, *Why Are Some International Agreements Informal?*, 45 Int'l Org. 495, 508 (1991) (stating that countries use

72. *See* Guzman, *supra* note 62 (explaining with a similar argument why states who enter into a treaty may not always want a dispute-settlement provision).

73. *See* Kal Raustiala, *Form & Substance in International Agreements* (2002) (unpublished manuscript, on file with author).

74. *See* Lipson, *supra* note 72, at 511.

75. *See* Goldsmith & Posner, *supra* note 5, at 1127–28.

76. *See* George W. Downs & Michael A. Jones, *Reputation, Compliance, and International Law*, 31 J. Legal. Stud. S95 (2002).

77. Although this article tends to speak of "a state's reputation," it is important to keep in mind that the reputation of a state may vary from one issue area to another and may depend on the identity of its counterparty.

78. This list is not intended to be exhaustive. Other factors may also be relevant.

79. *See* Chayes & Chayes, *supra* note 4, at 18 ("Flouting a cease-fire under a peace agreement or refusing to allow inspection of nuclear reactors under the NPT would be expected to evoke very different responses from a failure to meet the reporting requirements of an environmental treaty.").

80. Note that this is a claim about how nations view a violation, not how traditional conceptions of international law view it.

81. *See* Polinsky, *supra* note 56, at 31. In other words, if courts adopt expectation damages, contracts are breached if and only if breach is the value-maximizing outcome.

82. *See* Thomas D. Grant, *Foreign Takeovers of United States Airlines: Free Trade Process, Problems, and Progress*, 31 Harv. J. on Legis. 63, 139–40 (1994).

83. *Cf.* Simmons, *supra* note 2, at 325 ("[T]here is suggestive evidence that the more a polity has invested in such a reputation, the less willing a government will be to tarnish its reputation through non-compliance. . . .").

84. *See* Downs & Jones, *supra* note 77.

85. Even states with complex bilateral relationships violate their agreements with one another, of course, and the theory presented in this article does not predict perfect compliance. The model merely predicts that such violations will be less common, all else equal, in a complex, ongoing bilateral relationship than in simple or multilateral relationships.

86. Even if no BIT is cancelled, a failure to honor the dispute-settlement obligation under a BIT will harm the country's efforts to attract new investment.

87. *Id.*, art. 22.

88. *Id.*, arts. 21–22.

89. *See* Lipson, *supra* note 72, at 506.

90. Treaties are also the focus of most theories of compliance with international law. *See* Koh, *supra* note 3; Oscar Schachter, *Towards a Theory of International Obligation*, 8 Va. J. Int'l L. 300, 301 (1968).

91. *See* Guzman, *supra* note 62.

92. *See* Lipson, *supra* note 72, at 508.

93. *See* Vienna Convention on the Law of Treaties, *supra* note 21, art. 18.

94. One can certainly imagine cases in which the decision to honor or violate a military treaty is such a close one that the reputational consequences will make a difference. The more important the issues at stake, however, the less likely it is that such a case will come about.

95. *See* Anthony D'Amato, The Concept of Custom in International Law 6–10 (1971).

96. *Id.*

97. *Id.* at 66.

98. *See* Byers, *supra* note 7, at 180–83.

99. *See* Ian Brownlie, Principles of Public International Law 512–15 (4th ed. 1990). *But see* Jonathan I. Charney, *Universal International Law*, 87 Am. J. Int'l L. 529, 538–39 (1993) (arguing that the persistent-objector rule is rarely used and may not be effective in practice).

100. *See, e.g.*, Boyle, *supra* note 31, at 198 ("International law is therefore irrelevant to those matters which count the most, or more forcefully, to those matters which count for anything in international relations.").

101. *See* Goldsmith & Posner, *supra* note 5; Jack L. Goldsmith & Eric A. Posner, *Understanding the Resemblance between Modern and Traditional Customary International Law*, 40 Va. J. Int'l L. 639 (2000) [hereinafter Goldsmith & Posner, *Understanding*].

102. *See* Goldsmith & Posner, *Understanding, supra* note 103, at 640, 641 ("CIL as an independent normative force has little if any impact on national behavior. . . ."). In earlier writing, they are less forceful in their claims, stating that "CIL has real content, but it is much less robust than traditional scholars think, and it operates in a different fashion." Goldsmith & Posner, *supra* note 5, at 1177.

103. *See* Goldsmith & Posner, *supra* note 5, at 1135 ("[I]t is hard to see why reputation would play an important role in explaining compliance with CIL norms beyond the limited sense in which it describes tit-for-tat and related strategies in the repeat bilateral prisoner's dilemma.").

104. "[I]t is hard to see why reputation would play an important role in explaining compliance . . . ." *Id.* This view of reputational arguments fails to consider that reputation, like any enforcement mechanism, operates at the margins. Other national objectives remain relevant and may trump reputation even if reputation exerts some compliance pull. Goldsmith and Posner seem to agree, stating "[o]ne might conclude that all things equal, nations will strive to have a reputation for compliance with international law, but a reputation for compliance will not always be of paramount concern because all things are not equal." *Id.* at 1136. This statement is essentially the same as this article's observation that reputation is relevant to decision-making.

105. Goldsmith & Posner, *Understanding, supra* note, 103, at 640.

106. For a critique of Goldsmith and Posner and a detailed discussion of why CIL can exist within a rational choice framework, see Edward T. Swaine, *Rational Custom*, Duke L.J. (2002).

107. Notice that under this new definition, it no longer makes sense to ask whether or not CIL affects state behavior—it does so by definition. Instead, one can ask whether CIL exists.

108. For more about "soft law," see Tadeusz Gruchalla-Wesierski, *A Framework for Understanding "Soft Law"*, 30 McGill L.J. 37 (1984);

Gunther F. Handl et al., *A Hard Look at Soft Law*, 82 Am. Soc'y Int'l L. Proc. 371 (1988); K.C. Wellens & G.M. Borchardt, *Soft Law in European Community Law*, 14 Eur. L. Rev. 267 (1989). The term "soft law" is used herein to denote law that falls short of the classical definition of international law.

109. *See* Steven R. Ratner, *Does International Law Matter in Preventing Ethnic Conflict?*, 32 N.Y.U.J. Int'l L. & Pol. 591, 652 (2000).

110. F. van Dijk, *Normative Force and Effectiveness of International Norms*, 30 German Y.B. Int'l L. 9, 20 (1987). Perhaps the most traditional position views agreements other than treaties as nothing more than evidence of custom. *See* Pierre-Marie Dupuy, *Soft Law and the International Law of the Environment*, 12 Mich. J. Int'l L. 420, 432 (1991).

111. *See supra* note 21 and accompanying text.

Harold Hongju Koh

HOW IS INTERNATIONAL HUMAN RIGHTS LAW ENFORCED?

I am greatly honored to deliver this distinguished lecture, particularly given the illustrious list of lecturers who have preceded me to this podium.[1] My own path to this podium began in Washington, D.C., where as a private lawyer I specialized in issues of international business and trade law: what most American law schools now think of as "international business transactions."[2] But even while working on these matters, I became increasingly diverted toward the novel, growing field of international human rights. While in private practice in the early 1980s, I became involved in the representation of the American hostages who had been held for 444 days in the U.S. embassy in Tehran.[3] Once starting an academic career, I took occasional forays into international human rights advocacy,[4] but my main focus remained on the law of international business transactions and United States foreign policy, two examples of what Henry Steiner and Detlev Vagts have felicitously dubbed "Transnational Legal Problems."[5]

As this decade began, international human rights law became the primary focus of both my theoretical and academic work, when I became involved with my students in a number of lawsuits in U.S. courts against human rights violators. In 1992, my students and I brought suits on behalf of the Haitian and Cuban refugees against the U.S. government[6] and a number of lawsuits against foreign human rights violators who had come to the United States—the former Guatemalan Minister of

Defense, the former dictator of Haiti, an Indonesian general responsible for the 1991 Dili massacre in East Timor, and most recently a suit that is still ongoing in the Southern District of New York against Radovan Karadzic, the leader of the Bosnian Serbs.[7]

In each of these legal lives, as a scholar and a lawyer, I have asked the question that titles this lecture, namely, "How is International Human Rights Law Enforced?" I wouldn't be surprised if many of you hearing that question were to give a pessimistic answer: international human rights law is *not* enforced, you might say. Just take a look at the massive human rights violations in Bosnia, violations that have gone unredressed in Cambodia and Iraq; the continuing crises in the Congo, Sierra Leone, Algeria, and Burundi. Look at indicted war criminals, like Radovan Karadzic in Republica Srpska, who continue to flout the jurisdictions of the Bosnian war crimes tribunal. Look, you might say, at the world's willingness to overlook human rights violations committed by more powerful nations, such as Russia's activities in Chechnya, or China's continuing repression after Tienanmen Square. International human rights law is not enforced, you might say, because human rights norms are vague and aspirational, because enforcement mechanisms are toothless, because treaty regimes are notoriously weak, and because national governments lack the economic self-interest or the political will to restrain their own human rights violations. So if the question is "how is international human rights law enforced?," many of you might answer: "not at all, or hardly

From *Indiana Law Journal* 74, no. 4 (Fall 1991): 1397–1417.

at all." If you hold to this common, skeptical view of human rights enforcement, you would say that international human rights law is not enforced, like "real" domestic law; instead, it is only occasionally "complied with," by nation-states acting out of transparent convenience or self-interest.

In this lecture, let me take a somewhat different tack, asking first, "What do we mean when we say that *any* laws are enforced?" Are any laws perfectly enforced? Even here in Bloomington, Indiana, the height of civilization, are the parking laws or burglary laws perfectly enforced? Of course, you would concede, parking violations occur here in Bloomington, and burglaries occur, perhaps even daily; sometimes egregiously. But those facts alone hardly mean that there is no enforcement of laws against parking violations or burglary. Here in Indiana, the laws against burglary may be under-enforced, they may be imperfectly enforced, but they are enforced, through a well-understood *domestic legal process* of legislation, adjudication, and executive action. That process involves prosecutors, statutes, judges, police officers, and penalties that interact, interpret legal norms, and work to internalize those norms into the value sets of citizens like ourselves.

But if we are willing to give that answer to the question "how is domestic law enforced?", why not similarly answer the question whether *international human rights* law is enforced? In this lecture, I will argue that in much the same way, these international norms of international human rights law are underenforced, imperfectly enforced; but they *are* enforced through a complex, little-understood legal process that I call *transnational legal process*. As I have elaborated in other writing,[8] for shorthand purposes, transnational legal process can be thought of in three phases: the institutional *interaction* whereby global norms of international human rights law are debated, *interpreted*, and ultimately *internalized* by domestic legal systems. To claim that this complex transnational legal process of enforcing international human rights law via

interaction, interpretation, and *internalization* exists is not to say that it always works or even that it works very well. As I will be the first to concede, this process works sporadically, and that we often most clearly see its spectacular failures, as in Cambodia, Bosnia, and Rwanda. But the process of enforcing international human rights law also sometimes has its successes, which gives us reason not to ignore that process, but to try to develop and nurture it. Just as doctors used early successes in addressing polio to push our understanding of how the prevention and healing process works, lawyers can try to globalize the lessons of human rights enforcement. So if the question is "how is international human rights enforced?", my short answer is through a transnational legal process of institutional *interaction, interpretation* of legal norms, and attempts to *internalize* those norms into domestic legal systems.

With that introduction, let me divide the balance of these remarks into two parts: First, how, in theory, does transnational legal process promote national obedience of international human rights law? Second, how does transnational legal process—this process that I call "interaction, interpretation and internalization"—work in real cases?

The Theory of Transnational Legal Process

The first question, why do nations obey international human rights law, is really a subset of a much broader question: why do nations obey international law of any kind? That timeless question has troubled thinkers over historical eras dating back to the Roman Empire. * * * "Why Nations Obey?". My forthcoming book examines both the theoretical and the historical answers to that question.[9]

From Compliance to Obedience

Let us start by asking what it means to "obey" international law at all. Imagine four kinds of relationships between rules and conduct: coincidence, conformity, compliance, and obedience. For example, I have lived my whole life in the United States; but a few years ago, I took a sabbatical year in England. While there, I noticed that everybody drives on the left side of the road, as a matter of both practice and of law. Yet what is the relationship between the law and the observed practice?

One remote possibility is *coincidence*. It could be coincidence that the law is that everyone must drive on the left and that in practice everybody follows that norm. Yet coincidence might explain why one person follows a rule, but not why millions of people throughout the country do the same. That suggests a second possibility: *conformity*. If people know of the rule that you must drive on the left, they may well choose to conform their conduct to that rule when convenient; but feel no obligation to do so when inconvenient. (Perhaps some Scots, for example, swerve over and drive on the right, in remote unpopulated areas of the Hebrides). But, is there a third possibility, *compliance*? Perhaps people are both aware of the rule and accept the rule for a variety of external reasons, for example, to get specific rewards, to receive insurance benefits, or to avoid certain kinds of bad results, such as traffic tickets, or getting hit by an oncoming car. These are instrumental reasons why someone might decide to comply with a rule even if they felt no moral obligation to obey it. Finally, there is a fourth possibility, *obedience:* the notion that a person or an organization adopts the behavior that is prescribed by the rule because he or it has somehow internalized that rule and made it a part of their internal value system.

Notice that as we move down this scale from coincidence to conformity to compliance to obedience, we see an increase of what I will call "norm-internalization." As you move from grudgingly accepting a rule one time only to habitually obeying it, the rule transforms from being some kind of external sanction to becoming an internal imperative. We see this evolutionary process regularly in our daily lives: when you put on a bicycle helmet; when you snap on your seatbelt; when you recycle a tin can; when you do not smoke in the law school cafeteria. All of these are examples of people moving from conformity with a rule to compliance and gradually obedience, which is driven by a sense of an internalized norm. Over time, we also witness a rise in what one might call "normativity." If you see someone driving 100 mph, and then suddenly they see a police car and slow dramatically to 60 mph, you might say they are complying with; but not really obeying the speed limit. But, if one witnesses people routinely driving at the speed limit (without witnesses around), or routinely disposing of litter, or recycling without being told, we are seeing an *internalized normative form of behavior*—an increase in normativity, if you will—which derives from the incorporation of external norms or values into a person's or organization's internal value set.

There is a further point as well: namely, that the most effective form of *law-enforcement* is not the imposition of external sanction, but the inculcation of internal obedience. Most traffic laws, litter laws, tax laws and the like are enforced primarily not by enforcement officers, but by the social internalization of norms of obedience! Indeed, enforcement is maximized when a norm is so widely obeyed that external sanctions become virtually unnecessary. As my Yale colleague Bob Ellickson has demonstrated, when everyone in a community follows certain social norms out of felt internal normativity, order can be maintained without rigid systems of external legal enforcement, because self-enforcement is both more effective and more efficient than third-party controls.[10] Social psychologists who study why individuals obey the law have reached the same conclusion.[11]

The Relationship Between Enforcement and Obedience

With this background, let us now turn to the question of how *international human rights law* is enforced, which is a subset of the larger question: why do nations obey international law of any kind? In earlier writing, I have suggested that, over time, five distinct explanations have emerged to answer the question "why nations obey?": *power*; *self-interest* or rational choice; *liberal explanations* based on rule-legitimacy or political identity; *communitarian explanations*; and *legal process explanations* at the state-to-state level (what I will call "horizontal" or "international legal process" explanations) and from the international-to-national level (what I will call "vertical" or "transnational legal process explanations").[12]

In their current form, each of these five approaches gives their own short answer to the question "how is international human rights law enforced?" Let me start with the realists, who date back to Thomas Hobbes, but include such modern-day theorists as George Kennan, Hans Morgenthau, and Henry Kissinger. To the question "why do nations obey international law?", their short answer is *power*: nations never truly "obey" international law, they only comply with it, because someone else makes them. Why, for example, why did Iraq ultimately respect the borders of Kuwait? In the end, because the other nations of the world came in and drove Saddam out! Under this view, nations can be coerced or bribed to follow certain rules, or even induced to bargain in the shadow of such incentives. But in the end, the critical factor is neither altruistic or normative, only the realist values of power and coercion.[13] Thus, the familiar power explanation traces back to Thucydides: the strong states do what they can, the weak states suffer what they must, but in the end there is no real "obedience" of international law, only such coincidence between national conduct and international rules that results from power and coercion.

There is a second, kinder and gentler explanation, based on the self-interest rationales favored by the vibrant school of "rational choice" theory.[14] Under this explanation, nations may choose rationally to follow certain global rules out of a sense of self-interest. After participating in game-theoretic discussions, to avoid multi-party prisoners' dilemma, nations may decide to cooperate around certain rules, which lead them to establish what international relations theorists call "regimes": governing arrangements in which certain governing norms, rules, and decisionmaking procedures come to predominate because the nations in their long-term self-interests have calculated that they should follow a presumption favoring compliance with such rules.

This "self-interest" rationale helps explains why, for example, complex global rules have emerged in a whole variety of international areas in which nations have established regimes structured around legal rules born of self-interested cooperation. In the contemporary era, for example, talented international relations scholars such as Robert Keohane, Duncan Snidal, and Oran Young have applied increasingly sophisticated rational choice techniques to argue for such an instrumental, interest-based view of international law. Recently, a number of legal scholars, most prominently Kenneth Abbott, Alan Sykes, and John Setear have espoused a similar, "rationalistic" legal vision. Under the rationalist account, participants in a given issue area will develop a set of governing arrangements, along with a set of expectations, rules, and decisionmaking procedures—in other words, a regime—both to restrain the participants and to provide means for achieving their common aims. Within these regimes, international law stabilizes expectations and promotes compliance by reducing transaction costs, providing dispute-resolution procedures, performing signaling functions, triggering negative responses, and promoting information disclosure.

Recently, more sophisticated instrumentalists have begun to disaggregate the state into its component parts, to introduce international institutions and transnational actors, to incorporate long-term self-interest, and to consider the issue within massively iterated multi-party games.[15] Subtler instrumentalists even recognize that global rules form part of the environment faced by a state and thus alter the incentives of domestic interest groups and organizations. But even so, their analysis remains thin.

The rationalists recognize *nonstate actors* as players in the transnational system, but too often ignore them because of the complexity their inclusion adds to their *game-theoretic* analysis. Nor do these analysts tell much of a domestic politics story, because they tend to operate largely at the horizontal level of the international system. Their chosen issue areas thus tend to be areas like trade and arms control, where nation-states remain the primary players and traditional realist assumptions still largely prevail. Such rationalistic, state-centric theories thus work less well, for example, in such areas as human rights, debt restructuring, or international commercial transactions, where nonstate actors abound, pursue multiple goals in complex nonzero-sum games, and interact repeatedly within institutions nested within broader informal regimes. Rationalists see law as regulating behavior by changing incentives, not altering interests or identities. The role of norms, in their view, is to reduce transactions costs in dynamic interactions among exogenously constituted actors. Shared norms, and the interactive processes by which those norms are interpreted, have little effect on state policies. In effect, they see international law as a kind of mechanical device, a switching mechanism, which facilitates the interactions of autonomous states, not as a communal decisionmaking structure that helps generate options, modify preferences, and build a normative interpretive community.

In short, my major complaint about the self-interest explanation is that it does not take account of what I consider to be an important factor—the "vertical" internalization of international norms into domestic legal systems. The rationalists' picture takes too little account of the internalizing, normative, or constitutive impact of participating in the transnational legal process. For the rationalists, the decision to obey the law remains perpetually calculated, never internally felt. Compliance always remains an instrumental computation, never an internalized normative imperative.[16]

This brings me to a third possible explanation for why international human rights laws are enforced, so-called "liberal" theories, which I divide into those scholars who follow principles of "rule legitimacy" and those who focus on national "political identity." Both sets of theorists derive their analysis from Immanuel Kant's pamphlet in 1795, *Perpetual Peace*. Rule-legitimacy theorists, led by Thomas Franck of NYU, argue that nations do feel some sort of internal "compliance pull" toward certain rules that they feel are legitimate; for example, the rules against genocide or the rules favoring diplomatic immunity. When nations perceive that rules are legitimate, either because they meet some procedural standard of legitimacy or some substantive notion of due process or distributive justice, they will obey that rule because they are "normatively pulled" toward that rule by its legitimacy.[17]

In my view, this rule-legitimacy approach is problematic because it claims to draw its power from the legitimacy of rules themselves, rather than from communitarian and legal process pressures. In fact, most of us do not litter when others are watching, but not because the no-littering *rule* itself has such compliance pull, but because of a combination of internal impulse and felt peer pressure. In the same way, Franck's rule-legitimacy ends up being another way of saying that a state obeys a norm because it has been both internalized, and is being enforced by "communitarian peer pressure" (which, I will argue below, is really a form of transnational legal process).[18]

A second view, pressed strongly by other members of this liberal school, argues that whether or not nations comply with international law depends crucially on the extent to which their political identity is based on liberal democracy. This approach derives from a branch of international relations literature known as the "Democratic Peace" literature, pioneered by Michael Doyle of Princeton, my Yale colleague Bruce Russett, and many others who have sought to verify a basic tenet of Kant's writing that liberal democracies do not go to war with each other. The many adherents of this view include President Clinton, who in October of 1995 opined that promoting democracies that participate in the new global marketplace is the right thing to do because we know that these democracies are less likely to go to war.

Transposing this basic maxim to international law, several Harvard theorists, Anne-Marie Slaughter and Andrew Moravcsik, have flipped this maxim, arguing not so much that democracies do not fight each other, but rather, that democracies are more inclined to "do law" with one another. For these analysts, the key variable for whether a nation will or will not obey international law is whether they can be characterized as "liberal" in identity, i.e., having certain democratic attributes such as a form of representative government, civil and political rights, and an independent judicial system dedicated to the rule of law. Not surprisingly, many liberal scholars focus on European Union law, noting that the European system of human rights works because it is largely composed of liberal democracies, who share reasons for collective obedience. This helps explain why, for example, the embryonic African human rights system—a collection of democracies and authoritarian systems—does not work nearly as well.

What is troubling about this view is that it suggests that liberal states interact mainly in a zone of law, while liberal and illiberal states interact in a zone of politics. But in my view, any analysis that treats a state's identity as somehow exogenously or permanently given, is overly essentialist. National identities, like national interests, are socially constructed products of culture, ideology, learning, and knowledge. As we have witnessed, nations like South Africa, Nigeria, Indonesia, Poland, Argentina, Chile, and the Czech Republic are neither permanently liberal nor illiberal, but transition back and forth from dictatorship to democracy. As Laurence Whitehead has argued, democratization has powerful international dimensions, potentially spreading from one country to another by contagion, control, or consent.[19] Liberal identity analysis does not directly address the impact of compliance on democratization, and thus leaves unanswered a critical, constructivist question: to what extent does compliance with international law itself help *constitute the identity* of a state as law-abiding, and hence, as "liberal" or not? The notion that "only liberal states do law with one another" can be empirically falsified, particularly in such areas as international commercial law, where even rogue states like Libya tend to abide fastidiously by private international law rules on letters of credit without regard to whether they are representative democracies. Finally, like the "cultural relativist" argument in human rights, the claim that nonliberal states somehow do *not* participate in a zone of law denies the universalism of international law and effectively condones dealing with nonliberal states within a realist world of power politics.

In more recent writings, some liberal authors have revised their positions to say that they view liberal states not as actors, but as representative *agents* for various institutions and groups within civil society. These institutions and groups are more likely to engage in transborder cooperation with one another, thus predicting greater levels of transnational legal relations among liberal states. But if this is so, what it suggests is that the density of a state's *interactions* in the transnational legal process—not its label as liberal or illiberal—is the key to explaining its level of compliance with international law.

A fourth possible explanation—"communitarian" reasons—can be found in the English "International Society" school of International Relations, particularly in the work of Martin Wight and Hedley Bull, who traced their international origins back to the Dutch international law scholar Grotius. These theorists argue that nations obey international law because of the values of the international society of which they are a part. So, for example, the Czech Republic, Poland and Hungary now feel peer pressure to obey international law because of their community ties, now as NATO nations. The idea is that one's membership in a community helps to define how one views the obligations of that community. So, for example, when someone becomes a member of a church, they decide they will conduct their lives differently because they now view themselves as Catholic, Jewish, or Muslim. Similarly, under this view, the governments of Russia, Ukraine, and Turkey should all feel communitarian pressure to obey the European Convention on Human Rights—the "rules of their church"—because they have all now become members of the Council of Europe.

Unlike a liberal approach, this communitarian, constructivist approach at least recognizes the *positive transformational effects* of a state's repeated participation in the legal process. At the same time, however, the approach gives too little study to the vertical "transmission belt" whereby the norms created by international society infiltrate into *domestic* society. The *existence* of international community may explain the *horizontal* pressures to compliance generated among nation-states on the global plane, but it does not clarify the *vertical process* whereby transnational actors interact in various fora, generate and interpret international norms, and then seek to internalize those norms domestically, as future determinants of why nations obey.

Fifth and finally, there are so-called "legal process" explanations for why nations obey international law. Let me distinguish here between what I call "international legal process" or horizontal reasons for compliance, which tend to function at a government-to-government level,[20] and the so-called "vertical" explanation, which focuses on the relationship between the international and the domestic legal systems. Suppose, for example, that the government of Canada wishes to urge Japan to join the global land mine treaty. Initially, the two governments will engage in government-to-government discussions at the "horizontal" nation-state level within an intergovernmental process organized by the United Nations. But at the same time, there is also a "vertical," transnational process whereby governments, intergovernmental organizations, nongovernmental organizations, and private citizens argue together about why nations should obey international human rights law. Through this vertical dynamic, international rules that are developed at a government-to-government level gradually work their way down and become internalized into domestic legal structure. Take, for example, recent legal enactments whereby global norms regarding genocide, war crimes, torture, and religious freedom have become internalized into American legal rules.

What I have just recounted is a very compressed version of a small bookshelf of political science and international law and literature. But my broader point, simply speaking, is that all five explanations—power, self-interest, liberal theories, communitarian theories, and legal process explanations—work together to help explain why nations obey international law. These five explanatory strands work together as complementary conceptual lenses to give a richer explanation of why compliance with international law does, or does not, occur in particular cases.

To clarify, let me ask the parallel question, how is domestic law enforced? What is the explanation, for example, for why we now buckle our seatbelts, even though nobody wore seatbelts only a quarter of a century ago? Of course, there are many reasons, but if you thought to explain the change in compliance, you probably would give a variety of explanations. If you organized those explanations in your own mind, they would likely fall under five headings: power or coercion, self-interest, liberal theories, communitarian explanations, and legal process explanations.

Why do I now wear a seatbelt, when I never did before? First, because after the seatbelt rule issued, a lot of tickets were given out and I felt coerced to comply: a power explanation. A second factor: self-interest. People calculated that it is more rational to wear your seatbelt to avoid injury, sanction, or to gain insurance benefits. Third, the seatbelt rule acquired "rule-legitimacy" and over time developed a compliance pull. Over time, this became part of one's sense of personal identity. Individuals calculated: "If I am a law-abiding person, I ought to obey the seatbelt laws." Partly, the rationale was communitarian. Authorities exhorted people with slogans such as "Seatbelts Save Lives." And fifth and finally, the seatbelt rule was inculcated via legal process. Seatbelts were required by state laws, required by federal highway standards; incorporated into federal automotive standards and became part of the way the automobiles were made. Now you cannot get into a car and drive without buckling your seatbelt without every bell and whistle and electronic voice in the car erupting into a cacophony of noise, making your life miserable until you buckle your seatbelt!

So in short, how are seatbelt laws enforced? Not by any one of these factors acting alone, but by all of them acting in combination. As we move through the five explanations—from power to legal process—we also move from external enforcement of legal rules to internal obedience with legal rules. True compliance is not so much the result of externally imposed sanctions so much as internally felt norms. In other words, as we move from external to internal factors, we also move from coercive to constitutive behavior. My children, who have been wholly socialized to wear seatbelts, have wholly internalized the norm. They view wearing seatbelts as an integral part of what it means to be a law-abiding person. As always, the best way to enforce legal norms is not to coerce action, not to impose sanctions, but to change the way that people think about themselves: whether as teetotalers, safe drivers, or regular taxpayers. In short, our prime way to enforce the law is to encourage people to bring rules home, to internalize rules inside themselves, to transform themselves from lawless into law-abiding individuals.

What does this have to do with international human rights law? I would argue that in the international arena, we are seeing the exact same process at work; a process by which norms and rules are generated and internalized and become internal rules, normative rules, and rules that constitute new nations. The best example we have is South Africa; a country which for many years was an outlaw, was subjected to tremendous external pressure and coercive mechanisms over a long period of time. Through a gradual process, South Africa has converted itself into a country that has undergone a fundamental political transformation. It has now reconstituted itself as a law-abiding country that through its constitutional processes has internalized new norms of international human rights law as domestic law.

In the same way, if the United States is attempting to encourage China to follow norms of international human rights law, the analysis above suggests the need to act at all five levels: at the level of power and coercion, to apply external and political sanctions; at the level of self-interest, to develop carrots that can be offered to China in terms of trade benefits or other kinds of economic incentives; at the level of liberal theory, to encourage Hong Kong's liberal legal identity to bubble up to the Beijing government; at the level of communitarian values, to seek to encourage China to ratify the International Covenant on Civil and Political Rights and other multilateral communities of international human rights observance; and finally, from a legal process perspective, to seek to engage the Chinese people and groups in civil society in a variety of international interactions that will cause them to internalize norms of international human rights law. As with the seatbelt example, our goal is not simply to coerce conduct. More fundamentally, we seek to encourage a change in the nature of the Chinese political identity to reconstitute China as a nation that abides by core norms of international human rights law. In short, a theory of transnational legal process seeks to enforce international norms by motivating nation-states to *obey* international human rights law—out of a sense of internal acceptance of international law—as opposed to merely conforming to or complying with specific international legal rules when the state finds it convenient.

How Is International Human Rights Law Enforced?

Against this background, how should we now understand the recent history of international human rights enforcement? Here let me contrast the two "process" stories, the one that everyone usually looks at and the one that I think people should look at. Let me contrast what I will call the horizontal story of enforcement with what I prefer: the vertical, transnational story of human rights enforcement.

The "Horizontal" Story

The conventional "horizontal" story about international human rights law enforcement is that international human rights law was born about fifty years ago, the product of the U.N. Charter, the Nuremberg and Tokyo war crimes trials, and the Universal Declaration of Human Rights. Under this view, the principal enforcers of human rights law have always been nation-states, who have always interacted with one another on an interstate,

government-to-government level. The U.N. Charter introduced into this picture U.N. organizations and U.N. norms, which soon led to regional human rights systems as well: in Europe, the Strasbourg (Council of Europe) and Helsinki (Organization of Security and Cooperation in Europe) process; in the Americas, the Inter-American Commission and Court of Human Rights; and far less well-developed regional human rights systems in Africa, the Middle East, and Asia.

In this post-war order, an international regime developed in which governments and intergovernmental organizations began to put pressure on each other—always at a horizontal, intergovernmental level—to comply with human rights, invoking such universal treaty norms as the international covenants on civil and political and economic, social and cultural rights. U.N. organizations, such as the U.N. Human Rights Commission, and treaty-based organizations, such as the U.N. Human Rights Committee, participated as intergovernmental actors in this horizontal international regime, which addressed all manner of global issues: worker rights, racial discrimination, the rights of children, women, and indigenous peoples. As we soon saw, the difficulties of this horizontal, state-to-state enforcement mechanism were legion: the rules were largely declaratory and precatory, and the few mechanisms created had virtually no enforcement. Occasionally new mechanisms would be created: judicial fora, such as the Yugoslav and Rwandan War Crimes Tribunal, or new executive actors, such as the U.N. High Commissioner on Human Rights, or new quasi-legislative fora, such as the Vienna Conference on Human Rights or the 1995 Beijing Women's Conference. Despite these occasional advances, the overall picture of this standard enforcement story is one of impotence, ineffectiveness, of a horizontal system where the key actors are nation-states and intergovernmental organizations, the key forums are governmental forums, and the key transactions are transactions between states and other states.

The "Vertical" Story

If one accepts the horizontal story as the entire picture of human rights enforcement, then the glass is indeed more than half empty. But what is the vertical picture? The "vertical" story of human rights enforcement, I would argue, is a much richer picture: one that focuses on a transnational legal process that includes a different set of actors, fora, and transactions. As I have recently argued in my Frankel Lecture, "Bringing International Law Home," the key agents in this transnational legal process are transnational norm entrepreneurs, governmental norm sponsors, transnational issue networks, interpretive communities and law-declaring fora, bureaucratic compliance procedures, and issue linkages among issue areas.[21]

Many efforts at human rights norm-internalization are begun not by nation-states, but by "transnational norm entrepreneurs," private transnational organizations or individuals who mobilize popular opinion and political support within their host country and abroad for the development of a universal human rights norm. Such norm entrepreneurs first became prominent in the nineteenth century, when activists such as Lord William Wilberforce and the British and Foreign Anti-Slavery Society pressed for treaties prohibiting the slave trade,[22] Jean-Henri Dunant founded the International Committee of the Red Cross,[23] and Christian peace activists, such as America's William Ladd and Elihu Burritt promoted public international arbitration and permanent international criminal courts.[24] Modern-day entrepreneurs have included individuals as diverse as Eleanor Roosevelt, Jesse Jackson, the Dalai Lama, Aung Sang Suu Kyi, and Princess Diana. These nongovernmental actors seek to develop *transnational issue networks*[25] to discuss and generate political solutions among concerned individuals at the domestic, regional and international levels, among government agencies, intergovernmental organizations,

international and domestic, academics, and private foundations. Moreover, these norm entrepreneurs seek national government officials and bureaucracies concerned with the same issue areas and seek to enlist them as allies in their transnational cause. These *governmental norm sponsors*—for example, U.N. Human Rights Commissioner Mary Robinson, Presidents Oscar Arias of Costa Rica, Jimmy Carter of the United States, and the Pope, to take just a few prominent ones, use their official positions to promote normative positions. These transnational actors then seek governmental and nongovernmental fora competent to declare both general norms of international law (e.g., treaties) and *specific interpretation* of those norms in particular circumstances (e.g., particular interpretations of treaties and customary international law rules). Such law-declaring fora thus include treaty regimes; domestic, regional, and international courts; ad hoc tribunals; domestic and regional legislatures; executive entities; international publicists; and nongovernmental organizations: law-declaring fora that create an "interpretive community" that is capable of defining, elaborating and testing the definition of particular norms and their violation.[26]

The next vertical step is for national governments to internalize norm-interpretations issued by the global interpretive community into their domestic bureaucratic and political structures. Within national governments and intergovernmental organizations, for example, in-house lawyers and legal advisers acquire institutional mandates to ensure that the government's policies conform to international legal standards that have become imbedded in domestic law. Such institutional mandates to justify noncompliance with international legal norms may be found within the legal advising apparatus of national governments, in the Executive Branch, (e.g., the Legal Adviser's Office at the U.S. State Department), the legislature, as well as in intergovernmental organizations (e.g., the United Nations, the OAS, etc.).[27]

In the same way as corporations develop standard operating procedures to address new domestic mandates regarding corporate sentencing guidelines, occupational health and safety, and sexual harassment, domestic institutions adopt standard operating procedures, and other internal mechanisms to maintain habitual compliance with the internalized international norms. These institutions evolve in path-dependent routes that avoid conflict with the internalized norms.[28] Thus, over time, domestic decisionmaking structures become "enmeshed" with international legal norms, so that institutional arrangements for the making and maintenance of an international commitment become entrenched in domestic legal and political processes.[29] Gradually, legal ideologies come to prevail among domestic decisionmakers so that they seek to avoid perceptions that their actions will be perceived as domestically unlawful. Finally, strong process linkages exist across issue areas. Thus, when the United States adopts a twelve-mile limit in the ocean law area, for example, it is bound by it when dealing with refugees sailing toward U.S. shores.[30] Because international legal obligations tend to be closely interconnected, even a single deviation tends to lead noncompliant nations into vicious cycles of treaty violation. These institutional habits soon lead nations into default patterns of compliance. These patterns act like riverbeds, which channel conduct along compliant pathways. When a nation deviates from that pattern of presumptive compliance, frictions are created.

By so saying, I do not mean to suggest that international legal violations never occur. I merely suggest viewing human rights enforcement through vertical, "transnational legal process" lenses can help explain why in Louis Henkin's famous phrase, "almost all nations observe almost all principles of international law almost all of the time."[31] To avoid such frictions in its continuing interactions, a nation's bureaucracies or interest groups may press their leaders to shift over time from a policy of violation into one of compliance. Thus it is through this repeated cycle of interaction, interpretation, and internalization—this transnational legal process—that international law acquires its "stickiness," and that nations come to "obey" international human rights law out of a perceived self-interest that becomes institutional habit.

The Pattern Illustrated

By telling the vertical story of transnational legal enforcement, I am not saying that the "horizontal," international legal process picture is wrong. I am just saying it is incomplete. A state-to-state process account simply does not capture the full picture of how international human rights norms are currently generated, brought into domestic systems, and then brought back up to the international level. Take, for example, the recent international drive to limit the use of landmines, which began almost twenty years ago.[32] Despite the development and ratification of a treaty earlier this century banning the use of landmines against civilians, an international norm against the practice had not developed.

Instead, the key step toward a global ban on landmines was taken by nongovernmental organizations in conjunction with the efforts of one U.S. senator. At the end of 1991, a group of nongovernmental activists met in Washington, D.C. and decided to create the International Campaign to Ban Landmines, which had the elimination of landmines as its goal.[33] The organization enlisted the support of a governmental norm entrepreneur, Sen. Patrick J. Leahy, who introduced a measure, passed by the Congress and signed by President Bush in 1992, which prohibited the export of landmines by the United States for one year.[34] Soon, the nongovernmental organizations received the support of other transnational figures, including Pope John Paul II,[35] Princess Diana,[36] and the

International Committee of the Red Cross. Frustrated with what they perceived to be a lack of progress toward a total ban through the U.N.-sponsored efforts, nongovernmental organizations and other countries created a new law-declaring forum, the so-called "Ottawa process," in the process enlisting another governmental sponsor, Canadian Foreign Minister Lloyd Axworthy. In the end, the Ottawa process reached agreement on the Convention on the Prohibition of the Use, Stockpiling, Production and Transfer of Anti-Personnel Mines and on Their Destruction,[37] which has now been signed by more than 120 countries. Although the United States initially declined to sign the Convention, the new regime prodded the United States to enact a moratorium on the sale of landmines, to develop new technologies to aid in mine detection and demining, and to increase the amount of money that it spends on these programs to at least $100 million per year.[38] The United States further committed itself to stop using all antipersonnel mines except in Korea by 2003, and to sign the treaty itself by the year 2006. Although it remains to be seen whether the Senate will soon ratify the Convention, the United States government may, within the next decade, *obey* the Convention by fully internalizing the Convention's norms into the governing practices of the U.S. government.

Note that under the vertical, transnational enforcement story that I have told, the central actors are not so much governmental entities as nongovernmental organizations and individuals. Today, modern transnational norm entrepreneurs include most of our recent Nobel Peace Prize winners: Burma's Aung San Suu Kyi, East Timor's Bishop Belo and Jose Ramos-Horta, Tibet's Dalai Lama, Britain's Amnesty International, and America's Martin Luther King Jr. and Jody Williams of the Landmines Coalition. These are people who without governmental portfolio are able to transact a different kind of process,

focusing at times on creating new forums to develop new international norms. Their focus is less on the horizontal process among nation-states as upon what I call "vertical" or transnational process. Their effort is to try to bring human rights law home, by trying to internalize it into domestic systems through a process of interaction, interpretation, and internalization.

How, precisely, is this internalization accomplished? In earlier work, I have sought to distinguish among social, political and legal internalization:

- *Social internalization*, I argue, occurs when a norm acquires so much public legitimacy that there is widespread general adherence to it.
- *Political internalization* occurs when the political elites accept an international norm, and advocate its adoption as a matter of government policy.
- *Legal internalization* occurs when an international norm is incorporated into the domestic legal system through executive action, legislative action, judicial interpretation, or some combination of the three. Some legal systems establish their receptivity to internalization of international norms through constitutional law rules regarding the extent to which treaties are or are not self-executing and rules of customary international law are or are not automatically incorporated into domestic law.[39] Virtually all legal systems also have explicit mechanisms whereby executive, legislative, and judicial institutions may domesticate international norms. Thus, the landmines case exemplified the incorporation of an emerging norm of international law into U.S. law and policy largely through the *executive action* of the President and his agencies. *Legislative* internalization occurs when international law norms are embedded into constitutional norms or binding domestic

legislation that officials of a noncomplying government must obey as part of the domestic legal fabric. *Judicial internalization* occurs when litigation in domestic courts provokes judicial incorporation of international law norms into domestic law, statutes, or constitutional norms.

The precise sequencing among political, legal, and social internalization, and among the different forms of legal internalization, will vary from case to case. Sometimes an international norm is socially internalized long before it is politically or legally internalized. Thus, for example, the United States was the moving force behind the drafting and signature of the Genocide Convention in 1948, but the U.S. Senate did not formally ratify the Convention and implement it as U.S. domestic law until November 1988, long after the norm against genocide had acquired widespread social legitimacy.[40] In other cases, *legal* norm-internalization prompted by a transnational legal process of interaction and internalization helps to trigger the process of political and social internalization of global norms. By domesticating international rules, transnational legal process thereby spurs internal acceptance of international human rights principles.

The process can be viewed as having four phases: interaction, interpretation, internalization, and obedience. One or more transnational actors provokes an *interaction* (or series of interactions) with another in a law-declaring forum, which forces an *interpretation* or enunciation of the global norm applicable to the situation. By so doing, the moving party seeks not simply to coerce the other party, but to *internalize* the new interpretation of the international norm into the other party's internal normative system. Its aim is to "bind" that other party to obey the interpretation as part of its internal value set. That party's perception that it now has an internal obligation to follow the international norm as it has been domestically interpreted leads it to step four: *obedience to* the newly interpreted norm.

Take, for example, the efforts of U.S. courts to define a U.S. law of torture under the Alien Tort Statute since *Filartiga v. Pena-Irala*.[41] The U.S. Senate has been traditionally reluctant to ratify human rights treaties, even though the U.S. government was one of the primary drafters of these treaties in the postwar era. The Torture Convention, the Genocide Convention, and many others lay unratified by the U.S. government despite this initial input. In 1980, beginning with *Filartiga*, private U.S. human rights lawyers began to bring a series of domestic lawsuits against foreign violators to promote domestic judicial incorporation of the norm against torture under a little-known eighteenth-century statute, the Alien Tort Statute. Over fifteen decades, a string of U.S. courts have ruled that torture is a violation not only of international law, but also of U.S. law. In the early 1990s, these legal internalizations of the norm against torture were cited as precedents for Congress to enact a Torture Victim Protection Act,[42] a statute whose drafting and enactment helped persuade skeptical officials of the Bush Administration to acquiesce in U.S. ratification of the U.N. Torture Convention. Once again, an international law norm trickled down, was internalized, and bubbled back up into new international law.

In the United Kingdom, the issue of legislative internalization has similarly been brought to the forefront in recent years by the election of the Labour party, which promised, if elected, to incorporate the European Convention on Human Rights into United Kingdom law. This issue has been a major human rights issue in British politics since the Clement Attlee Government first ratified the Convention in the early 1950's. Since then, the Convention has been internalized in part through judicial construction. When total judicial incorporation efforts failed, a political internalization movement arose, which at this writing will shortly bring about *legal* internalization of the European Convention into U.K. law by an act of Parliament.[43]

Or, take finally the cases of the Haitian and Cuban boat people, in which my students and I were involved for serveral years. The United States had signed and ratified the Refugee Convention of 1951,[44] a multilateral treaty at the "horizontal" level whereby it agreed not to return refugees to their persecutors. But when the Haitian refugees began fleeing to the United States in 1991, it effectively reneged on that commitment and began to return the refugees, claiming that the Refugee Convention did not bar extraterritorial repatriations. In fact, Congress had passed a statute as part of the Immigration and Nationality Act which required unequivocally that refugees not be returned to their persecutors, thus ostensibly internalizing the treaty into domestic statute. And so on behalf of the Haitian refugees my students and I brought a lawsuit in which we argued that the courts should enforce the extraterritorial nonreturn rule as a matter of U.S. domestic law. We used a "judicialization strategy" to try to reinforce the concept of legal internalization of the international norm against extraterritorial repatriations.

In the end, the Supreme Court rejected our arguments, leaving the United States legally free to continue the extraterritorial return policy.[45] But other international forums, such as the U.N. High Commission on Refugees, the Inter-American Commission on Human Rights, and other bodies began to condemn the U.S. action. Various legislative efforts were made to overturn the Supreme Court's ruling, and the issue later became the subject of domestic political pressure from the African-American community, the Congressional Black Caucus, and Trans-Africa, all of whom began to promote the notion of a safe haven for Haitian refugees. Finally, in the fall of 1994, the U.S. government changed its Haitian policy, and intervened to return the refugees. When the issue arose again the following year, with regard to fleeing Cuban refugees, the Administration first resisted, then ultimately admitted into the United States those Cuban refugees being detained at offshore refugee camps. Although the U.S. stated policy remains problematic, at this writing, the actual practice of the U.S. government has moved into greater compliance with international law.

Conclusion

Let me close with two thoughts. First, the foregoing analysis teaches something about our duty, as citizens, to participate in transnational legal process. It is sometimes said that someone who, by acquiring medical training, comes to understand the human body acquires as well a moral duty not just to observe disease, but to try to cure it. In the same way, I would argue, a lawyer who acquires knowledge of the body politic acquires a duty not simply to observe transnational legal process, but to try to influence it. Once one comes to understand the process by which international human rights norms can be generated and internalized into domestic legal systems, one acquires a concomitant duty, I believe, to try to influence that process, to try to change the feelings of that body politic to promote greater obedience with international human rights norms.

In that effort, every citizen counts. To this, many Americans might say, "What can one person really do? Isn't such influence beyond the capacity of any one person?" But if you look at these people I have mentioned in this lecture—Aung Sun Suu Kyi, Jody Williams, Nelson Mandela, Martin Luther King Jr.—could they have not said the same thing? In response, many students might say: "But surely, I am not such a world historical figure," to which I would answer, "You don't need to be a Nobel Prize winner to make a difference. Just look at Rosa Parks, or Linda Brown, or Fred Korematsu, ordinary people who simply said that they would not go to the back of the bus, or attend a segregated school, or live in a Japanese internment camp." In short, we need look no further than those individuals who have triggered these legal processes in our own lifetime to promote the enforcement of human rights norms.

The struggle of these individuals reminds us again of the remarkable words of Robert Kennedy, which are etched on his grave in Arlington Cemetery:

> Each time a man stands up for an ideal, or acts to improve the lot of others, or strikes out against injustice, he sends forth a tiny ripple of hope, and crossing each other from a million different centers of energy and daring, those ripples build a current that can sweep down the mightiest walls of oppression and resistance.

What he is talking about, in the end, is the need for individuals to activate transnational legal process. As proof that what he says is indeed possible, one need look only at the country in which he said those words: South Africa, in 1966, a country which only three decades later has now been totally transformed by international human rights law.

So, in closing, if my question is "how is international human rights law enforced?", my answer is simple. International human rights law is enforced, I would say, not just by nation-states, not just by government officials, not just by world historical figures, but by people like us, by people with the courage and commitment to bring international human rights law home through a transnational legal process of interaction, interpretation, and internalization.[46] Thank you very much.

NOTES

1. Past Harris lecturers include my former Harvard professors Paul Bator and Charles Fried, as well as my current Yale colleagues Guido Calabresi, Owen Fiss, Jules Coleman, and Robert Gordon.

2. *See generally* Harold Hongju Koh, *International Business Transactions in United States Courts*, 261 Recueil des Cours 13 (1996).

3. *See* Persinger v. Islamic Republic of Iran, 729 F.2d 835 (D.C. Cir. 1984).

4. *See, e.g.,* David Cole et al., *Interpreting the Alien Tort Statute: Amicus Curiae Memorandum of International Law Scholars and Practitioners in* Trajano v. Marcos, 12 Hastings Int'l & Comp. L. Rev. 1 (1988).

5. *See generally* Henry J. Steiner et al., Transnational Legal Problems (4th ed. 1994).

6. *See* Cuban-American Bar Ass'n v. Christopher, 43 F.3d 1413 (11th Cir. 1995); Haitian Ctrs. Council, Inc. v. McNary, 969 F.2d 1326 (2d Cir. 1992), *vacated as moot sub nom.* Sale v. Haitian Ctrs. Council, Inc., 509 U.S. 155 (1993); Haitian Ctrs. Council, Inc. v. Sale, 823 F. Supp. 1028 (E.D.N.Y. 1993). For an account of these cases, written by three of my students, see Victoria Clawson et al., *Litigating as Law Students: An Inside Look at* Haitian Centers Council, 103 Yale L.J. 2337 (1994).

7. *See* Xuncax v. Gramajo, 886 F. Supp. 162 (D. Mass. 1995); Todd v. Panjaitan, No. 92-12255WD (D. Mass. decided Oct. 25, 1994) ($14 million judgment awarded); Doe v. Karadzic, 886, F. Supp. 734 (S.D.N.Y. 1994), *rev'd sub nom.* Kadic v. Karadzic, 70 F.3d 232 (2d Cir. 1995); Paul v. Avril, 812 F. Supp. 207 (S.D. Fla. 1993) ($41 million judgment awarded); Ortiz v. Gramajo, No. 91-11612WD (D. Mass. filed Sept. 17, 1992) ($47.5 million judgment awarded).

8. For fuller discussion of transnational legal process, see Harold Hongju Koh, *Transnational Legal Process*, 75 Neb. L. Rev. 181 (1996); Harold Hongju Koh, *The 1998 Frankel Lecture: Bringing International Law Home*, 35 Hous. L. Rev. 623 (1998) [hereinafter Koh, *Frankel Lecture*], and Harold Hongju Koh, *Why Do Nations Obey International Law?*, 106 Yale L.J. 2599 (1997) [hereinafter Koh, *Why Do Nations Obey International Law?*].

9. For the gist of [the] answer, see Koh, *Why Do Nations Obey International Law?, supra* note 8.

10. *See* Robert C. Ellickson, Order Without Law: How Neighbors Settle Disputes 132 (1991) ("A person who has 'internalized' a social norm is by definition committed to self-enforcement of a rule. . . ."); *id.* at 126 n.8 (1991) ("Whatever the origin of self-enforced moral rules, there is broad agreement that the overall system of social control must depend vitally on achieving cooperation through self-enforcement."); Robert C. Ellickson, *Bringing Culture and Human Frailty to Rational Actors: A Critique of Classical Law and Economics*, 65 Chi-Kent L. Rev. 23, 44 (1989) (arguing that the primary system of social control is a *"first-party* system of social control that would operate without external enforcers") (emphasis in original).

11. *See, e.g.,* Tom R. Tyler, Why People Obey the Law (1990) (concluding, after extensive empirical study, that people comply with law not so much because they fear punishment as because they feel that legal authorities are legitimate); *see also id.* at 4 (urging authorities who seek to promote voluntary compliance with laws to apply "[a] normative perspective [which] leads to a focus on people's internalized norms of justice and obligation," rather than "an instrumental perspective [which] regards compliance as a form of behavior occurring in response to external factors").

12. Both the historical and theoretical analysis are fleshed out in Koh, *Why Do Nations Obey International Law?, supra* note 8, from which this portion of the lecture derives.

13. The "power" rationale is captured in a famous joke often told about Henry Kissinger, who after he ceased to be the Secretary of State, reportedly went to work as a zoo keeper. After the first day, zoo patrons noticed an amazing phenomenon: that after all of these centuries, the lion was finally lying down with the lamb. The patrons ran excitedly to Dr. Kissinger, and asked, "How have you

achieved this miraculous result?" The famous realist replied, "It's simple. A lamb a day!"

14. *See, e.g.*, Kenneth W. Abbott, *Modern International Relations Theory: A Prospectus for International Lawyers*, 14 Yale J. Int'l L. 335 (1989); Kenneth W. Abbott, *The Trading Nation's Dilemma: The Functions of the Law of International Trade*, 26 Harv. Int'l L.J. 501 (1985); Kenneth W. Abbott, *'Trust But Verify': The Production of Information in Arms Control Treaties and Other International Agreements*, 26 Cornell Int'l L.J. 1 (1993).

15. Duke's Robert Keohane is the leading exemplar of such a sophisticated approach. *See* Robert O. Keohane, *When Does International Law Come Home?*, 35 Hous. L. Rev. 699 (1998).

16. It would be as if every time you got into a car, you calculated *for the first time* whether or not to put on a seat belt or to stop for a red light, rather than relying upon internalized norms of obedience.

17. Franck calls this the "compliance pull" of particular international legal rules. *See generally* Thomas M. Franck, The Power of Legitimacy Among Nations (1990).

18. Franck defines rule-legitimacy as "a property of a rule which exerts a pull towards compliance on those addressed normatively, because they believe that the rule has come into being and operates in accordance with generally accepted principles of right process," that is, an internalized view of fair legal process. *Id.* at 24 (emphasis omitted).

19. Laurence Whitehead, *Three International Dimensions of Democratization, in* The International Dimensions of Democratization 3, 5–22 (Laurence Whitehead ed., 1996) ("In the contemporary world, there is no such thing as democratization in one country, and perhaps there never was.").

20. The best exemplar of this international process view is Abram Chayes & Antonia Handler Chayes, The New Sovereignty: Compliance with International Regulatory Agreements (1995), which treats the primary instrument for maintaining compliance with treaties as "an *iterative process of discourse* among the parties, the treaty organization, and the wider public," *id.* at 4 (emphasis added).

21. *See* Koh, *Frankel Lecture, supra* note 8, at 647–70.

22. On the transnational work of Wilberforce and the British anti-slavery movement, see generally Betty Fladeland, Men and Brothers: Anglo-American Anti-Slavery Cooperation (1972), and Ethan A. Nadelmann, *Global Prohibition Regimes: The Evolution of Norms in International Society*, 44 Int'l Org. 479, 495 (1990).

23. On the work of Dunant and the International Committee of the Red Cross, which spurred the Geneva Convention of 1864 and the Hague Convention of 1899 and the movement toward codified rules of conduct in warfare, see generally Pierce Boissier, History of the International Committee of the Red Cross: From Solferino to Tsushima (1985), and Martha Finnemore, National Interests in International Society 69–88 (1996).

24. On the work of Ladd and Burritt, see Mark W. Janis, *Protestants, Progress and Peace in the Influence of Religion, in* The Influence of Religion on the Development of International Law 223 (Mark W. Janis ed., 1991).

25. *See* Kathryn Sikkink, *Human Rights, Principled Issue-Networks, and Sovereignty in Latin America*, 47 Int'l Org. 411 (1993).

26. The norm with respect to the recent genocide in Bosnia, for example, has been interpreted before such law-declaring fora as the U.N. General Assembly, the U.N. Security Council, the International Court of Justice, the International Criminal Tribunal for the Former Yugoslavia and Rwanda; the International Court of Justice, numerous scholarly groups, human rights organizations, as well as both the Congress of the United States and a U.S. federal appellate court.

27. *See* Antonio Cassese, *The Role of Legal Advisers in Ensuring that Foreign Policy Conforms to International Legal Standards*, 14 Mich. J. Int'l L. 139 (1992); Robert C. Clark, *Why So Many Lawyers? Are They Good or Bad?*, 61 Fordham L. Rev. 275, 282 (1992) (calling lawyers "specialists in normative ordering").

28. *See* Mark J. Roe, *Chaos and Evolution in Law and Economics*, 109 Harv. L. Rev. 641, 643–44 (1996) (explaining path-dependence).

29. *See* Robert O. Keohane, *Compliance with International Commitments: Politics Within a Framework of Law, International Law and International Relations Theory: Building Bridges,* 86 Am. Soc'y Int'l L. Proc. 167, 179 (1992) (discussing "institutional enmeshment," which "occurs when domestic decision making with respect to an international commitment is affected by the institutional arrangements established in the course of making or maintaining the commitment").

30. For example, Presidential Proclamation 5928, which extended the U.S. territorial sea from three to twelve miles in breadth, has since been followed throughout the U.S. executive branch as if it were internal law, and has become the basis for binding, internal Coast Guard standard operating procedures. In May 1992, the United States adopted a policy of interdicting fleeing Haitians on the high seas and repatriating them summarily to Haiti, while bringing into the United States for exclusion proceedings those Haitians who entered territorial waters. In November 1992, the U.S. Coast Guard interdicted a boat containing fleeing Haitian refugees ten miles off the coast of Florida, and began making plans to repatriate the occupants. When the 1988 opinion of the Justice Department's Office of Legal Counsel was drawn to the Deputy Associate Attorney General's attention, the Coast Guard consulted with the State and Justice Departments and brought the boat into shore, rather than repatriating the occupants. *See* Harold Hongju Koh, *Protecting the Office of Legal Counsel from Itself,* 15 Cardozo L. Rev. 513, 517–18 (1993).

31. Louis Henkin, How Nations Behave 47 (2d ed. 1979).

32. For a fuller account of this campaign, see Koh, *Frankel Lecture, supra* note 8, at 655–63.

33. *See* Raymond Bonner, *How a Group of Outsiders Moved Nations to Ban Land Mines*, N.Y. Times, Sept. 20, 1997, at A5.

34. *See id.*

35. *See id.*

36. *See, e.g.,* Roxanne Roberts, *From London, a Blitz with Glitz; Princess Diana Dazzles a Red Cross Benefit for Land Mine Victims,* Wash. Post, June 18, 1997, at D1. Princess Diana visited landmine victims in Angola and Bosnia in early 1997. *See* Raymond Bonner, *Pentagon Weighs Ending Opposition to a Ban on Mines*, N.Y. Times, Mar. 17, 1996, at A1.

37. Sept. 18, 1997, 36 I.L.M. 1507 (1997).

38. *See* Anthony DePalma, *Some See Opportunity in Global Push to Remove Land Mines*, N.Y. Times, Dec. 7, 1997, at A14.

39. The national constitutions of Ireland, the Netherlands, and Italy, for example, refer to the recognition of international legal principles as a broad policy goal, thereby requiring policymakers to take account of foreign policy guidelines deriving from international law. *See* Irish Const. art. 29, § 3; Grondwet [Constitution] [Grw. Ned.] art. 90 (Netherlands); Constituzione [Constitution] [Cost.] art. 10 (Italy).

40. *See* Genocide Convention Implementation Act of 1987 (The Proxmire Act), Pub. L. No. 100–606, 102 Stat. 3045 (codified in 18 U.S.C. §§ 1091–1093 (1994)).

41. Filartiga v. Pena-Irala, 630 F.2d 876 (2d Cir. 1980) (holding that Paraguayan human rights victims may sue Paraguayan official under Alien Tort Statute, 28 U.S.C. § 1350 (1994), in U.S. court for civil damages arising from official torture). For a theoretical analysis of this line of doctrine, see Harold Hongju Koh, *Transnational Public Law Litigation*, 100 Yale L.J. 2347 (1991).

42. Pub. L. No. 102–256, 106 Stat. 73 (1992) (codified at 28 U.S.C. § 1350 (1994)).

43. The debate over incorporation of the European Human Rights Convention is the subject of a voluminous literature. For a political history of the incorporation effort, see generally Michael Zander, A Bill of Rights? (4th ed. 1997). For a comparative study, see Andrew Z. Drzemczewski, European Human Rights Convention in Domestic Law: A Comparative Study 177–87 (1983); Aspects of Incorporation of the European Convention of Human Rights into Domestic Law (J.P. Gardner ed., 1993); Jorg Polakiewicz &Valerie Jacob-Foltzer, *The European Human Rights Convention in Domestic Law*, 12 Hum. Rts. J. 65, 65–85, 125–42 (1991). For discussion of compliance without incorporation, see David Kinley, The European Convention on Human Rights: Compliance Without Incorporation

(1993). *See also* 8(2) Halsbury's Laws of England (4th ed. 1996) (including human rights law as part of constitutional law). For bills urging incorporation, see Human Rights Bill, *as approved by the House of Lords*, 577 Parl. Deb., H.L. (5th Ser.) 1726 (1997). For arguments as to why the Convention should be incorporated, see generally Human Rights in the United Kingdom (Richard Gordon & Richard Wilmot-Smith eds., 1996); Hon. Sir John Laws, *Is the High Court the Guardian of Fundamental Constitutional Rights?*, 1992 Pub. L. 59; Lord Lester, *The Mouse that Roared: The Human Rights Bill 1995*, 1995 Pub. L. 198; Rt. Hon. Lord Browne-Wilkinson, *The Infiltration of a Bill of Rights*, 1992 Pub. L. 397.

44. Convention Relating to the Status of Refugees, July 28, 1951, 19 U.S.T. 6259, 189 U.N.T.S. 137.

45. For analysis of the opinions, see Clawson et al., *supra* note 6.

46. Author's note: Since I wrote these words, my life has fundamentally changed. In November 1998, I took an oath as our nation's chief human rights official. At this writing, I have now spent eight months in office, traveling to some twenty-five countries. As I have traveled from Belgrade to Beijing, Colombia to Kosovo, I have become increasingly convinced of the correctness of the basic thesis I have expressed in this lecture. Although I now spend my time as a "governmental norm sponsor," rather than as a private "transnational norm entrepreneur," I continue to witness, and to attempt to influence, the transnational legal process described herein. I look forward to returning to academic life before too long, not only to finish my book manuscript on "Why Nations Obey," but also to illustrate my basic thesis with reference to my governmental experiences in Kosovo, China, Colombia, Indonesia, and elsewhere.

8 INTERNATIONAL POLITICAL ECONOMY

Economic issues are critical to understanding international relations in the twenty-first century. In the first selection here, a classic from *U.S. Power and the Multinational Corporation* (1975), Robert Gilpin concisely discusses the relationship between economics and politics. He examines the three basic conceptions of political economy (liberalism, radicalism, and mercantilism), comparing their perspectives on the nature of economic relations, their theories of change, and how they characterize the relationship between economics and politics. With trade rivalries among the major economic powers on the rise, Gilpin's classic analysis of mercantilism is more timely ever.

Edward Alden explains how the failure of the United States to adjust to long-term changes in the structure of economic productivity has led to deindustrialization and job losses in the traditional U.S. working class. Fareed Zakaria discusses the political consequences of these economic trends and anti-immigration backlash in fueling the rise of populist movements in the United States and Europe. These movements in turn have consequences for international relations, sharpening trade rivalries, undermining support for international regimes governing refugees, challenging liberal democratic norms, and strengthening nationalist political forces that are skeptical about the European Union and accustomed forms of international cooperation.

Complicating this turmoil is the fear that the major liberal market economies are retreating from their efforts to correct the governance pathologies that contributed to the near-collapse of the global financial system in 2008. Emphasizing the resilience of the institutions of global capitalism, Daniel W. Drezner's essay argues that the governance system for the international economic system worked effectively to contain the global financial crisis.

Robert Gilpin
THE NATURE
OF POLITICAL ECONOMY

The international corporations have evidently declared ideological war on the "antiquated" nation state.... The charge that materialism, modernization and internationalism is the new liberal creed of corporate capitalism is a valid one. The implication is clear: the nation state as a political unit of democratic decision-making must, in the interest of "progress," yield control to the new mercantile mini-powers.[1]

While the structure of the multinational corporation is a modern concept, designed to meet the requirements of a modern age, the nation state is a very old-fashioned idea and badly adapted to serve the needs of our present complex world.[2]

These two statements—the first by Kari Levitt, a Canadian nationalist, the second by George Ball, a former United States undersecretary of state—express a dominant theme of contemporary writings on international relations. International society, we are told, is increasingly rent between its economic and its political organization. On the one hand, powerful economic and technological forces are creating a highly interdependent world economy, thus diminishing the traditional significance of national boundaries. On the other hand, the nation-state continues to command men's loyalties and to be the basic unit of political decision making. As one writer has put the issue, "The conflict of our era is between ethnocentric nationalism and geocentric technology."[3]

Ball and Levitt represent two contending positions with respect to this conflict. Whereas Ball advocates the diminution of the power of the nation-state in order to give full rein to the productive potentialities of the multinational corporation, Levitt argues for a powerful nationalism which could counterbalance American corporate domination. What appears to one as the logical and desirable consequence of economic rationality seems to the other to be an effort on the part of American imperialism to eliminate all contending centers of power.

Although the advent of the multinational corporation has put the question of the relationship between economics and politics in a new guise, it is an old issue. In the nineteenth century, for example, it was this issue that divided classical liberals like John Stuart Mill from economic nationalists, represented by Georg Friedrich List. Whereas the former gave primacy in the organization of society to economics and the production of wealth, the latter emphasized the political determination of economic relations. As this issue is central both to the contemporary debate on the multinational corporation and to the argument of this study, this chapter analyzes the three major treatments of the relationship between economics and politics—that is, the three major ideologies of political economy.

From Robert Gilpin, *U.S. Power and the Multinational Corporation* (New York: Basic Books, 1975), chap. 1.

The Meaning of Political Economy

The argument of this study is that the relationship between economics and politics, at least in the modern world, is a reciprocal one. On the one hand, politics largely determines the framework of economic activity and channels it in directions intended to serve the interests of dominant groups; the exercise of power in all its forms is a major determinant of the nature of an economic system. On the other hand, the economic process itself tends to redistribute power and wealth; it transforms the power relationships among groups. This in turn leads to a transformation of the political system, thereby giving rise to a new structure of economic relationships. Thus, the dynamics of international relations in the modern world is largely a function of the reciprocal interaction between economics and politics.

First of all, what do I mean by "politics" or "economics"? Charles Kindleberger speaks of economics and politics as two different methods of allocating scarce resources: the first through a market mechanism, the latter through a budget.[4] Robert Keohane and Joseph Nye, in an excellent analysis of international political economy, define economics and politics in terms of two levels of analysis: those of structure and of process.[5] Politics is the domain "having to do with the establishment of an order of relations, a structure. . . ."[6] Economics deals with "short-term allocative behavior (i.e., holding institutions, fundamental assumptions, and expectations constant). . . ."[7] Like Kindleberger's definition, however, this definition tends to isolate economic and political phenomena except under certain conditions, which Keohane and Nye define as the "politicization" of the economic system. Neither formulation comes to terms adequately with the dynamic and intimate nature of the relationship between the two.

In this study, the issue of the relationship between economics and politics translates into that between wealth and power. According to this statement of the problem, economics takes as its province the creation and distribution of wealth; politics is the realm of power. I shall examine their relationship from several ideological perspectives, including my own. But what is wealth? What is power?

In response to the question, What is wealth?, an economist-colleague responded, "What do you want, my thirty-second or thirty-volume answer?" Basic concepts are elusive in economics, as in any field of inquiry. No unchallengeable definitions are possible. Ask a physicist for his definition of the nature of space, time, and matter, and you will not get a very satisfying response. What you will get is an *operational* definition, one which is usable: it permits the physicist to build an intellectual edifice whose foundations would crumble under the scrutiny of the philosopher.

Similarly, the concept of wealth, upon which the science of economics ultimately rests, cannot be clarified in a definitive way. Paul Samuelson, in his textbook, doesn't even try, though he provides a clue in his definition of economics as "the study of how men and society *choose* . . . to employ *scarce* productive resources . . . to produce various commodities . . . and distribute them for consumption."[8] Following this lead, we can say that wealth is anything (capital, land, or labor) that can generate future income; it is composed of physical assets and human capital (including embodied knowledge).

The basic concept of political science is power. Most political scientists would not stop here; they would include in the definition of political science the purpose for which power is used, whether this be the advancement of the public welfare or the domination of one group over another. In any case, few would dissent from the following statement of Harold Lasswell and Abraham Kaplan:

The concept of power is perhaps the most fundamental in the whole of political science:

the political process is the shaping, distribution, and exercise of power (in a wider sense, of all the deference values, or of influence in general.)[9]

Power as such is not the sole or even the principal goal of state behavior. Other goals or values constitute the objectives pursued by nation-states: welfare, security, prestige. But power in its several forms (military, economic, psychological) is ultimately the necessary means to achieve these goals. For this reason, nation-states are intensely jealous of and sensitive to their relative power position. The distribution of power is important because it profoundly affects the ability of states to achieve what they perceive to be their interests.

The nature of power, however, is even more elusive than that of wealth. The number and variety of definitions should be an embarrassment to political scientists. Unfortunately, this study cannot bring the intradisciplinary squabble to an end. Rather, it adopts the definition used by Hans Morgenthau in his influential *Politics among Nations*: "man's control over the minds and actions of other men."[10] Thus, power, like wealth, is the capacity to produce certain results.

Unlike wealth, however, power cannot be quantified; indeed, it cannot be overemphasized that power has an important psychological dimension. Perceptions of power relations are of critical importance; as a consequence, a fundamental task of statesmen is to manipulate the perceptions of other statesmen regarding the distribution of power. Moreover, power is relative to a specific situation or set of circumstances; there is no single hierarchy of power in international relations. Power may take many forms—military, economic, or psychological—though, in the final analysis, force is the ultimate form of power. Finally, the inability to predict the behavior of others or the outcome of events is of great significance. Uncertainty regarding the distribution of power and the ability of the statesmen to control events plays an important role in international relations.

Ultimately, the determination of the distribution of power can be made only in retrospect as a consequence of war. It is precisely for this reason that war has had, unfortunately, such a central place in the history of international relations. In short, power is an elusive concept indeed upon which to erect a science of politics.

■   ■   ■

The distinction * * * between economics as the science of wealth and politics as the science of power is essentially an analytical one. In the real world, wealth and power are ultimately joined. This, in fact, is the basic rationale for a political economy of international relations. But in order to develop the argument of this study, wealth and power will be treated, at least for the moment, as analytically distinct.

To provide a perspective on the nature of political economy, the next section of the chapter will discuss the three prevailing conceptions of political economy: liberalism, Marxism, and mercantilism. Liberalism regards politics and economics as relatively separable and autonomous spheres of activities; I associate most professional economists as well as many other academics, businessmen, and American officials with this outlook. Marxism refers to the radical critique of capitalism identified with Karl Marx and his contemporary disciples; according to this conception, economics determines politics and political structure. Mercantilism is a more questionable term because of its historical association with the desire of nation-states for a trade surplus and for treasure (money). One must distinguish, however, between the specific form mercantilism took in the seventeenth and eighteenth centuries and the general outlook of mercantilistic thought. The essence of the mercantilistic perspective, whether it is labeled economic nationalism, protectionism, or the doctrine of the German Historical School, is the subservience of the economy to the state and its interests—interests that range from matters of domestic welfare to those of international security. It is this more general meaning of mercantilism that is implied by the use of the term in this study.

■ ■ ■

Three Conceptions of Political Economy

The three prevailing conceptions of political economy differ on many points. Several critical differences will be examined in this brief comparison. (See Table 8.1.)

The Nature of Economic Relations

The basic assumption of liberalism is that the nature of international economic relations is essentially harmonious. Herein lay the great intellectual innovation of Adam Smith. Disputing his mercantilist predecessors, Smith argued that international economic relations could be made a positive-sum game; that is to say, everyone could gain, and no one need lose, from a proper ordering of economic relations, albeit the distribution of these gains may not be equal. Following Smith, liberalism assumes that there is a basic harmony between true national interest and cosmopolitan economic interest. Thus, a prominent member of this school of thought has written, in response to a radical critique, that the economic efficiency of the sterling standard in the nineteenth century and that of the dollar standard in the twentieth century serve "the cosmopolitan interest in a national form."[11] Although Great Britain and the United States gained the most from the international role of their respective currencies, everyone else gained as well.

Liberals argue that, given this underlying identity of national and cosmopolitan interests in a free market, the state should not interfere with economic transactions across national boundaries.

Table 8.1. Comparison of the Three Conceptions of Political Economy

	LIBERALISM	MARXISM	MERCANTILISM
Nature of economic relations	Harmonious	Conflictual	Conflictual
Nature of the actors	Households and firms	Economic classes	Nation-states
Goal of economic activity	Maximization of global welfare	Maximization of class interests	Maximization of national interest
Relationship between economics and politics	Economics should determine politics	Economics does determine politics	Politics determines economics
Theory of change	Dynamic equilibrium	Tendency toward disequilibrium	Shifts in the distribution of power

Through free exchange of commodities, removal of restrictions on the flow of investment, and an international division of labor, everyone will benefit in the long run as a result of a more efficient utilization of the world's scarce resources. The national interest is therefore best served, liberals maintain, by a generous and cooperative attitude regarding economic relations with other countries. In essence, the pursuit of self-interest in a free, competitive economy achieves the greatest good for the greatest number in international no less than in the national society.

Both mercantilists and Marxists, on the other hand, begin with the premise that the essence of economic relations is conflictual. There is no underlying harmony; indeed, one group's gain is another's loss. Thus, in the language of game theory, whereas liberals regard economic relations as a nonzero-sum game, Marxists and mercantilists view economic relations as essentially a zero-sum game.

The Goal of Economic Activity

For the liberal, the goal of economic activity is the optimum or efficient use of the world's scarce resources and the maximization of world welfare. While most liberals refuse to make value judgments regarding income distribution, Marxists and mercantilists stress the distributive effects of economic relations. For the Marxist the distribution of wealth among social classess is central; for the mercantilist it is the distribution of employment, industry, and military power among nation-states that is most significant. Thus, the goal of economic (and political) activity for both Marxists and mercantilists is the redistribution of wealth and power.

The State and Public Policy

These three perspectives differ decisively in their views regarding the nature of the economic actors.

In Marxist analysis, the basic actors in both domestic and international relations are economic classes; the interests of the dominant class determine the foreign policy of the state. For mercantilists, the real actors in international economic relations are nation-states; national interest determines foreign policy. National interest may at times be influenced by the peculiar economic interests of classes, elites, or other subgroups of the society; but factors of geography, external configurations of power, and the exigencies of national survival are primary in determining foreign policy. Thus, whereas liberals speak of world welfare and Marxists of class interests, mercantilists recognize only the interests of particular nation-states.

Although liberal economists such as David Ricardo and Joseph Schumpeter recognized the importance of class conflict and neoclassical liberals analyze economic growth and policy in terms of national economies, the liberal emphasis is on the individual consumer, firm, or entrepreneur. The liberal ideal is summarized in the view of Harry Johnson that the nation-state has no meaning as an economic entity.[12]

Underlying these contrasting views are differing conceptions of the nature of the state and public policy. For liberals, the state represents an aggregation of private interests: public policy is but the outcome of a pluralistic struggle among interest groups. Marxists, on the other hand, regard the state as simply the "executive committee of the ruling class," and public policy reflects its interests. Mercantilists, however, regard the state as an organic unit in its own right: the whole is greater than the sum of its parts. Public policy, therefore, embodies the national interest or Rousseau's "general will" as conceived by the political élite.

The Relationship between Economics and Politics; Theories of Change

Liberalism, Marxism, and mercantilism also have differing views on the relationship between economics and politics. And their differences on this issue are directly relevant to their contrasting theories of international political change.

Although the liberal ideal is the separation of economics from politics in the interest of maximizing world welfare, the fulfillment of this ideal would have important political implications. The classical statement of these implications was that of Adam Smith in *The Wealth of Nations*.[13] Economic growth, Smith argued, is primarily a function of the extent of the division of labor, which in turn is dependent upon the scale of the market. Thus he attacked the barriers erected by feudal principalities and mercantilistic states against the exchange of goods and the enlargement of markets. If men were to multiply their wealth, Smith argued, the contradiction between political organization and economic rationality had to be resolved in favor of the latter. That is, the pursuit of wealth should determine the nature of the political order.

Subsequently, from nineteenth-century economic liberals to twentieth-century writers on economic integration, there has existed "the dream . . . of a great republic of world commerce, in which national boundaries would cease to have any great economic importance and the web of trade would bind all the people of the world in the prosperity of peace."[14] For liberals the long-term trend is toward world integration, wherein functions, authority, and loyalties will be transferred from "smaller units to larger ones; from states to federalism; from federalism to supranational unions and from these to superstates."[15] The logic of economic and technological development, it is argued, has set mankind on an inexorable course toward global political unification and world peace.

In Marxism, the concept of the contradiction between economic and political relations was enacted into historical law. Whereas classical liberals—although Smith less than others—held that the requirements of economic rationality *ought* to determine political relations, the Marxist position was that the mode of production does in fact determine the superstructure of political relations. Therefore, it is argued, history can be understood as the product of the dialectical process—the contradiction between the evolving techniques of production and the resistant sociopolitical system.

Although Marx and Engels wrote remarkably little on international economics, Engels, in his famous polemic, *Anti-Duhring*, explicitly considers whether economics or politics is primary in determining the structure of international relations.[16] E. K. Duhring, a minor figure in the German Historical School, had argued, in contradiction to Marxism, that property and market relations resulted less from the economic logic of capitalism than from extraeconomic political factors: "The basis of the exploitation of man by man was an historical act of force which created an exploitative economic system for the benefit of the stronger man or class."[17] Since Engels, in his attack on Duhring, used the example of the unification of Germany through the Zollverein or customs union of 1833, his analysis is directly relevant to this discussion of the relationship between economics and political organization.

Engels argued that when contradictions arise between economic and political structures, political power adapts itself to the changes in the balance of economic forces; politics yields to the dictates of economic development. Thus, in the case of nineteenth-century Germany, the requirements of industrial production had become incompatible with its feudal, politically fragmented structure. "Though political reaction was victorious in 1815 and again in 1848," he argued, "it was unable to prevent the growth of large-scale industry in Germany and the growing participation of German commerce in the world market."[18] In summary, Engels wrote, "German unity had become an economic necessity."[19]

In the view of both Smith and Engels, the nation-state represented a progressive stage in human development, because it enlarged the political realm of economic activity. In each successive economic epoch, advances in technology and an increasing scale of production necessitate an enlargement of political organization. Because the city-state and feudalism restricted the scale of production and the division of labor made possible by the Industrial Revolution, they prevented the efficient utilization of resources and were, therefore, superseded by larger political units. Smith considered this to be a desirable objective; for Engels it was an historical necessity. Thus, in the opinion of liberals, the establishment of the Zollverein was a movement toward maximizing world economic welfare;[20] for Marxists it was the unavoidable triumph of the German industrialists over the feudal aristocracy.

Mercantilist writers from Alexander Hamilton to Frederich List to Charles de Gaulle, on the other hand, have emphasized the primacy of politics; politics, in this view, determines economic organization. Whereas Marxists and liberals have pointed to the production of wealth as the basic determinant of social and political organization, the mercantilists of the German Historical School, for example, stressed the primacy of national security, industrial development, and national sentiment in international political and economic dynamics.

In response to Engels's interpretation of the unification of Germany, mercantilists would no doubt agree with Jacob Viner that "Prussia engineered the customs union primarily for political reasons, in order to gain hegemony or at least influence over the lesser German states. It was largely in order to make certain that the hegemony should be Prussian and not Austrian that Prussia continually opposed Austrian entry into the Union, either openly or by pressing for a customs union tariff lower than highly protectionist Austria could stomach."[21] In pursuit of this strategic interest, it was "Prussian might, rather than a common zeal for political unification arising out of economic partnership, (that) . . . played the major role."[22]

In contrast to Marxism, neither liberalism nor mercantilism has a developed theory of dynamics. The basic assumption of orthodox economic analysis (liberalism) is the tendency toward equilibrium; liberalism takes for granted the existing social order and given institutions. Change is assumed to be gradual and adaptive—a continuous process of dynamic equilibrium. There is no necessary connection between such political phenomena as war and revolution and the evolution of the economic system, although they would not deny that misguided statesmen can blunder into war over economic issues or that revolutions are conflicts over the distribution of wealth; but neither is inevitably linked to the evolution of the productive system. As for mercantilism, it sees change as taking place owing to shifts in the balance of power; yet, mercantilist writers such as members of the German Historical School and contemporary political realists have not developed a systematic theory of how this shift occurs.

On the other hand, dynamics is central to Marxism; indeed Marxism is essentially a theory of social *change*. It emphasizes the tendency toward *dis*equilibrium owing to changes in the means of production, and the consequent effects on the everpresent class conflict. When these tendencies can no longer be contained, the sociopolitical system breaks down through violent upheaval. Thus war and revolution are seen as an integral part of the economic process. Politics and economics are intimately joined.

Why an International Economy?

From these differences among the three ideologies, one can get a sense of their respective explanations for the existence and functioning of the international economy.

An interdependent world economy constitutes the normal state of affairs for most liberal economists. Responding to technological advances in transportation and communications, the scope of the market mechanism, according to this analysis, continuously expands. Thus, despite temporary setbacks, the long-term trend is toward global economic integration. The functioning of the international economy is determined primarily by considerations of efficiency. The role of the dollar as the basis of the international monetary system, for example, is explained by the preference for it among traders and nations as the vehicle of international commerce.[23] The system is maintained by the mutuality of the benefits provided by trade, monetary arrangements, and investment.

A second view—one shared by Marxists and mercantilists alike—is that every interdependent international economy is essentially an imperial or hierarchical system. The imperial or hegemonic power organizes trade, monetary, and investment relations in order to advance its own economic and political interests. In the absence of the economic and especially the political influence of the hegemonic power, the system would fragment into autarkic economies or regional blocs. Whereas for liberalism maintenance of harmonious international market relations is the norm, for Marxism and mercantilism conflicts of class or national interests are the norm.

■ ■ ■

NOTES

1. Kari Levitt, "The Hinterland Economy," *Canadian Forum* 50 (July–August 1970): 163.
2. George W. Ball, "The Promise of the Multinational Corporation," *Fortune*, June 1, 1967, p. 80.
3. Sidney Rolfe, "Updating Adam Smith," *Interplay* (November 1968): 15.
4. Charles Kindleberger, *Power and Money: The Economics of International Politics and the Politics of International Economics* (New York: Basic Books, 1970), p. 5.
5. Robert Keohane and Joseph Nye, "World Politics and the International Economic System," in *The Future of the International Economic Order: An Agenda for Research*, ed. C. Fred Bergsten (Lexington, MA: D. C. Heath, 1973), p. 116.
6. Ibid.
7. Ibid., p. 117.
8. Paul Samuelson, *Economics: An Introductory Analysis* (New York: McGraw-Hill, 1967), p. 5.
9. Harold Lasswell and Abraham Kaplan, *Power and Society: A Framework for Political Inquiry* (New Haven: Yale University Press, 1950), p. 75.
10. Hans Morgenthau, *Politics among Nations* (New York: Alfred A. Knopf), p. 26. For a more complex but essentially identical view, see Robert Dahl, *Modern Political Analysis* (Englewood Cliffs, NJ: Prentice-Hall, 1963).
11. Kindleberger, *Power and Money*, p. 227.
12. For Johnson's critique of economic nationalism, see Harry Johnson, ed., *Economic Nationalism in Old and New States* (Chicago: University of Chicago Press, 1967).
13. Adam Smith, *The Wealth of Nations* (New York: Modem Library, 1937).
14. J. B. Condliffe, *The Commerce of Nations* (New York: W. W. Norton, 1950), p. 136.
15. Amitai Etzioni, "The Dialectics of Supernational Unification" in *International Political Communities* (New York: Doubleday, 1966), p. 147.
16. The relevant sections appear in Ernst Wangerman, ed., *The Role of Force in History: A Study of Bismarck's Policy of Blood and Iron*, trans. Jack Cohen (New York: International Publishers, 1968).
17. Ibid., p. 12.
18. Ibid., p. 13.
19. Ibid., p. 14.
20. Gustav Stopler, *The German Economy* (New York: Harcourt, Brace and World, 1967), p. 11.
21. Jacob Viner, *The Customs Union Issue*, Studies in the Administration of International Law and Organization, no. 10 (New York: Carnegie Endowment for International Peace, 1950), pp. 98–99.
22. Ibid., p. 101.
23. Richard Cooper, "Eurodollars, Reserve Dollars, and Asymmetrics in the International Monetary System," *Journal of International Economics* 2 (September 1972): 325–44.

Edward Alden

FROM *FAILURE TO ADJUST*
How Americans Got Left Behind in the Global Economy

I was born into the most prosperous autarky in the history of mankind. Wikipedia, which has replaced Webster's as our go-to source for definitions, says that "autarky" is derived from the Greek αὐτάρκεια, which means self-sufficiency. "Autarky exists whenever an entity can survive or continue its activities without external assistance or international trade." The listing cites several recent examples, including Albania under Communist Party leader Enver Hoxha in the 1970s and 1980s, Burma from 1962 to 1988 under dictator Ne Win, and North Korea to this day. What sets the autarky into which I was born apart from those cited by Wikipedia is that its people were generally well-off and growing wealthier. In the other great autarkies of the day—the Soviet Union and China—most people were poor, and opportunities for economic advancement were few. My autarky, in contrast, was one in which a large middle class bought houses, drove cars, took vacations, and saved for retirement. A lucky and ambitious few even became rich.

Unlike the countries in the Wikipedia examples, the United States had not become self-sufficient out of ideological conviction; indeed, its leaders had for some years believed strongly in trade with the world and encouraged it. It was just that it had no particular need to buy much of anything from anywhere else and plenty of customers at home to purchase the things it made. The "Survey of Current Business" for April 1961, the month I was born, made only passing reference to imports and exports and instead focused on the state of internal demand for domestically produced manufactured goods such as steel, automobiles, textiles, television sets, radios, and vacuum cleaners. In the first two months of that year, overall steel production averaged 151,000 short tons daily—about enough to build two Golden Gate Bridges—of which just 6,000 tons were exported. Of the nearly $6 billion in cars and car parts made in those two months, less than $200 million worth, or just 3 percent of total output, was exported. There were almost no imports of cars and trucks. Gross national product for the previous year had been just over $500 billion, and all exports and imports combined had amounted to less than $50 billion, or just under 10 percent of the size of the total economy.

Economists will probably object that a trade-to-GDP (gross domestic product) ratio of nearly 10 percent does not constitute a true autarky, and that is certainly true. But it was pretty close. Trade-to-GDP is the standard measure of an economy's openness to trade. China, which was then pursuing autarky as a matter of national policy, had a trade-to-GDP ratio of about 5 percent. In the Soviet Union, which also had a policy of self-sufficiency, it was about 4 percent. No other wealthy country of the time traded so little as did the United States. In France, trade was equal to more than 25 percent of GDP; in Canada it was more than

From *Failure to Adjust: How Americans Got Left Behind in the Global Economy* (Lanham, MD: Rowman and Littlefield, 2016), 1–20.

35 percent; in the United Kingdom it was 41 percent.[1] Smaller countries depended even more on trade. In the United States of the early 1960s, foreign markets mattered only at the margins. All of the big economic questions—employment, incomes, inflation, and profits—depended on conditions at home. Foreign economic policy was primarily a matter of diplomacy and defense, of encouraging trade as a means of strengthening overseas alliances and bolstering the economies of allies.

Autarky has acquired a bad name because authoritarian political leaders have used it to increase their control over society. Keeping out foreign goods also helps dictators keep out unwanted foreign ideas and influences. But high self-sufficiency in a large country with relatively free markets and a liberal political system is not a bad thing. Such a market can still be highly competitive internally, and its size allows for economies of scale that generate improvements in productivity—making more with less—which is how a country's wealth grows. International trade allows smaller countries to replicate the advantages of size, but it comes at a cost. Competition within a single country permits adjustments that are not possible with competition across borders. Historically, for example, the northern US states were more industrialized than those in the South, and the need for employees was stronger. The result was an enormous internal migration that raised overall living standards by relocating people from poorer regions with few jobs to richer ones where labor demand was strong. By the 1960s, the flow had shifted and was going in the other direction, with jobs moving from a higher-wage North to the lower-wage but more rapidly growing southern states. In contrast, Europe today has faced repeated economic turmoil in part because it has both freed up trade and created a common currency, but labor mobility remains limited due to language and skill barriers. In any given year, just 0.2 percent of Europeans move to another

country, compared with nearly 3 percent who move each year to another US state.[2] Greece and Spain have endured crippling unemployment rates for years, and while there has been some movement of their peoples north, it has not been nearly enough to compensate for their weak domestic economies.

Such mobility tended to level wages within the United States as well since industry was just as mobile as labor—though, very importantly, not more so. While people could move to take advantage of higher wages, companies could also move to take advantage of lower labor costs. Labor-intensive industries such as clothing and shoe making, for instance, were already heading to the southern states in the 1950s and 1960s. Between 1959 and 1970, the northern states lost more than 200,000 jobs in textile and apparel manufacturing, while the southern states added nearly 250,000 jobs in those same industries.[3] While such jobs were not high paying, they offered a decent income in many smaller cities and towns where the cost of living was much lower than in the big cities. As with labor migration, the effect of this capital mobility within a single national territory was to smooth out economic adjustments. Those who lost their jobs in the inevitable churn of a competitive market generally found other jobs, even if they had to move to do so. Wages had risen steadily as well. Real average hourly earnings rose by some 75 percent between 1947 and 1973, an extraordinarily rapid gain. Productivity growth was similarly strong, indicating that a highly competitive internal market was driving both efficiency and innovation.[4]

By the time I went off to college in the fall of 1979, however, the conditions that had produced this self-sufficiency had largely disappeared. In the decade from 1970 to 1980, international trade as a share of the US economy had nearly doubled to more than 20 percent. In 1982, one of the country's most respected economic analysts wrote, "Job growth, price stability and economic security . . .

all depend substantially on events abroad and the interaction with them of internal economic developments and policies," a claim that would have seemed ludicrous just fifteen or twenty years earlier.[5] Two big things had changed. First, the other large industrial economies that were still recovering from World War II had again become producers of such core industrial goods as steel and cars. US steel imports, for example, began to rise sharply beginning in the mid-1960s and by the end of the 1970s accounted for about 20 percent of steel consumption; steel exports, in contrast, remained very small.[6] Imports of automobiles followed a similar pattern. In 1955, imports were less than 1 percent of all registered cars; by 1978, however, that number had grown to nearly 20 percent.[7] A similar story was taking place for simpler goods like textiles, clothing, radios, and televisions, with imports rising from close to zero in the early 1960s to capture a significant market share by the end of the 1970s.

Second, companies began moving across borders as well. In 1960, all American direct investment overseas was less than $34 billion, about 6 percent of GDP. Over the next two decades, it rose steadily, reaching $216 billion by 1980; by the mid-2000s US foreign investment was worth more than 20 percent of GDP annually.

Unlike with the earlier moves from north to south, however, when companies moved to other countries, their employees could not follow. While all Americans benefited from the lower-cost and often higher-quality consumer goods that were increasingly imported, those who lost their jobs to import competition had a harder time finding new jobs at similar wages. Real wages stopped growing and even began to fall for many, especially men, who comprised most of the manufacturing labor force. The job and wage effects could possibly have been coincidental. Growing integration into the global economy coincided with two recessions and a spike in energy costs that slowed overall growth. But the shift from a full-employment economy with few economic links to the rest of the world to a volatile economy that was more integrated with the world touched off an inevitable public debate over whether such growing integration was a good thing. By the late 1970s, one of the country's largest carmakers, Chrysler, teetered on the verge of bankruptcy and had to be bailed out by the government to avoid a collapse that would have thrown hundreds of thousands out of work. Other major industries were facing cutthroat competition from imports. The governor of California warned that these were "signs that the basis of our industrial prosperity—sustained economic growth that has allowed for a certain liberal politics in this country—is seriously eroding."[8]

The debate was often cast as a struggle between proponents of "free trade" and "protectionism," but that was always misleading. The nearly self-sufficient United States of the early 1960s was not a "protectionist" country; by the standards of the time, it was one of the more open economies in the world. It simply had few competitors. As competition grew, presidents and Congress continued to favor open trade, even as some beleaguered industries demanded and occasionally received government protection from imports. The problem, rather, was how best to adjust to the new economic competition. In a relatively closed economy, the concept of national "competitiveness" is meaningless. If an economy produces most of the goods and services needed by its people, competition is something that concerns individuals and companies but not the entire country. Like other young people, I had gone to college to learn a skill (journalism) that would allow me to compete with other young people for jobs in my field. My employers (mostly newspapers) were competing with other newspapers and magazines, as well as television and radio stations, for the market share and advertising revenue that would allow them to pay salaries and turn a profit. The question of whether the country was "competitive" in journalism, however, was nonsensical, because there was virtually no foreign competition. If one newspaper went out of business, I could always go work for another or branch out into radio or television, as long as my skills were attractive to employers. If they weren't, then I was the one with the competitiveness problem, not my country.

Two decades previously, that had been true for nearly every sector of the economy; by the end of the 1970s, it was not. For those who earned their livings making steel or stitching clothing or assembling TV sets, the nature of competition had changed profoundly. If one domestic car company gained market share at the expense of another, it had little impact on those who made cars; the employees let go by one company would likely be hired by another. But if the competitor was in another country, the impact was not so benign. Given the tight immigration restrictions in place in most countries, not to mention generally insurmountable cultural and linguistic barriers, laid-off auto workers could not simply pick up and move to another country where carmakers were hiring. The "adjustment costs," in the antiseptic language of economists, were much higher than in a closed economy.

Technology was in theory equally disruptive— and would greatly disrupt my chosen profession when the Internet undermined the advertising model for many newspapers. If companies invested in machinery that required fewer workers, or if new technologies made some jobs obsolete, then those workers would not likely find jobs doing the same type of work they had done previously. But if the companies reinvested their profits domestically, other sorts of jobs would be created that would at least partly compensate. Technology would also improve the productivity of the workers who remained in those industries, thereby increasing their earnings. When those earnings were spent on consumer goods or services, this would create additional domestic employment. In a more global market, however, the circle could be less virtuous. If corporate profits were invested in other countries, or if the additional earnings of workers were spent largely on imported goods, or if competition from lower-paid workers abroad held down wages, the jobs lost from technology were less likely to be offset by jobs created elsewhere in the economy. Recent economic research suggests that import competition and technology have quite different impacts on the US workforce; while technology and trade are both disruptive, import competition has a much bigger impact on labor markets. Those who lose their jobs to computers are likely to find new ones, while those who lose their jobs to imports are much less likely to do so.[9]

For several decades now, these challenges created by America's growing integration into the world economy have been at the center of a highly divisive debate. The United States has faced increased import competition in a growing number of economic sectors that once employed millions of people at generally higher wages than they could earn at other jobs. And the competition is not just over trade but over investment as well. The ease with which companies can move across international borders has given them enormous leverage over their workforces; capital is far freer to move in search of investment opportunities, but labor cannot follow. That has given business far more power than it had enjoyed in the more self-sufficient economy of a generation ago. Finally, the scale of the disruption has called into question many of the country's institutions. Education, science, universities, and government itself are now all judged in good part by whether they strengthen or weaken the country's international competitive position. The question of how best to adjust to the competitive pressures of a global economy has moved from irrelevance to the center of a debate over the performance and prospects of the United States that still rages today.

Failure to Adjust: The Competitiveness Challenge

For most of my life, the United States has faced a deep schism over how to respond to the competitive pressures of the global economy. As a reporter, I covered the negotiations that concluded in the North American Free Trade Agreement (NAFTA) in 1993 and the bitter fight that followed over its ratification in Congress. I spent many sleepless nights in hotels in Geneva reporting on the talks that led to the creation of the World Trade Organization (WTO) in 1995. I watched the wrenching debate that finally led Congress to support China's admission to the WTO in 2001. And that same year I got tear-gassed in Quebec City at a "Summit of the Americas," where leaders were talking about expanding NAFTA across the Western Hemisphere, and those locked outside the old city walls were protesting. Today these issues have become, if anything, even more divisive, with some leaders in both the Democratic and Republican parties calling for a halt to further trade liberalization and even a reversion to protectionist tariffs on imports from big developing countries like China and Mexico. The same fears that turned so many Americans against NAFTA were on full display as President Barack Obama tried to persuade Congress—and in particular the skeptical members of his own Democratic Party—to support the Trans-Pacific Partnership (TPP) trade agreement with Japan and ten other countries. The debates have a depressing similarity. Supporters of the trade agreements promise more jobs, higher wages from exports, and a consumer cornucopia, while opponents warn that trade will send away jobs, drive down wages, and increase inequality.

Americans can't quite make up their minds about which side to believe. When asked by pollsters whether America's integration into the global economy over the past two decades "is good because it has opened up new markets for American products and resulted in more jobs, or bad because it has subjected American companies and employees to unfair competition and cheap labor," about half have responded each way. Other poll questions about trade produce similarly mixed results.[10] The pessimists gained a bit of ground during the deep recession that followed the 2008 financial crisis, and the optimists later recovered along with the economy, but there has been no clear trend up or down over time. It's almost like Americans are telling the pollsters to ask a different question. The right question is not whether trade is good or bad for the United States; a better question is whether the United States has used the new opportunities created by international trade to boost American living standards while minimizing the costs for those who lose out to import competition or outsourcing. Trade remains highly contentious because the United States has done rather poorly at both.

How poorly? In 1983, at a time when rising imports of cars and consumer electronics from Japan had created a deep pessimism about the US ability to compete globally, President Ronald Reagan appointed the chief executive of one of the country's most successful technology companies, John Young of Hewlett-Packard, to lead a national commission to examine the problem. The commission came up with a definition of "competitiveness" that remains the standard one today. "Competitiveness," Young's team wrote, "is the degree to which a nation can, under free and fair market conditions, produce goods and services that meet the test of international markets while simultaneously maintaining or expanding the real income of its citizens." In other words, a competitive economy is one whose companies do very well in global markets *and* whose people also do very well and reap the benefits both of rising wages and falling real prices. By that definition, the US economy is, as Michael Porter and his Harvard Business School colleagues have said, doing only half its job.

Porter, the country's most respected authority on US competitiveness and a member of the Young commission, argues, "America's leading companies are thriving, but the prosperity they are producing is not being shared broadly among U.S. citizens."[11]

US corporate profits have been at or near record highs for several years, though they weakened slightly in the first half of 2016. US companies like Apple, Google, Amazon, and Facebook account for more than half of the top one hundred companies in the world by market value, and US firms have gained ground over the past five years. But for Americans, the picture has been far more mixed. Even as the price of many consumer goods has fallen, the real income of the median American household (which takes into account falling prices) has scarcely budged in the past four decades. Since 1970 the real, inflation-adjusted income for families in the middle fifth—a decent definition of the middle class—has risen from about $48,000 (in 2014 dollars) to just over $53,000, an increase of 13 percent.[12] And even that small increase was primarily the result of longer working hours, mostly because many more women have entered the workforce and two-income households are more common (though offset to some degree by a growing number of single-parent households). Even before the Great Recession hit in 2008 and further eroded incomes, men in their thirties were earning significantly less in real terms than their fathers had earned a generation before.[13] The only strong wage gains came in the late 1990s, and those proved fleeting. Over the last decade, even with the recovery from the Great Recession finally kicking in, median family income has fallen back to where it was in the late 1980s.

While weaker overall growth is part of the story, US growth has been stronger than that of most other advanced economies in recent years, and the United States overall remains one of a handful of the wealthiest countries in the world. But US workers and their families have nonetheless lost ground, even compared to economies whose overall economic performance has been weaker. From 2000 to 2014, the median income in Canada and Great Britain grew by nearly 20 percent, with Ireland and the Netherlands not far behind. In the United States, median incomes were up just 0.3 percent. "The idea that the median American has so much more income than the middle class in all other parts of the world is not true these days," Harvard economist Lawrence Katz told the *New York Times.* "In 1960, we were massively richer than anyone else. In 1980, we were richer. In the 1990s, we were still richer."[14] But today, he said, the US edge has disappeared. Since the mid-1980s, income inequality in the United States has also risen faster than in any other major advanced economy, and the level of inequality today is higher than in any other country in the Organization for Economic Cooperation and Development (OECD) except for Chile, Mexico, and Turkey.[15] And since the mid-1980s, the percentage of those living in poverty has risen more in the United States than in any other advanced economy in the OECD, with the sole exception of Israel.[16] A recent study from Stanford University put the United States at the back of the pack among the larger wealthy economies in terms of spreading wealth to citizens. While much of that was a reflection of growing income inequality and the weak US social safety net, the United States was near last even in economic mobility and the percentage of working-age individuals who have jobs.[17]

Cause and effect are notoriously difficult to sort out in economics, of course, and there is a robust business in trying to explain that uncertainty. The coincidence between the stagnation of median incomes over the past four decades and America's growing integration into the global economy in no way means that one necessarily caused the other. There are simply too many other things going on in the economy to have any certainty. But what is clear is that the gap between promise and performance has been enormous. Americans have been told by a succession of presidents—including a once skeptical President Barack Obama—that the liberalization of trade and investment would produce big economic gains for most Americans. That has not happened. The price of many goods has certainly fallen as a result of global competition. The average American household now spends just over 3 percent of its annual budget on clothing, shoes, and linens, compared to more than 7 percent in the early 1970s. The real costs of other household goods are down as well, and the variety of goods available is certainly far larger.[18] But those gains have been offset by international competitive pressures that have held down wages and limited the number of better-paying middle-class jobs. The US Commerce Department notes that jobs in exporting industries pay on average nearly 20 percent more than jobs in purely domestic industries. But the number of those jobs has remained flat.

The failure of the United States to nurture its competitiveness as a business location and to help more of its citizens build the skills to continue to prosper in a more competitive world has come with a big cost. As Harvard Business School professors Gary Pisano and Willy Shih have put it, "The competitiveness of a place matters most to the people who work and live there because, unlike investors, they cannot readily redeploy their [human] capital." Changes in competitive advantage, both within a country and across nations, can have big effects on prosperity, they argue. The expansion of software engineering in the Indian cities of Hyderabad and Bangalore, they note, has produced a rising middle class of engineers and managers and made those two of the most livable cities in India. In contrast, when Michigan and other upper midwestern states became less attractive places to make automobiles, "unemployment soared, real estate prices fell, buildings deteriorated, public services eroded, and life became terribly difficult for many people."[19] In his provocative book *Our Kids: The American Dream in Crisis*, Harvard sociologist Robert Putnam tells the story of his hometown of Port Clinton, Ohio, where manufacturing

employment fell from 55 percent of all jobs in 1965 to 25 percent by 1995 and to just 16 percent in 2012. Incomes fell from slightly above the national average in the mid-1970s to 25 percent below by 2012. Divorce rates, unwed births, and child poverty all climbed precipitously.[20]

Responding to a more competitive global economy has been one of the great challenges facing political leaders in the United States for the past half century. While there are many critics of globalization, the problem is not globalization itself; indeed, given technological advances and the aspirations of poorer countries across the world, growing global trade and investment were both inevitable and desirable. US leadership in building the rules for global commerce is one of the great success stories of the past fifty years. The problem has been the domestic political response to globalization, which in too many ways has been deeply irresponsible. A central task of any government is to provide the tools to help people to adjust and succeed in the face of economic change, but the story of the last half century has instead been the failure by governments to ease that adjustment. America's political leadership, weighted down by the habits of a country that had been nearly self-sufficient and highly competitive in the few things it did trade, has done far too little to help Americans make the adjustment. Rather than thinking carefully about the competitive implications of growing trade and the freer flow of investment dollars—trying to maximize the benefits and minimize the costs—Washington has left most Americans to fend for themselves. Some have flourished in the more competitive global economy, but far too many have not.

The Peterson Memo

In February 1971, the United States was facing the first big economic crisis of the modern era of globalization. The postwar Bretton Woods economic system, named for the New Hampshire resort town where the agreement was reached by the major Allied powers in 1944, was crumbling. In an effort to end the "beggar-thy-neighbor" currency devaluations of the Great Depression, the agreement had fixed the value of major currencies to the US dollar, while the dollar was made fully convertible to gold at a price of $35 per ounce. That stability, coupled with American foresight in spending generously to rebuild war-damaged Europe and Asia, had helped trade and investment flourish in the years that followed. But by the late 1960s, the arrangement had become increasingly untenable for the United States. The costs of the Vietnam War, rising overseas investment by US multinational corporations, and growing currency speculation had created a chronic balance-of-payments deficit. The link to gold also meant that foreign holders could freely exchange dollars for gold at the fixed price, draining US gold reserves. One consequence was an increasingly overvalued US dollar as productivity soared in countries like Japan and Germany but currency values did not adjust, hurting American companies competing with rivals selling their products in discounted currencies. A working group on monetary policy led by Paul Volcker, President Richard Nixon's undersecretary of Treasury for international monetary affairs, had warned nearly two years before that the United States was likely to face repeated crises that could force Washington to end gold convertibility unless allies like Germany and Japan let their currencies rise in value against the dollar.[21]

As the economic pressures continued to grow, Nixon asked his newly appointed White House advisor for international economics to prepare "a review and analysis of the changing world economy" to help set future directions for US foreign economic policy. The resulting 133-page memo, titled *The United States in a Changing World Economy*, set out to persuade the president that the United States was at the end of one economic era and on the cusp of a new one that required a radical change in direction to ensure its future prosperity. The memo would be well received by the president, and it would contribute to Nixon's decision on August 15, 1971, to stop gold convertibility, slap a temporary tariff on imports, and begin the move toward floating currencies—steps that brought an end to the Bretton Woods system. It was lauded in the press when it was published later in the year and brought some small measure of fame to its author, who would go on to a highly lucrative Wall Street career (and a prominent role in supporting many research institutions, including the Council on Foreign Relations, where I work). But its warnings about the competitive challenges facing the United States would be largely ignored and the problems it raised poorly addressed. Indeed, much of the memo could still be written today with only modest amendments.

The author was a forty-four-year-old business executive named Peter George Peterson, who was appointed January 19, 1971, by Nixon as the first-ever White House assistant to the president for international economic affairs. Peterson, born in Kearney, Nebraska, was the son of Greek parents. His father had changed his name from Petropoulos when he immigrated to the United States as a young man. After graduating at the top of his high school class, Peterson earned admission to the Massachusetts Institute of Technology and later graduated from Northwestern University in 1947, finally going on to receive an MBA from the University of Chicago. He went to work in advertising at the McCann-Erickson agency in Chicago and was recruited to the number three executive slot at Bell & Howell, then one of the biggest US makers of professional and consumer movie cameras. Just three years later, at age thirty-eight, he became chief executive and chairman of the board. While Nixon would introduce him as "the greatest CEO of his generation," Peterson later gave himself only a B for his time with the company. He had cut costs, introduced popular new consumer products, and maintained the company's market share. But he had failed, he admitted, to recognize the fast-arriving future of digital cameras and recorders that would transform the consumer video industry. Within a decade, that business would be dominated by Japanese companies such as Sony, Samsung, and Panasonic, while Bell & Howell was left struggling in a series of modestly profitable enterprises.[22]

Peterson was recommended to Nixon by George Shultz, director of the Office of Management and Budget and an old friend from their University of Chicago days. As assistant to the president, Peterson directed the newly created cabinet-level White House Council on International Economic Policy (CIEP). Like the National Economic Council formed by President Bill Clinton two decades later, the CIEP was charged with ensuring that economic concerns would have a stronger voice in the foreign policy-making process. Nixon and his national security advisor, Henry Kissinger, were largely uninterested in international economics, their hands full with the Vietnam War and the secret negotiations to reopen diplomatic ties with China. Nixon told Peterson, "Henry doesn't know a damn thing about economics. What's worse, he doesn't know what he doesn't know."[23] And one of Kissinger's top aides would later conclude that Kissinger's record on economic issues was "dismal," writing that "on most issues he has totally abstained," and when he did reluctantly get involved, "he usually bungled badly."[24]

Peterson's memo was aimed at ending that neglect. For too long, he warned the president, Americans had lived with the comfortable belief that "the international competitive superiority of the U.S. was an unalterable fact of life." In 1971 the United States was still producing almost a third of the world's output, but Peterson argued that the era of singular American economic dominance had already come to an end. "The central fact of the past twenty-five years had been the conviction—ours as much as that of other countries—that the U.S. was dominant, both in size and competitiveness, in the

international economy," he wrote. "The practices, institutions and rules governing international trade and payments were structured to fit that fact. We as a nation and the world as a whole were too slow to realize that basic structural and competitive changes were occurring."

That was a message that few American leaders wanted to hear then—and to a surprising degree, they do not wish to hear it even today. The assumption of US competitive dominance makes both foreign and domestic policy much easier for presidents to manage. It means that trade negotiations can focus on shoring up alliances or strengthening the economies of potential allies rather than on squeezing out maximum advantage for the US economy. It means that Treasury officials need not be especially concerned with the value of the dollar, assuming that US companies can prosper even when an overvalued currency offers price advantages to foreign competitors. It means that US corporate tax policies can be structured in ways that encourage companies to invest overseas rather than favoring investment at home. And it means that the US government's role is limited to setting the rules for international competition, assuming that more liberal trade and open competition will mostly favor American companies and workers. There is little need for anyone in the government to think strategically about how to help some sector or other of the economy respond to foreign competition. And it absolves the government from thinking about adjustment issues—if US companies and workers are almost always winners in global economic competition, why worry about how to help the losers?

Peterson's memo tried to turn those assumptions on their head. First, he argued that the weakening competitive position of the United States meant that other countries simply had to carry more of the burden for international growth by opening their markets to imports and maintaining appropriately valued currencies. Second, he asserted that the government needed to promote the United

States as a business location, using tax policies and other tools to encourage investment and bolster exports. Third, while open trade would create many winners, he maintained, there would also be losers, and policies were needed to help workers retrain and find new jobs. And finally, he argued that the United States needed an ambitious, sustained effort to strengthen its own competitiveness through education, investment, and new scientific research.

The first cause of America's weakening competitive position—the "rise of the rest," as it later came to be called—took up much of the memo. While the same story could have been told in the 2000s about China, Peterson's worry at the time was Japan and, to a lesser extent, Europe. Over the previous two decades, Japan's economy had been growing at 10 percent per year on the strength of rising exports, "the most dramatic rate of economic progress in the world" and more than twice the US growth rate. A decade before scholars like Ezra Vogel and Chalmers Johnson would explain the "Japanese miracle" to a broader audience, Peterson had grasped its essential characteristics. Japan's economy, he noted, was "consciously shaped to meet long-range objectives" under the guidance of powerful bureaucracies. International trade was not an end in itself but rather an instrument to promote domestic production and employment. The Japanese bureaucracy was not, as in the United States, an "umpire of private business"; rather it was a partner in advancing economic goals. That partnership had already brought Japan the largest steel mills in the world and a dominant role in shipbuilding, and future targets included computers, petrochemicals, aluminum, and aircraft. Japan had also exported its model to less developed countries in East Asia, leading Peterson to foresee the rise of the "East Asian rim" as an economic competitor to the United States. In Europe, the creation of the European Economic Community—which was supported by the United States as a bulwark against the advance of Soviet communism—had left US companies at a competitive disadvantage. Trade preferences within Europe meant that companies producing outside the European economic zone faced higher tariffs than those inside the zone, encouraging US companies to invest directly in Europe rather than exporting from the United States. And Europe had in 1967 implemented a value-added tax, a production tax that is rebated to producers for exports and added to the price of imports, further hurting US companies trying to export to the European market.[25]

Peterson did not bemoan European or Japanese success. US foreign policy had been aimed at achieving exactly that result. Nor did he predict, as later commentators would do with both Japan and China, that the United States would be overtaken economically by any of its competitors. Instead, what worried him was the impact on the economic well-being of many Americans. The United States had also been disappointed, he wrote, by the failure of those countries to accept their new economic strength. Instead of opening up to imports from the United States, "it seemed to many Americans that the interests of those countries which had benefitted most from American policies were increasingly concentrating on regional or nationalistic arrangements, which were too often either restrictive or discriminatory or both." These countries had also provided "a wide variety of aids to producers and exporters over the years to help them compete against external pressures" and had negotiated more firmly for their own interests in trade talks. In moderation, such practices could be tolerated by the United States. But carried to the extreme, he warned in language that could be used today to describe the gyrations of the Chinese economy, the "internal preoccupations of any developed world power center can become externally provocative and ultimately self-destructive." Peterson argued for a more robust US posture to promote and defend its economic interests. He rejected the view that "our competitive advantage was so great that we could easily afford concessions here and there, in an ad hoc fashion, in the interest of maintaining flexible and friendly relations with our international partners and developing a prospering world market." Instead, he predicted that the new era was "likely to be an era of great competition among countries." In order to respond to those new realities, "not only our policies but our methods of diplomacy will have to be changed. Our international negotiating stance will have to meet its trading partners with a clearer, more assertive version of new national interest. This will make us more predictable in the eyes of our trading partners. I believe we must dispel any 'Marshall Plan psychology' or relatively unconstrained generosity that may remain. . . . [T]his is not just a matter of choice but of necessity."

Peterson worried as well about overseas investment by American corporations and what this would mean for the US economy and American workers. By 1971, foreign sales by affiliates of US companies were twice as large as US exports. Scholars had only just begun to explore the significance of the new multinational business models. Most saw the companies bringing significant gains both to the United States and to other countries by lowering consumer prices and spreading technology and industrial knowledge. But labor unions feared that the ability of these companies to invest anywhere in the world would not be in the interests of the world's highest-paid industrial workers, those in the United States. The labor movement, which had supported free trade well into the 1960s, had done an about-face as the US trade surplus eroded. The shift in labor's stance was not due to cyclical economic factors. Unemployment had fallen from nearly 7 percent in 1961, when the unions were in favor of freer trade, to just 3.5 percent by 1969, when unions were leading the charge for Congress to block imports. Instead, the unions saw a fundamental threat to their members from growing offshore investment. The American Federation of Labor and Congress of Industrial Organizations, the umbrella labor organization,

warned that the new global production models would harm US workers. "A U.S.-based multinational corporate can produce components in widely separated plants in Korea, Taiwan and the United States, assemble the product in a plant on the Mexican side of the border and sell the goods in the United States at American prices—perhaps with a U.S. brand name."[26] The companies in question—household names like IBM and Xerox, along with chemical, oil, and mining companies—had mounted a fierce rebuttal, commissioning their own studies that concluded that expansion overseas actually boosted growth and job creation at home. The newly formed Emergency Committee for American Trade, a lobbying group for the multinationals that was founded with President Lyndon Johnson's encouragement in 1967 as protectionist pressures began to rise, asserted, "American multinational companies do not export jobs. They outperform other companies in making jobs." Peterson was skeptical of the union claims but acknowledged that "little is publicly known about the interlocking effects of these corporations on U.S. jobs, trade and the balance of payments, and the effects on the economies of other countries." Refusing to draw any firm conclusions about the multinationals, he suggested, "The sheer volume of their activities requires us to take a new look."

He was much less equivocal in arguing for a generous program of "adjustment assistance" for those Americans harmed by rising imports and overseas investment. While trade would generally benefit most Americans, he believed, there would be some sectors and industries that would lose out in the face of rising import competition, hurting employees and their communities. He told the president, "A program to build on America's strengths by enhancing its international competitiveness cannot be indifferent to the fate of those industries, and especially those groups of workers, which are not meeting the demands of a truly competitive world economy. It is unreasonable to say that a liberal trade policy is in the interest of the entire country and then allow particular industries, workers, and communities to pay the whole price." Congress had tackled this problem in 1962 when it created the first "trade adjustment assistance" program as part of President John F. Kennedy's Trade Expansion Act, which was critical to winning labor support for the bill. But the unions came to feel they had been sold a bill of goods instead. The act required that workers prove they had been harmed by import competition that was explicitly the result of a trade concession made by the United States. From 1962 to 1969, though twenty-five petitions were filed with the Labor Department, not a single American worker received help through the program.[27] Peterson urged a far more ambitious scheme of adjustment assistance that would "facilitate the processes of economic and social change brought about by foreign competition." That would require temporary income support and job retraining for workers and might even require broader federal assistance to affected communities. Certain industries might need temporary protection from imports or other trade restrictions to help them adjust rather than permitting huge job losses to occur. And greater efforts to promote exports would be needed to help offset the jobs lost from imports. He called for a program "which can be accepted by unions" and would persuade them that "their workers will enjoy real benefits" even if they had to be retrained for new occupations.

While the rising economies of Europe and Japan needed to import more and the multinational companies needed to be closely watched, the major sources of America's economic challenges, Peterson told Nixon, were homegrown. Prosperity in the new era of global competition "depends mainly *on our own efforts* rather than on the actions of other countries," he wrote. The United States must undertake a concerted effort "to increase our competitiveness, our productivity and, in general, enlarge the areas of comparative advantage vis-a-vis

the rest of the world. The way to do this is to concentrate on the things we do best. This in turn will increase our international competitiveness." Higher productivity would come from greater investments in plant and equipment and public infrastructure. It would require greater focus on research and development, including a more active federal government role in identifying and nurturing promising technologies. And it would require better educating and training Americans in the skills that the emerging industrial and services economy required, a "fundamental reorientation" to ensure that the American workforce was prepared for the coming, highly competitive global economy.

Nixon was delighted with the memo. Peterson presented his findings to the cabinet in a color slide show, and the president asked him to share the report with business, labor unions, the press, and congressional leaders. He ended up on the cover of *Businessweek*, and the *New York Times* called him "an economic Kissinger." The report, which was published later in 1971, sold over ten thousand copies.[28] But those inside the administration, who better understood its implications, were far less persuaded by his arguments. Peterson was the leading figure in the Nixon White House calling for a more assertive foreign economic policy. "The view more people are taking is you shouldn't abandon vital economic interests merely to improve your relations with another government," a senior National Security Council official told the *National Journal*. "We are willing now to push harder on economic interests," he said, adding that for too long "we bent over backwards" to accommodate the economic interests of Europe and Japan. But the State Department in particular saw the memo as far too nationalistic and worried that its aggressive tone would jeopardize political relations with close allies. Others feared its publication would encourage Congress to pass protectionist legislation to block imports. One high-level State Department official said there were "sharp differences of opinion on [the] substantive issues" raised by Peterson and that he lacked understanding of the implications for US foreign policy.[29] Fred Bergsten, a young economist who was Kissinger's advisor on international economic issues, cautioned his boss that while US trade and other foreign economic policies had long been used to serve broader foreign policy goals, "there is now great and increasing pressure to change this relationship." While a degree of rebalancing made sense, Bergsten wrote to Kissinger, "some go so far as to say that foreign policy should now become the handmaiden of foreign economic policy, that we should use our political and military muscle to pursue basically economic objectives. Pete himself believes that a trend in this direction is inevitable. There is certainly widespread support for it in Congress." He urged Kissinger to resist and to make clear to Peterson that "you are not prepared to see economic issues dominate foreign policy in areas where our political interests are sufficiently important."[30]

Peterson himself would prove unable to see the fight through. A year after he came to Washington, Nixon "promoted" him to secretary of commerce, removing him from a White House in which a handful of the president's most loyal aides jealously controlled all major policy matters. Following Nixon's 1972 reelection, with the president increasingly distracted by the growing Watergate scandal, Peterson was not reappointed as secretary and turned down an offer to take the newly created post of ambassador to Europe, headquartered in Brussels. Five years later, the White House Council on International Economic Policy was abolished by President Jimmy Carter. Nothing similar would exist until President Bill Clinton created the National Economic Council in 1993, promising that it would finally develop a coordinated response to America's competitive challenges.

Lessons Not Learned

Peterson's memo to Nixon had urged the president to see trade in a broader context. While he was a strong supporter of trade liberalization and better international trade rules, he did not assume that growing trade alone would automatically benefit most Americans. Instead, the gains would come only if the United States was vigilant in ensuring that the new rules were followed and that the playing field was a level one for American companies and workers. They would come only if the United States invested in its own future by building better infrastructure, educating its young people, and leading in technological breakthroughs. The federal government would need to adjust its tax policies and take other steps to boost exports, attract more investment, and ensure that Americans got their share of the growing global pie. It would need a strategy for rising to meet the competition. In short, along with international trade and financial policies, the United States needed a competitiveness policy.

The idea of competitiveness is an elusive one. Indeed, many economists insist that only companies, not countries, compete economically. They point out, quite rightly, that international trade and investment are not zero-sum and that a well-functioning global economy can raise prosperity for all. Indeed, over the past two decades, global trade has helped lift more people out of poverty worldwide than at any time in human history. But saying that international economic competition is not "win-lose" is quite different from saying there is no competition at all. Even as trade and investment have been freed up across much of the world over the past half century, countries are competing aggressively for a bigger share—for investment, for exports, and for the jobs they create. Sometimes the tools they use are trade-distorting ones such as subsidies or currency manipulation or regulations that discourage imports; in effect, these are "beggar-thy-neighbor" policies that serve to boost a country's share of global trade and investment beyond what the market would otherwise allocate. Left unchecked, these practices are not only harmful to other countries but produce lopsided economies that are overly dependent on investment and exports, eventually harming the countries that are doing the distorting. But competition can also be an incentive for countries to raise their game—by investing in education, in world-class infrastructure, and in cutting-edge research and development. It can force countries to think carefully about the competitive implications of their tax policies and their monetary and fiscal policies. Trade and investment liberalization, while necessary, are only the first step, one that sets the rules for international economic competition. Equally—perhaps more—important is what governments do next, how they try to ensure that both their companies and their citizens are prepared to prosper in the more competitive world that the new rules have helped to create.

For decades now the United States has been a remarkably successful leader in building rules to free up trade and investment globally. From the end of World War II through the mid-1990s, it led successive rounds of global trade liberalization, culminating in the creation of the WTO in 1995. More recently, as global trade liberalization has stalled, it has led the completion of the TPP in Asia and the negotiations for a Transatlantic Trade and Investment Partnership with the European Union. The TPP is designed as an open agreement, one that could be joined later by countries like Korea, Indonesia, the Philippines, and perhaps eventually China. And despite the stalemate in the WTO, the United States has pursued other avenues for liberalization, including services negotiations with a willing group of countries and the negotiation of an investment treaty with China.

But the United States has done much less to shape trade rules, to encourage public and private investment, and to support its own workforce in order to help Americans secure a bigger share of the gains. On trade and international investment, it has too often looked the other way while competitors manipulated currency values, subsidized their companies, or blocked imports to gain a competitive advantage. At home, the quality of the roads, bridges, and ports that bring US products to overseas markets has badly deteriorated; today the United States ranks sixteenth in the world in the quality of its infrastructure, behind even countries like Spain and Portugal.[31] Americans between the ages of fifty-five and sixty-four are better educated than their counterparts anywhere in the world, but Americans aged twenty-five to thirty-four have slipped to thirteenth.[32] The United States has been a laggard in exports, losing more ground to new competitors like China than have the Europeans or most other advanced economies. And the United States has done much less than almost any of its competitors to help out citizens who find themselves getting the short end of the stick with regard to global competition, those who have lost their jobs to cheap imports or whose factories have relocated to Mexico or China. For example, the United States today spends far, far less on retraining workers than any other advanced economy, even as employers complain of a skills shortage that makes it hard to find employees with the abilities they need.

To caricature only slightly, the US approach to the global economy for the last half century has been "Build it, and we will succeed." In other words, if trade and investment rules are liberalized, then competition alone will lift up Americans. Few other countries behave that way. China, Korea, Japan, and most other Asian countries subsidize their companies or protect their markets through discriminatory regulations to gain an edge in global competition. Germany nurtures its competitive manufacturing industries, trains its workforce, and heavily promotes its exports around the world. Denmark and the Nordic economies have generous schemes for upgrading the skills and education of their employees to help them move to new careers.

For some Americans—those with the right mixture of education, ambition, and connections—the lack of support doesn't matter very much. Highly educated Americans have been enormously successful in the more open global economy, building and staffing some of the world's most innovative and dynamic companies. And the United States, largely because of its unmatched universities, continues to attract the lion's share of the brightest, most ambitious immigrants. But far too many Americans are simply unprepared for the competition they are now in. They are like overmatched boxers who keep getting knocked down, only to be told by their corner that they just have to get back in the ring and keep taking the punches in the hope that eventually they will become better fighters. It would make more sense to pull them out of the ring for a year of training and conditioning before sending them back again.

Peterson had warned that the consequences of failing to respond to the new competitive challenges would be severe. With capital moving more freely and transportation costs falling, the pressures for adjustment would "come faster and harder than anything experienced in earlier years," he wrote. "The rising pace of change poses adjustment policy problems which simply cannot be ignored." Failure to adjust, he warned, would be "paid for in abnormal unemployment and wasted opportunity." Today, even with the strong job growth of recent years, fewer Americans are working than at any time since the mid-1970s, and wage growth continues to be anemic. For more Americans to prosper in the hypercompetitive global economy, governments need to recognize that they are in a competition. Peterson had hoped that Washington would take the lead. For the most part it has not, but fortunately there are signs that state and local governments are recognizing and responding to at least some of the challenges. With greater support from Washington, they have the potential to build the sort of competitiveness strategies that the United States has been lacking for far too long.

Facing the Competitive Challenge

In early 2015, Sweden's flagship car producer Volvo (now owned by a Chinese billionaire) announced that it would build its first North American plant just outside Charleston, South Carolina. The $500 million plant is scheduled to open in 2018 and employ about two thousand people. It comes at the same time that Germany's BMW has announced plans to expand in the state and create its largest production facility in the world in nearby Spartanburg. The state government of South Carolina has established permanent foreign offices in Shanghai, Tokyo, and Munich. Exports have doubled as a percentage of the state's output over the past decade, and the state has a higher percentage than any other of employees working for foreign-owned companies.[33] Nearby, Daimler, the maker of Mercedes, has its largest SUV production facility in Alabama. Tennessee lured the South Korean tire maker Hankook Tire in 2014, and the company is expected to invest $800 million and create nearly two thousand jobs. Chattanooga is already home to Germany's Volkswagen, which chose the state based on a package of expensive incentives that included the creation of a new job-training program tailored to the factory's needs. For decades now the US share of global investment has been shrinking in the face of competition from Asia. But led by the states and many cities, America is fighting back.

More than two dozen American cities, from large ones like San Diego and Los Angeles to midsize ones like Portland and Columbus, have developed their own strategies to boost exports, attract investment, and gain jobs in the traded sectors. The most successful ones are busily promoting businesses in which they are already world leaders—medical devices in Minneapolis–St. Paul, aircraft and parts in Wichita, life sciences in San Diego. Portland, which has long been a hub for exports because of chipmaker Intel, has launched a new initiative for boosting exports of clean technology and has undertaken trade missions to promote its athletic and outdoor industry, built around Nike. The athletic footwear company, which became the poster child for outsourcing to low-wage countries like Vietnam, has recently announced that it could create as many as ten thousand new jobs in the United States based on new advanced manufacturing techniques like 3-D printing that could revolutionize how the soles of athletic shoes are made.

These are some of the encouraging signs that at least some American political leaders are finally waking up to what it will take to prosper in the competitive global economy that the United States itself did so much to create. Some of the response is coming from Washington. The federal government, for the first time since the late 1980s, when the semiconductor industry was facing crippling competition, has become serious about boosting advanced manufacturing in the United States. The Obama administration expanded the first real national effort to attract foreign investment in US history. And the government has become more aggressive in demanding that other countries adhere to negotiated trade rules. But for the most part Washington remains mired in foundational disputes over the proper role of government that have prevented an effective response. Once noncontroversial policies—like incremental increases in the gas tax to pay for roads, bridges, and rail lines—have become impossible to enact. Even as other countries are aggressively promoting their exports on global markets, the US Congress shut down for nearly six months the US Export-Import Bank, which helps American companies sell in developing-country markets, and refused to make a needed appointment to the bank's board of directors, which blocked it from making any new large loans. And even as other countries are trying to educate their citizens for the jobs of the future, US public education is hostage to constant skirmishes over national versus local control. In a competitive world, such ideological battles are a luxury that the United States can ill afford.

The real progress has been not in Washington—where the idea of an active government role in promoting economic competitiveness remains suspect—but in the states and the largest cities. More and more local governments have taken the lead in developing competitiveness strategies that start from the premise that local prosperity depends in good part on success in international economic competition. Nearly every state—from the biggest, like Texas and California, to smaller ones, like Tennessee and Nevada—is now competing aggressively for job-creating investments, promoting exports, and trying to build a stronger foundation for future job growth. Too often this is a competition only with other states that does little to benefit the US economy as a whole and instead simply diverts business from one state to another. And too often as well, governments dole out costly tax breaks and other incentives only to discover that the promised benefits fall short. But despite some blunders, more and more states are going global in their search for both investment and new markets, especially for advanced manufacturing that creates higher-paying jobs with a range of spin-off benefits for the local economy. The most successful states and regions are boosting their competitiveness not just, and sometimes not even, by cutting business costs through low taxation or subsidies but instead by investing in infrastructure to help get products to market, by encouraging the commercialization of university research, and by working with companies to ensure they will have the trained workforce they need.

Washington should follow their lead. For the past half century, the federal government has seen its role almost solely as the champion of rules that allow large corporations to invest and move goods freely around the globe. Successive trade agreements—under terms devised largely by the United States—have eliminated quotas and import taxes on most imported goods and offered unprecedented protection for the investments that companies make almost anywhere in the world. But the federal government has done little to help the United States actually compete for those investments and for export market share. Washington needs to follow the lead of the states and cities, standing behind them to help build, attract, and retain businesses in the internationally competitive sectors that provide many of the best jobs in our economy. The timing is right—with its lead in innovation, the falling price of energy, and labor costs that are highly competitive compared to Europe or Japan, the United States is becoming one of the most attractive places to invest in the world.

The federal government needs to go further, however, by negotiating with other countries to create better rules for international economic competition and enforcing those rules vigorously. The trade and investment agreements of the past have made it easier for goods and capital to move around the world, which has brought gains in productivity and efficiency. But those same rules have too often made it easier for large corporations to simply play one country off against another. Companies have enormous leverage to demand government subsidies, tax cuts, or a compliant, low-wage workforce as a condition for investment. Even as it competes fiercely for investment, the United States must lead a new international effort to curb the destructive effects of unbridled competition. New rules should be put in place to set higher standards for business around the world, to discourage corporations from racing to the lowest tax jurisdictions, and to create the conditions for fairer global economic competition. And those rules must be enforced with a vigor that has too often been lacking. The United States needs to launch a new effort to negotiate and enforce rules that will bring the benefits of a global economy to the many rather than the few.

Americans have been told too often by their political leaders that the global economy is something beyond control, that the United States has no choice but to bow to the creative destruction of the market. In his memo to Nixon, Pete Peterson roundly rejected that view. The United States, he argued, must "meet head-on the essential—if demanding—task of improving our productivity and competitiveness in an increasingly competitive world, to seize the initiative in designing a new, comprehensive program designed to build on America's strengths, and to encourage a competitive world trading system that comes from having a sense of our future." In short, he wrote, the United States must lead "a conscious effort to shape our own future rather than resign ourselves to whatever it may bring." That same challenge remains today.

NOTES

1. Anthanasios Vamvakidis, "How Robust Is the Growth-Openness Connection? Historical Evidence," *Journal of Economic Growth* 7 (2002): 57–80, http://www.cer.ethz.ch/resec/teaching/seminar_aussenwirtschaft_wt_04_05/vamvakidis_JEG.pdf.

2. "On the Move," *Economist*, January 13, 2014, http://www.economist.com/blogs/freeexchange/2014/01/european-labour-mobility.

3. Anne O. Krueger, "Protectionist Pressures, Imports, and Employment in the United States," National Bureau of Economic Research, March 1980, http://www.nber.org/papers/w0461.pdf.

4. "Employment, Wage, and Benefits," US Department of Labor, http://www.dol.gov/oasam/programs/history/herman/reports/futurework/report/chapter2/#chart2–1.

5. C. Fred Bergsten, "The United States and the World Economy," *Annals of the American Academy of Political and Social Science* 460 (March 1982): 11–20, http://www.jstor.org/stable/1044592?seq=2.

6. Bureau of Economics, Staff Report, "The United States Steel Industry and Its International Rivals," Federal Trade Commission, November 1977, https://www.ftc.gov/sites/default/files/documents/reports/u.s.steel-industry-and-its-international-rivals-trends-and-factors-determining-international/197711steelindustry.pdf.

7. "International Competition: Trade Flows and Industry Structure," in Automobile Panel, Committee on Technology and International and Trade Issues of the Office of the Foreign Secretary, National Academy of Engineering, and the Commission on Engineering and Technical Systems, National Research Council, *The Competitive Status of the U.S. Auto Industry: A Study of the Influences of Technology in Determining International Industrial Competitive Advantage* (Washington, DC: National Academies Press, 1982), http://www.nap.edu/openbook.php?record_id=291&page=52.

8. "Jerry Brown on the 'Reindustrialization of America,'" *Washington Post*, January 14, 1980, http://search.proquest.com/news/docview/147148532/1375113D4C761DEE5DD/6?accountid=37722.

9. David H. Autor, David Dorn, and Gordon H. Hanson, "Untangling Trade and Technology: Evidence from Local Labor Markets," National Bureau of Economic Research, Working Paper No. 19838, April 2013, http://www.nber.org/papers/w18938.

10. "International Trade/Global Economy," PollingReport.com, http://www.pollingreport.com/trade.htm.

11. Jan W. Rivkin, Karen G. Mills, and Michael E. Porter, with contributions from Michael I. Norton and Mitchell B. Weiss, "The Challenge of Shared Prosperity: Findings of Harvard Business School's 2015 Survey on U.S. Competitiveness," Harvard Business School, September 2015, http://www.hbs.edu/competitiveness/Documents/challenge-of-shared-prosperity.pdf.

12. "Historical Income Tables: Households," US Census Bureau, http://www.census.gov/hhes/www/income/data/historical/household. See also Carmen DeNavas-Walt and Bernadette D. Proctor, "Income and Poverty in the United States: 2014," *Current Population Reports*, US Census, September 2015. http://www.census.gov/content/dam/Census/library/publications/2015/demo/p60-252.pdf.

13. Molly Selvin, "Study: Men's Earnings Shrink," *Los Angeles Times*, May 26, 2007, http://articles.latimes.com/2007/may/26/business/fi-men26.

14. David Leonhardt and Kevin Quealy, "The American Middle Class Is No Longer the World's Richest," *New York Times*, April 22, 2014.

15. "United States: Tackling High Inequalities, Creating Opportunities for All," OECD, June 2014, http://www.oecd.org/unitedstates/Tackling-high-inequalities.pdf.

16. Brian Keeley, "Income Inequality: The Gap between Rich and Poor," December 15, 2015, OECD Insights, http://www.oecd-library.org/docserver/download/0115391e.pdf?expires=1453488804&id=id&accname=guest&checksum=2EF4A6746AEC627825860E7300708125.

17. Stanford Center on Poverty and Inequality, *State of the Union: The Poverty and Inequality Report 2016*, special issues of *Pathways* (2016), http://inequality.stanford.edu/sites/default/files/Pathways-SOTU-2016.pdf.

18. Edward Gresser, "American Families Have Cut Their Bills for Food and Home Goods by 40 Percent since the 1970s," *Progressive Economy*, http://www.progressive-economy.org/trade_facts/american-families-have-cut-their-bills-for-food-home-goods-by-40-percent-since-the-1970s.

19. Gary P. Pisano and Willy Shih, *Producing Prosperity: Why America Needs a Manufacturing Renaissance* (Boston: Harvard Business Review Press, 2012).

20. Robert D. Putnam, *Our Kids: The American Dream in Crisis* (New York: Simon & Schuster, 2015).

21. See Daniel J. Sargent, *A Superpower Transformed: The Remaking of American Foreign Policy in the 1970s* (Oxford: Oxford University Press, 2014).

22. Peter G. Peterson, *The Education of an American Dreamer: How a Son of Greek Immigrants Learned His Way from a Nebraska Diner to Washington, Wall Street, and Beyond* (New York: Twelve, 2009).

23. Peterson, *The Education of an American Dreamer*.

24. C. Fred Bergsten, *Towards a New International Economic Order: Selected Papers of C. Fred Bergsten, 1971–1974* (Lexington, MA: Lexington Books, 1975), 499.

25. Robert A. Pastor, *Congress and the Politics of U.S. Foreign Economic Policy, 1929–1976* (Berkeley: University of California Press, 1980).

26. AFL-CIO, "An American Trade Union View on International Trade and Investment," February 21, 1971, in *Multinational Corporations: A Compendium of Papers Submitted to the Subcommittee on International Trade of the Committee on Finance in the United States Senate*, ed. US Senate, Committee on Finance, Subcommittee on International Trade (Washington, DC: US Government Printing Office, 1973), 71.

27. Howard Rosen, "Trade Adjustment Assistance: The More We Change, the More It Stays the Same," in *C. Fred Bergsten and the World Economy*, ed. Michael Mussa (Washington, DC: Peterson Institute for International Economics, 2006), 81.

28. Peterson, *The Education of an American Dreamer*.

29. Dom Bonafede, "Peterson Unit Helps Shape Tough International Economic Policy," *National Journal* 3, no. 46 (November 13, 1971): 2238–48.

30. "Memorandum from C. Fred Bergsten of the National Security Council Staff to the President's Special Assistant for National Security Affairs (Kissinger)," Washington, DC, April 21, 1971, in *Foreign Relations of the United States, 1969–1976*, Vol. 3: *Foreign Economic Policy; International Monetary Policy, 1969–1972*, ed. Bruce F. Duncombe (Washington, DC: United States Government Printing Office, 2001), document 64.

31. See Edward Alden and Rebecca Strauss, *How America Stacks Up: Economic Competitiveness and U.S. Policy* (New York: Council on Foreign Relations, February 2016).

32. Alden and Strauss, *How America Stacks Up*.

33. Bob Davis and Valerie Bauerlein, "South Carolina GOP Voters Feel the Benefits of Free Trade—but Also the Scars," *Wall Street Journal*, February 17, 2016.

Fareed Zakaria

POPULISM ON THE MARCH

Donald Trump's admirers and critics would probably agree on one thing: he is different. One of his chief Republican supporters, Newt Gingrich, describes him as a "unique, extraordinary experience." And of course, in some ways—his celebrity, his flexibility with the facts—Trump is unusual. But in an important sense, he is not: Trump is part of a broad populist upsurge running through the Western world. It can be seen in countries of widely varying circumstances, from prosperous Sweden to crisis-ridden Greece. In most, populism remains an opposition movement, although one that is growing in strength; in others, such as Hungary, it is now the reigning ideology. But almost everywhere, populism has captured the public's attention.

What is populism? It means different things to different groups, but all versions share a suspicion of and hostility toward elites, mainstream politics, and established institutions. Populism sees itself as speaking for the forgotten "ordinary" person and often imagines itself as the voice of genuine patriotism. "The only antidote to decades of ruinous rule by a small handful of elites is a bold infusion of popular will. On every major issue affecting this country, the people are right and the governing elite are wrong," Trump wrote in the *Wall Street Journal* in April 2016. Norbert Hofer, who ran an "Austria first" presidential campaign in 2016, explained to his opponent—conveniently, a former professor—"You have the *haute volée* [high society] behind you; I have the people with me."

Historically, populism has come in left- and right-wing variants, and both are flourishing today,

from Bernie Sanders to Trump, and from Syriza, the leftist party currently in power in Greece, to the National Front, in France. But today's left-wing populism is neither distinctive nor particularly puzzling. Western countries have long had a far left that critiques mainstream left-wing parties as too market-oriented and accommodating of big business. In the wake of the Cold War, center-left parties moved much closer toward the center—think of Bill Clinton in the United States and Tony Blair in the United Kingdom—thus opening up a gap that could be filled by populists. That gap remained empty, however, until the financial crisis of 2007–8. The subsequent downturn caused households in the United States to lose trillions in wealth and led unemployment in countries such as Greece and Spain to rise to 20 percent and above, where it has remained ever since. It is hardly surprising that following the worst economic crisis since the Great Depression, the populist left experienced a surge of energy.

The new left's agenda is not so different from the old left's. If anything, in many European countries, left-wing populist parties are now closer to the center than they were 30 years ago. Syriza, for example, is not nearly as socialist as was the main Greek socialist party, PASOK, in the 1970s and 1980s. In power, it has implemented market reforms and austerity, an agenda with only slight variations from that of the governing party that preceded it. Were Podemos, Spain's version of Syriza, to come to power—and it gained only about 20 percent of the vote in the country's most recent election—it would probably find itself in a similar position.

Right-wing populist parties, on the other hand, are experiencing a new and striking rise in

From *Foreign Affairs* (November/December 2016): 9–15.

country after country across Europe. France's National Front is positioned to make the runoff in next year's presidential election. Austria's Freedom Party almost won the presidency this year and still might, since the final round of the election was annulled and rescheduled for December. Not every nation has succumbed to the temptation. Spain, with its recent history of right-wing dictatorship, has shown little appetite for these kinds of parties. But Germany, a country that has grappled with its history of extremism more than any other, now has a right-wing populist party, Alternative for Germany, growing in strength. And of course, there is Trump. While many Americans believe that Trump is a singular phenomenon, representative of no larger, lasting agenda, accumulating evidence suggests otherwise. The political scientist Justin Gest adapted the basic platform of the far-right British National Party and asked white Americans whether they would support a party dedicated to "stopping mass immigration, providing American jobs to American workers, preserving America's Christian heritage and stopping the threat of Islam." Sixty-five percent of those polled said they would. Trumpism, Gest concluded, would outlast Trump.

Why the West, and Why Now?

In searching for the sources of the new populism, one should follow Sherlock Holmes' advice and pay attention to the dog that didn't bark. Populism is largely absent in Asia, even in the advanced economies of Japan and South Korea. It is actually in retreat in Latin America, where left-wing populists in Argentina, Bolivia, and Venezuela ran their countries into the ground over the last decade. In Europe, however, not only has there been a steady and strong rise in populism almost everywhere, but it has deeper roots than one might imagine. In

an important research paper for Harvard's Kennedy School of Government, Ronald Inglehart and Pippa Norris calculate that since the 1960s, populist parties of the right have doubled their share of the vote in European countries and populists of the left have seen more than a fivefold increase. By the second decade of this century, the average share of seats for right-wing populist parties had risen to 13.7 percent, and it had risen to 11.5 percent for left-wing ones.

The most striking findings of the paper are about the decline of economics as the pivot of politics. The way politics are thought about today is still shaped by the basic twentieth-century left-right divide. Left-wing parties are associated with increased government spending, a larger welfare state, and regulations on business. Right-wing parties have wanted limited government, fewer safety nets, and more laissez-faire policies. Voting patterns traditionally reinforced this ideological divide, with the working class opting for the left and middle and upper classes for the right. Income was usually the best predictor of a person's political choices.

A convergence in economic policy has contributed to a situation in which the crucial difference between the left and the right is cultural.

Inglehart and Norris point out that this old voting pattern has been waning for decades. "By the 1980s," they write, "class voting had fallen to the lowest levels ever recorded in Britain, France, Sweden and West Germany. . . . In the U.S., it had fallen so low [by the 1990s] that there was virtually no room for further decline." Today, an American's economic status is a bad predictor of his or her voting preferences. His or her views on social issues—say, same-sex marriage—are a much more accurate guide to whether he or she will support Republicans or Democrats. Inglehart and Norris also analyzed party platforms in recent decades and found that since the 1980s, economic issues have become less important. Noneconomic issues—such as those related to gender, race, the environment—have greatly increased in importance.

What can explain this shift, and why is it happening almost entirely in the Western world? Europe and North America include countries with widely varying economic, social, and political conditions. But they face a common challenge—economic stasis. Despite the variety of economic policies they have adopted, all Western countries have seen a drop-off in growth since the 1970s. There have been brief booms, but the secular shift is real, even including the United States. What could account for this decline? In his recent book, *The Rise and Fall of Nations,* Ruchir Sharma notes that a broad trend like this stagnation must have an equally broad cause. He identifies one factor above all others: demographics. Western counties, from the United States to Poland, Sweden to Greece, have all seen a decline in their fertility rates. The extent varies, but everywhere, families are smaller, fewer workers are entering the labor force, and the ranks of retirees swell by the year. This has a fundamental and negative impact on economic growth.

That slower growth is coupled with challenges that relate to the new global economy. Globalization is now pervasive and entrenched, and the markets of the West are (broadly speaking) the most open in the world. Goods can easily be manufactured in lower-wage economies and shipped to advanced industrial ones. While the effect of increased global trade is positive for economies as a whole, specific sectors get battered, and large swaths of unskilled and semiskilled workers find themselves unemployed or underemployed.

Another trend working its way through the Western world is the information revolution. This is not the place to debate whether new technologies are raising productivity. Suffice it to say, they reinforce the effects of globalization and, in many cases, do more than trade to render certain kinds of jobs obsolete. Take, for example, the new and wondrous technologies pursued by companies such as Google and Uber that are making driverless cars possible. Whatever the other effects of this trend, it cannot be positive for the more than three million Americans who are professional truck drivers. (The most widely held job for an American male today is driving a car, bus, or truck, as *The Atlantic's* Derek Thompson has noted.)

The final challenge is fiscal. Almost every Western country faces a large fiscal burden. The net debt-to-GDP ratio in the European Union in 2015 was 67 percent. In the United States, it was 81 percent. These numbers are not crippling, but they do place constraints on the ability of governments to act. Debts have to be financed, and as expenditures on the elderly rise through pensions and health care, the debt burden will soar. If one secure path to stronger growth is investment—spending on infrastructure, education, science, and technology—this path is made more difficult by the ever-growing fiscal burdens of an aging population.

These constraints—demographics, globalization, technology, and budgets—mean that policymakers have a limited set of options from which to choose. The sensible solutions to the problems of advanced economies these days are inevitably a series of targeted efforts that will collectively improve things: more investments, better worker retraining, reforms of health care. But this incrementalism produces a deep sense of frustration among many voters who want more dramatic solutions and a bold, decisive leader willing to decree them. In the United States and elsewhere, there is rising support for just such a leader, who would dispense with the checks and balances of liberal democracy.

From Economics to Culture

In part because of the broader forces at work in the global economy, there has been a convergence in economic policy around the world in recent decades. In the 1960s, the difference between the left and the right was vast, with the left seeking to nationalize entire industries and the right seeking to get the government out of the economy. When François Mitterrand came to power in France in the early 1980s, for example, he enacted policies that were identifiably socialist, whereas Margaret Thatcher and Ronald Reagan sought to cut taxes, privatize industries and government services, and radically deregulate the private sector.

The end of the Cold War discredited socialism in all forms, and left-wing parties everywhere moved to the center, most successfully under Clinton in the United States and Blair in the United Kingdom. And although politicians on the right continue to make the laissez-faire case today, it is largely theoretical. In power, especially after the global financial crisis, conservatives have accommodated themselves to the mixed economy, as liberals have to the market. The difference between Blair's policies and David Cameron's was real, but in historical perspective, it was rather marginal. Trump's plans for the economy, meanwhile, include massive infrastructure spending, high tariffs, and a new entitlement for working mothers. He has employed the usual rhetoric about slashing regulations and taxes, but what he has actually promised—let alone what he could actually deliver—has been less different from Hillary Clinton's agenda than one might assume. In fact, he has boasted that his infrastructure program would be twice as large as hers.

This convergence in economic policy has contributed to a situation in which the crucial difference between the left and the right today is cultural. Despite what one sometimes hears, most analyses of voters for Brexit, Trump, or populist candidates across Europe find that economic factors (such as rising inequality or the effects of trade) are not the most powerful drivers of their support. Cultural values are. The shift began, as Inglehart and Norris note, in the 1970s, when young people embraced a postmaterialist politics centered on self-expression and issues related to gender, race, and the environment. They challenged authority and established institutions and norms, and they were largely

successful in introducing new ideas and recasting politics and society. But they also produced a counterreaction. The older generation, particularly men, was traumatized by what it saw as an assault on the civilization and values it cherished and had grown up with. These people began to vote for parties and candidates that they believed would, above all, hold at bay these forces of cultural and social change.

In Europe, that led to the rise of new parties. In the United States, it meant that Republicans began to vote more on the basis of these cultural issues than on economic ones. The Republican Party had lived uneasily as a coalition of disparate groups for decades, finding a fusion between cultural and economic conservatives and foreign policy hawks. But then, the Democrats under Clinton moved to the center, bringing many professionals and white-collar workers into the party's fold. Working-class whites, on the other hand, found themselves increasingly alienated by the cosmopolitan Democrats and more comfortable with a Republican Party that promised to reflect their values on "the three Gs"—guns, God, and gays. In President Barack Obama's first term, a new movement, the Tea Party, bubbled up on the right, seemingly as a reaction to the government's rescue efforts in response to the financial crisis. A comprehensive study by Theda Skocpol and Vanessa Williamson, however, based on hundreds of interviews with Tea Party followers, concluded that their core motivations were not economic but cultural. As the virulent hostility to Obama has shown, race also plays a role in this cultural reaction.

For a few more years, the conservative establishment in Washington remained focused on economics, not least because its most important financial supporters tended toward libertarianism. But behind the scenes, the gap between it and the party's base was growing, and Trump's success has brought that division into the open. Trump's political genius was to realize that many Republican voters were unmoved by the standard party gospel of free trade, low taxes, deregulation, and entitlement reform but would respond well to a different appeal based on cultural fears and nationalist sentiment.

Nation vs. Migration

Unsurprisingly, the initial and most important issue Trump exploited was immigration. On many other social issues, such as gay rights, even right-wing populists are divided and recognize that the tide is against them. Few conservative politicians today argue for the recriminalization of homosexuality, for instance. But immigration is an explosive issue on which populists are united among themselves and opposed to their elite antagonists.

There is a reality behind the rhetoric, for we are indeed living in an age of mass migration. The world has been transformed by the globalization of goods, services, and information, all of which have produced their share of pain and rejection. But we are now witnessing the globalization of people, and public reaction to that is stronger, more visceral, and more emotional. Western populations have come to understand and accept the influx of foreign goods, ideas, art, and cuisine, but they are far less willing to understand and accept the influx of foreigners themselves—and today there are many of those to notice.

For the vast majority of human history, people lived, traveled, worked, and died within a few miles of their birthplace. In recent decades, however, Western societies have seen large influxes of people from different lands and alien cultures. In 2015, there were around 250 million international migrants and 65 million forcibly displaced people worldwide. Europe has received the largest share, 76 million immigrants, and it is the continent with the greatest anxiety. That anxiety is proving a better guide to voters' choices than issues such as inequality or slow growth. As a counterexample, consider Japan. The country has had 25 years of sluggish growth and is aging even faster than others, but it doesn't have many immigrants—and in part as a result, it has not caught the populist fever.

Levels of public anxiety are not directly related to the total number of immigrants in a country or even to the concentration of immigrants in different areas, and polls show some surprising findings. The French, for example, are relatively less concerned about the link between refugees and terrorism than other Europeans are, and negative attitudes toward Muslims have fallen substantially in Germany over the past decade. Still, there does seem to be a correlation between public fears and the pace of immigration. This suggests that the crucial element in the mix is politics: countries where mainstream politicians have failed to heed or address citizens' concerns have seen rising populism driven by political entrepreneurs fanning fear and latent prejudice. Those countries that have managed immigration and integration better, in contrast, with leadership that is engaged, confident, and practical, have not seen a rise in populist anger. Canada is the role model in this regard, with large numbers of immigrants and a fair number of refugees and yet little backlash.

To be sure, populists have often distorted or even invented facts in order to make their case. In the United States, for example, net immigration from Mexico has been negative for several years. Instead of the illegal immigrant problem growing, in other words, it is actually shrinking. Brexit advocates, similarly, used many misleading or outright false statistics to scare the public. Yet it would be wrong to dismiss the problem as one simply concocted by demagogues (as opposed to merely exploited by them). The number of immigrants entering many European countries is historically high. In the United States, the proportion of Americans who were foreign-born increased from less than five percent in 1970 to almost 14 percent today. And the problem of illegal immigration to the United States remains real, even though it has slowed recently. In many countries, the systems designed to manage immigration and provide services for integrating immigrants have broken down. And yet all too often, governments have refused to fix them, whether because powerful economic interests benefit from cheap labor or because officials fear appearing uncaring or xenophobic.

Immigration is the final frontier of globalization. It is the most intrusive and disruptive because as a result of it, people are dealing not with objects or abstractions; instead, they come face-to-face with other human beings, ones who look, sound, and feel different. And this can give rise to fear, racism, and xenophobia. But not all the reaction is noxious. It must be recognized that the pace of change can move too fast for society to digest. The ideas of disruption and creative destruction have been celebrated so much that it is easy to forget that they look very different to the people being disrupted.

Western societies will have to focus directly on the dangers of too rapid cultural change. That might involve some limits on the rate of immigration and on the kinds of immigrants who are permitted to enter. It should involve much greater efforts and resources devoted to integration and assimilation, as well as better safety nets. Most Western countries need much stronger retraining programs for displaced workers, ones more on the scale of the GI Bill: easily available to all, with government, the private sector, and educational institutions all participating. More effort also needs to be devoted to highlighting the realities of immigration, so that the public is dealing with facts and not phobias. But in the end, there is no substitute for enlightened leadership, the kind that, instead of pandering to people's worst instincts, appeals to their better angels.

Eventually, we will cross this frontier as well. The most significant divide on the issue of immigration is generational. Young people are the least anxious or fearful of foreigners of any group in society. They understand that they are enriched—economically, socially, culturally—by living in diverse, dynamic countries. They take for granted that they should live in an open and connected world, and that is the future they seek. The challenge for the West is to make sure the road to that future is not so rocky that it causes catastrophe along the way.

Daniel W. Drezner

THE IRONY OF GLOBAL ECONOMIC GOVERNANCE
The System Worked

Introduction

The 2008 financial crisis posed the biggest challenge to the global economy since the Great Depression and provided a severe "stress test" for global economic governance. A review of economic outcomes, policy outputs, and institutional resilience reveals that these regimes performed well during the acute phase of the crisis, ensuring the continuation of an open global economy. Even though some policy outcomes have been less than optimal, international institutions and frameworks performed contrary to expectations. Simply put, the system worked.

During the first ten months of the Great Recession, global stock market capitalization plummeted lower as a percentage of its precrisis level than during the first ten months of the Great Depression.[1] Housing prices in the United States declined more than twice as much as they did during the Great Depression.[2] The global decline in asset values led to aggregate losses of $27 trillion in 2008—a half-year's worth of global economic output.[3] Global unemployment increased by an estimated fourteen million people in 2008 alone.[4] Nearly four years after the crisis, concerns about systemic risk still continue.[5]

The demand for global economic governance structures to perform effectively is at its greatest during crises. An open global economy lessens the stagnation that comes from a financial crisis, preventing a downturn from metastasizing into another Great Depression. One of the primary purposes of multilateral economic institutions is to provide global public goods—such as keeping barriers to cross-border exchange low. Even if states are the primary actors in world politics, they rely on a bevy of acronym-laden institutions—the International Monetary Fund (IMF), World Trade Organization (WTO), Bank for International Settlements (BIS), and Group of Twenty (G20)—to coordinate action on the global scale. International institutions can be the policymaker's pacifier. In an anarchic world, these structures reduce uncertainty for all participating actors. When they function well, they facilitate communication and foster shared understanding between policy principals. When they function poorly, a lack of trust and a surfeit of uncertainty stymies responsible authorities from cooperating.

Since the Great Recession began, there has been no shortage of scorn for the state of global economic governance among pundits and scholars.[6] Nevertheless, a closer look at the global response to the financial crisis reveals a more optimistic picture. Despite initial shocks that were more severe than the 1929 financial crisis, national policy elites and multilateral economic institutions responded quickly and robustly. Whether one looks at economic outcomes, policy outputs, or institutional resilience, global economic

Working Paper, Council on Foreign Relations, International Institutions and Global Governance Program (Oct. 2012).

governance structures have either reinforced or improved upon the status quo since the collapse of the subprime mortgage bubble. To be sure, there remain areas where governance has either faltered or failed, but on the whole, the global regime worked.

How Does Global Economic Governance Work?

Debates about whether global governance works or not usually do not suffer from an abundance of data. More typically, critics of the current system tend to rely on a few stylized facts that are meant to suggest general dysfunction. In recent years, the three events most commonly cited are:[7]

- *The collapse of the Doha round.* Just before the financial crisis hit its acute phase, last-gasp efforts to the Doha round of WTO negotiations stalled out. Subsequent G20 pledges to abstain from protectionism and complete the Doha round of world trade talks have been as common as they have been toothless. Within the first six months of the financial crisis, seventeen of the twenty countries had violated that pledge, implementing a combined forty-seven measures to restrict trade at the expense of other countries.[8] The current status of the Doha round is so moribund that the Bush administration's last U.S. trade representative advocated abandoning the effort.[9]
- *The breakdown of macroeconomic policy consensus at the 2010 Toronto G20 summit.* Prior to the Toronto summit, there was a rough consensus among the G20 in favor of government stimulus to keep the global economy afloat. The United States went into that summit to argue for more expansionary monetary and fiscal policy, but came out of it with no consensus. Other countries embraced austerity

policies instead. In the subsequent eighteen months, numerous G20 members accused each other of starting a currency war.
- *The escalation of Europe's sovereign debt crisis.* As an increasing number of eurozone economies have found their fiscal fortunes collapsing, European institutions have appeared powerless to stop the spreading financial contagion. If the European Union, the single most powerful regional institution in existence, cannot cope with this crisis, why should we expect global governance structures to do better with bigger problems?

These facts are true, but they are not the whole truth. To ascertain the effectiveness of global economic governance after the 2008 financial crisis, it is useful to look at three different levels of analysis. First, what do the policy outcomes look like? How have global output, trade, and other capital flows responded since the start of the Great Recession? Second, what do the policy outputs look like? Have important international institutions provided policies that experts would consider significant and useful in response to the global financial crisis? Finally, have these governance structures demonstrated institutional resiliency and flexibility? A common complaint prior to 2008 was that these institutions had not adapted to the shifting distribution of power. Have these structures maintained their relevance and authority? Have they responded to the shifts in the distribution of power to ensure that the powerful actors continue to buy into existing arrangements?

Policy Outcomes

In looking at outcomes, the obvious question is how well the global economy has recovered from the 2008 crisis, The current literature on economic downturns suggests two factors that impose significant barriers to a strong recovery from the

Great Recession: it was triggered by a financial crisis and it was global in scope. Whether measuring output, per capita income, or employment, financial crashes trigger downturns that last longer and have far weaker recoveries than standard business cycle downturns.[10] Furthermore, the global nature of the crisis makes it extremely difficult for countries to export their way out of the problem. Countries that have experienced severe banking crises since World War II have usually done so when the global economy was largely unaffected. That was not the case for the Great Recession.

The global economy has rebounded much better than during the Great Depression. Economists Barry Eichengreen and Kevin O'Rourke have compiled data to compare global economic performance from the start of the crises (see Figures 8.1 and 8.2).[11] Two facts stand out in their comparisons. First, the percentage drop in global industrial output and world trade levels at the start of the 2008 financial crisis was more precipitous than the falloffs following the October 1929 stock market crash. The drop in industrial output was greater in 2008 nine months into the crisis than it was eighty years earlier after the same amount of time. The drop in trade flows was more than twice as large. Second, the post-2008 rebound has been far more robust. Four years after the onset of the Great Recession, global industrial output is 10 percent higher than when the recession began. In contrast, four years after the 1929 stock market crash, industrial output was at only two-thirds of precrisis levels.

A similar story can be told with aggregate economic growth. According to World Bank figures, global economic output rebounded in 2010 with 2.3 percent growth, followed up in 2011 with 4.2 percent growth. The global growth rate in 2011 was 44 percent higher than the average of the previous decade. Even more intriguing, the

Figure 8.1. World Industrial Production: Great Depression vs. Great Recession

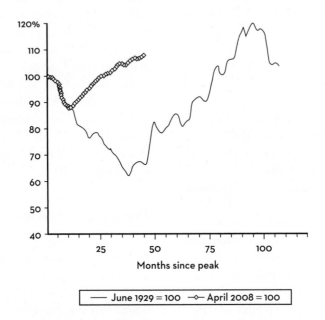

Source: Eichengreen and O'Rourke, "A tale of two depressions redux"

Figure 8.2. World Trade Volumes: Great Depression vs. Great Recession

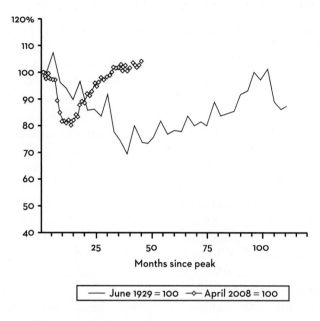

Months since peak

— June 1929 = 100   ◇ April 2008 = 100

Source: Eichengreen and O'Rourke, "A tale of two depressions redux"

growth continued to be poverty reducing.[12] The World Bank's latest figures suggest that despite the 2008 financial crisis, extreme poverty continued to decline across all the major regions of the globe. And the developing world achieved its first Millennium Development Goal of halving the 1990 levels of extreme poverty.[13]

An important reason for the quick return to positive economic growth is that cross-border flows did not dry up after the 2008 crisis. Again, compared to the Great Depression, trade flows have rebounded extremely well.[14] Four years after the 1929 stock market crash, trade flows were off by 25 percent compared to precrisis levels. Current trade flows, in contrast, are more than 5 percent higher than in 2008. Even compared to other postwar recessions, the current period has seen robust cross-border exchange. Indeed, as a report from CFR's Maurice R. Greenberg Center for Geoeconomic Studies concluded in May 2012, "The

growth in world trade since the start of the [current] recovery exceeds even the best of the prior postwar experiences."[15]

Other cross-border flows have also rebounded from 2008–2009 lows. Global foreign direct investment (FDI) has returned to robust levels. FDI inflows rose by 17 percent in 2011 alone. This put annual FDI levels at $1.5 trillion, surpassing the three-year precrisis average, though still approximately 25 percent below the 2007 peak. More generally, global foreign investment assets reached $96 trillion, a 5 percent increase from precrisis highs. Remittances from migrant workers have become an increasingly important revenue stream to the developing world—and the 2008 financial crisis did not dampen that income stream. Cross-border remittances to developing countries quickly rebounded to precrisis levels and then rose to an estimated all-time high of $372 billion in 2011, with growth rates in 2011 that exceeded those in 2010. Total cross-border remittances were more than $501 billion last year, and are estimated to reach $615 billion by 2014.[16]

Another salient outcome is mass public attitudes about the global economy. A general assumption in public opinion research is that during a downturn, demand for greater economic closure should spike, as individuals scapegoat foreigners for domestic woes. The global nature of the 2008 crisis, combined with anxiety about the shifting distribution of power, should have triggered a fall in support for an open global economy. Somewhat surprisingly, however, the reverse is true. Pew's Global Attitudes Project has surveyed a wide spectrum of countries since 2002, asking people about their opinions on both international trade and the free market more generally.[17] The results show resilient support for expanding trade and business ties with other countries. Twenty-four countries were surveyed both in 2007 and at least one year after 2008, including a majority of the G20 economies. Overall, eighteen of those twenty-four countries showed equal or greater support for trade in 2009 than two years earlier. By 2011, twenty of twenty-four countries showed greater or equal support for trade compared to 2007. Indeed, between 2007 and 2012, the unweighted average support for more trade in these countries increased from 78.5 percent to 83.6 percent. Contrary to expectation, there has been no mass public rejection of the open global economy. Indeed, public support for the open trading system has strengthened, despite softening public support for free-market economics more generally.[18]

The final outcome addresses a dog that hasn't barked: the effect of the Great Recession on cross-border conflict and violence. During the initial stages of the crisis, multiple analysts asserted that the financial crisis would lead states to increase their use of force as a tool for staying in power.[19] Whether through greater internal repression, diversionary wars, arms races, or a ratcheting up of great power conflict, there were genuine concerns that the global economic downturn would lead to an increase in conflict. Violence in the Middle East, border disputes in the South China Sea, and even the disruptions of the Occupy movement fuel impressions of surge in global public disorder.

The aggregate data suggests otherwise, however. A fundamental conclusion from a recent report by the Institute for Economics and Peace is that "the average level of peacefulness in 2012 is approximately the same as it was in 2007."[20] Interstate violence in particular has declined since the start of the financial crisis—as have military expenditures in most sampled countries. Other studies confirm that the Great Recession has not triggered any increase in violent conflict; the secular decline in violence that started with the end of the Cold War has not been reversed.[21]

None of these data suggest that the global economy is operating swimmingly. Growth remains unbalanced and fragile, and has clearly slowed in 2012. Transnational capital flows remain depressed compared to precrisis levels—primarily due to a drying up of cross-border interbank lending in Europe. Currency volatility remains an ongoing concern. Compared to the aftermath of other postwar recessions, growth in output, investment, and employment in the developed world have all lagged behind. But the Great Recession is not like other postwar recessions in either scope or kind; expecting a standard V-shaped recovery was unreasonable. One financial analyst characterizes the current global economy as in a state of "contained depression."[22] The operative word is contained, however. Given the severity, reach, and depth of the 2008 financial crisis, the proper comparison is with the Great Depression. And by that standard, the outcome variables look impressive.

Policy Outputs

It could be that the global economy has experienced a moderate bounce back in spite rather than because of the global policy response. Economists like Paul Krugman and Joseph Stiglitz have been particularly scornful of policymakers and central bankers.[23] In assessing policy outputs, Charles Kindleberger provided the classic definition of what should be done to stabilize the global economy during a severe financial crisis: "(a) maintaining a relatively open market for distress goods; (b) providing countercyclical long-term lending; and (c) discounting in crisis."[24] Serious concerns were voiced in late 2008 and early 2009 about the inability of anyone to provide these kinds of public goods, threatening a repeat of the trade protectionism and beggar-thy-neighbor policies of the 1930s.[25]

By Kindleberger's criteria, however, public goods provision has been quite robust since 2008. On the surface, the open market for distressed goods seemed under threat. The death of the Doha round, the rise of G20 protectionism after the fall 2008 summit, and the explosion of anti-dumping cases that occurred at the onset of the financial crisis suggested that markets were drifting toward closure. According to the WTO's data, anti-dumping initiations surged by 30 percent in 2008 alone. This surge quickly receded, however. Figure 8.3 shows that by 2011, antidumping initiations had declined dramatically to precrisis levels. Indeed, these cases have fallen to their lowest levels since the WTO's founding in 1995. Both countervailing duty complaints and safeguards initiations have also fallen to precrisis levels.

Some post-2008 measures aren't captured in these traditional metrics of nontariff barriers, but similar results hold. Most of those implemented measures were concentrated in countries that already possessed higher barriers to global economic integration, such as Russia and Argentina. Even including these additional measures, the combined effect of protectionist actions for the first year after the peak of the financial crisis

Figure 8.3. Trade Restrictions, 2006–2011

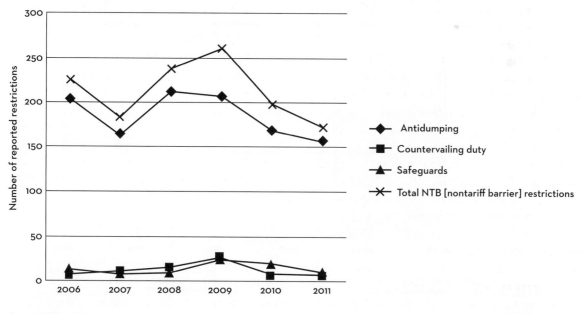

Source: WTO

affected less than 0.8 percent of global trade.[26] Furthermore, the use of these protectionist measures declined additionally in 2010 to cover only 0.2 percent of global trade. Protectionist actions rose again in 2012, but again, the effect of these measures remains modest.[27] The quick turnaround and growth in trade levels show that these measures have not seriously impeded market access.[28] In part, accelerated steps toward trade liberalization at the bilateral and regional levels have blunted the effect of these protectionist actions.

Proponents of trade liberalization embrace the bicycle theory—the belief that unless multilateral trade liberalization moves forward, the entire global trade regime will collapse because of a lack of forward momentum. The past four years suggest that there are limits to that rule of thumb. Recent surveys of global business leaders reveal that concerns about protectionism have stayed at

a low level.[29] At a minimum, the bicycle of world trade is still coasting forward at high speed.

From the earliest stages of the financial crisis, there was also concerted and coordinated action among central banks to ensure both discounting and countercyclical lending. The central banks of the major economics began cutting interest rates slowly after the fall of 2007. By the fall of 2008 they were cutting rates ruthlessly and in a coordinated fashion, as Figure 8.4 indicates. According to BIS estimates, global real interest rates fell from an average of 3 percent prior to the crisis to zero in 2012—in the advanced industrialized economies, the real interest rate was effectively negative.[30] At present, the highest interest rate among the major advanced economies is 0.75 percent, offered by the European Central Bank. Not content with lowering interest rates, most of the major central banks also expanded other credit facilities and

Figure 8.4. Major Policy Interest Rates, 2007–2012

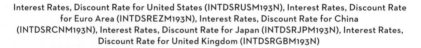

Interest Rates, Discount Rate for United States (INTDSRUSM193N), Interest Rates, Discount Rate for Euro Area (INTDSREZM193N), Interest Rates, Discount Rate for China (INTDSRCNM193N), Interest Rates, Discount Rate for Japan (INTDSRJPM193N), Interest Rates, Discount Rate for United Kingdom (INTDSRGBM193N)

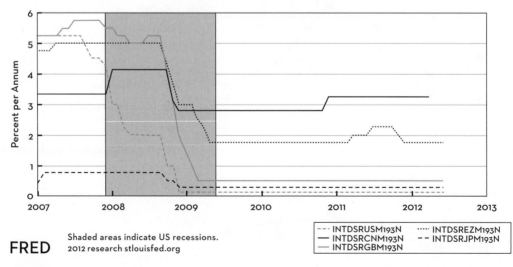

FRED   Shaded areas indicate US recessions.
        2012 research stlouisfed.org

INTDSRUSM193N   INTDSREZM193N
INTDSRCNM193N   INTDSRJPM193N
INTDSRGBM193N

Source: St. Louis Federal Reserve Bank

engaged in more creative forms of quantitative easing. Between 2007 and 2012, the balance sheets of the central banks in the advanced industrialized economies more than doubled. BIS acknowledged in its 2012 annual report that "decisive action by central banks during the global financial crisis was probably crucial in preventing a repeat of the experiences of the Great Depression."[31]

Central banks and finance ministries also took coordinated action during the fall of 2008 to try to ensure cross-border lending as to avert currency and solvency crises. In October of that year, the Group of Seven (G7) economies plus Switzerland agreed to unlimited currency swaps in order to ensure liquidity would be maintained in the system. The United States then extended its currency-swap facility to Brazil, Singapore, Mexico, and South Korea. The European Central Bank expanded its swap arrangements for euros with Hungary, Denmark, and Poland. China, Japan, South Korea, and the Association of Southeast Asian Nations (ASEAN) economics broadened the Chang Mai Initiative into an $80 billion swap arrangement to ensure liquidity. The IMF created the Short-Term Liquidity Facility designed to "establish quick-disbursing financing for countries with strong economic policies that are facing temporary liquidity problems."[32] The fund also negotiated emergency financing for Hungary, Pakistan, Iceland, and Ukraine.

Over the longer term, the great powers bulked up the resources of the international financial institutions to provide for further countercyclical lending. In 2009 the G20 agreed to triple the IMF's reserves to $750 billion. In 2012, in response to the worsening European sovereign debt crisis, G20 countries combined to pledge more than $430 billion in additional resources. The World Bank's International Development Association (IDA), which offers up the most concessionary form of lending, also increased its resources. The sixteenth IDA replenishment was a record $49.3 billion—an 18 percent increase of IDA resources from three years earlier. By Kindleberger's criteria, global economic governance worked reasonably well in response to the 2008 financial crisis.

To be sure, there exist global public goods that go beyond Kindleberger's criteria. Macroeconomic policy coordination would be an additional area of possible cooperation, as would coordinating and clarifying cross-border financial regulations. Again, however, the international system acted in these areas after 2008. Between late 2007 and the June 2010 G20 Toronto summit, the major economies agreed on the need for aggressive and expansionary fiscal and monetary policies in the wake of the financial crisis. Even reluctant contributors like Germany—whose finance minister blasted the "crass Keynesianism" of these policies in December 2008—eventually bowed to pressure from economists and G20 peers. Indeed, in 2009, Germany enacted the third-largest fiscal stimulus in the world.[33]

Progress has also been made on regulatory coordination in finance and investment rules. There were developments in two areas in particular: banking regulation and investor protectionism. In the former area, international regulators have significantly revised the Basel core banking principles. At the November 2010 Seoul summit, the G20 approved the Basel III banking standards. Basel III took only two years to negotiate—an extraordinarily brief period given that the Basel II standards took more than six years to hammer out. The new rules, scheduled to be phased in over the rest of this decade, increase the amount of reserve capital banks need to keep on hand and add additional countercyclical capital buffers to prevent financial institutions from engaging in pro-cyclical lending.

Financial sector scholars have debated whether Basel III is a sufficient upgrade in regulatory stringency and whether it will be implemented too slowly or not at all. There is consensus, however, on two points. First, Basel III clearly represents an upgrade over the Basel II standards in preventing bank failures.[34] Second, the dampening effects of the new standards on economic growth are negligible. Furthermore, these standards were approved despite fierce resistance from the global banking industry. In November 2011 the Financial Stability Board designated global systemically important banks that will be required to keep additional capital on hand, and it plans to identify global systemically important nonfinancial institutions by the end of 2012.[35]

Progress was also made in investor protectionism against state-owned enterprises and funds. The rise of sovereign wealth funds prior to 2008 had precipitated a ratcheting up of restrictions to cross-border investment by state-owned enterprises and funds. The Organization of Economic Cooperation and Development (OECD) articulated its own guidelines for recipient countries but warned that unless these funds demonstrated greater transparency, barriers to investment would likely rise even further. In September 2008 an IMF-brokered process approved a set of Generally Accepted Principles and Practices (GAPP) for sovereign wealth funds. These voluntary guidelines—also called the Santiago Principles—consisted of twenty-four guidelines addressing the legal and institutional frameworks, governance issues, and risk management of these funds. Contemporaneous press reports characterized the new rules as "a rare triumph for IMF financial diplomacy."[36] The expert consensus among financial analysts, regulators, and academics was that these principles—if fully implemented—address most recipient country concerns.[37] Since the IMF approved the Santiago Principles, furthermore, investor protectionism has declined.[38]

Institutional Resilience and Flexibility

The degree of institutional resiliency and flexibility at the global level has been rather remarkable. Once the acute phase of the 2008 financial crisis began, the G20 quickly supplanted the G7 and Group of Eight (G8) as the focal point for global economic governance. At the September 2009 G20 summit in Pittsburgh, the member countries explicitly avowed that they had "designated the G20 to be the premier forum for our international economic cooperation."[39] This move addressed the worsening problem of the G8's waning power and relevancy—a problem of which G8 members were painfully aware.[40] The G20 grouping comprises 85 percent of global economic output, 80 percent of global trade, and 66 percent of global population. The G20 is not perfectly inclusive, and it has a somewhat idiosyncratic membership at the margins, but it is a far more legitimate and representative body than the G8.[41] As Geoffrey Garrett puts it, "the G20 is globally representative yet small enough to make consensual decision-making feasible."[42] As a club of great powers, consensus within the G20 should lead to effective policy coordination across a wide range of issues.[43]

To be sure, having the capacity to be an effective body and actually *being* effective are two different things. The perception is that the G20's political momentum stalled out years ago after countries disagreed on macroeconomic imbalances and the virtues of austerity. The reality is a bit more complex. According to the University of Toronto's G20 Information Centre, compliance with G20 commitments actually increased over time. They measured G20 adherence to "chosen priority commitments." Measured on a per country average, G20 members have steadily improved since the 61.5 percent compliance rate for the April 2009 London Summit commitments, rising all the way to 77 percent for the November 2011 Cannes Summit.[44]

An obvious rejoinder is that this kind of assessment inflates compliance because the pledges made at these summits are increasingly modest.[45] It could be that the G20 has simply scaled back its ambitions—even in its "priority commitments"—making compliance easier. There are examples, however, of great powers using the G20 as a means of blunting domestic pressures for greater protectionism—at precisely the moment when the group was thought to be losing its momentum. For example, the G20 has served as a useful mechanism to defuse tensions concerning China's undervalued currency. In response to congressional pressure for more robust action, in April 2010 Treasury secretary Timothy Geithner cited the G20 meetings as "the best avenue for advancing U. S. interests" on China's manipulation of its exchange rate.[46] In June of that year, President Barack Obama sent a letter to his G20 colleagues stressing the importance of "market-determined exchange rates." Three days after the president's letter was sent, the People's Bank of China announced that it would "enhance the RMB exchange rate flexibility." For the next two years, the renminbi nominally appreciated at a rate of 5 percent a year—more so if one factors in the differences in national inflation rates.[47]

Other important financial bodies also strengthened their membership and authority as a response to the 2008 crisis. In March 2009, the Basel Committee on Banking Supervision expanded its membership from thirteen advanced industrialized states to twenty-seven countries by adding the developing country members of the G20. The Financial Stability Forum was renamed the Financial Stability Board in April 2009, was given greater responsibilities for regulatory coordination, and similarly expanded to include the developing country members of the G20 in its membership. During this period the Committee of the Global Financial System also grew in size from thirteen countries to twenty-two members, adding Brazil, China, and India, among others. The Financial Action Task Force on money laundering has added China, India, and South Korea to its grouping over the past five years. Prior to 2008, the G7 countries dominated most of these financial standard-setting agencies.[48] In terms of membership, that is no longer the case.

The International Monetary Fund and World Bank have also changed after the financial crisis, though on the surface that might not appear to be the case. The implicit compact in which a European is given the IMF managing director slot and an American the World Bank presidency has

continued over the past two years. Despite the scandals that engulfed Dominique Strauss-Kahn in 2011 and Paul Wolfowitz five years earlier, former French finance minister Christine Lagarde replaced Strauss-Kahn in 2011 and American Jim Yong Kim became the new World Bank president in 2012.

Beneath the surface, however, the bank and the fund have witnessed significant evolution. Power within the IMF is based on quota size, calculated using a complex formula of economic variables. Prior to 2007, the allotment of quotas in the IMF bore little resemblance to the distribution of economic power. This has changed. The most significant step has been two rounds of quota reform in the IMF, the first enacted in 2008 and the second to be completed by the end of this year. The explicit goal of the quota reform was to expand the voting power of advanced developing economies to better reflect the distribution of economic power. Once completed, China will possess the third-largest voting share in the fund and all four of the BRIC (Brazil, Russia, India, and China) economies will be among the ten largest shareholders in the IMF.[49] The World Bank Group underwent a parallel set of reforms. Between 2008 and 2010, the voting power of developing and transition economies within the main World Bank institution (the International Bank for Reconstruction and Development) had been increased by 4.59 percentage points, and China became the third-largest voting member. The International Finance Corporation (IFC) approved an even larger shift of 6.09 percentage points. More important, the bank's development committee agreed that bank and IFC shareholding would be reviewed every five years beginning in 2015, routinizing the process.[50]

While the appointments of Lagarde and Kim might seem retrograde, they came with political bargaining that reflected the greater influence of the advanced developing countries. In both cases, the nominee had to woo developing countries to secure political support in advance of voting. The appointment of Chinese national Min Zhu to be a deputy managing director of the IMF at the same time that Lagarde took over shows a shift in the distribution of senior-level appointments toward the advanced developing economies.

The content of the bank and fund policies has also shifted to better reflect developing country concerns. In a staff paper, the IMF acknowledged that "capital controls may be useful in addressing both macroeconomic and financial stability concerns in the face of inflow surges," a shift from the Washington consensus.[51] As for the bank, Kim's appointment to the presidency in 2012 highlights the shift in priorities. Trained as a doctor and an anthropologist, Kim's entire career has focused entirely on health policy until now. This suggests that the bank will use a more capacious notion of development going forward.

The trade and investment regimes have displayed somewhat less resiliency than global financial governance—but these regimes have not withered on the vine either. The multilateral trade regime in particular would appear to have suffered the most from the Great Recession. The collapse of the Doha round was a severe blow to the World Trade Organization. Nevertheless, the WTO as an institution has endured. Indeed, it has expanded its reach in several ways. Geographically, the WTO finally secured the accession of the Russian Federation, the last G20 nonmember, after a slow-motion, fifteen-year negotiation process. The WTO's dispute settlement mechanism helped contain the spread of protectionist measures that the Great Recession triggered. There is no evidence that compliance with these rulings has waned since 2008; the available evidence suggests that the WTO's dispute settlement arm is still playing a valuable role.[52] The WTO's Government Procurement Agreement (GPA) helped blunt the most blatant parts of the "Buy American" provisions of the 2009 fiscal stimulus, thereby preventing a cascade of fiscal protectionism. Although the GPA is only plurilateral, China is now negotiating to join the agreement. The United States, European Union, and China are also accelerating talks on a services liberalization agreement that would encompass most of the OECD economies as well as developing countries.

In truth, the Doha round had lost its momentum long before the 2007–2008 financial crisis, and it was effectively moribund before the Great Recession started. What is interesting to note is that the enthusiasm for greater trade liberalization has not lost its momentum, but rather found a new outlet: the explosion of regional and bilateral free trade agreements (FTAs). The traditional expectation that an economic downturn would dampen enthusiasm for greater openness has not been borne out by the data on FTAs. In the four years prior to the collapse of Lehman Brothers, fifty-one FTAs were reported to the World Trade Organization. In the four years since Lehman, fifty-eight free trade agreements have been registered.[53] A transpacific partnership and a transatlantic free trade zone are at preliminary stages of negotiation as well. To be sure, not all of these FTAs were created equal. Some of them have greater coverage of goods than others. Some of them might promote more trade diversion than trade creation. Nevertheless, the patterned growth of these FTAs mirrors how they spread in the late nineteenth century.[54] Although these FTAs do not possess the "most-favored nation" provision that accelerated trade liberalization in the nineteenth century, the political economy of trade diversion still generates competitive incentives for a growth in FTAs, thereby leading to a similar outcome.[55] Through their own shared understandings and dispute settlement mechanisms, they act as an additional brake on protectionist policies.[56]

There is no multilateral investment regime to display resiliency. Instead, investment is governed by a network of bilateral investment treaties (BITs). Compared to the data on free trade agreements, it would appear that the pace of BITs has slowed since 2008. According to United Nations Conference on Trade and Development (UNCTAD) data, an annual average of seventy-eight BITs were

Figure 8.5. Annual Count of Bilateral Investment Treaties, 1960–2011

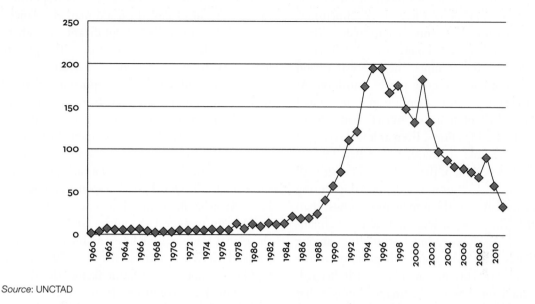

Source: UNCTAD

completed in the three years prior to 2008; only an average of sixty-one per annum were negotiated in the three years after 2008. That indicates a slowdown. A look at the series over the longer term, however, reveals that this slowdown is not surprising. As Figure 8.5 shows, the peak of BIT negotiations took place in the decade after the end of the Cold War. From 1992 to 2001, an annual average of 160 BITs were negotiated. After 2001, however, the number of negotiated BITs declined, following a standard diffusion pattern. Based on that kind of pattern of diffusion, the past three years have seen expected levels of BIT growth.

Why Has the System Worked?

Global economic governance did what was necessary during the Great Recession—but why did the system work? The precrisis observations about sclerotic international institutions and waning American power did not seem off the mark. How did these actors manage to produce the necessary policy outputs and reforms to stave off systemic collapse? The most commonly provided answer is that the shared sense of crisis spurred the major economies into joint action. The crisis mentality did not lead to sustained cooperation during the Great Depression, however. Significant postwar economic downturns—such as the end of the Bretton Woods regime, the oil shocks of the 1970s, and the failure of the European Exchange Rate Mechanism in the early 1990s—also failed to spur meaningful great power cooperation during the immediate crisis moments. What caused powerful actors to think of the 2008 crisis as a shared one?

A fuller answer will require additional research, but some tentative answers can be proffered here. Power, institutions, and ideas are among the primary building blocks of international relations theory, and each of these factors offers a partial explanation for the performance of global economic governance. Comparing the current situation with the analogous moment during the Great Depression along these three dimensions can help explain why events have unfolded differently this time around. Looking at the distribution of power, for example, the interwar period was truly a moment of great power transition. At the start of the Great Depression, the United Kingdom's lack of financial muscle badly hampered its leadership efforts. Even as it was trying to maintain the gold standard, Great Britain possessed only 4 percent of the world's gold reserves.[57]

In contrast, U.S. power and leadership during the recent crisis turned out to be more robust than expected. This was particularly true in the financial realm. Despite occasional grumblings among the BRICs, the U.S. dollar's hegemony as the world's reserve currency remains unchallenged, giving the United States the financial power that the United Kingdom lacked eight decades ago. Capital surplus countries—such as China—exaggerated the leverage they could obtain from holding large amounts of dollar-denominated reserves.[58] They rapidly discovered that U.S. dollar hegemony bound their interests to the United States on financial issues. While domestic politics might have prevented a more robust U.S. policy response, partisan gridlock did not prevent the United States from pursuing emergency rescue packages (via the 2008 Troubled Assets Relief Program), expansionary fiscal policy (via the 2009 American Recovery and Reinvestment Act), expansionary monetary policy (via interest rate cuts, two rounds of quantitative easing, and Operation Twist), and financial regulatory reform (via the Dodd-Frank Act). These deeds of U.S. leadership helped secure multilateral cooperation on macroeconomic policy coordination for two years, as well as Basel III.

Another way to demonstrate the significance of U.S. leadership is to compare and contrast the finance and trade dimensions. As just noted, U.S. power in the financial realm remained significant even after the crisis; according to the IMF, in 2010 the United States was responsible for 25 percent of global capital markets. American policy outputs were significant enough to display leadership on these issues. The picture looks very different on trade. U.S. relative power on this issue had faded: U.S. imports as a share of total world imports declined from 18.1 percent of total imports in 2001 to 12.3 percent a decade later. U.S. policy on this issue was inert.[59] The executive branch's trade promotion authority expired, and legislative demands for protectionism spiked. Not surprisingly, the global policy response on trade has been somewhat more muted than on finance.

Despite weaker U.S. power and leadership, the global trade regime has remained resilient—particularly when compared to the 1930s. This highlights another significant factor: the thicker institutional environment. There were very few multilateral economic institutions of relevance during the Great Depression. No multilateral trade regime existed, and international financial structures remained nascent. The last major effort to rewrite the global rules—the 1933 London Monetary and Economic Conference—ended in acrimony.[60] Newly inaugurated president Franklin D. Roosevelt unilaterally took the United States off the gold standard, signaling an end to any attempt at multilateral cooperation.

In contrast, the current institutional environment is much thicker, with status-quo policies focused on promoting greater economic openness. A panoply of preexisting informal and formal regimes was able to supply needed services during a time of global economic crisis. At a minimum, institutions like the G20 functioned as useful focal points for the major economies to coordinate policy responses. International institutions like the Bank of International Settlements further provided crucial expertise to rewrite the global rules of the game. Even if the Doha round petered out, the WTO's dispute settlement mechanism remained in place to coordinate and adjudicate monitoring and enforcement. Furthermore, the status-quo preference for each element of these regimes was to promote greater cross-border exchange within the rule of law. It is easier for international institutions to reinforce existing global economic norms than to devise new ones. Even if these structures were operating on autopilot, they had already been pointed in the right direction.

The final difference between the interwar era and the current day is the state of economic ideas. As the Great Depression worsened during the decade of the 1930s, there was no expert consensus about the best way to resuscitate the economy. Prominent economists like John Maynard Keynes, who had been staunch advocates of free trade a decade earlier, reversed themselves as the depression worsened. There was no agreement on the proper macroeconomic policy response to the downturn, nor was there any agreement about how to fix the broken gold standard.

There has also been a rethinking of causal beliefs after the 2008 financial crisis, but this rethink has been much less severe. Former Federal Reserve chairman Alan Greenspan made headlines when he admitted that his faith in the intellectual edifice of self-correcting markets had collapsed. As previously noted, the IMF has reversed course on the utility of temporary capital controls. Though the Washington consensus might be fraying, it has not been dissolved or replaced by a "Beijing consensus"—indeed, it is far from clear that a Beijing consensus actually exists.[61] Postcrisis surveys of leading economists suggest that a powerful consensus remains on several essential international policy dimensions. For example, the University of Chicago has run an economic experts panel for the past few years. The survey results show a strong consensus on the virtues of freer trade and a rejection of returning to the gold standard to regulate international exchange rates. On the other hand, there is much less consensus on monetary policy and the benefits of further quantitative easing.[62] This absence of agreement reflects a much greater policy debate on

the subject, helping to explain why macroeconomic policy coordination has been less robust.

Why the Misperception?

Why is there such a profound gap between perceptions and reality in evaluating the performance of multilateral economic institutions? The simplest explanation is that the core economies—the advanced industrialized democracies—have not rebounded as vigorously as expected. Two trends have marked most postwar global business cycles: economies rebound as vigorously as they drop, and the advanced industrialized states suffer less than the economic periphery. Neither of these trends has held during the Great Recession. As previously noted, the recovery from a financial crisis tends to be longer and slower than standard business-cycle recessions. After the 2008 financial crisis, the recovery has been particularly weak in the advanced industrialized economies. According to the Economist Intelligence Unit, the OECD economies have averaged GDP growth of 0.5 percent between 2008 and 2012. The non-OECD economies have averaged 5.2 percent during the same period. A weak economy feeds perceptions of institutional breakdown. The 2012 Edelman Trust Barometer reflects this phenomenon; contrary to traditional numbers, trust of elite institutions is significantly higher among developing countries than in the developed democracies.[63] Since most analyses of global governance structures have been anchored in the developed world, it is not surprising that this literature suffers from a pessimistic bias.

Pessimism about current economic conditions in the developed world might also be causing analysts to conflate poor domestic and regional governance with poor global governance. The primary causes for domestic economic weakness in the United States, Europe, and Japan are not global in origin—and neither are the best policy responses, Japan's current economic woes are a function of two decades of slack economic growth combined with the aftereffects of the Fukushima disaster. American economic misfortunes have little to do with either the global economy or global economic governance. Indeed, the United States has benefited from the current state of international affairs through lower borrowing costs and higher exports. Domestic political deadlock and uncertainty, on the other hand, have contributed to the anemic U.S. recovery. Already, concerns about the coming fiscal cliff have dampened economic activity.[64] Eroding policy consensus within the Federal Reserve has not helped either. Without more expansionary fiscal and monetary policies, it will take even longer for the necessary private-sector deleveraging to play itself out.

Europe's situation is more complex. To be sure, the Great Recession was the trigger for the eurozone's sovereign debt crisis. The international response to the crisis has been that of a modest supporting role. The IMF has proffered both its technical expertise and financial support in excess of $100 billion to Greece, Portugal, and Ireland. The United States and other major economies have offered to reopen swap lines with the European Central Bank to ensure liquidity. European and national policy responses to the crisis, however, have badly exacerbated the economic situation. Greece's reckless precrisis levels of government spending and borrowing made that economy a ripe target for market pessimism. The initial European bailout package for Greece was woefully inadequate, allowing the crisis to fester. The austerity policies advocated in some quarters have not panned out as expected. The European Central Bank's decision to prematurely raise interest rates in early 2010 helped stall out the nascent recovery on the continent. On the fiscal side of the equation, austerity-related policies have led to a double-dip recession in Great Britain, higher borrowing costs in Spain and Italy, and continued uncertainty about the future of the euro. Europe's fiscal and monetary policies have been less expansionary than in the United States. This, in turn,

has prevented any appreciable private-sector deleveraging in Europe, thereby guaranteeing a longer downturn before any sustained recovery is possible.[65]

The IMF has come under criticism for failing to exert more influence over the eurozone crisis. One official recently resigned, blasting the fund for its European bias and the consensus culture that keeps it from criticizing countries in the middle of lending programs. There are two counterpoints to this argument, however. First, the IMF *has* been critical at various moments during the eurozone crisis. Fund staff issued warnings about the health of the European banks in August 2011, and IMF managing director Lagarde called explicitly for debt sharing among the eurozone in June 2012.[66] The first criticism received significant pushback from the European Central Bank and eurozone governments, and Germany ignored the second criticism. This leads to the second point: it is highly unlikely that national governments would feel compelled to respond to IMF criticism in the absence of a market response. The fund must walk a tightrope between transparent criticism and setting off market panic. This is hardly an ideal vantage point for strong-arming governments with sizable IMF quotas.

A final reason for misperception about global economic governance is exaggerated nostalgia for the past eras of global economic governance. The presumption in much of the commentary on the current global political economy is that both governance structures and hegemonic leadership were better and stronger in the past. Much of this commentary evokes the 1940s, when the creation of the Bretton Woods institutions, backstopped by the United States, ushered in a new era of global governance. The contrast between U.S. leadership then and now seems stark.

This comparison elides some inconvenient facts, however. The late 1940s were indeed the acme of American hegemonic leadership. Even during that peak, however, the United States failed to ratify the Havana Charter that would have created an

International Trade Organization with wider scope than the current WTO. With the Marshall Plan, the United States decided to act outside the purview of Bretton Woods institutions, weakening their influence. After the late forties, American leadership and global financial governance experienced as many misses as hits. The logic of the Bretton Woods system rested on an economic contradiction that became known as the Triffin dilemma. Extravagant macroeconomic policies in the United States, combined with a growing reluctance to accommodate the U.S. position, eroded that global financial order. As the logical contradictions of the Bretton Woods regime became more evident, existing policy coordination mechanisms failed to correct the problem. By 1971, when the United States unilaterally decided to close the gold window, all of the major economies had chosen to ameliorate domestic interests rather than coordinate action at the global level.[67] In ending Bretton Woods, the United States also undercut the IMF's original purpose for existence.

Post–Bretton Woods global economic governance was equally haphazard. An increase in antidumping, countervailing duties, and nontariff barriers weakened the rules of the global trading system over the next two decades. Neither the United States nor any global governance structure was able to prevent the Organization of the Petroleum Exporting Countries (OPEC) from raising energy prices from 1973 to 1986.[68] Exchange rates and macroeconomic policy coordination devolved from the IMF to the G7. A predictable cycle emerged: other G7 countries would pressure the United States to scale back its fiscal deficits. In turn, the United States would pressure Japan and West Germany to expand their domestic consumption in order to act as locomotives of growth. Not surprisingly, the most common outcome on the macroeconomic front was a stalemate.[69]

Even perceived successes in macroeconomic policy coordination have had mixed results. The 1985 Plaza Accord helped depreciate the value of the dollar while allowing the yen to rise in value, but it was also the beginning of an unsustainable asset bubble in Japan. In Europe, the creation of the euro would seem to count as an example of successful coordination. The Growth and Stability Pact that was attached to the creation of the common European currency, however, was less successful. Within a year of the euro's birth, five of the eleven member countries were not in compliance; by 2005, the three largest countries in the eurozone were ignoring the pact.[70] Regardless of the distribution of power or the robustness of international institutions, the history of macroeconomic policy coordination is not a distinguished one.[71]

None of this is to deny that global economic governance was useful and stabilizing at various points after 1945. Rather, it is to observe that even during the heyday of American hegemony, the ability of global economic governance to solve ongoing global economic problems was limited.[72] The original point of Kindleberger's analysis of the Great Depression was to discuss what needed to be done during a global economic crisis. By that standard, the post-2008 performance of vital institutions has been far better than extant commentary suggests. Expecting more than an effective crisis response might be unrealistic.

Conclusion

Five years ago, there were rampant fears that waning American power would paralyze global economic regimes. The crisis of the Great Recession exacerbated those fears even further. A review of policy outcomes, policy outputs, and institutional resilience shows a different picture. Global trade and investment levels have recovered from the plunge that occurred in late 2008. A mélange of international coordination mechanisms facilitated the provision of policy outputs from 2008 onward. Existing global governance structures, particularly in finance, have revamped themselves to accommodate shifts in the distribution of power. The World Economic Forum's survey of global experts shows rising confidence in global governance and global cooperation.[73] The evidence suggests that global governance structures adapted and responded to the 2008 financial crisis in a robust fashion. They passed the stress test. The picture presented here is at odds with prevailing conventional wisdom on this subject.

This does not mean that global economic governance will continue to function effectively going forward. It is worth remembering that there were genuine efforts to provide global public goods in 1929 as well, but they eventually fizzled out. The failure of the major economies to assist Austria after the Credit Anstalt bank crashed in 1931 led to a cascade of bank failures across Europe and the United States. The collapse of the 1933 London conference guaranteed an ongoing absence of policy coordination for the next several years.

The start of the Great Depression was bad. International policy coordination failures made it worse. Such a scenario could play out again. There is no shortage of latent or ongoing crises that could lead to a serious breakdown in global economic governance. The IMF's reluctance to take more critical actions to address the curozone crisis have already prompted one angry resignation letter from an IMF staffer. The summer 2012 drought in the midwestern United States could trigger another spike in food prices. The heated protectionist rhetoric of the 2012 presidential campaign in the United States, or the nationalist rhetoric accompanying China's 2012 leadership transition, could spark a Sino-American trade war. If global economic growth continues to be mediocre, the surprising effectiveness of global economic governance could peter out. Incipient signs of backsliding in the WTO and G20 might mushroom into a true "G-Zero" world.[74]

It is equally possible, however, that a renewed crisis would trigger a renewed surge in policy coordination. As scholar G. John Ikenberry has observed, "the complex interdependence that is unleashed in an open and loosely rule-based order generates some expanding realms of exchange and investment that result in a growing array of firms, interest groups and other sorts of political stakeholders who seek to preserve the stability and openness of the system."[75] The post-2008 economic order has remained open, entrenching these interests even more across the globe. Despite uncertain times, the open economic system that has been in operation since 1945 does not appear to be closing anytime soon.

NOTES

1. Barry Eichengreen and Kevin O'Rourke, "A tale of two depressions," VoxEU.org, March 8, 2010, http://www.voxeu.org/index.php?q=node/3421.

2. Carmen Reinhart and Kenneth Rogoff, *This Time Is Different: Eight Centuries of Financial Folly* (Princeton: Princeton University Press, 2009), p. 226.

3. Charles Roxburgh, Susan Lund, and John Piotrowski, *Mapping global capital markets 2011*, McKinsey Global Institute, August 2011. An Asian Development Bank report also estimates the 2008 decline in asset values to have been twice as large. See Claudio Loser, "Global Financial Turmoil and Emerging Market Economies," Asian Development Bank, March 2009, p. 7.

4. *The Financial and Economic Crisis: A Decent Work Response* (Geneva: International Labour Organization, 2009), p. v.

5. See, for example, the *Financial Times-Economist* Business Barometer, August 2012.

6. See, for example, Richard Samans, Klaus Schwab, and Mark Malloch-Brown, "Running the World, After the Crash," *Foreign Policy* 184 (January/February 2011), pp. 80–83. See also Lee Howell, "The Failure of Governance in a Hyperconnected World," *New York Times*, January 10, 2012.

7. These are by no means the only facts mentioned when talking about the perceived failure of global economic governance. Other examples include the PBOC chairman's March 2009 call for a "supersovereign currency" to replace the dollar, the failure of the Copenhagen climate change summit in December 2009, and the continuation of the norm whereby a European heads the IMF and an American helms the World Bank. Quite often haplessness at the United Nations is also cited as evidence of the failure of global governance more generally.

8. Elisa Gamberoni and Richard Newfarmer, "Trade Protection: Incipient but Worrisome Trends," World Bank Trade Note No. 37, March 2, 2009.

9. Susan Schwab, "After Doha," *Foreign Affairs*, vol. 90, May/June 2011.

10. Carmen Reinhart and Kenneth Rogoff, "The Aftermath of Financial Crises," in Reinhart and Rogoff, *This Time Is Different: Eight Centuries of Financial Folly* (Princeton: Princeton University Press, 2009); Claessens, Kose, and Terrones, "Financial Cycles: What? How? When?" IMF Working Paper 11/76, April 2011;

Carmen Reinhart and Vincent Reinhart, "After the Fall," NBER Working Paper No. 16334, September 2010; Barry Eichengreen, "Crisis and Growth in the Advanced Economies: What We Know, What We Don't Know, and What We Can Learn from the 1930s," *Comparative Economic Studies* 53 (March 2011), pp. 383–406.

11. Eichengreen and O'Rourke, "A tale of two depressions"; Eichengreen and O'Rourke, "A tale of two depressions redux," VoxEU.org, March 6, 2012, http://www.voxeu.org/article/tale-two-depressions-redux.

12. *World Development Indicators*, World Bank, July 9, 2012.

13. Ibid. See also Shaochua Chen and Martin Rayallion, "An update to the World Bank's Estimate of consumption poverty in the developing world," March 1, 2012; Annie Lowrey, "Dire Poverty Falls Despite Global Slump, Report Finds," *New York Times*, March 6, 2012.

14. Data in this paragraph comes from Eichengreen and O'Rourke, "A tale of two depressions redux."

15. Dinah Walker, "Quarterly Update: The Economic Recovery in Historical Context," Council on Foreign Relations, August 13, 2012.

16. For FDI data, see the OECD/UNCTAD report "Seventh report on G20 investment measures," July 2012. For foreign investment assets, sec Roxburgh, Lund, and Piotrowski, *Mapping Global Capital Markets 2011*, p. 31. For remittance flows, see Dilip Ratha and Ani Silwal, "Remittances flows in 2011: An Update," *Migration and Development Brief* 18, World Bank, April 23, 2012.

17. See data gathered by the Pew Global Attitudes Project, Pew Research Center, 2012, http://www.pewglobal.org/database/?indicator=16&survey=13 &response=Good&20thing&mode=table.

18. On the latter, see data gathered by the Pew Global Attitudes Project, Pew Research Center, 2012, http://www.pewglobal.org/database/?indicator=18 &survey=12&response=Agree&mode=table.

19. See, for example, Paul Rogers, "The Tipping Point?" Oxford Research Group, November 2008; Joshua Kurlantzick, "The World is Bumpy," *New Republic*, July 15, 2009; Rogers Brubaker, "Economic Crisis, Nationalism, and Politicized Ethnicity," in Craig Calhoun and Georgi Derlugian, eds., *The Deepening Crisis: Governance Challenges After Neoliberalism* (New York: New York University Press, 2011), p. 93.

20. Institute for Economics and Peace, *Global Peace Index 2012*, June 2012, p. 37.

21. See, for example, the Human Security Report Project, *Human Security Report 2009/2010: The Causes of Peace and the Shrinking Costs of War* (New York: Oxford University Press, 2010).

22. David Levy, "The Contained Depression," Jerome Levy Forecasting Center, April 2012.

23. Paul Krugman, *End This Depression Now!* (New York: W. W. Norton, 2012); Joseph Stiglitz, *The Price of Inequality* (New York: W. W. Norton, 2012).

24. Kindleberger, *The World In Depression*, 292.

25. "The Return of Economic Nationalism," *Economist*, February 5, 2009; Kurlantzick, "The World is Bumpy"; Michael Sesit, "Smoot-Hawley's Ghost Appears as Economy Tanks," *Bloomberg News*, February 19, 2009; Rawi Abdelal and Adam Segal, "Yes, Globalization Passed Its Peak," ForeignAffairs.com, March 17, 2009.

26. Uri Dadush, Shimelse Ali, and Rachel Esplin Odell, "Is Protectionism Dying?" Carnegie Papers in International Economics, May 2011. Furthermore, while these measures are undeniably restrictive in nature, a case can be made that they represent a form of "efficient protectionism": small and symbolic measures that mollify protectionist constituencies in exchange for preserving and strengthening the overall level of economic openness. See C. Fred Bergsten, "A Renaissance for U.S. Trade Policy?" *Foreign Affairs*, vol. 81, November/December 2002.

27. See Simon Evenett, "Débacle," VoxEU.org, June 14, 2012. As a counter, however, see also Chad Bown, "Import Protection Update," VoxEU.org. August 18, 2012.

28. Dadush, Ali, and Odell, "Is Protectionism Dying?"; Matthieu Bussiere, Emilia Perez-Barreiro, Roland Straub, and Daria Taglioni, "Protectionist Responses to the Crisis: Global Trends and Implications," *World Economy*, vol. 34, May 2011.

29. Between May 2011 and August 2012, a maximum of 13 percent of business executives cited trade protectionism as a serious concern. See the *Financial Times-Economist* Business Barometer, http://www.ft.com/intl/cms/s/0/2648032c-c78d-1IeI-8686-00144feab49a.html#axzz23kj5DEaP.

30. Bank of International Settlements, *82nd Annual Report*, June 24, 2012, p. 39.

31. Ibid., p. 41.

32. "IMF Creates Short-Term Liquidity Facility for Market-Access Countries," IMF Press Release No. 08/262, October 29, 2008.

33. Eswar Prasad and Isaac Sorkin, "Assessing the G-20 Stimulus Plans: A Deeper Look," Brookings Institution, March 2009.

34. Adrian Blundell-Wignall and Paul Atkinson, "Thinking Beyond Basel III: Necessary Solutions for Capital and Liquidity," *OECD Journal: Financial Market Trends*, vol. 1, 2010; Nicolas Verou, "Financial Reform after the Crisis: An Early Assessment," Peterson Institute for International Economics Working Paper 12–2, January 2012.

35. It should be noted that some scholars have questioned whether the FSB has the capability and flexibility to impose more rigorous standards on the global financial system. See Stephany Griffith-Jones, Eric Helleiner, and Ngaire Woods, eds., *The Financial Stability Board: An Effective Fourth Pillar of Global Economic Governance?* (Waterloo: Centre for International Governance Innovation, June 2010).

36. Bob Davis, "Foreign Funds Agree to Set of Guiding Principles," *Wall Street Journal*, September 3, 2008.

37. *Minding the GAPP: Sovereign wealth, transparency and the "Santiago Principles,"* Deloitte Touche Tohmatsu, October 2008; Edward Truman, "Making the World Safe for Sovereign Wealth Funds," *Real Time Economic Issues Watch*, October 14, 2008; Cohen and DeLong, *The End of Influence*, p. 89.

38. OECD/UNCTAD, "Seventh Report on G20 investment measures."

39. "G20 to become main economic forum," al-Jazeera, September 28, 2009, http://www.aljazeera.com/news/americas/2009/09/20099252124936203.html.

40. Mark Sobel and Louellen Stedman, "The Evolution of the G-7 and Economic Policy Coordination," U.S. Treasury Department Occasional Paper No. 3, July 2006; Drezner, "The New New World Order," *Foreign Affairs*, vol. 86, March/April 2007.

41. The G20 also has no treaty status or permanent secretariat, but there are theoretical arguments in favor of this informal status. See, for

example, Charles Lipson, "Why are some international agreements informal?" *International Organization*, vol. 45, September 1991.

42. Geoffrey Garrett, "G2 in G20: China, the United States, and the World after the Global Financial Crisis," *Global Policy*, vol. 1, January 2010, p. 29.

43. Daniel W. Drezner, *All Politics is Global: Explaining International Regulatory Regimes* (Princeton: Princeton University Press, 2007).

44. *2011 Cannes G20 Summit Final Compliance Report*, G20 Information Centre, p. 12.

45. George Downs, David Rocke, and Peter Barsoom, "Is the Good News About Compliance Good News About Cooperation?" *International Organization*, vol. 50, June 1996.

46. "Geithner Statement on Delay of Report on China Currency Policies," Real Time Economics, *Wall Street Journal*, April 3, 2010, http://blogs.wsj.com/economics/2010/04/03/geithner-statement-on -delay-of-report-on-china-currency-policies/.

47. David Leonhardt, "As U.S. Currency Rises, U.S. Keeps Up the Pressure," *New York Times*, February 15, 2012. It should be noted, however, that the yuan has depreciated against the dollar for much of 2012.

48. Daniel W. Drezner, "Club Standards and International Finance," in Daniel W. Drezner, *All Politics Is Global.*

49. For more on IMF quota reform, see "IMF Quotas," International Monetary Fund, August 24, 2012.

50. "World Bank Group Reform: An Update," World Bank Group Development Committee, September 30, 2010.

51. Jonathan D. Ostry, Atish R. Ghosh, Karl Habermeier, Marcos Chamon, Mahvash S. Qureshi, and Dennis B.S. Reinhardt, "Capital Inflows: The Role of Controls," IMF Staff Position Note SPN/10/04, International Monetary Fund, February 19, 2010.

52. Alan Beattie, "Decommission the weapons of trade warfare," *Financial Times*, August 8, 2012.

53. "Regional Trade Agreements Information System," World Trade Organization, August 27, 2012, http://rtais.wto.org/UI/Public PreDefRepByEIF.aspx.

54. David Lazer, "The Free Trade Epidemic of the 1860s and Other Outbreaks of Economic Discrimination," *World Politics*, vol. 51, July 1999.

55. See Daniel W. Drezner, *U.S. Trade Strategy: Free Versus Fair?* (New York: Council on Foreign Relations Press, 2006), pp. 71–92, for more on this dynamic.

56. Dadush et al., "Is Protectionism Dying?" pp. 8–9.

57. Jeffry Frieden, "The established order collapses," in Jeffry Frieden, *Global Capitalism: Its Fall and Rise in the Twentieth Century* (New York: W. W. Norton, 2006); Liquat Ahamed, *Lords of Finance: The Bankers Who Broke The World* (New York Penguin, 2009).

58. The arguments in this paragraph draw from Daniel W. Drezner, "Bad Debts: Assessing China's Financial Influence in Great Power Politics," *International Security*, vol. 34, Fall 2009; and Daniel W. Drezner, "Will Currency Follow the Flag?" *International Relations of the Asia-Pacific*, vol. 10, September 2010.

59. Data from WTO: http://stat.wto.org/StatisticalProgram/WSDBStat ProgramHome.aspx, accessed August 2012.

60. Herbert Feis, *1933: Characters in Crisis* (Boston: Little Brown and Company, 1966).

61. Matt Ferchen, "Whose China Model is it Anyway? The contentious search for consensus," *Review of International Political Economy*, forthcoming.

62. On the gold standard and free trade, see "Gold Standard," IGM Forum, University of Chicago Booth School of Business, January 12, 2012; and "Free Trade," IGM Forum, University of Chicago Booth School of Business, March 13, 2012. On monetary policy, see "Monetary Policy," IGM Forum, University of Chicago Booth School of Business, September 29, 2011. For further evidence of the absence of consensus on monetary policy, compare Martin Wolf, "We still have that sinking feeling," *Financial Times*, July 10, 2012, with Mohamed El-Erian, "Central Bankers Can't Save the World," *Bloomberg View*, August 2, 2012. See also Joe Weisenthal, "The Biggest Tragedy in Economics," *Business Insider*, September 7, 2012.

63. Data from the Edelman Trust Barometer can be accessed at http:// trust.edelman.com/trust-download/global-results/.

64. Nelson D. Schwartz, "Fearing an Impasse in Congress, Industry Cuts Spending," *New York Times*, August 5, 2012.

65. Reinhart and Rogoff, *This Time Is Different*; Charles Roxburgh, Susan Lund, Toos Daruvala, James Manyika, Richard Dobbs, Ramon Forn, and Karen Croxson, *Debt and Deleveraging: Uneven Progress on the Path to Growth*, McKinsey Global Institute, January 2012.

66. Alan Beattie and Chris Giles, "IMF and curozone clash over estimates," *Financial Times*, August 31, 2011; James Kanter, "IMF Urges Europe's Strongest to Shoulder Burdens of Currency Bloc," *New York Times*, June 21, 2012.

67. Joanne Gowa, *Closing the Gold Window: Domestic Politics and the End of Bretton Woods* (Ithaca: Cornell University Press, 1984).

68. Robert Keohane, "Theory of Hegemonic Stability and Changes in International Economic Regimes, 1967–1977," in Ole Holsti, Randolph Siverson, and Alexander George, eds., *Change in the International System* (Boulder: Westview Press, 1980), pp. 131–62.

69. Robert Putnam and Nicholas Bayne, *Hanging Together: Cooperation and Conflict in the Seven-Power Summits* (Cambridge: Harvard University Press, 1987); David M. Andrews, ed., *International Monetary Power* (Ithaca: Cornell University Press, 2005).

70. Kathryn Dominguez, "The European Central Bank, the Euro, and Global Financial Markets," *Journal of Economic Perspectives*, vol. 20, Fall 2006.

71. Thomas Willett, "Developments in the Political Economy of Policy Coordination," *Open Economies Review*, vol. 10, May 1999.

72. This parallels the recent argument by Robert Kagan that people exaggerate the effectiveness of American hegemony in the past as well. Robert Kagan, *The World America Made* (New York: Knopf, 2012).

73. "Global Confidence Index," World Economic Forum, August 22, 2012, http://www.weforum.org/content/pages/global-confidence -index.

74. Ian Bremmer and Nouriel Roubini, "A G-Zero World," *Foreign Affairs*, vol. 90, March/April 2011; Ian Bremmer, *Every Nation for Itself* (New York: Portfolio/Penguin, 2012).

75. G. John Ikenberry, *Liberal Leviathan* (Princeton: Princeton University Press, 2011), p. 340.

9 INTERGOVERNMENTAL ORGANIZATIONS AND NONGOVERNMENTAL ORGANIZATIONS

International organizations such as the United Nations (UN) are major actors in international relations. Samantha Power argued in her Pulitzer Prize–winning book *A Problem from Hell* (2002), as excerpted here from *The Atlantic*, that one of the key tasks of international organizations and powerful states should be to prevent massive atrocities. This policy objective, called the "responsibility to protect," or R2P, has subsequently been formally adopted by the United Nations. Power explains why neither the UN nor the United States did more to stop the 1994 genocide in Rwanda. Despite the adoption of R2P, some of her explanations still resonate in light of the international community's more recent failure to intervene to stop atrocities in the Syrian civil war.

What explains how international institutions facilitate cooperation more generally? Robert O. Keohane, in his highly influential book *After Hegemony: Cooperation and Discord in the World Political Economy* (1984), lays out the theory of liberal institutionalism to explain how such institutions make cooperation possible despite the absence of a sovereign enforcement power standing above states. He explains that international institutions (or "international regimes") establish rules around which expectations converge. Rules reduce the costs of transactions, facilitate bargaining across different issue areas, and provide information that reduces the risk of cheating. By way of contrast, John J. Mearsheimer, the quintessential realist, is skeptical about the impact of international institutions. He delineates the flaws of liberal institutionalist theory, arguing that international institutions exert no independent influence of their own because they simply reflect the underlying power and interests of states.

In addition to intergovernmental organizations (IGOs) and international law, research on nongovernmental organizations (NGOs), social movements, and transnational advocacy networks has expanded since the 1990s. Using a constructivist approach, Margaret E. Keck and Kathryn Sikkink, in an excerpt from their award-winning book *Activists beyond Borders: Advocacy Networks in International Politics* (1998), show how such networks develop by "building new links among actors in civil societies, states, and international organizations."

Finally, Michael N. Barnett and Martha Finnemore draw on constructivism to study the "pathologies" of international organizations that can lead to unintended consequences. Erik Voeten explains the often misunderstood nature of deliberations in the United Nations Security Council. Its task is not mainly to apply international law to disputes or to bring specialized technical or analytic expertise to political problem solving. Rather, says Voeten, the value and effectiveness of the Security Council is as a venue for forging a broader consensus around major powers' desired projects for regional security and interventions, stipulating acceptable limits on goals and means.

Samantha Power

BYSTANDERS TO GENOCIDE
Why the United States Let the Rwandan Tragedy Happen

I. People Sitting in Offices

In the course of a hundred days in 1994 the Hutu government of Rwanda and its extremist allies very nearly succeeded in exterminating the country's Tutsi minority. Using firearms, machetes, and a variety of garden implements, Hutu militiamen, soldiers, and ordinary citizens murdered some 800,000 Tutsi and politically moderate Hutu. It was the fastest, most efficient killing spree of the twentieth century.

A few years later, in a series in *The New Yorker*, Philip Gourevitch recounted in horrific detail the story of the genocide and the world's failure to stop it. President Bill Clinton, a famously avid reader, expressed shock. He sent copies of Gourevitch's articles to his second-term national-security adviser, Sandy Berger. The articles bore confused, angry, searching queries in the margins. "Is what he's saying true?" Clinton wrote with a thick black felt-tip pen beside heavily underlined paragraphs. "How did this happen?" he asked, adding, "I want to get to the bottom of this." The President's urgency and outrage were oddly timed. As the terror in Rwanda had unfolded, Clinton had shown virtually no interest in stopping the genocide, and his Administration had stood by as the death toll rose into the hundreds of thousands.

Why did the United States not do more for the Rwandans at the time of the killings? Did the President really not know about the genocide, as his marginalia suggested? Who were the people in his Administration who made the life-and-death decisions that dictated U.S. policy? Why did they decide (or decide not to decide) as they did? Were any voices inside or outside the U.S. government demanding that the United States do more? If so, why weren't they heeded? And most crucial, what could the United States have done to save lives?

So far people have explained the U.S. failure to respond to the Rwandan genocide by claiming that the United States didn't know what was happening, that it knew but didn't care, or that regardless of what it knew there was nothing useful to be done. The account that follows is based on a three-year investigation involving sixty interviews with senior, mid-level, and junior State Department, Defense Department, and National Security Council officials who helped to shape or inform U.S. policy. It also reflects dozens of interviews with Rwandan, European, and United Nations officials and with peacekeepers, journalists, and nongovernmental workers in Rwanda. Thanks to the National Security Archive (www.nsarchive.org), a nonprofit organization that uses the Freedom of Information Act to secure the release of classified U.S. documents, this account also draws on hundreds of pages of newly available government records. This material provides a clearer picture than was previously possible of the interplay among people, motives, and events. It reveals that the U.S. government knew enough about the genocide early on to save lives, but passed up countless opportunities to intervene.

From *The Atlantic* (Sept. 2001), 84–108.

In March of 1998, on a visit to Rwanda, President Clinton issued what would later be known as the "Clinton apology," which was actually a carefully hedged acknowledgment. He spoke to the crowd assembled on the tarmac at Kigali Airport: "We come here today partly in recognition of the fact that we in the United States and the world community did not do as much as we could have and should have done to try to limit what occurred" in Rwanda.

This implied that the United States had done a good deal but not quite enough. In reality the United States did much more than fail to send troops. It led a successful effort to remove most of the UN peacekeepers who were already in Rwanda. It aggressively worked to block the subsequent authorization of UN reinforcements. It refused to use its technology to jam radio broadcasts that were a crucial instrument in the coordination and perpetuation of the genocide. And even as, on average, 8,000 Rwandans were being butchered each day, U.S. officials shunned the term "genocide," for fear of being obliged to act. The United States in fact did virtually nothing "to try to limit what occurred." Indeed, staying out of Rwanda was an explicit U.S. policy objective.

With the grace of one grown practiced at public remorse, the President gripped the lectern with both hands and looked across the dais at the Rwandan officials and survivors who surrounded him. Making eye contact and shaking his head, he explained, "It may seem strange to you here, especially the many of you who lost members of your family, but all over the world there were people like me sitting in offices, day after day after day, who *did not fully appreciate* [pause] the depth [pause] and the speed [pause] with which you were being engulfed by this *unimaginable* terror."

Clinton chose his words with characteristic care. It was true that although top U.S. officials could not help knowing the basic facts—thousands of Rwandans were dying every day—that were being reported in the morning papers, many did not

"fully appreciate" the meaning. In the first three weeks of the genocide the most influential American policymakers portrayed (and, they insist, perceived) the deaths not as astrocities or the components and symptoms of genocide but as wartime "casualties"—the deaths of combatants or those caught between them in a civil war.

Yet this formulation avoids the critical issue of whether Clinton and his close advisers might reasonably have been expected to "fully appreciate" the true dimensions and nature of the massacres. During the first three days of the killings U.S. diplomats in Rwanda reported back to Washington that well-armed extremists were intent on eliminating the Tutsi. And the American press spoke of the door-to-door hunting of unarmed civilians. By the end of the second week informed nongovernmental groups had already begun to call on the Administration to use the term "genocide," causing diplomats and lawyers at the State Department to begin debating the word's applicability soon thereafter. In order not to appreciate that genocide or something close to it was under way, U.S. officials had to ignore public reports and internal intelligence and debate.

The story of U.S. policy during the genocide in Rwanda is not a story of willful complicity with evil. U.S. officials did not sit around and conspire to allow genocide to happen. But whatever their convictions about "never again," many of them did sit around, and they most certainly did allow genocide to happen. In examining how and why the United States failed Rwanda, we see that without strong leadership the system will incline toward risk-averse policy choices. We also see that with the possibility of deploying U.S. troops to Rwanda taken off the table early on—and with crises elsewhere in the world unfolding—the slaughter never received the top-level attention it deserved. Domestic political forces that might have pressed for action were absent. And most U.S. officials opposed to American involvement in Rwanda were firmly convinced that they were doing all they could—and, most important, all they *should*—in light of competing American interests and a highly circumscribed understanding of what was "possible" for the United States to do.

One of the most thoughtful analyses of how the American system can remain predicated on the noblest of values while allowing the vilest of crimes was offered in 1971 by a brilliant and earnest young foreign-service officer who had just resigned from the National Security Council to protest the 1970 U.S. invasion of Cambodia. In an article in *Foreign Policy*, "The Human Reality of Realpolitik," he and a colleague analyzed the process whereby American policymakers with moral sensibilities could have waged a war of such immoral consequence as the one in Vietnam. They wrote,

> The answer to that question begins with a basic intellectual approach which views foreign policy as a lifeless, bloodless set of abstractions. "Nations," "interests," "influence," "prestige"—all are disembodied and dehumanized terms which encourage easy inattention to the real people whose lives our decisions affect or even end.

Policy analysis excluded discussion of human consequences. "It simply is not *done*," the authors wrote. "Policy—good, steady policy—is made by the 'tough-minded.' To talk of suffering is to lose 'effectiveness,' almost to lose one's grip. It is seen as a sign that one's 'rational' arguments are weak."

In 1994, fifty years after the Holocaust and twenty years after America's retreat from Vietnam, it was possible to believe that the system had changed and that talk of human consequences had become admissible. Indeed, when the machetes were raised in Central Africa, the White House official primarily responsible for the shaping of U.S. foreign policy was one of the authors of that 1971 critique: Anthony Lake, President Clinton's first-term national-security adviser. The genocide in Rwanda presented Lake and the rest of the Clinton team with an opportunity to prove that "good, steady policy" could be made in the interest of saving lives.

II. The Peacekeepers

Rwanda was a test for another man as well: Romeo Dallaire, then a major general in the Canadian army who at the time of the genocide was the commander of the UN Assistance Mission in Rwanda. If ever there was a peacekeeper who believed wholeheartedly in the promise of humanitarian action, it was Dallaire. A broad-shouldered French-Canadian with deep-set sky-blue eyes, Dallaire has the thick, calloused hands of one brought up in a culture that prizes soldiering, service, and sacrifice. He saw the United Nations as the embodiment of all three.

Before his posting to Rwanda Dallaire had served as the commandant of an army brigade that sent peacekeeping battalions to Cambodia and Bosnia, but he had never seen actual combat himself. "I was like a fireman who has never been to a fire, but has dreamed for years about how he would fare when the fire came," the fifty-five-year-old Dallaire recalls. When, in the summer of 1993, he received the phone call from UN headquarters offering him the Rwanda posting, he was ecstatic. "It was answering the aim of my life," he says. "It's *all* you've been waiting for."

Dallaire was sent to command a UN force that would help to keep the peace in Rwanda, a nation the size of Vermont, which was known as "the land of a thousand hills" for its rolling terrain. Before Rwanda achieved independence from Belgium, in 1962, the Tutsi, who made up 15 percent of the populace, had enjoyed a privileged status. But independence ushered in three decades of Hutu rule, under which Tutsi were systematically discriminated against and periodically subjected to waves of killing and ethnic cleansing. In 1990 a group of armed exiles, mainly Tutsi, who had been clustered on the Ugandan border, invaded

Rwanda. Over the next several years the rebels, known as the Rwandan Patriotic Front, gained ground against Hutu government forces. In 1993 Tanzania brokered peace talks, which resulted in a power-sharing agreement known as the Arusha Accords. Under its terms the Rwandan government agreed to share power with Hutu opposition parties and the Tutsi minority. UN peacekeepers would be deployed to patrol a cease-fire and assist in demilitarization and demobilization as well as to help provide a secure environment, so that exiled Tutsi could return. The hope among moderate Rwandans and Western observers was that Hutu and Tutsi would at last be able to coexist in harmony.

Hutu extremists rejected these terms and set out to terrorize Tutsi and also those Hutu politicians supportive of the peace process. In 1993 several thousand Rwandans were killed, and some 9,000 were detained. Guns, grenades, and machetes began arriving by the planeload. A pair of international commissions—one sent by the United Nations, the other by an independent collection of human-rights organizations—warned explicitly of a possible genocide.

But Dallaire knew nothing of the precariousness of the Arusha Accords. When he made a preliminary reconnaissance trip to Rwanda, in August of 1993, he was told that the country was committed to peace and that a UN presence was essential. A visit with extremists, who preferred to eradicate Tutsi rather than cede power, was not on Dallaire's itinerary. Remarkably, no UN officials in New York thought to give Dallaire copies of the alarming reports from the international investigators.

The sum total of Dallaire's intelligence data before that first trip to Rwanda consisted of one encyclopedia's summary of Rwandan history, which Major Brent Beardsley, Dallaire's executive assistant, had snatched at the last minute from his local public library. Beardsley says, "We flew to Rwanda with a Michelin road map, a copy of the Arusha agreement, and that was it. We were under the impression that the situation was quite straightforward: there was one cohesive government side and one cohesive rebel side, and they had come together to sign the peace agreement and had then requested that we come in to help them implement it."

Though Dallaire gravely underestimated the tensions brewing in Rwanda, he still felt that he would need a force of 5,000 to help the parties implement the terms of the Arusha Accords. But when his superiors warned him that the United States would never agree to pay for such a large deployment, Dallaire reluctantly trimmed his written request to 2,500. He remembers, "I was told, 'Don't ask for a brigade, because it ain't there.'"

Once he was actually posted to Rwanda, in October of 1993, Dallaire lacked not merely intelligence data and manpower but also institutional support. The small Department of Peacekeeping Operations in New York, run by the Ghanaian diplomat Kofi Annan, now the UN secretary general, was overwhelmed. Madeleine Albright, then the U.S. ambassador to the UN, recalls, "The global nine-one-one was always either busy or nobody was there." At the time of the Rwanda deployment, with a staff of a few hundred, the UN was posting 70,000 peacekeepers on seventeen missions around the world. Amid these widespread crises and logistical headaches the Rwanda mission had a very low status.

Life was not made easier for Dallaire or the UN peacekeeping office by the fact that American patience for peacekeeping was thinning. Congress owed half a billion dollars in UN dues and peacekeeping costs. It had tired of its obligation to foot a third of the bill for what had come to feel like an insatiable global appetite for mischief and an equally insatiable UN appetite for missions. The Clinton Administration had taken office better disposed toward peacekeeping than any other Administration in U.S. history. But it felt that the Department of Peacekeeping Operations needed fixing and demanded that the UN "learn to say no" to chancy or costly missions.

Every aspect of the UN Assistance Mission in Rwanda was run on a shoestring. UNAMIR (the acronym by which it was known) was equipped with hand-me-down vehicles from the UN's Cambodia mission, and only eighty of the 300 that turned up were usable. When the medical supplies ran out, in March of 1994, New York said there was no cash for resupply. Very little could be procured locally, given that Rwanda was one of Africa's poorest nations. Replacement spare parts, batteries, and even ammunition could rarely be found. Dallaire spent some 70 percent of his time battling UN logistics.

Dallaire had major problems with his personnel, as well. He commanded troops, military observers, and civilian personnel from twenty-six countries. Though multinationality is meant to be a virtue of UN missions, the diversity yielded grave discrepancies in resources. Whereas Belgian troops turned up well armed and ready to perform the tasks assigned to them, the poorer contingents showed up "bare-assed," in Dallaire's words, and demanded that the United Nations suit them up. "Since nobody else was offering to send troops, we had to take what we could get," he says. When Dallaire expressed concern, he was instructed by a senior UN official to lower his expectations. He recalls, "I was told, 'Listen, General, you are NATO-trained. This is not NATO.'" Although some 2,500 UNAMIR personnel had arrived by early April of 1994, few of the soldiers had the kit they needed to perform even basic tasks.

The signs of militarization in Rwanda were so widespread that even without much of an intelligence-gathering capacity, Dallaire was able to learn of the extremists' sinister intentions. In January of 1994 an anonymous Hutu informant, said to be high up in the inner circles of the Rwandan government, had come forward to describe the rapid arming and training of local militias. In what is now referred to as the "Dallaire fax," Dallaire relayed to New York the informant's claim that Hutu extremists "had been ordered to register all the Tutsi in Kigali." "He suspects it is for their extermination," Dallaire wrote. "Example he gave was that in 20 minutes his personnel could kill up to 1000 Tutsis." "Jean-Pierre," as the informant became known, had said that the militia planned first to provoke and murder a number of Belgian peacekeepers, to "thus guarantee Belgian withdrawal from Rwanda." When Dallaire notified Kofi Annan's office that UNAMIR was poised to raid Hutu arms caches, Annan's deputy forbade him to do so. Instead Dallaire was instructed to notify the Rwandan President, Juvénal Habyarimana, and the Western ambassadors of the informant's claims. Though Dallaire battled by phone with New York, and confirmed the reliability of the informant, his political masters told him plainly and consistently that the United States in particular would not support aggressive peacekeeping. (A request by the Belgians for reinforcements was also turned down.) In Washington, Dallaire's alarm was discounted. Lieutenant Colonel Tony Marley, the U.S. military liaison to the Arusha process, respected Dallaire but knew he was operating in Africa for the first time. "I thought that the neophyte meant well, but I questioned whether he knew what he was talking about," Marley recalls.

III. The Early Killings

On the evening of April 6, 1994, Romeo Dallaire was sitting on the couch in his bungalow residence in Kigali, watching CNN with Brent Beardsley. Beardsley was preparing plans for a national Sports Day that would match Tutsi rebel soldiers against Hutu government soldiers in a soccer game. Dallaire said, "You know, Brent, if the shit ever hit the fan here, none of this stuff would really matter, would it?" The next instant the phone rang. Rwandan President Habyarimana's Mystère Falcon jet, a gift from French President François Mitterrand, had just been shot down, with

Habyarimana and Burundian President Cyprien Ntaryamira aboard. Dallaire and Beardsley raced in their UN jeep to Rwandan army headquarters, where a crisis meeting was under way.

Back in Washington, Kevin Aiston, the Rwanda desk officer, knocked on the door of Deputy Assistant Secretary of State Prudence Bushnell and told her that the Presidents of Rwanda and Burundi had gone down in a plane crash. "Oh, shit," she said. "Are you sure?" In fact nobody was sure at first, but Dallaire's forces supplied confirmation within the hour. The Rwandan authorities quickly announced a curfew, and Hutu militias and government soldiers erected roadblocks around the capital.

Bushnell drafted an urgent memo to Secretary of State Warren Christopher. She was concerned about a probable outbreak of killing in both Rwanda and its neighbor Burundi. The memo read,

> If, as it appears, both Presidents have been killed, there is a strong likelihood that widespread violence could break out in either or both countries, particularly if it is confirmed that the plane was shot down. Our strategy is to appeal for calm in both countries, both through public statements and in other ways.

A few public statements proved to be virtually the only strategy that Washington would muster in the weeks ahead.

Lieutenant General Wesley Clark, who later commanded the NATO air war in Kosovo, was the director of strategic plans and policy for the Joint Chiefs of Staff at the Pentagon. On learning of the crash, Clark remembers, staff officers asked, "Is it Hutu and Tutsi or Tutu and Hutsi?" He frantically called for insight into the ethnic dimension of events in Rwanda. Unfortunately, Rwanda had never been of more than marginal concern to Washington's most influential planners.

America's best-informed Rwanda observer was not a government official but a private citizen, Alison Des Forges, a historian and a board member of Human Rights Watch, who lived in Buffalo, New York. Des Forges had been visiting Rwanda since 1963. She had received a Ph.D. from Yale in African history, specializing in Rwanda, and she could speak the Rwandan language, Kinyarwanda. Half an hour after the plane crash Des Forges got a phone call from a close friend in Kigali, the human-rights activist Monique Mujawamariya. Des Forges had been worried about Mujawamariya for weeks, because the Hutu extremist radio station, Radio Mille Collines, had branded her "a bad patriot who deserves to die." Mujawamariya had sent Human Rights Watch a chilling warning a week earlier: "For the last two weeks, all of Kigali has lived under the threat of an instantaneous, carefully prepared operation to eliminate all those who give trouble to President Habyarimana."

Now Habyarimana was dead, and Mujawamariya knew instantly that the hard-line Hutu would use the crash as a pretext to begin mass killing. "This is it," she told Des Forges on the phone. For the next twenty-four hours Des Forges called her friend's home every half hour. With each conversation Des Forges could hear the gunfire grow louder as the militia drew closer. Finally the gunmen entered Mujawamariya's home. "I don't want you to hear this," Mujawamariya said softly. "Take care of my children." She hung up the phone.

Mujawamariya's instincts were correct. Within hours of the plane crash Hutu militiamen took command of the streets of Kigali. Dallaire quickly grasped that supporters of the Arusha peace process were being targeted. His phone at UNAMIR headquarters rang constantly as Rwandans around the capital pleaded for help. Dallaire was especially concerned about Prime Minister Agathe Uwilingiyimana, a reformer who with the President's death had become the titular head of state. Just after dawn on April 7 five Ghanaian and ten Belgian peacekeepers arrived at the Prime Minister's home in order to deliver her to Radio Rwanda, so that she could broadcast an emergency appeal for calm.

Joyce Leader, the second-in-command at the U.S. embassy, lived next door to Uwilingiyimana. She spent the early hours of the morning behind the steel-barred gates of her embassy-owned house as Hutu killers hunted and dispatched their first victims. Leader's phone rang. Uwilingiyimana was on the other end. "Please hide me," she begged.

Minutes after the phone call a UN peacekeeper attempted to hike the Prime Minister over the wall separating their compounds. When Leader heard shots fired, she urged the peacekeeper to abandon the effort. "They can see you!" she shouted. Uwilingiyimana managed to slip with her husband and children into another compound, which was occupied by the UN Development Program. But the militiamen hunted them down in the yard, where the couple surrendered. There were more shots. Leader recalls, "We heard her screaming and then, suddenly, after the gunfire the screaming stopped, and we heard people cheering." Hutu gunmen in the Presidential Guard that day systematically tracked down and eliminated Rwanda's moderate leadership.

The raid on Uwilingiyimana's compound not only cost Rwanda a prominent supporter of the Arusha Accords; it also triggered the collapse of Dallaire's mission. In keeping with the plan to target the Belgians which the informant Jean-Pierre had relayed to UNAMIR in January, Hutu soldiers rounded up the peacekeepers at Uwilingiyimana's home, took them to a military camp, led the Ghanaians to safety, and then killed and savagely mutilated the ten Belgians. In Belgium the cry for either expanding UNAMIR's mandate or immediately withdrawing was prompt and loud.

In response to the initial killings by the Hutu government, Tutsi rebels of the Rwandan Patriotic Front—stationed in Kigali under the terms of the Arusha Accords—surged out of their barracks and resumed their civil war against the Hutu regime.

But under the cover of that war were early and strong indications that systematic genocide was taking place. From April 7 onward the Hutu-controlled army, the gendarmerie, and the militias worked together to wipe out Rwanda's Tutsi. Many of the early Tutsi victims found themselves specifically, not spontaneously, pursued: lists of targets had been prepared in advance, and Radio Mille Collines broadcast names, addresses, and even license-plate numbers. Killers often carried a machete in one hand and a transistor radio in the other. Tens of thousands of Tutsi fled their homes in panic and were snared and butchered at checkpoints. Little care was given to their disposal. Some were shoveled into landfills. Human flesh rotted in the sunshine. In churches bodies mingled with scattered hosts. If the killers had taken the time to tend to sanitation, it would have slowed their "sanitization" campaign.

IV. The "Last War"

The two tracks of events in Rwanda—simultaneous war and genocide—confused policymakers who had scant prior understanding of the country. Atrocities are often carried out in places that are not commonly visited, where outside expertise is limited. When country-specific knowledge is lacking, foreign governments become all the more likely to employ faulty analogies and to "fight the last war." The analogy employed by many of those who confronted the outbreak of killing in Rwanda was a peacekeeping intervention that had gone horribly wrong in Somalia.

On October 3, 1993, ten months after President Bush had sent U.S. troops to Somalia as part of what had seemed a low-risk humanitarian mission, U.S. Army Rangers and Delta special forces in Somalia attempted to seize several top advisers to the warlord Mohammed Farah Aideed. Aideed's faction had ambushed and killed two dozen Pakistani peacekeepers, and the United States was striking back. But in the firefight that ensued the Somali militia killed eighteen Americans, wounded seventy-three, and captured one Black Hawk helicopter pilot. Somali television broadcast both a video interview with the trembling, disoriented pilot and a gory procession in which the corpse of a U.S. Ranger was dragged through a Mogadishu street.

On receiving word of these events, President Clinton cut short a trip to California and convened an urgent crisis-management meeting at the White House. When an aide began recapping the situation, an angry President interrupted him. "Cut the bullshit," Clinton snapped. "Let's work this out." "Work it out" meant walk out. Republican Congressional pressure was intense. Clinton appeared on American television the next day, called off the manhunt for Aideed, temporarily reinforced the troop presence, and announced that all U.S. forces would be home within six months. The Pentagon leadership concluded that peacekeeping in Africa meant trouble and that neither the White House nor Congress would stand by it when the chips were down.

Even before the deadly blowup in Somalia the United States had resisted deploying a UN mission to Rwanda. "Anytime you mentioned peacekeeping in Africa," one U.S. official remembers, "the crucifixes and garlic would come up on every door." Having lost much of its early enthusiasm for peacekeeping and for the United Nations itself, Washington was nervous that the Rwanda mission would sour like so many others. But President Habyarimana had traveled to Washington in 1993 to offer assurances that his government was committed to carrying out the terms of the Arusha Accords. In the end, after strenuous lobbying by France (Rwanda's chief diplomatic and military patron), U.S. officials accepted the proposition that UNAMIR could be the rare "UN winner." On October 5, 1993, two days after the Somalia firefight, the United States reluctantly voted in the Security Council to authorize Dallaire's mission.

Even so, U.S. officials made it clear that Washington would give no consideration to sending U.S. troops to Rwanda. Somalia and another recent embarrassment in Haiti indicated that multilateral initiatives for humanitarian purposes would likely bring the United States all loss and no gain.

Against this backdrop, and under the leadership of Anthony Lake, the national-security adviser, the Clinton Administration accelerated the development of a formal U.S. peacekeeping doctrine. The job was given to Richard Clarke, of the National Security Council, a special assistant to the President who was known as one of the most effective bureaucrats in Washington. In an interagency process that lasted more than a year, Clarke managed the production of a presidential decision directive, PDD-25, which listed sixteen factors that policymakers needed to consider when deciding whether to support peacekeeping activities: seven factors if the United States was to vote in the UN Security Council on peace operations carried out by non-American soldiers, six additional and more stringent factors if U.S. forces were to participate in UN peacekeeping missions, and three final factors if U.S. troops were likely to engage in actual combat. In the words of Representative David Obey, of Wisconsin, the restrictive checklist tried to satisfy the American desire for "zero degree of involvement, and zero degree of risk, and zero degree of pain and confusion." The architects of the doctrine remain its strongest defenders. "Many say PDD-25 was some evil thing designed to kill peacekeeping, when in fact it was there to save peacekeeping," Clarke says. "Peacekeeping was almost dead. There was no support for it in the U.S. government, and the peacekeepers were not effective in the field." Although the directive was not publicly released until May 3, 1994, a month into the genocide, the considerations encapsulated in the doctrine and the Administration's frustration with peacekeeping greatly influenced the thinking of U.S. officials involved in shaping Rwanda policy.

V. The Peace Processors

Each of the American actors dealing with Rwanda brought particular institutional interests and biases to his or her handling of the crisis. Secretary of State Warren Christopher knew little about Africa. At one meeting with his top advisers, several weeks after the plane crash, he pulled an atlas off his shelf to help him locate the country. Belgian Foreign Minister Willie Claes recalls trying to discuss Rwanda with his American counterpart and being told, "I have other responsibilities." Officials in the State Department's Africa Bureau were, of course, better informed. Prudence Bushnell, the deputy assistant secretary, was one of them. The daughter of a diplomat, Bushnell had joined the foreign service in 1981, at the age of thirty-five. With her agile mind and sharp tongue, she had earned the attention of George Moose when she served under him at the U.S. embassy in Senegal. When Moose was named the assistant secretary of state for African affairs, in 1993, he made Bushnell his deputy. Just two weeks before the plane crash the State Department had dispatched Bushnell and a colleague to Rwanda in an effort to contain the escalating violence and to spur the stalled peace process.

Unfortunately, for all the concern of the Americans familiar with Rwanda, their diplomacy suffered from three weaknesses. First, ahead of the plane crash diplomats had repeatedly threatened to pull out UN peacekeepers in retaliation for the parties' failure to implement Arusha. These threats were of course counterproductive, because the very Hutu who opposed power-sharing wanted nothing more than a UN withdrawal. One senior U.S. official remembers, "The first response to trouble is 'Let's yank the peacekeepers.' But that is like believing that when children are misbehaving, the proper response is 'Let's send the baby-sitter home.'"

Second, before and during the massacres U.S. diplomacy revealed its natural bias toward states and toward negotiations. Because most official contact occurs between representatives of states, U.S. officials were predisposed to trust the assurances of Rwandan officials, several of whom were plotting genocide behind the scenes. Those in the U.S. government who knew Rwanda best viewed the escalating violence with a diplomatic prejudice that left them both institutionally oriented toward the Rwandan government and reluctant to do anything to disrupt the peace process. An examination of the cable traffic from the U.S. embassy in Kigali to Washington between the signing of the Arusha agreement and the downing of the presidential plane reveals that setbacks were perceived as "dangers to the peace process" more than as "dangers to Rwandans." American criticisms were deliberately and steadfastly leveled at "both sides," though Hutu government and militia forces were usually responsible.

The U.S. ambassador in Kigali, David Rawson, proved especially vulnerable to such bias. Rawson had grown up in Burundi, where his father, an American missionary, had set up a Quaker hospital. He entered the foreign service in 1971. When, in 1993, at age fifty-two, he was given the embassy in Rwanda, his first, he could not have been more intimate with the region, the culture, or the peril. He spoke the local language—almost unprecedented for an ambassador in Central Africa. But Rawson found it difficult to imagine the Rwandans who surrounded the President as conspirators in genocide. He issued pro forma demarches over Habyarimana's obstruction of power-sharing, but the cable traffic shows that he accepted the President's assurances that he was doing all he could. The U.S. investment in the peace process gave rise to a wishful tendency to see peace "around the corner." Rawson remembers, "We were naive policy optimists, I suppose. The fact that negotiations can't work is almost not one of the options open to people who care about peace. We were looking for the hopeful signs, not the dark signs. In fact, we were looking away from the dark signs . . . One of the things I learned and should have already known is that once you launch a process, it takes on its own momentum. I had said, 'Let's try this, and then if it doesn't work, we can back away.' But bureaucracies don't allow that. Once the Washington side buys into a process, it gets pursued, almost blindly." Even after the Hutu government began exterminating Tutsi, U.S. diplomats focused most of their efforts on "re-establishing a cease-fire" and "getting Arusha back on track."

The third problematic feature of U.S. diplomacy before and during the genocide was a tendency toward blindness bred by familiarity: the few people in Washington who were paying attention to Rwanda before Habyarimana's plane was shot down were those who had been tracking Rwanda for some time and had thus come to expect a certain level of ethnic violence from the region. And because the U.S. government had done little when some 40,000 people had been killed in Hutu-Tutsi violence in Burundi in October of 1993, these officials also knew that Washington was prepared to tolerate substantial bloodshed. When the massacres began in April, some U.S. regional specialists initially suspected that Rwanda was undergoing "another flare-up" that would involve another "acceptable" (if tragic) round of ethnic murder.

Rawson had read up on genocide before his posting to Rwanda, surveying what had become a relatively extensive scholarly literature on its causes. But although he expected internecine killing, he did not anticipate the scale at which it occurred. "Nothing in Rwandan culture or history could have led a person to that forecast," he says. "Most of us thought that if a war broke out, it would be quick, that these poor people didn't have the resources, the means, to fight a sophisticated war. I couldn't have known that they would do each other in with the most economic means." George Moose agrees: "We were psychologically and imaginatively too limited."

■   ■   ■

VII. Genocide? What Genocide?

Just when did Washington know of the sinister Hutu designs on Rwanda's Tutsi? Writing in *Foreign Affairs* last year [2000], Alan Kuperman argued that President Clinton "could not have known that a nationwide genocide was under way" until about two weeks into the killing. It is true that the precise nature and extent of the slaughter was obscured by the civil war, the withdrawal of U.S. diplomatic sources, some confused press reporting, and the lies of the Rwandan government. Nonetheless, both the testimony of U.S. officials who worked the issue day to day and the declassified documents indicate that plenty was known about the killers' intentions.

A determination of genocide turns not on the numbers killed, which is always difficult to ascertain at a time of crisis, but on the perpetrators' intent: Were Hutu forces attempting to destroy Rwanda's Tutsi? The answer to this question was available early on. "By eight AM the morning after the plane crash we knew what was happening, that there was systematic killing of Tutsi," Joyce Leader recalls. "People were calling me and telling me who was getting killed. I knew they were going door to door." Back at the State Department she explained to her colleagues that three kinds of killing were going on: war, politically motivated murder, and genocide. Dallaire's early cables to New York likewise described the armed conflict that had resumed between rebels and government forces, and also stated plainly that savage "ethnic cleansing" of Tutsi was occurring. U.S. analysts warned that mass killings would increase. In an April 11 memo prepared for Frank Wisner, the undersecretary of defense for policy, in advance of a dinner with Henry Kissinger, a key talking point was "Unless both sides can be convinced to return to the peace process, a massive (hundreds of thousands of deaths) bloodbath will ensue."

Whatever the inevitable imperfections of U.S. intelligence early on, the reports from Rwanda were severe enough to distinguish Hutu killers from ordinary combatants in civil war. And they certainly warranted directing additional U.S. intelligence assets toward the region—to snap satellite photos of large gatherings of Rwandan civilians or of mass graves, to intercept military communications, or to infiltrate the country in person. Though there is no evidence that senior policymakers deployed such assets, routine intelligence continued to pour in. On April 26 an unattributed intelligence memo titled "Responsibility for Massacres in Rwanda" reported that the ringleaders of the genocide, Colonel Théoneste Bagosora and his crisis committee, were determined to liquidate their opposition and exterminate the Tutsi populace. A May 9 Defense Intelligence Agency report stated plainly that the Rwandan violence was not spontaneous but was directed by the government, with lists of victims prepared well in advance. The DIA observed that an "organized parallel effort of *genocide* [was] being implemented by the army to destroy the leadership of the Tutsi community."

From April 8 onward media coverage featured eyewitness accounts describing the widespread targeting of Tutsi and the corpses piling up on Kigali's streets. American reporters relayed stories of missionaries and embassy officials who had been unable to save their Rwandan friends and neighbors from death. On April 9 a front-page *Washington Post* story quoted reports that the Rwandan employees of the major international relief agencies had been executed "in front of horrified expatriate staffers." On April 10 a *New York Times* front-page article quoted the Red Cross claim that "tens of thousands" were dead, 8,000 in Kigali alone, and that corpses were "in the houses, in the streets, everywhere." The *Post* the same day led its front-page story with a description of "a pile of corpses six feet high" outside the main hospital. On April 14 the *New York Times* reported the shooting and hacking to death of nearly 1,200

men, women, and children in the church where they had sought refuge. On April 19 Human Rights Watch, which had excellent sources on the ground in Rwanda, estimated the number of dead at 100,000 and called for use of the term "genocide." The 100,000 figure (which proved to be a gross underestimate) was picked up immediately by the Western media, endorsed by the Red Cross, and featured on the front page of the *Washington Post*. On April 24 the *Post* reported how "the heads and limbs of victims were sorted and piled neatly, a bone-chilling order in the midst of chaos that harked back to the Holocaust." President Clinton certainly could have known that a genocide was under way, if he had wanted to know.

Even after the reality of genocide in Rwanda had become irrefutable, when bodies were shown choking the Kagera River on the nightly news, the brute fact of the slaughter failed to influence U.S. policy except in a negative way. American officials, for a variety of reasons, shunned the use of what became known as "the g-word." They felt that using it would have obliged the United States to act, under the terms of the 1948 Genocide Convention. They also believed, understandably, that it would harm U.S. credibility to name the crime and then do nothing to stop it. A discussion paper on Rwanda, prepared by an official in the Office of the Secretary of Defense and dated May 1, testifies to the nature of official thinking. Regarding issues that might be brought up at the next interagency working group, it stated,

1. Genocide Investigation: Language that calls for an international investigation of human rights abuses and possible violations of the genocide convention. *Be Careful. Legal at State was worried about this yesterday—Genocide finding could commit [the U.S. government] to actually "do something."* [Emphasis added.]

At an interagency teleconference in late April, Susan Rice, a rising star on the NSC who worked under Richard Clarke, stunned a few of the officials present when she asked, "If we use the word 'genocide' and are seen as doing nothing, what will be the effect on the November [congressional] election?" Lieutenant Colonel Tony Marley remembers the incredulity of his colleagues at the State Department. "We could believe that people would wonder that," he says, "but not that they would actually voice it." Rice does not recall the incident but concedes, "If I said it, it was completely inappropriate, as well as irrelevant."

The genocide debate in U.S. government circles began the last week of April, but it was not until May 21, six weeks after the killing began, that Secretary Christopher gave his diplomats permission to use the term "genocide"—sort of. The UN Human Rights Commission was about to meet in special session, and the U.S. representative, Geraldine Ferraro, needed guidance on whether to join a resolution stating that genocide had occurred. The stubborn U.S. stand had become untenable internationally.

The case for a label of genocide was straightforward, according to a May 18 confidential analysis prepared by the State Department's assistant secretary for intelligence and research, Toby Gati: lists of Tutsi victims' names and addresses had reportedly been prepared; Rwandan government troops and Hutu militia and youth squads were the main perpetrators; massacres were reported all over the country; humanitarian agencies were now "claiming from 200,000 to 500,000 lives" lost. Gati offered the intelligence bureau's view: "We believe 500,000 may be an exaggerated estimate, but no accurate figures are available. Systematic killings began within hours of Habyarimana's death. Most of those killed have been Tutsi civilians, including women and children." The terms of the Genocide Convention had been met. "We weren't quibbling about these numbers," Gati says. "We can never know precise figures, but our analysts had been reporting huge numbers of deaths for weeks. We were basically saying, 'A rose by any other name . . .'"

Despite this straightforward assessment, Christopher remained reluctant to speak the obvious truth. When he issued his guidance, on May 21, fully a month after Human Rights Watch had put a name to the tragedy, Christopher's instructions were hopelessly muddied.

> The delegation is authorized to agree to a resolution that states that "acts of genocide" have occurred in Rwanda or that "genocide has occurred in Rwanda." Other formulations that suggest that some, but not all of the killings in Rwanda are genocide . . . e.g. "genocide is taking place in Rwanda"—are authorized. Delegation is not authorized to agree to the characterization of any specific incident as genocide or to agree to any formulation that indicates that all killings in Rwanda are genocide.

Notably, Christopher confined permission to acknowledge full-fledged genocide to the upcoming session of the Human Rights Commission. Outside that venue State Department officials were authorized to state publicly only that *acts* of genocide had occurred.

Christine Shelly, a State Department spokesperson, had long been charged with publicly articulating the U.S. position on whether events in Rwanda counted as genocide. For two months she had avoided the term, and as her June 10 exchange with the Reuters correspondent Alan Elsner reveals, her semantic dance continued.

ELSNER: How would you describe the events taking place in Rwanda?

SHELLY: Based on the evidence we have seen from observations on the ground, we have every reason to believe that acts of genocide have occurred in Rwanda.

ELSNER: What's the difference between "acts of genocide" and "genocide"?

SHELLY: Well, I think the—as you know, there's a legal definition of this . . . clearly not all of the killings that have taken place in Rwanda are killings to which you might apply that label . . . But as to the distinctions between the words, we're trying to call what we have seen so far as best as we can; and based, again, on the evidence, we have every reason to believe that acts of genocide have occurred.

ELSNER: How many acts of genocide does it take to make genocide?

SHELLY: Alan, that's just not a question that I'm in a position to answer.

The same day, in Istanbul, Warren Christopher, by then under severe internal and external pressure, relented: "If there is any particular magic in calling it genocide, I have no hesitancy in saying that."

VIII. "Not Even a Sideshow"

Once the Americans had been evacuated, Rwanda largely dropped off the radar of most senior Clinton Administration officials. In the situation room on the seventh floor of the State Department a map of Rwanda had been hurriedly pinned to the wall in the aftermath of the plane crash, and eight banks of phones had rung off the hook. Now, with U.S. citizens safely home, the State Department chaired a daily interagency meeting, often by teleconference, designed to coordinate mid-level diplomatic and humanitarian responses. Cabinet-level officials focused on crises elsewhere. Anthony Lake recalls, "I was obsessed with Haiti and Bosnia during that period, so Rwanda was, in William Shawcross's words, a 'sideshow,' but not even a sideshow—a no-show." At the NSC the person who managed Rwanda policy was not Lake, the national-security adviser, who happened to know Africa, but Richard Clarke, who oversaw peace-keeping policy, and for whom the news from Rwanda only confirmed a deep skepticism about the viability of UN deployments. Clarke believed that another UN failure could doom relations between Congress and the United Nations. He also sought to shield the President from congressional and public criticism. Donald Steinberg managed the Africa portfolio at the NSC and tried to look out for the dying Rwandans, but he was not an experienced infighter and, colleagues say, he "never won a single argument" with Clarke.

■   ■   ■

During the entire three months of the genocide Clinton never assembled his top policy advisers to discuss the killings. Anthony Lake likewise never gathered the "principals"—the Cabinet-level members of the foreign-policy team. Rwanda was never thought to warrant its own top-level meeting. When the subject came up, it did so along with, and subordinate to, discussions of Somalia, Haiti, and Bosnia. Whereas these crises involved U.S. personnel and stirred some public interest, Rwanda generated no sense of urgency and could safely be avoided by Clinton at no political cost. The editorial boards of the major American newspapers discouraged U.S. intervention during the genocide. They, like the Administration, lamented the killings but believed, in the words of an April 17 *Washington Post* editorial, "The United States has no recognizable national interest in taking a role, certainly not a leading role." Capitol Hill was quiet. Some in Congress were glad to be free of the expense of another flawed UN mission. Others, including a few members of the Africa subcommittees and the Congressional Black Caucus, eventually appealed tamely for the United States to play a role in ending the violence—but again, they did not dare urge U.S. involvement on the ground, and they did not kick up a public fuss. Members of Congress weren't hearing from their constituents. Pat Schroeder, of Colorado, said on April 30, "There are some groups terribly concerned about the gorillas . . . But—it sounds terrible—people just don't know what can be done about the people." Randall Robinson, of the nongovernmental organization TransAfrica, was preoccupied, staging a hunger strike to protest the U.S. repatriation of Haitian refugees. Human Rights Watch supplied exemplary intelligence and established important one-on-one contacts in the Administration, but the organization lacks a grassroots base from which to mobilize a broader segment of American society.

IX. The UN Withdrawal

When the killing began, Romeo Dallaire expected and appealed for reinforcements. Within hours of the plane crash he had cabled UN headquarters in New York: "Give me the means and I can do more." He was sending peacekeepers on rescue missions around the city, and he felt it was essential to increase the size and improve the quality of the UN's presence. But the United States opposed the idea of sending reinforcements, no matter where they were from. The fear, articulated mainly at the Pentagon but felt throughout the bureaucracy, was that what would start as a small engagement by foreign troops would end as a large and costly one by Americans. This was the lesson of Somalia, where U.S. troops had gotten into trouble in an effort to bail out the beleaguered Pakistanis. The logical outgrowth of this fear was an effort to steer clear of Rwanda entirely and be sure others did the same. Only by yanking Dallaire's entire peacekeeping force could the United States protect itself from involvement down the road.

One senior U.S. official remembers, "When the reports of the deaths of the ten Belgians came in, it was clear that it was Somalia redux, and the sense was that there would be an expectation everywhere that the U.S. would get involved. We thought leaving the peacekeepers in Rwanda and having them confront the violence would take us where we'd been before. It was a foregone conclusion that the United States wouldn't intervene and that the concept of UN peacekeeping could not be sacrificed again."

A foregone conclusion. What is most remarkable about the American response to the Rwandan genocide is not so much the absence of U.S. military action as that during the entire genocide the possibility of U.S. military intervention was never even debated. Indeed, the United States resisted intervention of any kind.

The bodies of the slain Belgian soldiers were returned to Brussels on April 14. One of the pivotal conversations in the course of the genocide took place around that time, when Willie Claes, the Belgian Foreign Minister, called the State Department to request "cover." "We are pulling out, but we don't want to be seen to be doing it alone," Claes said, asking the Americans to support a full UN withdrawal. Dallaire had not anticipated that Belgium would extract its soldiers, removing the backbone of his mission and stranding Rwandans in their hour of greatest need. "I expected the excolonial white countries would stick it out even if they took casualties," he remembers. "I thought their pride would have led them to stay to try to sort the place out. The Belgian decision caught me totally off guard. I was truly stunned."

Belgium did not want to leave ignominiously, by itself. Warren Christopher agreed to back Belgian requests for a full UN exit. Policy over the next month or so can be described simply: no U.S. military intervention, robust demands for a withdrawal of all of Dallaire's forces, and no support for a new UN mission that would challenge the killers. Belgium had the cover it needed.

On April 15 Christopher sent one of the most forceful documents to be produced in the entire three months of the genocide to Madeleine Albright at the UN—a cable instructing her to demand a full UN withdrawal. The cable, which was heavily influenced by Richard Clarke at the NSC, and which bypassed Donald Steinberg and was never seen by Anthony Lake, was unequivocal about the next steps. Saying that he had "fully" taken into account the "humanitarian reasons put forth for retention of UNAMIR elements in Rwanda,"

Christopher wrote that there was "insufficient justification" to retain a UN presence.

> The international community must give highest priority to full, orderly withdrawal of all UNAMIR personnel as soon as possible . . . We will oppose any effort at this time to preserve a UNAMIR presence in Rwanda . . . Our opposition to retaining a UNAMIR presence in Rwanda is firm. It is based on our conviction that the Security Council has an obligation to ensure that peacekeeping operations are viable, that they are capable of fulfilling their mandates, and that UN peacekeeping personnel are not placed or retained, knowingly, in an untenable situation.

"Once we knew the Belgians were leaving, we were left with a rump mission incapable of doing anything to help people," Clarke remembers. "They were doing nothing to stop the killings."

But Clarke underestimated the deterrent effect that Dallaire's very few peacekeepers were having. Although some soldiers hunkered down, terrified, others scoured Kigali, rescuing Tutsi, and later established defensive positions in the city, opening their doors to the fortunate Tutsi who made it through roadblocks to reach them. One Senegalese captain saved a hundred or so lives single-handedly. Some 25,000 Rwandans eventually assembled at positions manned by UNAMIR personnel. The Hutu were generally reluctant to massacre large groups of Tutsi if foreigners (armed or unarmed) were present. It did not take many UN soldiers to dissuade the Hutu from attacking. At the Hotel des Mille Collines ten peacekeepers and four UN military observers helped to protect the several hundred civilians sheltered there for the duration of the crisis. About 10,000 Rwandans gathered at the Amohoro Stadium under light UN cover. Brent Beardsley, Dallaire's executive assistant, remembers, "If there was any determined resistance at close quarters, the government guys tended to back

off." Kevin Aiston, the Rwanda desk officer at the State Department, was keeping track of Rwandan civilians under UN protection. When Prudence Bushnell told him of the U.S. decision to demand a UNAMIR withdrawal, he turned pale. "We can't," he said. Bushnell replied, "The train has already left the station."

On April 19 the Belgian Colonel Luc Marchal delivered his final salute and departed with the last of his soldiers. The Belgian withdrawal reduced Dallaire's troop strength to 2,100. More crucially, he lost his best troops. Command and control among Dallaire's remaining forces became tenuous. Dallaire soon lost every line of communication to the countryside. He had only a single satellite phone link to the outside world.

The UN Security Council now made a decision that sealed the Tutsi's fate and signaled the militia that it would have free rein. The U.S. demand for a full UN withdrawal had been opposed by some African nations, and even by Madeleine Albright; so the United States lobbied instead for a dramatic drawdown in troop strength. On April 21, amid press reports of some 100,000 dead in Rwanda, the Security Council voted to slash UNAMIR's forces to 270 men. Albright went along, publicly declaring that a "small, skeletal" operation would be left in Kigali to "show the will of the international community."

After the UN vote Clarke sent a memorandum to Lake reporting that language about "the safety and security of Rwandans under UN protection had been inserted by US/UN at the end of the day to prevent an otherwise unanimous UNSC from walking away from the at-risk Rwandans under UN protection as the peacekeepers drew down to 270." In other words, the memorandum suggested that the United States was *leading* efforts to ensure that the Rwandans under UN protection were not abandoned. The opposite was true.

Most of Dallaire's troops were evacuated by April 25. Though he was supposed to reduce the size of his force to 270, he ended up keeping 503 peacekeepers. By this time Dallaire was trying to deal with a bloody frenzy. "My force was standing knee-deep in mutilated bodies, surrounded by the guttural moans of dying people, looking into the eyes of children bleeding to death with their wounds burning in the sun and being invaded by maggots and flies," he later wrote. "I found myself walking through villages where the only sign of life was a goat, or a chicken, or a songbird, as all the people were dead, their bodies being eaten by voracious packs of wild dogs."

Dallaire had to work within narrow limits. He attempted simply to keep the positions he held and to protect the 25,000 Rwandans under UN supervision while hoping that the member states on the Security Council would change their minds and send him some help while it still mattered.

By coincidence Rwanda held one of the rotating seats on the Security Council at the time of the genocide. Neither the United States nor any other UN member state ever suggested that the representative of the genocidal government be expelled from the council. Nor did any Security Council country offer to provide safe haven to Rwandan refugees who escaped the carnage. In one instance Dallaire's forces succeeded in evacuating a group of Rwandans by plane to Kenya. The Nairobi authorities allowed the plane to land, sequestered it in a hangar, and, echoing the American decision to turn back the *S.S. St. Louis* during the Holocaust, then forced the plane to return to Rwanda. The fate of the passengers is unknown.

Throughout this period the Clinton Administration was largely silent. The closest it came to a public denunciation of the Rwandan government occurred after personal lobbying by Human Rights Watch, when Anthony Lake issued a statement calling on Rwandan military leaders by name to "do everything in their power to end the violence immediately." When I spoke with Lake six years later, and informed him that human-rights groups and U.S. officials point to this statement as the sum total of official public attempts to shame the Rwandan government in this period, he seemed stunned. "You're kidding," he said. "That's truly pathetic."

At the State Department the diplomacy was conducted privately, by telephone. Prudence Bushnell regularly set her alarm for 2:00 AM and phoned Rwandan government officials. She spoke several times with Augustin Bizimungu, the Rwandan military chief of staff. "These were the most bizarre phone calls," she says. "He spoke in perfectly charming French. 'Oh, it's so nice to hear from you,' he said. I told him, 'I am calling to tell you President Clinton is going to hold you accountable for the killings.' He said, 'Oh, how nice it is that your President is thinking of me.'"

X. The Pentagon "Chop"

The daily meeting of the Rwanda interagency working group was attended, either in person or by teleconference, by representatives from the various State Department bureaus, the Pentagon, the National Security Council, and the intelligence community. Any proposal that originated in the working group had to survive the Pentagon "chop." "Hard intervention," meaning U.S. military action, was obviously out of the question. But Pentagon officials routinely stymied initiatives for "soft intervention" as well.

The Pentagon discussion paper on Rwanda, referred to earlier, ran down a list of the working group's six short-term policy objectives and carped at most of them. The fear of a slippery slope was persuasive. Next to the seemingly innocuous suggestion that the United States "support the UN and others in attempts to achieve a cease-fire" the Pentagon official responded, "Need to change 'attempts' to 'political efforts'—without 'political' there is a danger of signing up to troop contributions."

The one policy move the Defense Department supported was a U.S. effort to achieve an arms embargo. But the same discussion paper acknowledged the ineffectiveness of this step: "We do not envision it will have a significant impact on the killings because machetes, knives and other hand implements have been the most common weapons."

Dallaire never spoke to Bushnell or to Tony Marley, the U.S. military liaison to the Arusha process, during the genocide, but they all reached the same conclusions. Seeing that no troops were forthcoming, they turned their attention to measures short of full-scale deployment which might alleviate the suffering. Dallaire pleaded with New York, and Bushnell and her team recommended in Washington, that something be done to "neutralize" Radio Mille Collines.

The country best equipped to prevent the genocide planners from broadcasting murderous instructions directly to the population was the United States. Marley offered three possibilities. The United States could destroy the antenna. It could transmit "counter-broadcasts" urging perpetrators to stop the genocide. Or it could jam the hate radio station's broadcasts. This could have been done from an airborne platform such as the Air Force's Commando Solo airplane. Anthony Lake raised the matter with Secretary of Defense William Perry at the end of April. Pentagon officials considered all the proposals non-starters. On May 5 Frank Wisner, the undersecretary of defense for policy, prepared a memo for Sandy Berger, then the deputy national-security adviser. Wisner's memo testifies to the unwillingness of the U.S. government to make even financial sacrifices to diminish the killing.

> We have looked at options to stop the broadcasts within the Pentagon, discussed them interagency and concluded jamming is an ineffective and expensive mechanism that will not accomplish the objective the NSC Advisor seeks.
>
> International legal conventions complicate airborne or ground based jamming and the mountainous terrain reduces the effectiveness of either

option. Commando Solo, an Air National Guard asset, is the only suitable DOD jamming platform. It costs approximately $8500 per flight hour and requires a semi-secure area of operations due to its vulnerability and limited self-protection.

> I believe it would be wiser to use air to assist in Rwanda in the [food] relief effort . . .

The plane would have needed to remain in Rwandan airspace while it waited for radio transmissions to begin. "First we would have had to figure out whether it made sense to use Commando Solo," Wisner recalls. "Then we had to get it from where it was already and be sure it could be moved. Then we would have needed flight clearance from all the countries nearby. And then we would need the political go-ahead. By the time we got all this, weeks would have passed. And it was not going to solve the fundamental problem, which was one that needed to be addressed militarily." Pentagon planners understood that stopping the genocide required a military solution. Neither they nor the White House wanted any part in a military solution. Yet instead of undertaking other forms of intervention that might have at least saved some lives, they justified inaction by arguing that a military solution was required.

Whatever the limitations of radio jamming, which clearly would have been no panacea, most of the delays Wisner cites could have been avoided if senior Administration officials had followed through. But Rwanda was not their problem. Instead justifications for standing by abounded. In early May the State Department Legal Advisor's Office issued a finding against radio jamming, citing international broadcasting agreements and the American commitment to free speech. When Bushnell raised radio jamming yet again at a meeting, one Pentagon official chided her for naiveté: "Pru, radios don't kill people. *People* kill people!"

■   ■   ■

However significant and obstructionist the role of the Pentagon in April and May, Defense Department officials were stepping into a vacuum. As one U.S. official put it, "Look, nobody senior was paying any attention to this mess. And in the absence of any political leadership from the top, when you have one group that feels pretty strongly about what *shouldn't* be done, it is extremely likely they are going to end up shaping U.S. policy." Lieutenant General Wesley Clark looked to the White House for leadership. "The Pentagon is always going to be the last to want to intervene," he says. "It is up to the civilians to tell us they want to do something and we'll figure out how to do it."

■　■　■

XI. PDD-25 in Action

No sooner had most of Dallaire's forces been withdrawn, in late April, than a handful of nonpermanent members of the Security Council, aghast at the scale of the slaughter, pressed the major powers to send a new, beefed-up force (UNAMIR II) to Rwanda.

When Dallaire's troops had first arrived, in the fall of 1993, they had done so under a fairly traditional peacekeeping mandate known as a Chapter VI deployment—a mission that assumes a ceasefire and a desire on both sides to comply with a peace accord. The Security Council now had to decide whether it was prepared to move from peacekeeping to peace *enforcement*—that is, to a Chapter VII mission in a hostile environment. This would demand more peacekeepers with far greater resources, more-aggressive rules of engagement, and an explicit recognition that the UN soldiers were there to protect civilians.

Two proposals emerged. Dallaire submitted a plan that called for joining his remaining peacekeepers with about 5,000 well-armed soldiers he hoped could be gathered quickly by the Security Council. He wanted to secure Kigali and then fan outward to create safe havens for Rwandans who had gathered in large numbers at churches and schools and on hillsides around the country. The United States was one of the few countries that could supply the rapid airlift and logistic support needed to move reinforcements to the region. In a meeting with UN Secretary General Boutros Boutros-Ghali on May 10, Vice President Al Gore pledged U.S. help with transport.

Richard Clarke, at the NSC, and representatives of the Joint Chiefs challenged Dallaire's plan. "How do you plan to take control of the airport in Kigali so that the reinforcements will be able to land?" Clarke asked. He argued instead for an "outside-in" strategy, as opposed to Dallaire's "inside-out" approach. The U.S. proposal would have created protected zones for refugees at Rwanda's borders. It would have kept any U.S. pilots involved in airlifting the peacekeepers safely out of Rwanda. "Our proposal was the most feasible, doable thing that could have been done in the short term," Clarke insists. Dallaire's proposal, in contrast, "could not be done in the short term and could not attract peacekeepers." The U.S. plan—which was modeled on Operation Provide Comfort, for the Kurds of northern Iraq—seemed to assume that the people in need were refugees fleeing to the border, but most endangered Tutsi could not make it to the border. The most vulnerable Rwandans were those clustered together, awaiting salvation, deep inside Rwanda. Dallaire's plan would have had UN soldiers move to the Tutsi in hiding. The U.S. plan would have required civilians to move to the safe zones, negotiating murderous roadblocks on the way. "The two plans had very different objectives," Dallaire says. "My mission was to save Rwandans. Their mission was to put on a show at no risk."

America's new peacekeeping doctrine, of which Clarke was the primary architect, was unveiled on May 3, and U.S. officials applied its criteria zealously. PDD-25 did not merely circumscribe U.S. participation in UN missions; it also limited U.S.

support for other states that hoped to carry out UN missions. Before such missions could garner U.S. approval, policymakers had to answer certain questions: Were U.S. interests at stake? Was there a threat to world peace? A clear mission goal? Acceptable costs? Congressional, public, and allied support? A working cease-fire? A clear command-and-control arrangement? And, finally, what was the exit strategy?

The United States haggled at the Security Council and with the UN Department of Peacekeeping Operations for the first two weeks of May. U.S. officials pointed to the flaws in Dallaire's proposal without offering the resources that would have helped him to overcome them. On May 13 Deputy Secretary of State Strobe Talbott sent Madeleine Albright instructions on how the United States should respond to Dallaire's plan. Noting the logistic hazards of airlifting troops into the capital, Talbott wrote, "The U.S. is not prepared at this point to lift heavy equipment and troops into Kigali." The "more manageable" operation would be to create the protected zones at the border, secure humanitarian-aid deliveries, and "promot[e] restoration of a ceasefire and return to the Arusha Peace Process." Talbott acknowledged that even the minimalist American proposal contained "many unanswered questions":

> Where will the needed forces come from; how will they be transported . . . where precisely should these safe zones be created; . . . would UN forces be authorized to move out of the zones to assist affected populations not in the zones . . . will the fighting parties in Rwanda agree to this arrangement . . . what conditions would need to obtain for the operation to end successfully?

Nonetheless, Talbott concluded, "We would urge the UN to explore and refine this alternative and present the Council with a menu of at least two options in a formal report from the [Secretary General] along with cost estimates before the Security Council votes on changing UNAMIR's mandate." U.S. policymakers were asking valid questions. Dallaire's plan certainly would have required the intervening troops to take risks in an effort to reach the targeted Rwandans or to confront the Hutu militia and government forces. But the business-as-usual tone of the American inquiry did not seem appropriate to the unprecedented and utterly unconventional crisis that was under way.

On May 17, by which time most of the Tutsi victims of the genocide were already dead, the United States finally acceded to a version of Dallaire's plan. However, few African countries stepped forward to offer troops. Even if troops had been immediately available, the lethargy of the major powers would have hindered their use. Though the Administration had committed the United States to provide armored support if the African nations provided soldiers, Pentagon stalling resumed. On May 19 the UN formally requested fifty American armored personnel carriers. On May 31 the United States agreed to send the APCs from Germany to Entebbe, Uganda. But squabbles between the Pentagon and UN planners arose. Who would pay for the vehicles? Should the vehicles be tracked or wheeled? Would the UN buy them or simply lease them? And who would pay the shipping costs? Compounding the disputes was the fact that Department of Defense regulations prevented the U.S. Army from preparing the vehicles for transport until contracts had been signed. The Defense Department demanded that it be reimbursed $15 million for shipping spare parts and equipment to and from Rwanda. In mid-June the White House finally intervened. On June 19, a month after the UN request, the United States began transporting the APCs, but they were missing the radios and heavy machine guns that would be needed if UN troops came under fire. By the time the APCs arrived, the genocide was over— halted by Rwandan Patriotic Front forces under the command of the Tutsi leader, Paul Kagame.

XII. The Stories We Tell

It is not hard to conceive of how the United States might have done things differently. Ahead of the plane crash, as violence escalated, it could have agreed to Belgian pleas for UN reinforcements. Once the killing of thousands of Rwandans a day had begun, the President could have deployed U.S. troops to Rwanda. The United States could have joined Dallaire's beleaguered UNAMIR forces or, if it feared associating with shoddy UN peacekeeping, it could have intervened unilaterally with the Security Council's backing, as France eventually did in late June. The United States could also have acted without the UN's blessing, as it did five years later in Kosovo. Securing congressional support for U.S. intervention would have been extremely difficult, but by the second week of the killing Clinton could have made the case that something approximating genocide was under way, that a supreme American value was imperiled by its occurrence, and that U.S. contingents at relatively low risk could stop the extermination of a people.

Alan Kuperman wrote in *Foreign Affairs* that President Clinton was in the dark for two weeks; by the time a large U.S. force could deploy, it would not have saved "even half of the ultimate victims." The evidence indicates that the killers' intentions were known by mid-level officials and knowable by their bosses within a week of the plane crash. Any failure to fully appreciate the genocide stemmed from political, moral, and imaginative weaknesses, not informational ones. As for what force could have accomplished, Kuperman's claims are purely speculative. We cannot know how the announcement of a robust or even a limited U.S. deployment would have affected the perpetrators' behavior. It is worth noting that even Kuperman concedes that belated intervention would have saved 75,000 to 125,000—no small achievement. A more serious challenge comes from the U.S. officials who argue that no amount of leadership from the White House would have overcome congressional opposition to

sending U.S. troops to Africa. But even if that highly debatable point was true, the United States still had a variety of options. Instead of leaving it to mid-level officials to communicate with the Rwandan leadership behind the scenes, senior officials in the Administration could have taken control of the process. They could have publicly and frequently denounced the slaughter. They could have branded the crimes "genocide" at a far earlier stage. They could have called for the expulsion of the Rwandan delegation from the Security Council. On the telephone, at the UN, and on the Voice of America they could have threatened to prosecute those complicit in the genocide, naming names when possible. They could have deployed Pentagon assets to jam—even temporarily—the crucial, deadly radio broadcasts.

Instead of demanding a UN withdrawal, quibbling over costs, and coming forward (belatedly) with a plan better suited to caring for refugees than to stopping massacres, U.S. officials could have worked to make UNAMIR a force to contend with. They could have urged their Belgian allies to stay and protect Rwandan civilians. If the Belgians insisted on withdrawing, the White House could have done everything within its power to make sure that Dallaire was immediately reinforced. Senior officials could have spent U.S. political capital rallying troops from other nations and could have supplied strategic airlift and logistic support to a coalition that it had helped to create. In short, the United States could have led the world.

Why did none of these things happen? One reason is that all possible sources of pressure—U.S. allies, Congress, editorial boards, and the American people—were mute when it mattered for Rwanda. American leaders have a circular and deliberate relationship to public opinion. It is circular because public opinion is rarely if ever aroused by foreign crises, even genocidal ones, in the absence of political leadership, and yet at the same time, American leaders continually cite the absence of public support as grounds for inaction. The relationship is deliberate because American leadership is not absent in such circumstances: it was present regarding Rwanda, but devoted mainly to suppressing public outrage and thwarting UN initiatives so as to avoid acting.

Strikingly, most officials involved in shaping U.S. policy were able to define the decision not to stop genocide as ethical and moral. The Administration employed several devices to keep down enthusiasm for action and to preserve the public's sense—and, more important, its own—that U.S. policy choices were not merely politically astute but also morally acceptable. First, Administration officials exaggerated the extremity of the possible responses. Time and again U.S. leaders posed the choice as between staying out of Rwanda and "getting involved everywhere." In addition, they often presented the choice as one between doing nothing and sending in the Marines. On May 25, at the Naval Academy graduation ceremony, Clinton described America's relationship to ethnic trouble spots: "We cannot turn away from them, but our interests are not sufficiently at stake in so many of them to justify a commitment of our folks."

Second, Administration policymakers appealed to notions of the greater good. They did not simply frame U.S. policy as one contrived in order to advance the national interest or avoid U.S. casualties. Rather, they often argued against intervention from the standpoint of people committed to protecting human life. Owing to recent failures in UN peacekeeping, many humanitarian interventionists in the U.S. government were concerned about the future of America's relationship with the United Nations generally and peacekeeping specifically. They believed that the UN and humanitarianism could not afford another Somalia. Many internalized the belief that the UN had more to lose by sending reinforcements and failing than by allowing the killings to proceed. Their chief priority, after the evacuation of the Americans, was

looking after UN peacekeepers, and they justified the withdrawal of the peacekeepers on the grounds that it would ensure a future for humanitarian intervention. In other words, Dallaire's peacekeeping mission in Rwanda had to be destroyed so that peacekeeping might be saved for use elsewhere.

A third feature of the response that helped to console U.S. officials at the time was the sheer flurry of Rwanda-related activity. U.S. officials with a special concern for Rwanda took their solace from mini-victories—working on behalf of specific individuals or groups (Monique Mujawamariya; the Rwandans gathered at the hotel). Government officials involved in policy met constantly and remained "seized of the matter"; they neither appeared nor felt indifferent. Although little in the way of effective intervention emerged from midlevel meetings in Washington or New York, an abundance of memoranda and other documents did.

Finally, the almost willful delusion that what was happening in Rwanda did not amount to genocide created a nurturing ethical framework for inaction. "War" was "tragic" but created no moral imperative.

What is most frightening about this story is that it testifies to a system that in effect worked. President Clinton and his advisers had several aims. First, they wanted to avoid engagement in a conflict that posed little threat to American interests, narrowly defined. Second, they sought to appease a restless Congress by showing that they were cautious in their approach to peacekeeping. And third, they hoped to contain the political costs and avoid the moral stigma associated with allowing genocide. By and large, they achieved all three objectives. The normal operations of the foreign-policy bureaucracy and the international community permitted an illusion of continual deliberation, complex activity, and intense concern, even as Rwandans were left to die.

Robert O. Keohane

FROM *AFTER HEGEMONY*
Cooperation and Discord in the World Political Economy

Realism, Institutionalism, and Cooperation

Impressed with the difficulties of cooperation, observers have often compared world politics to a "state of war." In this conception, international politics is "a competition of units in the kind of state of nature that knows no restraints other than those which the changing necessities of the game and the shallow conveniences of the players impose" (Hoffmann, 1965, p. vii). It is anarchic in the sense that it lacks an authoritative government that can enact and enforce rules of behavior. States must rely on "the means they can generate and the arrangements they can make for themselves" (Waltz, 1979, p. 111). Conflict and war result, since each state is judge in its own cause and can use force to carry out its judgments (Waltz, 1959, p. 159). The discord that prevails is accounted for by fundamental conflicts of interest (Waltz, 1959; Tucker, 1977).

Were this portrayal of world politics correct, any cooperation that occurs would be derivative from overall patterns of conflict. Alliance cooperation would be easy to explain as a result of the operation of a balance of power, but system-wide patterns of cooperation that benefit many countries without being tied to an alliance system directed against an adversary would not. If international politics were a state of war, institutionalized patterns of cooperation on the basis of shared purposes should not exist except as part of a larger struggle for power. The extensive patterns of international agreement that we observe on issues as diverse as trade, financial relations, health, telecommunications, and environmental protection would be absent.

At the other extreme from these "Realists" are writers who see cooperation as essential in a world of economic interdependence, and who argue that shared economic interests create a demand for international institutions and rules (Mitrany, 1975). Such an approach, which I refer to as "Institutionalist" because of its adherents' emphasis on the functions performed by international institutions, runs the risk of being naive about power and conflict. Too often its proponents incorporate in their theories excessively optimistic assumptions about the role of ideals in world politics, or about the ability of statesmen to learn what the theorist considers the "right lessons." But sophisticated students of institutions and rules have a good deal to teach us. They view institutions not simply as formal organizations with headquarters buildings and specialized staffs, but more broadly as "recognized patterns of practice around which expectations converge" (Young, 1980, p. 337). They regard these patterns of practice as significant because they affect state behavior. Sophisticated institutionalists do not expect cooperation always to prevail, but they are aware of the

From Robert O. Keohane, *After Hegemony: Cooperation and Discord in the World Political Economy* (Princeton, NJ: Princeton University Press, 1984), Chaps. 1, 6, 7. Some of the author's notes have been omitted.

malleability of interests and they argue that interdependence creates interests in cooperation.

During the first twenty years or so after World War II, these views, though very different in their intellectual origins and their broader implications about human society, made similar predictions about the world political economy, and particularly about the subject of this [discussion], the political economy of the advanced market-economy countries. Institutionalists expected successful cooperation in one field to "spill over" into others (Haas, 1958). Realists anticipated a relatively stable international economic order as a result of the dominance of the United States. Neither set of observers was surprised by what happened, although they interpreted events differently.

Institutionalists could interpret the liberal international arrangements for trade and international finance as responses to the need for policy coordination created by the fact of interdependence. These arrangements, which we will call "international regimes," contained rules, norms, principles, and decisionmaking procedures. Realists could reply that these regimes were constructed on the basis of principles espoused by the United States, and that American power was essential for their construction and maintenance. For Realists, in other words, the early postwar regimes rested on the *political hegemony* of the United States. Thus Realists and Institutionalists could both regard early postwar developments as supporting their theories.

After the mid-1960s, however, U.S. dominance in the world political economy was challenged by the economic recovery and increasing unity of Europe and by the rapid economic growth of Japan. Yet economic interdependence continued to grow, and the pace of increased U.S. involvement in the world economy even accelerated after 1970. At this point, therefore, the Institutionalist and Realist predictions began to diverge. From a strict Institutionalist standpoint, the increasing need for coordination of policy, created by interdependence, should have led to more cooperation. From

a Realist perspective, by contrast, the diffusion of power should have undermined the ability of anyone to create order.

On the surface, the Realists would seem to have made the better forecast. Since the late 1960s there have been signs of decline in the extent and efficacy of efforts to cooperate in the world political economy. As American power eroded, so did international regimes. The erosion of these regimes after World War II certainly refutes a naive version of the Institutionalist faith in interdependence as a solvent of conflict and a creator of cooperation. But it does not prove that only the Realist emphasis on power as a creator of order is valid. It might be possible, after the decline of hegemonic regimes, for more symmetrical patterns of cooperation to evolve after a transitional period of discord. Indeed, the persistence of attempts at cooperation during the 1970s suggests that the decline of hegemony does not necessarily sound cooperation's death knell.

International cooperation and discord thus remain puzzling. Under what conditions can independent countries cooperate in the world political economy? In particular, can cooperation take place without hegemony and, if so, how? This [project] is designed to help us find answers to these questions. I begin with Realist insights about the role of power and the effects of hegemony. But my central arguments draw more on the Institutionalist tradition, arguing that cooperation can under some conditions develop on the basis of complementary interests, and that institutions, broadly defined, affect the patterns of cooperation that emerge.

Hegemonic leadership is unlikely to be revived in this century for the United States or any other country. Hegemonic powers have historically only emerged after world wars; during peacetime, weaker countries have tended to gain on the hegemon rather than vice versa (Gilpin, 1981). It is difficult to believe that world civilization, much less a complex international economy, would survive such a war in the nuclear age. Certainly no prosperous hegemonic power is likely to emerge from such a cataclysm. As long as a world political economy persists, therefore, its central political dilemma will be how to organize cooperation without hegemony.

■   ■   ■

A Functional Theory of International Regimes

* * * [I]nternational regimes could be created and emphasized their value for overcoming what could be called "political market failure." * * * [Following is a] detailed examination of this argument by exploring why political market failure occurs and how international regimes can help to overcome it. This investigation will help us understand both why states often comply with regime rules and why international regimes can be maintained even after the conditions that facilitated their creation have disappeared. The functional theory developed in this chapter will therefore suggest some reasons to believe that even if U.S. hegemonic leadership may have been a crucial factor in the creation of some contemporary international economic regimes, the continuation of hegemony is not necessarily essential for their continued viability.

Political Market Failure and the Coase Theorem

Like imperfect markets, world politics is characterized by institutional deficiencies that inhibit mutually advantageous cooperation. * * * [I]n this self-help system, [there are] conflicts of interest between actors. In economic terms, these conflicts can be regarded as arising in part from the existence of externalities: actors do not bear the full costs, or receive the full benefits, of their own actions.[1] Yet in a famous article Ronald Coase (1960) argued that the presence of externalities alone does not necessarily prevent effective coordination among independent actors. Under certain conditions, declared Coase, bargaining among these actors could lead to solutions that are Pareto-optimal regardless of the rules of legal liability.

To illustrate the Coase theorem and its counter-intuitive result, suppose that soot emitted by a paint factory is deposited by the wind onto clothing hanging outdoors in the yard of an old-fashioned laundry. Assume that the damage to the laundry is greater than the $20,000 it would cost the laundry to enclose its yard and install indoor drying equipment; so if no other alternative were available, it would be worthwhile for the laundry to take these actions. Assume also, however, that it would cost the paint factory only $10,000 to eliminate its emissions of air pollutants. Social welfare would clearly be enhanced by eliminating the pollution rather than by installing indoor drying equipment, but in the absence of either governmental enforcement or bargaining, the egoistic owner of the paint factory would have no incentive to spend anything to achieve this result.

It has frequently been argued that this sort of situation requires centralized governmental authority to provide the public good of clean air. Thus if the laundry had an enforceable legal right to demand compensation, the factory owner would have an incentive to invest $10,000 in pollution control devices to avoid a $20,000 court judgment. Coase argued, however, that the pollution would be cleaned up equally efficiently even if the laundry had no such recourse. If the law, or the existence of a decentralized self-help system, gave the factory a right to pollute, the laundry owner could simply pay the factory owner a sum greater than $10,000, but less than $20,000, to install anti-soot equipment. Both parties would agree to some such bargain, since both would benefit.

In either case, the externality of pollution would be eliminated. The key difference would not be one of economic efficiency, but of distribution of benefits between the factory and the laundry. In a self-help system, the laundry would have to pay between $10,000 and $20,000 and the factory would reap a profit from its capacity to pollute. But if legal liability rules were based on "the polluter pays principle," the laundry would pay nothing and the factory would have to invest $10,000 without reaping a financial return. Coase did not dispute that rules of liability could be evaluated on grounds of fairness, but insisted that, given his assumptions, efficient arrangements could be consummated even where the rules of liability favored producers of externalities rather than their victims.

The Coase theorem has frequently been used to show the efficacy of bargaining without central authority, and it has occasionally been applied specifically to international relations (Conybeare, 1980). The principle of sovereignty in effect establishes rules of liability that put the burden of externalities on those who suffer from them. The Coase theorem could be interpreted, therefore, as predicting that problems of collective action could easily be overcome in international politics through bargaining and mutual adjustment—that is, through cooperation * * *. The further inference could be drawn that the discord observed must be the result of fundamental conflicts of interest rather than problems of coordination. The Coase theorem, in other words, could be taken as minimizing the importance of [Mancur] Olson's [1965] perverse logic of collective action or of the problems of coordination emphasized by game theory. However, such a conclusion would be incorrect for two compelling sets of reasons.

In the first place, Coase specified three crucial conditions for his conclusion to hold. These were: a legal framework establishing liability for actions, presumably supported by governmental authority; perfect information; and zero transaction costs (including organization costs and the costs of making side-payments). It is absolutely clear that none of these conditions is met in world politics. World government does not exist, making property rights and rules of legal liability fragile; information is extremely costly and often held unequally by different actors; transaction costs, including costs of organization and side-payments, are often very high. Thus an *inversion* of the Coase theorem would seem more appropriate to our subject. In the absence of the conditions that Coase specified, coordination will often be thwarted by dilemmas of collective action.

Second, recent critiques of Coase's argument reinforce the conclusion that it cannot simply be applied to world politics, and suggest further interesting implications about the functions of international regimes. It has been shown on the basis of game theory that, with more than two participants, the Coase theorem cannot necessarily be demonstrated. Under certain conditions, there will be no stable solution: any coalition that forms will be inferior, for at least one of its members, to another possible coalition. The result is an infinite regress. In game-theoretic terminology, the "core" of the game is empty. When the core is empty, the assumption of zero transaction costs means that agreement is hindered rather than facilitated: "in a world of zero transaction costs, the inherent instability of all coalitions could result in endless recontracting among the firms" (Aivazian and Callen, 1981, p. 179; Veljanovski, 1982).

What do Coase and his critics together suggest about the conditions for international cooperation through bargaining? First, it appears that approximating Coase's first two conditions—that is, having a clear legal framework establishing property rights and low-cost information available in a roughly equal way to all parties—will tend to facilitate cooperative solutions. But the implications of reducing transaction costs are more complex. If transaction costs are too high, no bargains will take place; but if they are too low, under certain conditions an infinite series of unstable coalitions may form.

Inverting the Coase theorem allows us to analyze international institutions largely as responses to problems of property rights, uncertainty, and transaction costs. Without consciously designed institutions, these problems will thwart attempts to cooperate in world politics even when actors' interests are complementary. From the deficiency of the "self-help system" (even from the perspective of purely self-interested national actors) we derive a need for international regimes. Insofar as they fill this need, international regimes perform the functions of establishing patterns of legal liability, providing relatively symmetrical information, and arranging the costs of bargaining so that specific agreements can more easily be made. Regimes are developed in part because actors in world politics believe that with such arrangements they will be able to make mutually beneficial agreements that would otherwise be difficult or impossible to attain.

This is to say that the architects of regimes anticipate that the regimes will facilitate cooperation. Within the functional argument being constructed here, these expectations explain the formation of the regimes: the *anticipated effects* of the regimes account for the actions of governments that establish them. Governments believe that *ad hoc* attempts to construct particular agreements, without a regime framework, will yield inferior results compared to negotiations within the framework of regimes. Following our inversion of the Coase theorem, we can classify the reasons for this belief under the categories of legal liability (property rights), transaction costs, and problems of uncertainty. We will consider these issues in turn.

LEGAL LIABILITY

Since governments put a high value on the maintenance of their own autonomy, it is usually impossible to establish international institutions that exercise authority over states. This fact is widely recognized by officials of international organizations and their advocates in national governments as well as by scholars. It would therefore be mistaken to regard international regimes, or the organizations that constitute elements of them, as characteristically unsuccessful attempts to institutionalize centralized authority in world politics. They cannot establish patterns of legal liability that are as solid as those developed within well-ordered societies, and their architects are well aware of this limitation.

Of course, the lack of a hierarchical structure of world politics does not prevent regimes from developing bits and pieces of law (Henkin, 1979, pp. 13–22). But the principal significance of international regimes does not lie in their formal legal status, since any patterns of legal liability and property rights established in world politics are subject to being overturned by the actions of sovereign states. International regimes are more like the "quasi-agreements" that William Fellner (1949) discusses when analyzing the behavior of oligopolistic firms than they are like governments. These quasi-agreements are legally unenforceable but, like contracts, help to organize relationships in mutually beneficial ways (Lowry, 1979, p. 276). Regimes also resemble conventions: practices, regarded as common knowledge in a community, that actors conform to not because they are uniquely best, but because others conform to them as well (Hardin, 1982; Lewis, 1969; Young, 1983). What these arrangements have in common is that they are designed not to implement centralized enforcement of agreements, but rather to establish stable mutual expectations about others' patterns of behavior and to develop working relationships that will allow the parties to adapt their practices to new situations. Contracts, conventions, and quasi-agreements provide information and generate patterns of transaction costs: costs of reneging on commitments are increased, and the costs of operating within these frameworks are reduced.

Both these arrangements and international regimes are often weak and fragile. Like contracts and quasi-agreements, international regimes are frequently altered: their rules are changed, bent, or broken to meet the exigencies of the moment. They are rarely enforced automatically, and they are not self-executing. Indeed, they are often matters for negotiation and renegotiation. As [Donald] Puchala has argued, "attempts to enforce EEC regulations open political cleavages up and down the supranational-to-local continuum and spark intense politicking along the cleavage lines" (1975, p. 509).

TRANSACTION COSTS

Like oligopolistic quasi-agreements, international regimes alter the relative costs of transactions. Certain agreements are forbidden. Under the provisions of the General Agreement on Tariffs and Trade (GATT), for instance, it is not permitted to make discriminatory trade arrangements except under specific conditions. Since there is no centralized government, states can nevertheless implement such actions, but their lack of legitimacy means that such measures are likely to be costly. Under GATT rules, for instance, retaliation against such behavior is justified. By elevating injunctions to the level of principles and rules, furthermore, regimes construct linkages between issues. No longer does a specific discriminatory agreement constitute merely a particular act without general significance; on the contrary, it becomes a "violation of GATT" with serious implications for a large number of other issues. In the terms of Prisoners' Dilemma, the situation has been transformed from a single-play to an iterated game. In market-failure terms, the transaction costs of certain possible bargains have been increased, while the costs of others have been reduced. In either case, the result is the same: incentives to violate regime principles are reduced. International regimes reduce transaction costs of legitimate bargains and increase them for illegitimate ones.

International regimes also affect transaction costs in the more mundane sense of making it cheaper for governments to get together to negotiate agreements. It is more convenient to make agreements within a regime than outside of one. International economic regimes usually incorporate international organizations that provide forums for meetings and secretariats that can act as catalysts for agreement. Insofar as their principles and rules can be applied to a wide variety of particular issues, they are efficient: establishing the rules and principles at the outset makes it unnecessary to renegotiate them each time a specific question arises.

International regimes thus allow governments to take advantage of potential economics of scale. Once a regime has been established, the marginal cost of dealing with each additional issue will be lower than it would be without a regime. * * * [I]f a policy area is sufficiently dense, establishing a regime will be worthwhile. Up to a point there may even be what economists call "increasing returns to scale." In such a situation, each additional issue could be included under the regime at lower cost than the previous one. As [Paul] Samuelson notes, in modern economies, "increasing returns is the prime case of deviations from perfect competition" (1967, p. 117). In world politics, we should expect increasing returns to scale to lead to more extensive international regimes.

In view of the benefits of economies of scale, it is not surprising that specific agreements tend to be "nested" within regimes. For instance, an agreement by the United States, Japan, and the European Community in the Multilateral Trade Negotiations to reduce a particular tariff will be affected by the rules and principles of GATT—that is, by the trade regime. The trade regime, in turn, is nested within a set of other arrangements, including those for monetary relations, energy, foreign investment, aid to developing countries, and other issues, which together constitute a complex and interlinked pattern of relations among the advanced market-economy countries. These, in turn, are related to military-security relations among the major states.[2]

The nesting patterns of international regimes affect transaction costs by making it easier or more difficult to link particular issues and to arrange side-payments, giving someone something on one issue in return for her help on another.[3] Clustering of issues under a regime facilitates side-payments among these issues: more potential *quids* are available for the *quo*. Without international regimes linking clusters of issues to one another, side-payments and linkages would be difficult to arrange in world politics; in the absence of a price system for the exchange of favors, institutional barriers would hinder the construction of mutually beneficial bargains.

Suppose, for instance, that each issue were handled separately from all others, by a different governmental bureau in each country. Since a side-payment or linkage always means that a government must give up something on one dimension to get something on another, there would always be a bureaucratic loser within each government. Bureaus that would lose from proposed side-payments, on issues that matter to them, would be unlikely to bear the costs of these linkages willingly on the basis of other agencies' claims that the national interest required it.

Of course, each issue is not considered separately by a different governmental department or bureau. On the contrary, issues are grouped together, in functionally organized departments such as Treasury, Commerce, and Energy (in the United States). Furthermore, how governments organize themselves to deal with foreign policy is affected by how issues are organized internationally; issues considered by different regimes are often dealt with by different bureaucracies at home. Linkages and side-payments among issues grouped in the same regime thus become easier, since the necessary internal tradeoffs will tend to take place within

rather than across bureaus; but linkages among issues falling into different regimes will remain difficult, or even become more so (since the natural linkages on those issues will be with issues within the same regime).

Insofar as issues are dealt with separately from one another on the international level, it is often hard, in simply bureaucratic terms, to arrange for them to be considered together. There are bound to be difficulties in coordinating policies of different international organizations—GATT, the IMF [International Monetary Fund], and the IEA [International Energy Agency] all have different memberships and different operating styles—in addition to the resistance that will appear to such a move within member governments. Within regimes, by contrast, side-payments are facilitated by the fact that regimes bring together negotiators to consider sets of issues that may well lie within the negotiators' bureaucratic bailiwicks at home. GATT negotiations, as well as deliberations on the international monetary system, have been characterized by extensive bargaining over side-payments and the politics of issue-linkage (Hutton, 1975). The well-known literature on "spillover" in bargaining, relating to the European Community and other integration schemes, can also be interpreted as concerned with side-payments. According to these writings, expectations that an integration arrangement can be expanded to new issue-areas permit the broadening of potential side-payments, thus facilitating agreement (Haas, 1958).

We conclude that international regimes affect the costs of transactions. The value of a potential agreement to its prospective participants will depend, in part, on how consistent it is with principles of legitimacy embodied in international regimes. Transactions that violate these principles will be costly. Regimes also affect bureaucratic costs of transactions: successful regimes organize issue-areas so that productive linkages (those that facilitate agreements consistent with the principles of the regime) are facilitated, while destructive linkages and bargains that are inconsistent with regime principles are discouraged.

UNCERTAINTY AND INFORMATION

From the perspective of market-failure theories, the informational functions of regimes are the most important of all. * * * [W]hat Akerlof [1970] called "quality uncertainty" was the crucial problem in [a] "market for lemons" example. Even in games of pure coordination with stable equilibria, this may be a problem. Conventions—commuters meeting under the clock at Grand Central Station, suburban families on a shopping trip "meeting at the car"—become important. But in simple games of coordination, severe information problems are not embedded in the structure of relationships, since actors have incentives to reveal information and their own preferences fully to one another. In these games the problem is to reach some point of agreement; but it may not matter much which of several possible points is chosen (Schelling, 1960/1978). Conventions are important and ingenuity may be required, but serious systemic impediments to the acquisition and exchange of information are lacking (Lewis, 1969; Young, 1983).

Yet as we have seen in * * * discussions of collective action and Prisoners' Dilemma, many situations—both in game theory and in world politics—are characterized by conflicts of interest as well as common interests. In such situations, actors have to worry about being deceived and double-crossed, just as the buyer of a used car has to guard against purchasing a "lemon." The literature on market failure elaborates on its most fundamental contention—that, in the absence of appropriate institutions, some mutually advantageous bargains will not be made because of uncertainty—by pointing to three particularly important sources of difficulty: *asymmetrical information; moral hazard;* and *irresponsibility.*

ASYMMETRICAL INFORMATION   Some actors may know more about a situation than others. Expecting that the resulting bargains would be unfair, "outsiders" will be reluctant to make agreements with "insiders" (Williamson, 1975, pp. 31–33). This is essentially the problem of "quality uncertainty" as discussed by Akerlof. Recall that this is a problem not merely of insufficient information, but rather of *systematically biased* patterns of information, which are recognized in advance of any agreement both by the holder of more information (the seller of the used car) and by its less well-informed prospective partner (the potential buyer of the "lemon" or "creampuff," as the case may be). Awareness that others have greater knowledge than oneself, and are therefore capable of manipulating a relationship or even engaging successful deception and double-cross, is a barrier to making agreements. When this suspicion is unfounded—that is, the agreement would be mutually beneficial—it is an obstacle to improving welfare through cooperation.

This problem of asymmetrical information only appears when dishonest behavior is possible. In a society of saints, communication would be open and no one would take advantage of superior information. In our imperfect world, however, asymmetries of information are not rectified simply by communication. Not all communication reduces uncertainty, since communication may lead to asymmetrical or unfair bargaining outcomes as a result of deception. Effective communication is not measured well by the amount of talking that used-car salespersons do to customers or that governmental officials do to one another in negotiating international regimes! The information that is required in entering into an international regime is not merely information about other governments' resources and formal negotiating positions, but also accurate knowledge of their future positions. In part, this is a matter of estimating whether they will keep their commitments. As the "market for lemons" example suggests, and as we will see in more detail below, a government's reputation therefore becomes an important asset in persuading others to enter into agreements with it. International regimes help governments to assess others' reputations by providing standards of behavior against which performance can be measured, by linking these standards to specific issues, and by providing forums, often through international organizations, in which these evaluations can be made.[4] Regimes may also include international organizations whose secretariats act not only as mediators but as providers of unbiased information that is made available, more or less equally to all members. By reducing asymmetries of information through a process of upgrading the general level of available information, international regimes reduce uncertainty. Agreements based on misapprehension and deception may be avoided; mutually beneficial agreements are more likely to be made.

Regimes provide information to members, thereby reducing risks of making agreements. But the information provided by a regime may be insufficiently detailed. A government may require precise information about its prospective partners' internal evaluations of a particular situation, their intentions, the intensity of their preferences, and their willingness to adhere to an agreement even in adverse future circumstances. Governments also need to know whether other participants will follow the spirit as well as the letter of agreements, whether they will share the burden of adjustment to unexpected adverse change, and whether they are likely to seek to strengthen the regime in the future.

The significance of asymmetrical information and quality uncertainty in theories of market failure therefore calls attention to the importance not only of international regimes but also of variations in the degree of closure of different states' decisionmaking processes. Some governments maintain secrecy much more zealously than others. American officials, for example, often lament that

the U.S. government leaks information "like a sieve" and claim that this openness puts the United States at a disadvantage vis-à-vis its rivals.

Surely there are disadvantages in openness. The real or apparent incoherence in policy that often accompanies it may lead the open government's partners to view it as unreliable because its top leaders, whatever their intentions, are incapable of carrying out their agreements. A cacophony of messages may render all of them uninterpretable. But some reflection on the problem of making agreements in world politics suggests that there are advantages for the open government that cannot be duplicated by countries with more tightly closed bureaucracies. Governments that cannot provide detailed and reliable information about their intentions—for instance, because their decisionmaking processes are closed to the outside world and their officials are prevented from developing frank informal relationships with their foreign counterparts—may be unable convincingly to persuade their potential partners of their commitment to the contemplated arrangements. Observers from other countries will be uncertain about the genuineness of officials' enthusiasm or the depth of their support for the cooperative scheme under consideration. These potential partners will therefore insist on discounting the value of prospective agreements to take account of their uncertainty. As in the "market for lemons," some potential agreements, which would be beneficial to all parties, will not be made because of "quality uncertainty"—about the quality of the closed government's commitment to the accord.[5]

MORAL HAZARD Agreements may alter incentives in such a way as to encourage less cooperative behavior. Insurance companies face this problem of "moral hazard." Property insurance, for instance, may make people less careful with their property and therefore increase the risk of loss (Arrow, 1974). The problem of moral hazard arises quite sharply in international banking. The solvency of a major country's largest banks may be essential to its financial system, or even to the stability of the entire international banking network. As a result, the country's central bank may have to intervene if one of these banks is threatened. The U.S. Federal Reserve, for instance, could hardly stand idly by while the Bank of America or Citibank became unable to meet its liabilities. Yet this responsibility creates a problem of moral hazard, since the largest banks, in effect, have automatic insurance against disastrous consequences of risky but (in the short-run at least) profitable loans. They have incentives to follow risk-seeking rather than risk-averse behavior at the expense of the central bank (Hirsch, 1977).

IRRESPONSIBILITY Some actors may be irresponsible, making commitments that they may not be able to carry out. Governments or firms may enter into agreements that they intend to keep, assuming that the environment will continue to be benign; if adversity sets in, they may be unable to keep their commitments. Banks regularly face this problem, leading them to devise standards of creditworthiness. Large governments trying to gain adherents to international agreements may face similar difficulties: countries that are enthusiastic about cooperation are likely to be those that expect to gain more, proportionately, than they contribute. This is a problem of self-selection, as discussed in the market-failure literature. For instance, if rates are not properly adjusted, people with high risks of heart attack will seek life insurance more avidly than those with longer life expectancies; people who purchased "lemons" will tend to sell them earlier on the used-car market than people with "creampuffs" (Akerlof, 1970; Arrow, 1974). In international politics, self-selection means that for certain types of activities—such as sharing research and development information—weak states (with much to gain but little to give) may

have more incentive to participate than strong ones, but less incentive actually to spend funds on research and developments.[6] Without the strong states, the enterprise as a whole will fail.

From the perspective of the outside observer, irresponsibility is an aspect of the problem of public goods and free-riding; but from the standpoint of the actor trying to determine whether to rely on a potentially irresponsible partner, it is a problem of uncertainty. Either way, informational costs and asymmetries may prevent mutually beneficial agreement.

REGIMES AND MARKET FAILURE

International regimes help states to deal with all of these problems. As the principles and rules of a regime reduce the range of expected behavior, uncertainty declines, and as information becomes more widely available, the asymmetry of its distribution is likely to lessen. Arrangements within regimes to monitor actors' behavior * * * mitigate problems of moral hazard. Linkages among particular issues within the context of regimes raise the costs of deception and irresponsibility, since the consequences of such behavior are likely to extend beyond the issue on which they are manifested. Close ties among officials involved in managing international regimes increase the ability of governments to make mutually beneficial agreements, because intergovernmental relationships characterized by ongoing communication among working-level officials, informal as well as formal, are inherently more conducive to exchange of information than are traditional relationships between closed bureaucracies. In general, regimes make it more sensible to cooperate by lowering the likelihood of being double-crossed. Whether we view this problem through the lens of game theory or that of market failure, the central conclusion is the same: international regimes can facilitate cooperation by reducing uncertainty. Like international law, broadly defined, their function is "to make human actions conform to predictable patterns so that contemplated actions can go forward with some hope of achieving a rational relationship between means and ends" (Barkun, 1968, p. 154).

Thus international regimes are useful to governments. Far from being threats to governments (in which case it would be hard to understand why they exist at all), they permit governments to attain objectives that would otherwise be unattainable. They do so in part by facilitating intergovernmental agreements. Regimes facilitate agreements by raising the anticipated costs of violating others' property rights, by altering transaction costs through the clustering of issues, and by providing reliable information to members. Regimes are relatively efficient institutions, compared with the alternative of having a myriad of unrelated agreements, since their principles, rules, and institutions create linkages among issues that give actors incentives to reach mutually beneficial agreements. They thrive in situations where states have common as well as conflicting interests on multiple, overlapping issues and where externalities are difficult but not impossible to deal with through bargaining. Where these conditions exist, international regimes can be of value to states.

We have seen that it does not follow from this argument that regimes necessarily increase global welfare. They can be used to pursue particularistic and parochial interests as well as more widely shared objectives. Nor should we conclude that all potentially valuable regimes will necessarily be instituted. * * * [E]ven regimes that promise substantial overall benefits may be difficult to invent.

■　■　■

Bounded Rationality and Redefinitions of Self-Interest

The perfectly rational decisionmaker * * * may face uncertainty as a result of the behavior of others, or the forces of nature, but she is assumed to make her own calculations costlessly. Yet this individual, familiar in textbooks, is not made of human flesh and blood. Even the shrewdest speculator or the most brilliant scientist faces limitations on her capacity for calculation. To imagine that all available information will be used by a decisionmaker is to exaggerate the intelligence of the human species.

Decisionmakers are in practice subject to limitations on their own cognitive abilities, quite apart from the uncertainties inherent in their environments. Herbert Simon has made this point with his usual lucidity (1982, p. 162):

> Particularly important is the distinction between those theories that locate all the conditions and constraints in the environment, outside the skin of the rational actor, and those theories that postulate important constraints arising from the limitations of the actor himself as an information processor. Theories that incorporate constraints on the information-processing capacities of the actor may be called *theories of bounded rationality*.

Actors subject to bounded rationality cannot maximize in the classical sense, because they are not capable of using all the information that is potentially available. They cannot compile exhaustive lists of alternative courses of action, ascertaining the value of each alternative and accurately judging the probability of each possible outcome (Simon, 1955/1979a, p. 10). It is crucial to emphasize that the source of their difficulties in calculation lies not merely in the complexity of the external world, but in their own cognitive limitations. In this respect, behavioral theories of bounded rationality are quite different from recent neoclassical theories, such as the theories of market failure * * *, which retain the assumption of perfect maximization:

> [In new neoclassical theories] limits and costs of information are introduced, not as psychological characteristics of the decision maker, but as part of his technological environment. Hence, the new theories do nothing to alleviate the computational complexities facing the decision maker—do not see him coping with them by heroic approximation, simplifying and satisficing, but simply magnify and multiply them. Now he needs to compute not merely the shapes of his supply and demand curves, but in addition, the costs and benefits of computing those shapes to greater accuracy as well. Hence, to some extent, the impression that these new theories deal with the hitherto ignored phenomena of uncertainty and information transmission is illusory. (Simon, 1979b, p. 504)

In Simon's own theory, people "satisfice" rather than maximize. That is, they economize on information by searching only until they find a course of action that falls above a satisfactory level—their "aspiration level." Aspiration levels are adjusted from time to time in response to new information about the environment (Simon, 1972, p. 168). In view of people's knowledge of their own cognitive limitations, this is often a sensible strategy; it is by no means irrational and may well be the best way to make most decisions.

In ordinary life, we satisfice all the time. We economize on information by developing habits, by devising operating rules to simplify calculation in situations that repeat themselves, and by adopting general principles that we expect, in the long run, to yield satisfactory results. I do not normally calculate whether to brush my teeth in the morning, whether to hit a tennis ball directed at me with my backhand or my forehand, or whether to tell the truth when asked on the telephone whether Robert Keohane is home. On the contrary, even apart from any moral scruples I might have (for instance, about lying), I assume that my interests will be furthered better by habitually brushing my teeth, applying the rule "when in doubt, hit it with your forehand because you have a lousy backhand," and adopting the general principle of telling the truth than by calculating the costs and benefits of every alternative in each case. I do not mean to deny that I might occasionally be advantaged by pursuing a new idea at my desk rather than brushing my teeth, hitting a particular shot with my backhand, or lying to an obnoxious salesman on the telephone. If I could costlessly compute the value of each alternative, it might indeed be preferable to make the necessary calculations each time I faced a choice. But since this is not feasible, given the costs of processing information, it is in my long-run interest to eschew calculation in these situations.

Simon's analysis of bounded rationality bears some resemblance to the argument made for rule-utilitarianism in philosophy, which emphasizes the value of rules in contributing to the general happiness.[7] Rule-utilitarianism was defined by John Austin in a dictum: "Our rules would be fashioned on utility; our conduct, on our rules" (Mackie, 1977, p. 136). The rule-utilitarian adopts these rules, or "secondary principles," in John Stuart Mill's terms, in the belief that they will lead, in general, to better results than a series of *ad hoc* decisions based each time on first principles.[8] A major reason for formulating and following such rules is the limited calculating ability of human beings. In explicating his doctrine of utilitarianism, Mill therefore anticipated much of Simon's argument about bounded rationality (1861/1951, p. 30):

> Nobody argues that the art of navigation is not founded on astronomy, because sailors cannot wait to calculate the Nautical Almanack. Being

rational creatures, they go to sea with it ready calculated; and all rational creatures go out upon the sea of life with their minds made up on the common questions of right and wrong, as well as on many of the far more difficult questions of wise and foolish. And this, as long as foresight is a human quality, it is to be presumed they will continue to do.

If individuals typically satisfice rather than maximize, all the more so do governments and other large organizations (Allison, 1971; Steinbruner, 1974; Snyder and Diesing, 1977). Organizational decision-making processes hardly meet the requirements of classical rationality. Organizations have multiple goals, defined in terms of aspiration levels; they search until satisfactory courses of action are found; they resort to feedback rather than systematically forecasting future conditions; and they use "standard operating procedures and rules of thumb" to make and implement decisions (Cyert and March, 1963, p. 113; March and Simon, 1958).

The behavioral theory of the firm has made it clear that satisficing does not constitute aberrant behavior that should be rectified where possible; on the contrary, it is intelligent. The leader of a large organization who demanded that the organization meet the criteria of classical rationality would herself be foolish, perhaps irrationally so. An organization whose leaders behaved in this way would become paralyzed unless their subordinates found ways to fool them into believing that impossible standards were being met. This assertion holds even more for governments than for business firms, since governments' constituencies are more varied, their goals more diverse (and frequently contradictory), and success or failure more difficult to measure. Assumptions of unbounded rationality, however dear they may be to the hearts of classical Realist theorists (Morgenthau, 1948/1966) and writers on foreign policy, are idealizations. A large, complex government would tie itself in knots by "keeping its options open," since

middle-level bureaucrats would not know how to behave and the top policymakers would be overwhelmed by minor problems. The search for complete flexibility is as quixotic as looking for the Holy Grail or the fountain of youth.

If governments are viewed as constrained by bounded rationality, what are the implications for the functional argument * * * about the value of international regimes? * * * [U]nder rational-choice assumptions, international regimes are valuable to governments because they reduce transaction costs and particularly because they reduce uncertainty in the external environment. Each government is better able, with regimes in place, to predict that its counterparts will follow predictably cooperative policies. According to this theory, governments sacrifice the ability to maximize their myopic self-interest by making calculations on each issue as it arises, in return for acquiring greater certainty about others' behavior.

Under bounded rationality, the inclination of governments to join or support international regimes will be reinforced by the fact that the alternatives to regimes are less attractive than they would be if the assumptions of classical rationality were valid. Actors laboring under bounded rationality cannot calculate the costs and benefits of each alternative course of action on each issue. On the contrary, they need to simplify their own decisionmaking processes in order to function effectively at all. The rules of thumb they devise will not yield better, and will generally yield worse, results (apart from decisionmaking costs) than classically rational action—whether these rules of thumb are adopted unilaterally or as part of an international regime. Thus a comparison between the value of a unilateral rule of thumb and that of a regime rule will normally be more favorable to the regime rule than a comparison between the value of costless, perfectly rational calculation and the regime rule.

When we abandon the assumption of classical rationality, we see that it is not international regimes that deny governments the ability to make classically rational calculations. The obstacle is rather the nature of governments as large, complex organizations composed of human beings with limited problem-solving capabilities. The choice that governments actually face with respect to international regimes is not whether to adhere to regimes at the expense of maximizing utility through continuous calculation, but rather on what rules of thumb to rely. Normally, unilateral rules will fit the individual country's situation better than rules devised multilaterally. Regime rules, however, have the advantage of constraining the actions of others. The question is whether the value of the constraints imposed on others justifies the costs of accepting regime rules in place of the rules of thumb that the country would have adopted on its own.

Thus if we accept that governments must adopt rules of thumb, the costs of adhering to international regimes appear less severe than they would be if classical rationality were a realistic possibility. Regimes merely substitute multilateral rules (presumably somewhat less congenial per se) for unilateral ones, with the advantage that other actors' behavior thereby becomes more predictably cooperative. International regimes neither enforce hierarchical rules on governments nor substitute their own rules for autonomous calculation; instead, they provide rules of thumb in place of those that governments would otherwise adopt.

* * * [W]e can see how different our conception of international regimes is from the self-help system that is often taken as revealing the essence of international politics. In a pure self-help system, each actor calculates its interests on each particular issue, preserving its options until that decision has been made. The rational response to another actor's distress in such a system is to take advantage of it by driving a hard bargain, demanding as much as "the traffic will bear" in return for one's money, one's oil, or one's military support. Many such bargains are in fact struck in world

politics, especially among adversaries; but one of the key features of international regimes is that they limit the ability of countries in a particularly strong bargaining position (however transitory) to take advantage of that situation. This limitation, as we have stressed, is not the result of altruism but of the fact that joining a regime changes calculations of long-run self-interest. To a government that values its ability to make future agreements, reputation is a crucial resource; and the most important aspect of an actor's reputation in world politics is the belief of others that it will keep its future commitments even when a particular situation, myopically viewed, makes it appear disadvantageous to do so. Thus even classically rational governments will sometimes join regimes and comply with their rules. To a government seeking to economize on decisionmaking costs, the regime is also valuable for providing rules of thumb; discarding it would require establishing a new set of rules to guide one's bureaucracy. The convenience of rules of thumb combines with the superiority of long-run calculations of self-interest over myopic ones to reinforce adherence to rules by egoistic governments, particularly when they labor under the constraints of bounded rationality.

■ ■ ■

NOTES

1. For an elaborated version of this definition, see Davis and North (1971, p. 16).
2. For the idea of "nesting," I am indebted to Aggarwal (1981). Snidal (1981) also relies on this concept, which was used in a similar context some years ago by Barkun (1968, p. 17).
3. On linkage, see especially the work of Kenneth A. Oye (1979, 1983). See also Stein (1980) and Tollison and Willett (1979).
4. This point was suggested to me by reading Elizabeth Colson's account of how stateless societies reach consensus on the character of individuals: through discussions and gossip that allow people to "apply the standards of performance in particular roles in making an overall judgement about the total person; this in turn allows them to predict future behavior" (1974, p. 53).
5. In 1960 Thomas Schelling made a similar argument about the problem of surprise attack. Asking how we would prove that we

were not planning a surprise attack if the Russians suspected we were, he observed that "evidently it is not going to be enough just to tell the truth. . . . There has to be some way of authenticating certain facts, the facts presumably involving the disposition of forces" (p. 247). To authenticate facts requires becoming more open to external monitoring as a way of alleviating what Akerlof [1970] later called "quality uncertainty."

6. Bobrow and Kudrle found evidence of severe problems of collective goods in the IEA's energy research and development program, suggesting that "commercial interests and other national rivalries appear to have blocked extensive international cooperation" (1979, p. 170).

7. In philosophy, utilitarianism refers to an ethical theory that purports to provide generalizable principles for moral human action. Since my argument here is a positive one, seeking to explain the behavior of egoistic actors rather than to develop or criticize an ethical theory, its relationship to rule-utilitarianism in philosophy, as my colleague Susan Okin has pointed out to me, is only tangential.

8. John Mackie argues that even act-utilitarians "regularly admit the use of rules of thumb," and that whether one follows rules therefore does not distinguish act- from rule-utilitarianism (1977, p. 137). Conversely, Joseph Nye has pointed out to me that even rule-utilitarians must depart at some point from their rules for consequentialist reasons. The point here is not to draw a hard-and-fast dichotomy between the two forms of utilitarianism, but rather to point out the similarities between Mill's notion of relying on rules and Simon's conception of bounded rationality. If all utilitarians have to resort to rules of thumb to some extent, this only strengthens the point I am making about the importance of rules in affecting, but not determining, the behavior of governments. For a succinct discussion of utilitarianism in philosophy, see Urmson (1968).

BIBLIOGRAPHY

*** Where a date is given for an original as well as a later edition, the latter was used; page references in the text refer to it.

Aggarwal, Vinod, 1981. Hanging by a Thread: International Regime Change in the Textile/Apparel System, 1950–1979 (Ph.D. dissertation. Stanford University).

Aivazian, Varouj A., and Jeffrey L. Callen, 1981. The Coase theorem and the empty core. *Journal of Law and Economics*, vol. 24, no. 1 (April), pp. 175–81.

Akerlof, George A., 1970. The market for "lemons." *Quarterly Journal of Economics*, vol. 84, no. 3 (August), pp. 488–500.

Allison, Graham, 1971. *Essence of Decision: Explaining the Cuban Missile Crisis* (Boston: Little, Brown).

Arrow, Kenneth J., 1974. *Essays in the Theory of Risk-Bearing* (New York: North-Holland/American Elsevier).

Barkun, Michael, 1968. *Law without Sanctions: Order in Primitive Societies and the World Community* (New Haven: Yale University Press).

Bobrow, Davis W., and Robert Kudrle, 1979. Energy R & D: in tepid pursuit of collective goods. *International Organization*, vol. 33, no. 2 (Spring), pp. 149–76.

Coase, Ronald, 1960. The problem of social cost. *Journal of Law and Economics*, vol. 3, pp. 1–44.

Colson, Elizabeth, 1974. *Tradition and Contract: The Problem of Order* (Chicago: Aldine Publishing Company).

Conybeare, John A.C., 1980. International organization and the theory of property rights. *International Organization*, vol. 34, no. 3 (Summer), pp. 307–34.

Cyert, Richard, and James G. March, 1963. *The Behavioral Theory of the Firm* (Englewood Cliffs, NJ: Prentice-Hall).

Davis, Lance, and Douglass C. North, 1971. *Institutional Change and American Economic Growth* (Cambridge: Cambridge University Press).

Fellner, William, 1949. *Competition among the Few* (New York: Knopf).

Gilpin, Robert, 1981. *War and Change in World Politics* (Cambridge: Cambridge University Press).

Haas, Ernst B., 1958. *The Uniting of Europe* (Stanford: Stanford University Press).

Hardin, Russell, 1982. *Collective Action* (Baltimore: The Johns Hopkins University Press for Resources for the Future).

Henkin, Louis, 1979. *How Nations Behave: Law and Foreign Policy*, 2nd edition (New York: Columbia University Press for the Council on Foreign Relations).

Hirsch, Fred, 1977. The Bagehot problem. *The Manchester School*, vol. 45, no. 3 (September), pp. 241–57.

Hoffmann, Stanley, 1965. *The State of War: Essays on the Theory and Practice of International Politics* (New York: Praeger).

Hutton, Nicholas, 1975. The salience of linkage in international economic negotiations. *Journal of Common Market Studies*, vol. 13, nos. 1–2, pp. 136–60.

Lewis, David K., 1969. *Convention: A Philosophical Study* (Cambridge: Harvard University Press).

Lowry, S. Todd, 1979. Bargain and contract theory in law and economics. In Samuels, 1979, pp. 261–82.

Mackie, J. L., 1977. *Ethics: Inventing Right and Wrong* (Harmondsworth, England: Penguin Books).

March, James G., and Herbert Simon, 1958. *Organizations* (New York: John Wiley & Sons).

Mill, John Stuart, 1861/1951. *Utilitarianism* (New York: E. P. Dutton).

Mitrany, David, 1975. *The Functional Theory of Politics* (London: St. Martin's Press for the London School of Economics and Political Science).

Morgenthau, Hans J., 1948/1966. *Politics among Nations*, 4th edition (New York: Knopf).

Olson, Mancur, 1965. *The Logic of Collective Action* (Cambridge: Harvard University Press).

Oye, Kenneth A., 1979. The domain of choice. In Oye et al., 1979, pp. 3–33.

Oye, Kenneth A., 1983. Belief Systems, Bargaining and Breakdown: International Political Economy 1929–1934 (Ph.D. dissertation, Harvard University).

Puchala, Donald J., 1975. Domestic politics and regional harmonization in the European Communities. *World Politics*, vol. 27, no. 4 (July), pp. 496–520.

Samuelson, Paul A., 1967. The monopolistic competition revolution. In R. E. Kuenne, ed., *Monopolistic Competition Theory* (New York: John Wiley & Sons).

Schelling, Thomas C., 1960/1980. *The Strategy of Conflict* (Cambridge: Harvard University Press).

Schelling, Thomas C., 1978. *Micromotives and Macrobehavior* (New York: W. W. Norton).

Simon, Herbert A., 1955. A behavioral model of rational choice. *Quarterly Journal of Economics*, vol. 69, no. 1 (February), pp. 99–118. Reprinted in Simon, 1979a, pp. 7–19.

Simon, Herbert A., 1972. Theories of bounded rationality. In Radner and Radner, 1972, pp. 161–76. Reprinted in Simon, 1982, pp. 408–23.

Simon, Herbert A., 1979a. *Models of Thought* (New Haven: Yale University Press).

Simon, Herbert A., 1979b. Rational decision making in business organizations. *American Economic Review*, vol. 69, no. 4 (September), pp. 493–513. Reprinted in Simon, 1982, pp. 474–94.

Simon, Herbert A., 1982. *Models of Bounded Rationality*, 2 vols. (Cambridge: MIT Press).

Snidal, Duncan, 1981. Interdependence, Regimes and International Cooperation (unpublished manuscript).

Snyder, Glenn H., and Paul Diesing, 1977. *Conflict among Nations: Bargaining, Decision making, and System Structure in International Crises* (Princeton: Princeton University Press).

Stein, Arthur A., 1980. The politics of linkage. *World Politics*, vol. 33, no. 1 (October), pp. 62–81.

Steinbruner, John D., 1974. *The Cybernetic Theory of Decision: New Dimensions of Political Analysis* (Princeton: Princeton University Press).

Tollison, Robert D., and Thomas D. Willett, 1979. An economic theory of mutually advantageous issue linkages in international negotiations. *International Organization*, vol. 33, no. 4 (Autumn), pp. 425–49.

Tucker, Robert W., 1977. *The Inequality of Nations* (New York: Basic Books).

Urmson, J. O., 1968. Utilitarianism. *International Encyclopedia of the Social Sciences* (New York: Macmillan), pp. 224–29.

Veljanovski, Cento G., 1982. The Coase theorems and the economic theory of markets and law. *Kyklos*, vol. 35, fasc. 1, pp. 53–74.

Waltz, Kenneth, 1959. *Man, the State and War* (New York: Columbia University Press).

Waltz, Kenneth, 1979. *Theory of World Politics* (Reading, MA: Addison-Wesley).

Williamson, Oliver, 1975. *Markets and Hierarchies: Analysis and Anti-Trust Implications* (New York: The Free Press).

Young, Oran R., 1980. International regimes: problems of concept formation. *World Politics*, vol. 32, no. 3 (April), pp. 331–56.

Young, Oran R., 1983. Regime dynamics: the rise and fall of international regimes. In Krasner, 1983, pp. 93–114.

John J. Mearsheimer

THE FALSE PROMISE OF INTERNATIONAL INSTITUTIONS

■ ■ ■

What Are Institutions?

There is no widely-agreed upon definition of institutions in the international relations literature.[1] The concept is sometimes defined so broadly as to encompass all of international relations, which gives it little analytical bite.[2] For example, defining institutions as "recognized patterns of behavior or practice around which expectations converge" allows the concept to cover almost every regularized pattern of activity between states, from war to tariff bindings negotiated under the General Agreement on Tariffs and Trade (GATT), thus rendering it largely meaningless.[3] Still, it is possible to devise a useful definition that is consistent with how most institutionalist scholars employ the concept.

I define institutions as a set of rules that stipulate the ways in which states should cooperate and compete with each other.[4] They prescribe acceptable forms of state behavior, and proscribe unacceptable kinds of behavior. These rules are negotiated by states, and according to many prominent theorists, they entail the mutual acceptance of higher norms, which are "standards of behavior defined in terms of rights and obligations."[5] These rules are typically formalized in international agreements, and are usually embodied in organizations with their own personnel and budgets.[6] Although rules are usually incorporated into a formal international

From *International Security* 19, no. 3 (Winter 1994/95): 5–49. Some of the author's notes have been edited.

organization, it is not the organization *per se* that compels states to obey the rules. Institutions are not a form of world government. States themselves must choose to obey the rules they created. Institutions, in short, call for the "decentralized cooperation of individual sovereign states, without any effective mechanism of command."[7]

■ ■ ■

Institutions in a Realist World

Realists * * * recognize that states sometimes operate through institutions. However, they believe that those rules reflect state calculations of self-interest based primarily on the international distribution of power. The most powerful states in the system create and shape institutions so that they can maintain their share of world power, or even increase it. In this view, institutions are essentially "arenas for acting out power relationships."[8] For realists, the causes of war and peace are mainly a function of the balance of power, and institutions largely mirror the distribution of power in the system. In short, the balance of power is the independent variable that explains war; institutions are merely an intervening variable in the process.

NATO provides a good example of realist thinking about institutions. NATO is an institution, and it certainly played a role in preventing World War III and helping the West win the Cold War. Nevertheless, NATO was basically a manifestation of the bipolar distribution of power in Europe during the

Cold War, and it was that balance of power, not NATO *per se*, that provided the key to maintaining stability on the continent. NATO was essentially an American tool for managing power in the face of the Soviet threat. Now, with the collapse of the Soviet Union, realists argue that NATO must either disappear or reconstitute itself on the basis of the new distribution of power in Europe.[9] NATO cannot remain as it was during the Cold War.

■   ■   ■

Liberal Institutionalism

Liberal institutionalism does not directly address the question of whether institutions cause peace, but instead focuses on the less ambitious goal of explaining cooperation in cases where state interests are not fundamentally opposed.[10] Specifically, the theory looks at cases where states are having difficulty cooperating because they have "mixed" interests; in other words, each side has incentives both to cooperate and not to cooperate.[11] Each side can benefit from cooperation, however, which liberal institutionalists define as "goal-directed behavior that entails mutual policy adjustments so that all sides end up better off than they would otherwise be."[12] The theory is of little relevance in situations where states' interests are fundamentally conflictual and neither side thinks it has much to gain from cooperation. In these circumstances, states aim to gain advantage over each other. They think in terms of winning and losing, and this invariably leads to intense security competition, and sometimes war. But liberal institutionalism does not deal directly with these situations, and thus says little about how to resolve or even ameliorate them.

Therefore, the theory largely ignores security issues and concentrates instead on economic and, to a lesser extent, environmental issues.[13] In fact, the theory is built on the assumption that international politics can be divided into two realms—security and political economy—and that liberal institutionalism mainly applies to the latter, but not the former. * * *

■   ■   ■

According to liberal institutionalists, the principal obstacle to cooperation among states with mutual interests is the threat of cheating.[14] The famous "prisoners' dilemma," which is the analytical centerpiece of most of the liberal institutionalist literature, captures the essence of the problem that states must solve to achieve cooperation.[15] Each of two states can either cheat or cooperate with the other. Each side wants to maximize its own gain, but does not care about the size of the other side's gain; each side cares about the other side only so far as the other side's chosen strategy affects its own prospects for maximizing gain. The most attractive strategy for each state is to cheat and hope the other state pursues a cooperative strategy. In other words, a state's ideal outcome is to "sucker" the other side into thinking it is going to cooperate, and then cheat. But both sides understand this logic, and therefore both sides will try to cheat the other. Consequently, both sides will end up worse off than if they had cooperated, since mutual cheating leads to the worst possible outcome. Even though mutual cooperation is not as attractive as suckering the other side, it is certainly better than the outcome when both sides cheat.

The key to solving this dilemma is for each side to convince the other that they have a collective interest in making what appear to be short-term sacrifices (the gain that might result from successful cheating) for the sake of long-term benefits (the substantial payoff from mutual long-term cooperation). This means convincing states to accept the second-best outcome, which is mutual collaboration. The principal obstacle to reaching this cooperative outcome will be fear of getting suckered, should the other side cheat. This, in a nutshell, is the problem that institutions must solve.

To deal with this problem of "political market failure," institutions must deter cheaters and protect victims.[16] Three messages must be sent to potential cheaters: you will be caught, you will be punished immediately, and you will jeopardize future cooperative efforts. Potential victims, on the other hand, need early warning of cheating to avoid serious injury, and need the means to punish cheaters.

Liberal institutionalists do not aim to deal with cheaters and victims by changing fundamental norms of state behavior. Nor do they suggest transforming the anarchical nature of the international system. They accept the assumption that states operate in an anarchic environment and behave in a self-interested manner.[17] * * * Liberal institutionalists instead concentrate on showing how rules can work to counter the cheating problem, even while states seek to maximize their own welfare. They argue that institutions can change a state's calculations about how to maximize gains. Specifically, rules can get states to make the short-term sacrifices needed to resolve the prisoners' dilemma and thus to realize long-term gains. Institutions, in short, can produce cooperation.

Rules can ideally be employed to make four major changes in "the contractual environment."[18] First, rules can increase the number of transactions between particular states over time.[19] This *institutionalized iteration* discourages cheating in three ways. It raises the costs of cheating by creating the prospect of future gains through cooperation, thereby invoking "the shadow of the future" to deter cheating today. A state caught cheating would jeopardize its prospects of benefiting from future cooperation, since the victim would probably retaliate. In addition, iteration gives the victim the opportunity to pay back the cheater: it allows for reciprocation, the tit-for-tat strategy, which works to punish cheaters and not allow them to get away with their transgression. Finally, it rewards states that develop a reputation for faithful adherence to agreements, and punishes states that acquire a reputation for cheating.[20]

Second, rules can tie together interactions between states in different issue areas. *Issue-linkage* aims to create greater interdependence between states, who will then be reluctant to cheat in one issue area for fear that the victim—and perhaps other states as well—will retaliate in another issue area. It discourages cheating in much the same way as iteration: it raises the costs of cheating and provides a way for the victim to retaliate against the cheater.

Third, a structure of rules can increase the amount of *information* available to participants in cooperative agreements so that close monitoring is possible. Raising the level of information discourages cheating in two ways: it increases the likelihood that cheaters will be caught, and more importantly, it provides victims with early warning of cheating, thereby enabling them to take protective measures before they are badly hurt.

Fourth, rules can reduce the *transaction costs* of individual agreements.[21] When institutions perform the tasks described above, states can devote less effort to negotiating and monitoring cooperative agreements, and to hedging against possible defections. By increasing the efficiency of international cooperation, institutions make it more profitable and thus more attractive for self-interested states.

Liberal institutionalism is generally thought to be of limited utility in the security realm, because fear of cheating is considered a much greater obstacle to cooperation when military issues are at stake.[22] There is the constant threat that betrayal will result in a devastating military defeat. This threat of "swift, decisive defection" is simply not present when dealing with international economics. Given that "the costs of betrayal" are potentially much graver in the military than the economic sphere, states will be very reluctant to accept the "one step backward, two steps forward" logic which underpins the tit-for-tat strategy of conditional cooperation. One step backward in the security realm might mean destruction, in which case there will be no next step—backward or forward.[23]

* * * There is an important theoretical failing in the liberal institutionalist logic, even as it applies

to economic issues. The theory is correct as far as it goes: cheating can be a serious barrier to cooperation. It ignores, however, the other major obstacle to cooperation: relative-gains concerns. As Joseph Grieco has shown, liberal institutionalists assume that states are not concerned about relative gains, but focus exclusively on absolute gains.[24] * * *

This oversight is revealed by the assumed order of preference in the prisoners' dilemma game: each state cares about how its opponent's strategy will affect its own (absolute) gains, but not about how much one side gains relative to the other. In other words, each side simply wants to get the best deal for itself, and does not pay attention to how well the other side fares in the process.[25] Nevertheless, liberal institutionalists cannot ignore relative-gains considerations, because they assume that states are self-interested actors in an anarchic system, and they recognize that military power matters to states. A theory that explicitly accepts realism's core assumptions—and liberal institutionalism does that—must confront the issue of relative gains if it hopes to develop a sound explanation for why states cooperate.

One might expect liberal institutionalists to offer the counterargument that relative-gains logic applies only to the security realm, while absolute-gains logic applies to the economic realm. Given that they are mainly concerned with explaining economic and environmental cooperation, leaving relative-gains concerns out of the theory does not matter.

There are two problems with this argument. First, if cheating were the only significant obstacle to cooperation, liberal institutionalists could argue that their theory applies to the economic, but not the military realm. In fact, they do make that argument. However, once relative-gains considerations are factored into the equation, it becomes impossible to maintain the neat dividing line between economic and military issues, mainly because military might is significantly dependent on economic might. The relative size of a state's economy has profound consequences for its standing in the international balance of military power. Therefore, relative-gains concerns must be taken into account for security reasons when looking at the economic as well as military domain. The neat dividing line that liberal institutionalists employ to specify when their theory applies has little utility when one accepts that states worry about relative gains.[26]

Second, there are non-realist (i.e., non-security) logics that might explain why states worry about relative gains. Strategic trade theory, for example, provides a straightforward economic logic for why states should care about relative gains.[27] It argues that states should help their own firms gain comparative advantage over the firms of rival states, because that is the best way to insure national economic prosperity. There is also a psychological logic, which portrays individuals as caring about how well they do (or their state does) in a cooperative agreement, not for material reasons, but because it is human nature to compare one's progress with that of others.[28]

Another possible liberal institutionalist counterargument is that solving the cheating problem renders the relative-gains problem irrelevant. If states cannot cheat each other, they need not fear each other, and therefore, states would not have to worry about relative power. The problem with this argument, however, is that even if the cheating problem were solved, states would still have to worry about relative gains because gaps in gains can be translated into military advantage that can be used for coercion or aggression. And in the international system, states sometimes have conflicting interests that lead to aggression.

There is also empirical evidence that relative-gains considerations mattered during the Cold War even in economic relations among the advanced industrialized democracies in the Organization for Economic Cooperation and Development (OECD). One would not expect realist logic about relative gains to be influential in this case: the United States was a superpower with little to fear militarily from the other OECD states, and those states were unlikely to use a relative-gains advantage to threaten the United States.[29] Furthermore, the OECD states were important American allies during the Cold War, and thus the United States benefited strategically when they gained substantially in size and strength.

Nonetheless, relative gains appear to have mattered in economic relations among the advanced industrial states. Consider three prominent studies. Stephen Krasner considered efforts at cooperation in different sectors of the international communications industry. He found that states were remarkably unconcerned about cheating but deeply worried about relative gains, which led him to conclude that liberal institutionalism "is not relevant for global communications." Grieco examined American and EC efforts to implement, under the auspices of GATT, a number of agreements relating to non-tariff barriers to trade. He found that the level of success was not a function of concerns about cheating but was influenced primarily by concern about the distribution of gains. Similarly, Michael Mastanduno found that concern about relative gains, not about cheating, was an important factor in shaping American policy towards Japan in three cases: the FSX fighter aircraft, satellites, and high-definition television.[30]

I am not suggesting that relative-gains considerations make cooperation impossible; my point is simply that they can pose a serious impediment to cooperation and must therefore be taken into account when developing a theory of cooperation among states. This point is apparently now recognized by liberal institutionalists. Keohane, for example, acknowledges that he "did make a major mistake by underemphasizing distributive issues and the complexities they create for international cooperation."[31]

CAN LIBERAL INSTITUTIONALISM BE REPAIRED?

Liberal institutionalists must address two questions if they are to repair their theory. First, can institutions facilitate cooperation when states seriously care about relative gains, or do institutions only matter when states can ignore relative-gains considerations and focus instead on absolute gains?

I find no evidence that liberal institutionalists believe that institutions facilitate cooperation when states care deeply about relative gains. They apparently concede that their theory only applies when relative-gains considerations matter little or hardly at all.[32] Thus the second question: when do states not worry about relative gains? The answer to this question would ultimately define the realm in which liberal institutionalism applies.

Liberal institutionalists have not addressed this important question in a systematic fashion, so any assessment of their efforts to repair the theory must be preliminary. * * *

■　■　■

PROBLEMS WITH THE EMPIRICAL RECORD

Although there is much evidence of cooperation among states, this alone does not constitute support for liberal institutionalism. What is needed is evidence of cooperation that would not have occurred in the absence of institutions because of fear of cheating, or its actual presence. But scholars have provided little evidence of cooperation of that sort, nor of cooperation failing because of cheating. Moreover, as discussed above, there is considerable evidence that states worry much about relative gains not only in security matters, but in the economic realm as well.

This dearth of empirical support for liberal institutionalism is acknowledged by proponents of that theory.[33] The empirical record is not completely blank, however, but the few historical cases that liberal institutionalists have studied provide scant support for the theory. Consider two prominent examples.

Keohane looked at the performance of the International Energy Agency (IEA) in 1974–81, a period that included the 1979 oil crisis.[34] This case does not appear to lend the theory much support. First, Keohane concedes that the IEA failed outright when put to the test in 1979: "regime-oriented efforts at cooperation do not always succeed, as the fiasco of IEA actions in 1979 illustrates."[35] He claims, however, that in 1980 the IEA had a minor success "under relatively favorable conditions" in responding to the outbreak of the Iran-Iraq War. Although he admits it is difficult to specify how much the IEA mattered in the 1980 case, he notes that "it seems clear that 'it [the IEA] leaned in the right direction,'" a claim that hardly constitutes strong support for the theory.[36] Second, it does not appear from Keohane's analysis that either fear of cheating or actual cheating hindered cooperation in the 1979 case, as the theory would predict. Third, Keohane chose the IEA case precisely because it involved relations among advanced Western democracies with market economies, where the prospects for cooperation were excellent.[37] The modest impact of institutions in this case is thus all the more damning to the theory.

Lisa Martin examined the role that the European Community (EC) played during the Falklands War in helping Britain coax its reluctant allies to continue economic sanctions against Argentina after military action started.[38] She concludes that the EC helped Britain win its allies' cooperation by lowering transaction costs and facilitating issue linkage. Specifically, Britain made concessions on the EC budget and the Common Agricultural Policy (CAP); Britain's allies agreed in return to keep sanctions on Argentina.

This case, too, is less than a ringing endorsement for liberal institutionalism. First, British efforts to maintain EC sanctions against Argentina were not impeded by fears of possible cheating, which the theory identifies as the central impediment to cooperation. So this case does not present an important test of liberal institutionalism, and thus the cooperative outcome does not tell us much about the theory's explanatory power. Second, it was relatively easy for Britain and her allies to strike a deal in this case. Neither side's core interests were threatened, and neither side had to make significant sacrifices to reach an agreement. Forging an accord to continue sanctions was not a

difficult undertaking. A stronger test for liberal institutionalism would require states to cooperate when doing so entailed significant costs and risks. Third, the EC was not essential to an agreement. Issues could have been linked without the EC, and although the EC may have lowered transaction costs somewhat, there is no reason to think these costs were a serious impediment to striking a deal.[39] It is noteworthy that Britain and America were able to cooperate during the Falklands War, even though the United States did not belong to the EC.

There is also evidence that directly challenges liberal institutionalism in issue areas where one would expect the theory to operate successfully. The studies discussed above by Grieco, Krasner, and Mastanduno test the institutionalist argument in a number of different political economy cases, and each finds the theory has little explanatory power. More empirical work is needed before a final judgment is rendered on the explanatory power of liberal institutionalism. Nevertheless, the evidence gathered so far is unpromising at best.

In summary, liberal institutionalism does not provide a sound basis for understanding international relations and promoting stability in the post–Cold War world. It makes modest claims about the impact of institutions, and steers clear of war and peace issues, focusing instead on the less ambitious task of explaining economic cooperation. Furthermore, the theory's causal logic is flawed, as proponents of the theory now admit. Having overlooked the relative-gains problem, they are now attempting to repair the theory, but their initial efforts are not promising. Finally, the available empirical evidence provides little support for the theory.

Conclusion

■ ■ ■

The attraction of institutionalist theories for both policymakers and scholars is explained, I believe, not by their intrinsic value, but by their relationship to realism, and especially to core elements of American political ideology. Realism has long been and continues to be an influential theory in the United States.[40] Leading realist thinkers such as George Kennan and Henry Kissinger, for example, occupied key policymaking positions during the Cold War. The impact of realism in the academic world is amply demonstrated in the institutionalist literature, where discussions of realism are pervasive.[41] Yet despite its influence, Americans who think seriously about foreign policy issues tend to dislike realism intensely, mainly because it clashes with their basic values. The theory stands opposed to how most Americans prefer to think about themselves and the wider world.[42]

There are four principal reasons why American elites, as well as the American public, tend to regard realism with hostility. First, realism is a pessimistic theory. It depicts a world of stark and harsh competition, and it holds out little promise of making that world more benign. Realists, as Hans Morgenthau wrote, are resigned to the fact that "there is no escape from the evil of power, regardless of what one does."[43] Such pessimism, of course, runs up against the deep-seated American belief that with time and effort, reasonable individuals can solve important social problems. Americans regard progress as both desirable and possible in politics, and they are therefore uncomfortable with realism's claim that security competition and war will persist despite our best efforts to eliminate them.[44]

Second, realism treats war as an inevitable, and indeed sometimes necessary, form of state activity. For realists, war is an extension of politics by other means. Realists are very cautious in their prescriptions about the use of force: wars should not be fought for idealistic purposes, but instead for balance-of-power reasons. Most Americans, however, tend to think of war as a hideous enterprise that should ultimately be abolished. For the time being, however, it can only justifiably be used for lofty moral goals, like "making the world safe for democracy"; it is morally incorrect to fight wars to change or preserve the balance of power. This makes the realist conception of warfare anathema to many Americans.

Third, as an analytical matter, realism does not distinguish between "good" states and "bad" states, but essentially treats them like billiard balls of varying size. In realist theory, all states are forced to seek the same goal: maximum relative power.[45] A purely realist interpretation of the Cold War, for example, allows for no meaningful difference in the motives behind American and Soviet behavior during that conflict. According to the theory, both sides must have been driven by concerns about the balance of power, and must have done what was necessary to try to achieve a favorable balance. Most Americans would recoil at such a description of the Cold War, because they believe the United States was motivated by good intentions while the Soviet Union was not.[46]

Fourth, America has a rich history of thumbing its nose at realism. For its first 140 years of existence, geography and the British navy allowed the United States to avoid serious involvement in the power politics of Europe. America had an isolationist foreign policy for most of this period, and its rhetoric explicitly emphasized the evils of entangling alliances and balancing behavior. Even as the United States finally entered its first European war in 1917, Woodrow Wilson railed against realist thinking. America has a long tradition of anti-realist rhetoric, which continues to influence us today.

Given that realism is largely alien to American culture, there is a powerful demand in the United States for alternative ways of looking at the world, and especially for theories that square with basic American values. Institutionalist theories nicely meet these requirements, and that is the main source of their appeal to policymakers and scholars. Whatever else one might say about these theories, they have one undeniable advantage in the eyes of their supporters: they are not realism. Not only do institutionalist theories offer an alternative to realism, but they explicitly seek to undermine it. Moreover, institutionalists offer arguments that reflect basic American values. For example, they are optimistic about the possibility of greatly reducing, if not eliminating, security competition among states and creating a more peaceful world. They certainly do not accept the realist stricture that war is politics by other means. Institutionalists, in short, purvey a message that Americans long to hear.

There is, however, a downside for policymakers who rely on institutionalist theories: these theories do not accurately describe the world, hence policies based on them are bound to fail. The international system strongly shapes the behavior of states, limiting the amount of damage that false faith in institutional theories can cause. The constraints of the system notwithstanding, however, states still have considerable freedom of action, and their policy choices can succeed or fail in protecting American national interests and the interests of vulnerable people around the globe. The failure of the League of Nations to address German and Japanese aggression in the 1930s is a case in point. The failure of institutions to prevent or stop the war in Bosnia offers a more recent example. These cases illustrate that institutions have mattered rather little in the past; they also suggest that the false belief that institutions matter has mattered more, and has had pernicious effects. Unfortunately, misplaced reliance on institutional solutions is likely to lead to more failures in the future.

NOTES

1. Regimes and institutions are treated as synonymous concepts in this article. They are also used interchangeably in the institutionalist literature. See Robert O. Keohane, "International Institutions: Two Approaches," *International Studies Quarterly,* Vol. 32, No. 4 (December 1988), p. 384; Robert O. Keohane, *International Institutions and State Power: Essays in International Relations Theory* (Boulder, CO: Westview Press, 1989), pp. 3–4; and Oran R. Young, *International Cooperation: Building Regimes for Natural Resources and the Environment* (Ithaca, NY: Cornell University Press, 1989),

chaps. 1 and 8. The term "multilateralism" is also virtually synonymous with institutions.

2. See Arthur A. Stein, *Why Nations Cooperate: Circumstance and Choice in International Relations* (Ithaca, NY: Cornell University Press, 1990), pp. 25–27. Also see Susan Strange, "*Cave! Hic Dragones:* A Critique of Regime Analysis," in Stephen D. Krasner, ed., *International Regimes,* special issue of *International Organization,* Vol. 36, No. 2 (Spring 1982), pp. 479–96.

3. Oran R. Young, "Regime Dynamics: The Rise and Fall of International Regimes," in Krasner, *International Regimes,* p. 277.

4. See Douglass C. North and Robert P. Thomas, "An Economic Theory of the Growth of the Western World," *The Economic History Review,* 2nd series, Vol. 23, No. 1 (April 1970), p. 5.

5. Krasner, *International Regimes,* p. 186. Non-realist institutions are often based on higher norms, while few, if any, realist institutions are based on norms. The dividing line between norms and rules is not sharply defined in the institutionalist literature. See Robert O. Keohane, *After Hegemony: Cooperation and Discord in the World Political Economy* (Princeton, NJ: Princeton University Press, 1984), pp. 57–58. For example, one might argue that rules, not just norms, are concerned with rights and obligations. The key point, however, is that for many institutionalists, norms, which are core beliefs about standards of appropriate state behavior, are the foundation on which more specific rules are constructed. This distinction between norms and rules applies in a rather straightforward way in the subsequent discussion. Both collective security and critical theory challenge the realist belief that states behave in a self-interested way, and argue instead for developing norms that require states to act more altruistically. Liberal institutionalism, on the other hand, accepts the realist view that states act on the basis of self-interest, and concentrates on devising rules that facilitate cooperation among states.

6. International organizations are public agencies established through the cooperative efforts of two or more states. These administrative structures have their own budget, personnel, and buildings. John Ruggie defines them as "palpable entities with headquarters and letterheads, voting procedures, and generous pension plans." Ruggie, "Multilateralism[: The Anatomy of an Institution]," [*International Organization,* Vol. 46, No. 3 (Summer 1992),] p. 573. Once rules are incorporated into an international organization, "they may seem almost coterminous," even though they are "distinguishable analytically." Keohane, *International Institutions and State Power,* p. 5.

7. Charles Lipson, "Is the Future of Collective Security Like the Past?" in George W. Downs, ed., *Collective Security beyond the Cold War* (Ann Arbor: University of Michigan Press), p. 114.

8. Tony Evans and Peter Wilson, "Regime Theory and the English School of International Relations: A Comparison," *Millennium: Journal of International Studies,* Vol. 21, No. 3 (Winter 1992), p. 330.

9. See Gunther Hellmann and Reinhard Wolf, "Neorealism, Neoliberal Institutionalism, and the Future of NATO," *Security Studies,* Vol. 3, No. 1 (Autumn 1993), pp. 3–43.

10. Among the key liberal institutionalist works are: Robert Axelrod and Robert O. Keohane, "Achieving Cooperation under Anarchy:

Strategies and Institutions," *World Politics,* Vol. 38, No. 1 (October 1985), pp. 226–54; Keohane, *After Hegemony;* Keohane, "International Institutions: Two Approaches," pp. 379–96; Keohane, *International Institutions and State Power,* chap. 1; Lisa L. Martin, *Coercive Cooperation: Explaining Multilateral Economic Sanctions* (Princeton, NJ: Princeton University Press, 1992); Kenneth A. Oye, "Explaining Cooperation Under Anarchy: Hypotheses and Strategies," *World Politics,* Vol. 38, No. 1 (October 1985), pp. 1–24; and Stein, *Why Nations Cooperate.*

11. Stein, *Why Nations Cooperate,* chap. 2. Also see Keohane, *After Hegemony,* pp. 6–7, 12–13, 67–69.

12. Milner, "International Theories of Cooperation [among Nations: Strengths and Weakness]," [*World Politics,* Vol. 44, No. 3 (April 1992),] p. 468.

13. For examples of the theory at work in the environmental realm, see Peter M. Haas, Robert O. Keohane, and Marc A. Levy, eds., *Institutions for the Earth: Sources of Effective International Environmental Protection* (Cambridge, MA: MIT Press, 1993), especially chaps. 1 and 9.

14. Cheating is basically a "breach of promise." Oye, "Explaining Cooperation Under Anarchy," p. 1. It usually implies unobserved non-compliance, although there can be observed cheating as well. Defection is a synonym for cheating in the institutionalist literature.

15. The centrality of the prisoners' dilemma and cheating to the liberal institutionalist literature is clearly reflected in virtually all the works cited in footnote 10. As Helen Milner notes in her review essay on this literature: "The focus is primarily on the role of regimes [institutions] in solving the defection [cheating] problem." Milner, "International Theories of Cooperation," p. 475.

16. The phrase is from Keohane, *After Hegemony,* p. 85.

17. Kenneth Oye, for example, writes in the introduction to an issue of *World Politics* containing a number of liberal institutionalist essays: "Our focus is on non-altruistic cooperation among states dwelling in international anarchy." Oye, "Explaining Cooperation Under Anarchy," p. 2. Also see Keohane, "International Institutions: Two Approaches," pp. 380–81; and Keohane, *International Institutions and State Power,* p. 3.

18. Haas, Keohane, and Levy, *Institutions for the Earth,* p. 11. For general discussions of how rules work, which inform my subsequent discussion of the matter, see Keohane, *After Hegemony,* chaps. 5–6; Lisa L. Martin, "Institutions and Cooperation: Sanctions During the Falkland Islands Conflict," *International Security,* Vol. 16, No. 4 (Spring 1992), pp. 143–78; and Milner, "International Theories of Cooperation," pp. 474–78.

19. See Axelrod and Keohane, "Achieving Cooperation Under Anarchy," pp. 248–50; [Charles] Lipson, "International Cooperation [in Economic and Security Affairs]," [*World Politics,* Vol. 37, No. 1 (October 1984),] pp. 4–18.

20. Lipson, "International Cooperation," p. 5.

21. See Keohane, *After Hegemony,* pp. 89–92.

22. This point is clearly articulated in Lipson, "International Cooperation," especially pp. 12–18. The subsequent quotations in this paragraph are from ibid. Also see Axelrod and Keohane, "Achieving Cooperation Under Anarchy," pp. 232–33.

23. See Roger B. Parks, "What if 'Fools Die'? A Comment on Axelrod," Letter to *American Political Science Review,* Vol. 79, No. 4 (December 1985), pp. 1173–74.

24. See Grieco, "Anarchy and the Limits of Cooperation[: A Realist Critique of the Newest Liberal Institutionalism,]" [*International Organization,* Vol. 42, No. 3 (Summer 1988)]. Other works by Grieco bearing on the subject include: Joseph M. Grieco, *Cooperation among Nations: Europe, America, and Non-Tariff Barriers to Trade* (Ithaca, NY: Cornell University Press, 1990).

25. Lipson writes: "The Prisoner's Dilemma, in its simplest form, involves two players. Each is assumed to be a self-interested, self-reliant maximizer of his own utility, an assumption that clearly parallels the Realist conception of sovereign states in international politics." Lipson, "International Cooperation," p. 2. Realists, however, do not accept this conception of international politics and, not surprisingly, have questioned the relevance of the prisoners' dilemma (at least in its common form) for explaining much of international relations. See Stephen D. Krasner, "Global Communications and National Power: Life on the Pareto Frontier," *World Politics,* Vol. 43, No. 3 (April 1991), pp. 336–66.

26. My thinking on this matter has been markedly influenced by Sean Lynn-Jones, in his June 19, 1994, correspondence with me.

27. For a short discussion of strategic trade theory, see Robert Gilpin, *The Political Economy of International Relations* (Princeton, NJ: Princeton University Press, 1987), pp. 215–21. The most commonly cited reference on the subject is Paul R. Krugman, ed., *Strategic Trade Policy and the New International Economics* (Cambridge, MA: MIT Press, 1986).

28. See Robert Axelrod, *The Evolution of Cooperation* (New York: Basic Books, 1984), pp. 110–13.

29. Grieco maintains in *Cooperation among Nations* that realist logic should apply here. Robert Powell, however, points out that "in the context of negotiations between the European Community and the United States . . . it is difficult to attribute any concern for relative gains to the effects that a relative loss may have on the probability of survival." Robert Powell, "Absolute and Relative Gains in International Relations Theory," *American Political Science Review,* Vol. 85, No. 4 (December 1991), p. 1319, footnote 26. I agree with Powell. It is clear from Grieco's response to Powell that Grieco includes non-military logics like strategic trade theory in the realist tent, whereas Powell and I do not. See Grieco's contribution to "The Relative-Gains Problem for International Relations," *American Political Science Review,* Vol. 87, No. 3 (September 1993), pp. 733–35.

30. Krasner, "Global Communications and National Power," pp. 336–66; Grieco, *Cooperation among Nations;* and Michael Mastanduno, "Do Relative Gains Matter? America's Response to Japanese Industrial Policy," *International Security,* Vol. 16, No. 1 (Summer 1991), pp. 73–113.

31. Keohane, "Institutional Theory and the Realist Challenge," [in Baldwin, *Neorealism and Neoliberalism,*] p. 292.

32. For example, Keohane wrote after becoming aware of Grieco's argument about relative gains: "Under specified conditions—where mutual interests are low and relative gains are therefore particularly important to states—neoliberal theory expects neorealism to

explain elements of state behavior." Keohane, *International Institutions and State Power*, pp. 15–16.

33. For example, Lisa Martin writes that "scholars working in the realist tradition maintain a well-founded skepticism about the empirical impact of institutional factors on state behavior. This skepticism is grounded in a lack of studies that show precisely how and when institutions have constrained state decisionmaking." Martin, "Institutions and Cooperation," p. 144.

34. Keohane, *After Hegemony*, chap. 10.

35. Ibid., p. 16.

36. Ibid., p. 236. A U.S. Department of Energy review of the IEA's performance in the 1980 crisis concluded that it had "failed to fulfill its promise." Ethan B. Kapstein, *The Insecure Alliance: Energy Crises and Western Politics Since 1944* (New York: Oxford University Press, 1990), p. 198.

37. Keohane, *After Hegemony*, p. 7.

38. Martin, "Institutions and Cooperation." Martin looks closely at three other cases in *Coercive Cooperation* to determine the effect of institutions on cooperation. I have concentrated on the Falklands War case, however, because it is, by her own admission, her strongest case. See ibid., p. 96.

39. Martin does not claim that agreement would not have been possible without the EC. Indeed, she appears to concede that even without the EC, Britain still could have fashioned "separate bilateral agreements with each EEC member in order to gain its cooperation, [although] this would have involved much higher transaction costs." Martin, "Institutions and Cooperation," pp. 174–75. However, transaction costs among the advanced industrial democracies are not very high in an era of rapid communications and permanent diplomatic establishments.

40. See Michael J. Smith, *Realist Thought from Weber to Kissinger* (Baton Rouge: Louisiana State University Press, 1986), chap. 1.

41. Summing up the autobiographical essays of 34 international relations scholars, Joseph Kruzel notes that "Hans Morgenthau is more frequently cited than any other name in these memoirs." Joseph Kruzel, "Reflections on the Journeys," in Joseph Kruzel and James N. Rosenau, eds., *Journeys through World Politics: Autobiographical Reflections of Thirty-four Academic Travelers* (Lexington, MA: Lexington Books, 1989), p. 505. Although "Morgenthau is often cited, many of the references in these pages are negative in tone. He seems to have inspired his critics even more than his supporters." Ibid.

42. See Keith L. Shimko, "Realism, Neorealism, and American Liberalism," *Review of Politics*, Vol. 54, No. 2 (Spring 1992), pp. 281–301.

43. Hans J. Morgenthau, *Scientific Man vs. Power Politics* (Chicago: University of Chicago Press, 1974), p. 201. Nevertheless, Keith Shimko convincingly argues that the shift within realism, away from Morgenthau's belief that states are motivated by an unalterable will to power, and toward Waltz's view that states are motivated by the desire for security, provides "a residual, though subdued optimism, or at least a possible basis for optimism [about international politics]. The extent to which this optimism is stressed or suppressed varies, but it is there if one wants it to be." Shimko, "Realism, Neorealism, and American Liberalism," p. 297. Realists like Stephen Van Evera, for example, point out that although states operate in a dangerous world, they can take steps to dampen security competition and minimize the danger of war. See Van Evera, *Causes of War* [Vol. II: *National Misperception and the Origins of War*, forthcoming].

44. See Reinhold Niebuhr, *The Children of Light and the Children of Darkness: A Vindication of Democracy and a Critique of Its Traditional Defense* (New York: Charles Scribner's, 1944), especially pp. 153–90. See also Samuel P. Huntington, *The Soldier and the State: The Theory and Politics of Civil-Military Relations* (New York: Vintage Books, 1964).

45. It should be emphasized that many realists have strong moral preferences and are driven by deep moral convictions. Realism is not a normative theory, however, and it provides no criteria for moral judgment. Instead, realism merely seeks to explain how the world works. Virtually all realists would prefer a world without security competition and war, but they believe that goal is unrealistic given the structure of the international system. See, for example, Robert G. Gilpin, "The Richness of the Tradition of Political Realism," in Keohane, ed., *Neorealism and Its Critics* [New York: Columbia University Press, 1986], p. 321.

46. Realism's treatment of states as billiard balls of different sizes tends to raise the hackles of comparative politics scholars, who believe that domestic political and economic factors matter greatly for explaining foreign policy behavior.

Margaret E. Keck and Kathryn Sikkink

TRANSNATIONAL ADVOCACY NETWORKS IN INTERNATIONAL POLITICS

World politics at the end of the twentieth century involves, alongside states, many nonstate actors that interact with each other, with states, and with international organizations. These interactions are structured in terms of networks, and transnational networks are increasingly visible in international politics. [Networks are forms of organization characterized by voluntary, reciprocal, and horizontal patterns of communication and exchange.] Some involve economic actors and firms. Some are networks of scientists and experts whose professional ties and shared causal ideas underpin their efforts to influence policy.[1] Others are networks of activists, distinguishable largely by the centrality of principled ideas or values in motivating their formation.[2] We will call these *transnational advocacy networks*. [A transnational advocacy network includes those relevant actors working internationally on an issue who are bound together by shared values, a common discourse, and dense exchanges of information and services.]

Advocacy networks are significant transnationally and domestically. By building new links among actors in civil societies, states, and international organizations, they multiply the channels of access to the international system. In such issue areas as the environment and human rights, they also make international resources available to new actors in domestic political and social struggles. By thus blurring the boundaries between a state's relations with its own nationals and the recourse both citizens and states have to the international system, advocacy networks are helping to transform the practice of national sovereignty.

■　■　■

Transnational advocacy networks are proliferating, and their goal is to change the behavior of states and of international organizations. Simultaneously principled and strategic actors, they "frame" issues to make them comprehensible to target audiences, to attract attention and encourage action, and to "fit" with favorable institutional venues.[3] Network actors bring new ideas, norms, and discourses into policy debates, and serve as sources of information and testimony. * * *

They also promote norm implementation, by pressuring target actors to adopt new policies, and by monitoring compliance with international standards. Insofar as is possible, they seek to maximize their influence or leverage over the target of their actions. In doing so they contribute to changing perceptions that both state and societal actors may have of their identities, interests, and preferences, to transforming their discursive positions, and ultimately to changing procedures, policies, and behavior.[4]

Networks are communicative structures. To influence discourse, procedures, and policy, activists

From *Activists beyond Borders: Advocacy Networks in International Politics* (Ithaca, NY: Cornell University Press, 1998), Chaps. 1, 3.

may engage and become part of larger policy communities that group actors working on an issue from a variety of institutional and value perspectives. Transnational advocacy networks must also be understood as political spaces, in which differently situated actors negotiate—formally or informally—the social, cultural, and political meanings of their joint enterprise.

■ ■ ■

Major actors in advocacy networks may include the following: (1) international and domestic nongovernmental research and advocacy organizations; (2) local social movements; (3) foundations; (4) the media; (5) churches, trade unions, consumer organizations, and intellectuals; (6) parts of regional and

Table 9.1. International Nongovernmental Social Change Organizations (Categorized by the Major Issue Focus of their Work)

ISSUE AREA (N)	1953 (N = 110)	1963 (N = 141)	1973 (N = 183)	1983 (N = 348)	1993 (N = 631)
Human rights	33	38	41	79	168
	30.0%	27.0%	22.4%	22.7%	26.6%
World order	8	4	12	31	48
	7.3%	2.8%	6.6%	8.9%	7.6%
International law	14	19	25	26	26
	12.7%	13.4%	13.7%	7.4%	4.1%
Peace	11	20	14	22	59
	10.0%	14.2%	7.7%	6.3%	9.4%
Women's rights	10	14	16	25	61
	9.1%	9.9%	8.7%	7.2%	9.7%
Environment	2	5	10	26	90
	1.8%	3.5%	5.5%	7.5%	14.3%
Development	3	3	7	13	34
	2.7%	2.1%	3.8%	3.7%	5.4%
Ethnic unity/ Group rts.	10	12	18	37	29
	9.1%	8.5%	9.8%	10.6%	4.6%
Esperanto	11	18	28	41	54
	10.0%	12.8%	15.3%	11.8%	8.6%

Source: Union of International Associations, *Yearbook of International Organizations* (1953, 1963, 1973, 1983, 1993). We are indebted to Jackie Smith, University of Notre Dame, for the use of her data from 1983 and 1993, and the use of her coding form and codebook for our data collection for the period 1953–73.

international intergovernmental organizations; and (7) parts of the executive and/or parliamentary branches of governments. Not all these will be present in each advocacy network. Initial research suggests, however, that international and domestic NGOs play a central role in all advocacy networks, usually initiating actions and pressuring more powerful actors to take positions. NGOs introduce new ideas, provide information, and lobby for policy changes.

Groups in a network share values and frequently exchange information and services. The flow of information among actors in the network reveals a dense web of connections among these groups, both formal and informal. The movement of funds and services is especially notable between foundations and NGOs, and some NGOs provide services such as training for other NGOs in the same and sometimes other advocacy networks. Personnel also circulate within and among networks, as relevant players move from one to another in a version of the "revolving door."

■ ■ ■

We cannot accurately count transnational advocacy networks to measure their growth over time, but one proxy is the increase in the number of international NGOs committed to social change. Because international NGOs are key components of any advocacy network, this increase suggests broader trends in the number, size, and density of advocacy networks generally. Table 9.1 suggests that the number of international nongovernmental social change groups has increased across all issues, though to varying degrees in different issue areas. There are five times as many organizations working primarily on human rights as there were in 1950, but proportionally human rights groups have remained roughly a quarter of all such groups. Similarly, groups working on women's rights accounted for 9 percent of all groups in 1953 and in 1993. Transnational environmental organizations have grown most dramatically in absolute and relative terms, increasing from two groups in 1953 to ninety in 1993, and from 1.8 percent of total groups in 1953 to 14.3 percent in 1993. The percentage share of groups in such issue areas as international law, peace, ethnic unity, and Esperanto, has declined.[5]

■ ■ ■

How Do Transnational Advocacy Networks Work?

Transnational advocacy networks seek influence in many of the same ways that other political groups or social movements do. Since they are not powerful in a traditional sense of the word, they must use the power of their information, ideas, and strategies to alter the information and value contexts within which states make policies. The bulk of what networks do might be termed persuasion or socialization, but neither process is devoid of conflict. Persuasion and socialization often involve not just reasoning with opponents, but also bringing pressure, arm-twisting, encouraging sanctions, and shaming. * * *

Our typology of tactics that networks use in their efforts at persuasion, socialization, and pressure includes (1) *information politics*, or the ability to quickly and credibly generate politically usable information and move it to where it will have the most impact; (2) *symbolic politics*, or the ability to call upon symbols, actions, or stories that make sense of a situation for an audience that is frequently far away;[6] (3) *leverage politics*, or the ability to call upon powerful actors to affect a situation where weaker members of a network are unlikely to have influence; and (4) *accountability politics*, or the effort to hold powerful actors to their previously stated policies or principles.

A single campaign may contain many of these elements simultaneously. For example, the human rights network disseminated information about human rights abuses in Argentina in the period 1976–83. The Mothers of the Plaza de Mayo marched in circles in the central square in Buenos Aires wearing white handkerchiefs to draw symbolic attention to the plight of their missing children. The network also tried to use both material and moral leverage against the Argentine regime, by pressuring the United States and other governments to cut off military and economic aid, and by efforts to get the UN and the Inter-American Commission on Human Rights to condemn Argentina's human rights practices. Monitoring is a variation on information politics, in which activists use information strategically to ensure accountability with public statements, existing legislation and international standards.

■ ■ ■

Network members actively seek ways to bring issues to the public agenda by framing them in innovative ways and by seeking hospitable venues. Sometimes they create issues by framing old problems in new ways; occasionally they help transform other actors' understanding of their identities and their interests. Land use rights in the Amazon, for example, took on an entirely different character and gained quite different allies viewed in a deforestation frame than they did in either social justice or regional development frames. In the 1970s and 1980s many states decided for the first time that promotion of human rights in other countries was a legitimate foreign policy goal and an authentic expression of national interest. This decision came in part from interaction with an emerging global human rights network. We argue that this represents not the victory of morality over self-interest, but a transformed understanding of national interest, possible in part because of structured interactions between state components and networks. * * *

■ ■ ■

Under What Conditions Do Advocacy Networks Have Influence?

To assess the influence of advocacy networks we must look at goal achievement at several different levels. We identify the following types or stages of network influence: (1) issue creation and agenda setting; (2) influence on discursive positions of states and international organizations; (3) influence on institutional procedures; (4) influence on policy change in "target actors" which may be states, international organizations like the World Bank, or private actors like the Nestlé Corporation; and (5) influence on state behavior.

Networks generate attention to new issues and help set agendas when they provoke media attention, debates, hearings, and meetings on issues that previously had not been a matter of public debate. Because values are the essence of advocacy networks, this stage of influence may require a modification of the "value context" in which policy debates takes place. The UN's theme years and decades, such as International Women's Decade and the Year of Indigenous Peoples, were international events promoted by networks that heightened awareness of issues.

Networks influence discursive positions when they help persuade states and international organizations to support international declarations or to change stated domestic policy positions. The role environmental networks played in shaping state positions and conference declarations at the 1992 "Earth Summit" in Rio de Janeiro is an example of this kind of impact. They may also pressure states to make more binding commitments by signing conventions and codes of conduct.

The targets of network campaigns frequently respond to demands for policy change with changes in procedures (which may affect policies in the future). The multilateral bank campaign is largely responsible for a number of changes in internal bank directives mandating greater NGO and local participation in discussions of projects. It also opened access to formerly restricted information, and led to the establishment of an independent inspection panel for World Bank projects. Procedural changes can greatly increase the opportunity for advocacy organizations to develop regular contact with other key players on an issue, and they sometimes offer the opportunity to move from outside to inside pressure strategies.

A network's activities may produce changes in policies, not only of the target states, but also of other states and/or international institutions. Explicit policy shifts seem to denote success, but even here both their causes and meanings may be elusive. We can point with some confidence to network impact where human rights network pressures have achieved cutoffs of military aid to repressive regimes, or a curtailment of repressive practices. Sometimes human rights activity even affects regime stability. But we must take care to distinguish between policy change and change in behavior; official policies regarding timber extraction in Sarawak, Malaysia, for example, may say little about how timber companies behave on the ground in the absence of enforcement.

We speak of stages of impact, and not merely types of impact, because we believe that increased attention, followed by changes in discursive positions, make governments more vulnerable to the claims that networks raise. (Discursive changes can also have a powerfully divisive effect on networks themselves, splitting insiders from outsiders, reformers from radicals.[7]) A government that claims to be protecting indigenous areas or ecological reserves is potentially more vulnerable to charges that such areas are endangered than one that makes no such claim. At that point the effort is not to make governments change their position but to hold them to their word. Meaningful policy change is thus more likely when the first three types or stages of impact have occurred.

Both issue characteristics and actor characteristics are important parts of our explanation of how networks affect political outcomes and the conditions under which networks can be effective. Issue characteristics such as salience and resonance within existing national or institutional agendas can tell us something about where networks are likely to be able to insert new ideas and discourses into policy debates. Success in influencing policy also depends on the strength and density of the network and its ability to achieve leverage. * * *

■   ■   ■

Toward a Global Civil Society?

Many other scholars now recognize that "the state does not monopolize the public sphere,"[8] and are seeking, as we are, ways to describe the sphere of international interactions under a variety of names: transnational relations, international civil society, and global civil society.[9] In these views, states no longer look unitary from the outside. Increasingly dense interactions among individuals, groups, actors from states, and international institutions appear to involve much more than representing interests on a world stage.

We contend that the advocacy network concept cannot be subsumed under notions of transnational social movements or global civil society. In particular, theorists who suggest that a global civil society will inevitably emerge from economic globalization or from revolutions in communication and transportation technologies ignore the issues of agency and political opportunity that we find central for understanding the evolution of new international institutions and relationships.

■   ■   ■

We lack convincing studies of the sustained and specific processes through which individuals and organizations create (or resist the creation of) something resembling a global civil society. Our research leads us to believe that these interactions involve much more agency than a pure diffusionist perspective suggests. Even though the implications of our findings are much broader than most political scientists would admit, the findings themselves do not yet support the strong claims about an emerging global civil society.[10] We are much more comfortable with a conception of transnational civil society as an arena of struggle, a fragmented and contested area where "the politics of transnational civil society is centrally about the way in which certain groups emerge and are legitimized (by governments, institutions, and other groups)."[11]

■　■　■

HUMAN RIGHTS ADVOCACY NETWORKS IN LATIN AMERICA

Argentina

Even before the military coup of March 1976, international human rights pressures had influenced the Argentine military's decision to cause political opponents to "disappear," rather than imprisoning them or executing them publicly.[12] (The technique led to the widespread use of the verb "to disappear" in a transitive sense.) The Argentine military believed they had "learned" from the international reaction to the human rights abuses after the Chilean coup. When the Chilean military executed and imprisoned large numbers of people, the ensuing uproar led to the international isolation of the regime of Augusto Pinochet. Hoping to maintain a moderate international image, the Argentine military decided to secretly kidnap, detain, and execute its victims, while denying any knowledge of their whereabouts.[13]

Although this method did initially mute the international response to the coup, Amnesty International and groups staffed by Argentine political exiles eventually were able to document and condemn the new forms of repressive practices. To counteract the rising tide of criticism, the Argentina junta invited AI for an on-site visit in 1976. In March 1977, on the first anniversary of the military coup, AI published the report on its visit, a well-documented denunciation of the abuses of the regime with emphasis on the problem of the disappeared. Amnesty estimated that the regime had taken six thousand political prisoners, most without specifying charges, and had abducted between two and ten thousand people. The report helped demonstrate that the disappearances were part of a deliberate government policy by which the military and the police kidnapped perceived opponents, took them to secret detention centers where they tortured, interrogated, and killed them, then secretly disposed of their bodies.[14] Amnesty International's denunciations of the Argentine regime were legitimized when it won the Nobel Peace Prize later that year.

Such information led the Carter administration and the French, Italian, and Swedish governments to denounce rights violations by the junta. France, Italy, and Sweden each had citizens who had been victims of Argentine repression, but their concerns extended beyond their own citizens. Although the Argentine government claimed that such attacks constituted unacceptable intervention in their internal affairs and violated Argentine sovereignty, U.S. and European officials persisted. In 1977 the U.S. government reduced the planned level of military aid for Argentina because of human rights abuses. Congress later passed a bill eliminating all military assistance to Argentina, which went into effect on 30 September 1978.[15] A number of high-level U.S. delegations met with junta members during this period to discuss human rights.

Early U.S. action on Argentina was based primarily on the human rights documentation provided by AI and other NGOs, not on information received through official channels at the embassy or the State Department.[16] For example, during a 1977 visit, Secretary of State Cyrus Vance carried a list of disappeared people prepared by human rights NGOs to present to members of the junta.[17] When Patricia Derian met with junta member Admiral Emilio Massera during a visit in 1977, she brought up the navy's use of torture. In response to Massera's denial, Derian said she had seen a rudimentary map of a secret detention center in the Navy Mechanical School, where their meeting was being held, and asked whether perhaps under their feet someone was being tortured. Among Derian's key sources of information were NGOs and especially the families of the disappeared, with whom she met frequently during her visits to Buenos Aires.[18]

Within a year of the coup, Argentine domestic human rights organizations began to develop significant external contacts. Their members traveled frequently to the United States and Europe, where they met with human rights organizations, talked to the press, and met with parliamentarians and government officials. These groups sought foreign contacts to publicize the human rights situation, to fund their activities, and to help protect themselves from further repression by their government, and

they provided evidence to U.S. and European policymakers. Much of their funding came from European and U.S.-based foundations.[19]

Two key events that served to keep the case of Argentine human rights in the minds of U.S. and European policymakers reflect the impact of transnational linkages on policy. In 1979 the Argentine authorities released Jacobo Timerman, whose memoir describing his disappearance and torture by the Argentine military helped human rights organizations, members of the U.S. Jewish community, and U.S. journalists to make his case a cause célèbre in U.S. policy circles.[20] Then in 1980 the Nobel Peace Prize was awarded to an Argentine human rights activist, Adolfo Pérez Esquivel. Peace and human rights groups in the United States and Europe helped sponsor Pérez Esquivel's speaking tour to the United States exactly at the time that the OAS was considering the IACHR report on Argentina and Congress was debating the end of the arms embargo to Argentina.

The Argentine military government wanted to avoid international human rights censure. Scholars have long recognized that even authoritarian regimes depend on a combination of coercion and consent to stay in power. Without the legitimacy conferred by elections, they rely heavily on claims about their political efficacy and on nationalism.[21] Although the Argentine military mobilized nationalist rhetoric against foreign criticism, a sticking point was that Argentines, especially the groups that most supported the military regime, thought of themselves as the most European of Latin American countries. The military junta claimed to be carrying out the repression in the name of "our Western and Christian civilization."[22] But the military's intent to integrate Argentina more fully into the liberal global economic order was being jeopardized by deteriorating relations with countries most identified with that economic order, and with "Western and Christian civilization."

The junta adopted a sequence of responses to international pressures. From 1976 to 1978 the military pursued an initial strategy of denying the legitimacy of international concern over human rights in Argentina. At the same time it took actions that appear to have contradicted this strategy, such as permitting the visit of the Amnesty International mission to Argentina in 1976. The "failure" of the Amnesty visit, from the military point of view, appeared to reaffirm the junta's resistance to human rights pressures. This strategy was most obvious at the UN, where the Argentine government worked to silence international condemnation in the UN Commission on Human Rights. Ironically, the rabidly anticommunist Argentine regime found a diplomatic ally in the Soviet Union, an importer of Argentine wheat, and the two countries collaborated to block UN consideration of the Argentine human rights situation.[23] Concerned states circumvented this blockage by creating the UN Working Group on Disappearances in 1980. Human rights NGOs provided information, lobbied government delegations, and pursued joint strategies with sympathetic UN delegations.

By 1978 the Argentine government recognized that something had to be done to improve its international image in the United States and Europe, and to restore the flow of military and economic aid.[24] To these ends the junta invited the Inter-American Commission on Human Rights for an on-site visit, in exchange for a U.S. commitment to release Export-Import Bank funds and otherwise improve U.S.-Argentine relations.[25] During 1978 the human rights situation in Argentina improved significantly. [T]he practice of disappearance as a tool of state policy was curtailed only after 1978, when the government began to take the "international variable" seriously.[26]

The value of the network perspective in the Argentine case is in highlighting the fact that international pressures did not work independently, but rather in coordination with national actors. Rapid change occurred because strong domestic human rights organizations documented abuses and protested against repression, and international pressures helped protect domestic monitors and open spaces for their protest. International groups amplified both information and symbolic politics of domestic groups and projected them onto an international stage, from which they echoed back into Argentina. This classic boomerang process was executed nowhere more skillfully than in Argentina, in large part due to the courage and ability of domestic human rights organizations.

Some argue that repression stopped because the military had finally killed all the people that they thought they needed to kill. This argument disregards disagreements within the regime about the size and nature of the "enemy." International pressures affected particular factions within the military regime that had differing ideas about how much repression was "necessary." Although by the military's admission 90 percent of the *armed* opposition had been eliminated by April 1977, this did not lead to an immediate change in human rights practices.[27] By 1978 there were splits within the military about what it should do in the future. One faction was led by Admiral Massera, a right-wing populist, another by Generals Carlos Suarez Mason and Luciano Menéndez, who supported indefinite military dictatorship and unrelenting war against the left, and a third by Generals Jorge Videla and Roberto Viola, who hoped for eventual political liberalization under a military president. Over time, the Videla-Viola faction won out, and by late 1978 Videla had gained increased control over the Ministry of Foreign Affairs, previously under the influence of the navy.[28] Videla's ascendancy in the fall of 1978, combined with U.S. pressure, helps explain his ability to deliver on his promise to allow the Inter-American Commission on Human Rights visit in December.

The Argentine military government thus moved from initial refusal to accept international human rights interventions, to cosmetic cooperation with the human rights network, and eventually to concrete improvements in response to increased international pressures. Once it had invited IACHR and discovered that the commission could not be co-opted or confused, the government ended the practice of disappearance, released political prisoners, and restored some semblance of political participation. Full restoration of human rights in Argentina did not come until after the Malvinas War and the transition to democracy in 1983, but after 1980 the worst abuses had been curtailed.

In 1985, after democratization, Argentina tried the top military leaders of the juntas for human rights abuses, and a number of key network members testified: Theo Van Boven and Patricia Derian spoke about international awareness of the Argentine human rights situation, and a member of the IACHR delegation to Argentina discussed the OAS report. Clyde Snow and Eric Stover provided information about the exhumation of cadavers from mass graves. Snow's testimony, corroborated by witnesses, was a key part of the prosecutor's success in establishing that top military officers were guilty of murder.[29] A public opinion poll taken during the trials showed that 92 percent of Argentines were in favor of the trials of the military juntas.[30] The tribunal convicted five of the nine defendants, though only two—ex-president Videla, and Admiral Massera—were given life sentences. The trials were the first of their kind in Latin America, and among the very few in the world ever to try former leaders for human rights abuses during their rule. In 1990 President Carlos Menem pardoned the former officers. By the mid-1990s, however, democratic rule in Argentina was firmly entrenched, civilian authority over the military was well established, and the military had been weakened by internal disputes and severe cuts in funding.[31]

The Argentine case set important precedents for other international and regional human rights action, and shows the intricate interactions of groups and individuals within the network and the repercussions of these interactions. The story of the Grandmothers of the Plaza de Mayo is an exemplar of network interaction and unanticipated effects. The persistence of the Grandmothers helped create a new profession—what one might call "human rights forensic science." (The scientific skills existed before, but they had never been put to the service of human rights.) Once the Argentine case had demonstrated that forensic science could illuminate mass murder and lead to convictions, these skills were diffused and legitimized. Eric Stover, Clyde Snow, and the Argentine forensic anthropology team they helped create were the prime agents of international diffusion. The team later carried out exhumations and training in Chile, Bolivia, Brazil, Venezuela, and Guatemala.[32] Forensic science is being used to prosecute mass murderers in El Salvador, Honduras, Rwanda, and Bosnia. By 1996 the UN International Criminal Tribunal for the former Yugoslavia had contracted with two veterans of the Argentine forensic experiment, Stover and Dr. Robert Kirschner, to do forensic investigations for its war crimes tribunal. " 'A war crime creates a crime scene,' said Dr. Kirschner, 'That's how we treat it. We recover forensic evidence for prosecution and create a record which cannot be successfully challenged in court.' "[33]

■ ■ ■

Conclusions

A realist approach to international relations would have trouble attributing significance either to the network's activities or to the adoption and implementation of state human rights policies. Realism offers no convincing explanation for why relatively weak nonstate actors could affect state policy, or why states would concern themselves with the internal human rights practices of other states even when doing so interferes with the pursuit of other goals. For example, the U.S. government's pressure on Argentina on human rights led Argentina to defect from the grain embargo of the Soviet Union. Raising human rights issues with Mexico could have undermined the successful completion of the free trade agreement and cooperation with Mexico on antidrug operations. Human rights pressures have costs, even in strategically less important countries of Latin America.

In liberal versions of international relations theory, states and nonstate actors cooperate to realize joint gains or avoid mutually undesirable outcomes when they face problems they cannot resolve alone. These situations have been characterized as cooperation or coordination games with particular payoff structures.[34] But human rights issues are not easily modeled as such. Usually states can ignore the internal human rights practices of other states without incurring undesirable economic or security costs.

In the issue of human rights it is primarily principled ideas that drive change and cooperation. We cannot understand why countries, organizations, and individuals are concerned about human rights or why countries respond to human rights pressures without taking into account the role of norms and ideas in international life. Jack Donnelly has argued that such moral interests are as real as material interests, and that a sense of moral interdependence has led to the emergence of human rights regimes.[35] For human rights * * * the primary movers behind this form of principled international action are international networks.

NOTES

1. Peter Haas has called these "knowledge-based" or "epistemic communities." See Peter Haas, "Introduction: Epistemic Communities and International Policy Coordination," *Knowledge, Power and International Policy Coordination,* special issue, *International Organization* 46 (Winter 1992), pp. 1–36.
2. Ideas that specify criteria for determining whether actions are right and wrong and whether outcomes are just or unjust are shared principled beliefs or values. Beliefs about cause-effect relationships are shared casual beliefs. Judith Goldstein and Robert Keohane, eds., *Ideas and Foreign Policy: Beliefs, Institutions, and Political Change* (Ithaca: Cornell University Press, 1993), pp. 8–10.
3. David Snow and his colleagues have adapted Erving Goffman's concept of framing. We use it to mean "conscious strategic efforts by groups of people to fashion shared understandings of the world and of themselves that legitimate and motivate collective action." Definition from Doug McAdam, John D. McCarthy, and Mayer N. Zald, "Introduction," *Comparative Perspectives on Social Movements: Political Opportunities, Mobilizing Structures, and Cultural Framings,* ed. McAdam, McCarthy, and Zald (New York: Cambridge University Press, 1996), p. 6. See also Frank Baumgartner and Bryan Jones, "Agenda Dynamics and Policy Subsystems," *Journal of Politics* 53:4 (1991): 1044–74.
4. With the "constructivists" in international relations theory, we take actors and interests to be constituted in interaction. See Martha Finnemore, *National Interests in International Society* (Ithaca: Cornell University Press, 1996), who argues that "states are embedded in dense networks of transnational and international social relations that shape their perceptions of the world and their role in that world. States are *socialized* to want certain things by the international society in which they and the people in them live" (p. 2).
5. Data from a collaborative research project with Jackie G. Smith. We thank her for the use of her data from the period 1983–93, whose results are presented in Jackie G. Smith, "Characteristics of the Modern Transnational Social Movement Sector," in Jackie G. Smith, et al., eds. *Transnational Social Movements and World Politics: Solidarity beyond the State* (Syracuse: Syracuse University Press 1997), and for permission to use her coding form and codebook for our data collection for the period 1953–73. All data were coded from Union of International Associations, *The Yearbook of International Organizations,* 1948–95 (published annually).
6. Alison Brysk uses the categories "information politics" and "symbolic politics" to discuss strategies of transnational actors, especially networks around Indian rights. See "Acting Globally: Indian Rights and International Politics in Latin America," in *Indigenous Peoples and Democracy in Latin America,* ed. Donna Lee Van Cott (New York: St. Martin's Press/Inter-American Dialogue, 1994), pp. 29–51; and "Hearts and Minds: Bringing Symbolic Politics Back In," *Polity* 27 (Summer 1995): 559–85.
7. We thank Jonathan Fox for reminding us of this point.
8. M. J. Peterson, "Transnational Activity, International Society, and World Politics," *Millennium* 21:3 (1992): 375–76.
9. See, for example, Ronnie Lipschutz, "Reconstructing World Politics: The Emergence of Global Civil Society," *Millennium* 21:3 (1992): 389–420; Paul Wapner, "Politics beyond the State: Environmental Activism and World Civic Politics," *World Politics* 47 (April 1995): 311–40; and the special issue of *Millennium* on social movements and world politics, 23:3 (Winter 1994).
10. Sidney Tarrow, *Power in Movement: Social Movements and Contentious Politics,* rev. ed. (Cambridge: Cambridge University Press 1998), Chapter 11. An earlier version appeared as "Fishnets, Internets and Catnets: Globalization and Transnational Collective Action," Instituto Juan March de Estudios e Investigaciones, Madrid: Working Papers 1996/78, March 1996; and Peterson, "Transnational Activity."

11. Andrew Hurrell and Ngaire Woods, "Globalisation and Inequality," *Millennium* 24:3 (1995), p. 468.

12. This section draws upon some material from an earlier co-authored work: Lisa L. Martin and Kathryn Sikkink, "U.S. Policy and Human Rights in Argentina and Guatemala, 1973–1980," in *Double-Edged Diplomacy: International Bargaining and Domestic Politics,* ed., Peter B. Evans, Harold K. Jacobson, and Robert D. Putnam (Berkeley: University of California Press, 1993), pp. 330–62.

13. See Emilio Mignone, *Derechos humanos y sociedad: el caso argentino* (Buenos Aires: Ediciones del Pensamiento Nacional and Centro de Estudios Legales y Sociales, 1991), p. 66; Claudio Uriarte, *Almirante Cero: Biografía No Autorizada de Emilio Eduardo Massera* (Buenos Aires: Planeta, 1992), p. 97; and Carlos H. Acuña and Catalina Smulovitz, "Adjusting the Armed Forces to Democracy: Successes, Failures, and Ambiguities in the Southern Cone," in *Constructing Democracy: Human Rights, Citizenship, and Society in Latin America,* ed. Elizabeth Jelin and Eric Hershberg (Boulder, CO: Westview, 1993), p. 15.

14. Amnesty International, *Report of an Amnesty International Mission to Argentina* (London: Amnesty International, 1977).

15. Congressional Research Service, Foreign Affairs and National Defense Division, *Human Rights and U.S. Foreign Assistance: Experiences and Issues in Policy Implementation (1977–1978),* report prepared for U.S. Senate Committee on Foreign Relations, November 1979, p. 106.

16. After the 1976 coup, Argentine political exiles set up branches of the Argentine Human Rights Commission (CADHU) in Paris, Mexico, Rome, Geneva, and Washington, DC. In October two of its members testified on human rights abuses before the U.S. House Subcommittee on Human Rights and International Organization. Iain Guest, *Behind the Disappearances: Argentina's Dirty War against Human Rights and the United Nations* (Philadelphia: University of Pennsylvania Press, 1990), pp. 66–67.

17. Interview with Robert Pastor, Wianno, Massachusetts, 28 June 1990.

18. Testimony given by Patricia Derian to the National Criminal Appeals Court in Buenos Aires during the trials of junta members. "Massera sonrió y me dijo: Sabe qué pasó con Poncio Pilatos . . . ?" *Diario del Juicio,* 18 June 1985, p. 3; Guest, *Behind the Disappearances,* pp. 161–63. Later it was confirmed that the Navy Mechanical School was one of the most notorious secret torture and detention centers. *Nunca Más: The Report of the Argentine National Commission for the Disappeared* (New York: Farrar, Straus & Giroux, 1986), pp. 79–84.

19. The Mothers of the Plaza de Mayo received grants from Dutch churches and the Norwegian Parliament, and the Ford Foundation provided funds for the Center for Legal and Social Studies (CELS) and the Grandmothers of the Plaza de Mayo.

20. Jacobo Timerman, *Prisoner without a Name, Cell without a Number* (New York: Random House, 1981).

21. See Guillermo O'Donnell, "Tensions in the Bureaucratic Authoritarian State and the Question of Democracy," in *The New Authoritarianism in Latin America,* ed. David Collier (Princeton: Princeton University Press, 1979), pp. 288, 292–94.

22. Daniel Frontalini and Maria Cristina Caiati, *El Mito de la Guerra Sucia* (Buenos Aires: Centro de Estudios Legales y Sociales, 1984), p. 24.

23. Guest, *Behind the Disappearances,* pp. 118–19, 182–83.

24. *Carta Política,* a news magazine considered to reflect the junta's views concluded in 1978 that "the principal problem facing the Argentine State has now become the international siege (*cerco internacional*)." "Cuadro de Situación," *Carta Política* 57 (August 1978): 8.

25. Interviews with Walter Mondale, Minneapolis, Minnesota, 20 June 1989, and Ricardo Yofre, Buenos Aires, 1 August 1990.

26. See Asamblea Permanente por los Derechos Humanos, *Las Cifras de la Guerra Sucia* (Buenos Aires, 1988), pp. 26–32.

27. According to a memorandum signed by General Jorge Videla, the objectives of the military government "go well beyond the simple defeat of subversion." The memorandum called for a continuation and intensification of the "general offensive against subversion," including "intense military action." "Directivo 504," 20 April 1977, in "La orden secreta de Videla," *Diario del Juicio* 28 (3 December 1985): 5–8.

28. David Rock, *Argentina, 1516–1987: From Spanish Colonization to Alfonsín* (Berkeley: University of California Press, 1985), pp. 370–71; Timerman, *Prisoner without a Name,* p. 163.

29. *Diario del Juicio* 1 (27 May 1985), and 9 (23 July 1985).

30. *Diario del Juicio* 25 (12 November 1985).

31. Acuña and Smulovitz, "Adjusting the Armed Forces to Democracy," pp. 20–21.

32. Cohen Salama, *Tumbas anónimas [informe sobre la identificación de restos de víctimas de la represión* (Buenos Aires: Catálogos Editora, 1992)], p. 275.

33. Mike O'Connor, "Harvesting Evidence in Bosnia's Killing Fields," *New York Times,* 7 April 1996, p. E3.

34. See, e.g., Arthur A. Stein, "Coordination and Collaboration: Regimes in an Anarchic World," *International Organization* 36:2 (Spring 1982): 299–324.

35. Donnelly, *Universal Human Rights [in Theory and Practice* (Ithaca: Cornell University Press, 1989)], pp. 211–12.

Michael N. Barnett and Martha Finnemore

THE POLITICS, POWER, AND PATHOLOGIES OF INTERNATIONAL ORGANIZATIONS

Do international organizations really do what their creators intend them to do? In the past century the number of international organizations (IOs) has increased exponentially, and we have a variety of vigorous theories to explain why they have been created. Most of these theories explain IO creation as a response to problems of incomplete information, transaction costs, and other barriers to Pareto efficiency and welfare improvement for their members. Research flowing from these theories, however, has paid little attention to how IOs actually behave after they are created. Closer scrutiny would reveal that many IOs stray from the efficiency goals these theories impute and that many IOs exercise power autonomously in ways unintended and unanticipated by states at their creation. Understanding how this is so requires a reconsideration of IOs and what they do.

In this article we develop a constructivist approach rooted in sociological institutionalism to explain both the power of IOs and their propensity for dysfunctional, even pathological, behavior. Drawing on long-standing Weberian arguments about bureaucracy and sociological institutionalist approaches to organizational behavior, we argue that the rational-legal authority that IOs embody gives them power independent of the states that created them and channels that power in particular directions. Bureaucracies, by definition, make rules, but in so doing they also create social knowledge.

They define shared international tasks (like "development"), create and define new categories of actors (like "refugee"), create new interests for actors (like "promoting human rights"), and transfer models of political organization around the world (like markets and democracy). However, the same normative valuation on impersonal, generalized rules that defines bureaucracies and makes them powerful in modern life can also make them unresponsive to their environments, obsessed with their own rules at the expense of primary missions, and ultimately lead to inefficient, self-defeating behavior. We are not the first to suggest that IOs are more than the reflection of state preferences and that they can be autonomous and powerful actors in global politics.[1] Nor are we the first to note that IOs, like all organizations, can be dysfunctional and inefficient.[2] However, our emphasis on the way that characteristics of bureaucracy as a generic cultural form shape IO behavior provides a different and very broad basis for thinking about how IOs influence world politics.[3]

Developing an alternative approach to thinking about IOs is only worthwhile if it produces significant insights and new opportunities for research on major debates in the field. Our approach allows us to weigh in with new perspectives on at least three such debates. First, it offers a different view of the power of IOs and whether or how they matter in world politics. This issue has been at the core of the neoliberal-institutionalists' debate with neorealists for years.[4] We show in this

From *International Organization* 53, no. 4 (Autumn 1999): 699–732.

article how neoliberal-institutionalists actually disadvantage themselves in their argument with realists by looking at only one facet of IO power. Global organizations do more than just facilitate cooperation by helping states to overcome market failures, collective action dilemmas, and problems associated with interdependent social choice. They also create actors, specify responsibilities and authority among them, and define the work these actors should do, giving it meaning and normative value. Even when they lack material resources, IOs exercise power as they constitute and construct the social world.[5]

Second and related, our perspective provides a theoretical basis for treating IOs as autonomous actors in world politics and thus presents a challenge to the statist ontology prevailing in international relations theories. Despite all their attention to international institutions, one result of the theoretical orientation of neoliberal institutionalists and regimes theorists is that they treat IOs the way pluralists treat the state. IOs are mechanisms through which others (usually states) act; they are not purposive actors. The regimes literature is particularly clear on this point. Regimes are "principles, norms, rules, and decision-making procedures"; they are not actors.[6] Weber's insights about the normative power of the rational-legal authority that bureaucracies embody and its implications for the ways bureaucracies produce and control social knowledge provide a basis for challenging this view and treating IOs as agents, not just as structure.

Third, our perspective offers a different vantage point from which to assess the desirability of IOs. While realists and some policymakers have taken up this issue, surprisingly few other students of IOs have been critical of their performance or desirability.[7] Part of this optimism stems from central tenets of classical liberalism, which has long viewed IOs as a peaceful way to manage rapid technological change and globalization, far preferable to the obvious alternative—war.[8] Also contributing to this uncritical stance is the normative judgment about IOs that is built into the theoretical assumptions of most neoliberal and regimes scholars and the economic organization theories on which they draw. IOs exist, in this view, only because they are Pareto improving and solve problems for states. Consequently, if an IO exists, it must be because it is more useful than other alternatives since, by theoretical axiom, states will pull the plug on any IO that does not perform. We find this assumption unsatisfying. IOs often produce undesirable and even self-defeating outcomes repeatedly, without punishment much less dismantlement, and we, as theorists, want to understand why. International relations scholars are familiar with principal-agent problems and the ways in which bureaucratic politics can compromise organizational effectiveness, but these approaches have rarely been applied to IOs. Further, these approaches by no means exhaust sources of dysfunction. We examine one such source that flows from the same rational-legal characteristics that make IOs authoritative and powerful. Drawing from research in sociology and anthropology, we show how the very features that make bureaucracies powerful can also be their weakness.

The claims we make in this article flow from an analysis of the "social stuff" of which bureaucracy is made. We are asking a standard constructivist question about what makes the world hang together or, as Alexander Wendt puts it, "how are things in the world put together so that they have the properties they do."[9] In this sense, our explanation of IO behavior is constitutive and differs from most other international relations approaches. This approach does not make our explanation "mere description," since understanding the constitution of things does essential work in explaining how those things behave and what causes outcomes. Just as understanding how the double-helix DNA molecule is constituted materially makes possible causal arguments about genetics, disease, and other biological processes, so understanding how bureaucracies are constituted socially allows us to hypothesize about the behavior of IOs and the effects this social form might have in world politics. This type of constitutive explanation does not allow us to offer law-like statements such as "if X happens, then Y must follow." Rather, by providing a more complete understanding of what bureaucracy is, we can provide explanations of how certain kinds of bureaucratic behavior are possible, or even probable, and why.[10]

We begin by examining the assumptions underlying different branches of organization theory and exploring their implications for the study of IOs. We argue that assumptions drawn from economics that undergird neoliberal and neorealist treatments of IOs do not always reflect the empirical situation of most IOs commonly studied by political scientists. Further, they provide research hypotheses about only some aspects of IOs (like why they are created) and not others (like what they do). We then introduce sociological arguments that help remedy these problems.

In the second section we develop a constructivist approach from these sociological arguments to examine the power wielded by IOs and the sources of their influence. Liberal and realist theories only make predictions about, and consequently only look for, a very limited range of welfare-improving effects caused by IOs. Sociological theories, however, expect and explain a much broader range of impacts organizations can have and specifically highlight their role in constructing actors, interests, and social purpose. We provide illustrations from the UN system to show how IOs do, in fact, have such powerful effects in contemporary world politics. In the third section we explore the dysfunctional behavior of IOs, which we define as behavior that undermines the stated goals of the organization. International relations theorists are familiar with several types of theories that might explain such behavior. Some locate the source of dysfunction in material factors, others focus on cultural factors. Some theories locate the source of dysfunction outside the organization, others locate

it inside. We construct a typology, mapping these theories according to the source of dysfunction they emphasize, and show that the same internally generated cultural forces that give IOs their power and autonomy can also be a source of dysfunctional behavior. We use the term *pathologies* to describe such instances when IO dysfunction can be traced to bureaucratic culture. We conclude by discussing how our perspective helps to widen the research agenda for IOs.

Theoretical Approaches to Organizations

Within social science there are two broad strands of theorizing about organizations. One is economistic and rooted in assumptions of instrumental rationality and efficiency concerns; the other is sociological and focused on issues of legitimacy and power.[11] The different assumptions embedded within each type of theory focus attention on different kinds of questions about organizations and provide insights on different kinds of problems.

The economistic approach comes, not surprisingly, out of economics departments and business schools for whom the fundamental theoretical problem, laid out first by Ronald Coase and more recently by Oliver Williamson, is why we have business firms. Within standard microeconomic logic, it should be much more efficient to conduct all transactions through markets rather than "hierarchies" or organizations. Consequently, the fact that economic life is dominated by huge organizations (business firms) is an anomaly. The body of theory developed to explain the existence and power of firms focuses on organizations as efficient solutions to contracting problems, incomplete information, and other market imperfections.[12]

This body of organization theory informs neoliberal and neorealist debates over international institutions. Following Kenneth Waltz, neoliberals and neorealists understand world politics to be analogous to a market filled with utility-maximizing competitors.[13] Thus, like the economists, they see organizations as welfare-improving solutions to problems of incomplete information and high transaction costs.[14] Neoliberals and realists disagree about the degree to which constraints of anarchy, an interest in relative versus absolute gains, and fears of cheating will scuttle international institutional arrangements or hobble their effectiveness, but both agree, implicitly or explicitly, that IOs help states further their interests where they are allowed to work.[15] State power may be exercised in political battles inside IOs over where, on the Pareto frontier, political bargains fall, but the notion that IOs are instruments created to serve state interests is not much questioned by neorealist or neoliberal scholars.[16] After all, why else would states set up these organizations and continue to support them if they did not serve state interests?

Approaches from sociology provide one set of answers to this question. They provide reasons why, in fact, organizations that are not efficient or effective servants of member interests might exist. In so doing, they lead us to look for kinds of power and sources of autonomy in organizations that economists overlook. Different approaches within sociology treat organizations in different ways, but as a group they stand in sharp contrast to the economists' approaches in at least two important respects: they offer a different conception of the relationship between organizations and their environments, and they provide a basis for understanding organizational autonomy.

IOS AND THEIR ENVIRONMENT

The environment assumed by economic approaches to organizations is socially very thin and devoid of social rules, cultural content, or even other actors beyond those constructing the organization. Competition, exchange, and consequent pressures for efficiency are the dominant environmental characteristics driving the formation and behavior of organizations. Sociologists, by contrast, study organizations in a wider world of nonmarket situations, and, consequently, they begin with no such assumptions. Organizations are treated as "social facts" to be investigated; whether they do what they claim or do it efficiently is an empirical question, not a theoretical assumption of these approaches. Organizations respond not only to other actors pursuing material interests in the environment but also to normative and cultural forces that shape how organizations see the world and conceptualize their own missions. Environments can "select" or favor organizations for reasons other than efficient or responsive behavior. For example, organizations may be created and supported for reasons of legitimacy and normative fit rather than efficient output; they may be created not for what they do but for what they are—for what they represent symbolically and the values they embody.[17]

Empirically, organizational environments can take many forms. Some organizations exist in competitive environments that create strong pressures for efficient or responsive behavior, but many do not. Some organizations operate with clear criteria for "success" (like firms that have balance sheets), whereas others (like political science departments) operate with much vaguer missions, with few clear criteria for success or failure and no serious threat of elimination. Our point is simply that when we choose a theoretical framework, we should choose one whose assumptions approximate the empirical conditions of the IO we are analyzing, and that we should be aware of the biases created by those assumptions. Economistic approaches make certain assumptions about the environment in which IOs are embedded that drive researchers who use them to look for certain kinds of effects and not others. Specifying different or more varied environments for IOs would lead us to look for different and more varied effects in world politics.[18]

IO AUTONOMY

Following economistic logic, regime theory and the broad range of scholars working within it generally treat IOs as creations of states designed to further state interests.[19] Analysis of subsequent IO behavior focuses on processes of aggregating member state preferences through strategic interaction within the structure of the IO. IOs, then, are simply epiphenomena of state interaction; they are, to quote Waltz's definition of reductionism, "understood by knowing the attributes and the interactions of [their] parts."[20]

These theories thus treat IOs as empty shells or impersonal policy machinery to be manipulated by other actors. Political bargains shape the machinery at its creation, states may politick hard within the machinery in pursuit of their policy goals, and the machinery's norms and rules may constrain what states can do, but the machinery itself is passive. IOs are not purposive political actors in their own right and have no ontological independence. To the extent that IOs do, in fact, take on a life of their own, they breach the "limits of realism" as well as of neoliberalism by violating the ontological structures of these theories.[21]

The regimes concept spawned a huge literature on interstate cooperation that is remarkably consistent in its treatment of IOs as structure rather than agents. Much of the neoliberal institutionalist literature has been devoted to exploring the ways in which regimes (and IOs) can act as intervening variables, mediating between states' pursuit of self-interest and political outcomes by changing the structure of opportunities and constraints facing states through their control over information, in particular.[22] Although this line of scholarship accords IOs some causal status (since they demonstrably change outcomes), it does not grant them autonomy and purpose independent of the states that comprise them. Another branch of liberalism has recently divorced itself from the statist ontology and focuses instead on the preferences of social groups as the causal engine of world politics, but, again, this view simply argues for attention to a different group of agents involved in the construction of IOs and competing for access to IO mechanisms. It does not offer a fundamentally different conception of IOs.[23]

The relevant question to ask about this conceptualization is whether it is a reasonable approximation of the empirical condition of most IOs. Our reading of detailed empirical case studies of IO activity suggests not. Yes, IOs are constrained by states, but the notion that they are passive mechanisms with no independent agendas of their own is not borne out by any detailed empirical study of an IO that we have found. Field studies of the European Union provide evidence of independent roles for "eurocrats."[24] Studies of the World Bank consistently identify an independent culture and agendas for action.[25] Studies of recent UN peacekeeping and reconstruction efforts similarly document a UN agenda that frequently leads to conflict with member states.[26] Accounts of the UN High Commission on Refugees (UNHCR) routinely note how its autonomy and authority has grown over the years. Not only are IOs independent actors with their own agendas, but they may embody multiple agendas and contain multiple sources of agency—a problem we take up later.

Principal-agent analysis, which has been increasingly employed by students of international relations to examine organizational dynamics, could potentially provide a sophisticated approach to understanding IO autonomy.[27] Building on theories of rational choice and of representation, these analysts understand IOs as "agents" of states ("principals"). The analysis is concerned with whether agents are responsible delegates of their principals, whether agents smuggle in and pursue their own preferences, and how principals can construct various mechanisms to keep their agents honest.[28] This framework provides a means of treating IOs as actors in their own right with independent interests and capabilities. Autonomous action by IOs is to be expected in this perspective. It would also explain a number of the nonresponsive and pathological behaviors that concern us because we know that monitoring and shirking problems are pervasive in these principal-agent relationships and that these relationships can often get stuck at suboptimal equilibria.

The problem with applying principal-agent analysis to the study of IOs is that it requires a priori theoretical specification of what IOs want. Principal-agent dynamics are fueled by the disjuncture between what agents want and what principals want. To produce any insights, those two sets of interests cannot be identical. In economics this type of analysis is usually applied to preexisting agents and principals (clients hiring lawyers, patients visiting doctors) whose ongoing independent existence makes specification of independent interests relatively straightforward. The lawyer or the doctor would probably be in business even if you and I did not take our problems to them. IOs, on the other hand, are often created by the principals (states) and given mission statements written by the principals. How, then, can we impute independent preferences a priori?

Scholars of American politics have made some progress in producing substantive theoretical propositions about what U.S. bureaucratic agencies want. Beginning with the pioneering work of William Niskanen, scholars theorized that bureaucracies had interests defined by the absolute or relative size of their budget and the expansion or protection of their turf. At first these interests were imputed, and later they became more closely investigated, substantiated, and in some cases modified or rejected altogether.[29]

Realism and liberalism, however, provide no basis for asserting independent utility functions for IOs. Ontologically, these are theories about states. They provide no basis for imputing interests to IOs beyond the goals states (that is, principals) give them. Simply adopting the rather battered Niskanen hypothesis seems less than promising given the glaring anomalies—for example, the opposition of many NATO and OSCE (Organization for Security and Cooperation in Europe) bureaucrats to those organizations' recent expansion and institutionalization. There are good reasons to assume that organizations care about their resource base and turf, but there is no reason to presume that such matters exhaust or even dominate their interests. Indeed, ethnographic studies of IOs describe a world in which organizational goals are strongly shaped by norms of the profession that dominate the bureaucracy and in which interests themselves are varied, often in flux, debated, and worked out through interactions between the staff of the bureaucracy and the world in which they are embedded.[30]

Various strands of sociological theory can help us investigate the goals and behavior of IOs by offering a very different analytical orientation than the one used by economists. Beginning with Weber, sociologists have explored the notion that bureaucracy is a peculiarly modern cultural form that embodies certain values and can have its own distinct agenda and behavioral dispositions. Rather than treating organizations as mere arenas or mechanisms through which other actors pursue interests, many sociological approaches explore the social content of the organization—its culture, its legitimacy concerns, dominant norms that govern behavior and shape interests, and the relationship of these to a larger normative and cultural environment. Rather than assuming behavior that corresponds to efficiency criteria alone, these approaches recognize that organizations also are bound up with power and social control in ways that can eclipse efficiency concerns.

The Power of IOs

IOs can become autonomous sites of authority, independent from the state "principals" who may have created them, because of power flowing from at least two sources: (1) the legitimacy of the rational-legal authority they embody, and (2) control over technical expertise and information. The first of these is almost entirely neglected by the political science literature, and the second, we argue, has been conceived of very narrowly, leading scholars to overlook some of the most basic and consequential forms of IO influence. Taken together, these two features provide a theoretical basis for treating IOs as autonomous actors in contemporary world politics by identifying sources of support for them, independent of states, in the larger social environment. Since rational-legal authority and control over expertise are part of what defines and constitutes any bureaucracy (a bureaucracy would not be a bureaucracy without them), the autonomy that flows from them is best understood as a constitutive effect, an effect of the way bureaucracy is constituted, which, in turn, makes possible (and in that sense causes) other processes and effects in global politics.

Sources of IO Autonomy and Authority

To understand how IOs can become autonomous sites of authority we turn to Weber and his classic study of bureaucratization. Weber was deeply ambivalent about the increasingly bureaucratic world in which he lived and was well-attuned to the vices as well as the virtues of this new social form of authority.[31] Bureaucracies are rightly considered a grand achievement, he thought. They provide a framework for social interaction that can respond to the increasingly technical demands of modern life in a stable, predictable, and nonviolent way; they exemplify rationality and are technically superior to previous forms of rule because they bring precision, knowledge, and continuity to increasingly complex social tasks.[32] But such technical and rational achievements, according to Weber, come at a steep price. Bureaucracies are

political creatures that can be autonomous from their creators and can come to dominate the societies they were created to serve, because of both the normative appeal of rational-legal authority in modern life and the bureaucracy's control over technical expertise and information. We consider each in turn.

Bureaucracies embody a form of authority, rational-legal authority, that modernity views as particularly legitimate and good. In contrast to earlier forms of authority that were invested in a leader, legitimate modern authority is invested in legalities, procedures, and rules and thus rendered impersonal. This authority is "rational" in that it deploys socially recognized relevant knowledge to create rules that determine how goals will be pursued. The very fact that they embody rationality is what makes bureaucracies powerful and makes people willing to submit to this kind of authority. According to Weber,

> in legal authority, submission does not rest upon the belief and devotion to charismatically gifted persons . . . or upon piety toward a personal lord and master who is defined by an ordered tradition. . . . Rather submission under legal authority is based upon an *impersonal* bond to the generally defined and functional "duty of office." The official duty—like the corresponding right to exercise authority: the "jurisdictional competency"—is fixed by *rationally established* norms, by enactments, decrees, and regulations in such a manner that the legitimacy of the authority becomes the legality of the general rule, which is purposely thought out, enacted, and announced with formal correctness.[33]

When bureaucrats do something contrary to your interests or that you do not like, they defend themselves by saying "Sorry, those are the rules" or "just doing my job." "The rules" and "the job" are the source of great power in modern society. It is because bureaucrats in IOs are performing "duties of office" and implementing "rationally established norms" that they are powerful.

A second basis of autonomy and authority, intimately connected to the first, is bureaucratic control over information and expertise. A bureaucracy's autonomy derives from specialized technical knowledge, training, and experience that is not immediately available to other actors. While such knowledge might help the bureaucracy carry out the directives of politicians more efficiently, Weber stressed that it also gives bureaucracies power over politicians (and other actors). It invites and at times requires bureaucracies to shape policy, not just implement it.[34]

The irony in both of these features of authority is that they make bureaucracies powerful precisely by creating the appearance of depoliticization. The power of IOs, and bureaucracies generally, is that they present themselves as impersonal, technocratic, and neutral—as not exercising power but instead as serving others; the presentation and acceptance of these claims is critical to their legitimacy and authority.[35] Weber, however, saw through these claims. According to him, the depoliticized character of bureaucracy that legitimates it could be a myth: "Behind the functional purposes [of bureaucracy], of course, 'ideas of culture-values' usually stand."[36] Bureaucracies always serve some social purpose or set of cultural values. That purpose may be normatively "good," as Weber believed the Prussian nationalism around him was, but there was no a priori reason to assume this.

In addition to embodying cultural values from the larger environment that might be desirable or not, bureaucracies also carry with them behavioral dispositions and values flowing from the rationality that legitimates them as a cultural form. Some of these, like the celebration of knowledge and expertise, Weber admired. Others concerned him greatly, and his descriptions of bureaucracy as an "iron cage" and bureaucrats as "specialists without spirit" are hardly an endorsement of the bureaucratic form.[37] Bureaucracy can undermine personal freedom in important ways. The very impersonal, rule-bound character that empowers bureaucracy also dehumanizes it. Bureaucracies often exercise their power in repressive ways, in the name of general rules because rules are their raison d'être. This tendency is exacerbated by the way bureaucracies select and reward narrowed professionals seeking secure careers internally—people who are "lacking in heroism, human spontaneity, and inventiveness."[38] Following Weber, we investigate rather than assume the "goodness" of bureaucracy.

Weber's insights provide a powerful critique of the ways in which international relations scholars have treated IOs. The legitimacy of rational-legal authority suggests that IOs may have an authority independent of the policies and interests of states that create them, a possibility obscured by the technical and apolitical treatment of IOs by both realists and neoliberals. * * *

Examples of the ways in which IOs have become autonomous because of their embodiment of technical rationality and control over information are not hard to find. The UN's peacekeepers derive part of their authority from the claim that they are independent, objective, neutral actors who simply implement Security Council resolutions. UN officials routinely use this language to describe their role and are explicit that they understand this to be the basis of their influence. As a consequence, UN officials spend considerable time and energy attempting to maintain the image that they are not the instrument of any great power and must be seen as representatives of "the international community" as embodied in the rules and resolutions of the UN.[39] The World Bank is widely recognized to have exercised power over development policies far greater than its budget, as a percentage of North/South aid flows, would suggest because of the expertise it houses. While competing sites of expertise in development have proliferated in recent years, for decades after its founding the World Bank was a magnet for the "best and brightest" among "development experts." Its staff had and continues to have impressive credentials from the most prestigious universities and the elaborate models, reports, and research groups it has sponsored over the years were widely influential among the "development experts" in the field. This expertise, coupled with its claim to "neutrality" and its "apolitical" technocratic decision-making style, have given the World Bank an authoritative voice with which it has successfully dictated the content, direction, and scope of global development over the past fifty years.[40] Similarly, official standing and long experience with relief efforts have endowed the UNHCR with "expert" status and consequent authority in refugee matters. This expertise, coupled with its role in implementing international refugee conventions and law ("the rules" regarding refugees), has allowed the UNHCR to make life and death decisions about refugees without consulting the refugees, themselves, and to compromise the authority of states in various ways in setting up refugee camps.[41] Note that, as these examples show, technical knowledge and expertise need not be "scientific" in nature to create autonomy and power for IOs.

The Power of IOs

If IOs have autonomy and authority in the world, what do they do with it? A growing body of research in sociology and anthropology has examined ways in which IOs exercise power by virtue of their culturally constructed status as sites of authority; we distill from this research three broad types of IO power. We examine how IOs (1) classify the world, creating categories of actors and action; (2) fix meanings in the social world; and (3) articulate and diffuse new norms, principles, and actors around the globe. All of these sources of power flow from the ability of IOs to structure knowledge.[42]

CLASSIFICATION

An elementary feature of bureaucracies is that they classify and organize information and knowledge. This classification process is bound up with power. "Bureaucracies," writes Don Handelman, "are ways of making, ordering, and knowing social worlds." They do this by "moving persons among social categories or by inventing and applying such categories."[43] The ability to classify objects, to shift their very definition and identity, is one of bureaucracy's greatest sources of power. This power is frequently treated by the objects of that power as accomplished through caprice and without regard to their circumstances but is legitimated and justified by bureaucrats with reference to the rules and regulations of the bureaucracy. Consequences of this bureaucratic exercise of power may be identity defining, or even life threatening.

Consider the evolving definition of "refugee." The category "refugee" is not at all straightforward and must be distinguished from other categories of individuals who are "temporarily" and "involuntarily" living outside their country of origin— displaced persons, exiles, economic migrants, guest workers, diaspora communities, and those seeking political asylum. The debate over the meaning of "refugee" has been waged in and around the UNHCR. The UNHCR's legal and operational definition of the category strongly influences decisions about who is a refugee and shapes UNHCR staff decisions in the field— decisions that have a tremendous effect on the life circumstance of thousands of people.[44] These categories are not only political and legal but also discursive, shaping a view among UNHCR officials that refugees must, by definition, be powerless, and that as powerless actors they do not have to be consulted in decisions such as asylum and repatriation that will directly and dramatically affect them.[45] Guy Gran similarly describes how the World Bank sets up criteria to define someone as a peasant in order to distinguish them from a farmer, day laborer, and other categories. The classification matters because only certain classes of people are recognized by the World Bank's development machinery as having knowledge that is relevant in solving development problems.[46] Categorization and classification are a ubiquitous feature of bureaucratization that has potentially important implications for those being classified. To classify is to engage in an act of power.

THE FIXING OF MEANINGS

IOs exercise power by virtue of their ability to fix meanings, which is related to classification.[47] Naming or labeling the social context establishes the parameters, the very boundaries, of acceptable action. Because actors are oriented toward objects and objectives on the basis of the meaning that they have for them, being able to invest situations with a particular meaning constitutes an important source of power.[48] IOs do not act alone in this regard, but their organizational resources contribute mightily to this end.

There is strong evidence of this power from development studies. Arturo Escobar explores how the institutionalization of the concept of "development" after World War II spawned a huge international apparatus and how this apparatus has now spread its tentacles in domestic and international politics through the discourse of development. The discourse of development, created and arbitrated in large part by IOs, determines not only what constitutes the activity (what development is) but also who (or what) is considered powerful and privileged, that is, who gets to do the developing (usually the state or IOs) and who is the object of development (local groups).[49]

Similarly, the end of the Cold War encouraged a reexamination of the definition of security.[50] IOs have been at the forefront of this debate, arguing that security pertains not only to states but also to individuals and that the threats to security may be economic, environmental, and political as well as military.[51] In forwarding these alternative definitions of security, officials from various IOs are empowering a different set of actors and legitimating an alternative set of practices. Specifically, when security meant safety from invading national armies, it privileged state officials and invested power in military establishments. These alternative definitions of security shift attention away from states and toward the individuals who are frequently threatened by their own government, away from military practices and toward other features of social life that might represent a more immediate and daily danger to the lives of individuals.

One consequence of these redefined meanings of development and security is that they legitimate, and even require, increased levels of IO intervention in the domestic affairs of states— particularly Third World states. This is fairly obvious in the realm of development. The World Bank, the International Monetary Fund (IMF), and other development institutions have established a web of interventions that affect nearly every phase of the economy and polity in many Third World states. As "rural development," "basic human needs," and "structural adjustment" became incorporated into the meaning of development, IOs were permitted, even required, to become intimately involved in the domestic workings of developing polities by posting in-house "advisors" to run monetary policy, reorganizing the political economy of entire rural regions, regulating family and reproductive practices, and mediating between governments and their citizens in a variety of ways.[52]

■ ■ ■

DIFFUSION OF NORMS

Having established rules and norms, IOs are eager to spread the benefits of their expertise and often act as conveyor belts for the transmission of norms and models of "good" political behavior.[53] There is nothing accidental or unintended about this role.

Officials in IOs often insist that part of their mission is to spread, inculcate, and enforce global values and norms. They are the "missionaries" of our time. Armed with a notion of progress, an idea of how to create the better life, and some understanding of the conversion process, many IO elites have as their stated purpose a desire to shape state practices by establishing, articulating, and transmitting norms that define what constitutes acceptable and legitimate state behavior. To be sure, their success depends on more than their persuasive capacities, for their rhetoric must be supported by power, sometimes (but not always) state power. But to overlook how state power and organizational missionaries work in tandem and the ways in which IO officials channel and shape states' exercise of power is to disregard a fundamental feature of value diffusion.[54]

Consider decolonization as an example. The UN Charter announced an intent to universalize sovereignty as a constitutive principle of the society of states at a time when over half the globe was under some kind of colonial rule; it also established an institutional apparatus to achieve that end (most prominently the Trusteeship Council and the Special Committee on Colonialism). These actions had several consequences. One was to eliminate certain categories of acceptable action for powerful states. Those states that attempted to retain their colonial privileges were increasingly viewed as illegitimate by other states. Another consequence was to empower international bureaucrats (at the Trusteeship Council) to set norms and standards for "stateness." Finally, the UN helped to ensure that throughout decolonization the sovereignty of these new states was coupled with territorial inviolability. Colonial boundaries often divided ethnic and tribal groups, and the UN was quite concerned that in the process of "self-determination," these governments containing "multiple" or "partial" selves might attempt to create a whole personality through territorial adjustment—a fear shared by many of these newly decolonized

states. The UN encouraged the acceptance of the norm of sovereignty-as-territorial-integrity through resolutions, monitoring devices, commissions, and one famous peacekeeping episode in Congo in the 1960s.[55]

Note that, as with other IO powers, norm diffusion, too, has an expansionary dynamic. Developing states continue to be popular targets for norm diffusion by IOs, even after they are independent. The UN and the European Union are now actively involved in police training in non-Western states because they believe Western policing practices will be more conducive to democratization processes and the establishment of civil society. But having a professional police establishment assumes that there is a professional judiciary and penal system where criminals can be tried and jailed; and a professional judiciary, in turn, presupposes that there are lawyers that can come before the court. Trained lawyers presuppose a code of law. The result is a package of reforms sponsored by IOs aimed at transforming non-Western societies into Western societies.[56] Again, while Western states are involved in these activities and therefore their values and interests are part of the reasons for this process, international bureaucrats involved in these activities may not see themselves as doing the bidding for these states but rather as expressing the interests and values of the bureaucracy.

Other examples of this kind of norm diffusion are not hard to find. The IMF and the World Bank are explicit about their role as transmitters of norms and principles from advanced market economies to less-developed economies.[57] The IMF's Articles of Agreement specifically assign it this task of incorporating less-developed economies into the world economy, which turns out to mean teaching them how to "be" market economies. The World Bank, similarly, has a major role in arbitrating the meaning of development and norms of behavior appropriate to the task of developing oneself, as was discussed earlier. The end of the Cold War has opened up a whole new set of states to this kind of norm diffusion task for IOs. According to former Secretary of Defense William Perry, one of the functions of NATO expansion is to inculcate "modern" values and norms into the Eastern European countries and their militaries.[58]

■ ■ ■

The Pathologies of IOs

Bureaucracies are created, propagated, and valued in modern society because of their supposed rationality and effectiveness in carrying out social tasks. These same considerations presumably also apply to IOs. Ironically, though, the folk wisdom about bureaucracies is that they are inefficient and unresponsive. Bureaucracies are infamous for creating and implementing policies that defy rational logic, for acting in ways that are at odds with their stated mission, and for refusing requests of and turning their backs on those to whom they are officially responsible.[59] Scholars of U.S. bureaucracy have recognized this problem and have devoted considerable energy to understanding a wide range of undesirable and inefficient bureaucratic behaviors caused by bureaucratic capture and slack and to exploring the conditions under which "suboptimal equilibria" may arise in organizational structures. Similarly, scholars researching foreign policy decision making and, more recently, those interested in learning in foreign policy have investigated organizational dynamics that produce self-defeating and inefficient behavior in those contexts.[60]

IOs, too, are prone to dysfunctional behaviors, but international relations scholars have rarely investigated this, in part, we suspect, because the theoretical apparatus they use provides few grounds for expecting undesirable IO behavior.[61] The state-centric utility-maximizing frameworks most international relations scholars have borrowed from economics simply assume that IOs are reasonably responsive to state interests (or, at least, more responsive than alternatives), otherwise states would withdraw from them. This assumption, however, is a necessary theoretical axiom of these frameworks; it is rarely treated as a hypothesis subject to empirical investigation.[62] With little theoretical reason to expect suboptimal or self-defeating behavior in IOs, these scholars do not look for it and have had little to say about it. Policymakers, however, have been quicker to perceive and address these problems and are putting them on the political agenda. It is time for scholars, too, to begin to explore these issues more fully.

In this section we present several bodies of theorizing that might explain dysfunctional IO behavior, which we define as behavior that undermines the IO's stated objectives. Thus our vantage point for judging dysfunction (and later pathology) is the publicly proclaimed mission of the organization. There may be occasions when overall organizational dysfunction is, in fact, functional for certain members or others involved in the IO's work, but given our analysis of the way claims of efficiency and effectiveness act to legitimate rational-legal authority in our culture, whether organizations actually do what they claim and accomplish their missions is a particularly important issue to examine. Several bodies of theory provide some basis for understanding dysfunctional behavior by IOs, each of which emphasizes a different locus of causality for such behavior. Analyzing these causes, we construct a typology of these explanations that locates them in relation to one another. Then, drawing on the work of James March and Johan Olsen, Paul DiMaggio, and Walter Powell, and other sociological institutionalists, we elaborate how the same sources of bureaucratic power, sketched earlier, can cause dysfunctional behavior. We term this particular type of dysfunction *pathology*.[63] We identify five features of bureaucracy that might produce pathology, and using examples from the UN system we illustrate the way these might work in IOs.

Extant theories about dysfunction can be categorized in two dimensions: (1) whether they locate the cause of IO dysfunction inside or outside the organization, and (2) whether they trace the causes to material or cultural forces. Mapping theories on these dimensions creates the typology shown in Figure 9.1.

Within each cell we have identified a representative body of theory familiar to most international relations scholars. Explanations of IO dysfunction that emphasize the pursuit of material interests within an organization typically examine how competition among subunits over material resources leads the organization to make decisions and engage in behaviors that are inefficient or undesirable as judged against some ideal policy that would better allow the IO to achieve its stated goals. Bureaucratic politics is the best-known theory here, and though current scholars of international politics have not widely adopted this perspective to explain IO behavior, it is relatively well developed in the older IO literature.[64] Graham Allison's central argument is that the "name of the game is politics: bargaining along regularized circuits among players positioned hierarchically within the government. Government behavior can thus be understood as . . . results of these bargaining games."[65] In this view, decisions are not made after a rational decision process but rather through a competitive bargaining process over turf,

budgets, and staff that may benefit parts of the organization at the expense of overall goals.

Another body of literature traces IO dysfunctional behavior to the material forces located outside the organization. Realist and neoliberal theories might posit that state preferences and constraints are responsible for understanding IO dysfunctional behavior. In this view IOs are not to blame for bad outcomes, states are. IOs do not have the luxury of choosing the optimal policy but rather are frequently forced to chose between the bad and the awful because more desirable policies are denied to them by states who do not agree among themselves and/or do not wish to see the IO fulfill its mandate in some particular instance. As Robert Keohane observed, IOs often engage in policies not because they are strong and have autonomy but because they are weak and have none.[66] The important point of these theories is that they trace IO dysfunctional behavior back to the environmental conditions established by, or the explicit preferences of, states.

Cultural theories also have internal and external variants. We should note that many advocates of cultural theories would reject the claim that an organization can be understood apart from its environment or that culture is separable from the material world. Instead they would stress how

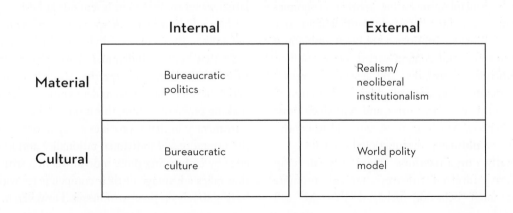

Figure 9.1. Theories of International Organization Dysfunction

	Internal	External
Material	Bureaucratic politics	Realism/ neoliberal institutionalism
Cultural	Bureaucratic culture	World polity model

the organization is permeated by that environment, defined in both material and cultural terms, in which it is embedded. Many are also quite sensitive to the ways in which resource constraints and the material power of important actors will shape organizational culture. That said, these arguments clearly differ from the previous two types in their emphasis on ideational and cultural factors and clearly differ among themselves in the motors of behavior emphasized. For analytical clarity we divide cultural theories according to whether they see the primary causes of the IO's dysfunctional behavior as deriving from the culture of the organization (internal) or of the environment (external).

The world polity model exemplifies theories that look to external culture to understand an IO's dysfunctional behavior. There are two reasons to expect dysfunctional behavior here. First, because IO practices reflect a search for symbolic legitimacy rather than efficiency, IO behavior might be only remotely connected to the efficient implementation of its goals and more closely coupled to legitimacy criteria that come from the cultural environment.[67] For instance, many arms-export control regimes now have a multilateral character not because of any evidence that this architecture is the most efficient way to monitor and prevent arms exports but rather because multilateralism has attained a degree of legitimacy that is not empirically connected to any efficiency criteria.[68] Second, the world polity is full of contradictions; for instance, a liberal world polity has several defining principles, including market economics and human equality, that might conflict at any one moment. Thus, environments are often ambiguous about missions and contain varied, often conflicting, functional, normative, and legitimacy imperatives.[69] Because they are embedded in that cultural environment, IOs can mirror and reproduce those contradictions, which, in turn, can lead to contradictory and ultimately dysfunctional behavior.

Finally, organizations frequently develop distinctive internal cultures that can promote dysfunctional behavior, behavior that we call "pathological." The basic logic of this argument flows directly from our previous observations about the nature of bureaucracy as a social form. Bureaucracies are established as rationalized means to accomplish collective goals and to spread particular values. To do this, bureaucracies create social knowledge and develop expertise as they act upon the world (and thus exercise power). But the way bureaucracies are constituted to accomplish these ends can, ironically, create a cultural disposition toward undesirable and ultimately self-defeating behavior.[70] Two features of the modern bureaucratic form are particularly important in this regard. The first is the simple fact that bureaucracies are organized around rules, routines, and standard operating procedures designed to trigger a standard and predictable response to environmental stimuli. These rules can be formal or informal, but in either case they tell actors which action is appropriate in response to a specific stimuli, request, or demand. This kind of routinization is, after all, precisely what bureaucracies are supposed to exhibit—it is what makes them effective and competent in performing complex social tasks. However, the presence of such rules also compromises the extent to which means-ends rationality drives organizational behavior. Rules and routines may come to obscure overall missions and larger social goals. They may create "ritualized behavior" in bureaucrats and construct a very parochial normative environment within the organization whose connection to the larger social environment is tenuous at best.[71]

Second, bureaucracies specialize and compartmentalize. They create a division of labor on the logic that because individuals have only so much time, knowledge, and expertise, specialization will allow the organization to emulate a rational decision-making process.[72] Again, this is one of the virtues of bureaucracy in that it provides a way of overcoming the limitations of individual rationality and knowledge by embedding those individuals in a structure that takes advantage of their competencies without having to rely on their weaknesses. However, it, too, has some negative consequences. Just as rules can eclipse goals, concentrated expertise and specialization can (and perhaps must) limit bureaucrats' field of vision and create subcultures within bureaucracy that are distinct from those of the larger environment. Professional training plays a particularly strong role here since this is one widespread way we disseminate specialized knowledge and credential "experts." Such training often gives experts, indeed is designed to give them, a distinctive worldview and normative commitments, which, when concentrated in a subunit of an organization, can have pronounced effects on behavior.[73]

Once in place, an organization's culture, understood as the rules, rituals, and beliefs that are embedded in the organization (and its subunits), has important consequences for the way individuals who inhabit that organization make sense of the world. It provides interpretive frames that individuals use to generate meaning.[74] This is more than just bounded rationality; in this view, actors' rationality itself, the very means and ends that they value, are shaped by the organizational culture.[75] Divisions and subunits within the organization may develop their own cognitive frameworks that are consistent with but still distinct from the larger organization, further complicating this process.

All organizations have their own culture (or cultures) that shape their behavior. The effects of bureaucratic culture, however, need not be dysfunctional. Indeed, specific organizational cultures may be valued and actively promoted as a source of "good" behavior, as students of business culture know very well. Organizational culture is tied to "good" and "bad" behavior, alike, and the effects of organizational culture on behavior are an empirical question to be researched.

To further such research, we draw from studies in sociology and anthropology to explore five mechanisms by which bureaucratic culture can breed pathologies in IOs: the irrationality of rationalization, universalism, normalization of deviance, organizational insulation, and cultural contestation.

The first three of these mechanisms all flow from defining features of bureaucracy itself. Consequently, we expect them to be present in any bureaucracy to a limited degree. Their severity may be increased, however, by specific empirical conditions of the organization. Vague mission, weak feedback from the environment, and strong professionalism all have the potential to exacerbate these mechanisms and to create two others, organizational insulation and cultural contestation, through processes we describe later. Our claim, therefore, is that the very nature of bureaucracy—the "social stuff" of which it is made—creates behavioral predispositions that make bureaucracy prone to these kinds of behaviors.[76] But the connection between these mechanisms and pathological behavior is probabilistic, not deterministic, and is consistent with our constitutive analysis. Whether, in fact, mission-defeating behavior occurs depends on empirical conditions. We identify three such conditions that are particularly important (mission, feedback, and professionals) and discuss how they intensify these inherent predispositions and activate or create additional ones.

IRRATIONALITY OF RATIONALIZATION

Weber recognized that the "rationalization" processes at which bureaucracies excelled could be taken to extremes and ultimately become irrational if the rules and procedures that enabled bureaucracies to do their jobs became ends in themselves. Rather than designing the most appropriate and efficient rules and procedures to accomplish their missions, bureaucracies often tailor their missions to fit the existing, well-known, and comfortable rulebook.[77] Thus, means (rules and procedures) may become so embedded and powerful that they determine ends and the way the organization defines its goals. One observer of the World Bank noted how, at an operational level, the bank did not decide on development goals and collect data necessary to pursue them. Rather, it continued to use existing data-collection procedures and formulated goals and development plans from those data alone.[78] UN-mandated elections may be another instance where means become ends in themselves. The "end" pursued in the many troubled states where the UN has been involved in reconstruction is presumably some kind of peaceful, stable, just government. Toward that end, the UN has developed a repertoire of instruments and responses that are largely intended to promote something akin to a democratic government. Among those various repertoires, elections have become privileged as a measure of "success" and a signal of an operation's successful conclusion. Consequently, UN (and other IO) officials have conducted elections even when evidence suggests that such elections are either premature or perhaps even counterproductive (frequently acknowledged as much by state and UN officials).[79] In places like Bosnia elections have ratified precisely the outcome the UN and Outside powers had intervened to prevent—ethnic cleansing—and in places like Africa elections are criticized as exacerbating the very ethnic tensions they were ostensibly designed to quell.

■　■　■

BUREAUCRATIC UNIVERSALISM

A second source of pathology in IOs derives from the fact that bureaucracies "orchestrate numerous local contexts at once."[80] Bureaucrats necessarily flatten diversity because they are supposed to generate universal rules and categories that are, by design, inattentive to contextual and particularistic concerns. Part of the justification for this, of course, is the bureaucratic view that technical knowledge is transferable across circumstances. Sometimes this is a good assumption, but not always; when particular circumstances are not appropriate to the generalized knowledge being applied, the results can be disastrous.[81]

Many critics of the IMF's handling of the Asian financial crises have argued that the IMF inappropriately applied a standardized formula of budget cuts plus high interest rates to combat rapid currency depreciation without appreciating the unique and local causes of this depreciation. These governments were not profligate spenders, and austerity policies did little to reassure investors, yet the IMF prescribed roughly the same remedy that it had in Latin America. The result, by the IMF's later admission, was to make matters worse.[82]

■　■　■

NORMALIZATION OF DEVIANCE

We derive a third type of pathology from Diane Vaughan's study of the space shuttle *Challenger* disaster in which she chronicles the way exceptions to rules (deviance) over time become routinized and normal parts of procedures.[83] Bureaucracies establish rules to provide a predictable response to environmental stimuli in ways that safeguard against decisions that might lead to accidents and faulty decisions. At times, however, bureaucracies make small, calculated deviations from established rules because of new environmental or institutional developments, explicitly calculating that bending the rules in this instance does not create excessive risk of policy failure. Over time, these exceptions can become the rule—they become normal, not exceptions at all: they can become institutionalized to the point where deviance is "normalized." The result of this process is that what at time t_1 might be weighed seriously and debated as a potentially unacceptable risk or dangerous procedure comes to be treated as normal at time t_n. Indeed, because of staff turnover, those making decisions at a later point in time might be unaware that the now-routine behavior was ever viewed as risky or dangerous.

We are unaware of any studies that have examined this normalization of deviance in IO decision making, though one example of deviance normalization comes to mind. Before 1980 the UNHCR viewed repatriation as only one of three durable solutions to refugee crises (the others being third-country asylum and host-country integration). In its view, repatriation had to be both safe and voluntary because forced repatriation violates the international legal principle of nonrefoulement, which is the cornerstone of international refugee law and codified in the UNHCR's convention. Prior to 1980, UNHCR's discussions of repatriation emphasized that the principles of safety and voluntariness must be safeguarded at all costs. According to many commentators, however, the UNHCR has steadily lowered the barriers to repatriation over the years. Evidence for this can be found in international protection manuals, the UNHCR Executive Committee resolutions, and discourse that now weighs repatriation and the principle of nonrefoulement against other goals such a peace building. This was a steady and incremental development as initial deviations from organizational norms accumulated over time and led to a normalization of deviance. The result was a lowering of the barriers to repatriation and an increase in the frequency of involuntary repatriation.[84]

INSULATION

Organizations vary greatly in the degree to which they receive and process feedback from their environment about performance. Those insulated from such feedback often develop internal cultures and worldviews that do not promote the goals and expectations of those outside the organization who created it and whom it serves. These distinctive worldviews can create the conditions for pathological behavior when parochial classification and categorization schemes come to define reality—how bureaucrats understand the world—such that they routinely ignore information that is essential to the accomplishment of their goals.[85]

Two causes of insulation seem particularly applicable to IOs. The first is professionalism. Professional training does more than impart technical knowledge. It actively seeks to shape the normative orientation and worldviews of those who are trained. Doctors are trained to value life

above all else, soldiers are trained to sacrifice life for certain strategic objectives, and economists are trained to value efficiency. Bureaucracies, by their nature, concentrate professionals inside organizations, and concentrations of people with the same expertise or professional training can create an organizational worldview distinct from the larger environment. Second, organizations for whom "successful performance" is difficult to measure—that is, they are valued for what they represent rather than for what they do and do not "compete" with other organizations on the basis of output—are protected from selection and performance pressures that economistic models simply assume will operate. The absence of a competitive environment that selects out inefficient practices coupled with already existing tendencies toward institutionalization of rules and procedures insulates the organization from feedback and increases the likelihood of pathologies.

■   ■   ■

Conclusion

■   ■   ■

Viewing IOs through a constructivist or sociological lens, as we suggest here, reveals features of IO behavior that should concern international relations scholars because they bear on debates central to our field—debates about whether and how international institutions matter and debates about the adequacy of a statist ontology in an era of globalization and political change. Three implications of this alternative approach are particularly important. First, this approach provides a basis for treating IOs as purposive actors. Mainstream approaches in political science that are informed by economic theories have tended to locate agency in the states that comprise IO membership and treat IOs as mere arenas in which states pursue their policies. By exploring the normative support for bureaucratic authority in the broader international culture and the way IOs use that authority to construct the social world, we provide reasons why IOs may have autonomy from state members and why it may make sense analytically to treat them as ontologically independent. Second, by providing a basis for that autonomy we also open up the possibility that IOs are powerful actors who can have independent effects on the world. We have suggested various ways to think about how IOs are powerful actors in global politics, all of which encourage greater consideration of how IOs affect not only discrete outcomes but also the constitutive basis of global politics.

Third, this approach also draws attention to normative evaluations of IOs and questions what appears to us to be rather uncritical optimism about IO behavior. Contemporary international relations scholars have been quick to recognize the positive contributions that IOs can make, and we, too, are similarly impressed. But for all their desirable qualities, bureaucracies can also be inefficient, ineffective, repressive, and unaccountable. International relations scholars, however, have shown little interest in investigating these less savory and more distressing effects. The liberal Wilsonian tradition tends to see IOs as promoters of peace, engines of progress, and agents for emancipation. Neoliberals have focused on the impressive way in which IOs help states to overcome collective action problems and achieve durable cooperation. Realists have focused on their role as stabilizing forces in world politics. Constructivists, too, have tended to focus on the more humane and other-regarding features of IOs, but there is nothing about social construction that necessitates "good" outcomes. We do not mean to imply that IOs are "bad"; we mean only to point out theoretical reasons why undesirable behavior may occur and suggest that normative evaluation of IO behavior should be an empirical and ethical matter, not an analytic assumption.

NOTES

1. For Gramscian approaches, see Cox 1980, 1992, and 1996; and Murphy 1994. For Society of States approaches, see Hurrell and Woods 1995. For the epistemic communities literature, see Haas 1992. For IO decision-making literature, see Cox et al. 1974; Cox and Jacobson 1977; Cox 1996; and Ness and Brechin 1988. For a rational choice perspective, see Snidal 1996.
2. Haas 1990.
3. Because the neorealist and neoliberal arguments we engage have focused on intergovernmental organizations rather than nongovernmental ones, and because Weberian arguments from which we draw deal primarily with public bureaucracy, we, too, focus on intergovernmental organizations in this article and use the term *international organizations* in that way.
4. Baldwin 1993.
5. See Finnemore 1993 and 1996b; and McNeely 1995.
6. Krasner 1983b.
7. See Mearsheimer 1994; and Helms 1996.
8. See Commission on Global Governance 1995; Jacobson 1979, 1; and Doyle 1997.
9. See Ruggie 1998; and Wendt 1998.
10. Wendt 1998.
11. See Powell and DiMaggio 1991, chap. 1; and Grandori 1993.
12. See Williamson 1975 and 1985; and Coase 1937.
13. Waltz 1979.
14. See Vaubel 1991, 27; and Dillon, Ilgen, and Willett 1991.
15. Baldwin 1993.
16. Krasner 1991.
17. See DiMaggio and Powell 1983; Scott 1992; Meyer and Scott 1992, 1–5; Powell and DiMaggio 1991; Weber 1994; and Finnemore 1996a.
18. Researchers applying these economistic approaches have become increasingly aware of the mismatch between the assumptions of their models and the empirics of IOs. See Snidal 1996.
19. Note that empirically this is not the case; most IOs now are created by other IOs. See Shanks, Jacobson, and Kaplan 1996.
20. Waltz 1979, 18.
21. Krasner 1983a, 355–68; but see Finnemore 1996b; and Rittberger 1993.
22. See Keohane 1984; and Baldwin 1993.
23. Moravcsik 1997.
24. See Pollack 1997; Ross 1995; and Zabusky 1995; but see Moravcsik 1999.
25. See Ascher 1983; Ayres 1983; Ferguson 1990; Escobar 1995; Wade 1996; Nelson 1995; and Finnemore 1996a.
26. Joint Evaluation of Emergency Assistance to Rwanda 1996.
27. See Pollack 1997; Lake 1996; Vaubel 1991; and Dillon, Ilgen, and Willett 1991.
28. See Pratt and Zeckhauser 1985; and Kiewit and McCubbins 1991.
29. See Niskanen 1971; Miller and Moe 1983; Weingast and Moran 1983; Moe 1984; and Sigelman 1986.
30. See Ascher 1983; Zabusky 1995; Barnett 1997b; and Wade 1996.
31. See Weber 1978, 196–97; Weber 1947; Mouzelis 1967; and Beetham 1985 and 1996.

32. See Schaar 1984, 120; Weber 1978, 973; and Beetham 1985, 69.

33. Gerth and Mills 1978, 299 (italics in original).

34. See Gerth and Mills 1978, 233; Beetham 1985, 74–75; and Schaar 1984, 120.

35. We thank John Boli for this insight. Also see Fisher 1997; Ferguson 1990; Shore and Wright 1997; and Burley and Mattli 1993.

36. Gerth and Mills 1978, 199.

37. See Weber [1930] 1968, 181–83; and Clegg 1994a, 152–55.

38. Gerth and Mills 1978, 216, 50, 299. For the extreme manifestation of this bureaucratic characteristic, see Arendt 1977.

39. See David Rieff, "The Institution that Saw No Evil," *The New Republic,* 12 February 1996, 19–24; and Barnett 1997b.

40. See Wade 1996; Ayres 1983; Ascher 1983; Finnemore 1996b; and Nelson 1995.

41. See Malkki 1996; Hartigan 1992; and Harrell-Bond 1989.

42. See Foucault 1977, 27; and Clegg 1994b, 156–59. International relations theory typically disregards the negative side of the knowledge and power equation. For an example, see Haas 1992.

43. Handelman 1995, 280. See also Starr 1992; and Wright 1994, 22.

44. See Weiss and Pasic 1997; Goodwin-Gill 1996; and Anonymous 1997.

45. See Harrell-Bond 1989; Walkup 1997; and Malkki 1996.

46. Gran 1986.

47. See Williams 1996; Clegg 1994b; Bourdieu 1994; Carr [1939] 1964; and Keeley 1990.

48. Blumer 1969.

49. See Gupta 1998; Escobar 1995; Cooper and Packard 1998; Gran 1986; Ferguson 1990; and Wade 1996.

50. See Matthews 1989; and Krause and Williams 1996.

51. See UN Development Program 1994; and Boutros-Ghali 1995.

52. See Escobar 1995; Ferguson 1990; and Feldstein 1998.

53. See Katzenstein 1996; Finnemore 1996b; and Legro 1997.

54. See Alger 1963, 425; and Claude 1966, 373.

55. See McNeely 1995; and Jackson 1993.

56. Call and Barnett [1999].

57. Wade 1996.

58. See Perry 1996; and Ruggie 1996.

59. March and Olsen 1989, chap. 5.

60. See Haas 1990; Haas and Haas 1995; and Sagan 1993.

61. Two exceptions are Gallaroti 1991; and Snidal 1996.

62. Snidal 1996.

63. Karl Deutsch used the concept of pathology in a way similar to our usage. We thank Hayward Alker for this point. Deutsch 1963, 170.

64. See Allison 1971; Haas 1990; Cox et al. 1974; and Cox and Jacobson 1977.

65. See Allison 1971, 144; and Bendor and Hammond 1992.

66. Personal communication to the authors.

67. See Meyer and Rowan 1977; Meyer and Zucker 1989; Weber 1994; and Finnemore 1996a.

68. Lipson 1999.

69. McNeely 1995.

70. See Vaughan 1996; and Lipartito 1995.

71. See March and Olsen 1989, 21–27; and Meyer and Rowan 1977.

72. See March and Olsen 1989, 26–27; and March 1997.

73. See DiMaggio and Powell 1983; and Schien 1996.

74. See Starr 1992, 160; Douglas 1986; and Berger and Luckmann 1966, chap. 1.

75. See Campbell 1998, 378; Alvesson 1996; Burrell and Morgan 1979; Dobbin 1994; and Immergut 1998, 14–19.

76. Wendt 1998.

77. Beetham 1985, 76.

78. See Ferguson 1990; and Nelson 1995.

79. Paris 1997.

80. Heyman 1995, 262.

81. Haas 1990, chap. 3.

82. See Feldstein 1998; Radelet and Sach 1999; and Kapur 1998.

83. Vaughan 1996.

84. See Chimni 1993, 447; Amnesty International 1997a,b; Human Rights Watch 1997; Zieck 1997, 433, 434, 438–39; and Barbara Crossette, "The Shield for Exiles Is Lowered, *The New York Times,* 22 December 1996, 4–1."

85. See Berger and Luckmann 1966, chap. 1; Douglas 1986; Bruner 1990; March and Olsen 1989; and Starr 1992.

REFERENCES

Alger, Chadwick. 1963. United Nations Participation as a Learning Process. *Public Opinion Quarterly* 27 (3):411–26.

Allison, Graham. 1971. *Essence of Decision.* Boston: Little, Brown.

Alvesson, Mats. 1996. *Cultural Perspectives on Organizations.* New York: Cambridge University Press.

Amnesty International. 1997a. In Search of Safety: The Forcibly Displaced and Human Rights in Africa. AI Index, 20 June, AFR 01/05/97. Available from www.amnesty.org/ailib/aipub/1997/10100597.htm.

———. 1997b. Rwanda: Human Rights Overlooked in Mass Repatriation. Available from www.amnesty.org/ailib/aipub/1997/AFR/147002797.htm.

Anonymous. 1997. The UNHCR Note on International Protection You Won't See. *International Journal of Refugee Law* 9 (2):267–73.

Arendt, Hannah. 1977. *Eichmann in Jerusalem: A Report on the Banality of Evil.* New York: Penguin.

Ascher, William. 1983. New Development Approaches and the Adaptability of International Agencies: The Case of the World Bank. *International Organization* 37 (3):415–39.

Ayres, Robert L. 1983. *Banking on the Poor: The World Bank and World Poverty.* Cambridge, MA: MIT Press.

Baldwin, David, ed. 1993. *Neorealism and Neoliberalism.* New York: Columbia University Press.

Barnett, Michael, 1997a. The Politics of Indifference at the United Nations and Genocide in Rwanda and Bosnia. In *This Time We Knew: Western Responses to Genocide in Bosnia,* edited by Thomas Cushman and Stjepan Mestrovic, 128–62. New York: New York University Press.

———. 1997b. The UN Security Council, Indifference, and Genocide in Rwanda. *Cultural Anthropology* 12 (4):55–78.

Beetham, David. 1985. *Max Weber and the Theory of Modern Politics.* New York: Polity.

———. 1996. *Bureaucracy.* 2d ed. Minneapolis: University of Minnesota Press.

Bendor, Jonathan, and Thomas Hammond. 1992. Rethinking Allison's Models. *American Political Science Review* 82 (2):301–22.

Berger, Peter, and Thomas Luckmann. 1966. *The Social Construction of Reality.* New York: Doubleday.

Blumer, Herbert. 1969. *Symbolic Interactionism: Perspective and Method.* Englewood Cliffs, NJ: Prentice-Hall.

Bourdieu, Pierre. 1994. On Symbolic Power. In *Language and Symbolic Power,* edited by Pierre Bourdieu, 163–70. Chicago: University of Chicago Press.

Boutros-Ghali, Boutros. 1995. *Agenda for Peace.* 2d ed. New York: UN Press.

Bruner, Jerome. 1990. *Acts of Meaning.* Cambridge, MA: Harvard University Press.

Burley, Anne-Marie, and Walter Mattli. 1993. Europe Before the Court: A Political Theory of Integration. *International Organization* 47 (1):41–76.

Burrell, Gibson, and Gareth Morgan. 1979. *Sociological Paradigms and Organizational Analysis.* London: Heinemann.

Call, Chuck, and Michael Barnett. [1999]. Looking for a Few Good Cops: Peacekeeping, Peacebuilding, and [CIVPOL]. *International Peacekeeping* [6 (4):43–68].

Campbell, John. 1998. Institutional Analysis and the Role of Ideas in Political Economy. *Theory and Society* 27:377–409.

Carr, Edward H. [1939] 1964. *The Twenty Year's Crisis.* New York: Harper Torchbooks.

Chimni, B. 1993. The Meaning of Words and the Role of UNHCR in Voluntary Repatriation. *International Journal of Refugee Law* 5 (3):442–60.

Claude, Inis L., Jr. 1966. Collective Legitimization as a Political Function of the United Nations. *International Organization* 20 (3):337–67.

Clegg, Stewart. 1994a. Power and Institutions in the Theory of Organizations. In *Toward a New Theory of Organizations*, edited by John Hassard and Martin Parker, 24–49. New York: Routledge.

———. 1994b. Weber and Foucault: Social Theory for the Study of Organizations. *Organization* 1 (1): 149–78.

Coase, Ronald. 1937. The Nature of the Firm. *Economica* 4 (November):386–405.

Commission on Global Governance. 1995. *Our Global Neighborhood.* New York: Oxford University Press.

Cooper, Frederick, and Randy Packard, eds. 1998. *International Development and the Social Sciences.* Berkeley: University of California Press.

Cox, Robert. 1980. The Crisis of World Order and the Problem of International Organization in the 1980s. *International Journal* 35 (2):370–95.

———. 1992. Multilateralism and World Order. *Review of International Studies* 18 (2):161–80.

———. 1996. The Executive Head: An Essay on Leadership in International Organization. In *Approaches to World Order*, edited by Robert Cox, 317–48. New York: Cambridge University Press.

Cox, Robert, and Harold Jacobson. 1977. Decision Making. *International Social Science Journal* 29 (1):115–33.

Cox, Robert, Harold Jacobson, Gerard Curzon, Victoria Curzon, Joseph Nye, Lawrence Scheinman, James Sewell, and Susan Strange. 1974. *The Anatomy of Influence: Decision Making in International Organization.* New Haven, CT: Yale University Press.

Deutsch, Karl. 1963. *The Nerves of Government: Models of Political Communication and Control.* Glencoe, IL: Free Press.

Dillon, Patricia, Thomas Ilgen, and Thomas Willett. 1991. Approaches to the Study of International Organizations: Major Paradigms in Economics and Political Science. In *The Political Economy of International Organizations: A Public Choice Approach,* edited by Ronald Vaubel and Thomas Willett, 79–99. Boulder, CO: Westview Press.

DiMaggio, Paul J., and Walter W. Powell. 1983. The Iron Cage Revisited: Institutional Isomorphism and Collective Rationality in Organizational Fields. *American Sociological Review* 48:147–60.

Dobbin, Frank. 1994. Cultural Models of Organization: The Social Construction of Rational Organizing Principles. In *The Sociology of Culture,* edited by Diana Crane, 117–42. Boston: Basil Blackwell.

Douglas, Mary. 1986. *How Institutions Think.* Syracuse, NY: Syracuse University Press.

Doyle, Michael. 1997. *Ways of War and Peace.* New York: Norton.

Escobar, Arturo. 1995. *Encountering Development: The Making and Unmaking of the Third World.* Princeton, NJ: Princeton University Press.

Feld, Werner J., and Robert S. Jordan, with Leon Hurwitz. 1988. *International Organizations: A Comparative Approach.* 2d ed. New York: Praeger.

Feldstein, Martin. 1998. Refocusing the IMF. *Foreign Affairs* 77 (2):20–33.

Ferguson, James. 1990. *The Anti-Politics Machine: "Development," Depoliticization, and Bureaucratic Domination in Lesotho.* New York: Cambridge University Press.

Finnemore, Martha. 1993. International Organizations as Teachers of Norms: The United Nations Educational, Scientific, and Cultural Organization and Science Policy. *International Organization* 47:565–97.

———. 1996a. Norms, Culture, and World Politics: Insights from Sociology's Institutionalism. *International Organization* 50 (2):325–47.

———. 1996b. *National Interests in International Society.* Ithaca, NY: Cornell University Press.

Fisher, William. 1997. Doing Good? The Politics and Antipolitics of NGO Practices. *Annual Review of Anthropology* 26:439–64.

Foucault, Michel. 1977. *Discipline and Punish.* New York: Vintage Press.

Gallaroti, Guilio. 1991. The Limits of International Organization. *International Organization* 45 (2):183–220.

Gerth, H. H., and C. Wright Mills. 1978. *From Max Weber: Essays in Sociology.* New York: Oxford University Press.

Goodwin-Gill, Guy. 1996. *Refugee in International Law.* New York: Oxford Clarendon.

Gran, Guy. 1986. Beyond African Famines: Whose Knowledge Matters? *Alternatives* 11:275–96.

Grandori, Anna. 1993. Notes on the Use of Power and Efficiency Constructs in the Economics and Sociology of Organizations. In *Interdisciplinary Perspectives on Organizational Studies*, edited by S. Lindenberg and H. Schreuder, 61–78. New York: Pergamon.

Gupta, Akhil. 1998. *Postcolonial Developments: Agriculture in the Making of Modern India.* Durham, NC: Duke University Press.

Haas, Ernst. 1990. *When Knowledge Is Power*. Berkeley: University of California Press.

Haas, Ernst, and Peter Haas. 1995. Learning to Learn: Improving International Governance. *Global Governance* 1 (3):255–85.

Haas, Peter, ed. 1992. Epistemic Communities. *International Organization* 46 (1). Special issue.

Handelman, Don. 1995. Comment. *Current Anthropology* 36 (2):280–8l.

Harrell-Bond, Barbara. 1989. Repatriation: Under What Conditions Is It the Most Desirable Solution for Refugees? *African Studies Review* 32 (1):41–69.

Hartigan, Kevin. 1992. Matching Humanitarian Norms with Cold, Hard Interests: The Making of Refugee Policies in Mexico and Honduras, 1980–89. *International Organization* 46:709–30.

Helms, Jesse. 1996. Saving the UN. *Foreign Affairs* 75 (5):2–7.

Heyman, Josiah McC. 1995. Putting Power in the Anthropology of Bureaucracy. *Current Anthropology* 36 (2):261–77.

Hirsch, John, and Robert Oakley. 1995. *Somalia and Operation Restore Hope: Reflections on Peacemaking and Peacekeeping*. Washington, DC: USIP Press.

Human Rights Watch. 1997. Uncertain Refuge: International Failures to Protect Refugees. Vol. 1, no. 9 (April).

Hurrell, Andrew, and Ngaire Woods. 1995. Globalisation and Inequality. *Millennium* 24 (3):447–70.

Immergut, Ellen. 1998. The Theoretical Core of the New Institutionalism. *Politics and Society* 26 (1):5–34.

Jackson, Robert. 1993. The Weight of Ideas in Decolonization: Normative Change in International Relations. In *Ideas and Foreign Policy*, edited by Judith Goldstein and Robert O. Keohane, 111–38. Ithaca, NY: Cornell University Press.

Jacobson, Harold. 1979. *Networks of Interdependence*. New York: Alfred A. Knopf.

Joint Evaluation of Emergency Assistance to Rwanda. 1996. *The International Response to Conflict and Genocide: Lessons from the Rwanda Experience*. 5 vols. Copenhagen: Steering Committee of the Joint Evaluation of Emergency Assistance to Rwanda.

Kapur, Devesh. 1998. The IMF: A Cure or a Curse? *Foreign Policy* 111:114–29.

Katzenstein, Peter J., ed. 1996. *The Culture of National Security: Identity and Norms in World Politics*. New York: Columbia University Press.

Keeley, James. 1990. Toward a Foucauldian Analysis of International Regimes. *International Organization* 44 (1):83–105.

Keohane, Robert O. 1984. *After Hegemony*. Princeton, NJ: Princeton University Press.

Kiewiet, D. Roderick, and Matthew McCubbins. 1991. *The Logic of Delegation*. Chicago: University of Chicago Press.

Krasner, Stephen D. 1991. Global Communications and National Power: Life on the Pareto Frontier. *World Politics* 43 (3):336–66.

———. 1983a. Regimes and the Limits of Realism: Regimes as Autonomous Variables. In *International Regimes*, edited by Stephen Krasner, 355–68. Ithaca, NY: Cornell University Press.

Krasner, Stephen D., ed. 1983b. *International Regimes*. Ithaca, NY: Cornell University Press.

Krause, Keith, and Michael Williams. 1996. Broadening the Agenda of Security Studies: Politics and Methods. *Mershon International Studies Review* 40 (2):229–54.

Lake, David. 1996. Anarchy, Hierarchy, and the Variety of International Relations. *International Organization* 50 (1):1–34.

Legro, Jeffrey. 1997. Which Norms Matter? Revisiting the "Failure" of Internationalism. *International Organization* 51 (1):31–64.

Lipartito, Kenneth. 1995. Culture and the Practice of Business History. *Business and Economic History* 24 (2):1–41.

Lipson, Michael. 1999. International Cooperation on Export Controls: Nonproliferation, Globalization, and Multilateralism. Ph.D. diss., University of Wisconsin, Madison.

Malkki, Liisa. 1996. Speechless Emissaries: Refugees, Humanitarianism, and Dehistoricization. *Cultural Anthropology* 11 (3):377–404.

March, James. 1988. *Decisions and Organizations*. Boston: Basil Blackwell.

———. 1997. Understanding How Decisions Happen in Organizations. In *Organizational Decision Making*, edited by Z. Shapira, 9–33. New York: Cambridge University Press.

March, James, and Johan P. Olsen. 1989. *Rediscovering Institutions: The Organizational Basis of Politics*. New York: Free Press.

Matthews, Jessica Tuchman. 1989. Redefining Security. *Foreign Affairs* 68 (2):162–77.

McNeely, Connie. 1995. *Constructing the Nation-State: International Organization and Prescriptive Action*. Westport, CT: Greenwood Press.

Mearsheimer, John. 1994. The False Promise of International Institutions. *International Security* 19 (3):5–49.

Meyer, John W., and Brian Rowan. 1977. Institutionalized Organizations: Formal Structure as Myth and Ceremony. *American Journal of Sociology* 83:340–63.

Meyer, John W., and W. Richard Scott. 1992. *Organizational Environments: Ritual and Rationality*. Newbury Park, CA: Sage.

Meyer, Marshall, and Lynne Zucker. 1989. *Permanently Failing Organizations*. Newbury Park: Sage Press.

Miller, Gary, and Terry M. Moe. 1983. Bureaucrats, Legislators, and the Size of Government. *American Political Science Review* 77 (June):297–322.

Moe, Terry M. 1984. The New Economics of Organization. *American Journal of Political Science* 28: 739–77.

Moravcsik, Andrew. 1997. Taking Preferences Seriously: Liberal Theory and International Politics. *International Organization* 51 (4):513–54.

———. 1999. A New Statecraft? Supranational Entrepreneurs and International Cooperation. *International Organization* 53 (2):267–306.

Mouzelis, Nicos. 1967. *Organization and Bureaucracy*. Chicago: Aldine.

Murphy, Craig. 1994. *International Organizations and Industrial Change*. New York: Oxford University Press.

Nelson, Paul. 1995. *The World Bank and Non-Governmental Organizations*. New York: St. Martin's Press.

Ness, Gayl, and Steven Brechin. 1988. Bridging the Gap: International Organizations as Organizations. *International Organization* 42 (2):245–73.

Niskanen, William A. 1971. *Bureaucracy and Representative Government*. Chicago: Aldine.

Paris, Roland. 1997. Peacebuilding and the Limits of Liberal Internationalism. *International Security* 22 (2):54–89.

Perry, William. 1996. Defense in an Age of Hope. *Foreign Affairs* 75 (6):64–79.

Pollack, Mark. 1997. Delegation, Agency, and Agenda-Setting in the European Community. *International Organization* 51 (1):99–134.

Powell, Walter W., and Paul J. DiMaggio, eds. 1991. *The New Institutionalism in Organizational Analysis.* Chicago: University of Chicago Press.

Pratt, John, and Richard J. Zeckhauser. 1985. *Principals and Agents: The Structure of Business.* Boston: Harvard Business School Press.

Radelet, Steven, and Jeffrey Sach. 1999. What Have We Learned, So Far, from the Asian Financial Crisis? Harvard Institute for International Development, 4 January. Available from www.hiid.harvard.edu/pub /other/aea122.pdf.

Rittberger, Volker, ed. 1993. *Regime Theory and International Relations.* Oxford: Clarendon Press.

Ross, George. 1995. *Jacques Delors and European Integration.* New York: Oxford University Press.

Ruggie, John. 1996. *Winning the Peace.* New York: Columbia University Press.

———. 1998. What Makes the World Hang Together. *International Organization* 52 (3):855–86.

Sagan, Scott. 1993. *The Limits of Safety: Organizations, Accidents, and Nuclear Weapons.* Princeton, NJ: Princeton University Press.

Schaar, John. 1984. Legitimacy in the Modern State. In *Legitimacy and the State,* edited by William Connolly, 104–33. Oxford: Basil Blackwell.

Schien, Edgar. 1996. Culture: The Missing Concept in Organization Studies. *Administrative Studies Quarterly* 41:229–40.

Scott, W. Richard. 1992. *Organizations: Rational, Natural, and Open Systems.* 3d ed. Englewood Cliffs, NJ: Prentice-Hall.

Shanks, Cheryl, Harold K. Jacobson, and Jeffrey H. Kaplan. 1996. Inertia and Change in the Constellation of Intergovernmental Organizations, 1981–1992. *International Organization* 50 (4):593–627.

Shapira, Zur, ed. 1997. *Organizational Decision.* New York: Cambridge University Press.

Shore, Cris, and Susan Wright. 1997. Policy: A New Field of Anthropology. In *Anthropology of Policy: Critical Perspectives on Governance and Power,* edited by Cris Shore and Susan Wright, 3–41. New York: Routledge Press.

Sigelman, Lee. 1986. The Bureaucratic Budget Maximizer: An Assumption Examined. *Public Budgeting and Finance* (spring):50–59.

Snidal, Duncan. 1996. Political Economy and International Institutions. *International Review of Law and Economics* 16:121–37.

Starr, Paul. 1992. Social Categories and Claims in the Liberal State. In *How Classification Works: Nelson Goodman Among the Social Sciences,* edited by Mary Douglas and David Hull, 154–79. Edinburgh: Edinburgh University Press.

UN Development Program. 1994. *Human Development Report 1994.* New York: Oxford University Press.

UN Peacekeeping Missions. 1994. The Lessons from Cambodia. Asia Pacific Issues, Analysis from the East-West Center, No. 11, March.

Vaubel, Roland. 1991. A Public Choice View of International Organization. In *The Political Economy of International Organizations,* edited

by Roland Vaubel and Thomas Willett, 27–45. Boulder, CO: Westview Press.

Vaughan, Diane. 1996. *The Challenger Launch Decision.* Chicago: University of Chicago Press.

Wade, Robert. 1996. Japan, the World Bank, and the Art of Paradigm Maintenance: The East Asian Miracle in Political Perspective. *New Left Review* 217:3–36.

Walkup, Mark. 1997. Policy Dysfunction in Humanitarian Organizations: The Role of Coping Strategies, Institutions, and Organizational Culture. *Journal of Refugee Studies* 10 (1):37–60.

Waltz, Kenneth. 1979. *Theory of International Politics.* Reading, MA: Addison-Wesley.

Weber, Max. 1947. *Theory of Social and Economic Organization.* New York: Oxford University Press.

———. [1930] 1968. *The Protestant Ethic and the Spirit of Capitalism.* New York: Routledge.

———. 1978. Bureaucracy. In *From Max Weber: Essays in Sociology,* edited by H. H. Gerth and C. Wright Mills. New York: Oxford.

Weber, Steven. 1994. Origins of the European Bank for Reconstruction and Development. *International Organization* 48 (1):1–38.

Weingast, Barry R., and Mark Moran. 1983. Bureaucratic Discretion or Congressional Control: Regulatory Policymaking by the Federal Trade Commission. *Journal of Political Economy* 91 (October):765–800.

Weiss, Thomas. 1996. Collective Spinelessness: U.N. Actions in the Former Yugoslavia. In *The World and Yugoslavia's Wars,* edited by Richard Ullman, 59–96. New York: Council on Foreign Relations Press.

Weiss, Tom, and Amir Pasic. 1997. Reinventing UNHCR: Enterprising Humanitarians in the Former Yugoslavia, 1991–95. *Global Governance* 3 (1):41–58.

Wendt, Alexander. 1995. Constructing International Politics. *International Security* 20 (1):71–81.

———. 1998. Constitution and Causation in International Relations. *Review of International Studies* 24 (4):101–17. Special issue.

Williams, Michael. 1996. Hobbes and International Relations: A Reconsideration. *International Organization* 50 (2):213–37.

Williamson, Oliver. 1975. *Markets and Hierarchies, Analysis and Antitrust Implications: A Study in the Economics of Internal Organization.* New York: Free Press.

———. 1985. *The Economic Institutions of Capitalism: Firms, Markets, Relational Contracting.* New York: Free Press.

Wright, Susan. 1994. "Culture" in Anthropology and Organizational Studies. In *Anthropology of Organizations,* edited by Susan Wright, 1–31. New York: Routledge.

Zabusky, Stacia. 1995. *Launching Europe.* Princeton, NJ: Princeton University Press.

Zieck, Marjoleine. 1997. *UNHCR and Voluntary Repatriation of Refugees: A Legal Analysis.* The Hague: Martinus Nijhoff.

Erik Voeten

THE POLITICAL ORIGINS OF THE UN SECURITY COUNCIL'S ABILITY TO LEGITIMIZE THE USE OF FORCE

In a 1966 article, Claude observed that the function of collective legitimization in global politics is increasingly conferred on international organizations (IOs), and that the United Nations (UN) has become the primary custodian of this legitimacy. Claude argued that "the world organization has come to be regarded, and used, as a dispenser of politically significant approval and disapproval of the claims, policies, and actions of states."[1] This assertion is even more relevant now than it was in 1966. States, including the United States, have shown the willingness to incur significant cost in terms of time, policy compromise, and side-payments simply to obtain the stamp of approval from the UN Security Council (SC) for military actions. To be sure, if the attempt to achieve a SC compromise proved unsuccessful, the United States has not shied away from using other means to pursue its ends. Nevertheless, the failure to acquire SC approval is generally perceived as costly, giving SC decisions considerable clout in international politics.

Given its lack of enforcement capabilities, the SC's leverage resides almost entirely in the perceived legitimacy its decisions grant to forceful actions.[2] Governments across the globe appear more willing to cooperate voluntarily once the SC has conferred its blessing on a use of force. Why has the SC become the most impressive source of international

legitimacy for the use of military force? That it would be so is far from obvious. Claude, for instance, thought of the UN General Assembly (GA) as the ultimate conferrer of legitimacy.[3] Franck argued in his influential 1990 treatise on legitimacy that if one were interested in identifying rules in the international system with a strong compliance pull, the provisions in the UN Charter that grant the SC military enforcement powers (Chapter VII) should be set aside.[4] Since then, these provisions have been invoked with great regularity to legitimize uses of force.

The development is also puzzling from a theoretical perspective. Most theorists seek the origins of modern institutional legitimacy in legal or moral principles. However, the SC has been inconsistent at best in applying legal principles; its decision-making procedures are not inclusive, transparent, or based on egalitarian principles; its decisions are frequently clouded by the threat of outside action; and the morality of its (non-) actions is widely debated. Hence, it is unlikely that the institution has the ability to appear depoliticized, an argument that motivates most constructivist accounts of institutional legitimacy in the international arena.[5]

On the other hand, scholars who study the strategic aspects of international politics have largely dismissed the UN from their analyses.[6] This article provides a firmer base for the role of the SC in strategic interactions. I argue that when governments and citizens look for an authority to legitimize the

From *International Organization* 59 (Summer 2005): 527–57. Some of the author's notes have been omitted.

use of force, they generally do not seek an independent judgment on the appropriateness of an intervention; rather, they want political reassurance about the consequences of proposed military adventures. The rationale is based on an analysis of the strategic dilemmas that impede cooperation in a unipolar world. In the absence of credible limits to power, fears of exploitation stifle cooperation. Because no single state can credibly check the superpower, enforcing limits on the superpower's behavior involves overcoming a complex coordination dilemma. A cooperative equilibrium that implies self-enforcing limits to the exercise of power exists but is unlikely to emerge spontaneously given that governments have conflicting perceptions about what constitute legitimate actions and fundamental transgressions by the superpower. The SC provides a focal solution that has the characteristics of an elite pact: an agreement among a select set of actors that seeks to neutralize threats to stability by institutionalizing nonmajoritarian mechanisms for conflict resolution. The elite pact's authority depends on the operation of a social norm in which SC approval provides a green light for states to cooperate, whereas its absence triggers a coordinated response that imposes costs on violators. The observance of this norm allows for more cooperation and restraint than can be achieved in the absence of coordination on the SC as the proper institutional device. Hence the extent to which the SC confers legitimacy on uses of force depends not on the perceived normative qualities of the institution, but on the extent to which actors in international politics believe that norm compliance produces favorable outcomes.

The attractiveness of the elite pact account resides partly in its ability to explain the emergence of a limited degree of governance in the international system without assuming the existence of a collective global identity that generates an ideological consensus over appropriate forms of global governance. There is little evidence that such a consensus exists. Thus accounts that require

only a limited set of a priori common values appear more plausible. Furthermore, the elite pact model better fits the SC's institutional design than alternative accounts and provides a plausible explanation for the sudden surge in authority following the Gulf War. Finally, the model stresses that elite pacts need to be self-enforcing. This opens a more promising avenue for analyzing norm stability than the constructivist assumption that norms are internalized.

The article proceeds with a broad overview of temporal fluctuations in the extent to which states have historically put weight on SC decisions. The next section explains why SC authority stems from its ability to legitimize uses of force and provides an operational definition. While there is a large literature that asserts that SC decisions confer legitimacy on uses of force, explanations for this phenomenon are rarely made explicit. One of the contributions of this article is to more precisely identify the various plausible roles of the SC in the international system. After discussing the four most common (though often implicit) explanations, the elite pact argument is introduced more elaborately. The conclusion discusses the implications for theories of international legitimacy and the future of SC legitimacy.

The Security Council and Its Authority over Uses of Force

When states sign the UN Charter, they pledge not to use or threaten force "against the territorial integrity or political independence of any state, or in any manner inconsistent with the Purposes of the United Nations."[7] The Charter delegates significant authority to the SC to decide whether particular uses of force meet these purposes. This delegation is necessitated by the incompleteness of any contract that seeks to regulate the use of force but falls short of forbidding it outright. The Charter provides some guidance by explicitly specifying two general circumstances in which force may be exercised.

First, Article 51 of the Charter affirms the inherent right of states to use force in individual or collective self-defense against armed attacks. In principle, states are not obliged to obtain the approval of the SC for invoking this right.[8] However, states routinely resort to expanded conceptions of self-defense in attempts to justify unilateral uses of force. SC resolutions conceivably provide judgments on the merit of self-defense claims. An example is Resolution 1373, which reaffirms the right of the United States to act forcefully in its self-defense against terrorist activities and de facto legitimized the U.S. military action in Afghanistan.[9] This resolution, however, was quite exceptional. In nearly all other controversial claims to self-defense the SC has been unable or unwilling to rule on the legitimacy of self-defense claims; instead allowing the GA to adopt highly politicized and mostly ignored resolutions about the legitimacy of uses of force.[10]

Second, Chapter VII of the Charter defines a more active role for the SC in the management of international security. This chapter lays out a set of procedures through which the SC can authorize uses of force in response to the "existence of any threat to the peace, breach of the peace, or act of aggression."[11] Before 1990, the SC adopted only twenty-two resolutions under Chapter VII, most of which authorized sanctions rather than uses of force.[12] The two most important exceptions were the Congo peacekeeping force and the Korean War (1950). In the latter case, authorization was possible only because of the temporary absence of the Union of Soviet Socialist Republics (USSR) to protest the exclusion of the People's Republic of China from the Council. In anticipation of deadlock when the USSR would retake its seat, the SC adopted the 1950 "Uniting for Peace Resolution,"

which allowed the GA to take responsibility in security affairs if the SC were unable to act. It has been invoked ten times, most notably in 1956 to order the French and British to stop their military intervention in the Suez Canal and to create the UN Emergency Force to provide a buffer between Egyptian and Israeli forces.

Although the UN's effectiveness and decisiveness were often limited, the UN was actively involved in the management of many international conflicts in the first twenty-five years of its existence. Decisions by the UN's political organs carried some weight, even to realists such as Hans Morgenthau, who argued that the United States should be willing to compromise to "to keep the United Nations in existence and make it an effective instrument of international government."[13] Between the late-1960s and 1989, however, neither the GA nor the SC exercised much influence over when or whether states resorted to force, a development characterized by Haas as evidence for "regime decay."[14] States, including the great powers, repeatedly intervened militarily without considering UN authorization and routinely ignored resolutions condemning their actions. Most obviously, this holds for major Cold War interventions, such as the Soviet invasion of Afghanistan and the U.S. military action in Vietnam. But it also pertains to smaller conflicts. U.S. President Ronald Reagan famously claimed that the 1983 GA resolution condemning the United States for its intervention in Grenada "didn't upset his breakfast at all."[15] This disregard for the authority of the UN over uses of force continued at least until December 1989, when the United States invaded Panama without considering asking approval from any IO. A GA resolution deploring the intervention had no discernable impact on domestic public or elite support for the intervention, and neither did a SC resolution that the United States vetoed.[16]

The successful cooperation between states in the first Persian Gulf War abruptly turned the SC into the natural first stop for coalition building.[17] It is important to appreciate the magnitude of the sudden shift in SC activity immediately after operation Desert Storm. Between 1977 and the start of the Gulf War, the SC had adopted only two resolutions under Chapter VII.[18] Between 1990 and 1998, the Council approved 145 Chapter VII resolutions.[19] The number of UN commanded missions that used force beyond traditional peacekeeping principles went from one (Congo) before 1990 to five thereafter.[20] The number of missions where the authority to exercise force was delegated to interested parties went from one (Korea) to twelve.[21] Since 1990, the SC has authorized uses of force by coalitions of able and willing states in Europe (for example, the former Yugoslavia), Africa (for example, Sierra Leone, Somalia, the Great Lakes Region), Latin America (for example, Haiti), Oceania (for example, East-Timor), and Asia (for example, Afghanistan).

This spurt in activity does not simply reflect a newfound harmony in the preferences of the five veto powers. China and Russia frequently abstained from SC votes and often accompanied their abstentions with statements of discontent.[22] Reaching agreement often involved difficult compromises that had a noticeable impact on the implementation of operations, as exemplified most prolifically by the Bosnia case.[23] On several occasions, the United States made significant side-payments to obtain SC blessing for operations it could easily, and de facto did, execute alone or with a few allies. For instance, in exchange for consent for the U.S. intervention in Haiti, China and Russia obtained sizeable concessions, including a favorable World Bank loan and U.S. support for peacekeeping in Georgia.[24] Thus, attaining SC approval for a use of force is no easy task.

Governments outside the United States have also placed considerable weight on SC decisions. SC authorization was crucial to Australia's willingness to intervene in East-Timor.[25] India has since 1992 committed to a "pro-active" approach toward UN peacekeeping missions, providing generous troop contributions across the globe to UN-approved missions while refusing to supply troops for non-UN approved missions.[26] New interpretations of Basic Law provisions that restrict German military activity abroad have made exceptions for German participation in UN peacekeeping and peacemaking missions, as well as North Atlantic Treaty Organization (NATO) and West European Union (WEU) operations directed at implementing SC resolutions.[27] Japan has adopted a law that makes military contributions of most kinds conditional on SC authorization.[28] Thus even for these powerful states that lack permanent membership, SC approval has become almost imperative for participation in cooperative military endeavors.

The increased significance of SC authorization is also apparent in public opinion, both in the United States and elsewhere. There is a wealth of evidence that Americans consistently prefer UN actions to other types of multilateral interventions and even more so to unilateral initiatives. For example, in a January 2003 poll, the Program on International Policy Attitudes (PIPA) asked respondents whether they "think the UN Security Council has the right to authorize the use of military force to prevent a country that does not have nuclear weapons from acquiring them." Of all respondents, 76 percent answered affirmatively to this question, whereas only 48 percent believes the United States without UN approval has this right.[29] What is impressive about these findings is their consistency across interventions, question formats, and time.[30] Public opinion outside the United States tends to insist even more strongly on UN authorization.[31] This suggests that SC authorization may facilitate foreign leaders to participate in military actions.

The observation that, since the Persian Gulf War, it has become costly to circumvent the authority of the SC is not completely undermined by the two main cases where this authority has been ignored: the Kosovo intervention and the 2003 Iraq intervention. The absence of SC authorization for the Kosovo intervention was generally (and explicitly) perceived as unfortunate by the U.S. administration and even more so by its allies in the North Atlantic Treaty Organization (NATO).[32] NATO motivated its actions by referring to previous SC resolutions and obtained SC authorization for the peacekeeping mission and transitional authority that were set up in the immediate aftermath of the military campaign. Similarly, the United States went to considerable length to persuade the SC to authorize the Iraq intervention, argued repeatedly that it was implementing past SC resolutions, and returned to the SC in the immediate aftermath of the intervention.[33] Moreover, the absence of SC authorization is often used domestically in the argument that the lack of allies makes the war unnecessarily expensive. That NATO and the United States eventually went ahead without SC authorization does demonstrate, however, that the SC may raise the costs of unilateral action but cannot prevent it altogether.[34] As former U.S. Secretary of Defense William Cohen said about SC authorization for the Kosovo intervention: "It's desirable, not imperative."[35]

Legitimacy

The previous section illustrates that since the Persian Gulf War, the main states in world politics have behaved "as if" it is costly to circumvent the authority of the SC when deciding on uses of force. How can one explain this observation given that the SC lacks independent capabilities to enforce its decisions? Several commonplace explanations for IO authority apply poorly to the SC. There are few, if any, institutional mechanisms that allow states to create credible long-term commitments to the institution, making it an unlikely candidate for locking in policies, along the lines suggested by Ikenberry.[36] The tasks that the SC performs are not routine and do not require high

levels of specific expertise or knowledge. Thus, delegation of decision-making authority to the SC does not result in similar gains from specialization that plausibly explain why states are willing to delegate authority to IOs such as the World Bank[37] and the International Monetary Fund (IMF).[38]

In the absence of obvious alternative sources, the origins of the SC authority are usually assumed to lie in the legitimacy it confers on forceful actions.[39] Actions that are perceived as legitimate are obeyed voluntarily rather than challenged. Hence, obtaining legitimacy for proposed interventions is valuable. This clearly implies that legitimacy resides entirely in the subjective beliefs of actors.[40] This contrasts with the conception that legitimacy properly signifies an evaluation on normative grounds, usually derived from democratic theory. In this view, if an institution fails to meet a set of specified standards it is illegitimate, regardless of how individual actors perceive the institution. While it is important to evaluate how democratic principles ought to be extended to a global arena,[41] such a normative approach is unlikely to generate much insight into the question why SC decisions confer the legitimacy they do.

I define legitimacy perceptions as the beliefs of actors that the convention or social norm that the SC authorizes and forbids discretionary uses of force by states against states should be upheld. Discretionary uses of force are those that do not involve direct and undisputed self-defense against an attack. Thus the authority of the SC resides in the beliefs of actors that violating this social norm is costly, undesirable, or inappropriate. This focus on perceptions and on the social aspect of legitimacy is consistent with constructivist approaches.[42] It also fits rationalist accounts of self-enforcing conventions and social norms.[43]

The primary actors are governments, who decide on uses of force and are the members of the UN. However, because governments, especially democratically elected ones, rely on the support of citizens, the perceptions of individuals also matter in an indirect way. In addition, it may well be that actors in the state with the intent to use force, most often the United States in our examples, and actors in other states may have different motivations for insisting on SC authorization.[44]

Explanations

Why do state actors believe that a failure to achieve SC authorization is undesirable? What sustains these beliefs? To find convincing answers to these questions one needs to appreciate not only why states demand some form of multilateralism, but also the reasons that would lead actors to rely on the SC rather than alternatives, such as the GA, regional institutions (for example, NATO), or multilateral coalitions that are not embedded in formal IOs. Thus, pointing to a general inclination toward multilateralism does not form a satisfactory explanation of the empirical pattern.[45] Besides institutional form, a persuasive account must provide useful insights about the sources for temporal variation in the authority of the SC, including its sudden surge following the Gulf War. Moreover, it should give a plausible explanation for how these beliefs can be sustained given the behavior of the SC.

Most theoretical accounts argue that the legitimacy of international institutions resides in their ability to appear depoliticized by faithfully applying a set of rules, procedures, and norms that are deemed desirable by the international community.[46] I discuss three variants of this general argument that each stresses a different role for institutions: consistently applying legal rules, facilitating deliberation, and increasing accountability and fairness. Alternatively, the origins of the SC's legitimacy may lie in beliefs that granting the SC the authority to legitimize force generally lead to more desirable outcomes. The public goods explanation discussed below fits this mold, as does the elite pact account.

Legal Consistency

Much legal scholarship assumes that the SC derives its ability to legitimize and delegitimize the use of force from its capacity to form judgments about the extent to which proposed actions fit a legal framework that defines a system of collective security. Although the SC is explicitly a political institution rather than a court, there is a body of customary and written international law that provides a basis for determinations about the legality of self-defense actions and other uses of force.[47] The indiscriminatory nature of legal norms potentially makes legal uses of force more acceptable to governments and citizens than actions that do not meet legal standards. To maintain its standing as a legitimate conferrer of legal judgments, an institution must thus strive for consistency in its rulings and motivate deviations from past practice with (developing) legal principles. This standard has usefully been applied to other bodies, such as dispute resolution mechanisms in trade organizations[48] and the European Court of Justice (ECJ).[49] That legal consistency is the institutional behavior that reinforces legitimacy beliefs also motivates concerns by legal scholars that the SC squanders its legitimacy when it behaves in ways that are inconsistent with general principles of international law.[50]

There is, however, no empirical evidence that legal consistency has been a driving force behind SC decisions. During the Cold War, the judgments by UN bodies on the legality of self-defense actions were widely perceived as politically motivated and not persuasive on the issue of lawfulness.[51] The SC has not developed a consistent doctrine on this matter since the end of the Cold War. The most noteworthy decision is the previously noted Resolution 1373, which affirms the right of the United States to act forcefully in its self-defense against terrorist activities. The extensive scope of the resolution has led some to question its legal foundations.

As Farer puts it: "At this point, there is simply no cosmopolitan body of respectable legal opinion that could be invoked to support so broad a conception of self-defense."[52]

With regard to Chapter VII authorizations, the most basic determination is whether a situation presents a threat to international peace and security. Such "Article 39 determinations" have been stretched on multiple occasions to accommodate immediate political objectives. For example, Iraqi actions in Kurdish areas in 1991, the humanitarian tragedy in Somalia in 1992, the civil war in Angola in 1993, the failure to implement election results in Haiti in 1994, and Libya's unwillingness to surrender its citizens accused of terrorism have all been deemed threats to international peace.[53] Most importantly, there has been no serious effort at motivating the Article 39 determination on these resolutions. As Kirgis points out: "[I]f we are concerned about the responsible use of power by a marginally representative international organ that at present is not subject to recall or judicial review, we should expect the Security Council to be conscious of how and why it is expanding the definition. It should also contemplate the limits to be applied to the broader definition. It should, in other words, make principled Article 39 determinations, publicly explicated, that do not set unlimited or unintended precedents."[54]

Legal scholars have noted a variety of other difficulties considering SC decisions, including the common practice to delegate the use of force to individual states or groupings of states, the failure to define a greater role for judicial review through the International Court of Justice, and the extent to which the Charter obliges states to seek peaceful resolutions before authorizing force.[55] Glennon has concluded that coherent international law concerning intervention by states no longer exists.[56] Others counter that the Charter does not impose meaningful restrictions on the set of cases in which the SC can legally authorize forceful means.[57] Clearly, either view precludes that legal consistency

is the driving force behind the SC's legitimizing ability. This does not mean that legal norms do not affect the use of force. The norm to ask for approval from the SC for the use of force can itself be understood as a legal norm. The observation that this norm is mostly obeyed even though the SC itself has shown little regard for legal principles warrants an explanation.

Forum for Deliberation

A second set of scholars claim that while legal arguments are not decisive in the SC, law plays a broader role in the process of justificatory discourse.[58] This view relies on the notion that governments generally feel compelled to justify their actions on something other than self-interest. This may be so because governments seek to acquire the support of other governments, domestic political actors, or public opinion. Or, it may be that governments have internalized standards for appropriate behavior that are embedded in international legal norms. The importance of law in persuasion resides in its ability to put limits on the set of arguments that can acceptably be invoked.[59] Moreover, professional experts (international lawyers) help distinguish good arguments from poor ones in the evaluation of truth claims. Of course, the extent to which legal specialists can perform this function depends on the presence of a relatively coherent body of international law that regulates uses of force.

Alternatively, discourse in the SC may be guided by rules that the international community collectively understands to guide the process of acquiring approval for uses of force, even if not codified by law.[60] This thesis relies on the presence of easily recognizable common values that facilitate the evaluation of arguments.

The above view provides a promising account for why states frequently appeal to legal arguments, precedents, and collective security rules, even if final decisions often violate those rules. However, this view does not provide a plausible explanation for the role of the SC in this discursive process. It is widely recognized that the SC falls far short of Habermasian conditions for effective communicative action.[61] There is only a shallow set of common values, participants are unequal, and the SC relies extensively on unrecorded and informal consultations between subsets of the permanent members.[62] U.S. Secretary of State Colin Powell's public exposition of evidence for the case against Iraq was highly unusual and of questionable efficacy as a persuasive effort.[63] More frequently, the most visible efforts at persuasion occur outside of the institutional context of the SC. SC debates are usually recitations by representatives of statements prepared by their state departments. Strategic incentives further impede deliberation. There are clear and obvious incentives for states to misrepresent their positions, as the stakes are clear and the relevant actors few. In short, it is hard to see how the institutional setting of the SC contributes to the process of justificatory discourse and why, if deliberation were so important, institutional reforms have not been undertaken or alternative venues such as the GA have not grown more relevant.

Appropriate Procedures

An institution's decisions may be seen as legitimate because the institution's decision-making process corresponds to practice deemed desirable by members of the community. Beliefs about the appropriateness of a decision-making process constitute an important source of authority for domestic political institutions, particularly in democracies. Citizens may attach inherent value to procedures that conform to principles widely shared in a society. As a consequence, decisions of an institution may be perceived as legitimate even if these produce outcomes deemed undesirable.[64]

In a similar vein, accountability, procedural fairness, and broad participation are often seen as inherent elements of the legitimacy of IOs.[65] This assumption underlies the common argument that the main threat to SC legitimacy is that the institution is dominated by a few countries and that its procedures are opaque and unfair.[66] The assertion is that the SC's decision would carry greater legitimacy if its procedures more closely matched liberal norms, which allegedly have become increasingly important in international society.[67]

The many attempts to reform the SC indicate that the legitimacy of the SC may be enhanced from the perspective of some if its decision-making procedures more closely corresponded to liberal principles. But one cannot plausibly explain the legitimacy the SC does confer on uses of force from the assumption that governments and citizens demand appropriate process. As outlined earlier, SC practice sets a low standard if measured against any reasonable set of liberal principles. One may object that a use of force authorized by the SC more closely approximates standards of appropriate procedure than unilateral actions. But if demands for appropriate procedure were strong, one would surely expect a greater use of more inclusive IOs, such as a return to the "uniting for peace" procedure popular in the 1950s and 1960s, perhaps under a weighted voting system. Instead, the GA has grown increasingly irrelevant for legitimizing uses of force. Alternatively, one might have expected reforms that increase transparency and accountability, which have been moderately successful in international financial institutions. Some argue that accountability has worsened in the 1990s, as the GA can no longer hold the SC accountable through the budget by qualified majority rule,[68] and because of the increasingly common practice of delegating the authority to use force to states and regional organizations.[69]

It is equally implausible that the general public appreciates the SC for its procedures. The public knows little about how the SC makes its decisions.

Even in the midst of the Iraq controversy, 32 percent of the U.S. public claimed that the United States does not have the right to veto SC decisions,[70] and only 16 percent could name the five members with veto power.[71] Knowledge is not much better elsewhere, with correct identification of permanent members varying in a nine-country study from 5 percent in Portugal to 24 percent in Germany.[72]

Finally and most fundamentally, there is no set of common values that generate consensus about what constitutes appropriate global governance. Disagreements have become especially apparent in debates about voting rules and membership questions, but they have also surfaced in virtually any other area where meaningful reforms have been proposed.[73] Even liberal democracies generally disagree on if and how liberal principles ought to be extended to global governance.[74] Explanations that emphasize strong common values are less likely to be successful for a diverse global organization than for an institution with more homogenous membership.

Global Public Goods

An alternative view is that the SC helps solve collective action problems that arise in the production of global public goods.[75] Successful peacekeeping operations reduce suffering and save lives. Globalization and the end of the Cold War may have increased demands for international actions that produce such effects.[76] In addition, UN-authorized interventions may provide a measure of stability and security that benefits virtually all nations. For example, the first Gulf War reinforced the norm that state borders not be changed forcibly and secured the stability of the global oil supply.[77] These benefits accrue to all status quo powers and are not easily excludable.

Models of public good provision predict that poor nations will be able to free ride off the contributions of wealthier nations and that the public good will be underprovided because contributors do not take into account the spillover benefits that their support confers to others. The SC may help alleviate underprovision and free riding in three ways. First, the fixed burden-sharing mechanism for peacekeeping operations provides an institutional solution that helps reduce risks of bargaining failures and lessens transaction costs.[78] Second, the delegation of decision-making authority to a small number of states may facilitate compromise on the amount of public good that ought to be produced.[79] Third, the SC helps states pool resources.[80] The existence of selective incentives induces some states to incur more than their required share of the peacekeeping burden. For example, Kuwait paid two-thirds of the bill for the UN Iraq-Kuwait Observation Mission through voluntary contributions. Australia proved willing to shoulder a disproportionate share of the peacekeeping burden in East-Timor. States are more likely to make such contributions when these add to the efforts of others in a predictable manner.

The absence of enforcement mechanisms implies that the survival of this cooperative solution depends on a social norm. This norm first and foremost requires states to pay their share of the burden. The more states believe that this norm is followed, the fewer incentives they have to free ride in any particular case. In individual instances, states must be willing to shoulder a larger share of the burden than they would with a voluntary mechanism, because they believe that the benefits from upholding the social norm (greater public good production in the long run) exceed the short-term benefits of shirking. Hence, interventions authorized by the SC could be perceived as more legitimate in the sense that they signal a longer-term commitment to global public good production.

Although this argument is plausible theoretically, it fails to account for some noticeable empirical patterns. First, the belief among rational actors that the SC plays this role should and probably has weakened considerably since the early 1990s. The much-publicized failures in Somalia, Rwanda, and Bosnia should have reduced beliefs that the SC is the appropriate mechanism for coordination that helps solve problems of public good production. Moreover, several wealthy states, most notably the United States, have failed repeatedly to meet their peacekeeping assessments. As of 31 January 2003, the United States had $789 million in peacekeeping arrears.[81] Other states owe the UN $1.4 billion in payments for peacekeeping. These arrears constitute a sizeable portion of the total peacekeeping budget.[82] Under the collective action model, the failure of states to meet their assessments gives other states clear incentives to shirk.

Second, the public goods rationale does not explain why states value SC authorization even when they do not use its fixed burden-sharing mechanism. Between 1996 and 2000, estimated expenditures on non–UN-financed peacekeeping missions have exceeded spending on UN-financed operations by $11.5 billion.[83] Interestingly, many of these non–UN-financed operations have taken place with the explicit authorization of the SC. For example, the mandates of the various peacekeeping and peacemaking forces in Bosnia, Kosovo, and Afghanistan were all authorized at some point by SC resolutions,[84] but none of them are financed primarily through the UN system or executed by the UN.

Third, the decision-making procedures grant veto power to states that contribute little to UN operations and exclude some of the most significant contributors. Japan and Germany are the second and third largest contributors but have no permanent seat at the table. China contributes less than small European states such as Belgium, Sweden, and the Netherlands, but has the right to veto any resolution.[85] If public good provision were the prime concern, reform of these decision-making mechanisms would be in every state's best interest. It would prevent large contributors from abandoning the institution or refusing to pay their dues.

International financial institutions, such as the World Bank and the IMF, have adopted weighted voting rules that better fit these objectives.

The value states attach to SC authorization rests not entirely in the extent to which it forms an institutional solution to free-rider problems that lead to under-production of public goods. However, the public good argument is not completely without merit. Several SC-authorized peacekeeping missions have helped resolve conflicts and have contributed to the implementation of peace agreements.[86] Moreover, a global alternative is not readily available. The elite pact rationale suggests that the main function of the SC in this may be that it addresses a distributional issue that frequently impedes successful collective action.

The Security Council as an Elite Pact

An alternative perspective is that the SC is an institutional manifestation of a central coalition of great powers.[87] This view does not proclaim that the SC enforces a broad system of collective security, but rather that it may serve as a useful mechanism that facilitates cooperative efforts in an anarchic world characterized by the security dilemma.[88] Concerts were historically designed to deal with situations of multipolarity that followed the defeat of hegemony. However, similar incentives for cooperation exist in a unipolar world characterized by interdependence. There are substantial potential gains from cooperation between the superpower and other states on economic issues such as trade and financial stability. Moreover, many governments face common security threats such as terrorism and states with the capacity and intention to challenge status quo boundaries or produce nuclear weapons. The main impediment to cooperation under the security dilemma is fear of exploitation.[89] Such fears are also relevant in a unipolar world where the superpower can use its preponderant capabilities to extract concessions, set the terms for cooperation, and act against the interests of individual states without being checked by a single credible power.

In such asymmetrical situations, credible limits to the use of force potentially benefit both the superpower and the rest of the world.[90] In the absence of credible guarantees, one observes suboptimal levels of cooperation as states pay a risk premium, captured for instance by increased military expenditure or other actions targeted at limiting the superpower's relative primacy. Institutions, such as NATO, help increase the credibility of security guarantees by raising the cost of reneging from a commitment. However, the absence of an outside threat and strong collective identity make such arrangements much more difficult to achieve at the global level.

Game-theoretic analyses that treat institutions as self-enforcing equilibria suggest an alternative route by which institutions help achieve better outcomes: they aid in solving the coordination dilemma among those actors that fear exploitation. Potential individual challenges are unlikely to deter a superpower from engaging in transgressions. However, the prospect of a coordinated challenge may well persuade the superpower to follow restraint. For this to succeed, states would have to agree on a mechanism that credibly triggers a coordinated response. For example, Greif, Milgrom, and Weingast argue that merchant guilds during the late medieval period provided a credible threat of costly boycotts if trade centers violated merchants' property rights.[91] Without these guilds, trade centers were unable to credibly commit to not exploit individual merchants and consequentially, merchants traded less than desired by the trade centers. As such, cooperation with the guilds became self-enforcing: it was in the self-interest of all actors to abide by the cooperative norm and defend against violations of the norm. Therefore, breaches of the norm came to be seen as illegitimate actions.

There is, however, a complicating factor in applying this analogy to the international arena. One can reasonably assume that merchants agreed on a common definition of what constituted a fundamental transgression by a trade center. Such consensus surely does not exist in the global arena. As the recent conflict over Iraq illustrates, what some states perceive as a proper use of force, others see as an encroachment. This introduces a political component to the problem. The strategic dilemma in the international system therefore more closely resembles that of achieving limited governance and rule of law in the context of ethnically, linguistically, and religiously heterogeneous societies, as analyzed by Weingast.[92]

In heterogeneous societies, actors usually have conflicting interests about many aspects of governance. Weingast's model assumes that each actor can classify each move by the superpower[93] as either a transgression or a legitimate action. However, actors do not necessarily agree on these classifications. A superpower can exploit this by rewarding a subset of actors and infringing on the interests of the others. Although there are many such uncooperative equilibria, in a dynamic setting the Pareto-optimal cooperative outcome is also an equilibrium. In this equilibrium, no transgressions occur and states can cooperate beneficially. However, this equilibrium entails that states agree on a mechanism that triggers a coordinated response against an identifiable action by the superpower. It also requires that states use trigger strategies to punish one another for failing to cooperate in a coordinated challenge. The heterogeneous actors that occupy the international system are unlikely to resolve their coordination dilemma in a wholly decentralized manner.

In accordance with the literature on comparative politics, Weingast suggests that the most effective manner to induce limited governance in divided societies is through elite pacts.[94] An elite pact is an agreement among a select set of actors that seeks to neutralize threats to stability by institutionalizing nonmajoritarian mechanisms for conflict resolution. The SC can usefully be understood as such a pact that functions as a focal point that helps state actors coordinate what limits to the exercise of power should be defended. If the SC authorizes a use of force, the superpower and the states that cooperate should not be challenged. If, however, the United States exercises force in the absence of SC authorization, other states should challenge it and its allies, for instance, by reducing cooperation elsewhere. This equilibrium behavior can be understood as a social norm or convention. For a convention to be successful, it needs to be self-enforcing. This means that actors should find it in their interest to punish unilateral defections from the pact, for example, because they believe that deviations have the potential to steer international society down a conflict-ridden path. SC authorizations thus legitimize uses of force in that they form widely accepted political judgments that signal whether a use of force transgresses a limit that should be defended. This fits with the conventional interpretation that legitimate power is limited power.

To domestic publics this convention performs a signaling function. Citizens are generally unprepared to make accurate inferences about the likely consequences of forceful actions. If the convention operates as specified above, SC agreement provides the public with a shortcut on the likely consequences of foreign adventures. SC authorization indicates that no costly challenges will result from the action. The absence of SC authorization on the other hand, signals the possibility of costly challenges and reduced cooperation. A U.S. public that generally wants the United States to be involved internationally but is fearful of overextension[95] may value such a signaling function. To foreign publics, SC approval signals that a particular use of force does not constitute an abuse of power that should lead to a coordinated, costly response.[96] Clearly this conception of the SC poses fewer informational demands on general publics than

alternatives. Moreover, it does not rely on the assumption that citizens share common values about the normative qualities of global governance. All citizens need to understand is that SC authorization implies some measure of consent and cooperation, whereas the absence of authorization signals potential challenges. The symbolic (focal point) aspect of SC approval allows for analogies to past experiences in a way that cooperative efforts through ad hoc coalitions do not.

More generally, the elite pact account does not depend on the existence of a broad set of common values that generates a consensus about what global governance should look like. For a cooperative equilibrium to survive, it is not necessary that each actor believe that the norm that sustains the equilibrium is morally appropriate, as long as most nonbelievers assume that other actors would react to violations. This is consistent with Weber's view on why a social order is binding on an individual level.[97] It helps explain the observation that governments insist on SC authorizations of uses of force even if they challenge the normative qualities of the institution. As observed earlier, powerful states such as Germany, Japan, and India, as well as many developing countries, regularly criticize the SC for its composition and decision-making procedures. Yet, they also insist on SC authorization of uses of force and in some cases even adjust their domestic laws to make cooperation conditional on SC.

■ ■ ■

Conclusions

The ability of the SC to successfully restrain the United States is at the heart of its aptitude to play a legitimizing role in international politics. In this conception, a legitimate exercise of power abides by certain accepted limits. SC authorization signals the observance of these limits, which are defined not by legal, moral, or efficiency standards, but by an undemocratic political process that seeks to achieve compromise among elite actors. It is important to understand that although the role of the SC depends entirely on the configuration of state interests, this fact does not make the institution epiphenomenal. There are many potential equilibria and convergence on a particular (semicooperative) equilibrium has important implications. This is true even if the restraint on the exercise of power is limited to raising the cost of unilateralism.

Theoretically, this conception of legitimacy corresponds best to those classical realists who did not consider power and legitimacy to be antithetical, but complementary.[98] Legitimacy, these theorists argued, helps convert power into authority. Authority is a much cheaper regulatory device than the constant exercise of coercion. Therefore, attempts to legitimize power are a persistent feature of political life, even in the anarchical global arena. However, these realists had little faith in legalities or moral values as the source for legitimacy. Instead, the process of legitimation primarily involves the acquisition of political judgments about the proper way in which the exercise of power ought to be limited. As Claude wrote in 1966: "[T]he process of legitimization is ultimately a political phenomenon, a crystallization of judgment that may be influenced but is unlikely to be wholly determined by legal norms and moral principles."[99] This statement contrasts sharply with the view that IOs derive their legitimacy precisely from their ability to appear depoliticized. One way of reconciling these views is that the latter focuses mostly on the role of IOs as bureaucracies or courts, whereas the first stresses their political arena role. The UN encompasses both roles, but the ability of the SC to legitimize the use of force stems from its function as a political meeting place. This political arena function of IOs has hitherto received too little attention in the theoretical literature.

The implications of this argument differ in important ways from alternative accounts. The common claim among scholars of international law that the SC threatens to lose its legitimacy if it adopts resolutions that do not fit a broader legal framework depends strongly on the (usually implicit) assumption that its legitimacy depends primarily on its ability to fulfill the role of legal adjudicator. This is the premise of Glennon's argument that the SC was a "grand attempt to subject the use of force to the rule of law," which has "fallen victim to geopolitical forces too strong for a legalist institution to withstand."[100] If the SC's legitimacy does not critically depend on its functioning as a guardian of a legal system, as I argue here, the legal consistency of SC resolutions should not per se be of great consequence to the legitimacy of the institution.[101]

Others claim that the gravest threat to the legitimacy of the SC is that a few countries dominate it and that its procedures are opaque and unfair.[102] If demand for proper procedures were the motivating factor behind the SC's authority, secretive backroom deals among the great powers would be considered illegitimate. Such deals are part of the elite pact account of legitimacy. This does not imply that actors view the procedural aspects of elite politics as desirable per se, but that these are useful to the higher purpose of stability. This situation suggests that successful reforms to make the SC more transparent may actually have adverse effects in that powerful states may flee the forum.[103] In the public goods rationale, the legitimacy of the SC depends critically on preventing free riding and effectiveness in producing global public goods. This is not necessarily the primary concern in the elite pact rationale, although the proper functioning of the elite pact increases public good production in comparison to uncooperative equilibria. Nevertheless, the failures of the SC in Rwanda and other places and the failure of the United States to meet its peacekeeping burden may have diminished esteem for the institution, but these failures appear to have had little effect on the belief that the SC is the proper authority to legitimize force.

The conclusion from this study should not be that states are not concerned with legal and moral principles or global public goods, but that the existing and persistent belief that the SC is the most desirable institution to approve the use of force cannot be explained persuasively from the assumption that states do. Legitimacy that relies on the effectiveness of an institution to resolve a particular dilemma is often thought to be inherently unstable. For example, it depends on outcomes that could be caused by a multitude of factors, not just the decisions of the institution. I agree that if the SC's legitimacy were based on a convergence of opinions on its normative properties, its legitimacy would be more stable than it is today. However, such agreement does not exist and is unlikely to emerge in the near future. The collective legitimation function of the UN helps shape state behavior because state officials have made it important by their actions and statements.[104] Those actions and statements could also undermine the Council's legitimacy.

NOTES

1. Claude 1966, 367.
2. See Barnett 1997; Caron 1993; and Hurd 1999 and 2002.
3. Claude 1966, 373.
4. Franck 1990, 42.
5. See especially Barnett and Finnemore 1999.
6. Hoffmann 1998, 179.
7. UN Charter, Article 2(4).
8. See Schachter 1989; and Franck 2001. Under the Charter, states do have an obligation to notify the SC.
9. SC Resolution 1373, 28 September 2001.
10. Schachter 1989.
11. UN Charter, Article 39.
12. Bailey and Daws 1998, 271.
13. Morgenthau 1954, 11.
14. Haas 1983.
15. Cited in Luck 2002, 63.
16. Luck 2002, 64.
17. Baker 1995, 278.
18. See SC Resolution 502, 3 April 1982; SC Resolution 598, 20 July 1987; and Bailey and Daws 1998, 272.
19. Bailey and Daws 1998, 271.
20. Jakobsen 2002.
21. Ibid.
22. Voeten 2001.
23. See Christopher 1998.
24. Malone 1998.
25. Coleman 2004.
26. Krishnasamy 2003.
27. Bundesverfassungsgericht [Federal Constitutional Court] 90, 286, 12 July 1994.
28. Law Concerning Cooperation for United Nations Peacekeeping Operations and Other Operations (the International Peace Cooperation Law) originally passed in June 1992. For other examples, see Hurd 1999.
29. PIPA 2003a. Poll conducted among 1,063 American adults, margin of error +/−3 percent. The order of the questions was randomized.
30. Kull 2002.
31. See German Marshall Fund and Compagnia di San Paolo 2003; and Thompson 2004.
32. Daalder and O'Hanlon 2000, 218–19.
33. See also Frederking 2003.
34. See also Hurd 2003, 205.
35. See New York Times, 12 June 1998, A1.
36. Ikenberry 2001. Accordingly, Ikenberry focuses on NATO and GATT/WTO.
37. Nielson and Tierney 2003.
38. Martin 2003.
39. See Caron 1993; and Hurd 1999.
40. Weber 1978.
41. For example, Held 1995.
42. See especially Hurd 1999.
43. See Lewis 1969; and Young 1993.
44. See also Thompson 2004.
45. See Ruggie 1993.
46. Barnett and Finnemore 1999, 708.
47. See Murphy 1997 for an overview.
48. Kelemen 2001.
49. Burley and Mattli 1993.
50. See Alvarez 1995; Farer 2002; Glennon 2001; and Kirgis 1995.
51. Schachter 1989.
52. Farer 2002, 359.
53. See SC Resolution 688, 5 April 1991; SC Resolution 794, 3 December 1992; and SC Resolution 940, 31 July 1994.
54. Kirgis 1995, 517. See also Gordon 1994.
55. See Alvarez 1995; Glennon 2001; and Kirgis 1995.
56. Glennon 1999 and 2001.
57. Franck 1999.
58. See Johnstone 2003; and Sandholtz and Stone Sweet 2004.
59. Johnstone 2003.
60. Frederking 2003.
61. See Johnstone 2003; and Risse 2000.
62. See Bailey and Daws 1998; Woods 1999; and Wood 1996.
63. Colin Powell, "Remarks to the United Nations Security Council," New York City, 5 February 2003.
64. Gibson 1989.
65. For example, see Keohane and Nye 2001; and Woods 1999.
66. See especially Caron 1993.
67. See the discussion in Barnett 1997.
68. Woods 1999.
69. Blokker 2000.

70. According to PIPA 2003b, 55 percent thought that the United States does have that right.
71. German Marshall Fund and Compagnia di San Paolo 2003.
72. Ibid.
73. Luck 2003.
74. See Schmitz and Sikkink 2002, 521; and Slaughter 1995.
75. For analyses along these lines see Khanna, Sandler, and Shimizu 1998; Bobrow and Boyer 1997; and Shimizu and Sandler 2002.
76. Jakobsen 2002.
77. Bennett, Lepgold, and Unger 1994.
78. This system was put in place in 1973 by General Assembly Resolution 310.
79. Martin 1992, 773.
80. Abbott and Snidal 1998.
81. See (http://www.globalpolicy.org/finance/tables/core/un-us-03.htm). Accessed 10 March 2005.
82. In the 2000–2002 period, yearly peacekeeping budgets were around $2.6 billion.
83. Based on data from Shimizu and Sandler 2002.
84. Initial SC resolutions for respective missions were SC Resolution 1031, 15 December 1995; SC Resolution 1088, 12 December 1996; SC Resolution 1244, 10 June 1999; and SC Resolution 1386, 20 December 2001.
85. Based on data in Shimizu and Sandler 2002.
86. Doyle and Sambanis 2000.
87. Rosecrance 1992.
88. Jervis 1985. Other realists believe that concerts were mostly epiphenomenal. See Downs and Iida 1994.
89. Jervis 1985, 69.
90. Ikenberry 2001.
91. Greif, Milgrom, and Weingast 1994.
92. The informal discussion here relies on the formal analysis provided by Weingast 1997.
93. Sovereign in Weingast's case.
94. For example, see Lijphart 1969; Rustow 1970; and Tsebelis 1990.
95. Holsti 2004.
96. For a similar argument, see Thompson 2004.
97. Weber 1978.
98. On the UN see: Claude 1964, 1966; and Morgenthau 1954, 10–11. Unfortunately, contemporary Realists have mostly ignored legitimacy. See Barnett 1997, 529.
99. Claude 1966, 369.
100. Glennon 2003, 16.
101. Slaughter 2003; and Hurd 2003 make similar arguments in response to Glennon.
102. Caron 1993.
103. Drezner 2003 argues that reforms in the IMF have had such an effect. For a proposal of procedural reform that takes such incentives into account, see Buchanan and Keohane 2004.
104. See also Claude 1966, 543.

REFERENCES

Abbot, Kenneth, and Duncan Snidal. 1998. Why States Act Through Formal International Organizations. *Journal of Conflict Resolution* 42 (1):3–32.

Alvarez, Jose E. 1995. The Once and Future Security Council. *The Washington Quarterly* (spring): 3–20.

Bailey, Sidney D., and Sam Daws. 1998. *The Procedure of the UN Security Council.* 3d ed. Oxford: Clarendon Press.

Baker, James A. III. 1995. *The Politics of Diplomacy: Revolution, War and Peace 1989–1992.* New York: Putnam's Sons.

Barnett, Michael N. 1997. Bringing in the New World Order: Liberalism, Legitimacy, and the United Nations. *World Politics* 49 (4):526–51.

Barnett, Michael N., and Martha Finnemore. 1999. The Politics, Power, and Pathologies of International Organizations. *International Organization* 53 (4):699–732.

Bennett, Andrew, and Joseph Lepgold. 1993. Reinventing Collective Security after the Cold War and the Gulf Conflict. *Political Science Quarterly* 108 (2):213–237.

Bennett, Andrew, and Joseph Lepgold, and Danny Unger. 1994. Burden-Sharing in the Persian Gulf War. *International Organization* 48 (1):39–75.

Blokker, Niels. 2000. Is the Authorization Authorized? Powers and Practice of the UN Security Council to Authorize the Use of Force by 'Coalitions of the Able and Willing.' *European Journal of International Law* 11 (3):541–68.

Bobrow, Davis B., and Mark A. Boyer. 1997. Maintaining System Stability: Contributions to Peace keeping Operations. *Journal of Conflict Resolution* 41 (6):723–48.

Buchanan, Allen, and Robert O. Keohane. 2004. The Preventive Use of Force: A Cosmopolitan Institutional Proposal. *Ethics and International Affairs* 18 (1):1–23.

Burley, Anne-Marie, and Walter Mattli. 1993. Europe Before the Court: A Political Theory of Legal Integration. *International Organization* 47 (1):41–76.

Caron, David C. 1993. The Legitimacy of the Collective Authority of the Security Council. *American Journal of International Law* 87 (4):552–88.

Christopher, Warren. 1998. *In the Stream of History: Shaping Foreign Policy for a New Era.* Stanford, Calif.: Stanford University Press.

Claude, Inis L. 1964. *Swords into Plowshares: The Problems and Progress of International Organization.* 3d ed. New York: Random House.

———. 1966. Collective Legitimation as a Political Function of the United Nations. *International Organization* 20 (3):367–79.

Coleman, Katharina P. 2004. States, International Organizations, and Legitimacy: The Role of International Organizations in Contemporary Peace Enforcement Operations. Ph.D. diss., Princeton University, Princeton, N.J.

Daalder, Ivo H., and Michael E. O'Hanlon. 2000. *Winning Ugly: NATO's War to Save Kosovo.* Washington, D.C.: Brookings Institution.

Downs, George, and Keisuke Iida, eds. 1994. *Collective Security Beyond the Cold War.* Ann Arbor: University of Michigan Press.

Doyle, Michael W., and Nicholas Sambanis. 2000. International Peace-building: A Theoretical and Quantitative Analysis, *American Political Science Review* 94 (4):779–801.

Drezner, Daniel. 2003. Clubs, Neighborhoods, and Universes: The Governance of Global Finance. Unpublished manuscript, University of Chicago, Chicago.

Farer, Tom. 2002. Beyond the Charter Frame: Unilateralism or Condominium Frame? *American Journal of International Law* 96 (2):359–64.

Franck, Thomas M. 1990. *The Power of Legitimacy Among Nations*. Oxford: Oxford University Press.

———. 1999. Sidelined in Kosovo? The United Nation's Demise Has Been Exaggerated. *Foreign Affairs* 78 (4):116–18.

———. 2001. Terrorism and the Right of Self-Defense. *American Journal of International Law* 95 (4):839–43.

Frederking, Brian. 2003. Constructing Post–Cold War Collective Security *American Political Science Review* 97 (3):363–78.

German Marshall Fund and Compagnia di San Paolo. 2003. *Transatlantic Trends 2003*. Washington, D.C.: German Marshall Fund of the United States.

Gibson, James L. 1989. Understandings of Justice: Institutional Legitimacy, Procedural Justice and Political Tolerance. *Law and Society Review* 23 (3):469–96.

Glennon, Michael J. 1999. The New Interventionism. *Foreign Affairs* 78 (3):2–7.

———. 2001. *Limits of Law, Prerogatives of Power: Intervention After Kosovo*. New York: Palgrave.

———. 2003. Why the Security Council Failed. *Foreign Affairs* 82 (3):16–35.

Gordon, Ruth. 1994. United Nations Intervention in Internal Conflicts: Iraq, Somalia, and Beyond. *Michigan Journal of International Law* 15(2):519–89.

Greif, Avner, and David Laitin. 2004. A Theory of Endogenous Institutional Change. *American Political Science Review* 98 (4):633–52.

Greif, Avner, Paul Milgrom, and Barry R. Weingast, 1994. Coordination, Commitment, and Enforcement: The Case of the Merchant Guild. *Journal of Political Economy* 102 (4):745–76.

Haas, Ernst B. 1983. Regime Decay: Conflict Management and International Organizations, 1945–1981. *International Organization* 37 (2): 189–256.

Held, David, 1995. *Democracy and the Global Order: From the Modern State to Cosmopolitan Governance*. Cambridge: Polity Press.

Hoffmann, Stanley. 1998. *World Disorders: Troubled Peace in the Post–Cold War Era*. Lanham, Md.: Rowman & Littlefield.

Holsti, Ole. 2004. *Public Opinion and American Foreign Policy*. Ann Arbor: University of Michigan Press.

Hurd, Ian. 1997. Security Council Reform: Informal Membership and Practice. In *The Once and Future Security Council*, edited by Bruce Russett and Ian Hurd, 135–52, New York: St. Martin's Press.

———. 1999. Legitimacy and Authority in International Politics. *International Organization* 53 (2):379–408.

———. 2002. Legitimacy, Power, and the Symbolic Life of the UN Security Council. *Global Governance* 8(1):35–51.

———. 2003. Stayin' Alive: The Rumours of the UN's Death Have Been Exaggerated: Too Legit to Quit. *Foreign Affairs* 82 (4):204–5.

Ikenberry, John. 2001. *After Victory*. Princeton, N.J.: Princeton University Press.

Jakobsen, Peter Viggo. 2002. The Transformation of United Nations Peace Operations in the 1990s. *Cooperation and Conflict* 37 (3):267–82.

Jervis, Robert. 1985. From Balance to Concert: A Study of International Security Cooperation. *World Politics* 38 (1):58–79.

Johnstone, Ian. 2003. Security Council Deliberations: The Power of the Better Argument. *European Journal of International Law* 14 (3):437–80.

Kelemen, R. Daniel. 2001. The Limits of Judicial Power: Trade-Environment Disputes in the GATT/WTO and the EU *Comparative Political Studies* 34 (6):622–50.

Keohane, Robert O., and Joseph S. Nye Jr. 2001. Democracy, Accountability, and Global Governance. Politics Research Group Working Paper 01–04. Cambridge, Mass.: Harvard University.

Khanna, Jyoti, Todd Sandler, and Hirofumi Shimizu. 1998. Sharing the Financial Burden for U.N. and NATO Peacekeeping, 1976–1996. *The Journal of Conflict Resolution* 42 (2):176–95.

Kirgis, Frederic L. 1995. The Security Council's First Fifty Years. *The American Journal of International Law* 89 (3):506–39.

Krishnasamy, Kabilan. 2003. The Paradox of India's Peacekeeping. *Contemporary South Asia* 12 (2):263–64.

Kull. Steven. 2002. Public Attitudes Towards Multilateralism. In *Multilateralism and U.S. Foreign Policy*, edited by Stewart Patrick and Shepard Forman, 99–120. London: Lynne Rienner.

Lesch, Ann M. 1991. Contrasting Reactions to the Persian Gulf Crisis: Egypt, Syria, Jordan, and the Palestinians. *Middle East Journal* 45 (1):30–50.

Lewis, David. 1969. *Convention, A Philosophical Study*. Cambridge, Mass.: Harvard University Press.

Lijphart, Arend. 1969. Consociational Democracy. *World Politics* 21 (2):207–25.

Luck, Edward C. 2002. The United States, International Organizations, and the Quest for Legitimacy. In *Multilateralism and U.S. Foreign Policy*, edited by Stewart Patrick and Shepard Forman, 47–74, London: Lynne Rienner.

———. 2003. Reforming the United Nations: Lessons from a History in Progress. International Relations Studies and the United Nations Occasional Paper 2003:1. Waterloo, Canada: Academic Council on the United Nations System.

Malone, David M. 1998. *Decision-Making in the UN Security Council: The Case of Haiti, 1990–1997*. New York: Oxford University Press.

Martin, Lisa L. 1992. Interests, Power, and Multilateralism. *International Organization* 46 (4): 765–92.

———. 2003. Distribution, Information, and Delegation to International Organizations: The Case of IMF Conditionality. Unpublished manuscript, Harvard University, Cambridge, Mass.

Morgenthau, Hans. 1954. The United Nations and the Revision of the Charter. *Review of Politics* 16 (1):3–21.

Morrow, James D. 1994. Modeling the Forms of International Cooperation: Distribution Versus Information. *International Organization* 48 (3):387–423.

Murphy, John F. 1997. Force and Arms. In *The United Nations and International Law*, edited by Christopher C. Joyner, 97–130. Cambridge: Cambridge University Press.

Nielson, Daniel, and Michael Tierney. 2003. Delegation to International Organizations: Agency Theory and World Bank Environmental Reform. *International Organization* 57 (2):241–76.

Program on International Policy Attitudes (PIPA). 2003a. PIPA Knowledge Networks Poll: Americans on Iraq and the UN Inspections I, 21–26 January 2003.

PIPA. 2003b. PIPA Knowledge Networks Poll: Americans on Iraq and the UN Inspections II, 21 February 2003.

Risse, Thomas. 2000. "Let's Argue!": Communicative Action in World Politics. *International Organization* 54 (1):1–40.

Rosecrance, Richard. 1992. A New Concert of Powers. *Foreign Affairs* 71 (2):64–82.

Ruggie, John Gerard. 1993. Multilateralism: The Anatomy of an Institution. In *Multilateralism Matters*, edited by John G. Ruggie, 3–48. New York: Columbia University Press.

Russett, Bruce, and James Sutterlin. 1991. The UN in a New World Order. *Foreign Affairs* 70 (2):69–83.

Rustow, Dankwart. 1970. Transitions to Democracy: Toward a Dynamic Model. *Comparative Politics* 2 (3):337–63.

Sandholtz, Wayne, and Alec Stone Sweet. 2004. Law, Politics and International Governance In *The Politics of International Law*, edited by Christian Reus-Smit, 238–71. Cambridge: Cambridge University Press.

Schachter, Oscar. 1989. Self-Defense and the Rule of Law. *American Journal of International Law* 83(2):259–77.

Schmitz, Hans Peter, and Kathryn Sikkink. 2002. International Human Rights. In *Handbook of International Relations*, edited by Walter Carlisnaes, Thomas Risse-Kappen, and Beth A. Simmons, 517–37, London: Sage Publications.

Shimizu, Hirofumi, and Todd Sandler. 2002. Peacekeeping and Burden-Sharing, 1994–2000. *Journal of Peace Research* 39 (6):651–68.

Slaughter, Anne-Marie. 1995. International Law in a World of Liberal States. *The European Journal of International Law* 6 (4):503–38.

———. 2003. Misreading the Record. *Foreign Affairs* 82 (4):202–4.

Thompson, Alexander. 2004. Understanding IO Legitimation. Unpublished paper, Ohio State University, Columbus.

Tsebelis, George. 1990. *Nested Games: Rational Choice in Comparative Politics*. Berkeley: University of California Press.

Urquhart, Brian. 1991. Learning from the Gulf. *New York Review of Books* 38 (5):34–37.

Voeten, Erik. 2001. Outside Options and the Logic of Security Council Action. *American Political Science Review* 95 (4):845–58.

Weber, Max. 1978. The Types of Legitimate Domination. In *Economy and Society: An Outline of Interpretive Sociology*, edited by Guenther Roth and Claus Wittich, 212–301. Berkeley: University of California Press.

Weingast, Barry. 1997. The Political Foundations of Democracy and the Rule of Law. *American Political Science Review* 91 (2):245–63.

Weingast, Barry, and William J. Marshall. 1988. The Industrial Organization of Congress; or, Why Legislatures, like Firms, Are Not Organized as Markets. *Journal of Political Economy* 96 (1):132–63.

Wood, Michael. 1996. Security Council Working Methods and Procedure: Recent Developments. *International and Comparative Law Quarterly* 45 (1):150–61.

Woods, Ngaire. 1999. Good Governance in International Organizations. *Global Governance* 5 (1):39–61.

Young, H. Peyton. 1993. The Evolution of Conventions. *Econometrica* 61 (1):57–84.

10   HUMAN RIGHTS

For generations, the idea of human rights has been contested. Which rights should be included? Which are excluded? How are rights determined in a culturally diverse world? Amartya Sen develops the argument that human rights need to be viewed as entitlements to capability—the opportunity to have freedom. Eschewing the idea of a fixed listing of capabilities, Sen suggests a process of public reasoning to arrive at an understanding of capability.

Jack Donnelly, in a chapter from *Universal Human Rights in Theory and Practice* (2003), probes whether there can be universal human rights. At the level of concepts, he sees an extensive consensus on a limited set of obligations defined in the Universal Declaration of Human Rights. But, he suggests, the ways these rights are implemented may vary, thus offering logical explanations for the persistence of arguments that rights should vary by culture.

Beth A. Simmons's *Mobilizing for Human Rights* (2009) is a meticulous study of whether signing human rights treaties does any good, or whether it is just cheap talk in an effort to distract attention from misbehavior. Mixing statistical evidence with case studies of allegations of Israeli torture of Palestinian detainees and of abuses under a Chilean military dictatorship, this excerpt from Simmons's magisterial book shows that treaties do indeed promote rights compliance, but mainly in partially democratic countries with somewhat independent courts and active civil society organizations. This finding is noteworthy, and so is the impeccable research design that she uses to derive the finding.

Much human rights activism in wealthy countries focuses on civil and political rights. Responding to criticism that Human Rights Watch has neglected economic and social rights, that organization's executive director, Kenneth Roth, lays out criteria for deciding when to treat economic and social demands as rights questions and when not to.

Amartya Sen

HUMAN RIGHTS AND CAPABILITIES

Introduction

The moral appeal of human rights has been used for varying purposes, from resisting torture and arbitrary incarceration to demanding the end of hunger and of medical neglect. There is hardly any country in the world—from China, South Africa and Egypt to Mexico, Britain and the United States—in which arguments involving human rights have not been raised in one context or another in contemporary political debates.

However, despite the tremendous appeal of the idea of human rights, it is also seen by many as being intellectually frail—lacking in foundation and perhaps even in coherence and cogency. The remarkable co-existence of stirring appeal and deep conceptual scepticism is not new. The American Declaration of Independence took it to be 'self-evident' that everyone is "endowed by their Creator with certain inalienable rights," and 13 years later, in 1789, the French declaration of 'the rights of man' asserted that "men are born and remain free and equal in rights." But it did not take Jeremy Bentham long to insist, in *Anarchical Fallacies*, written during 1791–1792, that "natural rights is simple nonsense: natural and imprescriptible rights [an American phrase], rhetorical nonsense, nonsense upon stilts" (Bentham, 1792/1843, p. 501). That division remains very alive today, and there are many who see the idea of human rights as no more than "bawling upon paper" (to use another of Bentham's barbed descriptions).

The concepts of human rights and human capabilities have something of a common motivation,

From *Journal of Human Development* 6, no. 2 (July 2005), 151–66.

but they differ in many distinct ways. It is useful to ask whether considering the two concepts together—capabilities and human rights—can help the understanding of each. I will divide the exercise into four specific questions. First, can human rights be seen as entitlements to certain basic capabilities, and will this be a good way of thinking about human rights? Second, can the capability perspective provide a comprehensive coverage of the content of human rights? Third, since human rights need specificity, does the use of the capability perspective for elucidating human rights require a full articulation of the list of capabilities? And finally, how can we go about ascertaining the content of human rights and of basic capabilities when our values are supposed to be quite divergent, especially across borders of nationality and community? Can we have anything like a universalist approach to these ideas, in a world where cultures differ and practical preoccupations are also diverse?

Human Rights as Entitlements to Capabilities

It is possible to argue that human rights are best seen as rights to certain specific freedoms, and that the correlate obligation to consider the associated duties must also be centred around what others can do to safeguard and expand these freedoms. Since capabilities can be seen, broadly, as freedoms of particular kinds, this would seem to establish a basic connection between the two categories of ideas.

We run, however, into an immediate difficulty here. I have argued elsewhere that 'opportunity' and 'process' are two aspects of freedom that require distinction, with the importance of each deserving specific acknowledgment.[1] While the opportunity aspect of freedoms would seem to belong to the same kind of territory as capabilities, it is not at all clear that the same can be said about the process aspect of freedom.

An example can bring out the *separate* (although not necessarily independent) relevance of both *substantive opportunities* and *freedom of processes.* Consider a woman, let us call her Natasha, who decides that she would like to go out in the evening. To take care of some considerations that are not central to the issues involved here (but which could make the discussion more complex), it is assumed that there are no particular safety risks involved in her going out, and that she has critically reflected on this decision and judged that going out would be the sensible—indeed the ideal—thing to do.

Now consider the threat of a violation of this freedom if some authoritarian guardians of society decide that she must not go out ('it is most unseemly'), and if they force her, in one way or another, to stay indoors. To see that there are two distinct issues involved in this one violation, consider an alternative case in which the authoritarian bosses decide that she must—absolutely *must*—go out ('you are expelled for the evening—just obey'). There is clearly a violation of freedom even here though Natasha is being forced to do exactly what she would have chosen to do anyway, and this is readily seen when we compare the two alternatives 'choosing freely to go out' and 'being forced to go out'. The latter involves an immediate violation of the *process aspect* of Natasha's freedom, since an action is being forced on her (even though it is an action she would have freely chosen also).

The opportunity aspect may also be affected, since a plausible accounting of opportunities can include having options and it can *inter alia*

include valuing free choice. However, the violation of the opportunity aspect would be more substantial and manifest if she were not only forced to do something chosen by another, but in fact forced to do something she would not otherwise choose to do. The comparison between 'being forced to go out' (when she would have gone out anyway, if free) and, say, 'being forced to polish the shoes of others at home' (not her favorite way of spending time, I should explain) brings out this contrast, which is primarily one of the opportunity aspect, rather than the process aspect. In the incarceration of Natasha, we can see two different ways in which she is losing her freedom: first, she is being forced to do something, with no freedom of choice (a violation of her process freedom); and second, what Natasha is being obliged to do is not something she would choose to do, if she had any plausible alternative (a violation of her substantive opportunity to do what she would like to do).[2]

It is important to recognize that both processes and opportunities can figure powerfully in the content of human rights. A denial of 'due process' in being, say, sentenced without a proper trial can be an infringement of human rights (no matter what the outcome of the fair trial might be), and so can be the denial of opportunity of medical treatment, or the opportunity of living without the danger of being assaulted (going beyond the exact process through which these opportunities are made real).

The idea of 'capability' (i.e., the opportunity to achieve valuable combinations of human functionings—what a person is able to do or be) can be very helpful in understanding the opportunity aspect of freedom and human rights.[3] Indeed, even though the concept of opportunity is often invoked, it does require considerable elaboration, and capability can help in this elucidation. For example, seeing opportunity in terms of capability allows us to distinguish appropriately between (i) whether a person is actually able to do things she would value *doing*, and (ii) whether she possesses the *means or instruments or permissions* to pursue what she would like to do (her actual ability to do that pursuing may depend on many contingent circumstances). By shifting attention, in particular, toward the former, the capability-based approach resists an overconcentration on means (such as incomes and primary goods) that can be found in some theories of justice (e.g. in the Rawlsian Difference Principle). The capability approach can help to identify the possibility that two persons can have very different substantial opportunities even when they have exactly the same set of means: for example, a disabled person can do far less than an able-bodied person can, with exactly the same income and other 'primary goods.' The disabled person cannot, thus, be judged to be equally advantaged—with the same opportunities—as the person without any physical handicap but with the same set of means or instruments (such as income and wealth and other primary goods and resources).

The capability perspective allows us to take into account the parametric variability in the relation between the means, on the one hand, and the actual opportunities, on the other.[4] Differences in the capability to function can arise even with the same set of personal means (such as primary goods) for a variety of reasons, such as: (1) *physical or mental heterogeneities among persons* (related, for example, to disability, or proneness to illness); (2) *variations in non-personal resources* (such as the nature of public health care, or societal cohesion and the helpfulness of the community); (3) *environmental diversities* (such as climatic conditions, or varying threats from epidemic diseases or from local crime); or (4) *different relative positions vis-à-vis others* (well illustrated by Adam Smith's discussion, in the *Wealth of Nations*, of the fact that the clothing and other resources one needs "to appear in public without shame" depends on what other people standardly wear, which in turn could be more expensive in rich societies than in poorer ones).

I should, however, note here that there has been some serious criticism of describing these substantive opportunities (such as the capability to live one kind of a life or another) as 'freedoms,' and it has been argued that this makes the idea of freedom too inclusive. For example, in her illuminating and sympathetic critique of my *Development as Freedom*, Susan Okin has presented arguments to suggest that I tend "to overextend the concept of freedom."[5] She has argued: "It is hard to conceive of some human functionings, or the fulfilment of some needs and wants, such as good health and nourishment, as freedoms without stretching the term until it seems to refer to everything that is of central value to human beings" (Okin, 2003, p. 292).

There is, certainly, considerable scope for argument on how extensively the term freedom should be used. But the particular example considered in Okin's counter-argument reflects a misinterpretation. There is no suggestion whatever that a functioning (e.g. being in good health or being well nourished) should be seen as freedom of any kind, such as capability. Rather, capability concentrates on the *opportunity* to be able to have combinations of functionings (including, in this case, the opportunity to be well-nourished), and the person is free to make use of this opportunity or not. A capability reflects the alternative combinations of functionings from which the person can choose one combination. It is, therefore, not being suggested at all that being well-nourished is to be seen as a freedom. The term freedom, in the form of capability, is used here to refer to the extent to which the person is free to choose particular levels of functionings (such as being well-nourished), and that is not the same thing as what the person actually decides to choose. During India's struggle for independence from the Raj, Mahatma Gandhi famously did not use that opportunity to be well fed when he chose to fast, as a protest against the policies of the Raj. In terms of the actual functioning of being well-nourished, the fasting Gandhi did not differ from a starving famine victim, but the freedoms and opportunities they respectively had were quite different.

Indeed, the *freedom to have* any particular thing can be substantially distinguished from actually *having* that thing. What a person is free to have—not just what he actually has—is relevant, I have argued, to a theory of justice.[6] A theory of rights also has reason to be involved with substantive freedoms.

Many of the terrible deprivations in the world have arisen from a lack of freedom to escape destitution. Even though indolence and inactivity had been classic themes in the old literature on poverty, people have starved and suffered because of a lack of alternative possibilities. It is the connection of poverty with unfreedom that led Marx to argue passionately for the need to replace "the domination of circumstances and chance over individuals by the domination of individuals over chance and circumstances."[7]

The importance of freedom can be brought out also by considering other types of issues that are also central to human rights. Consider the freedom of immigrants to retain their ancestral cultural customs and lifestyles. This complex subject cannot be adequately assessed without distinguishing between *doing* something and being free to do that thing. A strong argument can be constructed in favor of an immigrant's having the freedom to retain her ancestral lifestyle, but this must not be seen as an argument in favor of her pursuing that ancestral lifestyle whether she herself chooses that pursuit or not. The central issue, in this argument, is the person's freedom to choose how she should live—including the *opportunity* to pursue ancestral customs—and it cannot be turned into an argument for that person specifically pursuing those customs in particular, irrespective of the alternatives she has.[8] The importance of capability—reflecting opportunities—is central to this distinction.

The Process Aspect of Freedom and Information Pluralism

In the discussion so far I have been concentrating on what the capability perspective can do for a theory of justice or of human rights, but I would now like to turn to what it *cannot* do. While the idea of capability has considerable merit in the assessment of the opportunity aspect of freedom, it cannot possibly deal adequately with the process aspect of freedom, since capabilities are characteristics of individual advantages, and they fall short of telling us enough about the fairness or equity of the processes involved, or about the freedom of citizens to invoke and utilise procedures that are equitable.

The contrast of perspectives can be brought out with many different types of illustrations; let me choose a rather harsh example. It is, by now, fairly well established that, given symmetric care, women tend to live longer than men. If one were concerned only with capabilities (and nothing else), and in particular with equality of the capability to live long, it would have been possible to construct an argument for giving men more medical attention than women to counteract the natural masculine handicap. But giving women less medical attention than men for the same health problems would clearly violate an important requirement of process equity, and it seems reasonable to argue, in cases of this kind, that demands of equity in process freedom could sensibly override a single-minded concentration on the opportunity aspect of freedom (and on the requirements of capability equality in particular). While it is important to emphasise the relevance of the capability perspective in judging people's substantive opportunities (particularly in comparison with alternative approaches that focus on incomes, or primary goods, or resources), that point does not, in any way, go against seeing the relevance also of the process aspect of freedom in a theory of human rights—or, for that matter, in a theory of justice.

In this context, I should comment briefly also on a misinterpretation of the general relevance of the capability perspective in a theory of justice. A theory of justice—or more generally an adequate theory of normative social choice—has to be alive both to the fairness of the processes involved and to the equity and efficiency of the substantive opportunities that people can enjoy.[9] In dealing with the latter, capability can indeed provide a very helpful perspective, in comparison with, say, the Rawlsian concentration on 'primary goods.' But capability can hardly serve as the sole informational basis for the *other* considerations, related to processes, that must also be accommodated in normative social choice theory.

Consider the different components of Rawls's (1971) theory of justice. Rawls's 'first principle' of justice involves the priority of liberty, and the first part of the 'second principle' involves process fairness, through demanding that 'positions and offices be open to all.' The force and cogency of these Rawlsian concerns (underlying his first principle and the first part of the second principle) can neither be ignored nor be adequately addressed through relying only on the informational base of capabilities. We may not agree with Rawls's own way of dealing with these issues, but these issues have to be addressed, and they cannot be sensibly addressed within the substantive boundaries of capability accounting.

On the other hand, the capability perspective comes into its own in dealing with the *remainder* of the second principle; namely, 'the Difference Principle'—a principle that is particularly concerned with the distribution of advantages that different people enjoy (a consideration that Rawls tried to capture, I believe inadequately, within the confines of the accounting of 'primary goods'). The territory that Rawls reserved for primary goods, as used in his Difference Principle, would

indeed, I argue, be better served by the capability perspective. That does not, however, obliterate in any way the relevance of the rest of the territory of justice (related to the first principle and the first part of the second principle), in which process considerations, including liberty and procedural equity, figure.

A similar plurality of informational base has to be invoked in dealing with the multiplicity of considerations that underlie a theory of human rights. Capabilities and the opportunity aspect of freedom, important as they are, have to be supplemented by considerations of fair processes and the lack of violation of people's right to invoke and utilize them.

Listing Capabilities

I turn now to the controversial question of the listing of capabilities. In its application, the capability approach allows considerable variations in application. Martha Nussbaum has discussed powerfully the advantages of identifying an overarching 'list of capabilities,' with given priorities. My own reluctance to join the search for such a canonical list arises partly from my difficulty in seeing how the exact lists and weights would be chosen without appropriate specification of the context of their use (which could vary), but also from a disinclination to accept any substantive diminution of the domain of public reasoning. The framework of capabilities helps, in my judgement, to clarify and illuminate the subject matter of public reasoning, which can involve epistemic issues (including claims of objective importance) as well as ethical and political ones. It cannot, I would argue, sensibly aim at displacing the need for continued public reasoning.

Indeed, I would submit that one of the uses of the capability perspective is to bring out the need for transparent valuational scrutiny of individual advantages and adversities, since the different *functionings* have to be assessed and weighted in relation to each other, and the opportunities of having different *combinations* of functionings also have to be evaluated.[10] The richness of the capability perspective broadly interpreted, thus, includes its insistence on the need for open valuational scrutiny for making social judgments, and in this sense it fits in well with the importance of public reasoning. This openness of transparent valuation contrasts with burying the evaluative exercise in some mechanical—and valuationally opaque—convention (e.g. by taking market-evaluated income to be the invariable standard of individual advantage, thereby giving implicit normative priority to institutionally determined market prices).

The problem is not with listing important capabilities, but with insisting on one predetermined canonical list of capabilities, chosen by theorists without any general social discussion or public reasoning. To have such a fixed list, emanating entirely from pure theory, is to deny the possibility of fruitful public participation on what should be included and why.

I have, of course, discussed various lists of capabilities that would seem to demand attention in theories of justice and more generally in social assessment, such as the freedom to be well nourished, to live disease-free lives, to be able to move around, to be educated, to participate in public life, and so on. Indeed, right from my first writings on using the capability perspective (for example, the 1979 Tanner Lecture 'Equality of what?'; Sen, 1980), I have tried to discuss the relevance of specific capabilities that are important in a particular exercise. The 1979 Tanner Lecture went into the relevance of "the ability to move about" (I discussed why disabilities can be a central concern in a way that an income-centered approach may not be able to grasp), along with other basic capabilities, such as "the ability to meet one's nutritional requirements, the wherewithal to be clothed and sheltered, the power to participate in the social life of the community." The contrast between lists of capabilities and commodities was a central concern

in *Commodities and Capabilities* (Sen, 1985a). The relevance of many capabilities that are often neglected were discussed in my second set of Tanner Lectures, given at Cambridge University under the title *The Standard of Living* (Hawthorn, 1987).

My skepticism is about fixing a cemented list of capabilities that is seen as being absolutely complete (nothing could be added to it) and totally fixed (it could not respond to public reasoning and to the formation of social values). I am a great believer in theory, and certainly accept that a good theory of evaluation and assessment has to bring out the relevance of what we are free to do and free to be (the capabilities in general), as opposed to the material goods we have and the commodities we can command. But I must also argue that pure theory cannot 'freeze' a list of capabilities for all societies for all time to come, irrespective of what the citizens come to understand and value. That would be not only a denial of the reach of democracy, but also a misunderstanding of what pure theory can do, completely divorced from the particular social reality that any particular society faces.

Along with the exercise of listing the relevant capabilities, there is also the problem of determining the relative weights and importance of the different capabilities included in the relevant list. Even with a given list, the question of valuation cannot be avoided. There is sometimes a temptation not only to have one fixed list, but also to have the elements of the list ordered in a lexicographic way. But this can hardly work. For example, the ability to be well-nourished cannot in general be put invariably *above* or *below* the ability to be well-sheltered (with the implication that the tiniest improvement of the higher ranked capability will always count as more important than a large change in the lower ranked one). The judgment must take into account the extent to which the different abilities are being realized or violated. Also, the weighting must be contingent on circumstances. We may have to give priority to the ability to be well-nourished when people are dying of hunger in their homes, whereas the freedom to be sheltered may rightly receive more weight when people are in general well-fed, but lack shelter and protection from the elements.

Some of the basic capabilities (with which my 1979 Tanner Lecture was particularly concerned) will no doubt figure in every list of relevant capabilities in every society. But the exact list to be used will have to take note of the purpose of the exercise. There is often good sense in narrowing the coverage of capabilities for a specific purpose. Jean Drèze and I have tried to invoke such lists of elementary capabilities in dealing with 'hunger and public action,' and in a different context, in dealing with India's economic and social achievements and failures (Drèze and Sen, 1989, 2002). I see Martha Nussbaum's powerful use of a given list of capabilities for some minimal rights against deprivation as being extremely useful, in the same practical way. For another practical purpose, we may need quite a different list.

For example, when my friend Mahbub ul Haq asked me, in 1989, to work with him on indicators of human development, and in particular to help develop a general index for global assessment and critique, it was clear to me that we were involved in a particular exercise of specific relevance. So the 'Human Development Index' was based on a very minimal listing of capabilities, with a particular focus on getting at a minimally basic quality of life, calculable from available statistics, in a way that the Gross National Product or Gross Domestic Product failed to capture (United Nations Development Programme, 1990). Lists of capabilities have to be used for various purposes, and so long as we understand what we are doing (and, in particular, that we are getting a list for a particular reason, related to assessment, evaluation, or critique), we do not put ourselves against other lists that may be relevant or useful for other purposes.

All this has to be contrasted with insisting on one 'final list of capabilities that matter.' To decide that some capability will not figure in the list of relevant capabilities at all amounts to putting a zero weight on that capability for every exercise, no matter what the exercise is concerned with, and no matter what the social conditions are. This could be very dogmatic, for many distinct reasons.

First, we use capabilities for different purposes. What we focus on cannot be independent of what we are doing and why (e.g. whether we are evaluating poverty, specifying certain basic human rights, getting a rough and ready measure of human development, and so on).

Second, social conditions and the priorities that they suggest may vary. For example, given the nature of poverty in India as well as the nature of available technology, it was not unreasonable in 1947 (when India became independent) to concentrate on elementary education, basic health, and so on, and to not worry too much about whether everyone can effectively communicate across the country and beyond. However, with the development of the internet and its wide-ranging applications, and the advance made in information technology (not least in India), access to the web and the freedom of general communication has become a very important capability that is of interest and relevance to all Indians.

Third, even with given social conditions, public discussion and reasoning can lead to a better understanding of the role, reach, and the significance of particular capabilities. For example, one of the many contributions of feminist economics has precisely been to bring out the importance of certain freedoms that were not recognized very clearly—or at all—earlier on; for example, freedom from the imposition of fixed and time-honored family roles, or immunity from implicit derogation through the rhetoric of social communication.

To insist on a 'fixed forever' list of capabilities would deny the possibility of progress in social understanding, and also go against the productive role of public discussion, social agitation, and open debates. I have nothing against the listing of capabilities (and take part in that activity often enough), but I have to stand up against any proposal of a grand mausoleum to one fixed and final list of capabilities.

Public Reasoning, Cultural Diversity, and Universality

I turn now to the final question. If the listing of capabilities must be subject to the test of public reasoning, how can we proceed in a world of differing values and disparate cultures? How can we judge the acceptability of claims to human rights and to relevant capabilities, and assess the challenges they may face? How would such a disputation—or a defence—proceed? I would argue that, like the assessment of other ethical claims, there must be some test of open and informed scrutiny, and it is to such a scrutiny that we have to look in order to proceed to a disavowal or an affirmation. The status that these ethical claims have must be ultimately dependent on their survivability in unobstructed discussion. In this sense, the viability of human rights is linked with what John Rawls has called 'public reasoning' and its role in 'ethical objectivity.'[11]

Indeed, the role of public reasoning in the formulation and vindication of human rights is extremely important to understand. Any general plausibility that these ethical claims—or their denials—have is, on this theory, dependent on their ability to survive and flourish when they encounter unobstructed discussion and scrutiny (along with adequately wide informational availability). The force of a claim for a human right would be seriously undermined if it were possible to show that they are unlikely to survive open public scrutiny. But contrary to a commonly offered reason for skepticism and rejection, the case for human rights cannot be discarded simply by pointing to the possibility that in politically and socially repressive regimes, which do not allow open public discussion, many of these human rights are not taken seriously at all.

Open critical scrutiny is essential for dismissal as well as for defence. The fact that monitoring of violations of human rights and the procedure of 'naming and shaming' can be so effective (at least, in putting the violators on the defensive) is some indication of the wide reach of public reasoning when information becomes available and ethical arguments are allowed rather than suppressed.

It is, however, important not to keep the domain of public reasoning confined to a given society only, especially in the case of human rights, in view of the inescapably universalist nature of these rights. This is in contrast with Rawls's inclination, particularly in his later works, to limit such public confrontation within the boundaries of each particular nation (or each 'people,' as Rawls calls this regional collectivity), for determining what would be just, at least in domestic affairs.[12] We can demand, on the contrary, that the discussion has to include, even for domestic justice (if only to avoid parochial prejudices and to examine a broader range of counter-arguments), views also from 'a certain distance.' The necessity of this was powerfully identified by Adam Smith:

> We can never survey our own sentiments and motives, we can never form any judgment concerning them; unless we remove ourselves, as it were, from our own natural station, and endeavour to view them as at a certain distance from us. But we can do this in no other way than by endeavouring to view them with the eyes of other people, or as other people are likely to view them.[13]

Questions are often raised about whether distant people can, in fact, provide useful scrutiny of local issues, given what are taken to be 'uncrossable' barriers of culture. One of Edmund Burke's criticisms of the French declaration of the 'rights of man' and its universalist spirit was concerned with disputing the acceptability of that notion in other cultures. Burke argued that "the liberties and the restrictions vary with times and circumstances, and admit of infinite modifications, that cannot be settled upon any abstract rule."[14] The belief that the universality that is meant to underlie the notion of human rights is profoundly mistaken has, for this reason, found expression in many other writings as well.

A belief in uncrossable barriers between the values of different cultures has surfaced and resurfaced repeatedly over the centuries, and they are forcefully articulated today. The claim of magnificent uniqueness—and often of superiority—has sometimes come from critics of 'Western values,' varying from champions of regional ethics (well illustrated by the fuss in the 1990s about the peerless excellence of 'Asian values'), or religious or cultural separatists (with or without being accompanied by fundamentalism of one kind or another). Sometimes, however, the claim of uniqueness has come from Western particularists. A good example is Samuel Huntington's (1996) insistence that the "West was West long before it was modern," and his claim that "a sense of individualism and a tradition of individual rights and liberties" are "unique among civilized societies." Similarly, no less a historian of ideas than Gertrude Himmelfarb has argued that ideas of 'justice,' 'right,' 'reason,' and 'love of humanity' are "predominantly, perhaps even uniquely, Western values" (1996, pp. 74–75).

I have discussed these diagnoses elsewhere (for example Sen, 1999). Contrary to cultural stereotypes, the histories of different countries in the world have shown considerable variations over time as well as between different groups within the same country. When, in the twelfth century, the Jewish philosopher Maimonedes had to flee an intolerant Europe and its Inquisitions to try to safeguard his human right to stick to his own religious beliefs and practice, he sought shelter in Emperor Saladin's Egypt (via Fez and Palestine),

and found an honored position in the court of this Muslim emperor. Several hundred years later, when, in Agra, the Moghal emperor of India, Akbar, was arguing—and legislating—on the government's duty to uphold the right to religious freedom of all citizens, the European Inquisitions were still going on, and Giordano Bruno was burnt at the stake in Rome, in 1600.

In his autobiography, *Long Walk to Freedom*, Nelson Mandela (1994, p. 21) describes how he learned about democracy and individual rights, as a young boy, by seeing the proceedings of the local meetings held in the regent's house in Mqhekezweni:

> Everyone who wanted to speak did so. It was democracy in its purest form. There may have been a hierarchy of importance among the speakers, but everyone was heard, chief and subject, warrior and medicine man, shopkeeper and farmer, landowner and laborer.

Not only are the differences on the subject of freedoms and rights that actually exist between different societies often much exaggerated, but also there is, typically, little note taken of substantial variations *within* each local culture—over time and even at a point of time (in particular, right now). What are taken to be 'foreign' criticisms often correspond to internal criticisms from non-mainstream groups.[15] If, say, Iranian dissidents are imprisoned by an authoritarian regime precisely because of their heterodoxy, any suggestion that they should be seen as 'ambassadors of Western values' rather than as 'Iranian dissidents' would only add serious insult to manifest injury. Being culturally non-partisan requires respecting the participation of people from any corner of the earth, which is not the same thing as accepting the prevailing priorities, especially among dominant groups in particular societies, when information is extremely restricted and discussions and disagreements are not permitted.

Scrutiny from a 'distance' may have something to offer in the assessment of practices as different from each other as the stoning of adulterous women in the Taliban's Afghanistan and the abounding use of capital punishment (sometimes with mass jubilation) in parts of the United States. This is the kind of issue that made Smith insist that "the eyes of the rest of mankind" must be invoked to understand whether "a punishment appears equitable."[16] Ultimately, the discipline of critical moral scrutiny requires, among other things, "endeavoring to view [our sentiments and beliefs] with the eyes of other people, or as other people are likely to view them" (*The Theory of Moral Sentiments*, III, 1, 2; in Smith, 1976, p. 110).

Intellectual interactions across the borders can be as important in rich societies as they are in poorer ones. The point to note here is not so much whether we are *allowed* to chat across borders and to make cross-boundary scrutiny, but that the discipline of critical assessment of moral sentiments—no matter how locally established they are—*requires* that we view our practices *inter alia* from a certain distance.

Both the understanding of human rights and of the adequacy of a list of basic capabilities, I would argue, are intimately linked with the reach of public discussion—between persons and across borders. The viability and universality of human rights and of an acceptable specification of capabilities are dependent on their ability to survive open critical scrutiny in public reasoning.

Conclusions

To conclude, the two concepts—human rights and capabilities—go well with each other, so long as we do not try to subsume either entirely within the other. There are many human rights for which the capability perspective has much to offer. However, human rights to important process freedoms cannot be adequately analyzed within the capability approach.

Furthermore, both human rights and capabilities have to depend on the process of public reasoning, which neither can lose without serious impoverishment of its respective intellectual content. The methodology of public scrutiny draws on Rawlsian understanding of 'objectivity' in ethics, but the impartiality that is needed cannot be confined within the borders of a nation. We have to go much beyond Rawls for that reason, just as we also have to go beyond the enlightenment provided by his use of 'primary goods,' and invoke, in that context, the more articulate framework of capabilities. The need for extension does not, of course, reduce our debt to John Rawls. Neither human rights nor capabilities would have been easy to understand without his pioneering departures.

NOTES

1. See Sen (2002a), particularly the Arrow Lectures ('Freedom and Social Choice') included there (essays 20–22).
2. An investigation of more complex features of the opportunity aspect and the process aspect of freedoms can be found in the Arrow Lectures ('Freedom and Social Choice') in Sen (2002a, essays 20–22).
3. On the concept of capability, see Sen (1980, 1985a, 1985b), Nussbaum and Sen (1993), and Nussbaum (2000). See also the related theories of substantial opportunities developed by Arneson (1989), Cohen (1989), and Roemer (1996), among other contributions.
4. The relevance of such parametric variability for a theory of justice is discussed in Sen (1990).
5. See Okin (2003, p. 293). On related issues see also Joshua Cohen (1994, especially pp. 278–80), and G. A. Cohen (1995, especially pp. 120–25).
6. See Sen (1980, 1985a, 1985b). In contrast, G. A. Cohen has presented arguments in favor of focusing on achieved functionings—related to his concept of 'midfare'—rather than on capability (see Cohen, 1989, 1993).
7. See Marx (1845–1846/1977, p. 190).
8. There is a substantial difference between: (1) valuing multiculturalism because of the way—and to the extent that—it enhances the freedoms of the people involved to choose to live as they would like (and have reason to like); and (2) valuing cultural diversity *per se*, which focuses on the descriptive characteristics of a social pattern, rather than on the freedoms of the people involved. The contrast receives investigation in the *Human Development Report 2004* (United Nations Development Programme, 2004).

9. On the plurality of concerns that include processes as well as opportunities, which is inescapably involved in normative social choice (including theories of justice), see Sen (1970, 1985b). Since I have often encountered the diagnosis that I propound a "capability-based theory of justice," I should make it clear that this could be true only in the very limited sense of naming something according to one *principal* part of it (comparable with, say, using England for Britain). It is only one part of the informational base of a theory of justice that the capability perspective can expect to fill.

10. I cannot emphasise adequately how important I believe it is to understand that the need for an explicit valuational exercise is an advantage, rather than a limitation, of the capability approach, because valuational decisions have to be explicitly discussed, rather than being derived from some mechanical formula that is used, without scrutiny and assessment. For arguments *against* my position on this issue, see Beitz (1986) and Williams (1987). My own position is more fully discussed in Sen (1999, 2004).

11. See Rawls (1971, 1993, especially pp. 110–13).

12. See particularly John Rawls (1999). See also Rawls's formulation of the original position in *Political Liberalism* (Rawls, 1993, p. 12): "I assume that the basic structure is that of a closed society: that is, we are to regard it as self-contained and as having no relations with other societies. . . . That a society is closed is a considerable abstraction, justified only because it enables us to focus on certain main questions free from distracting details."

13. See Smith (1759/1790, III, 1, 2). Smith (1976, p. 110). I have tried to discuss and extend the Smithian perspective on moral reasoning in Sen (2002b).

14. Quoted in Lukes (1997, p. 238).

15. On this see Nussbaum and Sen (1988).

16. Smith (1978/1982, p. 104).

REFERENCES

Arneson, R. (1989) 'Equality and equal opportunity for welfare,' *Philosophical Studies*, 56, pp. 77–93.

Beitz, C. (1986) 'Amartya Sen's resources, values and development,' *Economics and Philosophy*, 2, pp. 282–90.

Bentham, J. (1792) *Anarchical Fallacies; Being an Examination of the Declaration of Rights Issued during the French Revolution* [Republished in J. Bowring (Ed.) (1843) *The Works of Jeremy Bentham*, volume II, William Talt, Edinburgh].

Cohen, G.A. (1989) 'On the currency of egalitarian Justice,' *Ethics*, 99, pp. 906–44.

Cohen, G.A. (1993) 'Equality of what? On welfare, resources and capabilities,' in M. Nussbaum and A. Sen (Eds.), *The Quality of Life*, Clarendon Press, Oxford.

Cohen, G.A. (1995) 'Review: Amartya Sen's unequal world,' *The New Left Review*, January, pp. 117–29.

Cohen, J. (1994) 'Review of Sen's *Inequality Reexamined*,' *Journal of Philosophy*, 92, pp. 275–88.

Drèze, J. and Sen, A. (1989) *Hunger and Public Action*, Clarendon Press, Oxford.

Drèze, J. and Sen, A. (2002) *India: Participation and Development*, Oxford University Press, Delhi.

Hawthorn, G. (Ed.) (1987) *Amartya Sen et al., The Standard of Living*, Cambridge University Press, Cambridge.

Himmelfarb, G. (1996) 'The illusions of cosmopolitanism,' in M. Nussbaum with respondents (Ed.), *For Love of Country*, Beacon Press, Boston.

Huntington, S. (1996) *The Clash of Civilizations and the Remaking of World Order*, Simon and Schuster, New York.

Lukes, S. (1997) 'Five fabies about human rights,' in M. Ishay (Ed.), *The Human Rights Reader*, Routledge, London.

Mandela, N. (1994) *Long Walk to Freedom*, Little, Brown & Co., Boston.

Marx, K. (1845–1846) *The German Ideology*, with F. Engels [Republished in D. McLellan (Ed.) (1977) *Karl Marx: Selected Writings*, Oxford University Press, Oxford].

Nussbaum, M. (2000) *Women and Human Development: The Capabilities Approach*, Cambridge University Press, Cambridge.

Nussbaum, M. and Sen, A. (1988) 'Internal criticism and Indian rationalist traditions,' in M. Krausz (Ed.), *Relativism: Interpretation and Confrontation*, University of Notre Dame Press, Notre Dame.

Nussbaum, M. and Sen, A. (Eds.) (1993) *The Quality of Life*, Clarendon Press, Oxford.

Okin, S. (2003) 'Poverty, Well-being and gender: what counts, who's heard?,' *Philosophy and Public Affairs*, 31, pp. 280–316.

Rawls, J. (1971) *A Theory of Justice*, Harvard University Press, Cambridge, MA.

Rawls, J. (1993) *Political Liberalism*, Columbia University Press, New York.

Rawls, J. (1999) *The Law of Peoples*, Harvard University Press, Cambridge, MA.

Roemer, J.E. (1996) *Theories of Distributive Justice*, Harvard University Press, Cambridge, MA.

Sen, A. (1970) *Collective Choice and Social Welfare*, Holden-Day, San Francisco [Republished by North-Holland, Amsterdam].

Sen, A. (1980) 'Equality of what?,' in S. McMurrin (Ed.), *Tanner Lectures on Human Values*, volume I, Cambridge University Press, Cambridge: University of Utah Press, Cambridge.

Sen, A. (1985a) *Commodities and Capabilities*, North-Holland, Amsterdam.

Sen, A. (1985b) 'Well-being, agency and freedom: the Dewey Lectures 1984,' *Journal of Philosophy*, 82, pp. 169–221.

Sen, A. (1985/1987) *The Standard of Living*, Tanner Lectures, Cambridge University Press, Cambridge.

Sen, A. (1990) 'Justice: means versus freedoms,' *Philosophy and Public Affairs*, 19, pp. 111–21.

Sen, A. (1999) *Development as Freedom*, Knopf, New York: Oxford University Press, New York.

Sen, A. (2002a) *Rationality and Freedom*, Harvard University Press, Cambridge, MA.

Sen, A. (2002b) 'Open and closed impartiality,' *The Journal of Philosophy*, 99, pp. 445–69.

Sen, A. (2004) 'Elements of a theory of human rights,' *Philosophy and Public Affairs*, 32(4), pp. 315–56.

Smith, A. (1759/1790/1976) *The Theory of Moral Sentiments*, revised edition 1790 [Republished by Clarendon Press, Oxford].

Smith, A. (1776/1979) *An Inquiry into the Nature and Causes of the Wealth of Nations*, Clarendon Press, Oxford [Reprinted by Liberty Press, 1981].

Smith, A. (1978/1982) in R. L. Meek, D. D. Raphael and P. G. Stein (Eds.), *Lectures on Jurisprudence*, Clarendon Press, Oxford [Reprinted by Liberty Press, Indianapolis].

United Nations Development Programme (1990) *Human Development Report 1990*, Oxford University Press, Oxford.

United Nations Development Programme (2004) *Human Development Report 2004*, Oxford University Press, Oxford.

Williams, B. (1987) 'The standard of living: interests and capabilities,' in G. Hawthorn (Ed.), *Amartya Sen et al., The Standard of Living*, Cambridge University Press, Cambridge.

Jack Donnelly

HUMAN RIGHTS AND CULTURAL RELATIVISM

Cultural relativity is an undeniable fact; moral rules and social institutions evidence astonishing cultural and historical variability. The doctrine of cultural relativism holds that some such variations cannot be legitimately criticized by outsiders. I argue, instead, for a fundamentally universalistic approach to internationally recognized human rights.

In most recent discussions of cultures or civilizations[1]—whether they are seen as clashing, converging, or conversing—the emphasis has been on differences, especially differences between the West and the rest. From a broad cross-cultural or intercivilizational perspective, however, the most striking fact about human rights in the contemporary world is the extensive overlapping consensus on the Universal Declaration of Human Rights. * * * Real conflicts do indeed exist over a few internationally recognized human rights. There are numerous variations in interpretations and modes of implementing internationally recognized human rights. Nonetheless, I argue that culture[2] poses only a modest challenge to the contemporary normative universality of human rights.

1. Defining Cultural Relativism

When internal and external judgments of a practice diverge, cultural relativists give priority to the internal judgments of a society. In its most extreme form, what we can call *radical cultural relativism* holds that culture is the sole source of the validity of a moral right or rule.[3] *Radical universalism*, by contrast, would hold that culture is irrelevant to the (universal) validity, of moral rights and rules. The body of the continuum defined by these end points can be roughly divided into what we can call strong and weak cultural relativism.

Strong cultural relativism holds that culture is the principal source of the validity of a right or rule. At its furthest extreme, strong cultural relativism accepts a few basic rights with virtually universal application but allows such a wide range of variation that two entirely justifiable sets of rights might overlap only slightly.

Weak cultural relativism, which might also be called strong universalism, considers culture a secondary source of the validity of a right or rule. Universality is initially presumed, but the relativity of human nature, communities, and rules checks potential excesses of universalism. At its furthest extreme, weak cultural relativism recognizes a comprehensive set of prima facie universal human rights but allows limited local variations.

We can also distinguish a qualitative dimension to relativist claims. Legitimate cultural divergences from international human rights norms might be advocated concerning the *substance* of lists of human rights, the *interpretation* of particular rights, and the *form* in which those rights are implemented. * * * I will defend a weak cultural relativist (strong universalist) position that permits deviations from international human

From *Universal Human Rights in Theory and Practice* (Ithaca: Cornell University Press, 2003), Chap. 6, 89–106.

rights norms primarily at the level of form or implementation.

2. Relativity and Universality: A Necessary Tension

Beyond the obvious dangers of moral imperialism, radical universalism requires a rigid hierarchical ordering of the multiple moral communities to which we belong. The radical universalist would give absolute priority to the demands of the cosmopolitan moral community over other ("lower") communities. Such a complete denial of national and subnational ethical autonomy, however, is rare and implausible. There is no compelling moral reason why peoples cannot accept, say, the nation-state, as a major locus of extrafamilial moral and political commitments. And at least certain choices of a variety of moral communities demand respect from outsiders—not uncritical acceptance, let alone emulation, but, in some cases at least, tolerance.

But if human rights are based in human nature, on the fact that one is a human being, how can human rights be relative in any fundamental way? The simple answer is that human nature is itself relative. * * * There is a sense in which this is true even biologically. For example, if marriage partners are chosen on the basis of cultural preferences for certain physical attributes, the gene pool in a community may be altered. More important, culture can significantly influence the presence and expression of many aspects of human nature by encouraging or discouraging the development or perpetuation of certain personality traits and types. Whether we stress the "unalterable" core or the variability around it—and however we judge their relative size and importance—"human nature," the realized nature of real human beings, is as much a social project as a natural given.

But if human nature were infinitely variable, or if all moral values were determined solely by culture (as radical cultural relativism holds), there could be no human rights (rights that one has "simply as a human being") because the concept "human being" would have no specificity or moral significance. As we saw in the case of Hindu India, * * * some societies have not even recognized "human being" as a descriptive category. The very names of many cultures mean simply "the people" (e.g., Hopi, Arapahoe), and their origin myths define them as separate from outsiders, who are somehow "not-human."

Such views, however, are almost universally rejected in the contemporary world. For example, chattel slavery and caste-based legal and political systems, which implicitly deny the existence of a morally significant common humanity, are almost universally condemned, even in the most rigid class societies.

The radical relativist response that consensus is morally irrelevant is logically impeccable. But many people do believe that such consensus strengthens a rule, and most think that it increases the justifiability of certain sorts of international action. In effect, a moral analogue to customary international law seems to operate. If a practice is nearly universal and generally perceived as obligatory, it is required of all members of the community. Even a weak cosmopolitan moral community imposes substantive limitations on the range of permissible moral variation.

Notice, however, that I contend only that there are a few cross-culturally valid moral *values*. This still leaves open, the possibility of a radical cultural relativist denial of human *rights*. Plausible arguments can be (and have been) advanced to justify alternative mechanisms to guarantee human dignity. But few states today attempt such an argument. In all regions of the world, a strong commitment to human *rights* is almost universally proclaimed. Even where practice throws that commitment into question, such a widespread rhetorical "fashion" must have some substantive basis.

That basis * * * lies in the hazards to human dignity posed by modern markets and states. The political power of traditional rulers usually was substantially limited by customs and laws that were entirely independent of human rights. The relative technological and administrative weakness of traditional political institutions further restrained abuses of power. In such a world, inalienable entitlements of individuals held against state and society might plausibly be held to be superfluous (because dignity was guaranteed by alternative mechanisms), if not positively dangerous to important and well-established values and practices.

Such a world, however, exists today only in a relatively small number of isolated areas. The modern state, even in the Third World, not only has been freed from many of the moral constraints of custom but also has a far greater administrative and technological reach. It thus represents a serious threat to basic human dignity, whether that dignity is defined in "traditional" or "modern" terms. In such circumstances, human rights seem necessary rather than optional. Radical or unrestricted relativism thus is as inappropriate as radical universalism.[4] Some kind of intermediate position is required.

3. Internal Versus External Judgments

Respect for autonomous moral communities would seem to demand a certain deference to a society's internal evaluations of its practices, but to commit ourselves to acting on the basis of the moral judgments of others would abrogate our own moral responsibilities. The choice between internal and external evaluations is a moral one, and whatever choice we make will be problematic.

Where internal and external judgments conflict, assessing the relative importance attached to those judgments may be a reasonable place to start in seeking to resolve them. Figure 10.1 offers a simple typology.

Case 1—morally unimportant both externally and internally—is uninteresting. Whether or not one maintains one's initial external condemnation is of little intrinsic interest to anyone. Case 2—externally unimportant, internally very important—is probably best handled by refusing to press the negative external judgment. To press a negative external judgment that one feels is relatively unimportant when the issue is of great importance internally usually will be, at best insensitive. By the same token, Case 3—externally very important, internally unimportant—presents the best occasion to press an external judgment (with some tact).

Case 4, in which the practice is of great moral importance to both sides, is the most difficult to handle, but even here we may have good reasons to press a negative external judgment. Consider, for example, slavery. Most people today would agree that no matter how ancient and well established the practice may be, to turn one's back on the enslavement of human beings in the name of cultural relativity would reflect moral obtuseness, not sensitivity. Human sacrifice, trial by ordeal, extrajudicial execution, and female infanticide are other cultural practices that are (in my view rightly) condemned by almost all external observers today.

Underlying such judgments is the inherent universality of basic moral precepts, at least as we understand morality in the West. We simply do not believe that our moral precepts are for us and us alone. This is most evident in Kant's deontological universalism. But it is no less true of the principle of utility. And, of course, human rights are also inherently universal.

Figure 10.1. Type Conflicts over Culturally Relative Practices

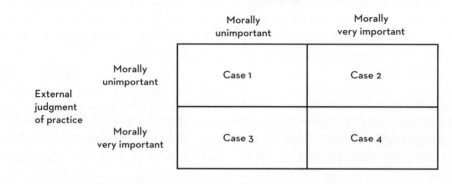

In any case, our moral precepts are *our* moral precepts. As such, they demand our obedience. To abandon them simply because others reject them is to fail to give proper weight to our own moral beliefs (at least where they involve central moral precepts such as the equality of all human beings and the protection of innocents).

Finally, no matter how firmly someone else, or even a whole culture, believes differently, at some point—slavery and untouchability come to mind—we simply must say that those contrary beliefs are wrong. Negative external judgments may be problematic. In some cases, however, they are not merely permissible but demanded.

4. Concepts, Interpretations, Implementations

In evaluating arguments of cultural relativism, we must distinguish between variations in substance, interpretation, and form. Even very weak cultural relativists—that is, strong universalists—are likely

to allow considerable variation in the form in which rights are implemented. For example, whether free legal assistance is required by the right to equal protection of the laws usually will best be viewed as largely beyond the legitimate reach of universal standards. Important differences between strong and weak relativists are likely to arise, however, at the levels of interpretation and, especially, substance.

A. Substance or Concept

The Universal Declaration generally formulates rights at the level of what I will call the *concept,* an abstract, general statement of an orienting value. "Everyone has the right to work, to free choice of employment, to just and favorable conditions of work and to protection against unemployment" (Art. 23). *Only* at this level do I claim that there is a consensus on the rights of the Universal Declaration, and at this level, most appeals to cultural relativism fail.

It is difficult to imagine arguments against recognizing the rights of Articles 3–12, which include life, liberty, and security of the person; the guarantee of legal personality, equality before the law, and privacy, and protections against slavery, arbitrary arrest, detention, or exile, and inhuman or degrading treatment. These are so clearly connected to basic requirements of human dignity, and are stated in sufficiently general terms, that virtually every morally defensible contemporary form of social organization must recognize them (although perhaps not necessarily as inalienable rights). I am even tempted to say that conceptions of human nature or society that are incompatible with such rights are almost by definition indefensible in contemporary international society.

Civil rights such as freedom of conscience, speech, and association may be a bit more relative. Because they assume the existence and positive evaluation of relatively autonomous individuals, they may be of questionable applicability in strong, thriving traditional communities. In such communities, however, they would rarely be at issue. If traditional practices truly are based on and protect culturally accepted conceptions of human dignity, then members of such a community will not have the desire or the need to claim such rights. In the more typical contemporary case, however, in which relatively autonomous individuals face modern states, it is hard for me to imagine a defensible conception of human dignity that does not include almost all of these rights. A similar argument can be made for the economic and social rights of the Universal Declaration.

In twenty years of working with issues of cultural relativism, I have developed a simple test that I pose to skeptical audiences. Which rights in the Universal Declaration, I ask, does your society or culture reject? Rarely has a single full right (other than the right to private property) been rejected. Never has it been suggested to me that as many as four should be eliminated.

Typical was the experience I had in Iran in early 2001, where I posed this question to three different audiences. In each case, discussion moved quickly to freedom of religion, and in particular atheism and apostasy by Muslims (which the Universal Declaration permits but Iran prohibits).[5] Given the continuing repression of Iranian Bahais—although, for the moment at least, the apparent end to executions—this was quite a sensitive issue. Even here, though, the challenge was not to the principle, or even the right, of freedom of religion (which almost all Muslims support) but to competing "Western" and "Muslim" conceptions of its limits. And we must remember that *every* society places some limits on religious liberty. In the United States, for example, recent court cases have dealt with forced medical treatment for the children of Christian Scientists, live animal sacrifice by practitioners of santaria, and the rights of Jehovah's Witnesses to evangelize at private residences.

We must be careful, however, not to read too much into this consensus at the level of the concept, which may obscure important disagreements concerning definitions and implicit limitations. Consider Article 5 of the Universal Declaration: "No one shall be subjected to torture or to cruel, inhuman or degrading treatment or punishment." The real controversy comes over definitions of terms such as "cruel." Is the death penalty cruel, inhuman, or degrading? Most European states consider it to be. The United States does not. We must recognize and address such differences without overstating their importance or misrepresenting their character.

Implicit limits on rights may also pose challenges to universalist arguments. Most of the rights in the Universal Declaration are formulated in categorical terms. For example, Article 19 begins: "Everyone has the right to freedom of opinion and expression." To use the hackneyed American example, this does not mean that one can scream "Fire!" in a crowded theater. All rights have limits.[6] But if these limits differ widely and systematically across civilizations, the resulting differences in human rights practices might indeed be considerable.

Are there systematic differences in definitions of terms across civilizations? Do cultures differ systematically in the standard limits they put on the exercises of rights? And if these differences are systematic, how significant are they? I have suggested that the answers to these questions are largely negative. For reasons of space—as well as the fact that such negative arguments cannot be conclusively established—I leave this claim as a challenge. Critics may refute my argument with several well-chosen examples of substantial cultural variation either at the level of concepts or in systematic variations at the level of interpretation that undermine the apparent conceptual consensus. So far, at least, I have not encountered anyone capable of presenting such, a pattern of contradictory evidence, except in the case of small and relatively isolated communities.[7]

B. Interpretations

What ought to count, for example, as adequate protection against unemployment? Does it mean a guaranteed job, or is it enough to provide compensation to those who are unemployed? Both seem to me plausible interpretations. Some such variations in interpreting rights seem not merely defensible but desirable, and even necessary.

Particular human rights are like "essentially contested concepts," in which there is a substantial but rather general consensus on basic meaning coupled with no less important, systematic, and apparently irresolvable conflicts of interpretations (Gallie 1968). In such circumstances, culture provides one plausible and defensible mechanism for selecting interpretations (and forms).

We should also note that the Universal Declaration lists some rights that are best viewed as interpretations. For example, the right of free and full consent of intending spouses reflects an interpretation of marriage over which legitimate controversy is possible. Notice, however, that the right (as stated in Sec. 2 of Art. 16) is subordinate to the right to marry and to found a family (over which, at this highest level of generality, there is little international dispute). Furthermore, some traditional customs, such as bride price, provide alternative protections for women that address at least some of the underlying concerns that gave rise to the norm of free and full consent.

I would suggest, however, that defensible variations in interpretations are likely to be relatively modest in number. And not all "interpretations" are equally plausible or defensible. They are *interpretations* not free associations or arbitrary, let alone self-interested, stipulations. The meaning of, for example, "the right to political participation" is controversial, but an election in which a people were allowed to choose an absolute dictator for life ("one man, one vote, once," as a West African quip put it) is simply indefensible.

We must also note that considerable divergences in interpretation exist not only between but also *within* cultures or civilizations. Consider, for example, differences within the West between Europe and the United States on the death penalty and the welfare state. Japan and Vietnam have rather different interpretations of the rights to freedom of speech and association, despite being East Asians.

Even where there are variations between two cultures, we still need to ask whether culture in fact is the source of cause of these differences. I doubt that we are actually saying much of interest or importance when we talk of, say, Japan as Asian. Consider the common claim that Asian societies are communitarian and consensual and Western societies are individualistic and competitive. What exactly is this supposed to explain, or even refer to, in any particular Asian or Western country? Dutch or Norwegian politics is at least as consensual as Thai politics. The Dutch welfare state is in its own way as caring and paternalistic as the most traditional of Japanese employers. Such examples, which are easily multiplied, suggest that even where variations in practice exist, culture does much less explanatory work than most relativists suggest—or at least that the "culture" in question is more local or national rather than regional or a matter of civilization.

C. Implementation or Form

Just as concepts need to be interpreted, interpretations need to be implemented in law and political practice. To continue with the example of the right to work, what rate of unemployment compensation should be provided, for how long, in what circumstances? The range of actual and defensible variation here is considerable—although limited by the governing concept and interpretation.

Even a number of rights in the International Human Rights Covenants involve specifications at the level of form. For example, Article 10(2)(b) of the International Covenant on Civil and Political Rights requires the segregation of juvenile defendants. In some cultures the very notion of a juvenile criminal defendant (or a penitentiary system) does not exist Although there are good reasons to suggest such rules, to demand them in the face of strong reasoned opposition seems to me to make little sense—so long as the underlying objectives are realized in some other fashion.

Differences in implementations, however, often seem to have little to do with culture. And even where they do, it is not obvious that cultural differences deserve more (or less) respect than differing implementations attributable to other causes (e.g., levels of economic development or unique national historical experiences).

I stress this three-level scheme to avoid a common misconception. My argument is for universality only at the level of the concept. The Universal Declaration insists that all states share a limited but important range of obligations. It is, in its own

words, "a common standard of achievement for all peoples and all nations." The ways in which these rights are implemented, however, so long as they fall within the range of variation consistent with the overarching concept, are matters of legitimate variation. * * *

This is particularly important because most of the "hot button" issues in recent discussions have occurred at the level of implementation. For example, debates about pornography are about the limits—interpretation or implementation—of freedom of expression. Most Western countries permit the graphic depiction of virtually any sex act (so long as it does not involve and is not shown to children). Many others countries punish those who produce, distribute, or consume such material. This dispute, however, does not suggest a rejection of human rights, the idea of personal autonomy, or even the right to freedom of speech.

We should also note that controversy over pornography rages internally in many countries. Every country criminalizes some forms of pornography, and most countries—Taliban Afghanistan being the exception that proves the rule—permit some depictions of sexual behavior or the display of erotic images that another country has within living memory banned as pornographic. Wherever one draws the line, it leaves intact both the basic internationally recognized human right to freedom of speech and the underlying value of personal autonomy.

D. Universality within Diversity

There are at least three ways in which rights that vary in form and interpretation can still be plausibly described as "universal." First, and most important, there may be an overlapping consensus * * * on the substance of the list, despite diversity in interpretations and implementations. Second, even where there are differences at the level of substance or concept, a large common core may exist with relatively few differences "around the edges." Third, even where substantial substantive disagreements occur, we might still be justified in speaking of universal rights if there are strong statistical regularities and the outliers are few and clearly overshadowed by the central tendency.

In contemporary international society, I think that we can say that there are few far outliers (e.g., North Korea) at least at the level of agreed-on concepts. I would admit that overlapping conceptual consensus often is thin. Nonetheless, I think that we can fairly (although not without controversy) say that variations at the level of concepts are infrequent. Somewhat more contentious is the claim that I would also advance that the range of diversity in standard interpretations is modest and poses relatively few serious international political disputes.

We do not face an either-or choice between cultural relativism and universal human rights. Rather, we need to recognize both the universality of human rights and their particularity and thus accept a certain *limited* relativity, especially with respect to forms of implementation. We must take seriously the initially paradoxical idea of the relative universality of internationally recognized human rights.[8]

5. Explaining the Persistence of Culturalist Arguments

If my argument for relative universality is even close to correct, how can we explain the persistence of foundational appeals to culture? If we could explain this puzzle, both for the relativist arguments * * * and for the claims about human rights in traditional societies, * * * the plausibility of a universalist perspective would be enhanced. At least six explanations come to mind.

First, it is surprisingly common for even otherwise sophisticated individuals to take the particular institutions associated with the realization of a right in their country or culture to be essential to that right. Americans, in particular, seem to have unusually great difficulty in realizing that the way we do things here is not necessarily what international human rights norms require.

Second, narrow-minded and ham-handed (Western, and especially American) international human rights policies and statements exacerbate these confusions. Consider Michael Fay, an American teenager who vandalized hundreds of thousands of dollars worth of property in Singapore. When he was sentenced to be publicly caned, there was a furor in the United States. President Clinton argued, with apparently genuine indignation, that it was abominable to cane someone, but he failed to find it even notable that in his own country people are being fried in the electric chair. If this indeed is what universalism means—and I hasten to repeat that it is not—then of course relativism looks far more attractive.

The legacy of colonialism provides a third important explanation for the popularity of relativist arguments. African, Asian, and Muslim (as well as Latin American) leaders and citizens have vivid, sometimes personal, recollections of their sufferings under colonial masters. Even when the statements and actions of great powers stay within the range of the overlapping consensus on the Universal Declaration, there is understandable (although not necessarily justifiable) sensitivity to external pressure. (Compare the sensitivity of the United States to external criticism even in the absence of such a historical legacy.) When international pressures exceed the bounds of the overlapping consensus, that sensitivity often becomes (justifiably) very intense.

Fourth, arguments of relativism are often rooted in a desire to express and foster national, regional, cultural, or civilizational pride. It is no coincidence that the "Asian values" debate * * * took off in the wake of the Asian economic miracle and dramatically subsided after the 1977 financial crisis.

The belief that such arguments have instrumental efficacy in promoting internationally recognized human rights is a fifth important reason. For example, Daniel Bell plausibly argues that building human rights implementation strategies on local traditions (1) is "more likely to lead to long term commitment to human rights"; (2) "may shed light on the groups most likely to bring about desirable social and political change"; (3) "allows the human rights activist to draw on the most compelling justifications"; (4) "may shed light on the appropriate attitude to be employed by human rights activists"; and (5) "may also make one more sensitive to the possibility of alternative" mechanisms for protecting rights (1996: 657–59). I would insist only that we be clear that this is a practical, not a theoretical, argument; that we operate with a plausible theory of culture and an accurate understanding of the culture in question; and that we not assume that culture trumps international norms. "To realize greater social justice on an international scale, activists and intellectuals must take culture seriously, but not in the totalizing, undifferentiated way in which some leaders of non-Western nations have used it as a trump card" (L. Bell 2001: 21).

This leads to the sixth, and perhaps the most important, explanation for the prevalence of culturalist arguments, namely, that they are used by vicious elites as a way to attempt to deflect attention from their repressive policies. And well-meaning Westerners with a well-developed sense of the legacy of Western colonialism indirectly support such arguments when they shy away from criticizing arguments advanced by non-Westerners even when they are empirically inaccurate or morally absurd.

6. Culture and Politics

So far I have proceeded, in line with the standard assumption of cultural relativists, by treating "cultures" as homogenous, static, all-encompassing, and voluntarily accepted "things," the substance of which can be relatively easily and uncontroversially determined. None of these assumptions is defensible.

A. Identifying a "Culture"

Cultures are anything but homogenous. In fact, differences *within* civilizations often are as striking and as important as those between civilizations. "The Western tradition," for example, includes both Caligula and Marcus Aurelius, Francis of Assisi and Torquemada, Leopold II of Belgium and Albert Schweitzer, Jesus and Hitler—and just about everything in between.

We thus face a difficult problem even in determining what is to count as evidence for a claim of the form "civilization *x* holds belief *y*." Political authorities are but one (very problematic) source of evidence of the views and practices of a civilization. Nor can we rely on authoritative texts. For example, the Christian Bible has significantly shaped Western civilization. But even when particular practices do not diverge from what one might expect from reading this "foundational" text and setting aside the fact that such expectations change with time, place, and reader—few Western practices are adequately explained in terms of, let alone reducible to, those texts.[9]

Even the long-established practice of leading states may diverge significantly from the norms and values of the civilization of which they are a part. The United States, for example, is in many ways a very *atypical* Western country in its approach to economic and social rights. In characterizing and comparing civilizations, we must not mistake some particular expressions, however characteristic, for the whole. For example, Christianity and secularism are arguably equally important to modern Western civilization. And the balance between secular and religious forces, values, and orientations varies dramatically with time, place, and issue in "the West."

Such cautions are especially important because culturalist arguments regularly rely on appeals to a distant past, such as the precolonial African village, Native American tribes, and traditional Islamic societies. The traditional culture advanced to justify cultural relativism far too often no longer exists—if it ever did in the idealized form in which it is typically presented. In the Third World today we usually see not the persistence of "traditional" culture in the face of "modern" intrusions, or even the development of syncretic cultures and values, but rather disruptive "Westernization," rapid cultural change, or people enthusiastically embracing "modern" practices and values.[10] And the modern nation-states and contemporary nationalist regimes that have replaced traditional communities and practices cannot be judged by standards of a bygone era.

We must also be careful to distinguish "civilization" or "culture" from religion and politics. The United States is a state, a political entity, not a civilization. Islam is not a civilization but a religion, or, as many believers would put it, a true and comprehensive way of life that transcends culture or civilization. An "Islamic civilization"—centered on Mecca and running, say, from the Maghreb to the Indus—does not include all Muslims, or even all majority Muslim countries. The broader Muslim world, running from Dakar to Jakarta, may be an international political unit of growing interest or importance, but it certainly is not a culture or civilization. And tens of millions of Muslims live outside of even this community.

B. The Politics of Cultural Relativism

Cultures are not merely diverse but are contested. In fact, contemporary anthropologists increasingly depict "cultures" not as "things" but as sites of contestation. "Rather than simply a domain of sharing and commonality, culture figures here more as a site of difference and contestation, simultaneously ground and stake of a rich field of cultural-political practices" (Gupta and Ferguson 1997: 5).

> Culture is usually viewed by the new cultural theorists as contested—a social context in which power struggles are constantly waged over the meaning and control of what Pierre Bourdieu has called "symbolic capital" as well as over more overtly material forms of wealth and power. In short, culture is not a given, but rather a congeries of ways of thinking, believing, and acting that are constantly in the state of being produced; it is contingent and always unstable, especially as the forces of "modernity" have barreled down upon most people throughout the world over the course of the twentieth century. (Bell, Nathan, and Peleg 2001: 11)

All forms of cultural relativism fundamentally fail to recognize culture as an ongoing historic and institutional process where the existence of a given custom does not mean that the custom is either adaptive, optimal, or consented to by a majority of its adherents. Culture is far more effectively characterized as an ongoing adaptation to a changing environment rather than as a static superorganic entity. In a changing environment, cultural practices routinely outlive their usefulness, and cultural values change either through internal dialogue within the cultural group or through cross-cultural influences. (Zechenter 1997: 332–33)

"Culture" is constructed through selective appropriations from a diverse and contested past and present. Those appropriations are rarely neutral in process, intent, or consequences. Cultural relativist arguments thus regularly obscure often troubling realities of power and politics.

Arguments of cultural relativism are far too often made by (or on behalf of) economic and political elites that have long since left traditional culture behind. Even when this represents an admirable effort to retain or recapture cherished traditional values, it is at least ironic to see "Westernized" elites warning against the values and practices they have adopted. There is also more than a hint of a troubling, even tragic, paternalism. For example, "villagization" in Tanzania, which was supposed to reflect traditional African conceptions, was accomplished only by force, against the strong opposition of much of the population.

Even such troubling sincerity is unfortunately rare. Government officials denounce the corrosive individualism of Western values—while they line their pockets with the proceeds of massive corruption, drive imported luxury automobiles, and plan European or American vacations. Leaders sing the praises of traditional communities—while they wield arbitrary power antithetical to traditional values, pursue development policies that systematically undermine traditional communities, and replace traditional leaders with corrupt cronies and party hacks. Rigged elections, military dictatorships, and malnutrition caused by government incentives to produce cash crops rather than food are just a few of the widespread abuses of internationally recognized human rights that do not express, but rather infringe, indigenous cultural values.

In traditional cultures—at least the kinds of traditional cultures that might justify deviations from international human rights standards—people are not victims of the arbitrary decisions of rulers whose principal claim to power is their control of modern instruments of force and administration. Traditional customs and practices usually provide each person with a place in society and a certain amount of dignity and protection. Furthermore, rulers and ruled (and rich and poor) usually are linked by reciprocal bonds. The human rights violations of most Third World regimes are as antithetical to such cultural traditions as they are to "Western" human rights conceptions.

Relativist arguments became particularly perverse when they support a small elite that has arrogated to itself the "right" to speak for "its" culture or civilization, and then imposes its own self-interested views and practices on the broader society—invoking cultural relativism abroad while ruthlessly trampling on local customs. Consider, for example, Suharto and his cronies in Indonesia, who sought to cloak their version of modern state-based repression and crony capitalism in the aura of traditional culture. In Zaire, President Mobutu created the practice of *salongo*, a form of communal labor with a supposedly traditional basis, which was in fact essentially a revival of the colonial, practice of corvee labor (Callaghy 1980: 490). Macias Nguema of Equatorial Guinea, perhaps the most vicious ruler independent black Africa has seen, called himself "Grand Master of Popular Education, Science, and Traditional Culture," a title that might be comical were the situation not so tragic.

7. Dialogue over Real Differences

The above discussion is intentionally one-sided. I have drawn attention to commonalities and minimized (real) differences. But even if I am correct about the extent of those differences, we must not confuse overlapping consensus with homogeneity.

Furthermore, the fact that differences are *relatively* minor, in the context of the full body of internationally recognized human rights, does not mean that they are unimportant, especially at the level of day-to-day polities. Question about such issues as capital and corporal punishment, the limits of religious liberty, and the dimensions of gender equality merit intensive discussions both within and between states and civilizations.

Should traditional notions of "family values" and gender roles be emphasized in the interest of children and society, or should families be conceived in more individualistic and egalitarian terms? What is the proper balance between rewarding individual economic initiative and redistributive taxation in the interest of social harmony and support for disadvantaged individuals and groups? At what point should the words or behaviors of deviant or dissident individuals be forced to give way the interests or desires of society?

Questions such as these, which in my terminology involve conflicting interpretations, involve vital issues of political controversy in virtually all societies. In discussing them we must often walk the difficult line between respect for the other and respect for one's own values. * * * Here I want to consider a relatively easy case—slavery—in an unconventional way.

Suppose that in contemporary Saudi Arabia a group were to emerge arguing that because slavery was accepted in the early Muslim world it should be reinstituted in contemporary Saudi Arabia. I am certain that almost all Saudis, from the most learned clerics to the most ordinary citizens, would reject this view. But how should these individuals be dealt with?

Dialogue seems to me the appropriate route, so long as they do not attempt to *practice* slavery. Those in the majority who would remonstrate these individuals for their despicable views have, I think, an obligation to use precisely such forceful moral terms. Nonetheless, freedom of belief and speech requires the majority to tolerate these views, in the minimal sense of not imposing legal liabilities on those who hold or express

them. Should they attempt to practice slavery, however, the force of the law is appropriately applied to suppress and punish this practice. Condemnation by outsiders also seems appropriate, although so long as the problem is restricted to expressions of beliefs only in Saudi Arabia there probably will be few occasions for such condemnations.

But suppose that the unthinkable were to occur and the practice of slavery were reintroduced in Saudi Arabia—not, let us imagine, as a matter of law, but rather through the state refusing to prosecute slave-holders. Here we run up against the state system and the fact that international human rights law gives states near total discretion to implement internationally recognized human rights within their own territories.

One might argue that slavery is legally prohibited as a matter of *jus cogens*, general principles of law, and customary (as well as treaty) law. But coercive international enforcement is extraordinarily contentious and without much legal precedent. Outsiders, however, remain bound by their own moral principles (as well as by international human rights norms) to condemn such practices in the strongest possible terms. And foreign states would be entirely justified in putting whatever pressure, short of force, they could mobilize on Saudi Arabia to halt the practice.

This hypothetical example illustrates the fact that *some* cultural practices, rather than deserve our respect, demand our condemnation. It also indicates, though, that some beliefs, however despicable, demand our toleration—because freedom of opinion and belief is an internationally recognized human right. So long as one stays within the limits of internationally recognized human rights, one is entitled to at least a limited and grudging toleration and the personal space that comes with that. But such individuals are *owed* nothing more.

Many cases, however, are not so easy. This is especially true where cultures are undergoing substantial or unusually rapid transformation. In much of the Third World we regularly face the problem of "modern" individuals or groups who reject traditional practices. Should we give priority to the idea of community self-determination and permit the enforcement of customary practices against modern "deviants" even if this violates "universal" human rights? Or should individual self-determination prevail, thus sanctioning claims of universal human rights against traditional society?

In discussing women's rights in Africa, Rhoda Howard suggests an attractive and widely applicable compromise strategy (1984: 66–68). On a combination of practical and moral grounds, she argues against an outright ban on such practices as child betrothal and widow inheritance, but she also argues strongly for national legislation that permits women (and the families of female children) to "opt out" of traditional practices. This would permit individuals and families to, in effect, choose the terms on which they participate in the cultures that are of value to their lives. Unless we think of culture as an oppressive external force, this seems entirely appropriate.

Conflicting practices, however, may sometimes be irreconcilable. For example, a right to private ownership of the means of production is incompatible with the maintenance of a village society in which families hold only rights of use to communally owned land. Allowing individuals to opt out and fully own their land would destroy the traditional system. Even such conflicts, however, may sometimes be resolved, or at least minimized, by the physical or legal separation of adherents of old and new values, particularly with practices that are not material to the maintenance or integrity of either culture.

Nevertheless, a choice must sometimes be made, at least by default, between irreconcilable practices. Such cases take us out of the realm in which useful general guidelines are possible. Fortunately, though, they are the exception rather than the rule—although no easier for that fact to deal with when they do arise.

It would be dangerous either to deny differences between civilizations where they do exist or to exaggerate their extent or practical importance. Whatever the situation in other issue areas, in the case of human rights, for all the undeniable differences, it is the similarities across civilizations that are more striking and important Whatever our differences, now or in the past, all contemporary civilizations are linked by the growing recognition of the Universal Declaration as, in its own words, "a common standard of achievement for all peoples and all nations." Or, as I prefer to put it, human rights are relatively universal.

NOTES

1. Civilizations seems to be emerging as the term of choice in UN-based discussions. 2001 was designated the United Nations Year of Dialogue Among Civilizations. For a sampling of UNESCO sources, see http://www.unesco.org/dialogue2001/en/culturer.htm. I use "culture" and "civilization" more or less interchangeably, although I think that a useful convention would be to treat civilizations as larger or broader: for example, French culture but Western civilization.

2. * * * I begin by taking at face value the common understanding of culture as static, unitary, and integral. * * *

3. I am concerned here only with cultural relativist views as they apply to human rights, although my argument probably has applicability to other relativist claims.

4. We can also note that radical relativism is descriptively inaccurate. Few people anywhere believe that their moral beliefs rest on nothing more than tradition. The radical relativist insistence that they do offers an implausible (and unattractive) account of the nature and meaning of morality.

5. Gender equality, perhaps surprisingly, did not come up (although these were elite, English-speaking audiences, and Iran has, self-consciously, made considerable progress on women's rights issues in recent years). But even when it does, dispute usually focuses on the meaning of nondiscrimination or on particular practices, such as equal rights in marriage.

6. Logically, there can be at most one absolute right (unless we implausibly assume that rights never conflict with one another).

7. The general similarity of regional human rights instruments underscores this argument. Even the African Charter of Human and Peoples' Rights, the most heterodox regional treaty, differs largely at the level of interpretation and, in substance or concept, by addition (of peoples' rights) rather than by subtraction.

8. Coming at a similar perspective from the other end of the spectrum, Richard Wilson notes that human rights, and struggles over their implementation, "are embedded in local normative orders and yet are caught within webs of power and meaning which extend beyond the local" (1997: 23). Andrew Nathan has recently described this orientation as "tempered universalism" (2001).

9. To cite one example of misplaced textualism, Roger Ames (1997) manages to devote an entire article to "the conversation on Chinese human rights" that manages to make only a few passing, exceedingly delicate, mentions of events since 1949. China and its culture would seem to have been unaffected by such forces as decades of brutal party dictatorship or the impact of both socialism and capitalism on land tenure and residence patterns. In fact, although he cites a number of passages from Confucius, Ames does not even attempt to show how traditional Confucian ideas express themselves in contemporary Chinese human rights debates.

10. None of this should be surprising when we compare the legal, political, and cultural practices of the contemporary West with those of ancient Athens, medieval Paris, Renaissance Florence, or even Victorian London.

REFERENCES

Ames, Roger. 1997. "Continuing the Conversation on Chinese Human Rights." *Ethics and International Affairs* 11: 177–205.

Bell, Daniel A. 1996. "The East Asian Challenge to Human Rights: Reflections on an East-West Dialogue." *Human Rights Quarterly* 18 (August): 641–67.

Bell, Lynda, Andrew J. Nathan, and Ilan Peleg. 2001. "Introduction: Culture and Human Rights." In *Negotiating Culture and Human Rights*. Edited by Lynda Bell, Andrew J. Nathan, and Ilan Peleg. New York: Columbia University Press.

Bell, Lynda S. 2001. "Who Produces Asian Identity? Discourses, Discrimination, and Chinese Peasant Women in the Quest for Human Rights." In *Negotiating Culture and Human Rights*. Edited by Lynda Bell, Andrew J. Nathan, and Ilan Peleg. New York: Columbia University Press.

Gallie, W. B. 1968. "Essentially Contested Concepts." In *Philosophy and the Historical Understanding*. New York: Schocken Books.

Gupta, Akhil, and James Ferguson. 1997. "Culture, Power, Place: Ethnography at the End of an Era." In *Culture, Power, Place: Explorations in Critical Anthropology*. Edited by Akhil Gupta and James Ferguson. Durham: Duke University Press.

Howard, Rhoda E. 1984. "Women's Rights in English-Speaking Sub-Saharan Africa." In *Human Rights and Development in Africa*. Edited by Claude E. Welch Jr. and Ronald I. Meltzer. Albany: State University of New York Press.

Kant, Immanuel. 1983. *Perpetual Peace and Other Essays*. Translated by Ted Humphrey. Indianapolis: Hackett.

Nathan, Andrew J. 2001. "Universalism: A Particularistic Account." In *Negotiating Culture and Human Rights*. Edited by Lynda Bell, Andrew J. Nathan, and Ilan Peleg. New York: Columbia University Press.

Wilson, Richard. 1997. "Introduction." In *Human Rights, Culture and Context: Anthropological Perspectives*. Edited by Richard Wilson. London: Pluto Press.

Zechenter, Elizabeth M. 1997. "In the Name of Cultural Relativism and the Abuse of the Individual." *Journal of Anthropological Research* 53 (Fall): 319–47.

Beth A. Simmons

FROM *MOBILIZING FOR HUMAN RIGHTS*

Human rights underwent a widespread revolution internationally over the course of the twentieth century. The most striking change is the fact that it is no longer acceptable for a government to make sovereignty claims in defense of egregious rights abuses. The legitimacy of a broad range of rights of individuals vis-à-vis their own government stands in contrast to a long-standing presumption of internal sovereignty: the right of each state to determine its own domestic social, legal, and political arrangements free from outside interference. And yet, the construction of a new approach has taken place largely at governments' own hands. It has taken place partially through the development of international legal institutions to which governments themselves have, often in quite explicit terms, consented.

■   ■   ■

* * * Treaties are the clearest statements available about the content of globally sanctioned decent rights practices. * * * Treaties serve notice that governments are *accountable*—domestically and externally—for refraining from the abuses proscribed by their own mutual agreements. Treaties signal a seriousness of intent that is difficult to replicate in other ways. They reflect politics but they also shape political behavior, setting the

stage for new political alliances, empowering new political actors, and heightening public scrutiny.

When treaties alter politics in these ways, they have the potential to change government behaviors and public policies. It is precisely because of their potential power to constrain that treaty commitments are contentious in domestic and international politics. Were they but scraps of paper, one might expect every universal treaty to be ratified swiftly by every government on earth, which has simply not happened. Rather, human rights treaties are pushed by passionate advocates—domestically and transnationally—and are opposed just as strenuously by those who feel the most threatened by their acceptance. This study deals with both the politics of treaty commitment and the politics of compliance. It is the latter, of course, that has the potential to change the prospects for human dignity around the world.

■   ■   ■

The Argument in Brief

Treaties reflect politics. Their negotiation and ratification reflect the power, organization, and aspirations of the governments that negotiate and sign them, the legislatures that ratify them, and the groups that lobby on their behalf. But treaties also *alter politics,* especially in fluid domestic political settings. Treaties set visible goals for public policy and practice that alter political coalitions and the strength, clarity, and legitimacy of their demands.

From *Mobilizing for Human Rights: International Law in Domestic Politics* (New York: Cambridge University Press, 2009). Some of the author's notes have been omitted.

Human rights treaties matter most where they have domestic political and legal traction. This * * * is largely about the conditions under which such traction is possible.

Why should a government commit itself to an international legal agreement to respect the rights of its own people? The primary reason is that the government anticipates its ability and willingness to comply. Governments participate in negotiations, sign drafts, and expend political capital on ratification in most cases because they support the treaty goals and generally want to implement them. They tend to drag their feet in negotiating treaties they find threatening, potentially costly, or socially alienating. Polities participate most readily and enthusiastically in treaty regimes that reflect values consonant with their own. In this sense, the treaty-making and ratifying processes "screen" the participants themselves, leaving a pool of adherents that *generally* are likely to support their goals. Were this not the case, treaty ratification would be empirically random and theoretically uninteresting—a meaningless gesture to which it would be impossible to attach political, social, or legal significance. If we expect treaties to have effects, we should expect them to be something other than random noise on the international political landscape.[1]

Treaties are not perfect screens, however—far from it. Motives other than anticipated compliance influence some governments to ratify, even if their commitments to the social purposes of the agreement are weak. The single strongest motive for ratification in the absence of a strong value commitment is the preference that nearly all governments have to avoid the social and political pressures of remaining aloof from a multilateral agreement to which most of their peers have already committed themselves. As more countries—especially regional peers—ratify human rights accords, it becomes more difficult to justify nonadherence and to deflect criticism for remaining a nonparty. Figuratively, a treaty's mesh widens as more and more governments pass through the ratification screen.

Treaties are also imperfect screens because countries vary widely in their treaty-relevant national institutions. Legal traditions, ratification procedures, and the degree of decentralization impact the politics of the treaty-acceptance process. Because governments sometimes anticipate that ratification will impose political costs that they are not ready to bear, they sometimes self-screen. Despite general support for the goals of a human rights accord, opposition may form in powerful political subunits (states or provinces) that have traditionally had jurisdiction in a particular area (e.g., the death penalty in the United States). Sympathetic governments may self-screen if the costs of legal incorporation are viewed as too high or too uncertain. They may also self-screen if the ratification hurdle is high relative to the value they place on joining a particular treaty regime. The point is this: Two governments with similar values may appear on opposite sides of the ratification divide because of their domestic institutions rather than their preferences for the content of the treaty itself. Treaties may act as screens, but domestic institutions can do so as well.

The most significant claim [made here] is that, regardless of their acknowledged role in generally separating the committed human rights defenders from the worst offenders, treaties also play a crucial constraining role. As in the case of their screening function, they constrain imperfectly but perceptibly. The political world differs in important ways on either side of the ratification act. The main reason is one that institutionalists have recognized since the publication of Robert Keohane's seminal work: Regimes focus actors' expectations. To be sure, the focus can begin to shift during the treaty negotiations.[2] Expectations can begin to solidify further as more governments express commitment to an emerging standard— the process of legitimation emphasized by scholars of international norms and their spread.[3] But expectations regarding a particular government's behavior change qualitatively when that government publicly expresses its commitment to be legally bound to a specific set of rules. Treaties are perhaps the best instrument available to sovereign states to sharpen the focus on particular accepted and proscribed behaviors. Indeed, they are valued by sovereign states as well as nongovernmental actors for precisely this reason. Treaties constrain governments because they help define the size of the *expectations gap* when governments fail to live up to their provisions. This expectations gap has the power to alter political demands for compliance, primarily from domestic constituencies, but sometimes by the international community as well.

The three domestic mechanisms I explore in the following pages are the ability of a treaty to effect elite-initiated agendas, to support litigation, and to spark political mobilization. I think of these mechanisms as ranging from the most to the least elite of processes. In the simplest case, treaties can change the national agenda simply because they raise questions of ratification and hence implementation. International law raises the question: Do we move to ratify and to implement? In many cases, treaties insert issues into national politics that would not have been there in the absence of international politics. Governing elites can initiate compliance, with practically no public participation, if they value international cooperation on the issue the treaty addresses. Treaties are important in these cases, because the national agenda would have been different in the absence of international negotiations.

International treaties also provide a resource in litigation should the government be less than eager to comply. The availability of this mechanism depends on the nature of the domestic legal system and the quality of the courts. Litigation is a possibility where treaties have the status of law in the domestic legal system (or where they have been implemented through enforceable domestic statutes) and where the courts have a degree of political independence. Even in these cases, litigation cannot force compliance. It can only raise the political costs of government resistance by legitimating through indigenous legal institutions the demand to comply. In countries with a strong rule of law tradition, an adverse court ruling can add weight to the pressures a government will experience to comply.

Finally, a public treaty commitment can be important to popular mobilization to demand compliance. Treaties provide political, legal, and social resources to individuals and groups whose goal is to hold governments to their promises. In these pages, I will argue that explicit legal commitments raise the expected value of social mobilization by providing a crucial tangible resource for nascent groups and by increasing the size of the coalition with stakes in compliance. What is more, this effect is greatest in countries that are neither stable democracies (where most rights are already protected and the motive to mobilize is relatively low) nor stable autocracies (where the likelihood of successful mobilization is low if the rights the treaty addresses are seen in any way as challenging status quo governing arrangements). Key here is the legitimating function of an explicit public commitment to a global standard. That commitment is used strategically by demandeurs to improve the rights in which they have an interest.

The central point is this: The political environment most (though not all) governments face differs on either side of the ratification divide. These changes are subtle, and they are often conditional. They involve changes that give relatively weak political actors important tangible and intangible resources that raise the political costs governments pay for foot-dragging or for noncompliance. These changes are not drastic, but they may be enough to encourage women's groups in Japan, supported by a few Diet members who otherwise might not have seized the cause, to press for legislation to address the most egregious forms of employment discrimination in that country. These changes are sometimes just enough to give a small rights interest group in Israel enough legal ammunition to argue before the Supreme Court that "moderate physical pressure" is not allowed under the Convention Against Torture and Other Cruel, Inhumane or Degrading Treatment or Punishment (CAT) and to turn the political tables by requiring the Israeli legislature explicitly (and, one can assume, to their embarrassment) to pass legislation to the contrary. No one, this author in particular, believes that signing a treaty will render a demonic government angelic. But under some circumstances, a public international legal commitment can alter the political costs in ways that make improvements to the human condition more likely.

The argument developed [here] is also conditional. Treaties vary by virtue of the rights practices they are attempting to influence. Some can directly impact the perceived ability of the government to maintain political control. The International Covenant on Civil and Political Rights (ICCPR) and the CAT are two examples that potentially have serious governing consequences for a ruling regime. Broad political rights can empower political opposition; the use of torture can be strategically employed to retain political control or to glean information from various enemies of the state. Governments are much more likely to disregard an international commitment if doing so is perceived in any way to endanger their grip on power or the "stability" of the broader polity. Other accords are less likely to threaten a government's political or security goals. The Convention on the Elimination of All Forms of Discrimination Against Women (CEDAW) and the Convention on the Rights of the Child (CRC) are much more important for their social impact than their direct political implications. Most governments—with the possible exception of theocracies whose doctrines embrace the political and social subordination of women—are far less likely to have a crucial political stake in assuring or withholding rights for women and children than they are to have the uninhibited freedom to oppress political opposition. The more a treaty addresses issues clearly related to the ability of the government to achieve its central political goals, the weaker we should expect the treaty's effect to be.

Finally, quintessentially political treaties, such as the CAT and the ICCPR, are likely to have their greatest mobilization effects precisely where the conditions exist to gain significant domestic political traction. Treaties alter politics; they do not cause miracles. They supplement and interact with domestic political and legal institutions; they do not replace them. Extremely stable domestic political institutions will not be much affected by a political human rights treaty commitment. On the one hand, in stable autocracies, they are largely irrelevant. Potential political actors simply do not have the resources to effectively demand change. Treaties may have effects if transnational coalitions are thereby empowered,[4] but the chain of demands is attenuated and likely to be weak. This obvious fact is what causes some scholars to conclude that human rights treaties do not have positive effects.[5] On the other hand, in stable democracies, treaties may be readily accepted, but they are often redundant. Because political rights are largely protected—and have been in living memory—treaty ratification adds very little political activity to that already established around domestically guaranteed protections. The point is that treaties have significant effects, but they do not have the same effects everywhere.

I argue that even the most politically sensitive human rights treaties have significant positive effects in those countries where political institutions have been unstable. Treaties alter politics through the channel of social mobilization, where domestic actors have the motive and the means to form and to demand their effective implementation. In stable autocracies, citizens have the motive to mobilize but not the means. In stable democracies, they have the means but generally lack a motive. Where institutions are most fluid, however, the expected value of importing external political rights agreements is quite high.[6] Rights beneficiaries have a clear incentive to reach for a legal instrument the content and status of which are unlikely to change regardless of the liberality of the current government. They also have a basic capacity to organize and to press for treaty compliance. In many cases, these more volatile polities have experienced at least a degree of political participation and enjoyed some modicum of democratic governance. It is precisely in these polities that we should expect ratification of the more political human rights treaties to influence political coalitions, demands, and ultimately government practices. One of my most significant findings * * * is that even the most politically sensitive human rights treaties have positive effects on torture and repression for the significant number of countries that are neither stable democracies nor stable autocracies. International law matters most where domestic institutions raise the expected value of mobilization, that is, where domestic groups have the motive and the means to demand the protection of their rights as reflected in ratified treaties.

■ ■ ■

Humane Treatment: The Prevalence and Prevention of Torture

Cruelty is perhaps the most difficult human interaction to regulate. Whether inflicted on alleged criminals, ethnic minorities, political opposition, or enemies of the nation, torture and inhumane treatment involve relationships of power and vulnerability that frequently resist external intervention. Torture is often one despicable act in a broader, frequently violent, political drama. Perpetrators sometimes view their actions as justified when placed in their broader context. What hope is there for international legal commitments to influence the torture and inhumane treatment of detainees held by public authorities? * * *

The previous [sections] have demonstrated that international legal agreements have had a positive, though limited, effect on the human rights practices of some governments. The crucial difference between gender or children's issues * * * and torture is that the latter is often perceived to have a critical bearing on the ability of the government to maintain order, security, and its own political power. [These sections] will examine whether, and under what conditions, international legal commitments can influence governments' most repressive and coercive tactics to achieve political goals. As we shall see, this is an area in which even the most democratic governments have preferred to retain a degree of discretion, though the ban in international law is absolute.

* * * The first section discusses the problem of torture. Unfortunately, torture is widespread and, for reasons to be discussed, extremely difficult to detect and eliminate. The next section discusses international legal efforts to address this problem. While the prohibition against torture is now widely considered a part of customary international law, one global treaty in particular—the Convention Against Torture and Other Cruel, Inhuman or Degrading Treatment or Punishment (the CAT)—defines and *categorically proscribes* the kinds of practices with which we are concerned here. The third section reviews what researchers now know about the scourge of officially sanctioned or permitted torture. Thanks to data that have been systematically gathered by such NGOs as Amnesty International and by some government agencies (the U.S. Department of State,[7] for example), it has been possible to research the coercive tactics that most governments would prefer to keep hidden from the broader international community.

The centerpiece * * * is an empirical investigation of what role, if any, international law has played in conditioning governmental use of torture. Few scholars or practitioners would expect an external legal obligation to have much leverage over a government intent on coercively cowing its own people into submission by employing extreme physical or psychological cruelty. But the findings * * * are surprising in this regard. As many skeptics would assume, there are certainly conditions under which treaty commitments matter not a (statistically detectable) whit to the governments that use these horrific political practices. But probing deeper reveals something quite interesting: Governments of polities that are partially accountable or in democratic transition are much less likely to use torture if they have made a public CAT commitment than similarly situated governments that have not. This process is examined in the context of Chile, where a brutal regime ratified the CAT before an election and then discovered just how powerful a tool it could be in the hands of activists. I then turn to the case of Israel, a democratic country but one embattled and conflicted over the issue of how to treat individuals held in detention by state security forces. In both of these cases, the evidence suggests that explicit international legal commitments can provide a mechanism allowing citizens to grasp their rights when their governments might prefer harsh repression. International law has its most important consequences in those—by now quite numerous—polities that have had at least a taste of democratic accountability and refuse to allow their governments to turn back.

Torture and International Law

THE NATURE OF THE PROBLEM

Without a doubt, the use of torture by state officials is one of the most horrifying human rights violations imaginable.[8] The use of severe physical or psychological coercion can be sensational but more often it is insidious, as officials deny or minimize and justify their practices in the name of a higher national or political purpose. Despite offending states' efforts to obscure such practices, the right to be free from torture is often listed as one of the physical integrity rights most commonly violated.[9] By some accounts, despite a decade-long campaign by NGOs to expose such practices, by the early 1990s torture continued to be practiced in more than half of the world's countries.[10] The fates of torturers' victims are not usually well known. Some are (intentionally) made to disappear; others remain at a vicious government's mercy for years. Some survive to see a new regime that effectively renounces such policies. Others flee, looking for sanctuary in a new location. By some estimates, 5 to 35 percent of the world's 20 million refugees have experienced torture.[11] And lest we imagine torture to be limited to a few brutal areas of the world, it is important to note that no region is immune. Appalling photos from the Abu Graib prison in Iraq have reminded Americans of the crucial importance of vigilance against the insidious abuse of prisoners. Even Europe, with the strongest legal regime of any region, still presents some surprisingly disturbing cases.[12]

The practice of torture is centuries old[13] and calls for explanation. Torture is broadly understood to mean the deliberate infliction of violence involving severe mental or physical suffering. The purpose of torturing an individual can vary: Jack Donnelly and others have noted that such explanations range from sadism to national security.[14] Psychologists and social psychologists concentrate on the immediate environmental and personal conditions that stimulate individuals to intentionally inflict pain on others. Social psychologists have analyzed the use of torture as they do other forms of human aggression, noting that stress, risk, group conflict, physical discomfort, and the belief that cherished values are at stake are conditions that can provoke the use of intentional pain on detainees.[15] Sociologists have analyzed torture as an institution used to "deculturate" a society by silencing the dominant group's cultural enemies and breaking down rival cultural identities.[16] Perhaps this is why some studies suggest that physically harsh repression is more prevalent in culturally and racially diverse societies than in more homogeneous ones.[17] Political scientists have tended to analyze torture as a practice used to achieve particular political or governing goals, especially as a means of maintaining order, security, or power by cowing political opposition. In the United States, torture has most recently been discussed as a way to "exploit [detainees] for actionable intelligence"[18] essential to the country's national security.[19] Social scientists have tried to explain why torture is appallingly widespread and to model the conditions under which it can become increasingly sadistic.[20]

The use of torture is a very difficult phenomenon to study in an objective and systematic way. Given the negative connotation modern societies attach to the use of intentionally painful coercive practices, completely frank discussions about official torture are extraordinarily rare. Even governments that have accepted the obligation under the CAT to report to the Committee Against Torture hardly expose their shortcomings gladly; more complete disclosures are usually left to "shadow reports" submitted by various nongovernmental human rights organizations.[21] Simply put: Every government has an incentive to minimize the seriousness of their own abuses; ironically, it is the most open governments that are most likely to allow the kind of access from which the more highly critical shadow reports can be written.[22] Furthermore, even if we can all agree that torture is abhorrent, people differ over exactly what it is. Whether a particular practice constitutes "maltreatment," "abuse," or is serious enough to be termed "torture" can be highly contentious in all but the most extreme cases.

Controlling the practice of torture—even among governments willing to do so—is quite difficult because of the highly decentralized way in which it is carried out. Certainly, torture is more likely to be systematic and widespread where governments encourage or condone such practices. But even when they do not, even when official policy actively opposes torture, the act of torture itself may be carried out in innumerable police stations, detention centers, or prisons around a country. It can be very difficult to make official policy effective in such highly decentralized settings. In their study of Latin American transitions, Ellen Lutz and Kathryn Sikkink found that although torture was explicitly prohibited by treaty and implemented in domestic legislation, eliminating such practices lagged behind progress in other, less legalized but more public areas, such as democratic elections. They point precisely to this problem of decentralization, noting that even a government that *wants* to comply with legal prohibitions against torture may find it difficult to control the actions taken in multiple police precincts across a country.[23]

INTERNATIONAL LEGAL EFFORTS TO PROHIBIT TORTURE

The prohibition against torture has been a part of the international human rights regime since its post–World War II inception. The UDHR addressed torture in Article 5, which states, "No one shall be subjected to torture or to cruel, inhuman or degrading treatment or punishment."[24] But because the declaration is a broad statement of principles, it neither defines torture nor provides any hint of enforcement. The first treaty to mention torture in peacetime was the ICCPR, whose Article 7 provides that "No one shall be subjected to torture or to cruel, inhuman or degrading treatment or punishment." In light of Nazi practices in the 1930s and 1940s, Article 7 went on to provide that "In particular, no one shall be subjected without his free consent to medical or scientific experimentation." The ICCPR created the Human Rights Committee and, for the first time, began a system of oversight (largely through state reporting). The ICCPR did not enter into force until 1976, however, and by that time, a concerted effort was underway, led by Amnesty International, to draft and promulgate a convention specifically designed to eliminate torture.[25]

From 1972, Amnesty International was a central advocate for, and ultimately an influential architect of, the international legal regime to ban torture.[26] Amnesty's campaign focused on key national legislatures (for example, the U.S. Congress), as well as the UN, in essence urging these bodies to take the problem much more seriously. Amnesty succeeded in arranging a joint UN–NGO Conference for the Abolition of Torture in 1973, which by most accounts was successful in publicizing the issue.[27] Soon thereafter, the governments of Sweden and the Netherlands took an especially active role, urging the UNGA to pass the Declaration on the Protection of All Persons from Being Subjected to Torture and Other Cruel, Inhuman, or Degrading Treatment or Punishment in December 1975.[28] The first article contained, in embryonic form, the definition of torture that would eventually make its way into the world's first binding treaty devoted to the subject. This declaration also proclaimed torture to be unjustifiable under any circumstances[29]—language that eventually became enshrined in treaty law.

The CAT is without doubt the premiere universal effort on the part of the international community to guarantee individuals a right to be free from torture and to ban its practice. On 4 February 1985, the convention was opened for signature at UN headquarters in New York City. Representatives of twenty-five states signed early that year.[30]

The CAT is the first international and legally binding effort to define torture. Article 1, paragraph 1 says:

> Torture means any act by which severe pain or suffering, whether physical or mental, is intentionally inflicted on a person for such purposes as obtaining from him or a third person information or a confession, punishing him for an act he or a third person has committed or is suspected of having committed, or intimidating

or coercing him or a third person, or for any reason based on discrimination of any kind, when such pain or suffering is inflicted by or at the instigation of or with the consent or acquiescence of a public official or other person acting in an official capacity. It does not include pain or suffering arising only from, inherent in or incidental to lawful sanctions.[31]

Article 2 makes it clear that the prohibition contained in the treaty is absolute. The convention is aimed at *official* or *officially condoned* or permitted torture.[32] Torture cannot be justified under any circumstances, including war, internal political instability, or any other public emergency,[33] nor can it be justified by orders from a superior public authority.[34]

■ ■ ■

The CAT takes three approaches to enforcement. First, it establishes universal jurisdiction for the crime of torture. Article 5 of the treaty requires nations either to extradite or to prosecute alleged torturers within their boundaries, *regardless of where their crimes took place*.[35] In theory, this means that torturers have no place to hide; they can be held legally accountable for their actions if they enter the jurisdiction of any party to the treaty. Article 5 was successfully used in Pinochet's prosecution, for example, illustrating that heads of state are not immune from the CAT's provisions.[36] In practice, of course, governments may be reluctant to prosecute torturers for political reasons, especially if they are former heads of state.[37] Nonetheless, most analysts have hailed universal jurisdiction as an important and innovative way to enforce the treaty's provisions.[38]

The CAT also contains two optional enforcement mechanisms. First, any state party may declare under Article 21 that it "recognizes the competence of the Committee to receive and consider communications to the effect that a State Party claims that another State Party is not fulfilling its obligations under this Convention." The committee is directed under Article 21 to handle such complaints in a dispute settlement rather than an enforcement mode. Its decisions are not binding on either party. Despite the fact that 53 states have to date made an Article 21 declaration,[39] this procedure has *never* been invoked.

The second optional enforcement mechanism is for state parties to declare themselves bound under Article 22 ". . . to recognize the competence of the Committee to receive and consider communications from or on behalf of individuals subject to its jurisdiction who claim to be victims of a violation by a State Party of the provisions of the Convention."[40] Such a declaration, in effect, gives individuals standing to complain about a state's behavior to the Committee Against Torture. Some 56 states have made such a declaration, and as of April 2004, the committee has received 241 complaints. Sweden, Switzerland, and Canada head the list of countries complained against, indicating that this provision may be most relevant to those individuals already in possession of a fairly strong sense of their rights.[41]

THE STATE OF RESEARCH

Relatively little cross-national research has been done to try to explain the prevalence and patterns of state-sponsored torture, and attention to the role of international legal commitments has been even more scant. * * *

Only two studies have addressed the role of international law in affecting governments' physical integrity rights violations, and only one of these deals specifically with torture. Linda Camp Keith's study of the ICCPR found differences across signatories and nonsignatories, but found no improvement in physical integrity rights among signatories before and after treaty ratification.[42] The only study

to directly examine the effect of the CAT on practices that are specifically banned by that convention is that of Oona Hathaway. Her work does not support the proposition that making a commitment to the CAT has much effect on the propensity to torture. Quite the contrary: She concluded her study by noting that "the torture and genocide conventions appear to have the smallest impact on human rights practices of all the universal conventions."[43] * * *

Hathaway's explanation for the CAT's null effect is that governments ratify human rights conventions to express their symbolic support for their principles as well as to reduce criticism attendant upon remaining formally outside the conventions. But compliance theorists have noted the logical oddities in such an argument, at least as a general explanation. The single most puzzling problem is why any government would sign an international treaty thinking that this would be sufficient to deflect criticism from their practices.[44] As I have [previously] argued, the empirical record with respect to treaty ratification seems to suggest a completely different dynamic: NGOs have campaigned hard for ratification (notably Amnesty International in the case of the CAT)[45] because they believe it will give them greater moral, legal, and political leverage over states than would have been the case otherwise. The evidence does not seem to support the contention that ratification alone satisfies antitorture groups that their mission has been accomplished.

A more reasonable expectation is that an international commitment to eschew the practice of torture is effective under some conditions and not under others. *Some* governments may ratify the CAT for expressive purposes; these are likely to be those polities already quite committed to the treaty's provisions. They do not need an international commitment to influence their policies: A credible commitment to abstain from torture can be generated from within the domestic political system itself.

The Swedens, Netherlands, and Costa Ricas of the world may sign as an expression of their commitment to humane treatment and their desire to influence others to do the same,[46] but so many internal checks on torture are in place that an international treaty is superfluous. On the other hand, *some* governments may believe (wrongly in many if not most cases) that ratification will earn them some cheap credit with the international community. In both cases, ratification should not be expected to alter behavior significantly: Those with the best records will continue to eschew torture, while the few looking for cheap international kudos will continue to behave badly. Under these conditions, the motives for signing and the propensity to torture will differ radically, but the behavioral observation—no apparent treaty effect—will be the same.

Many governments are neither stable compliers nor cynical signers. They rule polities with *some* experience with democratic principles and human rights. Their populations have in many cases had *some* exposure to the rule of law, as well as a degree of governmental accountability, and value international obligations as a way to help secure greater human rights guarantees. As I have argued [earlier], international legal instruments can mobilize individuals and groups to demand their rights under the treaty's provision. This is especially true in the case of torture. Experiences of pain and loss cut to the core of everyday lives, and when such suffering is the result of torture, these feelings can occupy a prominent place in the domains of public opinion and issue activism.[47] Civil society is *provokable* in these countries, and citizens have enough freedom to be able to act according to their values and in their perceived interests. In these cases, one might expect a convention against torture to have real effects on government practices.

There are good theoretical reasons to take another look at the effect of ratification of the CAT, specifying clearly the conditions under which we might expect it to have real consequences for the polity. Torture is about political and social control. The CAT should have its strongest positive effects in places where control is contested—where politics are most unstable and precarious for the governing elite. Neither stable democracies nor complete autocracies fit this description. Rather, we should expect a commitment to the CAT to matter most where political regimes are in flux. The next section tests this idea and reveals treaty effects that earlier studies have obscured.

Data and Methods

THE DEPENDENT VARIABLE: TORTURE SCALE

As defined by the CAT, torture is the intentional and coercive inflicting of severe pain or suffering by a government authority acting in his or her official capacity on another person or persons. The CAT specifically excludes pain or suffering caused by "lawful sanctions." Two sources have long collected information useful in developing a torture measure: NGOs (Amnesty International, in particular) and the U.S. Department of State. Oona Hathaway's work depended on the latter, which does not differ significantly from information collected by nongovernmental sources. Indeed, the Department of State to a large extent bases its own reports on information supplied at least in part by NGOs.[48] Since her measure is designed specifically to tap compliance with the CAT, I have extended Hathaway's data through 2002.

The dependent variable is a five-category measure that captures the pervasiveness of the practice of torture by government officials.[49] The worst cases (Category 1) are those in which torture (including severe beatings) was considered "prevalent" and "widespread."[50] The next category (Category 2) includes cases in which torture was considered "common," there were widespread reports of beatings to death, or other beatings and other forms of abusive treatment were quite routine. The third category involves those cases in which there was some reference (without specified frequency) to maltreatment, or common beatings or isolated reports of severe beatings (e.g., to death). The fourth category includes those cases in which abuses were occasional or there were possible cases of beatings (though never to death). And finally, the fifth category involves the best cases, those in which serious abuses were never reported, though isolated cases of a less serious nature were on rare occasions reported and responded to with disciplinary action. Table 10.1 summarizes the criteria used for the torture scale.

Figure 10.2 gives a sense of how torture practices have compared with CAT ratification since 1985. Apparently, the number of treaty adherents has increased even as the global average of torture practices has deteriorated. The question addressed here, though, is whether committing to the CAT improves practices among the committed or whether there are any conditions under which commitment improves practices, controlling for other explanations and influences. If governments are influenced by their international legal commitments, we should see a positive relationship, indicative of improvement, when countries ratify the CAT.

CONDITIONING EFFECTS: REGIME TYPE AND JUDICIAL INSTITUTIONS

The central hypothesis of this chapter is that human rights treaties need at least some domestic political traction to have significant positive effects. They are not likely to change behavior in countries with stable dictatorships or in countries that reliably ensure the political accountability of leaders and other agents of the state. Legal constraints are largely ignored in the former and are redundant in the latter. * * * I distinguish three kinds of historical

regime experiences. First, I distinguish countries that have been stable democracies for the entire post–World War II period or, if newly independent since 1945, democratic for their whole independent existence. I code them as "stable democracies" if their democracy score never goes below 8 in the polity dataset during the post–World War II period. Next, countries are never democratic if they have never had a democracy score above 5. I would expect a treaty commitment to have very little effect in either of these cases. That leaves the unstable, transitionally or partially democratic "middle"—a category that includes a large number of countries * * *. Many of these are countries transitioning toward democracy; a smaller number are moving in the opposite direction. A few are fairly stable partial democracies. I run additional tests later to see whether volatility or partial democracy seems to account most fully for the observed effects of the CAT in this cluster of regimes.

THE STATISTICAL MODELS

One of the most serious problems associated with trying to estimate treaty effects accurately is that, with a few exceptions, the same factors that lead to ratification are likely to explain compliance * * *. Thus, it is important to use a statistical model that endogenizes the ratification choice itself and to "identify" the model with instruments that can help distinguish ratification from compliance. Two of the most reliable factors that influence ratification, as we have seen, are the nature of the legal system[51] and treaty ratification of other states in the region. These are the two variables I use to explain ratification in the first equation of a two-stage least squares model. The second-stage equation tests the hypotheses for the CAT's influence that were developed previously. I expect the CAT to improve torture practices; hence, we should expect a positive relationship between the CAT and the torture scale. * * *

Table 10.1. Torture Prevalence: The Dependent Variable

NOTE: IN EACH CASE, AT LEAST ONE OF THE FOLLOWING MUST BE TRUE:

Type of Activity	Category 1	Category 2	Category 3	Category 4	Category 5
Psychological mistreatment		Frequent, often	Used without reference to frequency	Sometimes, occasional	Isolated reports with disciplinary response
Rough handling, other abuse		Frequent, routine	Regular brutality, severe maltreatment of prisoners	Sometimes, occasional	Isolated reports with disciplinary response
Beatings		Frequent, routine	Common (or not uncommon), numerous reports	Allegations or indications (any reported—regardless of redress)	Isolated reports with disciplinary response
Torture	Prevalent, widespread, repeated, methodical	Common, several reports, numerous allegations	Some, occasional (unless redressed)	Unsubstantiated; unlikely true; isolated, with redress	None
Abused to death	Common, frequent, many, widespread	Some, occasional incidents, several reports	Isolated reports	None	None

Note: This presentation inverts the original scale so that higher scores represent better practices.

Source: Hathaway 2002.

Figure 10.2. CAT Ratifications and the Torture Scale

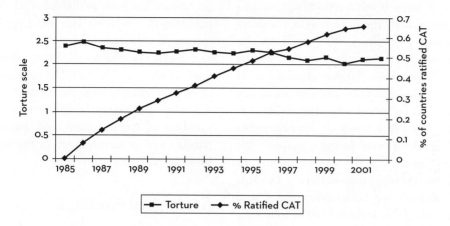

Source: Ratification status for the CAT: Office of the UN Commission for Human Rights, http://www.ohchr.org/english/countries/ratification /9.htm. Torture Scale (measuring torture prevalence): Hathaway 2002 (inverted scale).

■ ■ ■

CONTROLS

A series of control variables are included in all specifications to reduce the possibility of erroneously attributing causal significance to ratification of the CAT. Certainly, the basic causal explanations for the prevalence of torture are not likely to be an international legal commitment, but rather institutional and social features of each country, as well as each government's perceived threats to national security or to its hold on political power. No one should expect international law to overcome these basic conditions; rather, the question is, once we control for these conditions, does a treaty commitment make any difference to the prevalence of torture on the margins?

A first set of controls speaks to the country's domestic institutions. The primary hypotheses have to do with degree of democratic accountability and the rule of law, but other domestic institutions could matter as well. Most important here are institutions that make it difficult for a government to torture its citizens without some resistance. Besides regime

characteristics, accountability could plausibly be influenced by a free press. Torture is much less likely to be widespread in countries in which the press can expose and criticize the government without censorship or fear of reprisals or harassment. A free press can both expose abuse and remind a people that its government is violating international accords to which it is legally committed.[52] * * *

National truth commissions can be used in exceptional circumstances to try to address the widespread use of torture and related rights abuses. A truth commission is a domestically generated effort to come to terms with an oppressive and violent past. The creation of such a commission presumably signals a commitment to acknowledge past abuses, set the record straight, and place the country on a more just path. Truth commissions can certainly be aimed at injustices other than torture, but they are frequently set up specifically to address egregious human rights abuses.[53] If they are successful, we might expect torture practices to be ameliorated once a commission is established. * * *

The second set of controls relate to a country's security situation. One of the classic justifications for using coercive tactics against detainees is either to silence or to wrench information from various groups or individuals the government considers its or the country's enemies. War also gives rise to physical and social conditions that are linked to individual aggression.[54] Even countries that eschew torture under normal circumstances can find justifications for its use when the nation is at war.[55] Practically every study on human rights notes that they deteriorate during wartime.[56] We should therefore expect the use of torture to spread and become more intense during a violent conflict. Indicators for both international and civil wars are therefore included in the following analysis. * * *

A third set of controls relate to potential external levers of influence over a country's torture practices. Countries that receive large amounts of foreign aid or that trade extensively with wealthy democracies could be discouraged from using brutal interrogation practices if these partners publicize these practices and/or threaten sanctions. I therefore include overseas development aid as a proportion of GDP and the total number of preferential trade agreements as potential sources of external leverage over rights practices.

Among potential external levers, the international community working through the UN has developed mechanisms to investigate, expose, and embarrass governments about their repressive practices. Three major UN mechanisms could potentially have an influence on a country's propensity to torture.[57] The first is the UNGA's use of specific resolutions criticizing a country by name for some aspect of its human rights record. * * *

The second mechanism the international community has at its disposal for influencing countries' most egregious human rights practices is what is known as a 1503 Investigation. * * *

[The aim of this procedure] is to identify countries in which serious abuses are occurring rather than provide a remedy for those complaining of human rights violations.[58]

Third, since the 1980s, the special rapporteur on torture has been available to provide visits to countries that evidence indicates have indulged in torture on a systematic basis. * * *

Finally, I control for a country's developmental level, as measured by its GDP per capita, the size of its population (a large population could explain Amnesty International's ability to tally up large numbers of torture cases), and average regional trends (average torture score in the region in the previous period).

Statistical Findings

PARTIALLY DEMOCRATIC/ TRANSITION REGIMES

The first point that these analyses confirm is that committing one's state to honor the CAT does not have a positive effect on torture practices in all kinds of regimes. *The CAT does not have unconditional effects.*[59] In fact, in a lightly controlled model * * *, the CAT appears to be mildly *negative* (though not significantly so). But if ratifying the CAT appears to have no positive effect across the board, it does seem to have important effects *under certain political conditions.* Whereas we might not expect a CAT commitment to have much of an effect in a stable democracy—with well-developed and highly stable channels of political accountability—and while it may not be realistic to expect an international legal obligation to matter much in a polity that has never experienced any degree of political accountability, we can test the proposition that *ratifying the CAT helps significantly to reduce torture in polities with some experience with or prospect for a degree of political accountability.* These are the regimes in which domestic groups and stakeholders have both the motive and the means to organize to demand compliance with the CAT.

[Analysis suggests] that the CAT may indeed have an important impact on the severity of torture practices for countries with only moderately accountable institutions. * * * There is practically no influence of ratifying the CAT in stable democracies * * * and countries that have never been democratic * * *. It is fairly clear that ratifying the CAT does not help much in stable democracies or stable autocracies. For the most part, there is no significant difference within these categories between ratifiers and nonratifiers.[60] In fact, for countries that have never been democratic, the model with a full set of controls suggests that ratification likely has no effect whatsoever. Evidently, these are the governments most likely to believe that they can ratify the CAT strategically.

The results for countries in transition provide a sharp contrast. For these countries, it is fairly clear that those that ratify the CAT are much more likely to improve their practices (reduce their incidence of torture) than transitional countries that do not. Statistically speaking, we can be fairly confident (about 94 percent confident) that among transitional countries, CAT ratifiers' practices become much better than those of nonratifiers. Ratification of the CAT is associated with almost a 40 percent increase in the likelihood that a country will improve by one category on the torture scale. Among the control variables, the only consistent explanation appears to be the importance of information, as indicated by the strong positive effect of a relatively free press. The use of truth commissions may also be associated with future reductions in the use of torture, increasing the chances of moving from one category on the scale by about 15 percent. Surprisingly, neither international nor civil wars mattered significantly in these specifications for the transition countries. Nor did any of the UN mechanisms have much impact in these countries.

■   ■   ■

It is natural to wonder, what drives the "transitional" result: the fact that the country is partially democratic, and thus individuals and groups have both the motives and the means to demand greater respect and protection from their government? Or is it that they are unstable, and treaties—especially treaties guaranteeing a right not to be tortured—are a way to stabilize antitorture norms? In order to get at the mechanism involved, we can implement two further tests. The first tests for the hypothesis that the CAT has most traction under moderate levels of democratic accountability. I created an interaction term for moderate levels of democracy and interacted it with CAT ratification.[61] Moderate democracies thus defined were much more likely to improve their torture practices than moderate democracies without such a commitment* * *. The same relationship did not hold for either full democracies or full autocracies. * * *

THE COURTS: POSSIBILITIES FOR LITIGATION

The data suggest—they of course do not prove—that when a government makes a formal and public commitment to abide by the provisions of the CAT, under certain conditions it is likely to do so. The conditions under which CAT ratification was most likely to affect actual practices were conditions of partial democratization. I have theorized that these are the conditions under which groups and individuals have both the motive and the means to mobilize to demand that their rights be respected.

A second mechanism * * * was litigation. Treaties are law in most countries; as such, they are available at least in theory as a way to make a legal case against practices state agents use to hold "dangerous" persons while in custody. This should be true, however, only if a country's courts are not a sham. If they are politically controlled by the government, no citizen or activist would consider it worthwhile to launch a case to try to get the CAT enforced against a brutal government able to pull all judicial strings.

It is possible to test for the plausibility of litigation as a mechanism by examining the relationship between CAT ratification, torture practices, and judicial independence. The proxy used here for judicial independence is * * * a measure of the rule of law collected by the World Bank broadly reflecting perceptions of the quality of judicial institutions as well as law and order in each country. While we should be cognizant of its weaknesses as a measure of judicial independence, this proxy provides one (noisy) cut at the question of whether the CAT is more likely to matter in countries where the courts are more likely to be respected.

A certain degree of judicial independence, competence, and credibility is necessary if the courts are to be a mechanism available for the enforcement of international treaty commitments. To be sure, countries with the most highly developed rule of law norms are unlikely to be among the worst torturers in the first place. If we see large improvements in torture practices in countries with the weakest court systems, we should seek the explanation outside of the court system itself. If the courts are an important enforcement mechanism, we should see the top tier and possibly the middle tier of high-scoring rule of law countries making improvements after ratification.[62]

[Analysis] shows that ratification is associated with significant improvements in torture practices—but not universally. * * * Among countries with very weak legal systems, ratification makes no difference whatsoever * * *. Similarly, there is not much difference within high rule of law countries between those that have ratified and those that have not * * *. In fact, if anything, it looks like nonratifiers have better torture records among high rule of law states than nonratifiers, but the relationship is inconsistent and not statistically reliable. The picture is very different among the mid-level set of countries * * *. Where the rule of law is reasonably well developed and the courts are fairly independent of governmental control, chances are good that CAT ratification has indeed served

to improve practices on average and controlling for many other alternative explanations. * * *

Thus, there may be some basis to conclude that the CAT has had an important impact on a considerable subset of countries in which stakeholders and other activists have the motive and the means to mobilize politically to demand compliance with the CAT and to use the CAT in domestic legal struggles over the meaning and use of torture. The following section discusses two examples of how this treaty became important in domestic law and politics, eventually contributing to the amelioration of torture practices on the part of government agents.

Chile and Israel: Experiences with the CAT

To illustrate the kinds of political and legal dynamics that could be behind the broad trends documented previously, it is useful to look at an example of how the CAT has made its way into domestic politics and litigation. The case of Chile illustrates the role that this convention can play in a partial or transitional democracy. First, it shows that human rights activists strategically deployed international legal norms to gain adherents and to strengthen the legitimacy of their opposition to Augusto Pinochet's military regime. However, they were hobbled in this early effort by a paucity of ratified treaties and the uselessness of litigation by a conservative, regime-controlled court system. Second, it illustrates that rights activists did want international legal commitments to bind their government. In fact, by the mid-1980s, several groups were specifically and publicly demanding CAT ratification—often at significant personal risk. Third, the CAT was highly relevant to local law development well into the transition period and beyond. Once the courts were reformed (circa 1997), and particularly once the CAT's power was demonstrated by the arrest and extradition of Pinochet himself, litigation involving the CAT grew significantly. Furthermore, there is some evidence that torture practices in Chile were ameliorated at around this time as well. Overall, the case is useful in suggesting the importance of both the mobilization and litigation mechanisms discussed earlier.

Israel, of course, is a fairly stable democracy, and activists were motivated almost immediately upon Israel's ratification to use the CAT to bolster court cases alleging the use of torture and to embarrass the government by pointing to the treaty as an authoritative statement regarding the definition and the unconditional prohibition of torture. Crucial here was the Committee Against Torture's official view that many of the practices used in detention did in fact constitute torture. Once the Supreme Court of Israel rendered its landmark decision (1999) incorporating this view, the ball was back in the Israeli politician's court: They could choose to legalize those practices, but at the peril of making Israel the only country in the world to legalize torture. In both of these cases, the treaty was important in changing the way in which individuals held in government detention were treated.

CHILE: DEMOCRATIC TRANSITION, JUDICIAL REFORM, AND THE LEGAL EMPOWERMENT OF THE CAT

Chile is a case in which the treaty's commitments interact with democratic transition and institutional reform. Despite a comparatively long history of democratic governance, Chile is a country whose recent past has been marred by widespread use of torture perpetrated by the military and sanctioned by the highest levels of government. In 1973, a military junta led by General Augusto Pinochet overthrew the government of Salvador Allende and ruthlessly rooted out—tortured and murdered—political opponents and sympathizers with the left. For most of its rule, Pinochet's junta was not formally constrained by international human rights treaties, although throughout the period his government was accused of grave breaches of customary international law related to crimes against humanity and serious human rights abuses. Yet, human rights organizers—and, significantly, the political opposition to the junta—drew to a considerable extent on international law norms and rhetoric to legitimate demands for an end to human rights abuses and torture. The junta ratified the CAT in 1988—just before the election in which Pinochet would lose his official grasp on government. Not only would the CAT be the legal instrument responsible for Pinochet's extradition to face torture charges, it would also inspire litigation in Chilean courts that would cumulatively contribute to significant improvements in Chilean law and ultimately practice. Torture has not been eradicated from the country, but the CAT has been very useful in bringing attention to the problem, reducing the overt reliance on "states of exception," and reducing torturers' calculations that they will escape responsibility for their actions through amnesty, statutes of limitations, or protection in sympathetic military courts.

The domestic opposition to the repressive tactics of the junta, whose goal was to crush socialism, was led by the moral authority of the outspoken Catholic Church. The church early on had a legal strategy for responding to the crushing repression of Pinochet's military dictatorship.[63] As early as October 1973, a religious-cum-legal alliance against the repression developed under the coleadership of Catholic and Lutheran bishops. They founded the Cooperative Committee for Peace in Chile (COPACHI), which focused initially on providing legal defense in the courts-martial cases as well as in cases of political firings. Expanding from a mere 8 employees to over 100 less than a year after its founding, COPACHI began to investigate a broad range of rights violations. By 1974, when a Mexican newspaper reported that COPACHI was keeping records on fundamental human rights violations, the organization was viewed by the government as in a threatening alliance with the political opposition.

That year, COPACHI filed some 1,568 habeas corpus petitions on behalf of persons held in government detention, with the intent of both documenting these cases and delegitimating the government's practices. * * *

■   ■   ■

* * * In the 1970s, however, the international human rights regime was far less developed than it would become toward century's end. To be sure, the UDHR was available, and human rights organizations in Chile made reference to its norms on a regular basis. But in Chile, the status of the ICCPR was contested. ICCPR ratification was one of the last actions taken by Allende's regime before its overthrow. The UN records the date of Chile's ratification as 1972, but the position of the junta was that it had never been implemented in Chilean law and therefore was not a legally constraining document. Furthermore, the CAT did not exist when Pinochet came to power, though some accounts credit the widespread torture and disappearance under his rule with provoking the international community to address torture specifically. The international legal and institutional environment for human rights was fairly thin in the mid-1970s; still, rights groups appealed to an international audience to apply pressure directly on the Chilean government, as described well by Margaret Keck and Kathryn Sikkink.[64]

■   ■   ■

Activists continued to appeal to whatever international legal instruments were available to them to oppose civil rights violations and brutal treatment by government agents. Almost every December in the 1980s, activists from several rights organizations demonstrated in Santiago to commemorate the anniversary of the UDHR, reading the charter aloud in public and demanding the government's adherence.[65] * * *

■   ■   ■

For reasons that scholars have not yet been able to document convincingly, Chile finally did ratify the CAT in September 1988. General Pinochet himself signed the instrument of ratification. Three important reservations were entered upon ratification: that the convention would not be enacted until after 11 March 1990; that it would not be applied retroactively; and that Chile did not recognize the commission's jurisdiction over its internal affairs. Spain and other countries formally objected to these reservations, complaining that they were contrary to the objectives and intention of the international agreement.

Why did a regime infamous for the torture of detainees ratify a convention that bars these practices under all circumstances? No scholar has yet analyzed the ratification specifically, but Darren Hawkins's research implies that it may have been yet another legitimacy-seeking tactic by a junta that was in any case split on how much to concede to its political opposition.[66] The government's public justification was that ratification merely reflected its long-term commitment to human rights. According to the presidential secretary, the decision was "consistent with the principles of the government, maintaining an unchanged policy of preventing and punishing those illegal actions, and with preserving the Constitution and the law."[67] Coming only weeks before the national plebiscite that would determine whether Pinochet would remain in power another eight years, there is a good chance that ratification was a tactic (ultimately unsuccessful) to gain electoral support.[68] Furthermore, the government may have thought that its treaty reservations as well as the national amnesty laws would protect any government or military officials from being held accountable. * * *

It is probably safe to infer that Pinochet's government ratified the CAT anticipating that it would pose no serious threat to his freedom or his mode of governance. If so, his miscalculation began with the results of the plebiscite itself. Despite harassment of the opposition and attacks on the critical media, on 5 October 1988, Pinochet lost the national plebiscite, with nearly 55 percent of Chilean voters rejecting his plan to remain in power. Within weeks, the opposition coalesced around Patricio Aylwin as its candidate for the coming year's presidential elections.

Aylwin was among the leaders of the opposition that as early as 1978 had explicitly built their vision of Chilean political life around the UDHR. The UDHR was integrated into the opposition coalition's platform and represented a clear break with Chile's compromised rights practices.[69] The opposition party proposed several key judicial reforms meant to protect the rights of the detained, including the jurisdiction of ordinary courts in human rights cases, amnesty for political prisoners, and pardons for those who had not committed blood crimes. They also proposed that ratified international human rights treaties be raised to the status of constitutional law in Chile.[70] In 1989, one of the 54 constitutional changes introduced by the opposition added a line to Article 5 making it a duty of the state to respect and promote the human rights guaranteed by the constitution and by international treaties ratified by Chile.[71] On 30 July 1989, these constitutional reforms were approved by a whopping 85.7 percent of the Chilean electorate.[72]

The electoral success of the opposition did not make the democratic transition easy or human rights unquestionably secure. After all that dissidents had endured, Pinochet was still quite popular in Chile: He had won about 40 percent of the recent vote, and the political right still held the balance of power in the legislature. Moreover, the opposition was faced with an essentially hostile judiciary; the Supreme Court, in particular, was sympathetic to right-wing ideology and to the goals if not all of the methods of the military government.[73] * * *

The watershed year for the litigation of torture cases was 1998. In 1997, the Eduardo Frei government moved to propose and implement a number of reforms, and important shifts in the nature of court decisions began to surface in a very short time.[74] Most importantly, General Pinochet was arrested in London in 1998 while on a fleeting visit there. He was arrested and held, ironically, only because Chile had in 1988 ratified the CAT, which required either the prosecution or the extradition of alleged torturers to jurisdictions willing to prosecute. As a result of judicial reform and the example of the extraordinary reach of the CAT, litigation in Chilean courts began to change drastically. The number of cases alleging or in some way related to torture increased significantly.[75] Torture cases began appearing in much greater numbers in the Supreme Court and the Appeals Court of Santiago by 2003. In many more cases, the courts are relying on the CAT to make decisions. * * *

■   ■   ■

Did the possibility of torture litigation—appealing to the CAT in Chilean courts—have any effect on torture practices in the country? It will never be possible to know the definitive answer to that question. But the evidence is suggestive. The torture index does begin to improve in Chile in 1999—just as it becomes clear that the CAT is highly relevant to how international and hence Chilean law is equipped to deal with the atrocities of the Pinochet regime.[76] The most noticeable improvement on the torture scale did not come in the first decade of the country's democratic transition. Rather, it came when the utility of the CAT became clear and the courts had undergone crucial reforms. Under these circumstances, international law became available to Chilean activists to hold their government accountable for torture, past and current.

ISRAEL: AN EMBATTLED DEMOCRACY

Israel is an interesting case: It is a highly democratic country and a country that the World Bank scores well but not at or near the top of the countries they have rated on their rule of law scale. Israel also faces security threats that make interrogation of terrorist and criminal suspects a serious issue. It is a good case for illustrating the ways in which international treaty commitment can gain traction through the mobilization of activists employing a strategy of litigation. The fact that the Israeli Supreme Court is so easy for individuals to access made the strategy possible. This combination of factors gave the CAT special traction in Israeli domestic politics and institutions, which in turn provided some impetus for revising coercive practices that the international community had described as torture.

Israel is a democracy, and there is no particular reason to think that a treaty banning torture should have much impact in a democratic country, which is far less likely to practice torture in the first place. Israel provides an interesting case study because it is an outlier: a stable democracy with a recent history of harsh interrogation practices that many would describe as torture. It is a good case to compare with those of transitioning and politically unstable regimes. In particular, it is interesting to observe the ways in which ratification of the CAT opened up political as well as legal space within Israel for critics of government practices. Once Israel had ratified the CAT (in 1991), domestic political groups mobilized and made strategic use of Israel's own institutional strengths: relatively independent and competent courts. As a result, Israeli interrogation practices have moderated, though they are still far from perfect.

Israeli law has addressed the issue of torture since passage of the Prevention of Terrorism Act (1948) shortly after the inception of the state. Controversial regulations dating from 1977 permitted "moderate physical pressure" in the interrogation of terrorist suspects, but it was not until 1987—and the eruption of the intifada—that the government's policies were systematically assessed by the Landau Commission Report. After an investigation undertaken in response to a five-year prison sentence for a Palestinian man that was based largely on a forced confession, the commission controversially concluded that the use of "moderate physical" and "non-violent psychological" pressure by the General Security Services (Shin Bet) was acceptable against Palestinians suspected of security offences. The report—details of which were never made public—contained interrogation guidelines allowing for "a moderate measure of physical pressure," which nonetheless "must never reach the level of torture."[77]

Meanwhile, allegations of abusive interrogation practices were becoming a more common feature of the nightly news.[78] In 1993, the evening news told the story of Hassan Zubeidi, a 34-year-old grocer from Anabta on the West Bank, who had allegedly been beaten comatose by Shin Bet. This case and others sent the government into a flurry of activity that it hoped would deflect concern. In April the government announced that a ministerial committee had tightened up the 1987 Landau Commission guidelines for Shin Bet interrogators. In June a bill banning torture was proposed by several members of parliament, and the justice minister, David Libai, appointed a committee to study the proposal. Public protest was limited, partly because Israelis continued to view Shin Bet as crucial to Israel's security.[79]

While hardly sparking a mass social movement, the human rights issues—raised in stark fashion in the aftermath of the intifada—fueled a burst of organized activism. By one count, only one human rights NGO existed in Israel before December 1987, and about fifteen of the twenty-five rights NGOs currently operating in Israel were established in the years immediately following.[80] In the Occupied Territories, only one rights organization existed before the intifada, and about six other rights organizations were established within a very short period following its eruption.[81] One of the most important groups formed was the Public Committee Against Torture, which spearheaded much of the legal activity discussed below. Links with international rights groups were forged, from

Amnesty International and Middle East Watch to the International Commission of Jurists and Physicians for Human Rights.[82] International rights discourse peppered their press releases, human rights reports, and correspondence with Israeli authorities (government, military, civil administration).[83]

Israeli activists chose an explicit strategy of legal contestation in their efforts to stamp out their government's practice of what many considered torture. "Politically motivated Palestinian and Israeli lawyers used the legal terrain as a site of resistance to reform or to transform the way the state exercises power," according to one astute observer.[84] This strategy is clearly reflected in the number of cases alleging torture that were brought to the Israeli Supreme Court in the 1990s. * * *

■　■　■

Israel's struggle with terrorism over the course of the 1990s made it hard for the government to eschew completely the continued use of moderate physical pressure against suspects. In September 1994, critics of such practices gained support from some politicians on the right when members of an alleged Jewish terror cell were arrested and some alleged physical or mental violence while under interrogation.[85]

The Israeli government responded to its critics in two ways: necessity and compliance. "The main duty of the government is to protect its citizens," said Uri Dromi, the chief government spokesman in late 1995, "and therefore we have to resort to methods that are not so nice. In other circumstances we would not do it, but we are faced with a very dangerous enemy, and it is the enemy not only of Israel but of the free world."[86] At the same time, the government expressed its desire to comply with the CAT it had ratified five years before. In defending a legislative proposal to set guidelines on the use of physical pressure in interrogations in early 1996, Minister of Justice David Libai noted that "The [proposed] methods used during interrogations

will be in line with the International Convention against torture and will not lead to suffering or great pain. . . . This law will give clear regulations on acceptable methods, which will help Shin Bet agents avoid mistaken initiatives."[87] * * *

In a short while, the experts comprising the Committee Against Torture were to allege otherwise. Israel's techniques became a target of the committee's concern after a 1996 Israeli Supreme Court ruling gave interrogators more leeway in using physical means to uncover information on terrorism.[88] * * *

By 1998, the government and activists in alliance with the UN Committee Against Torture were at an impasse, with the former claiming that specific Israeli practices did not and the latter claiming that they did constitute torture. The most decisive way remaining to settle the issue was to apply to the highest legal authority in Israel to decide this very issue. * * *

■　■　■

The landmark case came on 7 September 1999, and the decision was unanimous. The court held that:

> . . . a reasonable investigation is necessarily one free of torture, free of cruel, inhuman treatment of the subject and free of any degrading handling whatsoever. There is a prohibition on the use of "brutal or inhuman means" in the course of an investigation. . . . Human dignity also includes the dignity of the suspect being interrogated. . . . This conclusion is in perfect accord with (various) International Law treaties—to which Israel is a signatory—which prohibit the use of torture, "cruel, inhuman treatment" and "degrading treatment." . . . These prohibitions are "absolute." There are no exceptions to them and there is no room for balancing. Indeed, violence directed at a suspect's body or spirit does not constitute a reasonable investigation practice.[89]

The court went on to say that particular practices were not permitted according to these prohibitions:

> . . . we declare that the GSS does not have the authority to "shake" a man, hold him in the "Shabach" position . . . , force him into a "frog crouch" position and deprive him of sleep in a manner other than that which is inherently required by the interrogation.[90]

Initial reactions to the ruling were very optimistic, almost ebullient.[91] The Israeli human rights organization B'Tselem characterized the decision as putting "an end to torture in Israel,"[92] while the Palestinian human rights group LAW declared that the decision "outlawed torture."[93] Once the amazement wore off, reactions to the High Court decision were much more restrained.[94] While certain practices—such as violent shaking, certain painful positions, and prolonged hooding—were declared to be torture by the court, the door was also left open for these issues to be legalized through parliamentary legislation.

It was only a matter of months before conservative members of the Knesset moved to do so. In November 1999 approximately 64 members of the 120-member Israeli parliament introduced a bill specifically authorizing the GSS to use physical pressure in interrogation. The author of the bill acknowledged that the bill would be "introducing torture into the law of the State of Israel" and that the provisions he proposed violated international law and Israel's treaty obligations.[95] As it turns out, however, legislating torture in a democratic forum is politically not very feasible. Antitorture lobbyists turned out in numbers, and the bill did not pass.

What are the larger implications of torture litigation in Israel? The Israeli Supreme Court did not ban torture, as many would have liked to see it do. On the other hand, torture has never been legitimated through a parliamentary decision of the Knesset, despite security threats that might

have made it expedient to do so. Activists and monitors continue to criticize certain aspects of Israel's interrogation practices. And yet, even Israel's critics recognize that practices have improved. Peter Burns of the ten-member UN Committee Against Torture told reporters in 2001 that "There is absolutely no question that the high court ruling has had an impact."[96] * * *

International law played a crucial supporting role in this episode. Mobilization in Israel on the issue of the treatment of detainees followed ratification of the CAT, and used the fact and language of that commitment to articulate an undeniable proposition: Israel was obligated by international convention not to engage in torture. The key problem was that the government disagreed that that is what its agents were doing. And here the convention played another crucial role: It bolstered the judgment that particular practices were beyond the pale. * * *

Conclusions

The ban on torture is the strongest international legal prohibition contained in any human rights treaty. By ratifying the CAT, governments expressly acknowledge that there are no conditions under which the use of severe physical or psychological pain by public authorities is justified. Yet, despite such clear prohibitory language, there is little quantifiable evidence that signing a treaty makes it so. Torture is appallingly widespread. Even if we take into account the likelihood that information on torture has improved over the course of the past two decades, and even if we concede that standards of what constitutes torture may be getting tougher, there are still far too many cases in which governments are willing to ignore or even to condone detainee treatment that is illegally harsh.

The initial evidence casts some doubt on the ability of treaty commitments to alter this basic reality. Indicators of torture seem to have gotten worse over time even as the number of CAT signatories increased. The *unconditional* effects of ratifying the CAT were, if anything, negative, indicating that it is quite common for governments to perform *worse* on this scale once they have ratified the CAT. It is important to reiterate the opening observations * * *: The decentralized and secretive nature of this offense makes it difficult to study, let alone to stop. Some governments practice torture out of self-constructed "necessity," justifying their practices with references to security and the public or national interest.

It is wrong to conclude, however, that the CAT has failed to improve the treatment of government-held detainees. This [analysis] revealed the ability of a treaty commitment to influence positively government behavior in moderately democratic and transitional regimes, of which there are many. Chile is a good example of how this can work out in practice. This [analysis] has also found some impact in countries whose legal systems are at least moderately well equipped to enforce international treaty commitments. Israel is a good example of how this can happen. The main finding * * * is that a CAT commitment significantly improves the treatment of detainees in countries with at least moderate levels of public accountability. CAT ratification resonates in those polities; individuals and groups who may have good reason to fear mistreatment of themselves, their families, their countrymen, or other humans by the government have strong incentives to mobilize to implement the international ban in domestic law. The domestic politics that mobilize around the issue are likely key to the treaty's gaining traction in the local polity.

The factors that drive torture are many, and many are far more important than a treaty commitment. The use of torture can become distressingly embedded in a local culture of brutality and can be very difficult to dislodge. Consistently, the most significant explanation for torture in every model in this [analysis] was practices in past years.

Governments often continue their "law enforcement" efforts as they have for decades, unless demands from a mobilized public begin to elicit a reexamination of policy. Then, too, governments tend to maintain good practices until a national security threat justifies the rougher handling of detainees. It is clear that many factors conspire to create an environment where torture flourishes, from military conflicts to a gagged press.

As Jack Donnelly has written, ". . . the key to change in state practices probably lies not in any one type or forum of activity but in the mobilization of multiple, complementary channels of influence."[97] A treaty commitment has an important role to play in polities where complementary channels of influence—public demands, foreign pressures, powerful and well-respected courts—come together to demand an end to torture. As this [analysis] has shown, that is most likely to be the case in polities that have experienced both public accountability and its breach. For many countries over the course of the past three decades, the CAT has provided a focal norm and a stabilizing standard from which vigilant polities have insisted their governments not retreat.

NOTES

1. Simmons and Hopkins 2005.
2. Chayes and Chayes 1993.
3. Finnemore and Sikkink 1998.
4. Keck and Sikkink 1998.
5. Hathaway 2002.
6. Moravcsik 2000.
7. Some of the practices that the State Department reports have condemned in other countries have, ironically, been approved by the United States in the interrogation of alleged terrorists. See Malinowski 2005.
8. Several books provide an account of the history of torture; see, for example, Dunér 1998.
9. Cingranelli and Richards 1999a.
10. Basoglu 1993.
11. Baker 1992; Kane and Peterson 1995.
12. Cassese 1996.
13. See Ross 2005.
14. Becker and Becker 2001; Donnelly 1998; Worden 2005.
15. Dunér 1998.

16. Sironi and Branche 2002; Slaughter 1997.

17. Walker and Poe 2002.

18. Article 15–16, Investigation of the 800th Military Police Brigade, paragraph 6. Text of the report, investigated under the direction of Maj. Gen. Antonio M. Taguba, can be found at http://www.msnbc.msn.com/id/4894001/ (accessed 30 June 2008).

19. Danner 2004.

20. Wantchekon and Healy 1999.

21. The United Kingdom's report to the Committee Against Torture is criticized by Amnesty International for not acknowledging that authorities had "violated the prohibition against the use of statements obtained through torture as evidence in any proceedings, except against a person accused of torture." See http://web.amnesty.org/library/Index/ENGEUR450292004?open&;of=ENG-GBR (accessed 30 June 2008). The U.S. report to the Committee Against Torture, for example, is criticized by the World Organization for Human Rights USA for "side-step[ping] and downplay[ing] the reality that as a matter of official policy the United States has been encouraging the use of torture of detainees on a systematic and widespread basis, and seeking to justify these major violations of international human rights standards as a necessary tool to combat terrorism." See http://www.humanrightsusa.org/modules.php?op=modload&name=News&file=article&sid=32 [inactive link].

22. Goodman and Jinks 2003.

23. Lutz and Sikkink 2000.

24. UDHR, Article 5.

25. For a discussion of the development of the UN regime with respect to torture, see Clark 2001:37–69.

26. On the role of NGOs in drafting the CAT, see Baehr 1989; Burgers 1989; Burgers and Danelius 1988; Clark 2001; Korey 1998; Lippman 1994; Tolley 1989. Korey describes this campaign as ". . . one of the most successful initiatives ever undertaken by an NGO" (1998:171).

27. See, for example, Leary 1979.

28. UNGA 9 December 1975 (resolution 3452 [XXX]). Text can be found at http://unhchr.ch/html/menu3/b/h_comp38.htm (accessed 23 August 2005).

29. CAT, Article 3.

30. Afghanistan, Argentina, Belgium, Bolivia, Costa Rica, Denmark, Dominican Republic, Ecuador, Finland, France, Greece, Iceland, Italy, Luxembourg, Netherlands, Norway, Panama, Portugal, Senegal, Spain, Sweden, Switzerland, United Kingdom, Uruguay, and Venezuela.

31. CAT, Article 1, para. 1.

32. On the other hand, the Tokyo declaration, adopted by the World Medical Association in 1975, defines torture as ". . . the deliberate, systematic, or wanton infliction of physical or mental suffering by one or more persons acting alone or on the orders of any authority, to force another person to yield information, to make a confession, or for any other reason." World Medical Association Declaration Guidelines for Medical Doctors Concerning Torture and Other Cruel, Inhuman, or Degrading Treatment or Punishment in Relation to Detention and Imprisonment (Declaration of Tokyo). Adopted by the 29th World Medical Assembly, Tokyo, Japan, October 1975.

33. CAT, Article 2.2. Text of the CAT can be found at http://www.hrweb.org/legal/cat.html.

34. CAT, Article 2.3. For a defense of the nonderogable nature of this prohibition, see Lukes 2006.

35. CAT, Article 5. Sweden and a group of NGOs—notably the International Association of Penal Law and the ICJ—were especially influential in including universal jurisdiction language in the CAT. See Burgers and Danelius 1988; Hawkins 2004; Rodley 1999.

36. Bosco 2000.

37. See Solomon 2001.

38. On the importance of universal jurisdiction in the CAT, see Boulesbaa 1999; Hawkins 2004; Rodley 1999.

39. Declarations can be found at http://www.unhchr.ch/html/menu2/6/cat/treaties/convention-reserv.htm (accessed 30 June 2008).

40. CAT, Article 22.

41. Statistics (current as of 30 April 2004) on individual complaints under Article 22 can be found at http://www.unhchr.ch/html/menu2/8/stat3.htm (accessed 30 June 2008).

42. Keith 1999.

43. Hathaway 2002:1988.

44. Goodman and Jinks 2003.

45. A point made by many observers of NGO priorities and the CAT ratification record; see Claude and Weston 1992; Forsythe 1985; van Boven 1989–1990.

46. See, for example, the discussion regarding the desire to influence others to sign as a motivation in Ratner 2004.

47. Jennings 1999.

48. For a discussion of how the U.S. Department of State reports are compiled, see De Neufville 1986; Valencia-Weber and Weber 1986.

49. For a detailed discussion of the criteria used, see Hathaway 2002. These categories are greatly preferable to counting instances of torture or abuse, which several researchers have noted give a false [sense] of accuracy; see Goldstein 1986; Stohl et al. 1986. The use of this scale comports with Thomas Pogge's notion of individuals' right to institutions that secure access to a particular right. Pogge asserts, for example, that whether an individual enjoys the human right against torture turns not on whether the individual is actually tortured, but rather on the probability that that individual will be tortured under the prevailing social conditions, which are roughly what this scale captures (2002:65).

50. Hathaway's (2002) coders also looked for terms such as "repeated," "methodical," "routine," and "frequent."

51. Common law countries are much less likely to ratify a human rights treaty * * *, but they are no more or less likely to engage in torture. In fact, common law countries average 2.3 on the torture scale, while all other counties average 2.2—a statistically indistinguishable and substantively insignificant difference.

52. On the role of the press generally in exposing human rights abuses, see Husarska 2000.

53. Bronkhorst 1995; Hayner 1994, 2001.

54. Sironi and Branche 2002.

55. For an excellent book on the French use of and justification for torture during the Algerian War, see Maran 1989.

56. See, for example, Apodaca 2001; Haas 1994; Hamburg 2000; Ignatieff 2001; Poe and Tate 1994; Poe et al. 1999.

57. For a discussion of these and other "enforcement" mechanisms, see Donnelly 1998. Legal scholars have considered these mechanisms "international secondary soft law"; see Shelton 1997.

58. For a general discussion of these mechanisms, see Tardu 1980. For a case study that provides some evidence that debate and resolutions adopted by the Human Rights Commission under these procedures has had some influence on China, see Kent 1999.

59. This confirms the reported findings in Hathaway 2002.

60. It is important to note, though, that stable democracies still tend to be at the very good end of the torture scale: about 85 percent of stable democracies' torture observations were in the top two categories. Among stable democracies, not a single observation fell in the worst category. Lithuania, Jamaica, and Israel were the only stable democracies to have had more than one observation in the second to the lowest category. Neither Lithuania nor Jamaica had ratified the CAT; Israel, on the other hand, had.

61. For purposes of this test, moderate democracies are those years scoring between 3 and 8 on the polity scale, inclusive. Full autocracies are those that scored 1 or 2, and full democracies are those that scored 9 or 10.

62. Kaufmann et al. 2008:10. See the description at http://papers.ssrn .com/so13/papers.cfm?abstract_id=1148386.

63. The Catholic Church in Chile's role in defending human rights deserves much more attention than can be devoted to it in these pages. In Mara Loveman's words, "The Church as an institution provided a 'moral shield' for human rights work through its domestic influence as a source of legitimacy and its international symbolic, moral, and political weight" (1998:494).

64. Keck and Sikkink 1998.

65. "Demonstrations Mark Human Rights Day in Santiago," Porto Alegre Radio Guiaba, FBIS PY110149. See also "Human Rights Demonstration Prompts Arrest," Santiago Radio Chilena, 10 December 1985. FBIS PY110135.

66. Hawkins 2002:4–5.

67. "Chile: Pinochet Signs OAS and UN Conventions on Torture," BBC Summary of World Broadcasts, 17 September 1988, part 4.

68. This was the view of the Chilean Human Rights Commission, as reported by Shirley Christian. "Violent Scenes as Torture Is Banned," *Sydney Morning Herald* (Australia); source: *New York Times*, 17 September 1988.

69. Brito 1997:110.

70. Brito 1997:120.

71. Hilbink 2007:179–80, fn 6.

72. Brito 1997:102.

73. Brito 1997:108.

74. Hilbink 2007:185.

75. Lutz and Sikkink 2001.

76. The torture scale improves from 3 to 2 in 1999, indicating a move from fairly regularized brutality to cases of isolated incidents.

77. For a discussion of the contents of the Landau Commission Report, see Grosso 2000.

78. In general, the relative openness of the Israeli political system, with its lack of press censorship, meant that many of the most egregious abuses were in fact fairly easy to document. In 1992,

five reports showed that, since the intifada began, between 2,000 and 3,000 detainees had been beaten, hooded, deprived of sleep, or made to stand in boxes no bigger than their bodies for hours. See Caroline Moorehead, "The Court to Rule on Use of Torture in Israel," *The Independent* (London), 21 April 1993; International news, p. 11.

79. Joel Greenberg, "Israel Rethinks Interrogation of Arabs," *New York Times,* Section 1, p. 3, 14 August 1993.

80. Gordon 2004.

81. Hanafi and Tabar 2004.

82. In the summer of 1993, a series of physicians' organizations— including the Israeli Medical Association and the Association of Israeli-Palestinian Physicians for human rights—publicly refused to cooperate with the government in its interrogation practices. See Joel Greenberg, "Israel Rethinks Interrogation of Arabs," *New York Times,* Section 1, p. 3, 14 August 1993.

83. Gordon and Berkovitch n.d.:12.

84. Hajjar 2001:24.

85. *The Economist,* 1 October 1994, p. 58.

86. Derek Brown, "Making Torture Legal," *The Guardian,* foreign page, p. 9, 23 October 1995.

87. Agence France Presse, "Israel to Legalise Use of Force Against Palestinian Prisoners," International news, 23 January 1996.

88. *New York Times,* "UN Panel Rules Israel Uses Torture." 10 May 1997, p. A6.

89. Judgment on the Interrogation Methods applied by the GSS; The Supreme Court of Israel, sitting as the High Court of Justice; Cases H.C. 5100/94, H.C. 4054/95, H.C. 6536/95, H.C. 5188/96, H.C. 7563/97, H.C. 7628/97, H.C. 1043/99, para. 23. Text available at http://www.derechos.org/human-rights/mena/doc /torture.html (accessed 14 August 2008).

90. Id., paragraph 40 (accessed 14 August 2008).

91. "The High Court decision brings an end to an inglorious chapter in Israel's history, in which the state authorized Shin Bet interrogators to use torture methods in their work on the grounds of security needs." *Ha'aretz,* editorial, 7 September 1999. See also Deborah Sontag, "Court Bans Most Use of Force in Interrogations," *New York Times,* 7 September 1999, p. A1.

92. Press Release, B'Tselem, 6 September 1999.

93. LAW, "After 18 Months, Israeli High Court Outlaws Torture," 7 September 1999.

94. St. Amand (1999–2000:683) asserts that the decision was a tiny legal step and notes that there was no explicit reference to the international prohibition contained in the CAT; see also Mandel 1999:313.

95. Aryeh Dayan, "A Ticking Time Bomb in the Knesset: Some 64 MKs Have Signed a Bill Specifically Authorizing the Shin Bet to Use Torture Under Certain Conditions—Despite the Fact That Israel Has Signed an International Treaty Prohibiting It," *Ha'aretz,* 1 November 1999.

96. Peter Capella, "UN Panel Urges Israel to Eliminate Torture." Agence France Presse, 23 November 2001. See also Elizabeth Olson, "Citing Some Progress, U.N. Panel on Torture Urges Israel to Take More Steps," *New York Times,* 24 November 2001, p. A8.

97. Donnelly 1998:85.

REFERENCES

Apodaca, Claire. 2001. Global Economic Patterns and Personal Integrity Rights after the Cold War. *International Studies Quarterly* 45(4): 587–602.

Baehr, P. R. 1989. The General Assembly: Negotiating the Convention on Torture. In *The United Nations in the World Political Economy: Essays in Honour of Leon Gordenker*, edited by David P. Forsythe and Leon Gordenker, 36–53. Basingstoke, England: Macmillan.

Baker, R. 1992. Psychological Consequences for Tortured Refugees Seeking Asylum and Refugee Status in Europe. In *Torture and Its Consequences: Current Treatment Approaches*, edited by Metin Basoglu, 83–106. Cambridge: Cambridge University Press.

Basoglu, Metin. 1993. Prevention of Torture and Care of Survivors: An Integrated Approach. *Journal of the American Medical Association* 270(5): 606–11.

Becker, Lawrence C., and Charlotte B. Becker. 2001. *Encyclopedia of Ethics,* 2nd ed. New York: Routledge.

Bosco, David. 2000. Dictators in the Dock. *The American Prospect*: 14 August 2000, 26–29.

Boulesbaa, Ahcene. 1999. *The U.N. Convention on Torture and the Prospects for Enforcement.* International Studies in Human Rights, V. 51. The Hague: Martinus Nijhoff.

Brito, Alexandra Batahona de. 1997. *Human Rights and Democratization in Latin America: Uruguay and Chile.* Oxford, New York: Oxford University Press.

Bronkhorst, Daan. 1995. *Truth and Reconciliation: Obstacles and Opportunities for Human Rights.* Amsterdam: Amnesty International, Dutch Section.

Burgers, Jan Herman, 1989. An Arduous Delivery: The United Nations Convention against Torture. In *Effective Negotiation: Case Studies in Conference Diplomacy,* edited by Johan Kaufmann, 45–52. Dordrecht, the Netherlands: Martinus Nijhoff.

Burgers, Jan Herman, and Hans Danelius. 1988. *The United Nations Convention Against Torture: A Handbook on the Convention Against Torture and Other Cruel, Inhuman, or Degrading Treatment or Punishment.* Dordrecht, the Netherlands: Martinus Nijhoff.

Cassese, Antonio. 1996. *Inhuman States: Imprisonment, Detention and Torture in Europe Today.* Oxford: Polity Press.

Chayes, Abram, and Antonia Handler Chayes. 1993. On Compliance. *International Organization* 47(2): 175–205.

Cingranelli, David L., and David L. Richards. 1999. Measuring the Level, Pattern, and Sequence of Government Respect for Physical Integrity Rights. *International Studies Quarterly* 43(2): 407–18.

———. 1999b. Respect for Human Rights after the End of the Cold War. *Journal of Peace Research* 36(5): 511–34.

Clark, Ann Marie. 2001. *Diplomacy of Conscience; Amnesty International and Changing Human Rights Norms.* Princeton, NJ: Princeton University Press.

Clark, Melissa. 2000–1. Israel's High Court of Justice Ruling on the General Security Service Use of "Moderate Physical Pressure": An End to the Sanctioned Use of Torture? *Indiana Comparative and International Law Review* 11(1): 145–82.

Claude, Richard Pierre, and Burns H. Weston. 1992. *Human Rights in the World Community: Issues and Action,* 2nd ed. Philadelphia: University of Pennsylvania Press.

Danner, Mark. 2004. *Torture and Truth: America, Abu Ghraib, and the War on Terror.* New York: New York Review of Books.

De Neufville, Judith Innes. 1986. Human Rights Reporting as a Policy Tool—An Examination of the State Department Country Reports. *Human Rights Quarterly* 8(4): 681–99.

Donnelly, Jack. 1998. *International Human Rights,* 2nd ed. Boulder, CO: Westview Press.

Dunér, Bertil, ed. 1998. *An End to Torture: Strategies for Its Eradication.* London, New York: Zed Books; St. Martin's Press.

Finnemore, Martha, and Kathryn Sikkink. 1998. International Norm Dynamics and Political Change. *International Organization* 52(4): 887–918.

Forsythe, David P. 1985. The United Nations and Human Rights. *Political Science Quarterly* 100(2): 249–69.

Goldstein, Judith. 1986. The Political Economy of Trade: Institutions of Protection. *American Political Science Review* 80(1): 161–84.

Goldstein, Robert J. 1986. The Limitations of Using Quantitative Data in Studying Human Rights Abuses. *Human Rights Quarterly* 8(4): 607–27.

Goodman, Ryan, and Derek Jinks. 2003. Measuring the Effects of Human Rights Treaties. *European Journal of International Law* 13:171–83.

Gordon, Neve, ed. 2004. *From the Margins of Globalization: Critical Perspectives on Human Rights.* Lanham, MD: Lexington Books.

Grosso, Catherine M. 2000. International Law in the Domestic Arena: The Case of Torture in Israel. *Iowa Law Review* 86:305–37.

Haas, Michael. 1994. *Improving Human Rights.* Westport, CT: Praeger.

Hajjar, Lisa. 2001. Human Rights in Israel/Palestine: The History and Politics of a Movement. *Journal of Palestine Studies* 30(4): 21–38.

Hamburg, David. 2000. Human Rights and Warfare: An Ounce of Prevention Is Worth a Pound of Cure. In *Realizing Human Rights: Moving from Inspiration to Impact,* edited by Samantha Power and Graham T. Allison, 321–36. New York: St. Martin's Press.

Hanafi, Sari, and Linda Tabar. 2004. Donor Assistance, Rent-Seeking and Elite Formation. In *State Formation in Palestine: Viability and Governance During a Social Transformation*, edited by Mushtaq H. Khan, 215–38. London, New York: Routledge.

Hathaway, Oona. 2002. Do Human Rights Treaties Make a Difference? *Yale Law Journal* III: 1935–2042.

Hawkins, Darren G. 2002. *International Human Rights and Authoritarian Rule in Chile: Human Rights in International Perspective V. 6.* Lincoln: University of Nebraska Press.

———. 2004. Explaining Costly International Institutions: Persuasion and Enforceable Human Rights Norms. *International Studies Quarterly* 48(4): 779–804.

Hayner, Priscilla B. 1994. Fifteen Truth Commissions—1974 to 1994: A Comparative Study. *Human Rights Quarterly* 16(4): 597–655.

———. 2001. *Unspeakable Truths: Confronting State Terror and Atrocity.* New York: Routledge.

Hilbink, Lisa. 2007. *Judges Beyond Politics in Democracy and Dictatorship: Lessons from Chile.* Cambridge: Cambridge University Press.

Husarska, Anna. 2000. "Conscience Trigger": The Press and Human Rights. In *Realizing Human Rights: Moving from Inspiration to Impact,* edited by Samantha Power and Graham T. Allison, 337–50. New York: St. Martin's Press.

Ignatieff, Michael. 2001. Human Rights as Politics. In *Human Rights as Politics and Idolatry,* edited by Michael Ignatieff and Amy Gutmann, 3–52. Princeton, NJ: Princeton University Press.

Jennings, M. Kent. 1999. Political Responses to Pain and Loss. *American Political Science Review* 92(113): 1–13.

Kane, Hal, and Jane A. Peterson. 1995. *The Hour of Departure: Forces That Create Refugees and Migrants.* Worldwatch Paper 125. Washington, DC: Worldwatch Institute.

Kaufmann, Daniel, Aart Kraay, and Massimo Mastruzzi. 2008. *Governance Matters VII: Aggregate and Individual Governance Indicators, 1996–2007.* Washington, DC: World Bank. Available at http://papers.ssrn.com/sol3/papers.cfm?abstract_id=1148386 (accessed 8 June 2009).

Keck, Margaret E., and Kathryn Sikkink. 1998. *Activists Beyond Borders: Advocacy Networks in International Politics.* Ithaca, NY: Cornell University Press.

Keith, Linda Camp. 1999. The United Nations International Covenant on Civil and Political Rights: Does It Make a Difference in Human Rights Behavior? *Journal of Peace Research* 36(1): 95–118.

Kent, Ann. 1999. *China, the United Nations, and Human Rights.* Philadelphia: University of Pennsylvania Press.

Korey, William. 1998. *NGOs and the Universal Declaration of Human Rights: A Curious Grapevine.* New York: St. Martin's Press.

Leary, Virginia A. 1979. A New Role for Non-Governmental Organizations in Human Rights: A Case Study of Non-Governmental Participation in the Development of Norms of Torture. In *UN Law/Fundamental Rights,* edited by Antonio Cassese, 197–210. Alphen aan den Rijn, the Netherlands: Sitjhoff & Noordhoff.

Lippman, Matthew. 1994. The Development and Drafting of the United Nations Convention Against Torture and Other Cruel, Inhuman or Degrading Treatment or Punishment. *Boston College International and Comparative Law Review* 17:275–335.

Loveman, Mara. 1998. High-Risk Collective Action: Defending Human Rights in Chile, Uruguay, and Argentina. *The American Journal of Sociology* 104(2): 477–525.

Lukes, Steven. 2006. Liberal Democratic Torture. *British Journal of Political Science* 36:1–16.

Lutz, Ellen L., and Kathryn Sikkink. 2000. International Human Rights Law and Practice in Latin America. *International Organization* 54(3): 633–59.

———. 2001. The Justice Cascade: The Evolution and Impact of Foreign Human Rights Trials in Latin America. *Chicago Journal of International Law* 2(1): 1–33.

Malinowski, Tom. 2005. Banned State Department Practices. In *Torture: Does It Make Us Safer? Is It Ever OK? A Human Rights Perspective,* edited by Kenneth Roth, Minky Worden, and Amy D. Bernstein, 139–44. New York: New Press.

Mandel, Michael. 1999. Democracy and the New Constitutionalism in Israel. *Israel Law Review* 33(2): 259–321.

Maran, Rita. 1989. *Torture: The Role of Ideology in the French–Algerian War.* New York: Praeger.

Moravcsik, Andrew. 2000. The Origins of Human Rights Regimes: Democratic Delegation in Postwar Europe. *International Organizations* 54(2): 217–52.

Poe, Steven C., and C. Neal Tate. 1994. Repression of Human Rights to Personal Integrity in the 1980s: A Global Analysis. *American Political Science Review* 88(4): 853–72.

Poe, Steven C., Neal Tate, and Linda Camp Keith. 1999. Repression of the Human Right to Personal Integrity Revisited: A Global Crossnational Study Covering the Years 1976–1993. *International Studies Quarterly* 43:291–315.

Pogge, Thomas Winfried Menko. 2002. *World Poverty and Human Rights: Cosmopolitan Responsibilities and Reforms.* Malden, MA: Blackwell.

Ratner, Steven R. 2004. Overcoming Temptations to Violate Human Dignity in Times of Crisis: On the Possibilities for Meaningful Self-Restraint. *Theoretical Inquiries in Law (Online Edition)* 5(1): Article 3. Available at http://www.bepress.com/til/default/vol5/iss1/art3 (accessed 8 June 2009).

Rodley, Nigel S. 1999. *The Treatment of Prisoners Under International Law,* 2nd ed. New York: Oxford University Press.

Ross, James. 2005. A History of Torture. In *Torture: Does It Make Us Safer? Is It Ever OK? A Human Rights Perspective,* edited by Kenneth Roth, Minky Worden, and Amy D. Bernstein, 3–17. New York: New Press. Distributed by W. W. Norton.

Schou, Nina. 2000. Instances of Human Rights Regimes. In *Delegating State Powers: The Effect of Treaty Regimes on Democracy and Sovereignty,* edited by Thomas M. Franck, 209–54. Ardsley, NY: Transnational Publishers.

Shelton, Dinah. 1997. Compliance with International Human Rights Soft Law. In *International Compliance with Nonbinding Accords,* edited by Edith Brown Weiss, 119–43. Washington, DC: American Society of International Law.

Simmons, Beth A., and Daniel J. Hopkins. 2005. The Constraining Power of International Treaties: Theory and Methods. *American Political Science Review* 99(4): 623–31.

Sironi, Francoise, and Raphaelle Branche. 2002. Torture and the Borders of Humanity. *International Social Science Journal* 54(174): 539–48.

Slaughter, Joseph. 1997. A Question of Narration: The Voice in International Human Rights Law. *Human Rights Quarterly* 19(2): 406–30.

Solomon, Aaron. 2001. The Politics of Prosecutions Under the Convention Against Torture. *Chicago Journal of International Law* 20(2): 309–13.

St. Amand, Matthew G. 1999–2000. Public Committee Against Torture in *Israel v. The State of Israel et al.:* Landmark Human Rights Decision by the Israeli High Court of Justice or Status Quo Maintained? *North Carolina Journal of International and Comparative Regulation* 25:655–84.

Stohl, Michael, David Carleton, George A. Lopez, and Stephen Samuels. 1986. State Violation of Human Rights: Issues and Problems of Measurement. *Human Rights Quarterly* 8(4): 592–606.

Tardu, Maxime. 1980. United Nations Responses to Gross Violations of Human Rights: The 1503 Procedure. *Santa Clara Law Review* 20:559.

Tolley, Howard. 1989. Popular Sovereignty and International Law—ICJ Strategies for Human Rights Standard Setting. *Human Rights Quarterly* 11(4): 561–85.

USIP. 2001a. *U.S. Human Rights Policy toward Africa.* Washington, DC: United States Institute of Peace.

———. 2001b. *U.S. Human Rights Policy toward Latin America.* Washington, DC: United States Institute of Peace.

Valencia-Weber, Gloria, and Robert J. Weber. 1986. El-Salvador: Methods Used to Document Human-Rights Violations. *Human Rights Quarterly* 8(4): 731–70.

van Boven, Theo. 1989–1990. The Role of Non-Governmental Organizations in International Human Rights Standard Setting: A Prerequisite of Democracy. *California Western International Law Journal* 20(2): 207–25.

Walker, Scott, and Steven C. Poe. 2002. Does Cultural Diversity Affect Countries' Respect for Human Rights? *Human Rights Quarterly* 24(1): 237–63.

Wantchekon, Leonard, and Andrew Healy. 1999. The "Game" of Torture. *Journal of Conflict Resolution* 43(5): 596–609.

Worden, Minky. 2005. Torture Spoken Here: Ending Global Torture. In *Torture: Does It Make Us Safer? Is It Ever OK? A Human Rights Perspective,* edited by Kenneth Roth, Minky Worden, and Amy D. Bernstein, 79–105. New York: New Press.

Kenneth Roth

DEFENDING ECONOMIC, SOCIAL, AND CULTURAL RIGHTS

Practical Issues Faced by an International Human Rights Organization

Over the last decade, many have urged international human rights organizations to pay more attention to economic, social and cultural (ESC) rights. I agree with this prescription, and for several years Human Rights Watch has been doing significant work in this realm.[1] However, many who urge international groups to take on ESC rights have a fairly simplistic sense of how this is done. Human Rights Watch's experience has led me to believe that there are certain types of ESC issues for which our methodology works well and others for which it does not. In my view, understanding this distinction is key for an international human rights organization such as Human Rights Watch to address ESC rights effectively. Other approaches may work for other types of human rights groups, but organizations such as Human Rights Watch that rely foremost on shaming and the generation of public pressure to defend rights should remain attentive to this distinction.

During the Cold War, ESC rights tended to be debated in ideological terms. This consisted of the West stressing civil and political rights while the Soviet bloc (in principle if not in practice) stressed ESC rights. Many in the West went so far as to deny the very legitimacy of ESC issues as rights. Aryeh Neier, the former head of Human Rights Watch and now the president of the Open Society Institute, is perhaps the leading proponent of this view—most recently in his memoirs, *Taking Liberties*.[2] Certainly, interesting philosophical debates can be had about whether the concept of human rights should embrace positive as well as negative rights.[3] Since consensus in such debates is probably unattainable, the international human rights movement, in my view, has no choice but to rest on a positive-law justification for its work. That is, unless there are concrete and broadly understandable reasons to deviate from existing law, we must defend human rights law largely as written if we are to have any legitimacy and force to our work. That law, of course, codifies civil and political as well as ESC rights.[4]

That said, I must admit to finding the typical discussion of ESC rights rather sterile. I have been to countless conferences and debates in which advice is freely offered about how international human rights organizations must do more to protect ESC rights. Fair enough. Usually, the advice reduces to little more than sloganeering. People lack medical care; therefore, we should say that their right to health has been violated. People lack shelter; therefore, we should say that their right to housing has been violated. People are hungry; therefore, we should say that their right to food has been violated. Such "analysis," of course, wholly ignores such key issues as who is responsible for the impoverished state of a population, whether

From *Human Rights Quarterly* 26, no. 1 (February 2004): 63–73.

the government in question is taking steps to progressively realize the relevant rights, and what the remedy should be for any violation that is found. More to the point, for our purposes, it also ignores which issues can effectively be taken up by international human rights organizations that rely on shaming and public pressure and which cannot.

There are obviously various ways to promote ESC rights. One way is simply to encourage people to insist on respect for these rights. The language of rights can be a powerful organizing tool. But given that respect for ESC rights often requires the reallocation of resources, the people who have the clearest standing to insist on a particular allocation are usually the residents of the country in question. Outsiders such as international human rights organizations are certainly free to have a say in such matters. In an imperfect world in which the fulfillment of one ESC right is often at the expense of another, however, their voice insisting on a particular tradeoff has less legitimacy than that of the country's residents. Why should outsiders be listened to when they counsel, for example, that less be spent on health care and more on education—or even that less be spent on roads, bridges or other infrastructure deemed important for long-term economic development, and more on immediate needs?

I would suggest that merely advocating greater respect for ESC rights—simply adding our voice to that of many others demanding a particular allocation of scarce resources—is not a terribly effective role for international human rights groups such as Human Rights Watch. By expending our accumulated moral capital, we may well be listened to more than others in the short term, but that moral capital does not accumulate through our voice alone (why should our opinion count more than others?) but through our investigative and reporting methodology. It is a finite resource that can dissipate rapidly if not grounded in our methodological strength.

I am aware that similar tradeoffs of scarce resources can arise in the realm of civil and political rights. Building prisons or creating a judicial system can be expensive. However, my experience has been that international human rights organizations implicitly recognize these tradeoffs by avoiding recommendations that are costly. For example, Human Rights Watch in its work on prison conditions routinely avoids recommending large infrastructure investments. Instead, we focus on improvements in the treatment of prisoners that would involve relatively inexpensive policy changes.[5] Similarly, our advocacy of due process in places such as Rwanda with weak and impoverished judicial systems implicitly takes account of the practical limitations facing the country leading us to be more tolerant of prosecutorial compromises such as *gacaca* courts than we would be in a richer country.[6]

A second way to promote ESC rights is through litigation—or, of greater relevance to most countries, by promoting the legislation that would make it possible to enforce ESC rights in court. It is clearly in the interest of those who believe in ESC rights that these rights be codified in enforceable national law. Many countries have such laws in various forms—be they guarantees of a minimum level of income (minimum wage or welfare), food, housing, or health care—but too many countries do not. International human rights organizations might press governments to adopt the legislation— the statutory rights—needed to make litigation a meaningful tool to enforce ESC rights. That is inevitably useful, but it is a procedural device that still falls significantly short of actual implementation. When it comes to deciding which ESC rights should be implemented first, or which tradeoffs among competing economic demands should be made, the advocacy of legislation does not give international human rights organizations any greater standing to address the concrete realization of ESC rights.

Similar shortcomings plague efforts by international human rights organizations to press governments to adopt national plans to progressively realize ESC rights.[7] Even though such plans would facilitate enforcement through public shaming for failure to live up to the plan, the international human rights movement is poorly placed to insist on the specifics of the plan.

Another way to promote ESC rights is by providing technical assistance to governments. Many development organizations perform this service, and presumably international human rights organizations could as well. But as in the realm of civil and political rights, technical assistance works only when governments have the will to respect ESC rights but lack the means or know-how to do so. This assistance thus is ill-suited to address the most egregious cases of ESC rights abuse—the area where, as in the civil and political rights realm, international human rights organizations would presumably want to focus. Indeed, the provision of technical assistance to a government that lacks a good-faith desire to respect rights can be counter-productive by providing a facade of conscientious striving that enables a government to deflect pressure to end abusive practices.

In my view, the most productive way for international human rights organizations, like Human Rights Watch, to address ESC rights is by building on the power of our methodology. The essence of that methodology, as I have suggested, is not the ability to mobilize people in the streets, to engage in litigation, to press for broad national plans, or to provide technical assistance. Rather, the core of our methodology is our ability to investigate, expose, and shame. We are at our most effective when we can hold governmental (or, in some cases, nongovernmental) conduct up to a disapproving public. Of course, we do not have to wait passively for public morality to coalesce on a particular issue; we can do much to shape public views by exposing sympathetic cases of injustice and suggesting a moral analysis for understanding them. In the end, the principal power of groups like Human Rights Watch is our ability to hold official conduct up to scrutiny and to generate public outrage. The relevant public is best when it is a local one—that is, the public of the country in question. Surrogate publics can also be used if they have the power to shape the policies of a government or institution with influence over the officials in question, such as by conditioning international assistance or trade benefits, imposing sanctions, or pursuing prosecution.

Although there are various forms of public outrage, only certain types are sufficiently targeted to shame officials into action. That is, the public might be outraged about a state of affairs—for example, poverty in a region—but have no idea whom to blame. Or it might feel that blame is dispersed among a wide variety of actors. In such cases of diffuse responsibility, the stigma attached to any person, government, or institution is lessened, and with it the power of international human rights organizations to effect change. Similarly, stigma weakens even in the case of a single violator if the remedy to a violation—what the government should do to correct it—is unclear.

In my view, to shame a government effectively—to maximize the power of international human rights organizations like Human Rights Watch—clarity is needed around three issues: violation, violator, and remedy. We must be able to show persuasively that a particular state of affairs amounts to a violation of human rights standards, that a particular violator is principally or significantly responsible, and that a widely accepted remedy for the violation exists. If any of these three elements is missing, our capacity to shame is greatly diminished. We tend to take these conditions for granted in the realm of civil and political rights because they usually coincide. For example, one can quibble about whether a particular form of mistreatment rises to the level of torture, but once a reasonable case is made that torture has occurred, it is fairly easy to determine the violator (the torturer as well as the governments or institutions that permit the torturer to operate with impunity) and the remedy (clear directions to stop torture, prosecution to back these up, and various prophylactic measures, such as ending incommunicado detention).

In the realm of ESC rights, the three preconditions for effective shaming operate much more independently. (For these purposes, I exclude the right to form labor unions and bargain collectively since while codified in the International Covenant on Economic, Social and Cultural Rights (ICESCR), this right functions more as a subset of the civil and political right to freedom of association.)[8] I accept, for the sake of this argument, that indicia have been developed for subsistence levels of food, housing, medical care, education, etc.[9] When steady progress is not being made toward realizing these subsistence levels, one can presumptively say that a "violation" has occurred.

But who is responsible for the violation, and what is the remedy? These answers flow much less directly from the mere documentation of an ESC rights violation than they do in the civil and political rights realm. For example, does responsibility for a substandard public health system lie with the government (through its corruption or mismanagement) or with the international community (through its stinginess or indifference). If the latter, which part of the international community? The answer is usually all of the above, which naturally reduces the potential to stigmatize any single actor.

Similar confusion surrounds discussions of appropriate remedies. Vigorously contested views about "structural adjustment" are illustrative. Is structural adjustment the cause of poverty, through its forced slashing of public investment in basic needs, or is it the solution by laying the groundwork for economic development? Supporting evidence can be found on both sides of this debate. When the target of a shaming effort can marshal respectable arguments in its defense, shaming usually fails.

The lesson I draw from these observations is that when international human rights organizations such as Human Rights Watch take on ESC rights,

we should look for situations in which there is relative clarity about violation, violator, and remedy.

Broadly speaking, I would suggest that the nature of the violation, violator, and remedy is clearest when it is possible to identify arbitrary or discriminatory governmental conduct that causes or substantially contributes to an ESC rights violation. These three dimensions are less clear when the ESC shortcoming is largely a problem of distributive justice. If all an international human rights organization can do is argue that more money be spent to uphold an ESC right—that a fixed economic pie be divided differently—our voice is relatively weak. We can argue that money should be diverted from less acute needs to the fulfillment of more pressing ESC rights, but little reason exists for a government to give our voice greater weight than domestic voices. On the other hand, if we can show that the government (or other relevant actor) is contributing to the ESC shortfall through arbitrary or discriminatory conduct, we are in a relatively powerful position to shame: we can show a violation (the rights shortfall), the violator (the government or other actor through its arbitrary or discriminatory conduct), and the remedy (reversing that conduct).

What does this mean in practice? To illustrate, let us assume we could demonstrate that a government was building medical clinics only in areas populated by ethnic groups that tended to vote for it, leaving other ethnic groups with substandard medical care. In such a case, an international human rights organization would be in a good position to argue that the disfavored ethnic groups' right to health care is being denied. This argument does not necessarily increase the resources being made available for health care, but it at least ensures a more equitable distribution. Since defenders of ESC rights should be concerned foremost with the worst-off segments of society, that redistribution would be an advance. Moreover, given that the government's supporters are not likely to be happy about a cutback in medical care, enforcement of a nondiscriminatory approach stands a reasonable chance of increasing health-related resources overall.

To cite another example, imagine a government that refuses to apply available resources for the benefit of its population's health. (South African President Thebo Mbeki's long refusal to allow donated nevirapine or AZT to be given to HIV-infected mothers to prevent mother-to-child transmission of the disease comes to mind.) A credible case can be made that such a government is acting arbitrarily—that it is not making a sincere effort to deploy available resources to progressively realize the ESC rights of its people. Again, by investigating and exposing this arbitrary conduct, an international human rights organization would have all the elements it needs to maximize the impact of its shaming methodology—a violation (the ESC shortcoming), a violator (the government acting arbitrarily), and the remedy (end the arbitrary conduct). Once more, there is no need to argue for more money to be spent or for a different allocation of available money (areas where there is little special power to the voice of international rights organizations), since in the case of arbitrary conduct the money is available but is being clearly misspent.

To cite yet another example, Human Rights Watch recently investigated conditions facing child farm workers in the United States. Had we been forced to delve into details about the appropriate maximum level of danger or pesticide exposure, or the appropriate number of working hours per day, we would have been in the amorphous realm of costs and benefits and thus lacked the clarity needed for effective shaming. However, we were able to show that child farm workers stand virtually alone in being excluded from the laws regulating working conditions for children in the United States. In making this revelation, we were able to demonstrate that U.S. laws governing child farm workers were both arbitrary (the exception was written in an era when the family farm was predominant; it has little relevance to the agribusiness that typifies the field today) and discriminatory (most of the parents of today's farmworker children are immigrants, politically an easy category to ignore).[10]

Education has been a productive area for this approach as well. For example, Human Rights Watch has been able to show that governments' failure to address violence against certain students (girls in South Africa, gays and lesbians in the United States) or bonded child labor (in India and Egypt) discriminatorily deprives these disfavored children of their right to education.[11]

If one accepts that international human rights organizations like Human Rights Watch are at our most powerful in the realm of ESC rights when we focus on discriminatory or arbitrary conduct rather than matters of pure distributive justice, guidance for our ESC work is provided. An important part of our work should be to shape public opinion gradually so that it tends to see ESC issues not only in terms of distributive justice but also in terms of discriminatory or arbitrary conduct. For example, governments' failure to provide universal primary education would seem to be a classic case of distributive justice—there is not enough money to go around, so governments cannot provide education to all children. Human Rights Watch is considering a project that would focus on the practice of funding education in such circumstances through school fees. We would hope to argue that this is a discriminatory and arbitrary way of funding education because it has the foreseeable effect of excluding children from poor families. If we succeed in promoting this perspective, we hope to transform the debate from one on which international human rights organizations have had little if any impact to one in which our ability to stigmatize and hence shape public policy on education would be much enhanced.

We used the same approach to highlight the neglect of "AIDS orphans" in Kenya. The provision of care for children without parents, while classically a state responsibility, is frequently limited by scarce resources. In Kenya, as in many African countries, the responsibility was typically delegated to, and accepted by, the extended family. However, given the devastation of the AIDS crisis, extended families increasingly are unable to bear this burden, leaving many of these orphans destitute. By demonstrating that the classic state approach to the problem had become arbitrary (it was no longer working in light of the AIDS pandemic) and discriminatory (it falls on a group of people who are already stigmatized, AIDS-affected families), Human Rights Watch succeeded in generating significant pressure on the Kenyan government and international organizations to recognize and address the problem.[12]

Similar efforts might be made to address issues of corruption. For example, if it can be shown that government officials are pocketing scarce public resources or wasting them on self-aggrandizing projects rather than meeting ESC needs, international human rights organizations can use our shaming capacity to enlarge the size of the economic pie without entering into more detailed discussions about how that pie should be divided to realize ESC rights.

In making these observations, I recognize that there are certain realms where international human rights organizations might be able to take on distributive justice questions more directly. If the issue is not how a foreign government divides a limited economic pie, but rather how much money a Northern government or an international financial institution spends on international assistance for the realization of ESC rights, Northern-based international human rights organizations speak less as an outside voice and more as a domestic constituent. Even then, given our relative weakness at mobilizing large numbers of people at this stage in our evolution, pressure simply to spend more, rather than stigmatization over arbitrary or discriminatory spending, is less likely to resonate with

decision makers. That is all the more true when Northern governments point to the failure of many needy governments to establish sufficient transparency and public accountability to reasonably assure that international assistance will be well spent. As noted, the international human rights movement's ability to shame diminishes significantly if the target has a credible rebuttal.

To conclude, let me offer a hypothesis about the conduct of international human rights organizations working on ESC rights. It has been clear for many years that the movement would like to do more in the ESC realm. Yet despite repeated professions of interest, its work in this area remains limited. Part of the reason, of course, is expertise; the movement must staff itself somewhat differently to document shortfalls in such matters as health or housing than to record instances of torture or political imprisonment. But much of the reason, I suspect, is a sense of futility. International human rights activists see how little impact they have in taking on matters of pure distributive justice so they have a hard time justifying devoting scarce institutional resources for such limited ends. However, if we focus our attention on ESC policy that can fairly be characterized as arbitrary or discriminatory, I believe our impact will be substantially larger. And there is nothing like success to breed emulation.

Thus, when outsiders ask international human rights organizations such as Human Rights Watch to expand our work on ESC rights, we should insist on a more sophisticated and realistic conversation than has been typical so far. It is not enough, we should point out, to document ESC shortcomings and to declare a rights violation. Rather, we should ask our interlocutors to help us identify ESC shortcomings in which there is relative clarity about the nature of the violation, violator, and remedy, so that our shaming methodology will be most effective. As we succeed in broadening the number of governmental actions that can be seen in this way, we will go a long way toward enhancing the ESC work of the international human rights movements—work that, we all realize, is essential to our credibility.

Coincidentally, international development and humanitarian organizations are increasingly adopting the view that poverty and severe deprivation is a product less of a lack of public goods than of officially promoted or tolerated policies of social exclusion. That insight meshes well with the approach I have outlined for promoting ESC rights. A lack of public goods tends to be a matter of distributive justice. In ESC right terms, however, policies of social exclusion tend to have a relatively clear violation, violator, and remedy. If development and humanitarian organizations indeed move in this direction, it portends useful partnerships with international human rights organizations such as Human Rights Watch.

NOTES

1. *See* the Human Rights Watch website on Economic, Social, and Cultural Rights at www.hrw.org/esc.
2. Aryeh Neier, Taking Liberties: Four Decades in the Struggle for Rights xxix–xxx (2003).
3. See Isaiah Berlin, Four Essays on Liberty 122–34 (1969) for more on the concepts of positive and negative freedom. See also, e.g., Amartya Sen, Development as Freedom (1999); Martha Nussbaum, Women and Human Development: The Capabilities Approach (2000) (discussing this debate within a contemporary human rights framework).
4. See International Covenant on Civil and Political Rights, adopted 16 Dec. 1966, G.A. Res. 2200 (XXI), U.N. GAOR, 21st Sess., Supp. No. 16, U.N. Doc. A/6316 (1966), 999 U.N.T.S. 171 (entered into force 23 Mar 1976); International Covenant on Economic, Social, and Cultural Rights, adopted 16 Dec. 1966, G.A. Res. 2200 (XXI), U.N. GAOR, 21st Sess., Supp. No. 16, U.N. Doc. A/6316 (1966), 993 U.N.T.S. 3 (entered into force 3 Jan. 1976) (hereinafter ICESCR); see also Universal Declaration of Human Rights, adopted 10 Dec. 1948, G.A. Res. 217A (III), U.N. GAOR, 3d Sess. (Resolutions, part 1), at 71, U.N. Doc. A/810 (1948), reprinted in 43 *Am. J. Int'l L.* Supp. 127 (1949).
5. See, e.g., Human Rights Watch, Prison Conditions in South Africa (1994); Human Rights Watch, Out of Sight: Super-Maximum Security Confinement in the United States Vol. 12 (2000); Human Rights Watch, Prison Conditions in Japan (1995); Human Rights Watch, Prison Conditions in Czechoslovakia (1989); Human Rights Watch, Prison Conditions in Czechoslovakia: An Update (1991); Human Rights Watch, Prison Conditions in Poland: An Update (1988); Human Rights Watch, Prison Conditions in Poland: An Update (1991).
6. See, e.g., Press Release, Human Rights Watch, Rwanda: Elections May Speed Genocide Trials: But New System Lacks Guarantees of Rights (4 Oct. 2001) available at www.hrw.org/press/2001/10/rwanda1004.
7. *See* ICESCR, *supra* note 4, art. 2:
   > Each State Party to the present Covenant undertakes to take steps, individually and through international assistance and co-operation, especially economic and technical, to the maximum of its available resources, with a view to achieving progressively the full realization of the rights recognized in the present Covenant by all appropriate means, including particularly the adoption of legislative measures.

   See also General Comment No. 3, Comm. on Econ., Soc. Cultural Rts., 5th Sess., Annex III, UN Doc. E/1991/23 (1990) (interpreting the meaning of the progressive-realization requirement).
8. See ICESCR, *supra* note 4.
9. See, e.g., Masstricht Guidelines on Violations of Economic, Social and Cultural Rights, adopted 22–26 Jan. 1997, reprinted in The Masstricht Guidelines on Violations of Economic, Social and Cultural Rights, 20 *Hum. Rts. Q.* 691 (1998); The Limburg Principles on the Implementation of the International Covenant on Economic, Social and Cultural Rights, adopted 8 Jan. 1987, U.N. ESCOR, Comm'n on Hum. Rts., 43rd Sess., Agenda Item 8, U.N. Doc. E/CN.4/1987/17/Annex (1987), reprinted in The Limburg Principles on the Implementation of the International Covenant on Economic, Social and Cultural Rights, 9 *Hum. Rts. Q.* 122 (1987); Draft Guidelines: A Human Rights Approach to Poverty Reduction Strategies, adopted 10 Oct. 2002, U.N. OHCHR.
10. Human Rights Watch, Fingers to the Bone: United States Failure to Protect Child Farmworkers 55–73 (2000).
11. Human Rights Watch, Hatred in the Hallways: Violence and Discrimination Against Lesbian, Gay, Bisexual, and Transgender Students in U.S. Schools 3–7 (2001); Press Release, Human Rights Watch, South Africa: Sexual Violence Rampant in Schools: Harassment and Rape Hampering Girls' Education (27 Mar. 2001) available at www.hrw.org/press/2001/03/sa–0327; Human Rights Watch, Underage and Unprotected: Child Labor in Egypt's Cotton Fields (2001); Human Rights Watch, The Small Hands of Slavery: Bonded Child Labor in India 14–19 (1996).
12. Human Rights Watch, In the Shadow of Death: HIV/AIDS and Children's Rights in Kenya (2001).

11 HUMAN SECURITY: MIGRATION, GLOBAL HEALTH, AND THE ENVIRONMENT

Reflecting the worldwide interconnectedness that is now called "globalization," transnational concerns have become part of the global agenda. Such concerns include the environment, pollution, population, health, and international crime. For many transnational issues, the interests, rights, and responsibilities of the individual, the state, and the international community may be incompatible or even diverge. Do the rights of the individual take precedence over the rights of the community in the use of land and natural resources? Does a couple have the right of unlimited procreation when resources are limited? In his pathbreaking 1968 article, Garrett Hardin posits in unequivocal terms that the pursuit of individual interests may not necessarily lead to the common good.

Climate change is a quintessential example of a "tragedy of the commons." The whole earth is affected, and the efforts of people and governments worldwide are needed to solve the problem. Scott Barrett asks, "Why Have Climate Negotiations Proved So Disappointing?" (2015). He argues that the temptation of states to "free ride" on the efforts of others is exacerbated by the high cost of the remedies, uncertainty about the point at which the climate will tip to disaster, and the difficulty of organizing reciprocity when cooperation of many stakeholders is needed. Barrett thinks the successful Montreal agreement banning gases that deplete the atmosphere's ozone layer offers a model of how to create incentives to limit carbon emissions that cause global climate change.

Global problems may also be caused by misguided social practices. Valerie M. Hudson and Hilary Matfess trace how, under conditions of economic and demographic change, traditions such as brideprice—the payments a groom must make to a bride's family—can constrict marriage opportunities for young men, in turn creating a disgruntled, socially disconnected pool of recruits for terrorism. Kate Cronin-Furman discusses the reasons for the persecution and expulsion of Myanmar's Muslim Rohingya minority. These atrocities were doubly shocking to observers in the West because they took place on the watch of the newly elected leader and Nobel Peace Prize winner Aung San Suu Kyi, erstwhile darling of the international human rights and democracy-promotion community.

Garrett Hardin

THE TRAGEDY OF THE COMMONS

The population problem has no technical solution; it requires a fundamental extension in morality.

At the end of a thoughtful article on the future of nuclear war, Wiesner and York[1] concluded that: "Both sides in the arms race are . . . confronted by the dilemma of steadily increasing military power and steadily decreasing national security. *It is our considered professional judgment that this dilemma has no technical solution.* If the great powers continue to look for solutions in the area of science and technology only, the result will be to worsen the situation."

I would like to focus your attention not on the subject of the article (national security in a nuclear world) but on the kind of conclusion they reached, namely that there is no technical solution to the problem. An implicit and almost universal assumption of discussions published in professional and semipopular scientific journals is that the problem under discussion has a technical solution. A technical solution may be defined as one that requires a change only in the techniques of the natural sciences, demanding little or nothing in the way of change in human values or ideas of morality.

In our day (though not in earlier times) technical solutions are always welcome. Because of previous failures in prophecy, it takes courage to assert that a desired technical solution is not possible. Wiesner and York exhibited this courage; publishing in a science journal, they insisted that the solution to the problem was not to be found in the natural sciences. They cautiously qualified their

statement with the phrase, "It is our considered professional judgment. . . ." Whether they were right or not is not the concern of the present article. Rather, the concern here is with the important concept of a class of human problems which can be called "no technical solution problems," and, more specifically, with the identification and discussion of one of these.

It is easy to show that the class is not a null class. Recall the game of tick-tack-toe. Consider the problem, "How can I win the game of tick-tack-toe?" It is well known that I cannot, if I assume (in keeping with the conventions of game theory) that my opponent understands the game perfectly. Put another way, there is no "technical solution" to the problem. I can win only by giving a radical meaning to the word "win." I can hit my opponent over the head; or I can drug him; or I can falsify the records. Every way in which I "win" involves, in some sense, an abandonment of the game, as we intuitively understand it. (I can also, of course, openly abandon the game—refuse to play it. This is what most adults do.)

The class of "No technical solution problems" has members. My thesis is that the "population problem," as conventionally conceived, is a member of this class. How it is conventionally conceived needs some comment. It is fair to say that most people who anguish over the population problem are trying to find a way to avoid the evils of overpopulation without relinquishing any of the privileges they now enjoy. They think that farming the seas or developing new strains of wheat will solve the problem—technologically. I try to show here that the solution they seek cannot be found. The population problem cannot be solved

From *Science* 162, no. 3859 (Dec. 13, 1968), 1243–48.

in a technical way, any more than can the problem of winning the game of tick-tack-toe.

What Shall We Maximize?

Population, as Malthus said, naturally tends to grow "geometrically," or, as we would now say, exponentially. In a finite world this means that the per capita share of the world's goods must steadily decrease. Is ours a finite world?

A fair defense can be put forward for the view that the world is infinite; or that we do not know that it is not. But, in terms of the practical problems that we must face in the next few generations with the foreseeable technology, it is clear that we will greatly increase human misery if we do not, during the immediate future, assume that the world available to the terrestrial human population is finite. "Space" is no escape.[2]

A finite world can support only a finite population; therefore, population growth must eventually equal zero. (The case of perpetual wide fluctuations above and below zero is a trivial variant that need not be discussed.) When this condition is met, what will be the situation of mankind? Specifically, can Bentham's goal of "the greatest good for the greatest number" be realized?

No—for two reasons, each sufficient by itself. The first is a theoretical one. It is not mathematically possible to maximize for two (or more) variables at the same time. This was clearly stated by von Neumann and Morgenstern,[3] but the principle is implicit in the theory of partial differential equations, dating back at least to D'Alembert (1717–1783).

The second reason springs directly from biological facts. To live, any organism must have a source of energy (for example, food). This energy is utilized for two purposes: mere maintenance and work. For man, maintenance of life requires about 1600 kilo-calories a day ("maintenance calories"). Anything that he does over and above merely staying alive will be defined as work, and is supported by "work calories" which he takes in. Work calories are used not only for what we call work in common speech; they are also required for all forms of enjoyment, from swimming and automobile racing to playing music and writing poetry. If our goal is to maximize population it is obvious what we must do: We must make the work calories per person approach as close to zero as possible. No gourmet meals, no vacations, no sports, no music, no literature, no art. . . . I think that everyone will grant, without argument or proof, that maximizing population does not maximize goods. Bentham's goal is impossible.

In reaching this conclusion I have made the usual assumption that it is the acquisition of energy that is the problem. The appearance of atomic energy has led some to question this assumption. However, given an infinite source of energy, population growth still produces an inescapable problem. The problem of the acquisition of energy is replaced by the problem of its dissipation, as J. H. Fremlin has so wittily shown.[4] The arithmetic signs in the analysis are, as it were, reversed; but Bentham's goal is still unobtainable.

The optimum population is, then, less than the maximum. The difficulty of defining the optimum is enormous; so far as I know, no one has seriously tackled this problem. Reaching an acceptable and stable solution will surely require more than one generation of hard analytical work—and much persuasion.

We want the maximum good per person; but what is good? To one person it is wilderness, to another it is ski lodges for thousands. To one it is estuaries to nourish ducks for hunters to shoot; to another it is factory land. Comparing one good with another is, we usually say, impossible because goods are incommensurable. Incommensurables cannot be compared.

Theoretically this may be true; but in real life incommensurables *are* commensurable. Only a criterion of judgment and a system of weighting are needed. In nature the criterion is survival. Is it better for a species to be small and hide-able, or large and powerful? Natural selection commensurates the incommensurables. The compromise achieved depends on a natural weighting of the values of the variables.

Man must imitate this process. There is no doubt that in fact he already does, but unconsciously. It is when the hidden decisions are made explicit that the arguments begin. The problem for the years ahead is to work out an acceptable theory of weighting. Synergistic effects, nonlinear variation, and difficulties in discounting the future make the intellectual problem difficult, but not (in principle) insoluble.

Has any cultural group solved this practical problem at the present time, even on an intuitive level? One simple fact proves that none has: there is no prosperous population in the world today that has, and has had for some time, a growth rate of zero. Any people that has intuitively identified its optimum point will soon reach it, after which its growth rate becomes and remains zero.

Of course, a positive growth rate might be taken as evidence that a population is below its optimum. However, by any reasonable standards, the most rapidly growing populations on earth today are (in general) the most miserable. This association (which need not be invariable) casts doubt on the optimistic assumption that the positive growth rate of a population is evidence that it has yet to reach its optimum.

We can make little progress in working toward optimum poulation size until we explicitly exorcize the spirit of Adam Smith in the field of practical demography. In economic affairs, *The Wealth of Nations* (1776) popularized the "invisible hand," the idea that an individual who "intends only his own gain," is, as it were, "led by an invisible hand to promote . . . the public interest."[5] Adam Smith did not assert that this was invariably true, and perhaps neither did any of his followers. But he contributed to a dominant tendency of thought that has ever since interfered with positive action based on rational analysis, namely, the tendency to assume that decisions reached individually will, in fact, be the best decisions for an entire society. If this assumption is correct it justifies the continuance of our present policy of laissez-faire in reproduction. If it is correct we can assume that men will control their individual fecundity so as to produce the optimum population. If the assumption is not correct, we need to reexamine our individual freedoms to see which ones are defensible.

Tragedy of Freedom in a Commons

The rebuttal to the invisible hand in population control is to be found in a scenario first sketched in a little-known pamphlet[6] in 1833 by a mathematical amateur named William Forster Lloyd (1794–1852). We may well call it "the tragedy of the commons," using the word "tragedy" as the philosopher Whitehead used it[7]: "The essence of dramatic tragedy is not unhappiness. It resides in the solemnity of the remorseless working of things:" He then goes on to say, "This inevitableness of destiny can only be illustrated in terms of human life by incidents which in fact involve unhappiness. For it is only by them that the futility of escape can be made evident in the drama."

The tragedy of the commons develops in this way. Picture a pasture open to all. It is to be expected that each herdsman will try to keep as many cattle as possible on the commons. Such an arrangement may work reasonably satisfactorily for centuries because tribal wars, poaching, and disease keep the numbers of both man and beast well below the carrying capacity of the land. Finally, however, comes the day of reckoning, that is, the day when the long-desired goal of social stability becomes a reality. At this point, the inherent logic of the commons remorselessly generates tragedy.

As a rational being, each herdsman seeks to maximize his gain. Explicitly or implicitly, more or less consciously, he asks, "What is the utility *to me* of adding one more animal to my herd?" This utility has one negative and one positive component.

1) The positive component is a function of the increment of one animal. Since the herdsman receives all the proceeds from the sale of the additional animal, the positive utility is nearly +1.

2) The negative component is a function of the additional overgrazing created by one more animal. Since, however, the effects of overgrazing are shared by all the herdsmen, the negative utility for any particular decision-making herdsman is only a fraction of −1.

Adding together the component partial utilities, the rational herdsman concludes that the only sensible course for him to pursue is to add another animal to his herd. And another; and another. . . . But this is the conclusion reached by each and every rational herdsman sharing a commons. Therein is the tragedy. Each man is locked into a system that compels him to increase his herd without limit—in a world that is limited. Ruin is the destination toward which all men rush, each pursuing his own best interest in a society that believes in the freedom of the commons. Freedom in a commons brings ruin to all.

Some would say that this is a platitude. Would that it were! In a sense, it was learned thousands of years ago, but natural selection favors the forces of psychological denial.[8] The individual benefits as an individual from his ability to deny the truth even though society as a whole, of which he is a part, suffers. Education can counteract the natural tendency to do the wrong thing, but the inexorable succession of generations requires that the basis for this knowledge be constantly refreshed.

A simple incident that occurred a few years ago in Leominster, Massachusetts, shows how perishable the knowledge is. During the Christmas shopping season the parking meters downtown were covered with plastic bags that bore tags reading: "Do not open until after Christmas. Free parking courtesy of the mayor and city council." In other words, facing the prospect of an increased demand for already scarce space, the city fathers reinstituted the system of the commons. (Cynically, we suspect that they gained more votes than they lost by this retrogressive act.)

In an approximate way, the logic of the commons has been understood for a long time, perhaps since the discovery of agriculture or the invention of private property in real estate. But it is understood mostly only in special cases which are not sufficiently generalized. Even at this late date, cattlemen leasing national land on the western ranges demonstrate no more than an ambivalent understanding, in constantly pressuring federal authorities to increase the head count to the point where overgrazing produces erosion and weed-dominance. Likewise, the oceans of the world continue to suffer from the survival of the philosophy of the commons. Maritime nations still respond automatically to the shibboleth of the "freedom of the seas." Professing to believe in the "inexhaustible resources of the oceans," they bring species after species of fish and whales closer to extinction.[9]

The National Parks present another instance of the working out of the tragedy of the commons. At present, they are open to all, without limit. The parks themselves are limited in extent—there is only one Yosemite Valley—whereas population seems to grow without limit. The values that visitors seek in the parks are steadily eroded. Plainly, we must soon cease to treat the parks as commons or they will be of no value to anyone.

What shall we do? We have several options. We might sell them off as private property. We might keep them as public property, but allocate the right to enter them. The allocation might be on the basis of wealth, by the use of an auction system. It might be on the basis of merit, as defined by some agreed-upon standards. It might be by lottery. Or it might be on a first-come, first-served basis, administered to long queues. These, I think, are all the reasonable possibilities. They are all objectionable. But we must choose—or acquiesce in the destruction of the commons that we call our National Parks.

Pollution

In a reverse way, the tragedy of the commons reappears in problems of pollution. Here it is not a question of taking something out of the commons, but of putting something in—sewage, or chemical, radioactive, and heat wastes into water; noxious and dangerous fumes into the air; and distracting and unpleasant advertising signs into the line of sight. The calculations of utility are much the same as before. The rational man finds that his share of the cost of the wastes he discharges into the commons is less than the cost of purifying his wastes before releasing them. Since this is true for everyone, we are locked into a system of "fouling our own nest," so long as we behave only as independent, rational, free-enterprisers.

The tragedy of the commons as a food basket is averted by private property, or something formally like it. But the air and waters surrounding us cannot readily be fenced, and so the tragedy of the commons as a cesspool must be prevented by different means, by coercive laws or taxing devices that make it cheaper for the polluter to treat his pollutants than to discharge them untreated. We have not progressed as far with the solution of this problem as we have with the first. Indeed, our particular concept of private property, which deters us from exhausting the positive resources of the earth, favors pollution. The owner of a factory on the bank of a stream—whose property extends to the middle of the stream—often has difficulty seeing why it is not his natural right to muddy the waters flowing past his door. The law, always behind the times, requires elaborate stitching and fitting to adapt it to this newly perceived aspect of the commons.

The pollution problem is a consequence of population. It did not much matter how a lonely American frontiersman disposed of his waste. "Flowing water purifies itself every 10 miles," my grandfather used to say, and the myth was near enough to the truth when he was a boy, for there were not too many people. But as population became denser, the natural chemical and biological recycling processes became overloaded, calling for a redefinition of property rights.

How to Legislate Temperance?

Analysis of the pollution problem as a function of population density uncovers a not generally recognized principle of morality, namely: *the morality of an act is a function of the state of the system at the time it is performed.*[10] Using the commons as a cesspool does not harm the general public under frontier conditions, because there is no public; the same behavior in a metropolis is unbearable. A hundred and fifty years ago a plainsman could kill an American bison, cut out only the tongue for his dinner, and discard the rest of the animal. He was not in any important sense being wasteful. Today, with only a few thousand bison left, we would be appalled at such behavior.

In passing, it is worth noting that the morality of an act cannot be determined from a photograph. One does not know whether a man killing an elephant or setting fire to the grassland is harming others until one knows the total system in which his act appears. "One picture is worth a thousand words," said an ancient Chinese; but it may take 10,000 words to validate it. It is as tempting to ecologists as it is to reformers in general to try to persuade others by way of the photographic shortcut. But the essen[c]e of an argument cannot be photographed: it must be presented rationally—in words.

That morality is system-sensitive escaped the attention of most codifiers of ethics in the past. "Thou shalt not . . ." is the form of traditional ethical directives which make no allowance for particular circumstances. The laws of our society follow the pattern of ancient ethics, and therefore are poorly suited to governing a complex, crowded, changeable world. Our epicyclic solution is to augment statutory law with administrative law. Since it is practically impossible to spell out all the conditions under which it is safe to burn trash in the back yard or to run an automobile without smog-control, by law we delegate the details to bureaus. The result is administrative law, which is rightly feared for an ancient reason—*Quis custodiet ipsos custodes?*— "Who shall watch the watchers themselves?" John Adams said that we must have "a government of laws and not men." Bureau administrators, trying to evaluate the morality of acts in the total system, are singularly liable to corruption, producing a government by men, not laws.

Prohibition is easy to legislate (though not necessarily to enforce); but how do we legislate temperance? Experience indicates that it can be accomplished best through the mediation of administrative law. We limit possibilities unnecessarily if we suppose that the sentiment of *Quis custodiet* denies us the use of administrative law. We should rather retain the phrase as a perpetual reminder of fearful dangers we cannot avoid. The great challenge facing us now is to invent the corrective feedbacks that are needed to keep custodians honest. We must find ways to legitimate the needed authority of both the custodians and the corrective feedbacks.

Freedom to Breed Is Intolerable

The tragedy of the commons is involved in population problems in another way. In a world governed solely by the principle of "dog eat dog"—if indeed there ever was such a world—how many children a family had would not be a matter of public concern. Parents who bred too exuberantly would leave fewer descendants, not more, because they would be unable to care adequately for their children. David Lack and others have found that such a negative feedback demonstrably controls the fecundity of birds.[11] But men are not birds, and have not acted like them for millenniums, at least.

If each human family were dependent only on its own resources; *if* the children of improvident parents starved to death; *if*, thus, overbreeding brought its own "punishment" to the germ line— *then* there would be no public interest in controlling the breeding of families. But our society is deeply committed to the welfare state,[12] and hence is confronted with another aspect of the tragedy of the commons.

In a welfare state, how shall we deal with the family, the religion, the race, or the class (or indeed any distinguishable and cohesive group) that adopts overbreeding as a policy to secure its own aggrandizement?[13] To couple the concept of freedom to breed with the belief that everyone born has an equal right to the commons is to lock the world into a tragic course of action.

Unfortunately this is just the course of action that is being pursued by the United Nations. In late 1967, some 30 nations agreed to the following[14]:

> The Universal Declaration of Human Rights describes the family as the natural and fundamental unit of society. It follows that any choice and decision with regard to the size of the family must irrevocably rest with the family itself, and cannot be made by anyone else.

It is painful to have to deny categorically the validity of this right; denying it, one feels as uncomfortable as a resident of Salem, Massachusetts, who denied the reality of witches in the seventeenth century. At the present time, in liberal quarters, something like a taboo acts to inhibit criticism of the United Nations. There is a feeling that the United Nations is "our last and best hope," that we shouldn't find fault with it; we shouldn't play into the hands of the archconservatives. However, let us not forget what Robert Louis Stevenson said: "The truth that is suppressed by friends is the readiest weapon of the enemy." If we love the truth we must openly deny the validity of the Universal Declaration of Human Rights, even though it is promoted by the United Nations. We should also join with Kingsley Davis[15] in attempting to get Planned Parenthood-World Population to see the error of its ways in embracing the same tragic ideal.

Conscience Is Self-Eliminating

It is a mistake to think that we can control the breeding of mankind in the long run by an appeal to conscience. Charles Galton Darwin made this point when he spoke on the centennial of the publication of his grandfather's great book. The argument is straightforward and Darwinian.

People vary. Confronted with appeals to limit breeding, some people will undoubtedly respond to the plea more than others. Those who have more children will produce a larger fraction of the next generation than those with more susceptible consciences. The difference will be accentuated, generation by generation.

In C. G. Darwin's words: "It may well be that it would take hundreds of generations for the progenitive instinct to develop in this way, but if it should do so, nature would have taken her revenge, and the variety *Homo contracipiens* would become extinct and would be replaced by the variety *Homo progenitivus*."[16]

The argument assumes that conscience or the desire for children (no matter which) is hereditary—but hereditary only in the most general formal sense. The result will be the same whether the attitude is transmitted through germ cells, or exosomatically, to use A. J. Lotka's term. (If one denies the latter possibility as well as the former, then what's the point of education?) The argument has here been stated in the context of the population problem, but it applies equally well to any instance in which society appeals to an individual exploiting a commons to restrain himself for the general good—by means of his conscience. To make such an appeal is to set up a selective system that works toward the elimination of conscience from the race.

Pathogenic Effects of Conscience

The long-term disadvantage of an appeal to conscience should be enough to condemn it; but has serious short-term disadvantages as well. If we ask a man who is exploiting a commons to desist "in the name of conscience," what are we saying to him? What does he hear?—not only at the moment but also in the wee small hours of the night when, half asleep, he remembers not merely the words we used but also the nonverbal communication cues we gave him unawares? Sooner or later, consciously or subconsciously, he senses that he has received two communications, and that they are contradictory: (i) (intended communication) "If you don't do as we ask, we will openly condemn you for not acting like a responsible citizen"; (ii) (the unintended communication) "If you *do* behave as we ask, we will secretly condemn you for a simpleton who can be shamed into standing aside while the rest of us exploit the commons."

Everyman then is caught in what Bateson has called a "double bind." Bateson and his co-workers have made a plausible case for viewing the double bind as an important causative factor in the genesis of schizophrenia.[17] The double bind may not always be so damaging, but it always endangers the mental health of anyone to whom it is applied. "A bad conscience," said Nietzsche, "is a kind of illness."

To conjure up a conscience in others is tempting to anyone who wishes to extend his control beyond the legal limits. Leaders at the highest level succumb to this temptation. Has any President during the past generation failed to call on labor unions to moderate voluntarily their demands for higher wages, or to steel companies to honor voluntary guidelines on prices? I can recall none. The rhetoric used on such occasions is designed to produce feelings of guilt in noncooperators.

For centuries it was assumed without proof that guilt was a valuable, perhaps even an indispensable, ingredient of the civilized life. Now, in this post-Freudian world, we doubt it.

Paul Goodman speaks from the modern point of view when he says: "No good has ever come from feeling guilty, neither intelligence, policy, nor compassion. The guilty do not pay attention to the object but only to themselves, and not even to their own interests, which might make sense, but to their anxieties."[18]

One does not have to be a professional psychiatrist to see the consequences of anxiety. We in the Western world are just emerging from a dreadful two-centuries-long Dark Ages of Eros that was sustained partly by prohibition laws, but perhaps more effectively by the anxiety-generating mechanisms of education. Alex Comfort has told the story well in *The Anxiety Makers*[19]; it is not a pretty one.

Since proof is difficult, we may even concede that the results of anxiety may sometimes, from certain points of view, be desirable. The larger question we should ask is whether, as a matter of policy, we should ever encourage the use of a technique the tendency (if not the intention) of which is psychologically pathogenic. We hear much talk these days of responsible parenthood; the coupled words are incorporated into the titles of some organizations devoted to birth control. Some people have proposed massive propaganda campaigns to instill responsibility into the nation's (or the world's) breeders. But what is the meaning of the word responsibility in this context? Is it not merely a synonym for the word conscience? When we use the word responsibility in the absence of substantial sanctions are we not trying to browbeat a free man in a commons into acting against his own interest? Responsibility is a verbal counterfeit for a substantial *quid pro quo*. It is an attempt to get something for nothing.

If the word responsibility is to be used at all, I suggest that it be in the sense Charles Frankel uses it.[20] "Responsibility," says this philosopher, "is the product of definite social arrangements." Notice that Frankel calls for social arrangements—not propaganda.

Mutual Coercion Mutually Agreed Upon

The social arrangements that produce responsibility are arrangements that create coercion, of some sort. Consider bank-robbing. The man who takes money from a bank acts as if the bank were a commons. How do we prevent such action? Certainly not by trying to control his behavior solely by a verbal appeal to his sense of responsibility. Rather than rely on propaganda we follow Frankel's lead and insist that a bank is not a commons; we seek the definite social arrangements that will keep it from becoming a commons. That we thereby infringe on the freedom of would-be robbers we neither deny nor regret.

The morality of bank-robbing is particularly easy to understand because we accept complete prohibition of this activity. We are willing to say "Thou shalt not rob banks," without providing for exceptions. But temperance also can be created by coercion. Taxing is a good coercive device. To keep downtown shoppers temperate in their use of parking space we introduce parking meters for short periods, and traffic fines for longer ones. We need not actually forbid a citizen to park as long as he wants to; we need merely make it increasingly expensive for him to do so. Not prohibition, but carefully biased options are what we offer him. A Madison Avenue man might call this persuasion; I prefer the greater candor of the word coercion.

Coercion is a dirty word to most liberals now, but it need not forever be so. As with the four-letter words, its dirtiness can be cleansed away by exposure to the light, by saying it over and over without apology or embarrassment. To many, the word coercion implies arbitrary decisions of distant and irresponsible bureaucrats; but this is not a necessary part of its meaning. The only kind of coercion I recommend is mutual coercion, mutually agreed upon by the majority of the people affected.

To say that we mutually agree to coercion is not to say that we are required to enjoy it, or even to pretend we enjoy it. Who enjoys taxes? We all grumble about them. But we accept compulsory taxes because we recognize that voluntary taxes would favor the conscienceless. We institute and (grumblingly) support taxes and other coercive devices to escape the horror of the commons.

An alternative to the commons need not be perfectly just to be preferable. With real estate and other material goods, the alternative we have chosen is the institution of private property coupled with legal inheritance. Is this system perfectly just? As a genetically trained biologist I deny that it is. It seems to me that, if there are to be differences in individual inheritance, legal possession should be perfectly correlated with biological inheritance—that those who are biologically more fit to be the custodians of property and power should legally inherit more. But genetic recombination continually makes a mockery of the doctrine of "like father, like son" implicit in our laws of legal inheritance. An idiot can inherit millions, and a

trust fund can keep his estate intact. We must admit that our legal system of private property plus inheritance is unjust—but we put up with it because we are not convinced, at the moment, that anyone has invented a better system. The alternative of the commons is too horrifying to contemplate. Injustice is preferable to total ruin.

It is one of the peculiarities of the warfare between reform and the status quo that it is thoughtlessly governed by a double standard. Whenever a reform measure is proposed it is often defeated when its opponents triumphantly discover a flaw in it. As Kingsley Davis has pointed out,[21] worshippers of the status quo sometimes imply that no reform is possible without unanimous agreement, an implication contrary to historical fact. As nearly as I can make out, automatic rejection of proposed reforms is based on one of two unconscious assumptions: (i) that the status quo is perfect; or (ii) that the choice we face is between reform and no action; if the proposed reform is imperfect, we presumably should take no action at all, while we wait for a perfect proposal.

But we can never do nothing. That which we have done for thousands of years is also action. It also produces evils. Once we are aware that the status quo is action, we can then compare its discoverable advantages and disadvantages with the predicted advantages and disadvantages of the proposed reform, discounting as best we can for our lack of experience. On the basis of such a comparison, we can make a rational decision which will not involve the unworkable assumption that only perfect systems are tolerable.

Recognition of Necessity

Perhaps the simplest summary of this analysis of man's population problems is this: the commons, if justifiable at all, is justifiable only under conditions of low-population density. As the human population has increased, the commons has had to be abandoned in one aspect after another.

First we abandoned the commons in food gathering, enclosing farm land and restricting pastures and hunting and fishing areas. These restrictions are still not complete throughout the world.

Somewhat later we saw that the commons as a place for waste disposal would also have to be abandoned. Restrictions on the disposal of domestic sewage are widely accepted in the Western world; we are still struggling to close the commons to pollution by automobiles, factories, insecticide sprayers, fertilizing operations, and atomic energy installations.

In a still more embryonic state is our recognition of the evils of the commons in matters of pleasure. There is almost no restriction on the propagation of sound waves in the public medium. The shopping public is assaulted with mindless music, without its consent. Our government is paying out billions of dollars to create supersonic transport which will disturb 50,000 people for every one person who is whisked from coast to coast three hours faster. Advertisers muddy the airwaves of radio and television and pollute the view of travelers. We are a long way from outlawing the commons in matters of pleasure. Is this because our Puritan inheritance makes us view pleasure as something of a sin, and pain (that is, the pollution of advertising) as the sign of virtue?

Every new enclosure of the commons involves the infringement of somebody's personal liberty. Infringements made in the distant past are accepted because no contemporary complains of a loss. It is the newly proposed infringements that we vigorously oppose; cries of "rights" and "freedom" fill the air. But what does "freedom" mean? When men mutually agreed to pass laws against robbing, mankind became more free, not less so. Individuals locked into the logic of the commons are free only to bring on universal ruin; once they see the necessity of mutual coercion, they become free to

pursue other goals. I believe it was Hegel who said, "Freedom is the recognition of necessity."

The most important aspect of necessity that we must now recognize, is the necessity of abandoning the commons in breeding. No technical solution can rescue us from the misery of overpopulation. Freedom to breed will bring ruin to all. At the moment, to avoid hard decisions many of us are tempted to propagandize for conscience and responsible parenthood. The temptation must be resisted, because an appeal to independently acting consciences selects for the disappearance of all conscience in the long run, and an increase in anxiety in the short.

The only way we can preserve and nurture other and more precious freedoms is by relinquishing the freedom to breed, and that very soon. "Freedom is the recognition of necessity"—and it is the role of education to reveal to all the necessity of abandoning the freedom to breed. Only so, can we put an end to this aspect of the tragedy of the commons.

NOTES

1. J. B. Wiesner and H. F. York, *Sci. Amer.* 211 (No. 4), 27 (1964).
2. G. Hardin, *J. Hered.* 50, 68 (1959); S. von Hoernor, *Science* 137, 18 (1962).
3. J. von Neumann and O. Morgenstern, *Theory of Games and Economic Behavior* (Princeton Univ. Press, Princeton, NJ, 1947), p. 11.
4. J. H. Fremlin, *New Sci.,* No. 415 (1964), p. 285.
5. A. Smith, *The Wealth of Nations* (Modern Library, New York, 1937), p. 423.
6. W. F. Lloyd, *Two Lectures on the Checks to Population* (Oxford Univ. Press, Oxford, England, 1833), reprinted (in part) in *Population, Evolution, and Birth Control*, G. Hardin, Ed. (Freeman, San Francisco, 1964), p. 37.
7. A. N. Whitehead, *Science and the Modern World* (Mentor, New York, 1948), p. 17.
8. G. Hardin, Ed., *Population, Evolution, and Birth Control* (Freeman, San Francisco, 1964), p. 56.
9. S. McVay, *Sci. Amer.* 216 (No. 8), 13 (1966).
10. J. Fletcher, *Situation Ethics* (Westminster, Philadelphia, 1966).
11. D. Lack, *The Natural Regulation of Animal Numbers* (Clarendon Press, Oxford, 1954).

12. H. Girvetz, *From Wealth to Welfare* (Stanford Univ. Press, Stanford, CA, 1950).
13. G. Hardin, *Perspec. Biol. Med.* 6, 366 (1963).
14. U. Thant, *Int. Planned Parenthood News*, No. 168 (February 1968), p. 3.
15. K. Davis, *Science* 158, 730 (1967).
16. S. Tax, Ed., *Evolution after Darwin* (Univ. of Chicago Press, Chicago, 1960), vol. 2, p. 469.
17. G. Bateson, D. D. Jackson, J. Haley, J. Weakland, *Behav. Sci.* 1, 251 (1956).
18. P. Goodman, *New York Rev. Books* 10(8), 22 (23 May 1968).
19. A. Comfort, *The Anxiety Makers* (Nelson, London, 1967).
20. C. Frankel, *The Case for Modern Man* (Harper, New York, 1955), p. 203.
21. J. D. Roslansky, *Genetics and the Future of Man* (Appleton-Century-Crofts, New York, 1966), p. 177.

Scott Barrett

WHY HAVE CLIMATE NEGOTIATIONS PROVED SO DISAPPOINTING?

I'm grateful to the organizers for proposing this question for my title, because it's important. People often complain that the climate negotiations have been disappointing, only to wring their hands and say that we must do better. But unless we know the *reasons* why the negotiations have been disappointing, we won't know *how* to do better. Using a medical metaphor, if our diagnosis of the illness is wrong, our recommended treatment is unlikely to heal the patient. Indeed, the wrong treatment may only make the patient sicker.

One of the striking things about the climate negotiations is that the negotiators have admitted that they have failed to meet their own goal.

In the Framework Convention on Climate Change, adopted in 1992, parties agreed that atmospheric concentrations of greenhouse gases should be stabilized "at a level that would prevent dangerous anthropogenic interference with the climate system." Later, in the non-binding Copenhagen Accord adopted in 2009, countries recognized "the scientific view that the increase in global temperature should be below 2 degrees Celsius." Finally, in Cancun in 2010, the parties to the Framework Convention reaffirmed this goal, but added that it may need to be strengthened, limiting temperature rise to 1.5°C.

After Copenhagen, countries submitted pledges for reducing their emissions. However, analysis by Rogelj et al. (2010) shows that even an optimistic reading of these pledges implies that mean global temperature will surpass the 2°C temperature change target.

The negotiators agree with this assessment. In Durban in 2011, they noted "*with grave concern* the significant gap between the aggregate effect of Parties' mitigation pledges in terms of global annual emissions of greenhouse gases by 2020 and aggregate emission pathways consistent with having a likely chance of holding the increase in global average temperature below" the agreed threshold. Rogelj et al. (2010: 1128) describe this behavior as being "equivalent to racing toward a cliff and hoping to stop just before it."

Note that the Copenhagen pledges are voluntary. It's possible that they'll be exceeded. As bad as things look now, they could turn out to be worse.

The problem isn't disagreement about what should be done. Support for the 2°C goal is universal. The problem is that this is a global goal. Everyone is responsible for meeting it, meaning that no country is responsible for meeting it. Limiting climate change requires very broad cooperation. It requires *collective action*.

The reason collective action has eluded us so far is that reducing emissions is a prisoners' dilemma game. Each country is better off when *all* countries reduce their emissions substantially. But each

From "Sustainable Humanity, Sustainable Nature: Our Responsibility." Proceedings of the Joint Workshop 2–6 May, 2014. Extra Series 41. Vatican City, 2015, 261–76.

country has only a small incentive to reduce its *own* emissions.

The Kyoto Protocol asks some countries to reduce their emissions beyond "business as usual," and so confronts the prisoners' dilemma head on. But Kyoto has failed in its mission to limit emissions.[1] The Copenhagen Accord, by focusing on the need to avoid "dangerous" climate change, has tried to reframe the problem. Will Copenhagen succeed? Reframing is the right strategy. But we need a different framing. Although my main purpose is to explain why the negotiations have been disappointing, I also want to suggest how an understanding of this failure can provide insights into how we might do better. Countries are currently trying to negotiate a new kind of climate agreement for adoption in 2015. My paper ends by suggesting how a different framing of the climate collective action problem could turn the negotiations around. The climate negotiations needn't be as disappointing as they have been so far.

The "Dangerous" Climate Change Game

Here is a way to think about the "dangerous" climate change game. Let's say that there exists a red line for "danger," and that countries know what this red line is. For example, it might be the 2°C goal. Let's also say that the impact of crossing this threshold is expected to be so severe relative to the costs of staying clear of it that all countries, collectively, prefer to stay clear of it. Then it's obvious what countries should do if they act collectively: they should limit concentrations of greenhouse gases to avoid crossing the red line.

The problem, of course, is that countries don't act collectively. They're sovereign. They act independently. So, we should ask: What *incentives* do countries have to stay within the good side of the red line?

Under reasonable assumptions, the game I have just described is not a prisoners' dilemma. It's a "coordination game" with two Nash equilibria (Barrett 2013).[2] In one, countries stay just within the "safe" zone. In the other, they breeze past the tipping point, making catastrophe inevitable. In general, game theory has trouble predicting how countries will behave in a coordination game. However, since the "bad" Nash equilibrium is so obviously bad, staying within the red line is focal (Schelling 1960). Moreover, with the help of a treaty, countries can virtually guarantee that they will coordinate around the "good" Nash equilibrium.

Here is how the treaty should be written. It should assign to every country an emission limit, with each country's limit chosen to ensure that, when all the limits are added up, concentrations stay within the "safe" zone. The limits should also be chosen to ensure that every country is better off staying within its assigned limit, given that all the other countries stay within *their* assigned limits. Finally, the agreement should only enter into force if ratified by every country.

The beauty of such a treaty is that it makes every country pivotal. If every other country behaves as required, each country has an incentive to behave as required. The reason: even the slightest slip up guarantees catastrophe.

This treaty, like all good treaties, transforms the game. In the treaty participation game, every country has a dominant strategy to participate. Why? Every country has nothing to lose by joining. If the agreement fails to enter into force, each country would be free to act as it pleased. If the agreement were to enter into force, however, then it would be binding on all parties, and catastrophe would be avoided—the outcome every country prefers. Every country is thus always better off participating.

How would the emission limits for individual countries be chosen? This is the bargaining problem. If countries were "symmetric," bargaining would be simple. Technically, a wide variety of allocations would satisfy the requirements I described above, but an equal allocation would be focal, and for that reason is to be expected. Asymmetry makes bargaining more complex, but so long as collective action promises all countries an aggregate gain, there will exist an allocation of responsibility that will be acceptable to every country (this allocation won't be unique and may require side payments, but these are relatively minor points compared with the imperative to avoid catastrophe).

The threat of catastrophe simplifies the negotiation problem. It makes each county's promise to stay within its agreed limits *credible*.

The vulnerability in this game isn't the behavior of the countries. It is the credibility of the *science*—in particular, the science of locating the critical tipping point.

In the dangerous climate change game, it would be irrational for any country to exceed its assigned amount of emissions when doing so would cause atmospheric concentrations to cross the catastrophic tipping point. In this case, free rider deterrence depends on the credibility of *Nature's* threat to tip a critical geophysical system. Yes, in the dangerous climate change game, Nature is an important player.

The Importance of Scientific Uncertainty

What would countries need to do collectively to prevent dangerous climate change?

The Copenhagen Accord says:

> To achieve the ultimate objective of the Convention to stabilize greenhouse gas concentration in the atmosphere at a level that would prevent dangerous anthropogenic interference with the climate system, we shall, recognizing *the scientific view that the increase in global temperature*

should be below 2 degrees Celsius [emphasis added], on the basis of equity and in the context of sustainable development, enhance our long-term cooperative action to combat climate change.[3]

Why defer to the "scientific view"? The reason is that it simplifies the negotiations. It allows negotiators to bargain over individual country shares.

However, while scientists warned of "climate disaster" before the Framework Convention was adopted (see, in particular, Mercer 1978), I think the Framework Convention caused scientists to focus on this question at least as much as previous scientific research caused negotiators to focus on it.

Reference to *"the* scientific view" [emphasis added] implies that there is strong agreement among scientists about the threshold. There isn't. The only "scientific view" that I detect in the literature is that thresholds are likely to exist.[4]

Although temperature thresholds are uncertain, the uncertainties involved in choosing a target are even greater than this. The Framework Convention specifies the target in terms of concentrations, not temperature, and converting temperature to concentrations introduces an additional layer of uncertainty—something known as "climate sensitivity" (Roe and Baker 2007). Moreover, we don't know the quantity of global emissions (expressed, perhaps, as a cumulative sum) needed to meet any particular concentration target, due to uncertainty in the carbon cycle. For example, there is uncertainty about how much of the CO_2 emitted will be taken up by soils and the oceans. The fifth assessment report by the Intergovernmental Panel on Climate Change calculates a global "budget" in terms of cumulative emissions that will keep temperature change within 2°C, but all of these values are probabilistic. Even if we knew for certain that 2°C were the true red line for climate change (and we don't know this), countries would have to decide how to balance the cost of reducing emissions with reductions in the risk of crossing the red line.

The Dangerous Climate Change Game with Uncertain Thresholds

Uncertainty about the threshold for "danger" changes the climate change game fundamentally.

Consider a very simple game—no treaty. In stage 1, countries choose their emission levels independently. In stage 2, Nature chooses the tipping point. When making their choices in stage 1, the players know the probability density function for the tipping point. What they don't know is which value under this function will be chosen by Nature—the "true" value for the tipping point.

An example will make this clear. Rockström et al. (2009) argue that atmospheric CO_2 concentrations should be constrained "to *ensure* [emphasis added] the continued existence of the large polar ice sheets." They note that the paleoclimatic record implies "that there is a critical threshold between 350 and 550 ppmv," and interpret this as saying that if concentrations are limited to 350 ppmv, then the ice sheets will be preserved, whereas if concentrations rise to 550 ppmv, then the ice sheets will be lost. In between these values there is a chance that the ice sheets will disappear, with the probability increasing with the concentration level. (For reference, last month's reading from Mona Loa was about 399.65 ppmv; at the start of the industrial revolution, concentrations were about 280 ppmv; when the Framework Convention was adopted they were 356 ppmv).

Assume that the probability density function is uniform over the range (350,550).[5] Assume also that the expected aggregate benefit of reducing the threat of catastrophe exceeds the cost. What should countries do? Under reasonable assumptions (Barrett 2013), the collective-best outcome is to limit concentrations to 350 ppmv. This implements the "precautionary principle." Acting independently, however, countries have incentives to reduce emissions only up to the point where their expected *individual* marginal benefit equals marginal cost— under reasonable assumptions, a substantially smaller value. Indeed, very simple calculations show that it will probably pay individual countries to abate so little that will they blow right past the critical threshold. They will cross the 550 ppmv line, guaranteeing catastrophe.

You might think this is just theory and that country representatives wouldn't be this dumb. I think there are good reasons to take the prediction seriously.

Astrid Dannenberg and I have tested these predictions in the experimental lab with real people playing for real money (Barrett and Dannenberg 2012). Putting people into groups of 10, we find that when the threshold is certain, 18 out of 20 groups avoid catastrophe.[6] By contrast, when the threshold is uncertain, catastrophe occurs with probability 100% for 16 out of 20 groups and with probability no less than 80% for the rest.[7]

How sensitive are these results? Intuitively, there should exist a critical amount of uncertainty such that if uncertainty were greater than this amount, catastrophe would be bound to occur, whereas if uncertainty were less than this, catastrophe would be avoided. This is exactly what the theory predicts (Barrett 2013), and in further experiments (Barrett and Dannenberg 2014a), Astrid Dannenberg and I have shown that this result is also robust. To the left of a critical "dividing line" for threshold uncertainty, we find that catastrophe is avoided with high probability almost all the time. Just to the right of the dividing line, by contrast, catastrophe occurs with probability 100% This research suggests that negotiators can't rely on science to solve their collective action problem. Even the new science of "early warning signals" won't be able to shrink uncertainty by enough to transform the behavior of nation states.

This research is helpful, I think, because it is completely consistent with the behavior we are observing in the real world. As noted before, countries have agreed to limit temperature change to 2°C, but they have pledged emission reductions that virtually guarantee overshooting of this target.

If the science of climate change were much more certain, the prospect of catastrophe would give countries the discipline they needed to act in their collective-best interest. It would make the dangerous climate change game a coordination game. Scientific uncertainty makes the emission reductions game a prisoners' dilemma. The most important thing about a prisoners' dilemma is that the collective-best outcome cannot be sustained by non-cooperative behavior. It requires enforcement, something that the international system is very bad at doing.

A Climate Doomsday Machine

It is tempting to consider an analogy to nuclear arms control. Herman Kahn (1961: 107) proposed construction of a Doomsday Machine,

> a device whose function is to destroy the world. This device is protected from enemy action (perhaps by being situated thousands of feet underground) and then connected to a computer, in turn connected to thousands of sensory devices all over the United States. The computer would be programmed so that if, say, five nuclear bombs exploded over the United States, the device would be triggered and the world destroyed. Barring such problems as coding errors (an important technical consideration), this machine would seem to be the 'ideal' [deterrent]. If Khrushchev ordered an attack, both Khrushchev and the Soviet population would be automatically and efficiently annihilated.

A Climate Doomsday Machine would connect all the world's nuclear bombs to a computer, which in turn would be linked to a sensor at the top of Mona Loa in Hawaii. This is where readings are taken of atmospheric concentrations of greenhouse gases. Today, as noted before, the concentration level is about 400 ppmv. The computer could be programmed to destroy the world should this level top, say, 500 ppmv. With the trigger for catastrophe being certain, theory and experimental evidence strongly suggest that this device would give the world all the encouragement needed to stay within 500.

Of course, I'm not seriously proposing this. The proposal is unacceptable.[8] However, the idea behind it is worth thinking about. The Doomsday Machine is a purely strategic device. Its sole purpose is to change the incentives countries have to rein in their emissions and save the world from dangerous climate change. It works by transforming the prisoners' dilemma into a coordination game. Thinking about it begs the question: Are there *acceptable* strategic approaches that could have a similar effect? I shall return to this point later in the paper.

Framing Reconsidered

Has a focus on "dangerous" climate change really made no difference? Under certain conditions, theory suggests that uncertainty about the threshold could mean that behavior won't change at all, even though the consequences of failing to act will be much worse because of the threat of catastrophic climate change (Barrett 2012).

But is this result to be believed? Many predictions of analytical game theory are disproved in the experimental lab. For example, cooperation in a prisoners' dilemma typically exceeds the Nash equilibrium prediction (though the level of cooperation declines rapidly as the players learn that their efforts to cooperate are not reciprocated). In a one-shot test of the theory, Astrid Dannenberg and I found that cooperation was higher for the prisoners' dilemma with an uncertain threshold for "catastrophe" compared to a prisoners' dilemma without any risk of "catastrophe" (Barrett and Danenberg 2014b). This suggests that, given the risk from "dangerous" climate change, the wording of Article II of the Framework Convention has probably helped (though it is the real risk rather than the wording that would affect behavior). Unfortunately, our experiment also showed that the additional cooperation wasn't enough to prevent catastrophe from occurring.

Strategies of Reciprocity

My description of the dangerous climate change game left out the role of an international agreement. I explained before that a treaty could change the incentives in the game with a certain threshold, ensuring coordination. Could a treaty help overcome the incentive to free ride when the threshold is very uncertain? Theory suggests that an agreement would help very little (Barrett 2013). The reason is the difficulty of enforcing an agreement to limit emissions.

Atmospheric concentrations of CO_2 are determined by the aggregate behavior of *all* countries (as mediated by the carbon cycle). Strategies of reciprocity work very well in two-player games. They work less well when the number of players is large.

In the climate change game, how many players really matter? Some countries are bigger emitters than others. However, the top ten emitters account for only about two-thirds of total emissions, and stabilizing concentrations requires driving global net emissions to zero, necessitating the engagement of nearly *all* countries.[9]

The temptation to free ride is further aggravated by the high marginal cost of reducing emissions substantially. It is sometimes argued that reducing emissions is cheap. If this were true, however, collective action would be easy.

Another problem is the lack of correlation between a country's contribution to emissions and its vulnerability to climate change. To illustrate, William Nordhaus (2011) has calculated that the "social cost of carbon" is more than twice as large for Africa, a continent of more than 50 states, as it is for the United States. Moreover, this gap is growing. Yet, Africa's emissions are tiny when compared to those of the United States. Africa is both more vulnerable to climate change and less able to prevent it from occurring.

Finally, globalization amplifies the incentives to free ride. Abatement by a single country or coalition of countries will tend to shift emissions toward the countries that fail to act—a phenomenon known as "leakage."

It is well known that infinitely repeated play of the prisoners' dilemma can allow the full cooperative outcome to be sustained as a (subgame perfect) Nash equilibrium, provided discount rates are sufficiently low. The reason is that, should a country "cheat" on an agreement to limit emissions, the others can reciprocate. This suggests that cooperation should be easy.

The flaw in this perspective is that it considers only the interests of individual countries. It ignores these countries' collective interests.

Imagine that all the world's countries come together and negotiate an agreement that maximizes their collective interests. Later, one country announces that it will withdraw. This withdrawal would harm the other states, and they would like to punish this country (or, better yet, threaten to punish it, hoping to deter its withdrawal). In the context of a treaty, they would naturally *cooperate* to punish the deviant country. To deter a deviation, their punishment must be big enough that the deviant would be better off remaining in the agreement than withdrawing and facing the punishment. But the punishment must also be credible. Given that this country has withdrawn, the remaining $N-1$ countries must be better off when they impose the punishment than when they do not impose it (or when they impose a weaker punishment). Because so many countries remain in the agreement, it will only pay these countries to cut their abatement a little. A larger punishment wouldn't be credible. A small punishment, however, would be too little to deter a defection. Continuing in this way, it is easy to see that an agreement to limit emissions is only self-enforcing if the number of countries participating is very small. For then, should one country withdraw, the remaining countries would have an incentive to drop their abatement significantly. However, once participation shrinks to such a low level, the treaty achieves very little.

It may be possible for countries to sustain a high level of participation, but this would only be true if the gains to cooperation were small. It may also be possible to sustain a high level of participation if the ambition of the treaty were set very low. What isn't possible is for countries to sustain a high degree of cooperation when the gains from cooperation are very large.[10]

I have so far focused on participation. What about compliance? A flaw in the approaches to enforcement taken previously is that they either ignore participation (as in Chayes and Chayes 1995) or fail to distinguish between participation and compliance (as in Downs, Rocke, and Barsoon 1996). Under the rules of international law, countries are free to choose whether or not to participate in a treaty. However, the countries that choose to participate are legally obligated to comply with it (*pacta sunt servanda,* meaning "agreements must be kept"). The easiest way to avoid needing to comply is therefore not to participate in the first place—or to withdraw after becoming a party. From the perspective of game theory, the problem is coming up with a credible punishment that is large enough to deter non-participation. Once this is done, deterring non-compliance is easy. Remember, larger deviations can only be deterred by larger punishments, and larger punishments are less credible. What's the biggest harm a party could ever do?

Behaving as it would were it not a party to the agreement (any bigger harm would not be credible). So, if the parties can deter non-participation, they can easily deter a smaller deviation of non-compliance. From both perspectives, then, deterring non-participation is the binding constraint on enforcement (Barrett 2003).

This is theory. Is the reasoning compelling? I know of no example from international cooperation that challenges this perspective. The World Trade Organization might appear to be an exception, but trade isn't a global public good. Trade is a bilateral activity, and strategies of reciprocity are very effective in sustaining cooperation amongst pairs of players. The Montreal Protocol on protecting the ozone layer might appear to be another exception, but as I shall explain later, this treaty works very differently.

Enforcement of the Kyoto Protocol

The Kyoto Protocol looks at climate change as a prisoners' dilemma, demands that certain countries cooperate, and then does nothing about enforcement.

How do we know this? The United States participated in the Kyoto negotiations. President Clinton signed the treaty. However, the United States never ratified Kyoto. One reason for this is that there were no consequences to the United States for not ratifying the agreement. Non-participation by the United States was not deterred.

Canada ratified Kyoto, but failed to adopt the domestic legislation needed to implement its obligations. As a consequence, Canada's emissions exceeded the limit set by Kyoto limit. Once in this situation, Canada had three options. It could buy permits or offsets to stay in compliance; it could stay in the agreement and be in non-compliance; or it could withdraw from the agreement. In contrast to the first option, withdrawal would be costless. In contrast to the second option, withdrawal would not violate international law. Not surprisingly, Canada decided to withdraw. The Kyoto Protocol could not deter Canada from withdrawing.

Compliance with the Kyoto Protocol by other parties is uneven (Haita 2012). However, there are ways to get around compliance. For example, Japan is maneuvering to achieve compliance partly by purchasing "assigned amount units" from Ukraine, when Ukraine's emissions are well below its "assigned amounts." In other words, in buying these units from Ukraine, Japan can comply without emissions being reduced anywhere. This may seem crazy but the treaty was written to allow this trading in "hot air."

Finally, countries like China and India are not subject to limits on their emissions. They participate in Kyoto. They comply with it. But Kyoto does not require that these countries do anything.

Overall, did Kyoto contribute to meeting the objectives of the Framework Convention? Did it reduce global emissions? Econometric analysis of the Kyoto Protocol by Rahel Aichele and Gabriel Felbermayr (2012: 351) shows that Kyoto did reduce the emissions of participating countries. However, its effect on *global* carbon emissions "has been statistically indistinguishable from zero."

The most important indicator of whether the objectives of the Framework Convention are being met is whether the growth in atmospheric concentrations is slowing. It isn't. If anything, the rate of increase has gone up.[11] We are no closer now to addressing this great problem than we were more than twenty years ago when the Framework Convention was adopted.

Pivot: From Kyoto to Paris

The Copenhagen talks were supposed to provide a successor agreement to the Kyoto Protocol. They failed.

A new agreement is now being negotiated under the "Durban Platform." It is supposed to be ready for adoption by 2015, when the parties to the Framework Convention meet in Paris. It is supposed to be implemented by 2020.

Since Kyoto's emission limits ended in 2012, this leaves a gap of eight years. To fill the gap, Kyoto was given an extension in the form of the Doha Amendment (which has yet to enter into force). However, it is a further sign of Kyoto's failings that Japan, New Zealand, and Russia declared their intention not to participate this time around.[12]

The new agreement being negotiated now won't repeat all of Kyoto's mistakes, but there is no indication yet that it will improve much on what countries would have done in the absence of cooperation. Kyoto referred to its emission limits as "commitments." However, countries were never truly committed to meeting these limits; they couldn't be committed to meeting these limits so long as Kyoto lacked the means to compel parties to do more than they were willing to do unilaterally. It is a sign of where the current round of negotiations are going that in Durban countries agreed to negotiate a new "protocol, legal instrument or agreed outcome with legal force," and that in the recent Warsaw talks they agreed to negotiate "contributions" rather than "commitments."

The world clearly needs a new model for cooperation on climate change.

Why the Montreal Protocol Succeeded

Kyoto lacks a strategic design. The emissions targets and timetables were chosen in the expectation that they would be met. No consideration was given to whether the treaty created *incentives* for them to be met.

The Montreal Protocol, negotiated to protect the stratospheric ozone layer, was designed very differently. Remarkably, while the Montreal Protocol was not intended to reduce greenhouse gases, it has been much more successful at doing this than the Kyoto Protocol. It turns out that ozone in the stratosphere is a greenhouse gas (protecting the ozone layer will thus add to climate change), as are the chemicals that deplete stratospheric ozone (reducing these emissions will thus help mitigate climate change) and many of their substitutes (use of these will thus add to climate change). Calculations by Velders et al. (2007) show that, by phasing out the ozone-depleting substances that double as greenhouse gases, the Montreal Protocol has done four times as much to limit atmospheric concentrations as the Kyoto Protocol aimed to do.

Why did Montreal succeed where Kyoto failed? A key reason for its success is the threat to restrict trade—in particular, a ban on trade in controlled substances between parties and non-parties (Barrett 2003). The most important motive for the trade restriction was to enforce participation in the agreement (Benedick 1998:91). If participation could be enforced, then trade leakage would be eliminated; moreover, compliance could also be enforced (Barrett 2003). Crucially, the trade restrictions in the Montreal Protocol are a strategic device. Their purpose was not to be used; their purpose was to change behavior.

How do the trade restrictions work? Imagine that very few countries are parties to an agreement to limit emissions, and your country is contemplating whether or not to join. If you join, you will have to reduce your emissions. Your country will pay the cost, and the benefits will be diffused; the incentives to free ride will not be blunted. If, in addition, you are now also prohibited from trading with non-parties—the vast majority of countries— then you will be doubly harmed. By joining, you not only forfeit the benefits of free riding; you also lose the gains from trade.

Now imagine that almost every other country is a party to the same agreement. If you join, you still lose the benefits of free riding. But now you are able to trade with the vast majority of countries. If the gains from trade exceed the loss from free riding, your country will be better off joining. Put differently, if every country is a party to such an agreement, none will wish to withdraw. The agreement will sustain full participation by means of a self-enforcing mechanism—the trade restriction. Most remarkably, in equilibrium, trade will never be restricted, just as the Doomsday Device would never be detonated. It is the credible threat to restrict trade (detonate the device) that disciplines behavior.

Notice that a key feature of this strategy is that "enough" countries participate in the agreement. If too few participate, none will want to participate. If enough participate, everyone will want to participate. Somewhere in between there exists a "tipping point" for participation. Once this tipping point has been identified, the treaty only needs to coordinate participation—something treaties can do very easily. As I said before, treaties need to ensure that countries are steered towards the desired outcome. In the Montreal Protocol, this was achieved by the minimum participation clause (Barrett 2003).

The trade restrictions are an acceptable alternative to the Doomsday Machine. Like the Doomsday Machine, trade restrictions transform the prisoners' dilemma into a coordination game.

Coordination in Climate Treaties

The Montreal Protocol could be amended to achieve more for the climate. Hydrofluorocarbons (HFCs) do not deplete the ozone layer, and so are not currently regulated by the Montreal Protocol. However, HFCs are a very potent greenhouse gas— one of the six gases controlled by the Kyoto Protocol. Kyoto has done very little to limit HFCs. In May 2011, the United States, Canada, and Mexico proposed amending the Montreal Protocol to control HFCs. If adopted, such an amendment would represent a significant departure from the approach taken so far to address climate change. It would mean addressing one piece of the problem, rather than all of it in a comprehensive way. And it would likely involve using trade restrictions for purposes of enforcement. I want to underline that the application of trade restrictions is purely strategic. Other proposals for trade restrictions in climate policy are very different; their purpose is to be *used,* not to alter behavior strategically (Barrett 2011).

There are other opportunities for transforming the climate change game from a prisoners' dilemma into a coordination game, especially the application of technology standards (Barrett 2003, 2006).

Let me give one example. Another greenhouse gas known as perfluorocarbons or PFCs is emitted in the process of manufacturing aluminum. Apparently, these emissions can be eliminated if the anodes being used now are replaced with inert anodes. According to the United States Environmental Protection Agency's webpage, "This technology is being pursued aggressively through a joint R&D program that has been established between the aluminum industry and the U.S. Department of Energy in its Industrial Technology Program."[13] The new anode is expected to be available in ten to fifteen years.

Here, then, is a suggestion. A new agreement should be negotiated requiring that producers adopt the new technology, and that all parties agree to import aluminum only from countries that participate in the agreement. This approach creates a "tipping" phenomenon. Provided enough countries join the agreement, all will want to join it. Why? To be outside the agreement when most countries are inside means not being able to trade in aluminum with most of the world.

This proposal for aluminum would be different from Montreal. The trade restriction would be based on a process standard, not a product standard. However, I believe it would still be effective.

I also believe it would be compatible with the WTO, partly because of the exemptions allowed under Article XX, but also because it would be adopted by a multilateral agreement.

A final point. Another reason Montreal works is that it includes side payments to address related equity issues. Side payments could also be included in an agreement establishing an aluminum production standard. As in Montreal, any side payments should be based on the "incremental costs" of adopting the standard. Transfers should be small, and the countries giving the money should know what they are getting for their money.

Again, this is just one example of how the negotiations could be made more effective.[14] My aim here is not to develop a comprehensive approach to future climate negotiations but to suggest a new direction. If the negotiators understood their job as needing to achieve coordination, and to think strategically, they would achieve more—and the climate negotiations wouldn't prove so disappointing.

NOTES

1. See, especially, research by Aichele and Felbermayr (2012), discussed later in this paper, which takes into account the effect of Kyoto on trade "leakage."

2. In a coordination game, people want to do what others are doing. A car may be driven on the left or right side of the road. So, on which side of the road should you drive? The answer depends on where everyone else is driving. In Italy, it's obvious that you should drive on the right. In the UK, it's obvious that you should drive on the left. These different outcomes (driving on the left and driving on the right) are each a "Nash equilibrium." Given that others are driving on the left (right), each driver chooses to drive on the left (right).

3. The Copenhagen Accord was written somewhat hastily, and this temperature target is identified without reference to a base level of temperature. In Cancun the following year, negotiators clarified that the temperature reference target was the pre-industrial level.

4. Rapid changes in temperature have been observed in the paleoclimatic record, an example being the Younger Dryas; see Broecker (1997).

5. This means that the probability that the threshold lies between 350 and 400 ppmv is the same as the probability that the threshold lies between 400 and 450 ppmv, between 450 and 500 ppmv, and

between 500 and 550 ppmv. It also means that the probability that the threshold lies below 350 or above 550 ppmv is zero.

6. In each of the two failing groups, just one individual, a bad apple, caused the trouble, pledging to contribute his or her fair share and then choosing to contribute nothing.

7. Interestingly, theory predicts that uncertainty about the *impact* of crossing a critical threshold should make no difference to collective action (Barrett 2013), another prediction confirmed in the experimental lab (Barrett and Dannenberg 2012). It is only uncertainty about the tipping point that matters, and this is a purely scientific matter.

8. Nor did Kahn recommend the Doomsday Machine: "If one were presenting a military briefing advocating some special weapon system as a deterrent . . . the Doomsday Machine might seem better than any alternative system; nevertheless, it is unacceptable" (Kahn 1961: 104–05).

9. Unless, that is, substantial amounts of carbon are removed from the atmosphere.

10. All of these points are developed in detail in Barrett (2003).

11. The data can be found at http://www.esrl.noaa.gov/gmd/ccgg/trends/.

12. The European Union will participate, because this agreement only requires that Europe meet the target it declared it would meet unilaterally. The new government in Australia has introduced legislation to repeal the previous government's climate legislation, a sign that Australia may not ratify the Doha Amendment.

13. http://www.epa.gov/aluminum-pfc/resources.html.

14. For other examples of sectoral approaches to reducing emissions, see Barrett (2011).

REFERENCES

Aichele, Rahel and Gabriel Felbermayr (2012). "Kyoto and the Carbon Footprint of Nations," *Journal of Environmental Economics and Management* 63: 336–54.

Barrett, Scott (2003). *Environment and Statecraft: The Strategy of Environmental Treaty-Making,* Oxford: Oxford University Press.

Barrett, S. (2006). "Climate Treaties and 'Breakthrough' Technologies," *American Economic Review (Papers and Proceedings)* 96(2): 22–25.

Barrett, Scott (2011). "Rethinking Climate Change Governance and Its Relationship to the World Trading System," *The World Economy* 34(11): 1863–82.

Barrett, Scott (2013). "Climate Treaties and Approaching Catastrophes," *Journal of Environmental Economics and Management,* 66(2): 235–50.

Barrett, Scott and Astrid Dannenberg (2012). "Climate Negotiations Under Scientific Uncertainty," *Proceedings of the National Academy of Sciences,* 109(43): 17372–376.

Barrett, Scott and Astrid Dannenberg (2014a). "Sensitivity of Collective Action to Uncertainty about Climate Tipping Points," *Nature Climate Change* 4: 36–39.

Barrett, Scott and Astrid Dannenberg (2014b). "Negotiating to Avoid 'Gradual' versus 'Dangerous' Climate Change: An Experimental Test of Two Prisoners' Dilemmas," in Todd L. Cherry, Jon Hovi, and Dave McEvoy (eds.), *Toward a New Climate Agreement: Conflict, Resolution, and Governance,* London: Routledge.

Benedick, R. E. (1998). *Ozone Diplomacy: New Directions in Safeguarding the Planet,* Enlarged Edition, Cambridge, MA: Harvard University Press.

Broecker, W. S. (1997). "Thermohaline Circulation, the Achilles Heel of Our Climate System: Will Man-Made CO_2 Upset the Current Balance?" *Science* 278:1582–88.

Chayes, A. and A. H. Chayes (1995). *The New Sovereignty,* Cambridge, MA: Harvard University Press.

Downs, G. W., D. M. Rocke, and P. N. Barsoon (1996). "Is the Good News About Compliance Good News About Cooperation?" *International Organization* 50: 379–406.

Environmental Protection Agency (2006). *Global Mitigation of Non-CO_2 Greenhouse Gases,* Washington, DC: EPA.

Haita, Corina (2012). "The State of Compliance in the Kyoto Protocol," International Center for Climate Governance; http://www.iccgov .org/FilePagineStatiche/Files/Publications/Reflections/12 _Reflection_December_2012.pdf.

Kahn, Herman (1961). "The Arms Race and Some of Its Hazards," in Donald G. Brennan (ed.), *Arms Control, Disarmament, and National Security,* New York: George Braziller, pp. 89–121.

Mercer, J. H. (1978). "West Antarctic Ice Sheet and CO2 Greenhouse Effect: A Threat of Disaster," *Nature* 271: 321–25.

Nordhaus, William (2011). "Estimates of the Social Cost of Carbon: Background and Results from the RICE-2011 Model." Cowles Foundation Discussion Paper No. 1826, Yale University.

Rockström, J., W. Steffen, K. Noone, Å. Persson, S. Chapin III, E. F. Lambin, T. M. Lenton, M. Scheffer, C. Folke, H. J. Schellnhuber, B. Nykvist, C. A. de Wit, T. Hughes, S. van der Leeuw, H. Rodhe, S. Sörlin, P. K. Snyder, R. Costanza, U. Svedin, M. Falkenmark, L. Karlberg, R. W. Corell, V. J. Fabry, J. Hansen, B. Walker, D. Liverman, K. Richardson, P. Crutzen, and J. A. Foley (2009). "A Safe Operating Safe for Humanity," *Nature* 461: 472–75.

Roe, G. H. and M. B. Baker (2007). "Why Is Climate Sensitivity So Unpredictable?" *Science* 318: 629–32.

Rogelj, J., J. Nabel, C. Chen, W. Hare, K. Markmann, M. Meinshausen, M. Schaeffer, K. Macey, and N. Höhne (2010). "Copenhagen Accord Pledges are Paltry," *Nature* 464: 1126–28.

Schelling, T. C. (1960). *The Strategy of Conflict,* Cambridge, MA: Harvard University Press.

Velders, G.J.M., S. O. Anderson, J. S. Daniel, D. W. Fahey, and M. McFarland (2007). "The Importance of the Montreal Protocol in Protecting Climate," *Proceedings of the National Academy of Sciences* 104 (12): 4814–19.

Valerie M. Hudson and Hilary Matfess

IN PLAIN SIGHT
The Neglected Linkage between Brideprice and Violent Conflict

Strapped to a gurney and visibly shaken by the bloodied bodies of his fellow terrorists strewn about, Mohammed Jamal Amir Kasab, aged twenty-one, begged his police interrogators to turn off their cameras. They refused, and Kasab's recorded confession provided the world with a glimpse into the individual motivations of the young men behind the four days of attacks in Mumbai, India. Kasab explained that he "joined the militant group Lashkar-e-Taiba only for money."[1] His was not solely an individual decision, however, and the money he earned from participating in the attacks was not intended to be discretionary income. According to Kasab, his father had urged him to join so that Kasab and his siblings could afford to marry.[2] Kasab recounted that his father had told him that his participation would mean that the family would no longer be poor and that they would be able to pay the costs required to finalize a marriage contract. One of the police officers, seemingly ignoring Kasab's response, pressed, "So you came here for jihad? Is that right?" Crying, Kasab asked, "What jihad?" Lashkar-e-Taiba deposited the promised money in his father's account after the successful attack; for his participation, Kasab was hanged in 2012 by the Indian government. Whether his siblings were subsequently able to contract marriages as a result of the funds provided by Lashkar-e-Taiba remains unknown.

In many ways, Kasab's story lends itself to the narrative that terrorist recruitment is a function of poverty and a lack of opportunity for young men. Indeed, Kasab joined Lashkar-e-Taiba's network while engaged in petty criminality and working as a laborer for a mere 60 cents a day. While in custody, he told police, "If you give me regular meals and money I will do the same for you that I did for them."[3] Kasab's decision to join Lashkar-e-Taiba, his motivations for participating in the Mumbai attack, and his confession after being captured all suggest that the appeal of membership in a terrorist organization was material, rather than ideological.

Yet there is something else in this anecdote that helps explain the motivations of young men who take up arms not only for terrorist groups, but for the broader purpose of engaging in group violence for political ends. Kasab's story casts light on something hidden in plain sight: poverty alone cannot explain participation in such organized groups because the vast majority of poor people do not turn to violence.[4] Rather, poverty and social marginalization must manifest themselves in particularly vexing ways for grievances to lead to such terrible violence. Kasab's confession points to one such factor, which we explore in this article. Across much of the world, especially in the shatter belts of the Global South, customary law requires that young men and their families pay a brideprice to marry.[5] In this article, we identify the role of marriage market obstruction caused by inflationary brideprice as an additional factor beyond

From *International Security* 42, no. 1 (Summer 2017): 7–40. Some of the authors' notes have been omitted.

Figure 11.1. Brideprice/Dowry/Wedding Costs (Type and Prevalence) Scaled 2016

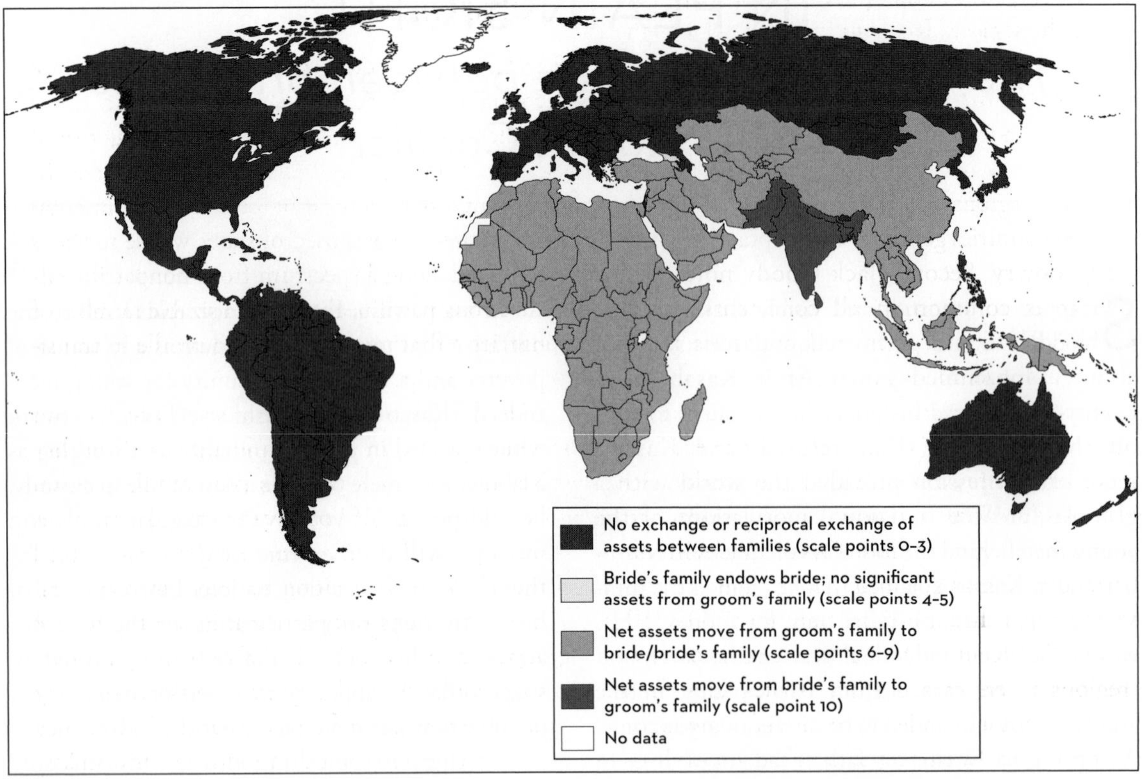

- No exchange or reciprocal exchange of assets between families (scale points 0–3)
- Bride's family endows bride; no significant assets from groom's family (scale points 4–5)
- Net assets move from groom's family to bride/bride's family (scale points 6–9)
- Net assets move from bride's family to groom's family (scale point 10)
- No data

those already identified in the literature as predisposing young men to become involved in organized group violence for political purposes, including terrorism, rebellion, intergroup aggression, raiding, and insurrection. Furthermore, we argue that this factor is critical not only in a theoretical sense but also in a policy context.

The extant literature points to deprivation, identity, and socialization as primary risk factors for why young men take up arms. Most modern analysis posits that it is not absolute poverty that motivates rebellion, but rather relative deprivation.[6] Some scholars theorize that greed, rather than grievance, animates conflict entrepreneurs to rebel against governments when it is financially viable or

beneficial to do so, thereby tying natural resource wealth to conflict.[7] Micro-level explanations also suggest that peer-group pressure to join armed groups is a significant motivating factor for young men; in-group members are able to justify otherwise unacceptable actions through the benefits thereby obtained by the group.[8] This new sense of identity, in turn, incentivizes rebellious activity.[9]

Our research adds to this literature by analyzing how inflationary brideprice contributes to marriage market obstruction. In many cultures, marriage is much more than a social formality; it marks the transition to culturally defined manhood. When marriage includes brideprice, it is also an expensive economic transaction. In these cultures, females are exchanged between kinship groups in return for assets, whether those assets be cash, cattle, gold, or other goods that serve as currency in the society. The map in Figure 11.1 highlights the prevalence of this arrangement in the twenty-first century; in a sense, the world is divided by this custom into two almost equal parts.

The map suggests three patterns: one economic, one regional, and one cultural. First, more developed countries generally do not practice brideprice or dowry. Second, Jack Goody notes that brideprice is common in all continents except America.[10] Third, the practice of brideprice is less common in predominantly Christian cultures. Sub-Saharan Africa is an interesting case in this regard; despite a strong Christian presence (38 percent), the practice of brideprice is endemic to the region (see Figure 11.1). With minority status, brideprice, though discouraged by most Christian denominations in Africa, may be a practical necessity to contract marriage through customary law.[11] Overall, roughly 75 percent of the world's population lives in regions where this practice is prevalent. It is important not to underestimate the prevalence and importance of this custom in the twenty-first century; although the United States and many of its closest security partners do not practice brideprice, they have security interests in many societies that do.[12]

Brideprice and its trajectory are an important cause of marriage market obstruction, producing grievances among young males that have been linked to violence and political instability.[13] We begin our examination of this phenomenon with a discussion of the logic and dynamics of brideprice and its potential to obstruct marriage markets. We then illustrate our argument using three case studies of countries that have been grappling with rising brideprice—Nigeria, South Sudan, and Saudi Arabia. We conclude with recommendations for policymakers interested in tracking and mitigating the risks associated with brideprice, and we offer suggestions for further scholarly research.

Marriage in Patrilineal Cultures

Patrilineality is a social system wherein persons are accounted kin through the male, or agnatic, line.[14] A millennium ago, the overwhelming majority of societies were organized along patrilineal lines. In the twenty-first century, by contrast, the international system is composed of states whose societies are arrayed along a spectrum from nonpatrilineality to strong patrilineality, with a sizable number of countries reflecting a more mixed profile in transition from one pole to the other.

Patrilineality is, at heart, a security-provision mechanism. In an anarchic world, patrilineality solves the social cooperation problem for a given group of men, providing them with natural allies in conflict situations because of the trust created through blood ties among male group members. That is, the first priority in assuring security for the group requires managing males' propensity for risk-taking, violence, and aggression and harnessing these predispositions for pro-group ends, lest they destroy the group. With its focus on prioritizing male kinship, patrilineality is the solution to which human societies have, generally speaking, historically resorted, with the vast majority of traditional societies organized along agnatic lines. In a sense, the purpose of patrilineality is to create a fraternal alliance system of brothers, cousins, sons, uncles, and fathers capable of countering threats to the group. Although it is not the only means of creating fraternity—fraternity can also be created in matrilineal societies or, somewhat less successfully, through ideological ties—patrilineality is the most straightforward and robust means of achieving the fraternal alliance necessary to provide group security.[15]

Women, however, move between kinship groups in exogamous marriage and thus, in a sense, are not full kin in patrilineal societies. Patrilocal marriage, in which a bride moves to her in-laws' household, becomes the norm, and the patriline acts to retain all significant assets, particularly land and livestock. This situation typically precludes the conferral of significant property rights or marital rights on women. Not just physical security for men, then, but economic security is afforded by the system of extended male kin groups. Women, on the other hand, suffer from a lack of both physical and economic security.

This system of social organization is still in use today. In a context in which the state is virtually nonexistent and cannot provide security for its citizens (e.g., Somalia), or in which it is profoundly indifferent to human security, the most viable alternative for an individual is to rely on extended kin groups for basic security needs.

The status of males in patrilineal societies is strongly linked to marriage. Not only does marriage mark the transition to manhood in patrilineal societies, but it establishes the male as a source of lineage and inheritance within the larger patriline. The marriage imperative is thus deeply felt among males in such cultures. And yet, marriage is unobtainable without assets. In *The Other Half of Gender: Men's Issues in Development*, the World Bank observed: "The main social requirement for achieving manhood in Sub-Saharan Africa—for being a man—is attaining some level of financial independence, employment, or income, and subsequently starting a family. In much of Sub-Saharan Africa, brideprice is commonplace, and thus marriage and family formation are directly tied to having income or property."[16]

These descriptions and conclusions are generalizable to many societies, but they take on an intensified meaning in more strongly patrilineal societies. Although it is possible to be unmarried and still be regarded as an adult man in, say, the United States, it is not possible in a strongly patrilineal society. Marriage, then, is obligatory for men living in such societies. It is through marriage and having legitimate male offspring that men maintain into the future a kindred "presence" in the lineage. It is also the only way to claim a just share of the patriline's assets and rents, which are distributed to families and not individuals. Further, in this context males are not considered to be full adults until they marry. Only then will they have a significant voice in the male collective, making marriage an important socialization ritual in addition to a valuable economic practice.

Marriage in patrilineal societies is accompanied by asset exchange, wherein brideprice offsets the cost to the natal family of raising the bride.[17] The consequences for women that grow out of this system, however, are deeply detrimental to their security and status. In addition to patrilocal marriage and the lack of female property rights mentioned above, these societies are characterized by arranged marriage in the patriline's interest; a relatively low age of marriage for girls; profound underinvestment in female human capital; intense son preference, resulting in passive neglect of girl children or active female infanticide/sex-selective abortion; highly inequitable family and personal status law favoring men; and chronically high levels of violence against women as a means to enforce the imposition of the patrilineal system on often recalcitrant women. Consider the findings of a report by a Tanzanian women's organization following an extensive survey that, "due to brideprice," women suffer "insults, sexual abuse, battery, denial of their rights to own property, being overworked and having to bear a large number of children." The report notes that "women also complained of some men's tendency to reclaim the bride price when marriages broke up, saying fear of this outcome forced women to cling to their marriages even when abused."[18]

There are two variants of this patrilineal syndrome that are worthy of analysts' attention, given their effects on the status of women overall. First, where women's work is considered productively valuable, such as when women provide the preponderance of agricultural labor, brideprice and polygyny are often prevalent. Given that marriage is patrilocal and inheritance passes through the patriline, buying or exchanging women between kinship groups becomes essential, and brideprice becomes established. Goody finds that 78 percent of the patrilineal cultures he has studied practice brideprice, and a further 6 percent practice bride-service, a variant thereof in which a young man works off the brideprice to compensate his father-in-law.[19] Richer men within the kin group can afford to pay the brideprice for more than one wife, and thus are assured even greater returns on their investment than poorer men. This brideprice-with-polygyny-for-the-rich system is by far the most prevalent variant of patrilineality, according to Goody.[20]

A second, less frequent variant of the patrilineal system occurs when women are not valued for their productive labor; in this case, women are seen as a burden, and the family providing the bride must be prepared to compensate the groom and his family for assuming this burden through payment of a dowry. Goody explains that brideprice "is more commonly found where women make the major contribution to agriculture, whereas dowry is restricted to those societies where males contribute most; this is the difference between hoe agriculture and the use of the plough, which is almost invariably in male hands."[21] The practice of brideprice differs from that of dowry in its effects on the status of women; tellingly, dowry is often associated with female infanticide because families can be bankrupted by the birth of daughters whose dowries they will be required to pay in future years.[22]

Patrilineality, therefore, cannot exist without the subordination of women to the interests of the patriline. Women are either economic boons or burdens, passed from one man to another with compensation for the economic loss incurred by her birth family if her labor is considered valuable or by the groom's family if it is lacking in value. A woman who wants to choose her marriage partner, divorce, own land, or invest in her daughters is, in a very real sense, undermining patrilineality and the security mechanism it offers male kin groups.

A fierce and often violent reaction against such women is typical.[23]

Elsewhere, Valerie Hudson and others have argued that patrilineality, though arguably effective in providing individual security for men in many circumstances, produces, generally speaking, an inherently unstable society prone to violent conflict and rentierism.[24] While historically prevalent, patrilineality is linked to a host of destabilizing tendencies that have also been historically prevalent, including food insecurity, demographic insecurity, annihilative violence, economic predation, and corruption.[25] Both this system of security provision and the instability and violence it inevitably creates have existed through millennia. The linkage we document here is not new or hidden, but has to date been rendered invisible by conventional explanations. Although the broad-ranging effects of patrilineality on security is our overall research aim, we focus in this article on the patrilineal custom of brideprice and trace its destabilizing effects on society.[26]

Brideprice and Marriage Market Obstruction

In patrilineal systems, brideprice is essentially an obligatory tax on young men, payable to older men. The young man's father and male kindred may help him pay the tax, but the intergenerational nature of the tax should be understood, especially as regards poor young men whose male relatives may likewise be too poor to help. The framing of brideprice as a tax and of marital exchange as a market eschews the kind of moralizing that often accompanies discussions of unfamiliar social rituals and clarifies the functioning of this market.

Important in this conceptualization is evidence that brideprice acts as a flat tax—for the most part, brideprice is pegged to what is considered the "going rate" for a bride in a particular society at a given point in time. The brideprice is nudged slightly upward or downward at the margin according to the status of the bride's kin, but it is not influenced greatly by the status of the man responsible for paying it. If the cost of brideprice rises, it will rise for every man, rich or poor. The flat-tax nature of brideprice has been noted across such geographically diverse states as Afghanistan, China, and Kenya.[27]

The tendency toward a consistent brideprice within a community is understandable. As Goody suggests, "In bridewealth systems, standard payments are more common; their role in a societal exchange puts pressure towards similarity."[28] The reason is that men pay for their sons' brideprices by first collecting the brideprice for their daughters. Such transactions are another force pushing down the age of marriage among girls in brideprice societies, in addition to the desire to stop providing for daughters who, socially, will become the responsibility of another family. Unless a family is very wealthy, daughters in general must be married off first, so that the family can accumulate enough assets to pay the sons' brideprices. Quoting anthropologist Lucy Mair, Goody remarks, "'When cattle payments are made, the marriage of girls tends to be early for the same reason that that of men is late—that a girl's marriage increases her father's herd while that of a young man diminishes it.' . . . [M]en chafe at the delay, girls at the speed."[29] If brideprice were not standardized within the society, families could not count on the brideprices brought in by their daughters being sufficient to cover the costs of their sons' marriages. Thus, over time, a fairly consistent brideprice emerges for the community at any given time, though the actual cost may vary somewhat over time depending on local conditions.

Many accounts suggest that men are highly sensitive to new trends in brideprice, and that the societal brideprice level is easily pushed upward but very difficult to push downward. Quoting Mair once more, Goody notes, "Every father fears being left in the lurch by finding that the bridewealth which he has accepted for his daughter will not suffice to get him a daughter-in-law; therefore, he is always on the lookout for any signs of a rise in the rate, and tends to raise his demands whenever he hears of other fathers doing so. This means in general terms that *individual* cases of over-payment produce a *general* rise in the rate all around."[30]

Almost universally, then, the amount required for an acceptable brideprice rises continually over time. The result of this persistent brideprice inflation is that marriage is either delayed or even put out of reach for many young men, particularly in situations of economic stagnation, rising inequality, or both. A summary of the average brideprice from a number of different periods and countries found that the burden equated to as much as twelve to twenty times the per capita holdings of large livestock or two to four times gross household income.[31] As Bradley Thayer and Valerie Hudson note in an article on marriage market obstruction and suicide terrorism in Islamic societies:

Delayed marriage has become a new norm in the Middle East. For example, in Egypt, one study documents that families of young adult males must save five to seven years to pay for their sons' marriages. From 2000 to 2004, wedding costs in Egypt rose 25 percent. As a result, the average marriage age for Egyptian men has risen sharply, from the early twenties to the late twenties and early thirties. In one study, nearly 25 percent of young adult males in Egypt had not married by age twenty-seven; the average age was thirty-one. In poverty-stricken Afghanistan, wedding costs for young men average $12,000–$20,000. . . . In Saudi Arabia, men usually are unable to marry before age twenty-nine; often they marry only in their mid-thirties. In Iran, 38 percent of twenty-five-year-old to twenty-nine-year-old men are unmarried. Across the Middle East, only about 50 percent of twenty-five-year-old to twenty-nine-year-old men are married, the lowest percentage for this group in the developing world. Whether in Afghanistan, Iran, Lebanon, or the United Arab Emirates, the exorbitant costs of marriage have delayed the age at which Muslim men marry.[32]

Given the tendency toward brideprice inflation, an unequal distribution of wealth will amplify market distortions by facilitating polygyny.[33] Wealthy men are able to pay even when poor men cannot. Because additional wives produce greater wealth for their husband both through their productive labor and through the birth of additional daughters who will fetch a brideprice for their father, brideprice inflation may cause a rise in the average number of wives in the households of such wealthy men. This, too, feeds into the predisposition to push down the age of marriage for girls where brideprice is present. Goody remarks, "Polygyny . . . is made possible by the differential marriage age, early for girls, later for men. Bridewealth and polygyny play into each other's hands. . . . [T]he two institutions appear to reinforce each other."[34] Polygyny is also a marker of higher social status, and it is practiced even in societies where women's labor is not considered valuable (e.g., in the United Arab Emirates).

A final source of marriage market distortion often found in brideprice societies is higher female mortality. To the degree that patrilineal-based societies profoundly devalue the lives of women and girls, resulting in significant underinvestment in women's health when resources are scarce and poverty is endemic, one sees higher rates of morbidity and mortality for females after marriage. In no area is this more evident than in that of maternal mortality. Given both low investments in women's health and the early age of marriage for girls in these societies, maternal mortality rates in most patrilineal societies tend to be egregiously high.[35] If a young wife dies in childbirth, the logic of the patrilineal syndrome dictates that she will need to be replaced, usually by a girl the same age the first wife was when she married. Despite the economic cost of having to pay brideprice once again when a woman dies in childbirth, adequate attention to the physical well-being of women and girls is often not culturally supported within the society.[36] Indeed, brideprice helps to reinforce and justify this underinvestment in women: as a women's rights activist in Uganda noted, women "cannot negotiate safer sex because of brideprice. They cannot limit the number of children that they have because of brideprice. They cannot go to school and do their own thing because they were bought."[37]

Thus, both polygyny and higher rates of postmarriage female mortality increase the ratio of marriageable males to marriageable females. Sometimes this scarcity produces extreme downward pressure on the marriage age of girls in a given society, with some marrying off girls as young as eight.[38] In most societies, however, the alteration in sex ratio results in a greater number of young men unable to find wives, even if they could afford the brideprice.

The patrilineal syndrome, therefore, is primed to produce chronic marriage market obstruction because (1) brideprice acts as a flat tax on young men that they cannot refuse to pay without suffering profoundly adverse social consequences; (2) brideprice catalyzes polygyny among the wealthier segments of society; and (3) the devaluation of women's lives leads to high female mortality.

Marriage market obstruction, in turn, can be an important factor driving young men to join violent groups. The flat and inflationary nature of brideprice guarantees that poor young men will be hard-pressed to marry. Like Jamal Kasab, they may not be able to raise the funds for brideprice without resorting to desperate measures. These young men are not taking up arms against the institution of brideprice. Rather, at the individual level, a young man engages in violence to become more successful within the patrilineal system. At the group level, it is merely the identity of the men who dominate the sociopolitical system that the group wishes to change, and not the system of male-bonded security provision itself: the recruits hope one day to replace those wealthy, powerful men themselves.

Furthermore, if a family has many sons, it may strive mightily to get the first son married, but then the younger, higher birth-order sons (such as the third, fourth and fifth sons) are typically expected to find their own sources of funding to pay brideprice. As Goody notes, these younger sons often "leav[e] the countryside to swell the growing population of the towns. . . . [I]t is people with a high bridewealth payment that have the highest rates of labor migration."[39] In sum, then, the marriage market in brideprice societies is obstructed for poor young men and sons of higher birth orders.

Young Male Grievance

The destabilizing effects of a "youth bulge" in some countries have received scholarly attention, but would profit from a concomitant analysis of marriage markets.[40] According to scholars investigating this phenomenon, a large cohort of young adults may feel aggrieved when they experience high unemployment and diminished future prospects. What is left unsaid is that the young for whom such grievances may turn explosive are overwhelmingly male. Furthermore, to have a youth bulge in the first place, a country must have a high fertility rate. Only in certain countries—that is, predominantly patrilineally based cultures where women enjoy few rights of possession, even over their own bodies—will one find such high fertility rates.[41] If such destabilization is found primarily in patrilineally organized countries, we argue that the youth bulge literature would benefit from examining the close relationship between young male grievance and obstructed marriage markets in patrilineal cultures. * * *

Glimpses of the linkage between young male grievance and marriage market obstruction do occasionally surface. For example, one commentator noted in 2011, "Communications recently made public by WikiLeaks reveal that U.S. diplomats identified delayed marriage as a source of discontent in Libya two years ago. Other scholars have called the problem a regional 'marriage crisis,' born out of low incomes and the high cost of marriage. They point out that in conservative Middle Eastern countries, unmarried young adults are generally denied intimate relationships, and the social status that comes along with being an adult."[42] Without an understanding of the dynamics of brideprice, explanations of the sources of instability in societies that practice brideprice are woefully incomplete. Being unemployed is never good, but being unemployed in a society where you can only become an adult man by marrying and in which marriage requires significant financial resources produces a clear intensification of vexation and desperation.[43]

Journalist Michael Slackman notes that "in Egypt and across the Middle East, many young people are being forced to put off marriage, the gateway to independence, sexual activity, and social respect. . . . In their frustration, the young are turning to religion for solace and purpose, pulling their parents and their governments with them."[44] One Egyptian young man whom Slackman interviewed, stated, "Sometimes, I can see how it [this frustration] does not make you closer to God, but pushes you toward terrorism. Practically, it killed my ambition. I can't think of a future."[45] The competition to fund brideprice, though most immediately an economic one, often translates into intergenerational resentment because it is older men who are typically in a financial position to acquire more wives. According to the World Bank, "The concentration of power in the hands of big men and male elders leads to power struggles between older and young men, and is related to some insurgencies in Sub-Saharan Africa. The institutionalized stratification of age groups frequently puts younger men at the service of elders, and the control of property and women by older men creates a structural conflict between younger and older generations of men. A major tension is over access to women."[46]

High levels of grievance open up an opportunity for anti-establishment groups to exploit young men attempting to gain the status and the assets needed to marry. Delayed marriage and, importantly, the threat that one may never father a son in a culture defined by patrilineality are common elements exploited by groups seeking young adult men interested in redressing the injustice they feel on a personal level, by force if necessary.

It is fascinating to see how many terrorist and rebel groups are so concerned about the marriage prospects of the young men in their ranks. For example, Diane Singerman notes, "To mobilize supporters, there were many reports of radical Islamist groups in Egypt in the 1990s arranging extremely low-cost marriages among the group's members."[47] In the 1970s, Black September, a terrorist offshoot of the Palestine Liberation Organization, offered its members brides, cash, apartments in Beirut, and even a baby bonus of $5,000 if they had a baby within a year of marriage.[48] In 2008 Taghreed el-Khodary wrote that "Hamas leaders have turned to matchmaking, bringing together single fighters and widows, and providing dowries and wedding parties for the many here who cannot afford such trappings of matrimony."[49] The Islamic State also provides its foreign fighters with opportunities to marry that they may not have had in their own country. In one such campaign, the group offered "its fighters a $1,500 bonus to go towards a starter home along with a free honeymoon in their stronghold city of Raqqa."[50] Ariel Ahram found that "ISIS foreign fighters paid $10,000 dowries to the families of their brides," suggesting that the group was attracting foreign fighters by promising resources (and available women) to marry.[51] Esther Mokuwa and her colleagues have described the great success of rebel-group recruitment in those areas of Sierra Leone with high rates of polygyny. In such areas, where wealthy older men can easily afford multiple wives, impoverished young men have little hope of marrying.[52]

Summary

Having identified patterns of patrilineality, brideprice, marriage market obstruction, and young male grievance, we illustrate in the next section how these forces have played out in three recent conflicts. To set the stage for the case studies, we performed a prefatory exploratory empirical analysis. The associations are significant: for example, in a one-way ANOVA using as the dependent variable the 2016 multivariate Global Peace Index score operationalized by Vision of Humanity to

Table 11.1. Cross Tabulation of Brideprice (Yes/No) with (Rounded) Global Peace Index, 2016 (N = 163)

BRIDEPRICE	Global Peace Index (1 Is Most Peaceful)				
	1	2	3	4	TOTAL
No (0)	16	53	8	0	77
Yes (1)	0	68	14	4	86
Total	16	121	22	4	163

scale how stable and peaceful a society is,[53] and the four-point version of the 2016 WomanStats Brideprice Scale as the independent grouping variable (N = 163),[54] the results were significant at the 0.0001 level.[55]

We also performed a cross tabulation between those same variables, with brideprice here discretized as a simple "no" or "yes" indicating whether any form of brideprice is practiced, and the Global Peace Index discretized by rounding to the nearest whole-number scale point.

The results of this cross tabulation are striking (see Table 11. 1): no society with brideprice fell into the most peaceful quartile of this sample of 163 nation-states. No society without brideprice fell into the least peaceful quartile of the sample. Additional exploratory statistical results can be found in the supplemental material online.[56]

These exploratory empirical results are interesting, but only suggestive. Process tracing is required to understand the casual mechanisms at work, prior to conducting any confirmatory analysis, and that requires a more detailed examination of relevant cases.

Case Studies

In this section, we describe the linkages between marriage market obstruction and the resort to organized violence with the help of three case studies. We chose these cases as plausibility probes of the thesis that brideprice can destabilize societies. The first two cases, Boko Haram in the Lake Chad Basin and various militias in South Sudan, illustrate the dynamics of brideprice and rebellion in practice. These are cases in which observers and participants have explicitly acknowledged the role of brideprice in the emergence of group-based violence. The third case, Saudi Arabia, demonstrates how some states, having recognized the risk posed by brideprice, are attempting to mitigate that risk through the creation of programs and policies to prevent or ameliorate the destabilizing effects of brideprice inflation.

How Brideprice Bolsters Boko Haram's Recruitment in Nigeria

Inflationary brideprice in northern Nigeria led to, and then continued to fuel, the rise of the Salafi-jihadist group Boko Haram. The group first gained international attention following its abduction of 276 schoolgirls from Chibok, a town in the northeastern state of Borno in Nigeria, in April 2014. Although this episode, and the international community's rallying behind efforts to free the girls, thrust Boko Haram onto the global agendas of Western countries and human rights advocates for the first time, the group has been active for more than a decade. Thus far, Boko Haram–related actions have claimed more than 35,000 lives and have led to the displacement of an estimated 2.5 million people throughout the Lake Chad Basin. As one of the most lethal insurgencies in Africa, Boko Haram is responsible for one of the world's worst humanitarian disasters.[57]

Despite a renewed military offensive against the group in 2015, the conflict is ongoing. Boko Haram continues to engage in bombing campaigns and has thwarted the government's efforts to exercise control over much of Borno State. It also has expanded its activities into neighboring Chad, Niger, and Cameroon, drawing on existing trade and kinship networks.

As part of its recruitment strategy, Boko Haram has continued to organize inexpensive weddings for its members, a practice dating back to the group's founder, Muhammad Yusuf. Given rising brideprice, underemployment, and polygamy-related bride scarcity, many of the young men who marry in these weddings would have probably remained bachelors.[58]

According to S.P. Reyna, brideprice in Nigeria's Lake Chad Basin serves to "partially socialize younger men into their mature economic roles."[59] The region's marriage market constitutes a reward system in which men are incentivized to become economically productive and thus socially significant. Although the past three decades have witnessed changes in Lake Chad Basin social norms, Reyna's 1985 observation about the town of Bama, in Borno State, still holds true for the larger region. He writes, "The crucial point is that the spoils of deference cannot begin to accrue to a man until he has married."[60] Within the social strata, the older, married men receive the most respect, then younger, married men, and lastly unmarried men. As Reyna describes, "There are gatherings of men that convene in each ward every day. Though informal, these sessions play a vital role in communicating information and formulating opinions about affairs that touch village and ward. Mature, married men sit on cushions or stools in the center of large mats laid out beneath trees. Younger, married men sit on these mats, but on the edges and without stools or cushions. Young, unmarried men sit in the dirt beside the mat."[61]

This sort of social hierarchy also appears in anthropological accounts of the Kanuri ethnic group, whose members are thought to have made up a significant proportion of Boko Haram's organization and leadership, particularly in its early years. Among the Kanuri and other ethnic groups in the Lake Chad Basin, prestige is tied to the size of a man's family and household unit, which includes his family and other members of the community who live under his care. This system further incentivizes the taking of multiple wives and the expansion of patronage systems. Young men are often taken under the wing of a local "big man," whose wealth and social status facilitate the process of finding them wives. In return, the young men pledge loyalty to their patron—a commitment that often entails the younger men providing labor.[62] Only after taking a wife is a young man able to act as a "real man," exercising autonomy and accumulating social capital.[63]

In northern Nigeria, obtaining the financial resources to pay brideprice has become increasingly difficult. The country's oil wealth has disincentivized investment in the manufacturing sector and made non-agricultural, non-oil sector employment difficult to obtain. Youth unemployment remains a constant concern; less discussed is the impact of the lack of jobs on the psychology of unemployed young men. A 2015 survey found that, for 57 percent of Nigerian men, "insufficient income" was a source of stress; 44 percent experienced stress as a result of "not having enough work." Despite these economic stressors, 98 percent of the men surveyed reported that "bride price is important and should remain [so]"; 29 percent reported that "a real man in Nigeria is one with many wives."[64] These high percentages are all the more striking when one considers that the survey included regions in Nigeria where polygamy is not widely practiced, as well as regions with higher employment statistics and annual incomes.[65]

According to the spiritual leader Khalifa Abulfathi, in the communities surrounding Maiduguri, where Boko Haram was founded, the cost of "items required for [a] successful [marriage] celebration kept changing in tune with inflation over the years."[66] The Kanuri and Shuwa Arabs, two prominent ethnic groups in the area, "primarily demand payment of dowries in gold coins."[67] Increases in the price of gold over time have made it difficult for young men to pay brideprice, further adding to their strain.

Maiduguri has also witnessed shifts in the marriage practice known as *Toshi* (literally, "blocking"), in which the fiancé, often with his family's support, provides gifts to his fiancée and her family to ward off other suitors. According to Abulfathi, "the Toshi became monetized and progressively included the funding for the Turaren wuta (scents) and kayan lalle (henna)," which women use in the wedding ceremony.[68] He noted that "these were later included in the brideprice that resulted in a spike in the bride-price in the 2000s."[69] It was during this period that "economic hardship began playing a role in the marriage processes in Borno."[70]

It was also during this period that Boko Haram came into its own, with founder Mohammed Yusuf breaking away from his patron, Ja'far Adams, and establishing his own mosque in 2002. Yusuf had been put in charge of the youth wing of Adams's politically connected Salafist group because of his skill in mobilizing young men. In exchange for building political support for the governor of Borno State, Adams and Yusuf influenced the terms under which Borno State adopted and implemented Sharia law. Over time, however, Yusuf became increasingly frustrated with what he perceived as the government's inadequate implementation of Sharia law. This frustration would eventually lead him to reject the legitimacy of the government at both the state and federal levels, as well as Western institutions and influences.

In the early days of Boko Haram, Yusuf provided the types of social services that Borno State, the federal government, and traditional authorities had failed to supply. In addition to increasing access to education and farmland, the group helped to arrange marriages for young men. A resident of the Railroad neighborhood of Maiduguri, where Yusuf established his mosque, recalled that in just a few years, Yusuf had facilitated more than 500 weddings. The group also provided support for young men to become "okada drivers," who gained popularity for their affordable motorbike taxi services. Some even saved enough to marry. At this time, Boko Haram was a relatively nonviolent group that focused its aggression toward local political and religious figures who criticized the group's rejection of the government's legitimacy on religious grounds. Violence ramped up, however, when the police began targeting okada drivers for not wearing protective helmets, which the drivers argued interfered with their religious head-dressings. In 2009, government forces killed 700 suspected Boko Haram members in a massive security sweep in Maiduguri that included door-to-door raids and the extrajudicial killing of Mohammed Yusuf. Following this crackdown, the group went underground for a year or so before re-emerging with a deepened sense of grievance and a new leader, Abubakar Shekau.[71]

Under Shekau, Boko Haram has engaged in a wholesale war against the Nigerian state. Through raids in rural areas, suicide bombings, attacks on military posts, and the bombings of cities, the insurgency has killed more than 35,000 people and displaced more than 2.5 million.[72] Hundreds of suicide bombers have detonated their devices against civilian targets such as bus stations and markets, killing thousands.[73] In rural areas, fear of Boko Haram has been so pervasive that farmers have left their fields fallow, contributing to a regional food security crisis thought to have affected 11 million people in the Lake Chad Basin. The World Bank estimates that Boko Haram has caused $9 billion worth of damage throughout the country's north since 2010.[74]

Under Shekau, Boko Haram also has begun to abduct women to be "wives" for its members. In many cases, these women are essentially sex slaves. Amnesty International estimated in 2015 that the group had abducted more than 2,000 women, and it is likely that this figure has risen since then. In interviews, women who voluntarily joined Boko Haram reported that they were often attracted to the group because the brideprice, though smaller than those accompanying "traditional" weddings, was paid directly to the women, not to their fathers. At least in the beginning, however, a token brideprice was left for the fathers of kidnapped girls: one man recounted how Boko Haram kidnapped girls in his community, "tossing 5,000 naira [about $25] on the floor as a brideprice." Another offered the following account:

> Bawagana, a shy 15-year-old living in Sanda Kyarimi camp, one of the official Internally Displaced People sites, said that a Boko Haram

fighter had come to her home in Dikwa, 90 kilometres east of Maiduguri, and asked, "Do you love me?"

Of course I answered, "No!" she said, with her eyes fixed on the ground. The boy got very angry and said, "If you do not come with me, I will kill your father, but if you come with me I will let him live."

I followed to save my father. The boy left 10,000 naira (about $50) on the floor. It was a bride price in Boko Haram's eyes.[75]

Those familiar with Boko Haram's practices state that women are given to fighters to reward them for their service and to cultivate loyalty. A fifteen-year-old who worked as a driver for Boko Haram before defecting to the Civilian Joint Task Force (a vigilante group that assists the government's forces against Boko Haram) reported that "wives are 'earned,' they are a reward for those who stay six months." Once you have proven your commitment to the group, "if you see someone who you like, you can pick the wife you want."[76] The women are often groomed before becoming wives, a process that can involve days of "Quranic education," in which they are subjected to lectures on Boko Haram's ideology. Women who were married before being abducted are told to forget their "infidel" husbands and accept a Boko Haram husband. Although the media often describe the abductions of women and girls who later become wives of insurgents as cases of purely sexual and physical violence, reports suggest that the process of marrying an insurgent is always formalized for purposes of legitimation. The fifteen-year-old driver-turned-vigilante reported that marriages are often accompanied by a large ceremony; the young man observed that a Boko Haram wedding is "like a regular marriage."[77]

Since its founding as a dissident sect through its transformation into one of the most lethal insurgencies in sub-Saharan Africa, Boko Haram has recognized the importance of marriage to young men, and has capitalized on male grievances related to brideprice inflation. By providing members access to wives, and thus a sense of self as "real men," Boko Haram has gained a following of 3,000–5,000 young men, with shockingly few reports of defection. "These men can take a wife at no extra charge," explained Kaka, a young woman orphaned, captured, and raped by Boko Haram members. "Usually it is very expensive to take a wife, very hard to get married, but not now."[78]

In sum, the intergenerational nature of the brideprice tax in Nigeria's Lake Chad Basin, coupled with other grievances common to the region's young men, has galvanized some of these men to obtain wives (and social standing) in ways that have destabilized the state and augmented the power of anti-state groups. The most visible of these groups is Boko Haram. Without taking into account the effect of brideprice, one cannot fully understand why Boko Haram emerged, why it persists, and how it could be successfully challenged.

Brideprice, Cattle Raiding, and Civil War in South Sudan

South Sudan is another state where brideprice inflation has had destabilizing effects by incentivizing violence. It is the world's newest state, its population having voted overwhelmingly to declare independence from Sudan in a 2011 referendum after decades of violence and instability. Even before the referendum, the dynamics of marriage markets in the region had contributed to insecurity in areas now a part of South Sudan by incentivizing young men's participation in armed groups. One such group, the Sudanese People's Liberation Army (SPLA)—a key participant in the 1983–2005 Second Sudanese Civil War—acknowledged the importance of marriage to its members. Although the SPLA's recruitment efforts might not have been explicitly predicated on access to women, in practice, members were rewarded with wives.

In the context of South Sudan's post-independence civil war, cattle raiding has become even more deadly, driven not only by the militarization of the region but also by skyrocketing brideprice and ensuing economic desperation. Where once a bride would cost twelve cows, marrying an educated woman in South Sudan after the referendum would require fifty cows, in addition to 60 goats and 30,000 Sudanese pounds (in 2011, the equivalent of $12,000 in cash).[79]

Cattle, masculinity, and livelihoods have been inexorably connected in the region's history; the civil war is now being woven into this political and economic tapestry. According to Hannah Wright, "Owning a gun and participating in a cattle raid are rites of passage for adolescent boys, and for men these are symbols of manhood and virility which confer social status."[80] Those who successfully carry out cattle raids are doubly rewarded: first, stealing cattle gives them the ability to afford a now-exorbitant brideprice. Additionally, those who steal another tribe's cattle enjoy the social standing conferred through livestock ownership, including being honored in public ceremonies in which women praise them in song.

Although brideprice is sometimes paid in cash or through a mixture of livestock, the use of cattle as the primary measurement of brideprice remains widespread. One pastoralist in South Sudan states simply, "You cannot marry without cows, and you cannot be called a man without cows."[81] According to the ECC [Environment, Conflict, and Cooperation] Platform, "Traditionally, cattle raids are a livelihood sustaining practice, which allows restocking herds after droughts" and also serves an important social function, "as it provides the means for young men to get married."[82] * * *

In South Sudan, brideprice inflation and the wide availability of small arms have resulted in increasingly violent cattle raids and facilitated the proliferation of militias. Together, these forces have fueled an intercommunal conflict that has destabilized the young country. A comprehensive security analysis would of necessity acknowledge the significant role that brideprice has played in fostering instability in South Sudan since independence. Policymakers in South Sudan and its international partners must find a way to circumvent the instability resulting from brideprice inflation if the country is to break the cycle of violence.

Stabilization Efforts in Saudi Arabia's Marriage Market

There is at least one state that takes brideprice inflation as a serious policy issue: Saudi Arabia. And arguably, the Saudi regime has seen some measure of success from its efforts in addressing this concern. Despite the intersection of regime characteristics and population indicators that would suggest Saudi Arabia is ripe for violent rebellion, the country has been remarkably stable. Saudi Arabia's stability is rightly puzzling, given the thesis of this article. Although there are a number of important differences between Saudi Arabia, on the one hand, and Nigeria and South Sudan, on the other, all three countries have strong brideprice traditions. Additionally, as in the Nigeria and South Sudan case studies, concepts of masculinity and social standing in Saudi Arabia are deeply connected to a man's ability to take a wife. Polygyny is also a feature of the marriage market in Saudi Arabia, which could be expected to have the same sorts of effects on the distribution of potential wives as in Nigeria and South Sudan—and thus to pose the same threat to intergenerational relations. Similarly, all of these countries have experienced the inflationary pressures in brideprice that threaten obstruction of marriage markets.

There is, however, at least one critical difference between Saudi Arabia and Nigeria and South Sudan: the Saudi regime's activism on the issue of brideprice inflation and its recognition of the threat to national stability from marriage market obstruction. Unlike the Nigerian and South Sudanese governments which have largely refrained from intervening in the marriage market to dampen brideprice inflation—whether because of a lack of interest or a lack of capacity—Saudi Arabia, through both the government and civil-society groups, has undertaken vigorous efforts to cap brideprice and reduce the cost of weddings. Although marriage and marriage markets are infrequently discussed in purely economic terms by governments, it is clear from the Saudi Arabian case that, just as in other economic markets (e.g., housing and credit), targeted governmental intervention is possible and helpful.[83]

In the early 2000s, brideprice in Saudi Arabia was on the rise. One anecdotal account reported that the average price for a virgin bride was 70,000 SAR (more than $18,500). By 2015, there were reports of brideprice payments "as high as SR100,000."[84] Following consultations with religious leaders, the government released a decree asking for local cooperation with enforcement of a ceiling for brideprice. Ostensibly the government framed its legislative cap on brideprice—limiting the payment for a virgin bride to 50,000 SAR and a previously married woman to 30,000 SAR—as a means of combating the rise in unmarried women. The government claimed that "the number of spinsters in Saudi Arabia [had] surged from around 1.5 million at the end of 2010 to more than four million" in 2015.[85]

■　■　■

To further ameliorate the destabilizing effects of brideprice, the government has begun to promote the concept that brideprice must be proportional to the man's economic situation, thus dampening somewhat the regressive nature of brideprice. In 2015, Morgan Windsor reported that "the average dowry for middle-class families in Saudi Arabia is SR30,000 or $8,000, but it can be hundreds of thousands of riyals for the wealthy."[86] Although this sum still constitutes a significant burden, a sliding scale of brideprice would reduce the concentration of wives in the hands of the few and the obstruction of marriage markets by opening up the possibility of marriage to a wider range of social classes. * * *

Some analysts would suggest that the relatively high number of Saudi Arabians joining terrorist organizations undermines the thesis of this article. It was estimated in 2016 that more than 2,500 Saudis were fighting for the Islamic State.[87] Although the Saudi government has taken steps to address brideprice's destabilizing effects, the capped level is still relatively burdensome even for middle-class families. Brideprice is certainly not the only reason a young Saudi man would join an insurgent group, but in the absence of the government's efforts to cap brideprice, the figure cited above could be much higher.

Conclusion

The brideprice system associated with patrilineality is an important underlying cause of chronic instability within some societies. Like other marketized commodities, brideprice is subject to destabilizing inflation, obstructing marriage markets by pricing marriage out of the reach of many young men. This tendency toward marriage market obstruction is aggravated by polygyny, an early age of marriage for girls, and the high post-marriage female mortality rates that typically accompany brideprice systems. These structural problems incentivize violence to obtain brideprice resources, as we have demonstrated in the case of South Sudan, and offer insurgent groups a ready-made recruitment tool, as we have shown in the case of Boko Haram in northern Nigeria.

Brideprice functions as a profoundly regressive tax, disproportionately affecting poorer and higher birth-order young men and creating a large, aggrieved base from which violent groups can more easily recruit. The demands of brideprice in places where the economy is stagnating or jobs are scarce leave young men with few options. Without an income, they cannot get a wife; without a wife, they cannot be regarded as so-called real men in their patrilineal society. For many young men, the only means to accumulate the assets needed to marry may be looting, raiding, or joining a rebel or terrorist group.

This analysis offers two important takeaways. First, no comprehensive security analysis of many of today's conflicts can be complete without an examination of how the structuration of male/female relations affects those conflicts. How those relations are structured has cascading effects on macro-level state phenomena, as the case of brideprice demonstrates. Marriage market obstruction, fueled by brideprice and polygyny, can destabilize nations by incentivizing violence and facilitating recruitment into insurgent groups. As former Secretary of State Hillary Clinton has asserted, "The subjugation of women is a threat to the common security of our world and to the national security of our country."[88]

Scholars in the field of security studies and analysts in the state security sector must begin to gather the type of information necessary to include these important factors in their analysis, and consider the linkages between the security concepts conventionally employed and the structuration of male/female relations. Given the role of brideprice inflation in facilitating grievance, violent conflict, raiding, and even insurrection, monitoring fluctuations in marriage markets is a critical task for the security analyst—and yet such monitoring is not taking place. That must change. Part of this neglect no doubt stems from conventions in security analysis circles, which assign what are too often considered "soft" social issues a lower priority. Marriage, with all of its associations with women and family, perhaps seems to those in these circles to be a far cry from the logic of conflict. Concerned with

the movements and weapons of violent nonstate actors, national security scholars and analysts in the United States and around the globe may thus unintentionally overlook the social forces that prompt so many young men to take up arms.

■   ■   ■

The second major takeaway of our analysis is that even though marriage is a deeply socialized practice, governments are not powerless; they can act to mitigate the heightened risk of destabilization caused by brideprice inflation, as the Saudi case makes plain. Given the linkages among brideprice inflation, grievance, and violent conflict, governments can, for example, place caps on brideprices or subsidize marriage costs to avoid marriage market obstruction. Initiatives to end child marriage and make it harder to contract polygynous marriages take on even greater significance once their relevance for national stability and security are recognized. This sort of regulation represents a market intervention that not only protects the rights of girls and women, but inhibits the market's tendency toward concentration and inequality.

Civil society groups also play an important role in curbing harmful brideprice practices. In Uganda, a fifteen-year campaign to end harmful brideprice practices marked a victory when in 2015, the high court ruled that the practice of refunding brideprice in order for a woman to get a divorce was unconstitutional. The campaign continues with the hope that brideprice, which has hurt the status of women and made "marriage a competition that many young people cannot afford to enter," will be banned entirely one day.[89] * * *

All these initiatives are worth resourcing from national security funding. Not only will affected nations benefit from this expenditure, but also third-party governments concerned with international and regional flashpoints. Efforts to cap brideprice, raise the marriage age of girls, and curb polygyny are hard security matters in many shatter belts where spillover threats easily destabilize entire regions and where military intervention by great powers may one day be contemplated. The time has come to recognize what has been hiding in plain sight.

NOTES

1. Vikas Bajaj and Lydia Polgreen, "Suspect Stirs Mumbai Court by Confessing," *New York Times,* July 20, 2009, www.nytimes.com /2009/07/21/world/asia/21 india.html.

2. Mumbai Gunman Video, Channel 4 (India), n.d., http://link .brightcove.com/services/player/bcpid1184614595?bctid =27874456001.

3. "Know More about Ajmal Amir Kasab," *India TV,* November 21, 2012, http://www.indiatvnews.com/news/india/know-more-about -ajmal-amir-kasab-18703.html?page=3.

4. Alan B. Krueger and Jitka Maleckova, "Education, Poverty, and Terrorism: Is There a Causal Connection?" *Journal of Economic Perspectives,* Vol. 17, No. 4 (November 2003), pp. 119–144, doi:10.3386/w9074.

5. The term "brideprice" refers to an overall net transfer of assets from the groom's family to the bride's family. This includes brideprice, bridewealth, and bride-service. It also includes dower, which should not be confused with dowry. Dowry refers to an overall net transfer of assets from the bride's family to the groom's family.

6. See the seminal work by Ted Robert Gurr, *Why Men Rebel* (Princeton, N.J.: Princeton University Press, 1970).

7. Paul Collier and Anke Hoeffler, "Greed and Grievance in Civil Wars" (Washington, D.C.: World Bank, 2001), doi:10.1093/oep/ gpf064.

8. Scott Atran, *Talking to the Enemy: Faith, Brotherhood, and the (Un) Making of Terrorists* (New York: Ecco, 2010).

9. See, among others, John Horgan, *Walking Away from Terrorism: Accounts of Disengagement from Radical and Extremist Movements* (New York: Routledge, 2009).

10. Jack Goody, "Bridewealth and Dowry in Africa and Eurasia," in Goody and S.J. Tambiah, *Bridewealth and Dowry* (Cambridge: Cambridge University Press, 1973), p. 51.

11. Bob Seidensticker, "Christianity Becomes an African Religion, Islam Overtakes Christianity, and Other Upcoming Changes," *Patheos,* May 11, 2015, http://www.patheos.com/blogs /crossexamined/2015/05/christianity-becomes-an-african-religion -islam-overtakes-christianity-and-other-upcoming-changes/.

12. This statistic comes from our estimates of the percentage distribution of world populations by continent, which tally nearly 60 percent of the world's population as residing in Asia and more than 16 percent as residing in sub-Saharan Africa.

13. See, for example, Valerie M. Hudson and Andrea M. Den Boer, *Bare Branches: The Security Implications of Asia's Surplus Male Population* (Cambridge, Mass.: MIT Press, 2004); and Bradley A. Thayer

and Valerie M. Hudson, "Sex and the Shaheed: Insights from the Life Sciences on Islamic Suicide Terrorism," *International Security,* Vol. 34, No. 4 (Spring 2010), pp. 37–62, doi:10.1162/ isec.2010.34.4.37. Raiding for resources to marry is typical in societies with obstructed marriage markets. Because the obstruction is worst for poor, unskilled young men, less violent types of resource raiding are not feasible alternatives.

14. Linda Stone, *Kinship and Gender: An Introduction* (Boulder, Colo: Westview, 2013).

15. For example, some matrilineal systems, such as those in Melanesia, also practice brideprice. Although patrilineality makes male control over assets, women, and power more straightforward, males are still able to exert almost the same level of control in brideprice-practicing matrilineal societies, and brideprice plays a role in creating grievances that lead violence in these societies, as well. We are indebted to Sue Ingram of the Australian National University for this insight. Additionally, ideology is not as sturdy a basis for fraternity as kinship is, which is why some ideologically based groups attempt to shore up that fraternity with marriages that make men not only ideological brothers, but in-laws and therefore kin. Osama bin Laden, for example, attempted to have his top lieutenants marry sisters to better ensure they would remain loyal to each other. See Thayer and Hudson, "Sex and the Shaheed."

16. Ian Bannon and Maria C. Correia, *The Other Half of Gender: Men's Issues in Development* (Washington, D.C.: World Bank, 2006), p. 161, https://openknowledge.worldbank.org/handle/10986/7029.

17. If we turn our attention from brideprice to dowry, dowry is intended to offset the cost to the groom's family of feeding and sheltering the bride, who is viewed as nonproductive (i.e., only reproductive).

18. "Human Rights Study Links Payment of Bride Price to Abuse of Women," *IRIN,* May 16, 2006, http://www.irinnews.org/report /59032/tanzania-study-links-payment-bride-price-abuse-women.

19. Goody, "Bridewealth and Dowry in Africa and Eurasia," p. 50.

20. Ibid.

21. Ibid., p. 52.

22. Hudson and Den Boer, *Bare Branches.*

23. See, for example, David Jacobson, *Of Virgins and Martyrs: Women and Sexuality in Global Conflict* (Baltimore, Md.: Johns Hopkins University Press, 2013).

24. Valerie M. Hudson, Donna Lee Bowen, and Perpetua Lynne Nielsen, "Clan Governance and State Stability: The Relationship between Female Subordination and Political Order," *American Political Science Review,* Vol. 109, No. 3 (August 2015), pp. 535–555, doi:10.1017/S0003055415000271. "Rentierism" refers to an economic system based on appropriation of resources that produce rents, which are then used to govern and control society. Rentier powers govern, in the first place, through corruption.

25. Ibid.

26. Valerie M. Hudson et al., *The First Political Order: Sex, Governance, and National Security,* Texas A&M University and Brigham Young University, 2017.

27. Hudson, Bowen, and Nielsen, "Clan Governance and State Stability."

28. Goody, "Bridewealth and Dowry in Africa and Eurasia," p. 18.

29. Ibid, p. 10.

30. Ibid, p. 5 (emphasis in the original).

31. Siwan Anderson, "The Economics of Dowry and Brideprice," *Journal of Economic Perspectives*, Vol. 21, No. 4 (Fall 2007), pp. 151–174, doi:10.1257/jep.21.4.151.

32. Thayer and Hudson, "Sex and the Shaheed," p. 54.

33. Polygyny is also a custom that has not died out to the extent that some would imagine. For a visual representation of the prevalence of polygyny in the world today, see "Prevalence and Legal Status of Polygyny," WomanStats Project, 2016, http://www.womanstats .org/substatics/PW-SCALE-1-2016.png.

34. Goody, "Bridewealth and Dowry in Africa and Eurasia," p. 10.

35. That is not the case in some patrilineal societies. For example, in Saudi Arabia and the United Arab Emirates, there are sufficient resources to justify the expense of investing in maternal health care. Furthermore, the average age of marriage has been creeping upward in these societies. For both these reasons, maternal mortality in these Gulf States tends to be lower than in other patrilineal cultures. China, too, has made a successful push toward lowering maternal mortality rates, and it strictly regulates both fertility and age of marriage.

36. This phenomenon is difficult to explain in solely economic terms. Whereas in some regions with brideprice (such as sub-Saharan Africa), childhood sex ratios are normal, indicating that families understand the economic value of keeping girls alive until married, in other regions with brideprice (e.g., Pakistan and Albania), childhood sex ratios are abnormal and favor males.

37. Jessica Heckert and Madeline Short Fabic, "Improving Data Concerning Women's Empowerment in Sub-Saharan Africa," *Studies in Family Planning*, Vol. 44, No. 3 (September 2013), p. 335, doi:10.1111/j.1728-4465.2013.00360.x.

38. Cynthia Gorney, "Too Young to Wed: The Secret World of Child Brides," *National Geographic*, June 2011, http://ngm.national geographic.com/2011/06/child-brides/gorney-text/1; and George Thomas, "India's Innocent: Secret Weddings of Child Brides," *CBN News*, August 24, 2015, http://www1.cbn.com/cbnnews/world /2012/June/Innocence-Lost-Indias-Children-Marrying-at-Age-8.

39. Goody, "Bridewealth and Dowry in Africa and Eurasia," pp. 8–9.

40. Henrik Urdal, "A Clash of Generations? Youth Bulges and Political Violence," *International Studies Quarterly*, Vol. 50, No. 3 (September 2006), pp. 607–629, doi:10.1111/j.1468-2478.2006.00416.x; Justin Yifu Lin, "Youth Bulge: A Demographic Dividend or a Demographic Bomb in Developing Countries?" (Washington, D.C.: World Bank, 2012); and Ragnhild Nordås and Christian Davenport, "Fight the Youth: Youth Bulges and State Repression," *American Journal of Political Science*, Vol. 57, No. 4 (April 2013), pp. 926–940, doi:10.1111/ajps.12025.

41. Compare our scaling of birth rates and our scaling of patrilineal clan governance in the following two maps: "Birth Rates, Scaled 2015," WomanStats Project, 2015, http://www.womanstats.org /substatics/BirthRates2015correctedstatic.png; and "Clan Governance Index (Degree of Female Subordination in Marriage/ Family), Scaled 2015," WomanStats Project, 2015, http://www .womanstats.org/substatics/ClanGovernanceIndex _2correctstaticmiddle.png. All countries in the highest two

categories of birth rates also score in the highest category of patrilineal clan governance.

42. Heather Murdock, "'Delayed' Marriage Frustrates Middle East Youth," *Voice of America*, February 22, 2011, http://www.voanews .com/a/delayed-marriage-frustrates-middle-east-youth-116744384 /172742.html.

43. Interestingly, a report by Nava Ashraf, Natalie Bau, Nathan Nunn, and Alessandra Voena found that increasing girls' education may raise the rate of brideprice in the community. Noting this unintended side-effect is not meant to discredit girls' education as a development objective, but rather highlights how girls' gains may feed other sources of female oppression as well as marriage market obstruction. See Ashraf et al., "Bride Price and Female Education" (Cambridge, Mass.: National Bureau of Economic Research, 2016), http://www .nber.org/papers/w22417.pdf.

44. Michael Slackman, "Stifled, Egypt's Youth Turn to Islamic Fervor," *New York Times*, February 17, 2008, www.nytimes.com/2008/02/17 /world/middleeast/17youth.html.

45. Ibid.

46. Bannon and Correia, *The Other Half of Gender*.

47. Diane Singerman, "The Economic Imperatives of Marriage: Emerging Practices and Identities among Youth in the Middle East" (Dubai: Wolfensohn Center for Development at the Dubai School of Government, 2007), p. 49, http://www.meyi.org/uploads/3/2/0/1 /32012989/singerman_-_the_economic_imperatives_of_marriage -_emerging_practices_and_identities_among_youth_in_the _middle_east.pdf.

48. Bruce Hoffman, "Gaza City, All You Need Is Love: How the Terrorists Stopped Terrorism," *Atlantic*, December 2001, https:// www.theatlantic.com/past/docs/issues/2001/12/hoffman.htm.

49. Taghreed El-Khodary, "For War Widows, Hamas Recruits Army of Husbands," *New York Times*, October 31, 2008, www.nytimes.com /2008/10/31/world/middleeast/31gaza.html.

50. "ISIS Fighters Get Marriage Bonus, Including Honeymoon," *CBSNews*, May 26, 2015, http://www.cbsnews.com/news/isis -fighters-get-marriage-bonuses-including-honeymoon/.

51. Ariel I. Ahram, "Sexual Violence and the Making of ISIS," *Survival*, Vol. 57, No. 3 (May 2015), pp. 57–78, at p. 69.

52. Esther Mokuwa et al., "Peasant Grievance and Insurgency in Sierra Leone: Judicial Serfdom as a Driver of Conflict," *African Affairs*, July 2011, pp. 339–366, doi:10.1093/afraf/adr019.

53. "Global Peace Index, 2016" (New York: Vision of Humanity, Institute for Economics and Peace, 2016), http://visionofhumanity .org/indexes/global-peace-index/.

54. "Brideprice/Dowry/Wedding Costs (Type and Prevalence), Scaled 2016," WomanStats Project, 2016, http://www.womanstats.org /substatics/Brideprice_Dowry_Wedding_Costs_2correctstatic.png.

55. Results can be found at doi:10.7910/DVN/SPZSJZ/.

56. Ibid.

57. Nigerian Social Violence Project dataset, Johns Hopkins School of Advanced International Studies, Washington, D.C., http://www .connectsaisafrica.org/research/african-studies-publications/social -violence-nigeria/.

58. Hilary Matfess, interviews with persons who wish to remain anonymous, North East Region, Nigeria, 2015–16.

59. S.P. Reyna, "Bridewealth Revisited: Socialization and the Reproduction of Labor in a Domestic African Economy" (Durham: University of New Hampshire, 1985), p. 1, http://pdf.usaid.gov/pdf_docs/PNAAX355.pdf.

60. Ibid, p. 9.

61. Ibid, p. 8.

62. Ronald Cohen, "Marriage Instability among the Kanuri of Northern Nigeria," *American Anthropologist,* Vol. 63, No. 6 (December 1961), pp. 1231–1249.

63. Ronald Cohen, "The Analysis of Conflict in Hierarchical Systems: An Example from Kanuri Political Organization," *Anthropologica,* Vol. 4, No. 1 (1962), pp. 87–120.

64. If brideprice is quick to rise, why is it so resistant to falling? First, individuals and families want to maintain social face and standing in the male hierarchy. Which man wants to be the first to accept a lower-than-normal brideprice for his daughter? Similarly, perhaps to a lesser degree, which family wants to be the first to pay a lower price for a bride, signaling potential economic woes? Second, an economic calculus helps maintain high brideprices: those who have already paid the going rate, and those who have daughters of marriageable age, will see their investment degraded by lowered brideprice and will resist any decrease. Voices 4 Change, *Being a Man in Nigeria: Perceptions and Realities* (London: UKAID, 2015), p. 22, www.v4c-nigeria.com/being-a-man-in-nigeria-perceptions-and-realities/.

65. Ibid.

66. Hilary Matfess interview with Khalifa Abulfathi, email correspondence, 2016.

67. Ibid.

68. Ibid.

69. Ibid.

70. Ibid.

71. The description of the sect's evolution is drawn from author fieldwork and from Andrew Walker, *"Eat the Heart of the Infidel": The Harrowing of Nigeria and the Rise of Boko Haram* (London: Hurst, 2016).

72. Nigerian Social Violence Project dataset.

73. Jason Warner and Hilary Matfess, "Trends and Demography in Boko Haram's Suicide Bombings," Harvard University and Center for Democracy and Development, Abuja, Nigeria, 2017.

74. Michael Olukayode and Yinka Ibukun, "Boko Haram Caused $9 Billion Damage in Nigeria's North," *Bloomberg,* March 6, 2017, https://www.bloomberg.com/news/articles/2017-03-06/boko-haram-caused-9-billion-damage-in-nigeria-s-north-un-says.

75. Hilary Matfess, "Boko Haram Is Enslaving Women, Making Them Join the War," *Newsweek,* February 8, 2016, http://www.newsweek.com/2016/02/19/nigeria-boko-haram-buhari-chibok-girls-424091.html.

76. Hilary Matfess, fieldwork, North East Region, Nigeria, 2015–16.

77. Ibid.

78. Matfess, "Boko Haram Is Enslaving Women, Making Them Join the War."

79. Matt Richmond and Flavia Krause-Jackson, "Cows-for-Bride Inflation Spurs Cattle Theft in South Sudan," *Bloomberg,* July 26, 2011, www.bloomberg.com/news/2011-07-26/cows-for-bride-inflation-spurs-cattle-theft-among-mundari-in-south-sudan.html.

80. Hannah Wright, *Masculinities, Conflict, and Peacebuilding: Perspectives on Men through a Gender Lens* (London: Saferworld, 2014), p. 7, www.saferworld.org.uk/resources/view-resource/862-masculinities-conflict-and-peacebuilding-perspectives-on-men-through-a-gender-lens.

81. Marc Sommers and Stephanie Schwartz, "Dowry and Division: Youth and State Building in South Sudan" (Washington, D.C.: United States Institute of Peace, 2011), p. 4, https://www.usip.org/publications/2011/11/dowry-and-division-yough-and-state-building-south-sudan.

82. "Conflict between Dinka and Nuer in South Sudan."

83. Although both Nigeria and Saudi Arabia subsidize fuel, and South Sudan has subsidized food in the past, only Saudi Arabia has intervened to control the rising costs of this other critical household expenditure.

84. Carol Fleming, "What Is a Typical Dowry in the Kingdom?" *American Bedu,* June 23, 2008, https://delhi4cats.wordpress.com/2008/06/23/what-is-a-typical-dowry-in-the-kingdom/. "Dowry" is the wrong term here; "dower" or "brideprice" would be more accurate.

85. Mugdha Variyar, "Saudi Arabia Sets Dowry Limit for Virgin Brides to Combat Rise in Spinsters," *International Business Times,* August 19, 2015, http://www.ibtimes.co.in/saudi-arabia-sets-dowry-limit-virgin-brides-combat-rise-spinsters-643419. Again, "dowry" is the wrong term here; "dower" or "brideprice" would be more accurate.

86. Morgan Windsor, "Saudi Brides Demanding Lowest Dowry Are Rewarded with Cash Prize at Mass Wedding," *International Business Times,* June 3, 2015, http://www.ibtimes.com/saudi-brides-demanding-lowest-dowry-are-rewarded-cash-prize-mass-wedding-1951522. Again, "dowry" is the wrong term here; "dower" or "brideprice" would be more accurate.

87. Ashley Kirk, "Iraq and Syria: How Many Foreign Fighters Are Fighting for ISIL?" *Telegraph,* March 24, 2016, http://www.telegraph.co.uk/news/2016/03/29/iraq-and-syria-how-many-foreign-fighters-are-fighting-for-isil/.

88. Hillary Clinton, "Remarks at the TEDWomen Conference," Washington, D.C., December 8, 2010.

89. Eliza Anyan, "Imagine Having to Pay to Divorce Your Abuser," *CNN,* August 19, 2015, http://edition.cnn.com/2015/08/19/africa/bride-price-uganda-mifumi-atuki-turner/.

Kate Cronin-Furman

SIX QUESTIONS ABOUT THE ROHINGYA CRISIS

Nearly three-quarters of a million Burmese Rohingya have crossed the border into Bangladesh in the last six months, driven out of their homes by brutal violence unleashed upon them by the military. The rate of population displacement is remarkable, rivaled in recent memory only by the mass exoduses from Rwanda and Kosovo in the 1990s. These refugees bring with them stories of atrocities so horrifying that experienced human rights workers and UN officials have consistently described them as "among the worst we've ever seen."[1] Traumatized survivors tell of the mass rape of women and girls, the slaughter of infants, and wholesale destruction of villages. From the earliest days of the crisis, human rights reporting has documented "a clear and systematic pattern" to the abuses.[2] Despite the Burmese government's denials of attacks on civilians, satellite imagery has attested to the deliberate burning, then bulldozing, of Rohingya villages.

1. Why are the Rohingya being attacked?

The violence is shocking, but it is utterly unsurprising. The Rohingya are often described as the "the world's most persecuted minority." Muslims in a Buddhist state, they have suffered decades of discrimination and abuse at the hands of their neighbors and the Burmese security forces. Although

Written by the author for *Essential Readings in World Politics* (2018).

the Rohingya have lived in Burma's Rakhine State since the era of British colonial rule, Burma does not recognize their citizenship and insists that they are illegal migrants from Bangladesh. A 1982 citizenship law formally deprived them of nationality, resulting in systematic discrimination and denial of access to state services. Local policies in northern Rakhine, where many Rohingya live, add additional burdens. Rohingya there are subject to restrictions on their ability to marry, bear children, pursue an education, and travel.

Burmese security forces have twice before launched significant attacks on the Rohingya population. In 1977–78, abuses committed during a joint operation by the military and immigration authorities in Rakhine State sparked mass displacement, with approximately 200,000 fleeing into Bangladesh. And in 1991–92, a second military operation in northern Rakhine State displaced another 200,000–250,000 Rohingya across the border. While many of these refugees returned to Burma, at least 100,000 of them remained in Bangladesh when the current crisis began.

The Rohingya's precarious legal status has also made them particularly vulnerable to violence from other groups. In 2012, reports that three Muslim men had raped and murdered a Buddhist woman led to rioting between the two communities. As the violence spread, the authorities did little to calm the situation. Despite increased security measures, police stood aside as Rakhine Buddhists attacked Rohingya, looted their possessions, and burned their homes. Credible reports suggest that members of the security forces armed Rakhine mobs and arranged buses to transport them to Rohingya villages.[3] Although the violence was described as "clashes" between the two communities, the collusion of state forces suggests that the Rohingya's subsequent forced relocation to squalid displacement camps and urban ghettos in the name of security was part of a deliberate plan to further restrict their freedom of movement.

In the aftermath of the 2012 riots, there have been several more flare-ups of communal violence, accompanied by worsening state repression of the Rohingya. Additional riots in Rakhine State in January 2014 left more than 40 Rohingya dead and contributed to a crisis on the Andaman Sea when thousands of Rohingya boarded rickety boats in search of asylum.

These developments raised alarm bells for many observers. For the past three years, the U.S. Holocaust Memorial Museum's Early Warning Project has identified Burma as one of three countries most at risk for a mass atrocity. In a 2015 report, "Early Warning Signs of Genocide in Burma," the museum's researchers pronounced themselves "deeply concerned that so many preconditions for genocide are already in place."[4] They described the Rohingya's precarious situation within Burma as "an especially alarming problem that has received inadequate international attention."[5] A legal analysis conducted by Yale Law School in late 2015 went further, finding "strong evidence that genocide [was] being committed against Rohingya."[6] And a study by the International State Crime Initiative argued that the Rohingya were in fact in "the final stages" of a genocidal process.[7]

Bearing out these warnings, the security forces responded with unrestrained fury when a feeble Rohingya insurgency attacked several border posts in October 2016. Openly invoking the hate speech propagated by militant Buddhist months, government officials have characterized the Rohingya as "dirty," as illegal immigrants, and liars. The government, including its Nobel Peace laureate civilian leader, Aung San Suu Kyi, has made a concerted push to brand the Rohingya as Islamic militants and to dismiss all claims of abuses as "fabricated news" and "propaganda for Muslim groups." But by November 2016, human rights groups were warning that the military was systematically employing extrajudicial killings, torture, and sexual violence against the civilian population in the name of counterinsurgency. And in February 2017, a UN report concluded that the so-called clearance operations likely amounted to crimes against humanity.[8]

The violence, already severe, escalated sharply following the deaths of 12 security officers on August 25, 2017. In response, the military launched an all-out attack on the Rohingya. Credible estimates suggest that over half of the Rohingya population of Rakhine State has now fled. Thousands more attempt to cross the border into Bangladesh every day. And as the death toll mounted throughout late 2017, many began to ask whether Burma is expelling the Rohingya or exterminating them.

2. Is Burma committing genocide against the Rohingya?

Government officials from France, Turkey, Malaysia, Pakistan, the Philippines, and Bangladesh have all described what's happening to the Rohingya as genocide. But the question of whether a mass atrocity constitutes genocide hinges on intent, not scale. The torture, rape, and murder of huge numbers of civilians in both the Democratic Republic of Congo and Syria, for instance, are war crimes and/or crimes against humanity, but not genocide. Although the violence in both cases is systematic and devastating, civilians are not being targeted on the basis of their group identity.

The Rohingya, on the other hand, clearly *are* being targeted because of their ethnicity. And numerous international actors have noted that the

Burmese military's actions look like a "textbook example of ethnic cleansing."[9] The methodical commission of sexual violence, the burning of villages the Rohingya have fled, and the laying of land mines to prevent their return all support this claim. Ethnic cleansing—the use of violence or terror to remove an ethnic group from an area—is not itself a defined crime under international law. But when committed systematically, many of the tactics that militaries and militias use to "cleanse" territory are crimes against humanity. And they may also constitute genocide if committed with the goal of destroying that group "in whole or in part." Without that intent, no matter how brutal the violence, it does not qualify as genocide.

It can be hard to identify genocidal intent even in cases of severe ethnic violence. For instance, in both the Central African Republic and South Sudan, widespread and brutal violence is being inflicted on civilians, clearly on the basis of their ethnicity. But whether these attacks are genocide or another crime depends on what's inside the perpetrators' heads. Was the slaughter of 500 members of an ethnic minority part of an effort to wipe the group out, discourage them from supporting a rival armed group, or scare them into fleeing the country? It's difficult to distinguish among these possibilities without knowing what the perpetrators were thinking.

The Nazi regime kept extensive records documenting its plans to wipe out the Jews, but most atrocity perpetrators aren't so meticulous. Because of this, international courts have repeatedly ruled that genocidal intent can be inferred from context. The tribunal that convened after the genocide in Rwanda convicted perpetrators of genocide based on the huge numbers of Tutsi victims and the systematic nature of their targeting. And the Yugoslavia tribunal looked to "the general political doctrine which gave rise to the acts" to establish intent.[10]

As we witness the horrors being unleashed in Rakhine State, the contextual clues that international courts look for are abundant. A leaked 1988 policy document tellingly titled "Rohingya Extermination Plan" outlines the government's intent to limit the Rohingya's population growth "by application of all possible methods of oppression and suppression against them."[11] Among the measures listed were forbidding Rohingya access to higher education, preventing them from owning property or engaging in trade, and banning the construction of mosques. Together with ominous comments from high-ranking military officials that refer to the Rohingya as "an unfinished job,"[12] these measures suggest the existence of a long-standing plan to eliminate the group. They make up exactly the sort of sociopolitical context in which international courts have inferred in the past that mass atrocities were committed with genocidal intent.

Viewed against this background, many of the Burmese military's actions that could have plausibly been interpreted as efforts to terrorize the Rohingya into fleeing instead look like measures in pursuit of their destruction. The targeting of teachers and religious leaders, the systematic burning of homes, and the particular brutality inflicted on women and very young children appear calculated to erase Rohingya culture, eliminate all traces of their presence, and prevent the survival of future generations.

Furthermore, aid workers on the ground report that security forces have surrounded a number of villages blocking both the delivery of supplies and any escape routes while the inhabitants starve to death. Others have documented multiple instances of soldiers shooting people as they attempt to flee across the border. And finally, international media reports confirm that the military has laid land mines in the border area, causing those attempting to seek refuge in Bangladesh to be killed and maimed. These look less like efforts to coerce the Rohingya population into flight than to pen them in and eradicate them.

3. If the international community knew the Rohingya were at risk for genocide, why didn't it do anything?

A vast apparatus of international law and policy is dedicated to protecting civilians from mass atrocities in general, and genocide specifically. The "crime of crimes," as genocide is known, was named and outlawed in 1948 by an international community still reeling from the shock of the Holocaust. Nearly 150 countries have signed the Convention on the Prevention and Punishment of the Crime of Genocide, accepting an obligation to prevent genocide from happening and punish those who commit it. Although the convention doesn't explicitly say anything about stopping ongoing violence, the mandate "Never Again" echoes in the minds of policymakers and the public. Famously, during the Rwandan genocide, the Clinton administration was so convinced that designating it as such would carry a moral obligation to intervene that it instructed its officials not to say the word.

The international community's failures to stop mass slaughter in Rwanda and Bosnia in the 1990s sparked an effort to institute better atrocity response protocols. In 2005, the member states of the United Nations endorsed the responsibility to protect framework (R2P), which obligates the international community to protect civilians from mass atrocities when their governments are "unwilling or unable" to keep them safe. R2P promised a new era of "timely and decisive" atrocity response.[13] In pursuit of this goal, early warning efforts to identify the precursors of mass atrocities became a focus for both international organizations and Western governments.

The logic of these efforts was that, in the words of the U.S. government's Genocide Prevention Task Force cochaired by Madeleine Albright and William Cohen, "the earlier the United States can recognize risks of mass atrocities, the wider the range of preventive options will be."[14] The establishment of the interagency Atrocities Prevention Board reflected this analysis. Its mandate was to "support more focused monitoring and response to potential atrocity risks," with the expectation that the United States could then engage "early, proactively, and decisively."[15]

Yet the plight of the Rohingya suggests that the early warning logic is flawed. The high risk of mass atrocities was clear from the escalating communitarian violence, the documented uptick in online hate speech beginning in 2012, and the tightening of official restrictions on their movement and activities. Nor are the Rohingya the only post-R2P victims of long-telegraphed mass atrocities.

In 2009, Sri Lanka slaughtered tens of thousands of Tamil civilians in the final phase of its war against the Liberation Tigers of Tamil Eelam. The bloodbath was neither sudden nor unpredictable. The security forces had committed systematic abuses throughout the conflict and had expelled aid workers and journalists from the field of combat in late 2008. More recently, South Sudan's descent into violence and anarchy was preceded by the breakdown of a power-sharing agreement and rumors of ethnic militias forming. In both cases, the threat of atrocities was clear, yet the international community took no action to prevent them. These examples underscore the fact that a lack of advance notice is not the critical obstacle to preventing mass atrocities.

4. Why is it so hard to prevent mass atrocities?

Although neither the academic nor the policy literature frames it this way, atrocity prevention is a deterrence challenge. International actors attempt to use the threat of consequences to prevent potential atrocity perpetrators from attacking civilians. There is a range of potential measures they can threaten: diplomatic censure, suspension of aid and trade, financial (targeted sanctions) or criminal (prosecutions) consequences for individual perpetrators, or the use of force to protect civilian populations or pursue the military defeat of the perpetrators.

The incentive structures of potential atrocity perpetrators and members of the international community contrive to make all of these threats inadequate to reliably deter mass atrocities. Those that do not involve the use of force are generally not severe enough to alter potential perpetrators' cost-benefit calculations. Atrocities are not committed on a whim. They are motivated by the need to win wars or elections. The loss of Western development aid, or condemnation by the UN Human Rights Council, simply does not stack up against these existential concerns.

Meanwhile, deterrent threats that do involve the use of force are not credible because members of the international community do not have compelling interests at stake. In fact, many powerful members of the international community have strong interests *against* permitting action that infringes on another state's sovereignty. This is particularly true for countries like China, India, and Russia that are fighting insurgencies within their own territory. And for those who lack these disincentives, the costs of action may still present a barrier. International actors are aware that humanitarian interventions are rarely simple exercises and often presage long-term commitments. And likewise, potential atrocity perpetrators know that military intervention is extremely rare. Faced with strong incentives to attack civilians, they may reasonably gamble that the international community is unlikely to use force to stop them.

Burma is a particularly hard case for the deterrence of mass atrocities. The military enjoys broad popular support for its campaign against the Rohingya, providing strong domestic political incentives for the commission of atrocities. Having partially transitioned from military rule only six years ago, Burma is incompletely linked into the international community. This means that informal pathways for exerting human rights pressure are limited. Additionally, its hybrid regime is unlikely to be as sensitive to reputational costs as a full democracy eager to maintain its status as a human rights–respecting member of the international community. Furthermore, Burma is not heavily dependent on Western aid or trade and has already lived through crippling sanctions, making the threat of reductions less compelling. It also has the support of China, minimizing the possibility that it might find itself the target of a UN Security Council resolution authorizing either the use of force or the criminal investigation of its leaders by the International Criminal Court.

Burma's decision to pursue a campaign of mass atrocities also took place against the backdrop of an international system whose structural dynamics made international intervention particularly unlikely. The international community is already struggling to respond to crises elsewhere, most prominently in Syria, but also in the often overlooked wars in Yemen, the Central African Republic, and South Sudan. And in the aftermath of the Libyan intervention, where R2P was explicitly invoked, members of the international community are particularly leery of intervention, wary of the potential for making a bad situation worse.

Additionally, the fact that the attacks on the Rohingya are taking place with a singularly apathetic U.S. administration in power further reduces the likelihood of intervention on their behalf. Under President Trump, the United States has removed human rights conditions on arms sales, gutted the State Department's human rights and democracy promotion mission, and threatened to withdraw from the UN Human Rights Council. However vulnerable to charges of hypocrisy that the United States has been, its rhetorical commitment to human rights and willingness to exert pressure has provided a constraint on repressive states who seek the support of the West. But a world in which the United States downplays the importance of human rights constitutes a permissive environment for the commission of atrocities.

All of these factors conspired to make robust international attempts to prevent atrocities against the Rohingya both unlikely to occur and unlikely to succeed. Early warning didn't save the Rohingya because it couldn't offset the countervailing interests or cooperation challenges that make preventing mass atrocities difficult. But today, the question is no longer one of prevention, but of intervention into an ongoing atrocity.

5. Why hasn't anyone intervened to stop the atrocities against the Rohingya?

There is no longer any doubt that Burma is perpetrating an atrocity on a massive scale. And as the numbers of dead and displaced mount, it is clear that without intervention, the Rohingya are doomed—either to extermination or exile. But the dynamics precluding deterrence only became more pronounced as the crisis escalated.

Once atrocities are underway, with strategic goals in sight and reputational loss already incurred, perpetrators' incentives to commit them strengthen. Halting ongoing atrocities is therefore significantly more difficult than preventing them. In the case of Burma, which has very nearly achieved its apparent goal of ridding itself of the Rohingya entirely, this is particularly true. While it is conceivable that the credible threat of targeted sanctions might have impacted military leaders' cost-benefit calculation in October 2016 and defused the crisis, by the time such sanctions were imposed by the United States and EU in late 2017, it was far too late.

The goal of international action is also far less straightforward this late in the game. Responding

to the crisis is no longer reducible to a deterrence challenge. In 2015, when international organizations warned of oncoming atrocities, the objective of any international action undertaken would have been clear: coerce Burma's government into allowing the Rohingya to remain in their homes safely and with improved human rights protections. But once a significant number of Rohingya had fled, the cessation of attacks became an increasingly incomplete response to the crisis.

More than 700,000 people have now crossed into Bangladesh. Many of them are understandably reluctant to ever return to Burma. They have suffered intense trauma and need psychosocial services in addition to food, shelter, and medical care. Bangladesh is unwilling to grant them asylum and allow them to integrate into the local population. The options are bleak: allowing hundreds of thousands of people to live out their lives in squalid refugee camps or undertaking an international military intervention and ongoing presence to secure their safety in Rakhine State.

6. What does the failure to save the Rohingya mean for the future of atrocity prevention and response efforts?

Despite the soaring rhetoric surrounding the adoption of R2P, or the simple promise of "Never Again," intervention to prevent or stop mass atrocities remains rare. Cases like the Syrian Civil War and the Rohingya Crisis test the limits of the international community's commitment and capacity to protect civilians from serious abuses. The default rule of the international system remains reciprocal respect for sovereignty. Generating the political will to violate a fellow state's sovereignty is challenging, even when the justification for intervention is clear.

Faced with similar situations of ongoing mass atrocities and limited political will to engage, the international community has often shifted focus from intervention to accountability. In 1993, as ethnic violence engulfed the Balkans, the UN Security Council created the International Criminal Tribunal for Yugoslavia (ICTY). Likewise, efforts to prosecute mass rape in Congo have substituted for solutions to the problem of ongoing violence.

There is no easy path to justice for crimes against the Rohingya. The creation of an ad hoc tribunal like the ICTY is almost certainly precluded by the Chinese veto. And Burma is not a member of the Rome Statute, meaning that any investigation into its actions on its own territory by the permanent International Criminal Court (ICC) would also require a Security Council resolution. The ICC may be able to take jurisdiction over the forced deportation of Rohingya into Bangladesh, which, unlike Burma, *is* a member state, but that would not extend to investigating the mass slaughter, systematic rape, and enforced starvation that have occurred within Burma's borders.

Notably, after Russia's veto prevented an ICC referral of the situation in Syria, the UN General Assembly created a special mechanism to investigate atrocities there. A similar mechanism may be the most likely case for accountability for Burmese atrocities but would still leave open the question of when, if ever, these crimes might actually be prosecuted and by whom.

NOTES

1. Fatma Tanis, "U.N. Rights Chief: Myanmar's Treatment of Rohingya Includes 'Almost ISIS-Type Crimes,'" October 24, 2017, https://www.npr.org/sections/parallels/2017/10/24/559546982/u-n-rights-chief-myanmars-treatment-of-rohingya-includes-almost-isis-type-crimes.

2. Amnesty International, "Myanmar: Scorched-earth campaign fuels ethnic cleansing of Rohingya from Rakhine State," September 14, 2017, https://www.amnesty.org/en/latest/news/2017/09/myanmar-scorched-earth-campaign-fuels-ethnic-cleansing-of-rohingya-from-rakhine-state/.

3. Francis Wade, *Myanmar's Enemy Within: Buddhist Violence and the Making of a Muslim 'Other'* (London: Zed Books, 2017).

4. Simon-Skjodt Center for the Prevention of Genocide, United States Holocaust Memorial Museum, "'They Want Us All to Go Away': Early Warning Signs of Genocide in Burma," May 2015, https://www.ushmm.org/m/pdfs/20150505-Burma-Report.pdf.

5. Simon-Skjodt Center, "Early Warning Signs."

6. Allard K. Lowenstein International Human Rights Clinic, Yale Law School, "Persecution of the Rohingya Muslims: Is Genocide Occurring in Myanmar's Rakhine State? A Legal Analysis," October 2015, http://www.fortifyrights.org/downloads/Yale_Persecution_of_the_Rohingya_October_2015.pdf.

7. Penny Green, Thomas Mac Marius, and Alicia de la Cour Venning, *Countdown to Annihilation: Genocide in Myanmar* (London: International State Crime Initiative, 2015), http://statecrime.org/data/2015/10/ISCI-Rohingya-Report-PUBLISHED-VERSION.pdf.

8. Office of the High Commission for Human Rights, Mission to Bangladesh, "Flash Report: Interviews with Rohingyas fleeing from Myanmar since 9 October 2016," February 3, 2017, http://www.ohchr.org/Documents/Countries/MM/FlashReport3Feb2017.pdf.

9. Office of the High Commissioner for Human Rights "Darker and more dangerous: High Commissioner updates the Human Rights Council on human rights issue in 40 countries," 2017, http://www.ohchr.org/EN/NewsEvents/Pages/DisplayNews.aspx?NewsID=22041.

10. *Prosecutor v. Radovan Karadžić & Ratko Mladić*, Review of the Indictments Pursuant to Rule 61 of the Rules of Procedure and Evidence (July 11, 1996), http://www.icty.org/x/cases/mladic/related/en/rev-ii960716-e.pdf.

11. Green et al., *Countdown to Annihilation*.

12. Nirmal Ghosh, "Myanmar's 'Bengali problem' threatens to embroil the region," *Straits Times*, September 6, 2017, http://www.straitstimes.com/opinion/myanmars-bengali-problem-threatens-to-embroil-the-region.

13. International Commission on Intervention and State Sovereignty, *The Responsibility to Protect* (Ottawa: International Development Research Centre, 2001).

14. Genocide Prevention Task Force, *Preventing Genocide: A Blueprint for U.S. Policymakers,* 2008, https://www.ushmm.org/m/pdfs/20081124-genocide-prevention-report.pdf.

15. U.S. Department of State, "Atrocities Prevention," August 15, 2011, https://www.state.gov/j/atrocitiesprevention/.

CREDITS

Press. Reprinted with the permission of Cambridge University Press.

Kenneth Waltz: "Why Iran Should Get the Bomb," reprinted with permission of the Council on Foreign Relations, from *Foreign Affairs* Vol. 91, No. 4 (July/August 2012). Copyright © 2012 by the Council on Foreign Relations, Inc.

Alexander Wendt: Excerpts from "Anarchy Is What States Make of It: The Social Construction of Power Politics." *International Organization*, 46:2 (Spring 1992), pp. 391–425. © 1992 by the World Peace Foundation and the Massachusetts Institute of Technology. Reprinted with permission.

Keren Yarhi-Milo: Excerpts from "In the Eye of the Beholder: How Leaders and Intelligence Communities Assess the Intentions of Adversaries." *International Security* 38:1 (Summer 2013), pp. 7–51. © 2013 by the President and Fellows of Harvard College and the Massachusetts Institute of Technology. Reprinted with permission.

Fareed Zakaria: "Populism on the March: Why the West is in Trouble," reprinted with permission of the Council on Foreign Relations, from *Foreign Affairs* Vol. 95, No. 6 (November/December 2016). Copyright © 2016 by the Council on Foreign Relations, Inc.